PRINCIPLES OF
INTERNATIONAL LAW

3rd edition

In Memoriam

Professor George Winterton (1946–2008)
scholar, mentor, friend

PRINCIPLES OF
INTERNATIONAL LAW

3rd edition

Stephen Hall

LLB (Queensland), LLM (Hons) (UTS), DPhil (Oxford)

Professor, Faculty of Law
The Chinese University of Hong Kong

LexisNexis Butterworths
Australia
2011

LexisNexis

AUSTRALIA	LexisNexis Butterworths
	475–495 Victoria Avenue, Chatswood NSW 2067
	On the internet at: www.lexisnexis.com.au
ARGENTINA	LexisNexis Argentina, BUENOS AIRES
AUSTRIA	LexisNexis Verlag ARD Orac GmbH & Co KG, VIENNA
BRAZIL	LexisNexis Latin America, SAO PAULO
CANADA	LexisNexis Canada, Markham, ONTARIO
CHILE	LexisNexis Chile, SANTIAGO
CHINA	LexisNexis China, BEIJING, SHANGHAI
CZECH REPUBLIC	Nakladatelství Orac sro, PRAGUE
FRANCE	LexisNexis SA, PARIS
GERMANY	LexisNexis Germany, FRANKFURT
HONG KONG	LexisNexis Hong Kong, HONG KONG
HUNGARY	HVG-Orac, BUDAPEST
INDIA	LexisNexis, NEW DELHI
ITALY	Dott A Giuffrè Editore SpA, MILAN
JAPAN	LexisNexis Japan KK, TOKYO
KOREA	LexisNexis, SEOUL
MALAYSIA	LexisNexis Malaysia Sdn Bhd, PETALING JAYA, SELANGOR
NEW ZEALAND	LexisNexis, WELLINGTON
POLAND	Wydawnictwo Prawnicze LexisNexis, WARSAW
SINGAPORE	LexisNexis, SINGAPORE
SOUTH AFRICA	LexisNexis Butterworths, DURBAN
SWITZERLAND	Staempfli Verlag AG, BERNE
TAIWAN	LexisNexis, TAIWAN
UNITED KINGDOM	LexisNexis UK, LONDON, EDINBURGH
USA	LexisNexis Group, New York, NEW YORK
	LexisNexis, Miamisburg, OHIO

National Library of Australia Cataloguing-in-Publication entry

Author:	Hall, Stephen.
Title:	International Law.
Edition:	3rd edition.
ISBN:	9780409327724 (pbk).
Notes:	Includes index.
Subjects:	International law.
Dewey Number:	341.

Typeset in Sabon and Myriad.

Printed in Australia by Ligare Pty Ltd (NSW).

Visit LexisNexis Butterworths at www.lexisnexis.com.au

Publisher's note

The United Nations is the author of the original material reproduced in the Appendix: Basic Documents and owns the copyright in that material. It is reproduced with the kind permission of the United Nations. For more information, see www.un.org.

Contents

11 International human rights   531

Preface

This book has been written with a specific objective in view. It seeks to explain and illustrate the cardinal concepts of international law to practising and academic lawyers, to students of law and international relations, and to anyone interested in developing their understanding of the rules of the international system. It also seeks to bring a clarity to international law that is occasionally missing from some specialist works, and a comprehensiveness which is always missing from basic introductions. Finally, it seeks to advance an understanding of the international legal order based on a vision of international law as a natural authority called into existence by the demands of the common good of peoples organised into States. It strives to avoid both globalist utopianism and the left and right varieties of cynical 'realism' that sometimes haunt international law.

The book deals with the main topics covered in most general university courses in international law, with an emphasis on the legal system itself and other core systemic areas which are not usually the subject of specialised courses in most Australian law schools: the nature and sources of international law, the law of treaties, statehood, legal personality, State responsibility, treatment of foreign nationals, jurisdiction, immunities, territory, dispute settlement, the international use of force, and the place of international law in Australian domestic law. It also traverses three more specialised but important fields which occupy highly strategic positions in contemporary international relations: the law of the sea, human rights, and international criminal law. These additional specialised areas are not only important in themselves, they also serve to illustrate the international legal system in action. It is hoped that this book will repay the reader with a sound grasp of the structure and systemic requirements of international law and an appreciation of international law as a system constantly adapting to new international realities.

The reader's understanding will be extended by the inclusion, at the beginning of each chapter, of a statement of clear objectives and a table of the most important cases, treaties and other instruments relevant to the topics under consideration. At each chapter's conclusion, illustrative problem scenarios and suggested answers aim to apply and deepen the reader's understanding, while a menu of further questions is designed to stimulate further reflection and a deeper understanding of international law.

I would like to thank Professor Mike McConville, Dean of the Faculty of Law at The Chinese University of Hong Kong, for his extraordinary patience and cooperation in helping to make it possible for me to write this edition. All my other colleagues at the same Faculty also deserve considerable credit for putting up with me.

This edition was substantially completed as a guest of the Faculty of Law at the University of Sydney. In this connection I am most grateful to the Dean, Professor Gillian Triggs (one of Australia's pre-eminent international law scholars), for her hospitality. Dr Peter Gerangelos kindly sponsored my visits and made them possible. I am most grateful to him for these efforts and for his companionship. I am also thankful for the lively and instructive discussions with Dr Brett Williams of the Sydney Centre for International Law who, I am sure, had more pressing matters to deal with. David Corey and Patrick Lui provided splendid administrative and technical support.

On the production side, I would like to thank Jocelyn Holmes, commissioning editor at LexisNexis Butterworths, for her support for and faith in the project. Michelle Nichols performed simply peerless editorial work which made my task much easier.

I owe a special debt to Stankie Yap Hong Chai for all-round support in Hong Kong, which greatly assisted in the manuscript's finalisation.

Finally, I feel compelled to thank my students at The Chinese University of Hong Kong, the University of New South Wales, and the City University of Hong Kong, from whom I have learned much.

Stephen Hall
Sha Tin
Hong Kong
24 November 2010

Cases

Treaties and instruments

References are to paragraphs

This index includes conventions, charters, covenants, declarations and statutes.

Nature and sources of international law

1

Objectives

After completing this chapter, you should:

(1) understand the material scope of international law;
(2) have a basic understanding of the historical origins of modern international law;
(3) understand and be able to explain the structure of the international legal system;
(4) understand and be able to explain the juridical character of international law;
(5) understand and be able to identify the sources of international law;
(6) have a basic understanding of treaties and 'soft law';
(7) understand and be able to explain the salient characteristics of customary international law;
(8) understand and be able to explain the salient characteristics of the general principles of law;
(9) understand and be able to explain the role played by judicial and arbitral decisions and the teachings of eminent publicists;
(10) understand and be able to identify the modes by which acts of public international organisations affect the normative requirements of international law; and
(11) understand and be able to identify the way in which unilateral declarations by States can create legally binding obligations.

Key cases

Anglo-Norwegian Fisheries case *(United Kingdom v Norway)* ICJ Rep (1951) 116
Asylum case *(Colombia v Peru)* ICJ Rep (1950) 266
North Sea Continental Shelf cases *(Germany v Denmark, Germany v The Netherlands)* ICJ Rep (1969) 3
Right of Passage case *(Portugal v India)* ICJ Rep (1960) 6
Case Concerning the Factory at Chorzów (Indemnity) (Merits) (Germany v Poland), PCIJ Rep (1928) Series A No 17
Diversion of Water from the River Meuse case *(The Netherlands v Belgium)* PCIJ Rep (1937) Series A/B No 70
Nuclear Tests cases *(Australia v France, New Zealand v France)* ICJ Rep (1974) 253
Frontier Dispute case *(Burkina Faso v Mali)* ICJ Rep (1986) 554

Key treaties and instruments

Charter of the United Nations (1945): Art 1, Art 103
Statute of the International Court of Justice (1945): Art 38(1)

Concept of international law

1.1   Until comparatively recent times, international law was regarded as a system of legally binding rules and principles which regulated relations exclusively among sovereign States. These States were held to be the only subjects of international law and the only entities possessing legal personality on the international plane. This meant that only States could enjoy legal rights and be under legal obligations at the international level. For the purposes of international law, the word 'State' denotes a country which exhibits certain specific features: an independent government, a definite territory, a permanent population, and a capacity to enter into legal relations with other States.[1] States, in other words, are independent countries.

1.2   Other entities, such as natural persons or corporations, fell within the ambit of international law only by virtue of having a designated relationship to a State. These non-State entities were regarded as 'objects' of international law, whose affairs were of concern to international lawyers only to the extent that a State was either responsible for their actions or entitled to protect them against the actions of other States.[2]

1.3   Since the First World War, the concept of international law has broadened to include among its subjects public international organisations and individuals. Thus, international organisations established by agreement among States, such as the United Nations, may also have certain rights, obligations and capacities under international law.[3] Individuals have increasingly become subjects of international law in certain fields, as States have concluded agreements codifying and conferring human rights and establishing direct individual responsibility for international crimes.[4]

1.4   International law can now be defined as a body of rules and principles which regulates relations:

(i)   among States and public international organisations inter se;

(ii)   between States and individuals in the field of international human rights; and

(iii)   between the international society and individuals who have committed international crimes.

1.5   International law is frequently called 'public international law' in order to distinguish it from private international law (also sometimes called 'conflict of laws'). Whereas public international law is a uniform and autonomous system of norms regulating relations among its subjects, private international law consists of norms developed within States as part of their own domestic legal orders to resolve disputes between

---

1.   See **4.4–4.17**.
2.   See **chapter 5**.
3.   See **4.57–4.61**.
4.   See **1.21**.

private parties where a foreign element is involved. Private international law determines the choice of law applicable to a legal dispute, whether a particular domestic court or tribunal has jurisdiction where there is a cross-border element and whether it should exercise any such jurisdiction, and whether a domestic court may order the enforcement of a foreign court's judgment.

A clash between public international law and private international law may arise in a number of ways. There may, for example, be a simple failure to comply with a treaty coordinating or harmonising rules of private international law among the contracting States. In such a case, the State that has failed to maintain or reform its domestic law or practices in accordance with its treaty obligations has committed a breach of the treaty in question. Such a breach would be a violation of the delinquent State's duties under public international law — namely, the duty to perform treaty obligations in good faith. A more familiar cause of conflict between the two systems is the existence of a domestic rule of private international law that affirms or denies a domestic court's jurisdiction inconsistently with a customary norm of public international law. Once again, by applying such a domestic rule, the delinquent State violates its duty under public international law — in this case, the duty to comply with applicable customary legal obligations.

Development and scope of international law

1.6 International law, understood simply as a body of norms regulating relations among political rulers, can be traced back to the period of antiquity. Indeed, archaeologists have discovered treaties between kings of city-states in ancient Mesopotamia, the cradle of civilisation, dating from around 3000 BC. Treaty relations among rulers remained a feature of political life throughout the ancient history of the Middle East and the Mediterranean, with most civilisations recognising the binding force of treaties and respecting the persons of diplomatic envoys.

1.7 Medieval Europe enjoyed a more elaborate form of international law, though the structure of feudal realms was not well suited to the emergence of a distinctly separate legal system for the regulation of relations among sovereigns.

These feudal kingdoms, principalities and duchies were not States in the modern sense. There was usually no sovereign exercising undisputed authority within the realm's boundaries. Feudal princes shared power internally with an aristocratic class who often maintained their own armies and legal systems. Furthermore, the rulers, and sometimes their vassals, frequently owed political allegiance to external authorities such as the Church or the Holy Roman Emperor. There was, therefore, an absence of that specifically modern concept of sovereignty which is emblematic of modern statehood and which makes possible an autonomous body of international law: the exercise of political authority over a definite territory and population, unrestricted by any external political authority, and limited only by the requirements of international law.

In relation to any parcel of territory, there might easily have been a number of overlapping, and sometimes conflicting, political authorities — more than one of which participated directly in Europe's 'international' life. During this period, the law governing relations among European rulers was an expression mostly of the *jus gentium:* the 'law of nations' or the 'common law of all mankind', which has conceptual roots in both Roman law and the natural law. Thus, the principle *pacta sunt servanda* (agreements are to be observed) applied equally to treaties and to private commercial contracts as an expression of the *jus gentium.* Medieval princes were bound like everyone to observe the universal principles of the *jus gentium* in their dealings with all people, regardless of whether they were commoners, nobles or other princes.

1.8 During the course of the 15th and 16th centuries, several powerful States emerged (Spain, Portugal, England, France, the Netherlands and Sweden) in which internal authority became more centralised. These States, and especially those in Northern Europe where the Protestant revolution was most influential, refused to accept the political authority of entities beyond themselves. This development prepared the ground for the modern autonomous system of international law.

1.9 In its origins, the modern system of international law was concerned almost exclusively with regulating relations among States as armed actors on the European stage. Emerging from the turmoil of Europe's religious wars in the 16th and 17th centuries, modern international law was long dominated by norms regulating the conduct of war and clarifying matters about which disagreements might lead to war. Indeed, the most influential book in international law's early modern period was *De jure belli ac pacis (On the Law of War and Peace)*, published in 1625 and written by the Dutch jurist and diplomat Hugo Grotius (1583–1645). This definitive work in three volumes was concerned with the lawfulness or justice of war itself, the causes of just war, and the legal status of particular acts performed in the course of waging war. Grotius also expounded upon issues such as the property of States and their freedom on the high seas, which provided notorious points of friction potentially leading to armed conflict between States.

Grotius explained the reason for his focus on the law of international armed conflict and security, and underscored modern international law's essentially European origins, in the following terms:[5]

> I saw prevailing throughout the Christian world a license in making war of which even barbarous nations would have been ashamed; recourse being had to arms for slight reasons or no reason; and when arms were once taken up, all reverence for divine and human law was thrown away, just as if men were thenceforth authorized to commit all crimes without restraint.

---

5.   Hugo Grotius, *De jure belli ac pacis libri tres,* with an abridged translation by William Whewell, John W Parker, London, 1853, Vol I, lix (Prolegomena, 28).

For the next 300 years, international law was largely a matter of working through the terrain mapped by Grotius, although the precise content of the norms that emerged often departed substantially from those propounded by the great pioneer.

1.10 The emergence of the modern conception of statehood was a lengthy process with origins traceable to England and France in the 15th century. The treaties concluding the Peace of Westphalia at the end of the Thirty Years War (1618–48) confirmed the modern State system, and feudal conceptions of international order were extinguished as a potent force animating intra-European relations. The treaties established the rights of numerous small States to participate directly in the international system, with only symbolic concessions to the pre-modern order represented chiefly by the Holy Roman Empire. The peace treaties confirmed the legitimacy of States based on differing versions of Christianity, established that no political authority existed over States, and enshrined the principle of religious tolerance for minorities in some parts of Europe.

The sovereignty of States was, thus, simultaneously established and limited in a way that dimly foreshadowed the later emergence of international human rights law. The treaties of Westphalia also established diplomatic machinery for the peaceful settlement of international disputes, though this system remained dormant.

The peace treaties of Westphalia, at whose negotiations over 190 established or nascent States were represented, settled and regulated many of the issues which had ignited the most destructive and exhausting series of wars Europe had yet endured. As a result, religion was largely eliminated as a cause likely to stir the European powers to open warfare among themselves.

1.11 The Final Act of the Congress of Vienna (1815) and related international agreements sought to adapt the Westphalian State system to substantially new circumstances. The task of the Act and agreements was to maintain international peace in the situation brought about by the insistent movement within many European States away from monarchical despotism, under which territories and populations could be transferred at will, towards various forms of democratic control based on nationalism and national self-determination. This movement, whatever its merits in other regards, was revolutionary in character and proved highly disruptive to peace within Europe, as the recently concluded wars against Napoleonic France amply demonstrated.

The principal European powers established a formal system of collective security against revolutionary turmoil anywhere within Europe, which system was successfully employed on several occasions. The concept of formalised collective security would become a familiar refrain in international law. Other potential flashpoints of armed conflict were also addressed by, among other things, extending freedom of navigation to international rivers within Europe and codifying certain rules relating to diplomats. The Final Act's formal condemnation of the slave trade was also a significant development in international law, and made another important conceptual link between human rights concerns and the maintenance of international peace.

1.12   The increasingly destructive power of military technology during the course of the 19th century, and the emergence of mass military mobilisation, posed new challenges for international law, with its continuing focus on the law of war and peace.

The American Civil War (1861–65), which up to that point was the world's most destructive war, killed more than 600,000 people and wounded more than 500,000 more. The Geneva Convention of 1864 gave legal protection to the wounded in international military conflicts and to those seeking to assist the wounded. The Brussels Conference of 1874 and the Hague Peace Conferences of 1899 and 1907 formulated and agreed upon rules protecting non-combatant civilians, as well as rules for the treatment of prisoners of war, in international armed conflicts. The 1899 conference also established the Permanent Court of Arbitration in an attempt to provide a standing mechanism for the peaceful settlement of international disputes.

1.13   While international law, at this stage, retained its overriding focus on the law of war and peace, there was also an increasing interdependence of international life in the fields of transport, communications and economics. Indeed, the first great era of globalisation occurred in the late 19th and very early 20th centuries.

This period saw international law begin to broaden its domain beyond issues of war and peace, and turn its attention to facilitating international cooperation in a range of technical areas. Significant achievements during this period include the Paris Convention establishing the International Telegraph Union (1865), the Berne Convention establishing the General Postal Union (1874), the Paris Convention for the Protection of Industrial Property (1883), the Berne Convention for the Protection of Literary and Artistic Works (1886), the Brussels Convention for the Publication of Customs Tariffs (1890) and the Madrid Agreement for the Repression of False or Deceptive Indications of Source on Goods (1891). All these, and other similar, agreements foreshadowed the wide cooperation in technical matters that was to become a major feature of international law in the late 20th century.

1.14   Just as the Thirty Years War and the Napoleonic Wars ended in peace conferences that changed the course of international law, so too did the First World War. The Versailles Peace Conference (1919) established the League of Nations, a bold experiment in international order. The traumatic experience of the war, in which more than 16 million people died, prompted the victors to establish the League with a view to preventing the recurrence of any similar conflict. It was thought that a principal catalyst of hostilities was the rush to war by several States in the summer of 1914, while martial passions remained high. The remedy contained in the Covenant of the League of Nations was a mandatory cooling-off period of three months before resorting to war.

The Covenant did not, therefore, prohibit resort to war as an instrument of national policy; on the contrary, war was conditionally preserved as a remedy of last resort among the League's member States.[6] The League of Nations ultimately failed in its primary mission to prevent the recurrence of another world war.

1.15 In 1928, an attempt was made to outlaw resort to war completely by the General Treaty for the Renunciation of War as an Instrument of National Policy (the Kellogg–Briand Treaty, or Pact of Paris).[7] Consisting of two brief Articles, it is one of the shortest treaties in history. Article I provides: 'The High Contracting Parties solemnly declare in the names of their respective peoples that they condemn recourse to war for the solution of international controversies, and renounce it, as an instrument of national policy in their relations with one another.' Article II provides: 'The High Contracting Parties agree that the settlement or solution of all disputes or conflicts of whatever nature or of whatever origin they may be, which may arise among them, shall never be sought except by pacific means.' No attempt was made to define 'war', which left open the question of whether it applied to prohibit the use of armed force without a formal declaration of war.[8]

1.16 A substantially more successful development was the establishment of the Permanent Court of International Justice (PCIJ) by the League of Nations in 1921. The PCIJ lasted until 1945, handing down 32 judgments in contentious cases between States and giving 27 advisory opinions at the request of League institutions. Many of these judgments made lasting contributions to the development of international law in a variety of fields. The years between the world wars were, indeed, something of a springtime for the international arbitration of disputes. In addition to the outpourings of the PCIJ, numerous ad hoc arbitral tribunals and commissions produced awards which, likewise, made important contributions to the development of international law, even if the awards themselves were sometimes ignored by participating States. The International Court of Justice (ICJ) replaced the PCIJ in 1945 upon the establishment of the United Nations (UN).

1.17 In the immediate aftermath of the Second World War, international law's spotlight remained, understandably, principally trained on the perennial questions of war and peace. The UN Charter was opened for signature while the war against Japan was still being fought (26 June 1945). By the time the Charter entered into force (24 October 1945), two Japanese cities had been devastated by atomic bombs, the war had finally ended, and the International Military Tribunal for the Punishment of War Criminals had held its first session in Germany.

---

6. See **9.5**.
7. League of Nations Treaty Series, Vol 94, p 57. The original parties were Australia, Belgium, Canada, Czechoslovakia, France, Germany, India, Ireland, Italy, Japan, New Zealand, Poland, South Africa, the United Kingdom and the United States. A further 39 States (including China and the Soviet Union) subsequently became parties.
8. See **9.6**.

1.18   The UN architecture for preserving and restoring international peace will be considered in more detail in **chapters 8** and **9**. For present purposes, it is sufficient to observe that a serious attempt was made to improve upon the legal mechanisms that existed in the years between the world wars. In particular, the League Covenant's highly qualified restriction on resort to 'war' was replaced by a more comprehensive UN Charter prohibition 'on the threat or use of force',[9] subject to an 'inherent right of individual or collective self-defence if an armed attack occurs'.[10] The UN Security Council is, furthermore, able to authorise or require the use of economic sanctions and to authorise armed force in order to maintain or restore international peace and security.[11]

The result was that, for the first time, the customary international law right of States to resort to armed force as a means of resolving disputes was apparently superseded for those States which became a party to the Charter. Furthermore, the customary right itself disappeared either immediately upon the entry into force of the Charter, or over time as States aligned their practice to the Charter's requirements.

An interesting question is whether the continuing non-occurrence of another global war is primarily due to this newer legal architecture, or whether other factors have been decisive. In particular and in contrast to the League of Nations, the UN has not had to deal with a multi-polar system in which several of the world powers were totalitarian States determined to establish empires by force of arms, and where no other State or alliance of States was sufficiently resolute to deter them.

1.19   The trial and conviction of many of the National Socialist leaders for crimes against the peace, crimes against humanity and war crimes was of monumental significance in demonstrating that responsibility for the most serious offences against international law could attach to political and military leaders and not simply to the State whose affairs they directed. This was reaffirmed by the 1948 Convention on the Prevention and Punishment of the Crime of Genocide,[12] which provides for punishment of individual offenders after conviction by a national court or an international criminal tribunal.

1.20   Since the First World War, there has been an unprecedented expansion in the material scope of international law beyond its traditional concern with issues of war and peace. While the law of armed force remains of central concern to many international lawyers, a range of political and technological developments have, over the last 90 years, provided a climate in which there has been a dramatic expansion of the subject matter over which international law exercises authority. This process has gathered even further pace since the end of the Cold War,

---

9.   UN Charter, Art 2(4).
10.   Ibid, Art 51.
11.   Ibid, Arts 39, 41 and 42.
12.   UNTS, Vol 999, p 171.

with increased opportunities for international economic and political cooperation.

1.21   As noted above, the personal scope of international law has expanded to embrace individuals, at least for some purposes.[13] This has been primarily in the areas of human rights protection and the law relating to international crimes, such as crimes against the peace, crimes against humanity, war crimes and genocide. In the case of human rights protection, international law's traditional link with the maintenance of international peace is recognised in the preambles to the 1948 Universal Declaration of Human Rights (UDHR),[14] the 1950 Convention for the Protection of Human Rights and Fundamental Freedoms (European Convention on Human Rights, or ECHR),[15] the 1966 International Covenant on Economic, Social and Cultural Rights (ICESCR)[16] and the 1966 International Covenant on Civil and Political Rights (ICCPR).[17]

1.22   As Grotius and other early publicists recognised, competition for the use of the seas, which cover more than 70 per cent of the Earth's surface, was also intimately connected with the maintenance of international peace. It followed that the Law of the Sea was one of the earliest areas of international law to be developed.

This is also an area that has been the subject of extensive development and refinement since the Second World War.[18]

1.23   As the factual interdependence of international society has increased, so has the material scope of international law naturally expanded to provide a framework within which States and other members of international society may fruitfully coordinate their joint and competing activities for the benefit of the common good.

1.24   As with domestic law, international law frequently lags behind developments in the society to which it corresponds. Forces with vested or sectional interests may periodically retard developments in international law that would be beneficial to the society as a whole, just as such forces might sponsor new developments which undermine the common good.

The risk of such distortions appearing is generally increased wherever political authority is not, in some real sense, representative of the whole of the society that it governs. International society has, since the Peace of Westphalia and the transmission of the European State system to the rest of the world, been under the political authority of the society of States. The activities of these States generate the treaties and customs that constitute positive international law.[19]

---

13.   See **1.3**.
14.   General Assembly Resolution 217A (III); UN Doc A/810, 71 (1948).
15.   UNTS, Vol 213, p 221; Council of Europe Treaty Series, No 5.
16.   UNTS, Vol 993, p 3.
17.   UNTS, Vol 999, p 171.
18.   See **chapter 12**.
19.   See **1.27**.

It is notorious, however, that many States that participate in the exercise of this international political authority are not representative of their populations. These States frequently exercise domestic power and use their international authority directly against their people's fundamental interests and without their consent. Not being concerned with their own people's welfare or consent, such States have only limited interest in the development of international law in directions genuinely beneficial to international society as a whole. Furthermore, the continuing participation of such dysfunctional or dictatorial States in the generation of international law sometimes creates a reluctance on the part of other States to entrust international law with a major role in the solution of international problems.

1.25 Notwithstanding this serious weakness in the international legal system, there has emerged a universal system of legal cooperation in a large number of fields. These include areas which might be regarded as essentially systemic or constitutional to international law itself, such as a more fully developed conception of international law's sources,[20] the law relating to States and intergovernmental organisations,[21] title to territory,[22] the law of the sea,[23] the law relating to jurisdiction and immunities of States,[24] and peaceful dispute settlement.[25] So central has the law on the use of force been to the development of international law that this area, with its many important developments since the Second World War, might also be regarded as forming part of the international legal system's constitutional structure.[26]

This development towards universal cooperation also extends to numerous substantive subjects, many of which fell entirely or mostly within the domestic jurisdiction of States until relatively recently, and which have only an indirect connection to the maintenance of international peace. These subjects include protection of the environment, the regulation of trade, development and monetary stability, aerospace, communications, transport, health, natural resources and nuclear energy.

International law will continue to provide indispensable tools wherever there is a need for States or their peoples to coordinate activities in relation to the preservation of the peace or the distribution or preservation of the world's resources, or where, for other reasons, stable and predictable frameworks are required for the advancement of the international common good.

---

20. See **1.79–1.204** and **chapter 2**.
21. See **chapter 4**.
22. See **chapter 7**.
23. See **chapter 6**.
24. See **chapter 8**.
25. See **chapter 8**.
26. See **chapters 9** and **10**.

Structure of the international system

Legal norms

1.26   The single most striking feature of the international legal system is its decentralised and consensual character. On the international legal plane, and in contrast to domestic legal systems, it is not possible to point to institutions endowed with readily identifiable legislative and executive functions. Furthermore, such international judicial organs as exist are not endowed with compulsory jurisdiction. Indeed, it is not even possible to point to international legal instruments that possess the unambiguously normative character of domestic constitutions or legislation. In this limited sense, there is no international government and no system of international legislation. There are, however, two notable exceptions. First, certain resolutions adopted by the UN Security Council will impose legally binding obligations on all States.[27] Second, the European Union, while founded on a number of constitutive treaties, possesses most of the characteristics of a federal legal system, so that the Union's legislative organs may adopt laws which are effective in the member States in such a way that they may be directly relied upon by litigants in national courts and tribunals.

1.27   The absence of an international legislature does not, however, result in international society being without the means of generating and modifying international legal rules. International law is primarily a system of customary law, increasingly supplemented by rules and principles that are agreed upon in treaties. These two sources of law are 'positive international law' in the sense that the norms that they generate have been chosen or agreed upon by States in their dealings with each other. Positive international law co-exists with, and is conditioned by, numerous general principles of law that also find expression in most of the world's domestic legal systems.[28]

1.28   Customary systems of law are generally characterised by their stability and high levels of compliance. Customary international law is no exception. Its stability results from the usually gradual method of its development. Ordinarily, though not invariably, a new customary norm requires considerable time to emerge through changing State practice, as well as for its obligatory character to be widely recognised by States. It will not come into existence without such widespread practice and recognition, and its modification is dependent upon a similar process occurring. This feature of customary law helps explain why violations are rare. By its nature, a customary norm will be one that enjoys widespread support among States. Typically, such norms do not impose onerous burdens and States find compliance convenient.

---

27.   See **9.49–9.59**.
28.   See **1.152–1.174**.

1.29   It is possible that States which persistently object to an emerging customary law rule, and which maintain their objection after its emergence, will not be bound by the rule.[29]

1.30   Most norms of customary international law are 'universal' in character — that is, they apply to the entire society of States. Exceptionally, norms of customary international law may be 'local', 'regional' or 'special' in character, which means that they apply only as between two or several States.[30]

1.31   Treaties are agreements between States, or between States and intergovernmental organisations, which the parties intend to be legally binding under international law.[31] They are almost always in writing, but may be concluded orally. Indeed, even unilateral declarations may be legally binding in certain circumstances.[32] Treaties are analogous to domestic law contracts and typically bind only those States or intergovernmental organisations that are a party to them.

1.32   Sometimes, however, a treaty can be so widely adhered to and observed that its norms assume the character of customary international law. In that case, even States that are not party to the treaty can be bound by one or more of the norms that the treaty contains.[33] Treaties of this kind are analogous to domestic legislation in that they produce norms of general application binding even on States that have not signified their consent. Indeed, treaties that attract significant numbers of States parties are sometimes informally, if somewhat inaccurately, referred to as 'legislative treaties'.

1.33   A norm contained in an applicable treaty takes priority over a customary norm, so that in the event of an inconsistency the treaty norm prevails. However, there are some customary law norms of a peremptory character, usually known as *jus cogens* norms, from which treaties may not derogate and which will cause any inconsistent treaty to be void.[34]

1.34   The general principles of law provide a reservoir from which international lawyers may draw in order to fill gaps in the network of treaty and customary norms.[35] In this way, international law is able to function as a complete system in which lawyers are able to find a legal solution to every problem which may arise in international relations. The general principles are frequently employed to fill gaps in matters of international judicial administration so that, for example, the doctrine of *res judicata* and the entitlement to reparations for unlawful injury will be applied to international judicial or arbitral proceedings, even without express authorisation.

---

29.   See **1.119–1.123**.
30.   See **1.147–1.151**.
31.   See **2.16–2.18**.
32.   See **1.199–1.201**.
33.   See **1.138–1.146**.
34.   See **2.106–2.110**.
35.   See **1.152–1.174**.

1.35   The term 'evidence' in international law has a somewhat different meaning from that which it normally bears in domestic law. In domestic legal systems, lawyers usually speak of material tending to establish facts as 'evidence' of those facts. In international law, 'evidence' is usually material which tends to establish the content and scope of particular norms derived from custom, treaties or the general principles.

Thus, the text of a treaty is evidence of what a treaty requires and a historical incident may be evidence of a customary norm's requirement. By contrast, it would be most unusual for a lawyer in a common law jurisdiction to speak of a statute as constituting evidence of what the legislature requires.

Occasionally, international lawyers will also use the term 'evidence' in the fact-establishing sense familiar to domestic lawyers, so that attention to context is needed in order to determine the sense in which the term 'evidence' is employed.

1.36   There is no doctrine of *stare decisis* in international law. Consequently, international courts and tribunals are not bound by earlier judicial decisions. Nevertheless, decisions of international and domestic courts and tribunals are often highly persuasive evidence for determining the content and scope of international norms derived from treaties, custom and the general principles.[36] These norms may change over time so that, generally speaking, the older the judicial decision, the more cautious one should be in using it as evidence of a particular norm.

1.37   The writings of acknowledged experts in international law may also provide means for determining the existence, content and scope of international norms derived from custom, treaties and the general principles.[37] These experts (usually referred to by internationals lawyers as 'publicists') will normally be eminent academics, though the published works of diplomats or statesmen may also occasionally feature. Whereas judicial precedent plays a somewhat lesser role in international law as compared to common law systems, academic writings figure more prominently in resolving international legal problems than they do in most domestic legal systems. The evidential value of academic writings will vary according to the reputation of the author, the quality of the reasoning, and the degree of relevance and the age of the publication in question.

1.38   Resolutions of the UN General Assembly and other gatherings of State representatives in international organisations and conferences do not create norms per se. Nevertheless, if certain conditions are met, they may be evidence of an international customary norm.[38]

---

36.   See **1.175–1.180**.
37.   See **1.181–1.187**.
38.   See **1.188–1.198**.

1.39   There is also a category of material that is sometimes referred to as 'soft law',[39] which includes such materials as non-binding guidelines formulated by international organisations or hortatory resolutions of conferences or assemblies of States. The term is also sometimes used in reference to resolutions or guidelines adopted by certain international non-governmental organisations where they perform functions officially recognised by treaties. Not in itself legally binding, soft law may, nevertheless, provide guidance in relation to international law's future development, or in helping to provide more precise shape to norms couched in general terms.

Institutions

1.40   Ever since the emergence of the modern State system, the most frequently used method of conducting international relations has been bilateral contact between diplomats of States. The embassies that States maintain in the capital cities of other States have traditionally been the principal agents of official communication, discussion, cooperation, negotiation and agreement between the States concerned. Less frequently, these same functions are performed by diplomats on special missions to other States, especially where no permanent embassies are maintained between the States concerned.

The emergence of more efficient means of transport and communications has, over time, diminished somewhat the critical role played by diplomats, as national leaders are increasingly able to communicate swiftly with their diplomats abroad and directly with the leaders of other States. Nevertheless, the vast bulk of State-to-State relations, which are the principal focus of international law, are still conducted by diplomats.

States are the basic units of the modern international system.[40] All the Earth's land territory, except possibly Antarctica, is under the authority of a State. States have either evolved (in the case of older States) or been consciously established in order to advance the common good of particular human communities. According to J L Brierly (1881–1955), a State:[41]

> ... is an institution, that is to say, it is a system of relations which men establish among themselves as a means of securing certain objects, of which the most fundamental is a system of order within which their activities can be carried on.

This functional view of a contingent State contrasts with the more romantic conception of writers such as G W F Hegel (1770–1831), according to whom the State is the 'realised ethical ideal or ethical spirit',[42] and the inevitable fruit of an objective historical process whose existence and vitality transcend human choice and other human purposes.

---

39.   See **1.202–1.204**.
40.   See **4.2**.
41.   J L Brierly, *The Law of Nations,* ed Sir Humphrey Waldock, 6th ed, Oxford University Press, New York, 1963, 126.
42.   G W F Hegel, *Philosophy of Right (Grundlinien der Philosophie des Rechts),* trans S W Dyde, Batoche, Kitchener, Ontario, 2001, § 257, 194.

1.41   There are, at present, no institutions other than States that exercise comprehensive political authority. Nevertheless, States are not the only institutions in the international system.

States themselves have established hundreds of bilateral, regional or universal organisations for the purposes of advancing the common good of their peoples in areas where unilateral State action would be less effective than international coordination or cooperation.

These organisations may be classified from the perspective of their scope *ratione materiae* (that is, their subject-matter competence) or their scope *ratione personae* (that is, the range of States legally affected by their exercise of competence). Some organisations are very limited both *ratione materiae* and *ratione personae* — for example, the Channel Tunnel Intergovernmental Commission, which was established by the governments of France and the United Kingdom in the 1986 Treaty of Canterbury to supervise operation of the undersea tunnel connecting the two countries. Some are narrowly constructed *ratione materiae,* but are nearly universal *ratione personae* — for example, the Universal Postal Union, which has 188 member States. Yet others are broadly endowed *ratione materiae* but relatively limited *ratione personae* — for example, the 35-member Organization of American States, which has a sweeping set of purposes including promoting economic, social and cultural development; preserving peace and security; promoting democracy; and eradicating poverty.

1.42   The UN is, however, the one international organisation which is almost universal in its membership (192 States) and whose purposes extend to regulating most matters of international concern. It is the institution that, more than any other, has shaped international relations and international law since the end of the Second World War.

1.43   Article 1 of the UN Charter sets out the ambitious scope of the organisation's purposes: These purposes are:

1. To maintain international peace and security, and to that end: to take effective collective measures for the prevention and removal of threats to the peace, and for the suppression of acts of aggression or other breaches of the peace, and to bring about by peaceful means, and in conformity with the principles of justice and international law, adjustment or settlement of international disputes or situations which might lead to a breach of the peace;

2. To develop friendly relations among the nations based on respect for the principle of equal rights and self-determination of peoples, and to take other appropriate measures to strengthen universal peace;

3. To achieve international co-operation in solving international problems of an economic, social, cultural, or humanitarian character, and in promoting and encouraging respect for human rights and for fundamental freedom for all without distinction as to race, sex, language, or religion; and

4. To be a centre for harmonizing the actions in the attainment of these common ends.

1.44   Equally important as its extensive scope *ratione materiae* and its near-universal scope *ratione personae,* the UN Charter makes a claim to international constitutional supremacy. Article 103 provides as follows:

> In the event of a conflict between the obligations of the Members of the UN under the present Charter and their obligations under any other international agreement, their obligations under the present Charter shall prevail.

1.45   The UN consists of six 'principal organs': the General Assembly, the Security Council, the Economic and Social Council, the Trusteeship Council, the International Court of Justice and the Secretariat.[43]

1.46   The General Assembly is the only principal organ on which all UN members are represented. It also has the broadest functions of any UN organ. The General Assembly is able to 'consider', 'discuss' and 'make recommendations' in relation to any matter within the Charter's scope, including the maintenance of international peace and security.[44]

1.47   The Security Council consists of 15 members, five of which are permanent members (China, France, Russia, the United Kingdom and the United States)[45] with a power of veto on all but procedural matters.[46] The other 10 members are elected for two-year terms by the General Assembly.[47] The Charter confers on the Security Council 'primary responsibility for the maintenance of international peace and security'.[48]

Although the range of the Security Council's competence is narrower than that of the General Assembly, the Security Council's powers are not limited to consideration, discussion and recommendation. In certain circumstances, the Security Council may adopt resolutions that legally bind all States to which the resolutions are addressed.[49]

The composition of the Security Council, and especially the current system of permanent membership, is widely criticised as being outdated because it reflects the international order as it existed in 1945. There are currently a number of proposals to reform the Security Council, most of which involve expanding the number of permanent members. The main contenders for inclusion in an expanded permanent membership are Brazil, Egypt, Germany, India, Japan, Nigeria and South Africa. Prospects for reform along these lines are limited owing mainly to the reluctance of some existing permanent members to dilute their influence.

1.48   The Economic and Social Council (Ecosoc) has 54 members which are elected for three-year terms by the General Assembly.[50] Ecosoc is empowered to 'make or initiate studies and reports', 'make

---

43.   UN Charter, Art 7(1).
44.   Ibid, Arts 9–11.
45.   Ibid, Art 23(1).
46.   Ibid, Art 27.
47.   Ibid, Art 23(2).
48.   Ibid, Art 24(1).
49.   See **9.49–9.59**.
50.   UN Charter, Art 61(1).

recommendations', 'prepare draft conventions' and call international conferences. It may do these things with respect to international economic, social, cultural, educational, health and 'related matters', including human rights.[51] Of particular significance to international law, the work of Ecosoc has led to the adoption of the International Covenant on Economic, Social and Cultural Rights (ICESCR)[52] and the International Covenant on Civil and Political Rights (ICCPR).[53]

1.49   The Trusteeship Council was established under Chapter XII (Arts 75–85) of the Charter. Its task was to supervise the administration by some member States of certain non-independent territories, known as 'trust territories', which had been placed under their control pursuant to Art 77 of the Charter. The last remaining trust territory — Palau — attained independence in 1994. The Trusteeship Council thereafter suspended its own operations and amended its rules of procedure so that it is no longer required to meet at least once annually. Any future meetings of the Trusteeship Council can be held on the decision of its President, or at the request of a majority of members of the General Assembly or Security Council.

1.50   The International Court of Justice is the 'principal judicial organ of the United Nations'.[54] The ICJ's Statute is annexed to the UN Charter and every member of the UN is automatically a party to the Statute.[55] States that are not members of the UN may also become parties to the Statute.[56] The ICJ consists of 15 judges who are elected by the General Assembly for renewable terms of nine years.[57] It may issue judgments in disputes between States[58] or advisory opinions on legal questions at the request of organs or specialised agencies of the United Nations.[59] Although the ICJ exercises no jurisdiction in contentious cases unless the parties have consented,[60] and although it issues, on average, only two or three judgments annually, the prestige of the Court is such that its judgments and advisory opinions have been of tremendous importance in the development of international law.

1.51   The Secretariat comprises 'a Secretary-General and such staff as the Organisation may require'. The Secretary-General, who is the 'chief administrative officer of the Organisation', is appointed by the General Assembly upon the Security Council's recommendation.[61] The Secretariat has a staff of approximately 40,000 people located at its headquarters in New York; in its major establishments in Addis Ababa, Bangkok,

---

51.   Ibid, Art 62.
52.   UNTS, Vol 993, p 3.
53.   UNTS, Vol 999, p 171.
54.   UN Charter, Art 92.
55.   Ibid, Art 93(1).
56.   Ibid, Art 93(2).
57.   ICJ Statute, Arts 2 and 13.
58.   Ibid, Arts 34–36; UN Charter, Art 92.
59.   UN Charter, Art 96; ICJ Statute, Art 65.
60.   ICJ Statute, Art 36.
61.   UN Charter, Art 97.

Beirut, Geneva, Nairobi, Santiago and Vienna; and in its numerous offices around the world.

The General Assembly, Security Council, Ecosoc and Trusteeship Council are all empowered to confer further functions on the Secretary-General,[62] and the incumbent is sometimes called upon to mediate international disputes and perform ad hoc executive functions on behalf of the United Nations. The Secretary-General also has a potentially important, though little-used, power to 'bring to the attention of the Security Council any matter which ... may threaten the maintenance of international peace and security'.[63] The post of Secretary-General is a potentially very influential one, though much depends on the personality and diplomatic skills of the person appointed.

1.52   In addition to the principal organs, the UN system also embraces 'subsidiary organs'[64] and 'specialised agencies'.[65]

1.53   Subsidiary organs are bodies that are not established by the UN Charter itself, but are established by organs of the UN in accordance with the Charter. The General Assembly, Security Council, Ecosoc and Trusteeship Council have all established subsidiary organs from time to time.

Some of the best-known subsidiary organs have been established by Ecosoc under Art 68 of the Charter and include the United Nations Children's Fund (UNICEF), the World Food Programme (WFP), the office of the United Nations High Commissioner for Refugees (UNHCR), and the United Nations Development Programme (UNDP). The Human Rights Council, replacing the Commission on Human Rights, was established in 2006 as a subsidiary organ by the General Assembly.[66]

1.54   The most significant subsidiary organ from the perspective of international law is the International Law Commission (ILC), which was established pursuant to Art 13(1)(a) of the UN Charter authorising the General Assembly to 'initiate studies ... encouraging the progressive development of international law and its codification'. The General Assembly established the ILC in 1947.[67]

The Statute of the ILC provides that its objective is the 'promotion of the progressive development of international law and its codification', and that it 'shall concern itself primarily with public international law, but is not precluded from entering the field of private international law'.[68] The ILC consists of 34 persons who are elected for renewable five-year terms by the General Assembly, from a list of candidates nominated by member State governments.[69] The General Assembly is required to ensure

---

62.   Ibid, Art 98.
63.   Ibid, Art 99.
64.   Ibid, Art 7(2).
65.   Ibid, Art 57.
66.   General Assembly Resolution 60/251.
67.   General Assembly Resolution 174 (II).
68.   ILC Statute, Art 1.
69.   Ibid, Arts 3 and 10.

that 'in the Commission as a whole representation of the main forms of civilisation and of the principal legal systems of the world should be assured'.[70]

The ILC has had a significant impact on the development of international law. Among its numerous important achievements are the preparation of the Vienna Convention on the Law of Treaties,[71] the Vienna Convention on Diplomatic Relations,[72] the Vienna Convention on Consular Relations,[73] the Rome Statute of the International Criminal Court,[74] a number of conventions on the Law of the Sea,[75] and the Draft Articles on State Responsibility for Internationally Wrongful Acts.[76]

1.55 The specialised agencies are neither principal organs nor subsidiary organs of the United Nations. They are, instead, autonomous international organisations affiliated to the UN. The Charter requires that the:[77]

> ... various specialised agencies, established by international agreement and having wide international responsibilities ... in economic, social, cultural, educational, health, and related fields, shall be brought into relationship with the United Nations.

Ecosoc is given the responsibility of entering into agreements with the specialised agencies 'defining the terms on which the agency concerned shall be brought into relationship with the United Nations'.[78] These agreements are subject to approval by the General Assembly. Among the most significant specialised agencies are the International Labour Organisation (ILO), the International Civil Aviation Organisation (ICAO), the International Monetary Fund (IMF), the World Bank, the World Health Organisation (WHO), the Food and Agriculture Organisation (FAO), and the United Nations Educational, Scientific and Cultural Organisation (UNESCO).

Legal character of international law

1.56 John Austin (1790–1859) was the University of London's first professor of Jurisprudence and the Law of Nations. He and his friend Jeremy Bentham (1748–1832) are widely regarded as the founders of a school of jurisprudence known as 'legal positivism', although they were building on foundations laid earlier by writers such as Niccolò Machiavelli (1469–1527), Jean Bodin (c 1520–1596) and Thomas Hobbes (1588–1679). Bentham was, indeed, the first writer to use the term

---

70. Ibid, Art 8.
71. UNTS, Vol 1155, p 331.
72. UNTS, Vol 500, p 95.
73. UNTS, Vol 596, p 261.
74. UNTS, Vol 2187, p 3.
75. See, generally, **chapter 12**.
76. *Yearbook of the International Law Commission*, 2001, Vol II, Pt 2.
77. UN Charter, Art 57.
78. Ibid, Art 63.

'international law'.[79] Austin's *The Province of Jurisprudence Determined*, containing his lectures on jurisprudence, inspired an eventual revolution in legal thought and remains one of the most influential law books ever published.[80] By the end of the 19th century, Austin's theories had assumed the status of jurisprudential orthodoxy, and his ideas continue to inform jurisprudential debates into the 21st century.

1.57   Before Bentham and Austin, it was generally accepted that the law comprised any rule or principle that was widely recognised by persons as binding upon them by virtue of their membership of a political community, and provided those rules and principles were enforceable. Consequently, the law could embrace royal decrees, legislative statutes, judicial decisions, customary rules or general legal principles if there was widespread acceptance of their binding authority by members of the political community.

The question of a rule's widespread acceptance, particularly in the case of customary norms, was also usually linked to a consideration of the putative legal rule's concordance with elementary or general legal principles, such as the requirement that no man be a judge in his own cause. Enforcement might be a responsibility of the political authority, but could also be effected by acts of self-help in any modes which were permitted by the political authority and which also conformed to general legal principles such as proportionality or reasonableness.

1.58   The jurisprudential revolution wrought by Austin and Bentham largely overturned these prevailing conceptions. Proceeding under the influence of the 19th century's industrial and scientific revolutions, and desiring to transform jurisprudence into a 'real' science resembling the burgeoning and increasingly prestigious physical sciences, Austin sought to extract from jurisprudence all elements that required evaluation of a norm's justice or rightness. This meant the exclusion of questions of an essentially 'conjectural' character — that is, those pertaining principally to the justice of a putative legal rule. Only those elements susceptible to descriptive analysis, as distinct from ethical evaluation, were to remain part of jurisprudence. A way had to be found to place jurisprudence on this newly scientific basis, and the key to the puzzle was sovereign will. A legislator's act of will was thought to be an object that can be observed and analysed without reference to questions of morality, ethics or metaphysics.

1.59   According to Austin, the 'matter of jurisprudence is positive law: law, simply and strictly so called: or law set by political superiors to political inferiors'. Positive law is 'contradistinguished to *natural law* or to the law of *nature*' and is 'law existing by *position*' — that is, law 'set by men to men'. Only sovereigns may set positive laws. A sovereign is a person, or a body of persons, to whom a political community is in the

---

79.   Jeremy Bentham, *Introduction to the Principles of Morals and Legislation*, T Payne & Son, London, 1789.
80.   John Austin, *The Province of Jurisprudence Determined*, J Murray, London, 1832.

habit of obedience or submission, and who is not in a habit of obedience or submission to any determinate human superior. The sovereign, in setting laws, must also have 'the power of affecting others with evil or pain, and of forcing them, through fear of that evil, to fashion their conduct' to the requirements of the sovereign's laws.[81]

1.60   In Austin's view, 'laws improperly so called' include '*laws set or imposed by general opinion*: that is to say, by the general opinion of any class or any society of persons'. In this connection, Austin remarks:

> A few species of the laws which are set by general opinion have gotten appropriate names. ... There are laws which regard the conduct of independent political societies in their various relations to one another: Or, rather, there are laws which regard the conduct of sovereigns or supreme governments in their various relations to one another. And laws or rules of this species, which are imposed upon nations or sovereigns by opinions current amongst nations, are usually styled *the law of nations or international law*.

Therefore, according to Austin, international law is not law properly so called, and does not belong to the science of jurisprudence. Into the same category, he argued, fall 'the rules of honour' and 'the law set by fashion'.

Furthermore, in Austin's view, international law fails the test of law strictly so called because it does not emanate from a sovereign to an independent political society.[82]

Austin posed a critical theoretical challenge to the legal ordering of international relations and inspired a continuing debate on the extent to which international law truly possesses a legal character.

1.61   Austin's challenge remained, however, confined mostly to the realm of theory. Nothing he or his followers have written has had much impact on the actual behaviour of States and other actors on the international plane.

Then, as now, States continued to regard international law as real law. They continued to abide by international law's requirements in the vast majority of cases. Their diplomatic communications continued to bristle with claims and counter-claims of legal right, for which purpose they usually maintained a corps of lawyers to provide legal advice on international relations. They continued to sign treaties by which they regarded themselves and other States as legally bound. International disputes continued increasingly to be submitted to judicial or arbitral tribunals for judgment or award made according to international legal norms. All this remained so, notwithstanding the absence of an international sovereign, the absence of an independent political community subject to such a sovereign, the absence of any commands set by the former to the latter, and (usually) the absence of a factual power of coercion in case of a violation of the law.

---

81.   Ibid, Lectures I and V (emphasis in original).
82.   Ibid, Lecture V (emphasis in original).

Indeed, the universal profession by States of fidelity to the compulsory requirements of international law is probably the most important obstacle to the Austinian challenge. It requires defenders of Austin's position to assert that this impressive unanimity across space and time is either delusional or rhetorically cynical.

1.62   Austin conceded that although international law did not belong to the science of jurisprudence, it might belong to a science of 'positive morality', being 'a science closely analogous to jurisprudence'.[83] This is a popular and recurring theme among sceptics of international law's legal character. It is frequently asserted — especially by adherents of the 'realist' school of international relations, which emphasises the function of national interest and power in international affairs — that international law is really just a code of international ethics which States observe when it is convenient or advantageous to do so.

1.63   As noted above, however, States themselves do not treat breaches of international law as though they were simply breaches of an ethical code. Rather, disputes about international law are invariably couched in the familiar terms of legal argument with liberal recourse to authorities, including judicial and arbitral precedent. It is also noteworthy that:[84]

> ... when a breach of international law is alleged by one party to a controversy, the act impugned is practically never defended by claiming a right of private judgment, which would be the natural defence if the issue concerned the morality of the act, but always by attempting to prove that no rule has been violated.

1.64   There are, moreover, many disputes that raise ethical or moral issues precisely because there is an applicable legal norm. This type of situation arises particularly where the legal norm is of a technical character, prescribing procedures, timeframes, distances, physical quantities, and so on. For instance, absent a legal norm on the subject, there is no determinative moral or ethical reason why a State's territorial sea should be three or 12 nautical miles wide, or even that there should be a territorial sea at all. However, once a legal norm emerges permitting States to set the width of their territorial seas at 12 nautical miles,[85] then a moral obligation to observe the requirements of that rule arises. This is because the rule is a reasonable determination duly established by widely accepted procedures for the peaceful and orderly conduct of international relations.

1.65   Furthermore, as Brierly points out, it is inconvenient in practical terms to deny international law's legal character on the basis that it is simply international morality:[86]

---

83.   Ibid.
84.   J L Brierly, *The Law of Nations,* ed Sir Humphrey Waldock, 6th ed, Oxford University Press, New York, 1963, 69–70.
85.   Convention on the Law of the Sea, Art 3, UNTS, Vol 1833, p 3; see **12.41**.
86.   J L Brierly, *The Law of Nations,* ed Sir Humphrey Waldock, 6th ed, Oxford University Press, New York, 1963, 69.

It is inconvenient because if international law is nothing but international morality, it is certainly not the whole of international morality, and it is difficult to see how we are to distinguish it from those other admittedly moral standards which we apply in formulating judgments on the conduct of states. Ordinary usage certainly uses two tests in judging the 'rightness' of a state's act, a moral test and one which is somehow felt to be independent of morality. Every state habitually commits acts of selfishness which are often gravely injurious to other states, and yet are not contrary to international law; but we do not on that account necessarily judge them to have been 'right'.

Accordingly, there are some breaches of ethical behaviour on the international plane that are regarded as being not 'simply' or 'merely' immoral or unethical. They involve something more: something which transforms or upgrades the ethical delinquency into a legal one.

1.66   The element that transforms a simple ethical or moral obligation into a fully legal one is the availability of enforcement. According to Lassa Oppenheim (1858–1919), law may be defined as 'a body of rules for human conduct within a community which by common consent of this community shall be enforced by external power' — that is, 'external to the person against whom they are enforced'.[87] Similarly, Hans Kelsen (1881–1973) observed that:[88]

> … the law is that specific social technique which consists in the attempt to bring about the desired social conduct of men through the threat of a measure of coercion which is to be taken in case of … legally wrong conduct.

1.67   The argument that international law is merely a code of international ethics is usually advanced by reference to two linked propositions. First, it is asserted that international law notoriously fails to constrain the behaviour of States, especially where important national interests are at stake. Second, there is said to be no effective and centralised enforcement mechanism of such a kind as to provide the required element of compulsion.

1.68   The first of these propositions is the easier to deal with. It is simply incorrect to claim that international law is ineffective in curtailing lawless behaviour by States. International law constantly exerts a decisive influence on relations between States. Every day, countless dealings between States occur which are fully in accordance with international law. It should not be forgotten that international law regulates numerous technical matters, such as international telecommunications and air transport, without which everyday life would be much more difficult and which States have very little incentive to disregard. Even with more overtly political and sensitive issues arising from international peace and national security, international law almost always furnishes States with conclusive reasons not to resort to armed force.

---

87.   Sir Robert Jennings and Sir Arthur Watts (eds), *Oppenheim's International Law*, 9th ed, Longman, New York, 1992, § 3, 9.
88.   Hans Kelsen, *Principles of International Law*, Rinehart, New York, 1952, 5.

When friction arises between States, it is usually because international law does not (yet) prescribe a relevant rule, or because the States concerned genuinely disagree over what the relevant rules require. This is also frequently true in the case of friction among individuals operating under the shadow of domestic law. In reality, flagrant violations are much less common in international law than in domestic law.

Egregiously unlawful international acts, such as Iraq's invasion of Kuwait in 1990, are sensational partly because they are so rare. These highly unusual events are more likely to occur where a State calculates that vital interests are at stake and there is a good likelihood of 'getting away with it' (that is, keeping whatever gains are planned, and avoiding unacceptably harsh consequences). The same is true of those planning a deliberate violation of domestic law. However, the delinquent State will invariably attempt to justify its conduct in terms consonant with international law, thereby signifying a realistic recognition of international law's effective authority in world affairs. Such attempts at justification also signify an understanding that naked violations of international law are likely to have serious repercussions for the delinquent State.

1.69   This brings us to the second proposition, that international law lacks an effective and centralised enforcement mechanism of such a kind as to provide the required element of compulsion. Enforcement is not the same thing as adjudication. Enforcement is the process by which the requirements of a legal right or entitlement are effected against the wishes of the party violating the right or denying the entitlement. In modern domestic legal orders, enforcement is usually the function of the police or other civilian authorities with certain compulsory powers. Sometimes, military forces may have a role in domestic law enforcement. Adjudication, by contrast, is a process by which the existence of a legal right or entitlement is authoritatively established, and it is usually performed by courts, tribunals, commissions and similar bodies.

1.70   The idea that the absence of a centralised enforcement apparatus deprives international law of its legal character is really just another way of formulating Austin's requirement for a political sovereign. Enforcement mechanisms in international law do exist, though it is true that very few of them are centralised in international institutions.

Indeed, the enforcement of international law remains overwhelmingly decentralised in character and much more dependent upon self-help than is the case with mature domestic legal orders.

This feature of the international legal system is, however, symptomatic of primitive legal systems generally and was common in domestic legal orders prior to the emergence of the modern European State system. Absent the availability of centralised enforcement machinery, these legal systems routinely left enforcement to those who had been injured by unlawful conduct. The distinctive feature of these acts of self-help was that they would have been legally prohibited but for the delict, breach of agreement, crime or other legal wrong in response to which they were performed. They also typically had to conform to general legal principles such as proportionality or reasonableness.[89]

1.71   At least until the 1928 General Treaty for the Renunciation of War as an Instrument of National Policy (Kellogg–Briand Treaty, or Pact of Paris),[90] international law regarded resort to war and retaliation (involving both armed and unarmed reprisals) as legitimate remedies available to States aggrieved by the violation of their international rights by another party. As mentioned above, the League of Nations Covenant expressly preserved war as a remedy of last resort in relations among States, though League members were under a primary duty to seek settlement by peaceful means.[91] The UN Charter has made resort to armed force unlawful except in self-defence and, possibly, for the purposes of humanitarian intervention.[92] Instead, States are now under an obligation to settle their disputes exclusively by peaceful means — that is, without resort to armed force.[93] To this extent, and absent effective centralised enforcement mechanisms, international law is less enforceable now than at any other time in its history, thereby diminishing somewhat its legal character.

1.72   Nevertheless, States may still resort to countermeasures — that is, acts of self-help not involving armed force — in enforcing their rights under international law.[94]

1.73   Sometimes, the taking of countermeasures may or must be authorised by international institutions — for example, the Dispute Settlement Body of the World Trade Organization (WTO). Nevertheless, the execution of countermeasures is always by States. Therefore, even where centralised international organs are involved, countermeasures remain a decentralised mode of enforcement. The Security Council's powers under Chapter VII of the UN Charter to authorise or require the use of force and other sanctions do not really constitute an exception to this general scheme.[95] The Chapter VII powers do not exist for the enforcement of international law generally, but only to 'maintain or restore international peace and security',[96] even where no breach of international law has actually occurred. Furthermore, execution of the Security Council's decisions currently remains the responsibility of States.

1.74   It is obvious that the enforcement mechanisms available at international law are weak compared to most domestic legal orders. Yet, this

---

89.   See **1.57**.
90.   See **1.15** and **9.6**.
91.   See **1.14** and **9.5**.
92.   See **chapter 9**.
93.   See **chapter 8**.
94.   See **5.66**.
95.   See **8.3–8.6** and **9.7–9.18**.
96.   UN Charter, Art 39.

weakness is a difference of degree and not of kind. Many domestic legal orders have weak or inefficient enforcement mechanisms, and most also permit acts of self-help in numerous circumstances (for example, the common law rules on rescission of contracts).

1.75   Moreover, it is easy to overestimate the significance of enforcement mechanisms in ensuring compliance with the law. If disrespect for the law were generalised in any system, then not even a vast and powerful police force could ensure widespread compliance without resorting to terror (and perhaps not even then). A State's police apparatus can hope to be effective only where the law is already generally respected and observed, so that enforcement is reserved for those at the margins who flout its requirements. The impressively high rate of compliance with international law reflects the extent of its political legitimacy and moral credibility in regulating relations among States.

1.76   Most States have populations numbering in the millions, and people living in such societies can hope to establish direct relations with only a very small fraction of their fellow citizens. The nature of human affairs is such that unlawful activities can be conducted clandestinely, and the interest and capacity of other individuals to detect and react to such behaviour is severely limited. In response, modern States have established specialist and centralised law enforcement agencies.

By contrast, the society of States is currently numbered at fewer than 200 and it is quite possible for States to maintain relationships with all other States, even in the absence of permanent embassies. With the notable exception of espionage, their conduct inter se is almost always either a matter of public record or easily discoverable. States are also equipped with political leaders and bureaucracies which specialise in monitoring international affairs and conducting relations with other States.

Many of the circumstances which call for the establishment of centralised law enforcement agencies by vast human communities are, therefore, absent in the society of States.

Each State has the opportunity to observe nearly all the actions of other States, and to raise concerns about unlawful conduct with both the delinquent State and any other State which may also be concerned about the delinquency. In this sense, the society of States more closely resembles a small self-governing village than a vast modern nation.

1.77   Viewed in this way, the international legal system, with its focus on custom, the keeping of promises (through treaties), general principles of justice, and enforcement by self-help, is reasonably well adapted to the society that it serves. It is a basic legal system serving a decentralised but interdependent society.

Most small self-governing human communities are regulated in just this way. As these communities become more populous and multifaceted, their political authority becomes more hierarchical. As a result, authority is exercised increasingly by persons or institutions (councils of elders, chiefs, kings, parliaments, and so on) that can more effectively coordinate affairs too dynamic to be handled solely by custom and promise making.

Generally speaking, the smaller the community in question, the less powerful and centralised will be the political institutions which arise to serve its interests. Furthermore, in the absence of coercion, centralised institutions can arise and continue only where there is a true community — that is, a shared culture and standards of conduct (sometimes called 'values').

The political, social and economic heterogeneity of States ensures that there is no worldwide 'international community'. Decentralised arrangements aimed at facilitating cooperation, coordination and peace are more likely to emerge and be viable in a society, such as the international society of States, which lacks the conditions of a true community.

1.78   The emergence of an increasing number of international institutions with responsibilities covering a widening range of topics is consistent with this pattern. Although the total number of States remains relatively small, there is now almost four times the number that existed when the UN was established.

Yet almost all these international institutions remain decentralised in the sense that, rather than exercising political authority directly, they provide forums in which States may conveniently reach agreement on joint or coordinated responses to matters of common concern. Some also provide formal machinery for the adjudication of disputes that arise in connection with agreements already made. The essentially consensual nature of international law is not, therefore, seriously challenged by the plethora of international organisations that now exist.

Necessity of sources

1.79   Whenever human beings live together in social contact, means must be found to coordinate their activities in pursuit of various human goods. There must be arrangements within which joint or cooperative activities can be efficiently pursued, with confidence, to their conclusion. There must also be arrangements which allow individuals or groups to pursue their own projects in a way which protects the just interests of those engaged in other, competing or unrelated, activities. These arrangements, taken together, constitute the common good of any society. The more effectively human activities are coordinated so as to produce a stable, just and harmonious social order, the better served is the common good of the society.

A failure to find the necessary means of coordinating the activities of human beings results in disorder or, beyond a certain level, chaos. In either case, there will be lost opportunities for individuals or groups to pursue their chosen goals with an efficient disposition of means to ends. Chaos also implies that the resulting conflicts can be resolved only by force. Both these consequences involve a significant or radical diminution of the common good for the society affected.

1.80   These problems of social coordination can be resolved in only two ways. The simplest approach is to leave the problem of coordination to unanimous agreement among those participating in, or standing to be affected by, an activity. The nature of human affairs, however, is such that unanimity is unlikely to be reached or long sustained where the activity has any complexity or longevity, or where the agreement of numerous persons is required.

1.81   The alternative to unanimity is authority. Political authority has the task, and the duty, to formulate solutions to problems of social coordination. Authority is justified by its ability to protect and advance the common good of the society it serves, provided it is established and exercised in accordance with procedures broadly accepted as valid within that society.

Primary among the manifestations of political authority are public institutions, including legal institutions. At least some legal institutions are necessary if the common good of a political society is to be well served. There are numerous problems of social coordination, especially involving the resolution of disputes arising out of past courses of conduct, that can be resolved non-arbitrarily only by resort to techniques which are unique to such institutions.

Furthermore, activities that can be efficiently pursued (that is, with an optimum application of resources to ends) only within a reasonably stable and predictable social framework are ideally suited to coordination by techniques characteristic of legal institutions. The law of contracts and the law of treaties, for instance, provide authoritative reasons to honour an undertaking covered by that law even if the giver of the undertaking is no longer inclined to do so.

1.82   When we hear the phrase 'legal institutions', we are, perhaps, inclined to think initially of law courts, police forces and other public organisations possessing functions specifically connected with the interpretation and enforcement of legal norms. Yet the legal norms themselves — that is, the rules, principles and doctrines of law — are the primary and most essential of all legal institutions.

These legal norms are human cultural objects which are created for the purpose of furnishing universally (or almost universally) accepted techniques for achieving authoritative solutions to disputes concerning problems of social coordination where unanimous agreement would otherwise be impracticable, and for providing sanctions in the event of their violation.

These techniques are especially valuable and necessary where, as is usual, more than one solution to a dispute or problem of social coordination is reasonably consistent with the requirements of the common good, but where a choice needs to be made because the available solutions are incompatible with each other. For instance, if there is to be a territorial sea, is it to be three miles or 12 miles wide? The institution of the positive law, either alone or in conjunction with certain general legal principles that are not entirely positive in character,[97] is, in theory, always capable of furnishing a single technically correct answer where unaided moral reasoning would be indecisive as among two or more incompatible options.

1.83   The posited cultural institution which is 'the law' typically consists of numerous elements: permitted and prohibited modes of reasoning and argument; a vocabulary to which has been assigned specific technical meanings; rules requiring, permitting, facilitating and prohibiting conduct; and relatively flexible principles which complement and temper the rules. At higher levels of development, there may also be processes and routines providing a practical framework in support of the other elements (specific forms of pleading, contract, trial, testamentary disposition, arbitration, deposition, and so on), along with public organisations such as courts and police forces.

1.84   Among the most essential elements, however, are secondary rules identifying and validating the applicable primary rules and principles. H L A Hart (1907–1992) called the primary norms 'rules of obligation'.[98] According to Hart, it is the existence of various categories of secondary rules that transforms a mere set of laws into a true legal system. Among the various types of secondary rules is a 'rule of recognition' which 'will specify some feature or features possession of which by a suggested rule is taken as a conclusive affirmative indication that it is a rule of the group to be supported by the social pressure it exerts'.[99]

Hart argued that for a set of laws to be a true legal system, there must be a single overarching rule of recognition which validates all the primary rules of obligation and which ranks them in a normative hierarchy in the event of a conflict between them (for example, statutes take precedence over common law rules).

Hart also taught that although international law is a set of real laws, it is not a legal system — partly because it apparently lacks an overarching rule of recognition which both provides an ultimate validation of all laws in the set and authoritatively creates a definite hierarchy among them. Nevertheless, in Hart's own view, different classes of primary rules (for example, enactments, customs, and so on) are capable of being validated by reference to different criteria. Different rules of recognition would, therefore, seem capable of existing even in the absence of a single overarching rule of recognition. Consequently, rather than asserting that there is no system of international law because it fails to replicate all the structures of most national legal systems, it is perhaps more accurate to say that international law is a less developed or less tightly structured system than most national legal systems.

---

97.   See **1.152–1.174**.
98.   H L A Hart, *The Concept of Law,* Clarendon Press, Oxford, 1961.
99.   Ibid, 92.

1.85   These secondary rules of recognition must exist even in the most primitive legal systems, if only to distinguish rules of law from non-legal standards of conduct (such as etiquette, tradition or fashion) which do not attract publicly recognised sanctions in the event of a breach. It is these rules of recognition that are the 'sources' of law possessed by every legal system, even where the system consists entirely of customary norms. If law provides reasons for action and decision, then the sources of law are the sources of reasoning in any legal system.

The sources of law are the cornerstone of every system of positive law, though their structure can take different forms across systems. Consequently, in some legal systems, judicial decisions, customs or royal decrees are sources of law, while in others they are not. What, then, are the sources of reasoning in international law?

Range of sources

1.86   Article 38(1) of the Statute of the International Court of Justice provides as follows:

> The Court, whose function is to decide in accordance with international law such disputes as are submitted to it, shall apply:
>
> a.   international conventions, whether general or particular, establishing rules recognised by the contesting states;
>
> b.   international custom, as evidence of a general practice accepted as law;
>
> c.   the general principles of law recognised by civilised nations;
>
> d.   subject to the provisions of Article 59, judicial decisions and the teachings of the most highly qualified publicists of the various nations, as subsidiary means for the determination of the rules of law.

1.87   Although Art 38(1) was adopted for the relatively limited purpose of specifying the sources of law which the ICJ is to use in deciding cases before it, the provision is widely regarded as identifying the sources of international law generally.

1.88   Many publicists draw a distinction between 'formal sources of law' and 'material sources of law'. A material source of law is that which specifies the content of a legal obligation or entitlement in a particular case, whereas a formal source of law is that which endows the obligation or entitlement with a legally binding character. A 'material source of law' is, therefore, perhaps better understood as a 'source of obligation' (which obligation might or might not be legally binding, depending on whether it is also encompassed by a formal source of law).

Thus, a treaty or contract, considered in itself as a litany of promises and undertakings, is a source of obligation; it specifies merely the content of certain obligations which the parties have freely assumed towards each other. Yet it is perfectly possible for States and individuals to undertake obligations that are not legally binding (for example, 'understandings' or social promises). The formal source of law for a treaty or contract is the general principle of law known as *pacta sunt servanda* (agreements are to be complied with), which general principle is enlivened when all the elements specified by the positive law for the creation of an enforceable treaty or contract are in existence.

Similarly, a social practice does not per se create a customary law obligation or right. Such a practice will tell us about the way States or people habitually behave on certain occasions — and even, perhaps, that there is a social expectation of conformity to that behaviour. It tells us what States or people habitually do and, perhaps, that they are in some sense obliged to do it. The widespread practice is, in itself, at most a source of obligation. That obligation assumes a legal character only when the positive law requirements relating to the consistency of the practice and the way in which the community regards it ('a general practice accepted as law') are in existence.

Only after an agreement or a social practice falls within the scope of a formal source of law is it really appropriate to speak of that agreement or practice as a 'material source of law' instead of a mere 'source of obligation'.

1.89   Only Art 38(1)(a)–(c) of the ICJ Statute specifies formal sources of international law. Consequently, only conventions (that is, treaties, understood as including all the positive law elements which enliven *pacta sunt servanda*), custom (understood as 'a general practice accepted as law'), and the general principles of law are formal sources of law.

1.90   The materials referred to in Art 38(1)(d) are, as the text itself makes plain, 'subsidiary means for the determination of the rules of law'. Judicial decisions and the teachings of publicists are not themselves sources of law. Rather, they can be used to help prove the existence and content of legal norms sourced in treaties, custom or the general principles. They are among the objects that constitute evidence of the legal status and content of putative norms of international law.

That judicial decisions do not create binding precedent in international law is underlined by the reference to Art 59 in 38(1)(d) of the ICJ Statute. Article 59 provides that the 'decision of the Court has no binding force except between the parties and in respect of the particular case'.

1.91   There is no formal hierarchy among the three sources of law identified in paras (a)–(c). Article 38(1) merely sets out a rational methodology for technical legal reasoning, proceeding from the specific to the general. In determining the rules applicable to a particular problem, it is legally sound first to look for any obligations established between the parties as a result of their own agreement — that is, treaties. Failing any such obligations, or failing their sufficiency in resolving the problem, it is then necessary to examine any applicable customary law. Customary law will also provide rules by which the treaties may be interpreted and applied. Failing a sufficient solution being found in customary law, the general principles of law should then be looked at, in order to avoid a *non liquet* (that is, an inability to render judgment because of lacunae in the law) and for principles underpinning and modulating our understanding of treaties and custom — for example, and most significantly, *pacta sunt servanda*.

It is also possible for a treaty to generate customary law binding on States which are not parties to the treaty,[100] for State practice to affect the interpretation of treaties,[101] and for customary norms of a peremptory character *(jus cogens)* to render inconsistent treaties void.[102]

Treaties

1.92   A treaty is a legally binding arrangement between two or more States or public international organisations by which they agree to regulate their conduct in accordance with its terms. It is, in other words, a contractual engagement between States or organisations established by States.

1.93   Article 38(1)(a) of the ICJ Statute speaks of 'international conventions, whether general or particular, establishing rules expressly recognised by the contesting states'.

'Convention' is a term sometimes used to mean a treaty. Other terms include 'covenant', 'pact', 'charter', 'Act', 'declaration', 'agreement', 'concordat' and 'protocol'. The term 'conventional law' is frequently used to refer to rights, obligations and processes prescribed by a treaty.

1.94   Treaties are often classified as either 'bilateral' or 'multilateral'. A bilateral treaty is concluded between two States or public international organisations, whereas a multilateral treaty is concluded among more than two States or public international organisations.

1.95   Furthermore, as the language of Art 38(1)(a) of the ICJ Statute indicates, treaties may be either 'general' or 'particular'. When a multilateral treaty is widely adhered to and represents the views of the States parties as to universal substantive legal principles, it may be regarded as possessing a general character. More commonly, such treaties are said to be 'legislative' or 'law-making' *(traités-lois)*. This means that they lay down standards of conduct that are common to all States parties, subject only to specific reservations.

Multilateral treaties are also sometimes described as 'legislative' or 'law making' when they create rules binding on all States, whether or not they are parties to the treaty. While it is entirely possible for States to be bound by rules that have their origins in multilateral treaties to which they are not parties, it would be a mistake to regard such a treaty as being a legislative Act in the same way as a legislative Act in a domestic legal order. It is possible for a multilateral treaty to reflect an existing

---

100. See **1.138–1.146**.
101. See **2.79**.
102. See **2.106–2.110**.

customary norm, to crystallise an emerging customary norm, or to generate a new customary norm where certain conditions are met.[103]

Whatever the precise relationship between the multilateral treaty and the parallel customary norm which it reflects, crystallises or generates, States which are not party to the treaty are bound by the customary norm and not by the treaty. The point is not entirely moot, as the treaty may possess a procedural, institutional or enforcement dimension that will be inapplicable to the parallel customary norm.

1.96 A 'particular' treaty is one in which States undertake obligations in relation to specific matters around which wide or universal agreement would be unattainable, or in relation to which States would not be willing to commit on a multilateral basis. Such treaties are usually bilateral, and most closely resemble a domestic law contract *(traités-contrat)*.

1.97 Since the end of the Second World War, treaties have assumed an increasingly important place in international law. Unlike custom, the evolution of which usually takes long periods of time and the precise requirements of which can often be unclear, treaties are capable of furnishing States with instant and clearly defined rights and obligations. Treaties are therefore an essential tool for keeping international law abreast of the requirements of an increasingly interdependent world society.

Treaties are, moreover, the real workhorses of international law because they are used for an array of indispensable tasks, ranging from the creation of commercial commitments, the regulation of technical matters, and the establishment of universal norms of conduct, through to founding international organisations.

1.98 The law of treaties is largely customary in character and deals with matters such as treaty-making capacity, formation, interpretation, impact on third parties, reservations, invalidity, breach and termination. The customary law of treaties has been extensively codified and developed by the Vienna Convention on the Law of Treaties (VCLT).[104]

Custom

Nature of customary law

1.99 Custom is the most basic source of positive law in any human community. It precedes all other sources of positive law or obligation — contracts, judicial decisions, decrees, legislation, constitutions, and so on. Even if a human community completely lacks any other formal sources of positive law or obligation, and if it is regulated by positive

---

103. See **1.138–1.146**.
104. See **chapter 2**.

law at all, it will possess customary law. Customary law is, indeed, the principal form taken by the positive law in primitive legal systems.

1.100   A practice will give rise to a customary legal norm when certain criteria, recognised in a community as transforming the practice into a legal obligation, are met. The precise contours of these criteria will vary from one community to another, but they will specify the extent to which the practice must be observed. A practice will not correspond to a customary legal norm unless it is widespread, although how widespread any particular practice must be may vary between communities. Once a practice is sufficiently widespread, the community will then need to regard it as engaging liability to a sanction in the event of non-observance. If the means for public enforcement is absent, the sanction need only be executable as an act of self-help. It must, however, be recognised by the community as a justified response to the non-observance.

Elements of custom

1.101   Although customary law has played a prominent role in relations between different political communities since antiquity, it was not until the 20th century that international law developed a definite doctrine sharply defining the requirements for a practice to qualify as a customary legal norm.

1.102   The first important step in this direction was the adoption in 1920 of the text of Art 38 of the Statute of the Permanent Court of International Justice. In 1945, this provision was readopted almost verbatim as the text of Art 38 of the ICJ Statute. Article 38 specified international custom as one of the sources of international law, and described it as 'evidence of a general practice accepted as law'.

It is on the basis of Art 38 that the PCIJ and the ICJ have elaborated the doctrine that customary international law consists of two distinct elements:

(i)   general practice (or *usus*); and

(ii)   *opinio juris sive necessitatis* (or *opinio juris et necessitatis*), usually referred to simply as *opinio juris* and meaning a belief that the practice is required as a matter of legal right or obligation.

State practice

1.103   International law has evolved in such a way as to treat States as the basic units of the system.[105] States are simultaneously the main subjects of international law and the entities whose choices and conduct generate positive international law. The choices and conduct of States are their 'practice', and the general practice of States is an essential element in the emergence, evolution, decline and disappearance of norms of customary international law.

---

105. See **4.2**.

1.104 A State is a legal person. As with all legal persons, its will is necessarily expressed through the choices and conduct of natural persons whose activities are legally attributable to it. In the case of States, this means their governments — broadly defined to include their executive, legislative and judicial branches and any other person, organ or institution exercising official public authority or exercising public functions at a national, regional or local level.

The choices and conduct of persons who are not officials of a State, or who are not acting on the instructions or under the control of State officials, cannot be regarded as evidence of State practice. Consequently, the choices and conduct of private natural persons, entities incorporated under domestic law for commercial or charitable purposes, and non-governmental organisations (NGOs) do not ordinarily furnish practice which is relevant to determining the existence or scope of a putative norm of customary international law.[106] According to Judge McNair of the ICJ in the *Anglo-Norwegian Fisheries* case:[107]

> ... the independent activity of private individuals is of little value unless it can be shown that they have acted in pursuance of a licence or some other authority received from their Government or that in some other way their Governments have asserted jurisdiction through them.

Evidence of State practice

1.105 Subject to this limitation, however, State practice may be evidenced by reference to a wide array of materials. Essentially, anything that demonstrates the choices and conduct of persons acting in their capacities as State officials, or under the instructions or control of State officials, will provide evidence of State practice. Examples include:

- speeches by State officials and diplomats;
- transcripts of parliamentary proceedings;
- domestic legislation;
- decisions of domestic courts and tribunals;
- diplomatic correspondence;
- historical records;
- press releases and communiqués;
- policy statements;
- reports of military and naval activities;
- comments by governments on the work of international bodies (for example, the ILC);
- voting records in international forums (for example, the UN General Assembly);
- official manuals issued to diplomats and armed forces; and
- treaties.

---

106. Semble Draft Articles on State Responsibility for Internationally Wrongful Acts, Arts 4–11. See **5.16–5.44**.
107. *Anglo-Norwegian Fisheries* case *(United Kingdom v Norway)* ICJ Rep (1951) 116, 184. See **1.119**.

These and other instances of State practice may be evidenced by official documents or, where appropriate, unofficial documents, such as newspaper reports and academic works.

1.106   It has sometimes been argued that mere statements and declarations by States are insufficient to establish State practice, and that they must be supported by actual conduct directed at physically exercising or defending claimed rights.[108] This remains, however, a minority view and the ICJ and other international tribunals regularly accept statements as evidence of State practice.

The weight to be attached to such statements may, however, be diminished where a State fails to take action in enforcement of its claims and no reasonable explanation exists for such failure.

1.107   State practice can also include omissions. This type of practice is particularly relevant where a customary rule involves a prohibition or requires forbearance, such as the obligation not to harm diplomatic personnel.

Consistency of State practice

1.108   The State practice element of a customary norm is not established merely because some States occasionally behave in a way that is approximately consistent with that putative norm. Article 38(1)(b) of the ICJ Statute specifies that the practice must be 'general'.

1.109   In the *Lotus* case,[109] the Permanent Court of International Justice rejected a submission that the infrequency with which States sought to prosecute criminal offences committed on the high seas aboard vessels flying another State's flag was proof of a customary law rule forbidding criminal prosecutions in those circumstances. In rejecting this submission, the Court was impressed by several reported cases which contradicted the alleged rule and which drew no protest from the flag State.

1.110   In the *Asylum* case,[110] the ICJ said that in order for a *usus* to help constitute custom, it must be 'in accordance with a constant and uniform practice'. The ICJ found that the State practices raised before it were too uncertain and contradictory to establish a general practice. Similarly, in the *Anglo-Norwegian Fisheries* case,[111] the ICJ rejected a British argument that customary international law precluded drawing baselines longer than 10 miles across bays for the purposes of mapping the territorial sea; there was too much State practice which was inconsistent with the asserted rule to regard it as reflecting a general practice.

---

108. For example, Judge John Read's dissenting opinion in the *Anglo-Norwegian Fisheries* case *(United Kingdom v Norway)* ICJ Rep (1951) 116, 191.
109. *Case of the SS Lotus (France v Turkey)* PCIJ Rep (1927) Series A No 10. See **6.11**.
110. *Asylum* case *(Colombia v Peru)* ICJ Rep (1950) 266. See **1.127**.
111. *Anglo-Norwegian Fisheries* case *(United Kingdom v Norway)* ICJ Rep (1951) 116. See **1.119**.

1.111   Does this mean that there needs to be an absolute conformity among States before a practice can be regarded as 'general' for the purposes of establishing a customary norm of international law? According to the American Law Institute:[112]

> A practice can be general even if it is not universally accepted; there is no precise formula to indicate how widespread a practice must be, but it should reflect wide acceptance among the states particularly involved in the relevant activity.

1.112   In the *North Sea Continental Shelf* cases, the ICJ remarked that, in order to help establish the existence of a new rule of customary international law, 'State practice, including that of States whose interests are specifically affected, should have been both extensive and virtually uniform'.[113] This suggests that occasional departures from an otherwise uniform practice will not be fatal to the emergence of a new customary rule of international law.

As the *North Sea Continental Shelf* cases themselves indicate, however, the fewer the instances of State practice said to support a new customary rule, the more significant will be occurrences of inconsistent or contradictory State practice.

1.113   In the *Nicaragua* case, the ICJ elaborated upon what constitutes 'general practice' in the context of discussing the existence of customary international law rules against the use of force and intervention:[114]

> It is not to be expected that in the practice of States the application of the rules in question should have been perfect, in the sense that States should have refrained, with complete consistency, from the use of force or from intervention in each other's internal affairs. The Court does not consider that, for a rule to be established as customary, the corresponding practice must be in absolutely rigorous conformity with the rule. In order to deduce the existence of customary rules, the Court deems it sufficient that the conduct of States should, in general, be consistent with such rules, and that instances of State conduct inconsistent with a given rule should generally have been treated as breaches of that rule, not as indications of the recognition of a new rule. If a State acts in a way prima facie incompatible with a recognized rule, but defends its conduct by appealing to exceptions or justifications contained within the rule itself, then whether or not the State's conduct is in fact justifiable on that basis, the significance of that attitude is to confirm rather than to weaken the rule.

1.114   Thus, occasional departures from an otherwise widespread and uniform practice will not deprive it of its customary character, provided such departures are generally either first, met with protest by other States; or second, justified by reference to exceptions allegedly forming part of the rule itself (even if such attempted justification is ill-founded).

---

112. American Law Institute, *Restatement (Third) of the Foreign Relations Law of the United States*, 1987, Vol 1, §102, 25.
113. *North Sea Continental Shelf* cases *(Germany v Denmark, Germany v The Netherlands)* ICJ Rep (1969) 3, para 74. See **1.140**.
114. *Military and Paramilitary Activities in and Against Nicaragua (Nicaragua v United States)* Merits, ICJ Rep (1986) 14, para 186.

Protest and acquiescence

1.115   Protest will be more significant in the case of alleged new rules of customary international law than in the case of established rules. In the former case, protest by just a few other States will weigh heavily against recognising the rule's emergence. In this situation, there will need to be much more evidence in support of the practice in order to establish its 'general' character.

1.116   Failure to protest is sometimes referred to as 'acquiescence', which has been defined as 'silence or absence of protest in circumstances which generally call for a positive reaction signifying objection'.[115] Acquiescence in the face of conduct inconsistent with an asserted new rule will count heavily against its recognition.[116]

In the case of an established customary rule, acquiescence in the face of departures from the rule will tend to erode its legal status and may, in time, lead to its disappearance or replacement by a different or modified rule. In the case of alleged new customary rules, acquiescence in the face of practice said to reflect the new putative rule may be treated as implied consent.

1.117   Furthermore — and whether dealing with practice, protest or acquiescence — greater weight will be given to the attitude of States which are specially affected by the putative rule or which are particularly involved in the activity it is said to regulate. Thus, in the *North Sea Continental Shelf* cases,[117] the ICJ, in seeking to ascertain the existence of an alleged new customary rule affecting the delimitation of disputed boundaries over the continental shelf, was more interested in the practice of States with extensive coastlines than in the practice of landlocked States.

Similarly, in the evolution of customary law regulating activities in outer space, the attitudes of the United States, Russia and other States with space programs are more significant than those of States without such programs.

1.118   As mentioned above, it is not necessary for every State to have actively participated in a *usus* for it to assume the status of general practice. It follows that a State is not able to assert the non-application to it of a customary rule corresponding to a general practice merely on the basis that the State did not adopt the *usus* in its own conduct. In the absence of protest against a new or developing *usus*, a State will usually be taken as having acquiesced in its emergence, and such acquiescence will count as assent.

---

115. I C MacGibbon, 'Customary international law and acquiescence' (1954) 31 *British Yearbook of International Law*, 143–86, 143.
116. *Case of the SS Lotus (France v Turkey)* PCIJ Rep (1927) Series A No 10. See **6.11**.
117. *North Sea Continental Shelf* cases *(Germany v Denmark, Germany v The Netherlands)* ICJ Rep (1969) 3. See **1.140**.

Persistent objection

1.119   Moreover, protest against a customary rule that has already emerged will not release a State from the obligation to comply with it. It is, however, possible for a State to remain free from the obligations of a customary law rule if the State has publicly maintained a persistent objection to the rule. This exception to the universally binding character of general customary international law is known as the 'persistent objector' principle.

> In the ***Anglo-Norwegian Fisheries* case *(United Kingdom v Norway)*,**[118] the United Kingdom argued that a Norwegian royal decree delimiting Norway's 'fishery zone' (which was meant to be co-extensive with the territorial sea) was incompatible with customary international law rules regulating the delimitation of territorial waters. Much of Norway's extensive coastline is highly punctuated by fjords and sounds, as well as by fringing islands and rocks (the *skjaergaard,* a Norwegian word meaning 'rock barrier') that are close to the mainland. Instead of delimiting its territorial sea by taking measurements from the low-water mark at every point along its coast, as was the usual practice of States, Norway employed straight baselines between the out-jutting headlands, islands and rocks, thereby enclosing a larger area of sea than would otherwise have been the case. Access by British fishing vessels to areas of sea near the Norwegian coast, which the United Kingdom claimed were part of international waters, was thus adversely affected. The United Kingdom objected, inter alia, to the length of many of the baselines used in the Norwegian decree, the longest of which measured 44 miles. The United Kingdom maintained that customary international law imposed a limit of 10 miles on the length of such baselines. The Court said:[119]
>
>> [T]he Court deems it necessary to point out that although the 10-mile rule has been adopted by certain States both in their national law and in their treaties and conventions, and although certain arbitral decisions have applied it as between these States, other States have adopted a different limit. Consequently, the 10-mile rule has not acquired the authority of a general rule of international law. In any event the 10-mile rule would appear to be inapplicable as against Norway inasmuch as she has always opposed any attempt to apply it to the Norwegian coast.

Furthermore, in its pleadings to the ICJ, the United Kingdom accepted that the customary law limit of three miles on the width of the territorial sea might not apply to Norway which, together with other members of the Scandinavian League, had long insisted on a limit of four miles.[120]

The terms of the Court's in-principle approval of the persistent objector principle make it clear that the objection must be maintained throughout the customary rule's life in order to shield the objecting State from its requirements. The moment a State drops its objections by, for instance, acquiescing in the face of conduct performed in reliance on the

---

118. *Anglo-Norwegian Fisheries* case *(United Kingdom v Norway)* ICJ Rep (1951) 116.
119. Ibid, 131.
120. Ibid, para 18 of the United Kingdom's pleadings.

rule or performing an act that expressly or tacitly accepts the rule, the State will, from then on, be bound by the rule, even if the objection is subsequently revived.

1.120   Similarly, in the *Asylum* case the ICJ found that there was no customary law rule permitting an asylum-granting State the right, unilaterally, to qualify an asylum seeker's offence as political. The Court said:[121]

> But even if it could be supposed that such a custom existed between certain Latin-American States only, it could not be invoked against Peru which, far from having by its attitude adhered to it, has, on the contrary, repudiated it by refraining from ratifying the Montevideo Conventions of 1933 and 1939, which were the first to include a rule concerning the qualification of the offence in matters of diplomatic asylum.

From this passage, it is possible to infer a view on the Court's part that when dealing with a local custom,[122] it is sufficient that repudiation or objection was made at the time the rule began to emerge. On this interpretation of the Court's decision, subsequent acquiescence in the face of conduct performed in reliance on the local customary rule would not deprive the State of the protection afforded by the initial objection or repudiation. This more expansive role for objection in relation to local customs can be justified by reference to the fact that customs that bind only a few States are an exceptional manifestation of the generally universal character of customary international law.

However, even if one were to accept this approach, it is difficult to see why an act expressing actual acceptance of a local customary rule would not remove the protection afforded by the initial objection or repudiation to that rule at the time it was emerging. Accordingly, the better view is that, in the case of local customary rules, any shielding effect attaching to an objection made at the time of the rule's emergence will be vitiated by a subsequent act that indicates acceptance of the rule.

1.121   The Court's opinion in the *Anglo-Norwegian Fisheries* case[123] that Norway's persistent objection to the asserted 10-mile rule precluded its application to the Norwegian coast was clearly *obiter,* given that no such rule was found to exist.

Also *obiter* in character were the Court's comments in the *Asylum* case[124] as to the effect of Peru's repudiation of the alleged offence-qualification rule. In fact, the ICJ has never decided a case in which a persistent objection was successfully made to a valid customary rule. This, combined with the paucity of State practice in support of the persistent objector principle, has led some publicists to doubt or deny the principle's very existence in international law. This scepticism is also sometimes based on a rejection of the State-consent model of customary international law in favour of more community-focused conceptions,

---

121. *Asylum* case *(Colombia v Peru)* ICJ Rep (1950) 266, 277–278. See **1.127**.
122. See **1.147–1.151**.
123. *Anglo-Norwegian Fisheries* case *(United Kingdom v Norway)* ICJ Rep (1951) 116. See **1.119**.
124. *Asylum* case *(Colombia v Peru)* ICJ Rep (1950) 266, 277–278. See **1.127**.

according to which States collectively seek integrated rules in order to resolve problems of common concern.[125]

1.122   The scarcity of State practice in support of the persistent objector principle can best be explained by reference to the realities of modern international relations. It is, in fact, extremely difficult for a single State to maintain its dissent from an otherwise universally observed rule unless, perhaps, that State is so strong as to be able to resist the political, diplomatic, economic and (possibly) military pressures which other States are likely to exert in order to bring it into compliance. Such realities lend some credence to the community-focused conception of customary international law. On the other hand, States and many publicists are reluctant to abandon either the State-consent model of customary international law or the notional validity of the persistent objector principle.[126]

1.123   In any event, it is clear that a State's persistent objection to a customary rule of *jus cogens* status will not operate to shield the objecting State from application of the rule against it.[127]

Opinio juris

1.124   If a general practice by States *(usus)* is the necessary objective element of customary international law, a belief that the practice is permitted or required as a matter of legal right or obligation *(opinio juris)* is the necessary subjective element.

A *usus* does not generate a rule of customary international law merely because it has become an extensive and virtually uniform practice of States. Many such practices are not reflective of legal rules but are simply the expression of international 'comity' — that is, courtesy among States. For example, the practice of greeting visiting Heads of State with military honours and displays of the visitor's national flag is an expression of international comity, but does not involve a legal obligation. Such practices may be expressive of a custom in the social sense, but are not required as a matter of customary law. It is the presence of an *opinio juris* that transforms an extensive and virtually uniform *usus* into a rule of customary international law.

1.125   In the *Lotus* case, the PCIJ, after commenting on the inadequacy of the State practice said to sustain a customary rule forbidding the commencement of criminal proceedings in certain circumstances, said:[128]

---

125. Antonio Cassese, *International Law*, 2nd ed, Oxford University Press, New York, 2005, 162–63.
126. For example, American Law Institute, *Restatement (Third) of the Foreign Relations Law of the United States*, 1987, Vol 1, at 18, 26 and 32.
127. See the separate opinion of Judge Lachs in the *North Sea Continental Shelf* cases *(Germany v Denmark, Germany v The Netherlands)* ICJ Rep (1969) 3.
128. *Case of the SS Lotus (France v Turkey)* PCIJ Rep (1927) Series A No 10, 28. See **6.11**.

Even if the rarity of the judicial decisions to be found among the reported cases were sufficient to prove in point of fact the circumstances alleged by the Agent for the French Government, it would merely show that States had often, in practice, abstained from instituting criminal proceedings, and not that they recognized themselves as being obliged to do so; for only if such abstention were based on their being conscious of having a duty to abstain would it be possible to speak of an international custom. The alleged fact does not allow one to infer that States have been conscious of having such a duty.

1.126   In the *North Sea Continental Shelf* cases, the ICJ considered the significance of adherence by States to a multilateral treaty (the 1958 Geneva Convention on the Continental Shelf) for the purposes of generating a rule of customary international law. According to the Court, State practice relied upon to support an alleged customary rule 'should ... have occurred in such a way as to show a general recognition that a rule of law or legal obligation is involved'.[129] In commenting on the conduct of States which were not parties to the treaty but were in apparent conformity to its requirements, the Court said:[130]

> [E]ven if these instances of action by non-parties to the Convention were much more numerous than they in fact are, they would not, even in the aggregate, suffice in themselves to constitute the *opinio juris* — for, in order to achieve that result, two conditions must be fulfilled. Not only must the acts concerned amount to a settled practice, but they must also be such, or be carried out in such a way, as to be evidence of a belief that this practice is rendered obligatory by the existence of a rule of law requiring it. The need for such a belief, i.e. the existence of a subjective element, is implicit in the very notion of the *opinio juris sive necessitatis*. The States concerned must therefore feel that they are conforming to what amounts to a legal obligation. The frequency, or even habitual character of the acts is not in itself enough.

1.127   Where there is reason to believe that a *usus* is motivated by political or other non-juridical considerations, it will be more difficult to establish the existence of the requisite *opinio juris*. In the *North Sea Continental Shelf* cases, the ICJ noted that there was 'not a shred of evidence' indicating that States which had applied the equidistance method of drawing international boundaries contained in the 1958 Geneva Convention on the Continental Shelf, but which were not parties to the Convention, 'believed themselves to be applying a mandatory rule of customary international law'. The Court also noted that there was 'no lack of other reasons for using the equidistance method, so that acting, or agreeing to act, in a certain way, does not of itself demonstrate anything of a juridical nature'.[131]

---

129. *North Sea Continental Shelf* cases *(Germany v Denmark, Germany v The Netherlands)* ICJ Rep (1969) 3, para 74.
130. Ibid, para 77. See **1.140**.
131. Ibid, para 76.

In the **Asylum case (Colombia v Peru),**[132] authorities in Peru issued an arrest warrant for a Peruvian national, Victor Raúl Haya de la Torre, who had been granted asylum as a political refugee in the premises of Colombia's embassy in Lima. Haya de la Torre was the leader of a Peruvian opposition political party (the American People's Revolutionary Alliance) that had been involved in an unsuccessful military rebellion against the Peruvian government. Colombia sought safe passage for Haya de la Torre so that he could leave Peru. The Peruvian government rejected the request on the grounds that Haya de la Torre had committed common crimes, and made it clear that he would be arrested the moment he left the grounds of the Colombian embassy. The Colombian ambassador in Peru claimed that Haya de la Torre qualified as a political refugee and was entitled to take up refuge abroad. The Colombian government claimed that there was a rule of 'American international law' (that is, a regional or local customary rule confined to Latin-American States) which permitted the State granting asylum to qualify the offence for the purposes of the asylum. The existence of this regional custom was contested by Peru. The ICJ said:[133]

> The Colombian Government has … invoked 'American international law in general' … it has relied on an alleged regional or local custom peculiar to Latin-American States. The Party which relies on a custom of this kind must prove that this custom is established in such a manner that it has become binding on the other Party. The Colombian Government must prove that the rule invoked by it is in accordance with a constant and uniform practice by the States in question, and that this usage is the expression of a right appertaining to the State granting asylum and a duty incumbent on the territorial State. This follows from Article 38 of the Statute of the Court, which refers to international custom 'as evidence of a general practice accepted as law'.

> … the Colombian Government has referred to a large number of cases in which diplomatic asylum was in fact granted and respected. But it has not shown that the alleged rule of unilateral and definitive qualification was invoked or … that it was, apart from conventional stipulations, exercised by the States granting asylum as a right appertaining to them and respected by the territorial State as a duty incumbent on them and not merely for reasons of political expediency. The facts brought to the knowledge of the Court disclose so much uncertainty and contradiction, so much fluctuation and discrepancy in the exercise of diplomatic asylum and in the official views expressed on various occasions, there has been so much inconsistency in the rapid succession of conventions on asylum, ratified by some States and rejected by others, and the practice has been so much influenced by considerations of political expediency in the various cases, that it is not possible to discern in all this any constant and uniform practice accepted as law, with regard to the alleged rule of unilateral and definitive qualification of the offence.

Evidence of *opinio juris*

1.128   There are passages from the judgments in the *Lotus* case,[134] the *Asylum* case,[135] and the *North Sea Continental Shelf* cases[136] which

---

132. *Asylum* case *(Colombia v Peru)* ICJ Rep (1950) 266.
133. Ibid, 276–277.
134. *Case of the SS Lotus (France v Turkey)* PCIJ Rep (1927) Series A No 10. See **6.11**.
135. *Asylum* case *(Colombia v Peru)* ICJ Rep (1950) 266. See **1.127**.
136. *North Sea Continental Shelf* cases *(Germany v Denmark, Germany v The Netherlands)* ICJ Rep (1969) 3. See **1.140**.

indicate that separate evidence is required of the *opinio juris* element, and that it is not permissible simply to infer *opinio juris* from State practice. These findings were made, however, in the context of related determinations that the evidence of State practice fell short of what was required to establish a general practice, and that there was reason to believe that the practice was motivated by political or other non-juridical considerations.

The dissenting opinions of Judge Kotaro Tanaka (1890–1974) and Judge ad hoc Max Sørenson (1913–1981) in the *North Sea Continental Shelf* cases, however, point to a different approach to proving *opinio juris* where the evidence indicates that a State practice has indeed become general. Both judges regarded the practice in issue as being sufficiently widespread as to be capable of supporting a customary rule. Judge Tanaka said:[137]

> [S]o far as ... *opinio juris sive necessitatis* is concerned, it is extremely difficult to get evidence of its existence in concrete cases. This factor, relating to international motivation and being of a psychological nature, cannot be ascertained very easily, particularly when diverse legislative and executive organs of a government participate in an internal process of decision-making in respect of ratification or other State acts. There is no other way than to ascertain the existence of *opinio juris* from the fact of the external existence of a certain custom and its necessity felt in the international community, rather than to seek evidence as to the subjective motive of each example of State practice, which is something which is impossible of achievement.

Judge ad hoc Sørenson quoted with approval from Sir Hersch Lauterpacht (1897–1960), who wrote that:[138]

> [T]he accurate principle ... consists in regarding all uniform conduct of governments (or, in appropriate cases, abstention therefrom) as evidencing the *opinio necessitatis juris* except when it is shown that the conduct in question was not accompanied by any such intention.

Although these dissenting opinions are rationally compelling, the ICJ has more recently reaffirmed the necessity of separately establishing *opinio juris*, even where the State practice to which it corresponds is widespread and virtually uniform.[139]

1.129   There are also occasions when a virtually unanimous and unequivocal *opinio juris* will be capable of sustaining a customary rule even in the absence of an 'extensive and virtually uniform' practice by States. For instance, the customary and *jus cogens* rule against torture retains its legal status notwithstanding that torture is widespread in the practice of States. Torture remains, however, universally condemned as unlawful in the pronouncements of States. When accused of torture, States almost always deny the charge, and never assert that torture is permitted by international law.

---

137. Ibid, 77.
138. Ibid, 248.
139. See **1.145**.

Temporal dimension

1.130   The very notion of custom implies a temporal element — that is, a custom is normally regarded as a practice that evolves and is widely observed over time. In this sense, custom is akin to tradition. Does this mean that a long period of time must expire before a practice can crystallise into custom?

1.131   Many customs have indeed emerged only after a long gestation period. For example, it took centuries for the customary rule supporting freedom of the high seas to become firmly established. The 20th century saw, however, an acceleration of the rate at which new customary international law emerged. In the *North Sea Continental Shelf* cases, the ICJ accepted, in principle, that 'the passage of only a short period of time is not necessarily or of itself a bar to the formation of a new rule of customary international law'.[140] The 'short period of time' in that case was as little as the several months which elapsed between the entry into force of the 1958 Geneva Convention on the Continental Shelf and the breakdown in negotiations between Germany, Denmark and the Netherlands over delimiting their boundaries.

The customary rule establishing that States do not have sovereignty over the outer space above their territories was established within days, or perhaps even within hours, of the launch of the first artificial satellite in 1957. No other States protested to the Soviet Union when *Sputnik I* traversed the outer space above them. Although the time was brief, it was sufficient in all the circumstances for an 'extensive and virtually uniform' practice to emerge.

1.132   A rule of customary international law can thus emerge without a long period of gestation. The critical factor is the preponderance of State practice and *opinio juris*, especially by States with a special interest in the subject matter of the rule. If such a preponderance of practice and *opinio juris* emerges quickly, a new customary rule can emerge with it. If there is widespread resistance to the new practice, a longer period of time may be required before it attracts sufficient adherence in the conduct and *opinio juris* of States to transform it into a new customary rule. Of course, such a widespread adherence may never emerge, and the States supporting the new practice may eventually accept a continuation of the established practice.

Custom and the positivist paradox

1.133   The requirement that a customary rule consists of two elements — 'general practice' and *opinio juris* — is frequently said to involve a paradox. It is often observed that, in order for an international custom to emerge, there must be a stage during which States are labouring under the

---

140. *North Sea Continental Shelf* cases *(Germany v Denmark, Germany v The Netherlands)* ICJ Rep (1969) 3, para 74.

necessarily false belief that the conduct is already required or permitted by international law. Where the false belief is that the conduct is already permitted, the paradox is said to be sharper and results in the act being grounded in an actual breach of the *lex lata*. Yet there is nothing in the text of Art 38(1)(b) of the ICJ Statute,[141] nor in the decisions of the ICJ or PCIJ, which requires that the 'general practice' must have been 'accepted as law' at all stages of its emergence. In Antonio Cassese's view:[142]

> It would seem that the two elements need not be both present from the outset. Usually, a practice evolves among certain States under the impulse of economic, political or military demands. At this stage the practice may thus be regarded as being imposed by social or economic or political needs *(opinio necessitatis)*. If it does not encounter strong and consistent opposition from other States but is increasingly accepted, or acquiesced in, a customary rule gradually crystallizes. At this later stage it may be held that the practice is dictated by international law *(opinio juris)*. In other words, now States begin to believe that they must conform to the practice not so much, or not only, out of economic, political, or military considerations, but because an international rule enjoins them to do so. At that moment — difficult to pinpoint exactly, since it is the result of a continuous process — a customary rule may be said to have evolved.

1.134   Thus, customary international law evolves and is recognised, or 'accepted' in the language of Art 38(1)(b) of the ICJ Statute, as being already binding. The *opinio necessitatis* element in relation to any particular practice is, in reality, a belief that first, it is necessary or desirable for the international common good that there be a binding rule governing a particular domain; second, this practice is an appropriate means of responding to the requirements of the international common good; and third, this practice would be normatively binding if the belief and practice were subscribed to, or acquiesced in, by a sufficient mass of States.

1.135   The *opinio* element in customary international law is, therefore, initially propositional — that is, it is a view that a particular practice is a suitable candidate for customary law status. Once the practice and the accompanying *opinio necessitatis* are sufficiently widespread, acceptance of the practice's legal status follows and the *opinio necessitatis* is transformed into an *opinio juris*. Similar conceptions of customary law's *opinio* element existed prior to the drafting of Art 38. John Westlake (1828–1913), for instance, taught:[143]

> Custom and reason are the two sources of international law. ... Reason is a source of international law ... for two causes. First, the rules already regarded as established, whatever their source, must be referred to their principles, applied, and their principles extended to new cases, by the methods of reasoning proper to jurisprudence, enlightened by a sound view of the necessities of international life. Secondly, the rules as yet

---

141. See **1.186**.
142. Antonio Cassese, *International Law*, 2nd ed, Oxford University Press, New York, 2005, 157–58.
143. John Westlake, *International Law*, Part I: *Peace*, 2nd ed, Cambridge University Press, 1910, 14–15.

established, even when so applied and extended, do not cover the whole field of international life, which is constantly developing in new directions. Therefore from time to time new rules have to be proposed on reasonable grounds, acted on provisionally, and ultimately adopted or rejected as may be determined by experience ...

1.136 How widespread the State practice and *opinio necessitatis* need to be before 'acceptance as law' occurs depends on the relationship of the putative customary rule to the requirements of the international common good, including especially the attitude of any subjects of international law whose interests are particularly affected.

1.137 This conception of *opinio juris sive necessitatis* also has the advantage of being more faithful to the language of Art 38(1)(b) than the classical positivist understanding. According to that understanding, *opinio juris sive necessitatis* and State practice are evidence of the existence of an international custom. Yet the text of Art 38(1)(b) puts the matter entirely the other way around: 'The Court ... shall apply ... international custom, as evidence of a general practice accepted as law'. According to the classical positivist understanding, Art 38(1)(b) inexplicably reverses the relationship between international custom and those elements (State practice and a conviction of its extant legal status) which are evidence of the custom.

On a proper conception of *opinio juris sive necessitatis*, however, there is no peculiarity in the drafting of Art 38(1)(b). *Opinio necessitatis* and 'acceptance as law' are different, albeit related, objects.

Therefore, Article 38(1)(b) accurately, and without paradox, expresses the true dynamic underlying customary international law: international custom, which consists of sufficiently widespread State conduct supported by *opinio necessitatis* (in the propositional sense), really is 'evidence' supporting the existence of a 'general practice' which is 'accepted as law' *(opinio juris)*.

Treaties generating custom

1.138 Activities relating to the conclusion of treaties — such as negotiation, signing, ratification and accession — may be evidence of State practice.[144] Sometimes treaties are concluded which substantially codify existing customary international law. When this occurs, signing, ratification and accession are acts which reinforce the customary rules codified in the treaty — not only because the customary rules become binding treaty obligations, but also because signing, ratification and accession provide further evidence of State practice in support of the customary rules.

1.139 This raises the possibility that a rule contained in a treaty provision might be transformed into a new customary rule if the treaty provision is adhered to by a sufficiently large number of States.

---

144. See **1.105–1.107**.

The new customary rule might arise either because the treaty crystallises a customary rule already in the process of formation, or because the treaty influences international behaviour to such an extent that a consistent and virtually uniform State practice emerges on its foundation. Thus transformed, the new rule would be binding, as custom, even on States that were not parties to the treaty.

1.140   In 1969, the ICJ took an important step in this direction.

In the **North Sea Continental Shelf cases (Germany v Denmark, Germany v The Netherlands),**[145] Germany had entered into separate agreements with Denmark and the Netherlands partially delimiting the continental shelves beneath the North Sea adjacent to their territories. The parties could not agree on a complete delimitation and submitted the dispute to the ICJ, seeking guidance as to the international law rules and principles applicable to a final delimitation in the absence of agreement. The Court dismissed Germany's submission that it was entitled to a 'just and reasonable share' of the continental shelf. It also dismissed submissions from Denmark and the Netherlands that Art 6(2) of the 1958 Geneva Convention on the Continental Shelf, which provided for an 'equidistance-special circumstance' principle in the absence of contrary agreement, had crystallised customary international law at the time of the Convention's adoption. The Court then turned its attention to submissions by Denmark and the Netherlands that Art 6(2), either by its own impact or by subsequent State practice under its influence, had generated a new rule of customary law. Germany had not ratified the Convention, and could be bound by the principle in Art 6(2) only if it existed also as a matter of customary law:

71. In so far as this contention is based on the view that Article 6 of the Convention has had the influence, and has produced the effect described, it clearly involves treating that Article as a norm-creating provision which has constituted the foundation of, or has generated a rule which, while only conventional or contractual in its origin, has since passed into the general *corpus* of international law, and is now accepted as such by the *opinio juris,* so as to have become binding even for countries which have never, and do not, become parties to the Convention. There is no doubt that this process is a perfectly possible one and does from time to time occur: it constitutes indeed one of the recognised methods by which new rules of customary international law may be formed. At the same time this result is not lightly to be regarded as having been attained.

The Court then specified three conditions that need to be satisfied before a treaty rule can be said to have generated a parallel customary law rule:

72. It would in the first place be necessary that the provision should, at all events potentially, be of a fundamentally norm-creating character such as could be regarded as forming the basis of a general rule of law. …

73. With respect to the other elements usually regarded as necessary before a conventional rule can be considered to have become a general rule of international law, it might be that, even without the passage of any considerable period of time, a very widespread and representative participation in the convention might suffice of itself, provided it included that of States whose interests were specially affected.

---

145. *North Sea Continental Shelf* cases *(Germany v Denmark, Germany v The Netherlands)* ICJ Rep (1969) 3.

> 74. As regards the time element ... Although the passage of only a short period of time is not necessarily, of itself, a bar to the formation of a new rule of customary international law on the basis of what was originally a purely conventional rule, an indispensable requirement would be that within the period in question, short though it might be, State practice including that of States whose interests are specially affected, should have been both extensive and virtually uniform in the sense of the provision invoked and should moreover have occurred in such a way as to show a general recognition that a rule of law or legal obligation is involved.

1.141   The ICJ took the view that Art 6(2) of the 1958 Geneva Convention on the Continental Shelf failed to satisfy all three conditions necessary for the generation of a parallel rule of customary international law.

1.142   In relation to the first condition, the Court gave three reasons for rejecting the provision's fundamentally norm-creating character:

> 72. ... Considered *in abstracto* the equidistance principle might be said to fulfil this requirement. Yet in the particular form in which it is embodied in Article 6 of the Geneva Convention, and having regard to the relationship of that Article to other provisions of the Convention, this must be open to some doubt. In the first place, Article 6 is so framed as to put second the obligation to make use of the equidistance method, causing it to come after a primary obligation to effect delimitation by agreement. ... Secondly the part played by the notion of special circumstances relative to the principle of equidistance as embodied in Article 6, and the very considerable, still unresolved controversies as to the exact meaning and scope of this notion, must raise further doubts as to the potentially norm-creating character of the rule. Finally, the faculty of making reservations to Article 6, while it might not of itself prevent the equidistance principle being eventually received as general law, does add considerably to the difficulty of regarding this result as having been brought about (or being potentially possible) on the basis of the Convention ...

Any other factor that tends to impede a treaty rule's capacity to form the basis of a general rule of law will also weigh against its capacity to generate a parallel customary rule. In particular, a treaty provision which is essentially procedural or institutional in character — such as a requirement to notify an international body of an event — will not ordinarily be fundamentally norm-creating: for example, the requirement to notify the Security Council of an armed attack before resorting to the inherent right of self-defence under Art 51 of the UN Charter.[146]

1.143   In relation to the second condition, requiring a widespread and representative participation in the treaty, the Court noted that only a small number of States had ratified or acceded to the 1958 Geneva Convention and said:

> 73. ... [E]ven if allowance is made for the existence of a number of States to whom participation in the Geneva Convention is not open, or which,

---

146. *Military and Paramilitary Activities in and Against Nicaragua (Nicaragua v United States)* Merits, ICJ Rep (1986) 14. See **9.10**.

by reason for instance of being land-locked States, would have no interest in becoming parties to it, the number of ratifications and accessions so far secured is, though respectable, hardly sufficient.

There is no magic number of signatures, ratifications or accessions which, when reached, furnishes the requisite 'widespread and representative participation' in a treaty provision such as to make it capable of founding a parallel rule of customary international law. The number in any particular case will depend upon the nature of the treaty rule, the subject matter of the treaty, and the extent to which 'specially affected' States are among the treaty's participants.

1.144   In relation to the third condition, requiring an 'extensive and virtually uniform' adherence to the treaty rule's requirements, the Court observed:

> 75. ... Some fifteen cases have been cited ... in which continental shelf boundaries have been delimited according to the equidistance principle ... [E]ven if these various cases constituted more than a very small proportion of those potentially calling for delimitation in the world as a whole, the Court would not think it necessary to enumerate or evaluate them separately, since there are, a priori, several grounds which deprive them of weight in the present context.

> 76. ... Over half the States concerned, whether acting unilaterally or conjointly, were or shortly became parties to the Geneva Convention, and were therefore presumably, so far as they were concerned, acting actually or potentially in the application of the Convention. But from that no inference could justifiably be drawn that they believed themselves to be applying a mandatory rule of customary international law. There is not a shred of evidence that they did and ... there is no lack of other reasons for using the equidistance method, so that acting, or agreeing to act in a certain way, does not of itself demonstrate anything of a juridical nature.

The Court was of the view that evidence of a rule's customary status cannot be derived from the fact that States comply with it, 'actually or potentially', as a treaty obligation. It therefore required evidence of practice by States which were not, and which were not proposing to become, parties to the treaty in question.

It should be noted, however, that this additional evidence was required because of the relatively small number of States that had adhered to the Geneva Convention. In the case of treaties which attracted 'a very widespread and representative participation' and which included 'States whose interests were specially affected', the Court said that they 'might suffice of themselves' to generate rules of customary international law.[147]

1.145   Nevertheless, in the more recent *Nicaragua* case, the ICJ considered it necessary to search for separate evidence of *opinio juris*

---

147. *North Sea Continental Shelf* cases *(Germany v Denmark, Germany v The Netherlands)* ICJ Rep (1969) 3, para 73.

in respect of the customary law rule against the threat or use of force in international relations against the territorial integrity or political independence of any State, or in any other manner inconsistent with the purposes of the UN.[148] This customary prohibition was found to 'correspond in essentials' to the prohibition contained in Art 2(4) of the UN Charter,[149] a treaty to which almost all States are party.

The better view would, therefore, seem to be that a very widespread and representative participation in a treaty is to be regarded as sufficing to establish 'general practice' corresponding to the treaty's rules, but that separate evidence of *opinio juris* will still be required in order to prove the existence of those rules in customary international law.

1.146 In the *Nicaragua* case, the ICJ held that a State may be bound by a conventional rule and a parallel customary rule simultaneously. In the Court's view, 'customary international law continues to exist and apply, separately from international treaty law, even where the two categories of law have an identical content'.[150]

Local custom

1.147 As a general rule, customary international law is universally applicable — that is, it legally binds all States. Occasionally, universally applicable customary international law is referred to as 'general customary law' or 'general international law' (which also includes the general principles of law[151]). Exceptionally, a rule of customary international law will bind only a particular group of States. This variety of customary international law is referred to variously and interchangeably as 'local', 'regional' or 'special' customary law.

1.148 In the *Asylum* case,[152] the ICJ accepted in principle that a regional custom binding only among Latin American States could exist, but held that evidence advanced in support was too uncertain and contradictory to warrant the recognition of a special rule in that case. The ICJ subsequently accepted the existence of a local customary rule binding as between only two States.

In the ***Right of Passage case (Portugal v India),***[153] Portugal possessed certain colonial territories on the Indian subcontinent (Goa, Daman and Diu) to which India laid claim. Two districts of Daman lay inland and were completely surrounded by Indian territory, so that access to them, and between them, was possible only by crossing Indian territory. In 1954, India denied passage over its territory to

---

148. *Military and Paramilitary Activities in and Against Nicaragua (Nicaragua v United States)* Merits, ICJ Rep (1986) 14, para 188.
149. See **9.9**.
150. *Military and Paramilitary Activities in and Against Nicaragua (Nicaragua v United States)* Merits, ICJ Rep (1986) 14, para 179.
151. See **1.152–1.174**.
152. *Asylum* case *(Colombia v Peru)* ICJ Rep (1950) 266. See **1.127**.
153. *Right of Passage* case *(Portugal v India)* ICJ Rep (1960) 6.

Portuguese officials, police, military personnel, other persons holding Portuguese nationality, and consignments of arms and ammunition. This move was part of newly independent India's campaign to annex the Portuguese territories. As a matter of general customary law, and as an incident of territorial sovereignty, States are under no obligation to permit the nationals, officials or military forces of other States, or any goods, to enter or traverse their land territory. Portugal complained, however, that the denial of passage violated a special rule of customary international law that had developed between it and the United Kingdom, the colonial administrator of India until 1949. The Court said:[154]

> With regard to Portugal's claim of right of passage as formulated by it on the basis of local custom, it is objected on behalf of India that no local custom could be established between only two States. It is difficult to see why the number of States between which a local custom may be established on the basis of long practice must necessarily be larger than two. The Court sees no reason why long continued practice between two States accepted by them as regulating their relations should not form the basis of mutual rights and obligations between the two States. ...

> The Court ... concludes that, with regard to private persons, civil officials and goods in general there existed during the British and post-British periods a constant and uniform practice allowing free passage between Daman and the enclaves. This practice having continued over a period extending beyond a century and a quarter unaffected by the change in regime in respect of the intervening territory which occurred when India became independent, the Court is, in view of all the circumstances of the case, satisfied that the practice was accepted as law by the Parties and has given rise to a right and a correlative obligation. ... The Court is ... of the view that no right of passage in favour of Portugal involving a correlative obligation on India has been established in respect of armed forces, armed police, and arms and ammunition.

> The course of dealings established between the Portuguese and British authorities with respect to the passage of these categories excludes the existence of any such right. The practice that was established shows that, with regard to these categories, it was well understood that passage could take place only by permission of the British authorities. This situation continued during the post-British period.

1.149   That there might be a higher standard of proof in order to establish a local customary rule is suggested by passages from the ICJ's judgments in the *Asylum* case[155] and the *Right of Passage* case.[156] According to Malcolm Shaw:[157]

> [L]ocal customs ... depend upon a particular activity by one state being accepted by the other state (or states) as an expression of a legal obligation or right. While in the case of a general customary rule the process of consensus is at work so that a majority or a substantial minority of interested states can be sufficient to create a new custom, a local custom needs the positive acceptance of both (or all) parties to the rule. This is because local customs are an exception to the general

---

154. Ibid, 49–53.
155. *Asylum* case *(Colombia v Peru)* ICJ Rep (1950) 266. See **1.127**.
156. *Right of Passage* case *(Portugal v India)* ICJ Rep (1960) 6. See **1.148**.
157. Malcolm N Shaw, *International Law*, 6th ed, Cambridge University Press, Cambridge, 2008, 93 (footnote omitted).

nature of customary law, which involves a fairly flexible approach to law-making by all states, and instead constitutes a reminder of the former theory of consent whereby states are bound only by what they assent to. Exceptions may prove the rule, but they need greater proof than the rule to establish themselves.

1.150   Where a local custom is established, it will, as between the States participating in the local custom, usually prevail over any inconsistent general custom. This will not, however, be the case where the general custom is also a peremptory norm of general international law. Frequently referred to as *'jus cogens'*, the Vienna Convention on the Law of Treaties defines a peremptory norm of general international law as:[158]

> ... a norm accepted and recognised by the international community of States as a whole as a norm from which no derogation is permitted and which can be modified only by a subsequent norm of general international law having the same character.

This definition indicates that *jus cogens* norms are customary in character.

1.151   Although the concept of *jus cogens* has its origins in the codification of treaty law in the Vienna Convention on the Law of Treaties, it is generally recognised that *jus cogens* also operates to override any inconsistent customary law. Because it is axiomatic that a *jus cogens* rule must be accepted and recognised as such by 'the international community of States as a whole', it is not easily conceivable how a direct conflict with another general customary rule might arise. In contrast, local customary rules have meaning precisely because they are inconsistent with an applicable general custom or because there is no applicable general custom. Where an applicable general customary rule is *jus cogens*, it will invalidate any contrary local customary rule. The content of *jus cogens* norms is discussed elsewhere.[159]

General principles of law

1.152   The 'general principles of law' recognised by civilised nations are the third, and final, source of law identified by Art 38(1) of the ICJ Statute.[160]

Legal status of general principles

1.153   The very existence of the general principles as a source of law indicates that treaty and custom do not provide an exhaustive source of legal norms in international law. The fact that the general principles are described as 'principles of law' demonstrates that they do not authorise

---

158. VCLT, Art 53. See **2.107**.
159. See **2.106–2.110**.
160. See **1.186**.

the ICJ to proceed on the basis of non-legal considerations that are thought to be fair and right in all the circumstances.

This conclusion is reinforced by the fact that Art 38(2) of the ICJ Statute provides separate authorisation for the ICJ to decide cases *ex aequo et bono* — that is, by reference to non-legal conceptions of equity and fairness — if the parties agree.[161] Such separate authorisation would not have been necessary had Art 38(1)(c) already authorised resort to non-legal considerations.

The same reasoning precludes the view that the reference to general principles of law in the ICJ Statute adds nothing to what is already indicated by the reference to treaty and custom: cf, the contrary Soviet view advanced by Grigory Tunkin (1906–1993).[162]

The result is that the general principles, which are of a legal nature and not merely manifestations of treaty and custom, are a source of real law for the regulation of international relations.

Origin of general principles

1.154   The general principles are merely 'recognised' by civilised nations, and not enacted or consented to by them. In the Advisory Committee of Jurists on the Statute of the Permanent Court of International Justice, Lord Phillimore (1845–1929), the provision's co-author, observed that:[163]

> … the general principles referred to … were those which were accepted
> by all nations *in foro domestico,* such as certain principles of procedure,
> the principle of good faith, and the principle of *res judicata,* etc.

In particular, he intended the general principles to mean 'maxims of law'.[164]

This suggests that those basic concepts and processes of legal justice that are observed in mature domestic legal systems are to serve as sources of international law. Again, what is required is recognition of existing basic legal ideas, not enactment of, or consent to, measures to be adopted on the plane of international law.

1.155   This approach is strengthened by reference to the fact that recognition of the general principles is by 'nations' and not by States. The terminology is not without significance. States are the international legal entities that are still the principal subjects of rights and duties in international law. Nations, by contrast, are the peoples themselves.

This interpretation is confirmed by the fact that, apart from the expression 'United Nations', the word 'nations' is used only twice in the ICJ Statute: in connection with the general principles of law in Art 38,

---

161. *Case Concerning the Frontier Dispute (Burkina Faso v Mali)* ICJ Rep (1986) 554, paras 27–28.
162. G I Tunkin, 'Coexistence and international law', *Rec Acad,* Vol 95, 1958, III, 25–26.
163. Permanent Court of International Justice, Advisory Committee of Jurists, 'Procés-verbaux of the Proceedings of the Committee', 1920, 335.
164. Ibid.

and in the phrase, 'the teachings of the most highly qualified publicists of the various nations', also in Art 38.

In the latter phrase, the intention appears to convey the idea that the publicists are not representatives of the States as such, but are simply members of the world's diverse peoples and emblematic of the world's various legal cultures. The nouns 'state' or 'states' appear 30 times, and uniformly signify the State as a sovereign legal entity in international law (for example, Art 34(1), which provides: 'Only states may be parties in cases before the Court'). Article 38 is, therefore, declaring that those general principles of law recognised by the peoples of the world, without necessarily being adopted or enacted into international law by States, are to be employed in international law.

General principles and the *jus gentium*

1.156   What one is dealing with in the general principles of law, then, is the *jus gentium*.[165] The term *'jus gentium'* is commonly translated as 'the law of nations', but is perhaps less ambiguously rendered as 'the law common to all peoples', or 'the common law of mankind'.

1.157   The *jus gentium* originated in Roman law as a supplement to the *jus civile*, which was the law regulating relations among Roman citizens. As Roman power expanded and Roman citizens had increasing contact with non-citizens, a law was developed to regulate relations among non-citizens and between citizens and non-citizens; this was the *jus gentium*. The Roman jurist Gaius (AD c 130–180) provides the following characterisation:[166]

> Every people that is governed by statutes and customs observes partly its own peculiar law and partly the common law of all mankind. That law which a people establishes for itself is peculiar to it, and is called *ius civile*, while the law that natural reason establishes among all mankind is followed by all peoples alike, and is called *ius gentium* as being observed by all mankind. Thus the Roman people observes partly its own peculiar law and partly the law of mankind.

1.158   The *jus gentium* did not regulate relations among sovereigns (formal equality between Rome and foreign sovereigns was not recognised) and was, therefore, not international law in the modern sense. Rather, it consisted of general principles governing relations among individuals in any civilised society, which principles would find differentiated manifestation as to detail in each society's functional equivalent of the *jus civile*. Accordingly, the:[167]

165. Semble Judge Tanaka (dissenting) in the *South West Africa* cases *(Ethiopia v South Africa, Liberia v South Africa)* Second Phase, ICJ Rep (1966) 6, 296. See also D P O'Connell, *International Law*, 2nd ed, Stevens, London, 1970, Vol 1, 10–14.
166. Gaius, *Institutiones,* as translated by Hans Julius Wolff in *Roman Law: An Historical Introduction,* University of Oklahoma Press, Norman, 1951, 82–83.
167. Arthur Nussbaum, *A Concise History of the Law of Nations,* 2nd ed, Macmillan, New York, 1958, 14.

> ... *ius gentium* as defined by Gaius is a comprehensive concept which
> includes rules and legal institutions ... found everywhere, such as
> matrimony, protection of property, or the wrongdoer's obligation for
> damages; it is a universal law.

The *jus gentium* included some principles of an international character,
such as the inviolability of envoys and the law on spoils in war, but
this was far from establishing an equivalence of the *jus gentium* to
international law.

1.159   The *jus gentium* became, over time, confused with the *jus
naturale* (eternal and universal principles of law discoverable by right
reason), which entered Roman law through Greek stoic philosophy. This
confusion was the result of both uncertainty and expositional lack of
clarity as to whether the *jus gentium* was based on the positive law, or
whether it was founded on reason alone. This confusion affected legal
and philosophical analysis in practical ways. For example, if the *jus
gentium* was identical with the natural law, it would follow that the
then-universal institution of slavery was part of the *jus naturale*, and
was truly eternal. If, on the other hand, the *jus gentium* was based on
the positive common law of mankind, then the possibility remained that
slavery was contrary to the *jus naturale*.

1.160   One of the great accomplishments of the scholastics, and especially
St Thomas Aquinas (1225–1274), lay in clarifying the ambiguities that
had long dogged thinking about the *jus gentium*. According to Aquinas,
'Every human positive law has the nature of law to the extent that it
is derived from the natural law'. Positive law can be derived from the
natural law in two ways and, he wrote:[168]

> ... in this respect human law is divided into the common law of mankind
> *[jus gentium]* and civil law *[jus civile]* according to the two ways in which
> things can be derived from the natural law ... For those things belong
> to the common law of mankind which are derived from the natural law
> as conclusions from principles, such as just buying and selling and the
> like without which men cannot live together ... But those things that
> are derived from the natural law by way of particular determination
> *[per modum particularis determinationis]* belong to the civil law according
> as each political community *[civitas]* determines something appropriate
> for itself.

1.161   Thus, both the *jus gentium* and the *jus civile* are derived from the
natural law — the former by a process of deduction from first principles,
the latter by particular determination. Aquinas compares the process of
deduction by which we arrive at the *jus gentium* to 'that by which, in
sciences, demonstrated conclusions are drawn from the principles'. The
act of particular determination leading to the *jus civile* is compared to
'that whereby, in the arts, general forms are particularised as to details',
just as 'the craftsman needs to determine the general form of a house to
some particular shape'.[169]

---

168. St Thomas Aquinas, *Summa Theologica*, I–II, Q 95, A 2, C and A 4, c 1266.
169. Ibid, Q 95, A 2, C.

1.162   The *jus gentium* and the *jus civile* are, according to Aquinas, both part of the human or positive law in that they are both the result of deliberate human choosing. As with all human or positive law, they both derive their obligatory force from the natural law. However, whereas the *jus civile* belongs solely to positive law, the principles of *jus gentium* belong simultaneously to the positive law and the natural law. They are 'part of the natural law by their mode of derivation (by deduction, not *determinatio*), and at the same time part of positive human law by their mode of promulgation'.[170] The *jus gentium* consists of deduced secondary principles derived from the precepts and first principles of the natural law; it is manifested in positive laws, which are themselves part of the *jus civile*.

1.163   John Finnis identifies 13 interrelated principles which constitute 'general principles of law', and which are (or are part of) the *jus gentium* in the sense explained by Aquinas:[171]

(i) compulsory acquisition of property rights to be compensated, in respect of *damnum emergens* (actual losses) if not of *lucrum cessans* (loss of expected profits); (ii) no liability for unintentional injury, without fault; (iii) no criminal liability without *mens rea;* (iv) estoppel *(nemo contra factum proprium venire potest);* (v) no judicial aid to one who pleads his own wrong (he who seeks equity must do equity); (vi) no aid to abuse of rights; (vii) fraud unravels everything; (viii) profits received without justification and at the expense of another must be restored; (ix) *pacta sunt şervanda* (contracts are to be performed); (x) relative freedom to change existing patterns of legal relationships by agreement; (xi) in assessments of the legal effects of purported acts-in-the-law, the weak to be protected against their weakness; (xii) disputes not to be resolved without giving both sides an opportunity to be heard; (xiii) no one to be allowed to judge his own cause.

These *jus gentium* principles really are principles in that 'they justify, rather than require, particular rules and determinations, and are qualified in their application to particular circumstances by other like principles'.[172] This is precisely how the general principles of law function in international law.

1.164   The *jus gentium* general principles of law identified by Finnis bear a striking resemblance to the general principles of law and of equity that feature prominently in the work of the ICJ and other tribunals applying international law.[173]

1.165   The application of the first of these general principles (compulsory acquisition of property rights to be compensated) is demonstrated by the following case before the Permanent Court of International Justice.

---

170. John Finnis, *Natural Law and Natural Rights*, Oxford University Press, Oxford, 1980, 296.
171. Ibid.
172. Ibid, 288.
173. Sir Robert Jennings and Sir Arthur Watts (eds), *Oppenheim's International Law,* 9th ed, Longman, New York, 1992, § 12, 36–40, § 15, 43–45; Ian Brownlie, *Principles of Public International Law,* 7th ed, Oxford University Press, Oxford, 2008, 16–18, 25–27.

In the ***Case Concerning the Factory at Chorzów (Indemnity) (Merits) (Germany v Poland)***,[174] Poland seized a factory at Chorzów that was the property of German nationals. Prior to the conclusion of the First World War, Chorzów had been in German territory, but it was transferred to Poland as part of the peace settlement. A treaty between Germany and Poland (the Geneva Convention of 1922 on Upper Silesia) would have regulated the payment of fair compensation had Poland engaged in an official act of expropriation, but the treaty did not regulate mere seizures of property. The Court said:[175]

> The essential principle contained in the notion of an illegal act — a principle which seems to be established by international practice and in particular by the decisions of arbitral tribunals — is that reparation must, as far as possible, wipe out all the consequences of the illegal act and re-establish the situation which would, in all probability, have existed if that act had not been committed. Restitution in kind, or, if this is not possible, payment of a sum corresponding to the value which a restitution in kind would bear; the award, if need be, of damages for loss sustained which would not be covered by restitution in kind or payment in place of it — such are the principles which should serve to determine the amount of compensation due for an act contrary to international law.

> ... The dispossession of an industrial undertaking — the expropriation of which is prohibited by the Geneva Convention — then involves the obligation to restore the undertaking and, if this not be possible, to pay its value at the time of the indemnification, which value is designed to take the place of restitution which has become impossible. To this obligation, in virtue of the general principles of international law, must be added that of compensating loss sustained as a result of the seizure.

1.166   The following case illustrates the fifth principle in Finnis's catalogue of general principles of law: no judicial aid to one who pleads his own wrong — he who seeks equity must do equity.

In the ***Diversion of Water from the River Meuse* case (*The Netherlands v Belgium*)**,[176] the Netherlands claimed that Belgium had violated a treaty undertaking by constructing canals that altered the volume of water flowing in the River Meuse. Belgium replied that the Netherlands was unable to maintain the claim because of prior similar conduct on its part. The dispute was referred to the Permanent Court of International Justice. The following passage is from Judge Hudson's individual opinion:[177]

> What are widely known as principles of equity have long been considered to constitute a part of international law, and as such they have often been applied by international tribunals. ... The Court has not been expressly authorised by its Statute to apply equity as distinguished from law. ... Article 38 of the Statute expressly directs the application of 'general principles of law recognised by civilised nations' and in more than one nation principles of equity have an

---

174. *Case Concerning the Factory at Chorzów (Indemnity) (Merits) (Germany v Poland)* PCIJ Rep (1928) Series A No 17.
175. Ibid, 47–48.
176. *Diversion of Water from the River Meuse* case (*The Netherlands v Belgium*) PCIJ Rep (1937) Series A/B No 70.
177. Ibid, 76–77.

established place in the legal system. The Court's recognition of equity as part of international law is in no way restricted by the special power conferred upon it 'to decide cases *ex aequo et bono,* if the parties agree thereto'. ... It must be concluded, therefore, that under Article 38 of the Statute, if not independently of that Article, the Court has some freedom to consider principles of equity as part of the international law it must apply.

It would seem to be an important principle of equity that where two parties have assumed an identical or reciprocal obligation, one party which is engaged in a continuing non-performance of that obligation should not be permitted to take advantage of a similar nonperformance by the other party. The principle finds expression in the so-called maxims of equity which exercised great influence in the creative period of the development of Anglo-American law. Some of these maxims are, 'Equality is equity'; 'He who seeks equity must do equity'. It is in line with such maxims that 'a court of equity refuses relief to a plaintiff whose conduct in regard to the subject-matter of the litigation has been improper'.

1.167   Other general principles of a primarily procedural character, such as *res judicata, effet utile* and denial of justice, have also figured among the general principles that international tribunals have applied in cases before them.

1.168   The foundational and pre-positive nature of the general principles was emphasised by Bin Cheng in his landmark work on the subject:[178]

This part of international law does not consist ... in specific rules formulated for practical purposes, but in general propositions underlying the various rules of law which express the essential qualities of juridical truth itself, in short of Law.

Non liquet

1.169   Furthermore, Baron Édouard Descamps (1847–1933), President of the Advisory Committee of Jurists on the Statute of the Permanent Court of International Justice, stated that the inclusion of general principles in the text of Art 38 'was necessary to meet the possibility of a *non liquet*'.[179] To pronounce a *non liquet* (a Latin phrase meaning 'not clear') is to 'invoke the absence of clear legal rules applicable to a dispute as a reason for declining to give judgment'.[180]

1.170   Consequently, the general principles of law provide a reservoir from which apparent gaps in the corpus of international law may be filled. They reinforce the view that international law should properly be regarded as a 'complete system' — that is, that every international situation is capable of being determined as a matter of law and that

---

178. Bin Cheng, *General Principles of Law as Applied by International Courts and Tribunals,* Stevens, London, 1953, 24.
179. Permanent Court of International Justice, Advisory Committee of Jurists, 'Procés-verbaux of the Proceedings of the Committee', 1920, 336.
180. Sir Robert Jennings and Sir Arthur Watts (eds), *Oppenheim's International Law,* 9th ed, Longman, New York, 1992, § 3, 13.

international tribunals may not pronounce a *non liquet*. Because they belong partly to the positive law, the *jus gentium* general principles do not provide a foundation for any arbitrary or capricious rejection of positive law rules. Rather, the positive law rules from which the general principles are partly derived furnish a basis upon which the *jus gentium* may be employed to fashion a rule to 'fit' the requirements of a case where no directly applicable conventional or customary rule provides an answer.

Natural law

1.171   Sir Gerald Fitzmaurice (1901–1982) proposed that at least some of the general principles of law falling within the scope of Art 38(1)(c) of the ICJ Statute 'involving inherently necessary principles of natural law, are such as to cause natural law, at any rate that aspect of it that relates to these principles, to be a formal, not merely a material source of law'.[181]

Judge Kotaro Tanaka, in his dissenting opinion in the *South West Africa* cases, observed that 'it is undeniable that in Article 38, para 1(c), some natural law elements are inherent'.[182] Sir Hersch Lauterpacht was even more forthright:[183]

> [T]he 'general principles of law' conceived as a source of international law are in many ways indistinguishable from the law of nature as often applied in the past in that sphere. There is no occasion for treating it, for that reason, with suspicion or embarrassment. The part of the law of nature in legal history — including the history of international law — is more enduring and more beneficent than that of positivism, which either identifies the law with, or considers it the result of, the mere will of the State and its agencies.

1.172   In the 'general principles of law recognised by civilised nations', we are not dealing with principles which States have willed into existence, or to whose application to international relations States have consented. They exist partly spontaneously in every civilised legal order, including international law.

Relationship to positive law

1.173   Because the general principles of law function primarily to fill lacunae in positive international law (treaties and custom), their practical significance has steadily declined as the corpus of conventional and customary international law has grown. In its earlier stages, modern international law relied heavily on the extrapolation of rules directly from the *jus gentium*.

---

181. Gerald Fitzmaurice, *Symbolae Verzijl: présentées au professeur J H W Verzijl à l'occasion de son LXXX-ième anniversaire*, Martinus Nijhoff, The Hague, 1958, 174.
182. Judge Tanaka (dissenting) in the *South West Africa* cases *(Ethiopia v South Africa, Liberia v South Africa)* Second Phase, ICJ Rep (1966) 6, 298.
183. Eli Lauterpacht (ed), *International Law, Being the Collected Works of Hersch Lauterpacht*, Cambridge University Press, Cambridge, 1970, Vol 1, 76.

The role of publicists from the time of Hugo Grotius (1583–1645) until well into the 19th century consisted largely of reasoning from first principles towards just solutions across the array of international legal problems. It is this feature of the earlier publicists' works which lends most of them a quality ranging from the rigorously rationalist to the flatly speculative, and which makes them seem so remote in style and substance from more recent works.

As conventional and customary law accumulated, the need to engage in reasoning directly from the general principles receded, and publicists began placing greater emphasis upon positive international law. This development was accelerated during the 19th century by the emergence of legal positivism as the dominant philosophy of law, according to which positive law is the only variety of law in the true sense.[184]

While legal positivism no longer enjoys the near-monopoly on legal theorising which it held in its heyday from the mid–19th to the mid–20th centuries, the fact remains that the general principles are only a reserve source from which new rules of international law may be fashioned.

That reserve function should not, however, be undervalued. In the words of a United States–United Kingdom Claims Tribunal:[185]

> Even assuming that there was ... no treaty and no specific rule of international law formulated as the expression of a universally recognized rule governing the case ..., it cannot be said that there is no principle of international law applicable. International law, as well as domestic law, may not contain, and generally does not contain, express rules decisive of particular cases; but the function of jurisprudence is to resolve the conflict of opposing rights and interests by applying, in default of any specific provision of law, the corollaries of general principles, and so to find ... the solution of the problem. This is the method of jurisprudence; it is the method by which the law has been gradually evolved in every country resulting in the definition and settlement of legal relations as well between States as between private individuals.

1.174 Furthermore, the general principles remain highly significant in providing a ratio for the positive law rules. The interpretation and application of conventional and customary rules will inevitably occur against the background of the general principles, which furnish a juridical foundation for the positive law.

Judicial decisions

1.175 Article 38(1)(d) of the ICJ Statute specifies that 'judicial decisions' are among the 'subsidiary means for the determination of the rules of law'. This means that judicial decisions are not themselves sources of law, but may be used to ascertain the existence and scope of rules sourced in treaties, custom and the general principles of law.

---

184. See **1.56–1.78**.
185. *Eastern Extension, Australasia and China Telegraph Co Ltd* (1923) 6 RIAA 112, 114–115.

1.176   Moreover, there is no doctrine of *stare decisis* in international law. In the case of the ICJ, the point is driven home by Art 59 of the Court's Statute, which specifies that the 'decision of the Court has no binding force except between the parties and in respect of that particular case'. Accordingly, prior decisions of courts and tribunals have no binding force in the determination of disputes before international courts. This is partly a consequence of the absence of a formal system and hierarchy of international courts and tribunals, but it also accords with the legal tradition to be found in most non-common law jurisdictions.

1.177   Nevertheless, the tendency by judges to have regard to the reported decisions of prior cases is a recurrent feature of almost all modern legal systems, even if it is not formalised in legal dogma. This is a natural product of the rule of law itself, which requires that like cases be treated alike. Accordingly, international courts and tribunals routinely have regard to earlier decisions by dispute-settlement bodies for the determination of rules of international law.

1.178   A 'judicial decision' may be the result of a hearing before either national or international courts and tribunals. Generally speaking, decisions of international tribunals are more persuasive, though the most superior courts or tribunals of several States are very highly regarded: for example, the Supreme Court of the United States, the English House of Lords and the High Court of Australia. The most prominent international tribunals are the International Court of Justice (and its predecessor, the Permanent Court of International Justice), the European Court of Human Rights, the Inter-American Court of Human Rights, the Human Rights Committee of the United Nations, the European Court of Justice, the Dispute Settlement Body and the Appeal Body of the World Trade Organisation, the Permanent Court of Arbitration, and the International Criminal Court.

All these tribunals are permanent or 'standing' in their constitution. However, a large volume of frequently important international adjudication or arbitration is conducted by ad hoc tribunals which are constituted, usually by special agreement between disputing States, to determine or arbitrate particular international disagreements of a legal character. Sometimes, ad hoc tribunals, such as the International Criminal Tribunal for Yugoslavia (and the corresponding tribunal for Rwanda), are established by an act of the United Nations or another international organisation.

1.179   The absence of a formal hierarchy among courts and tribunals in international law means that a number of other factors will assume greater importance in determining the extent to which a prior judicial decision is persuasive.

Obviously, relevance to the problem at hand is always the most important consideration. The next most important is the extent and quality of the reasoning. A brief or elliptical judgment will generally carry less weight than one that is thorough and well argued. A decision written by a judge or publicist of high repute in international law will generally carry more weight than decisions authored by lesser-known figures. Indeed, even a dissenting, but thorough and well-argued, opinion by a well-regarded judge or publicist can frequently be highly persuasive.

In the case of national courts or tribunals, the extent to which the decision really turns on issues of international law, as distinct from domestic law considerations, will be important. Finally, the age of the decision will be significant. Formally, courts and tribunals are merely ascertaining and applying rules sourced in treaties, customs and the general principles of law. As a general proposition, the older the decision, the more cautiously it should be treated as conventional, as customary laws are likely to change with the passage of time.

1.180 The formal absence of a judicial hierarchy notwithstanding, decisions of the International Court of Justice and its predecessor (the Permanent Court of International Justice) are afforded the very highest respect. Such are their influence in international law that their decisions have frequently had a decisive impact on the practice of States. It is no exaggeration to say that even where the courts have probably determined the law wrongly, States have generally accepted these courts' view of international law and altered their own practice accordingly. These courts have also routinely made liberal reference to their previous judgments in reaching decisions, according them a status which can only be regarded as falling not far short of binding. As Judge Philadelpho Azevedo (1894–1951) remarked in his dissenting opinion in the *Asylum* case:[186]

> It should be remembered ... that the [ICJ's] decision in a particular case has deep repercussions, particularly in international law, because views which have been confirmed by that decision acquire quasi-legislative value, in spite of the legal principle to the effect that the decision has no binding force except between parties and in respect of that particular case (Statute, Art 59).

Teachings of publicists

1.181 The 'teachings of the most highly qualified publicists of the various nations' are also among the 'subsidiary means for the determination of the rules of law'.[187] These teachings are frequently referred to as 'doctrine' or 'doctrinal writings'. This means that, as with judicial decisions, the teachings of publicists are not themselves sources of law, but may be used to ascertain the existence and scope of rules sourced in treaties, custom and the general principles of law.

1.182 As mentioned above,[188] 'publicists' will almost always be eminent academic experts in international law, though the published works of

---

186. *Asylum* case *(Colombia v Peru)* ICJ Rep (1950) 266, 332. See **1.127**.
187. ICJ Statute, Art 38(1)(d).
188. See **1.37**.

diplomats or statesmen may also occasionally feature. Their 'teachings' are generally found in published scholarly books and journals.

Analogous to the teachings of publicists, and often regarded as more authoritative, are the published works of bodies such as the International Law Commission,[189] the Institute of International Law, committees of jurists commissioned by international organisations, and other expert bodies.

1.183 With the decline in importance of the general principles of law relative to conventional and customary law,[190] the role of publicists in shaping international law also has declined. Nevertheless, whereas judicial precedent plays a somewhat lesser role in international law as compared to common law systems, academic writings continue to figure more prominently in resolving international legal problems than they do in common law systems and most other domestic legal systems.

1.184 The writings of publicists often feature prominently in legal argument before courts and tribunals determining issues of international law. Such writings are, however, only infrequently cited in judgments and opinions of the International Court of Justice. This is partly due to the fact that the ICJ's judgments and opinions are the result of collective drafting. The much greater prominence of doctrinal writings in the Court's separate and dissenting opinions probably better indicates the true extent of their influence.

1.185 The role of doctrinal writings in the process of international law adjudication before United States courts was described by United States Supreme Court Associate Justice Horace Gray (1828–1902) in the following terms:[191]

> International law is part of our law, and must be ascertained and administered by the courts of justice of appropriate jurisdiction, as often as questions of right depending upon it are duly presented for their determination. For this purpose, where there is no treaty, and no controlling executive or legislative act or judicial decision, resort must be had to the customs and usages of civilized nations; and as evidence of these, to the works of jurists and commentators who by years of labor, research and experience have made themselves particularly well acquainted with the subjects of which they treat. Such works are resorted to by judicial tribunals, not for the speculations of their authors concerning what the law ought to be, but for trustworthy evidence of what the law really is.

Justice Gray's formulation is too narrow for the purposes of adjudication before international courts and tribunals. Not only are the teachings of publicists relevant for the purpose of ascertaining the state of customary international law in relation to a particular point, but they are also helpful in interpreting and applying treaties and the general principles of law.

---

189. See **1.54**.
190. See **1.173**.
191. *The Paquete Habana* 175 US (1900) 677, 700–701.

1.186 The factors that are important in determining the relative persuasive weight to be attached to different doctrinal writings resemble those which apply to assessing the relative weight of judicial decisions. Accordingly, relevance to the applicable legal issues is always the most important factor, followed by the extent and quality of reasoning. The more thorough and well argued the writing, the more weight it will be given. The work of a publicist of high repute in international law will carry more weight than opinions authored by lesser-known figures. As with judicial decisions, the age of the doctrinal writing can also be significant. Formally, doctrinal writings help in ascertaining and applying rules sourced in treaties, customs and the general principles of law. Again, the older the writing, the more cautiously it should be treated, as conventional and customary laws are likely to change over time.

1.187 Generally speaking, doctrinal writings are afforded less persuasive weight than the decisions of courts and tribunals. As the corpus of reported judicial decisions expands, the relative importance of doctrinal writings gradually declines. This is partly the result simply of judicial habit, but also reflects the fact that judgments, decisions, awards or opinions issued by courts or tribunals are almost always the product of careful and collective consideration after taking into account extensive evidence and legal submissions from the parties.

Although eminent publicists frequently make significant contributions to the explication and development of international law, it is 'obvious that subjective factors enter into any assessment of juristic opinion, that individual writers reflect national and other prejudices, and, further, that some publicists see themselves to be propagating new and better views rather than providing a passive appraisal of the law'.[192]

Acts of international organisations

1.188 International organisations established by agreement among States provide forums within which international relations may be conducted. With the exception of certain acts adopted by the United Nations Security Council,[193] none of these organisations are capable of adopting acts that per se create rules applicable to all States in international law. Neither the United Nations nor any other international organisation is a world legislature.

1.189 The treaty establishing an international organisation is its constitution. Where the treaty provides that the organisation may adopt measures that bind its member States then, as a matter of conventional law, those States are obliged to comply with any such measures to the extent and in the manner prescribed by the conventional obligation.

---

192. J L Brierly, *The Law of Nations,* ed Sir Humphrey Waldock, 6th ed, Oxford University Press, New York, 1963, 24.
193. See **9.49–9.59**.

Usually, authorisation of this kind extends only to adopting measures affecting the organisation's internal operations, such as its finances or procedures.[194] Furthermore, and subject to any contrary provisions in the treaty itself, an organisation's constitutive treaty may be authoritatively interpreted by the practice of States operating within the treaty.[195]

Less commonly, a constitutive treaty will empower an international organisation to adopt measures which produce more general legal obligations among the member States inter se: for example, the power of the International Civil Aviation Organisation to adopt legally binding standards for air navigation under Chapter VI of the 1944 Convention on Civil Aviation.[196]

Much more rarely, however, a constitutive treaty might confer on the organisation powers to adopt measures which produce legal effects directly in the territory of its member States: for example, Art 249 of the 1957 Treaty Establishing the European Community.[197] In such a case, international law requires States to give effect to the more extensive obligation as a matter of *pacta sunt servanda*.

1.190   Although resolutions and similar acts of international organisations do not directly and per se generate rules that form part of general international law, it is possible for them indirectly to help create such rules. Acts of international organisations can provide useful and easily accessible evidence of *opinio juris*, and may, therefore, contribute to the emergence of rules of customary international law binding on all States. Similarly, the acts of regional organisations, such as the Council of Europe or the Organisation of American States, are capable of providing evidence of *opinio juris* in support of both general and regional customary international law.

In ascertaining the existence of the *opinio juris* element of the customary rule against the threat or use of force in international relations, the International Court of Justice in the *Nicaragua* case took account of several UN General Assembly resolutions, a resolution of the 1928 Sixth International Conference of American States, and a declaration of the 1975 Conference on Security and Co-operation in Europe.[198] Ten years later, in the *Nuclear Weapons* advisory opinion, the ICJ considered a series of General Assembly resolutions passed since 1961 and said:[199]

> General Assembly resolutions, even if they are not binding, may sometimes
> have normative value. They can, in certain circumstances, provide evidence
> important for establishing the existence of a rule or the emergence of an
> *opinio juris*. To establish whether this is true of a given General Assembly

---

194. For example, UN Charter, Arts 17 and 18.
195. *Reparation for Injuries Suffered in the Service of the United Nations* case, ICJ Rep (1949) 174. See **4.60**.
196. UNTS, Vol 15, p 295.
197. *Official Journal of the European Communities*, C 325/33, 24 December 2002.
198. *Military and Paramilitary Activities in and Against Nicaragua (Nicaragua v United States)* Merits, ICJ Rep (1986) 14, paras 188–189. See **9.10**.
199. *Legality of the Threat or Use of Nuclear Weapons* advisory opinion, ICJ Rep (1996) 226, para 70. See **8.51** and **9.27**.

resolution, it is necessary to look at its content and the conditions of its adoption; it is also necessary to see whether an *opinio juris* exists as to its normative character. Or a series of resolutions may show the gradual evolution of the *opinio juris* required for the establishment of a new rule.

1.191   Not all acts of international organisations are equally useful in helping to establish the existence of a customary rule. Among the factors to be taken into account are the following.

- The extent to which the act is supported by States from different political and economic groupings — support from only one group or bloc will tend to militate against its support for a customary rule.
- The extent to which the act is supported by States which are specially affected by the putative rule, or which are particularly involved in the activity it is said to regulate.[200]
- The language used in the act itself — language which declares or suggests that it is stating an existing legal right or obligation will be stronger evidence in support of a customary rule.
- The records of any proceedings leading up to the act's adoption — statements by State representatives indicating their view as to the provision's juridical character will be important.
- The frequency with which the provision in the Act has been reiterated in subsequent acts — a frequently reiterated provision will provide stronger evidence in support of a customary rule than a single statement.

1.192   The United Nations Security Council possesses an exceptional, and relatively narrow, power to adopt Acts which directly and per se create legal obligations in general international law.

1.193   The Security Council's powers under Chapter VII of the UN Charter to authorise the use of force by States in order to maintain or restore international peace and security are dealt with in detail elsewhere.[201] These powers include a power to require, with compulsory legal effect, a State to perform acts or refrain from acts in order that international peace and security might be maintained or restored. Thus, in its Chapter VII resolution of 25 June 1950, the Security Council called upon 'the authorities of North Korea to withdraw forthwith to the 38th parallel' and, in Resolution 1267 (1999), the Security Council demanded that Afghanistan turn over the terrorist leader Osama bin Laden to face trial.

1.194   Concomitant with those powers is a power conferred by Art 41 of the UN Charter:

> The Security Council may decide what measures not involving the use of armed force are to be employed to give effect to its decisions, and it may call upon the Members of the United Nations to apply such measures. They may include complete or partial interruption of economic relations and of rail, sea, air, postal, telegraphic, radio, and other means of communication, and the severance of diplomatic relations.

---

200. See **1.117**.
201. See **9.49–9.59**.

1.195 Article 41 enables the Security Council to 'call upon' States to impose a range of embargoes and sanctions in the areas of economic relations, transport, communications and diplomatic contacts. This may be done in order to 'maintain or restore international peace and security' where the Council has already determined that the situation to which the sanctions are directed constitutes a 'threat to the peace, breach of the peace or act of aggression'.[202]

1.196 A decision taken under Art 41 may require States, as a matter of legal obligation, to impose particular embargos and sanctions. Art 25 of the UN Charter provides that member States 'agree to accept and carry out decisions of the Security Council in accordance with the present Charter'. Article 103 goes on to provide that:[203]

> In the event of a conflict between the obligations of the Members of the United Nations under the present Charter and their obligations under any other international agreement, their obligations under the present Charter shall prevail.

1.197 The first use of the enforcement powers in Art 41 occurred in 1965 in response to Southern Rhodesia's Unilateral Declaration of Independence from the United Kingdom by the white minority government of that territory.

By two resolutions in that year, the Security Council called upon all States not to recognise the regime controlling Rhodesia, to break all economic relations with it, and to impose an arms embargo against it.[204] The following year, selective economic sanctions were imposed[205] and in 1968 those sanctions were made comprehensive.[206] All these measures were finally lifted upon the conclusion of agreements leading to the independence of Zimbabwe.

Since the end of the Cold War, increasing use has been made of Art 41. Sanctions or embargoes have been imposed on Iraq, Libya, Yugoslavia, Somalia, Liberia, Haiti, Rwanda, Sierra Leone, Afghanistan, Eritrea, Ethiopia, Iran, North Korea and UNITA (National Union for Total Independence of Angola) forces in Angola. The range of measures has included economic and trade sanctions, arms embargoes, travel bans, financial or diplomatic restrictions, and supply of material for the manufacture of nuclear weapons.

1.198 It should be emphasised that the Security Council is a political and not a judicial body. When acting under Chapter VII of the UN Charter, it does not need to make a determination that a breach of international law has occurred, though it will frequently do so where agreement on such a characterisation can be reached.[207] Conversely, not every breach of

---

202. UN Charter, Art 39.
203. On the effect of Arts 25 and 103 of the UN Charter, see *Case Concerning Questions of Interpretation and Application the 1971 Montreal Convention Arising from the Aerial Incident at Lockerbie (Provisional Measures) (Libya v United Kingdom)* ICJ Rep (1992) 3, paras 37, 39.
204. Resolution 216 (1965) and Resolution 217 (1965).
205. Resolution 232 (1966).
206. Resolution 253 (1968).
207. See **9.55**.

international law will justify resort to Chapter VII powers. The Security Council's powers to act under Chapter VII are enlivened only when it determines that there is a threat to the peace, a breach of the peace or an act of aggression.[208]

Unilateral declarations by States

1.199 An additional source of legal obligation, not mentioned in Art 38 of the ICJ Statute, is certain types of unilateral declarations made on behalf of States. These declarations may be made outside the context of any negotiations, without any requirement of reciprocity or quid pro quo, and even without the need for other States to either accept or acknowledge the declaration. This source of obligation is a relatively recent development in international law, and it originates in a judgment of the ICJ that was greeted with scepticism by many publicists and commentators.

In the ***Nuclear Tests* cases (*Australia v France, New Zealand v France*),**[209] Australia and New Zealand brought proceedings against France challenging the legality of the latter's atmospheric testing of nuclear weapons in the South Pacific Ocean. Before the matter could proceed to a hearing on the merits, France moved that the Court not proceed to give final judgment on the grounds that the claims no longer had an object. France made this move on the basis of several public utterances made by high officials of the French State in the preceding few months. In a communiqué issued by the President of the Republic, he declared that 'France will be in a position to pass on to the stage of underground explosions as soon as the series of tests planned for this summer is completed'. Subsequently, the President of the Republic made a statement at a press conference in which he repeated his commitment to ending France's atmospheric nuclear tests. France's Foreign Minister also made a speech at the UN General Assembly where he said that France has 'now reached a stage in our nuclear technology that makes it possible for us to continue our programme by underground testing, and we have taken steps to do so as early as next year'. Statements to similar effect were made to the media by the French Defence Minister. France contended that these statements had the effect of legally binding France to discontinue its program of atmospheric testing; there was, therefore, nothing left for the Court to decide. Australia and New Zealand, which wished to obtain a ruling from the Court on the legality of atmospheric testing of nuclear weapons, rejected France's argument that the unilateral statements made by the French officials could create a legal obligation binding on France. The Court said:

> 43. It is well recognised that declarations made by way of unilateral acts, concerning legal or factual situations, may have the effect of creating legal obligations. Declarations of this kind may be, and often are, very specific. When it is the intention of the State making the declaration that it should be bound according to its terms, that intention confers on the declaration the character

---

208. As to the possibility of judicial review of Security Council measures adopted under Chapter VII, see **9.56–9.57**.
209. *Nuclear Tests* cases *(Australia v France, New Zealand v France)* ICJ Rep (1974) 253.

of a legal undertaking, the State being thenceforth legally required to follow a course of conduct consistent with the declaration. An undertaking of this kind, if given publicly, and with an intent to be bound, even though not made within the context of international negotiations, is binding. In these circumstances, nothing in the nature of a *quid pro quo* nor any subsequent acceptance of the declaration, nor even any reply or reaction from other States, is required for the declaration to take effect …

44. Of course, not all unilateral acts imply obligation; but a State may choose to take up a certain position in relation to a particular matter with the intention of being bound the intention to be ascertained by interpretation of the act. When States make statements by which their freedom of action is to be limited, a restrictive interpretation is called for.

45. … Whether a statement is made orally or in writing makes no essential difference …

46. One of the basic principles governing the creation and performance of legal obligations, whatever their source, is the principle of good faith. Trust and confidence are inherent in international co-operation, in particular in an age when this co-operation in many fields is becoming increasingly essential. Just as the very rule of *pacta sunt servanda* in the law of treaties is based on good faith, so also is the binding character of an international obligation assumed by unilateral declaration. Thus interested States may take cognizance of unilateral declarations and place confidence in them, and are entitled to require that the obligation thus created be respected …

51. … The Court finds that the unilateral undertaking resulting from these statements cannot be interpreted as having been made in implicit reliance on an arbitrary power of reconsideration.

The Court stated its satisfaction that the declarations made by, and under the authority of, France's Head of State, having regard to their content and the circumstances in which they were made, were sufficient to bind France legally to observe their terms. France's motion was, accordingly, granted.

1.200   On the basis of the Court's reasoning in the *Nuclear Tests* cases, it appears that the formal source of law for a unilateral declaration is the general principle of good faith, and that the terms of the declaration furnish the source of obligation or the material source of law.[210] Good faith is, however, a general principle modulating the performance of existing legal obligations and is not normally seen as being a formal source of law itself. The ICJ itself later held that the principle of good faith is one of the basic principles governing the creation and performance of legal obligations, but 'is not in itself a source of obligation where none would otherwise exist'.[211]

1.201   The International Court of Justice has reaffirmed the doctrine that unilateral declarations can be legally binding, while simultaneously emphasising its limits.

---

210. See **1.88**.
211. *Border and Transborder Armed Actions* case *(Nicaragua v Costa Rica)* ICJ Rep (1988) 69, para 94.

In the ***Frontier Dispute* case (*Burkina Faso v Mali*),**[212] the ICJ was called upon to delimit a portion of the border separating Burkina Faso from Mali. It was part of Burkina Faso's case that the President of Mali had, in a media interview, made a unilateral statement binding Mali to accept the solution recommended by a Mediation Commission of the Organisation of African Unity. The Commission's recommendations were never formally published, but their contents were known to be more favourable to Burkina Faso than to Mali. The President of Mali had said: 'Mali extends over 1,240,000 square kilometres, and we cannot justify fighting for a scrap of territory 150 kilometres long. Even if the Organisation of African Unity Commission decides objectively that the frontier runs through Bamako [Mali's capital city], my government will comply with the decision.' The Court referred to passages from its judgment in the *Nuclear Tests* cases and said:

> 39. ... Thus it all depends on the intention of the State in question and the Court emphasized that it is for the Court to 'form its own view of the meaning and scope intended by the author of a unilateral declaration which may create a legal obligation' ...

> 40. In order to assess the intentions of the author of a unilateral act, account must be taken of all the factual circumstances in which the act occurred. For example, in the *Nuclear Tests cases,* the Court took the view that since the applicant States were not the only ones concerned at the possible continuance of atmospheric testing by the French Government, the Government's unilateral declarations 'conveyed to the world at large, including the Applicant, its intention effectively to terminate these tests' ... In the particular circumstances of those cases, the French Government could not express an intention to be bound otherwise than by unilateral declarations. ... The circumstances of the present case are radically different. Here, there was nothing to hinder the parties from manifesting an intention to accept the binding character of the conclusions of the Organisation of African Unity Mediation Commission by the normal method: a formal agreement on the basis of reciprocity. Since no agreement of this kind was concluded between the Parties, the Chamber finds that there are no grounds to interpret the declaration made by Mali's Head of State ... as a unilateral act with legal implications in regard to the present case.

The Court was not persuaded that the Mali President's comments were seriously intended to bind Mali as a matter of international law. This was partly due to the nature and circumstances of the comments themselves. A larger factor in the Court's reasoning, however, was the fact that only one other State had an interest in the declaration's subject matter and a unilateral declaration was not the only way in which a legal obligation could be effectively undertaken.

The more normal method of an agreement based on reciprocity was practicably open to the parties, and it could not be lightly assumed that Mali's President intended to adopt some other method of committing his State. It would, therefore, seem that unilateral declarations will not easily have the effect of binding a State where only one other State has an interest in the declaration's subject matter.

---

212. *Frontier Dispute* case *(Burkina Faso v Mali)* ICJ Rep (1986) 554.

Soft law

1.202   There is a category of legal materials that is often referred to, somewhat infelicitously, as 'soft law'. The reference is an unfortunate one because the material is not really law at all, and the label 'soft law' has a capacity to mislead the reader into ascribing to the materials a legal significance that they do not really possess.

1.203   Soft law is any material that is not intended to generate, or is not per se capable of generating, legal rules, but which may, nonetheless, produce certain legal effects. Those effects can range from providing the evidence of the State practice and *opinio juris* required to establish a rule of customary international law, through providing assistance in the interpretation and application of conventional and customary law, the precise requirements of which remain unclear, to indicating the likely future course of international law's development.

1.204   This rather amorphous category of materials is usually taken to mean non-binding instruments, such as declarations, resolutions and guidelines adopted by international organisations or assemblies of States. Occasionally, it can extend to similar instruments adopted by private associations, such as the International Committee of the Red Cross, where they are endowed with officially recognised functions by virtue of a treaty.[213]

Accordingly, although UN General Assembly resolutions are not usually per se capable of producing legal effects,[214] they may provide evidence of a customary rule[215] or point to the *lex ferenda* (the future development of the law). The same is true of expressly non-legally binding international agreements or declarations, such as the declaration on principles governing the mutual relations of States adopted at the 1975 Helsinki Conference on Security and Co-operation in Europe.[216]

These materials may also provide a foundation upon which States eventually conclude treaties.

---

213. Hilaire McCoubrey, *International Humanitarian Law*, 2nd ed, Ashgate, Dartmouth, 1999, 52–53.
214. But see **1.189**.
215. See **1.105–1.106**.
216. *Military and Paramilitary Activities in and Against Nicaragua (Nicaragua v United States)* Merits, ICJ Rep (1986) 14, para 189. See **9.10**.

Question

The only true sources of international law are treaties and custom, of which treaties are superior in that they always displace customary law. Discuss.

Suggested answer

Both parts of the proposition are inaccurate: treaties and custom are not the only true sources of law. Indeed, treaties are not truly a source of law at all. Furthermore, treaties are not inherently superior to custom. It is certainly true that treaties and custom are the only varieties of purely positive international law, in the sense that they are both the result of choices made by States. Yet there is a third source of international law that is not entirely positive in character and which provides binding legal norms on the plane of international relations.

The general principles of law recognised by civilised nations are explicitly identified as a source of law by Art 38(1)(c) of the ICJ Statute. The general principles are part of the positive law in the sense that they are manifested, often as positive law, in the domestic legal systems of States. They are part of the natural law inasmuch as their applicability to international legal relations is merely 'recognised', and not enacted or consented to, by States.

Their most practical function in modern international law is to fill gaps in the positive law network of customs and treaties, so that international law may furnish an answer to every dispute arising in international relations (for example, the *Chorzów Factory* case and the *River Meuse* case). As conventional and customary international law develop, the significance of this function of the general principles recedes because the general principles cannot replace requirements of the positive law.

Nevertheless, even if there were to be few remaining gaps in the positive law, the general principles would retain significance as foundational legal justifications of the positive law rules and principles. Indeed, requirements of conventional and customary law are frequently interpreted and applied in the context of the underlying general principles that justify them in juridical terms. Perhaps the most significant example is the general principle of law known as *pacta sunt servanda* that furnishes the juridical basis for the legal force of all treaties.

Indeed, it is the juridical dependency of treaties on *pacta sunt servanda* that makes it appropriate to say that treaties are not sources of law. Many publicists have observed that treaties are, in reality, sources of obligation rather than sources of law. This means that treaties specify the content of certain promises. Not all promises, however, are legally binding, and it is a formal source of law which endows promises made in treaties with a legally binding character — that is, *pacta sunt servanda*.

It would be easy to conclude, on the basis that treaties are listed prior to custom in Art 38(1) of the ICJ Statute, that treaties possess a superior legal quality to custom. Indeed, *pacta sunt servanda* operates so as to render treaty obligations legally superior to conflicting customary obligations in most cases, so that a State will ordinarily be obliged to comply with the treaty requirement and to disregard the conflicting customary rule.

Nevertheless, there are two sets of circumstances in which a treaty obligation will not override or negate a conflicting customary rule. First, a treaty will be void if it conflicts with any requirement of the *jus cogens,* which are customary rules from which no derogation is permitted. Second, State A will not escape its customary obligations with State B because it has entered into conflicting treaty obligations with State C; State A will need to choose which obligation it will observe and which it will breach, while recognising that it will be liable for whichever breach occurs. The relationship between treaty and custom is more complex than a straightforward hierarchical model would produce.

It should be noted that the rules by which we interpret treaties and ascertain their validity, continuance in force, and termination, and, therefore, by which we ascertain the scope of conventional rights and obligations, are based in custom. The Vienna Convention on the Law of Treaties does not apply to all treaties, and most of its provisions are reflective of customary law.

A striking feature of the international legal system is the capacity of certain multilateral treaties to generate customary rules binding on States that are not party to the treaty. This will occur where first, the treaty provision in question is 'of a fundamentally norm-creating character'; second, 'even without the passage of any considerable period of time, a very widespread and representative participation in the convention might suffice of itself, provided it included that of States whose interests were specially affected'; and third, 'State practice including that of States whose interests are specially affected, should have been both extensive and virtually uniform in the sense of the provision invoked — and should moreover have occurred in such a way as to show a general recognition that a rule of law or legal obligation is involved' (*North Sea Continental Shelf* cases).

Furthermore, in the *Nicaragua* case, the ICJ held that a State may be bound by a conventional rule and a parallel customary rule simultaneously. The treaty rule does not abolish or subsume the customary rule. In the Court's view, 'customary international law continues to exist and apply, separately from international treaty law, even where the two categories of law have an identical content'.

It can be seen, therefore, that there is no simple hierarchy among the three sources of law or obligation identified in paras (a)–(c) of Art 38(1) of the ICJ Statute. Article 38(1) merely sets out a rational methodology for technical legal reasoning, proceeding from the specific to the general. In determining the rules applicable to a particular problem, it is legally sound first to look for any obligations established between the parties as a result of their own agreement, and for that one must turn primarily to treaties. Failing any such obligations, or failing their sufficiency in resolving the problem, one should then look to any applicable customary law.

Customary law will also provide rules by which we interpret and apply treaties and may also furnish us with *jus cogens* norms that will void inconsistent treaties. The customary law may also have resulted from the widespread adherence to a treaty. Failing a sufficient solution being found in customary law, we should then look to the general principles of law in order to avoid a *non liquet* (that is, an inability to render judgment because of *lacunae* in the law), and for principles underpinning and modulating our understanding of treaties and custom — for example, *pacta sunt servanda*.

What one has, then, is an interlocking and mutually reinforcing system of sources, rather than a straightforward hierarchy.

Judicial decisions and the teachings of the most highly qualified publicists of the various nations are also identified by Art 38(1) as materials to which the ICJ may refer in deciding cases submitted to it. As para (d) of that provision makes clear, however, these materials are merely 'subsidiary means for the determination of the rules of law'. As such, they are not sources of law themselves, although they do assist in understanding the scope and meaning of treaties, custom and the general principles. Their usefulness depends on how well they perform this function. As a corollary, decisions of the ICJ do not create binding legal precedent (ICJ Statute, Art 59), and the same is true for decisions of other tribunals that pronounce upon issues of international law.

Decisions by the Security Council under Chapter VII of the UN Charter are capable of creating binding obligations on all States. The formal legal sources of these obligations are *pacta sunt servanda* and custom (for parties to the UN Charter) or custom alone (for all other States). In other words, Chapter VII resolutions are not themselves sources of law but, as with treaties, are sources of obligation. Similarly, resolutions of the General Assembly are never per se binding on States, although they may furnish evidence of customary law by demonstrating the existence of State practice and *opinion juris* (*Nicaragua* case and *Nuclear Weapons* advisory opinion).

Certain unilateral declarations made by States are a somewhat anomalous source of legal obligation. According to the innovative decision of the ICJ in the *Nuclear Tests* cases, where a unilateral declaration was made which contains precise undertakings and which was intended to create legal obligations, it will be binding according to its terms, even without a quid pro quo from any other State and even without an acceptance by any other State. Such declarations are not agreements between States and are, therefore, not treaties. They are probably not binding as a result of the general principle of law requiring good faith in the performance of international obligations, because that principle presupposes a pre-existing legal obligation to which it can be attached. Assuming that such declarations are indeed binding as a matter of international law, the best available basis for their binding legal character is probably custom.

Further tutorial discussion

Nature of international law

1. Given that international law's enforcement mechanisms are decentralised and weak compared to most domestic legal orders, why do States almost always comply with its requirements?
2. What is 'positive international law'? Is there any other kind of international law?
3. Many States that participate in the making of positive international law are internally undemocratic and repressive. Does this ever affect the content or legal character of international law?
4. Is the current international legal system well adapted to the requirements of international society? If you could make one reform to the structure of international law, what would it be?
5. Does international law serve an 'international community'?
6. Less powerful States will frequently be unable to engage in meaningful or effective countermeasures in response to a violation of their international rights by more powerful States. Does this mean that international law is less useful to weaker States? Does it affect the legal character of international law?

Sources of international law

7. Customary law is evidenced by State practice and *opinio juris*. When is separate evidence of *opinio juris* required, and how is it proved?
8. Would the international legal system be strengthened if the persistent objector principle were abandoned?
9. The general principles of law are not really a separate source of law; they do not have an existence separate from treaty and custom. Discuss.
10. The doctrine permitting multilateral treaties to generate customary norms binding on all States, including States not party to the treaty, is a significant encroachment on the sovereignty of States. Do you agree?
11. Treaties are often described as material sources of law or sources of obligation. Why is this so, and why is the claim important?
12. H L A Hart argued, in *The Concept of Law* (1961), that international law is not a legal system because it consists only of 'primary rules' of obligation while lacking 'secondary rules' by which the primary rules may be changed and compulsorily adjudicated. Do you agree?

Law of treaties

2

Objectives

After completing this chapter, you should:

(1) understand and be able to explain the principal similarities and differences between the law of treaties and domestic contract law;

(2) appreciate the relationship between the Vienna Convention on the Law of Treaties and customary international law as it regulates treaties;

(3) understand and be able to explain what constitutes a treaty;

(4) understand and be able to identify the modes by which a treaty may be validly concluded and enter into force;

(5) understand and be able to identify the effects of treaties on signatories, parties and certain third parties;

(6) understand and be able to navigate the conventional and customary rules and principles governing the making and effect of reservations to treaties;

(7) be able to interpret a treaty;

(8) understand and be able to explain how a treaty is amended or modified, and the difference between amendment and modification;

(9) be able to identify and explain the ways in which a treaty might be invalid, and the consequences of invalidity;

(10) understand and be able to explain how a treaty is denounced or withdrawn from, and the difference between denunciation and withdrawal;

(11) understand and be able to apply the rules and principles governing the termination and suspension of treaties and the consequences of termination and suspension; and

(12) understand and be able to describe the mandatory conventional procedures relating to invalidity, denunciation, withdrawal, termination and suspension of treaties.

Key cases

Legal Status of Eastern Greenland case *(Norway v Denmark)* PCIJ Rep (1933) Ser A/B No 53

Reservations to the Convention on the Prevention and Punishment of the Crime of Genocide advisory opinion, ICJ Rep (1951) 15

Case Concerning the Temple of Preah Vihear (Cambodia v Thailand) Merits, ICJ Rep (1962) 6

Legal Consequences for States of the Continued Presence of South Africa in Namibia (South West Africa) notwithstanding Security Council Resolution 276 (1970) advisory opinion, ICJ Rep (1971) 16

Fisheries Jurisdiction case *(United Kingdom v Iceland)* ICJ Rep (1973) 3
Appeal Relating to the Jurisdiction of the ICAO Council (India v Pakistan) ICJ Rep (1972) 46

Key treaties and instruments

Vienna Convention on the Law of Treaties (1969): Art 2(1)(a), Art 2(1)(d), Art 14, Art 18, Art 19, Art 20, Art 21, Art 24, Art 26, Art 27, Art 28, Art 29, Art 31, Art 32, Art 42, Art 44, Art 48, Art 52, Art 53, Art 56, Art 60, Art 62, Art 64, Art 65, Art 67
Human Rights Committee, General Comment 24, *General comment on issues relating to reservations made upon ratification or accession to the Covenant or the Optional Protocols thereto, or in relation to declarations under article 41 of the Covenant,* UN Doc CCPR/C/21/Rev.1/Add.6 (1994), (1995) 15 HRLJ 464, (1995) 2 IHRR 10, (1995) 34 ILM 839

Vienna Convention on the Law of Treaties and Customary Rules

2.1   The law of treaties is that branch of international law which regulates the formation, interpretation, application and termination of treaties. It is analogous to the law of contracts in domestic law. Treaties are not, however, perfectly analogous to domestic contracts; treaties perform a broader range of tasks than is normally expected of domestic contracts.[1] Furthermore, it is common for multilateral treaties to have large numbers of parties which, when the law on reservations is taken into account,[2] has the potential to complicate significantly the network of rights and obligations subsisting among the parties to such treaties. Every State is party to numerous treaties. Australia, for instance, is party to more than 900 treaties (not including treaty amendments and treaty actions).

2.2   Until the entry into force of the 1969 Vienna Convention on the Law of Treaties (VCLT)[3] on 27 January 1980, the law of treaties was governed exclusively by customary international law. The VCLT has 111 State parties, including Australia, and a further 15 signatories which have not yet ratified. Among the five permanent members of the Security Council, China, Russia and the United Kingdom are parties, while France and the United States are not.[4] A large minority of the world's States have declined, so far, to become parties to the VCLT.

2.3   The VCLT applies in respect of conventional relations between States where both of them are parties to the VCLT. It does not govern the operation of treaties between States in any of the following cases:

---

1.   See 1.97.
2.   See 2.53–2.74.
3.   UNTS, Vol 1155, p 331.
4.   As of October 2010.

- bilateral treaties where either contracting State is not a party to the VCLT;
- multilateral treaties, to the extent that they establish conventional relations between two States where either of them is not a party to the VCLT;
- treaties not concluded 'in written form'; and[5]
- treaties concluded or acceded to prior to entry into force of the VCLT, Art 4 of which denies retrospective effect to the VCLT.

In any of these cases, the treaty is governed by customary international law.

2.4   This bifurcation of the law of treaties into rules established in the VCLT and rules based in customary international law is not, however, as significant as one might expect.

Most of the VCLT's substantive provisions either codify pre-existing custom or have since crystallised into customary rules. Consequently, in relation to most issues of treaty law, the content of the applicable rule will be the same regardless of whether it is formally sourced in the VCLT or in custom. In the discussion that follows, VCLT provisions may be understood as reflecting customary international law unless the contrary is stated.

Definition of 'treaty'

2.5   Article 2(1)(a) of the VCLT contains a definition of 'treaty':

1. For the purposes of the present Convention:

   (a) 'treaty' means an international agreement concluded between States in written form and governed by international law, whether embodied in a single instrument or in two or more related instruments and whatever its particular designation;

If an agreement meets all the requirements of Art 2(1)(a), it will be a treaty whatever its formal designation.[6]

2.6   This definition is expressed to be applicable only for the purposes of the VCLT. Before an international agreement can constitute a treaty for the purposes of the VCLT, it must be:

- concluded between States;
- in written form; and
- governed by international law.

2.7   An arrangement may, however, constitute a treaty even if it fails to satisfy all the criteria in the VCLT definition. In such a case, the treaty will be governed not by the VCLT, but by rules based in customary law.

---

5.   See 2.11–2.15.
6.   See 2.15.

Concluded between States

2.8 Only treaties concluded between States may be regulated by the VCLT. As a matter of customary international law, however, intergovernmental organisations are also capable of entering into treaties. Sometimes, territorial units which are not States — such as semi-sovereign units within a federation — are capable of concluding treaties.[7] The VCLT cannot regulate treaties concluded between a State and these non-State entities or between these non-State entities. Article 3 of the VCLT, however, expressly preserves the legal force of such treaties, which will be regulated by customary international law.

2.9 The 1986 Vienna Convention on the Law of Treaties between States and International Organizations or between International Organizations (VCLTSIO)[8] is designed to regulate treaty relations not only between States and intergovernmental organisations, but also between intergovernmental organisations *inter se*. Although the VCLTSIO is not yet in force, many of its provisions are reflective of customary international law. This includes Art 6, which provides that the capacity of an intergovernmental organisation to conclude treaties with States or other intergovernmental organisations is governed by the constituent instrument or rules of that organisation. The VCLT, and not the VCLTSIO, applies to any treaty that is the constituent instrument of an intergovernmental organisation.[9]

2.10 Agreements concluded between States and private entities, such as companies incorporated under the domestic law of a foreign State, are not ordinarily regulated by the law of treaties.[10] The parties may, however, be able to 'internationalise' such an agreement by stipulating either that international law is the contract's proper law, or that any dispute shall be submitted to international arbitration. If the contract is concluded in this way, then the arbitrator will be able to apply international law in adjudication of the dispute under the contract.[11] This does not, however, transform the contract into a treaty.

In written form

2.11 The following case considered the status of an oral agreement made by persons representing their States.

> In the ***Legal Status of Eastern Greenland* case *(Norway v Denmark)*,**[12] a dispute between Norway and Denmark concerning sovereignty over the eastern part of Greenland was referred to the Permanent Court of International Justice. Denmark

---

7.   See **4.16**.
8.   Doc A/CONF129/15.
9.   VCLT, Art 5.
10.   *Anglo-Iranian Oil Co case (United Kingdom v Iran)* Preliminary Objection, ICJ Rep (1952) 93, 112.
11.   *Texaco Overseas Petroleum Co and California Asiatic Oil Co v Libya* (1977) 53 ILR 389.
12.   *Legal Status of Eastern Greenland case (Norway v Denmark)* PCIJ Rep (1933) Ser A/B No 53.

had established colonies in other parts of Greenland, and had long claimed sovereignty over the whole island. Eastern Greenland was uncolonised due mainly to its inhospitable climate and geography. After dispatching an expedition to eastern Greenland, Norway declared in 1931 that it had taken possession of the area. Part of Denmark's claim to sovereignty over the disputed territory was an alleged declaration made in 1919 by Nils Ihlen, the Norwegian Foreign Minister, in discussions with Denmark's Minister accredited to Norway. The discussions occurred in the context of the two States seeking to coordinate their positions at the Paris Peace Conference at the end of the First World War. The Danish Minister proposed that Denmark would make no objection to a Norwegian claim to sovereignty over Spitzbergen if Norway would not object to Denmark's claim to the whole of Greenland. At a subsequent meeting, the Norwegian Foreign Minister uttered the 'Ihlen declaration' to the Danish Minister. According to Mr Ihlen's own record of the conversation, he told the Danish Minister that 'the Norwegian Government would not make any difficulty' concerning Denmark's claim to the whole island. Denmark claimed that the Ihlen declaration constituted part of a binding agreement between the two States, which agreement had been breached by Norway's claim to sovereignty over eastern Greenland. The Court said:[13]

> This declaration by M. Ihlen has been relied on by Counsel for Denmark as a recognition of an existing Danish sovereignty over Greenland. The Court is unable to accept this point of view. A careful examination of the words used and of the circumstances in which they were used, as well as of the subsequent developments, shows that M. Ihlen cannot have meant to be giving then and there a definitive recognition of Danish sovereignty over Greenland, and shows also that he cannot have been understood by the Danish Government at the time as having done so …

> Nevertheless, the point which must now be considered is whether the Ihlen declaration even if not constituting a definitive recognition of Danish sovereignty did not constitute an engagement obliging Norway to refrain from occupying any part of Greenland. …

> What Denmark desired to obtain from Norway was that the latter should do nothing to obstruct the Danish plans in regard to Greenland. The declaration which the Minister for Foreign Affairs gave … on behalf of the Norwegian Government, was definitively affirmative …

> The Court considers it beyond all dispute that a reply of this nature given by the Minister for Foreign Affairs on behalf of his Government in response to a request by the diplomatic representative of a foreign Power, in regard to a question falling within his province, is binding upon the country to which the Minister belongs. …

> It follows that, as a result of the undertaking involved in the Ihlen declaration …, Norway is under an obligation to refrain from contesting Danish sovereignty over Greenland as a whole, and *a fortiori* to refrain from occupying a part of Greenland.

The PCIJ held that an oral undertaking made by a person with sufficient authority, and in the context of diplomatic negotiations, was capable of binding a State. Part of the context was the fact that Norway received a quid pro quo in respect of Mr Ihlen's declaration — that is, Denmark's acquiescence at the Paris Peace Conference in Norway's

---

13.   Ibid, 69–73.

claims to Spitzbergen. It is these factual elements — negotiations and the existence of a quid pro quo — which principally distinguish the Ihlen declaration from the declaration made in the *Nuclear Tests* cases.[14] The oral declaration by Mr Ihlen was, therefore, a treaty term between Norway and Denmark and, contrary to the view of some publicists, not a binding unilateral declaration. The VCLT expressly preserves the legal force of treaties which are not in written form.[15]

2.12   In an advisory opinion, the Permanent Court of International Justice also held that the participation by two States in the adoption of a resolution by the Council of the League of Nations calling upon them to enter into negotiations was capable of constituting a binding engagement between them.[16]

2.13   The VCLT prescribes no particular requirements for 'written form'. Customary international law is similarly silent in relation to the form of treaties which parties have reduced to writing. The International Court of Justice has remarked that where, 'as is generally the case in international law, which places the principal emphasis on the intention of the parties, the law prescribes no particular form, parties are free to choose what form they please provided their intention clearly results from it'.[17]

2.14   In the *Aegean Sea Continental Shelf* case *(Greece v Turkey)*,[18] the International Court of Justice considered whether an official joint communiqué issued at the end of a meeting in Brussels between the Prime Ministers of Greece and Turkey could constitute a binding international agreement to submit their dispute to arbitration or judicial settlement. The communiqué was issued to the media at the end of the meeting, but was neither signed nor initialled. The Court said that there was no rule of international law that precluded a document of the sort in question from constituting a binding international agreement. It then observed that whether the communiqué at issue constituted a binding agreement between Greece and Turkey:[19]

> ... essentially depends on the nature of the act or transaction to which the Communiqué gives expression; and it does not settle the matter simply to refer to the form — a communiqué — in which that act or transaction is embodied. On the contrary, in determining what was indeed the nature of the act or transaction embodied in the Brussels Communiqué, the Court must have regard above all to its actual terms and to the particular circumstances in which it was drawn up.

---

14. *Nuclear Tests* cases *(Australia v France, New Zealand v France)* ICJ Rep (1974) 253. See **1.199**.
15. VCLT, Art 3.
16. *Railway Traffic between Lithuania and Poland (Railway Sector Landwarów-Kaisiadorys)* advisory opinion, PCIJ Rep (1932) Series A/B No 42, 115–116.
17. *Case Concerning the Temple of Preah Vihear (Cambodia v Thailand)* Preliminary Objections, ICJ Rep (1961) 17, 31.
18. *Aegean Sea Continental Shelf* case *(Greece v Turkey)* ICJ Rep (1978) 3.
19. Ibid, para 96.

After construing the communiqué in light of this test, the Court concluded that the parties did not intend it to constitute an immediate commitment to submit their dispute to determination by the Court. Consequently, it could not constitute such a commitment.

2.15   In the *Case Concerning Maritime Delimitation and Territorial Questions between Qatar and Bahrain (Qatar v Bahrain)*,[20] the International Court of Justice held that an exchange of letters between the Heads of States of Qatar and Bahrain constituted a binding international agreement. Similarly, and having regard to their terms and the circumstances of their preparation, the minutes of a meeting between the Foreign Ministers of the two States in the presence of Saudi Arabia's Foreign Minister were held to constitute a binding agreement serving as the basis of the Court's jurisdiction.

Governed by international law

2.16   An essential element of a valid treaty in customary international law is the intention to create legal relations. Indeed, because no particular form is required for an international agreement to be regarded as a valid treaty, the intention to create legal relations is the decisive factor in deciding whether an oral statement or a particular document gives rise to treaty relations.[21] In construing an oral statement or a written document, international courts and tribunals look for evidence that the parties intended to create treaty relations. Such evidence may be found in the language employed in the oral or written statement, as well as all the surrounding circumstances of its execution.[22] However, the requirement of intention to create legal relations is not spelt out in Art 2(1)(a) of the VCLT. The International Law Commission, the work of which resulted in the VCLT, explains this apparent omission by commenting that the intention element is embraced by the phrase 'governed by international law'.[23]

2.17   Sometimes an intention not to create legal relations is manifest in the terms of the agreement itself — for example, the Final Act of the 1975 Helsinki Conference on Security and Co-operation in Europe, which specified in its final clauses that the agreement was 'not eligible for registration under Article 102 of the Charter of the United Nations'.[24] More commonly, however, the absence of the intention must be deduced from the nature of the agreement and the circumstances of its conclusion.[25]

---

20.   *Case Concerning Maritime Delimitation and Territorial Questions between Qatar and Bahrain (Qatar v Bahrain)* Jurisdiction and Admissibility, ICJ Rep (1994) 112.

21.   Sir Robert Jennings and Sir Arthur Watts (eds), *Oppenheim's International Law*, 9th ed, Longman, New York, 1992, § 582, 1202.

22.   *Legal Status of Eastern Greenland* case *(Norway v Denmark)* PCIJ Rep (1933) Series A/B No 53, see **2.11**; *Case Concerning Maritime Delimitation and Territorial Questions between Qatar and Bahrain (Qatar v Bahrain)* Jurisdiction and Admissibility, ICJ Rep (1994) 112, see **2.14**.

23.   *Yearbook of the International Law Commission*, 1966, Vol II, 189.

24.   See **2.52**.

25.   For example, *Aegean Sea Continental Shelf* case *(Greece v Turkey)* ICJ Rep (1978) 3; see **2.14**.

Provisions which express only political aspirations, which are highly vague, or which are couched in platitudinous terms are unlikely to have been adopted with the requisite intention. On the other hand, it is not necessary that every provision in a treaty should constitute legal obligations, and non-legally binding provisions may be used to interpret obligation-creating terms.[26]

2.18   States also sometimes conclude agreements among themselves which, although intended to be legally binding, are not necessarily intended to be governed by international law. Common among such agreements are contracts of a commercial character (for example, sale of goods and property, leasing arrangements, dealings in securities, and so on). In each case, careful attention to the form, terms and circumstances of the agreement may be required in order to determine whether parties intended the agreement to be governed by international law or domestic law. If the former, the agreement will be a treaty. If the latter, the agreement will be a contract under domestic law, the enforcement of which may involve issues of sovereign immunity.[27]

Formation of treaties

The capacity of States to conclude treaties

2.19   Article 6 of the VCLT provides: 'Every State possesses the capacity to conclude treaties.'

Not only are States capable of concluding treaties, but the capacity to conclude treaties is evidence of statehood.[28]

2.20   States may perform certain acts in the course of bringing a treaty into existence. Typically, there is a proposal for a treaty, followed by negotiations. Thereafter, if negotiations proceed fruitfully, the participating States may adopt a text of the treaty, which means that the negotiators settle upon a final text which is open for signature.[29] Adopting a text is more important in the case of multilateral treaties than in the case of bilateral treaties. The adopted text may sometimes require authentication, which means that States' representatives certify that a document faithfully reflects the text which the States agreed to adopt.[30] Finally, States may express their consent to be bound by a treaty, which almost always involves a signature, but which may also necessitate an exchange of instruments, as well as acts of ratification, acceptance, approval or accession.[31]

---

26.   *Case Concerning Oil Platforms (Iran v United States)* Preliminary Objection, ICJ Rep (1996) 803, para 52.
27.   See 6.37–6.49.
28.   See 4.12–4.14.
29.   See 2.24–2.26.
30.   See 2.27.
31.   See 2.28–2.35.

Full powers

2.21   Being legal persons, States can perform acts relating to the formation of treaties only through the agency of natural persons. Before a natural person can commit a State to an act of treaty formation, he or she must be legally authorised to do so. Sometimes, this will involve the production of 'full powers', which are defined in Art 2(1)(c) of the VCLT to mean:

> ... a document emanating from the competent authority of a State designating a person or persons to represent the State for negotiating, adopting or authenticating the text of a treaty, for expressing the consent of the State to be bound by a treaty, or for accomplishing any other act with respect to the treaty.

The function of full powers is specified by Art 7(1) of the VCLT:

1. A person is considered as representing a State for the purpose of adopting or authenticating the text of a treaty or for the purpose of expressing the consent of the State to be bound by a treaty if:

    (a) he produces full powers; or

    (b) it appears from the practice of the States concerned or from other circumstances that their intention was to consider that person as representing the State for such purposes and to dispense with full powers.

Consequently, any person may commit a State to any of the acts leading to treaty formation to the extent that the person is authorised by his or her full powers. The necessity for full powers may be impliedly dispensed with where circumstances justify concluding that the States involved considered the person as representing his or her State for the purposes of the acts he or she performed.

2.22   Certain classes of persons are, without the need to produce full powers, deemed to be capable of representing their State. The extent of their capacity depends on the nature of their official office. These rules are contained in Art 7(2) of the VCLT:

2. In virtue of their functions and without having to produce full powers, the following are considered as representing their State:

    (a) Heads of State, Heads of Government and Ministers for Foreign Affairs, for the purposes of performing all acts relating to the conclusion of a treaty;

    (b) heads of diplomatic missions, for the purpose of adopting the text of a treaty between the accrediting State and the State to which they are accredited;

    (c) representatives accredited by States to an international conference or to an international organization or one of its organs, for the purpose of adopting the text of a treaty in that conference, organization or organ.

Only Heads of State, Heads of Government and Foreign Ministers are deemed to be capable of representing a State for the purpose of performing all acts in the process of concluding a treaty. Therefore, if State A wishes to have its ambassador to State B sign a treaty with State B on its behalf, the ambassador must satisfy the requirements of Art 7(1): either he or she will need to be furnished with full powers, or there will need to be other evidence that States A and B regard the ambassador as representing State A for the purpose of signing the treaty. That other evidence could be provided by the past practice of the two States or by 'other circumstances', which might include diplomatic communications prior to the act of signing.

2.23   Article 8 of the VCLT specifies that an 'act relating to the conclusion of a treaty performed by a person who cannot be considered under Article 7 as authorised to represent a State for that purpose is without legal effect unless afterwards confirmed by that State'. Failures of the kind envisaged by Art 8 are rare. Where they occur, States are clearly permitted to disavow the *ultra vires* act and to regard it as lacking legal consequence.

On the other hand, the ILC is of the view that a subsequent confirmation which rectifies a person's lack of authority may be implied by conduct such as invoking the treaty's terms or otherwise acting 'in such a way as to appear to treat the act of its representative as effective'.[32]

Adoption of the text

2.24   Adoption of the text is an important step towards concluding a multilateral treaty. Numerous States might participate in the process of negotiating a particular treaty. If there is a large number of interested States, there will probably be an international conference at which the final phase of negotiations is conducted. Because of the large number of States involved, each with their own interests to protect and advance, much effort will frequently be expended in agreeing on a text which strikes a balance between advancing certain policy objectives and attracting the widest possible adherence to the treaty. At the end of the conference, if it is a success, a final text will be proposed on which the conference may vote. This text, if adopted, becomes the treaty that is thrown open for adherence by States. Article 9 of the VCLT provides:

1.   The adoption of the text of a treaty takes place by the consent of all the States participating in its drawing up except as provided in paragraph 2.

2.   The adoption of the text of a treaty at an international conference takes place by the vote of two-thirds of the States present and voting, unless by the same majority they shall decide to apply a different rule.

2.25   Where the adoption of a text occurs outside the context of an international conference, unanimity will be the rule unless the participating States unanimously agree to a different procedure. This generally arises only where there is a small number of participating States. At international

---

32.   *Yearbook of the International Law Commission*, 1966, Vol II, 192.

conferences, States are free to accept either the two-thirds rule as specified in Art 9(2) or any other rule (for example, simple majority, three-quarters majority, or a system of weighted voting), provided the alternative rule is approved by two-thirds of the States present and voting.

2.26   Sometimes, treaty texts are adopted within the framework of an intergovernmental organisation. Where this occurs, Art 9 of the VCLT will not apply if it is contradicted by the rules of that organisation.[33]

Authentication of the text

2.27   Once a text is adopted, a final version of the document is prepared, and then it is usually authenticated. However, a series of complicated votes may first be necessary, following debates conducted in different languages, in order that States can be certain that there is real agreement as to the document to which they will be invited to commit themselves. Article 10 of the VCLT provides:

> The text of a treaty is established as authentic and definitive:
>
> (a) by such procedure as may be provided for in the text or agreed upon by the States participating in its drawing up; or
>
> (b) failing such procedure, by the signature, signature ad referendum or initialing by the representatives of those States of the text of the treaty or of the Final Act of a conference incorporating the text.

Sometimes, authentication as a separate step is dispensed with. On other occasions, the adopted text may provide for a designated person or persons to authenticate the text (for example, the conference chairman). If the text was adopted within the framework of an intergovernmental organisation, any rules of that organisation as to authentication will be applicable.[34] Failing any such agreement, the procedure prescribed by Art 10(b) of the VCLT will apply.

Consent to be bound

2.28   Consenting to be bound by a treaty is the most critical step in a treaty's formation. It is an act which frequently helps activate the treaty and which causes it to produce legal effects for the consenting State. No State can be considered bound by a treaty unless it has manifested its consent to be bound thereby; in this respect, treaties are identical to contracts under domestic law. In the case of contracts, what constitutes a sufficient manifestation of consent to be bound varies from one jurisdiction to another. Usually, signature or the affixing of a corporate seal to a contract document is regarded as sufficient to indicate consent. Domestic legal systems also frequently specify that other acts, such as oral acceptance or acceptance implied by conduct, may be effective to manifest consent to be bound by a contract.

---

33.   VCLT, Art 5.
34.   Ibid.

2.29   States enjoy considerable freedom in deciding how their consent to be bound by a treaty will be manifested. Article 11 of the VCLT provides that a State's consent to be bound by a treaty 'may be expressed by signature, exchange of instruments constituting a treaty, ratification, acceptance, approval or accession, or by any other means if so agreed'.

Article 2(1)(b) of the VCLT provides as follows:

1. For the purposes of the present Convention: ...

    (b) 'ratification', 'acceptance', 'approval', and 'accession' mean in each case the international act so named whereby a State establishes on the international plane its consent to be bound by a treaty; ...

2.30   Consent to be bound by signature is dealt with by Art 12 of the VCLT, which provides:

1. The consent of a State to be bound by a treaty is expressed by the signature of its representative when:

    (a) the treaty provides that signature shall have that effect;

    (b) it is otherwise established that the negotiating States were agreed that signature should have that effect; or

    (c) the intention of the State to give that effect to the signature appears from the full powers of its representative or was expressed during the negotiation.

2. For the purposes of paragraph 1:

    (a) the initialing of a text constitutes a signature of the treaty when it is established that the negotiating States so agreed;

    (b) the signature ad referendum of a treaty by a representative, if confirmed by his State, constitutes a full signature of the treaty.

Sometimes a signature is appended *ad referendum* — that is, subject to confirmation by the representative's State. Where this is the case, and the State subsequently confirms the representative's act, the signature then operates to bind the State. A signature affixed, but expressed to be subject to ratification, will not be effective to bind the State until ratification occurs, even if the treaty specifies that signature is sufficient to bind the State.[35]

2.31   States may occasionally express their consent to be bound by an exchange of instruments.[36] This procedure is more suitable to a bilateral treaty than to a multilateral treaty. In practice, exchange of instruments usually means that a State signs its copy of the treaty and then exchanges it for the copy signed by the other State. When the exchange occurs, the States have consented to be bound. Consent by exchange of instruments is applicable where the instruments themselves specify the procedure, or where it is otherwise established that the States were agreed on using the procedure.

---

35.   VCLT, Art 14(1)(c). See **2.32**.
36.   VCLT, Art 13.

2.32   Consenting to be bound by ratification, acceptance or approval is governed by Art 14 of the VCLT:

1. The consent of a State to be bound by a treaty is expressed by ratification when:

   (a) the treaty provides for such consent to be expressed by means of ratification;

   (b) it is otherwise established that the negotiating States were agreed that ratification should be required;

   (c) the representatives of the States signed the treaty subject to ratification; or

   (d) the intention of the State to sign the treaty subject to ratification appears from the full powers of its representatives or was expressed during the negotiation.

2. The consent of a State to be bound by a treaty is expressed by acceptance or approval under conditions similar to those which apply to ratification.

Ratification is a procedure of long standing in international treaty relations. Originally, it was a device suited to an age prior to modern communications. Representatives would negotiate and sign treaties, frequently in foreign lands and with limited opportunity to consult with, or seek instructions from, their own States. By making their signatures subject to ratification, representatives ensured that their sovereigns would have an opportunity to review the treaty before accepting it as definitively binding.

The act of ratification was simply a confirmation by the sovereign that he or she approved of the treaty and accepted its binding character. Sometimes it was asserted that ratification could not be withheld unless the representatives had exceeded their powers or violated secret instructions. It was the act of ratification, and not the representative's signature, which had the effect of definitively binding the State to the treaty's obligations.

The original necessity for ratification has largely evaporated with the modern revolution in communications and transportation. Ratification survives, however, as a common procedure for concluding treaties due to political changes in many countries.

Whereas in earlier times ratification was mainly a means by which the sovereign audited the activities of his or her representatives to foreign powers, it now serves the purpose of permitting some measure of democratic control of the decision to be bound by treaties. Many States, while leaving the formal act of ratification to the Head of State, subject treaties to scrutiny by authorities designated for that purpose under domestic law (usually the legislature or some component thereof). Once those authorities express their approval, ratification may occur. Ratification is now undoubtedly optional; States are free to ratify or withhold ratification at their absolute discretion.

2.33   Treaties are sometimes expressed to be subject to 'acceptance' or 'approval'. These terms refer to less formal domestic procedures of review and endorsement of treaties than 'ratification', which often connotes formal constitutional procedures in many States. At the level of international law, nothing turns on the use of these three terms. Article 14 of the VCLT applies regardless of whether signatures by representatives are subject to ratification, acceptance or approval.

2.34   Article 16 of the VCLT provides:

> Unless the treaty otherwise provides, instruments of ratification, acceptance, approval or accession establish the consent of a State to be bound by a treaty upon:
>
> (a) their exchange between the contracting States;
>
> (b) their deposit with the depository; or
>
> (c) their notification to the contracting States or to the depository, if so agreed.

The treaty itself will normally specify the way in which an act of ratification is to generate a consent to be bound by international law. Usually, this will mean specifying one of the procedures mentioned in Art 16. An exchange of instruments of ratification will normally be specified in the case of bilateral treaties. In the case of multilateral treaties, a 'depository' is usually nominated as the authority to whom instruments of ratification are to be transmitted. The depository is frequently the Foreign Minister of one of the States participating in the treaty's negotiation. If the treaty is negotiated within the framework of an intergovernmental organisation, the nominated depository is usually the Secretary-General (or equivalent) of that organisation. Failure to complete an act of ratification on the international plane will result in the State failing to signify its consent to be bound, even if all the domestic law procedures for ratification have been properly concluded.[37]

2.35   A State may also accede to a treaty, thereby expressing its consent to be bound. This is the normal means by which a State becomes party to a multilateral treaty that it has not signed. Multilateral treaties will normally specify which States are eligible to become parties, and how many ratifications or other manifestations of consent to be bound are necessary for it to enter into force. Sometimes a treaty will specify that it is open for signature only until a specified date, whereafter States which wish to become parties will need to accede.

Usually, after a treaty enters into force it is no longer open for signature (though the treaty itself may specify a different rule). Thereafter, a State that is eligible to become party to the treaty, and which wishes to do so, must accede to the treaty. The mode of acceding will usually be specified by the treaty. Sometimes, it is sufficient for a State simply to transmit an instrument of accession to the treaty's depository. Other treaties have

---

37. *Case Concerning Military and Paramilitary Activities in and Against Nicaragua (Nicaragua v United States)* Jurisdiction and Admissibility, ICJ Rep (1984) 392, 398ff.

more rigorous requirements. For example, before a State can accede to the various treaties constituting the European Union, it must conclude a separate treaty of accession with all the existing States parties.[38]

Entry into force

2.36 States participating in the creation of a treaty enjoy a wide discretion in deciding when and by what means it will come into force. The chosen mode will usually be expressed in the text of the treaty instrument itself.

In the case of bilateral treaties, the usual practice is for parties to provide that the treaty enters into force when both States have definitively expressed their consent to be bound, or on some specified date thereafter. In the case of multilateral treaties, the usual practice is for the adopted text to designate the number of signatures, ratifications or accessions required before the treaty enters into force, and then to indicate either that the treaty enters into force when the requisite number of such acts is reached or on some specified date thereafter. For example, Art 308(1) of the 1982 Convention on the Law of the Sea[39] provides that the treaty 'shall enter into force 12 months after the date of deposit of the sixtieth instrument of ratification or accession'.

2.37 Article 24 of the VCLT acknowledges the freedom that States enjoy in determining the manner and date for a treaty's entry into force. The provision also furnishes rules in default of such provision being made, and makes necessary provision for the authoritative determination of certain procedural steps before the treaty enters into force:

1. A treaty enters into force in such manner and upon such date as it may provide or as the negotiating States may agree.

2. Failing any such provision or agreement, a treaty enters into force as soon as consent to be bound by the treaty has been established for all the negotiating States.

3. When the consent of a State to be bound by a treaty is established on a date after the treaty has come into force, the treaty enters into force for that State on that date, unless the treaty otherwise provides.

4. The provisions of a treaty regulating the authentication of its text, the establishment of the consent of States to be bound by the treaty, the manner or date of its entry into force, reservations, the functions of the depository and other matters arising necessarily before the entry into force of the treaty apply from the time of the adoption of its text.

---

38. Article 49 of the Treaty on European Union, *Official Journal of the European Union,* C 321 E/5, 29 December 2006.
39. UNTS, Vol 1833, p 3.

Effect of treaties

Effect of treaties before entry into force

2.38 A treaty is fully effective only after it has entered into force, and in respect of States that are parties to it. Sometimes, however, a State will signify its intention to be bound by a treaty subject to ratification.[40] A State may also signify its consent to be bound before the treaty has entered into force. A question arises, in these cases, as to whether the treaty produces any legal effect on the State.

Article 18 of the VCLT provides:

> A State is obliged to refrain from acts which would defeat the object and purpose of a treaty when:
>
> (a) it has signed the treaty or exchanged instruments constituting the treaty subject to ratification, acceptance or approval, until it shall have made its intention clear not to become a party to the treaty; or
>
> (b) it has expressed its consent to be bound by the treaty, pending the entry into force of the treaty and provided that such entry into force is not unduly delayed.

The position at customary international law prior to the VCLT was that the principle of good faith required States, prior to ratification, to refrain from acts 'intended substantially to impair the value of the undertaking as signed'.[41] The VCLT requires a State to refrain from acts that would defeat the treaty's 'object and purpose' once it has signed a treaty subject to ratification or once it has expressed a definitive consent to be bound pending the treaty's entry into force.

A State can escape from its obligation not to defeat the object and purpose of a treaty that it signed subject to ratification by manifesting a clear intention not to ratify the treaty. Politicians and journalists sometimes refer to this as 'un-signing' the treaty. Similarly, if a treaty's entry into force is 'unduly delayed', a State may revoke its consent to be bound before it enters into force. In either case, the State will thereafter be released from its obligation not to perform acts that would defeat the treaty's object and purpose. This will not affect the State's obligation to comply with identical legal requirements based in other treaties to which it is party, in customary law, or in the general principles of law.

Effect of treaty after entry into force

2.39 Once a treaty enters into force, it binds the parties thereto pursuant to the general principle of law known as *pacta sunt servanda*.[42] This principle finds expression in Art 26 of the VCLT as follows:

---

40. See **2.32**.
41. Sir Robert Jennings and Sir Arthur Watts (eds), *Oppenheim's International Law*, 9th ed, Longman, New York, 1992, § 612, 1239.
42. See **1.88**.

Every treaty in force is binding upon the parties to it and must be performed by them in good faith.

As between the parties, a rule contained in a treaty will prevail over any inconsistent rule of customary international law except rules of the *jus cogens*.[43] To the extent that a treaty-based rule is identical in its content to a customary rule, both rules will apply simultaneously as between the parties to the treaty.[44]

Effect on third States

2.40   As the terms of Art 26 of the VCLT indicate, a treaty is binding 'upon the parties to it'. However, it is exceptionally possible for parties to a treaty to confer rights, or impose obligations, on States which are not parties to the treaty. Article 34 of the VCLT provides:

> A treaty does not create either obligations or rights for a third State without its consent.

2.41   The consent of a State is, therefore, necessary to establish that a treaty to which it is not a party has created rights or obligations for that State. In addition to the third State's consent, it is also necessary to establish that the States parties to the treaty actually intended to create rights or obligations for the third State.

2.42   The rule for establishing the consent of a State to be bound by an obligation imposed by a treaty to which it is not a party is strict. Article 35 of the VCLT provides:

> An obligation arises for a third State from a provision of a treaty if the parties to the treaty intend the provision to be the means of establishing the obligation and the State expressly accepts that obligation in writing.

It is not possible for a third State to assume a binding obligation under a treaty by acquiescence, oral consent or implication from conduct. An obligation that has arisen for a third State under Art 35 of the VCLT may be revoked or modified only with the consent of the treaty's parties and of the third State, unless they have all agreed otherwise.[45]

2.43   It is comparatively easy to establish the consent of a State to accept the conferral of a right by a treaty to which it is not a party. The third State's consent will normally be presumed. Article 36 of the VCLT provides:

> 1.   A right arises for a third State from a provision of a treaty if the parties to the treaty intend the provision to accord that right either to the third State, or to a group of States to which it belongs, or to all States, and the third State assents thereto. Its assent shall be presumed so long as the contrary is not indicated, unless the treaty otherwise provides.
>
> 2.   A State exercising a right in accordance with paragraph 1 shall comply with the conditions for its exercise provided for in the treaty or established in conformity with the treaty.

---

43.   See **2.106–2.110**.
44.   See **1.146**.
45.   VCLT, Art 37(1).

The third State's consent will not be presumed where the contrary is indicated — that is, where the third State has expressly, or by implication, rejected the conferral of the right. Nor will it be presumed where the treaty itself requires the third State to perform an act signifying its acceptance of the conferred right; in that case, the third State will need to comply with the treaty's requirements in order for the right to be effectively conferred.

A right that has arisen for a third State under Art 36 of the VCLT may not be revoked or modified by subsequent agreement of the treaty's parties if it can be shown that the parties' original intention in conferring the right was that revocation or modification could occur only with the consent of the third State.[46]

Effect of national law on treaty obligations

2.44   On the plane of international law, a State party to a treaty may not invoke provisions of its internal law as justification for its failure to perform a treaty.[47] Accordingly, a national government may not plead that its State's failure to comply with a treaty is justified by an obstacle in national constitutional law, such as the constitutional inability of the executive branch to control the activities of the legislature, the judiciary or semi-sovereign federal units within the State. The obligation imposed by international law on the State as a whole, including all its official organs and constituent components, is to find the means to comply with its treaty obligations. This rule is subject to the operation of Art 46 of the VCLT on 'internal laws regarding competence to conclude treaties'.[48]

Temporal effect of treaties

2.45   Article 28 of the VCLT specifies that treaties do not, prima facie, produce retroactive effects:

> Unless a different intention appears from the treaty or is otherwise established, its provisions do not bind a party in relation to any act or fact which took place or any situation which ceased to exist before the date of the entry into force of the treaty with respect to that party.

Territorial effect of treaties

2.46   Article 29 of the VCLT provides as follows:

> Unless a different intention appears from the treaty or is otherwise established, a treaty is binding upon each party in respect of its entire territory.

A State will sometimes exercise its authority in respect of territories for whose international affairs it is responsible (for example, colonial possessions and dependent territories), or which are under the State's

---

46.   Ibid, Art 37(2).
47.   Ibid, Art 27. Semble Draft Articles on State Responsibility, Art 3; see **5.14**.
48.   See **2.96**.

effective control (for example, by military occupation). In such cases, a question arises as to whether a treaty to which the State is a party binds the State in respect of those territories.

It is common practice for States exercising these types of authority to specify in the treaty's text, or by reservation or declaration when expressing their consent to be bound, the extent to which the treaty applies to such territories. A provision of this kind is usually referred to as a 'territorial clause'. Where there is no territorial clause, and if the parties' intention cannot be otherwise established (for example, by reference to the *travaux préparatoires*[49]), the International Law Commission's Fourth Special Rapporteur on the law of treaties expressed the opinion that 'the general understanding today clearly is that ... a treaty is presumed to apply to all territories for which the contracting States are internationally responsible'.[50] The 1966 International Covenant on Civil and Political Rights (ICCPR)[51] applies 'in respect of acts done by a State in the exercise of its jurisdiction outside its own territory', such as jurisdiction pursuant to military occupation,[52] and the 1989 Convention on the Rights of the Child (CRC)[53] applies to territories under a State party's military occupation.[54]

Effect of inconsistent treaties

2.47   States sometimes enter into new treaty obligations that are inconsistent with existing treaty obligations. In such circumstances, questions arise as to the effect of both the earlier and the later treaty obligations.

2.48   Where all the parties to the earlier treaty are the same as the parties to the later, little difficulty is presented; the earlier treaty applies only to the extent that its provisions are compatible with those of the later treaty.[55] In other words, the later treaty overrides inconsistent provisions in the earlier treaty.

2.49   Where only some of the parties to the earlier treaty are parties to the later treaty, then as between those States *inter se* the later treaty overrides inconsistent provisions in the earlier treaty.[56]

2.50   It may be the case, however, that a State is party to both treaties, but another State is party to only one of them. In these circumstances, legal relations between the two States *inter se* are governed only by the

---

49.   See **2.82**.
50.   *Yearbook of the International Law Commission*, 1964, Vol II, 189.
51.   UNTS, Vol 999, p 171.
52.   *Legal Consequences of the Construction of a Wall in the Occupied Palestinian Territory* advisory opinion, ICJ Rep (2004) 136, para 111.
53.   UNTS, Vol 1577, p 3.
54.   *Legal Consequences of the Construction of a Wall in the Occupied Palestinian Territory* advisory opinion, ICJ Rep (2004) 136, para 113.
55.   VCLT, Art 30(3).
56.   Ibid, Art 30(4)(a).

treaty to which they are both parties.[57] No effect is given to the later treaty if both States are not parties to it.

2.51   If a State were to enter into mutually exclusive treaty obligations with two different States (for instance, by concluding separate treaties with both of them, promising to extend to each of them the same exclusive right), then the promising State will incur responsibility for breach of treaty to whichever of the other States in respect of which it chooses not to honour the treaty obligation.[58] For example, State A might conclude a treaty with State B under which companies incorporated in State B are given exclusive rights to exploit certain mineral resources in State A's territory. Subsequently, State A concludes a treaty with State C extending the same exclusive rights to companies incorporated in State C. Both treaties cannot be honoured, and State A decides to honour the treaty with State C. In these circumstances, State B will have a claim for breach of treaty against State A, notwithstanding that the inconsistent treaty upon which State A acted was concluded later in time.

Registration of treaties

2.52   Article 80 of the VCLT requires treaties to be transmitted to the United Nations Secretariat for registration or filing and recording, and for publication. This provision complements Art 102 of the UN Charter, which provides as follows:

1.   Every treaty and every international agreement entered into by any Member of the United Nations after the present Charter comes into force shall as soon as possible be registered with the Secretariat and published by it.

2.   No party to any such treaty or international agreement which has not been registered in accordance with the provisions of paragraph 1 of this Article may invoke that treaty or agreement before any organ of the United Nations.

Article 102 was included in the Charter in order to combat the practice of concluding and maintaining secret treaties. Treaties that do not comply with the registration requirement in Art 102(2) remain legally binding, although they may not be 'invoked' before any organ of the United Nations. Notwithstanding that the International Court of Justice is a principal organ of the United Nations,[59] unregistered treaties and international agreements may be pleaded before the Court, which will give legal effect to them.[60]

---

57.   Ibid, Art 30(4)(b).
58.   Ibid, Art 30(5).
59.   UN Charter, Art 7.
60.   *Case Concerning Maritime Delimitation and Territorial Questions between Qatar and Bahrain (Qatar v Bahrain)* Jurisdiction and Admissibility, ICJ Rep (1994) 112, para 29.

Reservations

Definition and function of reservations

2.53 A reservation is a device sometimes employed by States in the course of expressing their consent to be bound by a treaty. According to Art 2(1)(d) of the VCLT:

1. For the purposes of the present Convention: ...

    (d) 'reservation' means a unilateral statement, however phrased or named, made by a State, when signing, ratifying, accepting, approving or acceding to a treaty, or for accomplishing any other act with respect to a treaty, whereby it purports to exclude or to modify the legal effect of certain provisions of the treaty in their application to that State; ...

2.54 Not all unilateral statements made by States at the time of signing, ratifying or acceding to a treaty are reservations. It is not uncommon for States to make declarations concerning their understanding of the treaty's meaning or effect. Where such a declaration is not intended to exclude or modify the legal effect of any provisions of the treaty, it is not a reservation. These sorts of statements are usually referred to as 'interpretative declarations', and are not intended to signify that the declaring State's consent to be bound is contingent upon other States accepting the interpretation.

Sometimes, however, a unilateral statement in the form of an interpretative declaration is made with the intention of signifying that the declaring State's consent to be bound is contingent upon other States accepting the interpretation of the treaty contained in the statement. Where this occurs, the statement is a reservation, whatever the name formally attached to it by the State issuing the statement.[61]

2.55 Reservations provide a mechanism by which a State can tailor the terms of a treaty, the text of which has already been adopted, to its own will. A State may wish to become party to a treaty, but only on condition that a small number of its provisions are excluded or modified in the treaty's application to that State. Reservations are employed almost exclusively in relation to multilateral treaties, though reservations to bilateral treaties have been made on occasion.

2.56 The more common practice in relation to bilateral treaties is that a proposal to modify or amend its terms is taken as a proposal to amend the final text, which proposal is considered as part of the treaty's negotiation prior to signature. An attempted reservation to a bilateral treaty might occur where a State's signature is expressed to be subject to ratification, and ratification of the treaty is then accompanied by a reservation.

---

61.   *Belilos v Switzerland* [1988] ECHR Ser A No 132, 49.

In such a case, the traditional position was that a ratification could produce legal effects only if the accompanying reservation was accepted by the other State; otherwise, the treaty would not enter into force.

From custom to VCLT

2.57   The early modern law of reservations with respect to multilateral treaties, which prevailed almost unchallenged until the 1930s, was very similar. A State could not make reservation to a treaty unless the treaty permitted reservations and all other States which had already consented to be bound accepted it.

This amounted to a veto on reservations, and on the participation of States which wished to make reservations. It was this approach that prevailed in multilateral treaties prepared under League of Nations auspices.

2.58   Multilateral treaties are normally proposed in order to effect either a widespread or a universal change in the law relating to some aspect of international relations, or to codify and clarify existing customary law. Not infrequently, both purposes are pursued by different provisions of the same multilateral treaty. In any case, there will always be a tension between the need to maintain the integrity of the treaty's text and securing the most widespread adherence by States. Under the early modern law of reservations, priority was given to maintaining the integrity of treaty texts, at the expense of maximising the number of participating States.

2.59   In the 1930s, there began a shift away from text integrity and towards encouraging widespread adherence. Treaties concluded under the aegis of the Pan-American Union adopted a more flexible policy to reservations by which a reserving State could adhere to a treaty, but no treaty relationship would be established with any other State that objected to the reservation. Accordingly, it was possible for two States parties to the same multilateral treaty not to have any legal rights and obligations vis-à-vis each other under that treaty. The rights and obligations between the reserving State and other States which had not objected would be governed on each side by the treaty as modified by the reservation; both the accepting State and the reserving State would be entitled to invoke the reservation in their relations *inter se*. Multilateral treaties were, in effect, regarded as creating a potentially complex network of bilateral relationships. This encouraged a wider participation in the treaty by States, but at the expense of creating a non-uniform legal regime among the participants.

2.60   By 1951, the move towards the universalism of multilateral treaties, and away from text integrity, had gathered some momentum.

In the **Reservations to the Convention on the Prevention and Punishment of the Crime of Genocide advisory opinion,**[62] some States had made reservations to the 1948 Convention on the Prevention and Punishment of the Crime of Genocide.[63] No provision for reservations was made in the Convention's text. The UN General Assembly requested the International Court of Justice to furnish an advisory opinion with regard to the following questions:[64]

I. Can the reserving State be regarded as being a party to the Convention while still maintaining its reservation if the reservation is objected to by one or more of the parties to the Convention but not by others?

II. If the answer to Question I is in the affirmative, what is the effect of the reservation as between the reserving State and:

(a)   The parties which object to the reservation?

(b)   Those who accept it?

In answer to the first question, the Court said:

It is well established that in its treaty relations a State cannot be bound without its consent, and that consequently no reservation can be effective against any State without its agreement thereto. It is also a generally recognized principle that a multilateral convention is the result of an agreement freely concluded upon its clauses and that consequently none of the contracting parties is entitled to frustrate or impair, by means of unilateral decisions or particular agreements, the purpose and *raison d'être* of the convention. To this principle was linked the notion of the integrity of the convention as adopted, a notion which in its traditional concept involved the proposition that no reservation was valid unless it was accepted by all the contracting parties without exception, as would have been the case if it had been stated during the negotiations. ...

... Extensive participation in conventions of this type has already given rise to greater flexibility in the international practice concerning multilateral conventions. More general resort to reservations, very great allowance made for tacit assent to reservations, the existence of practices which go so far as to admit that the author of reservations which have been rejected by certain contracting parties is nevertheless to be regarded as a party to the convention in relation to those contracting parties that have accepted the reservations — all these factors are manifestations of a new need for flexibility in the operation of multilateral conventions.

It must also be pointed out that although the Genocide Convention was finally approved unanimously, it is nevertheless the result of a series of majority votes. The majority principle, while facilitating the conclusion of multilateral conventions, may also make it necessary for certain States to make reservations. This observation is confirmed by the great number of reservations which have been made of recent years to multilateral conventions.

In this state of international practice, it could certainly not be inferred from the absence of an article providing for reservations in a multilateral convention that the contracting States are prohibited from making certain reservations. ... The character of a multilateral convention, its purpose, provisions, mode of preparation and adoption, are factors which must be considered in determining,

---

62.   *Reservations to the Convention on the Prevention and Punishment of the Crime of Genocide* advisory opinion, ICJ Rep (1951) 15.
63.   UNTS, Vol 78, p 277.
64.   ICJ Rep (1951) 15, 16.

in the absence of any express provision on the subject, the possibility of making reservations, as well as their validity and effect. …

The object and purpose of the Genocide Convention imply that it was the intention of the General Assembly and of the States which adopted it that as many States as possible should participate. The complete exclusion from the Convention of one or more States would not only restrict the scope of its application, but would detract from the authority of the moral and humanitarian principles which are its basis. It is inconceivable that the contracting parties readily contemplated that an objection to a minor reservation should produce such a result. But even less could the contracting parties have intended to sacrifice the very object of the Convention in favour of a vain desire to secure as many participants as possible. The object and purpose of the Convention thus limit both the freedom of making reservations and that of objecting to them. It follows that it is the compatibility of a reservation with the object and purpose of the Convention that must furnish the criterion for the attitude of a State in making the reservation on accession as well as for the appraisal by a State in objecting to the reservation. Such is the rule of conduct which must guide every State in the appraisal which it must make, individually and from its own standpoint, of the admissibility of any reservation. …

Having replied to Question I, the Court will now examine Question II …

The considerations which form the basis of the Court's reply to Question I are to a large extent equally applicable here. As has been pointed out above, each State which is a party to the Convention is entitled to appraise the validity of the reservation, and it exercises this right individually and from its own standpoint. As no State can be bound by a reservation to which it has not consented, it necessarily follows that each State objecting to it will or will not, on the basis of its individual appraisal within the limits of the criterion of the object and purpose stated above, consider the reserving State to be a party to the Convention. In the ordinary course of events, such a decision will only affect the relationship between the State making the reservation and the objecting State; on the other hand, as will be pointed out later, such a decision might aim at the complete exclusion from the Convention in a case where it was expressed by the adoption of a position on the jurisdictional plane.

The disadvantages which result from this possible divergence of views — which an article concerning the making of reservations could have obviated — are real; they are mitigated by the common duty of the contracting States to be guided in their judgment by the compatibility or incompatibility of the reservation with the object and purpose of the Convention. …

It may be that the divergence of views between parties as to the admissibility of a reservation will not in fact have any consequences. On the other hand, it may be that certain parties who consider that the assent given by other parties to a reservation is incompatible with the purpose of the Convention, will decide to adopt a position on the jurisdictional plane in respect of this divergence and to settle the dispute which thus arises either by special agreement or by the procedure laid down in Article IX of the Convention.[65]

Finally, it may be that a State, whilst not claiming that a reservation is incompatible with the object and purpose of the Convention, will nevertheless object to it,

---

65. Article IX: 'Disputes between the Contracting Parties relating to the interpretation, application or fulfilment of the present Convention, including those relating to the responsibility of a State for genocide or for any of the other acts enumerated in article III, shall be submitted to the International Court of Justice at the request of any of the parties to the dispute.'

but that an understanding between that State and the reserving State will have the effect that the Convention will enter into force between them, except for the clauses affected by the reservation. ...

The Court is of the opinion, ... in so far as concerns the Convention on the Prevention and Punishment of the Crime of Genocide ...

On Question I:

... that a State which has made and maintained a reservation which has been objected to by one or more of the parties to the Convention but not by others, can be regarded as being a party to the Convention if the reservation is compatible with the object and purpose of the Convention; otherwise that State cannot be regarded as being party to the Convention.

On Question II: ...

(a) that if a party to the Convention objects to a reservation which it considers to be incompatible with the object and purpose of the Convention, it can in fact consider that the reserving State is not a party to the Convention;

(b) that if, on the other hand, a party accepts the reservation as being compatible with the object and purpose of the Convention, it can in fact consider that the reserving State is a party to the Convention.

2.61   In the *Reservations to the Genocide Convention* advisory opinion, the International Court of Justice not only embraced the universalism approach to reservations of the Pan-American Union, but extended it.

Care should, however, be exercised in drawing overly general conclusions from the case inasmuch as the judgment is heavily and expressly contingent upon the Convention's universal character and its special objects and purposes. A State making a reservation to a treaty of a universal character, where the reservation is compatible with the treaty's object and purpose, could be a party to the treaty even if some contracting States objected to the reservation.

On the other hand, only a reservation that was incompatible with the treaty's object and purpose deprived the reserving State of its participation in the treaty. The Court suggests, in relation to a treaty with a potentially universal membership such as the Genocide Convention, that a State could not validly object to another State's reservation unless the objecting State was bona fide of the view that the reservation contradicted the treaty's object and purpose. Until a determination of the reservation's compatibility with the object and purpose of the treaty was made 'on the jurisdictional plane', it would be for each State to form its own view as to the validity of the reservation.

2.62   The VCLT built upon the approach adopted by the Court in the *Reservations to the Genocide Convention* advisory opinion. Article 19 of the VCLT provides:

A State may, when signing, ratifying, accepting, approving or acceding to a treaty, formulate a reservation unless:

(a) the reservation is prohibited by the treaty;

(b) the treaty provides that only specified reservations, which do not include the reservation in question, may be made; or

(c) in cases not falling under sub-paragraphs (a) and (b), the reservation is incompatible with the object and purpose of the treaty.

Sometimes, multilateral treaties will specify that no reservations are permitted, or that reservations to certain provisions, or of a certain type, are not permitted. Where that is the case, a consent to be bound accompanied by a prohibited reservation will generally have the effect of preventing that State from becoming a party to the treaty. The same is true where a reservation is incompatible with the treaty's object and purpose.

That such a reservation is said to 'generally' have the effect of precluding participation indicates that there now exists some uncertainty as to whether the making of a prohibited reservation can preclude participation in a treaty for the protection of human rights, or whether the prohibited reservation to a human rights treaty must be severed from the consent to be bound.[66]

Incompatibility with object and purpose

2.63 Article 19 of the VCLT makes it plain that any reservation that is incompatible with any treaty's object and purpose will be invalid, and human rights treaties are not different in this regard.

As the *Reservations to the Genocide Convention* advisory opinion indicates, whether a reservation suffers from invalidity on this basis is an objective legal question. In the absence of an authoritative adjudicatory pronouncement, however, the attitude of the treaty's contracting States to a reservation will have practical evidentiary value. If no contracting State objects to a particular reservation, that will constitute strong evidence that the reservation does not contradict the treaty's object and purpose as understood by the contracting States. Acquiescence will be regarded as acceptance. Conversely, a large number of objections to a particular reservation on the grounds of its alleged inconsistency with a treaty's object and purpose will provide strong evidence in support of the allegation.

An interesting means of determining whether a provision contradicts a treaty's object and purpose is provided by Art 20(2) of the 1966 International Convention on the Elimination of All Forms of Racial Discrimination (ICERD):[67]

> A reservation incompatible with the object and purpose of this Convention shall not be permitted, nor shall a reservation the effect of which would inhibit the operation of any of the bodies established by this Convention be allowed. A reservation shall be considered incompatible or inhibitive if at least two-thirds of the States Parties to this Convention object to it.

---

66. See **2.68–2.71**.
67. UNTS, Vol 660, p 195.

Acceptance and objection

2.64   Article 20 of the VCLT regulates acceptance of and objection to reservations:

1. A reservation expressly authorized by a treaty does not require any subsequent acceptance by the other contracting States unless the treaty so provides.

2. When it appears from the limited number of the negotiating States and the object and purpose of a treaty that the application of the treaty in its entirety between all the States is an essential condition of the consent of each one to be bound by the treaty, a reservation requires acceptance by all the parties.

3. When a treaty is a constituent instrument of an international organization and unless it otherwise provides, a reservation requires the acceptance of the competent organ of that organization.

4. In cases not falling under the preceding paragraphs and unless the treaty otherwise provides:

    (a) acceptance by another contracting State of a reservation constitutes the reserving State a party to the treaty in relation to that other State if or when the treaty is in force for those States;

    (b) an objection by another contracting State to a reservation does not preclude the entry into force of the treaty as between the objecting and reserving States unless a contrary intention is definitely expressed by the objecting State;

    (c) an act expressing a State's consent to be bound by the treaty and containing a reservation is effective as soon as at least one other contracting State has accepted the reservation.

5. For the purposes of paragraphs 2 and 4 and unless the treaty otherwise provides, a reservation is considered to have been accepted by a State if it shall have raised no objection to the reservation by the end of a period of twelve months after it was notified of the reservation or by the date on which it expressed its consent to be bound by the treaty, whichever is later.

2.65   The traditional rule, whereby reservations must be accepted by all parties to a treaty, is preserved only where it appears that 'the application of the treaty in its entirety between all the States is an essential condition of the consent of each one to be bound by the treaty'. That essential condition can be deduced from 'the limited number of the negotiating States and the [treaty's] object and purpose'.[68] A regional free trade treaty, for instance, would be likely to require the approval of all existing parties before a reservation would be effective.

2.66   Under pre-existing customary international law, a State's objection to a reservation needed to be made within a reasonable time. Having regard to the traditional rule that a single objection could deny a reserving State the ability to adhere to the treaty, a long delay would rarely be

---

68.   VCLT, Art 20(2). See **2.64**.

reasonable. With the demise of that earlier rule for most treaties,[69] a more generous timeframe for making objections becomes possible. Article 20(5) of the VCLT now lays down a 12-month rule for making objections; unless a State objects to a reservation within 12 months of its notification of the reservation, or within 12 months of expressing its consent to be bound (whichever is the later), it will be taken to have accepted the reservation.

2.67 Article 20(4) of the VCLT deals with the *existence* of treaty relations between a reserving State on the one hand, and accepting and objecting States on the other. Reserving States and accepting States are parties to the treaty in relation to each other. Reserving States and objecting States are also parties to the treaty in relation to each other, unless the objecting State definitely expresses a contrary intention. The way in which their treaty relationships are *affected* by the reservation are discussed below.[70] Article 20(4) tempers the older customary rule that objection to a reservation precluded the existence of relations under the treaty between the two States. A reserving State's expression of consent to be bound by a treaty becomes effective as soon as one other contracting State accepts the reservation.

Reservations and human rights treaties

2.68 There is a body of opinion which contends that impermissible reservations to human rights treaties are severable from the reserving State's consent to be bound. According to this view, the reserving State remains bound by the treaty, and the impermissible reservation is simply disregarded. It is to be noted that Art 19(c) of the VCLT precludes the making of a reservation which is inconsistent with a treaty's object and purpose, but that Art 20 of the VCLT does not specify the consequences for a State's participation in a treaty if it makes such a reservation. The customary law position as articulated by the International Court of Justice in the *Reservations to the Genocide Convention* advisory opinion, however, is that the making of a prohibited reservation nullifies a State's consent to be bound even where the treaty has a universal and humanitarian object and purpose.

2.69 Nevertheless, in *Belilos v Switzerland* the European Court of Human Rights held that a reservation made by Switzerland to the European Convention on Human Rights 1950 was impermissible because it violated that treaty's prohibition on making reservations of a 'general character' and the requirement to make a 'brief statement' of the domestic laws necessitating the reservation. The Court said the reservation was 'invalid', but that 'Switzerland is, and regards itself as, bound by the Convention irrespective of the validity of the [reservation]'.[71] The Court effectively severed the impermissible reservation from Switzerland's

---

69. Ibid.
70. See 2.72–2.73.
71. *Belilos v Switzerland* [1988] ECHR Ser A No 132, para 60.

consent to be bound, but gave no further reasons for this apparent departure from customary international law.[72]

2.70 Reasons in defence of this approach were subsequently furnished by the Human Rights Committee, established by Art 28 of the 1966 International Covenant on Civil and Political Rights.[73] In 1994, the Committee issued General Comment No 24 dealing with reservations made to the ICCPR by States parties.[74] The Committee noted that there were 127 States parties, of which 46 had entered reservations. Altogether, there were 150 separate reservations 'of varying significance'. In the Committee's view, the number of reservations, as well as their content and scope, threatened 'to undermine the effective implementation of the Covenant' and tended 'to weaken respect for the obligations of States parties'.[75] According to the Committee:

> 8. ... Although treaties that are mere exchanges of obligations between States allow them to reserve *inter se* application of rules of general international law, it is otherwise in human rights treaties, which are for the benefit of persons within their jurisdiction. Accordingly, provisions in the Covenant that represent customary international law (and *a fortiori* when they have the character of peremptory norms) may not be the subject of reservations. ...

> 17. ... [T]he Committee believes that [the VCLT's] provisions on the role of State objections in relation to reservations are inappropriate to address the problem of reservations to human rights treaties. Such treaties, and the Covenant specifically, are not a web of inter-State exchanges of mutual obligations. They concern the endowment of individuals with rights. The principle of inter-State reciprocity has no place ... and because the operation of the classic rules on reservations is so inadequate for the Covenant, States have often not seen any legal interest in or need to object to reservations. The absence of protest by States cannot imply that a reservation is either compatible or incompatible with the object and purpose of the Covenant. ... In the view of the Committee, because of the special characteristics of the Covenant as a human rights treaty, it is open to question what effect objections have between States *inter se*.

> 18. ... The normal consequence of an unacceptable reservation is not that the Covenant will not be in effect at all for the reserving party. Rather, such a reservation will generally be severable, in the sense that the Covenant will be operative for the reserving party without benefit of the reservation.

2.71 Thus, the Human Rights Committee supported the approach of the European Court of Human Rights in severing impermissible reservations from a State's consent to be bound by a human rights

---

72. Semble *Weber v Switzerland* [1990] ECHR Ser A No 177; *Loizidou v Turkey* Preliminary Objections [1995] ECHR Ser A No 310.
73. UNTS, Vol 999, p 171.
74. Human Rights Committee, General Comment 24, *General comment on issues relating to reservations made upon ratification or accession to the Covenant or the Optional Protocols thereto, or in relation to declarations under article 41 of the Covenant*, UN Doc CCPR/C/21/Rev.1/Add.6 (1994), (1995) 15 HRLJ 464, (1995) 2 IHRR 10, (1995) 34 ILM 839.
75. Ibid, para 1.

treaty. The justification for this policy was said to rest upon the special nature of human rights treaties as being for the benefit of individuals and not merely expressing a bargain between States. The Human Rights Committee effectively sought to create a dual regime for reservations, with one set of rules applicable to human rights treaties and a different set for treaties dealing with other matters.

The principal weakness of the Committee's General Comment is its reliance on policy arguments without reference to authority in conventional or customary law. Many States — notably France, the United Kingdom and the United States — have rejected the Committee's attempt to establish a separate legal regime for reservations to human rights treaties, and expressed continuing support for the customary position as enunciated by the International Court of Justice in the *Reservations to the Genocide Convention* advisory opinion.[76] Indeed, 'to consider invalid reservations to human rights treaties as not formulated at all is, at the present time, a position not supported by state practice'.[77]

Effects of reservations

2.72   Article 21 of the VCLT regulates the legal effects of reservations between a reserving State on the one hand, and accepting and objecting States on the other:

1.   A reservation established with regard to another party in accordance with articles 19, 20 and 23:

(a)   modifies for the reserving State in its relations with that other party the provisions of the treaty to which the reservation relates to the extent of the reservation; and

(b)   modifies those provisions to the same extent for that other party in its relations with the reserving State.

2.   The reservation does not modify the provisions of the treaty for the other parties to the treaty *inter se*.

3.   When a State objecting to a reservation has not opposed the entry into force of the treaty between itself and the reserving State, the provisions to which the reservation relates do not apply as between the two States to the extent of the reservation.

Accordingly, as between a reserving State and an accepting State, their mutual relations are to be governed by the treaty as modified by the reservation; the accepting State will also be able to rely on the reservation in its dealings with the reserving State. The reservation has no impact on the relations among other parties to the treaty.

2.73   A State that objects to a reservation has the option of opposing or accepting the entry into force of the treaty as between itself and the reserving State.[78] Where the objecting State does not oppose the treaty's

---

76.   See **2.60**.
77.   Roberto Baratta, 'Should invalid reservations to human rights treaties be disregarded?' (2000) 11 *European Journal of International Law*, 413–25, 425.
78.   VCLT, Art 20(4)(b). See **2.64**.

entry into force between itself and the reserving State, the treaty applies between them without the provisions to which the reservation relates.[79] This does not mean that the subject matter of the excluded provisions is not regulated by law as between the two States. Any applicable customary rules and general principles of law will operate in place of the excised treaty provisions.[80] The provisions of any other treaty in force between the parties would also apply to the extent that they are relevant.

Withdrawal of reservations and objections

2.74   Article 22 of the VCLT regulates the withdrawal of reservations, the withdrawal of objections to reservations, and the point at which such withdrawals become operative:

1. Unless the treaty otherwise provides, a reservation may be withdrawn at any time and the consent of a State which has accepted the reservation is not required for its withdrawal.

2. Unless the treaty otherwise provides, an objection to a reservation may be withdrawn at any time.

3. Unless the treaty provides otherwise, or it is otherwise agreed:

    (a) the withdrawal of a reservation becomes operative in relation to another contracting State only when notice of it has been received by that State;

    (b) the withdrawal of an objection to a reservation becomes operative only when notice of it has been received by the State which formulated the reservation.

The rules in Art 22(3) are important because reservations can negate the existence, or vary the legal effect, of treaty relations between the reserving State and other States parties to the treaty. These consequences can be removed or altered by the withdrawal of a reservation and of an objection to a reservation, and Art 22(3) specifies the time from which these variations in legal relations take effect.

For example, the withdrawal by State A of an objection to a reservation by State B will establish the treaty as modified by the reservation as the basis of legal relations between the two States. Hitherto, relations between the States would have been governed either, first, by the treaty without the provision to which the reservation applied, if State A did not object to the treaty's entry into force between itself and State B, or, second, without reference to the treaty to which the reservation applied, if State A did object to the treaty's entry into force between itself and State B.[81] In either case, the change in legal relations becomes effective only from the time when State B receives notification of State A's withdrawal of objection, unless the treaty itself provides differently or unless the two States agree otherwise.[82]

---

79. VCLT, Art 21(3).
80. *English Channel Arbitration (United Kingdom v France)* (1977) 54 ILR 6; (1979) 18 ILM 397, para 62.
81. See **2.72**.
82. VCLT, Art 22(3)(b).

Interpretation

Schools of interpretation

2.75 Writing in 1951, Sir Gerald Fitzmaurice (1901–1982) identified three distinct schools of thought in connection with the interpretation of treaties.[83] He called these schools:

- the 'intentions of the parties' or 'founding fathers' school;
- the 'textual' or 'ordinary meaning of the words' school; and
- the 'teleological' or 'aims and objects' school.

In describing the approach of each of these schools, Fitzmaurice wrote:[84]

> The ideas of these three schools are not necessarily exclusive of one another, and the theories of treaty interpretation can be constructed (and are indeed normally held) compounded of all three. However, each tends to confer the primacy on one particular aspect of treaty interpretation, if not to the exclusion, certainly to the subordination of the others. Each, in any case, employs a different approach. For the 'intentions' school, the prime, indeed the only legitimate, object is to ascertain and give effect to the intentions, of the parties: the approach is therefore to discover what these were, or must be taken to have been. For the 'meaning of the text' school, the prime object is to establish what the text means according to the ordinary or apparent signification of its terms: the approach is therefore through the study and analysis of the text. For the 'aims and objects' school, it is the general purpose of the treaty itself that counts, considered to some extent as having … an existence of its own, independent of the original intentions of the framers. The main object is to establish this general purpose, and construe the particular clauses in the light of it: hence it is such matters as the general tenor and atmosphere of the treaty, the circumstances in which it was made, the place it has come to have in international life, which for this school indicate the approach to interpretation. It should be added that this last, the teleological, approach has its sphere of operation almost entirely in the field of general multilateral conventions, particularly those of the social, humanitarian, and law-making type.

General rule of interpretation

2.76 As Fitzmaurice himself pointed out, these three approaches to interpretation exist side by side. They are frequently employed simultaneously, albeit to differing degrees, in interpreting the same treaty. This composite approach to treaty interpretation is reflected in Art 31 of the VCLT, which sets out general rules for interpreting treaties:

1. A treaty shall be interpreted in good faith in accordance with the ordinary meaning to be given to the terms of the treaty in their context and in the light of its object and purpose.

---

83. Gerald Fitzmaurice, 'The law and procedure of the International Court of Justice: treaty interpretation and certain other treaty points' (1951) 28 *British Yearbook of International Law*, 1.
84. Ibid, 1–2.

2. The context for the purpose of the interpretation of a treaty shall comprise:

(a) any agreement relating to the treaty which was made between all the parties in connexion with the conclusion of the treaty;

(b) any instrument that was made by one or more parties in connexion with the conclusion of the treaty and accepted by the other parties as an instrument related to the treaty.

3. There shall be taken into account, together with the context:

(a) any subsequent agreement between the parties regarding the interpretation of the treaty or the application of its provisions;

(b) any subsequent practice in the application of the treaty which establishes the agreement of the parties regarding its interpretation;

(c) any relevant rules of international law applicable in the relations between the parties.

4. A special meaning shall be given to a term if it is established that the parties so intended.

2.77   The European Court of Human Rights has observed, on the basis of the presentation of the law in Art 31 of the VCLT, that 'the process of interpretation of a treaty is a unity, a single combined operation; this rule, closely integrated, places on the same footing the various elements enumerated in the four paragraphs of the article'.[85]

2.78   When concluding a multilateral treaty or a group of related treaties, it is not unusual for the contracting States also to conclude a 'final act' of the conference at which the treaties were negotiated. The terms of the final act, as well as the terms of any other treaties concluded at the same conference or negotiations, are part of a treaty's context by virtue of Art 31(2)(a) of the VCLT. Accordingly, they are agreements that may be referred to in interpreting the treaty.[86]

2.79   After a treaty enters into force, it sometimes happens that practices emerge which, while not in strict or literal compliance with the treaty's terms, are nevertheless performed in intended compliance with the treaty. Where this practice becomes established by the habitual performance of all parties, or by the habitual performance of one party and the acceptance or acquiescence of the others, it may be taken to have established an agreement regarding the treaty's interpretation. Where this is the case, the new practice shall be taken into account in interpreting the treaty.[87]

An example of this rule is provided by the interpretation now universally given to Art 27(3) of the UN Charter which provides, in relation to non-procedural matters, that '[d]ecisions of the Security Council ... shall be made by an affirmative vote of nine members including the concurring votes of the permanent members'. The text of Art 27(3) clearly stipulates

---

85. *Golder v United Kingdom* [1975] ECHR Ser A No 18, 14.
86. VCLT, Art 31(1).
87. Ibid, Art 31(3)(b).

that non-procedural decisions cannot be made unless all permanent members cast a vote in favour. Yet, a practice quickly emerged on the Security Council by which a decision could be made provided that none of the permanent members cast a vote against it, so that abstention would not defeat the making of the decision. This new formula may be characterised as a subsequent practice in the application of the UN Charter which establishes the agreement of the parties regarding its interpretation.

Supplementary means of interpretation

2.80   In certain relatively narrow circumstances, reference may be made to supplementary sources not mentioned in Art 31 of the VCLT for the purposes of interpreting a treaty. The relevant provision of the VCLT is Art 32:

> Recourse may be had to supplementary means of interpretation, including the preparatory work of the treaty and the circumstances of its conclusion, in order to confirm the meaning resulting from the application of Article 31, or to determine the meaning when the interpretation according to Article 31:
>
> (a) leaves the meaning ambiguous or obscure; or
>
> (b) leads to a result which is manifestly absurd or unreasonable.

2.81   Clearly, supplementary means of interpretation are available only in three circumstances: (i) to confirm the meaning resulting from the application of Art 31 of the VCLT; (ii) to determine the treaty's meaning where the interpretation according to the means prescribed by Art 31 results in ambiguity or obscurity; and (iii) to determine the treaty's meaning where interpretation according to the means prescribed by Art 31 results in absurdity or unreasonableness.

Absent ambiguity, obscurity, absurdity or unreasonableness, the supplementary means of interpretation are unavailable to contradict the interpretation of a treaty established in accordance with Art 31.

2.82   In practical terms, the 'preparatory work of the treaty' is pre-eminent among a treaty's supplementary means of interpretation. Most courts, tribunals and publicists habitually refer to the preparatory works by their French name, the *travaux préparatoires* (or sometimes simply the *travaux*). A wide range of materials falls within the scope of the *travaux préparatoires*, including all records of the negotiations, whether in the form of diplomatic correspondence or of public pronouncements, the proceedings of any international conference convened in connection with preparing the treaty, and the work of any expert or official body (such as the International Law Commission) whose work contributed to the treaty's adoption. In short, anything which indicates the intentions of the parties in the course of adopting the treaty will constitute its *travaux préparatoires*, and will be available as supplementary means of interpretation under Art 32 of the VCLT.

2.83   The strictly supplementary role of the *travaux préparatoires* was emphasised by the Permanent Court of International Justice in the

Lotus case, when it remarked that 'there is no occasion to have regard to preparatory work if the text of the convention is sufficiently clear in itself'.[88] The International Court of Justice in the *Territorial Dispute* case has similarly cautioned against hasty interpretational departures from the treaty's text:[89]

> The Court would recall that, in accordance with customary international law, reflected in Article 31 of the 1969 Vienna Convention on the Law of Treaties, a treaty must be interpreted in good faith in accordance with the ordinary meaning to be given to its terms in their context and in the light of its object and purpose. Interpretation must be based above all upon the text of the treaty. As a supplementary measure recourse may be had to means of interpretation such as the preparatory work of the treaty and the circumstances of its conclusion.

Treaties in different languages

2.84   Treaties are frequently prepared in more than one language. Usually, a treaty will appear in the languages of all the States participating in its preparation, although authentication of the text[90] may occur in a lesser number of languages if many States with different languages are involved.

2.85   The rules for interpreting treaties that appear in different languages are set out in Art 33 of the VCLT:

1. When a treaty has been authenticated in two or more languages, the text is equally authoritative in each language, unless the treaty provides or the parties agree that, in case of divergence, a particular text shall prevail.

2. A version of the treaty in a language other than one of those in which the text was authenticated shall be considered an authentic text only if the treaty so provides or the parties so agree.

3. The terms of the treaty are presumed to have the same meaning in each authentic text.

4. Except where a particular text prevails in accordance with paragraph 1, when a comparison of the authentic texts discloses a difference of meaning which the application of articles 31 and 32 does not remove, the meaning which best reconciles the texts, having regard to the object and purpose of the treaty, shall be adopted.

2.86   An ambiguity, obscurity, absurdity or unreasonableness in the interpretation of a treaty reached in accordance with Art 31 of the VCLT can sometimes be removed by referring to the other authoritative language versions of the treaty. Where this is the case, it would seem that recourse to the supplementary means of interpretation prescribed by Art 32 of the VCLT is not permissible, except to confirm the meaning reached in accordance with Arts 31 and 33. Where, however, the ambiguity or

---

88.   *Case of the SS Lotus (France v Turkey)* PCIJ Rep (1927) Series A No 10, 16. See **6.11**.
89.   *Case Concerning the Territorial Dispute (Libya v Chad)* ICJ Rep (1994) 6, para 41.
90.   See **2.27**.

obscurity arises because of differences in meaning between the languages employed in different authenticated texts, Art 33(4) of the VCLT permits recourse both to Art 31 and to the supplementary means of interpretation prescribed by Art 32.

2.87 In the *Mavrommatis Palestine Concessions* case *(Greece v United Kingdom)*, the Permanent Court of International Justice said, in the context of interpreting the Palestine Mandate from the League of Nations which was equally authentic in the English and French languages:[91]

> ... where two versions possessing equal authority exist one of which appears to have a wider bearing than the other, the Court is bound to adopt the more limited interpretation which can be made to harmonise with both versions and which, as far as it goes, is doubtless in accordance with the common intention of the Parties.

The proper approach may be somewhat different, however, where the issue of interpretation arises in respect of a 'law-making' treaty.[92] The European Court of Human Rights has remarked:[93]

> [C]onfronted with two versions of a treaty which are equally authentic but not exactly the same, the Court must, following established international law precedents, interpret them in a way that will reconcile them as far as possible. Given that it is a law-making treaty, it is also necessary to seek the interpretation that is most appropriate in order to realize the aim and achieve the objective of the treaty, not that which would restrict to the greatest possible degree the obligations undertaken by the Parties.

Amendment and modification

2.88 The realities of international life sometimes require that a treaty be revised in order to keep abreast of current requirements. A treaty may be revised by either amendment or modification. 'Amendment' refers to the formal alteration of treaty provisions that affects all the parties to the treaty. 'Modification', on the other hand, is a variation of a treaty's terms that affects only some of the parties.

2.89 A bilateral treaty may be amended by a subsequent agreement between the parties. Unless the treaty itself otherwise provides, the VCLT's rules governing the conclusion and entry into force of treaties apply to any amending agreement.[94]

2.90 A multilateral treaty may be amended, although the rules are somewhat more complex than for the amendment of a bilateral treaty.

Any proposal to amend a multilateral treaty must be notified to all the contracting States (that is, all States which have consented to be bound by the treaty even if it has not yet entered into force). These States

---

91. *Mavrommatis Palestine Concessions* case *(Greece v United Kingdom)* PCIJ Rep (1926) Series A No 2, 19. See **5.77**.
92. See **1.95** and **2.75**.
93. *Wemhoff v Germany* [1968] ECHR Ser A No 7, 23.
94. VCLT, Art 39.

each have a right to participate in the decision as to whether any action should be taken on the proposal, and to take part in the negotiation and conclusion of any agreement to amend the treaty.

Every State that was entitled to be a party to the treaty is also entitled to be a party to the treaty as amended. The treaty as amended does not bind any State which was already a party to the original treaty and which does not become a party to the amending agreement; in that case, relations between such a State and the other parties to the treaty are governed by Art 30(4)(b) of the VCLT.[95]

Any State which becomes a party to the treaty after it has been amended shall be considered bound by the treaty as amended, unless that State expresses a different intention. In its relations with States that have not become parties to the amending agreement, however, the new State party shall be regulated by the unamended treaty. Where the unamended treaty itself stipulates different procedures for, and consequences of, its amendment, those stipulations will prevail.[96]

2.91   A multilateral treaty might also be open to modification by agreement. The parties seeking to modify the treaty in their relations between themselves must first notify all the other parties of their intentions, unless the treaty itself provides for such a modification.[97]

A modification agreement can be made if the treaty itself provides for the making of such an agreement. If no such provision exists, the treaty can be modified only if the modification does not affect the rights and obligations of the other parties to the treaty and if it is compatible with the treaty's object and purpose as a whole.[98]

Invalidity

2.92   Although an agreement possesses all the elements necessary to qualify it as a treaty,[99] there might, nevertheless, be grounds upon which it will be regarded as invalid.

2.93   Article 42(1) of the VCLT provides that the 'validity of a treaty or of the consent to be bound by a treaty may be impeached only through the application of the present Convention'. The VCLT establishes both a substantive and a procedural code regulating the invalidity of treaties, which replaces the older and less certain customary rules on the subject. The substantive grounds of invalidity are set out at Arts 46–53 of the VCLT.

2.94   A State loses its right to invoke the invalidity of a treaty if it has expressly agreed that the treaty is valid, remains in force or continues in operation after becoming aware of the facts justifying invalidity.[100] A State

95. See 2.50.
96. VCLT, Art 40.
97. Ibid, Art 41(2).
98. Ibid, Art 41(1).
99. See 2.5–2.18.
100. VCLT, Art 45(a).

also loses its right to invoke the invalidity of a treaty if it acquiesces in the validity of the treaty, in its maintenance in force, or in its continuance in operation after becoming aware of the facts justifying invalidity.[101]

Express agreement or acquiescence does not, however, deprive a State of the right to invoke a treaty's invalidity if the grounds of invalidity are coercion[102] or a violation of the *jus cogens*.[103]

Constitutional *ultra vires*

2.95   Prior to the VCLT, international law accommodated in principle the invalidity of treaties where a State's consent to be bound had been expressed contrary to that State's internal constitutional requirements relating to the conclusion of treaties. Difficulty lay in determining the extent of the principle's application. In particular, there was disagreement over whether the violation of any constitutional requirement could invalidate a treaty, or whether the requirements of the violated constitutional law needed to be well-known and free from uncertainty. The theoretical difficulty was magnified by the absence of State practice on the subject. As Hans Blix wrote in a study completed shortly prior to the VCLT:[104]

> ... no treaty has been found that has been admitted to be invalid or held by an international tribunal to be invalid, because concluded by a constitutionally incompetent authority or in an unconstitutional manner.

In the *Legal Status of Eastern Greenland* case,[105] Norway contended that any treaty concluded with Denmark concerning the status of eastern Greenland was invalid because Norway's Foreign Minister lacked authority under Norwegian law to commit his State to such an agreement. According to Norway's submission, the Foreign Minister was forbidden under Norwegian law from committing Norway to international agreements on 'matters of importance' without the prior approval of the King in Council. The Permanent Court of International Justice regarded the violation of these domestic law constraints on the Foreign Minister's authority as irrelevant to the existence of a binding commitment to Denmark on the plane of international law.[106] Similarly, in the *Spanish Zone of Morocco Claims (United Kingdom v Spain)*, rapporteur Max Huber found it 'unnecessary' to address Spain's contention that an agreement with the United Kingdom in relation to one of the claims was invalid because it had not been approved in the manner required by the law of Morocco (Spain's protectorate).[107]

---

101. Ibid, Art 45(b).
102. See **2.102–2.105**.
103. See **2.106–2.110**.
104. Hans Blix, *Treaty-making Power*, Stevens, London, 1960, 373–74.
105. *Legal Status of Eastern Greenland* case *(Norway v Denmark)* PCIJ Rep (1933) Series A/B No 53. See **2.11**.
106. See also **2.22**.
107. *Spanish Zone of Morocco Claims (United Kingdom v Spain)* (1925) 2 RIAA 615, 724.

2.96   Article 46 of the VCLT deals with the issue of constitutional *ultra vires* in the making of treaties by providing as follows:

1.   A State may not invoke the fact that its consent to be bound by a treaty has been expressed in violation of a provision of its internal law regarding competence to conclude treaties as invalidating its consent unless that violation was manifest and concerned a rule of fundamental importance.

2.   A violation is manifest if it would be objectively evident to any State conducting itself in the manner in accordance with normal practice and good faith.

As the wording of Art 46 indicates, the rule may be invoked only by the State whose consent has been expressed in violation of its internal law. Therefore, States may not invoke a treaty's invalidity where the violation concerns the internal law of another State party.

The violated internal law must also be one regarding competence to conclude treaties, and would, therefore, normally be of a constitutional character. It would not, for instance, be possible to argue that a treaty is invalid merely for inconsistency with a State's ordinary criminal or civil law, or because some general constitutional rule or principle had been breached. Indeed, Art 27 of the VCLT expressly precludes reliance by a State on provisions of its internal law as justification for its failure to perform a treaty obligation.[108]

A State is, therefore, entitled to presume that another State's duly appointed representatives possess domestic legal authority to commit that other State to treaty relations.[109] The presumption is displaced only if the violation is both 'manifest' (within the meaning of Art 46(2)) and concerns a domestic rule 'of fundamental importance'. Where this is the case, the State whose internal laws were violated by those expressing its consent to be bound will be able to invoke the treaty's invalidity.

It is not, however, easy to demonstrate that a violation was 'manifest'. In the *Land and Maritime Boundary* case, Nigeria maintained that it was not bound by a treaty signed by its President as he had not complied with Nigeria's constitutional requirements for concluding international agreements. In dismissing this submission, the International Court of Justice said:[110]

> The rules concerning the authority to sign treaties for a State are constitutional rules of fundamental importance. However, a limitation of a Head of State's capacity in this respect is not manifest in the sense of Article 46, paragraph 2, unless at least properly publicized. This is particularly so because Heads of State belong to the group of persons who, in accordance with Article 7, paragraph 2, of the [VCLT] '[i]n virtue of their functions and without having to produce full powers' are considered as representing their State. ...

---

108. See **2.44**.
109. See **2.21–2.23**.
110. *Land and Maritime Boundary between Cameroon and Nigeria (Cameroon v Nigeria: Equatorial Guinea intervening)* ICJ Rep (2002) 303, paras 265–266.

Nigeria further argues that Cameroon knew, or ought to have known, that the Head of State of Nigeria had no power legally to bind Nigeria without consulting the Nigerian Government. In this regard the Court notes that there is no general legal obligation for States to keep themselves informed of legislative and constitutional developments in other States which are or may become important for the international relations of these States.

Ultra vires by representatives

2.97   It may be that a person who has been duly appointed to represent a State for the purpose of concluding a treaty has had his or her authority restricted in relation to certain matters. For example, in concluding a peace treaty, a State's delegation may be under specific instructions from its government not to concede a particular point. It could be argued that failure to observe the restriction by a State's representative invalidates that State's consent. Article 47 of the VCLT accepts this possibility, but only in narrowly defined circumstances:

> If the authority of a representative to express the consent of a State to be bound by a particular treaty has been made subject to a specific restriction, his omission to observe that restriction may not be invoked as invalidating the consent expressed by him unless the restriction was notified to the other negotiating States prior to his expressing such consent.

As with constitutional *ultra vires*, this variety of excess of authority is extremely rare.

Error

2.98   Error is of somewhat more frequent concern for the invalidity of treaties. In particular, it frequently manifests itself in the context of border disputes where the accuracy of a map is in issue.

In the **Case Concerning the Temple of Preah Vihear (Cambodia v Thailand)**,[111] a 1904 agreement between France and Siam settled the border between Cambodia (then a French protectorate) and Siam in the remote Preah Vihear region. The agreement stipulated that the border was to follow the watershed line, and left the details to be determined by a Mixed Franco–Siamese Commission. A map clearly placed a significant Buddhist temple on the Cambodian side of the border. The map itself was prepared by French technical experts, with the agreement of Siamese representatives. The map was not endorsed by the Commission, which ceased to function before the map was completed.

It was, however, received and accepted by French and Siamese authorities. Subsequently, Thailand (as Siam had been renamed) took possession of the temple with military forces, and removed certain artefacts from the temple into Thailand. The government of Thailand contended that the boundary displayed on the map

---

111. *Case Concerning the Temple of Preah Vihear (Cambodia v Thailand)* Merits, ICJ Rep (1962) 6.

contained an error in that it did not accurately follow the watershed line as agreed in 1904, and that the temple actually fell on the Thai side of that line. Cambodia relied upon the map and sought a ruling from the International Court of Justice that the temple lay within Cambodian territory in accordance with the 1904 treaty. The Court said:[112]

> [I]t is contended on behalf of Thailand that an error was committed, an error of which the Siamese authorities were unaware at the time they accepted the map. It is an established rule of law that the plea of error cannot be allowed as an element vitiating consent if the party advancing it contributed by its own conduct to the error, or could have avoided it or if the circumstances were such as to put that party on notice of a possible error. The Court considers that the character and qualifications of the persons who saw the map on the Siamese side would alone make it difficult for Thailand to plead error in law. These persons included the members of the very Commission of Delimitation within whose competence this sector of the frontier had lain. But even apart from this, the Court thinks that there were other circumstances relating to the map which make the plea of error difficult to receive.
>
> An inspection indicates that the map itself drew such pointed attention to the Preah Vihear region that no interested person, nor anyone charged with the duty of scrutinizing it, could have failed to see what the map was purporting to do in respect of that region. The Siamese authorities knew it was the work of French topographical officers to whom they had themselves entrusted the work of producing the maps. They accepted it without any independent investigation, and cannot therefore now plead any error vitiating the reality of their consent. The Court concludes that the plea of error has not been made out.

2.99 Article 48 of the VCLT deals with error in the following terms:

1. A State may invoke an error in a treaty as invalidating its consent to be bound by the treaty if the error relates to a fact or situation which was assumed by that State to exist at the time when the treaty was concluded and formed an essential basis of its consent to be bound by the treaty.

2. Paragraph 1 shall not apply if the State in question contributed by its own conduct to the error or if the circumstances were such as to put that State on notice of a possible error.

3. An error relating to the wording of the text of a treaty does not affect its validity; article 79 then applies.

This provision is not identical to the test employed by the International Court of Justice in the *Temple of Preah Vihear* case. In particular, the Court said that a State would not be able to plead error if it 'contributed by its own conduct to the error, or could have avoided it or if the circumstances were such as to put that party on notice of a possible error'. Article 48(2), on the other hand, omits the phrase 'or could have avoided it'. The International Law Commission's commentary reveals that this omission was intentional. The Commission said that the omitted phrase 'is so wide as to leave little room for the operation of the rule' set out in Art 48(1).[113]

---

112. Ibid, 26–27.
113. *Yearbook of the International Law Commission*, 1966, Vol II, 244.

Fraud

2.100   It is a general principle of law that fraud vitiates consent. In the context of the law of treaties, this principle finds expression in Art 49 of the VCLT:

> If a State has been induced to conclude a treaty by the fraudulent conduct of another negotiating State, the State may invoke the fraud as invalidating its consent to be bound by the treaty.

In its commentary, the International Law Commission indicated its understanding that the concept of fraud includes 'any false statements, misrepresentations or other deceitful proceedings by which a State is induced to give consent to a treaty which it would not otherwise have given'.[114]

Corruption

2.101   The corruption by a negotiating State of another State's representatives will provide grounds for invalidation of the treaty. Article 50 of the VCLT provides:

> If the expression of a State's consent to be bound by a treaty has been procured through the corruption of its representative directly or indirectly by another negotiating State, the State may invoke such corruption as invalidating its consent to be bound by the treaty.

The International Law Commission made the following comment on the scope of Art 50:[115]

> The strong term 'corruption' is used in the article expressly in order to indicate that only acts calculated to exercise a substantial influence on the disposition of the representative to conclude the treaty may be invoked as invalidating the expression of consent which he has purported to give on behalf of his State. The Commission did not mean to imply that under the present article a small courtesy or favour shown to a representative in connexion with the conclusion of a treaty may be invoked as a pretext for invalidating the treaty.

Coercion

2.102   A State's consent to be bound by a treaty must be freely given. If such consent is given only because the will of the State or its representative has been overborne as a result of coercive pressure, the legal validity of the consent will be adversely affected.

2.103   Coercion of a State's representative is covered by Art 51 of the VCLT:

> The expression of a State's consent to be bound by a treaty which has been procured by the coercion of its representative through acts or threats directed against him shall be without any legal effect.

---

114. Ibid, 245.
115. *Yearbook of the International Law Commission*, 1966, Vol II, 245.

In its commentary on Art 51, the International Law Commission remarked that coercion against a State representative includes threats of blackmail and threats against the representative's family.[116]

2.104 Coercion against a State's representatives has long been regarded as a ground for invalidating consent to a treaty. Of relatively more recent vintage, and of greater practical significance, is the rule relating to certain kinds of coercion against the State as such. Article 52 of the VCLT provides:

> A treaty is void if its conclusion has been procured by the threat or use of force in violation of the principles of international law embodied in the Charter of the United Nations.

In the *Fisheries Jurisdiction* case, the International Court of Justice remarked:[117]

> There can be little doubt, as is implied in the Charter of the United Nations and recognised in Article 52 of the Vienna Convention on the Law of Treaties, that under contemporary international law an agreement concluded under the threat or use of force is void. It is equally clear that a court cannot consider an accusation of this serious nature on the basis of a vague general charge unfortified by evidence in its support.

2.105 Not all forms of coercion will result in the invalidity of a treaty under Art 52. Pressures exerted on, or measures taken against, a State which do not constitute a violation of the Charter's prohibition on the threat or use of force[118] will not invalidate a treaty even if the State's consent was procured as a direct result of those pressures or measures. Therefore, a peace treaty forced upon an aggressor who has suffered a military defeat would not be invalid under Art 52. On the other hand, Art 52 would probably apply to a peace treaty forced upon a State that had been the victim of aggression.[119]

Jus cogens and obligations *erga omnes*

2.106 States are usually free to conclude treaties which, as between the contracting parties, modify or nullify the application of rules of international law that would otherwise be applicable in their relations. Contracting States are therefore usually free to exclude or modify general or local customary rules and, subject to the rules governing the effect of inconsistent treaties,[120] rules established by prior treaties. Two conspicuous exceptions are certain measures adopted by the Security Council under Chapter VII of the UN Charter[121] and rules of *jus cogens* — that is, peremptory norms of general international law from which derogations are not permitted. The *jus cogens* may be considered as the expression of an international public policy that the law upholds even in the face of inconsistent agreements between States.

---

116. Ibid, 246.
117. *Fisheries Jurisdiction* case *(United Kingdom v Iceland)* ICJ Rep (1973) 3, para 24. See **2.139**.
118. See, for example, **9.17**.
119. See **9.13–9.18**.
120. See **2.47–2.51**.
121. See **9.58**.

2.107   The *jus cogens* finds expression in Art 53 of the VCLT:

> A treaty is void if, at the time of its conclusion, it conflicts with a general norm of peremptory international law. For the purposes of the present Convention, a peremptory norm of general international law is a norm accepted and recognized by the international community of States as a whole as a norm from which no derogation is permitted and which can be modified only by a subsequent norm of general international law having the same character.

The International Law Commission made the following comment on *jus cogens*:[122]

> The emergence of rules having the character of *jus cogens* is comparatively recent while international law is in [the] process of rapid development. The Commission considered the right course to be to provide in general terms that a treaty is void if it conflicts with a rule of *jus cogens* and to leave the full content of this rule to be worked out in State practice and in the jurisprudence of international tribunals.

> Examples suggested included (a) a treaty contemplating an unlawful use of force contrary to the principles of the Charter, (b) a treaty contemplating the performance of any other act criminal under international law, and (c) a treaty contemplating or conniving at the commission of acts, such as trade in slaves, piracy or genocide, in the suppression of which every State is called upon to participate. The Commission decided against including any examples of rules of *jus cogens* in the article for two reasons. First, the mention of some cases of treaties void for conflict with a rule of *jus cogens* might, even with the most careful drafting, lead to misunderstanding as to the position concerning other cases not mentioned in the article. Secondly, if the Commission were to attempt to draw up, even on a selective basis, a list of the rules of international law which are to be regarded as having the character of *jus cogens*, it might find itself engaged in a prolonged study of matters which fall outside the scope of the present articles.

2.108   So far, no international tribunal has held a treaty void for violation of the *jus cogens*. However, in *Aloeboetoe v Suriname,* the Inter-American Court of Human Rights said that it was not necessary to consider the applicability of a 1762 treaty between a local tribe (to whose obligations Suriname had allegedly succeeded) and the Netherlands. The treaty included an obligation of capture and return of runaway slaves and the Court said: 'the treaty would today be null and void because it contradicts the norms of *jus cogens superveniens*'.[123] Furthermore, in the *Nicaragua* case, the International Court of Justice referred with approval to submissions that the principle against the use of force in international relations had become a matter of the *jus cogens*.[124]

2.109   In the *Barcelona Traction* case, the International Court of Justice identified the existence of obligations which are owed *erga omnes* (that

---

122. *Yearbook of the International Law Commission,* 1966, Vol II, 248.
123. *Aloeboetoe v Suriname* (1993) Inter-Am Ct HR Ser C No 15; (1994) 1 IHRR 208, para 57.
124. *Military and Paramilitary Activities in and Against Nicaragua (Nicaragua v United States)* Merits, ICJ Rep (1986) 14, para 190.

is, to all States) and which would appear largely to correspond to the *jus cogens*:[125]

> [A]n essential distinction should be drawn between the obligations of a State towards the international community as a whole, and those arising *vis-a-vis* another State in the field of diplomatic protection. By their very nature, the former are the concern of all States. In view of the importance of the rights involved, all States can be held to have a legal interest in their protection; they are obligations *erga omnes*.

> Such obligations derive, for example, in contemporary international law, from the outlawing of acts of aggression, and of genocide, as also from the principles and rules concerning basic rights of the human person including protection from slavery and racial discrimination. Some of the corresponding rights of protection have entered into the body of general international law; others are conferred by international instruments of a universal or quasi-universal character.

The ICJ has since observed, in the *East Timor* case, that 'the assertion that the rights of people to self-determination, as it evolved from the Charter and from UN practice has an *erga omnes* character, is irreproachable'.[126] Furthermore, in the *Security Wall* advisory opinion, the ICJ stated that both self-determination of peoples and certain rules of international humanitarian law constitute obligations owed *erga omnes*.[127]

2.110   It is to be expected that all rules possessing a *jus cogens* character will potentially give rise to obligations owed *erga omnes,* so that all States would potentially be able to make international claims for a breach of the *jus cogens*. This ability exists as a matter of customary international law, and does not pre-empt or supersede conventional rules relating to admissibility and jurisdiction prescribed in respect of particular international courts and tribunals: see the *East Timor* case.[128] State practice, however, indicates that not every violation of the *jus cogens* violates an obligation owed *erga omnes*. In practice, it is only widespread or systematic violations of the *jus cogens* that attract claims by other States. Some violations of the *jus cogens* are widespread and systematic by definition — for example, denials of self-determination of peoples and the prohibitions on genocide, apartheid and aggression. These violations of the *jus cogens* will always violate obligations owed *erga omnes*. On the other hand, State practice does not support a view that isolated or non-systematic violations of the *jus cogens* (such as isolated and domestically unlawful acts of racial discrimination or torture) entitle all other States to make international claims against the perpetrating State.

---

125. *Case Concerning the Barcelona Traction, Light and Power Company Ltd* Second Phase, ICJ Rep (1970) 4, paras 33–34. See **5.110**.
126. *Case Concerning East Timor (Portugal v Australia)* ICJ Rep (1995) 90, para 29. See **8.40**.
127. *Legal Consequences of the Construction of a Wall in the Occupied Palestinian Territory* advisory opinion, ICJ Rep (2004) 136, paras 88, 155–159.
128. *Case Concerning East Timor (Portugal v Australia)* ICJ Rep (1995) 90, para 29.

Unequal treaties

2.111   Many communist States advocated a doctrine which held that treaties were tainted by invalidity if they were concluded in violation of the principle of the sovereign equality of States. This violation was argued to have occurred whenever an economically or militarily stronger State concluded a treaty with a weaker State on terms said to be unfavourable to the weaker State. The terms on which a treaty was said to be 'unfavourable' were usually highly influenced by ideological conceptions advocated by communist States and their allies.

The doctrine did not find support among developed Western States and many developing States, and its status as customary international law must be regarded as highly doubtful. With the demise of the European communist regimes, much less is now heard of this alleged ground of invalidity. It is to be noted that the communist regime in China, once a champion of the doctrine, has in recent times ceased promoting it.

The doctrine of unequal treaties was not included as a discrete ground of invalidity in the VCLT, further discrediting the view that it ever formed part of customary international law. Nevertheless, some of its substantive content is subsumed within the rules relating to coercion, *jus cogens* (especially the principles of self-determination and non-use of force) and fundamental change of circumstances.

Consequences of invalidity

2.112   Antonio Cassese remarks that the VCLT has made a significant contribution to general international law by developing and clarifying rules with respect to the consequences of a treaty's invalidity. In particular, he observes that the VCLT has drawn a distinction between 'absolute' and 'relative' grounds of invalidity:[129]

> What is very novel, and marks a momentous advance in the field of the law of treaties, is the distinction drawn in the Convention between *'absolute' and 'relative' grounds of invalidity*. The former (coercion against a State representative; coercion against the State as a whole; incompatibility with *jus cogens* ...) implies that: (1) any State party to the treaty (that is, not merely the State which has suffered from possible coercion or which might be prejudiced by actions contrary to a peremptory rule) can invoke the invalidity of the treaty; (2) a treaty cannot be divided into valid and invalid clauses, but stands or falls as a whole (Article 44.5); and (3) possible acquiescence does not render the treaty valid (Article 45). If one of these grounds is established, the treaty is null and void *ex tunc*, that is since the moment it was concluded. In contrast, grounds of relative invalidity are: error, fraud, corruption, manifest violation of internal law or of the restrictions of the powers of the State representative who has concluded the treaty. These grounds may only be invoked by the State that has been the victim of error, fraud, corruption or whose representative has acted in manifest breach of internal law or of the restrictions on

---

129. Antonio Cassese, *International Law*, 2nd ed, Oxford University Press, New York, 2005, 177 (emphasis in original).

his powers. Further, these grounds may be *cured* by acquiescence or subsequent express consent of the aggrieved party.

Finally, these grounds of nullity may vitiate only *some provisions* of the treaty. Also these grounds of invalidity operate *ex tunc*, that is, they render the treaty or some of its provisions null and void as from the conclusion of the treaty. However, acts performed bona fide by the aggrieved party before the treaty is declared null and void may be regarded as valid and legally effective, depending upon the specific circumstances of each case.

2.113   Article 44(2) of the VCLT provides that, as a general rule, invalidity may be invoked only with respect to the whole treaty. Accordingly, the general position is that the invalidity of any part of the treaty operates to invalidate the whole treaty.

Article 44(3) ameliorates the impact of the general rule by providing an important exception. If the ground of invalidity relates solely to particular clauses, it may be invoked only with respect to those clauses. Such clauses are severable from the remainder of the treaty where three conditions are met: (a) the affected clauses are separable from the remainder of the treaty with regard to their application; (b) acceptance of those clauses was not an essential basis of the consent of the other parties to be bound by the treaty as a whole; and (c) continued performance of the remainder of the treaty would not be unjust.

According to Art 44(5) of the VCLT, no severance of clauses is ever permitted where the ground of invalidity is coercion of a State's representative,[130] coercion of the State itself,[131] or a violation of the *jus cogens*.[132] Article 8 of the VCLT also provides that a treaty is 'without legal effect' for a State if it was concluded by a person who lacked authorisation to commit the State and if the State does not subsequently confirm the person's act.[133]

2.114   A treaty or a severable treaty provision which has been established as invalid in accordance with the procedures prescribed by the VCLT[134] is void and has no legal force.[135] All such treaty provisions are, therefore, *void ab initio* and not merely from the time the invalidity is invoked or established.

2.115   If a State performs acts in good faith under a treaty before that treaty's invalidity is invoked, such acts are not rendered unlawful merely by reason of the invalidity.[136] On the other hand, if the acts were unlawful but for the treaty, or if the acts were not performed on the basis of a good faith belief in the treaty's validity, then the State performing those acts remains liable for their consequences under the general law of State responsibility.

---

130. See **2.103**.
131. See **2.104**.
132. See **2.106–2.110**.
133. See **2.23**.
134. See **2.147–2.153**.
135. VCLT, Art 69(1).
136. Ibid, Art 69(2)(b).

2.116 Where a treaty or one of its provisions has been established as invalid, 'each party may require any other party to establish as far as possible in their mutual relations the position that would have existed if the acts had not been performed'.[137] This obligation may, in particular cases, be capable of only limited fulfilment and is concurrent with the rule that acts performed in good faith are not rendered unlawful merely by reason of the treaty's subsequently established invalidity.

2.117 Where the invalidity of a treaty arises from its inconsistency with an existing requirement of the *jus cogens*,[138] the parties are required to 'eliminate as far as possible the consequences of any act performed in reliance on any provision which conflicts with' the *jus cogens* and to 'bring their mutual relations into conformity with' the *jus cogens*.[139]

Denunciation and withdrawal

2.118 There is a presumption in favour of the continuing validity of treaties once they have been properly concluded. This presumption finds expression in the general principle of law known as *pacta sunt servanda*.[140] However, in certain circumstances, States may withdraw from or denounce a treaty. Withdrawal is a term usually reserved for multilateral treaties, whereas denunciation is usually employed in connection with bilateral treaties. Denunciation of a bilateral treaty will result in the treaty's termination. Withdrawal from a multilateral treaty will not ordinarily terminate a treaty, but will terminate the withdrawing State's participation in it.

2.119 Article 42(2) of the VCLT provides that a treaty's 'denunciation or the withdrawal of a party, may take place only as a result of the application of the provisions of the treaty or of the present Convention'. However, any provisions contained within the treaty affected by the act of denunciation or withdrawal will take precedence over inconsistent rules relating to withdrawal and denunciation contained in the VCLT.

2.120 Article 56(1) of the VCLT prescribes a general rule that States may not denounce or withdraw from a treaty which contains no express provision for denunciation or withdrawal. This rule is tempered by two exceptions.

First, a treaty without a denunciation or withdrawal clause may be denounced or withdrawn from if 'it is established that the parties intended to admit the possibility of denunciation or withdrawal'.[141] This would appear to enable resort to materials such as the *travaux préparatoires* in order to establish the relevant intention.[142]

---

137. Ibid, Art 69(2)(a).
138. See 2.106–2.110.
139. VCLT, Art 71(1).
140. See 1.88 and 2.39.
141. VCLT, Art 56(1)(a).
142. See 2.82.

Second, 'a right of denunciation or withdrawal may be implied by the nature of the treaty'.[143] At the time of the VCLT's conclusion, this provision probably did not reflect customary international law. Although British publicists tended to favour an implied right of denunciation or withdrawal, most European publicists did not. At the United Nations Conference on the Law of Treaties, the provision was included in the final text of the VCLT only by the narrowest of margins (26:25, with 37 abstentions). Since then, however, the International Court of Justice appears to have accepted Art 56 of the VCLT as reflecting customary international law.[144]

J L Brierly taught that a *modus vivendi* (that is, an instrument recording an international agreement of temporary or provisional nature intended to be replaced by an arrangement of a more permanent and detailed character) is an 'obvious illustration', and that treaties of alliance and commercial treaties are among the types of international agreements in which a right of denunciation or withdrawal may be more readily implied.[145]

2.121 Where the treaty itself is silent on the period of notice required for a State to denounce or withdraw from a treaty, customary international law requires merely that notice be reasonable. The VCLT is more specific, and requires the denouncing or withdrawing State to give at least 12 months' notice to the other States parties.[146]

2.122 The consequences of a treaty's termination by denunciation and a State's withdrawal from a multilateral treaty are dealt with elsewhere.[147]

Termination and suspension

2.123 A treaty terminates when all rights and obligations under it come to an end. This can occur in a number of ways. A bilateral treaty can be terminated by a valid denunciation of one of the parties. Other means of termination include:

- the consent of all the parties to the treaty;
- the subsequent conclusion of an incompatible treaty;
- the occurrence of a material breach;
- a supervening impossibility of performance;
- a fundamental change of circumstances; and
- the emergence of a new rule of the *jus cogens* with which the treaty is in conflict.

---

143. VCLT, Art 56(1)(b).
144. *Case Concerning Military and Paramilitary Activities in and Against Nicaragua (Nicaragua v United States)* Jurisdiction and Admissibility, ICJ Rep (1984) 392, para 63.
145. J L Brierly, *The Law of Nations,* ed Sir Humphrey Waldock, 6th ed, Oxford University Press, New York, 1963, 331.
146. VCLT, Art 56(2).
147. See **2.144**.

A treaty does not terminate simply because all obligations prescribed under it have been complied with. Although there remain no executory provisions under such a treaty, it nevertheless continues in force until terminated. A boundary treaty, for instance, does not terminate once the parties have established markers and displays of State sovereignty in accordance with its terms. A treaty may also be suspended. Where this occurs, the treaty remains in force but the parties, as between which the suspension operates, are relieved of the obligation of performance while the treaty remains suspended.

Agreement or consent of the parties

2.124   The parties themselves may consent to the termination or suspension of a treaty.[148] This can occur in two ways.

First, the parties might provide in the treaty itself that it terminates or is suspended upon the occurrence of a specific event or set of events — typically, this will be the performance of a specified act by one or more of the parties — or the treaty might provide that it terminates after a certain date.

Alternatively, all the parties might simply consent to the treaty's termination or suspension at any time. Where the parties consent to a termination or suspension, all other 'contracting States'[149] must first be consulted. Two or more parties to a multilateral treaty may agree to suspend the operation of a treaty only as between themselves if the treaty itself provides for such a possibility.

They may also agree to suspend the treaty only as between themselves if the suspension is not prohibited by the treaty and it does not affect the rights or obligations of other parties under the treaty, and if the suspension is not incompatible with the treaty's object and purpose.[150] It would seem likely that multilateral disarmament treaties and multilateral human rights treaties would not be amenable to suspension as between only some of the parties, unless the treaty itself provided for such a possibility. Unless the treaty otherwise provides, parties intending to suspend the operation of a multilateral treaty as between themselves must first notify their intention to all the other parties.[151]

Incompatible later treaty

2.125   It sometimes happens that all the parties to a treaty subsequently conclude another treaty which covers the same subject matter as the earlier treaty. The earlier treaty will be terminated if the later treaty makes provision for such termination, or if it is established that the parties intended that the later treaty should govern that subject matter.[152]

---

148. VCLT, Arts 54 and 57.
149. That is, States which have 'consented to be bound by the treaty, whether or not the treaty has entered into force': VCLT, Art 2(1)(f).
150. VCLT, Art 58(1).
151. Ibid, Art 58(2).
152. Ibid, Art 59(1)(a).

This would appear to enable resort to materials such as the *travaux préparatoires*[153] in order to establish the relevant intention. The earlier treaty will also be terminated if 'the provisions of the later treaty are so far incompatible with those of the earlier one that the two treaties are not capable of being applied at the same time'.[154]

Suspension of the earlier treaty, rather than its termination, may result if such an intention appears from the later treaty or if the intention can be otherwise established.[155]

Material breach

2.126   The VCLT provides that a 'material breach of a bilateral treaty by one party entitles the other party to invoke the breach as a ground for terminating the treaty or suspending its operation in whole or in part'.[156]

2.127   The position with respect to multilateral treaties is, as usual, somewhat more complicated. The VCLT provides for a range of possible responses by the non-defaulting parties. The non-breaching parties may, by unanimous agreement among themselves, terminate the treaty or suspend it in whole or in part. They may do this in relations either between themselves and the breaching State, or between all the parties.[157]

It may be that one or more of the non-defaulting parties are more affected by a material breach than the other non-defaulting parties. In such a case, it might not be possible to obtain unanimous agreement among the non-defaulting parties to terminate or suspend the treaty. The VCLT nevertheless permits States specially affected by a material breach to protect their interests by invoking the breach as a ground for terminating or suspending the treaty in the relations between themselves and the defaulting State.[158] The treaty remains in force between all the non-defaulting States, and between the defaulting State and the non-defaulting States which do not terminate or suspend on the ground that they are specially affected by the material breach.

It might also happen that a material breach by one State radically changes the position of every other State with respect to the further performance of their obligations under the treaty. In this case, none of the non-defaulting States are necessarily 'specially affected' by the material breach vis-à-vis other non-defaulting States. In its commentary on the draft of the VCLT, the International Law Commission identified arms reduction treaties as an example of the types of treaty where this problem might arise.[159] The VCLT permits a non-defaulting State in

---

153. See **2.82**.
154. VCLT, Art 59(1)(b).
155. Ibid, Art 59(2).
156. Ibid, Art 60(1).
157. Ibid, Art 60(2)(a).
158. Ibid, Art 60(2)(b).
159. *Yearbook of the International Law Commission*, 1966, Vol II, 255.

such a position to suspend the treaty in whole or in part with respect to itself. No allowance is made for termination of the treaty in these circumstances.[160]

2.128   The occurrence of a material breach does not automatically terminate a treaty. Rather, the material breach must first be invoked, thereby furnishing the non-defaulting party or parties with an option to terminate or suspend. Furthermore, a non-defaulting State will lose its option to terminate or suspend on grounds of material breach if, after becoming aware of the facts, it expressly agrees to or acquiesces in the treaty's continuance in operation.[161] The option to terminate or suspend does not, therefore, continue to exist beyond the time when the non-defaulting party becomes aware of the breach. Once a material breach is invoked, the procedures prescribed by Arts 65–67 of the VCLT must be observed before the treaty can be effectively terminated or suspended, unless the treaty itself provides differently.[162]

2.129   A non-defaulting State will forfeit its entitlement to invoke a material breach of a treaty by another State if the non-defaulting State has, by some unlawful act on its own part, prevented the other State from fulfilling its obligations under the treaty.[163] The unlawful act by the non-defaulting State may involve a breach of a rule or obligation sourced in another treaty to which the other State is also a party, or in customary international law.

Furthermore, the International Court of Justice has expressed the view that conduct by the non-defaulting State, which contributes to the creation of a situation which is 'not conducive' to the performance by the defaulting State of its treaty obligations, may sometimes deprive the non-defaulting State of its entitlement to invoke the material breach. This is so, apparently, even if the non-defaulting State's conduct is not per se unlawful.[164]

2.130   A treaty may not be terminated because a State has breached a rule of international law located outside the treaty itself. In the *Gabcíkovo-Nagymaros Project* case, the International Court of Justice said:[165]

> [T]he Court is of the view that it is only a material breach of the treaty itself, by a State party to that treaty, which entitles the other party to rely on it as a ground for terminating the treaty. The violation of other treaty rules or of rules of general international law may justify the taking of certain measures, including countermeasures, by the injured State, but it does not constitute a ground for termination under the law of treaties.

---

160. VCLT, Art 60(2)(c).
161. Ibid, Art 45.
162. Ibid, Art 42(2). As to Arts 65–67, see **2.147–2.153**.
163. *Case Concerning the Factory at Chorzów (Indemnity) (Merits) (Germany v Poland)* PCIJ Rep (1928) Series A No 17, 31; *Case Concerning the Gabcíkovo-Nagymaros Project (Hungary v Slovakia)* ICJ Rep (1997) 7, para 110.
164. *Case Concerning the Gabcíkovo-Nagymaros Project (Hungary v Slovakia)* ICJ Rep (1997) 7, para 107.
165. Ibid, para 106.

2.131   Article 60(3) of the VCLT defines a material breach in the following terms:

A material breach of a treaty, for the purposes of this article, consists in:

(a) a repudiation of the treaty not sanctioned by the present Convention; or

(b) the violation of a provision essential to the accomplishment of the object or purpose of the treaty.

It is noteworthy that the VCLT refers to 'material' breaches and not 'fundamental' breaches. The International Law Commission's commentary discloses that the mode of expression was not accidental:[166]

Some authorities have in the past seemed to assume that any breach of any provision would suffice to justify the denunciation of the treaty. The Commission, however, was unanimous that the right to terminate or suspend must be limited to cases where the breach is of a serious character. It preferred the term material to fundamental to express the kind of breach which is required. The word fundamental might be understood as meaning that only the violation of a provision directly touching the central purposes of the treaty can ever justify the other party in terminating the treaty. But other provisions considered by a party to be essential to the effective execution of the treaty may have been very material in inducing it to enter into the treaty at all, even although these provisions may be of an ancillary character.

This passage explains why Art 60(3)(b) of the VCLT defines a material breach to include 'the violation of a provision essential to the accomplishment of the object or purpose of the treaty'. A material breach will occur not only where a State violates a provision directly touching the objects and purpose of the treaty, but also where it violates an ancillary provision essential to the effective execution of the treaty. Accordingly, an arms reduction treaty which makes provisions for inspections might be materially breached by a refusal to permit inspectors to carry out their tasks, even if there is no evidence of a failure to reduce armaments in accordance with the treaty.

2.132   The definition adopted in Art 60(3) of the VCLT is seemingly at odds with the International Law Commission's commentary in one notable respect. The Commission recorded its unanimous view that 'the right to terminate or suspend must be limited to cases where the breach is of a serious character'.

The text of Art 60(3)(b), on the other hand, provides merely that a 'violation of a provision essential to the accomplishment of the object or purpose of the treaty' is sufficient to constitute a material breach. The provision does not specify that the breach of the essential provision needs to be serious.

A literal reading of Art 60(3)(b) would lead one to conclude that even a minor breach of an essential provision would constitute a material breach, whereas the Commission itself was of the view that only serious

---

166. *Yearbook of the International Law Commission*, 1966, Vol II, 255.

infringements would fall within the scope of material breach. Would the delay by a State's customs authorities of a single trans-border movement of goods in violation of a free trade treaty, out of many thousands of such movements annually, constitute a material breach justifying termination or suspension of the treaty? The better view is that Art 60(3)(b) should be read as requiring a serious breach of a provision essential to the accomplishment of the object or purpose of the treaty.

This view is consistent with the *South West Africa* advisory opinion of the International Court of Justice. The Court remarked that South Africa had committed a material breach of its UN Mandate because it had engaged in a 'deliberate and persistent violation of obligations which destroys the very object and purpose' of the agreement.[167]

2.133 A treaty may, with complete legal effect, make provisions at variance with the VCLT with respect to what constitutes a material breach, and the ability of parties to terminate or suspend a treaty as a consequence of any such breach.[168] The parties may also contract out of the VCLT's procedural requirements concerning material breach.[169]

2.134 Shortly after the VCLT was opened for signature, the International Court of Justice considered the application and meaning of the Convention's provisions on material breach.

In the *Legal Consequences for States of the Continued Presence of South Africa in Namibia (South West Africa) notwithstanding Security Council Resolution 276 (1970)* advisory opinion,[170] South Africa was exercising on behalf of the United Kingdom a UN Mandate, following on from a League of Nations Mandate, over the territory known as Namibia or South West Africa. Following the implementation of South Africa's policy of apartheid, there was widespread concern in the General Assembly that South Africa was not discharging its obligations to the people of Namibia under the Mandate, which had the status of an international treaty. In 1966, the General Assembly adopted Resolution 2145 (XXI) in which it declared that 'South Africa has failed to fulfil its obligations in respect of the administration of the Mandated Territory and to ensure the moral and material well-being and security of the indigenous inhabitants of South West Africa and has, in fact, disavowed the Mandate'.[171] The Assembly further decided that 'the Mandate conferred upon His Britannic Majesty to be expressed on his behalf by the Government of the Union of South Africa is therefore terminated'.[172] South Africa refused to regard its Mandate over South West Africa as terminated, and declined to leave the territory or cease exercising the functions and powers of a mandatory power. In 1970, the Security Council adopted Resolution 276, in which it reaffirmed the Assembly's resolution

---

167. *Legal Consequences for States of the Continued Presence of South Africa in Namibia (South West Africa) notwithstanding Security Council Resolution 276 (1970)* advisory opinion, ICJ Rep (1971) 16, para 95.
168. VCLT, Art 60(4).
169. See **2.150**.
170. *Legal Consequences for States of the Continued Presence of South Africa in Namibia (South West Africa) notwithstanding Security Council Resolution 276 (1970)* advisory opinion, ICJ Rep (1971) 16.
171. Paragraph 2 of the resolution.
172. Ibid, para 4.

and declared 'that the continued presence of the South African authorities in Namibia is illegal and that consequently all acts taken by the Government of South Africa on behalf of or concerning Namibia after the termination of the Mandate are illegal and invalid'. South Africa continued to reject the termination of its rights under the Mandate and remained in occupation of Namibia. Subsequently, the Security Council sought an advisory opinion from the International Court of Justice in the following terms: 'What are the legal consequences for States of the continued presence of South Africa in Namibia, notwithstanding Security Council Resolution 276 (1970)?' The Court took the view that South Africa's Mandate had been validly terminated, and made the following remarks concerning breach of treaty obligations:

> 94. In examining this action [Resolution 2145 (XXI)] of the General Assembly it is appropriate to have regard to the general principles of international law regulating termination of a treaty relationship on account of breach. ... The rules laid down by the Vienna Convention on the Law of Treaties concerning termination of a treaty relationship on account of breach (adopted without a dissenting vote) may in many respects be considered as a codification of existing customary law on the subject. In the light of these rules, only a material breach of a treaty justifies termination.

> 95. General Assembly resolution 2145 (XXI) determines that both forms of material breach [set out in Article 60(3) VCLT] had occurred in this case. By stressing that South Africa 'has, in fact, disavowed the Mandate', the General Assembly declared in fact that it had repudiated it. The resolution in question is therefore to be viewed as the exercise of the right to terminate a relationship in case of a deliberate and persistent violation of obligations which destroys the very object and purpose of that relationship.

> 96. It has been contended that the Covenant of the League of Nations did not confer on the Council of the League power to terminate a mandate for misconduct of the mandatory and that no such power could therefore be exercised by the United Nations, since it could not derive from the League greater powers than the latter itself had. For this objection to prevail it would be necessary to show that the mandates system, as established under the League, excluded the application of the general principle of law that a right of termination on account of breach must be presumed to exist in respect of all treaties, except as regards provisions relating to the protection of the human person contained in treaties of a humanitarian character (as indicated in Art. 60, para. 5, of the Vienna Convention). The silence of a treaty as to the existence of such a right cannot be interpreted as implying the exclusion of a right which has its source outside the treaty, in general law, and is dependent on the occurrence of circumstances which are not normally envisaged when a treaty is concluded.

2.135 The VCLT's provisions relating to permitted responses by non-defaulting States to a material breach[173] and the definition of 'material breach' itself[174] 'do not apply to provisions relating to the protection of the human person contained in treaties of a humanitarian character, in particular to provisions prohibiting any form of reprisals against persons protected by such treaties'.[175] This paragraph was not included in the International Law Commission's draft, but was added

---

173. See **2.126–2.127**.
174. See **2.131**.
175. VCLT, Art 60(5).

by the United Nations Conference on the Law of Treaties which settled the final text.

The records of the UN Conference disclose an intention to preclude the possibility that a violation by one party of a treaty provision designed to protect fundamental interests of the human person would justify other parties in terminating or suspending the treaty. They also indicate that the provision was intended to apply to the prohibition on reprisals contained in the 1949 Geneva Conventions on the laws of war, and to treaties concerning slavery, refugees, genocide and human rights.

Supervening impossibility

2.136 It may occasionally happen that the subject matter of a treaty disappears or is destroyed. For instance, a river may dry up, an island may submerge or a dam may be destroyed. A consequence may be that performance of the treaty is rendered impossible. The International Law Commission noted that termination of treaties for impossibility finds few manifestations in State practice.[176] The VCLT deals with this ground for terminating treaties at Art 61:

1. A party may invoke the impossibility of performing a treaty as a ground for terminating or withdrawing from it if the impossibility results from the permanent disappearance or destruction of an object indispensable for the execution of the treaty. If the impossibility is temporary, it may be invoked only as a ground for suspending the operation of the treaty.

2. Impossibility of performance may not be invoked by a party as a ground for terminating, withdrawing from or suspending the operation of a treaty if the impossibility is the result of a breach by that party either of an obligation under the treaty or of any other international obligation owed to any other party to the treaty.

2.137 It is worth noting that a supervening impossibility does not automatically terminate the treaty. Rather, the impossibility must be invoked as a ground for termination, and the procedures prescribed in the VCLT for making such an invocation must be followed.[177]

Fundamental change of circumstances

2.138 The doctrine of *rebus sic stantibus* (things remaining as they are) was long part of the customary law of treaties. According to this doctrine, a treaty could be terminated if the circumstances providing the context for the treaty's conclusion had undergone a fundamental change, thereby rendering the agreement substantially different from the one originally contracted. There was, however, considerable uncertainty as to the precise requirements of the doctrine. The VCLT makes provision for this ground of termination by Art 62:

---

176. *Yearbook of the International Law Commission*, 1966, Vol II, 256.
177. VCLT, Art 42(2).

1. A fundamental change of circumstances which has occurred with regard to those existing at the time of the conclusion of a treaty, and which was not foreseen by the parties, may not be invoked as a ground for terminating or withdrawing from the treaty unless:

    (a) the existence of those circumstances constituted an essential basis of the consent of the parties to be bound by the treaty; and

    (b) the effect of the change is radically to transform the extent of obligations still to be performed under the treaty.

2. A fundamental change of circumstances may not be invoked as a ground for terminating or withdrawing from a treaty:

    (a) if the treaty establishes a boundary; or

    (b) if the fundamental change is the result of a breach by the party invoking it either of an obligation under the treaty or of any other international obligation owed to any other party to the treaty.

3. If, under the foregoing paragraphs, a party may invoke a fundamental change of circumstances as a ground for terminating or withdrawing from a treaty, it may also invoke the change as a ground for suspending the operation of the treaty.

2.139   Not long after the conclusion of the VCLT, the International Court of Justice considered the scope and application of *rebus sic stantibus*.

In the ***Fisheries Jurisdiction* case (*United Kingdom v Iceland*),**[178] the United Kingdom alleged a violation by Iceland of a 1961 agreement in which Iceland undertook not to extend its 'exclusive fisheries zone' beyond a distance of 12 miles from its coast. A compromissory clause in the agreement provided that disputes should be referred to the ICJ. In 1971, Iceland purported to extend the fisheries zone to 50 miles, and the United Kingdom brought proceedings before the ICJ. Iceland contended that the circumstances surrounding the conclusion of any agreement it had with the United Kingdom had fundamentally changed since 1961. In particular, Iceland argued, changes in fishing techniques meant that a 12-mile zone could no longer protect Iceland's vital interests as a country peculiarly dependent on fishing for its livelihood and development. According to Iceland, if the 1961 arrangement was a treaty, Iceland was justified in terminating it in accordance with the doctrine of *rebus sic stantibus*. It followed, Iceland argued, that the compromissory clause conferring jurisdiction on the ICJ was also terminated. The Court said:

> 36. ... the Government of Iceland is basing itself on the principle of termination of a treaty by reason of change of circumstances. International law admits that a fundamental change in the circumstances which determined the parties to accept a treaty, if it has resulted in a radical transformation of the extent of the obligations imposed by it, may, under certain conditions, afford the party affected a ground for invoking the termination or suspension of the treaty. This principle, and the conditions and exceptions to which it is subject, have been embodied in Article 62 of the Vienna Convention on the Law of Treaties, which may in many respects be considered as a codification of existing customary law on the subject of the termination of a treaty relationship on account of change of circumstances.

---

178. *Fisheries Jurisdiction* case (*United Kingdom v Iceland*) ICJ Rep (1973) 3.

37. One of the basic requirements embodied in that Article is that the change of circumstances must have been a fundamental one. In this respect the Government of Iceland has, with regard to developments in fishing techniques, referred to the increased exploitation of the fishery resources in the seas surrounding Iceland and to the danger of still further exploitation because of an increase in the catching capacity of fishing fleets. The Icelandic statements recall the exceptional dependence of that country on its fishing for its existence and economic development.

38. The invocation by Iceland of its vital interests, which were not made the subject of an express reservation to the acceptance of the jurisdictional obligation under the 1961 Exchange of Notes, must be interpreted, in the context of the assertion of changed circumstances, as an indication by Iceland of the reason why it regards as fundamental the changes which in its view have taken place in previously existing fishing techniques. This interpretation would correspond to the traditional view that the changes of circumstances which must be regarded as fundamental or vital are those which imperil the existence or vital development of one of the parties. ...

40. If, as contended by Iceland, there have been any fundamental changes in fishing techniques in the waters around Iceland, those changes might be relevant for the decision on the merits of the dispute. But the alleged changes could not affect in the least the obligation to submit to the Court's jurisdiction ... It follows that the apprehended dangers for the vital interests of Iceland, resulting from changes in fishing techniques, cannot constitute a fundamental change with respect to the lapse or subsistence of the compromissory clause establishing the Court's jurisdiction. ...

43. Moreover, *in order that a change of circumstances may give rise to a ground for invoking the termination of a treaty it is also necessary that it should have resulted in a radical transformation of the extent of the obligations still to be performed. The change must have increased the burden of the obligations to be executed to the extent of rendering the performance something essentially different from that originally undertaken.* In respect of the obligation with which the Court is here concerned, this condition is wholly unsatisfied; the change of circumstances alleged by Iceland cannot be said to have transformed radically the extent of the jurisdictional obligation which is imposed in the 1961 Exchange of Notes. The compromissory clause enabled either of the parties to submit to the Court any dispute between them relating to an extension of Icelandic fisheries jurisdiction in the waters above its continental shelf beyond the 12-mile limit. Not only has the jurisdictional obligation not been radically transformed in this extent; it has remained precisely what it was in 1961. [Emphasis added.]

2.140   Oppenheim observes that 'the doctrine *rebus sic stantibus*, when kept within proper limits, embodies a general principle of law as expressed in the doctrines of frustration, or supervening impossibility of performance, or the like, and known to the law of many countries'.[179] That its limits are narrow is necessitated by the imperative to maintain another important general principle: *pacta sunt servanda*.

Were *rebus sic stantibus* to be given a broad field of application, the bindingness of treaties would be seriously undermined. Many of the circumstances in whose general context most treaties are concluded are

---

179. Sir Robert Jennings and Sir Arthur Watts (eds), *Oppenheim's International Law,* 9th ed, Longman, New York, 1992, § 651, 1306.

constantly changing, and it would be exceedingly tempting for States to escape the obligations of an inconvenient treaty simply by asserting some change in those circumstances. This largely explains the care with which the International Court of Justice circumscribed the scope of the doctrine at para 43 of its judgment in the *Fisheries Jurisdiction* case.

2.141   More recently, the ICJ again dismissed an argument based on *rebus sic stantibus*. In the *Gabcíkovo-Nagymaros Project* case,[180] the Court rejected Hungary's submission that a treaty concluded between it and Slovakia in 1977, relating to an extensive development scheme spanning their mutual border, was affected by *rebus sic stantibus*.

According to Hungary, the changed circumstances were that both countries had ceased to operate socialist political and economic systems and abandoned their previous policy of socialist integration, the project had become much less economically viable, and new scientific knowledge relating to environmental protection raised serious concerns about the project's environmental impacts. The Court rejected these arguments while pointing out that, although the two countries' socialist orientation had been a material factor in concluding the treaty, its objects and purpose were not dependent on a continuation of the socialist system.

Furthermore, although the economic benefits of the agreed project had clearly diminished, they were not bound to diminish to such an extent that the treaty obligations of the parties would have been radically transformed as a result. Finally, the Court was not satisfied that the new scientific knowledge relating to environmental impacts was 'completely unforeseen' and noted provisions in the treaty for taking account of any such developments.

The Court amplified its earlier caution concerning *rebus sic stantibus* with the following passage from its judgment:[181]

> A fundamental change of circumstances must have been unforeseen; the existence of the circumstances at the time of the Treaty's conclusion must have constituted an essential basis of the consent of the parties to be bound by the Treaty. The negative and conditional wording of Article 62 of the Vienna Convention on the Law of Treaties is a clear indication moreover that the stability of treaty relations requires that the plea of fundamental change of circumstances be applied only in exceptional cases.

Severance of diplomatic relations

2.142   The VCLT provides that a severance of diplomatic or consular relations between parties to a treaty does not affect their legal relations under that treaty 'except in so far as the existence of diplomatic or consular relations is indispensable for the application of the treaty'.[182] Conversely, it is not necessary for States to have established diplomatic or consular relations in order to conclude a treaty between them.

---

180. *Case Concerning the Gabcíkovo-Nagymaros Project (Hungary v Slovakia)* ICJ Rep (1997) 7.
181. Ibid, para 104.
182. VCLT, Art 62.

New norm of the *jus cogens*

2.143   Article 64 of the VCLT provides as follows:

> If a new peremptory norm of general international law emerges, any existing treaty which is in conflict with that norm becomes void and terminates.

A treaty is void if, at the time of its conclusion, it conflicts with a norm of the *jus cogens* — that is, a peremptory norm of general international law.[183] Article 64 regulates the situation where a treaty was validly concluded, but subsequently comes into conflict with a newly emerged norm of *the jus cogens*. Where this occurs, the treaty is void.

Consequences of termination and suspension

2.144   A treaty may expressly provide for the consequences of its own termination or suspension. Similarly, the parties may reach agreement as to the consequences attendant upon the termination or suspension of a treaty. In either case, the terms settled by the parties themselves will determine the consequences of the treaty's termination or suspension.

Where the treaty itself does not provide for the consequences of its own termination and where the parties do not reach an agreement about such consequences, termination of a treaty releases all parties from any further obligations to perform the treaty, while leaving intact all rights, obligations and legal situations which were created under the treaty prior to its termination. If a State withdraws from a multilateral treaty, the same consequences apply as between the withdrawing State and each of the other parties from the date on which the withdrawal takes effect.[184]

Where the cause of termination is the treaty's inconsistency with a newly emerged norm of the *jus cogens*, all the rights, obligations and legal situations which were created under the treaty prior to its termination remain intact only insofar as their maintenance is not in itself inconsistent with the new requirement of the *jus cogens*.[185]

A treaty will probably not provide for the consequences of its own suspension. In such cases, and where the parties do not reach an agreement about such consequences, suspension releases the parties between which the treaty is suspended from their mutual obligations of performance while the treaty remains suspended. Suspension does not otherwise affect the legal relations established among the parties by the treaty. Furthermore, during the period of the treaty's suspension, all parties must refrain from acts tending to obstruct the treaty's resumption of operation.[186]

2.145   Nothing in the VCLT prejudges the application of the international law of State responsibility in relation to treaties.[187] Accordingly, States

---

183. See 2.106–2.110.
184. VCLT, Art 70.
185. Ibid, Art 71(2).
186. Ibid, Art 72.
187. Ibid, Art 73. On the law of State responsibility, see chapter 5.

remain liable for the consequences of violating treaty obligations in accordance with the rules and principles of State responsibility.

2.146 The VCLT provides for certain procedures to be followed before a treaty may be terminated or suspended if the parties to the treaty have not established an alternative procedural scheme.[188] If an alternative procedural scheme has been established, or if the parties are not bound by the VCLT,[189] a question may arise as to whether a purported unilateral termination or suspension of a treaty is effective to also terminate or suspend any jurisdiction clauses contained in the treaty.

In the ***Appeal Relating to the Jurisdiction of the ICAO Council (India v Pakistan),***[190] India unilaterally suspended the 1944 Chicago Convention on International Civil Aviation in its relations with Pakistan. India justified its decision on the basis of Pakistan's alleged involvement in the hijacking of an Indian aircraft in violation of the Convention. Pakistan challenged India's decision before the Council of the International Civil Aviation Organisation (ICAO), in putative compliance with the terms of the Convention. India replied by denying the Council's jurisdiction, arguing that the clauses permitting recourse to the Council were suspended together with the rest of the Convention. India appealed to the International Court of Justice against the Council's decision that the Council possessed jurisdiction to determine Pakistan's complaint. Pakistan, in turn, objected to the ICJ's jurisdiction, arguing that India could not simultaneously deny the operation of the Convention and rely on the Convention's clauses conferring jurisdiction on the Court. The ICJ rejected Pakistan's objection, and in so doing remarked:[191]

> 16. Nor in any case could a merely unilateral suspension per se render jurisdictional clauses inoperative, since one of their purposes might be, precisely, to enable the validity of the suspension to be tested. If a mere allegation, as yet unestablished, that a treaty was no longer operative, could be used to defeat its jurisdictional clauses, all such clauses would become potentially a dead letter, even in cases like the present, where one of the very questions at issue on the merits, and as yet undecided, is whether or not the treaty is operative — ie, whether it has been validly terminated or suspended. The result would be that means of defeating jurisdictional clauses would never be wanting.

Accordingly, jurisdiction clauses in a treaty, to the extent that they permit the adjudication of an issue as to the validity of a termination or suspension, are not terminated or suspended even if the rest of the treaty has been.

---

188. See **2.150**.
189. See **2.3**.
190. *Appeal Relating to the Jurisdiction of the ICAO Council (India v Pakistan)* ICJ Rep (1972) 46.
191. Ibid, 53–54.

Procedures relating to invalidity, denunciation, withdrawal, termination and suspension

2.147   The VCLT effected a useful reform of the position under customary international law by providing mandatory procedures to be observed in order to establish authoritatively that a treaty is invalid, terminated or suspended, or that it has been lawfully denounced or withdrawn from. As the ILC observed, it was essential that any treaty emerging from its Draft Articles on Treaties:[192]

> … should contain procedural safeguards against the possibility that the nullity, termination or suspension of the operation of a treaty may be arbitrarily asserted as a mere pretext for getting rid of an inconvenient obligation.

2.148   Article 42 of the VCLT provides as follows:

1. The validity of a treaty or of the consent of a State to be bound by a treaty may be impeached only through the application of the present convention.

2. The termination of a treaty, its denunciation or the withdrawal of a party, may take place only as a result of the application of the provisions of the treaty or of the present Convention. The same rule applies to suspension of the operation of a treaty.

This provision performs two tasks, one substantive and one procedural. In substantive terms, it indicates that the grounds specified in the VCLT may justify invalidity, termination, suspension, denunciation or withdrawal. In procedural terms, Art 42 points to the provisions contained in Arts 65–68. These provisions specify procedural requirements to be observed by a State invoking grounds in support of invalidity, termination, suspension, denunciation or withdrawal.

2.149   Article 42(1) of the VCLT specifies that only the grounds and procedures contained in the VCLT can support a treaty's invalidity. It would, in any event, be peculiar for a treaty to make provision for its own invalidity.

2.150   In the case of termination, suspension, denunciation and withdrawal, Art 42(2) of the VCLT indicates that the treaty itself may make provision displacing, replacing or supplementing the VCLT provisions. It follows that the treaty itself may validly make provision inconsistent with the VCLT in respect of the grounds justifying termination, suspension, denunciation and withdrawal, as well as the procedural requirements for invoking those grounds. Article 65(4) preserves 'provisions in force binding the parties with regards to the settlement of disputes'. In such a case, the treaty's provisions would prevail over inconsistent VCLT provisions, except to the extent that the VCLT provisions reflect the

---

192. *Yearbook of the International Law Commission*, 1966, Vol II, 262.

jus cogens (for example, the requirement in Art 65(3) of the VCLT that disputes be settled by peaceful means).

2.151   A party which invokes a ground for invalidating, terminating, suspending or withdrawing from a treaty must first notify in writing all other parties of its claim. The notification must indicate the measure that is proposed to be taken with respect to the treaty and the reasons for taking those measures.[193]

The other parties must then normally be given a period of at least three months to object to the invoking party's notice. A shorter period may be specified in cases of special emergency. If, at the end of the specified period, no other party has objected to the notice, the invoking party may carry out the measure which it has proposed. Any act by the invoking party which declares the treaty invalid, terminated, suspended or withdrawn from must be carried out through an instrument communicated to the other parties.[194]

It may be, however, that one or more of the other parties take objection to the invoking party's written notice within the specified time. Where that is so, Art 65(3) of the VCLT requires that the parties seek a solution to their dispute by the peaceful means prescribed by Art 33 of the UN Charter.[195]

2.152   The VCLT allows a 12-month period within which the dispute settlement mechanisms under Art 33 of the UN Charter may be allowed to work. If, at the end of that period, there is still no solution, two further dispute settlement procedures are potentially activated.

If the dispute concerns the application or interpretation of the VCLT's provisions on the *jus cogens*,[196] any party to the dispute may submit it to the International Court of Justice for a decision unless all parties to the dispute agree to submit it to arbitration.[197]

If the dispute concerns the application or interpretation of the other provisions under Part V of the VCLT (invalidity, denunciation, withdrawal, termination and suspension), any party to the dispute may require that it be settled by a Conciliation Commission established under the Annex to the VCLT.[198]

2.153   Unless a State's conduct brings it within the scope of Art 45 of the VCLT,[199] a failure to make a notification under Art 65(1) of the VCLT[200] does not prevent a State 'from making such notification in answer to another party claiming performance of the treaty or alleging its violation'.[201] Thus, if State A receives an Art 65(1) demand for performance or an allegation

---

193. VCLT, Arts 65(1) and 67(1).
194. Ibid, Arts 65(2) and 67(2).
195. See 8.4–8.6.
196. See 2.107 and 2.113.
197. VCLT, Art 66(a).
198. Ibid, Art 66(b).
199. See 2.94.
200. See 2.151.
201. VCLT, Art 65(5).

of breach from State B, then State A may respond to State B with its own notice under Art 65(1), unless State A has already expressly agreed to, or acquiesced in, the treaty's validity or continuance in force in respect of the circumstances said to justify State A's notice.

Question 1

Alpha, Beta, Gamma and Delta are neighbouring States. Alpha has for many years advocated establishing closer economic relations among all the neighbours.

In October 1996, Alpha's Foreign Minister and Beta's Foreign Minister had a meeting to discuss deepening economic ties between the two States. The Alphan Foreign Minister said that Alpha would abolish import duties on bananas grown in Beta, if Beta would give immediate support to Alpha in convening an intergovernmental conference to establish a free trade zone among the four neighbours.

The Betan Foreign Minister replied that Beta was delighted with the offer and would provide the requested support. Alpha abolished import duties on Betan bananas in November 1996.

In January 1997, Alpha formally called on the governments of Beta, Gamma and Delta to attend a conference in Alpha's capital city in order to establish a free trade zone. Gamma and Delta immediately communicated their readiness to attend on condition that Beta would also participate. Beta remained silent for 10 months before agreeing to attend the proposed conference, which was finally held in December 1997. In the meantime, Alpha repeatedly protested to Beta against Beta's delay in supporting the conference.

The text of a Free Trade Agreement (FTA) was adopted on the votes of Alpha, Beta and Gamma. The adopted FTA text was in the following terms.

1. The object of this agreement is to strengthen economic ties between the parties by establishing a zone of free trade.

2. Each party agrees to abolish, by not later than 31 December 2015, all import duties and customs duties on goods entering its territory from the territory of any other party.

3. Each party undertakes to ensure, within its own territory, that racial discrimination in all aspects of employment (including hiring, dismissal, promotion, remuneration and terms of retirement) is legally prohibited in places where goods are produced.

4. This agreement is open for signature until 31 December 1998. Thereafter, any State which is eligible to become a party to this agreement may accede by notifying all contracting States of its intention to do so.

5. Alpha, Beta, Gamma and Delta are eligible to become parties to this agreement.

6. This agreement shall enter into force when three States become party to the agreement, or on 1 January 2003, whichever is the later.

Alpha, Beta and Gamma signed the FTA at the conclusion of the conference in December 1997. Delta declined to sign the text as adopted. Gamma sent the other three States a note saying that Gamma's signature was subject to ratification in accordance with Gamma's constitution.

On 1 February 1999, Delta informed Alpha, Beta and Gamma that Delta now acceded to the FTA 'subject to the attached reservation'. The reservation specified that Delta did not consider itself bound by Art 3, except in relation to enterprises owned by the State. On the same day, Alpha wrote to Beta, Gamma and Delta formally objecting to Delta's reservation as being contrary to the object and purpose of the FTA. Neither Beta nor Gamma have ever made objection to Delta's reservation.

In July 2003, the Gamman parliament, against the wishes of the Gamman Council of Ministers, doubled import duties on all goods imported into its territory. On 1 September 2003, the King of Gamma wrote to the Heads of State of Alpha, Beta and Delta advising that his country's ratification formalities had been successfully completed and that Gamma now ratified its signature to the FTA.

Alpha seeks your advice on two questions:

■ Has any State violated international obligations owed to Alpha?
■ Are all four States bound by all the provisions of the FTA in their relations with each other?

You may assume that the four States are parties to the Vienna Convention on the Law of Treaties, but that they are not parties to any other treaty which might be relevant.

Suggested answer

The parole agreement between the Foreign Ministers of Alpha and Beta in October 1996 was binding on Beta. In the *Legal Status of Eastern Greenland* case, the Permanent Court of International Justice observed that a 'definitively affirmative' commitment given by a Foreign Minister:

> ... on behalf of his government in response to a request by the diplomatic representative of a foreign power, in regard to a question falling within his province, is binding upon the country to which the Minister belongs.

The context in which the undertaking was given is important. In the *Legal Status of Eastern Greenland* case, the undertakings made by the representatives of Norway and Denmark occurred in the course of discussing the adoption of a coordinated position at a forthcoming multilateral peace conference. The fact that the context in which Norway's Foreign Minister made his promise was a diplomatic negotiation, and the fact that Norway received a quid pro quo in respect of its undertaking, contributed to the finding that Norway was bound by that promise.

Although there is no requirement for valuable consideration or a quid pro quo in order for a treaty obligation to arise, its existence will strengthen the inference that the parties intended to be legally bound.

Beta's Foreign Minister made a definitively affirmative promise to Alpha's Foreign Minister in the context of diplomatic negotiations, and similarly received a benefit in return for that promise — that is, the abolition of Alphan import duties on Betan bananas.

Although the agreement is not covered by the VCLT because it is not in writing (VCLT, Art 2(1)(a)), such agreements between States are still binding in international law (VCLT, Art 3). Beta's failure, for a period of 10 months, to honour its binding undertaking to give immediate support to Alpha's call for a regional trade conference placed Beta in breach of its international legal obligations to Alpha.

In July 2003, Gamma was under a legal obligation owed to all other contracting States to the FTA, including Alpha, not to double import duties on goods imported into its territory from the territory of any other contracting State. Gamma did not become a party to the FTA until 1 September 2003. Although Gamma signed the FTA in December 1997, it did so expressly subject to ratification, with the result that its consent to be bound was not effective until its instrument of ratification was communicated to the other contracting States (VCLT, Arts 14(1)(c) and 16). Nevertheless, once Gamma signed the FTA subject to ratification, it fell under an obligation to refrain from acts which would defeat the FTA's object and purpose until such time as it made its intention clear not to become a party to the treaty (VCLT, Art 18).

The doubling of import duties on all goods entering its territory from the other contracting States clearly defeated the FTA's object, as stated in Art 1, to strengthen economic ties between the parties by establishing a free trade zone. The FTA was drafted to give effect to this purpose by requiring the eventual abolition of all import duties as between the parties (FTA, Art 2), and the Gamman measure contradicted that stipulation.

The fact that the Gamman government opposed the Gamman parliament's adoption of the offending national measure does not absolve the Gamman State from breaching the obligation it owed to the other contracting States. A State may not invoke provisions of its internal law, including its internal constitutional arrangements, as justification for its failure to comply with its obligations under a treaty (VCLT, Art 27).

If Art 20(2) of the VCLT is applicable: It is highly arguable that the application in its entirety of the FTA was an essential condition of each State to be bound. This may be inferred from the limited number of negotiating States, the fact that the FTA has only two substantive provisions, and the reciprocity upon which trade agreements depend. If this is right, then the consent of all the parties to Delta's reservation is required and Alpha's objection to the reservation prevented Delta from becoming a party to the FTA (VCLT, Art 20(2)). If this is correct, then Delta receives neither rights nor obligations under the FTA. Relations among Alpha, Beta and Gamma are regulated by all the provisions of the FTA since its entry into force (VCLT, Art 21(2)).

If Delta never became a party to the FTA, the treaty did not enter into force until 1 September 2003, when Gamma notified its ratification to the other contracting States and became the third State to be a party to the treaty (FTA, Art 6).

If Art 20(2) of the VCLT is not applicable: Effective from the entry into force of the FTA, Delta became a party to the treaty in its relations with any other State party which had accepted the reservation (VCLT, Art 20(4)(a)). Having raised no objection to Delta's reservation, Beta and Gamma are deemed to have accepted the reservation 12 months after their notification of the reservation or of their expression of consent to be bound by the treaty, whichever is later (VCLT, Art 20(5)). In Beta's case, this will be 1 February 1995 (12 months after receiving notification) and in Gamma's case it will be 1 September 1999 (12 months after ratification).

Delta's accession did not become effective until 1 February 2000, when Beta was deemed to have accepted Delta's reservation (VCLT, Art 20(4)(c)).

In this case, Delta became the third State party to the FTA, which entered into force on 1 January 2003 in accordance with Art 6 of the FTA.

Because Alpha did not definitely express an intention not to allow the FTA to enter into force between itself and Delta, the treaty has regulated relations between the two States since its entry into force on 1 January 2003 (VCLT, Art 20(4)(b)).

As between Delta on the one hand, and Beta and Gamma on the other, relations are governed by the FTA as modified by the reservation. Delta may rely on the reservation in its bilateral relations with Beta and Gamma, while Beta and Gamma may also rely on the reservation to exactly the same extent in their bilateral relations with Delta (VCLT, Art 21(1)). In other words, in relations between Delta and Beta and between Delta and Gamma, neither side will incur international responsibility for a non-observance of Art 3 of the FTA where non-State-owned enterprises are concerned.

As between Alpha and Delta, the situation is somewhat different. The provision to which the reservation relates (that is, FTA, Art 3) does not apply at all as between the two States (VCLT, Art 21(3)). This means that neither side incurs any international responsibility to the other in the event of any non-observance of Art 3 of the FTA, regardless of the ownership of the enterprise concerned.

These arrangements are tentative and remain valid until an authoritative determination is made 'on the jurisdictional plane' as to whether Delta's reservation is compatible with the FTA's object and purpose (*Reservations to the Genocide Convention* advisory opinion).

If a judicial determination is eventually made that Delta's reservation violates the FTA's object and purpose, then Delta could no longer be regarded as a party to the treaty as its consent would be based on a reservation which it was not entitled to make (VCLT, Art 19(c)).

If, on the other hand, an eventual judicial determination holds Delta's reservation to be consistent with the FTA's object and purpose, then Delta will continue to be party to the treaty. As Alpha's objection was based on the reservation's incompatibility with the FTA's object and purpose, the legal foundation for the objection would fall away and relations between the two States would be governed by the reservation; Alpha could also rely on the reservation to exactly the same extent in its relations with Delta (VCLT, Art 21(1)). In other words, in relations between Alpha and Delta, neither side would incur international responsibility for a non-observance of Art 3 of the FTA where non-State owned enterprises are concerned.

Relations among Alpha, Beta and Gamma are regulated by all the provisions of the FTA since its entry into force (VCLT, Art 21(2)).

Reservations to human rights treaties

Alpha might prefer to establish that Delta is a party to the FTA and that its relations with Delta are regulated by the FTA in its entirety. In that case, it would need to argue that the reservation is invalid but severable from Delta's consent to be bound. The general rule is that an invalid reservation attached to a consent to be bound invalidates that consent (*Reservations to the Genocide Convention* advisory opinion; VCLT, Art 19(c)).

Nevertheless, the European Court of Human Rights severs invalid reservations from a State's consent to be bound by the European Convention on Human Rights (ECHR) (for example, *Belilos v Switzerland*, *Weber v Switzerland*, *Loizidou v Turkey*). Similarly, the Human Rights Committee established under the International Covenant on Civil and Political Rights (ICCPR) supports the severance of invalid reservations from a State's consent to be bound by that Convention (General Comment No 24).

In neither the ECHR nor the ICCPR is there textual warrant for this departure from customary international law. The reason advanced for the departure is that treaty provisions protecting human rights are not classical exchanges of obligations between States, but endow individuals with rights. This unique feature of human rights treaties, it is argued, makes the general law on reservations inapplicable to such treaties.

Article 3 of the FTA is a provision for the protection of human rights. Alpha could, accordingly, argue that the reservation is incompatible with the FTA's object and purpose, but that it should be severed from Delta's consent to be bound because it affects a provision for the protection of human rights. The result would be, if the argument were to be accepted, that Delta's relations with Alpha would be governed by the FTA in its entirety.

One should, however, be circumspect in advancing this argument. Apart from the European Court of Human Rights and the Human Rights Committee, there is very little authority for it. Indeed, it directly contradicts the opinion of the International Court of Justice in the *Reservations to the Genocide Convention* advisory opinion, and numerous States are on record as opposing the views of the Human Rights Committee and reaffirming the customary law position as formulated by the ICJ in 1951.

Question 2

Epsilon, Zeta and Eta concluded an arms control treaty, known as the EZE Pact, in 2000. The Pact entered into force the same year, and contains only three substantive provisions.

According to Art 2, the parties are required to 'decommission and scuttle their existing fleets of naval submarines by 31 December 2005'. Article 3 specifies that the parties must 'refrain from acquiring or commencing the construction of any new naval submarines'. Article 4 authorises each State party to 'compel any of its citizens to participate in executing the obligations contained in Art 2, if such compulsion is deemed necessary for their timely completion'. Diplomatic correspondence prior to the EZE Pact's conclusion indicates that the treaty was contemplated by all three States to remain in force indefinitely.

Last week, the news media reported that between November 2005 and June 2006, Eta had been secretly constructing a naval submarine, but that the project had been terminated when a new government came to power in Eta. The President of Eta denies the report.

Zeta originally entered into the treaty because its intelligence service had determined that Epsilon had acquired the capacity to construct nuclear-powered submarines, a capacity which Zeta did not possess. Since 2008, it has been generally known that Epsilon was, in fact, never capable of constructing nuclear-powered submarines. In the meantime, Zeta has acquired the capacity to construct such submarines.

Zeta's Foreign Minister informs you that his government is considering an 'immediate abandonment' of the EZE Pact. He says this will probably be done at a news conference to be held next week. Advise the Foreign Minister as to Zeta's position in international law.

You may assume that Epsilon, Zeta and Eta are parties to the Vienna Convention on the Law of Treaties, but that they are not parties to any other treaty which might be relevant.

Suggested answer

All treaties in force are binding upon the parties and must be performed by them in good faith (VCLT, Art 26). Because the EZE Pact does not contain a provision providing for withdrawal, Zeta may not unilaterally withdraw from the EZE Pact simply by making an announcement to that effect unless an exception to the general rule applies. Zeta may withdraw from the EZE Pact only if it can be established that the parties intended to admit the possibility of withdrawal, or if a right of withdrawal may be implied from the nature of the treaty (VCLT, Art 56(1)).

An examination of the *travaux préparatoires* of the EZE Pact shows that the parties regarded the treaty as being concluded for an indefinite period, which does not assist an argument that the parties intended a unilateral right of withdrawal to exist. Furthermore, there would appear to be nothing special about the nature of the EZE Pact which would imply an exceptional right of withdrawal. In any event, Zeta would not be able to 'immediately abandon' the EZE Pact by an act of withdrawal; a State intending to withdraw from a treaty must give at least 12 months' notice of its intention to do so (VCLT, Art 56(2)).

In order to escape its obligations under the EZE Pact, Zeta must establish either that the treaty suffers from invalidity or that there are grounds for its termination. In either case, Zeta will need to observe certain procedural requirements before the treaty can be established as invalid or terminated (VCLT, Art 42).

There are two possible bases upon which Zeta might argue that the EZE Pact is invalid: error and violation of the *jus cogens*.

Zeta entered into the EZE Pact because its intelligence service concluded that Epsilon had acquired the potential to construct nuclear-powered submarines. This intelligence was in error, although it 'formed an essential basis' of Zeta's consent to be bound. Such an error is, in principle, capable of invalidating Zeta's consent (VCLT, Art 48(1)). However, Zeta will not be able to invoke the error for the purpose of invalidating its consent if it contributed by its own conduct to the error (VCLT, Art 48(2); *Temple of Preah Vihear* case). It would appear that Zeta's error was entirely due to its own failure to collect or assess, with accuracy, intelligence on Epsilon's naval capabilities.

In any event, Zeta has been aware since 2003 that Epsilon did not possess the capability to construct nuclear-powered submarines. Zeta has not, however, hitherto raised the possibility of the treaty's invalidity. This probably means that Zeta has, by acquiescence in the EZE Pact's validity, lost any right it might have possessed to invoke the treaty's invalidity (VCLT, Art 45(b)). Accordingly, it is unlikely that error could operate as a ground for invalidating the EZE Pact.

Article 4 of the EZE Pact authorises all States parties to 'compel any of its citizens to participate in executing the obligations contained in Art 2, if such compulsion is deemed necessary for their timely completion'. It is possible that this provision purports to authorise the establishment of slavery, servitude or forced labour in violation of the *jus cogens*. If this were the case, the EZE Pact would be void (VCLT, Art 53) and Zeta's possible acquiescence in the treaty's continuance would not deprive it of the right to invoke the treaty's invalidity (VCLT, Art 45). If Art 4 of the EZE Pact violated the *jus cogens,* it would not be severable from the rest of the treaty (VCLT, Art 44(5)) and the EZE Pact would be completely invalid.

Assuming that Eta did in fact attempt secretly to construct a naval submarine between November 1995 and June 1996, Eta breached the EZE Pact. This raises the prospect of the treaty's termination or suspension if the breach was of a material character.

Eta committed a material breach of the EZE Pact if its attempted construction of a submarine violated a provision essential to the accomplishment of the object or purpose of the treaty (VCLT, Art 60(3)(b)). Undertaking the construction project was a violation by Eta of Art 3 of the EZE Pact, and this would strengthen an argument that Eta's conduct constituted a sufficiently 'serious' breach as to characterise it as 'material' (see the ILC commentary on VCLT, Art 60).

On the other hand, Eta terminated the project before completion; no submarine was in fact ever built. This would tend to weaken an argument that Eta's conduct was sufficiently serious as to constitute a material breach of Art 3 of the EZE Pact. Furthermore, the fact that Eta engaged in only a single and uncompleted submarine construction project would suggest that it lacked the persistent character which may be necessary in order to categorise an act as a material breach (*South West Africa* advisory opinion).

Even if Eta's construction project is regarded as constituting a material breach of the EZE Pact, Zeta may be taken to have acquiesced in the continuance of the treaty by not having protested against Eta's conduct earlier. This will depend on when Zeta became aware of Eta's construction project. If Zeta has known of the project for a considerable period of time but said nothing until recently, it may be taken to have acquiesced in Eta's conduct and now be precluded from invoking the breach as a ground for terminating the EZE Pact (VCLT, Art 45(b)).

If Eta's construction project does constitute a material breach of the EZE Pact which Zeta is not estopped from invoking, what steps are open to Zeta? Whether it is invoking Eta's construction project as a material breach of the EZE Pact, or whether it is invoking Art 4 of the EZE Pact for inconsistency with the *jus cogens*, Zeta must comply with the procedural scheme contained in the VCLT (VCLT, Art 42). Zeta must first notify its claims in writing to both Eta and Epsilon (VCLT, Arts 65(1) and 67(1)). In the case of the *jus cogens* point, Zeta's claim can only be that the entire EZE Pact is invalid (VCLT, Arts 53 and 44(5)).

In the case of the possible material breach occasioned by Eta's construction project, and given that Zeta wishes to extricate itself from its obligations under the EZE Pact, Zeta would have two options. First, Zeta might persuade Epsilon to join it in terminating or suspending the treaty altogether (VCLT, Art 60(2)(a)). Second, it might claim a right to suspend unilaterally the treaty with respect to itself on the grounds that the alleged material breach by Eta radically changes the position of both Zeta and Epsilon with respect to their further obligations under the treaty (VCLT, Art 60(2)(c)). Given that Eta's breach was terminated prior to the construction of a single submarine, this would probably be a difficult submission to sustain.

Epsilon and Eta will then have three months to reply to Zeta's claims. If neither objects, Zeta may carry out the measures it has proposed. If either Epsilon or Eta objects, then the parties must seek to resolve their dispute by the peaceful means prescribed by Art 33 of the UN Charter (VCLT, Art 65(3)).

If the UN Charter processes do not result in a settlement within 12 months, the parties then have two further avenues to resolve the disputed claim. If the claim concerns a violation of the *jus cogens*, any party to the dispute may submit it for decision to the International Court of Justice unless they all agree to submit it to arbitration (VCLT,

Art 66(a)). If the claim concerns the alleged material breach occasioned by Eta's construction project, any party to the dispute may require it to be settled by a Conciliation Commission established under the Annex to the VCLT (VCLT, Art 66(b)).

Further tutorial discussion

1. Are the VCLT's rules on treaty interpretation well adapted to ascertaining the parties' intentions?

2. Will a breach of an *erga omnes* obligation always involve a violation of the *jus cogens*? Will a breach of the *jus cogens* always engage obligations *erga omnes*?

3. Why should a State be bound by a human rights treaty if its consent to the treaty was conditional upon the making of a reservation, and the reservation is held to be contrary to the treaty's object and purpose?

4. Treaties are nothing more than contracts between States; there can be no such thing as a 'legislative treaty'. Do you agree?

5. What is the significance of allowing termination of a treaty on grounds of 'material breach' instead of 'fundamental breach'

International law in Australian law

3

Objectives

After completing this chapter, you should:

(1) be aware of the traditional distinction between monist and dualist conceptions of international law, and understand that most domestic legal orders blend elements of both approaches;

(2) understand and be able to explain the extent to which rules of customary international law may be assimilated into the Australian common law;

(3) understand and be able to explain the extent to which rules of conventional international law may be assimilated into the Australian common law;

(4) understand and be able to explain the extent to which rules of customary international law may affect rights and obligations established by Australian legislation;

(5) understand and be able to explain the extent to which rules of conventional international law may affect rights and obligations established by Australian legislation;

(6) understand and be able to explain the nature and extent of the Commonwealth's power to legislate in order to implement international law in Australian domestic law; and

(7) appreciate that there remains uncertainty as to whether there is a denial of legitimate expectation and procedural fairness in Australian administrative law when a decision-maker fails to comply with an unincorporated Australian treaty obligation and has not given the aggrieved person a chance to be heard on the proposed departure from that obligation.

Key cases

Chow Hung Ching v The King (1948) 77 CLR 449
Mabo v Queensland (No 2) (1992) 175 CLR 1
Nulyarimma v Thompson (1999) 96 FCR 153; 165 ALR 621
Victoria v Commonwealth (ILO Case) (1996) 187 CLR 416
Polites v Commonwealth (1945) 70 CLR 60
Minister for Immigration and Ethnic Affairs v Teoh (1995) 183 CLR 273

Key instruments

Constitution of the Commonwealth of Australia: s 51(xxix)
Acts Interpretation Act 1901 (Cth): s 15AB

3.1   International law, understood as the rules and principles regulating relations among States and public international organisations on the plane of international relations, is a field in which only a very small proportion of lawyers will ever practice on a regular basis. The vast majority of lawyers spend almost all of their professional lives dealing with matters regulated by private or public domestic law. Nevertheless, international law has always impinged on the theory and practice of domestic law. The frontier between international law and Australian law is not perfectly watertight, and there are several strategic points at which there is significant seepage. It is at these points that international law acquires a practical significance for most practitioners and students of Australian domestic law.

Monism and dualism

3.2   It is traditional to discuss the relationship of international law to domestic law by reference to two theories known as 'monism' and 'dualism'.

According to the monist theory, frequently identified with the civil law tradition and some natural law theories, there is only one legal order of which international law and domestic law are different aspects. In this theory, as it is usually presented, domestic law derives its authority from international law, international law is automatically part of a State's domestic legal order, and any inconsistency between the two systems must be resolved in favour of international law.

According to the dualist theory, frequently identified with the common law tradition and varieties of legal positivism, international law and domestic law are completely distinct legal orders with different sources and different subjects. In this theory, as it is usually presented, inconsistencies between the two legal orders cannot really arise because international law regulates State-to-State relations on the international plane, while domestic law regulates relations among persons and institutions within the jurisdiction of States. In order for a rule of international law to enter the domestic legal order, a formal step of incorporation or transformation into domestic law (such as legislation) is required.

3.3   Thus very briefly outlined, the monist and dualist theories are presented in their starkest and most radical forms. These characterisations of the theories are useful intellectual starting points, but in reality pragmatic blends of the two theories characterise the relationship of international law to most domestic legal orders. Many States which adopt an officially or predominantly monist stance towards international law require a formal domestic act of transformation or recognition before some rules of international law can be made effective in domestic law. For instance, most democratic States which operate mainly within the monist tradition deny domestic effect to at least some treaties unless they have been authorised or approved by the legislature[1] (whereafter the Head of

---

1.   For example, Art 80 of the Constitution of the Italian Republic: 'Parliament shall authorise by law the ratification of such international treaties as have a political nature, require arbitration or a legal settlement, entail change of borders, spending or new legislation.'

State usually performs a formal act of ratification). Many States which operate mainly within the dualist tradition permit international law to affect the interpretation of domestic legislation (at least in circumstances of legislative ambiguity) and the development of non-legislated rules and principles.

3.4   More than pragmatism, however, is at work. The monist–dualist hybrid positions which actually prevail in most States are natural products of modern international law's doctrinal origins. Prior to the emergence of the modern State system in the 17th century, relations between sovereign princes were not understood in terms of an autonomous 'international law'.[2] Rather, and following Roman law conceptions, relations between sovereigns and their subjects were governed by the *jus civile* (customary and enacted laws specific to a given community), which were specific manifestations of the *jus gentium*. Sourced partly in custom and partly in natural law, the *jus gentium* consists of general legal precepts accepted by all civilised peoples.[3] As sovereigns could not legislate with binding force for each other, relations between sovereigns were regulated directly by the *jus gentium*. For example, just as all persons were obliged to honour their agreements *(pacta sunt servanda)* and were permitted to defend themselves from attack, so every sovereign prince was obliged to honour his agreements and to defend his realm from attack. Christendom's legal order was, in this sense, a unity.

3.5   With the emergence of the modern State system, of which the Peace of Westphalia (1648) was a major catalyst, inter-sovereign relations were progressively placed on a new footing. Sovereignty became less an attribute of individual princes, and more a feature of new corporate State entities. These corporate States were possessed of increasingly clear and exclusive sovereign rights and responsibilities within defined territories. They also began to constitute a new and distinct stratum of political, diplomatic, military and economic relations, relatively autonomous from relations among individual subjects, or between subjects and their State. The emergence of autonomous State interests, increasingly detached from the interests of individual princes, was accompanied by the diminishing political powers of princes within their realms and by their replacement with republican constitutional arrangements (even if monarchial forms were often preserved). There was also a steadily decreasing political significance of personal relations among those princes who retained a diminishing constitutional role within their States — dynastic princely marriages, for instance, eventually came to lose virtually all their former strategic importance.

In this new environment, States were able to engage with each other as fully sovereign corporate entities in their own right, free from the complications of overlapping sovereignties of individual princes which

2.   See 1.7.
3.   See 1.154–1.164.

characterised pre-modern Europe. Modern States gradually developed, in their relations with each other, customary and conventional rules giving a particular international form to the general precepts of the *jus gentium*.

3.6   Although the *jus gentium* thereby gradually retreats behind the curtain of customary and conventional rules, it remains important in two respects. It provides the *ratio juris* — the ultimate juridical justification — of rules sourced in custom and treaty. It also remains a direct source of law, as the 'general principles of law recognised by civilised nations',[4] where custom and convention have yet to provide a norm necessary to resolve a legal dispute on the international plane.

3.7   It is therefore not correct to say that domestic law derives its authority from international law. Nor is it correct to say that domestic law and international law are completely distinct legal orders. Rather, domestic law and international law are different legal orders (*contra* the pure monist theory) deriving their authority from a common source (*contra* the pure dualist theory).

In accommodating this reality, each State develops a set of rules and principles regulating the extent to which, and the modes by which, international law produces effects within its domestic legal order. These rules and principles are informed by each State's juridical and historical context. Some States, particularly those which share the civilian legal tradition, tend to emphasise the unity of the domestic and international legal orders. Other States, particularly those which share the common law tradition, tend to emphasise the separateness of the two legal orders. All States will, in fact, blend elements of both the monist and the dualist conceptions of international law into a doctrine which allows international law to play a role in the domestic legal order consistent with the latter's structure, fundamental values, and historical development.

3.8   International law itself is neither monist nor dualist. It requires simply that States comply with their international obligations. Failure to comply cannot be justified, from the perspective of international law, on the basis that international legal obligations are inconsistent with the requirements of domestic law.[5] Whether a State complies with international law by regarding it as automatically forming part of domestic law, or whether the State does so by a domestic act of incorporation or transformation, is a matter of indifference to international law.

3.9   The remainder of this chapter is concerned with the extent to which, and the modes by which, Australian law accommodates itself to international law. In Australia's federal, democratic and common law context, this task can be usefully approached by examining the relationship between international law and (i) the common law; (ii) legislation; (iii) the Commonwealth's constitutional power to legislate; and (iv) the exercise of executive discretion.

---

4.   See 1.154–1.174.
5.   See 5.14–5.15 concerning international legal obligations generally, and 2.44 concerning conventional obligations specifically.

International law and the common law

3.10   The common law is that portion of Australia's domestic law that is not sourced in the Commonwealth or state constitutions or in legislation. Although this definition is couched in residual terms, the common law (including equity) is the foundation of Australia's legal order and the immediate juridical spring from which constitutional law and legislation draw their legal force. The rule that legislation displaces inconsistent requirements of the common law is itself a common law rule which emerged in the 17th century.[6]

3.11   Although Australia's Constitution finds substantial expression in a written document, its sources are British. Many of the rules and conventions of Australian constitutional law, and especially those relating to executive power, derive from the rules and conventions of the British Constitution. Commenting on the relationship between the British Constitution and the common law, A V Dicey (1835–1922) remarked:[7]

> The 'rule of law' ... may be used as a formula for expressing the fact that with us the law of the constitution, the rules which in foreign countries naturally form part of a constitutional code, are not the source but the consequence of the rights of individuals, as defined and enforced by the courts; that, in short, the principles of private law have been with us by the action of the courts and Parliament so extended as to determine the position of the Crown and its servants; thus the constitution is the result of the ordinary law of the land.

It is therefore possible to define the common law as providing the totality of Australian law, except where constitutions and legislation make conflicting, supplemental or additional provision.

3.12   Frequently described as 'judge-made' law, the common law is more accurately understood as that body of a community's customary practices which the courts recognise as furnishing norms for the resolution of legal disputes, supplemented where necessary by a process of practical reasoning drawing heavily on analogy and universally recognised general principles of law. The proposition that the common law is an essentially customary system has a long and respectable pedigree. A full treatment of the common law's essentially customary nature is beyond the scope of this work, but for present purposes it is worth noting that an impressive consensus across epochal periods has subscribed to a vision of the common law as customary or essentially customary in character.

---

6.   As late as 1610, Coke CJ was able to say in *Dr Bonham's Case* (1610) 8 Co Rep 114a, 118a: 'And it appears in our books, that in many cases, the common law will controul Acts of Parliament, and sometime adjudge them to be utterly void: for when an Act of Parliament is against common right or reason, or repugnant, or impossible to be performed, the common law will control it, and adjudge such Act to be void.' See also Hobart CJ in *Day v Savadge* (1614) Hob 85, 80 ER 235, 237: '[E]ven an Act of Parliament, made against natural equity, as to make a man judge in his own case, is void in itself, for *jura naturae sunt immutabilia*, and they are *leges legume*.'
7.   A V Dicey, *Introduction to the Study of the Law of the Constitution*, 5th ed, MacMillan, London, 1897, 194–95.

As Sir Frederick Pollock (1845–1937) observed, 'the Common Law is a customary law if, in the course of about six centuries, the undoubting belief and uniform language of everybody who had occasion to consider the matter were able to make it so'.[8] Rather than being 'judge-made', the common law is more accurately described as 'judge-recognised'.

To what extent are the requirements of international law recognised by courts as forming part of Australia's common law?

Customary international law

3.13   The English common law is less dualist than might be supposed. As early as 1737, Lord Talbot LC in *Barbuit*'s *Case* ventured the opinion that the *jus gentium* immunity on foreign ambassadors would have been part of English law even without statutory incorporation.[9] More explicit still is a much more recent English Court of Appeal judgment in *Trendtex Trading Corp v Central Bank of Nigeria*. In deciding whether English courts are precluded by the doctrine of *stare decisis* from applying a new rule of customary international law in circumstances where an older displaced rule had been recognised and applied by higher judicial authority, Shaw LJ said:[10]

> May it not be that the true principle as to the application of international law is that the English courts must at any given time discover what the prevailing international rule is and apply that rule? This is not the same process as applying foreign law in our courts for that only comes into question when for a particular reason the proper law relating to the matter before the court is that foreign law. In the case of international law it is always part of the law to be applied irrespective of any intention or agreement of the parties in suit. This, so it seems to me, is the true distinction and not that the one is immutable as a rule of law while the other is always subject to investigation as a question of fact.
>
> What *is* immutable is the principle of English law that the law of nations (not what *was* the law of nations) must be applied in the courts of England. The rule of stare decisis operates to preclude a court from overriding a decision which binds it in regard to a particular rule of (international)

---

8.   Sir Frederick Pollock, *A First Book of Jurisprudence for Students of the Common Law*, Gaunt, Holmes Beach, Florida, 1994 (reprint of 6th ed, 1929), 254. See also James Coolidge Carter, *The Provinces of the Written and the Unwritten Law*, Banks & Brothers, New York, 1889; James Coolidge Carter, 'The ideal and the actual in the law', address to the American Bar Association, Dando, Philadelphia, 1890; James Coolidge Carter, *Law: Its Origins, Growth and Function*, G P Putnam, New York, 1907, 179–90; W Blake Odgers and Walter Blake Odgers, *The Common Law of England*, 2nd ed, Sweet & Maxwell, London, 1920, Vol I, ch VII; Pollock, supra, 247–60; Carleton Kemp Allen, *Law in the Making*, 7th ed, Clarendon, Oxford, 1964; Lon L Fuller, 'Human interaction and the law' (1969) 14 *American Journal of Jurisprudence* 1–36; T F T Plucknett, *Legislation of Edward I*, Oxford University Press, Oxford, 1970, 6–8; Friedrich A Hayek, *Law, Legislation and Liberty*, Vol I: *Rules and Order*, Chicago University Press, 1983, 72–93; Geoffrey de Q Walker, *The Rule of Law: Foundation of Constitutional Democracy*, Melbourne University Press, 1988; Leon Sheleff, 'Customary law as common law', in Leon Sheleff, *The Future of Tradition: Customary Law, Common Law and Legal Pluralism*, Frank Cass, London, 1999, 79–90; David VanDrunen, *Law & Custom: The Thought of Thomas Aquinas and the Future of the Common Law*, Peter Lang, New York, 2003, 5–15.
9.   *Barbuit's Case* (1737) Forr cases Talbot 281, 25 ER 777 (see note 1, 25 ER 778).
10.   *Trendtex Trading Corp v Central Bank of Nigeria* [1977] 1 QB 529, 578–579; 1 All ER 881, 910.

law, it does not prevent a court from applying a rule which did not exist when the earlier decision was made if the new rule has had the effect in international law of extinguishing the old rule.

3.14 The English common law therefore appears receptive to direct assimilation of customary international law. The common law in Australia, however, has proved somewhat more resistant.

In **Chow Hung Ching v The King,**[11] two Chinese nationals were convicted by the Supreme Court of the Territory of Papua-New Guinea on charges of assault causing bodily harm and then detaining the victim against his will. They were sentenced to periods of imprisonment with hard labour. At the time of the assaults, the perpetrators were members of a labour gang organised by the Chinese government and supervised by Chinese military officers. They were in the Australian-administered territory of Papua-New Guinea in order to relocate property sold to China by the United States after the end of the Second World War. The perpetrators appealed to the High Court of Australia against their convictions on grounds, inter alia, that they enjoyed, as a matter of customary international law, sovereign immunity as members of a foreign State's armed forces present in Australian territory with Australia's permission. The Court found, on the evidence, that the appellants were civilian labourers and not part of China's army. Consequently, they were not entitled to the protection of China's sovereign immunity under customary international law. Nevertheless, the Court considered whether the appellants would have been entitled to immunity if they had been members of China's armed forces:[12]

> Latham CJ: ... International law is not as such part of the law of Australia,[13] but a universally recognized principle of international law would be applied by our courts.[14]
>
> Where the rule with respect to armed forces applies as part of the municipal law it would give some degree of immunity from local jurisdiction. But there is a considerable conflict of opinion between authorities on international law as to the extent of the immunity given. Some writers limit it in respect of area, and to acts done while the members of the force are on duty and not engaged upon their own affairs, such as recreation or pleasure ...
>
> The uncertainty of the extent of immunity in the case of visiting armed forces is illustrated by the varying language used by authorities upon international law ...
>
> The result is that it has not been satisfactorily demonstrated that a general exemption from the application of local criminal law is implied in the permitted presence of foreign armed forces within Australia, though there is an implied exemption from such provisions of our law as are inconsistent with the existence of the force as an armed organized force: e.g., as Jordan C.J. said in *Wright v Cantrell,*[15] if a foreign force is admitted to the country there must be an implication that any restrictions which would otherwise be applicable under immigration laws are waived, and that the members of the forces will not be subject to prosecution for carrying arms in breach of local law. So much may be implied from the mere fact that the force is present with consent. ... There is

---

11. *Chow Hung Ching v The King* (1948) 77 CLR 449.
12. Ibid, 462–466, 470–472, 477–478. Footnotes in this extract refer to sources cited in the judgment.
13. *Chung Chi Cheung v The King* (1939) AC 160, and see *Polites v Commonwealth; Kandiliotes v Commonwealth* (1945) 70 CLR 60.
14. *West Rand Central Gold Mining Co v The King* (1905) 2 KB 391, 406, 407.
15. *Wright v Cantrell* (1943) 44 SR (NSW) 45.

general agreement that in matters of discipline and internal administration the foreign force is exempt from the jurisdiction of local courts. There is no general agreement that the exemption extends any further, and the weight of authority in Australia, Great Britain and Canada is that no wider principle has been clearly established as part of the municipal law to be recognized and enforced by the courts. In my opinion it is not the law that members of visiting forces in a country with the consent of the sovereign are exempt from local jurisdiction in respect of offences committed against the inhabitants of the country, and more especially this is not the case if those offences have no relation to the military activities of the armed forces. Accordingly, in my opinion, the principle which is relied upon for the purpose of excluding the jurisdiction of the Supreme Court of Papua-New Guinea has not been shown to exist as part of the municipal law of the Territory. Upon this ground, therefore, the appeals should in my opinion be dismissed in so far as they depend upon an objection to jurisdiction.

Starke J: ... The appellants in this case claim that the personnel of armed and military forces of a foreign state in amity with the territorial sovereign possess immunities from local jurisdiction in respect of their persons when in the territory of the territorial sovereign with its permission. And it was said that these immunities attach to these forces when passing through the territory or stationed in it for garrison duty or using the territory as a base for operations or other purposes. 'It must always be remembered,' observed the Judicial Committee in *Chung Chi Cheung v The King*,[16] 'that, so far, at any rate, as the Courts of this country are concerned, international law has no validity save in so far as its principles are accepted and adopted by our own domestic law. There is no external power that imposes its rules upon our own code of substantive law or procedure. The Courts acknowledge the existence of a body of rules which nations accept amongst themselves. On any judicial issue they seek to ascertain what the relevant rule is, and, having found it, they will treat it as incorporated into the domestic law, so far as it is not inconsistent with rules enacted by statues or finally declared by their tribunals.' What then are the immunities of armed and military forces of other nations accepted by our courts? It is by no means easy to answer that question, for in modern times those immunities are settled by conventions between the nations ...

The extent of these immunities is by no means settled. ...

Dixon J: ... The presence of a military force of a friendly foreign power is an exceptional thing. Apart from the visits of small bodies of troops by way of courtesy or to take part in ceremonies, celebrations or the like, it is unlikely to occur except in circumstances in which a full antecedent discussion between the two governments might be expected. Even if no more is involved than the movement in times of profound peace by one country of its troops through another country by a more convenient route to an outlying part of its own territory, it is not likely to be done except under an express arrangement. What therefore the principles of international law may be expected to deal with is the necessity of the permission, the terms on which it may be legitimately sought, the terms that are implied if the permission is granted and the obligations of neutrality, if a belligerent desires the passage of his troops through a neutral country.

It is obvious that the whole question involves in the case of the British Commonwealth the authority of the Crown in the conduct of foreign relations. It is a mistake to treat the question of the extent of the immunity as one depending upon the recognition by Great Britain of a rule of international law. In the first place the theory of Blackstone (Commentaries, (1809), vol. 4, p. 67) that 'the law of nations (whenever any question arises which is properly the object of its jurisdiction) is here adopted in its full extent by the common law,

---

16.   *Chung Chi Cheung v The King* (1939) AC 160, 167, 168.

> and is held to be a part of the law of the land' is now regarded as without foundation. The true view, it is held, is 'that international law is not a part, but is one of the sources, of English law' (Article by Prof. J. L. Brierly on International Law in England, (1935), 51 Law Quarterly Review, p. 31.). 'In each case in which the question arises the court must consider whether the particular rule of international law has been received into, and so become a source of, English law' (Sir William Holdsworth, Relation of English Law to International Law: Essays in Law and History, p. 267.).
>
> The appeal was unanimously dismissed, although neither McTiernan J nor Williams J commented on the relationship between international law and the common law.

3.15 According to the High Court in *Chow Hung Ching*, international law cannot be regarded as automatically part of Australia's common law. Customary international law is, however, one of the common law's sources. A rule of customary international law which is universally recognised will be applied in Australian courts. But an asserted rule of customary international law which is the subject of credible contention — such as the contentious 'rule' that members of foreign armed forces attract sovereign immunity in circumstances where they commit criminal offences while off duty — will not be automatically applied.

3.16 Being an essentially customary system, the common law reflects the customs and expectations of the community it serves — the 'reasonable person' is everywhere. The common law is thus simultaneously democratic and conservative. It is democratic because it emerges from the community's customs and expectations. It is conservative because it reflects the community and is not an instrument for remoulding it.

Precedent authority is the best, but not the only, evidence of what the community's customs are. Common law rules and doctrines evolve over time in order to keep pace with the community's customs and expectations. Because every political community is also part of a universal human society, customary international law can provide evidence of a particular community's customs and expectations. A universally acknowledged customary international law rule will furnish virtually conclusive evidence that it accords with the customs and expectations of a given political community. Where that political community is regulated by the common law, the universally acknowledged customary international law rule is able to enter the common law because customary international law is a 'source' of the common law.

3.17 Thus characterised, the relationship between the common law and customary international law contains two possibilities: a change in customary international law may precipitate a change in the common law where that change reflects the customs and expectations of the community served by the common law; and the common law will refrain from drawing on its customary international law 'source' when the latter is not in harmony with the customs and expectations of the community served by the common law.

In **Mabo v Queensland (No 2),**[17] the plaintiffs were members of the Meriam people who had occupied the Murray Islands in the Torres Strait. They sought several declarations against the State of Queensland. The relief sought was based partly on a claim that the Crown's sovereignty over three of the Murray Islands was subject to local customary and traditional native title rights of the Meriam people. It was part of Queensland's case that, when sovereignty over them was acquired by the Crown in 1879, the islands were *terra nullius* as a matter of international law and that English law applied to the land in such a way that no customary or native title rights survived.[18]

> Brennan J: ... In discharging its duty to declare the common law of Australia, this Court is not free to adopt rules that accord with contemporary notions of justice and human rights if their adoption would fracture the skeleton of principle which gives the body of our law its shape and internal consistency. Australian law is not only the historical successor of, but is an organic development from, the law of England. ... The law which governs Australia is Australian law. The Privy Council itself held that the common law of this country might legitimately develop independently of English precedent.[19] Increasingly since 1968,[20] the common law of Australia has been substantially in the hands of this Court. Here rests the ultimate responsibility of declaring the law of the nation. Although this Court is free to depart from English precedent which was earlier followed as stating the common law of this country,[21] it cannot do so where the departure would fracture what I have called the skeleton of principle. The Court is even more reluctant to depart from earlier decisions of its own.[22] The peace and order of Australian society is built on the legal system. It can be modified to bring it into conformity with contemporary notions of justice and human rights, but it cannot be destroyed. It is not possible, *a priori,* to distinguish between cases that express a skeletal principle and those which do not, but no case can command unquestioning adherence if the rule it expresses seriously offends the values of justice and human rights (especially equality before the law) which are aspirations of the contemporary Australian legal system. If a postulated rule of the common law expressed in earlier cases seriously offends those contemporary values, the question arises whether the rule should be maintained and applied. Whenever such a question arises, it is necessary to assess whether the particular rule is an essential doctrine of our legal system and whether, if the rule were to be overturned, the disturbance to be apprehended would be disproportionate to the benefit flowing from the overturning.
>
> ... By the common law, the law in force in a newly-acquired territory depends on the manner of its acquisition by the Crown. Although the manner in which a sovereign state might acquire new territory is a matter for international law, the common law has had to march in step with international law in order to provide the body of law to apply in a territory newly acquired by the Crown.

---

17. *Mabo v Queensland (No 2)* (1992) 175 CLR 1. Footnotes in this extract refer to sources cited in the judgment.
18. Ibid, 29–63.
19. See *Australian Consolidated Press Ltd v Uren* (1967) 117 CLR 221, 238, 241; [1969] AC 590, 641, 644.
20. See the *Privy Council (Limitation of Appeals) Act 1968* (Cth) and the *Privy Council (Appeals from the High Court) Act 1975* (Cth).
21. *Cook v Cook* (1986) 162 CLR 376, 390, 394; *Viro v The Queen* (1978) 141 CLR 88, 93, 120–121, 132, 135, 150–151, 166, 174.
22. *Jones v Commonwealth* (1987) 61 ALJR 348, 349; 71 ALR 497, 498–499; *John v Federal Commissioner of Taxation* (1989) 166 CLR 417, 438–439, 451–452; *McKinney v The Queen* (1991) 171 CLR 468, 481–482.

International law recognized conquest, cession, and occupation of territory that was *terra nullius* as three of the effective ways of acquiring sovereignty. No other way is presently relevant.[23] The great voyages of European discovery opened to European nations the prospect of occupying new and valuable territories that were already inhabited. As among themselves, the European nations parcelled out the territories newly discovered to the sovereigns of the respective discoverers,[24] provided the discovery was confirmed by occupation and provided the indigenous inhabitants were not organized in a society that was united permanently for political action.[25] To these territories the European colonial nations applied the doctrines relating to acquisition of territory that was *terra nullius*. They recognized the sovereignty of the respective European nations over the territory of 'backward peoples' and, by State practice, permitted the acquisition of sovereignty of such territory by occupation rather than by conquest.[26] ...

The enlarging of the concept of *terra nullius* by international law to justify the acquisition of inhabited territory by occupation on behalf of the acquiring sovereign raised some difficulties in the expounding of the common law doctrines as to the law to be applied when inhabited territories were acquired by occupation (or 'settlement', to use the term of the common law). Although Blackstone commended the practice of 'sending colonies [of settlers] to find out new habitations', he wrote:[27]

> so long as it was confined to the stocking and cultivation of desert uninhabited countries, it kept strictly within the limits of the law of nature. But how far the seising on countries already peopled, and driving out or massacring the innocent and defenceless natives, merely because they differed from their invaders in language, in religion, in customs, in government, or in colour; how far such a conduct was consonant to nature, to reason, or to christianity, deserved well to be considered by those, who have rendered their names immortal by thus civilizing mankind.

As we shall see, Blackstone's misgivings found a resonance in international law after two centuries.[28] But he was unable to declare any rule by which the laws of England became the laws of a territory which was not a 'desert uninhabited' country when the Crown acquired sovereignty over that territory by discovery and occupation as *terra nullius*. ...

According to Blackstone, English law would become the law of a country outside England either upon first settlement by English colonists of a 'desert uninhabited' country or by the exercise of the Sovereign's legislative power over a conquered or ceded country. Blackstone did not contemplate other ways by which sovereignty might be acquired. In the case of a conquered country, the general rule was that the laws of the country continued after the conquest until those laws were altered by the conqueror.[29] The Crown had a

---

23. See Elizabeth Evatt, 'The acquisition of territory in Australia and New Zealand', in C H Alexandrowicz (ed), *Grotian Society Papers 1968*, Martinus Nijhoff, The Hague, 1970, 16, which, the Court notes, 'mentions only cession and occupation as relevant to the Australasian colonies'.
24. *Worcester v Georgia* (1832) 6 Pet 515, 543–544 (31 US 350, 369).
25. M F Lindley, *The Acquisition and Government of Backward Territory in International Law*, 1926, chs III and IV.
26. Ibid, 47.
27. William Blackstone, *Commentaries on the Laws of England*, 17th ed, 1830, Bk II, ch 1, 7.
28. Western Sahara advisory opinion, ICJ Rep (1975) 12.
29. *Blankard v Galdy* (1693) Holt KB 341 (90 ER 1089); *Campbell v Hall* (1774) Lofft 655, 741 (98 ER 848, 895–896); *Beaumont v Barrett* (1836) 1 Moo PC 59 (12 ER 733).

prerogative power to make new laws for a conquered country although that power was subject to laws enacted by the Imperial Parliament.[30] The same rule applied to ceded colonies, though the prerogative may have been limited by the treaty of cession.[31] When 'desert uninhabited countries' were colonized by English settlers, however, they brought with them 'so much of the English law as [was] applicable to their own situation and the condition of an infant colony'.[32] ...

When British colonists went out to other inhabited parts of the world, including New South Wales, and settled there under the protection of the forces of the Crown, so that the Crown acquired sovereignty recognized by the European family of nations under the enlarged notion of *terra nullius,* it was necessary for the common law to prescribe a doctrine relating to the law to be applied in such colonies, for sovereignty imports supreme internal legal authority.[33] The view was taken that, when sovereignty of a territory could be acquired under the enlarged notion of *terra nullius,* for the purposes of the municipal law that territory (though inhabited) could be treated as a 'desert uninhabited' country. The hypothesis being that there was no local law already in existence in the territory,[34] the law of England became the law of the territory (and not merely the personal law of the colonists). Colonies of this kind were called 'settled colonies'. *Ex hypothesi,* the indigenous inhabitants of a settled colony had no recognized sovereign, else the territory could have been acquired only by conquest or cession. The indigenous people of a settled colony were thus taken to be without laws, without a sovereign and primitive in their social organization. ...

The facts as we know them today do not fit the 'absence of law' or 'barbarian' theory underpinning the colonial reception of the common law of England. That being so, there is no warrant for applying in these times rules of the English common law which were the product of that theory. ...

... This Court can either apply the existing authorities and proceed to inquire whether the Meriam people are higher 'in the scale of social organization' than the Australian Aborigines whose claims were 'utterly disregarded' by the existing authorities or the Court can overrule the existing authorities, discarding the distinction between inhabited colonies that were *terra nullius* and those which were not.

The theory of *terra nullius* has been critically examined in recent times by the International Court of Justice in its Advisory Opinion on Western Sahara.[35] There the majority judgment read:

'Occupation' being legally an original means of peaceably acquiring sovereignty over territory otherwise than by cession or succession, it was a cardinal condition of a valid 'occupation' that the territory should be *terra nullius* — a territory belonging to no-one — at the time of

---

30.   *Campbell v Hall* (1774) Lofft 741, 742 (98 ER 895, 896).
31.   See the discussion in Kenneth Roberts-Wray, *Commonwealth and Colonial Law,* Stevens, London, 1966, 214ff; *Sammut v Strickland* [1938] AC 678; *Blankard v Galdy* (1693) 2 Salk 411 (91 ER 356); and *Buchanan v Commonwealth* (1913) 16 CLR 315, 334.
32.   William Blackstone, *Commentaries on the Laws of England,* 17th ed, 1830, Bk I, ch 4, 107; *State Government Insurance Commission v Trigwell* (1979) 142 CLR 617, 625, 634.
33.   See Alan James, *Sovereign Statehood,* Allen and Unwin, London, 1986, 3ff, 203–09.
34.   *Lyons (Mayor of) v East India Co* (1836) 1 Moo PC 175, 272–273 (12 ER 782, 818); *Cooper v Stuart* (1889) 14 App Cas; *Lauderdale Peerage* (1885) 10 App Cas 692, 744–745; *Kielley v Carson* (1842) 4 Moo PC 63, 84–85 (13 ER 225, 233).
35.   *Western Sahara* advisory opinion, ICJ Rep (1975) 39.

the act alleged to constitute the 'occupation' (cf. *Legal Status of Eastern Greenland*, P.C.I.J., Series A/B, No. 53, pp. 44 f. and 63 f.). In the view of the Court, therefore, a determination that Western Sahara was a *'terra nullius'* at the time of colonization by Spain would be possible only if it were established that at that time the territory belonged to no-one in the sense that it was then open to acquisition through the legal process of 'occupation'.

80. Whatever differences of opinion there may have been among jurists, the State practice of the relevant period indicates that territories inhabited by tribes or peoples having a social and political organization were not regarded as *terrae nullius*. It shows that in the case of such territories the acquisition of sovereignty was not generally considered as effected unilaterally through 'occupation' of *terra nullius* by original title but through agreements concluded with local rulers. On occasion, it is true, the word 'occupation' was used in a non-technical sense denoting simply acquisition of sovereignty; but that did not signify that the acquisition of sovereignty through such agreements with authorities of the country was regarded as an 'occupation' of a *'terra nullius'* in the proper sense of these terms. On the contrary, such agreements with local rulers, whether or not considered as an actual 'cession' of the territory, were regarded as derivative roots of title, and not original titles obtained by occupation of *terrae nullius*. ...

If the international law notion that inhabited land may be classified as *terra nullius* no longer commands general support, the doctrines of the common law which depend on the notion that native peoples may be 'so low in the scale of social organization' that it is 'idle to impute to such people some shadow of the rights known to our law'[36] can hardly be retained. If it were permissible in past centuries to keep the common law in step with international law, it is imperative in today's world that the common law should neither be nor be seen to be frozen in an age of racial discrimination.

The fiction by which the rights and interests of indigenous inhabitants in land were treated as non-existent was justified by a policy which has no place in the contemporary law of this country. The policy appears explicitly in the judgment of the Privy Council in *In re Southern Rhodesia* in rejecting an argument[37] that the native people 'were the owners of the unalienated lands long before either the Company or the Crown became concerned with them and from time immemorial ... and that the unalienated lands belonged to them still'. Their Lordships replied:[38]

> the maintenance of their rights was fatally inconsistent with white settlement of the country, and yet white settlement was the object of the whole forward movement, pioneered by the Company and controlled by the Crown, and that object was successfully accomplished, with the result that the aboriginal system gave place to another prescribed by the Order in Council.

Whatever the justification advanced in earlier days for refusing to recognize the rights and interests in land of the indigenous inhabitants of settled colonies, an unjust and discriminatory doctrine of that kind can no longer be accepted. The expectations of the international community accord in this respect with the contemporary values of the Australian people. The opening up of international

36. *In re Southern Rhodesia* [1919] AC, 233–234.
37. Ibid, 232.
38. Ibid, 234.

remedies to individuals pursuant to Australia's accession to the Optional Protocol to the International Covenant on Civil and Political Rights[39] brings to bear on the common law the powerful influence of the Covenant and the international standards it imports. The common law does not necessarily conform with international law, but international law is a legitimate and important influence on the development of the common law, especially when international law declares the existence of universal human rights. A common law doctrine founded on unjust discrimination in the enjoyment of civil and political rights demands reconsideration. It is contrary both to international standards and to the fundamental values of our common law to entrench a discriminatory rule which, because of the supposed position on the scale of social organization of the indigenous inhabitants of a settled colony, denies them a right to occupy their traditional lands.

... [T]he common law of Australia rejects the notion that, when the Crown acquired sovereignty over territory which is now part of Australia it thereby acquired the absolute beneficial ownership of the land therein, and accepts that the antecedent rights and interests in land possessed by the indigenous inhabitants of the territory survived the change in sovereignty. Those antecedent rights and interests thus constitute a burden on the radical title of the Crown.

It must be acknowledged that, to state the common law in this way involves the overruling of cases which have held the contrary. To maintain the authority of those cases would destroy the equality of all Australian citizens before the law. The common law of this country would perpetuate injustice if it were to continue to embrace the enlarged notion of *terra nullius* and to persist in characterizing the indigenous inhabitants of the Australian colonies as people too low in the scale of social organization to be acknowledged as possessing rights and interests in land. ...

3.18   According to Brennan J (with whom Mason CJ and McHugh J agreed), the common law is a body of rules and principles whose content changes over time in order to keep abreast of the 'values of justice and human rights (especially equality before the law) which are aspirations of the contemporary Australian legal system' and the 'contemporary values of the Australian people'.

Precedent authority is very strong evidence of those prevailing values of justice, but it is not conclusive: 'If a postulated rule of the common law expressed in earlier cases seriously offends those contemporary values, the question arises whether the rule should be maintained and applied.'[40] Doctrines which are 'skeletal' or 'essential' to the Australian common law cannot be overturned (except, presumably, by legislation), but all others are subject to a process of evolutionary adaptation to the customs and expectations of the community which the common law serves and regulates. Among the sources of the common law is customary international law, which is a 'legitimate and important influence on the development of the common law'.[41]

---

39.   See Communication 78/1980 in *Selected Decisions of the Human Rights Committee under the Optional Protocol*, United Nations, New York, 1985–90, Vol 2, 23.
40.   *Mabo v Queensland (No 2)* (1992) 175 CLR 1, 29.
41.   Ibid, 42.

3.19   This is not to say, however, that international law automatically constitutes part of the common law. International law and the common law are separate legal systems and the 'common law does not necessarily conform with international law'.[42] The 'skeletal' or 'essential' common law doctrines cannot be overturned by international law. Nor could a requirement of customary international law be assimilated to the common law if the former were inconsistent with the contemporary values (that is, customs and expectations) of the Australian people.

3.20   There were essentially two bases upon which Brennan J concluded that the Meriam people's customary native title rights had not been extinguished upon acquisition of sovereignty by the Crown. First, the customary international law doctrine of *terra nullius* justifying sovereignty by occupation over certain inhabited territories 'no longer commands general support'.[43] Common law rules resting upon a defunct principle of *terra nullius* 'can hardly be retained', with the result that native title rights survived until the land was alienated by the Crown or by statute. Second, even if customary international law continued to support a principle of *terra nullius* applicable to inhabited territories, it could no longer justify the adoption of a common law doctrine which deprived native peoples of their customary title. Such a principle of international law would be inconsistent with the contemporary values (that is, customs and expectations) of the Australian people, and would be a source from which the common law could not draw.

   The final result was that the Meriam people's pre-British customary native title rights survived as if the Murray Islands had been conquered by or ceded to the Crown; customary native title remained intact until the Crown or Parliament acted in a way inconsistent with it.

3.21   Among the 'skeletal' or essential common law doctrines which would prevent adoption of an inconsistent requirement of customary international law is the rule against criminal liability without breach of an existing criminal law.

In ***Nulyarimma v Thompson,***[44] Crispin J in the Federal Court of Australia upheld a Magistrate's Court decision not to issue warrants for the arrest of the Prime Minister, the Deputy Prime Minister, a Senator, and a Member of the House of Representatives on charges of genocide. The offences were allegedly committed in connection with the formulation of the Commonwealth Government's native title 'Ten Point Plan' and support of the Bill that ultimately became the *Native Title Amendment Act 1998* (Cth). Genocide was not a crime under any Australian legislation, but the appellants argued that it had been adopted into Australia's common law because it was a crime enjoying *jus cogens* status under customary international law. Consequently, the appellants argued before the Full Court of

---

42.   Ibid, 42.
43.   Although Brennan J makes no express mention of it, *Chow Hung Ching* establishes that only uncontentious rules of customary international law can be assimilated to the common law.
44.   *Nulyarimma v Thompson* (1999) 96 FCR 153; 165 ALR 621.

the Federal Court of Australia, the defendants could be prosecuted in Australian courts for the common law crime of genocide.

> Wilcox J: … 18. I accept that the prohibition of genocide is a peremptory norm of customary international law, giving rise to a non-derogatable obligation by each nation State to the entire international community. … I accept, also, that the obligation imposed by customary law on each nation State is to extradite or prosecute any person, found within its territory, who appears to have committed any of the acts cited in the definition of genocide set out in the Convention. It is generally accepted this definition reflects the concept of genocide, as understood in customary international law.
>
> 19. It follows from the obligation to prosecute or extradite, imposed by international customary law on Australia as a nation State, that it would be constitutionally permissible for the Commonwealth Parliament to enact legislation providing for the trial within Australia of persons accused of genocide, wherever occurring. …
>
> 20. However, it is one thing to say Australia has an international legal obligation to prosecute or extradite a genocide suspect found within its territory, and that the Commonwealth Parliament may legislate to ensure that obligation is fulfilled; it is another thing to say that, without legislation to that effect, such a person may be put on trial for genocide before an Australian court. If this were the position, it would lead to the curious result that an international obligation incurred pursuant to customary law has greater domestic consequences than an obligation incurred, expressly and voluntarily, by Australia signing and ratifying an international convention. Ratification of a convention does not directly affect Australian domestic law unless and until implementing legislation is enacted.
>
> 22. … If genocide is to be regarded as punishable in Australia, on the basis that it is an international crime, it must be shown that *Australian law* permits that result. There being no relevant statute, that means Australian common law.
>
> 25. … [I]t is difficult to make a general statement covering all the diverse rules of international customary law. It is one thing, it seems to me, for courts of a particular country to be prepared to treat a civil law rule like the doctrine of foreign sovereign immunity as part of its domestic law, whether because it is accepted by those courts as being 'incorporated' in that law or because it has been 'transformed' by judicial act. It is another thing to say that a norm of international law criminalising conduct that is not made punishable by the domestic law entitles a domestic court to try and punish an offender against that law.
>
> 26. … [D]omestic courts face a policy issue in deciding whether to recognise and enforce a rule of international law. If there is a policy issue, I have no doubt it should be resolved in a criminal case by declining, in the absence of legislation, to enforce the international norm. As Shearer pointed out …, in the realm of criminal law 'the strong presumption *nullum crimen sine lege* (there is no crime unless expressly created by law) applies.'[45] In the case of serious criminal conduct, ground rules are needed. Which courts are to have jurisdiction to try the accused person? What procedures will govern the trial? What punishment may be imposed? These matters need to be resolved before a person is put on trial for an offence as horrendous as genocide. …

---

45.   Ivan Shearer, 'The relationship between international law and domestic law', in Brian R Opeskin and Donald R Rothwell (eds), *International Law and Australian Federalism,* Melbourne University Press, 1997, 42.

29. Although it is but a straw in the wind, *Pinochet (Regina v Bow Street Metropolitan Stipendiary Magistrate; Ex parte Pinochet (No 3)* [1999] 2 WLR 827)[46] suggests the same conclusion. This is not because of anything said by their Lordships or even anything argued; but rather because of what was not argued. Usually, a non-argument would have no significance; but this was a most exceptional case. The appeal was twice argued in the House of Lords, and those supporting the extradition of Pinochet to Spain were represented by leading international lawyers. On the view that prevailed (that the issue of double criminality must be addressed as at the date of the conduct, not the date of the extradition application), extradition on all charges would have been secured if counsel had been able to demonstrate that Pinochet would have been punishable in the United Kingdom before the commencement of the 1988 United Kingdom statute adopting and implementing the Torture Convention. Yet, although torture is an international crime, nobody suggested Pinochet would have been triable in the United Kingdom before that date by reason of the incorporation into United Kingdom law of the international customary law about torture. The only explanation of this omission can be that those arguing for extradition accepted that torture was not a triable offence in the United Kingdom until implementing legislation was enacted.

30. ... [T]he decision of the Supreme Court of Israel in *Attorney-General of Israel v Eichmann* (1962) ILR 277[47] furnishes no support for the view that torture would have been punishable in the United Kingdom, pursuant to international customary law, before September 1988. Eichmann was charged under an Israeli statute. It was contended before the District Court that the terms of the Israeli statute were inconsistent with the principles of international customary law concerning genocide. In a passage in its reasons approved by the Supreme Court at 280, the District Court responded: 'The Court has to give effect to the law of the Knesset, and we cannot entertain the contention that this law conflicts with the principles of international law'. On my reading of the case, the District Court did only give effect to the law of the Knesset, the Israeli Parliament. ...

32. It follows from what I have said that I am of the opinion that Mr Thompson was correct in refusing to issue the warrants sought by the appellants. In the absence of enabling legislation, the offence of genocide is not cognisable in the courts of the Australian Capital Territory. ...

Whitlam J: ... 57. ... The emergence after the Second World War of the international crime of genocide no doubt imposes non-derogable obligations on Australia under the law of nations. The exercise of universal jurisdiction to prosecute such an offence is a matter for the Commonwealth, yet Parliament has expressly abolished common law offences under Commonwealth law[48] The courts of the States and the Territories can have no authority for themselves to proscribe conduct as criminal under the common law simply because it has now become recognised as an international crime with the status of *jus cogens* under customary international law. In any event, common law offences are anathemas in the so-called Griffith Code jurisdictions: Queensland, Western Australia, Tasmania and the Northern Territory. It would be absurd if the common law countenanced the selective exercise by municipal courts of a universal jurisdiction under international law.

58. ... I would accordingly dismiss the appeal from Crispin J.

---

46. See **6.60**.
47. See **6.22**.
48. *Criminal Code 1995* (Cth), s 1.1.

Merkel J, in contrast to both Wilcox J and Whitlam J, was of the opinion that there was an Australian common law offence of genocide sourced in customary international law. He took the view, however, that the appeal should be dismissed on the grounds that none of the allegations made by the appellants were capable of raising an arguable case of genocide under international or Australian law.

Treaty law

3.22   As Wilcox J observed in *Nulyarimma,* one of the reasons that customary international law cannot always be adopted into the common law is that 'it would lead to the curious result that an international obligation incurred pursuant to customary law has greater domestic consequences than an obligation incurred, expressly and voluntarily, by Australia signing and ratifying an international convention'.

3.23   The established rule in the Australian common law is that participation in a treaty does not, without incorporation by legislative enactment, affect liberties, rights and obligations under the common law. This remains true even if the treaty recognises or establishes fundamental human rights. In *Dietrich v The Queen,*[49] the appellant argued before the High Court of Australia that he had been denied a fair trial in violation of Art 14(3) of the International Covenant on Civil and Political Rights (ICCPR) because he was unrepresented by legal counsel after the failure of his applications for legal aid. Mason CJ and McHugh J said:[50]

> Ratification of the I.C.C.P.R. as an executive act has no direct legal effect upon domestic law; the rights and obligations contained in the I.C.C.P.R. are not incorporated into Australian law unless and until specific legislation is passed implementing the provisions.[51] No such legislation has been passed. This position is not altered by Australia's accession to the First Optional Protocol to the I.C.C.P.R., effective as of 25 December 1991, by which Australia recognizes the competence of the Human Rights Committee of the United Nations to receive and consider communications from individuals subject to Australia's jurisdiction who claim to be victims of a violation by Australia of their covenanted rights. On one view, it may seem curious that the Executive Government has seen fit to expose Australia to the potential censure of the Human Rights Committee without endeavouring to ensure that the rights enshrined in the I.C.C.P.R. are incorporated into domestic law, but such an approach is clearly permissible.

3.24   The High Court unanimously re-affirmed the doctrine denying automatic adoption of treaty law into the common law in a constitutional challenge to Commonwealth legislation.

---

49.   *Dietrich v The Queen* (1992) 177 CLR 292.
50.   Ibid, 305.
51.   A footnote here in the judgment refers to *Bradley v Commonwealth* (1973) 128 CLR 557, 582; *Simsek v MacPhee* (1982) 148 CLR 636, 641–644; *Kioa v West* (1985) 159 CLR 550, 570–571.

In **Victoria v Commonwealth (ILO Case)**,[52] the Commonwealth enacted certain amendments to the *Industrial Relations Act 1988* (Cth) allowing for the imposition of, or imposing, obligations on employers with respect to minimum wages, equal pay, termination of employment, discrimination in employment and family leave, and providing for collective bargaining and the right to strike. The states of Victoria, South Australia and Western Australia commenced proceedings challenging the validity of the amendments on the grounds that they exceeded the Commonwealth's legislative powers under the Constitution. The Commonwealth justified the amendments partly on the basis that they gave effect to certain conventions of the International Labour Organization (ILO) binding Australia, and partly on the basis that they gave effect to recommendations adopted by the General Conference of the ILO. On the Commonwealth's view, the legislative amendments were thus a valid exercise of the external affairs power under the Constitution. The High Court of Australia took the opportunity to discuss the relationship between Australia's treaty obligations and domestic Australian law:[53]

> Brennan CJ, Toohey, Gaudron, McHugh and Gummow JJ: ... As a general proposition,[54] under the common law, entry by the Executive into a treaty is insufficient, without legislation to implement it, to modify the domestic or municipal legal order by creating or changing public and private legal rights and obligations. In 1892, in argument before the Judicial Committee in *Walker v Baird*,[55] the British Attorney-General had conceded that he could not maintain the proposition that the Crown could sanction an invasion by its officers of the rights of private individuals whenever it was necessary to compel obedience to the provisions of a treaty. In the first edition of Halsbury's Laws of England,[56] which stated the law in 1909, the prevailing view stated by contributors, who included the future Sir William Holdsworth, was:
>
>> Treaties ... are in general binding upon the subject without express parliamentary sanction; but the previous consent of, or subsequent ratification by, the legislature is legally necessary to their validity in certain cases.
>>
>> Thus, though treaties relating to war and peace, the cession of territory, or concluding alliances with foreign powers are generally conceded to be binding upon the nation without express parliamentary sanction, it is deemed safer to obtain such sanction in the case of an important cession of territory. And where taxation is imposed or a grant from the public funds rendered necessary, or where the existing laws of trade and navigation are affected, or where the private rights of the subject are interfered with by a treaty concluded in time of peace, it is apprehended that the previous or subsequent consent of Parliament is in all cases required to render the treaty binding upon the subject and enforceable by officers of the Crown.
>
> Later, in *Chow Hung Ching v The King*,[57] Dixon J said that a treaty, 'at all events one which does not terminate a state of war', has no legal effect upon the

---

52. *Victoria v Commonwealth; South Australia v Commonwealth; Western Australia v Commonwealth* (1996) 187 CLR 416; 70 ALJR 680; 138 ALR 129. Footnotes in this extract refer to sources cited in the judgment.
53. Ibid, 480–482.
54. The Court notes in a footnote here that '[c]ertain exceptions or qualifications are identified and discussed by J G Starke in "The High Court of Australia and the rule in Walker v Baird [1892] AC 491" (1974) 48 *Australian Law Journal* 368'.
55. *Walker v Baird* [1892] AC 491, 492.
56. *Halsbury's Laws of England*, Vol 6: *Constitutional Law*, 440–41.
57. *Chow Hung Ching v The King* (1948) 77 CLR 449, 478; see also *Brown v Lizars* (1905) 2 CLR 837, 851, 860; *Bradley v Commonwealth* (1973) 128 CLR 557, 582; *Simsek v Macphee* (1982) 148 CLR 636, 641–642.

> rights and duties of citizens and, 'speaking generally no power resides in the Crown to compel them to obey the provisions of a treaty'. His Honour cited *Walker v Baird*.[58]
>
> Thus, as matters stand in Australia, and as they stood in 1900, the conduct of external affairs by the Executive may produce agreements which the Executive wishes to translate into the domestic or municipal legal order. To do so, it must procure the passage of legislation implementing those agreements if it wishes to create individual rights and obligations or change existing rights and obligations under that legal order.[59] Of course, the pursuit of some aspects of external affairs by the Executive Government does not require enabling legislation. In *Barton*, Mason J concluded[60] that the making of a request to a foreign state for the surrender of a fugitive offender alleged to have committed an offence against the laws of Australia falls within the executive power of the Commonwealth, unless the prerogative be displaced by legislation. Another example is the preservation of friendly relations with other countries, including the sending or receiving of diplomatic representatives. This is 'an important part of the management of the external affairs of the Commonwealth'.[61]
>
> Where, as in the present case, the Executive ratifies a Convention which calls for action affecting powers and relationships governed by the domestic legal order, legislation is needed to implement the Convention. ...

3.25   There are only a few exceptions to the common law rule that conventional law does not affect liberties, rights and obligations under the common law without legislative enactment. Treaties of peace, treaties relating to war, treaties of alliance with foreign States, and cessions of territory are capable of affecting domestic law rights without legislative enactment.

3.26   The High Court has, albeit with considerable reserve, left open the possibility that conventional law may play a role in the development of the common law. In *Minister for Immigration and Ethnic Affairs v Teoh*, Mason CJ and Deane J made the following *obiter* remarks:[62]

> ... an international convention may play a part in the development by the courts of the common law. The provisions of an international convention to which Australia is a party, especially one which declares universal fundamental rights, may be used by the courts as a legitimate guide in developing the common law.[63] But the courts should act in this fashion with due circumspection when the Parliament itself has not seen

---

58.   *Walker v Baird* [1892] AC 491, 497.
59.   *Minister for Immigration and Ethnic Affairs v Teoh* (1995) 183 CLR 273, 286–288, 298, 315.
60.   *Barton v Commonwealth* (1974) 131 CLR 477, 498–499. A similar conclusion was reached by Barwick CJ (at 487–488), McTiernan and Menzies JJ (at 491) and Jacobs J (at 505).
61.   *R v Sharkey* (1949) 79 CLR 121, 136–137.
62.   *Minister of State for Immigration and Ethnic Affairs v Teoh* (1995) 183 CLR 273, 288. Footnotes in this extract refer to sources cited in the judgment.
63.   *Mabo v Queensland (No 2)* (1992) 175 CLR 1, 42, per Brennan J (with whom Mason CJ and McHugh J agreed); *Dietrich v The Queen* (1992) 177 CLR 292, 321, per Brennan J; 360, per Toohey J; *Jago v District Court (NSW)* (1988) 12 NSWLR 558, 569, per Kirby P; *Derbyshire County Council v Times Newspapers Ltd* [1992] QB 770.

fit to incorporate the provisions of a convention into our domestic law. Judicial development of the common law must not be seen as a backdoor means of importing an unincorporated convention into Australian law. A cautious approach to the development of the common law by reference to international conventions would be consistent with the approach which the courts have hitherto adopted to the development of the common law by reference to statutory policy and statutory materials.[64] Much will depend upon the nature of the relevant provision, the extent to which it has been accepted by the international community, the purpose which it is intended to serve and its relationship to the existing principles of our domestic law.

Mason CJ and Deane J were, in raising this possibility, right to be highly cautious as they effectively suggest a means of altering domestic law by the executive act of concluding treaties. Their observations can, however, be more easily harmonised with established doctrine and the well-trodden path of Australian courts if they are understood to mean that treaty rules which have entered into customary international law[65] may play a part in the development of the common law.

Otherwise, Australia's common law is unaffected by treaty obligations absent legislation giving them domestic effect.

International law and legislation

3.27 Legislation is that portion of Australia's domestic law that is enacted by the Commonwealth Parliament, a state Parliament or a territory legislature,[66] or by persons or bodies authorised by those Parliaments or legislatures to enact subordinate legislation. The common law provides that legislation displaces — but does not repeal — an inconsistent common law rule. Similarly, obligations established by treaty displace inconsistent non-*jus cogens* norms of customary international law (although the mechanism producing this result is not a rule of customary international law, but the general principle of *pacta sunt servanda*).

Customary international law

3.28 We have seen that customary international law is, subject to important limitations, capable of adoption within the Australian legal system in such a way as to vary the effect of the common law. Can customary international law similarly vary the effect of legislation?

---

64. *Lamb v Cotogno* (1987) 164 CLR 1, 11–12.
65. See **1.138–1.146**.
66. Some imperial legislation also remains in force in Australia.

In **Polites v Commonwealth**,[67] the plaintiffs were nationals of Greece and not British subjects. They were in Australia when, in 1942, they were served by the Commonwealth with notices enlisting them into the Australian armed forces. The notices were issued pursuant to the *National Security (Aliens Service) Regulations*, authorising the compulsory enlistment of allied aliens into the Australian armed forces, made pursuant to s 13A of the *National Security Act 1939–1943*. Section 13A provided as follows:

> Notwithstanding anything contained in this Act, the Governor-General may make such regulations making provision for requiring persons to place themselves, their services and their property at the disposal of the Commonwealth, as appear to him to be necessary or expedient for securing the public safety, the defence of the Commonwealth and the Territories of the Commonwealth, or the efficient prosecution of any war in which His Majesty is or may be engaged.

The plaintiffs sought declarations from the High Court of Australia (Latham CJ, Rich, Starke, Dixon, McTiernan and Williams JJ) that the notices were invalid because the Act did not authorise the Regulations:[68]

> Latham CJ: … It is argued for the plaintiffs, first, that there is a general rule of construction of statutes according to which, unless the contrary intention is clear, it is to be presumed that they do not violate any recognized rule of international law; secondly, that there is a well-established rule of international law that aliens cannot be compelled to serve in the military forces of a foreign State in which they happen to be; thirdly, that the Regulations are made under a provision in the *National Security Act 1939* as amended, namely s. 13A, which refers to persons generally; that these general words must be limited in some way, as otherwise they would apply to all persons in the world, and that one proper limitation is to be found in the recognition and application of the rule of international law to which reference has been made. By this course of reasoning, it is sought to establish the propositions that the Regulations are a clear breach of an established rule of international law, and that s. 13A of the *National Security Act* should be construed as not intended to authorize such a violation of established principle.
>
> The first proposition for which the plaintiffs contend is well established by many authorities. Perhaps it is most conveniently stated in *Bloxam v Favre*,[69] where Sir James Hannen approved the statement in *Maxwell on Interpretation of Statutes*, 8th ed. (1937), p. 130, that 'every statute is to be so interpreted and applied, as far as its language admits, as not to be inconsistent with the comity of nations or with the established rules of international law.' See also *Craies* on *Statute Law*, 4th ed. (1936), p. 379, and *Oppenheim, International Law*, 5th ed. (1937), vol. *i.*, p. 37.
>
> But all the authorities in English law also recognize that courts are bound by the statute law of their country, even if that law should violate a rule of international law: See, e.g., *Croft v Dunphy*[70] where, after reference to the well-known authorities of *R v Burah*[71] and *Hodge v The Queen*,[72] establishing that Dominion Parliaments have, within the limits of their powers, authority as plenary and as ample as that of the Imperial Parliament, it is said that 'legislation of the Imperial

---

67. *Polites v Commonwealth; Kandiliotes v Commonwealth* (1945) 70 CLR 60.
68. Ibid, 68–73.
69. *Bloxam v Favre* (1883) 8 PD 101, 107.
70. *Croft v Dunphy* (1933) AC 156, 163, 164.
71. *R v Burah* (1878) 3 App Cas 889.
72. *Hodge v The Queen* (1883) 9 App Cas 117.

Parliament, even in contravention of generally acknowledged principles of international law, is binding upon and must be enforced by the Courts of this country, for in these Courts the legislation of the Imperial Parliament cannot be challenged as *ultra vires*,' that is, as *ultra vires* by reason of being inconsistent with international law.

It was not really argued, and it could not, I think, successfully be contended, that the powers conferred on the Commonwealth Parliament itself by the *Constitution*, s. 51 (vi.), relating to naval and military defence, and s. 51 (xix.), 'naturalization and aliens,' were limited in any other manner than by the description of the subject matter. The Commonwealth Parliament can legislate on these matters in breach of international law, taking the risk of international complications. This is recognized as being the position in Great Britain — cf. *Craies* on *Statute Law*, 4th ed. (1936), p. 393: 'Each State can, at its own international risks, reject the opinions of other States as to international law.' ... It must be held that legislation otherwise within the power of the Commonwealth Parliament does not become invalid because it conflicts with a rule of international law, though every effort should be made to construe Commonwealth statutes so as to avoid breaches of international law and of international comity. The question, therefore, is not a question of the power of the Commonwealth Parliament to legislate in breach of international law, but is a question whether in fact it has done so.

... The Regulations provide for compulsory service of aliens in Australian armed forces and place the aliens in the same position as British subjects in Australia. They must be held to be contrary to an established rule of international law.

The next question which arises is whether the *National Security Act* authorizes the making of regulations of this character. This is a question of the intention of Parliament, to be ascertained from the terms of the relevant legislation. ... [The] regulations with respect to aliens were clearly within the contemplation of Parliament when the Act was passed.

... They make specific provision for the imposition in the case of certain aliens of compulsory military service. ...

I agree that s. 13A must be limited in its operation: for example, it does not refer to all persons everywhere in the world, or to all property everywhere in the world. But ... the Commonwealth Parliament by s. 13A of the *National Security Act* intended to authorize the Governor-General to make regulations under which the service of any person in Australia, including aliens, may be compelled for defence purposes. It is not for a court to express an opinion upon the political propriety of this action. ...

In my opinion, the regulations are valid ... there should be judgment in the actions for the defendants.

The Court found unanimously for the defendants.

3.29 Legislation is, therefore, more resistant than the common law to alteration by customary international law. The *Polites* judgment reaffirmed the rule that legislatures do not intend to enact laws which violate established rules of customary international law and that legislation will, as far as its language permits, be construed in a way which avoids any such violation. However, where it is clear that Parliament intended to legislate contrary to a requirement of customary international law, full effect will be given to that legislative intention. This remains so notwithstanding that Australia would thus be in breach of its obligations on the plane of international law.

Treaty law

3.30   Similar principles prevail where there is a conflict between Australian legislation and a conventional rule binding Australia on the plane of international law.

Inconsistency of treaty and legislation

3.31   As a corollary of the rule that treaties unincorporated by legislation do not affect common law rights and obligations, a treaty-based rule of international law cannot displace an inconsistent rule expressed by legislation. In *Bradley v Commonwealth*,[73] the Commonwealth government suspended postal and telecommunications services to the 'Rhodesia Information Centre'. This was done in purported compliance with resolutions adopted by the Security Council under Art 41 of the UN Charter[74] requiring States to frustrate official acts of the internationally illegal regime controlling Rhodesia. The High Court found that Australian legislation, properly construed, required the Commonwealth to supply the suspended services. The legislation made no exceptions for obligations arising under the UN Charter. Security Council resolutions could not per se deprive these statutory obligations of their legal force:

> Since the Charter and the resolutions of the Security Council have not been carried into effect within Australia by appropriate legislation, they cannot be relied upon as a justification for executive acts that would otherwise be unjustified, or as grounds for resisting an injunction to restrain an excess of executive power, even if the acts were done with a view to complying with the resolutions of the Security Council.[75]

3.32   Even legislation which is intended to be the instrument by which Parliament gives effect to a treaty may be inconsistent with obligations stipulated by that treaty if such was Parliament's intention. This remains true even if the treaty recognises or establishes fundamental human rights. In *Minogue v HREOC*,[76] the Full Court of the Federal Court of Australia affirmed the validity of Commonwealth legislation excluding the states from the powers of the Human Rights and Equal Opportunity Commission (HREOC). This was so notwithstanding that the ICCPR applies, as a matter of international law, to all levels of government and that the Commonwealth established HREOC in order to facilitate observance of the ICCPR and other human rights treaties in Australia.

3.33   What this means in practical terms is that breaches by Australia of its treaty obligations are not justiciable before Australian courts. This is not to say that a failure to comply with a treaty obligation is lawful. Where a treaty obliges Australia to alter its domestic law but no legislation is enacted to produce such a result, there will be a breach

---

73.   *Bradley v Commonwealth* (1973) 128 CLR 557.
74.   See **9.51**.
75.   *Bradley v Commonwealth* (1973) 128 CLR 557, 582–583, per Barwick CJ and Gibbs J.
76.   *Minogue v Human Rights and Equal Opportunity Commission* (1999) 84 FCR 438.

of that treaty engaging Australia's responsibility as a State on the plane of international law.

3.34   That legislation should be more resistant than the common law to influence from the international legal order should not be surprising. The separation of powers is a well-established doctrine (in one form or another) in all democratic constitutional orders, with the Anglo-American common law providing its birthplace and nursery. In Australia, as in all Westminster-style democracies, the executive is primarily responsible for conducting foreign affairs and concluding treaties while the legislature is primarily responsible for enacting legislation. To permit an obligation enshrined in a treaty to take precedence over legislation, without parliamentary approval in some form, would be to elevate the executive and diminish the legislature, thereby prejudicing the Westminster conception of responsible government.

Treaties and legislative interpretation

3.35   Although treaties unincorporated by legislation cannot per se be given effect in Australian domestic law, they are not without domestic juridical consequences. The interpretation of legislation is very frequently a live issue in legal disputes, and treaties can play a role in assisting courts to interpret legislation. As Mason CJ and Deane J observed in *Minister for Immigration and Ethnic Affairs v Teoh* when discussing the status of the Convention on the Rights of the Child in Australian domestic law:[77]

> It is well established that the provisions of an international treaty to which Australia is a party do not form part of Australian law unless those provisions have been validly incorporated into our municipal law by statute.[78] This principle has its foundation in the proposition that in our constitutional system the making and ratification of treaties fall within the province of the Executive in the exercise of its prerogative power whereas the making and the alteration of the law fall within the province of Parliament, not the Executive.[79] So, a treaty which has not been incorporated into our municipal law cannot operate as a direct source of individual rights and obligations under that law. In this case, it is common ground that the provisions of the Convention have not been incorporated in this way. ...

> But the fact that the Convention has not been incorporated into Australian law does not mean that its ratification holds no significance for Australian law. Where a statute or subordinate legislation is ambiguous, the courts should favour that construction which accords with Australia's obligations under a treaty or international convention

---

77.   *Minister for Immigration and Ethnic Affairs v Teoh* (1995) 183 CLR 273, 287–288. Footnotes in this extract refer to sources cited in the judgment.
78.   *Chow Hung Ching v The King* (1948) 77 CLR 449, 478; *Bradley v Commonwealth* (1973) 128 CLR 557, 582; *Simsek v Macphee* (1982) 148 CLR 636, 641–642; *Koowarta v Bjelke-Petersen* (1982) 153 CLR 168, 211–212, 224–225; *Kioa v West* (1985) 159 CLR 550, 570; *Dietrich v The Queen* (1992) 177 CLR 292, 305; *J H Rayner (Mincing Lane) Ltd v Department of Trade and Industry* [1990] 2 AC 418, 500.
79.   *Simsek v Macphee* (1982) 148 CLR 636, 641–642.

to which Australia is a party,[80] at least in those cases in which the legislation is enacted after, or in contemplation of, entry into, or ratification of, the relevant international instrument. That is because Parliament, *prima facie*, intends to give effect to Australia's obligations under international law.

It is accepted that a statute is to be interpreted and applied, as far as its language permits, so that it is in conformity and not in conflict with the established rules of international law.[81] The form in which this principle has been expressed might be thought to lend support to the view that the proposition enunciated in the preceding paragraph should be stated so as to require the courts to favour a construction, as far as the language of the legislation permits, that is in conformity and not in conflict with Australia's international obligations. That indeed is how we would regard the proposition as stated in the preceding paragraph. In this context, there are strong reasons for rejecting a narrow conception of ambiguity. If the language of the legislation is susceptible of a construction which is consistent with the terms of the international instrument and the obligations which it imposes on Australia, then that construction should prevail. So expressed, the principle is no more than a canon of construction and does not import the terms of the treaty or convention into our municipal law as a source of individual rights and obligations.[82]

3.36   The interpretation of legislation in a common law jurisdiction is always a search for the legislator's intention. Where it is clear that an Australian legislator intended to enact a rule contrary to an obligation contained in a treaty binding on Australia, effect will be given to that intention. In the course of ascertaining the legislator's will, however, it is necessary to start with a rebuttable presumption that there was no intention to enact a rule placing Australia in breach of its conventional obligations. Thus, where the wording of legislation is reasonably capable of bearing a meaning that is in conformity with Australia's conventional obligations, effect should be given to that meaning in preference to another interpretation which would place Australia in breach of conventional international law.[83]

Given the rationale for this principle of interpretation, it should not apply where the legislation in question was enacted prior to a contemplated participation by Australia in the treaty said to be of relevance to the exercise of interpretation. We are concerned with the legislator's intention, which cannot logically be established by reference to a treaty uncontemplated at the time of the legislative enactment.

3.37   As far as the interpretation of Commonwealth legislation is concerned, s 15AB of the *Acts Interpretation Act 1901* (Cth) provides as follows:

---

80.   *Chu Kheng Lim v Minister for Immigration* (1992) 176 CLR 1, 38.
81.   *Polites v Commonwealth; Kandiliotes v Commonwealth* (1945) 70 CLR 60, 68–69, 77, 80–81.
82.   *R v Secretary of State for Home Department; Ex parte Brind* [1991] 1 AC 696, 748.
83.   In *AMS v AIF; AIF v AMS* (1999) 199 CLR 160, 180, Gleeson CJ, McHugh and Gummow JJ said that 'a statute of the Commonwealth or of a State is to be interpreted and applied, as far as its language permits, so that it is in conformity and not in conflict with established rules of international law'.

Use of Extrinsic Material in the Interpretation of an Act

(1) ... in the interpretation of a provision of an Act, if any material not forming part of the Act is capable of assisting in the ascertainment of the meaning of the provision, consideration may be given to that material:

    (a) to confirm that the meaning of the provision is the ordinary meaning conveyed by the text of the provision taking into account its context in the Act and the purpose or object underlying the Act; or

    (b) to determine the meaning of the provision when:

        (i) the provision is ambiguous or obscure; or

        (ii) the ordinary meaning conveyed by the text of the provision taking into account its context in the Act and the purpose or object underlying the Act leads to a result that is manifestly absurd or is unreasonable.

(2) Without limiting the generality of subsection (1), the material that may be considered in accordance with that subsection in the interpretation of a provision of an Act includes: ...

    (d) any treaty or other international agreement that is referred to in the Act; ...

3.38 Therefore, whenever Commonwealth legislation 'refers to' a treaty, that treaty may be used to assist in the interpretation of the legislation. But this may occur only for the purposes set out in s 15AB(1), including, most importantly from a practical perspective, 'to determine the meaning of the provision when ... the provision is ambiguous or obscure'.

Section 15AB does not replace, but rather supplements, the common law rules on statutory interpretation. Regard may thus be had to a treaty in order to resolve ambiguities in favour of compliance with the treaty, even where it is not 'referred to' in the legislation itself.

3.39 Where the legislation itself expressly incorporates the terms of a treaty, the correct approach is, subject to a contrary intention by the legislator, to interpret the incorporated terms in accordance with the principles of treaty interpretation at international law. In *Applicant A v Minister for Immigration and Ethnic Affairs*,[84] the High Court of Australia needed to determine the meaning of the term 'refugee' for the purposes of the *Migration Act 1958* (Cth). The statute defined the term by reference to its meaning in the Convention Relating to the Status of Refugees.[85] Dawson J said that the Court's task:[86]

> ... involves the construction of a domestic statute which incorporates a definition found in an international treaty. Such a provision, whether it is a definition or otherwise, should ordinarily be construed in accordance

---

84. *Applicant A v Minister for Immigration and Ethnic Affairs* (1997) 190 CLR 225.
85. UNTS, Vol 189, p 137.
86. *Applicant A v Minister for Immigration and Ethnic Affairs* (1997) 190 CLR 225, 239–240. Semble Brennan CJ (230–231), McHugh J (251–252), Gummow J (277), and Kirby J (292–294). As to the law on interpretation of treaties, see **2.75–2.87**.

with the meaning to be attributed to the treaty provision in international law. By transposing the provision of the treaty, the legislature discloses the *prima facie* intention that it have the same meaning in the statute as it does in the treaty. Absent a contrary intention, … such a statutory provision is to be construed according to the method applicable to the construction of the corresponding words in the treaty.

3.40   Interpretation of treaty terms according to the canons of treaty interpretation at international law would also seem appropriate whenever there is a need to ascertain the conformity of ambiguous legislation with Australia's conventional obligations (as in *Teoh*), or for the purposes of s 15AB of the *Acts Interpretation Act 1901* (Cth).

Treaties and constitutional interpretation

3.41   In contrast to the interpretation of legislation, it appears that international law has no role to play in the interpretation of the Australian Constitution. As Gleeson CJ, McHugh and Gummow JJ remarked in *AMS v AIF*:[87] 'As to the Constitution, its provisions are not to be construed as subject to an implication said to be derived from international law.' In *Polites v Commonwealth*,[88] Dixon J noted that, subject to a contrary intention by Parliament, legislation should be interpreted in a way which conforms to Australia's international legal obligations. There is, however, no similar rule of construction with respect to the Australian Constitution:[89]

> The contention that s. 51 (vi.) of the Constitution should be read as subject to the same implication, in my opinion, ought not to be countenanced. The purpose of Part V. of Chapter I. of the Constitution is to confer upon an autonomous government plenary legislative power over the assigned subjects. Within the matters placed under its authority, the power of the Parliament was intended to be supreme and to construe it down by reference to the presumption is to apply to the establishment of legislative power a rule for the construction of legislation passed in its exercise. It is nothing to the point that the Constitution derives its force from an Imperial enactment. It is none the less a constitution.

3.42   Nor can s 51(xxix) of the Constitution, which confers on the Commonwealth power to legislate with respect to 'external affairs', be interpreted to mean that the Commonwealth cannot give legislative effect to a treaty which violates international law. In *Horta v Commonwealth*,[90] some East Timor independence leaders challenged the constitutionality of two Commonwealth statutes giving effect to a treaty with Indonesia concerning exploitation of oil resources in the Timor Gap. The High Court of Australia unanimously said:[91]

---

87.   *AMS v AIF; AIF v AMS* (1999) 199 CLR 160, 180.
88.   *Polites v Commonwealth; Kandiliotes v Commonwealth* (1945) 70 CLR 60.
89.   Ibid, 78.
90.   *Horta v Commonwealth* (1994) 181 CLR 183.
91.   Ibid, 195 (Mason CJ, Brennan, Deane, Dawson, Toohey, Gaudron and McHugh JJ).

It was submitted on behalf of the plaintiffs that the enactment of the two Acts would be beyond the legislative power conferred by s. 51(xxix) if the Treaty were void under international law either on the ground that it was contrary to international law or on the ground that Australia's entry into or performance of it would be in breach of Australia's obligations under international law. There is, however, a short answer to that submission. That answer is that even if the Treaty were void or unlawful under international law or if Australia's entry into or performance of the Treaty involved a breach of Australia's obligations under international law, the Act and the Consequential Act would not thereby be deprived of their character as laws with respect to 'External affairs' for the purposes of s. 51(xxix). Neither s. 51(xxix) itself nor any other provision of the Constitution confines the legislative power with respect to 'External affairs' to the enactment of laws which are consistent with, or which relate to treaties or matters which are consistent with, the requirements of international law.[92] In particular, there is simply no basis either in s. 51(xxix) or in any other provision of the Constitution for the plaintiffs' submission that the legislative power conferred by s. 51(xxix) must be confined within the limits of 'Australia's legislative competence as recognized by international law'.

International law and legislative power

3.43 Australia is a federation in which the power to legislate is divided between the Commonwealth (federal) government and the six constituent state governments. Such an arrangement implies the need to demarcate subject matters about which the Commonwealth and the states are competent to legislate. In Canada, the Constitution enumerates the legislative powers of both the Dominion (federal) government and the provincial governments, leaving any residue to the Dominion government.[93] The Australian Constitution embraces almost the opposite approach, with the Commonwealth possessed of enumerated powers and the states enjoying legislative power in all other matters (including most matters in relation to which the Commonwealth has not exercised its legislative power[94]).

This means that the Commonwealth is an entity of limited legislative sovereignty. Its legislative powers, and those of the states, are subject to limitations arising from the federal structure of the Australian

---

92. A footnote here in the judgment refers to *Polites v Commonwealth; Kandiliotes v Commonwealth* (1945) 70 CLR 60, 68–69, per Latham CJ; 74, per Rich J; 75–76, per Starke J; 77–78, per Dixon J; 79, per McTiernan J; 81, per Williams J; *Fishwick v Cleland* (1960) 106 CLR 186, 196.
93. *Constitution Act,* ss 91, 92 and 92A.
94. A few legislative powers are exclusive to the Commonwealth, so that the states may not legislate even if the Commonwealth has not enacted legislation. These exclusive Commonwealth legislative powers are the power to regulate the Commonwealth public service, the Commonwealth's seat of government, and Commonwealth public places (s 52); the power to levy customs and excise duties (s 90); the power to regulate defence (s 114); and the power to coin money (s 115). All other legislative powers in the Constitution are concurrent — that is, they are powers which may be exercised by the states until the Commonwealth exercises its legislative power.

Constitution. Australia itself is legislatively fully sovereign, but the nation's legislative powers are divided among seven parliaments. As the High Court of Australia unanimously observed in one of its first few judgments: 'In considering the respective powers of the Commonwealth and of the States it is essential to bear in mind that each is, within the ambit of its authority, a sovereign State, subject only to the restrictions imposed by the Imperial connection and to the provisions of the Constitution, either expressed or necessarily implied.'[95]

3.44   Among the legislative powers of the Commonwealth enumerated in the Constitution is the 'external affairs' power in s 51:

Legislative powers of the Parliament

The Parliament shall, subject to this Constitution, have power to make laws for the peace, order, and good government of the Commonwealth with respect to: ...

(xxix.) External Affairs

3.45   Section 51(xxix) of the Constitution is one of the most wide-ranging sources of Commonwealth legislative power. It has several dimensions, empowering the Commonwealth to enact legislation with respect to persons, things, places or matters geographically external to Australia; relations with other States; the implementation of treaties; and matters of international concern, such as Australia's compliance with customary international law. It is with the last two of these dimensions that we are presently concerned.

Implementation of treaties and recommendations

3.46   The external affairs power confers on the Commonwealth broad authority to implement by legislation Australia's treaty obligations and the recommendations of international organisations.

The Commonwealth's power in this regard is not limited to implementing conventional rules and recommendations related to the Commonwealth's other enumerated powers. Rather, it enables the Commonwealth to enact legislation which, but for the external affairs power, would fall within the exclusive legislative power of the states. Using the external affairs power, the Commonwealth has successfully enacted legislation giving effect to international conventional rules concerning intra-state air navigation safety standards *(R v Burgess; Ex parte Henry (No 2)[96])*, racial discrimination *(Koowarta v Bjelke-Petersen[97])*, environmental protection *(Commonwealth v Tasmania (Tasmanian Dam Case),[98] Richardson v Forestry Commission[99])*,

---

95.   *D'Emden v Pedder* (1904) 1 CLR 91, 109.
96.   *R v Burgess; Ex parte Henry (No 2)* (1939) 61 CLR 634.
97.   *Koowarta v Bjelke-Petersen* (1982) 153 CLR 168.
98.   *Commonwealth v Tasmania; Attorney-General for Tasmania v Commonwealth; Commonwealth v Tasmania (Tasmanian Dam Case)* (1983) 158 CLR 1.
99.   *Richardson v Forestry Commission* (1988) 164 CLR 261.

and employment conditions and discrimination at work *(Victoria v Commonwealth (ILO Case)*[100]).

3.47 The scope of the Commonwealth's authority to legislatively implement treaties under the external affairs power was for a time thought to be subject to the treaty being a 'matter of international concern'. This theory was postulated on the possibility that some treaties, though giving rise to conventional obligations at international law, might not really deal with a matter of legitimate concern to the international society of States. This putative limitation on the scope of the external affairs power was indicated by Stephen J in his judgment in *Koowarta v Bjelke-Petersen*.[101] Stephen J agreed with Mason, Murphy and Brennan JJ that the *Racial Discrimination Act 1975* (Cth) was a valid exercise of the Commonwealth's external affairs powers, but added the following caveat:[102]

> ... [W]here the grant of power is with respect to 'external affairs' an examination of subject-matter, circumstance and parties will be relevant whenever a purported exercise of such power is challenged. It will not be enough that the challenged law gives effect to treaty obligations. A treaty with another country, whether or not the result of a collusive arrangement, which is on a topic neither of especial concern to the relationship between Australia and that other country nor of general international concern will not be likely to survive that scrutiny.

> ... [There is an] increasing awareness of the nations of the world that the state of society in other countries is very relevant to the state of their own society. Thus areas of what are of purely domestic concern are steadily contracting and those of international concern are ever expanding. Nevertheless the quality of being of international concern remains, no less than ever, a valid criterion of whether a particular subject-matter forms part of a nation's 'external affairs'. A subject-matter of international concern necessarily possesses the capacity to affect a country's relations with other nations and this quality is itself enough to make a subject-matter a part of a nation's 'external affairs'. And this being so, any attack upon validity, either in what must be the very exceptional circumstances which could found an allegation of lack of bona fides or where there is said to be an absence of international subject-matter, will still afford an appropriate safeguard against improper exercise of the 'External affairs' power.

3.48 This narrow concept of the external affairs power, dependent on the existence of a matter of genuine international concern, was rejected by the majority but kept alive by the minority in the High Court's *Tasmanian Dam Case*.[103] In *Richardson v Forestry Commission*,[104] however, the High Court unanimously put to rest the putative requirement of a 'matter of international concern' as a prerequisite for an exercise of the external affairs power. The matter now appears to be settled.

---

100. *Victoria v Commonwealth; South Australia v Commonwealth; Western Australia v Commonwealth* (1996) 187 CLR 416; 70 ALJR 680; 138 ALR 129.
101. *Koowarta v Bjelke-Petersen* (1982) 153 CLR 168.
102. Ibid, 216–217.
103. *Tasmanian Dam Case* (1983) 158 CLR 1.
104. *Richardson v Forestry Commission* (1988) 164 CLR 261.

In ***Victoria v Commonwealth (ILO Case),***[105] for the facts of which see 3.24, the High Court of Australia said:[106]

> Brennan CJ, Toohey, Gaudron, McHugh and Gummow JJ: ... Where, as in the present case, the Executive ratifies a Convention which calls for action affecting powers and relationships governed by the domestic legal order, legislation is needed to implement the Convention. The question then arises whether the law is supported by the legislative power with respect to external affairs. The spare text of s 51(xxix) must be construed to ascertain its scope.
>
> The phrase 'External affairs' was adopted in s 51(xxix) of the Constitution in preference to 'foreign affairs' so as to make it clear that the power comprehended both the relationship between the Commonwealth of Australia and other parts of the then British Empire and the relationship with foreign countries.[107] ... [T]he Commonwealth of Australia was established at a time of evolving law and practice in the external relations between sovereign powers and between the self-governing units of the Empire. It would be a serious error to construe par (xxix) as though the subject matter of those relations to which it applied in 1900 were not continually expanding. Rather, the external relations of the Australian colonies were in a condition of continuing evolution and, at that time, were regarded as such. Accordingly, it is difficult to see any justification for treating the content of the phrase 'external affairs' as crystallised at the commencement of federation, or as denying it a particular application on the ground that the application was not foreseen or could not have been foreseen a century ago.
>
> From the foundation of the Commonwealth ... informed observers took the view that the power to legislate with respect to external affairs included power to legislate with respect to treaties, in so far as they affected Australia, which had been concluded by the Imperial Government. Thus, in *McKelvey v Meagher,*[108] Barton J said that it was probable that the external affairs power 'includes power to legislate as to the observance of treaties between Great Britain and foreign nations'. Writing as Attorney-General in 1902,[109] Deakin dealt as follows with the omission of the words 'and treaties' from s 51(xxix):
>
>> The omission, as appears from the debates, was solely to prevent any assumption arising that the Commonwealth claimed an independent power of making treaties. Legislation with respect to the enforcement of treaty obligations is clearly within the scope of 'external affairs'.
>
> The legislative power was designed to authorise the implementation of treaty obligations which bound Australia. At the time of federation the source of such obligations was action taken by the Imperial authorities. However, given the scope of the legislative power, it was at least implicit that it would authorise the implementation of treaty obligations accepted independently by the Commonwealth of Australia, if and when the Executive Branch of government attained the competence to do so.

---

105. *Victoria v Commonwealth; South Australia v Commonwealth; Western Australia v Commonwealth* (1996) 187 CLR 416; 70 ALJR 680; 138 ALR 129.
106. *Victoria v Commonwealth; South Australia v Commonwealth; Western Australia v Commonwealth* (1996) 187 CLR 416, 482–485, 488–489. Footnotes in this extract refer to sources cited in the judgment.
107. *R v Burgess; Ex parte Henry* (1936) 55 CLR 608, 684–685; *New South Wales v Commonwealth (Seas and Submerged Lands Act Case)* (1975) 135 CLR 337, 360.
108. *McKelvey v Meagher* (1906) 4 CLR 265, 286.
109. Bevan Mitchell (ed), *Opinions of Attorneys-General of the Commonwealth of Australia,* 1981, Vol 1, 134.

There was some suggestion in the submissions of the plaintiff States in the present case that what has come to pass with the legislation they seek to impugn is something beyond contemplation at the time of the adoption of the Constitution. Any such proposition is, as we have endeavoured shortly to illustrate, too widely stated. The treaties which were part of the subject matter of foreign relations in 1900, and the treaties that have since been made, embrace an ever-expanding range of topics.

The content of the relevant executive power of the Commonwealth under s 61, and the legislative power of the Parliament under s 51(xxix), are to be understood accordingly. Thus, as long ago as 1936, Evatt and McTiernan JJ said:[110]

> But it is not to be assumed that the legislative power over 'external affairs' is limited to the execution of treaties or conventions; and … the Parliament may well be deemed competent to legislate for the carrying out of 'recommendations' as well as the 'draft international conventions' resolved upon by the International Labour Organisation or of other international recommendations or requests upon other subject matters of concern to Australia as a member of the family of nations.

Their Honours also said in that case:[111]

> [A] consequence of the closer connection between the nations of the world (which has been partly brought about by the modern revolutions in communication) and of the recognition by the nations of a common interest in many matters affecting the social welfare of their peoples and of the necessity of co-operation among them in dealing with such matters, that it is no longer possible to assert that there is any subject matter which must necessarily be excluded from the list of possible subjects of international negotiation, international dispute or international agreement.

The present case is said to be one in which the law of the Commonwealth enters upon a field which previously was the preserve of State legislative power. To preclude the supersession of State law by Commonwealth law, the States sought to confine the scope of Commonwealth power under s 51(xxix) by reference to what Stephen J said in *Koowarta v Bjelke-Petersen*.[112] … Stephen J said[113] that a treaty with another country on a topic neither of special concern to the relationship between Australia and that other country nor of general international concern would be unlikely to attract the external affairs power. The plaintiff States rely upon that circumstance as a ground for narrowing the proposition for which *Koowarta* is authority. From that foundation the plaintiff States then seek to attack the validity of the legislation now in question. In particular, the Solicitor-General for Victoria contended for a criterion of validity which resembled that adopted by Stephen J or alternatively that of the minority judges in *Koowarta*. He submitted that, even upon this limited footing, the result in the *Tasmanian Dam Case*[114] would have been the same. Therefore, the submission proceeded, there was no occasion to seek leave to reopen the correctness of the *Tasmanian Dam Case*.

The difficulty in the path of these submissions is that subsequently the majority in the *Tasmanian Dam Case* adopted the broader view. It is not to the point that

---

110. *R v Burgess; Ex parte Henry* (1936) 55 CLR 608, 687.
111. *Ex parte Henry* (1936) 55 CLR 608, 680–681; see to similar effect the comments of Wilson J in *Koowarta v Bjelke-Petersen* (1982) 153 CLR 168, 248–249.
112. *Koowarta v Bjelke-Petersen* (1982) 153 CLR 168.
113. Ibid, 216–217.
114. *Tasmanian Dam Case* (1983) 158 CLR 1.

the same result might have been achieved by application of the view previously taken by Stephen J. It is to seek to distort the principles of *stare decisis* and of *ratio decidendi*[115] to contend that a decision lacks authority because it might have been reached upon a different path of legal reasoning to that which was actually followed. That would be to replace what was decided by that which might have been decided. According to basic constitutional principle, and with qualifications not presently relevant, the intrusion of Commonwealth law into a field that has hitherto been the preserve of State law is not a reason to deny validity to the Commonwealth law provided it is, in truth, a law with respect to external affairs.

Of course the scope of the legislative power is not confined to the implementation of treaties. The modern doctrine as to the scope of the power conferred by s 51(xxix) was adopted in *Polyukhovich v The Commonwealth*.[116] Dawson J expressed the doctrine in these terms:[117]

> [T]he power extends to places, persons, matters or things physically external to Australia. The word 'affairs' is imprecise, but is wide enough to cover places, persons, matters or things. The word 'external' is precise and is unqualified. If a place, person, matter or thing lies outside the geographical limits of the country, then it is external to it and falls within the meaning of the phrase 'external affairs'.

Similar statements of the doctrine are to be found in the reasons for judgment of other Justices: Mason CJ,[118] Deane J,[119] Gaudron J[120] and McHugh J.[121] They must now be taken as representing the view of the Court.

In accordance with the principles of constitutional interpretation, the phrase 'external affairs' is to be construed with all the generality which the words admit.[122] And, as Brennan J pointed out in the *Tasmanian Dam Case*:[123]

> The application of that canon of construction to the affirmative grants of paramount legislative powers gives the Constitution a dynamic force which is incompatible with a static constitutional balance. The complexity of modern commercial, economic, social and political activities increases the connections between particular aspects of those activities and the heads of Commonwealth power and carries an expanding range of those activities into the sphere of Commonwealth legislative competence. This phenomenon is nowhere more manifest than in the field of external affairs.
>
> ...
>
> It would be a tenable proposition that legislation purporting to implement a treaty does not operate upon the subject which is an aspect of external affairs unless the legislation complies with all the obligations assumed under the

---

115. As to the distinction between these principles, see *Re Tyler; Ex parte Foley* (1994) 181 CLR 18, 37–38; cf as to *stare decisis* in constitutional law decisions of the United States Supreme Court, *Payne v Tennessee* (1991) 501 US 808, 827–830, 842–844, 848–855; *Seminole Tribe of Florida v Florida* (1996) 64 LW 4167, 4172–4173.
116. *Polyukhovich v Commonwealth* (1991) 172 CLR 501.
117. Ibid, 632.
118. Ibid, 528–531.
119. Ibid, 599–603.
120. Ibid, 695–696.
121. Ibid, 712–714.
122. *R v Coldham; Ex parte Australian Social Welfare Union* (1983) 153 CLR 297, 314; *Jumbunna Coal Mine NL v Victorian Coal Miners' Association* (1908) 6 CLR 309, 367–368.
123. *Tasmanian Dam Case* (1983) 158 CLR 1, 221.

treaty. That appears to have been the view taken by Evatt and McTiernan JJ in *R v Burgess; Ex parte Henry*.[124] But the *Tasmanian Dam Case* and later authorities confirm that this is not an essential requirement of validity.[125]

In the *Tasmanian Dam Case,* the Wilderness Regulations that were under attack implemented only in part the supporting Convention. They were nevertheless upheld. A criterion of validity expressed in *R v Burgess; Ex parte Henry* namely, whether the Regulations could fairly be regarded as 'sufficiently stamped with the purpose of carrying out the terms of the convention',[126] was applied by Brennan J.[127] Deane J dealt as follows with 'partial' legislative implementation:[128]

> It is competent for the Parliament, in a law under s 51(xxix), partly to carry a treaty into effect or partly to discharge treaty obligations leaving it to the States or to other Commonwealth legislative or executive action to carry into effect or discharge the outstanding provisions or obligations or leaving the outstanding provisions or obligations unimplemented or unperformed. On the other hand, if the relevant law 'partially' implements the treaty in the sense that it contains provisions which are consistent with the terms of the treaty and also contains significant provisions which are inconsistent with those terms, it would be extremely unlikely that the law could properly be characterised as a law with respect to external affairs on the basis that it was capable of being reasonably considered to be appropriate and adapted to giving effect to the treaty.

Deficiency in implementation of a supporting Convention is not necessarily fatal to the validity of a law; but a law will be held invalid if the deficiency is so substantial as to deny the law the character of a measure implementing the Convention or it is a deficiency which, when coupled with other provisions of the law, make it substantially inconsistent with the Convention.

The Court held some of the amendments valid, some valid if read down, and others invalid as exceeding the Commonwealth's external affairs power.

3.49 As the judgment in the *ILO Case* also establishes, it is not necessary that legislation implementing a treaty should enact all the obligations assumed under that treaty. Partial implementation will be sufficient to bring the legislation within s 51(xxix), provided it is 'sufficiently stamped with the purpose of carrying out the terms of the convention' and does not contain provisions inconsistent with the obligations undertaken under the treaty.

3.50 Although the Commonwealth's power to legislatively implement treaties or recommendations of international organisations under s 51(xxix) is broad, it is not without limits. The restrictions on the Commonwealth's power were succinctly summarised by Deane J in the *Tasmanian Dam Case:*[129]

---

124. *R v Burgess; Ex parte Henry* (1936) 55 CLR 608, 688.
125. See *Tasmanian Dam Case* (1983) 158 CLR 1, 172, 233–234, 268; *Chu Kheng Lim v Minister for Immigration* (1992) 176 CLR 1, 75.
126. *Ex parte Henry* (1936) 55 CLR 608, 688.
127. *Tasmanian Dam Case* (1983) 158 CLR 1, 234.
128. Ibid, 268.
129. Ibid, 259–260. Footnotes in this extract refer to sources cited in the judgment.

[A] law cannot properly be characterized as a law with respect to external affairs if its direct operation is upon a domestic subject-matter which is not in itself within the ambit of external affairs and if it lacks the particular operation which is said to justify such characterization. Thus, a law would not properly be characterized as a law with respect to external affairs if it failed to carry into effect or to comply with the particular provisions of a treaty which it was said to execute (see *Burgess' Case*; *Airlines of N.S.W.* [No. 2]) or if the treaty which the law was said to carry into effect was demonstrated to be no more than a device to attract domestic legislative power: *Burgess' Case*;[130] *Koowarta*.[131] More importantly, while the question of what is the appropriate method of achieving a desired result is a matter for the Parliament and not for the Court (see *Poole* [No. 2];[132] *Airlines of N.S.W.* [No. 2][133]), the law must be capable of being reasonably considered to be appropriate and adapted to achieving what is said to impress it with the character of a law with respect to external affairs; cf. per Starke J., speaking of the scope of the regulation-making power, in *Burgess' Case*[134] and in *Poole* [No. 2],[135] and per Barwick C.J. in *Airlines of N.S.W.* [No. 2].[136]

3.51   Although it is not necessary for the Commonwealth to demonstrate the existence of a 'matter of international concern', if a treaty is merely a sham or 'device' to exercise legislative power then it would be most unlikely to support a valid exercise of power under s 51(xxix). According to Brennan J in the *Tasmanian Dam Case*:[137]

[A] treaty obligation stamps the subject of the obligation with the character of an external affair unless there is some reason to think that the treaty had been entered into merely to give colour to an attempt to confer legislative power upon the Commonwealth Parliament. Only in such a case is it necessary to look at the subject-matter of the treaty, the manner of its formation, the extent of international participation in it and the nature of the obligations it imposes in order to ascertain whether there is an international obligation truly binding on Australia.

3.52   It is to be expected that a very heavy burden of proof would lie upon any party attempting to establish that the Commonwealth had entered into a treaty or other international obligation merely as an artificial device in order to acquire the appearance of legislative power under s 51(xxix) of the Constitution. Unless that burden is met, any treaty obligation will enliven the Commonwealth's external affairs power.

Implementation of customary international law

3.53   Section 51(xxix) of the Constitution does not restrict the Commonwealth to the enactment of legislation with respect to 'treaties'.

---

130. *R v Burgess; Ex parte Henry* (1936) 55 CLR 608, 687, 642, 669.
131. *Koowarta v Bjelke-Petersen* (1982) 153 CLR 168, 231, 260.
132. *Poole (No 2)* (1939) 61 CLR 644, 647–648, 655.
133. *Airlines of NSW Pty Ltd v New South Wales (No 2)* (1965) 113 CLR 136.
134. *R v Burgess; Ex parte Henry* (1936) 55 CLR 608, 659–660.
135. *Poole (No 2)* (1939) 61 CLR 644, 647.
136. *Airlines of NSW Pty Ltd v New South Wales (No 2)* (1965) 113 CLR 136, 86.
137. *Tasmanian Dam Case* (1983) 158 CLR 1, 218–219. Semble Brennan J in *Koowarta v Bjelke-Petersen* (1982) 153 CLR 168, 259–260.

Rather, it authorises Commonwealth legislation with respect to 'external affairs'. As the *ILO Case* indicates, this extends to legislating in order to give effect to the recommendations of international organisations. Does it also extend to authorise legislation giving effect to customary international law?

In *Koowarta v Bjelke-Petersen*,[138] Stephen J agreed with the majority that Australia's participation in the Convention for the Elimination of All Forms of Racial Discrimination engaged the external affairs power under the Constitution in such a way as to justify the *Racial Discrimination Act 1975* (Cth). To this he added the following observations:[139]

> Even were Australia not a party to the Convention, this would not necessarily exclude the topic as a part of its external affairs. It was contended on behalf of the Commonwealth that, quite apart from the Convention, Australia has an international obligation to suppress all forms of racial discrimination because respect for human dignity and fundamental rights, and thus the norm of non-discrimination on the grounds of race, is now part of customary international law, as both created and evidenced by state practice and as expounded by jurists and eminent publicists. There is, in my view, much to be said for this submission and for the conclusion that, the Convention apart, the subject of racial discrimination should be regarded as an important aspect of Australia's external affairs, so that legislation much in the present form of the Racial Discrimination Act would be supported by power conferred by s. 51(xxix). As with slavery and genocide, the failure of a nation to take steps to suppress racial discrimination has become of immediate relevance to its relations within the international community.

It would, furthermore, be anomalous if customary international law binding on Australia could be adopted as part of the Australian common law by a process of judicial recognition, but could not be imported into Australian law by Commonwealth statute. It would therefore seem that s 51(xxix) empowers the Commonwealth to enact legislation giving effect to customary international law.

International law and executive discretion

3.54   It is conceivable that a conventional obligation binding on Australia could affect the exercise of administrative discretions by Australian public authorities. In particular, it is conceivable that participation by Australia in a treaty could give rise to a legitimate expectation that executive discretion will be exercised in a way which conforms to Australia's international treaty obligations. Failure to comply with those obligations would, on this view, violate legitimate expectations in Australian administrative law, unless the person adversely affected by the decision were first given an opportunity to present a case against the decision maker's proposed departure from Australia's conventional obligations.

---

138. *Koowarta v Bjelke-Petersen* (1982) 153 CLR 168.
139. Ibid, 220.

In **Minister for Immigration and Ethnic Affairs v Teoh,**[140] a Malaysian national arrived in Australia on a temporary entry permit in May 1988. The following month, he married an Australian citizen by whom he fathered three children. At the time of the marriage, his wife also had four children from previous relationships. He applied for a permanent entry permit and, while that application was pending, was convicted of drug-related offences and sentenced to six years' imprisonment. His application for a permanent entry permit was denied on the basis that his criminal convictions caused him to fail the policy requirement that applicants be of good character. In reaching this decision, the Minister did not take into account Australia's obligations under the Convention on the Rights of the Child (CRC), Art 3(1) of which provides: 'In all actions concerning children, whether undertaken by public or private social welfare institutions, courts of law, administrative authorities or legislative bodies, the best interests of the child shall be a primary consideration.' The CRC had not been incorporated into Australian law by legislation. The applicant was unsuccessful before the Federal Court of Australia, but successfully appealed to the Full Court of the Federal Court. The Minister brought a further appeal to the High Court of Australia, where the applicant argued that the Minister had denied him procedural fairness by not giving him an opportunity to comment on the Minister's departure from Art 3(1) of the CRC.

> Mason CJ and Deane J:[141] ... Junior counsel for the appellant contended that a convention ratified by Australia but not incorporated into our law could never give rise to a legitimate expectation. No persuasive reason was offered to support this far-reaching proposition. The fact that the provisions of the Convention do not form part of our law is a less than compelling reason — legitimate expectations are not equated to rules or principles of law. Moreover, ratification by Australia of an international convention is not to be dismissed as a merely platitudinous or ineffectual act,[142] particularly when the instrument evidences internationally accepted standards to be applied by courts and administrative authorities in dealing with basic human rights affecting the family and children. Rather, ratification of a convention is a positive statement by the executive government of this country to the world and to the Australian people that the executive government and its agencies will act in accordance with the Convention. That positive statement is an adequate foundation for a legitimate expectation, absent statutory or executive indications to the contrary, that administrative decision-makers will act in conformity with the Convention[143] and treat the best interests of the children as 'a primary consideration'. It is not necessary that a person seeking to set up such a legitimate expectation should be aware of the Convention or should personally entertain the expectation; it is enough that the expectation is reasonable in the sense that there are adequate materials to support it. ...
>
> The existence of a legitimate expectation that a decision-maker will act in a particular way does not necessarily compel him or her to act in that way. That is the difference between a legitimate expectation and a binding rule of law. To regard a legitimate expectation as requiring the decision-maker to act in a particular way is tantamount to treating it as a rule of law. It incorporates the provisions of the unincorporated convention into our municipal law by the back door. ...

---

140. *Minister for Immigration and Ethnic Affairs v Teoh* (1995) 183 CLR 273.
141. Ibid, 290–292. Subsequent footnotes in this extract refer to sources cited in the judgment.
142. See *Minister for Foreign Affairs and Trade v Magno* (1992) 37 FCR 298, 343; *Tavita v Minister of Immigration* [1994] 2 NZLR 257, 266.
143. Cf *Simsek v Macphee* (1982) 148 CLR 636, 644.

But, if a decision-maker proposes to make a decision inconsistent with a legitimate expectation, procedural fairness requires that the persons affected should be given notice and an adequate opportunity of presenting a case against the taking of such a course. So, here, if the delegate proposed to give a decision which did not accord with the principle that the best interests of the children were to be a primary consideration, procedural fairness called for the delegate to take the steps just indicated.

The Court held (Mason CJ, Deane, Toohey and Gaudron JJ, McHugh J dissenting) that the appeal should be allowed on the basis that that the Minister had denied procedural fairness to the applicant by not providing him with an opportunity to comment on the proposed departure from Australia's obligations under Art 3(1) of the CRC.

3.55 In order to circumvent successful pleas that legitimate expectations have been violated, the Minister for Foreign Affairs and the Attorney-General issued a joint statement on 10 May 1995 which included the declaration: 'It is not legitimate, for the purpose of applying Australian law, to expect that the provisions of a treaty not incorporated by legislation should be applied by decision-makers.' After a change of government, the new Minister for Foreign Affairs and the Attorney-General issued a joint statement to similar effect on 25 February 1997. Some courts expressed scepticism as to the effectiveness of these declarations to deprive persons of their *Teoh*-style legitimate expectations.[144] The Commonwealth government also introduced three Bills into Parliament with the intention of removing this new species of legitimate expectation, but they all lapsed.[145]

3.56 The existence of *Teoh*-style legitimate expectations has remained controversial. In particular, there are questions from the perspective of administrative law as to how a person can have a legitimate expectation arising from a matter or state of affairs of which he or she is in fact ignorant. Furthermore, and contrary to the denial of Mason CJ and Deane J, it appears that this new species of legitimate expectations crosses the line which prevents a treaty from producing legal rights and obligations in Australian law without legislative incorporation.

3.57 Doubt has been cast on the correctness of this aspect of *Teoh* in a more recent decision of the High Court. In *Re Minister for Immigration and Multicultural Affairs; Ex parte Lam*,[146] McHugh and Gummow JJ said:

---

144. *Wu v Minister for Immigration and Multicultural Affairs* (1996) 64 FCR 245; *Department of Immigration and Ethnic Affairs v Ram* (1996) 69 FCR 431; *Browne v Minister for Immigration and Multicultural Affairs* (1998) 52 ALD 550; *Tien v Minister for Immigration and Multicultural Affairs* (1998) 53 ALD 32. Cf *Baldini v Minister for Immigration and Multicultural Affairs* (2000) 115 A Crim R 307.
145. Administrative Decisions (Effect of International Instruments) Bill 1995 (Cth), Administrative Decisions (Effect of International Instruments) Bill 1997 (Cth), and Administrative Decisions (Effect of International Instruments) Bill 1999 (Cth).
146. *Re Minister for Immigration and Multicultural Affairs; Ex parte Lam* (2003) 214 CLR 1, 98–102. Footnotes in this extract refer to sources cited in the judgment.

If *Teoh* is to have continued significance at a general level for the principles which inform the relationship between international obligations and the domestic constitutional structure, then further attention will be required to the basis upon which *Teoh* rests. The case involved ratification by the Executive of a treaty which had not been followed by any relevant exercise of legislative power to make laws with respect to external affairs. It was remarked in the *Industrial Relations Act Case*[147] [that is, the *ILO Case*] that there may be some treaties with a subject-matter identified in terms of aspiration which cannot enliven the power conferred by s 51(xxix) of the Constitution. But that does not necessarily mean that the executive act of ratification is to be dismissed as platitudinous; an international responsibility to the contracting state parties or other international institutions has been created.

In any event, it was not suggested that *Teoh* concerned a treaty of this limited nature. However, in general, ratification, as an executive act, did not in the domestic constitutional structure thereby confer rights upon citizens or impose liabilities upon them.[148] In that sense the ratified treaty was not 'self-executing' and lacked 'direct application' in that domestic system.

Nevertheless, in various respects, an unincorporated treaty, left in that state, may be invoked in various ways in the conduct of domestic affairs. For example, a peace treaty will, without legislation, change the status of enemy aliens in Australian courts.[149] Further, the taking of a step by the executive government in the conduct of external affairs, whilst of itself neither creating rights nor imposing liabilities, may supply a step in a broader process of resolution of justiciable disputes.[150] The so-called 'disguised extradition' cases are an example.[151] The treatment of public policy objections in the conflict of laws may be another.[152] More frequently encountered are the rules of statutory interpretation which favour construction which is in conformity and not in conflict with Australia's international obligations; this matter was discussed by Mason CJ and Deane J in *Teoh* (1995) 183 CLR 273 at 287–288. It is with such influences as these in domestic law that American scholars have been concerned in distinguishing, under the United States system, between 'self-executing' treaties and their 'invocability' without direct application.[153]

---

147. *Victoria v Commonwealth (ILO Case)* (1996) 187 CLR 416, 486.
148. Ibid, 480–482.
149. *Porter v Freudenberg* [1915] 1 KB 857, 871, 880; cf *Schering AG v Pharmedica Pty Ltd* (1950) 52 SR (NSW) 16.
150. *Re Ditfort; Ex parte Deputy Commissioner of Taxation* (1988) 19 FCR 347, 370.
151. See *Schlieske v Minister for Immigration and Ethnic Affairs* (1988) 84 ALR 719. Other examples are given in Mark Leeming, 'Federal treaty jurisdiction' (1999) 10 *Public Law Review* 173; see also Leslie Zines, *Cowen and Zines's Federal Jurisdiction in Australia*, 3rd ed, 2002 at 29–30.
152. See, for example, *Regie National des Usines Renault SA v Zhang* (2002) 76 ALJR 551, 562 [56]–[57]; 187 ALR 1, 16; *Kuwait Airways Corporation v Iraqi Airways Co (Nos 4 and 5)* [2002] 2 WLR 1353, 1363 [29], 1383–1384 [114], 1390 [137], 1393 [148]; [2002] 3 All ER 209, 219, 238, 245, 247.
153. Stefan A Riesenfeld, 'International agreements' (1989) 14 *Yale Journal of International Law* 455, 462–67; John Jackson, 'Status of treaties in domestic legal systems: a policy analysis' (1992) 86 *American Journal of International Law* 310, 315–19.

However, in the case law a line has been drawn which limits the normative effect of what are unenacted international obligations upon discretionary decision-making under powers conferred by statute and without specification of those obligations. The judgments in *Teoh* accepted the established doctrine that such obligations are not mandatory relevant considerations attracting judicial review for jurisdictional error. The curiosity is that, nevertheless, such matters are to be treated, if *Teoh* be taken as establishing any general proposition in this area, as mandatory relevant considerations for that species of judicial review concerned with procedural fairness.

The reasoning which as a matter of principle would sustain such an erratic application of 'invocation' doctrine remains for analysis and decision. Basic questions of the interaction between the three branches of government are involved. One consideration is that, under the Constitution (s 61), the task of the Executive is to execute and maintain statute law which confers discretionary powers upon the Executive. It is not for the judicial branch to add to or vary the content of those powers by taking a particular view of the conduct by the Executive of external affairs.[154] Rather, it is for the judicial branch to declare and enforce the limits of the power conferred by statute upon administrative decision-makers, but not, by reference to the conduct of external affairs, to supplement the criteria for the exercise of that power.

The validity of *Teoh*-style legitimate expectations in Australian administrative law therefore remains to be finally determined. If the view advanced by McHugh and Gummow JJ in *Lam* is correct, it would exclude the existence of *Teoh*-style legitimate expectations in both Commonwealth and state administrative law.

Question

Roger spends most weekends in the rivers, creeks and estuaries of country Victoria fishing for a species known as the golden catfish.

In January last year, the United Nations Convention for the Conservation of Freshwater Fish (CCFF) entered into force upon ratification by Australia. Article 2 of the CCFF provides that 'all State parties agree to make it a criminal offence to catch any of the fish species listed in Annex A'. Included in Annex A — among many other species, several of which are found in Australia — is the golden catfish. The definition of the offence in Art 2 makes it clear that it does not extend to catching fish in estuaries. The CCFF has 40 State parties. The opinions of eminent publicists in international law are sharply divided as to whether any part of the CCFF has attained the status of customary international law.

The Attorney-General has indicated his intention in January next year to introduce the Golden Catfish Preservation Bill into the Commonwealth Parliament. The Bill is expressed to implement the CCFF in Australia

---

154. Cf *Simsek v Macphee* (1982) 148 CLR 636, 641–642.

and, if passed in its current form, will make it a criminal offence to catch a golden catfish in Australia. In its current form, the Bill does not seek to prohibit or restrict the catching of any other fish species listed in Annex A of the CCFF.

The definition of the offence in the Bill is ambiguous as to whether it extends to catching fish in river estuaries, but otherwise unambiguously extends to catching golden catfish in rivers and creeks. The offence will be prosecuted before a Magistrate's Court and subject to a maximum penalty of $1,000 or three months' imprisonment. There is currently no prohibition on the catching or killing of golden catfish in any Commonwealth or Victorian legislation.

One weekend last month, Roger caught 20 golden catfish in a creek near Bendigo. After a report of Roger's feat in a local newspaper, a wildlife conservation activist took out a summons from the Bendigo Magistrate's Court against Roger on a charge of 'catching and killing golden catfish contrary to law'.

Roger seeks your advice on two questions:

- Is there currently any offence in Australia of 'catching and killing golden catfish contrary to law'? Would your answer be different if there was a consensus among eminent publicists that Art 2 of the CCFF has crystallised into a rule of customary international law? (You may assume that, if there is such an offence as specified in the summons, there are no procedural or jurisdictional issues preventing a trial before the Bendigo Magistrate's Court.)

- Will he be at liberty to continue catching golden catfish after the passage and entry into force of the Golden Catfish Preservation Bill? (You may assume that the CCFF provides the only basis upon which the Commonwealth could enact the Bill.)

Suggested answer

With regard to the first question, the CCFF, as a treaty, cannot be a source of legal rights or obligations in Australian domestic law without incorporation by legislation *(Dietrich; Teoh; ILO Case)*. The Golden Catfish Preservation Bill is yet to be enacted. There is currently no prohibition on the catching or killing of golden catfish in Commonwealth or Victorian legislation. Therefore, if Roger has committed an offence, it must be under the common law.

Customary international law is not part of the Australian common law, but it is one of the sources of the Australian common law. A rule of customary international law which has been universally recognised may be applied in Australian courts. However, an asserted but contentious rule of customary international law will not be applied in Australian law *(Chow Hung Ching)*. The prohibition on catching golden catfish appears, at best, to be a contentious rule of international law and will not be applied as part of the common law in Australian courts.

Even if there was a consensus as to the existence of a customary international law rule requiring States to prohibit the catching of golden catfish, it would not automatically apply as part of the common law in Australia. The Australian common law will not draw on the source of customary international law if the international rule in question is inconsistent with either an essential or a 'skeletal' principle of the common law or the 'contemporary values of the Australian people' *(Mabo)*. The presumption of *nullum crimen sine lege* is simultaneously an essential or 'skeletal' common law principle and, very arguably, situated firmly among the contemporary values of the Australian people *(Nulyarimma)*. This presumption operates to avoid criminal liability for conduct which was lawful at the time in which it was engaged. There is currently no legislative or common law prohibition on catching golden catfish. Consequently, the CCFF notwithstanding, there is no offence of 'catching golden catfish contrary to law'.

With regard to the second question, the Golden Catfish Preservation Bill will be effective to restrict Roger's liberty to catch golden catfish only if it is enacted pursuant to a valid Commonwealth legislative power. Section 51(xxix) of the Constitution empowers the Commonwealth to legislate with respect to 'external affairs'.

It is very arguable that the conservation of catfish in Australia's internal waters is not a matter of legitimate international concern. However, the very fact that such conservation is the subject of an international convention will be enough to bring it within the Commonwealth's external affairs power *(Richardson; ILO Case)*, unless Australia's participation is a mere sham or device in order to acquire legislative power *(Tasmanian Dam Case)*. The burden of proof to establish such a motive will be very heavy, and the fact that the CCFF is a United Nations convention with 40 States parties is almost certainly enough to dispel any suggestion that the treaty's subject matter is a mere device to confer legislative power on the Commonwealth.

It is to be noted that the Bill only partially implements the CCFF. Whereas the CCFF prohibits the catching of many species of fish found in Australia, the Bill prohibits the catching of only one species. It is not, however, necessary that legislation implementing a treaty should enact all the obligations assumed under that treaty. Partial implementation will be sufficient to bring the legislation within s 51(xxix), provided it is 'sufficiently stamped with the purpose of carrying out the terms of the convention' and does not contain provisions inconsistent with the obligations undertaken under the treaty *(ILO Case)*. Although the Bill only partially implements the CCFF, it does not appear to contain any provisions otherwise inconsistent with the CCFF. Enactment of the Bill would not, therefore, be removed from the ambit of the external affairs power on the basis of only partial implementation of the CCFF.

If the Golden Catfish Preservation Bill is enacted in its current form and validly enters onto force, it will prohibit the catching of golden catfish in rivers and creeks. The Bill is, however, ambiguous as to whether it will prohibit the catching of golden catfish in estuaries.

Where Commonwealth legislation refers to a treaty, it is permissible to consider that treaty in order to resolve an ambiguity in the legislation

(*Acts Interpretation Act 1901* (Cth), s 15AB). Furthermore, '[w]here a statute ... is ambiguous, the courts should favour that construction which accords with Australia's obligations under a treaty or international convention to which Australia is a party, at least in those cases in which the legislation is enacted after, or in contemplation of, entry into, or ratification of, the relevant international instrument' (*Teoh*, per Mason CJ and Deane J).

Even if, as seems almost certain, the Bill's enactment would be a valid exercise of legislative power by the Commonwealth, it would probably not operate to prohibit the catching of golden catfish in estuaries. Roger would not, however, remain at liberty to catch golden catfish in rivers and creeks.

Further tutorial discussion

1. In its stance towards international law, Australia adopts a predominantly dualist position. Why only 'predominantly'? Would Australia be better served by strengthening the monist or dualist aspects of its stance towards international law?

2. Rules of customary international law having *jus cogens* status should always be automatically assimilated to the Australian common law. Do you agree?

3. Why should customary international law be more readily assimilated to the common law than to conventional law?

4. Rules of customary international law having *jus cogens* status should take priority in Australian domestic law over inconsistent legislation. Do you agree?

5. Section 51(xxix) of the Constitution, without the safeguard of 'international concern', has the potential to reduce the Australian states to legislative irrelevance. Do you agree?

6. Were McHugh and Gummow JJ in *Lam* justified in casting doubt on the version of legitimate expectation postulated by Mason CJ and Deane J in *Teoh*?

Statehood and personality

4

Objectives

After completing this chapter, you should:

(1) understand the nature of and requirement for legal personality in international law;

(2) understand and be able to explain the customary international law criteria for statehood, with particular emphasis on the requirements of independent and effective government and capacity to enter into international relations;

(3) appreciate the non-juridical but evidentially significant nature of recognition of States, and the circumstances in which non-recognition of States is juridically required;

(4) understand the impact of the 'Estrada doctrine' on recognition of governments;

(5) understand the historical evolution of and be able to apply the principle of self-determination of peoples to claims of independent statehood in various contexts;

(6) know how to determine whether, and to what extent, an international public organisation possesses international legal personality; and

(7) appreciate and be able to explain how, and the extent to which, individuals can be subjects of international law.

Key cases

Aaland Islands case, LNOJ Special Supplement No 3 (1920)
Customs Régime between Germany and Austria (Protocol of March 19th, 1931) advisory opinion, PCIJ Rep (1931) Ser A/B No 41
Tinoco Arbitration (Great Britain v Costa Rica) (1923) 1 RIAA 369
Reference re Secession of Quebec [1998] 2 SCR 217
Reparation for Injuries Suffered in the Service of the United Nations advisory opinion, ICJ Rep (1949) 174

Key treaties and instruments

Convention on Rights and Duties of States, adopted by the Seventh International Conference of American States (Montevideo Convention) (1933): Art 1, Art 3
Charter of the United Nations (1945): Art 1(2), Art 55, Art 56
Declaration on the Granting of Independence to Colonial Territories and Peoples, General Assembly Resolution 1514 (XV) (1960): Arts 1–7

Principles which should guide Members in determining whether or not an obligation exists to transmit the information called for under Article 73 e of the Charter, General Assembly Resolution 1541 (XV) (1960): Principle IV, Principle V
International Covenant on Civil and Political Rights (ICCPR) (1966): Art 1
International Covenant on Economic, Social and Cultural Rights (ICESCR) (1966): Art 1
Declaration on Principles of International Law Concerning Friendly Relations and Co-operation among States in Accordance with the Charter of the United Nations, General Assembly Resolution 2625 (XXV) (1970)
Declaration on the Rights of Persons Belonging to National or Ethnic, Religious and Linguistic Minorities, General Assembly Resolution 47/135 (1992)
Final Report and Recommendations of an International Meeting of Experts on the Further Study of the Concept of the Rights of People for UNESCO, SNS 89/Conf 602/7 (1990)

Concept of personality

4.1 Every modern legal system possesses a concept of legal personality. Personality is a legal category under which entities may be assigned various combinations of legal rights, duties, powers, obligations and capacities. An entity which possesses any combination of such attributes also possesses legal personality. It is not, therefore, very instructive simply to say that a particular entity possesses legal personality. Such a statement reveals only that the entity possesses some combination of attributes, without indicating the extent of the attribution. The entity's capacity within the legal order might be complete, or it might be extremely limited.

In most domestic legal orders, individuals (or 'natural persons') are the entities who enjoy the most extensive legal personality. Unless they are subject to some special limitation (for example, minority, insanity, imprisonment, and so on), individuals are typically capable of exercising or acquiring the full range of rights, duties, powers and obligations available within a domestic legal order. In many national legal orders, this total package of capacities is described as 'citizenship', which only individuals may enjoy. Other entities are often granted more limited forms of legal personality. Incorporated and unincorporated associations, some government agencies, and the State itself are also frequently accorded a form of legal personality. Their legal capacities are generally more limited. They are never given the capacity, for instance, to marry, vote, seek election to public office, or make a testamentary disposition. Nor are they capable of being imprisoned (though they may often be dissolved or fined). Nevertheless, they are often capable of suing and being sued, acquiring and disposing of property, incurring and acquiring tortious and contractual obligations and rights, and supporting many other legal capacities also applicable to individuals.

4.2 In the international legal system, States are the most important subjects. States are independent countries. They are the entities which bear the most extensive form of legal personality. As the international legal system is currently constituted, States are also the sole generators of international law. All rules and principles of international law are the result of treaties between States, of State activity which generates custom, or of general principles which emerge within the framework provided by the legal orders of States. States are free to confer legal personality on other entities. This frequently occurs when States conclude a treaty establishing an international organisation.

These sorts of treaties usually result in the conferral of a limited range of legal capacities on the organisation.[1] Since the Second World War, States have also concluded a number of important treaties which have conferred limited legal personality on individuals.[2]

4.3 Every legal system contains rules about which entities are entitled to possess a legal personality, and the extent to which the conferred personality results in the attribution of legal capacities. International law stipulates that all States possess legal personality and that their capacity is complete. This stipulation does not, however, identify which entities are to be regarded as 'States'. International law has rules which serve to identify which entities are entitled to statehood.[3]

The decentralised and highly political character of the international society of States means that an entity which claims to be a State might have its putative statehood denied by one or more other States. Similarly, the right of a State's putative government to govern that State might be denied by another State. In international law, this failure or refusal to recognise another entity as a State or to recognise the legitimacy of its effective government is also subject to certain rules.[4]

Elements of statehood

4.4 The classical criteria for determining whether an entity possesses legal personality in international law are conveniently set out in Art 1 of the 1933 Convention on Rights and Duties of States adopted by the Seventh International Conference of American States (Montevideo Convention):[5]

> The State as a person of international law should possess the following qualifications: a) a permanent population; b) a defined territory; c) government; and d) capacity to enter into relations with other States.

The Montevideo Convention was adopted in 1933 by an international conference of States in North America and South America. The United States and 14 Latin American States are party to it. Notwithstanding this rather limited participation in the Convention, Art 1 is widely regarded as codifying the customary requirements for statehood as they stood at the time of the Convention's adoption. These requirements remain valid

---

1.   See **4.57–4.61**.
2.   See **4.62–4.70**.
3.   See **4.4–4.17**.
4.   See **4.18–4.36**.
5.   LNTS, Vol 165, p 19.

today, although it is sometimes suggested that additional customary criteria have since emerged. These additional criteria are, however, better regarded as relevant to issues of recognition of statehood rather than the existence of statehood.[6]

Permanent population

4.5 States cannot exist without people. Indeed, a State is primarily a legal construct which facilitates the establishment and maintenance of a system of government by, for or over a group of people. It is not necessary that the number of people be very large. Seychelles and Nauru are States with populations of 80,000 and 13,000 respectively.

The Vatican City (whose government is the Holy See) is also a State and has a permanent population of only around 1,000. Although a population need only be small, it must be permanent. Thus, Antarctica, with its entirely transient population of mainly scientists and tourists, cannot be a State.

Defined territory

4.6 States are territorial units. An essential attribute of statehood is that the State is entitled to exercise territorial sovereignty — that is, it has the right to exercise official authority within a given territory to the exclusion of any other State without the territorial State's consent.

There are many territorial disputes in the world. The fact that a State's borders are disputed does not mean that it lacks a 'defined territory'. It is enough that a State's territory possesses a 'sufficient consistency, even though its boundaries have not yet been accurately delimited'.[7]

Government

4.7 Every State must possess a government. There is no requirement that the government be established according to any particular constitutional pattern. Hence, the absence of an independent judiciary or of clearly identifiable legislative and executive branches is no barrier to satisfying this criterion. Nor is there, as yet, a requirement that the government be elected by or answerable to the population. Accordingly, States may be constitutional democracies, absolute monarchies, personal autocracies, oligarchies, one-party dictatorships, or theocracies.

The requirement of government is satisfied when two conditions are met. First, the administering authority must exercise effective control over a defined territory. Second, it must be independent in the sense that it is not subject to control by any other State or external political power.

---

6. See **4.23–4.26**.
7. *Deutsche Continental Gas-Gesellschaft v Polish State* (1929) 5 AD 11, 15.

4.8   The circumstances in which the requirement of effective control is satisfied were addressed in 1920 by the International Committee of Jurists in the course of reporting on a dispute between Finland and Sweden concerning sovereignty over the Aaland Islands. A material issue in the dispute was the date on which Finland attained independence from Russia in the aftermath of the Bolshevik coup in November 1917.

In the ***Aaland Islands case***,[8] the Finnish Diet (parliament) declared Finland's independence from Russia in December 1917. This declaration met with significant resistance from within Finland itself, and a civil war erupted. For several months, the pro-independence authorities asserted their control over the territory of Finland only with the assistance of troops from Soviet Russia. The Committee report said:

> In the midst of revolution and anarchy certain elements essential to the existence of a State, even some elements of fact, were lacking for a fairly considerable period. Political and social life was disorganised; the authorities were not strong enough to assert themselves; civil war was rife; further, the Diet, the legality of which had been disputed by a large section of the people, had been dispersed by the revolutionary party, and the Government had been chased from the capital and forcibly prevented from carrying out its duties; the armed camps and the police were divided into two opposing forces, and Russian troops, and after a time Germans also, took part in the civil war between the inhabitants and between the Red and White Finnish troops. It is, therefore, difficult to say at what exact date the Finnish Republic, in the legal sense of the term, actually became a definitely constituted sovereign State. This certainly did not take place until a stable political organisation had been created, and until the public authorities had been strong enough to assert themselves throughout the territories of the State without the assistance of foreign troops. It would appear that it was in May 1918, that the civil war ended and that the foreign troops began to leave the country, so that from that time onwards it was possible to re-establish order and normal political and social life, little by little.

The Committee report emphasises that Finland lacked a government in the sense required for statehood, until a stable political organisation came into existence and the public authorities were able to assert themselves throughout Finland's territory without foreign assistance. It was not necessary that order and normal life should have been perfectly restored.

4.9   The requirement that an entity must have an effective government in order to possess statehood is more important in determining the existence of a new State than in deciding whether an existing State has disappeared. Once a State has come into existence, and especially after it has already attracted wide recognition of its statehood, the collapse of effective government will not generally result in a loss of statehood. This point may be demonstrated by State practice. Somalia has almost certainly lacked an effective government — and, therefore, a theoretically essential attribute of statehood — since it fell into chronic internal

---

8.   *League of Nations Official Journal*, Special Supplement No 3, 1920.

disorder in 1991. Nevertheless, it remains recognised as a State by the vast majority of States and retains its membership of the United Nations and some other international organisations. A similar point can be made about numerous other States which have endured periods of civil war.

4.10   An entity cannot be a government for the purposes of establishing statehood unless it is independent. The meaning of 'independence' for a State was examined in an advisory opinion of the Permanent Court of International Justice.

In the ***Austro-German Customs Union* advisory opinion,**[9] Austria was required by the Treaty of Saint-Germain 1919 (part of the settlement of the First World War) to refrain from any act 'which might directly or indirectly or by any means whatever compromise her independence' without the permission of the Council of the League of Nations. A protocol concluded in 1922 reinforced this obligation with specific reference to Austria's 'economic independence'. In 1931, Germany and Austria agreed to negotiate for the establishment of a customs union between the two States. There was widespread concern that such a step would be a prelude to political unification, with adverse consequences for European peace and stability. The League of Nations requested an advisory opinion from the Permanent Court of International Justice on the question of the proposed customs union's compatibility with the 1919 and 1922 treaties. Eight of the Court's 15 judges thought the customs union would violate the 1922 treaty. All but one of the judges in the majority also thought the customs union would violate the 1919 treaty. Many of the opinions, including the individual opinion of Judge Dionisio Anzilotti (1869–1950), appear to be based upon the assumption that a customs union would, or would be likely to, lead to a subsequent political union.

> Judge Anzilotti: [T]he independence of Austria within the meaning of [the Treaty of Saint-Germain] is nothing else but the existence of Austria, within the frontiers laid down by the Treaty of Saint-Germain, as a separate State and not subject to the authority of any other State or group of States. Independence as thus understood is really no more than the usual condition of States according to international law; it may also be described as *sovereignty (suprema potestas)*, or *external sovereignty*, by which is meant that the State has over it no other authority than that of international law. The conception of independence, regarded as the normal characteristic of States as subjects of international law, cannot be better defined than by comparing it with the exceptional and, to some extent, abnormal class of States known as 'dependent States'. These are States subject to the authority of one or more States. The idea of dependence therefore necessarily implies a relation between a superior State (suzerain, protector, etc.) and an inferior or subject State (vassal, *protégé*, etc.); the relation between the State which can legally impose its will and the State which is legally compelled to submit to that will. Where there is no such relation of superiority and subordination, it is impossible to speak of dependence within the meaning of international law.
>
> It follows that the legal conception of independence has nothing to do with a State's subordination to international law or with the numerous and constantly increasing states of *de facto* dependence which characterize the relation of one country to other countries.

---

9.   *Customs Régime between Germany and Austria (Protocol of March 19th, 1931)* advisory opinion, PCIJ Rep (1931) Ser A/B No 41.

It also follows that the restrictions upon a State's liberty, whether arising out of ordinary international law or contractual engagements, do not as such in the least affect its independence. As long as those restrictions do not place the State under the legal authority of another State, the former remains an independent State however extensive or burdensome those obligations may be.

4.11 An entity can be independent for the purposes of proving statehood even if it is subject to numerous and far-reaching obligations under international law. Accordingly, the fact that Australia has committed itself to more than 900 treaties does not adversely affect its character as a State. Similarly, the fact that a State is economically reliant on international trade or foreign aid for its prosperity, or even for its necessities, does not affect its independence in international law. What matters is that the entity is not legally subject to the authority of any other State. Provided an entity is formally independent and is not formally a colony, protectorate, vassal, etcetera, it will satisfy the requirement of independent government for the purposes of proving statehood. This focus on the formalities accords with modern State practice.

Thus, between 1945 and 1989, many Eastern European States were clearly mere puppets of the Soviet Union, lacking any meaningful degree of political independence from Moscow. Nevertheless, they were all eventually recognised as States by almost all other States.

The question of recognising new 'puppet' States established as the result of an act of aggression is discussed elsewhere.[10]

Capacity to enter into relations with other States

4.12 An entity which lacks the 'capacity' to enter into relations with other States will not satisfy this criterion of statehood. 'Capacity', in this context, could mean one of two things. First, it could mean that the entity possesses the political, technical, financial and other material resources necessary to establish and maintain diplomatic contact with other States. Alternatively, it could simply mean that other States are willing to deal with the entity as a State on the plane of international relations — in other words, that other States do in fact recognise the entity as a State.

4.13 State practice and most publicists overwhelmingly support the view that an entity has 'capacity' in the relevant sense if it possesses the political, technical, financial and other material resources necessary to establish and maintain diplomatic contact with other States.[11] This view reflects the 'declaratory theory' of recognition. According to this theory, recognition by other States does not create, but merely acknowledges, an entity's statehood, which arises independently of recognition.

---

10. See **4.25**.
11. For example, American Law Institute, *Restatement (Third) of the Foreign Relations Law of the United States*, 1987, Vol 1, §201, comment e.

The view that 'capacity' is missing unless other States actually recognise the entity as a State is consistent with the 'constitutive theory' of recognition. According to this theory, recognition as a State by other States is a necessary precondition for statehood; recognition is essential to constitute a State in international law. The constitutive theory is today supported by few publicists and very little State practice.

Nevertheless, the constitutive theory is not entirely otiose. The realities of international life are such that States themselves are the authorities which decide claims to statehood. If very few States recognise an entity's statehood, that will be strong evidence that the entity lacks one or more of the essential attributes of statehood. If no State extends recognition, the evidence against statehood will be practically irresistible.

4.14   The significance of non-recognition for the purposes of establishing statehood is well illustrated by the results of an international arbitration between the United Kingdom and Costa Rica by William Howard Taft (1857–1930), Chief Justice of the United States. Although the facts of the arbitration involved the non-recognition of a government, the principles discussed are equally relevant to the non-recognition of States.

In the **Tinoco Arbitration (Great Britain v Costa Rica),**[12] Federico Tinoco (1868–1931) forcibly overthrew the government of Costa Rica in 1917. After elections were held, he led a government which exercised effective control over Costa Rica. He was, in turn, forcibly overthrown in 1919. In the meantime, the Tinoco administration had granted certain concessions to British nationals and issued banknotes, some of which were held by British nationals. The post-Tinoco government repudiated the concessions and declared the banknotes invalid. The United Kingdom brought a claim against Costa Rica for the allegedly unlawful treatment to which its nationals had been subjected by the post-Tinoco government. Costa Rica replied that, as the United Kingdom had refused to recognise the legitimacy of the Tinoco government, it was now estopped from urging claims on Costa Rica arising from official acts of that government. The arbitrator said:[13]

> I must hold from the evidence … the Tinoco government was an actual sovereign government. But it is argued that many leading Powers refused to recognize the Tinoco government, and that recognition by other nations is the chief and best evidence of the birth, existence and continuity of succession of a government. Undoubtedly recognition by other Powers is an important evidential factor in establishing proof of the existence of a government in the society of nations.

After observing that 20 States had recognised the Tinoco government, the arbitrator continued:[14]

> The non-recognition by other nations of a government claiming to be a national personality, is usually appropriate evidence that it has not attained the independence and control entitling it by international law to be classed as such. But when recognition *vel non* of a government is by such nations determined by inquiry, not into its *de facto* sovereignty and complete governmental control, but into its illegitimacy or irregularity of origin, their non-recognition loses

---

12. *Tinoco Arbitration (Great Britain v Costa Rica)* (1923) 1 RIAA 369.
13. Ibid, 380.
14. Ibid, 381–382.

something of evidential weight on the issue with which those applying the rules of international law are alone concerned. … Such non-recognition for any reason, however, cannot outweigh the evidence disclosed by this record before me as to the *de facto* character of Tinoco's government, according to the standard set by international law. … The contention here [as to estoppel] … precludes a government which did not recognize a *de facto* government from appearing in an international tribunal on behalf of its nationals to claim any rights based on the acts of such government. … Here the executive of Great Britain takes the position that the Tinoco government which it did not recognize, was nevertheless a *de facto* government that could create rights in British subjects which it now seeks to protect. Of course, as already emphasized, its failure to recognize the *de facto* government can be used against it to disprove the character it now attributes to that government, but this does not bar it from changing its position.

Membership of international organisations

4.15 Membership of international organisations which admit only States will be strong evidence that an entity possesses statehood. Membership of the United Nations is taken as particularly strong evidence of statehood. The UN Charter provides that membership of the UN is:[15]

> … open to all … peace-loving states which accept the obligations contained in the present Charter and, in the judgment of the Organization, are able and willing to carry out these obligations.

The admission of a new member is effected by a decision of the General Assembly upon the recommendation of the Security Council.[16] On the other hand, non-membership should not be taken as proof that an entity lacks statehood. Italy joined the UN only in 1955, Japan in 1956, Germany in 1973, North Korea in 1991, San Marino in 1992, Monaco in 1993, Nauru in 1999 and Switzerland in 2002. All these entities were States for many years before they joined. The Vatican City is still not a UN member, but is a State nevertheless; it is a member of some other international organisations, such as the World Health Organization and the International Labour Organization.

A UN member State may also be suspended[17] or expelled[18] in certain circumstances; in neither case does this entail a loss of statehood.

Federal states and colonies

4.16 Federal states normally vest the authority to conduct international relations in the hands of the federal government. It is the federal entity which is the 'State' for the purposes of international law. Accordingly, the semi-sovereign political units which exist within a federal state (for example, New South Wales, California or Ontario) do not normally enjoy international legal personality. As a matter of State responsibility,

---

15. UN Charter, Art 4(1).
16. Ibid, Art 4(2).
17. Ibid, Art 5.
18. Ibid, Art 6.

it will be the federal state which is liable for the acts of any of the federation's constituent units in violation of international law.[19]

Exceptionally, some federal constitutions bestow upon sub-federal political units a limited capacity to enter into international treaties (for example, Germany, Russia, Switzerland and the United States). Where a federal State's constitutional order permits the sub-federal political units to make international agreements, the sub-federal unit will have legal personality to the extent necessary to realise that constitutional competence.

4.17   There are some entities which, although they possess a defined territory and population, lack both an independent government and a capacity to enter into relations with States. Colonies fall into this category, as did trust territories.[20] Colonies possess limited legal personality if the colonial power permits the local authorities in the colony to enter into treaty relations with foreign States.

Recognition of States

4.18   In international law, recognition is a particular kind of act performed by a State. Normally, it takes the form of an official announcement, formal declaration, diplomatic message or express treaty provision. A State may recognise another entity as possessing statehood, in which case the recognising State is declaring its readiness to deal with the other entity as a State on the plane of international relations. A State may also refuse or withdraw recognition of statehood, thereby signalling the non-recognising State's unwillingness to deal with the entity as a State on the plane of international relations.

4.19   An act of recognition may also occur by implication from conduct. Thus, where diplomatic or consular relations are established or where a formal treaty is concluded, each entity will be taken to have recognised the other's statehood, even without an express declaration or statement to that effect. It is also possible that a State will be taken to have impliedly recognised the statehood of an entity if the State supports, without reservation or qualification, the entity's membership of an international organisation which is open only to States.

The important point is that the State's act must clearly demonstrate an intention to recognise. State practice indicates, however, that many common forms of contact on the plane of international relations cannot be understood as involving an implied act of recognition.

Therefore, there will be no implication of recognition where:

(i)   an entity attends an international conference at which non-recognising States are present;

(ii)   a non-recognising State establishes a 'trade mission', 'liaison office' or some other non-diplomatic or non-consular contact with an entity;

---

19.   See **5.20**.
20.   See **1.49**.

(iii) a non-recognising State remains, or becomes, party to a multilateral treaty to which the entity is also a party; or

(iv) a non-recognising State remains, or becomes, a member of an international organisation of which the entity is also a member.

4.20 Some commentators have adopted the position that once an entity fulfils all the requirements of statehood, it is legally entitled to recognition as a State by other States.[21] This approach is consistent with the constitutive theory of recognition.[22]

4.21 Most publicists, however, support the view that recognition is a political and discretionary act, not a legal duty. On this view, no entity is ever entitled to recognition as a State, even if it possesses all the legal attributes of statehood. States are, therefore, as a matter of general principle, free to extend, withhold or withdraw recognition whenever they please. This view is consistent with the declaratory theory of recognition and accords with the preponderance of State practice on the subject.

Implicit in this approach is an acceptance that recognition by other States is not a juridically necessary element of statehood. Indeed the Montevideo Convention, which is widely regarded as reflecting customary law, provides at Art 3:

> The political existence of the State is independent of recognition by other States. Even before recognition the State has the right to defend its integrity and independence, to provide for its conservation and prosperity, and consequently to organise itself as it sees fit, to legislate upon its interests, administer its services, and to define the jurisdiction and competence of its courts. The exercise of these rights has no other limitations than the exercise of the rights of other States according to international law.

4.22 The understanding that recognition of statehood is a discretionary and political act explains the behaviour of non-communist States in accepting the statehood of most, but not all, East European countries during part of the Cold War. Most of the East European countries lacked a truly independent government because of their de facto client relationship with Moscow. All of these countries, except East Germany (styling itself the 'German Democratic Republic'), already existed and were universally recognised as States before the Second World War. Those States which existed prior to the imposition of communist rule in the 1940s continued to be recognised as States by non-communist States.

East Germany provides an instructive contrast. Created by the Soviet Union as a completely new entity in 1949, East Germany in fact possessed all the attributes of statehood from the time of its formation, including a formally independent government. Nevertheless, many non-communist States refused to recognise East Germany's statehood

---

21. Hersch Lauterpacht, *Recognition in International Law*, Cambridge University Press, Cambridge, 1947, chs 3 and 11.
22. See **4.13**.

until the 1970s, because its establishment was regarded as being in violation of international agreements about Germany's status among the victorious allied States.

4.23   Although States are never under a legal duty to recognise an entity's statehood, there may be circumstances where there is a duty not to recognise statehood.

4.24   A separatist political movement may seek to break away from an existing State by establishing a new State on part of the existing State's territory. If a third State recognises the separatist entity as a new State before the separatist entity has established all the essential criteria for statehood, it is likely that the third State would be in breach of its obligation to refrain from intervening in the existing State's internal affairs.[23] Different considerations may, however, apply where an independence movement seeks to establish a new State in the territory of a colony or other dependent territory against the colonial power's wishes, but in accordance with a right of self-determination. In these circumstances, it may be lawful to recognise the new entity's statehood, provided the independence movement has the support of the local people and controls substantial territory.[24]

4.25   Customary international law forbids States from recognising any 'territorial acquisition or special advantage resulting from aggression'.[25] This requirement can be regarded as a specific manifestation of the general legal principle that illegal acts cannot become a source of legal rights for the malefactor *(ex iniuria jus non oritur)*.

If an aggressor State seizes control of territory and, rather than annexing it or simply occupying it, establishes a new State-like entity on the conquered territory, a question arises as to the permissibility of recognising that entity's statehood. The fact that the new State-like entity was established as a result of a violation of the *jus cogens* rule against the threat or use of force, as embodied in Art 2(4) of the UN Charter,[26] is enough to require that entity's non-recognition as a State.[27]

If the new entity is de facto dependent on the aggressor State, either because it is unable to assert its will without the assistance of invading forces or because its public authorities act at the direction of the aggressor State, then it is possible that this constitutes an additional ground for the compulsory non-recognition of the entity's statehood. In 1931, Japan

---

23.   Sir Robert Jennings and Sir Arthur Watts (eds), *Oppenheim's International Law*, 9th ed, Longman, New York, 1992, § 41, 143–46. As to the customary rule against intervention, see **9.41–9.48**.
24.   James Crawford, *The Creation of States in International Law*, Clarendon, New York, 2006, 387.
25.   *Resolution on the Definition of Aggression*, General Assembly Resolution 3314 (XXIX), 14 December 1974, Art 5(3).
26.   See **9.7–9.18**.
27.   See **7.31** on the non-recognition of title to territory acquired in violation of Art 2(4) of the UN Charter; Malcolm N Shaw, *International Law*, 6th ed, Cambridge University Press, Cambridge, 2008, 469; Sir Robert Jennings and Sir Arthur Watts (eds), *Oppenheim's International Law*, 9th ed, Longman, New York, 1992, § 54, 185–86.

conquered the Chinese province of Manchuria. Subsequently, Japan was instrumental in establishing a new State-like entity on Manchurian territory. The new entity was named 'Manchukuo'. The League of Nations refused to admit Manchukuo to membership after a fact-finding commission reported that Japanese officials, in reality, decided all important questions falling for determination by the government of Manchukuo, and that the government of Manchukuo was reliant on Japanese troops for the maintenance of internal order. The League determined that China retained legal sovereignty over Manchuria, notwithstanding the establishment of Manchukuo. Only five States (El Salvador, Germany, Hungary, Italy and Japan) ever recognised Manchukuo's statehood.

4.26   There is also State practice to suggest that it is unlawful to recognise the statehood of any entity which has been established in order to institute or consolidate a policy of apartheid. In 1965, the Security Council called upon all States to refrain from recognising Rhodesia as a State after it declared independence from the United Kingdom in order to preserve white minority rule.[28] No State recognised Rhodesia's statehood. Similarly, when South Africa established Transkei as a separate State for the Xhosa people in 1976, the General Assembly passed a resolution condemning apartheid and rejecting Transkei's independence, and called upon all States 'to deny any form of recognition to the so-called independent Transkei'.[29] The Security Council subsequently endorsed this call.[30] With the sole exception of South Africa, no State recognised Transkei's statehood. The establishment by South Africa of the other 'homelands' of Ciskei, Bophutatswana and Venda met a similar fate.

This customary rule of non-recognition, if it exists, does not apply to require non-recognition of existing States which implement a policy of apartheid. South Africa was recognised as a State by many other States, both before and after it implemented its apartheid policies.

4.27   Even if a State does not recognise another entity's statehood, relations between them may still be governed by international law — provided, of course, that the entity actually meets the requirements of statehood.

Accordingly, it is possible for a State to maintain an international legal claim against another State which the former does not recognise, and vice versa.[31] It is also possible for such States to conclude legally binding treaties. In 1953, for instance, the United States concluded an armistice agreement with North Korea (whose statehood the United States did not recognise) and mainland China (whose government the United States did not recognise).

In purely practical terms, however, a State which is subject to non-recognition by other States will find it much more difficult to have effective dealings with those other States. The refusal to have any official contact on a State-to-State basis places serious practical difficulties in

---

28.   Resolution 216 (1965) and Resolution 217 (1965).
29.   Resolution 31/6 A of 26 October 1976.
30.   Resolution 402 (1976).
31.   *Tinoco Arbitration (Great Britain v Costa Rica)* (1923) 1 RIAA 369. See **4.14**.

the way of those States establishing treaty relations, enforcing rights and obligations in international law, and conducting normal diplomatic life. The results can be inconvenient and costly for all concerned.

4.28   In practice, States rarely withdraw recognition of another entity's statehood once it has been granted, unless the State itself disappears. The case of Somalia illustrates the point.[32] States do occasionally disappear, either because they break up into smaller territorial units, none of which is a successor to the larger State, or because a State is absorbed into, or annexed by, another State. There are some relatively recent examples of these phenomena: the Soviet Union, the Socialist Federal Republic of Yugoslavia, and Czechoslovakia fragmented into distinct new States, while East Germany was absorbed into the Federal Republic of Germany.

Recognition of governments

4.29   A State may also recognise a controlling authority in another State as the government of that State. In this case, the recognising State is expressing a willingness to have diplomatic dealings with the other State on the basis that the controlling authority represents and binds that State. Conversely, a refusal to recognise a government involves a decision not to engage in any diplomatic dealings with that authority. As with non-recognition of States, this can place serious practical difficulties in the way of conducting normal international relations, with potentially inconvenient and costly results for those involved.

4.30   In practice, recognition is never an issue where a government assumes power constitutionally in an established State. Although it is traditional for many foreign States to congratulate a new constitutionally appointed government, the mere absence of such a message from any given State cannot be regarded as indicating non-recognition of the new government by that State.

4.31   Where a new State has been established, recognition of its statehood is normally taken to imply recognition of its government. This will especially be the case where the new State's government has assumed power in accordance with legal procedures in which the State formerly exercising authority over the new State's territory has participated. Thus, if a colonial power legally transfers independence to a new State and its first government, there will be no question of other States withholding recognition from the new State's government.

4.32   Different considerations have, however, operated where a new public authority unconstitutionally assumes power in a State (for example, by revolution or coup d'état).

In these cases, States have usually applied a test of effective control before extending recognition to a new government. Recognition of a

---

32.   See **4.9**.

constitutionally irregular public authority's right to govern will almost always be withheld, at least until it has established effective governmental authority over the State's territory.

Premature recognition of a constitutionally irregular government — that is, recognition before it has actually established its political control over the State — will involve an unlawful intervention in the State's internal affairs. An insurgency authority which effectively controls only part of a State's territory may be recognised as a de facto government in that territory so that limited official relations may be established with it, albeit falling short of full diplomatic contact.

4.33   In 1931, Mexico's Foreign Minister, Genaro Estrada (1887–1937), proposed the adoption of a policy whereby only States would be recognised. According to the Estrada doctrine, governments should never be formally recognised. This was because the act of recognition or non-recognition could be construed as a sign of approval or disapproval of a new regime in another State, and such a position might constitute an interference in the other State's internal affairs. A number of States adopted this policy, but many Western States continued with the established practice of formally recognising governments as well as States.

4.34   It is generally accepted that, as with recognition of States, recognition of governments is never obligatory and may be withheld for political reasons. An example is provided by China. For more than 20 years, many non-communist States refused recognition to the communist dictatorship in Peking, which was in effective control of China's mainland territory. These States preferred, for political reasons, to recognise the authorities located in Taiwan as China's government. It was not until the 1970s that the mainland regime attracted the recognition of many Western States as the government of China.

4.35   In more recent times, the significance of the law on formally recognising governments has markedly declined. This is a consequence of a policy adopted by a large and growing number of mainly Western States of abandoning formal recognition or non-recognition of governments. This shift is a belated victory for the Estrada doctrine. An impression is often created that a decision to recognise a non-constitutionally installed government is not just an acknowledgement of its effective control, but a sign of political approval by the recognising State. Sometimes this impression is accurate, but often it is not.

4.36   A number of civil law States, including Belgium and France, abandoned the policy of formally recognising governments in the 1960s.

In 1977, the United States declared that its policy had been, and would continue to be, to avoid recognising governments but to establish diplomatic relations in the absence of formal recognition.[33]

---

33.   John A Boyd (ed), *Digest of United States Practice in International Law*, United States Department of State, Washington DC, 1977, 19–21.

The United Kingdom expressly embraced a similar policy in 1980 when its Foreign Secretary announced in parliament that it would no longer formally recognise governments and that it would:[34]

> ... continue to decide the nature of dealings with regimes which came to power unconstitutionally in the light of our assessment of whether they are able of themselves to exercise effective control of the territory of the State concerned, and seem likely to continue to do so.

Many other States, including Australia, Canada, the Netherlands and New Zealand, have adopted similar policies. Australia's change of policy was enunciated by its Foreign Minister in 1988:[35]

> Previously Australia recognised (or did not recognise) both States and governments in existing States. We now recognise States only ...

> Under our old policy the recognition of a new [government] which had come to power in an existing State as the government of that State was technically a formal acknowledgement that the government was in effective control of that State and in a position to represent that State internationally. However, recognition of a new government inevitably led to public assumptions of approval or disapproval of the government concerned, and could thereby create domestic or other problems for the recognising government. On the other hand 'non-recognition' limited the non-recognising government's capacity to deal with the new regime.

> Considerations such as these have led a number of western governments to change to a policy of recognising States only. Australia now follows this policy ... In future, Australia will no longer announce that it recognises, or does not recognise, a new regime in an existing State. Australia's attitude to a new regime will be ascertained by the nature of our policies towards and relations with the new regime. Important indicators to Australia's attitude to a new regime will be: public statements; establishment of and/or the conduct of diplomatic relations with it; ministerial contact; and other contacts, such as entering into aid, economic or defence arrangements, technical and cultural exchanges.

Apart from abandoning the practice of formally recognising governments, very little has changed for these States. They still apply a test of effective control in deciding whether to have diplomatic contact or establish diplomatic relations with regimes that have assumed power unconstitutionally. Political factors also continue to influence whether, and to what extent, diplomatic relations should occur, so that the issue remains a matter for the discretion of States.

Self-determination of peoples

4.37   The self-determination of peoples emerged as a legal principle with the adoption of the United Nations Charter in 1945. Article 1(2) of the Charter provides that a purpose of the UN is to 'develop friendly

---

34.   House of Lords, *Hansard,* Vol 408, cols 1121–1122, 28 April 1980.
35.   Australian Department of Foreign Affairs and Trade, *Backgrounder,* No 611, 16 March 1988.

relations among nations based on respect for the principle of equal rights and self-determination of peoples'.

Article 55 of the Charter requires the United Nations to promote certain economic, social, health and human rights objectives with a view:

> ... to the creation of conditions of stability and well-being which are necessary for peaceful and friendly relations among nations based on respect for the principle of equal rights and self-determination of peoples.

Article 56 of the Charter requires all members of the United Nations to take action in cooperation with the UN to achieve the purposes contained in Art 55.

4.38 Both the content of the principle and the extent of its legal character remained unclear for a number of years after the Charter's adoption. The principle received no mention in the General Assembly's 1948 Universal Declaration of Human Rights.[36] In particular, it was not clear whether the principle conferred a right to statehood on any groups of people and how any such groups were to be identified.

4.39 After the end of the Second World War, the colonial possessions of European States began to assume independent statehood. The first significant case was India in 1947. By the late 1950s, the process of decolonisation was well underway and, through the 1960s, it progressed steadily. By the end of the 1970s, there were very few colonial possessions remaining. At its founding, the United Nations had 51 members. Largely as a result of new States having been created by decolonisation in Africa, Asia, the Middle East, the Carribbean Sea and the Pacific Ocean, the UN now has more than 190 members.

4.40 In the 1950s and 1960s, the UN Charter's principle of self-determination was frequently invoked in order to provide a legal impetus to the decolonisation process. In 1960, the General Assembly adopted Resolution 1514 (XV), entitled *Declaration on the Granting of Independence to Colonial Territories and Peoples*. The resolution was adopted by 89 votes to zero, with nine abstentions. The Assembly declared as follows:

1. The subjection of peoples to alien subjugation, domination and exploitation constitutes a denial of fundamental human rights, is contrary to the Charter of the United Nations and is an impediment to the promotion of world peace and co-operation;

2. All peoples have the right to self-determination; by virtue of that right they freely determine their political status and freely pursue their economic, social and cultural development;

3. Inadequacy of political, economic, social or education preparedness should never serve as a pretext for delaying independence;

4. All armed action or repressive measures of all kinds directed against dependent peoples shall cease in order to enable them to exercise

---

36. General Assembly Resolution 217A (III); UN Doc A/810, 71 (1948).

peacefully and freely their right to complete independence, and the integrity of their national territory shall be respected;

5.   Immediate steps shall be taken, in Trust and Non-Self-Governing territories or all other territories which have not yet attained independence, to transfer all powers to the peoples of those territories, without any conditions or reservations, in accordance with their freely expressed will and desire, without any distinction as to race, creed or colour, in order to enable them to enjoy complete independence and freedom;

6.   Any attempt at the partial or total disruption of the national unity and the territorial integrity of a country is incompatible with the Purposes and Principles of the Charter of the United Nations;

7.   All States shall observe faithfully and strictly the provisions of the Charter of the United Nations, the Universal Declaration of Human Rights and the present Declaration on the basis of equality, non-interference in the internal affairs of all States, and respect for the sovereign rights of all peoples and their territorial integrity.

4.41   Resolution 1514 is significant partly because it seeks to define and limit self-determination, and to confirm its status as a principle of law entailing certain rights and obligations.

In particular, Art 2 elaborates the requirements of self-determination: all peoples are entitled to 'freely determine their political status and freely pursue their economic, social and cultural development'. This clearly implies that the 'peoples' to whom the resolution refers may set up their own State with their own independent government.

This is confirmed by the references in Arts 3, 4 and 5 to 'independence' or 'complete independence'. These aspects of the resolution represent its clarifying function.

4.42   Resolution 1514 also has a limiting function. According to Art 6, the principle of self-determination may not be applied to disrupt the national unity and territorial integrity of a 'country'. Furthermore, Art 7 stipulates that the principle must be applied consistently with the requirement of non-interference in the internal affairs of States. These provisions strongly imply that self-determination does not operate so as to confer a right to separate statehood upon peoples inside an independent State. At least to the extent that self-determination confers a right to establish a separate State, it would appear to be limited to peoples occupying only colonial or other non-self-governing territories. Thus, the principle could not operate to confer a right to statehood on racial or ethnic minorities living inside a sovereign State.

Article 6 also furnishes a basis for the view that the principle of self-determination is subject to the principle of *uti possidetis juris*. Accordingly, the boundaries of colonial territories are to be upgraded to international frontiers when those territories attain independence, and are not to be altered except by agreement between the States sharing those boundaries. That the boundaries divide a racial or ethnic group into two or more new States does not affect their legal validity because of any alleged inconsistency with the right of peoples to self-determination.[37]

4.43   Having established that self-determination of peoples was a right attaching exclusively to the peoples of non-self-governing territories, a question quickly arose as to which territories lacked self-government for the purposes of attracting the right — in other words, which territories were colonial or dependent in such a way as to confer on their peoples a right of self-determination. The United Nations was reluctant to accept uncritically an administering State's unilateral characterisation of any particular territory. The question of which territories attracted the right of self-determination was answered through a procedural obligation imposed by Chapter XI (*Declaration Regarding Non-self-governing Territories*, Arts 73–74) of the UN Charter.

Article 73 provides that:

> Members of the United Nations which have or assume responsibilities for the administration of territories whose peoples have not yet attained a full measure of self-government recognize the principle that the interests of the inhabitants of these territories are paramount, and accept as a sacred trust the obligation to promote to the utmost, within the system of international peace and security established by the present Charter, the well-being of the inhabitants of these territories.

Among the obligations imposed by Chapter XI is a requirement of UN members under Art 73(e) 'to transmit regularly to the Secretary-General … statistical and other information of a technical nature relating to economic, social, and educational conditions in the territories for which they are respectively responsible'. But which were the non-self-governing territories for which UN members were responsible and in respect of which there was an obligation to make reports? Whoever could identify these territories would also identify the territories attracting a right of self-determination of peoples.

4.44   In 1960, the General Assembly adopted Resolution 1541 (XV) specifying certain principles that 'should be applied in the light of the facts and circumstances of each case to determine whether or not an obligation exists to transmit information under Article 73 e of the Charter'.[38] Among these principles are:

Principle IV

Prima facie there is an obligation to transmit information in respect of a territory which is geographically separate and is distinct ethnically and/or culturally from the country administering it.

Principle V

Once it has been established that such a *prima facie* case of geographical and ethnical or cultural distinctness of a territory exists, other elements

---

37.   *Case Concerning the Frontier Dispute (Burkina Faso v Mali)* ICJ Rep (1986) 554, paras 20–26.
38.   Resolution 1541 (XV) of 15 December 1960 *(Principles which should guide Members in determining whether or not an obligation exists to transmit the information called for under Article 73 e of the Charter)*, Art 3.

may then be brought into consideration. These additional elements may be, *inter alia*, of an administrative, political, juridical, economic or historical nature. If they affect the relationship between the metropolitan State and the territory concerned in a manner which arbitrarily places the latter in a position or status of subordination, they support the presumption that there is an obligation to transmit information under Article 73 e of the Charter.

The primary test of a territory's non-self-governing status, therefore, is its geographic separateness and its ethnic or cultural distinctiveness from the administering State. Where these criteria are satisfied, there arises a prima facie presumption that they are non-self-governing and therefore subject to the report-making obligation under Art 73(e) of the Charter. This would also imply that, prima facie, the territory attracts a right of self-determination of peoples. This presumption may be fortified by evidence that the territory has been arbitrarily subordinated administratively, politically, juridically, economically or historically. All these factors must also be considered in the context of the facts and circumstances relevant to each case.

4.45   In 1966, the International Covenant on Civil and Political Rights (ICCPR)[39] and the International Covenant on Economic, Social and Cultural Rights (ICESCR) enshrined common Art 1 as follows:[40]

Article 1

1. All peoples have the right of self-determination. By virtue of that right they freely determine their political status and freely pursue their economic, social and cultural development.

2. All peoples may, for their own ends, freely dispose of their natural wealth and resources without prejudice to any obligations arising out of international economic co-operation, based upon the principle of mutual benefit, and international law. In no case may a people be deprived of its own means of subsistence.

3. The States Parties to the present Covenant, including those having responsibility for the administration of Non-Self-Governing and Trust Territories, shall promote the realization of the right of self-determination, and shall respect that right, in conformity with the provisions of the Charter of the United Nations.

Consequently, the principle of self-determination of peoples was elevated to a position of primacy among the basic rights contained in the two most important human rights treaties in the United Nations system.

4.46   The General Assembly elaborated further on the entailments of the right to self-determination in 1970 by adopting Resolution 2625 (XXV), entitled *Declaration on Principles of International Law Concerning*

---

39.   UNTS, Vol 999, p 171.
40.   UNTS, Vol 993, p 3.

Friendly Relations and Co-operation among States in Accordance with the Charter of the United Nations. The Assembly declared that the:

> ... establishment of a sovereign and independent State, the free association or integration with an independent State or the emergence into any other political status freely determined by a people constitute modes of implementing the right of self-determination by that people.

Thus, statehood is only one possible result of a people's right of self-determination; any other status is also open to them, provided only that the status is freely chosen by the people concerned.[41]

4.47   The International Court of Justice stated in its *Namibia* advisory opinion that the principle of self-determination, at least in its application to colonial and similar dependent territories, had attained the status of customary international law.[42]

A few years later, in the *Western Sahara* advisory opinion,[43] the International Court of Justice reaffirmed that view largely on the basis of various General Assembly resolutions already adopted on the subject. In particular, the Court emphasised that the status chosen by a colonial people must be the result of a 'free and genuine expression of the will of the peoples concerned'.[44] The Court prescribed no single method for ascertaining that will. Rather, the General Assembly was left with 'a measure of discretion with respect to the forms and procedures by which the right is to be realized'.[45]

Finally, in the *East Timor* case[46] and in the *Security Wall* advisory opinion,[47] the International Court of Justice affirmed that the right of self-determination of peoples possesses an *erga omnes* character.[48]

4.48   The process of decolonisation is now almost complete. To the extent that the legal right of self-determination applies to colonial and other dependent territories, it has lost most of its former significance. Furthermore, self-determination limited in this way presents few problems in deciding who might be a 'people' for the purpose of exercising the right; a 'people' are all those persons living in a colonial or other dependent territory, regardless of differences in their race, language, religion, ethnicity or other criteria. The only possible exception is that an imported colonial population might not be regarded as the 'people' of a dependent territory. This was the approach taken by the UN's Decolonisation Committee and the General Assembly in rejecting the

---

41. See also Principles VI–IX, *Declaration Regarding Non-self-governing Territories,* General Assembly Resolution 1541 (XV) of 15 December 1960.
42. *Legal Consequences for States of the Continued Presence of South Africa in Namibia (South West Africa) notwithstanding Security Council Resolution 276 (1970)* advisory opinion, ICJ Rep (1971) 16, para 53.
43. *Western Sahara* advisory opinion, ICJ Rep (1975) 12. See **7.13**.
44. Ibid, para 55.
45. Ibid, para 71.
46. *Case Concerning East Timor (Portugal v Australia)* ICJ Rep (1995) 90, para 29. See **8.40**.
47. *Legal Consequences of the Construction of a Wall in the Occupied Palestinian Territory* advisory opinion, ICJ Rep (2004) 136, para 88.
48. As to obligations owed *erga omnes,* see **2.106–2.110**.

results of a 1967 referendum on Gibraltar's status. Gibraltar has been a British colony since its capture from Spain in 1704 or its formal cession by Spain in 1713. The population of Gibraltar voted overwhelmingly in favour of remaining under British rule. The Decolonisation Committee and the General Assembly nevertheless dismissed the result on the basis that the present population of Gibraltar had been imported to replace the earlier, mostly Spanish, population.

4.49   Although decolonisation is now a virtually completed process, the utility of self-determination has not been exhausted.

Since the end of the Cold War, there has been greater international attention focused on the position of racial, ethnic and religious minorities located inside States. In some cases, civil conflicts have erupted as a result of the adverse and discriminatory treatment received by minorities at the hands of the majority population and the authorities of the State. Increasingly, the principle of self-determination has been invoked by separatist movements to justify a claim to separate statehood for particular 'peoples' who claim to be the victims of discriminatory human rights abuses in a State in which they do not form a majority.

State practice has been, and continues largely to be, unreceptive to such claims (for example, the lack of international support for the Biafran rebels' claim to self-determination in the Nigerian civil war of 1967–70). However, there is some evidence that the principle of self-determination may be adapting to new international conditions.

4.50   During the violent break-up of the Socialist Federal Republic of Yugoslavia in the early 1990s, a question arose as to whether the minority Serbian population of Bosnia-Herzegovina and Croatia (two of the breakaway republics) was entitled to exercise a right of self-determination. Most of the Serbian minority would probably have preferred to have the lands on which they mostly lived transferred to the neighbouring republic of Serbia.

The Arbitration Committee established by the European Community Peace Conference on Yugoslavia (the Badinter Committee) was asked to give an opinion on the question. In its *Opinion No 2*,[49] the Committee said that the principle of *uti possidetis juris* applied to the collapse of federal States and that self-determination was subordinate to that principle. Accordingly, the Serbian population was not entitled to demand alteration of the frontiers of independent States such as Bosnia-Herzegovina, Croatia and Serbia in order to accommodate ethnic realities on the ground. Nor was it entitled to establish a separate Bosnian-Serb State or a separate Croatian-Serb State.

However, the Committee also concluded that the principle of self-determination was relevant to the position of the Serbian minorities. Although they were not entitled to alter the borders of Bosnia-Herzegovina or Croatia, self-determination required that the minority Serbs were entitled, under international law, to have their identity recognised by

---

49.   *Opinion No 2* (1992) 92 ILR 167.

Bosnia-Herzegovina and Croatia. Accordingly, the Commission said that 'the Serbian population in Bosnia-Herzegovina and Croatia is entitled to all the rights accorded to minorities and ethnic groups under international law'. These rights of minorities were, in the Commission's view, peremptory norms of international law.[50]

This more limited kind of self-determination is sometimes referred to as 'internal self-determination'. Conversely, the more extensive variety of self-determination which gives a right to separate statehood in colonial situations is sometimes referred to as 'external self-determination'.

4.51 In 1992, the General Assembly adopted Resolution 47/135, entitled *Declaration on the Rights of Persons Belonging to National or Ethnic, Religious and Linguistic Minorities*. This declaration provides that States must protect the existence and the national or ethnic, cultural, religious and linguistic identity of minorities within their territories. It also states that persons belonging to minorities have the right to enjoy their own culture, to practise and profess their own religion, and to use their own language both privately and publicly. Members of minorities must also have the right to participate in cultural, social, economic and public life.

4.52 Given that the principle of self-determination of peoples in its 'internal' mode has acquired a relevance for minorities inside sovereign States, a question arises as to who are the 'peoples' entitled to enjoy self-determination in such situations. They cannot be identified simply by the relatively easy technique of pointing to all the inhabitants of a particular colonial territory. Guidance may be obtained from the 1990 *Final Report and Recommendations of an International Meeting of Experts on the Further Study of the Concept of the Rights of People for UNESCO.*[51]

According to this report, a people, for the purposes of the right to self-determination, has the following characteristics:

(a) A group of individual human beings who enjoy some or all of the following common features:

    (i)   A common historical tradition;

    (ii) Racial or ethnic identity;

    (iii) Cultural homogeneity;

    (iv) Linguistic unity;

    (v) Religious or ideological affinity;

    (vi) Territorial connection;

    (vii) Common economic life.

(b) The group must be a certain number who need not be large (e.g. the people of micro States) but must be more than a mere association of individuals within a State.

---

50.   As to such norms, see **2.106–2.110**.
51.   SNS 89/Conf 602/7.

    (c) The group as a whole must have the will to be identified as a people or the consciousness of being a people — allowing that groups or some members of such groups, though sharing the foregoing characteristics, may not have the will or consciousness.

    (d) Possibly the group must have institutions or other means of expressing its common characteristics and will for identity.

The rights of minorities is an area of international law that is very far from being fully developed. There is still no comprehensive multilateral treaty on the subject and such law as exists is primarily customary in nature and relatively early in development.

4.53   This renaissance of the principle of self-determination of peoples, at the very moment that its significance seemed to be permanently passing away in the twilight of decolonisation, became important in the context of Quebec's status within the Canadian federation.

Originally a French colony called 'New France', Quebec was conquered by British military forces in 1759, formally ceded to Britain in 1763, and became a founding component of the Canadian federation in 1867. Since the 1960s, there has been a significant political movement for the secession of the mostly francophone province of Quebec from the remainder of Canada. After two referenda (in 1980 and 1995) failed to obtain majority support in Quebec for independence, the pro-independence provincial government adopted legislation laying out a roadmap for secession in the event of a future successful referendum on independence. This prompted the Canadian federal executive government to make a reference to the Supreme Court of Canada in *Reference re Secession of Quebec*.[52] The federal government sought an opinion on three questions, all relating to the lawfulness of a possible future unilateral secession by Quebec. The first and third questions dealt with issues of Canadian constitutional law, but the second question raised the principle of self-determination of peoples in international law:

B. Question 2

Does international law give the National Assembly, legislature or government of Quebec the right to effect the secession of Quebec from Canada unilaterally? In this regard, is there a right to self-determination under international law that would give the National Assembly, legislature or government of Quebec the right to effect the secession of Quebec from Canada unilaterally?

…

(1) Secession at International Law

111. It is clear that international law does not specifically grant component parts of sovereign states the legal right to secede unilaterally from their 'parent' state.
…

(a) Absence of a Specific Prohibition

112. International law contains neither a right of unilateral secession nor the explicit denial of such a right, although such a denial is, to some extent, implicit in the exceptional circumstances required for secession to be permitted under

---

52. *Reference re Secession of Quebec* [1998] 2 SCR 217.

the right of a people to self-determination, e.g., the right of secession that arises in the exceptional situation of an oppressed or colonial people, discussed below. As will be seen, international law places great importance on the territorial integrity of nation states and, by and large, leaves the creation of a new state to be determined by the domestic law of the existing state of which the seceding entity presently forms a part ...

(b) The Right of a People to Self-determination

113. While international law generally regulates the conduct of nation states, it does, in some specific circumstances, also recognize the 'rights' of entities other than nation states — such as the right of a *people* to self-determination. ...

122. ... [I]nternational law expects that the right to self-determination will be exercised by peoples within the framework of existing sovereign states and consistently with the maintenance of the territorial integrity of those states. Where this is not possible, in the exceptional circumstances discussed below, a right of secession may arise.

(i) Defining 'Peoples'

...

125. While much of the Quebec population certainly shares many of the characteristics (such as a common language and culture) that would be considered in determining whether a specific group is a 'people', as do other groups within Quebec and/or Canada, it is not necessary to explore this legal characterization to resolve Question 2 appropriately. Similarly, it is not necessary for the Court to determine whether, should a Quebec people exist within the definition of public international law, such a people encompasses the entirety of the provincial population or just a portion thereof. Nor is it necessary to examine the position of the aboriginal population within Quebec. As the following discussion of the scope of the right to self-determination will make clear, whatever be the correct application of the definition of people(s) in this context, their right of self-determination cannot in the present circumstances be said to ground a right to unilateral secession.

(ii) Scope of the Right to Self-Determination

126. The recognized sources of international law establish that the right to self-determination of a people is normally fulfilled through *internal* self-determination — a people's pursuit of its political, economic, social and cultural development within the framework of an existing state. A right to *external* self-determination (which in this case potentially takes the form of the assertion of a right to unilateral secession) arises in only the most extreme of cases and, even then, under carefully defined circumstances. *External* self-determination can be defined as in the following statement from the *Declaration on Friendly Relations*[53] as '[t]he establishment of a sovereign and independent State, the free association or integration with an independent State or the emergence into any other political status freely determined by a *people* constitute modes of implementing the right of self-determination by *that people*.' [Emphasis added.]

127. The international law principle of self-determination has evolved within a framework of respect for the territorial integrity of existing states. ... [T]he exercise of such a right must be sufficiently limited to prevent threats to an existing state's territorial integrity or the stability of relations between sovereign states.

---

53. *Declaration on Principles of International Law Concerning Friendly Relations and Co-operation among States in Accordance with the Charter of the United Nations,* General Assembly Resolution 2625 (XXV) of 24 October 1970.

...

130. ... There is no necessary incompatibility between the maintenance of the territorial integrity of existing states, including Canada, and the right of a 'people' to achieve a full measure of self-determination. A state whose government represents the whole of the people or peoples resident within its territory, on a basis of equality and without discrimination, and respects the principles of self-determination in its own internal arrangements, is entitled to the protection under international law of its territorial integrity.

(iii) Colonial and Oppressed Peoples

...

132. The right of colonial peoples to exercise their right to self-determination by breaking away from the 'imperial' power is now undisputed, but is irrelevant to this Reference.

133. The other clear case where a right to external self-determination accrues is where a people is subject to alien subjugation, domination or exploitation outside a colonial context. ...

134. A number of commentators have further asserted that the right to self-determination may ground a right to unilateral secession in a third circumstance. Although this third circumstance has been described in several ways, the underlying proposition is that, when a people is blocked from the meaningful exercise of its right to self-determination internally, it is entitled, as a last resort, to exercise it by secession. The *Vienna Declaration*[54] requirement that governments represent 'the whole people belonging to the territory without distinction of any kind' adds credence to the assertion that such a complete blockage may potentially give rise to a right of secession.

135. Clearly, such a circumstance parallels the other two recognized situations in that the ability of a people to exercise its right to self-determination internally is somehow being totally frustrated. While it remains unclear whether this third proposition actually reflects an established international law standard, it is unnecessary for present purposes to make that determination. Even assuming that the third circumstance is sufficient to create a right to unilateral secession under international law, the current Quebec context cannot be said to approach such a threshold. ...

136. The population of Quebec cannot plausibly be said to be denied access to government. Quebecers occupy prominent positions within the government of Canada. Residents of the province freely make political choices and pursue economic, social and cultural development within Quebec, across Canada, and throughout the world. The population of Quebec is equitably represented in legislative, executive and judicial institutions. In short, to reflect the phraseology of the international documents that address the right to self-determination of peoples, Canada is a 'sovereign and independent state conducting itself in compliance with the principle of equal rights and self-determination of peoples and thus possessed of a government representing the whole people belonging to the territory without distinction'.

...

138. In summary, the international law right to self-determination only generates, at best, a right to external self-determination in situations of former colonies; where a people is oppressed, as for example under foreign military occupation;

---

54.   United Nations World Conference on Human Rights, *Vienna Declaration and Programme of Action*, A/CONF 157/24 (Part I), 25 June 1993.

or where a definable group is denied meaningful access to government to pursue their political, economic, social and cultural development. In all three situations, the people in question are entitled to a right to external self-determination because they have been denied the ability to exert internally their right to self-determination. Such exceptional circumstances are manifestly inapplicable to Quebec under existing conditions. Accordingly, neither the population of the province of Quebec, even if characterized in terms of 'people' or 'peoples', nor its representative institutions, the National Assembly, the legislature or government of Quebec, possess a right, under international law, to secede unilaterally from Canada.

4.54   The Supreme Court of Canada in *Reference re Secession of Quebec* recognised that international law accepts only three circumstances in which the right of self-determination entitles a people to form a new State by unilaterally seceding from an existing State: (i) colonial status; (ii) oppression under foreign military occupation or similar circumstances of foreign domination; and (iii) denial to a 'people' (however properly defined) of their internal self-determination rights within an existing sovereign State.

The first two circumstances correspond to the familiar right of external self-determination as established since at least 1960, and attach to all the people of a given colonial or foreign-controlled non-self-governing territory. Such people are always entitled to 'secede' from the administering State in order to establish a new sovereign State.

The third circumstance corresponds to a newer right of external self-determination. Where the rights of a (minority) 'people' within a sovereign State to pursue their own internal self-determination rights to political, economic, social and cultural development are systematically frustrated by that State, they will acquire an external right of self-determination to secede and establish a new State. In the *Unilateral Declaration of Independence* advisory opinion, the International Court of Justice referred to this putative species of self-determination as 'remedial secession', but found a discussion of its status in customary international law beyond the scope of the question posed by the General Assembly.[55]

In the Supreme Court of Canada's opinion, it was simply implausible to argue that the people of Quebec had been denied their rights of internal self-determination within the Canadian federation. Quoting from the pleadings, the Court observed:[56]

For close to 40 of the last 50 years, the Prime Minister of Canada has been a Quebecer. During this period, Quebecers have held from time to time all the most important positions in the federal Cabinet. During the 8 years prior to June 1997, the Prime Minister and the Leader of the

---

55.   *Accordance with International Law of the Unilateral Declaration of Independence in Respect of Kosovo* advisory opinion, 22 July 2010, para 83.
56.   Para 135 of the opinion.

Official Opposition in the House of Commons were both Quebecers. At present, the Prime Minister of Canada, the Right Honourable Chief Justice and two other members of the Court, the Chief of Staff of the Canadian Armed Forces and the Canadian ambassador to the United States, not to mention the Deputy Secretary-General of the United Nations, are all Quebecers. The international achievements of Quebecers in most fields of human endeavour are too numerous to list. Since the dynamism of the Quebec people has been directed toward the business sector, it has been clearly successful in Quebec, the rest of Canada and abroad.

Being citizens within a sovereign State which respected their internal self-determination right to pursue their own political, economic, social and cultural development, international law gave the people of Quebec no right to secede unilaterally from Canada.

4.55 On the other hand, the Supreme Court of Canada accepted that the absence of an international law right to secede unilaterally did not mean that the people of Quebec could not effectively establish a new State on the basis of such a secession:[57]

Secession of a province from Canada, if successful in the streets, might well lead to the creation of a new state. Although recognition by other states is not, at least as a matter of theory, necessary to achieve statehood, the viability of a would-be state in the international community depends, as a practical matter, upon recognition by other states. That process of recognition is guided by legal norms. However, international recognition is not alone constitutive of statehood and, critically, does not relate back to the date of secession to serve retroactively as a source of a 'legal' right to secede in the first place. Recognition occurs only after a territorial unit has been successful, as a political fact, in achieving secession.

It would follow that a unilateral secession not based on an affirmative right of self-determination could nevertheless result in the formation of a new State if all the customary law criteria for statehood codified in Art 1 of the Montevideo Convention[58] were satisfied. That would not, however, mean that the secession was effected in pursuance of a right of self-determination: 'It may be that a unilateral secession by Quebec would eventually be accorded legal status by Canada and other states, and thus give rise to legal consequences; but this does not support the more radical contention that subsequent recognition of a state of affairs brought about by a unilateral declaration of independence could be taken to mean that secession was achieved under colour of a legal right.'[59]

4.56 Although no international law right of unilateral secession from a sovereign State exists in the absence of a denial of internal self-determination rights, neither does international law operate to delegitimise a State established by a unilateral secession in the absence of such a denial. Not only is this clearly implicit in *Reference re Secession*

---

57. Ibid, para 142.
58. See **4.4**.
59. *Reference re Secession of Quebec* [1998] 2 SCR 217, para 144.

of Quebec, but the International Court of Justice in the *Unilateral Declaration of Independence* advisory opinion said:[60]

> 79. During the eighteenth, nineteenth and early twentieth centuries, there were numerous instances of declarations of independence, often strenuously opposed by the State from which independence was being declared. Sometimes a declaration resulted in the creation of a new State, at others it did not. In no case, however, does the practice of States as a whole suggest that the act of promulgating the declaration was regarded as contrary to international law. On the contrary, State practice during this period points clearly to the conclusion that international law contained no prohibition of declarations of independence. During the second half of the 20th century, the international law of self-determination developed in such a way as to create a right to independence for the peoples of non-self-governing territories and peoples subject to alien subjugation, domination and exploitation ... A great many new States have come into existence as a result of the exercise of this right. There were, however, also instances of declarations of independence outside this context. The practice of States in these latter cases does not point to the emergence in international law of a new rule prohibiting the making of a declaration of independence in such cases.

> 80. Several participants in the proceedings before the Court have contended that a prohibition of unilateral declarations of independence is implicit in the principle of territorial integrity.

> The Court recalls that the principle of territorial integrity is an important part of the international legal order and is enshrined in the Charter of the United Nations, in particular in Article 2, paragraph 4, which provides that:

> > All Members shall refrain in their international relations from the threat or use of force against the territorial integrity or political independence of any State, or in any other manner inconsistent with the Purposes of the United Nations.

> In ... resolution 2625 (XXV), ... the General Assembly reiterated '[t]he principle that States shall refrain in their international relations from the threat or use of force against the territorial integrity or political independence of any State'. This resolution then enumerated various obligations incumbent upon States to refrain from violating the territorial integrity of other sovereign States. In the same vein, the Final Act of the Helsinki Conference on Security and Co-operation in Europe ... stipulated that '[t]he participating States will respect the territorial integrity of each of the participating States' (Art. IV). Thus, the scope of the principle of territorial integrity is confined to the sphere of relations between States.

Unilateral declarations of independence from sovereign States are therefore not per se unlawful. Furthermore, where such declarations are made without attribution to another State, there is no violation of the principle of territorial integrity because respect for that principle binds only States in their relations with each other. Accordingly, an

---

60.   *Accordance with International Law of the Unilateral Declaration of Independence in Respect of Kosovo* advisory opinion, 22 July 2010.

internal separatist movement is not bound to respect the principle of territorial integrity of States and may declare independence. Whether such a declaration results in the successful establishment of a new State will again depend on whether the entity resulting from the declaration satisfies all the requirements of statehood codified in Art 1 of the Montevideo Convention.[61]

International organisations

4.57 International organisations are entities established by agreement between two or more States. They are to be distinguished from international non-governmental organisations (NGOs) which have been established by non-State entities such as individuals or private associations and which draw their memberships from more than one country.

There are well over 100 international organisations in the world today, with wide-ranging variations as to their scope *ratione materiae* and *ratione personae*.[62] They range from multilateral organisations such as the United Nations, with more than 190 member States, to bilateral organisations set up and constituted by only two States.

4.58 International organisations are capable of possessing an international legal personality. Whereas States automatically possess complete international legal personality, the existence and extent of an international organisation's legal personality is dependent upon its constituent instruments (usually a treaty) and the practice of States.

4.59 Sometimes a treaty establishing an international organisation will specify that the organisation possesses international personality. Article 210 of the Treaty Establishing the European Community,[63] for instance, expressly confers legal personality on the European Community. Such a provision in a treaty will have the effect of conferring legal personality on any organisation constituted by the treaty, at least as far as member States of that organisation are concerned.

4.60 More commonly, however, an international organisation's constituent charter will not specify that it possesses international personality. This does not mean, however, that the international organisation necessarily lacks any legal personality. The UN Charter does not specify that the United Nations possesses legal personality. In its first advisory opinion, the International Court of Justice considered whether, and to what extent, the UN is a legal person in international law.

---

61. See **4.4**.
62. See **1.41–1.42**.
63. *Official Journal of the European Communities*, C 325/33, 24 December 2002.

In the **Reparation for Injuries Suffered in the Service of the United Nations advisory opinion**,[64] Count Folke Bernadotte (1895–1948) had been assassinated by terrorists in a part of Jerusalem controlled by Israeli authorities. The Count was a Swedish national and a United Nations official responsible for negotiating a truce between warring factions in the area. At the time of the assassination (September 1948), Israel was not a member of the United Nations. The UN considered that Israel was internationally responsible for the Count's death because it had negligently failed to prevent his murder or punish the murderers. Wishing to make a claim against Israel, the General Assembly asked the International Court of Justice whether the UN had capacity to bring a claim in respect of the Count's death. The Court said:[65]

> The subjects of law in any legal system are not necessarily identical in their nature or in the extent of their rights, and their nature depends upon the needs of the community. … [T]he progressive increase in the collective action of States has already given rise to instances of action upon the international plane by certain entities which are not States. This development culminated in the establishment … of an international organisation whose purposes and principles are specified in the Charter of the United Nations. But to achieve these ends the attribution of international personality is indispensable. The Charter has not been content to make the Organisation created by it merely a centre for 'harmonising the actions of nations in the attainment of these common ends' (Article 1, para. 4). It has equipped that centre with organs, and has given it special tasks. It has defined the position of Members in relation to the Organisation by requiring them to give it every assistance in any action undertaken by it (Article 2, para. 5), and to accept and carry out the decisions of the Security Council; by authorising the General Assembly to make recommendations to the Members; by giving the Organisation legal capacity and privileges and immunities in the territory of each of its Members; and by providing for the conclusion of agreements between the Organisation and its Members. Practice — in particular, the conclusions of conventions to which the Organisation is a party — has confirmed the character of the Organisation, which occupies a position in certain respects in detachment from its Members, and which is under a duty to remind them, if need be, of certain obligations.

> It must be added that the Organisation is a political body, charged with political tasks of an important character, and covering a wide field … The 'Convention on the Privileges and Immunities of the United Nations' of 1946 creates rights and duties between each of the signatories and the Organisation … It is difficult to see how such a convention could operate except upon the international plane and as between parties possessing international personality.

> In the opinion of the Court, the Organisation was intended to exercise and enjoy, and is in fact exercising and enjoying, functions and rights which can only be explained on the basis of the possession of a large measure of international personality and the capacity to operate upon an international plane.

> It is at present the supreme type of international organisation, and it could not carry out the intentions of its founders if it was devoid of international personality. It must be acknowledged that its Members, by entrusting certain functions to it, with the attendant duties and responsibilities, have clothed it with the competence required to enable those functions to be effectively discharged.

---

64. *Reparation for Injuries Suffered in the Service of the United Nations* advisory opinion, ICJ Rep (1949) 174.
65. Ibid, 178–185.

Accordingly, the Court has come to the conclusion that the Organisation is an international person. This is not the same thing as saying that it is a State, which it certainly is not, or that its legal personality and rights and duties are the same as those of a State. ... What it does mean is that it is a subject of international law and capable of possessing international rights and duties, and that it has capacity to maintain its rights by bringing international claims.

... Whereas a State possesses the totality of international rights and duties recognised by international law, the rights and duties of an entity such as the Organisation must depend upon its purposes and functions as specified or implied in its constituent documents and developed in practice. The functions of the Organisation are of such a character that they could not be effectively discharged if they involved the concurrent action, on the international plane, of fifty-eight or more Foreign Offices, and the Court concludes that the Members have endowed the Organisation with capacity to bring international claims when necessitated by the discharge of its functions. ...

Under international law, the Organisation must be deemed to have those powers which, though not expressly provided in the Charter, are conferred upon it by necessary implication as being essential to the performance of its duties. ...

[There is a question] whether the Organisation has capacity to bring a claim against the defendant State to cover reparation in respect of [the Count's murder] or whether, on the contrary, the defendant State, not being a member [of the United Nations], is justified in raising the objection that the Organisation lacks the capacity to bring an international claim.

On this point, the Court's opinion is that fifty States, representing the vast majority of the members of the international community, had the power, in conformity with international law, to bring into being an entity possessing objective international personality and not merely personality recognised by them alone, together with capacity to bring international claims.

Israel joined the United Nations before this advisory opinion was delivered. After receiving the Court's opinion, the Secretary-General made a claim against Israel for reparation in respect of Count Bernadotte's death. Israel paid the requested sum in settlement of the claim.

4.61   As a result of the *Reparation for Injuries Suffered in the Service of the United Nations* advisory opinion, international organisations may be regarded as having such legal personality as:

(i)   is expressly prescribed in their constituent instruments;

(ii)   arises by necessary implication in order to give effect to their specified or implied objects and purposes;

(iii)   arises by necessary implication as being essential to the performance of their duties; or

(iv)   conforms to the practice of States in their relations with the organisations in question.

An international organisation's legal personality determined in this way will be effective as against any States which are members of the organisation. As against non-members, an organisation's personality will be effective (that is, objectively effective) if a sufficiently large number of States are members of the organisation. Even if only a relatively small number of States are members of the organisation, it would nevertheless possess objective legal personality if a sufficiently large number of other States deal with it on the basis that it possesses international personality.

Individuals

4.62 Prior to the emergence of the modern State system and the creation of an extensive body of positive law based in custom and treaty, international law was viewed in Europe largely as a matter of the *jus gentium* transposed to the level of relations among different political communities.[66] In this setting, it was taken for granted that rules governing relations among sovereigns also extended to their subjects. There was no international legal order distinctly separate from domestic law; the former was an extension of, and adapted from, the latter.

4.63 By the 19th century, however, the present State-centred and autonomous system of international law had become firmly established. In this system, international law regulated only relations among States. This meant that generally only States could truly be subjects of international law and possess an international legal personality. With few exceptions, other entities such as individuals featured only as objects of international law — that is, as entities with which States could deal according to standards prescribed by international law, but which did not themselves possess rights and obligations. If an individual was mistreated at the hands of a foreign State, only the individual's State could take up the individual's claim at the international level under the rules of diplomatic protection. Similarly, individuals who were acting under the authority of their State were generally shielded by their State's sovereignty from personal liability under international law for their official acts.

Nevertheless, there remained, even into the 20th century, pockets of the older conceptions of international legal ordering. In particular, individuals continued to be held personally responsible for breaching international standards enshrined in the *jus in bello* (the law regulating the conduct of war), the rules and principles of which were frequently applied by national military tribunals. Similarly, the crime of piracy *jure gentium* has for centuries been an offence under international law and is subject to the universal principle of jurisdiction[67] so that individuals committing it may be tried by the courts of any State.

In more recent times, acts of terrorism, aircraft hijacking and drug trafficking have emerged as crimes against international law. They too fall within the scope of the universal principle of jurisdiction and render the perpetrators liable to punishment as individuals.

4.64 At the end of the Second World War, International Military Tribunals at Nuremberg and Tokyo were established by treaty among

---

66. See **1.156–1.174**.
67. See **6.24** and **10.22–10.25**.

the victorious States. They were responsible for trying individual defendants for war crimes, crimes against the peace, and crimes against humanity. These were all offences against customary international law which attracted personal liability for the individuals committing them. In its final judgment, the International Military Tribunal at Nuremberg remarked:[68]

> It was submitted that international law is concerned with the actions of sovereign States, and provides no punishment for individuals; and further, that where the act in question is an act of State, those who carry it out are not personally responsible but are protected by the doctrine of the sovereignty of the State. In the opinion of the Tribunal, both these submissions must be rejected. That international law imposes duties and liabilities upon individuals as upon States has long been recognised … Crimes against international law are committed by men, not by abstract entities, and only by punishing individuals who commit such crimes can the provisions of international law be enforced.

4.65   The Convention on the Prevention and Punishment of the Crime of Genocide was adopted in 1948,[69] and confirmed that genocide is a crime under international law. Individuals committing genocide are to be punished 'whether they are constitutionally responsible rulers, public officials or private individuals'.[70]

4.66   In 1993 and 1994, the UN Security Council established two tribunals to try individuals charged with certain serious crimes against international law in connection with civil conflicts occurring in the former Yugoslavia and Rwanda: the International Tribunal for the Prosecution of Persons Responsible for Serious Violations of International Humanitarian Law Committed in the Territory of the Former Yugoslavia (ICTY),[71] and the International Tribunal for the Prosecution of Persons Responsible for Genocide and Other Serious Violations of International Humanitarian Law Committed in the Territory of Rwanda and Rwandan Citizens Responsible for Genocide and Other Such Violations Committed in the Neighbouring States (ICTR).[72]

4.67   An international conference of States in 1998 adopted the Rome Statute of the International Criminal Court (ICC).[73] This treaty, which came into force in 2002 upon the ratification of 60 States, established the ICC and vests it with jurisdiction over 'persons for the most serious crimes of international concern'.[74] These offences are genocide, crimes against humanity, and war crimes; the crime of aggression may be added if and when the parties to the Statute agree on a definition of the crime

---

68.   Judgment of the Nuremberg International Military Tribunal (1947) 41 *American Journal of International Law* 172, 220–221.
69.   UNTS, Vol 78, p 277.
70.   Article IV.
71.   Security Council Resolution 827 (1993).
72.   Security Council Resolution 955 (1994).
73.   UNTS, Vol 2187, p 3.
74.   Article 1.

and the conditions under which the ICC may exercise jurisdiction with respect to it.[75] The ICC may exercise its jurisdiction if:[76]

> ... one or more of the parties involved is a state party; the accused is a national of a state party; the crime is committed on the territory of a state party; or a state not party to the statute [decides] to accept the court's jurisdiction over a specific crime that has been committed within its territory, or by its national.

4.68   By the 19th century, States had not only emerged as almost the sole subjects and persons of international law, but they had also become the sole law makers. Indeed, prior to the introduction of the *jus cogens,* their capacity to adopt binding rules by treaty was theoretically unlimited. This implied that States could, if they wished, confer on other entities any measure of legal personality they chose. Indeed, in the *Polish Postal Service in Danzig* advisory opinion,[77] the Permanent Court of International Justice affirmed that there was no barrier to States conferring rights directly on individuals by treaty. Such rights could also be made enforceable by national courts if States choose to do so by international agreement.[78]

4.69   In 1907, a treaty among five Central American States established the Central American Court of Justice and a right of individuals to bring actions directly before the Court.[79] This court lasted 11 years and received only five cases, four of which were ruled inadmissible. Article 304(b) of the 1919 Treaty of Versailles[80] authorised nationals of the allied and associated powers to bring claims for compensation in their own names against Germany before a Mixed Arbitral Tribunal. The peace treaties of 1919 also authorised individuals to bring international claims against States for violation of rights guaranteed to certain minority groups.

4.70   Since the Second World War, there has been an increase in the number of treaties which confer or affirm rights under international law directly on individuals and furnish a judicial or arbitral mechanism for their enforcement by individuals. The most conspicuous examples are:

- the (European) Convention for the Protection of Human Rights and Fundamental Freedoms,[81] and the European Court of Human Rights;
- the Treaty Establishing the European Community,[82] and the Court of Justice of the European Communities;

---

75. Article 5.
76. Article 12.
77. *Polish Postal Service in Danzig* advisory opinion, PCIJ Rep (1925) Ser B No 11.
78. *Jurisdiction of the Courts of Danzig (Pecuniary Claims of Danzig Railway Officials who have Passed into the Polish Service against the Polish Railways Administration)* advisory opinion, PCIJ Rep (1928) Ser B No 15.
79. Marjorie M Whiteman (ed), *Digest of International Law,* US Government Printing Office, 1963, Vol 1, 39.
80. Treaty of Peace between the Allied and Associated Powers and Germany, signed at Versailles, 28 June 1919, [1920] Australian Treaty Series 1.
81. UNTS, Vol 213, p 221; Council of Europe Treaty Series, No 5.
82. *Official Journal of the European Communities,* C 325/33, 24 December 2002.

- the International Convention for the Elimination of All Forms of Racial Discrimination,[83] and the Committee on the Elimination of Racial Discrimination;

- the Convention on the Settlement of Investment Disputes Between States and Nationals of Other States,[84] and the International Centre for the Settlement of Investment Disputes;

- the International Covenant on Civil and Political Rights,[85] and the Human Rights Committee; and

- the American Convention on Human Rights,[86] and the Inter-American Court of Human Rights.

Question

The Socialist Republic of Taiku (SRT) was established in 1964 and joined the United Nations the same year. It maintains diplomatic relations with well over 100 other States, including Australia.

Around 90 per cent of the SRT's population are members of the Taiku ethnic group. The remaining 10 per cent (about 300,000 people) are members of the Lorku ethnic group, with a language, religion, history and cultural tradition which distinguish them from the majority.

When the SRT was established, it created the Lorku Autonomous Region (LAR) located in the far south of the SRT. The LAR enjoyed a large measure of internal self-government through its own Regional Assembly, and the SRT's socialist economic policies did not apply in the LAR. Almost all the Lorku people lived in the LAR, where they comprised about 95 per cent of the population and enjoyed standards of living, health care, education, civil rights and economic freedom far higher than those of the population of the remainder of the SRT.

In October 2004, the Regional Assembly of the LAR met and by a large majority declared the region's independence as a new State to be known as Lorkunia. This declaration of independence expressly invoked 'the Lorku people's inherent right of self-determination'. The Regional Assembly also declared that the borders of Lorkunia were to be the same as the borders of the old LAR, and elected an interim President and Cabinet.

A pro-SRT faction walked out of the Regional Assembly and called upon SRT troops to 'safeguard national unity'. Widespread fighting erupted in the LAR between pro-independence militias and pro-SRT militias supported by SRT troops. The Regional Assembly dispersed for the safety of its members. The LAR police force and civil service were divided in their support for the two factions.

For almost three years, bitter fighting raged across the LAR. During this time, neither the SRT nor the pro-independence forces were able to

---

83.   UNTS, Vol 660, p 195.
84.   UNTS, Vol 575, p 160.
85.   UNTS, Vol 999, p 171.
86.   UNTS, Vol 1144, p 144.

assert effective control over most of the LAR's territory. Nevertheless, the pro-independence forces never controlled less than about one-third of the LAR. It was not until August 2007 that, growing weary of the struggle, the SRT withdrew all its forces from the LAR, thereby permitting the establishment of control over the LAR's entire territory by the Regional Assembly and the pro-independence militias.

By September 2007, over 20 States had recognised Lorkunia's statehood. The Australian Foreign Minister, however, announced that Australia was still considering whether to recognise Lorkunia. At the same time, a building in Lorkunia partly owned by the Australian government and partly owned by the United Nations was burned down by an angry group of pro-independence militias. The Lorkunian Foreign Minister publicly apologised for the incident, accepted responsibility on behalf of Lorkunia, and said that Lorkunia would pay full compensation to any State or organisation entitled to it, provided they recognised Lorkunia's statehood.

In October 2007, the United Nations received an application for membership from Lorkunia. The Lorkunian Foreign Minister wrote to the Australian Foreign Minister asking that Australia recognise Lorkunia's statehood and Lorkunia's government.

He also requested that Australia acknowledge that the Lorku people were legally entitled to their self-determination, and that Lorkunia had been a State since the formal declaration of independence in October 2004.

The SRT ambassador at the United Nations is opposing Lorkunia's bid for UN membership on the basis that no such State exists and that the LAR is part of the SRT's sovereign territory. Similarly, the SRT ambassador in Canberra is insisting that any Australian recognition of Lorkunia's statehood or government would constitute an unlawful interference in the SRT's internal affairs.

The Australian Foreign Minister seeks your legal advice. You may assume that Lorkunia is not a party to any treaties, and that the only treaty to which the SRT is a party is the UN Charter.

Suggested answer

There are several distinct issues here:

- Is Lorkunia a State?
- Is Australia obliged to recognise Lorkunia's statehood and government?
- May Australia or the United Nations bring an international claim against Lorkunia in respect of the building fire?
- Should Australia support Lorkunia's application for UN membership?

Lorkunia's statehood

Customary international law prescribes four criteria, all of which must be met in order for an entity to be regarded as a State. These criteria are conveniently codified in Art 1 of the Montevideo Convention on Rights and Duties of States. A State should have:

(a) a permanent population;

(b) a defined territory;

(c) a government; and

(d) the capacity to enter into relations with other States.

Population

Lorkunia has a permanent population of only about 300,000. This is a small number, but the number does not need to be large. There are already a few States with far smaller populations than Lorkunia — for example, Seychelles (80,000), Nauru (13,000) and the Vatican City (around 1,000).

Lorkunia satisfies this criterion.

Defined territory

Lorkunia claims that its territory is co-extensive with that of the old LAR. It appears, furthermore, to be exercising actual control over that territory. The SRT denies the existence of any international border between itself and Lorkunia. However, the fact that an international border is contested does not justify an assertion that the affected State lacks a defined territory. It is enough that the territory in question possesses a 'sufficient consistency, even though its boundaries have not yet been accurately delimited' *(Deutsche Continental Gas-Gesellschaft v Polish State)*.

In any event, if Lorkunia has indeed emerged as a State, then its territory would appear to be precisely defined. The principle of *uti posseditis juris* requires that when an entity emerges as a State, any applicable pre-independence administrative or colonial boundaries should remain intact until an agreement to alter them is reached. This principle was applied to preserve Spanish imperial administrative boundaries as international boundaries in the 19th century, and has been applied to post-colonial boundaries in the 20th century as a matter of customary international law *(Frontier Dispute* case). The principle has also been applied to transform the internal boundaries of a disintegrating federal State (Yugoslavia) into international borders for the new States which emerged: Badinter Committee, *Opinion No 2*. The principle of *uti posseditis juris* is almost certainly applicable to situations, such as the present, where internal administrative boundaries serve as the basis for a breakaway State's international frontier.

Lorkunia satisfies the criterion of defined territory.

Government

The requirement of government is not satisfied unless the governing authority is both formally independent and actually effective. There is no reason to believe that the Lorkunian government is not independent. The government was not, however, effective between the declaration of independence (October 2004) and the withdrawal of SRT troops (August 2007). During this time, the civil war prevented the Lorkunian authorities from asserting themselves. It was only after SRT troops departed that a stable political organisation was created, and the Lorkunian government became strong enough to assert itself throughout Lorkunia (*Aaland Islands* case).

Accordingly, Lorkunia satisfies the criterion of government, but only from August 2007.

Capacity to enter into relations with other States

Lorkunia's statehood has already been recognised by more than 20 States which, presumably, stand ready to establish diplomatic relations with it. Furthermore, the fact that these other States recognise Lorkunia is strong evidence, albeit not conclusive proof, that Lorkunia satisfies all the criteria of statehood *(Tinoco Arbitration)*. Whether one embraces the declaratory or the constitutive theory of recognition, it would appear that Lorkunia possesses the capacity to enter into relations with other States.

At the time of the declaration of Lorkunia's independence, the pro-independence forces in the LAR were not a State and there is no evidence that their conduct in declaring independence was attributable to a State. Consequently, the declaration of independence did not violate SRT's territorial integrity (*Unilateral Declaration of Independence* advisory opinion). It would, therefore, appear that Lorkunia satisfied all the criteria for statehood required by international law as from August 2007.

Recognition of Lorkunia's statehood and government

Recognition of statehood

It is occasionally suggested that a State is legally entitled to be recognised if it fulfils all the criteria of statehood. Were this true, Australia would currently be obliged to recognise Lorkunia as a State. However, the preponderance of State practice and most publicists support the view that recognition is a discretionary act which is validly subject to political considerations.

Australia is, therefore, free to recognise Lorkunia's statehood at its own discretion, and Lorkunia is not entitled to demand recognition from Australia as a matter of legal right.

If Lorkunia lacked any of the four essential indicia of statehood, the SRT would be justified in arguing that an act of recognition by Australia would be an unlawful intervention in the SRT's internal affairs. If this advice is correct in its conclusion that Lorkunia satisfies all the essential elements of statehood, then no unlawful violation of the SRT's sovereignty would result from Australia's recognition of Lorkunia.

Lorkunia also seeks an 'acknowledgement' that its statehood dates from the declaration of independence in October 2004. This request is linked to a claim to a right of self-determination by the Lorku people. We have already seen that the essential criterion of effective government was not satisfied for Lorkunia until August 2007. Granting the acknowledgement requested would, prima facie, constitute an unlawful intervention in the SRT's internal affairs.

Nevertheless, there is State practice to support the view that a new entity's statehood may be recognised where a movement enjoying popular support is fighting for independence in pursuit of a right of self-determination, and the movement controls 'substantial territory'. After the declaration of independence in this case, the pro-independence forces never controlled less than approximately one-third of Lorkunia's territory. This probably represents 'substantial territory'.

However, it must also be shown that the Lorku people enjoyed a right of self-determination. To the extent that the principle of the self-determination of peoples entails a right to choose independent statehood, it applies only to peoples inhabiting a colonial or other dependent territory, or to a 'people' within a sovereign State who are being systematically denied their rights of internal self-determination to pursue their own political, economic, social and cultural development. Undoubtedly, the Lorku are a 'people' for the purposes of self-determination *(Final Report and Recommendations of an International Meeting of Experts on the Further Study of the Concept of the Rights of People for UNESCO)*, but this entitles them only to respect for certain minority rights under customary international law and not to separate statehood (General Assembly Resolution 47/135; Badinter Committee, *Opinion No 2*) unless they are being systematically denied their rights of internal self-determination to pursue their own political, economic, social and cultural development *(Reference re Secession of Quebec)*. The LAR was part of a sovereign State and not a colonial or dependent territory. There is also no evidence that the Lorku people's internal rights of self-determination were being suppressed by the SRT. Therefore, Lorkunia's declaration of independence was not made in accordance with a right of self-determination.

Accordingly, Australia would probably commit an unlawful intervention in the SRT's internal affairs were it to acknowledge Lorkunia's statehood as dating from any time earlier than August 2007.

Recognition of government

As with the recognition of States, there is no general obligation in international law to recognise a foreign government. Australia may extend or withhold recognition of Lorkunia's government at its discretion, and may act on political considerations in making its choice.

Since 1988, Australia's policy has been not to engage in formal acts of recognition of governments. Unless the Australian government now wishes to depart from its policy, then Australia's attitude to the Lorkunian government will be ascertained by the nature of Australia's policies towards, and relations with, the Lorkunian government.

According to the existing policy:

... [i]mportant indicators to Australia's attitude to a new regime will be: public statements; establishment of and/or the conduct of diplomatic relations with it; ministerial contact; and other contacts, such as entering into aid, economic or defence arrangements, technical and cultural exchanges.

Lorkunia should be informed of Australia's current policy on recognising foreign governments so that offence may be avoided when formal recognition of Lorkunia's government is not forthcoming.

Claim against Lorkunia

The arson attack on the building owned partly by Australia and partly by the United Nations occurred after Lorkunia attained statehood, but at a time when that statehood remained unrecognised by Australia. Lorkunia has accepted international responsibility for the fire, and has indicated a willingness to satisfy international claims from States which recognise Lorkunia.

Australia

From Australia's perspective, two questions present themselves. First, can Australia make an international claim against Lorkunia before it recognises Lorkunia's statehood? Second, even if Australia recognises Lorkunia's statehood before making the claim, is Australia estopped from pressing the claim against Lorkunia by reason that it did not recognise Lorkunia at the time of the arson attack? As mentioned above, Lorkunia satisfied all the criteria for statehood and, therefore, became a State in August 2007. The arson attack occurred in September 2007. State practice supports the idea that States which do not recognise each other may nevertheless conclude binding treaties (for example, the 1953 armistice agreement between the United States and North Korea). It would appear to follow that breaches of such agreements, and international wrongs generally, can be the subject of legal claims between non-recognising States, and that no issue of estoppel arises from the fact of non-recognition *(Tinoco Arbitration)*.

The United Nations

The UN, like all international organisations, is endowed with as much international legal personality as is necessarily implied in order to give effect to its specified or implied objects and purposes. It is not known what object or purpose of the UN was being served by that organisation's part-ownership of the destroyed building in Lorkunia.

On the assumption that its interest in the building was not *ultra vires* its objects and purposes, the UN has sufficient legal personality to bring a claim in respect of the unlawful destruction of the property. The fact that Lorkunia is not yet a member of the UN does not prevent the organisation bringing a claim against Lorkunia.

The UN member States, 'representing the vast majority of the members of the international community, had the power, in conformity with international law, to bring into being an entity possessing objective international personality and not merely personality recognised by them alone, together with capacity to bring international claims' (*Reparation for Injuries Suffered in the Service of the United Nations* advisory opinion). Consequently, a claim may be brought against non-member States, including Lorkunia.

Lorkunia's application to join the United Nations

Article 4(1) of the UN Charter provides that membership of the UN is:

> ... open to all ... peace-loving states which accept the obligations contained in the present Charter and, in the judgment of the Organisation, are able and willing to carry out these obligations.

The admission of a new member is effected by a decision of the General Assembly upon the recommendation of the Security Council (UN Charter, Art 4(2)). A member State may also be suspended (Art 5) or expelled (Art 6) in certain circumstances.

These provisions indicate that membership of the United Nations is not a legal right for States — or, at least, that it is not an unconditional legal right. If Australia takes the view that Lorkunia is a State, it may, but is not compelled to, vote in favour of Lorkunia's application for membership.

If Lorkunia's application comes before a UN body on which Australia is represented and before a decision has been made formally to recognise Lorkunia, care should be taken. If Australia supports Lorkunia's application without reservation or qualification, it may be taken to have impliedly recognised Lorkunia. Therefore, if Australia wishes to support the application while still considering the question of recognition, it should make a clear statement that its support does not imply Australian recognition of Lorkunia's statehood.

Further tutorial discussion

1. In the *Reparation for Injuries Suffered in the Service of the United Nations* advisory opinion, the International Court of Justice said that the United Nations possesses objective international personality. Do any other international organisations possess this kind of personality? Do States possess only 'subjective international personality'?

2. Why are the criteria for statehood identified in Art 1 of the Montevideo Convention more strictly applied to entities claiming to be new States than to existing States?

3. Most publicists support the declaratory theory of recognition. However, if only a small number of States recognise an entity's statehood, can that entity be said to satisfy the requirement of 'capacity to enter into relations with other States'?

4. What sort of difficulties might arise between two States when neither of them recognises the other?

5. Can an international organisation lacking objective international personality bring a claim against a State which is not a member of that organisation?

6. If States are under a legal duty not to recognise an entity's statehood, can that entity be a State?

7. To what rights are a minority 'people' entitled inside a sovereign State? If they are denied those rights, will they acquire a right to establish their own State under the principle of self-determination?

8. The only way that an individual can acquire legal personality under international law is for States to bestow it on them by treaty or custom. Do you agree?

State responsibility and treatment of foreign nationals

5

Objectives

After completing this chapter, you should:

(1) understand the nature of and requirement for State responsibility in international law;

(2) be aware of the Draft Articles on State Responsibility and the Draft Articles on Diplomatic Protection and their relationship with customary international law;

(3) understand and be able to apply to concrete situations the basic principles of State responsibility;

(4) appreciate the requirement of attribution and be able to discern when conduct is attributable to a State, with particular regard to *ultra vires* conduct and conduct not exhibiting due diligence;

(5) understand the customary international law remedies for internationally wrongful acts, with particular reference to restitution, compensation and satisfaction;

(6) have a basic understanding of the general customary law rules precluding responsibility for conduct which is prima facie wrongful at international law;

(7) be able to explain the circumstances in which a State may protect its own nationals from certain kinds of mistreatment at the hands of other States, with particular reference to expropriation of property; and

(8) understand and be able to apply the rules on nationality of claims and exhaustion of local remedies as they affect a State's right to protect its own nationals from certain kinds of mistreatment at the hands of other States.

Key cases

Caire Claim (France v Mexico) (1929) 5 RIAA 516
Asian Agricultural Products Ltd (AAPL) v Sri Lanka (1990) 4 ICSID Rep 246
Yeager v Iran (1984) 17 Iran–US CTR 92
Mavrommatis Palestine Concessions case *(Jurisdiction) (Greece v United Kingdom)* PCIJ Rep (1924) Ser A No 2
Roberts Claim (United States v Mexico) (1926) 4 RIAA 77
Janes Claim (United States v Mexico) (1926) 4 RIAA 82
Noyes Claim (United States v Panama) (1933) 6 RIAA 308
Starrett Housing Corp v Iran (1984) 4 Iran–US CTR 122
Nottebohm case *(Liechtenstein v Guatemala)* ICJ Rep (1955) 4

Case Concerning the Barcelona Traction, Light and Power Company Ltd (Belgium v Spain) ICJ Rep (1970) 3

M/V 'Saiga' (No 2) case (Saint Vincent and the Grenadines v Guinea) (1999) 3 ITLOS Rep, No 2

Key treaties and instruments

Draft Articles on State Responsibility (2001): Art 1, Art 2, Art 3, Art 4, Art 5, Art 6, Art 7, Art 8, Art 9, Art 10, Art 11, Art 16, Art 20, Art 21, Art 22, Art 23, Art 24, Art 25, Art 31, Art 35, Art 36, Art 37, Art 44, Art 49, Art 50, Art 51

Resolution on Permanent Sovereignty over Natural Resources, General Assembly Resolution 1803 (XVII) (1962): Art 4

Hague Convention on Certain Questions Relating to the Conflict of Nationality Laws (1930): Art 1, Art 4

Draft Articles on Diplomatic Protection (2006): Art 4, Art 7, Art 9, Art 15

Convention on the Settlement of Investment Disputes between States and Nationals of Other States (1965): Art 27

Responsibility generally

5.1   States are the principal subjects of international law.[1] They are the entities which carry the most extensive form of legal personality. Indeed, only States are capable of exercising all the rights and bearing all the obligations available in international law (except for human rights and individual responsibility under international criminal law).

Although States have conferred a limited measure of legal personality on international organisations[2] and individuals,[3] it is States which, in practice, still bear primary responsibility for breaches of the rules prescribed by international law. Even where international law imposes liability directly on an individual (for example, for breaches of international criminal law and acts of piracy *jure gentium*), if the individual's unlawful conduct can be attributed to a State then that State will also bear international responsibility for the conduct.

5.2   Every legal system contains a class of primary rules which specify prohibited and permitted types of conduct (for example, rules relating to physical violence, protection from defamation, marriage, or breach of contractual promise). These might be called the primary rules of responsibility. Depending on the domestic legal system in question, these rules might be found in constitutions, legislation, decrees, customs or legally binding judicial precedents.

---

1.   See **1.1–1.5** and **4.1–4.3**.
2.   See **4.57–4.61**.
3.   See **4.62–4.70**.

The international legal system also contains primary rules of responsibility. These primary rules may be found in treaties, customs and general principles which commit States to certain standards of behaviour (for example, diplomatic immunity, non-intervention in each other's internal affairs, respecting the innocent passage of foreign vessels through territorial waters, and so on). Indeed, primary rules of responsibility are the principal subject matter of the remaining chapters of this book.

5.3 Unless a legal system is very primitive, there will also be complementary rules which specify particular legal consequences for any such breaches (for example, damages for violation of certain contractual and tortious obligations). These might be classified as secondary rules of responsibility. Further, where the entity apparently committing the breach is not a natural person (viz, an incorporated association or other legal person), there will also need to be secondary rules of responsibility which render the acts of individuals attributable to that entity before legal responsibility can be attached to it. In domestic legal systems, this is often dealt with as a matter of the law of agency or of special rules concerning authority and delegation in corporations law and administrative law.

The secondary rules of obligation in domestic law find an equivalent in the international legal order. International law, too, possesses rules concerning the consequences for breaching the system's primary rules of obligation.[4] Moreover, States are legal persons which are incapable of acting except through the conduct of natural persons associated with them, such as politicians, judges, police or military officers. Accordingly, international law has rules which determine the circumstances in which the conduct of such persons may be attributed to the States which they serve for the purpose of establishing the State's legal responsibility.[5]

Definition of State responsibility

5.4 Max Huber (1874–1960), in his capacity as arbitrator in the *Spanish Zone of Morocco Claims*, expressed the idea of State responsibility in the following terms:[6]

> Responsibility is the necessary corollary of a right. All rights of an international character involve international responsibility. If the obligation is not met, responsibility entails the duty to make reparations.

It is the secondary rules of responsibility in the international legal system which constitute the separate and relatively autonomous law of State responsibility. This law does not determine the content of primary legal obligations — that task is a matter of treaty interpretation, and of construing applicable customary rules and general legal principles.

---

4.   See **5.49–5.62**.
5.   See **5.16–5.48**.
6.   *Spanish Zone of Morocco Claims (United Kingdom v Spain)* (1925) 2 RIAA 615, 641.

Rather, the law of State responsibility is concerned with determining: (i) whether an act or omission which is inconsistent with a primary legal obligation can be attributed to a State so as to engage that State's responsibility for the violation; and (ii) the legal consequences for a State in respect of any act or omission which has been successfully attributed to it.

5.5 There are two further aspects of the law of State responsibility which do not find a ready analogy in domestic law.

First, States are not only subjects of international law, they are also possessed of domestic legal orders. Indeed, according to theorists such as Hans Kelsen (1881–1973), States are nothing but legal orders.[7] The law of State responsibility must, therefore, provide for the possibility that an act prohibited by international law is permitted or required by a State's domestic legal order. Conversely, an act required by international law may be forbidden by a State's domestic legal order. As will be seen,[8] the law of State responsibility gives supremacy to the obligation under international law. Consequently, the fact that an obligation under international law is inconsistent with domestic law is not, as far as international law is concerned, a defence to an alleged breach of an international legal obligation.

5.6 Second, the law of State responsibility was for a long time almost inseparable from the primary rules of obligation governing standards of treatment owed by States to nationals of other States. Indeed, many of the rules of State responsibility have their origin in disputes involving the treatment by States of aliens within their jurisdiction. The law of State responsibility evolved in such a way as to require a bond of nationality between the mistreated alien and the State which took diplomatic action in respect of that mistreatment. The importance of the primary rules regarding mistreatment of aliens has been somewhat diminished by the emergence of international human rights law. The requirements of international human rights law do not, with a few exceptions such as certain political rights and rights of migration, depend on the nationality of the affected individuals.

Nevertheless, when a State mistreats an alien, whether under the classical rules relating to treatment of aliens or under international human rights law, it remains necessary to establish a link of nationality between the alien and the State making any claim on his or her behalf,[9] unless the mistreatment involves breach of an obligation *erga omnes*.[10]

It is still traditional to consider the rules on nationality of claims and the primary rules of responsibility regarding treatment of aliens in the course of studying the law of State responsibility.

---

7.   Hans Kelsen, *Pure Theory of Law (Reine Rechtslehre)*, 2nd ed (1960), University of California Press, Berkeley, 1967, 285–90.
8.   See **5.14–5.15**.
9.   See **5.99–5.116**.
10. Draft Articles on State Responsibility, Art 48(1)(b). See **2.106–2.110**.

5.7   It should also be noted at the outset that the law of State responsibility is customary and residual. That is to say, it applies only if the State breaching the obligation and the State to which the obligation is owed have not made legally binding alternative arrangements.[11] It is always open to the States concerned, by treaty or local custom,[12] to modify the operation of the law of State responsibility in their relations *inter se*. States might, for instance, agree that a breach of a particular treaty obligation should engage a consequence different from that which would apply under the law of State responsibility. In such a case, the agreed alternative arrangement would prevail over the general customary rules of State responsibility.

Draft Articles on State Responsibility and Draft Articles on Diplomatic Protection

5.8   The law of State responsibility is found in customary international law and the general principles of law. There is, as yet, no multilateral treaty regulating or codifying the general rules and principles of State responsibility.

Until relatively recent times, establishing the requirements of State responsibility in any particular case usually involved an extensive consideration of numerous arbitral determinations and instances of State practice. Furthermore, there was frequently much disagreement about some fairly fundamental matters, such as whether the liability of States for breaching primary rules of responsibility depended on some fault or culpability on the part of that State (for example, wilful breach or negligence), or whether liability could be established strictly (that is, merely by demonstrating the fact of the breach).

5.9   Recognising the importance of this branch of international law, the International Law Commission (ILC)[13] approached its codification as an early priority. The ILC's work in studying the law of State responsibility commenced in 1949, and generated numerous reports on various aspects of State responsibility. Early hopes that the ILC's work would result in a multilateral convention proved misplaced. Disagreement about the substantive content of the relevant rules and principles remained difficult to resolve. It was not until 1980 that the ILC was able to adopt provisionally a reasonably comprehensive set of 35 Draft Articles dealing with the 'origins' of State responsibility. The ILC revised and expanded the provisional Draft Articles in 1996.

The ILC finally adopted a set of Draft Articles on the Responsibility of States for Internationally Wrongful Acts (Draft Articles) at its 53rd session in 2001.[14]

---

11.   Draft Articles on State Responsibility, Art 55.
12.   As to local custom, see **1.147–1.151**.
13.   See **1.54**.
14.   *Yearbook of the International Law Commission,* 2001, Vol II, Pt II.

5.10 Where State responsibility is incurred in the form of State A unlawfully mistreating a national of State B, then State B's response may take the form of diplomatically protecting its injured national. This right of diplomatic protection involves State B taking diplomatic action and/ or pursuing a claim against State A for reparation in respect of the injury. The claim can take any form that is lawful under international law, and typically manifests itself in the modes of peaceful dispute settlement sanctioned by Art 33(1) of the UN Charter — 'negotiation, enquiry, mediation, conciliation, arbitration, judicial settlement, resort to regional agencies or arrangements, or other peaceful means of their own choice'.[15]

Before State B may invoke a right of diplomatic protection, it must show that the individual was its national from the moment of the injury until the time the claim is made.[16] State B's claim will, furthermore, be defeated if State A can demonstrate that the injured individual has not exhausted all potentially effective legal remedies available under State A's domestic law.[17] The requirement of nationality and the defence of non-exhaustion of local remedies have been made the subject of a study by the International Law Commission, resulting in a set of Draft Articles on Diplomatic Protection (DADP) which were adopted at the ILC's 58th session in 2006.[18]

5.11 It is conceivable that the Draft Articles and the DADP might yet form the foundation of a multilateral convention on State responsibility and diplomatic protection. However, it is more likely that they will eventually be adopted as part of General Assembly resolutions on the law of State responsibility and diplomatic protection.

In the meantime, most of the Draft Articles, the DADP and their accompanying ILC Commentaries serve as a highly convenient and valuable statement of the applicable customary rules and general legal principles. They are the product of long and detailed study by many of the world's most eminent publicists of international law. It is to be anticipated that, as with many other landmark reports and studies of the ILC, even those provisions of the Draft Articles and the DADP which are strictly only *lex ferenda* will be so influential as to cause customary international law to coalesce in conformity with them. It is therefore difficult to overstate the importance of the Draft Articles and the DADP in understanding the contemporary law of State responsibility and diplomatic protection.

Basic principles of State Responsibility

Existence of responsibility

5.12 The cornerstone principle of State responsibility is codified in Art 1 of the Draft Articles on State Responsibility:

---

15. See **chapter 8**.
16. See **5.99–5.116**.
17. See **5.117–5.125**.
18. *Yearbook of the International Law Commission*, 2006, Vol II, Pt II.

Article 1

Responsibility of a State for its internationally wrongful acts

Every internationally wrongful act of a State entails the international responsibility of that State.

In its Commentaries, the International Law Commission says that Draft Art 1 states the basic principle underlying the Draft Articles as a whole. It reflects both a customary rule of international law and a general principle of law recognised by civilised nations (that is, that every person who is not subject to some special incapacity is legally responsible for his or her own unlawful acts).

In the *Rainbow Warrior* case, the arbitral tribunal observed that 'any violation by a State of any obligation, of whatever origin, gives rise to State responsibility'.[19]

Internationally wrongful act

5.13 The concept of 'internationally wrongful act' is defined in Draft Art 2:

Article 2

Elements of an internationally wrongful act of a State

There is an internationally wrongful act of a State when conduct consisting of an action or omission:

(a) Is attributable to the State under international law; and

(b) Constitutes a breach of an international obligation of the State.

There can be no internationally wrongful act, and therefore no State responsibility to make reparation, unless both elements of the definition are present — that is, conduct attributable to the State and a breach of an international obligation. The requirement of both elements is well established in customary international law and finds reflection in a number of international judicial decisions. In the *Tehran Hostages* case, the International Court of Justice remarked that in order for the Court to establish Iran's responsibility:[20]

First, it must determine how far, legally, the acts in question may be regarded as imputable to the Iranian State. Secondly, it must consider their compatibility or incompatibility with the obligations of Iran under treaties in force or under any other rules of international law that may be applicable.

The rules on attribution are dealt with in Draft Arts 4–11.[21] The question as to whether there has been a breach of an international

---

19. *Case Concerning the Difference between New Zealand and France concerning the Interpretation or Application of Two Agreements, concluded on 9 July 1986 between the Two States and which related to the Problems arising from the Rainbow Warrior Affair (New Zealand v France)* (1990) 20 RIAA 217, 251.

20. *United States Diplomatic and Consular Staff in Tehran case (United States v Iran)* ICJ Rep (1980) 3, para 56.

21. See **5.16–5.48**.

obligation is a matter for the primary rules of obligation under international law, and demands that attention be given to the applicable conventional or customary rule or general principle of law which is alleged to have been violated. Draft Art 12 provides that '[t]here is a breach of an international obligation by a State when an act of that State is not in conformity with what is required of it by that obligation, regardless of its origin or character'. Both acts and omissions are capable of breaching a conventional or customary obligation.

Competence to characterise act as wrongful

5.14   Draft Art 3 deals with the issue of which legal order — international or domestic — is competent to characterise an act or omission as internationally wrongful:

> Article 3
>
> *Characterization of an act of a State as internationally wrongful*
>
> The characterization of an act of State as internationally wrongful is governed by international law. Such characterization is not affected by the characterization of the same act as lawful by internal law.

There are two elements to Draft Art 3. In the words of the International Law Commission's Commentaries:[22]

> First, an act of a State cannot be characterized as internationally wrongful unless it constitutes a breach of an international obligation, even if it violates a provision of the State's own laws. Secondly, and most importantly, a State cannot, by pleading that its conduct conforms to the provision of its internal law, escape the characterization of that conduct as wrongful by international law. An act of a State must be characterized as internationally wrongful if it constitutes a breach of an international obligation, even if the act does not contravene the State's internal law — even if, under that law, the State was actually bound to act in that way.

5.15   That an act or omission has been held by a court to be consistent with domestic law does not, therefore, foreclose the question of its wrongfulness under international law; that issue falls to be determined solely by reference to the requirements of the relevant conventional or customary international rule. This is not to say, however, that a characterisation of an act under domestic law is without any relevance in international law. As the International Court of Justice observed in the *ELSI* case:[23]

> [T]he fact that an act of a public authority may have been unlawful in municipal law does not necessarily mean that that act was unlawful in international law, as a breach of treaty or otherwise. A finding of the local courts that an act was unlawful may well be relevant to an argument that it was also arbitrary; but by itself, and without more, unlawfulness

---

22.   *Yearbook of the International Law Commission*, 2001, Vol II, Pt II, 36.
23.   *Case Concerning Elettronica Sicula SpA (ELSI) (United States v Italy)* ICJ Rep (1989) 15, para 124.

cannot be said to amount to arbitrariness ... Nor does it follow from a finding by a municipal court that an act was unjustified, or unreasonable, or arbitrary, that the act is necessarily to be classified as arbitrary in international law, though the qualification given to an impugned act by a municipal authority may be a valuable indication.

A classification of conduct under domestic law by a domestic court or other competent authority may therefore be valuable evidence (but not conclusive proof) for an international tribunal determining a dispute concerning treatment of aliens or involving an issue of international human rights law. States are, in these areas, frequently required to conduct themselves 'according to law' or to avoid engaging in arbitrary behaviour.

Attribution

5.16 States are legal persons which are incapable of acting except through the agency of individuals. The rules on attribution in the Draft Articles determine the circumstances in which the conduct of individuals can be regarded as the conduct of a State.

It is possible to imagine a rule which makes States responsible for the conduct of any person who is their national. Such a rule would, however, be highly inconvenient inasmuch as the vast majority of States' nationals are not expressly or implicitly authorised to act on their State's behalf. States would thus be internationally responsible for conduct over which they had no control.

5.17 The law on State responsibility has, instead, developed rules which require some relationship between the individuals whose conduct is in issue and the government of the State which is said to be responsible for that conduct. International law has, in effect, developed its own doctrine of agency for the purpose of attributing the conduct of State officials, or persons performing certain official functions, to their State.

Organs of State

5.18 The official constitutional or other legal organs of a State present the least difficulty. Their conduct is the most easily attributable to their State. Draft Art 4 provides:

Article 4

Conduct of organs of a State

1. The conduct of any State organ shall be considered an act of that State under international law, whether the organ exercises legislative, executive, judicial or any other functions, whatever position it holds in the organization of the State, and whatever its character as an organ of the central government or of a territorial unit of the State.

2. An organ includes any person or entity which has that status in accordance with the internal law of the State.

5.19   It follows that all persons holding public office under a State's laws, and all collective bodies performing official functions under a State's laws, will engage the responsibility of the State when they perform an internationally wrongful act. Thus, orders or decrees issued, or non-private decisions made, by a Head of State or government minister will be regarded as the acts of their State for the purposes of State responsibility. Similarly, judgments of courts or administrative tribunals are capable of placing a State in breach of its international obligations. The non-private conduct of military personnel and police officers is also to be regarded as acts of their State for the purpose of establishing the State's responsibility. The existence of legislation, if it authorises or requires a situation or conduct contrary to international law, will likewise engage the State's international responsibility.[24]

5.20   Official acts of any level of government — central, regional or local — are also attributable to the State, even if they are performed by constitutionally or legally independent organs which are not subject to direction by the executive branch of the central government. In particular, the acts of organs of the constituent territorial elements of a federal State (for example, 'states' in Australia and the United States, provinces in Canada, *Länder* in Germany or *Bundesländer* in Austria) are attributable to the federal State. A constituent territorial unit's conduct may not, however, be attributable to the federal State where that territorial unit has entered into an international agreement on its own account and the wrongful act consists of a non-observance of that agreement.

Similarly, the federal State's responsibility may be limited by a treaty clause exempting the federal State from responsibility for breaches committed by its constituent territorial units. In the words of the ILC Commentaries:[25]

> In those cases where the constituent unit of a federation is able to enter into international agreements on its own account, the other party may well have agreed to limit itself to recourse against the constituent unit in the event of a breach. In that case the matter will not involve the responsibility of the federal State and will fall outside the scope of the present articles. Another possibility is that the responsibility of the federal State under a treaty may be limited by the terms of a federal clause in the treaty. This is clearly an exception to the general rule, applicable solely in relations between the States parties to the treaty and in the matters which the treaty covers.

5.21   Draft Art 4(2) makes it clear that if a person or entity is an organ of a State under the domestic law of a State, then its official acts will be attributable to the State. However, in some States a person or entity may exercise official authority by tradition or consent and the law may be

---

24.   For example, *Case Concerning Certain German Interests in Polish Upper Silesia* Merits, PCIJ Rep (1926) Ser A No 7, 19; *M/V 'Saiga' (No 2)* case *(Saint Vincent and the Grenadines v Guinea)* (1999) 3 ITLOS Rep, No 2, paras 119–120.
25.   *Yearbook of the International Law Commission*, 2001, Vol II, Pt II, 42 (footnote omitted).

silent even as to that person's or entity's existence. The ILC Commentaries deal with this situation:[26]

> [I]t is not sufficient to refer to internal law for the status of State organs. In some systems the status and functions of various entities are determined not only by law but also by practice, and reference exclusively to internal law would be misleading. The internal law of a State may not classify, exhaustively or at all, which entities have the status of 'organs'. In such cases, while the powers of an entity and its relation to other bodies under internal law will be relevant to its classification as an 'organ', internal law will not itself perform the task of classification. Even if it does so, the term 'organ' used in internal law may have a special meaning, and not the very broad meaning it has under article 4. For example, under some legal systems the term 'government' refers only to bodies at the highest level such as the head of State and the cabinet of ministers. In others, the police have a special status, independent of the executive; this cannot mean that for international law purposes they are not organs of the State. Accordingly, a State cannot avoid responsibility for the conduct of a body which does in truth act as one of its organs merely by denying it that status under its own law. This result is achieved by the use of the word 'includes' in paragraph 2.

Other persons exercising official authority

5.22   The problem of attribution is further complicated by the practice of many States of devolving governmental powers onto persons or bodies which are not 'State organs' within the meaning of Draft Art 4. For instance, a State might contract out to private security firms the task of supervising prisons. It might also impose on airlines or shipping companies certain official functions regarding immigration control and quarantine. This type of situation is dealt with by Draft Art 5:

> **Article 5**
>
> *Conduct of persons or entities exercising elements of governmental authority*
>
> The conduct of a person or entity which is not an organ of the State under article 4 but which is empowered by the law of that State to exercise elements of the governmental authority shall be considered an act of the State under international law, provided the person or entity is acting in that capacity in the particular instance.

5.23   As the ILC Commentaries indicate, the range of 'entities' which might be covered by Draft Art 5 is very wide:[27]

> They may include public corporations, semi-public entities, public agencies of various kinds and even, in special cases, private companies, provided that in each case the entity is empowered by the law of the State to exercise functions of a public character normally exercised by State organs, and the conduct of the entity relates to the exercise of the governmental authority concerned.

---

26.   Ibid (footnote omitted).
27.   Ibid, 43.

State organs at disposal of another State

5.24 A much less common problem of attribution arises where a State places its official organs at the disposal of another State. Will the State at whose disposal the organs are placed be responsible for the internationally wrongful acts of those organs? Such a situation might arise where, for instance, there is a natural disaster in State A. State B might 'lend' elements of its police force, government health service or government fire-fighting service to State A in order to deal with the emergency. If these organs of State B act in violation of State A's international obligations, a question arises as to whether State A is responsible for their conduct. This type of situation is covered by Draft Art 6:

> Article 6
>
> *Conduct of organs placed at the disposal of a State by another State*
>
> The conduct of an organ placed at the disposal of a State by another State shall be considered an act of the former State under international law if the organ is acting in the exercise of elements of the governmental authority of the State at whose disposal it is placed.

5.25 The scope of Draft Art 6 is relatively narrow. As the ILC Commentaries make clear, it is not enough that the organs of State B are performing functions for State A's benefit. Rather, the loaned organs must truly be 'placed at the disposal of' State A before State A will be responsible for their conduct. The loaned organs must be acting with the consent, under the authority, and for the purposes of State A.[28]

Furthermore, in performing the functions entrusted to it by State A, the organs must act in conjunction with State A's machinery and under its exclusive direction and control, rather than on instructions from State B. Draft Art 6 does not apply to ordinary instances of international cooperation or collaboration.[29]

If it can be established that the loaned organs are covered by Draft Art 6, then only State A will be responsible for their internationally wrongful conduct; State B will not be concurrently responsible. The ILC Commentaries give the example of the United Kingdom's Privy Council, which acts as a court of final appeal for a number of overseas Commonwealth States. According to the ILC, when the Privy Council is acting in this way, its conduct is attributable to the overseas State and not to the United Kingdom.[30]

Ultra vires acts

5.26 One of the most important and contentious areas of State responsibility has been the issue of *ultra vires* acts by an organ or agent whose conduct is attributable to the State. Historically, there were two schools of thought. On the one hand, it was sometimes maintained

---

28. Ibid, 44.
29. Ibid.
30. Ibid, 45.

that a State could not be held responsible for the conduct of its organs or agents where such conduct was in violation of the State's internal law or contrary to instructions. The opposing school maintained that liability was strict, and that a State was not excused from liability merely because the official had exceeded his or her authority under domestic law.

The overwhelming preponderance of State practice and scholarly opinion came to favour the strict liability school, and Draft Art 7 embraces this approach:

Article 7

Excess of authority or contravention of instructions

The conduct of an organ of a State or of a person or entity empowered to exercise elements of the governmental authority shall be considered an act of the State under international law if the organ, person or entity acts in that capacity, even if it exceeds its authority or contravenes instructions.

This provision is more consistent with the requirements of Draft Art 3 than a rule which makes State responsibility effectively dependent on the correct interpretation and application of domestic law.

5.27 Thus, a State does not escape responsibility merely because its organs or agents have exceeded their authority under domestic law. According to the ILC Commentaries, this remains so even if the conduct was overtly or manifestly unlawful. Nevertheless, it is still necessary that the organ or agent acted in an official capacity.

5.28 This clearly raises a question as to when conduct is to be regarded as having been performed in an official capacity. Some forms of conduct are so obviously and radically removed from a person's official capacity that they might reasonably be regarded as being purely private in character (for example, where a police officer commits an armed robbery). This type of problem was addressed by a French–Mexican Claims Commission in 1929, the decision of which is referred to with approval in the ILC Commentaries.[31]

In the **Caire Claim,**[32] a French national was murdered at a barracks by two Mexican military officers after they had attempted to extort money from him. The murder was a violation of Mexican law, and was committed without orders and against the wishes of the murderers' commanding officer. Mexico denied that it was responsible for the death of the French national. The Presiding Commissioner said:

> I am interpreting the … principles in accordance with the doctrine of 'objective responsibility' of the State, that is, the responsibility for the acts of the officials or organs of a State, which may devolve upon it even in the absence of any 'fault' of its own.

> It is widely known that theoretical conceptions in this sphere have advanced a great deal in recent times … Without going into the question of whether these

---

31.   Ibid, 46.
32.   *Caire Claim (France v Mexico)* (1929) 5 RIAA 516.

> new ideas … may require some modifications … I can say that I regard them as perfectly correct in that they tend to impute to the State, in international affairs, the responsibility for all the acts committed by its officials or organs which constitute offences from the point of view of the law of nations, whether the official or organ in question has acted within or exceeded the limits of his competence. 'It is generally agreed,' as M. Bourquin has rightly said, 'that acts committed by the officials and agents of a State entail the international responsibility of that State, even if the perpetrator did not have specific authorisation … The act of an official operating beyond his competence is not an act of State. It should not in principle, therefore, affect the responsibility of the State. If it is accepted in international law that the position is different, it is for reasons peculiar to the mechanisms of international life; it is because it is felt that international relations would become too difficult, too complicated and too insecure if foreign States were obliged to take into account the often complex judicial arrangements that regulate competence in the international affairs of a State. From this it is immediately clear that in the hypothesis under consideration the international responsibility of the State is purely *objective* in character, and that it rests on a *guarantee*, in which the subjective notion of fault plays no part. But in order to be able to admit this so-called objective responsibility of the State for acts committed by its officials or organs outside their competence, they must have acted at least to all appearances as competent officials or organs, or they must have used powers or methods appropriate to their official capacity.'

The Presiding Commissioner discussed the facts of the case, including especially that the murderers conducted themselves as military officers, and removed the victim to a military barracks before shooting him. The decision proceeded:

> Under these circumstances, there remains no doubt that, even if they are to be regarded as having acted outside their competence … and even if their superior officers issued a counter-order, these two officers have involved the responsibility of the State, in view of the fact that they acted in their capacity of officers and used the means placed at their disposition by virtue of that capacity.

It would, therefore, seem that a person is acting in an official capacity when he or she either:

(i)   holds himself or herself out as performing official functions; or

(ii) uses powers, methods or means placed at his or her disposal by virtue of an official capacity.

In either situation, the person's conduct is attributable to the State for the purposes of establishing its responsibility.[33]

Direction or control of a State

5.29   It is a general rule of State responsibility that States are not liable for the acts of private persons — that is, individuals or corporations which are neither officials nor organs of the State. However, it may happen that a private person performs acts which, because of the existence of special circumstances, are attributable to the State for the purpose of establishing the State's responsibility.

---

33.   See also the *Youmans Claim* (**5.85**).

Two of these special circumstances are mentioned in Draft Art 8:

Article 8

Conduct directed or controlled by a State

The conduct of a person or group of persons shall be considered an act of a State under international law if the person or group of persons is in fact acting on the instructions of, or under the direction or control of, that State in carrying out the conduct.

The conduct of private persons is attributable to a State under Draft Art 8 if they are either (i) acting on the State's instructions; or (ii) acting under the State's direction or control.

5.30   The ILC Commentaries contain the following discussion of the attribution to a State of conduct by private persons acting on the State's instructions:[34]

The attribution to the State of conduct in fact authorized by it is widely accepted in international jurisprudence. In such cases it does not matter that the person or persons involved are private individuals nor whether their conduct involves 'governmental activity'. Most commonly cases of this kind will arise where State organs supplement their own action by recruiting or instigating private persons or groups who act as 'auxiliaries' while remaining outside the official structure of the State. These include, for example, individuals or groups of private individuals who, though not specifically commissioned by the State and not forming part of its police or armed forces, are employed as auxiliaries or are sent as 'volunteers' to neighbouring countries, or who are instructed to carry out particular missions abroad.

5.31   It is possible for private persons to be acting under a State's direction and control without actually acting on its particular instructions. However, conduct of this character will be attributable to the State only if the State directed or controlled the specific operation and the conduct complained of was an integral part of that operation. The general dependence on, and support of, the State is insufficient. This was made clear in the *Nicaragua* case. The International Court of Justice rejected Nicaragua's submission that the United States was responsible for all the alleged violations of international humanitarian law by the Contra rebels because of the control which the United States was said to be exercising over them. The Court said:[35]

[D]espite the heavy subsidies and other support provided to them by the United States, there is no clear evidence of the United States having actually exercised such a degree of control in all fields as to justify treating the contras as acting on its behalf ...

All the forms of United States participation mentioned above, and even the general control by the respondent State over a force with a high degree of dependency on it, would not in themselves mean, without further evidence, that the United States directed or enforced the perpetration of the acts contrary to human rights and humanitarian law alleged by the applicant

---

34. *Yearbook of the International Law Commission*, 2001, Vol II, Pt II, 47 (footnote omitted).
35. *Military and Paramilitary Activities in and Against Nicaragua (Nicaragua v United States* Merits, ICJ Rep (1986) 14, paras 109 and 115. See **9.10**.

State. Such acts could well be committed by members of the contras without the control of the United States. For this conduct to give rise to legal responsibility of the United States, it would in principle have to be proved that that State had effective control of the military or paramilitary operations in the course of which the alleged violations were committed.

Lack of due diligence

5.32 A State may also be responsible for the consequences of unlawful conduct by private persons where the State has failed to exercise due diligence in preventing that conduct, such as where the State's police forces fail to take reasonable steps to prevent mob violence or the activities of insurrectionaries.[36]

In **Asian Agricultural Products Ltd (AAPL) v Sri Lanka,**[37] a Hong Kong company partly owned a shrimp farm in Sri Lanka that was destroyed in fighting between government forces and the rebel Tamil Tiger insurrectionaries. A tribunal established under the Convention on the Settlement of Investment Disputes Between States and Nationals of Other States[38] made the following remarks concerning the responsibility of a State in the context of terrorist activity or an armed rebellion:

72. It is a generally accepted rule of International Law, clearly stated in international arbitral awards and in the writings of the doctrinal authorities, that:

(i)   A State on whose territory an insurrection occurs is not responsible for loss or damage sustained by foreign investors unless it can be shown that the Government of that state failed to provide the standard of protection required, either by treaty, or under general customary law, as the case may be; and

(ii) Failure to provide the standard of protection required entails the state's international responsibility for losses suffered, regardless of whether the damages occurred during the insurgents' offensive act or resulting from governmental counter-insurgency activities.

73. The long established arbitral case law was adequately expressed by Max Huber, the *Rapporteur* in the *Spanish Zone of Morocco* claims (1923), in the following terms:

The principle of non-responsibility in no way excludes the duty to exercise a certain degree of vigilance. If a state is not responsible for the revolutionary events themselves, it may nevertheless be responsible, for what its authorities do or do not do to ward off the consequences, within the limits of possibility …

Furthermore, the famous arbitrator indicated that 'the degree of vigilance' required in providing the necessary protection and security would differ according to the circumstances. In the absence of any higher standard provided for by Treaty, the general international law standard was stated to reflect the 'degree of security reasonably expected'.

The Tribunal found that Sri Lanka had failed to exercise the necessary degree of vigilance in protecting AAPL, and decided that Sri Lanka should pay compensation to AAPL.

---

36. Ian Brownlie, *Principles of Public International Law,* 7th ed, Oxford University Press, Oxford, 2008, 454–56. See also the *Noyes Claim (Noyes (US) v Panama)* (1933) 6 RIAA 308 (**5.88**).
37. *Asian Agricultural Products Ltd v Sri Lanka* (1990) 4 ICSID Rep 246.
38. UNTS, Vol 575, p 160.

Absence or default of official authorities

5.33 There will be relatively rare circumstances where private persons perform elements of governmental functions without the authority of the State.

This might occur in times of turmoil created by foreign invasion, revolution or severe natural disaster where the legally constituted authorities are absent or non-functioning. In these circumstances, private persons may come forward in order to fill the vacuum and perform essential tasks (such as policing or defence) until legal authority is re-established.

When this occurs, a question may arise as to whether the State is responsible for any internationally wrongful acts committed by the private persons. This problem is addressed by Draft Art 9:

Article 9

Conduct carried out in the absence or default of the official authorities

The conduct of a person or group of persons shall be considered an act of a State under international law if the person or group of persons is in fact exercising elements of the governmental authority in the absence or default of the official authorities and in circumstances such as to call for the exercise of those elements of authority.

5.34 An instance of the species of attribution described by Draft Art 9 may be seen in an award of the Iran–United States Claims Tribunal.

In **Yeager v Iran**,[39] a United States national was employed by a United States company in Iran. In 1979, a revolutionary movement overthrew the government of the Shah and replaced it with one headed by Ayatollah Khomeini. Two days after the new government assumed power, and while widespread turmoil remained, two members of the armed 'Revolutionary Guards', or 'Komitehs', arrested the United States national at his apartment, gave him 30 minutes to pack his belongings, and forcibly detained him at the Hilton Hotel in Tehran. A few days later, the 'Guards' deported him from Iran. The proceedings concerned a claim of expulsion contrary to customary international law before the Iran–United States Claims Tribunal. Iran denied any responsibility for the conduct of the 'Guards', who, it argued, were a group of private persons whose activities the Iranian State had not authorised. The Tribunal said:

42. ... attributability of acts to the State is not limited to acts of organs formally recognized under internal law. Otherwise a State could avoid responsibility under international law merely by invoking its internal law. It is generally accepted in international law that a State is also responsible for acts of persons, if it is established that those persons were in fact acting on behalf of the State. ... An act is attributable even if a person or group of persons was in fact merely exercising elements of governmental authority in the absence of the official authorities and in circumstances which justified the exercise of those elements of authority. ...

---

39. *Yeager v Islamic Republic of Iran* (1984) 17 Iran–US CTR 92.

> 43. The Tribunal finds sufficient evidence in the record to establish a presumption that revolutionary 'Komitehs' or 'Guards' ... were acting in fact on behalf of the new Government, or at least exercising elements of governmental authority in the absence of official authorities, in operations of which the new Government must have had knowledge and to which it did not specifically object. ...
>
> 45. Nor has the Respondent established that it could not control the revolutionary 'Komitehs' or 'Guards' in this operation. Because the new government accepted their activity in principle and their role in the maintenance of public security, calls for more discipline phrased in general rather than specific terms, do not meet the standard of control required in order to effectively prevent these groups from committing wrongful acts against United States nationals. Under international law Iran cannot, on the one hand, tolerate the existence of governmental authority by revolutionary 'Komitehs' or 'Guards' and at the same time deny responsibility for wrongful acts committed by them. ... [T]he Tribunal finds the acts of the two men who took the Claimant to the Hilton Hotel attributable to Iran.

Insurrectional and secessionist movements

5.35　At any given time, there are a number of States within which insurrectional movements are active. These movements conduct armed activities for the purpose of either overthrowing a State's government and replacing it with a new government, or securing the secession of part of a State's territory so that a new State may be established on that territory. A political movement may also attempt, through non-violent means, to establish a new State on territory occupied by an existing State. Ordinarily, the State against which the acts of insurrection are directed is not responsible for the conduct of such movements because they are considered to be acts of private persons. Draft Art 10, however, prescribes some exceptional circumstances where a State will be responsible for the conduct of insurrectionaries or unlawful secessionist movements:

Article 10

Conduct of an insurrectional or other movement

1. The conduct of an insurrectional movement which becomes the new government of a State shall be considered an act of that State under international law.

2. The conduct of a movement, insurrectional or other, which succeeds in establishing a new State in part of the territory of a pre-existing State or in a territory under its administration shall be considered an act of the new State under international law.

3. This article is without prejudice to the attribution to a State of any conduct, however related to that of the movement concerned, which is to be considered an act of that State by virtue of articles 4 to 9.

5.36　Draft Art 10(1) indicates that the conduct of an insurrectional movement which has assumed control of an existing State is attributable to that State. Therefore, internationally wrongful acts of the insurrectional movement will be attributable to the State only if that movement becomes the State's new government. Otherwise, they remain acts of private persons for which the State is not responsible. This rule involves, in effect, a retrospective imposition of responsibility on a State for the conduct of a successful insurrectional movement.

5.37   The term 'insurrectional movement' is not defined by the Draft Articles. The ILC Commentaries, however, look to guidance from the 1977 first additional protocol to the Geneva Convention, which refers to 'dissident armed forces or other organized armed groups which, under responsible command, exercise such control over [the relevant State's] territory as to enable them to carry out sustained and concerted military operations'.[40] These examples are contrasted to 'situations of internal disturbances and tensions, such as riots, isolated and sporadic acts of violence and other acts of a similar character'.[41]

5.38   The ILC Commentaries make clear that the conduct of both the successful insurrectional movement and the organs of the government against which it was struggling are attributable to the State. What is not quite so clear from the Commentaries is whether the conduct of the insurrectional movement is attributable to the State if it assumes power by non-insurrectional means — for example, if the government of a State yields power to an armed rebel movement as the result of a democratic election. On the one hand, the wording of Draft Art 10(1) requires only that the insurrectional movement 'becomes' the new government, without specifying that power was seized by insurrection. On the other hand, the Commentaries specify that Draft Art 10(1):[42]

> ... covers the scenario in which the insurrectional movement, having triumphed, has substituted its structures for those of the previous government of the State in question. The phrase 'which becomes the new government' is used to describe this consequence.

The ILC Commentaries further specify that Draft Art 10(1) is not intended to apply to circumstances where an insurrectional movement is incorporated into a government of national reconciliation whereby the insurrectional movement and the existing government agree to share power. The better view would therefore appear to be that Draft Art 10(1) does not apply to make the State responsible for the activities of an insurrectional movement where that movement assumes power by non-insurrectional means.

5.39   It is the conduct of the insurrectional or other movement as such which becomes attributable to the State, 'not the individual acts of members of the movement, acting in their own capacity'.[43]

5.40   Draft Art 10(2) deals with the conduct of all movements which establish a new State in territory formerly belonging to another State or under another State's administration (for example, a colony).

---

40.   Article 1, Protocol Additional to the Geneva Conventions of 12 August 1949, and relating to the Protection of Victims of International Armed Conflicts (Protocol I), UNTS, Vol 1125, p 3.
41.   Ibid.
42.   *Yearbook of the International Law Commission*, 2001, Vol II, Pt II, 51.
43.   Ibid, 50.

It therefore covers the conduct of secessionist or anti-colonial movements, and draws no distinction between insurrectional and 'other' movements.

It is therefore not necessary, for the purposes of applying Draft Art 10, for a movement to be insurrectional if it establishes a new State, as distinct from seizing power in an existing State. This implies that the conduct of successful secessionist or independence movements which are peaceful, or which use force short of actual insurrection, is capable of being attributed to the new State.

The movement must, however, have been operating outside the normal legal procedures of the existing State; the ILC Commentaries make it clear that the words 'insurrectional or other movements' do not 'extend to encompass the actions of a group of citizens advocating separation or revolution where these are carried out within the framework of the predecessor State'.[44] A secessionist or anti-colonial movement waging a conventional political campaign within the parameters of the State's laws would not appear to be covered by Draft Art 10(2).

5.41 Another notable feature of Draft Art 10(2) is that, unlike Draft Art 10(1), there is no express requirement that the secessionist or anticolonial movement must have become the government of the new State before its conduct is attributable to the new State.

5.42 A State may, in exceptional circumstances, be responsible for the conduct of an insurrectional, separatist or anti-colonial movement, even where the movement is unsuccessful or not yet successful.

Draft Art 10(3) specifies a range of applicable exceptional circumstances. Of particular importance is the reference back to Draft Art 9. Thus, the conduct of a movement which has not succeeded, or not yet succeeded, will be attributable to the State if it is in fact exercising elements of governmental authority in the absence or default of the official authorities and in circumstances which call for the exercise of those elements of authority.

Adoption

5.43 States may 'acknowledge and adopt' the conduct of another entity (for example, private persons, other States or international organisations), with the consequence that the conduct is attributed to the State. Draft Art 11 provides:

Article 11

Conduct acknowledged and adopted by a State as its own

Conduct which is not attributable to a State under the preceding articles shall nevertheless be considered an act of that State under international law if and to the extent that the State acknowledges and adopts the conduct in question as its own.

---

44. Ibid, 51.

5.44   Instances of a State acknowledging and adopting another entity's conduct as its own are relatively rare. This is because the State must do more than merely express support and approval of the conduct. In the words of the ILC Commentaries:[45]

> The phrase 'acknowledges and adopts the conduct in question as its own' is intended to distinguish cases of acknowledgement and adoption from cases of mere support or endorsement. The Court in the *Diplomatic and Consular Staff* case[46] used phrases such as 'approval', 'endorsement', 'the seal of official governmental approval' and 'the decision to perpetuate [the situation]'. These were sufficient in the context of that case, but as a general matter, conduct will not be attributable to a State under article 11 where a State merely acknowledges the factual existence of conduct or expresses its verbal approval of it. In international controversies States often take positions which amount to 'approval' or 'endorsement' of conduct in some general sense but do not involve any assumption of responsibility. The language of 'adoption', on the other hand, carries with it the idea that the conduct is acknowledged by the State as, in effect, its own conduct. Indeed, provided the State's intention to accept responsibility for otherwise non-attributable conduct is clearly indicated, article 11 may cover cases in which a State has accepted responsibility for conduct of which it did not approve, had sought to prevent and deeply regretted. However such acceptance may be phrased in the particular case, the term 'acknowledges and adopts' in article 11 makes it clear that what is required is something more than a general acknowledgement of a factual situation, but rather that the State identifies the conduct in question and makes it its own.

Direction, control or coercion

5.45   According to Draft Arts 17 and 18, a State will also be responsible for the wrongful act of another State if it directs, controls or coerces the other State to commit an internationally wrongful act.

Aiding or assisting

5.46   A State will be responsible if it aids or assists another State in the commission of an internationally unlawful act. Draft Art 16 provides:

Article 16

Aid or assistance in the commission of an internationally wrongful act

A State which aids or assists another State in the commission of an internationally wrongful act by the latter is internationally responsible for doing so if:

(a) That State does so with knowledge of the circumstances of the internationally wrongful act; and

(b) The act would be internationally wrongful if committed by that State.

---

45.   Ibid, 53 (footnote omitted).
46.   *United States Diplomatic and Consular Staff in Tehran* case *(United States v Iran)* ICJ Rep (1980) 3.

The ILC Commentaries provide examples of the type of conduct covered by the concept of aid and assistance:[47]

> Such situations arise where a State voluntarily assists or aids another State in carrying out conduct which violates the international obligations of the latter, for example, by knowingly providing an essential facility or financing the activity in question. Other examples include providing means for the closing of an international waterway, facilitating the abduction of persons on foreign soil, or assisting in the destruction of property belonging to nationals of a third country. ...
>
> The obligation not to use force may also be breached by an assisting State through permitting the use of its territory by another State to carry out an armed attack against a third State. ...

5.47 It is important to note that a State which has aided or assisted another State in the commission of a wrongful act is not responsible for the unlawful act itself. This is evident from a careful reading of the text of Draft Art 16. The aiding or assisting State is 'internationally responsible for doing so' — that is, for aiding or assisting. The ILC Commentaries underscore this point by stressing that aiding or assisting is not to be confused with the responsibility of the acting State. Rather, the assisting State will be responsible only to the extent that its conduct has caused or contributed to the wrongful act. Indeed, the Commentaries clarify the situation in the following terms:[48]

> In accordance with article 16, the assisting State is responsible for its own act in deliberately assisting another State to breach an international obligation by which they are both bound. It is not responsible, as such, for the act of the assisted State. In some cases this may be a distinction without a difference: where the assistance is a necessary element in the wrongful act in absence of which it could not have occurred, the injury suffered can be concurrently attributed to the assisting and the acting State. In other cases, however, the difference may be very material: the assistance may have been only an incidental factor in the commission of the primary act, and may have contributed only to a minor degree, if at all, to the injury suffered. By assisting another State to commit an internationally wrongful act, a State should not necessarily be held to indemnify the victim for all the consequences of the act, but only for those which, in accordance with the principles stated in Part Two of the articles, flow from its own conduct.

5.48 According to Draft Art 16(b), the aiding or assisting State will not be internationally responsible for so doing unless the conduct which was aided or assisted would have been unlawful if committed by that State.

For example, State A will be internationally responsible for assisting State B to carry out terrorist attacks on State C where State A provides the terrorists with false passports in order to enter the territory of State C.

---

47. *Yearbook of the International Law Commission*, 2001, Vol II, Pt II, 66.
48. Ibid, 67 (footnote omitted).

This is because State A and State B are both required to respect State C's territorial sovereignty and to refrain from launching terrorist attacks against State C.

On the other hand, State A will not be internationally responsible for providing State B with the financial means to avoid a bilateral treaty obligation owed to State C. State A would be assisting State B to commit an internationally wrongful act but, unless State A was party to the treaty obligation in question or under another obligation to State C in materially identical terms, that act would not have been unlawful if it had been committed by State A.

Reparation

Reparation generally

5.49 Once it has been established that conduct constituting an internationally wrongful act has been committed and is attributable to a State, a question arises as to the appropriate consequences for that State. There are two principal obligations which arise in this regard. First, Draft Art 30 requires that the State cease the act if it is continuing and offer appropriate assurances of non-repetition if circumstances so require. Second, there is an obligation to make reparation, as indicated by Draft Art 31:

> Article 31
>
> *Reparation*
>
> 1. The responsible State is under an obligation to make full reparation for the injury caused by the internationally wrongful act.
>
> 2. Injury includes any damage, whether material or moral, caused by the internationally wrongful act of a State.

5.50 The Permanent Court of International Justice said in the jurisdiction stage of the *Chorzów Factory* case:[49]

> [I]t is a principle of international law, and even a general conception of law, that any breach of an engagement involves an obligation to make reparation. ... [R]eparation therefore is the indispensable complement of a failure to apply a convention, and there is no necessity for this to be stated in the convention itself.

At the merits stage of the same case, the Court added the following observations:[50]

> The essential principle contained in the notion of an illegal act — a principle which seems to be established by international practice and

---

49. *Case Concerning the Factory at Chorzów (Indemnity) (Jurisdiction) (Germany v Poland)* PCIJ Rep (1927) Series A No 9, 21.
50. *Case Concerning the Factory at Chorzów (Indemnity) (Merits) (Germany v Poland)* PCIJ Rep (1928) Series A No 17, 46.

in particular by the decisions of arbitral tribunals — is that reparation must, as far as possible, wipe out all the consequences of the illegal act and reestablish the situation which would, in all probability, have existed if that act had not been committed.

It follows that every performance of any internationally wrongful act entails the State's responsibility to make reparation.

This obligation is grounded both in customary international law and in the general principles of law recognised by civilised nations. The Court's understanding as to the requirements of an obligation to make reparation finds reflection in the Draft Articles.

5.51   In the *Chorzów Factory* case, the claim made by Germany was in respect of financial losses. Hence, the Court mentioned only restitution and monetary compensation or damages as entailments of an obligation to make reparation. It has long been accepted, however, that satisfaction is also a possible entailment of reparation. Draft Art 34 acknowledges this by providing that '[f]ull reparation for the injury caused by the internationally wrongful act shall take the form of restitution, compensation and satisfaction, either singly or in combination'.

Restitution

5.52   As the *Chorzów Factory* case makes clear, restitution is the primary form of reparation. According to Draft Art 35:

Article 35

Restitution

A State responsible for an internationally wrongful act is under an obligation to make restitution, that is, to re-establish the situation which existed before the wrongful act was committed, provided and to the extent that restitution:

(a) Is not materially impossible;

(b) Does not involve a burden out of all proportion to the benefit deriving from restitution instead of compensation.

There has been disagreement among publicists as to the scope of the requirements of restitution, as the ILC Commentaries make clear:[51]

The concept of restitution is not uniformly defined. According to one definition, restitution consists in re-establishing the status quo ante, ie, the situation that existed prior to the occurrence of the wrongful act. Under another definition, restitution is the establishment or re-establishment of the situation that would have existed if the wrongful act had not been committed. The former definition is the narrower one; it does not extend to the compensation which may be due to the injured party for loss suffered, for example for loss of the use of goods wrongfully detained but subsequently returned. The latter definition absorbs into the concept of restitution other elements of full reparation and tends to conflate

---

51.   *Yearbook of the International Law Commission*, 2001, Vol II, Pt II, 96, para (2).

restitution as a form of reparation and the underlying obligation of reparation itself. Article 35 adopts the narrower definition which has the advantage of focusing on the assessment of a factual situation and of not requiring a hypothetical inquiry into what the situation would have been if the wrongful act had not been committed. Restitution in this narrow sense may of course have to be completed by compensation in order to ensure full reparation for the damage caused ...

5.53 In the *Temple of Preah Vihear* case,[52] the International Court of Justice ordered restitutionary relief by requiring Thailand to return to Cambodia artefacts which had been unlawfully removed from a temple and its vicinity.

5.54 Restitution will be clearly impossible where the object of the obligation has ceased to exist, but may also extend to situations where third parties acting in good faith and without notice of the internationally wrongful act have acquired an interest in it.[53]

Compensation

5.55 Where restitution is not available, or is not sufficient to effect full reparation, compensation may be payable. This is provided for in Draft Art 36:

Article 36

Compensation

1. The State responsible for an internationally wrongful act is under an obligation to compensate for the damage caused thereby, insofar as such damage is not made good by restitution.

2. The compensation shall cover any financially assessable damage including loss of profits insofar as it is established.

5.56 As the wording of Draft Art 36(1) indicates, compensation is secondary to restitution as a form of reparation and is available only where damage is not made good by restitution. In practice, restitution is rarely sufficient to 'wipe out all the consequences of the illegal act and re-establish the situation which would, in all probability, have existed if that act had not been committed'.[54] Compensation normally accompanies restitution, and is frequently awarded instead of restitution. In fact, compensation is a more common remedy than restitution.

5.57 Compensation covers any financially assessable damage. The term 'damage' embraces both material and moral damage.[55] The ILC Commentaries explain these two types of damage in the following terms:[56]

---

52. *Case Concerning the Temple of Preah Vihear (Cambodia v Thailand)* Merits, ICJ Rep (1962) 6. See **2.98**.
53. *Forests of Central Rhodope* case (1933) 3 RIAA 1405.
54. See **5.50**.
55. Draft Articles on State Responsibility, Art 31(2). See **5.49**.
56. *Yearbook of the International Law Commission*, 2001, Vol II, Pt II, 92.

'Material' damage here refers to damage to property or other interests of the State and its nationals which is assessable in financial terms. 'Moral' damage includes such items as individual pain and suffering, loss of loved ones or personal affront associated with an intrusion on one's home or private life.

As Draft Art 36(2) makes clear, compensation also covers loss of profits where it has been established. This type of compensation will be most relevant where the internationally wrongful act takes the form of an unlawful expropriation by a State of income-producing property belonging to another State's national.

5.58   The role of compensation was addressed by the Permanent Court of International Justice in the *Chorzów Factory* case in the following terms:[57]

> Restitution in kind, or, if this is not possible, payment of a sum corresponding to the value which a restitution in kind would bear; the award, if need be, of damages for loss sustained which would not be covered by restitution in kind or payment in place of it — such are the principles which should serve to determine the amount of compensation due for an act contrary to international law.

5.59   Where compensation does not result in full reparation, the victim State shall be entitled, when necessary, to interest on any principal sum awarded to it. The interest rate and mode of its calculation must be set to achieve full reparation. Interest entitlements accumulate from the date when the principal sum should have been paid until the date the obligation to pay has been fulfilled.[58]

5.60   If a victim State has contributed to its injury by any wilful or negligent act or omission on its part, any reparation shall be adjusted to take account of that contribution.[59]

Satisfaction

5.61   The final form of reparation is satisfaction. Draft Art 37 makes the following stipulation:

Article 37

Satisfaction

1. The State responsible for an internationally wrongful act is under an obligation to give satisfaction for the injury caused by that act insofar as it cannot be made good by restitution or compensation.

2. Satisfaction may consist in an acknowledgement of the breach, an expression of regret, a formal apology or another appropriate modality.

3. Satisfaction shall not be out of proportion to the injury and may not take a form humiliating to the responsible State.

---

57.   *Case Concerning the Factory at Chorzów (Indemnity) (Merits) (Germany v Poland)* PCIJ Rep (1928) Series A No 17, 47.
58.   Draft Articles on State Responsibility, Art 38.
59.   Ibid, Art 39.

5.62   The ancillary nature of satisfaction is made clear by the language of Draft Art 37(1). In practice, States employ satisfaction as a remedy in circumstances where an internationally wrongful act is not financially assessable and constitutes an affront to the dignity of the victim State.

The practice was described by the arbitral tribunal in the *Rainbow Warrior* case in the following terms:[60]

> There is a long established practice of States and international Courts and Tribunals of using satisfaction as a remedy or form of reparation … for the breach of an international obligation. This practice relates particularly to the case of moral or legal damage done directly to the State, especially as opposed to the case of damage to persons involving international responsibilities.

The case involved a clandestine attack by agents of the French intelligence service on a civilian vessel within New Zealand's territorial waters. The Secretary-General of the United Nations ruled that 'the Prime Minister of France should convey to the Prime Minister of New Zealand a formal and unqualified apology for the attack'.[61]

Satisfaction may, in some circumstances, take the simple form of a finding by a court or tribunal that the obligation was breached. In the *Mutual Assistance in Criminal Matters* case,[62] France failed to comply with an obligation under Art 17 of the 1986 Convention on Mutual Assistance in Criminal Matters between France and Djibouti to give reasons for its refusal to execute a letter rogatory issued by Djibouti and addressed to a person in France. By the time of the ICJ's judgment, France's reasons had passed into the public domain and the Court found it unnecessary to order that they be provided to Djibouti. The Court determined, in these circumstances, that 'its finding that France has violated its obligation to Djibouti under Article 17 constitutes appropriate satisfaction'.[63]

Circumstances precluding wrongfulness

5.63   There is a range of circumstances in which the acts or omissions of a State are lawful, notwithstanding that they would ordinarily be internationally wrongful. In such cases, the State is not internationally responsible for the acts or omissions. These circumstances are consent, self-defence, the taking of countermeasures, *force majeure*, distress and necessity.

---

60.   *Case Concerning the Difference between New Zealand and France concerning the Interpretation or Application of Two Agreements, concluded on 9 July 1986 between the Two States and which related to the Problems arising from the Rainbow Warrior Affair (New Zealand v France)* (1990) 20 RIAA 217, 272–273.
61.   Ibid, 516.
62.   *Case Concerning Certain Questions of Mutual Assistance in Criminal Matters (Djibouti v France)* ICJ Rep (2008) 179.
63.   Ibid, para 204.

Consent

5.64   An act by a State will not be internationally wrongful if the State said to be the victim of that act has validly consented to it, and provided the act remains within the limits of any such consent.[64] Thus, if a person properly authorised by State A freely consents to having a diplomatic bag belonging to State A opened by officers of State B, then State A cannot afterwards claim that State B is responsible for violating diplomatic privilege in relation to any conduct which remained strictly within the limits of the consent given by State A.

Self-defence

5.65   An act of self-defence, taken in conformity with the United Nations Charter,[65] will not be internationally wrongful.[66]

Countermeasures

5.66   To the extent that an act by a State is a legitimate countermeasure against another State,[67] the act will not be internationally wrongful against that other State.[68] The act may still be internationally wrongful against third States if it also involves a breach of an obligation owed to them.[69]

Countermeasures taken by a State must be proportionate[70] and taken only in order to induce another State which is in breach of its obligations to comply with those obligations.[71] The countermeasures adopted must, as far as possible, be taken in such a way as to permit the resumption of performance of the obligations in question.[72]

Countermeasures must not affect the obligation to refrain from the threat or use of force, obligations for the protection of human rights, obligations prohibiting reprisals, or obligations of a *jus cogens* character.[73] Countermeasures must also be suspended once the internationally wrongful act has ceased or if the dispute is pending before a court or tribunal.[74]

Finally, termination of a treaty cannot constitute a lawful countermeasure.[75]

Force majeure

5.67   If an act is performed due to *force majeure*, its wrongfulness is precluded. *Force majeure* is the 'occurrence of an irresistible force or of

---

64. Draft Articles on State Responsibility, Art 20.
65. See **9.19–9.40**.
66. Draft Articles on State Responsibility, Art 21.
67. Ibid, Arts 49–53. See also **1.72–1.73**.
68. Draft Articles on State Responsibility, Art 22.
69. See also ibid, Art 49(2).
70. Ibid, Art 51.
71. Ibid, Art 49(1).
72. Ibid, Art 49(3).
73. Ibid, Art 50.
74. Ibid, Art 52(3).
75. *Case Concerning the Gabcíkovo-Nagymaros Project (Hungary v Slovakia)* ICJ Rep (1997) 7, para 107.

an unforeseen event, beyond the control of the State, making it materially impossible in the circumstances to perform the obligation'.[76]

The ILC Commentaries give the following example of situations that are, and are not, covered by the rule:[77]

> Material impossibility of performance giving rise to *force majeure* may be due to a natural or physical event (eg, stress of weather which may divert State aircraft into the territory of another State, earthquakes, floods or drought) or to human intervention (eg, loss of control over a portion of the State's territory as a result of an insurrection or devastation of an area by military operations carried out by a third State), or some combination of the two. Certain situations of duress or coercion involving force imposed on the State may also amount to *force majeure* if they meet the various requirements of article 23. In particular the situation must be irresistible, so that the State concerned has no real possibility of escaping its effects. *Force majeure* does not include circumstances in which performance of an obligation has become more difficult, for example due to some political or economic crisis. Nor does it cover situations brought about by the neglect or default of the State concerned, even if the resulting injury itself was accidental and unintended.

5.68   That *force majeure* will not arise only because performance of an obligation has become more onerous is made clear by the decision of the arbitral tribunal in the *Rainbow Warrior* case:[78]

> New Zealand is right in asserting that the excuse of *force majeure* is not of relevance in this case because the test of its applicability is of absolute and material impossibility, and because a circumstance rendering performance more difficult or burdensome does not constitute a case of *force majeure*.

Accordingly, the Tribunal concluded that France could not rely on *force majeure* in order to justify removing its intelligence agents from their place of detention in Hao for medical treatment and not returning them thereafter. This conduct was in violation of a 1986 agreement between France and New Zealand concerning the detention of the officers, who had been convicted of offences under New Zealand law.

5.69   A State is also not entitled to rely on *force majeure* if its conduct has contributed to the situation arising, or if the State has assumed the risk of the situation arising.[79]

Distress

5.70   A State may rely on distress where an individual whose acts are attributable to the State is in a situation of peril, either personally or in relation to persons under his or her care. Draft Art 24(1) precludes the

---

76. Draft Articles on State Responsibility, Art 23(1).
77. *Yearbook of the International Law Commission,* 2001, Vol II, Pt II, 76–77 (footnotes omitted).
78. *Case Concerning the Difference between New Zealand and France concerning the Interpretation or Application of Two Agreements, concluded on 9 July 1986 between the Two States and which related to the Problems arising from the Rainbow Warrior Affair (New Zealand v France)* (1990) 20 RIAA 217, 253.
79. Draft Articles on State Responsibility, Art 23(2).

wrongfulness of conduct adopted by the State agent in circumstances where the agent had no other reasonable way of saving life.

5.71 Most cases of distress have involved aircraft or ships entering another State's territory because of dangerous weather conditions or mechanical failure. The ILC Commentaries provide the following illustration of the principle:[80]

> An example is the entry of United States military aircraft into Yugoslavia's airspace in 1946. On two occasions, United States military aircraft entered Yugoslav airspace without authorization and were attacked by Yugoslav air defences.

> The United States Government protested [against] the Yugoslav action on the basis that the aircraft had entered Yugoslav airspace solely in order to escape extreme danger. The Yugoslav Government responded by denouncing the systematic violation of its airspace, which it claimed could only be intentional in view of its frequency. A later note from the Yugoslav Chargé d'Affaires informed the American Department of State that Marshal Tito [Yugoslavia's Head of State] had forbidden any firing on aircraft which flew over Yugoslav territory without authorization, presuming that, for its part, the United States Government 'would undertake the steps necessary to prevent these flights, except in the case of emergency or bad weather, for which arrangements could be made by agreement between American and Yugoslav authorities'. The reply of the American Acting Secretary of State reiterated the assertion that no American planes had flown over Yugoslavia intentionally without prior authorization from Yugoslav authorities 'unless forced to do so in an emergency'. However, the Acting Secretary of State added:

>> I presume that the Government of Yugoslavia recognizes that *in case a plane and its occupants are jeopardized, the aircraft may change its course so as to seek safety even though such action may result in flying over Yugoslav territory without prior clearance.*

5.72 A plea of distress was also made by France in the *Rainbow Warrior* case. France argued that, in removing its intelligence officers from their place of detention in Hao for medical and compassionate reasons, it was acting on 'circumstances of distress in a case of extreme urgency involving elementary humanitarian considerations affecting the acting organs of the State'. The Tribunal said that before France could succeed on the plea, it had to show three things:[81]

(1) The existence of very exceptional circumstances of extreme urgency involving medical or other considerations of an elementary nature, provided always that a prompt recognition of the existence of those exceptional circumstances is subsequently obtained from the other interested party or is clearly demonstrated.

---

80. *Yearbook of the International Law Commission*, 2001, Vol II, Pt II, 78–79 (footnotes omitted; emphasis in original).

81. *Case Concerning the Difference between New Zealand and France concerning the Interpretation or Application of Two Agreements, concluded on 9 July 1986 between the Two States and which related to the Problems arising from the Rainbow Warrior Affair (New Zealand v France)* (1990) 20 RIAA 217, 255.

(2) The re-establishment of the original situation of compliance with the assignment in Hao as soon as the reasons of emergency invoked to justify the repatriation had disappeared.

(3) The existence of a good-faith effort to try to obtain the consent of New Zealand in terms of the 1986 Agreement.

5.73 A State may not rely on distress if the State contributes to the situation arising or the act in question is likely to create a comparable or greater peril.[82]

Necessity

5.74 A State may be able to invoke necessity in order to justify an otherwise internationally wrongful act. It will, however, succeed only if the act was the only way for it to safeguard an essential interest against grave and imminent peril and if it did not impair an essential interest of other States.[83] The principle has rarely been successfully invoked.

In the *Security Wall* advisory opinion,[84] the International Court of Justice rejected a plea of necessity from Israel which sought to justify the erection of a wall or security fence through parts of the territories occupied by Israel after failed invasion attempts by it neighbours. Israel argued that the wall was necessary in order to prevent terrorist attacks, and the Court accepted that Israel was confronted with 'numerous indiscriminate and deadly acts of violence against its civilian population'.[85] The Court nevertheless rejected the plea on the basis that, in its assessment, the construction of the fence along the route chosen was not 'the only means to safeguard the interests of Israel against the peril which it has invoked as justification for that construction'.[86]

The ILC Commentaries refer to a case in which the principle, though not expressly invoked, was in fact successfully applied:[87]

In March 1967 the Liberian oil tanker *Torrey Canyon* went aground on submerged rocks off the coast of Cornwall outside British territorial waters, spilling large amounts of oil which threatened the English coastline. After various remedial attempts had failed, the British Government decided to bomb the ship to burn the remaining oil. This operation was carried out successfully. The British Government did not advance any legal justification for its conduct, but stressed the existence of a situation of extreme danger and claimed that the decision to bomb the ship had been taken only after all other means had failed. No international protest resulted.

5.75 A State may not rely on necessity if the obligation in question excludes the possibility of necessity (for example, treaties dealing

---

82. Draft Articles on State Responsibility, Art 24(2).
83. Ibid, Art 25(1).
84. *Legal Consequences of the Construction of a Wall in the Occupied Palestinian Territory* advisory opinion, ICJ Rep (2004) 136.
85. Ibid, para 141.
86. Ibid, para 140.
87. *Yearbook of the International Law Commission*, 2001, Vol II, Pt II, 82 (footnotes omitted).

with humanitarian and human rights issues often exclude necessity in certain situations), or where the State has contributed to the situation of necessity.[88]

Treatment of foreign nationals

5.76   Most internationally wrongful acts involve a State violating an obligation owed by it directly to another State or to a group of other States. Breaches of bilateral or multilateral treaties provide the most common instances. The wrongful act may also involve violation of a customary rule or principle owed directly to another State, such as the obligation to respect the other State's property or territorial sovereignty.

5.77   Sometimes, however, the internationally wrongful act consists in violating an obligation owed only indirectly to another State. Such will be the case where a State mistreats a national of another State in such a way as to violate standards prescribed by customary or conventional international law. Conduct of this kind does not operate directly on the other State, but engages the interest of the other State because of the bond of nationality existing between it and the victim of the unlawful conduct. When this occurs, the State whose nationality the mistreated private person possesses is regarded as having been the victim of an internationally wrongful act.

In the ***Mavrommatis Palestine Concessions* case,**[89] there was a dispute between a Greek national (Mr Mavrommatis) and the British government. Mr Mavrommatis was dissatisfied with the outcome in the British courts, whereafter Greece took up his case directly with the United Kingdom. The matter eventually reached the Permanent Court of International Justice, which said:[90]

It is an elementary principle of international law that a State is entitled to protect its subjects, when injured by acts contrary to international law committed by another State, from which they have been unable to claim satisfaction through the ordinary channels. By taking up the case of one of its subjects and by resorting to diplomatic action or international judicial proceedings on his behalf, a State is in reality asserting its own rights — its right to ensure, in the person of its subjects, respect for the rules of international law.

The question, therefore, whether the ... dispute originates in an injury to a private interest, which in point of fact is the case in many international disputes, is irrelevant from this standpoint. Once a State has taken up a case on behalf of one of its subjects before an international tribunal, in the eyes of the latter the State is sole claimant.

---

88.   Draft Articles on State Responsibility, Art 25(2).
89.   *Mavrommatis Palestine Concessions* case *(Jurisdiction) (Greece v United Kingdom)* PCIJ Rep (1924) Ser A No 2.
90.   Ibid, 12.

The idea that a State is advancing its own claims when it takes up the case of one of its nationals who has been unlawfully treated by another State has an air of unreality about it. It is one of those useful fictions which occur from time to time in every legal system. The International Law Commission, in its Commentaries on the Draft Articles on Diplomatic Protection, observed:[91]

> Obviously it is a fiction — and an exaggeration — to say that an injury to a national is an injury to the State itself. Many of the rules of diplomatic protection contradict the correctness of this fiction, notably the rule of continuous nationality which requires a State to prove that the injured national remained its national after the injury itself and up to the date of the presentation of the claim. A State does not 'in reality' — to quote *Mavrommatis* — assert its own right only. 'In reality' it also asserts the right of its injured national.

> ... The individual has rights under international law but remedies are few. Diplomatic protection conducted by a State at inter-State level remains an important remedy for the protection of persons whose human rights have been violated abroad.

5.78 States sometimes conclude treaties regulating how they will treat each other's nationals. There is, however, no general convention concerning the treatment to which foreign nationals are entitled (human rights treaties almost always apply to persons regardless of their nationality). Accordingly, and unless there is a relevant treaty in force between two States, one of whose nationals has been mistreated by the other, the content of the treatment depends on customary international law and the general principles of law. In practice, international lawyers usually turn to decisions of international tribunals and the writings of publicists in order to establish whether, in any particular case, a State has unlawfully treated a foreign national.

Standard of treatment

5.79 Just as there is frequently uncertainty about the existence and content of the rules affecting treatment of foreign nationals in particular cases, so too is there disagreement about the appropriate standard of treatment. Historically, there have been two schools of thought.

5.80 On the one hand, there are those who argue for a 'national treatment' standard. According to this view, advocated by some developing States in which respect for basic standards of justice is not always evident, a foreign national is entitled only to be treated no worse than a person possessing local nationality. The national treatment standard rests on the principle of non-discrimination. Provided the foreign national receives the same treatment as a local national, then, however harsh that treatment might be, no international wrong is committed.

5.81 The other school supports the 'international minimum' standard. According to this view, supported by developed States and many

---

91. *Yearbook of the International Law Commission*, 2006, Vol II, Pt II, 25, 26 (footnote omitted).

developing States, there is a minimum civilised standard of treatment to which foreigners are entitled regardless of how poorly a State treats its own nationals. A State's failure to extend that minimum standard of treatment to a foreigner engages the international responsibility of the State. The requirements of the international minimum standard are typically stated in fairly general terms.

In the *Neer Claim*, the United States–Mexican General Claims Commission said that in order for a State's treatment of a foreign national to incur international responsibility, it:[92]

> ... should amount to an outrage, to bad faith, to willful neglect of duty, or to an insufficiency of governmental action so far short of international standards that every reasonable and impartial man would readily recognise its insufficiency.

A stark illustration of this standard's application is provided by another decision of the same Commission:

In the **Roberts Claim,**[93] a claim was brought by the United States against Mexico in respect of, inter alia, the treatment to which a United States national was subjected while in a Mexican prison. The Commission said:

8. With respect to the charge of ill-treatment of Roberts, it appears from evidence submitted by the American Agency that the jail in which he was kept was a room thirty-five feet long and twenty feet wide with stone walls, earthen floor, straw roof, a single window, a single door and no sanitary accommodations, all the prisoners depositing their excrement in a barrel kept in a corner of the room; that thirty or forty men were at times thrown together in this single room; that the prisoners were given no facilities to clean themselves; that the room contained no furniture except that which the prisoners were able to obtain by their own means; that they were afforded no opportunity to take physical exercise; and that the food given them was scarce, unclean, and of the coarsest kind. The Mexican Agency did not present evidence disproving that such conditions existed in the jail. It was stated by the agency that Roberts was accorded the same treatment as that accorded to all other persons, and with respect to the food that Roberts received, it was observed in the Answer that he was given 'the food that was believed necessary, and within the means of the municipality'. ... Facts with respect to equality of treatment of aliens and nationals may be important in determining the merits of a complaint of mistreatment of an alien. But such equality is not the ultimate test of the propriety of the acts of authorities in the light of international law. That test is, broadly speaking, whether aliens are treated in accordance with ordinary standards of civilization. We do not hesitate to say that the treatment of Roberts was such as to warrant an indemnity on the ground of cruel and inhumane imprisonment.

The international minimum standard is now accepted as applicable by most publicists. Support for this standard has been strengthened by the emergence of international human rights law which lays down

---

92.   *Neer (USA) v United Mexican States* (1926) 4 RIAA 60, 61–62.
93.   *Roberts (USA) v United Mexican States* (1926) 4 RIAA 77.

universally applicable norms for the treatment of all persons regardless of their nationality. The international minimum standard is also more consonant with the rule that it is international law, and not domestic law, which determines whether a State's conduct is internationally wrongful.[94]

Instances of mistreatment

5.82   Because there is no general convention dealing with the situations in which States must not mistreat foreign nationals, the obligation's scope is best understood by reference to specific examples drawn from arbitral and judicial awards resulting from disputes between States. Many of these result from claims arising out of events occurring during the Mexican Revolution of 1917–18.

5.83   As the *Roberts Claim* indicates, States are obliged not to mistreat foreign nationals held in lawful custody.

5.84   A failure to punish persons who have committed serious crimes against foreign nationals may also engage a State's responsibility. In the *Massey Claim*,[95] the murderer of a United States national in Mexico was arrested and imprisoned pending trial. A Mexican prison officer allowed the murderer to escape from the prison. The prisoner eluded recapture. Although the prison officer was punished for his conduct, Mexico was held responsible for failing to capture and punish the killer.

> Similarly, in the **Janes Claim**,[96] the United States–Mexican General Claims Commission had to consider a claim by the United States against Mexico in respect of the murder of a United States national. The Commission said:
>
> > 17. Carbajal, the person who killed Janes, was well known in the community where the killing took place. Numerous persons witnessed the deed. The slayer, after killing his victim, left on foot. There is evidence that a Mexican police magistrate was informed of the shooting within five minutes after it took place. The official records with regard to the action taken to apprehend and punish the slayer speak for themselves. Eight years have elapsed since the murder, and it does not appear from the records that Carbajal has been apprehended at this time. Our conclusions to the effect that Mexican authorities did not take proper steps to apprehend and punish the slayer of Janes is based on the records before us consisting of evidence produced by both parties.
>
> The Commission ordered that Mexico pay financial compensation to the United States in respect of the failure to apprehend and punish the murderer.

---

94.   See **5.14**.
95.   *Massey (USA) v United Mexican States* (1927) 4 RIAA 155.
96.   *Janes (USA) v United Mexican States* (1926) 4 RIAA 82.

5.85   Where State officials themselves injure foreign nationals, even where the officials are acting *ultra vires* and contrary to instructions, the State's international responsibility will be engaged. In the *Youmans Claim*,[97] Mexico was held responsible to the United States for the murder of three United States nationals by a contingent of Mexican soldiers. This responsibility was not negatived by the fact that the soldiers acted contrary to their orders.[98]

5.86   States are potentially responsible for damage to property belonging to foreign nationals. Article 9(1) of the 1961 Harvard Draft Convention on the International Responsibility of States for Injuries to Aliens provides that '[d]eliberate destruction of or damage to the property of an alien is wrongful, unless it was required by circumstances of urgent necessity not reasonably admitting of any other course of action'.[99] The Harvard Draft is an unofficial document, but resulted from the work of eminent publicists. It further provides that 'destruction of the property of an alien resulting from the judgment of a competent tribunal or from the action of the competent authorities of the State in the maintenance of public order, health, or morality shall not be considered wrongful'.[100] Such judgment or action must not, however, be a 'clear and discriminatory violation of the law of the State concerned', an 'unreasonable departure from the principles of justice recognized by the principal legal systems of the world', or 'an abuse of powers … for the purpose of depriving an alien of his property'.[101]

5.87   A State may also commit an internationally wrongful act when it expels a foreign national from its territory. States are free to expel foreign nationals, but they must not act without giving sufficient notice.

In *Yeager v Iran*,[102] the Iran–United States Claims Tribunal said that giving the United States national 30 minutes' notice to pack a few personal belongings without any advance notice gave insufficient time for the foreigner to put his affairs in order. Iran was responsible for this internationally wrongful conduct. In *Rankin v Iran*, the same tribunal said:[103]

> According to the practice of States, the writings of scholars, the decisions of international tribunals, and bilateral treaty provisions … international law imposes certain restraints on the circumstances and the manner in which a State may expel aliens from its territory. A claimant alleging expulsion has the burden of proving the wrongfulness of the expelling State's action, in other words that it was arbitrary, discriminatory, or in breach of the expelling State's obligations.

5.88   A failure to take such steps as are reasonable to protect foreign nationals from the effects of mob violence, terrorism or insurrection will engage the State's responsibility.[104]

---

97.   *Youmans (USA) v United Mexican States* (1926) 4 RIAA 110.
98.   See also Draft Articles on State Responsibility, Art 7 (**5.26**) and the *Caire Claim* (**5.28**).
99.   (1961) 55 *American Journal of International Law* 548, 551.
100. Ibid, Art 9(2).
101. Ibid.
102. *Yeager v Islamic Republic of Iran* (1984) 17 Iran–US CTR 92. See **5.34**.
103. *Rankin v Islamic Republic of Iran* (1987) 17 Iran–US CTR 135, para 22.
104. For example, *Asian Agricultural Products Ltd v Sri Lanka* (1990) 4 ICSID Rep 246. See **5.32**.

In the **Noyes Claim,** the United States–Mexican General Claims Commission said of a claim for personal injuries allegedly caused by a failure of the Panama police to prevent an assault on a United States national by an unruly and intoxicated crowd:[105]

> The village of Juan Díaz [in Panama] has only a small population, but on June 19, 1927, several hundreds of adherents of the party then in control of the Government had gathered there for a meeting. The police on the spot had not been increased for the occasion; it consisted of the usual three policemen stationed there. In the course of the day the authorities in Panama City learned that the crowd in Juan Díaz had become unruly under the influence of liquor. The chief of the police, General Pretelt, thereupon drove thither with reinforcements. ...

> At about 3.00 p.m. the claimant [Mr Noyes] passed through the village in his automobile, on his return from Panama City from a trip to the Tapia River bridge. In the center of the village a crowd blocked the road and Mr Noyes stopped and sounded his horn, whereupon the crowd slowly opened. Whilst he was progressing very slowly through it, he had to stop again, because somebody lurched against the car and fell upon the running-board. Thereupon members of the crowd smashed the windows of the car and attacked Mr Noyes, who was stabbed in the wrist and hurt by fragments of glass. A police officer who had been giving orders that gangway should be made for the automobile, but who had not before been able to reach the car, then sprang upon the running-board and remained there, protecting the claimant and urging him to get away as quickly as possible. He remained with Mr Noyes, until the latter had got clear of the crowd. At some distance from Juan Díaz the claimant was further attacked by members of the same crowd, who pursued him in a bus and who forced him to drive his car off the road and into a ditch. He was then rescued by General Pretelt who, having come from the opposite direction, had, after reaching the plaza of the village, returned upon his way in order to protect Mr Noyes against his pursuers.

> The facts related above show that ... the police most actively protected the claimant against his assailants ... The contention of the American agent ... is, that the Panamanian Government incurred a liability under international law, because its officials had not taken the precaution of increasing for that day the police force at Juan Díaz, although they knew some time in advance that the meeting would assemble there.

> The mere fact that an alien has suffered at the hands of private persons an aggression, which could have been averted by the presence of a sufficient police force on the spot, does not make a government liable for damages under international law. There must be shown special circumstances from which the responsibility of the authorities arises: either their behavior in connection with the particular occurrence, or general failure to comply with their duty to maintain order, to prevent crimes or to prosecute and punish criminals.

> There were no such circumstances in the present case. Accordingly, a lack of protection has not been established. ...

> The claim is disallowed.

5.89   A State may also be held responsible for any denial of justice to foreign nationals. In the *Chattin Claim,*[106] the United States–Mexican General Claims Commission said that Mexico's handling of criminal

---

105. *Noyes (US) v Panama* (1933) 6 RIAA 308, 310–311.
106. *Chattin (USA) v United Mexican States* (1927) 4 RIAA 282.

proceedings against a United States national for embezzlement was 'highly insufficient' and referred particularly to 'an insufficiency of governmental action recognizable by every unbiased man'.

The Commission identified numerous deficiencies in the trial, including:[107]

> ... absence of proper investigations, an insufficiency of confrontations, withholding from the accused the opportunity to know all the charges against him, undue delay of the proceedings, [and] making the hearings in open Court a mere formality.

The Commission also said that 'the whole of the proceedings discloses a most astonishing lack of seriousness on the part of the Court'.[108] Mexico was held internationally responsible for its conduct towards the United States national.

Article 14 of the International Covenant on Civil and Political Rights (ICCPR)[109] contains reasonably detailed requirements for the conduct of criminal proceedings against all persons. These include a right to a fair and public hearing, to the presumption of innocence, to be informed of the charges, to adequate time and facilities to prepare the defence, to be tried without undue delay, to communicate with counsel, to be present at the trial, to examine prosecution witnesses and to call defence witnesses, to avoid giving self-incriminating evidence, to have convictions and sentences 'reviewed by a higher tribunal according to law', and not to be re-tried for any offence in respect of which there has already been a conviction or acquittal. Even where a State is not a party to the ICCPR, Art 14 is a useful guide as to the contents of the requirement to treat a foreign national fairly in the conduct of criminal proceedings.

The cases involving conditions of detention and failure to apprehend offenders[110] are also sometimes classified as denials of justice to foreign nationals.

Expropriation of property

5.90 A State will, in certain circumstances, be internationally responsible for taking property belonging to a foreign national. In practical terms, this situation most often arises where a foreign corporation's property has been nationalised by the State in whose territory that property is located. To nationalise property is to transfer its ownership to the State, normally by legislation or other official act.

5.91 As a matter of general international law, States are entitled in principle to nationalise any property, including property belonging to

---

107. Ibid, para 30.
108. Ibid, para 22.
109. UNTS, Vol 999, p 171.
110. See, for example, 5.81–5.84.

foreign nationals. In the General Assembly's Resolution on Permanent Sovereignty over Natural Resources,[111] it is declared that 'peoples and nations' enjoy 'permanent sovereignty over their natural wealth and resources'.[112] The resolution was adopted by 87:2, with 12 abstentions. It is now widely recognised as reflecting customary international law.[113] Article 4 of the resolution provides:

> Nationalization, expropriation or requisitioning shall be based on grounds or reasons of public utility, security or the national interest which are recognized as overriding purely individual or private interests, both domestic and foreign. In such cases, the owner shall be paid appropriate compensation in accordance with the rules in force in the State taking such measures in the exercise of its sovereignty and in accordance with international law. In any case where the question of compensation gives rise to a controversy, the national jurisdiction of the State taking such measures shall be exhausted. However, upon agreement by sovereign States and other parties concerned, settlement of the dispute should be made through arbitration or international adjudication.

5.92   The Resolution on Permanent Sovereignty over Natural Resources requires that any act of expropriation be carried out for a public purpose ('public utility, security or the national interest'). Thus, an expropriation for the purpose of enriching public officials or their associates would appear to be unlawful.[114] Customary international law also requires, as an extension of the same principle, that a nationalisation not be an act of political retaliation against the State whose nationality the property owner possesses.[115] Nevertheless, as the Iran–United States Claims Tribunal has observed:[116]

> A precise definition of the 'public purpose' for which an expropriation may be lawfully decided has neither been agreed upon in international law nor even suggested. It is clear that, as a result of the modern acceptance of the right to nationalize, this term is broadly interpreted, and that States, in practice, are granted extensive discretion. An expropriation, the only purpose of which would have been to avoid contractual obligations of the State or of an entity controlled by it, could not, nevertheless, be considered as lawful under international law.

5.93   A State may commit an act of expropriation even where there is no formal taking of property, and even where the object of the expropriation is a legal right as distinct from tangible property.

---

111. General Assembly Resolution 1803 (XVII) (1962).
112. Ibid, Art 1.
113. For example, *Texaco Overseas Petroleum Co and California Asiatic Oil Co v Libya* (1977) 53 ILR 389, para 88.
114. Cf *Libyan American Oil Company (LIAMCO) v Government of the Libyan Arab Republic* (1977) 62 ILR 140, 194, where a sole arbitrator took the view that 'the public utility principle is not a necessary requisite for the legality of a nationalization'.
115. *British Petroleum Exploration Company (Libya) Ltd v Libyan Arab Republic* (1974) 53 ILR 329.
116. *Amoco International Finance Corp v Iran* (1987) 15 Iran–US CTR 189, para 145.

In **Starrett Housing Corp v Iran,**[117] a subsidiary of the claimant United States company (Shah Goli) concluded a contractual arrangement with an Iranian bank under which the subsidiary purchased certain land in Iran for the purpose of building housing upon it (the Zomorod Project). During the period of revolutionary turmoil in 1979, the subsidiary was the subject of extensive harassment, resulting in the withdrawal of most United States and other non-Iranian personnel. The revolutionary authorities forced the subsidiary to surrender its entitlement to certain contractual payments and froze its bank account. Thereafter, the revolutionary authorities appointed a 'temporary manager' to run the subsidiary's affairs. The Iranian government argued that there had been no expropriation. The Iran–United States Claims Tribunal said:[118]

> It is undisputed in this case that the Government of Iran did not issue any law or decree according to which the Zomorod Project or Shah Goli expressly was nationalized or expropriated. However, it is recognized in international law that measures taken by a State can interfere with property rights to such an extent that these rights are rendered so useless that they must be deemed to have been expropriated, even though the State does not purport to have expropriated them and the legal title to the property formally remains with the original owner. ...

> There can be little doubt that ... the claimants had been deprived of the effective use, control and benefits of their property rights in Shah Goli. ... As a result of these measures the Claimants could no longer exercise their rights to manage Shah Goli and were deprived of their possibilities of effective use and control of it.

> It has, however, to be borne in mind that assumption of control over property by a government does not automatically and immediately justify a conclusion that the property has been taken by the government, thus requiring compensation under international law. In this case it cannot be disregarded that Starrett has been requested to resume the Project. The Government of Iran argues that it would have been possible for Starrett to appoint managers from any country other than the United States ... The completion of the Project was dependent upon a large number of American construction supervisors and subcontractors whom it would have been necessary to replace and the right freely to select management, supervisors and subcontractors is an essential element of the right to manage a project.

The Tribunal went on to hold that Iran had expropriated Starrett's property interests in the construction project, and that compensation was payable.

Article 10(7) of the Harvard Draft[119] defines 'property' as consisting of 'all movable and immovable property, whether tangible or intangible, including industrial, literary, and artistic property, as well as rights and interests in any property'. Further, the Iran–United States Claims Tribunal has remarked that expropriation 'may extend to any right which can be the object of a commercial transaction, ie, freely sold and bought, and thus has monetary value'.[120]

---

117. *Starrett Housing Corporation v Government of the Islamic Republic of Iran (Interlocutory Award)* (1984) 4 Iran–US CTR 122.
118. Ibid, 154–155.
119. See **5.86**.
120. *Amoco International Finance Corporation v Government of the Islamic Republic of Iran* (1987) 15 Iran–US CTR 189, para 108.

5.94 If an act of expropriation is not accompanied by the payment of compensation, it will be internationally wrongful. As Art 4 of the General Assembly's Resolution on Permanent Sovereignty over Natural Resources[121] makes clear, the expropriating State must pay the owner 'appropriate compensation in accordance with the rules in force in the State taking such measures in the exercise of its sovereignty and in accordance with international law'. There has been significant disagreement over what this requirement entails.

5.95 According to many States, especially developed States, appropriate compensation is restitution or payment which is 'prompt, adequate and effective'. This is widely known as the 'Hull formula', after former United States Secretary of State Cordell Hull (1871–1955). The Hull formula has been used in numerous bilateral commercial treaties. The United Kingdom's understanding of the formula was detailed in its pleadings in the *Anglo-Iranian Oil* case:[122]

> 30. ... it is clear that the nationalisation of the property of foreigners, even if not unlawful on any other grounds, becomes an unlawful confiscation unless provision is made for compensation which is adequate, prompt and effective. By 'adequate' compensation is meant 'the value of the undertaking at the moment of dispossession, plus interest to the day of payment [the phrase "to the day of judgment" appears mistakenly in the pleadings]' — per the Permanent Court of International Justice in the *Chorzów Factory (Claim for Indemnity) (Merits)* case, ... There have, in fact, been pronouncements that prompt compensation means immediate payment of cash. ... The Government of the United Kingdom is, however, prepared to admit that deferred payment may be interpreted as satisfying the requirement of payment in accordance with the rules of international law if:
>
> (a) the total amount to be paid is fixed promptly;
>
> (b) the allowance for interest for late payment is made;
>
> (c) the guarantees that the future payments will in fact be made are satisfactory, so that the person to be compensated may, if he so desires, raise the full sum at once on the security of the future payments. ...
>
> 30A. ... The third requirement is summed up in the word 'effective' and means that the recipient of the compensation must be able to make use of it. He must, for instance, be able, if he wishes, to use it to set up a new enterprise to replace the one that has been expropriated or to use it for such other purposes as he wishes. Monetary compensation that is in blocked currency is not effective because, where the person to be compensated is a foreigner, he is not in a position to use it or to obtain the benefit of it. The compensation must therefore be freely transferable from the country paying it and, so far as the country's restrictions are concerned, convertible into other currencies.

5.96 The Hull formula has, in the past, been rejected by a number of States, especially some developing States. They adopted a position which

---

121. General Assembly Resolution 1803 (XVII) (1962). See **5.91**.
122. *Anglo-Iranian Oil Co Case (United Kingdom v Iran)* Pleadings, Oral Arguments, Documents (1952), 105–107.

found reflection in the General Assembly's Charter of Economic Rights and Duties of States.[123] According to Art 2(2)(c) of the Charter, each State has the right:

> To nationalize, expropriate or transfer ownership of foreign property in which case appropriate compensation should be paid by the State adopting such measures, taking into account its relevant laws and regulations and all circumstances that the State considers pertinent. In any case where the question of compensation gives rise to a controversy, it shall be settled under the domestic law of the nationalizing State and by its tribunals, unless it is freely and mutually agreed by all States concerned that other peaceful means be sought on the basis of the sovereign equality of States and in accordance with the principle of free choice of means.

This approach effectively makes the question of compensation entirely a matter of domestic law. Article 2(2)(c) was adopted with widespread opposition or abstentions from developed States, and at a time when State-centred economic programs were disastrously widespread among developing States. The Tribunal in *Texaco v Libya* did not regard the provision as reflective of customary international law,[124] and the same view is widely shared by publicists. In more recent times, the approach in Art 2(2)(c) has lost support among developing States where there has been a significant switch to liberal economic policies and competition to attract foreign investment.

5.97 In *Amoco International Finance v Iran*,[125] the Iran–United States Claims Tribunal returned to the formulation of the Permanent Court of International Justice in the *Chorzów Factory* case:[126] a lawful expropriation gives rise to 'the payment of fair compensation' or of 'the just price of what was expropriated'. This means, according to the Tribunal, that the State must pay *damnum emergens* — that is, the value of the property, measured as the market value of the property as a going concern at the time of its taking. If the expropriation is unlawful (for example, for lack of public purpose or refusal to pay fair compensation), then the foreign national will also be entitled to an award of *lucrum cessans* — that is, lost profits — but only up to the time of judgment. In neither case, however, is the foreign national entitled to an award in the nature of punitive damages.

Diplomatic protection: admissibility of claims

5.98 When a foreign national has been mistreated by a State, that foreigner's own State may be entitled to take up the case on the plane of international relations. Action of this kind might take the form of

---

123. General Assembly Resolution 3281 (XXIX) (1974).
124. *Texaco Overseas Petroleum Co and California Asiatic Oil Co v Libyan Arab Republic* (1977) 53 ILR 389, paras 85–90.
125. *Amoco International Finance Corporation v Government of the Islamic Republic of Iran* (1987) 15 Iran–US CTR 189, paras 227–232.
126. *Case Concerning the Factory at Chorzów (Indemnity) (Merits) (Germany v Poland)* PCIJ Rep (1928) Series A No 17.

making claims through diplomatic channels or, if that fails, formal dispute settlement proceedings.[127] In either case, this type of action is often referred to as 'diplomatic protection'. There are, however, two conditions which must be met before a State will be entitled to take up the person's case. First, the person must be a national of the State. Second, the person must have exhausted all effective domestic remedies in the State alleged to be responsible for the mistreatment. These customary requirements find reflection in Art 44 of the Draft Articles on State Responsibility:

Article 44

Admissibility of claims

The responsibility of a State may not be invoked if:

(a) The claim is not brought in accordance with any applicable rule relating to the nationality of claims;

(b) The claim is one to which the rule of exhaustion of local remedies applies and any available and effective local remedy has not been exhausted.

Nationality of claims

5.99 The nature and rationale of a State's entitlement to protect diplomatically its own nationals, and only its own nationals, was addressed by the Permanent Court of International Justice in both the *Mavrommatis Palestine Concessions* case[128] and the *Panevezys Railway* case.[129] In the latter case, the Court said:[130]

> In the opinion of the Court, ... in taking up the case of one of its nationals, by resorting to diplomatic action or international judicial proceedings on his behalf, a State is in reality asserting its own right, the right to ensure in the person of its nationals respect for the rules of international law. This right is necessarily limited to intervention on behalf of its own nationals because, in the absence of a special agreement, it is the bond of nationality between the State and the individual which alone confers upon the State the right of diplomatic protection, and it is as a part of the function of diplomatic protection that the right to take up a claim and to ensure respect for the rules of international law must be envisaged. Where the injury was done to the national of some other State, no claim to which such injury may give rise falls within the scope of the diplomatic protection which a State is entitled to afford nor can it give rise to a claim which that State is entitled to espouse.

5.100 Every time a State seeks to protect diplomatically a private person, it is relevant to ask whether that person is a national of the State.

---

127. See chapter 8.
128. *Mavrommatis Palestine Concessions* case *(Jurisdiction) (Greece v United Kingdom)* PCIJ Rep (1924) Ser A No 2. See **5.77**.
129. *Panevezys-Saldutiskis Railway* case *(Estonia v Lithuania) (Preliminary Objections)* PCIJ Rep (1939) Ser A/B No 76, 4.
130. Ibid, 16.

The position at customary international law has long been that a State may assert its diplomatic protection only in respect of its own nationals. This found stark manifestation in *Dickson Car Wheel Co v Mexico*, in which the United States–Mexican General Claims Commission observed that a State 'does not commit an international delinquency in inflicting an injury upon an individual lacking nationality, and consequently, no State is empowered to intervene or complain on his behalf either before or after the injury'.[131]

The traditional view finds prima facie support in Art 1 of the Draft Articles on Diplomatic Protection (DADP), which defines 'diplomatic protection' as 'the invocation by a State, through diplomatic action or other means of peaceful settlement, of the responsibility of another State for an injury caused by an internationally wrongful act of that State to a natural or legal person that is a national of the former State with a view to the implementation of such responsibility'. Article 3(1) further provides that '[t]he State entitled to exercise diplomatic protection is the State of nationality'.

5.101   The DADP seek, however, to extend a State's right of diplomatic protection to two classes of persons who are not its own nationals but who are 'lawfully and habitually resident' in the State exercising the right of protection. These extended categories of resident-protectees are (i) stateless persons; and (ii) persons recognised by the protecting State as refugees 'in accordance with internationally accepted standards'. In each case, the person must have belonged to the extended class of protectee at both the date of injury and the date of presentation of the claim.[132] The DADP's extended right of diplomatic protection does not reach the refugee's State of nationality,[133] so that the refugee's host State is still prevented from diplomatically protecting him or her from mistreatment at the hands of the refugee's own State of nationality.

The International Law Commission's Commentaries on the DADP frankly acknowledge that the rules extending a host State's right of diplomatic protection to certain stateless persons and refugees are 'an exercise in progressive development of the law'.[134] It is therefore premature to regard them as being part of customary international law.

5.102   The relevant rules of customary international law concerning determination of the nationality of individuals are set out in the 1930 Hague Convention on Certain Questions Relating to the Conflict of Nationality Laws,[135] to which Australia and 19 other States are parties:

Article 1

It is for each State to determine under its own law who are its nationals. This law shall be recognised by other States in so far as it is consistent

---

131. *Dickson Car Wheel Co v Mexico* 4 RIAA (1931) 669, 678.
132. Draft Articles on Diplomatic Protection, Arts 8(1) and 8(2).
133. Ibid, Art 8(3).
134. *Yearbook of the International Law Commission*, 2006, Vol II, Pt II, 48.
135. LNTS, Vol 179, p 89.

with international conventions, international custom, and the principles of law generally recognised with regards to nationality. ...

Furthermore, Art 2 provides that any question as to whether a person possesses the nationality of a particular State 'shall be determined in accordance with the law of that State'.

5.103 International law does not determine whether an individual possesses the nationality of any particular State. That question is referred back to domestic law, with States being free to confer their nationality on any person they choose in accordance with their own laws. Conferring nationality on any person for domestic law purposes is one thing, but recognition of that conferral by other States for the purposes of diplomatic protection is another. As Art 1 of the 1930 Hague Convention indicates, other States are entitled to withhold recognition of a conferral of nationality where such conferral is inconsistent with 'international conventions, international custom, and the principles of law generally recognised with regards to nationality'. Other States are therefore entitled to reject a claim of diplomatic protection where the conferral of nationality on the injured person by the claimant State was inconsistent with the customary law position as articulated in Art 1.

In practice, the vast majority of individuals have their nationality conferred on them by State law at birth, either by virtue of the fact that they were born in the State's territory *(de jure soli)* or because one or both of their parents possessed the State's nationality *(de jure sanguinis)*. It is also common practice for individuals to acquire a State's nationality under the laws of that State by naturalisation, by marriage to a national of the State, upon adoption by adoptive parents who are nationals of the State, or where the State succeeds to another State (for example, the succession in 1991 of Russia to the former Soviet Union). The Draft Articles on Diplomatic Protection provide:

Article 4

State of nationality of a natural person

For the purposes of the diplomatic protection of a natural person, a State of nationality means a State whose nationality that person has acquired, in accordance with the law of that State, by birth, descent, naturalization, succession of States or in any other manner, not inconsistent with international law.

As a general rule, individuals may be diplomatically protected by any State which has conferred its nationality on them for any of these reasons.

5.104 It is also a well-established requirement of customary international law that the person being diplomatically protected must have possessed the protecting State's nationality 'continuously' — that is, at both the date of the injury and the date of the presentation of the claim.[136] Article 5(1) of the DADP seeks to 'progressively develop' this customary rule by

---

136. For example, *Kren Claim* (1953) 20 ILR 233, 234.

expressly requiring the person also to have continuously retained the protecting State's nationality *between* the date of injury and the date of the claim's presentation.[137]

5.105   Difficulties may arise in several situations: first, where an individual possesses the nationality of both the State which is alleged to have mistreated the person and the State which seeks to protect him or her diplomatically; second, where the injured individual is not a national of the State which has allegedly injured the person, but is a national of more than one other State; and third, where the individual possesses the nationality only of the State which seeks to protect the person diplomatically, but has stronger links to the State against which the claim is being made.

5.106   Where the injured individual is a national of both the State responsible for the injury and the State seeking to protect the person diplomatically, the classical view is set out in the 1930 Hague Convention:

> Article 4
>
> A State may not afford diplomatic protection to one of its nationals against a State whose nationality such person also possesses.

This view was supported by the International Court of Justice in the *Reparation* advisory opinion, in which the judgment referred in *obiter* to the 'ordinary practice whereby a State does not exercise protection on behalf of its nationals against a State which regards him as its own national'.[138]

There is also authority for the proposition that a dual national may not be diplomatically protected against the State to which the person has the stronger bond. Thus, in the *Canevaro* case,[139] the Permanent Court of Arbitration rejected Italy's standing to claim on behalf of Mr Canevaro against Peru. Mr Canevaro had Italian nationality by descent and Peruvian nationality by birth. The critical factor for the Court was Mr Canevaro's active participation in the public life of Peru, especially the seeking and holding of Peruvian public office. The Court also regarded as important the fact that Mr Canevaro sought and obtained the consent of the Peruvian Congress to act as a third State's Consul General in Peru, which consent was required under Peruvian law only for Peruvian nationals. The Court said that, in the circumstances, Peru could deny Mr Canevaro's status as an Italian national.

The reasoning in the *Canevaro* case was expressly rejected in the *Salem* case, in which the arbitral tribunal said in *obiter* that, 'if two powers are both entitled by international law to treat a person as their national, neither of these powers can raise a claim against the other in the name of such a person'.[140] However, in the *Mergé Claim*, the Italian–United

---

137. DADP, Art 5(1); *Yearbook of the International Law Commission*, 2006, Vol II, Pt II, 36.
138. *Reparation for Injuries Suffered in the Service of the United Nations* advisory opinion, ICJ Rep (1949) 174, para 186. See **4.60**.
139. *Canevaro* case *(Italy v Peru)* (1912) 11 RIAA 397.
140. *Salem* case *(Egypt v United States)* (1932) 2 RIAA 1161, 1187.

States Conciliation Commission said that the principle 'which excludes diplomatic protection in the case of dual nationality, must yield before the principle of effective nationality whenever such nationality is that of the claiming State'.[141] The Commission went on to say:[142]

> [I]t is considered that the Government of the United States of America shall be entitled to protect its nationals before this Commission in cases of dual nationality, United States and Italian, whenever the United States nationality is the effective nationality. In order to establish the prevalence of the United States nationality in individual cases, habitual residence can be one of the criteria of evaluation, but not the only one. The conduct of the individual in his economic, social, political, civic and family life, as well as the closer and more effective bond with one of the two States must also be considered.

Similarly, the Iran–United States Claims Tribunal expressly doubted the applicability of Art 4 of the 1930 Hague Convention to cases of diplomatic protection where the injured person possesses the nationality of both the claimant State and the defendant State. In *Iran–United States Case No A/18*,[143] the Full Tribunal had to rule on the standing of the United States to bring claims against Iran in respect of numerous individuals who possessed the nationality of both States. It said that it would allow such claims when the individual's 'dominant and effective' nationality was that of the United States. In determining the individual's dominant and effective nationality, the Tribunal said that it would 'consider all relevant factors, including habitual residence, centre of interests, family ties, participation in public life, and other evidence of attachment'.[144]

According to the International Law Commission, the older customary rule evidenced in Art 4 of the 1930 Hague Convention has been superseded by a more recent customary rule, as evidenced in cases such as the *Mergé Claim* and *Iran–United States Case No A/18* and as articulated in Art 7 of the DADP:

> **Article 7**
>
> *Multiple nationality and claim against a State of nationality*
>
> A State of nationality may not exercise diplomatic protection in respect of a person against a State of which that person is also a national unless the nationality of the former State is predominant, both at the date of injury and at the date of the official presentation of the claim.

The Draft Articles on Diplomatic Protection do not define 'predominance' in the context of a person's nationality. The ILC's Commentaries, however, make the following observations:[145]

> No attempt is made to describe the factors to be taken into account in deciding which nationality is predominant. The authorities indicate that such

141. *Mergé Claim (United States v Italy)* (1955) 22 ILR 443, 455.
142. Ibid.
143. *Iran–United States Case No A/18* (1984) 5 Iran–US CTR Rep 251.
144. Ibid, 265.
145. *Yearbook of the International Law Commission*, 2006, Vol II, Pt II, 46.

factors include habitual residence, the amount of time spent in each country of nationality, date of naturalization (i.e., the length of the period spent as a national of the protecting State before the claim arose); place, curricula and language of education; employment and financial interests; place of family life; family ties in each country; participation in social and public life; use of language; taxation, bank account, social security insurance; visits to the other State of nationality; possession and use of passport of the other State; and military service. None of these factors is decisive and the weight attributed to each factor will vary according to the circumstances of each case.

The current position at customary international law is, therefore, that State A can diplomatically protect a person against State B even where the person is a dual national of the two States, provided that the person's predominant nationality is that of State A. Predominance will be established by weighing the numerous factors referred to in the ILC's Commentaries in determining to which of the two States the person is more closely connected. If the person's predominant nationality is that of the claimant State, the nationality of claims requirement is satisfied; if the predominant nationality is that of the respondent State, the nationality of claims requirement is not satisfied and the claim must fail.

5.107   Where the injured person is not a national of the State which is responsible for the injury, but is a national of more than one other State, a question arises as to which of those other States can diplomatically protect the person. Can they all protect the injured person, or only the one whose nationality is predominant for the person? The decisions in the *Mergé Claim*,[146] the *Canevaro* case[147] and the *Nottebohm* case[148] would all suggest that only the State with which the injured person enjoyed the strongest effective bond could take up that person's claim. None of these cases, however, involved a situation where the injured individual was a national of both the claimant State and a third State. In contrast, the *Salem* case[149] involved a claim by the United States against Egypt in respect of mistreatment suffered by Mr Salem, who was a joint national of the United States and Persia (now Iran). Egypt argued that only Persia was entitled to claim on Salem's behalf, but the Tribunal said:[150]

> ... the Egyptian Government cannot set forth against the United States the eventual continuation of the Persian nationality of George Salem; the rule of international law being that in a case of dual nationality a third power is not entitled to contest the claim of one of the two powers whose national is interested in the case by referring to the nationality of the other power.

The position adopted in the *Salem* case accords, in the view of the International Law Commission, with current customary international law. According to Art 6(1) of the DADP, '[a]ny State of which a dual or multiple national is a national may exercise diplomatic protection in respect of that national against a State of which that person is not a

---

146. See **5.106**.
147. Ibid.
148. See **5.108**.
149. See **5.107**.
150. *Salem* case *(Egypt v United States)* (1932) 2 RIAA 1161, 1188.

national'. Thus, where State A injures a person who is a national of both State B and State C under their domestic laws, either State B or State C may seek to protect the person, regardless of which of them is the injured person's predominant nationality.

5.108 The International Court of Justice has addressed the law applicable in a situation where an allegedly injured individual possesses the nationality only of the State which seeks to protect him or her diplomatically, and has stronger links to the State against which the claim is being made.

In the **Nottebohm case,**[151] Mr Nottebohm was born in Germany in 1881 and acquired German nationality at birth. In 1905, he moved to Guatemala, where he remained domiciled and conducted his business affairs until 1943. At that time, Guatemala seized his property and expelled him as an enemy alien: Guatemala was at war with Germany. In 1939, one month after the Second World War commenced, Mr Nottebohm had travelled to Liechtenstein, where he applied for Liechtenstein nationality. His application was granted within a few days, and he quickly returned to Guatemala. When he acquired Liechtenstein nationality, he lost his German nationality by automatic operation of German law. After the war, Liechtenstein brought a claim against Guatemala before the International Court of Justice in respect of Mr Nottebohm's treatment at the hands of the Guatemalan authorities. Guatemala responded by challenging the admissibility of the claim on the grounds that Liechtenstein could not diplomatically protect Mr Nottebohm against Guatemala. The Court said:[152]

> ... the Court must ascertain whether the nationality conferred on Nottebohm by Liechtenstein by means of a naturalization which took place in the circumstances which have been described, can be validly invoked as against Guatemala, whether it bestows upon Liechtenstein a sufficient title to the exercise of protection in respect of Nottebohm as against Guatemala and therefore entitles it to seise the Court of a claim relating to him. In this connection, Counsel for Liechtenstein said: 'the essential question is whether Mr Nottebohm, having acquired the nationality of Liechtenstein, that acquisition of nationality is one which must be recognised by other States'. This formulation is accurate, subject to the twofold reservation that, in the first place, what is involved is not recognition for all purposes but merely for the purposes of the admissibility of the Application, and, secondly, that what is involved is not recognition by all States but only by Guatemala. ... It is for Liechtenstein, as it is for every sovereign State, to settle by its own legislation the rules relating to the acquisition of its nationality, and to confer that nationality by naturalization granted by its own organs in accordance with that legislation. It is not necessary to determine whether international law imposes any limitations on its freedom of decision in this domain. ... [N]ationality is within the domestic jurisdiction of the State.

> But the issue which the Court must decide is not one which pertains to the legal system of Liechtenstein. It does not depend on the law or on the decision of Liechtenstein whether that State is entitled to exercise its protection in the case under consideration. To exercise protection, to apply to the Court, is to place oneself on the plane of international law. It is international law which determines whether a State is entitled to exercise protection and to seise the Court. ...

---

151. *Nottebohm* case *(Liechtenstein v Guatemala)* Second Phase, ICJ Rep (1955) 4.
152. Ibid, 16–24.

The practice of certain States which refrain from exercising protection in favour of a naturalized person when the latter has in fact, by his prolonged absence, severed his links with what is no longer for him anything but his nominal country, manifests the view of these States that, in order to be capable of being invoked against another State, nationality must correspond with the factual situation. ...

... a State cannot claim that the rules it has ... laid down are entitled to recognition by another State unless it has acted in conformity with this general aim of making the legal bond of nationality accord with the individual's genuine connection with the State which assumes the defence of it citizens by means of protection as against other States. ... According to the practice of States, to arbitral and judicial decisions and to the opinions of writers, nationality is a legal bond having as its basis a social fact of attachment, a genuine connection of existence, interests and sentiments, together with the existence of reciprocal rights and duties. It may be said to constitute the juridical expression of the fact that the individual upon whom it is conferred, either directly by the law or as the result of an act of the authorities, is in fact more closely connected with the population of the State conferring nationality than with that of any other State. Conferred by a State, it only entitles that State to exercise protection *vis-à-vis* another State, if it constitutes a translation into juridical terms of the individual's connection with the State which has made him its national. ... the Court must ascertain whether the nationality granted to Nottebohm by means of naturalization is of this character or, in other words, whether the factual connection between Nottebohm and Liechtenstein in the period preceding, contemporaneous with and following his naturalization appears to be sufficiently close, so preponderant in relation to any connection which may have existed between him and any other State, that it is possible to regard the nationality conferred upon him as real and effective, as the exact juridical expression of a social fact of a connection which existed previously or came into existence thereafter. ...

At the time of his naturalization does Nottebohm appear to have been more closely attached by his tradition, his establishment, his interests, his activities, his family ties, his intentions for the near future to Liechtenstein than to any other State? ...

The Court noted Mr Nottebohm's extensive and longstanding business, residential, family and social connections to Guatemala and Germany, and then said:[153]

In contrast, his actual connections with Liechtenstein were extremely tenuous. No settled abode, no prolonged residence in that country at the time of his application for naturalization ... No intention of settling there was shown at that time or realized in the ensuing weeks, months or years.

On the contrary, he returned to Guatemala very shortly after his naturalization and showed every intention of remaining there. If Nottebohm went to Liechtenstein in 1946, this was because of the refusal of Guatemala to admit him. ... There is no allegation of any economic interest or of any activities exercised or to be exercised in Liechtenstein and no manifestation of any intention whatsoever to transfer all or some of his interests and business activities to Liechtenstein. ... Furthermore ... members of his family have asserted Nottebohm's desire to spend his old age in Guatemala.

These facts clearly establish, on the one hand, the absence of any bond of attachment between Nottebohm and Liechtenstein and, on the other hand, the existence of a long-standing and close connection between him and Guatemala, a link which his naturalization in no way weakened. That naturalization was not based on any real prior connection with Liechtenstein, nor did it in any way alter the manner of life of the person upon whom it was conferred in exceptional

---

153. Ibid, 25–26.

circumstances of speed and accommodation. In both respects, it was lacking in the genuineness requisite to an act of such importance ...

Naturalization was asked for not so much for the purpose of obtaining a legal recognition of Nottebohm's membership in fact of the population of Liechtenstein, as it was to enable him to substitute for his status as a national of a belligerent State that of a national of a neutral State, with the sole aim of thus coming within the protection of Liechtenstein but not of becoming wedded to its traditions, its interests, its way of life or of assuming the obligations ... and exercising the rights pertaining to the status thus acquired.

Guatemala is under no obligation to recognise a nationality granted in such circumstances. Liechtenstein consequently is not entitled to extend its protection to Nottebohm *vis-à-vis* Guatemala and its claim must, for this reason, be held to be inadmissible.

5.109 The *Nottebohm* case is undoubtedly the most significant decision on the international law relating to nationality of individuals ever to have issued from the Court. Nevertheless, it is easy to overestimate the importance of *Nottebohm*. The Court itself was at pains to point out that its judgment was not about nationality in a general sense, but only about the obligation to recognise another State's conferral of nationality by naturalisation in the context of diplomatic protection.

It is unlikely that its principles could be applied in cases of nationality acquired at birth either *de jure soli* or *de jure sanguinis,* or in situations involving recognition of foreign nationality outside the context of diplomatic protection. Further, the case is not even authority for the proposition that the lack of an effective bond between an individual and a naturalising State must always deprive that State of its standing to protect diplomatically the individual.

Rather, the Court's judgment recognises only that an individual without genuine bonds of attachment to the naturalising State will not be able to enjoy the benefit of that State's diplomatic protection against another State to which he or she does have such bonds. This understanding of the limited scope of the judgment in the *Nottebohm* case was soon expressly adopted by the Italian–United States Conciliation Commission in the *Flegenheimer Claim*.[154]

On this reading of the *Nottebohm* case, Liechtenstein's claim would have been admissible against any State except Guatemala and, perhaps, Germany.

5.110 States may diplomatically protect corporations as well as individuals. As with individuals, there must exist a bond of nationality between the State and the corporation before a right of diplomatic protection arises. Different considerations operate, however, in determining whether a corporation is a national of a State for the purposes of establishing a right of diplomatic protection.

---

154. *Flegenheimer Claim (United States v Italy)* (1958) 25 ILR 91, 147–150.

In the **Barcelona Traction case**,[155] the Barcelona Traction, Light and Power Company Ltd had been incorporated under the law of Canada and had its registered office in Canada, but 88 per cent of its share capital was owned by Belgian nationals. The company's business operations were in Spain. The company was subjected to allegedly arbitrary and discriminatory treatment at the hands of Spanish authorities, which treatment was alleged to be internationally wrongful. Having lost all its assets in Spain, the company was placed in receivership in Canada. Spain's conduct towards the company was originally the subject of diplomatic representations by Canada. However, Canada later withdrew from the matter. Belgium then made claims against Spain and commenced proceedings in the International Court of Justice. Spain denied that Belgium had standing on the grounds that the company was not a Belgian national, and that Belgium could not claim on behalf of the shareholders of an incorporated company possessing separate legal personality under domestic law. The Court said:

33. When a State admits into its territory foreign investments or foreign nationals, whether natural or juristic persons, it is bound to extend to them the protection of the law and assumes obligations concerning the treatment to be afforded them. ...

35. ... In order to bring a claim in respect of the breach of [an obligation which is the subject of diplomatic protection], a State must first establish its right to do so, for the rules on the subject rest on two suppositions:

'The first is that the defendant State has broken an obligation towards the national State in respect of its nationals. The second is that only the party to whom an international obligation is due can bring a claim in respect of its breach.' (*Reparation for Injuries Suffered in the Service of the United Nations, Advisory Opinion, ICJ Reports 1949*, pp 181–182).

In the present case it is therefore essential to establish whether the losses allegedly suffered by Belgian shareholders in Barcelona Traction were the consequence of the violation of obligations of which they were the beneficiaries. In other words: has a right of Belgium been violated on account of its nationals having suffered infringement of their rights as shareholders in a company not of Belgian nationality? ...

41. ... The concept and structure of the company are founded on and determined by a firm distinction between the separate entity of the company and that of the shareholder, each with a distinct set of rights. ...

44. ... [T]he mere fact that damage is sustained by both company and shareholder does not imply that both are entitled to claim compensation. ... [N]o doubt, the interests of the aggrieved are affected, but not their rights. Thus whenever a shareholder's interests are harmed by an act done to the company, it is to the latter that he must look to institute appropriate action; for although two separate entities may have suffered from the same wrong, it is only one entity whose rights have been infringed. ...

47. The situation is different if the act complained of is aimed at the direct rights of the shareholders as such. It is well known that there are rights which municipal law confers upon the latter distinct from those of the company, including the right to any declared dividend, the right to attend and vote at general meetings, the right to share in the residual assets of the company on liquidation. Whenever one of his direct rights is infringed, the shareholder has an independent right of action. ...

48. The Belgian Government claims that shareholders of Belgian nationality suffered damage in consequence of unlawful acts of the Spanish authorities

---

155. *Case Concerning the Barcelona Traction, Light and Power Company Ltd (Belgium v Spain)* Second Phase, ICJ Rep (1970) 3.

and, in particular, that the Barcelona Traction shares, though they did not cease to exist, were emptied of all real economic content. ... Thus the legal issue is reducible to the question of whether it is legitimate to identify an attack on company rights, resulting in damage to shareholders, with the violation of their direct rights. ...

66. ... Only in the event that of the legal demise of the company are the shareholders deprived of the possibility of a remedy available through the company; it is only if they became deprived of all such possibility that an independent right of action for them and their government could arise.

67. ... Though in receivership, the company continues to exist. ...

69. The Court will now turn to the second possibility, that of the lack of capacity of the company's national State to act on its behalf. The first question which must be asked here is whether Canada — the third apex of the triangular relationship — is, in law, the national State of Barcelona Traction.

70. In allocating corporate entities to States for purposes of diplomatic protection, international law is based, but only to a limited extent, on an analogy with the rules governing the nationality of individuals. The traditional rule attributes the right of diplomatic protection of a corporate entity to the State under whose laws of which it is incorporated and in whose territory it has its registered office. These two criteria have been confirmed by long practice and numerous international instruments. This notwithstanding, further or different links are at times said to be required in order that a right of diplomatic protection should exist. ... However, in the particular field of diplomatic protection of corporate entities, no absolute test of the 'genuine connection' has found general acceptance. ...

77. It is true that at a certain point the Canadian Government ceased to act on behalf of Barcelona Traction, for reasons which have not been fully revealed ... The Canadian Government has nonetheless retained its capacity to exercise diplomatic protection; no legal impediment has prevented it from doing so: no fact has arisen to render this protection impossible. It has discontinued its action of its own free will.

78. The Court would here observe that, within the limits prescribed by international law, a State may exercise diplomatic protection by whatever means and to whatever extent it thinks fit, for it is its own right that the State is asserting. Should the natural or legal persons on whose behalf it is acting consider that their rights are not adequately protected, they have no remedy in international law. All they can do is resort to municipal law if means are available ...

79. The State must be viewed as the sole judge to decide whether its protection will be granted, to what extent it is granted, and when it will cease. It remains in this respect a discretionary power the exercise of which may be determined by considerations of a political or other nature, unrelated to the particular case. ...

92. ... a theory has been developed to the effect that the State of the shareholders has a right of diplomatic protection when the State whose responsibility is invoked is the national State of the company. Whatever the validity of this theory may be, it is certainly not applicable to the present case, since Spain is not the national State of Barcelona Traction.

96. The Court considers that the adoption of the theory of diplomatic protection of shareholders as such, by opening the door of competing diplomatic claims, could create an atmosphere of confusion and insecurity in international economic relations. The danger would be all the greater inasmuch as the shares of companies whose activity is international are widely scattered and frequently change hands. ...

> 100. ... Barcelona Traction was never reduced to a position of impotence such that it could not have approached its national State, Canada, to ask for its diplomatic protection, and that, as far as appeared to the Court, there was nothing to prevent Canada from continuing to grant its diplomatic protection to Barcelona Traction if it had considered that it should do so. ...
>
> 103. Accordingly, the Court rejects the Belgian Government's claim ...

5.111   Consequently, the only State which has a right to protect a company diplomatically is the State under whose laws it was incorporated or in whose territory its registered office is located.

In adopting its Draft Articles on Diplomatic Protection, the International Law Commission seeks to extend the range of corporations which a State may legitimately regard as its nationals for the purposes of diplomatic protection. According to the DADP:

Article 9

State of nationality of a corporation

For the purposes of the diplomatic protection of a corporation, the State of nationality means the State under whose law the corporation was incorporated. However, when the corporation is controlled by nationals of another State or States and has no substantial business activities in the State of incorporation, and the seat of management and the financial control of the corporation are both located in another State, that State shall be regarded as the State of nationality.

By seeking to establish a new rule on nationality of claims for corporations in terms of Art 9, the ILC is effectively seeking to establish an 'effective link' test analogous to that sometimes operating in connection with the nationality of natural persons. Although the ILC Commentaries are somewhat equivocal on the subject as to whether Art 9 is *lex ferenda*, it seems most unlikely that it reflects current customary international law.

5.112   As *Barcelona Traction* indicates, a shareholder's State of nationality has a right to protect only where the company has ceased to exist (for example, by liquidation),[156] where the company's State of incorporation is legally incapacitated from exercising protection, or where the shareholder's direct legal rights have been attacked by another State.[157] According to Judge Oda's separate opinion in the *ELSI* case:[158]

> Shareholders' material rights remain confined to the area of participation in the disposal of company profits and, in the event of liquidation, sharing in the residuary property of the company. They may protect those rights by exercising their formal entitlement to vote at shareholders' meetings,

---

156. Semble DADP, Art 11(a):
> A State of nationality of shareholders in a corporation shall not be entitled to exercise diplomatic protection in respect of such shareholders in the case of an injury to the corporation unless ... (a) The corporation has ceased to exist according to the law of the State of incorporation for a reason unrelated to the injury.

157. Semble DADP, Art 12.

158. *Case Concerning Elettronica Sicula SpA (ELSI) (United States v Italy)* ICJ Rep (1989) 15, 84.

thus participating in the management and operation of a company. Indeed, shareholders' rights in relation to the company and its assets are limited as a corollary of the shareholders' limited liability.

5.113   There is also a suggestion in para 92 of the Court's judgment in *Barcelona Traction* that a shareholder's State may have a right of diplomatic protection when the State whose responsibility is invoked is the national State of the company. However, in the *ELSI* case,[159] Judge Oda wrote a separate opinion in which he rejected the possibility under customary international law that the United States could claim on behalf of US shareholders for treatment by Italy of a company incorporated under Italian law.

5.114   A variation on this idea, not directly broached by the judgment in *Barcelona Traction,* is that the State of nationality of shareholders could diplomatically protect the company against its own State of nationality 'by substitution' for the company's shareholders. In the *Diallo* case, however, the International Court of Justice rejected the idea that diplomatic protection 'by substitution' has become part of customary international law.[160]

5.115   The International law Commission has, at Art 11(b) of the DADP, proposed that a shareholder's State of nationality be able to diplomatically protect him or her where '[t]he corporation had, at the date of injury, the nationality of the State alleged to be responsible for causing the injury, and incorporation in that State was required by it as a precondition for doing business there'. The ILC's Commentaries suggest that Art 11(b) reflects customary international law,[161] but in the *Diallo* case the International Court of Justice expressly declined to comment on the putative rule's customary status.[162]

5.116   International law also permits a State to make claims in respect of another State's mistreatment of corporations and individuals associated with the activities of ships bearing the claimant State's nationality.

In the *Saiga* **case** (for the facts of which, see 12.71),[163] the International Tribunal for the Law of the Sea said:

103. In its last objection to admissibility, Guinea argues that certain claims of Saint Vincent and the Grenadines cannot be entertained by the Tribunal because they relate to violations of the rights of persons who are not nationals of Saint Vincent and the Grenadines. According to Guinea, the claims of Saint Vincent and the Grenadines in respect of loss or damage sustained by the ship, its owners, the Master and other members of the crew and other persons, including the owners of the cargo, are clearly claims of diplomatic protection. In its view, Saint Vincent and the Grenadines is not competent to institute these claims on behalf of the persons concerned since none of them is a national of Saint Vincent and the

---

159. Ibid, 83.
160. *Case Concerning Ahmadou Sadio Diallo (Guinea v Congo)* Preliminary Objections, ICJ Rep (2007), para 89.
161. *Yearbook of the International Law Commission,* 2006, Vol II, Pt II, 62.
162. *Case Concerning Ahmadou Sadio Diallo (Guinea v Congo)* Preliminary Objections, ICJ Rep (2007), para 93.
163. *M/V 'Saiga' (No 2) case (Saint Vincent and the Grenadines v Guinea)* (1999) 3 ITLOS Rep, No 2.

Grenadines. During the oral proceedings, Guinea withdrew its objection as far as it relates to the shipowners, but maintained it in respect of the other persons.

104. In opposing this objection, Saint Vincent and the Grenadines maintains that the rule of international law that a State is entitled to claim protection only for its nationals does not apply to claims in respect of persons and things on board a ship flying its flag. In such cases, the flag State has the right to bring claims in respect of violations against the ship and all persons on board or interested in its operation. Saint Vincent and the Grenadines, therefore, asserts that it has the right to protect the ship flying its flag and those who serve on board, irrespective of their nationality.

105. In dealing with this question, the Tribunal finds sufficient guidance in the Convention [on the Law of the Sea]. The Convention contains detailed provisions concerning the duties of flag States regarding ships flying their flag. Articles 94 and 217, in particular, set out the obligations of the flag State which can be discharged only through the exercise of appropriate jurisdiction and control over natural and juridical persons such as the Master and other members of the crew, the owners or operators and other persons involved in the activities of the ship.

No distinction is made in these provisions between nationals and non-nationals of a flag State. Additionally, articles 106, 110, paragraph 3, and 111, paragraph 8, of the Convention contain provisions applicable to cases in which measures have been taken by a State against a foreign ship. These measures are, respectively, seizure of a ship on suspicion of piracy, exercise of the right of visit on board the ship, and arrest of a ship in exercise of the right of hot pursuit. In these cases, the Convention provides that, if the measures are found not to be justified, the State taking the measures shall be obliged to pay compensation 'for any loss or damage' sustained. In these cases, the Convention does not relate the right to compensation to the nationality of persons suffering loss or damage. Furthermore, in relation to proceedings for prompt release under article 292 of the Convention, no significance is attached to the nationalities of persons involved in the operations of an arrested ship.

106. The provisions referred to in the preceding paragraph indicate that the Convention considers a ship as a unit, as regards the obligations of the flag State with respect to the ship and the right of a flag State to seek reparation for loss or damage caused to the ship by acts of other States and to institute proceedings under article 292 of the Convention. Thus the ship, every thing on it, and every person involved or interested in its operations are treated as an entity linked to the flag State. The nationalities of these persons are not relevant.

107. The Tribunal must also call attention to an aspect of the matter which is not without significance in this case. This relates to two basic characteristics of modern maritime transport: the transient and multinational composition of ships' crews and the multiplicity of interests that may be involved in the cargo on board a single ship. A container vessel carries a large number of containers, and the persons with interests in them may be of many different nationalities. This may also be true in relation to cargo on board a break-bulk carrier. Any of these ships could have a crew comprising persons of several nationalities. If each person sustaining damage were obliged to look for protection from the State of which such person is a national, undue hardship would ensue.

108. The Tribunal is, therefore, unable to accept Guinea's contention that Saint Vincent and the Grenadines is not entitled to present claims for damages in respect of natural and juridical persons who are not nationals of Saint Vincent and the Grenadines.

109. In the light of the above considerations, the Tribunal rejects the objection to admissibility based on nationality of claims.

The State of a ship's registration is, therefore, its State of nationality (that is, its 'flag State'). Consequently, the flag State is entitled to protect diplomatically the ship against unlawful treatment at the hands of other States. Not only that, but the flag State is also entitled to protect diplomatically others associated with the ship — such as its owners, officers, crew and passengers, and those with legal interests in any cargo — who have suffered injury resulting from the ship's unlawful treatment, even if those other persons are not nationals of the flag State.

Exhaustion of local remedies

5.117 It is a well-established rule of customary international law that international proceedings may not be commenced unless and until all the effective remedies available within the legal order of the defendant State have been exhausted. The obligation is on the foreign individual or company which has suffered internationally unlawful treatment attributable to the State to pursue all effective remedies under the law of that State. If the victim of the unlawful treatment fails to meet the requirement, that person's State of nationality will be precluded from raising an international claim on the victim's behalf.

The rationale for this requirement was articulated by the International Court of Justice in the *Interhandel Case:*[164]

> The rule that local remedies must be exhausted before international proceedings may be instituted is a well-established rule of customary international law; the rule has been generally observed in cases in which a State has adopted the cause of its national whose rights are claimed to have been disregarded in another State in violation of international law. Before resort may be had to an international court in such a situation, it has been considered necessary that the State where the violation occurred should have an opportunity to redress it by its own means, within the framework of its own domestic legal system.

5.118 This rule applies only in the domain of diplomatic protection. It does not apply where the injury results from a direct violation of another State's own rights. In the *Saiga* case,[165] the International Tribunal for the Law of the Sea considered the admissibility of a claim by Saint Vincent and the Grenadines against Guinea involving Guinea's mistreatment of the master of a ship flying the Vincentian flag. The ship's master was convicted before Guinea's *tribunal de première instance* and fined. On appeal to the *cour d'appel,* the conviction was upheld and the penalty increased by the addition of a six months' suspended prison sentence. The master did not exercise his right of appeal, either to the Criminal Chamber of the *cour d'appel* or to the *cour suprême.* Guinea argued that the ship's master had not exhausted all his avenues of appeal under Guinean law, and that the international claim was therefore inadmissible.

---

164. *Interhandel Case (Switzerland v United States)* ICJ Rep (1959) 6, 27.
165. *M/V 'Saiga' (No 2) case (Saint Vincent and the Grenadines v Guinea)* (1999) 3 ITLOS Rep, No 2.

The Convention on the Law of the Sea expressly applies the rule on exhaustion of local remedies to proceedings before the International Tribunal for the Law of the Sea 'where this is required by international law'.[166] The Tribunal noted that the criminal conviction involved 'direct violations of the rights of Saint Vincent and the Grenadines' (for example, the right to freedom of navigation) and that damage 'to the persons involved in the operation of the ship arises from those violations', with the consequence that 'the claims in respect of such damage are not subject to the rule that local remedies must be exhausted'.[167]

Wrongful conduct by a State against a foreign national will not, however, be regarded as a direct injury to the victim's State of nationality merely because the conduct occurs within the general framework of a treaty between the two States.

In the *ELSI* case,[168] the United States argued that Italy's mistreatment of two United States corporations was in breach of an applicable bilateral treaty of Friendship, Commerce and Navigation. Consequently, it was submitted, there was no need for the companies to have exhausted Italian domestic remedies because the obligation breached was owed directly to the United States. The International Court of Justice rejected this argument and emphasised that the matter 'which colours and pervades the US claim as a whole' was the alleged injury inflicted on the two corporations by Italy.[169] The wrong suffered by the United States was not distinct from, and independent of, the dispute regarding the treatment of the corporations. The Court took the view that such an important principle of customary international law could not be regarded as having been tacitly dispensed with; clear words evincing such an intention are necessary.

5.119   The requirement that local remedies be exhausted before the victim's State of nationality may pursue a claim does not apply where, as a matter of international law, there was no valid jurisdictional connection between the mistreating State and the victim. In the *Saiga* case, a plea that local remedies had not been exhausted was rejected because, inter alia, the mistreatment occurred during a customs-enforcement operation in the respondent State's exclusive economic zone, an area in which States are not internationally entitled to enforce their customs laws.[170]

5.120   The ILC Commentaries on the Draft Articles on State Responsibility discuss the scope of the requirement that local remedies be exhausted:[171]

> Only those local remedies which are 'available and effective' have to be exhausted before invoking the responsibility of a State. The mere existence

---

166. Convention on the Law of the Sea, Art 295.
167. *M/V 'Saiga' (No 2) case (Saint Vincent and the Grenadines v Guinea)* (1999) 3 ITLOS Rep, No 2, para 98.
168. *Case Concerning Elettronica Sicula SpA (ELSI) (United States v Italy)* ICJ Rep (1989) 15.
169. Ibid, para 52.
170. *M/V 'Saiga' (No 2) case (Saint Vincent and the Grenadines v Guinea)* (1999) 3 ITLOS Rep, No 2, paras 92, 99 and 100.
171. *Yearbook of the International Law Commission*, 2001, Vol II, Pt II, 121.

on paper of remedies under the internal law of a State does not impose a requirement to make use of those remedies in every case. In particular there is no requirement to use a remedy which offers no possibility of redressing the situation, for instance, where it is clear from the outset that the law which the local court would have to apply can lead only to the rejection of any appeal.

In the *Finnish Ships* arbitration,[172] an arbitrator ruled that local remedies had been exhausted notwithstanding that a Finnish national, aggrieved by his treatment at the hands of British authorities, had not appealed from the first instance decision of a British tribunal. This was because the tribunal had determined a critical issue of fact against the Finnish national, and the British appeal court lacked jurisdiction to set that finding aside. In these circumstances, launching appeal proceedings would have been futile. A commission of arbitration in the *Ambatielos Claim* discussed the range of possible ineffective local remedies in the following terms:[173]

> The ineffectiveness of local remedies may result clearly from the municipal law itself. That is the case, for example, when a Court of Appeal is not competent to reconsider the judgment given by a court of first instance on matters of fact, and when, failing such reconsideration, no redress can be obtained. ...
>
> Furthermore ... it is generally considered that the ineffectiveness of available remedies, without being legally uncertain, may also result from circumstances which do not permit any hope of redress to be placed in the use of those remedies. But in a case of that kind it is essential that such remedies, if they had been resorted to, would have proved to be *obviously futile*.

5.121   If a person fails to take advantage of procedural devices which would have assisted him or her before a State's courts or tribunals, the person may have failed to exhaust local remedies. Accordingly, in the *Ambatielos Claim*, a British trial court made findings of fact, and gave judgment, against a Greek national suing British authorities. The British appeal court lacked jurisdiction to review the critical findings of fact, and so an appeal would have been futile. Greece brought an international claim against the United Kingdom, but the commission of arbitration held Greece's claim to be inadmissible. This was because the Greek national had failed to call material witnesses who might have been able to establish the facts of the case in his favour. There was no legal or factual reason preventing him from calling those witnesses at first instance. The commission said:[174]

> The rule requires that 'local remedies' shall have been exhausted before an international action can be brought. These 'local remedies' include not only reference to the courts and tribunals, but also the use of the procedural facilities which municipal law makes available to litigants

---

172. *Claim of Finnish Shipowners against Great Britain in Respect of the Use of Certain Finnish Vessels during the War (Finland v United Kingdom)* (1934) 3 RIAA 1479.
173. *Ambatielos Claim (Greece v United Kingdom)* (1956) 12 RIAA 83, 119 (emphasis in original).
174. Ibid, 120.

before such courts and tribunals. It is the whole system of legal protection, as provided by municipal law, which must have been put to the test before a State, as the protector of its nationals, can prosecute the claim on the international plane.

5.122 The local remedies which must be exhausted include not only judicial relief, but also administrative procedures. An administrative appeal will not constitute an effective local remedy, however, unless its immediate or ultimate purpose is to vindicate a legal right. As the International Court of Justice observed in the *Diallo* case:[175]

> [W]hile the local remedies that must be exhausted include all remedies of a legal nature, judicial redress as well as redress before administrative bodies, administrative remedies can only be taken into consideration for purposes of the local remedies rule if they are aimed at vindicating a right and not at obtaining a favour, unless they constitute an essential prerequisite for the admissibility of subsequent contentious proceedings. Thus, the possibility open to Mr Diallo of submitting a request for reconsideration of the expulsion decision to the administrative authority having taken it — that is to say the Prime Minister — in the hope that he would retract his decision as a matter of grace cannot be deemed a local remedy to be exhausted.

5.123 The Draft Articles on Diplomatic Protection codify the circumstances in which customary international law regards an injured person as exempt from further pursuing domestic remedies within the jurisdiction of a foreign State that has injured him or her:

Article 15

Exceptions to the local remedies rule

Local remedies do not need to be exhausted where:

(a) There are no reasonably available local remedies to provide effective redress, or the local remedies provide no reasonable possibility of such redress;

(b) There is undue delay in the remedial process which is attributable to the State alleged to be responsible;

(c) There was no relevant connection between the injured person and the State alleged to be responsible at the date of injury;

(d) The injured person is manifestly precluded from pursuing local remedies; or

(e) The State alleged to be responsible has waived the requirement that local remedies be exhausted.

5.124 Non-exhaustion of local remedies is, in substance, a defence to an international claim. It is therefore unsurprising that the onus of showing the existence of unexhausted local remedies rests on the State against which the claim is made.[176]

---

175. *Case Concerning Ahmadou Sadio Diallo (Guinea v Congo)* Preliminary Objections, ICJ Rep (2007), para 47.
176. *Ambatielos Claim (Greece v United Kingdom)* (1956) 12 RIAA 83, 119; *Case Concerning Ahmadou Sadio Diallo (Guinea v Congo)* Preliminary Objections, ICJ Rep (2007), para 44.

5.125   Even where local remedies have been exhausted, it is still possible for States to agree to limit the right of diplomatic protection. An important case in point is the Convention on the Settlement of Investment Disputes between States and Nationals of Other States,[177] which has more than 150 States parties including Australia. On the subject of diplomatic protection, the Convention provides as follows:

> Article 27
>
> (1) No Contracting State shall give diplomatic protection, or bring an international claim, in respect of a dispute which one of its nationals and another Contracting State shall have consented to submit or shall have submitted to arbitration under this Convention, unless such other Contracting State shall have failed to abide by and comply with the award rendered in such dispute.
>
> (2) Diplomatic protection, for the purposes of paragraph (1), shall not include informal diplomatic exchanges for the sole purpose of facilitating a settlement of the dispute.

Question

Top Banana Ltd was a limited liability company incorporated under the law of the Republic of Baretta and had its registered office in Baretta. It was a wholly owned subsidiary of Federated Fruit Inc, a company incorporated under the law of the Federated Provinces of Arcadia. Top Banana Ltd operated a large banana plantation in a remote rural region of Baretta.

The Barettan Liberation Movement (BLM) was, until it took power in March 2007, a highly organised paramilitary organisation established to overthrow the Barettan government. It had been active in many of the rural regions of Baretta for a number of years.

In October 2005, a unit of six lightly armed BLM fighters attacked Top Banana Ltd's plantation with the purpose of destroying the plantation's crops; some crops were, in fact, destroyed by the fighters.

In the course of seizing the plantation, the BLM unit shot and seriously wounded Hugo, the plantation's manager, who spent the next few months in the intensive care ward of the Baretta General Hospital. Hugo was a citizen of Arcadia by birth according to the laws of Arcadia. He had lived in Arcadia his whole life until June 2005, when he moved to Baretta to take up his post at the plantation. His family and almost all his material assets were always located in Arcadia and he is registered to vote only in Arcadia.

Before Hugo could assume a management role at the plantation, Barettan law required him to become a naturalised Barettan citizen. He applied for naturalisation in May 2005 and, although he had never visited Baretta and did not speak its language, received his Barettan citizenship that same month.

---

177. UNTS, Vol 575, p 160.

A few days after the plantation's seizure, a company of Barettan government troops arrived to drive out the BLM. Although the company commander had express orders not to use heavy weapons, he ordered the use of heavy artillery to attack the plantation. The bombardment lasted an hour and destroyed almost all of the plantation's buildings. The six BLM fighters fled as soon as the artillery bombardment commenced.

The BLM launched a major offensive in early 2007, and succeeded in overthrowing the existing Barettan government in March. Baretta experienced several weeks of turmoil as the new BLM government struggled to establish a functioning administration.

The Secretary-General of the BLM, who held no official government post but who effectively controlled the government, ordered that all Arcadian nationals be expelled immediately from Baretta. Hugo was still in intensive care at Baretta General Hospital when two men in civilian clothing, calling themselves members of the 'Interim Police', removed Hugo from the hospital and immediately put him on a plane bound for Arcadia. The Interim Police had no official existence under Barettan law, but were organised by some supporters of the BLM during the period of turmoil when no regular police force was functioning. The Secretary-General, when informed of Hugo's expulsion, publicly said that the two men had 'done their patriotic duty'. The Interim Police have since been legally constituted as the Barettan People's Police.

In March 2007, the new Barettan President issued a decree simultaneously dissolving Top Banana Ltd and declaring its plantation 'the property of the Barettan people' because 'Arcadia is an enemy of the BLM'. He also rejected calls from Federated Fruit Inc for compensation, and directed Baretta's new system of Revolutionary Courts to refuse all attempts to reverse the decree. The same decree also directed the Revolutionary Courts to refuse payment to Arcadian nationals of 'any compensation arising out of incidents associated with the revolution'. The Revolutionary Courts always comply with presidential decrees.

Can Arcadia make any claims in respect of the treatment suffered by Hugo and Federated Fruit Inc? You may assume that neither Arcadia nor Baretta is a party to any treaty which might be relevant.

Suggested answer

Arcadia may exercise a right of diplomatic protection only in respect of treatment affecting its own nationals. When a State makes such a claim, it is asserting its own right to have its nationals treated in accordance with the requirements of international law (*Mavrommatis Palestine Concessions* case; *Panevezys Railway* case).

Nationality of claims

Hugo is an Arcadian national under Arcadian law, so that Arcadia is, prima facie, entitled to exercise diplomatic protection over him (Hague

Convention on Certain Questions Relating to the Conflict of Nationality Laws, Arts 1 and 2). Hugo is, however, also a national of Baretta by naturalisation. The classical view is that a State may not afford diplomatic protection to one of its nationals against a State whose nationality the person also possesses (Hague Convention on Certain Questions Relating to the Conflict of Nationality Laws, Art 4; *Salem* case). This approach has been described in *obiter* by the International Court of Justice as being in accordance with the 'ordinary practice' of States (*Reparation* case). However, current customary international law permits Arcadia to diplomatically protect Hugo against Baretta where it can be shown that his more effective links or predominant nationality lie with Arcadia (*Mergé Claim*; *Canevaro* case; *Iran–United States No A/18*; Draft Articles on Diplomatic Protection, Art 7).

Indicators of effective links include the place where the person exercises his or her political rights (*Canevaro* case); the place of habitual residence and locale of the person's economic, social, political, civic and family life *(Mergé Claim)*; the place of habitual residence, centre of interests, family ties, and participation in public life *(Iran–United States No A/18)*; and the place of establishment, interests, activities, family ties, and intentions for the near future (*Nottebohm* case). Applying these criteria to Hugo, it would appear that his links to Arcadia are substantially more genuine and effective than those to Baretta. It is, therefore, highly likely that Arcadia would be able to make a claim against Baretta in respect of the latter's treatment of Hugo.

The owner of the property damaged and expropriated by Baretta was Top Banana Ltd. The judgment of the International Court of Justice in the *Barcelona Traction* case provides valuable guidance on the requirements of customary international law concerning the nationality of limited liability corporations for the purposes of exercising diplomatic protection.

Top Banana Ltd was incorporated under the laws of Baretta and was, therefore, a Barettan national regardless of the nationality of its shareholders. Notwithstanding Art 9 of the Draft Articles on Diplomatic Protection, there is probably no rule of genuine and effective nationality when one is considering the nationality of limited liability companies. The general rule is that only the State under whose laws the company is incorporated may diplomatically protect it. That the State mistreating a company is also the State of its incorporation probably does not create an exception to the rule (Judge Oda's separate opinion in the *ELSI* case). It is also not possible to maintain that Arcadia can protect Top Banana Ltd 'by substitution' for Federated Fruit Inc (*Diallo* case).

However, the Court in the *Barcelona Traction* case said that a shareholder's State of nationality would be able to make a claim against the company's State of incorporation either where the latter unlawfully attacked the shareholder's direct rights, or where the company had ceased to exist. In the present case, Top Banana Ltd was dissolved by presidential decree. Consequently, Arcadia, as the State of nationality of the sole shareholder (Federated Fruit Inc), is entitled to make a claim against Baretta in respect of the latter's treatment of that shareholder.

Injury to Hugo

Hugo was shot and seriously wounded by a militia unit of the BLM. At the time of the attack, the BLM was an insurrectional movement against the government of Baretta. Therefore, its conduct was that of private persons and not attributable to Baretta. However, about five months after the shooting, the BLM seized power in Baretta and established itself as the new government. When this occurred, its acts became attributable to Baretta, notwithstanding that they occurred before the seizure of power (Draft Articles on State Responsibility, Art 10(1)). Provided the attack by the BLM unit was an act of the BLM as such, and 'not the individual acts of members of the movement acting in their own capacity' (ILC Commentaries), Baretta is now responsible for the shooting. Armed attacks on foreign nationals are internationally wrongful acts (for example, the *Caire Claim* and the *Youmans Claim*).

Hugo was also expelled from the country without any notice. States are free to expel foreign nationals, but must give reasonable notice of their intention to do so. In *Yeager v Iran*, 30 minutes' notice was regarded as unreasonable. Furthermore, the fact that Hugo was forcibly removed without notice from a hospital intensive care unit probably amounts to an 'outrage ... or to an insufficiency of governmental action so far short of international standards that every reasonable and impartial man would readily recognise its insufficiency' *(Neer Claim)*.

Hugo's expulsion was made pursuant to an order from the BLM Secretary-General for the immediate expulsion of all Arcadian nationals. Baretta is responsible for the conduct of all its State organs (Draft Articles on State Responsibility, Art 4(1)). A State organ includes any person or entity which has that status under Barettan law (Draft Articles on State Responsibility, Art 4(2)). The Secretary-General has no official status under Baretta's internal law, but the ILC Commentaries make clear that an entity can be a State organ even where the internal law is silent, provided it exercises official powers in practice. Because the Secretary-General effectively controlled the new Barettan government, his acts are attributable to Baretta.

The conduct of the 'Interim Police' may provide an additional basis upon which the expulsion may be attributable to Baretta. The Interim Police were a group of BLM supporters who had no status under Barettan law. A State is responsible for the conduct of its State organs, but the Interim Police were probably not organs of the State at the time of Hugo's expulsion. Nevertheless, because no regular police force was functioning, the Interim Police were probably 'exercising elements of the governmental authority in the absence or default of the official authorities and in circumstances such as to call for the exercise of those elements of authority' (Draft Articles on State Responsibility, Art 9). The conduct of such persons is attributable to the State. The fact that the Interim Police were carrying out orders from the Secretary-General provides an additional reason for regarding their actions as engaging the responsibility of Baretta *(Yeager v Iran)*.

The mere fact that the Secretary-General expressed approval of Hugo's expulsion is probably not sufficient to warrant a finding that Baretta has acknowledged and adopted the conduct of the Interim Police (Draft Articles on State Responsibility, Art 11). The ILC Commentaries make clear that adoption does not occur 'where a State merely acknowledges the factual existence of conduct or expresses its verbal approval of it'. Rather, 'what is required is something more than a general acknowledgement of a factual situation, but ... that the State identifies the conduct in question and makes it its own'. Adoption is probably not, therefore, an additional basis upon which the conduct of the Interim Police can be attributed to Baretta.

Arcadia would be entitled to seek compensation for damage suffered by Hugo for which Baretta is internationally responsible (Draft Articles on State Responsibility, Art 36(1)). The term 'damage' embraces both material and moral damage (Draft Articles on State Responsibility, Art 31(2)). As the ILC Commentaries make clear, material damage includes damage to property or other interests of a State's nationals which is assessable in financial terms. Moral damage includes individual pain and suffering and personal affront.

Injury to Federated Fruit Inc

Federated Fruit Inc's shareholder interest in Top Banana Ltd was damaged when:

(i)   the banana plantation was attacked by the BLM in October 2005;

(ii) plantation buildings were destroyed by the Barettan army's artillery bombardment a few days later; and

(iii) the plantation was expropriated by the new Barettan government in March 2007.

The BLM's attack on the banana plantation is attributable to Baretta on the same basis that the BLM's attack on Hugo is attributable to Baretta (Draft Articles on State Responsibility, Art 10(1)). Destruction of a foreign national's property engages the responsibility of a State unless it results from a lawful decision of the State's authorities and is not an 'unreasonable departure from the principles of justice recognized by the principal legal systems of the world' (Harvard Draft Convention on the International Responsibility of States for Injuries to Aliens, Art 9).

Baretta would also be liable for the BLM attack if it could be shown that its then security forces failed to provide the degree of security reasonably expected by Federated Fruit Inc *(Noyes Claim; Asian Agricultural Products Ltd (AAPL) v Sri Lanka)*. The facts of the present case, however, are probably not favourable to a claim on this basis; the BLM had not been active in that part of Baretta before and there is no evidence that the security forces knew, or should have known, that the attack on the plantation would occur.

Baretta may also be responsible for the army's artillery bombardment of the plantation a few days after the BLM attack. The army was undoubtedly an organ of the Barettan State under Art 4 of the Draft Articles on State Responsibility, and its conduct was therefore attributable to Baretta. The standard of protection reasonably required can be breached 'regardless of whether the damages occurred during the insurgents' offensive act or resulting from governmental counterinsurgency activities' *(Asian Agricultural Products Ltd (AAPL) v Sri Lanka)*. The heavy artillery bombardment lasted an hour, notwithstanding that the small number of BLM fighters fled as soon as it started. This disproportionate action was probably in breach of Baretta's standard of protection reasonably required by foreign nationals. The fact that the Barettan army's company commander acted in violation of his express orders will not preclude Baretta's responsibility. Conduct of a State organ is attributable to the State if the person acts in that capacity, and even if he or she exceeds his or her authority or contravenes instructions (Draft Articles on State Responsibility, Art 7). The company commander was undoubtedly acting in his capacity as an army officer, and he employed means placed at his disposal by virtue of his official capacity *(Caire Claim)*.

Baretta was, in principle, entitled to nationalise the banana plantation, provided it was done for a public purpose and appropriate compensation was paid (General Assembly Resolution 1803, Art 4). The requirement of public purpose will readily be inferred *(Amoco International Finance Corp v Iran)*, although the public purpose criterion would not be met where nationalisation is conducted as an act of political retaliation against the State whose nationality the property owner possesses *(British Petroleum Exploration Company (Libya) Ltd v Libya)*. Baretta's nationalisation of the banana plantation was expressly retaliatory and therefore unlawful. The refusal by Baretta to pay any form of compensation also renders the nationalisation unlawful.

Because the nationalisation is unlawful, Arcadia is entitled to claim both *damnum emergens* (the value of the property, measured as the market value of the property as a going concern at the time of its taking) and *lucrum cessans* (lost profits up to the time of any judgment) *(Amoco International Finance Corp v Iran)*.

Exhaustion of local remedies

Before Arcadia could make a claim against Baretta in respect of the treatment suffered by Hugo or Federated Fruit Inc, it must be established that they have both exhausted all effective remedies inside Baretta. If a remedy would be clearly ineffective because of the way the domestic law rules operate, then there is no obligation to pursue those remedies. Further, the onus of showing the existence of unexhausted local remedies rests on the defendant State — that is, Baretta *(Ambatielos Claim*; Draft Articles on Diplomatic Protection, Art 15(a),(d))).

Baretta's new President issued directions to the Revolutionary Courts not to reverse the nationality decree and to refuse payment to Arcadian nationals of 'any compensation arising out of incidents associated with the revolution'. Assuming the courts regard themselves as bound by the presidential direction, any recourse to the Barettan courts by Hugo or Federated Fruit Inc would appear to be futile.

Accordingly, their apparent failure to seek relief before Baretta's national courts would not prevent Arcadia from making an international claim on their behalf.

Further tutorial discussion

1. In discussing the law of State responsibility, Professor Cassese remarks that 'the international community is so primitive that the archaic concept of collective responsibility still prevails': Antonio Cassese, *International Law*, 2001, 182. Do you agree?

2. Do you think that the law on nationality of claims would be made more just if the principle of effective nationality were introduced for corporations?

3. Why should a State be obliged to treat foreign nationals better than its own citizens?

4. What are the reasons for and against retaining the rule that all effective local remedies must be exhausted before an international claim can be made?

5. Is it reasonable to require States to comply with their international obligations, even if it means violating their own constitutions? Should a State's liability to pay compensation on an international claim be mitigated by the existence of domestic constitutional barriers to compliance with international obligations?

6. The imperative of saving human life always negates the obligation to comply with a rule of international law which hinders that objective. True or false?

7. Are States ever internationally responsible for the conduct of their own citizens who are in open revolt against the government?

State jurisdiction and immunity

6

Objectives

After completing this chapter, you should:

(1) appreciate the need for limits on the jurisdictional sovereignty of States in international relations;

(2) understand and be able to explain the extent and limits of the four principles (territorial, nationality, protective and universal) upon which States may exert their jurisdictional sovereignty;

(3) appreciate the need for States to enjoy certain immunities from each other's jurisdictional sovereignty in their international relations;

(4) understand and be able to explain sovereign immunity and the way its material scope has narrowed over time;

(5) understand and be able to apply the most important rules conferring immunity of diplomats from the jurisdiction of the States to which they are accredited; and

(6) be aware of the special immunities enjoyed by Heads of State, Heads of Government and Foreign Ministers from the jurisdictional sovereignty of foreign States.

Key cases

Case of the SS Lotus (France v Turkey) PCIJ Rep (1927) Series A No 10
Attorney-General of the Government of Israel v Eichmann (1961) 36 ILR 5
R v Bow Street Metropolitan Stipendiary Magistrate; Ex parte Pinochet Ugarte (No 3) [2000] 1 AC 147
Case Concerning the Arrest Warrant of 11 April 2000 (Congo v Belgium) ICJ Rep (2002) 3

Key treaties and instruments

Charter of the International Military Tribunal (Nuremberg Tribunal) (1945): Art 6
Convention on the Prevention and Punishment of the Crime of Genocide (1948): Art II
Hague Convention for the Suppression of Unlawful Seizure of Aircraft (1970): Art 1, Art 4
Montreal Convention for the Suppression of Unlawful Acts against the Safety of Civil Aviation (1971): Art 1, Art 5
International Convention against the Taking of Hostages (1979): Art 1, Art 5(2)

International Convention for the Suppression of Terrorist Bombings (1977): Art 2, Art 6(4)
Convention against Torture and Other Cruel, Inhuman or Degrading Treatment or Punishment (1984): Art 1, Art 5(2)
Draft Articles on Jurisdictional Immunities of States and Their Property (1991): Art 1(c), Art 5, Art 6, Art 7, Art 8, Art 9, Art 10, Art 12, Art 13, Art 14, Art 16
United Nations Convention on Jurisdictional Immunities of States and Their Property (2005): Art 1(c), Art 5, Art 6, Art 7, Art 8, Art 9, Art 10, Art 11, Art 12, Art 13, Art 14, Art 16
Foreign States Immunities Act 1985 (Cth): s 9, s 10, s 11, s 12, s 13, s 14, s 15, s 18
Vienna Convention on Diplomatic Relations (1961): Art 9, Art 22, Art 24, Art 27(2), Art 27(3), Art 29, Art 31
Vienna Convention on Consular Relations (1963): Art 41, Art 43

Jurisdiction generally

6.1   Jurisdiction is a word with a multitude of meanings. It is commonly employed by lawyers to describe the scope of a court's legal authority to hear and determine a case before it. Lawyers might speak, for example, of a particular court's jurisdiction to hear a claim involving a certain sum of money, or involving certain parties, or involving events which occurred in a particular place, or arising from a specified statute. They might also discuss a court's jurisdiction to make a certain kind of order, or to impose a certain sentence, or even to adopt a particular procedure in the course of hearing a case. Lawyers and others might also consider a political authority's jurisdiction to make or enforce laws of a particular type or in relation to a certain place or subject matter. Sometimes the police are said to possess, or lack, jurisdiction in a certain kind of situation or in a particular place.

6.2   In international law, 'jurisdiction' is used to describe a crucial aspect of State sovereignty; indeed, it is sometimes referred to as 'jurisdictional sovereignty'. Jurisdictional sovereignty pertains to a State's sovereign right to exercise authority over persons, things and events by use of its domestic law and its State organs.

6.3   There are two types of jurisdiction: prescriptive and enforcement. A State's prescriptive jurisdiction is its power to lay down legal rules, and this usually refers to the activities of persons or bodies exercising legislative power. Enforcement jurisdiction is a State's power to enforce legal rules already prescribed, by either judicial or executive action (for example, a court hearing and judgment, or the arrest of persons or seizure of property by police).

6.4   International law concerns itself with the scope and limits of the jurisdictional sovereignty of States. These limits arise most frequently because each State co-exists with other States. If there were no limits to permissible exercises of jurisdictional sovereignty, the occasions for international conflict would be dramatically increased.

It is one thing for a court in State A to convict a person for exceeding the road speed limit of State A while driving in State A. It is another thing for a court in State A to convict a citizen of State B for exceeding the road speed limit of State A while driving in State B. In the latter situation, the conduct of the court in State A would call into question the sovereignty of State B to exercise authority over persons, things and events within its own territory by use of its domestic law.

As shall be seen, customary international law has developed rules and principles which define the limits of a State's enforcement jurisdiction by reference primarily to the State's territory, the nationality of the persons affected by the exercise of jurisdiction, certain vital security interests of the State, and the defence of the international legal order as a whole.

Another source of conflict would arise where the courts of State A sought to adjudicate and enforce a claim against State B against the latter's wishes, or where the police of State A sought to arrest State B's representatives. These sorts of situations are dealt with by international law rules on immunity, which grant exemptions to certain foreign persons and bodies from a State's exercise of jurisdictional sovereignty.

6.5 Most State practice and arbitral decisions relating to jurisdictional sovereignty have dealt with criminal jurisdiction. This is largely because of the public nature of criminal law; prosecutions are almost always brought by organs of State, and police forces are usually involved somewhere in the process.

There is disagreement among eminent publicists as to the extent to which international law principles on jurisdiction apply to non-criminal matters. The applicable principles of international law are less settled in the case of non-criminal matters. The exercise of civil jurisdiction where international elements are involved is governed primarily by private international law,[1] although what domestic courts and legislatures do in this domain provides evidence of State practice. On the other hand, and with the exception of administrative law matters, non-criminal matters involve executive State organs much less frequently than criminal matters and they rarely possess a public dimension.

6.6 There are traditionally four bases or principles upon which States are entitled to exercise their jurisdictional sovereignty in criminal matters. These are the:

- territorial principle;
- nationality principle;
- protective principle; and
- universality principle.

There is no hierarchy among these principles, and it is quite possible for several States to have a valid basis for exercising jurisdictional sovereignty in relation to the same criminal act. In such a case, and subject to any treaty obligations, whichever State actually possesses

---

1.   See **1.5**.

custody will have a perfectly valid right to prosecute and punish the offender, notwithstanding the competing claims of other States.

Territorial principle

6.7 Unless an entity has a government with the capacity to prescribe and enforce legal rules in its own defined territory, it cannot be described as a State.[2] Indeed, it is the territorial connection between a State on the one hand, and a person, thing or event on the other, which provides the surest and most usual foundation for the exercise of jurisdictional sovereignty.

Max Huber (1874–1960), as sole arbitrator in the *Island of Palmas Case,* put the relationship between State sovereignty and territorial sovereignty in the following terms:[3]

> Sovereignty in the relations between States signifies independence. Independence in regard to a portion of the globe is the right to exercise therein, to the exclusion of any other State, the functions of a State. The development of the national organization of States during the last few centuries and, as a corollary, the development of international law, have established this principle of the exclusive competence of the State in regard to its own territory in such a way as to make it the point of departure in settling most questions that concern international relations.

In describing the link between territorial sovereignty and jurisdictional sovereignty, Lord Macmillan in the House of Lords said that it:[4]

> … is an essential attribute of sovereignty of this realm, as of all sovereign independent states, that it should possess jurisdiction over all persons and things within its territorial limits and all causes civil and criminal arising within these limits.

6.8 If a person or thing is located in a State's territory, or if an event occurs in a State's territory, then international law normally permits a State to prescribe and enforce its domestic law in respect of that person, thing or event.

However, mere presence in the territory is not always enough; enforcement power can be exercised only on a recognised basis of prescriptive jurisdiction. Thus, international law does not permit a State to enforce a domestic law against a foreign national in respect of an act committed outside the State's territory and where the act concerned is covered by neither the universality principle (viz, certain serious crimes under international law) nor the protective principle (viz, acts aimed at destroying the security of the State).

Further, a State will not be permitted to exercise its jurisdictional sovereignty if the person, thing or event is protected by an immunity recognised by international law (for example, sovereign or diplomatic

---

2.   See **4.7–4.11**.
3.   *Island of Palmas Case (Netherlands v United States)* (1928) 2 RIAA 829, 838.
4.   *Compania Naviera Vascongado v Steamship 'Cristina'* [1938] AC 485, 496–497.

immunity), or if jurisdictional sovereignty is exercised in a way specifically forbidden by international law (for example, in violation of certain human rights obligations).

Subjective territorial principle

6.9   There are two dimensions to the territorial principle. The 'pure' or 'subjective' territorial principle provides that a State is free to prescribe and enforce rules for all conduct which actually takes place within its own territory, or affecting the status of persons or things located in its own territory. This is the simplest and most usual sense in which the territorial principle is understood.

The subjective territorial principle does not depend on conduct being concluded in the State's territory, or on the effects of the conduct being manifested in the State's territory, provided the conduct originates there.

In *Treacy v Director of Public Prosecutions*, Lord Diplock in the House of Lords remarked that there is:[5]

> ... no rule of comity to prevent Parliament from prohibiting under pain of punishment persons who are present in the United Kingdom ... from doing physical acts in England, notwithstanding that the consequences of those acts take effect outside the United Kingdom.

Accordingly, if a person standing in State A fires a gun across the border into State B and kills another person standing in State B, State A will be permitted to exercise its enforcement jurisdiction over the gunman. This remains so notwithstanding that the effects of the gunman's act were felt entirely within the territory of State B.

Objective territorial principle

6.10   There is also an 'objective' dimension to the territorial principle. Under this aspect of the principle, a State may exercise its jurisdictional sovereignty over conduct on the basis that some subsequent element of it occurs in that State, or provided its effects are felt in that State.

Accordingly, if a person standing in State A fires a gun across the border into State B and kills another person standing in State B, State B will be permitted to exercise its enforcement jurisdiction against the gunman. This remains so notwithstanding that all of the conduct apart from its effects occurred entirely within the territory of State A.

6.11   The Permanent Court of International Justice considered an application of the objective territorial principle in a case involving collision at sea.

---

5.   *Treacy v Director of Public Prosecutions* [1971] AC 537, 561–562.

In the **Lotus case,**[6] there was a collision on the high seas between a French steamship (the SS *Lotus*) and a Turkish steamship. As a result, eight sailors and passengers aboard the Turkish vessel perished. When the French vessel arrived in a Turkish port, its officer of the watch at the time of the collision, Lieutenant Demons, was arrested and charged with the criminal offence of involuntary manslaughter under Turkish law. France challenged the compatibility of the prosecution with international law on the grounds, inter alia, that Turkey could not demonstrate any basis of jurisdiction by which a State could prosecute a foreign national for acts committed outside its territory. The Court said:[7]

> International law governs relations between independent States. The rules of law binding upon States therefore emanate from their own free will as expressed in conventions and usages generally accepted as expressing principles of law and established in order to regulate the relations between those co-existing independent communities or with a view to the achievement of common aims. Restrictions upon the independence of States cannot therefore be presumed.

> Now the first and foremost restriction imposed by international law upon a State is that failing the existence of a permissive rule to the contrary it may not exercise its power in any form in the territory of another State. In this sense jurisdiction is certainly territorial; it cannot be exercised by a State outside its territory except by virtue of a permissive rule derived from international custom or from a convention.

> It does not, however, follow that international law prohibits a State from exercising in its own territory, in respect of any case which relates to acts which have taken place abroad, and in which it cannot rely on some permissive rule of international law.

> Such a rule would only be tenable if international law contained a general prohibition to States to extend the application of their laws and the jurisdiction of their courts to persons, property and acts outside their territory, and if, as an exception to this general prohibition, it allowed States to do so in certain specific cases. But this is certainly not the case as it stands under international law at present. Far from laying down a general prohibition to the effect that States may not extend the application of their laws and the jurisdiction of their courts to persons, property and acts outside their territory, it leaves them in this respect a wide measure of discretion which is only limited in certain cases by prohibitive rules. ...

> Though it is true in all systems of law that the principle of the territorial character of criminal law is fundamental, it is equally true that all or nearly all those systems of law extend their action to offences committed outside the territory of the State which adopts them ... The territoriality of criminal law, therefore, is not an absolute principle of international law and by no means coincides with territorial sovereignty. ...

> No argument has come to the knowledge of the Court from which it could be deduced that States recognize themselves to be under an obligation towards each other only to have regard to the place where the author of the offence happens to be at the time of the offence. On the contrary, it is certain that the courts of many countries, even of countries which have given their criminal legislation a strictly territorial character, interpret criminal law in the sense that offences, the authors of which at the moment of commission are in the territory

---

6.   *Case of the SS Lotus (France v Turkey)* PCIJ Rep (1927) Series A No 10.
7.   Ibid, 18–23.

of another State, are nevertheless to be regarded as having been committed in the national territory, if one of the constituent elements of the offence, and more especially its effects, have taken place there. ... Consequently, once it is admitted that the effects of the offence were produced on the Turkish vessel, it becomes impossible to hold that there is a rule of international law which prohibits Turkey from prosecuting Lieutenant Demons because of the fact that the author of the offence was on board the French ship.

The Court held that 'a ship on the high seas is assimilated to the territory of the State of the flag of which it flies' and that the Turkish vessel was therefore assimilated to the territory of Turkey.[8] Consequently, although all of Lieutenant Demons's conduct occurred outside Turkish territory, its effects were manifested within Turkish territory. Absent a prohibitive rule preventing Turkey from exercising its criminal jurisdiction in such circumstances, Turkey remained free to exercise its criminal jurisdiction over Lieutenant Demons.

It should be noted that in cases of collision on the high seas, the law is now that criminal jurisdiction may not be exercised except by the flag State of the vessel at fault or the State whose nationality the accused individual possesses.[9]

Scope of State territory

6.12   A State's territory consists of several components.[10] Most importantly, there are all the lands within its international frontiers, including the subsoil. To these must be added internal waters, the territorial sea,[11] and all lands directly beneath them. Finally, a State's territory includes the airspace directly above these areas, but does not extend to any part of outer space.

Nationality principle

Active nationality principle

6.13   States are free to exercise their criminal jurisdiction over persons who possess their nationality. Thus, a State may arrest and prosecute one of its nationals for offences against its laws even if all elements of the offence, including its effects, occurred outside its territory. Such an exercise of jurisdictional sovereignty is said to rest on the 'active nationality principle' or the 'active personality principle'.

8.   But see **6.18**.
9.   See **12.94**.
10.   See **7.5**.
11.   But see **12.42–12.56**.

6.14 States whose legal systems share in the civil law tradition make extensive use of the active nationality principle in criminal matters. Common law States — such as Australia, the United Kingdom and the United States — make much less use of it, but do not object to its employment by other States.

Even the common law States sometimes have resort to the active nationality principle in criminal matters. For example, Australian legislation makes use of the active nationality principle in respect of certain crimes committed by Australian citizens aboard foreign ships[12] and where Australian citizens have sexual relations outside Australia with persons under the age of 16 years.[13]

In *Joyce v Director of Public Prosecutions*,[14] the House of Lords upheld a conviction for treason against a radio broadcaster of German propaganda during the Second World War. The broadcaster had travelled to Germany on a British passport, but none of his treasonous acts had occurred in British territory.

Passive nationality principle

6.15 Some States — such as Brazil, Italy, Mexico and Turkey — assert jurisdictional sovereignty in criminal matters on the basis that the victim of the crime possessed the State's nationality. Thus, they seek to exercise jurisdictional sovereignty over criminal acts committed abroad against their own citizens. Such an exercise of jurisdictional sovereignty is said to rest on the 'passive nationality principle' or the 'passive personality principle'.

6.16 Many States, especially those which share in the common law tradition, reject the passive nationality principle as a basis for the exercise of jurisdictional sovereignty, at least insofar as ordinary crimes are concerned. All six dissenting judges in the *Lotus* case rejected the passive nationality principle as a basis for the exercise of jurisdictional sovereignty.

The majority in the case (six judges, including the President's casting vote) did not address the passive nationality principle, having decided the case on different grounds. In his dissenting opinion, Judge John Bassett Moore (1860–1947) dismissed the passive nationality principle, which he termed the 'system of protection', with the following words:[15]

> What, we may ask, is this system? In substance it means that the citizen of one country, when he visits another country, takes with him for his 'protection' the law of his own country and subjects those with whom he comes into contact to the operation of that law. In this way an inhabitant of a great commercial city, in which foreigners congregate, may in the course of an hour unconsciously fall under the operation of a number

---

12. *Crimes at Sea Act 1979* (Cth).
13. *Crimes (Child Sex Tourism) Act 1994* (Cth).
14. *Joyce v Director of Public Prosecutions* [1946] AC 347.
15. *Case of the SS Lotus (France v Turkey)* PCIJ Rep (1927) Series A No 10, 92–93.

of foreign criminal codes. ... It is evident that this claim is at variance not only with the principle of the exclusive jurisdiction of a State over its own territory, but also with the equally well-settled principle that a person visiting a foreign country, far from radiating for his protection the jurisdiction of his own country, falls under the dominion of the local law and, except so far as his government may diplomatically intervene in case of a denial of justice[16] must look to that law for his protection.

No one disputes the right of a State to subject its citizens abroad to the operations of its own penal laws, as it sees fit to do so. This concerns simply the citizen and his own government, and no other government can properly intervene. But the case is fundamentally different where a country claims either that its penal laws apply to other countries and to what takes place wholly within such countries or, if it does not claim this, that it may punish foreigners for alleged violations, even in their own country, of laws to which they were not subject.

Judge Moore's 'system of protection', by which he referred to the passive nationality principle, should not be confused with the protective principle of jurisdiction.[17]

6.17 In more recent times, there has been a slight shift in the attitude of some sceptical States to the passive nationality principle. This is largely a response to the rise of international terrorism, and the United States, in particular, has demonstrated a willingness to employ the passive nationality principle where its nationals are victims of acts of hostage-taking, or where they have been targeted by reason of their nationality. The American Law Institute's third restatement of United States foreign relations law provides as follows:[18]

The [passive nationality] principle has not been generally accepted for ordinary torts and crimes. But it is increasingly accepted as applied to terrorist and other organized attacks on a state's nationals by reason of their nationality, or to assassination of a state's diplomats or other officials.

In *United States v Yunis*,[19] the United States District Court for the District of Columbia relied partly on the passive nationality principle to uphold its own jurisdiction to hear a criminal charge against a Lebanese national for hijacking a foreign aircraft outside the United States with two United States citizens aboard. The District Court's decision was upheld on appeal to the United States Court of Appeal.[20]

Ships, aircraft and spacecraft

6.18 It is sometimes said that ships, aircraft and spacecraft are assimilated to the territory of the State under whose laws they are registered while they remain outside another State's territory (that is, when ships are

---

16. See **5.89**.
17. See **6.19–6.22**.
18. American Law Institute, *Restatement (Third) of the Foreign Relations Law of the United States,* 1987, Vol 1, §402, comment g.
19. *United States v Yunis* 681 F Supp 896 (1988).
20. *United States v Yunis* (1991) 30 ILM 463.

on the high seas, when aircraft or spacecraft are above the high seas, or when spacecraft are in outer space). This point was explicitly made, as far as ships are concerned, by the Permanent Court of International Justice in the *Lotus* case.[21] For certain purposes, such as determining a person's nationality at birth, this may be correct. It is doubtful, however, that the PCIJ's judgment on this point accurately reflected the position in customary international law for the purposes of jurisdiction.

Whether or not the Court's view was correct at the time of the *Lotus* judgment, the position is now that a State's criminal jurisdiction over ships, aircraft and spacecraft is governed by a theory more closely fitting the nationality principle of jurisdiction. A ship, aircraft or spacecraft is generally subject to the criminal jurisdiction both of the State under whose laws it is registered and of any State in whose territory it is located.[22]

When an object (or a component part of it) which was launched into outer space is found outside the territory of the State where the object is registered, it must be returned to that State.[23]

Protective principle

6.19 The protective principle (sometimes known as the 'security principle') permits a State to exercise its criminal jurisdiction over certain acts committed abroad by foreign nationals. This basis of jurisdiction therefore resembles the objective territorial principle.

The protective principle is different from the objective territorial principle in two important ways. Whereas the objective territorial principle permits a State to protect both State interests and private interests against an actual injury occurring within the State's territory, the protective principle permits a State to protect only the State's own security interests against either an actual injury or the threat of injury. Furthermore, it is not necessary that the actual or threatened injury should have a territorial connection with the State.

6.20 The actual or threatened injury must be directed at the State's security interests, and it must be generally recognised as a criminal offence among the community of States.[24]

Among the security interests generally recognised as falling within the scope of the protective principle are physical attacks on officers or organs

---

21.   See **6.11**. See also the judgment of the United States Supreme Court in *United States v Flores* 289 US 137 (1933), in which the United States was held to possess jurisdiction to try a defendant for murder aboard a US-registered vessel located in the internal waters of the Belgian Congo on the basis that the vessel was part of United States territory.

22.   For special rules relating to the exercise of coastal State jurisdiction over foreign ships in internal waters and the territorial sea, see **12.40** and **12.42–12.56**. For the law relating to the nationality of ships, see **12.90–12.95**.

23.   Treaty on Principles Governing the Activities of States in the Exploration and Use of Outer Space, Including the Moon and Other Celestial Bodies, Art 8, UNTS, Vol 610, p 205.

24.   American Law Institute, *Restatement (Third) of the Foreign Relations Law of the United States*, 1987, Vol 1, §402(3).

of the State, forgery of official documents (for example, passports), counterfeiting of currency, and acts of espionage against the State.

Accordingly, a conspiracy by nationals of State A to assassinate a government minister of State B while on a visit to State A would engage the protective principle enabling State B to exercise criminal jurisdiction over the conspirators.[25] Similarly, if a national of State A counterfeits State B's currency in State A, then, regardless of where he or she intends to use the forged notes, State B could exercise criminal jurisdiction over the counterfeiter.

6.21 The protective principle has also been extended to other serious crimes, such as conspiracy to import prohibited narcotics or conspiracy to commit an act of terrorism where no act has yet occurred in the State's territory.[26]

6.22 Furthermore, cases such as *Joyce v Director of Public Prosecutions* and *United States v Yunis* are also explicable partly on the basis of the protective principle. The protective principle is, in practice, rarely invoked by itself. Rather, it is generally raised to justify an exercise of jurisdiction together with one or more of the other principles: territorial, nationality or universality. Perhaps the clearest instance of an exercise of criminal jurisdiction on the basis of the protective principle is provided by an Israeli court in 1961.

In the **Eichmann case,**[27] the District Court of Jerusalem heard criminal charges against the former chief of the Jewish Office of the Gestapo, National Socialist Germany's secret police. Adolf Eichmann (1906–1962), who had administered the National Socialist regime's program of extermination against the Jewish population of Europe, was charged under Israeli law with war crimes, crimes against the Jewish people, and crimes against humanity. Eichmann's conduct had not occurred on Israeli territory, nor had Eichmann ever been an Israeli national — indeed, Israel did not exist at the time of Eichmann's conduct. In response to submissions that it lacked jurisdiction to try Eichmann, the Court said:

> 30. We have discussed at length the international character of the crimes in question because this offers the broadest possible, though not the only, basis for Israel's jurisdiction according to the law of nations. No less important from the point of view of international law is the special connection which the State of Israel has with such crimes, since the people of Israel ..., the Jewish people ..., constituted the target and the victim of most of the said crimes.

> The State of Israel's 'right to punish' the accused derives, in our view, from two cumulative sources: a universal source (pertaining to the whole of mankind), which vests the right to prosecute and punish crimes of this order in every State within the family of nations; and a specific or national source, which gives the victim nation the right to try any who assault its existence.

---

25. See also **6.36**.
26. *Liangsiriprasert v Government of the United States of America* [1991] AC 225 (Privy Council) — *ratio* for conspiracy to import prohibited narcotics, *obiter* for conspiracy to commit an act of terrorism.
27. *Attorney-General of the Government of Israel v Eichmann* (1961) 36 ILR 5.

> This second foundation of criminal jurisdiction conforms, according to accepted terminology, to the protective principle …
>
> 33. … The 'linking point' between Israel and the accused (and for that matter any person accused of a crime against the Jewish people under this Law) is striking in the case of 'crime against the Jewish people', a crime that postulates an intention to exterminate the Jewish people in whole or in part. …
>
> 34. The connection between the State of Israel and the Jewish people needs no explanation. The State of Israel was established and recognized as the State of the Jews. …
>
> 35. Indeed, this crime very deeply concerns the 'vital interests' of the State of Israel, and under the 'protective principle' this State has the right to punish the criminals. … The punishment of Nazi criminals does not derive from the arbitrariness of a country 'abusing' its sovereignty but is a legitimate and reasonable exercise of a right of penal jurisdiction. A people which can be murdered with impunity lives in danger, to say nothing of its 'honour and dignity' …
>
> 36. Defence Counsel contended that the protective principle cannot apply to this Law because that principle is designed to protect only an existing State, its security and its interests, whereas the State of Israel did not exist at the time of the commission of the said crimes. … The right of the injured group to punish offenders derives directly, as Grotius explained … from the crime committed against them by the offender, and it is only want of sovereignty that denies it the power to try and punish the offender. If the injured group or people thereafter achieves political sovereignty in any territory, it may exercise such sovereignty for the enforcement of its natural right to punish the offender who injured it. All this applies to the crime of genocide (including the 'crime against the Jewish people') which, although committed by the killing of individuals, was intended to exterminate the nation as a group.

The District Court identified the principal objection against the protective principle — namely, that it could be used abusively so as to render foreigners located outside the State's territory to the laws of the State. This objection is not fanciful, as many States regard conduct which is in complete accord with international human rights law — especially the freedoms of religion, speech, assembly and association — as subversive, seditious or otherwise contrary to State security.

The answer to this objection is that the protective principle can justify an exercise of State sovereignty in international law only if the impugned conduct is generally recognised as criminal by the community of States and if it is not protected by an applicable rule of international human rights law.

Universality principle

6.23   The universality principle exists in order to furnish all States with the jurisdiction to try and punish certain crimes which are so serious that they pose a threat to the international order as a whole. Any State which actually has custody of the offender may exercise its jurisdictional sovereignty over that offender, regardless of the offender's nationality or the location of the offence.

The principle is normally reserved to justify jurisdiction where the repression of acts committed outside a State's territory by foreign nationals is required as a matter of international public policy.

Piracy

6.24 The earliest application of the universality principle concerned pirates, whom customary international law has long described as *hostes humani generis* (enemies of mankind). At various times in history, piracy has posed a major threat to human life, property and economic activity. Any State into whose custody a pirate falls is entitled to punish the pirate. The Convention on the Law of the Sea defines piracy as follows:

> **Article 101**
>
> *Definition of Piracy*
>
> Piracy consists of any of the following acts:
>
> (a) any illegal acts of violence or detention, or any act of depredation, committed for private ends by the crew or passengers of a private ship or a private aircraft, and directed:
>
> > (i) on the high seas, against another ship or aircraft, or against persons or property on board such ship or aircraft;
> >
> > (ii) against a ship, aircraft, persons or property in a place outside the jurisdiction of any State;
>
> (b) any act of voluntary participation in the operation of a ship or of an aircraft with knowledge of facts making it a pirate ship or aircraft;
>
> (c) any act of inciting or of intentionally facilitating an act described in subparagraph (a) or (b).

Because piracy exists as an offence in various forms in numerous domestic legal orders, the term 'piracy *jure gentium*' is frequently used to designate the offence of piracy in its modality under customary international law.

Article 100 of the Convention on the Law of the Sea imposes an obligation on all States to 'co-operate to the fullest possible extent in the repression of piracy on the high seas or in any other place outside the jurisdiction of any State'.

War crimes and crimes against humanity

6.25 During the 20th century, the universality principle was extended to embrace war crimes, crimes against humanity, and genocide. Indeed, the Israeli court in the *Eichmann* case expressly invoked the universality principle in support of its jurisdiction.

6.26 War crimes and crimes against humanity were defined by the Statute of the Nuremberg International Military Tribunal[28] as follows:

---

28. Agreement for the Prosecution and Punishment of the Major War Criminals of the European Axis, and Charter of the International Military Tribunal (Nuremberg Tribunal), UNTS, Vol 82, p 279.

Article 6

... The following acts, or any of them, are crimes within the jurisdiction of the Tribunal for which there shall be individual responsibility: ...

(b)   War Crimes: namely, violations of the laws or customs of war. Such violations shall include, but not be limited to, murder, ill-treatment or deportation to slave labor or for any other purpose of civilian population of or in occupied territory, murder or ill-treatment of prisoners of war or persons on the seas, killing of hostages, plunder of public or private property, wanton destruction of cities, towns or villages, or devastation not justified by military necessity;

(c)   Crimes Against Humanity: namely, murder, extermination, enslavement, deportation, and other inhumane acts committed against any civilian population, before or during the war, or persecutions on political, racial or religious grounds in execution of or in connection with any crime within the jurisdiction of the Tribunal whether or not in violation of the domestic law of the country where perpetrated.

Leaders, organizers, instigators, and accomplices, participating in the formulation or execution of a common plan or conspiracy to commit any of the foregoing crimes are responsible for all acts performed by any persons in execution of such plan.

The United Nations General Assembly subsequently adopted a resolution affirming 'the principles of international law recognised by the Charter of the Nuremberg Tribunal and the judgment of the Tribunal'.[29]

The 1997 Rome Statute of the International Criminal Court[30] contains detailed definitions of war crimes[31] and crimes against humanity[32] which elaborate upon the Nuremberg principles. Similar definitions had already been included in the statutes of the international criminal tribunals for Yugoslavia and Rwanda, adopted by resolution of the United Nations Security Council. The Rome Statute — which is in fact a multilateral treaty — has more than 110 parties, including Australia.

Genocide

6.27 The international crime of genocide is defined in the 1948 Convention on the Prevention and Punishment of the Crime of Genocide:[33]

Article II

In the present Convention, genocide means any of the following acts committed with intent to destroy, in whole or in part, a national, ethnical, racial or religious group, as such:

(a) Killing members of the group;

(b) Causing serious bodily or mental harm to members of the group;

---

29.   General Assembly Resolution 95 (I) (1945).
30.   UNTS, Vol 2187, p 3.
31.   Article 8.
32.   Article 7.
33.   UNTS, Vol 999, p 171.

(c) Deliberately inflicting on the group conditions of life calculated to bring about its physical destruction in whole or in part;

(d) Imposing measures intended to prevent births within the group;

(e) Forcibly transferring children of the group to another group.

An attempt, conspiracy or direct and public incitement to commit genocide is also punishable, as is any complicity in genocide.[34] People committing these acts 'shall be punished, whether they are constitutionally responsible rulers, public officials or private individuals'.[35]

The Genocide Convention has more than 140 parties, including Australia. The Rome Statute of the International Criminal Court contains a definition of genocide materially identical to that of the Genocide Convention.[36]

Extradite or prosecute

6.28   Over the last 50 years, a number of multilateral treaties have extended the range of crimes to which a variant of the universality principle applies. These treaties adopt an *aut dedere aut judicare* approach to their offences — that is, they impose upon the State possessing custody of the alleged offender an obligation to either prosecute or extradite to another State with a specified interest in the offence.

This version of the universality principle may be found in multilateral conventions dealing with a range of offences, including aircraft hijacking and sabotage, hostage-taking, torture, drug trafficking and violent crimes against certain representatives of States and public international organisations. Some of these conventions, which are discussed below, are now so widely adhered to that their norm-creating provisions have almost certainly been transposed into requirements of customary international law.

Aircraft hijacking

6.29   Hijacking of aircraft is dealt with in the 1970 Hague Convention for the Suppression of Unlawful Seizure of Aircraft,[37] which defines the offence in the following terms:

Article 1

Any person who on board an aircraft in flight:

(a) unlawfully, by force or threat thereof, or by any other form of intimidation, seizes, or exercises control of, that aircraft, or attempts to perform any such act, or

(b) is an accomplice of a person who performs or attempts to perform any such act

commits an offence ...

---

34.   Article III.
35.   Article IV.
36.   Article 6.
37.   UNTS, Vol 860, p 105.

The 1970 Hague Convention requires that each State 'establish its jurisdiction over the offence and any other act of violence against passengers and crew committed by the alleged offender in connection with the offence' when, inter alia, 'the aircraft on board which the offence is committed lands in its territory with the alleged offender still on board'.[38]

A State is also required to establish its jurisdiction over the offence even where the offender is merely present in its territory, unless it extradites the offender to the State of the hijacked aircraft's registration, the State in whose territory it landed, or the State in whose territory any lessee of the aircraft has his or her principal place of business or permanent residence.[39] The Convention has more than 180 parties, including Australia.

Aircraft sabotage

6.30   Sabotage of aircraft is dealt with in the 1971 Montreal Convention for the Suppression of Unlawful Acts against the Safety of Civil Aviation,[40] which defines the offence as follows:

Article 1

1.   Any person commits an offence if he unlawfully and intentionally:

   (a)   performs an act of violence against a person on board an aircraft in flight if that act is likely to endanger the safety of that aircraft; or

   (b)   destroys an aircraft in service or causes damage to such an aircraft which renders it incapable of flight or which is likely to endanger its safety in flight; or

   (c)   places or causes to be placed on an aircraft in service, by any means whatsoever, a device or substance which is likely to destroy that aircraft, or to cause damage to it which renders it incapable of flight, or to cause damage to it which is likely to endanger its safety in flight; or

   (d)   destroys or damages air navigation facilities or interferes with their operation, if any such act is likely to endanger the safety of aircraft in flight; or

   (e)   communicates information which he knows to be false, thereby endangering the safety of an aircraft in flight.

2.   Any person also commits an offence if he:

   (a)   attempts to commit any of the offences mentioned in paragraph 1 of this Article; or

   (b)   is an accomplice of a person who commits or attempts to commit any such offence.

---

38.   Article 4(1)(b).
39.   Article 4(2).
40.   UNTS, Vol 974, p 177, and Vol 1217, p 404 (corrigendum).

The 1971 Montreal Convention requires States to establish their jurisdiction of the offence in substantially the same circumstances as apply under the 1970 Hague Convention.[41] It has more than 185 parties, including Australia.

Marine hijacking and sabotage

6.31 Hijacking and sabotage of non-military ships are governed by the 1988 Convention for the Suppression of Unlawful Acts against the Safety of Maritime Navigation,[42] which substantially transposes to civil navigation the regime applicable to civil aviation.[43] The Convention has more than 155 parties, including Australia.

A materially identical regime is also adopted in relation to certain fixed platforms under the 1988 Protocol for the Suppression of Unlawful Acts against the Safety of Fixed Platforms Located on the Continental Shelf.[44] The Protocol has more than 140 parties, including Australia.

Hostage-taking

6.32 The taking of hostages is regulated under international law primarily by the 1979 International Convention against the Taking of Hostages,[45] which provides:

Article 1

1. Any person who seizes or detains and threatens to kill, to injure or to continue to detain another person (hereinafter referred to as the 'hostage') in order to compel a third party, namely, a State, an international intergovernmental organization, a natural or juridical person, or a group of persons, to do or abstain from doing any act as an explicit or implicit condition for the release of the hostage commits the offence of taking of hostages ('hostage-taking') within the meaning of this Convention.

2. Any person who:

   (a) attempts to commit an act of hostage-taking, or

   (b) participates as an accomplice of anyone who commits or attempts to commit an act of hostage-taking likewise commits an offence for the purposes of this Convention.

Where a hostage-taker is present in the territory of a State, regardless of where the hostage-taking occurred or the nationality of any person involved, the State must either exercise its jurisdiction over the offence or extradite the offender to the State on whose territory the offence occurred, or whose nationality the offender or a victim possessed.[46] The Convention has more than 165 parties, including Australia.

---

41.   Articles 5(1)(c) and 5(2).
42.   UNTS, Vol 1678, p 201.
43.   See especially Arts 3 and 6.
44.   UNTS, Vol 1678, p 304. See especially Arts 2 and 3.
45.   UNTS, Vol 1316, p 205.
46.   Article 5(2).

Terrorist bombing and financing

6.33   Certain terrorist bombings are also subject to universal jurisdiction under the terms of the 1977 International Convention for the Suppression of Terrorist Bombings,[47] which defines the offence as follows:

Article 2

1. Any person commits an offence within the meaning of this Convention if that person unlawfully and intentionally delivers, places, discharges or detonates an explosive or other lethal device in, into or against a place of public use, a State or government facility, a public transportation system or an infrastructure facility:

    (a) With the intent to cause death or serious bodily injury; or

    (b) With the intent to cause extensive destruction of such a place, facility or system, where such destruction results in or is likely to result in major economic loss.

2. Any person also commits an offence if that person attempts to commit an offence as set forth in paragraph 1 of the present article.

3. Any person also commits an offence if that person:

    (a) Participates as an accomplice in an offence as set forth in paragraph 1 or 2 of the present article; or

    (b) Organizes or directs others to commit an offence as set forth in paragraph 1 or 2 of the present article; or

    (c) In any other way contributes to the commission of one or more offences as set forth in paragraph 1 or 2 of the present article by a group of persons acting with a common purpose; such contribution shall be intentional and either be made with the aim of furthering the general criminal activity or purpose of the group or be made in the knowledge of the intention of the group to commit the offence or offences concerned.

Where an offender is present in the territory of a State, regardless of where the offence occurred or the nationality of any person involved, the State must either exercise its jurisdiction over the offence or extradite the offender to the State on whose territory it occurred, or whose nationality the offender or a victim possessed, or against whose government facilities the offence was committed, or against whom the terrorists' demands were directed.[48] The Convention has more than 160 parties, including Australia.

6.34   A similar regime of universal jurisdiction is established under the 1999 International Convention for the Suppression of the Financing of Terrorism,[49] by which it is an offence to provide or collect funds with the intention, or in the knowledge, that they are to be used in order to carry out a wide range of specified terrorist activities.[50] The Convention has more than 170 parties, including Australia.

---

47.   UNTS, Vol 2149, p 284.
48.   Article 6(4).
49.   UNTS, Vol 2178, p 197.
50.   Articles 2 and 7.

Torture

6.35   Universal jurisdiction over acts of torture is provided for under the 1984 Convention against Torture and Other Cruel, Inhuman or Degrading Treatment or Punishment.[51] Torture is defined in the following terms:

> **Article 1**
>
> 1. For the purposes of this Convention, torture means any act by which severe pain or suffering, whether physical or mental, is intentionally inflicted on a person for such purposes as obtaining from him or a third person information or a confession, punishing him for an act he or a third person has committed or is suspected of having committed, or intimidating or coercing him or a third person, or for any reason based on discrimination of any kind, when such pain or suffering is inflicted by or at the instigation of or with the consent or acquiescence of a public official or other person acting in an official capacity. It does not include pain or suffering arising only from, inherent in or incidental to lawful sanctions.

Where a torturer is present in the territory of a State, regardless of where the act of torture occurred or the nationality of any person involved, the State must either exercise its jurisdiction over the offence or extradite the offender to the State on whose territory the offence occurred, or whose nationality the offender or a victim possessed.[52] The Convention has more than 145 parties, including Australia.

Violence against protected persons

6.36   Certain acts committed against the persons, premises or means of transport of Heads of State, Heads of Government and Foreign Ministers while they are abroad, or members of their accompanying families, will give rise to an obligation on any State which has custody of the offender to either prosecute the offender or extradite the offender to the victim's State. The prohibited acts include murder, kidnapping or other attacks, and any attempt or threat to commit such acts. Identical protection extends to any representative or official of a State or public international organisation who is legally entitled to special protection from any attack on his or her person, freedom or dignity.[53]

Sovereign immunity

6.37   International law postulates that all States are equal in their sovereignty. Indeed, Art 2(1) of the UN Charter provides that the organisation 'is based on the principle of the sovereign equality of all its

---

51.   UNTS, Vol 1465, p 85.
52.   Article 5(2).
53.   1973 Convention on the Prevention and Punishment of Crimes against Internationally Protected Persons, UNTS, Vol 1035, p 167, which has more than 170 parties, including Australia.

Members'. General Assembly Resolution 2625 (XXV) also emphasises that all States enjoy sovereign equality, that they have equal rights and duties, and that all States are required to respect the personality of other States.

As a corollary of this, international law contains a general principle that no State may be made subject to the jurisdiction of any other State against its will. This principle is a specific manifestation of the more general legal principle *par in parem non habat imperium* — one cannot exercise authority over one's equal. Sovereign immunity (or State immunity) is that body of rules and principles under international law which determines the extent to which a State is entitled to claim exemption from another State's jurisdiction.

6.38   The classical postulate of sovereign immunity under the common law was that neither a State, nor any of its emanations, nor a State's property could ever be subjected to the jurisdiction of a foreign State's courts unless the State consented. Thus, sovereign immunity conferred on a State absolute freedom from the jurisdiction of any other State.

The classical position was forcefully articulated by John Marshall (1755–1835), Chief Justice of the United States Supreme Court, in *Schooner Exchange v McFaddon:*[54]

> This full and absolute territorial jurisdiction being alike the attribute of every sovereign, and being incapable of conferring extra-territorial power, would not seem to contemplate foreign sovereigns nor their sovereign rights as its objects. One sovereign being in no respect amenable to another, and being bound by obligations of the highest character not to degrade the dignity of his nation, by placing himself or its sovereign rights within the jurisdiction of another, can be supposed to enter a foreign territory only under an express license, or in the confidence that the immunities belonging to his independent sovereign station, though not expressly stipulated, are reserved by implication, and will be extended to him.

> This perfect equality and absolute independence of sovereigns, and this common interest compelling them to mutual intercourse, and an interchange of good offices with each other, have given rise to a class of cases in which every sovereign is understood to waive the exercise of a part of that complete exclusive territorial jurisdiction, which has been stated to be the attribute of every nation.

6.39   The broad scope of classical sovereign immunity is starkly illustrated by a series of English cases. In *De Haber v Queen of Portugal,* Lord Campbell observed that 'to cite a foreign potentate in a municipal court ... is contrary to the law of nations and an insult which he is entitled to resent'.[55]

The Court of Appeal in *Parlement Belge* considered its jurisdiction to hear proceedings against a mail vessel owned by the King of Belgium and said that every State:[56]

---

54.   *Schooner Exchange v Mc Faddon* (1812) 7 Cranch 116, 137.
55.   *De Haber v Queen of Portugal* (1851) 17 QB 196, 207.
56.   *Parlement Belge* (1880) PD 197, 215.

... declines to exercise by means of its courts any of its territorial jurisdiction over the person of any sovereign or ambassador of any other state, or over the public property of any state, which is destined to public use ... even though such sovereign, ambassador or property be within its jurisdiction.

In *Porto Alexandre*,[57] the Court of Appeal held that Portugal was entitled to claim sovereign immunity for a State-owned vessel, notwithstanding that it was engaged in purely commercial activity. In *Krajina v Tass Agency*,[58] sovereign immunity was recognised by the Court of Appeal as applying to a news agency which was an organ of the Soviet government. Similarly, in *Baccus SRL v Servicio Nacional del Trigo*,[59] the defendant was found to be an organ of the Spanish State, and therefore entitled to sovereign immunity, notwithstanding that it possessed a separate legal personality under Spanish law.

6.40   During the course of the 20th century, and in response to the increasing involvement by many States in activities of an essentially commercial character, States began moving away from the absolute theory of sovereign immunity. This movement began in States possessing a civil law system, before spreading to common law States in the latter half of the century. The effect of this change was to extend sovereign immunity to foreign States only to the extent that their activities or property in question were for a governmental or public purpose *(jure imperii)*, and not for some commercial or other essentially private purpose *(jure gestionis)*. This move towards qualified sovereign immunity in common law jurisdictions received a statutory fillip with the passage of legislation such as the United States *Foreign Sovereign Immunities Act of 1976*, the British *State Immunity Act 1978*, and the Australian *Foreign States Immunities Act 1985* (Cth). States controlled by communist dictatorships continued to adhere to an absolute conception of sovereign immunity.

6.41   The qualified variant of sovereign immunity found expression in the 1972 European Convention on State Immunity,[60] which influenced the drafting of domestic legislation in Europe and beyond — including the Australian statute. In the meantime, the United Nations General Assembly decided in 1977 to include the topic of sovereign immunity in the work program of the International Law Commission.

At the 43rd session of the International Law Commission in 1991, the Draft Articles on Jurisdictional Immunities of States and Their Property were presented to the General Assembly. The Draft Articles drew heavily on State practice and the 1972 European Convention. The United Nations Convention on Jurisdictional Immunities of States and Their Property[61] is closely based on the Draft Articles and was opened for signature on 17 January 2005. This Convention will not enter into force

---

57.   *Porto Alexandre* [1920] P 30.
58.   *Krajina v Tass Agency* [1949] 2 All ER 274.
59.   *Baccus SRL v Servicio Nacional del Trigo* [1957] 1 QB 438.
60.   UNTS, Vol 1495, p 182; CETS, No 74.
61.   General Assembly Resolution 59/38 (2004).

until there are 30 parties. Australia is not yet a party. It is likely that the restrictive variant of sovereign immunity is now part of customary international law.[62]

6.42   The Draft Articles and the Convention commence with a presumption of immunity for States and their property from the jurisdiction of other States' courts.[63] A State will be taken to have waived its immunity if it commences the proceedings, if it counter-claims, or if it consented to the jurisdiction by international agreement, written contract or a communication to the court.[64] A proceeding shall be considered as having been commenced against a foreign State if either the State is named as a party to the proceeding, or the proceeding 'in effect seeks to affect the property, rights, interests or activities' of the foreign State.[65]

6.43   The most significant provisions of the Draft Articles and the Convention deal with the circumstances in which sovereign immunity may not be claimed. It is here that the Draft Articles and the Convention seek to codify the exclusion of acts and property *jure gestionis* from the scope of sovereign immunity.

6.44   States are not entitled to immunity in respect of disputes arising from 'commercial transactions'.[66] These are defined as any commercial contract or transaction for the sale of goods or supply of services, any contract for a loan or other transaction of a financial nature, or any other contract or transaction of a commercial, industrial, trading or professional nature, but not including employment contracts.[67] Nor may States invoke sovereign immunity where the commercial transaction involved a State enterprise or other entity established by the State which has an independent legal personality.[68] The immunity does, however, extend to commercial transactions between States.[69]

6.45   States are not entitled to immunity from proceedings in respect of contracts of employment for work carried out in the forum State, unless the 'employee has been recruited to perform particular functions in the exercise of governmental authority', or if the employee is a diplomatic agent, consular officer or other person entitled to diplomatic immunity,

---

62. *FG Hemisphere Associates LLC v Democratic Republic of the Congo* [2010] 2 HKLRD 66, 101–102 (Hong Kong Court of Appeal).
63. Draft Art 5; United Nations Convention on Jurisdictional Immunities of States and Their Property, Art 5; semble *Foreign States Immunities Act 1985*, s 9.
64. Draft Arts 7–9; United Nations Convention on Jurisdictional Immunities of States and Their Property, Arts 7–9; semble *Foreign States Immunities Act 1985*, s 10.
65. Draft Art 6; United Nations Convention on Jurisdictional Immunities of States and Their Property, Art 6.
66. Draft Art 10(1); United Nations Convention on Jurisdictional Immunities of States and Their Property, Art 10(1).
67. Draft Art 1(c); United Nations Convention on Jurisdictional Immunities of States and Their Property, Art 1(c).
68. Draft Art 10(3) (Alternative A); United Nations Convention on Jurisdictional Immunities of States and Their Property, Art 10(3).
69. Draft Art 10(2); United Nations Convention on Jurisdictional Immunities of States and Their Property, Art 10(3); semble *Foreign States Immunities Act 1985*, s 11.

or if the subject matter of the proceedings is the recruitment, renewal of employment or reinstatement of an individual.[70]

6.46   Immunity is also withheld where the proceedings are for pecuniary compensation for death or injury to the person, or damage to tangible property, caused by an act attributable to the defendant State, and if the author of the act was present in the forum State's territory at the time of the act.[71]

6.47   A State may not invoke immunity where the proceedings relate to the State's interest, rights or obligations concerning immovable property located in the forum State.[72]

6.48   Immunity will not apply where the proceedings relate to an infringement by the State, in the territory of the forum State, of an industrial or intellectual property right.[73]

6.49   A State which owns or operates a ship will not be able to claim sovereign immunity in proceedings relating to the operation of that ship unless, at the time the cause of action arises, it was being used for 'government non-commercial purposes'.[74]

Diplomatic and consular immunity

6.50   States which have established diplomatic relations with each other may be represented by ambassadors (or High Commissioners between Commonwealth countries) accredited in the receiving State.

The ambassador or High Commissioner may be assisted by persons who are also accredited in the receiving State as diplomats. Ambassadors and other diplomats have long played a crucial role in international relations, and their special status in the international system has given rise to rules of international law protecting them from the reach of the sovereign power to which they are sent. Indeed, the inviolability of the persons of ambassadors is one of the oldest customary rules governing relations among sovereigns, stretching back into pre-classical antiquity. The rationale for the special status of diplomats is that diplomatic functions, and thus international relations, could be severely prejudiced if the persons exercising them could be subjected to coercion or pressure by the local sovereign.

---

70.   United Nations Convention on Jurisdictional Immunities of States and Their Property, Art 11; cf, *Foreign States Immunities Act 1985*, s 12, in which immunity is somewhat more restricted.
71.   Draft Art 12; United Nations Convention on Jurisdictional Immunities of States and Their Property, Art 12; semble s 13, *Foreign States Immunities Act 1985*.
72.   Draft Art 13; United Nations Convention on Jurisdictional Immunities of States and Their Property, Art 13; semble *Foreign States Immunities Act 1985*, s 14.
73.   Draft Art 14; United Nations Convention on Jurisdictional Immunities of States and Their Property, Art 14; semble *Foreign States Immunities Act 1985*, s 15.
74.   Draft Art 16; United Nations Convention on Jurisdictional Immunities of States and Their Property, Art 16; semble *Foreign States Immunities Act 1985*, s 18.

6.51   The special status which international law extends to diplomats is largely contained within the corpus of rules known as 'diplomatic immunity'. The general effect of these customary rules is to render diplomats immune from the criminal, civil and administrative jurisdiction of the State to which they are accredited. The modern law of diplomatic immunity was simultaneously codified and developed in the 1961 Vienna Convention on Diplomatic Relations.[75] Australian domestic legislation on the subject is expressed in the *Diplomatic Privileges and Immunities Act 1967* (Cth).

6.52   The key provision of the 1961 Vienna Convention concerning the immunity of diplomats from legal proceedings is as follows:

Article 31

1. A diplomatic agent shall enjoy immunity from the criminal jurisdiction of the receiving State. He shall also enjoy immunity from its civil and administrative jurisdiction, except in the case of:

    (a) a real action relating to private immovable property situated in the territory of the receiving State, unless he holds it on behalf of the sending State for the purposes of the mission;

    (b) an action relating to succession in which the diplomatic agent is involved as executor, administrator, heir or legatee as a private person and not on behalf of the sending State;

    (c) an action relating to any professional or commercial activity exercised by the diplomatic agent in the receiving State outside his official functions.

2. A diplomatic agent is not obliged to give evidence as a witness.

3. No measures of execution may be taken in respect of a diplomatic agent except in the cases coming under sub-paragraphs (a), (b) and (c) of paragraph 1 of this Article, and provided that the measures concerned can be taken without infringing the inviolability of his person or of his residence.

4. The immunity of a diplomatic agent from the jurisdiction of the receiving State does not exempt him from the jurisdiction of the sending State.

6.53   The premises of a diplomatic mission are inviolable; agents of the receiving State may not enter them without the permission of the ambassador or the person acting as head of the mission. The receiving State is, furthermore, under an obligation to prevent intrusion or damage and to prevent any disturbance of the peace of the mission or any act impairing its dignity. Neither the mission's premises nor its means of transport may be searched, and the mission is immune from any attachment or act of execution.[76] The mission's archives and documents,[77] official correspondence,[78] and diplomatic bags[79] are also inviolable.

---

75.   UNTS, Vol 500, p 95.
76.   Vienna Convention on Diplomatic Relations, Art 22.
77.   Ibid, Art 24.
78.   Ibid, Art 27(2).
79.   Ibid, Art 27(3).

The premises of a diplomatic mission are not, however, part of the sending State's sovereign territory. It remains part of the receiving State's territory for the purposes of prescriptive and enforcement jurisdiction, albeit subject to a special regime of immunities. Thus, in *R v Turnbull; Ex parte Petroff*,[80] the Supreme Court of the Australian Capital Territory rejected an argument that it lacked jurisdiction over an incident involving explosive substances being thrown at the Soviet Union's embassy in Canberra on the ground that the offence took place on Soviet territory. Australian law applied to the premises of the embassy subject only to the privileges and immunities enjoyed by the diplomatic mission.

6.54 The person of a diplomat is also inviolable. An accredited diplomat may not be arrested or detained, and the receiving State is required to take all appropriate steps to prevent any attacks on his or her person, freedom or dignity.[81]

6.55 Diplomatic immunity is a procedural bar, not a defence. Accordingly, when a person ceases to be a diplomat, the person loses the protection which the immunity extended to him or her. Further, diplomatic immunity belongs to States and not diplomats individually. Accordingly, the sending State may waive the immunity of any of its diplomats.[82]

The receiving State may also, at any time and without explanation, declare a diplomat to be *persona non grata*. When this occurs, the sending State must recall the person or terminate the person's functions with the diplomatic mission.[83]

6.56 A diplomat represents his or her home State on political matters, whereas a consul is not a State representative. Rather, a consul's function is to protect the interests of his or her State's nationals in the receiving State (for example, passport and visa matters, the promotion of trade, tourism and cultural contacts, representations to local law enforcement agencies, and so on). Sometimes embassies also perform the functions of consulates — usually for reasons of economy — but this does not deprive an accredited diplomat of diplomatic status.

Consuls do not enjoy the same sweeping protections as diplomats. Their immunities are codified in the 1963 Vienna Convention on Consular Relations,[84] which finds Australian domestic expression in the *Consular Privileges and Immunities Act 1972* (Cth). A consul does not enjoy immunity from the jurisdiction of local courts and agencies, except in matters arising from the performance of his or her official functions.[85]

Consuls may not, however, be arrested or detained, except in the case of a grave crime and pursuant to a decision by a competent judicial authority.[86]

---

80. *R v Turnbull; Ex parte Petroff* (1971) 17 FLR 438.
81. Vienna Convention on Diplomatic Relations, Art 29.
82. Ibid, Art 32(1).
83. Ibid, Art 9.
84. UNTS, Vol 596, p 261.
85. Vienna Convention on Diplomatic Relations, Art 43.
86. Ibid, Art 41.

Heads of State, Heads of Government and Foreign Ministers

6.57   As mentioned above, diplomats enjoy sweeping immunity from the jurisdiction of the States to which they are accredited so that they may properly perform their functions on the plane of international relations without exposure to personal coercion or pressure from those States. Diplomatic immunity is an extension to certain accredited State representatives of the immunity enjoyed by States themselves. State immunity is often referred to as 'sovereign immunity', which is a reminder that it evolved from the immunity enjoyed personally by a Monarch before another Monarch's courts or law enforcement apparatus.

6.58   Heads of State continue to enjoy sovereign immunity in this older sense of the term. Monarchs, Presidents and other Heads of State are not, without their consent, subject to the jurisdiction of foreign States' courts or law enforcement apparatus. This immunity exists *ratione personae* while the individual is serving as Head of State, so that he or she is completely immune while in office. After leaving office, the immunity continues to exist *ratione materiae,* so that the former Head of State remains entitled to the shield of sovereign immunity in respect of his or her official conduct during the term of office.

The former Head of State may become exposed, however, to the jurisdiction of a foreign State's courts and law enforcement apparatus in respect of some forms of conduct performed while in office. It is often said that sovereign immunity *ratione materiae* does not extend to conduct of a 'private' character. This potentially raises difficult questions about whether particular conduct was official or private in character. In particular, will a violation of domestic law by the Head of State rob that conduct of its official character, thereby depriving him or her of the protection of sovereign immunity?

6.59   According to the international law of State responsibility, the mere fact that a State official violated domestic law does not automatically render the conduct 'private' in character. What matters is that the official either held himself or herself out as performing official functions, or employed powers, methods or means placed at the official's disposal by virtue of his or her official functions.[87]

In either case, the official's conduct will be official and attributable to his or her State, notwithstanding that it was *ultra vires* according to domestic law. It is not, therefore, to be expected that a breach of domestic law by a State's highest official will necessarily deprive the official's apparently official acts of their public character. A contrary approach would, furthermore, usually require national courts to enquire into the regularity of executive acts according to the laws of a foreign State.

---

87.   See **5.26–5.28**.

This would require a breach of the Act of State doctrine according to which a national court may not impugn the domestic validity within a foreign State of its legislative, executive and judicial acts.

6.60 Nevertheless, some forms of unlawful conduct in office will deprive a former Head of State of the protection of sovereign immunity *ratione materiae*. This situation will arise where a former Head of State engaged in conduct which, although non-private in character, violated international law in such a way as to attract universal jurisdiction.[88]

In the **Pinochet case**,[89] Senator Augusto Pinochet of Chile was arrested while visiting the United Kingdom for medical treatment in 1998. Senator Pinochet had been Chile's Head of State from 1973, or sometime soon thereafter, until 1990. His arrest was made pursuant to an English warrant after a Spanish court had issued an international arrest warrant on a number of charges, including torture allegedly inflicted upon Spanish nationals during his tenure as Head of State, as well as murder and conspiracy to murder. The English warrant was a prelude to the possible extradition to Spain of Senator Pinochet. Torture is a crime against international law and the subject of universal jurisdiction in accordance with the 1984 Convention against Torture and Other Cruel, Inhuman or Degrading Treatment or Punishment,[90] which entered into force on 8 December 1988. Murder has not been made an international crime. Senator Pinochet sought to have the lawfulness of his arrest in England set aside. On appeal to the House of Lords, the Court considered inter alia whether he was now entitled to sovereign immunity in respect of any acts of torture for which he might be responsible between 29 September 1988 (when the 1984 Convention was transposed into English law) and the time he left office as Chile's Head of State. The Court held by a majority of four to one that Senator Pinochet was not entitled to the protection of sovereign immunity in respect of any such acts after ceasing to be Head of State. Lord Browne-Wilkinson referred to State immunity and said:[91]

> This is the point around which most of the argument turned. It is of considerable general importance internationally since, if Senator Pinochet is not entitled to immunity in relation to the acts of torture alleged to have occurred after 29 September 1988, it will be the first time ... when a local domestic court has refused to afford immunity to a head of state or former head of state on the grounds that there can be no immunity against prosecution for certain international crimes.

> ... The issue is whether international law grants state immunity in relation to the international crime of torture and, if so, whether the Republic of Chile is entitled to claim such immunity even though Chile, Spain and the United Kingdom are all parties to the Torture Convention ...

> State immunity probably grew from the historical immunity of the person of the monarch. In any event, such personal immunity of the head of state persists to the present day: the head of state is entitled to the same immunity as the state

---

88. See **6.23–6.36**.
89. *R v Bow Street Metropolitan Stipendiary Magistrate; Ex parte Pinochet Ugarte (No 3)* [2000] 1 AC 147.
90. See **6.35**.
91. *R v Bow Street Metropolitan Stipendiary Magistrate; Ex parte Pinochet Ugarte (No 3)* [2000] 1 AC 147, 201–205.

itself. ... This immunity enjoyed by a head of state in power and an ambassador in post is a complete immunity attaching to the person of the head of state or ambassador and rendering him immune from all actions or prosecutions whether or not they relate to matters done for the benefit of his state. Such immunity is said to be granted ratione personae.

What then when the ambassador leaves his post or the head of state is deposed? ...

The continuing partial immunity of the ambassador after leaving post is of a different kind from that enjoyed ratione personae while he was in post. Since he is no longer the representative of the foreign state he merits no particular privileges or immunities as a person. However in order to preserve the integrity of the activities of the foreign state during the period when he was ambassador, it is necessary to provide that immunity is afforded to his *official* acts during his tenure in post. ... This limited immunity, ratione materiae, is to be contrasted with the former immunity ratione personae which gave complete immunity to all activities whether public or private.

In my judgment at common law a former head of state enjoys similar immunities, ratione materiae, once he ceases to be head of state. He too loses immunity ratione personae on ceasing to be head of state: see Watts *The Legal Position in International Law of Heads of States, Heads of Government and Foreign Ministers* p. 88 and the cases there cited. ...

... Senator Pinochet as former head of state enjoys immunity ratione materiae in relation to acts done by him as head of state as part of his official duties as head of state.

The question then which has to be answered is whether the alleged organisation of state torture by Senator Pinochet (if proved) would constitute an act committed by Senator Pinochet as part of his official functions as head of state. It is not enough to say that it cannot be part of the functions of the head of state to commit a crime. Actions which are criminal under the local law can still have been done officially and therefore give rise to immunity ratione materiae. ...

Can it be said that the commission of a crime which is an international crime against humanity[92] and jus cogens[93] is an act done in an official capacity on behalf of the state? I believe there to be strong ground for saying that the implementation of torture as defined by the Torture Convention cannot be a state function. ...

I have doubts whether, before the coming into force of the Torture Convention, the existence of the international crime of torture as jus cogens was enough to justify the conclusion that the organisation of state torture could not rank for immunity purposes as performance of an official function. At that stage there was no international tribunal to punish torture and no general jurisdiction to permit or require its punishment in domestic courts. ... But in my judgment the Torture Convention did provide what was missing: a worldwide universal jurisdiction. Further, it required all member states to ban and outlaw torture: Article 2. How can it be for international law purposes an official function to do something which international law itself prohibits and criminalises? ...

... [I]f, as alleged, Senator Pinochet organised and authorised torture after 8 December 1988, he was not acting in any capacity which gives rise to immunity ratione materiae because such actions were contrary to international law, Chile had agreed to outlaw such conduct and Chile had agreed with the other parties

---

92. See **6.25–6.26** and **chapter 10**.
93. See **2.106–2.110**.

> to the Torture Convention that all signatory states should have jurisdiction to try official torture (as defined in the Convention) even if such torture were committed in Chile.
>
> As to the charges of murder and conspiracy to murder, no one has advanced any reason why the ordinary rules of immunity should not apply and Senator Pinochet is entitled to such immunity.

On the basis of the House of Lords decision in the *Pinochet* case, it would appear that almost all apparently official conduct performed by a former Head of State while he or she was in office is protected by sovereign immunity. The sole exception would appear to be conduct which, at the time it occurred, constituted an international crime for which a form of universal jurisdiction was established.

6.61   The sovereign immunity enjoyed by a serving Head of State extends also to Heads of Government and Ministers of Foreign Affairs. A serving Minister of Foreign Affairs enjoys sovereign immunity *ratione personae* and in respect of any conduct, even if it was performed before assuming the office and even if it constituted an international crime for which universal jurisdiction was established at the time of its performance. It is not even material that the impugned conduct violated the *jus cogens*.[94]

In the **Arrest Warrant case,**[95] the International Court of Justice held that the Congolese Foreign Minister was entitled to the protection of Congo's sovereign immunity in respect of an arrest warrant issued against him by a Belgian court seeking to try him for alleged war crimes and crimes against humanity.[96] The ICJ remarked, however, that immunity does not equate to impunity. In this connection, the Court said:

> 61. ... [T]he immunities enjoyed under international law by an incumbent or former Minister of Foreign Affairs do not represent a bar to criminal prosecution in certain circumstances. First, such persons enjoy no criminal immunity under international law in their own countries, and may thus be tried by those countries' courts in accordance with the relevant rules of domestic law. Secondly, they will cease to enjoy immunity from foreign jurisdiction if the state which they represent or have represented decides to waive that immunity. Thirdly, after a person ceases to hold the office of Minister for Foreign Affairs, he or she will no longer enjoy all of the immunities accorded by international law in other States. Provided that it has jurisdiction under international law, a court of one State may try a former Minister for Foreign Affairs of another State in respect of acts committed prior or subsequent to his or her period of office, as well as in respect of acts committed during that period of office in a private capacity.
>
> Fourthly, an incumbent or former Minister for Foreign Affairs may be subject to criminal proceedings before certain international criminal courts, where they

---

94. Semble the judgment of the European Court of Human Rights in *Al-Adsani v United Kingdom* (2001) 34 EHRR 273.

95. *Case Concerning the Arrest Warrant of 11 April 2000 (Congo v Belgium)* ICJ Rep (2002) 3.

96. See **6.25–6.26** and **chapter 10**.

> have jurisdiction. Examples include the ... International Criminal Court created by the 1998 Rome Convention. The latter's Statute expressly provides, in Article 27, paragraph 2, that '[i]mmunities or special procedural rules which may attach to the official capacity of a person, whether under national or international law, shall not bar the Court from exercising its jurisdiction over such a person'.
>
> The Court also observed that sovereign immunity attaches to Heads of State, Heads of Government and Ministers of Foreign Affairs on the basis of an identical rationale, in order that they might effectively perform their functions as representatives of their respective States recognised under international law.[97] It is worth noting in this connection that only Heads of State, Heads of Government and Ministers of Foreign Affairs are automatically regarded as representing their States for the purpose of performing all acts leading to the conclusion of treaties.[98]

Question

Since January 2007, Oscar has been the ambassador from the Democratic Popular Republic of Remora accredited to Australia. Prior to this appointment, he was a colonel in the Remoran government's secret police force, the Committee for Public Security (CPS), with special responsibility for extracting confessions of 'counter-revolutionary agitation' from opponents of Remora's one-party dictatorship. Oscar regularly extracted confessions by subjecting the prisoners to severe beatings and electric shocks to sensitive parts of the body. In 2004, Oscar also had responsibility for organising 'Operation Clean Hills', the Remoran government's policy of forced sterilisations of an ethnic hill tribe in Remora. The tribe has produced no children since that time. All of the people affected by Oscar's conduct were nationals of Remora, and the acts all occurred in the territory of Remora.

Carla (widely known as 'Carla the Hyena') is a notorious professional assassin and terrorist who also leads a terrorist organisation known as the Remoran Hyenas. She is a national of France.

Last November, Carla boarded a crowded New Zealand-registered passenger aircraft on a scheduled flight from Auckland to Fiji. Apart from Carla, everyone on board the plane was a national of New Zealand or Australia. The aircraft belongs to a commercial airline company which is owned by the New Zealand government. While the aircraft was over international waters, Carla stood up and announced that she had planted a bomb on the aircraft and that she could detonate the bomb by remote control. She also produced a hand gun. Carla entered the aircraft's cockpit and ordered the pilot to divert the flight to Tuvalu.

---

97. *Case Concerning the Arrest Warrant of 11 April 2000 (Congo v Belgium)* ICJ Rep (2002) 3, para 53.
98. Vienna Convention on the Law of Treaties, Art 7(2)(a). See **2.22**.

When the Australian co-pilot tried to grab Carla's gun, she shot him, causing serious injury. The pilot flew the plane to Tuvalu, where it landed. Tuvalu police surrounded the aircraft at the airport. Carla announced on the plane's radio that she was holding the crew and passengers at gunpoint and would shoot one person every hour unless the Australian government agreed to release a number of Remoran Hyena terrorists imprisoned in Australia. She said that the Australians on board would be shot first. She also said that she would detonate the bomb if the Tuvalu police made any attempt to approach the plane. After one hour, Carla shot and killed Brenda, an Australian passenger.

Ten minutes later, a unit of New Zealand military commandos stormed the aircraft, capturing Carla. She was handed over to the Tuvalu police and detained. The commandos found a bomb in Carla's hand luggage.

The wounded co-pilot was placed on an emergency flight to Hawaii in order to receive medical treatment. He died in the ambulance between the airport and the hospital in Hawaii.

After two days, the Tuvalu Minister of Justice announced that, due to his country's limited resources, Tuvalu might not be able to properly prosecute Carla and that the government was considering its options. The Tuvalu government immediately received separate requests from the embassies of Australia, New Zealand, France and the United States for Carla's extradition to their countries in order to face criminal charges arising out of the recent hijacking.

Oscar appeared on Australian television declaring Carla a 'hero of the oppressed in every country' and speculating that Brenda must have provoked her.

Brenda's son wants to know if Australia is entitled to obtain Carla's extradition, and what steps can be taken against Oscar consistently with international law. He also wants to know if there are any obstacles in international law to suing the New Zealand airline in an Australian court for his mother's death, since the airline had allowed an armed and notorious terrorist to board the flight. Advise him. You may assume that Tuvalu is not party to any treaties which might be relevant.

Suggested answer

There are three issues to be considered:

(1) Oscar's conduct as a public official in Remora;
(2) Carla's extradition from Tuvalu; and
(3) the possibility of suing the New Zealand airline in an Australian court.

Oscar's conduct

Oscar's conduct as a colonel in Remora's CPS constituted a violation of international criminal law in at least two respects. In extracting confessions from prisoners, Oscar regularly administered severe beatings and electric shocks to sensitive parts of the body. This conduct constitutes torture within the meaning of Art 1 of the Convention against Torture and Other Cruel, Inhuman or Degrading Treatment or Punishment: severe pain or suffering intentionally for the purposes of obtaining a confession and inflicted by a public official. Australia is a party to the Torture Convention, but it is not clear whether Remora is also a party.

Even if Remora is not a party to the Torture Convention, the fact that it has more than 140 States parties strongly indicates that its norm-creating provisions are part of customary international law. Consequently, when a torturer is present in the territory of Australia, regardless of where the act of torture occurred or the nationality of any person involved, Australia must either prosecute the offence or extradite the torturer to the State on whose territory the offence occurred, or whose nationality the offender or a victim possessed (Art 5(2)). In this case, the only place to which Oscar might be extradited is Remora, but it is highly unlikely that he would be subjected to a serious trial there, even if Remora requested extradition.

Consequently, Australia is prima facie under an obligation to prosecute Oscar for his acts of torture while serving as an interrogating officer in the CPS.

Oscar was also in charge of Operation Clean Hills. In carrying out a policy of forced sterilisations against an ethnic group, Oscar's conduct constituted genocide within the meaning of Art II of the Convention on the Prevention and Punishment of the Crime of Genocide: the imposition of measures intended to prevent births within a national, ethnic or racial group with an intent to destroy that group in whole or in part. Conspiracies to commit genocide, direct and public incitement to genocide, attempts to commit genocide, and complicity in genocide are also punishable (Art III). Public officials are liable to prosecution for any of these crimes (Art IV). Article 6 of the Rome Statute of the International Criminal Court is to materially identical effect. The international crime of genocide attracts jurisdiction under the universality principle so that, regardless of the place the crime was committed or the nationality of any person involved, any State with custody of the offender may prosecute him or her (*Eichmann* case).

If Australian authorities were to take Oscar into custody, Australia would prima facie be entitled to prosecute him for his conduct in executing Operation Clean Hills.

Oscar is, however, currently accredited to the Australian government as Remora's ambassador. While this situation continues, international law confers diplomatic immunity on him from Australia's criminal jurisdiction (Art 31(1) of the Vienna Convention on Diplomatic Relations, given domestic effect by the *Diplomatic Privileges and Immunities Act 1967* (Cth)). Nor may he be arrested or detained (Art 29). The protection afforded to Oscar by diplomatic immunity may be waived by Remora (Art 32(1)), though such a course of action could hardly be expected in this case. Clearly, Oscar is a person whom the Australian government should regard as unsuitable to discharge the functions of a diplomat. Under Art 9 of the Vienna Convention on Diplomatic Relations, Australia may declare Oscar to be *persona non grata*. No reasons need be given for this declaration, and Remora would then be required either to recall Oscar to Remora or simply to terminate his functions with Remora's embassy. A recall would be likely, in which case Oscar would lose his diplomatic accreditation and Australia could prosecute him for torture and genocide if he subsequently came into Australia's custody.

Carla's extradition from Tuvalu

Australia does not presently have custody of Carla and there are four other States which have expressed an interest in possibly prosecuting her: France, the United States, Tuvalu and New Zealand. The claims of each State to exercise jurisdiction over Carla are examined below.

France

International law accepts that States are free to exercise their criminal jurisdiction over their own nationals, even where the violation of the State's laws occurs outside its territory (for example, Judge Moore's dissenting opinion in the *Lotus* case). In such cases, jurisdiction is said to rest on the active nationality principle (or the active personality principle). Carla is a national of France and, as a matter of international law, France is entitled to prosecute her for any violations of French criminal law committed in connection with the events on the aircraft.

United States

Although Carla shot the co-pilot outside United States territory, his resulting death occurred on United States territory. The courts of many States, even of States which have given their criminal legislation a strictly territorial character, interpret criminal law in the sense that offences, the authors of which at the moment of commission are in the territory of another State, are nevertheless to be regarded as having been committed in the national territory, if one of the constituent elements of the offence, and more especially its effects, have taken place there (*Lotus* case).

Assuming the American authorities intend charging Carla with an offence involving the co-pilot's unlawful killing (for example, murder), the United States could exercise jurisdiction in accordance with the objective territorial principle.

New Zealand and Tuvalu

Given that the co-pilot was shot in airspace above international waters, but on a New Zealand-registered aircraft, New Zealand could also exercise jurisdiction over the offence.

Carla shot and killed Brenda in the territory of Tuvalu, giving Tuvalu jurisdiction over that offence on the basis of the subjective territorial principle. Brenda's killing occurred aboard a New Zealand-registered aircraft, thereby also conferring jurisdiction on New Zealand.

Carla hijacked the aircraft. That conduct amounts to an offence within the meaning of Art 1 of the Hague Convention for the Suppression of Unlawful Seizure of Aircraft: while on board the aircraft in flight, she used force to seize or take control of the aircraft unlawfully.

Tuvalu is required to establish its jurisdiction over Carla's act of hijacking by virtue of Carla's presence in Tuvalu and because the hijacked aircraft landed on its territory with Carla still on board (Art 4). If Tuvalu chooses not to prosecute Carla, then its obligation in relation to the hijacking offence is to extradite her to the State in which the hijacked aircraft is registered — that is, New Zealand.

Carla also committed an act of aircraft sabotage. She did this by shooting the co-pilot, thereby performing 'an act of violence against a person on board an aircraft in flight ... likely to endanger the safety of that aircraft', and by bringing a bomb on board, thereby 'placing on an aircraft in service ... a device or substance which is likely to destroy that aircraft' (Montreal Convention for the Suppression of Unlawful Acts against the Safety of Civil Aviation, Art 1).

The Montreal Convention requires States to establish their jurisdiction over the offence in substantially the same circumstances as apply under the Hague Convention (Montreal Convention, Arts 5(1)(c) and 5(2)). Accordingly, Tuvalu must either prosecute Carla for the act of sabotage or extradite her to New Zealand, being the State of the aircraft's registration.

Once the aircraft landed in Tuvalu, Carla committed the crime of hostage-taking within the meaning of Art 1 of the International Convention against the Taking of Hostages: she seized and threatened to kill people in order to compel Australia to release the Remoran Hyena terrorists from prison.

Tuvalu may exercise jurisdiction over the act of hostage-taking by virtue of the subjective territorial principle, or simply by virtue of the fact that Carla is now in its custody. According to Art 6 of the International Convention against the Taking of Hostages, Tuvalu must either prosecute Carla for the hostage-taking or extradite her to Australia (the State against which her demands were directed), France (the State of her nationality), or any State whose nationality any of the hostages possessed (that is, Australia and New Zealand).

For the purposes of this exercise, Tuvalu is not a party to the Hague Convention, the Montreal Convention or the Torture Convention. However, the fact that the Hague and Montreal Conventions each has well over 170 parties and the Torture Convention has over 140 parties strongly indicates that their norm-creating provisions are part of customary international law.

Australia

There were Australian nationals aboard the hijacked flight — including the co-pilot and Brenda, who were both killed. Although some States regularly assert criminal jurisdiction over offences committed against their nationals abroad in accordance with the passive nationality principle, this basis of jurisdiction has traditionally been the most controversial and uncertain (for example, Judge Moore's dissenting opinion in the *Lotus* case). Nevertheless, in more recent times the passive nationality principle has been increasingly used to justify assertions of jurisdiction where the prosecuting State's nationals have been victims of terrorist acts (for example, *United States v Yunis*). Carla killed Brenda because she was an Australian national, and it appears that she intended to kill all the other Australians aboard the flight unless her demands were met. This probably justifies an assertion by Australia of criminal jurisdiction over Carla in connection with the two killings, the aircraft sabotage, the hijacking and the hostage-taking.

Australia would, as we have already seen, also have jurisdiction to prosecute Carla for the hostage-taking by reason of Tuvalu's obligations under customary rules reflected in the Montreal Convention.

Conclusion

There is no formal hierarchy among the various bases for exercising jurisdictional sovereignty. This means that if a State has actual custody of Carla and if it can invoke any one of the recognised bases for exercising jurisdiction, it is free to arrest, detain, prosecute and punish her, notwithstanding the existence of competing claims by other States.

Tuvalu must either prosecute Carla or extradite her to one of the States mentioned in the Hague, Montreal and Torture Conventions. New Zealand is the only State to which Tuvalu could extradite Carla consistently with the requirements of all three conventions. New Zealand also has its own bases for exercising jurisdiction in respect of all Carla's offences. If Tuvalu chooses not to prosecute Carla, it should extradite her to New Zealand in order to face charges there.

Suing the New Zealand airline in Australia

The New Zealand aircraft was owned by a commercial airline company which was, in turned, owned by the New Zealand government. This presents an issue as to whether New Zealand could raise a claim of sovereign immunity in respect of any suit brought against the airline in an Australian court.

Sovereign immunity prevents a State being subjected against its will to another State's jurisdiction. A State, including one of its courts, commits a violation of international law when it persists in exercising jurisdiction against another State in the face of a valid claim of sovereign immunity.

In States sharing a common law tradition, the view for much of the 20th century was that sovereign immunity was absolute. Any foreign State, organ of a State, State-owned property, or State-owned entity was completely immune from another State's jurisdiction, even if the entity had a separate legal personality *(Baccus SRL v Servicio Nacional del Trigo)* and even if its activities were purely commercial in character *(Porto Alexandre)*.

By the 1970s, however, most common law States had modified their approach and embraced a doctrine of qualified sovereign immunity closely resembling the model favoured by most civil law States. Qualified sovereign immunity protects foreign States from exercises of jurisdiction only where the activities or property in question were for a governmental or public purpose *(jure imperii)*, and not for some commercial or other essentially private purpose *(jure gestionis)*. By the early 1980s, it was possible to discern a broad international consensus in favour of qualified sovereign immunity.

To the extent that the proposed suit against the airline rests upon 'differences related to a commercial transaction', including a contract for the supply of services, New Zealand would probably not be able to invoke sovereign immunity as a matter of international law. Thus, a claim that the airline was in breach of its contract for services with Brenda — by allowing Carla aboard the flight while armed with a gun and a bomb, and by failing to protect her from Carla on board the aircraft — would not be covered by sovereign immunity (Draft Articles on Jurisdictional Immunities of States and Their Property and United Nations Convention on Jurisdictional Immunities of States and Their Property, Arts 10(1) and 1(c); semble *Foreign States Immunity Act 1985* (Cth), s 11).

To the extent, however, that the proposed suit is based on the law of torts, it would be more likely to attract a successful claim of sovereign immunity in international law. Common Art 12 of the Draft Articles and the Convention effectively preserves a State's right to claim sovereign immunity in a 'proceeding which relates to pecuniary compensation for death or injury to the person' unless the act or omission occurred in whole or in part in the territory of the forum State and if the author of the act or omission was present in that territory at the time of the act or omission (semble *Foreign States Immunity Act 1985*, s 13). All the relevant acts or omissions in this case appear to have occurred outside Australian territory by people who were likewise outside that territory.

Whether there is a cause of action and a competent Australian court for the proposed suit against the airline is a matter of Australian domestic law.

Further tutorial discussion

1. International law does not permit a State's court to assert jurisdiction over any matter unless there is an internationally recognised basis for the exercise of jurisdictional sovereignty. Do you agree?
2. Why should the passive nationality principle constitute a valid basis of jurisdiction only in cases of terrorist offences?
3. Look at the tutorial question and answer. Would the answer concerning Oscar's conduct be different if he were a consul and not an ambassador?
4. Who gets to make the final decision on whether conduct constitutes a threat to the State when the protective principle is employed to justify an exercise of jurisdiction? The State itself?

5. If a person guilty of genocide, war crimes, or crimes against humanity is present in a State's territory, is the State obliged to prosecute the person?

6. If a State is always entitled to exercise criminal jurisdiction over a person on the basis that he or she is a national of that State, why is a State not always entitled to exercise criminal jurisdiction over a person on the basis that he or she has entered the State's territory?

State territory

7

Objectives

After completing this chapter, you should:

(1) appreciate the importance of territory for States and statehood in international law;
(2) be aware of the scope of State territory;
(3) understand that disputes over title to territory are decided by establishing which State has the stronger claim;
(4) understand and be able to explain and apply the five principles by which all States may justify a claim to title over territory (cession, occupation, prescription, accretion and conquest); and
(5) understand and be able to explain and apply *uti possedetis juris* as a basis for determining the international borders of States established by decolonisation or by the secession from or dissolution of States.

Key cases

Western Sahara advisory opinion, ICJ Rep (1975) 12
Arbitral Award on the Subject of the Difference Relative to the Sovereignty over Clipperton Island (France v Mexico) (1932) 26 *American Journal of International Law* 390
Island of Palmas Case (Netherlands v United States) (1928) 2 RIAA 829
Case Concerning the Frontier Dispute (Burkina Faso v Mali) ICJ Rep (1986) 554

Nature and scope of State territory

7.1   State territory is that portion of the Earth which is subject to the sovereign authority of a State. Indeed, unless an entity has a government with the ability to prescribe and enforce its will in its own defined territory, it cannot be described as a State.[1]

Importance of territory

7.2   State territory is important in international law because it is the place in which a State's prescriptive and enforcement jurisdiction may be

---

1.   See 4.6–4.11.

exercised to the exclusion of all other States. According to Max Huber (1874–1960) in the *Island of Palmas Case:*[2]

> Sovereignty in the relations between States signifies independence. Independence in regard to a portion of the globe is the right to exercise therein, to the exclusion of any other State, the functions of a State. The development of the national organisation of States during the last few centuries and, as a corollary, the development of international law, have established this principle of the exclusive competence of the State in regard to its own territory in such a way as to make it the point of departure in settling most questions that concern international relations.

In the *Lotus* case, the Permanent Court of International Justice similarly remarked:[3]

> Now the first and foremost restriction imposed by international law upon a State is that — failing the existence of a permissive rule to the contrary — it may not exercise its power in any form in the territory of another State. In this sense, jurisdiction is certainly territorial; it cannot be exercised by a State outside its territory except by virtue of a permissive rule derived from international custom or from a convention.

7.3   This normally exclusive legal authority exercised by a State over its territory is, indeed, a cornerstone principle of the international legal system. Article 2(4) of the United Nations Charter provides, for example, that all members of the United Nations must 'refrain in their international relations from the threat or use of force against the territorial integrity or political independence of any state, or in any other manner inconsistent with the Purposes of the United Nations'.

7.4   A State may exercise its sovereign authority as it pleases in any part of its territory, subject only to the requirements of international law. In the *Corfu Channel Case*, the International Court of Justice observed that it is 'every State's obligation not to allow knowingly its territory to be used for acts contrary to the rights of other States'.[4] Other States may also acquire limited rights over a State's territory by treaty or local custom — for example, Portugal's restricted right of passage in parts of India's territory in the *Right of Passage* case.[5]

Scope of territory

7.5   A State's territory includes all lands and internal waters within its international boundaries, its territorial sea adjacent to its coast, the airspace above the State's land and territorial sea, the seabed and subsoil beneath the territorial sea, and all the resources thereof.[6] A State's territorial sea cannot be more than 12 nautical miles wide,[7] although

---

2.   *Island of Palmas Case (Netherlands v United States)* (1928) 2 RIAA 829, 838. See **7.19**.
3.   *Case of the SS Lotus (France v Turkey)* PCIJ Rep (1927) Series A No 10, 18.
4.   *Corfu Channel Case (Merits) (United Kingdom v Albania)* ICJ Rep (1949) 4, 22. See **12.51**.
5.   *Case Concerning Right of Passage over Indian Territory (Portugal v India)* Merits, ICJ Rep (1960) 6. See **1.148**.
6.   Chicago Convention on International Civil Aviation, Art 1, UNTS, Vol 15, p 295; Convention on the Law of the Sea, Art 2, UNTS, Vol 1833, p 3.
7.   Convention on the Law of the Sea, Art 3.

some States make more ambitious claims. The upper limit of a State's airspace is not certain, but it is clear that a State's territory does not extend as far as outer space, no part of which may be appropriated by any State.[8] A State's land territory extends downwards, in theory, to the Earth's core; a State's territorial jurisdiction therefore encompasses persons, things and events in mines and other underground locations.

Internal waters are treated in the same way as a State's land territory. They consist of all rivers, lakes, canals or other bodies of water which are surrounded by a State's land territory, and include all bodies of water to the landward side of any baselines used for measuring the territorial sea.[9] The territorial sea, however, is subject to a regime whereby ships of foreign States enjoy certain rights of transit (known as 'innocent passage').[10] Special rules apply to archipelagic States,[11] such as Indonesia, the Philippines and several micro-States in the Pacific Ocean.

Title to land territory is critical because title to other forms of territory depends on rules which make reference, directly or indirectly, to land territory. For example, a State will not possess a territorial sea, and will therefore have no title to airspace above it and land and resources below it, if the State does not possess title to any coastal land.

Disputes over territory

7.6 With the possible exception of Antarctica, virtually all the world's land territory is now under the sovereign authority of one of the almost 200 States currently in existence. Consequently, rules governing the establishment of first title to territories previously unpossessed by any State are now of practical value only where two or more States lay claim to the same piece of territory and the relative strengths of the competing claims need to be assessed. As the Permanent Court of International Justice remarked in the *Legal Status of Eastern Greenland* case, '[i]n most of the cases involving claims to territorial sovereignty which have come before an international tribunal, there have been two competing claims to sovereignty, and the tribunal has had to decide which of the two is stronger'.[12]

Antarctica

7.7 Antarctica is something of a special case and, as it occupies about 14 million square kilometres of land (Australia occupies 7.7 million square kilometres), its status is worth mentioning. The continent is the subject of partly overlapping claims by Argentina, Australia, Chile, France, New Zealand, Norway and the United Kingdom. Some other

---

8.   Treaty on Principles Governing the Activities of States in the Exploration and Use of Outer Space, including the Moon and Other Celestial Bodies, Art 2, UNTS, Vol 610, p 206.
9.   Convention on the Law of the Sea, Art 8. See **12.38–12.40**.
10. Convention on the Law of the Sea, Arts 17–32. See **12.47–12.56**.
11. Convention on the Law of the Sea, Arts 46–54. See **12.33–12.37**.
12. *Legal Status of Eastern Greenland case (Norway v Denmark)* PCIJ Rep (1933) Ser A/B No 53, 46.

States reject all these claims and favour instead an international status for the whole territory. The Antarctic area south of 60° S latitude is subject to a *sui generis* regime established by the 1959 Antarctic Treaty,[13] to which the seven territorial claimants are party together with Belgium, Japan, Russia, South Africa and the United States. The most important feature of the Treaty is a requirement that Antarctica be used for peaceful purposes only; there must be no military bases, military manoeuvres, weapons testing or any other measures of a military nature. Further, freedom of movement and scientific exploration is guaranteed throughout the territory. The Treaty specifically provides that it prejudices neither existing territorial claims nor the position of any party as regards its recognition or non-recognition of any other State's claim. While the Treaty remains in force, no new claim may be made, and no activities shall constitute a basis for asserting, supporting or denying any claim to territorial sovereignty. In 1991, the parties adopted a protocol concerning environmental protection of Antarctica and designating it a natural reserve devoted to peace and science.

Modes of establishing title

7.8   There are five customary law principles by which all States may justify a claim to title over territory:

- cession;
- occupation;
- prescription;
- accretion; and
- conquest.

For former colonial and sub-national territories that have achieved statehood, the customary international law principle of *uti possidetis juris* may also be relevant in determining their claims to territorial title.

Each of these principles will be considered in turn.

Cession

7.9   Cession is the transfer of sovereignty over territory by one sovereign to another. Transfer is effected by treaty, often at the conclusion of armed hostilities. One State must evince an intention to assume sovereignty over a territory, and the other State must evince an intention to relinquish it — an agreement to permit the exercise by a foreign State of certain State functions on the territory will not suffice. Thus, a treaty permitting

---

13.   Agreement between the Governments of Australia, Argentina, Chile, the French Republic, Japan, New Zealand, Norway, the Union of South Africa, the Union of the Soviet Socialist Republics, the United Kingdom of Great Britain and Northern Ireland and the United States of America concerning the Peaceful Uses of Antarctica, UNTS, Vol 402, p 71.

a foreign State to establish and maintain military bases on a State's territory will not effect a transfer of territorial sovereignty, even if the agreement permits the foreign State's domestic law to be applied in respect of events on the base.

7.10   An act of cession will be void if it was the result of a treaty procured by the threat or use of force in violation of the principles of international law embodied in the United Nations Charter.[14]

Such an act of cession will, however, be valid under the inter-temporal principle[15] if it was made prior to the emergence of the prohibition on the threat or use of force.

7.11   A ceding State can neither derogate from its own grant, nor pass a better title than it possessed. Consequently, if the territory, prior to cession, was affected by sovereign rights of third States (for example, rights of passage), such rights continue after cession has been effected and may also be enforced against the territory's new State sovereign. Similarly, no State may cede title to territory which does not belong to it. This limitation, an instance of the principle *nemo dat quod non habet,* was manifested in the *Island of Palmas Case,*[16] in which Spain's purported cession to the United States of an island by treaty was ineffective because the Netherlands possessed title at the time of the treaty's conclusion.

Occupation

7.12   Occupation was the means by which a State acquired title to a territory which lacked a State sovereign, either because there never was such a sovereign or because a sovereign had abandoned the territory. It was thus an original mode of acquisition inasmuch as title did not derive from the prior sovereignty of another State.

A territory was not considered abandoned unless the departing sovereign demonstrated an *animus relinquendi* — that is, an intention to relinquish sovereignty.[17] Occupation could occur only in relation to territory which was, at the time occupation commenced, *terra nullius*.

Terra nullius

7.13   In international law, the phrase '*terra nullius*' denotes a territory that is owned by no-one. The circumstances in which, for the purposes of international law in the 19th century, a territory could be considered *terra nullius* have been addressed by the International Court of Justice.

---

14.   Vienna Convention on the Law of Treaties, Art 52. See **2.104**.
15.   See **7.14**.
16.   *Island of Palmas Case (Netherlands v United States)* (1928) 2 RIAA 829, 838. See **7.19**.
17.   *Arbitral Award on the Subject of the Difference Relative to the Sovereignty over Clipperton Island (France v Mexico)* (1932) 26 *American Journal of International Law* 390 *(Clipperton Island case)*. See **7.16**.

In the **Western Sahara** **advisory opinion,**[18] Spain had decided to conduct a referendum in its colony of Western Sahara in order to allow its inhabitants to exercise their right of self-determination. The King of Morocco objected to Spain's plans, arguing that Morocco was entitled to exercise sovereignty over the territory of Western Sahara on the basis of 'historic title' predating Spain's colonisation. Mauritania made a similar claim. The UN General Assembly asked the International Court of Justice to furnish an advisory opinion in response to two questions:

I.   Was Western Sahara ... at the time of colonisation by Spain a territory belonging to no-one (terra nullius)? If the answer to the first question is in the negative,

II.   What were the legal ties between the territory and the Kingdom of Morocco and the Mauritanian entity?

The Court said:

79. ... The expression 'terra nullius' was a legal term of art employed in connection with 'occupation' as one of the accepted legal methods of acquiring sovereignty over territory.

'Occupation' being legally an original means of peaceably acquiring sovereignty over territory otherwise than by cession or succession, it was a cardinal condition of a valid 'occupation' that the territory should be terra nullius a territory belonging to no-one at the time of the act alleged to constitute the 'occupation' ... In the view of the Court, therefore, a determination that Western Sahara was a 'terra nullius' at the time of colonization by Spain would be possible only if it were established that at that time the territory belonged to no-one in the sense that it was then open to acquisition through the legal process of 'occupation'.

80. Whatever differences of opinion there may have been among jurists, the State practice of the relevant period indicates that territories inhabited by tribes or people having a social and political organization were not regarded as terrae nullius. It shows that in the case of such territories the acquisition of sovereignty was not generally considered as effected unilaterally through 'occupation' of terra nullius by original title but through agreements concluded with local rulers. On occasion, it is true, the word 'occupation' was used in a non-technical sense denoting simply acquisition of sovereignty; but that did not signify that the acquisition of sovereignty through such agreements with authorities of the country was regarded as an 'occupation' of a 'terra nullius' in the proper sense of these terms. On the contrary, such agreements with local rulers, whether or not considered as an actual 'cession' of the territory, were regarded as derivative roots of title, and not original titles obtained by occupation of terrae nullius.

81. In the present instance, the information furnished to the Court shows that at the time of colonization Western Sahara was inhabited by peoples which, if nomadic, were socially and politically organized in tribes and under chiefs competent to represent them. It also shows that, in colonizing Western Sahara, Spain did not proceed on the basis that it was establishing its sovereignty over terrae nullius. In its Royal Order of 26 December 1884, far from treating the case as one of occupation of terra nullius, Spain proclaimed that the King was taking the Rio de Oro under his protection on the basis of agreements which had been entered into with the chiefs of the local tribes. ...

---

18.   *Western Sahara* advisory opinion, ICJ Rep (1975) 12.

The Court needed to determine if Western Sahara (or Rio de Oro, as it was formerly known) was *terra nullius* at the time of Spain's colonisation in order to assess whether there could have been any pre-existing 'legal ties' between Western Sahara and Morocco. If the Court had determined that the territory was *terra nullius,* such ties would have been impossible. The Court concluded that the territory was not *terra nullius,* as that term was understood in 1884, because its inhabitants were 'socially and politically organized in tribes and under chiefs competent to represent them'. The Court then examined the claim to pre-existing 'legal ties', but concluded that they were not effective to establish legal title to the territory.

7.14 The Court's historical approach to the *terra nullius* doctrine in the *Western Sahara* case was required partly because of the way in which the General Assembly framed the request for an advisory opinion. It was also necessary because of the doctrine of inter-temporal law, according to which 'a juridical fact must be appreciated in the light of the law contemporary with it'.[19]

When assessing a claim to sovereignty over territory which depends on past events, the legal effect of those events must be assessed in the context of the law as it stood at the time they occurred.

7.15 If a territory was *terra nullius,* title by occupation would exist only if two elements were established: possession and administration.

Possession

7.16 Possession involved some formal act (for example, planting flags or making official proclamations) with an intention to occupy *(animus occupandi)* and, usually, actual settlement by a population under the authority of the possessing State. The requirement of *animus occupandi* by the State poses a problem where acts are performed by individuals without State authority because 'the independent activity of private individuals is of little value unless it can be shown that they have acted in pursuance of ... some ... authority received from their Governments or that in some other way their Governments have asserted jurisdiction through them'.[20]

The requirement of actual settlement was relaxed where the territory involved was particularly inaccessible or its climate especially inhospitable, to such an extent that the establishment of a permanent settlement would be practicably very difficult.

---

19. *Island of Palmas Case (Netherlands v United States)* (1928) 2 RIAA 829, 845. See **7.19**.
20. Dissenting opinion of Judge Sir Arnold McNair in the *Anglo-Norwegian Fisheries* case *(United Kingdom v Norway)* ICJ Rep (1951) 116, 184.

In the **Clipperton Island case,**[21] France sent a naval vessel to a small, remote and unpopulated coral island reef in the Pacific Ocean. Upon arrival, the vessel's commander made a proclamation of French sovereignty over the island and briefly landed some of the vessel's crew members on the reef. A French consul shortly thereafter notified a foreign government (Hawaii) of France's claim and made an announcement of the claim in a Hawaii newspaper. The arbitrator said:[22]

> ... [T]here is ground to admit that, when in November, 1858, France proclaimed her sovereignty over Clipperton, that island was in the legal situation of *territorium nullius,* and, therefore, susceptible of occupation. ...

> It is beyond doubt that by immemorial usage having the force of law, besides the *animus occupandi,* the actual, and not the nominal, taking of possession is a necessary condition of occupation. The taking of possession consists in the act, or series of acts, by which the occupying state reduces to its possession the territory in question and takes steps to exercise exclusive authority there. Strictly speaking, and in ordinary cases, that only takes place when the state establishes in the territory itself an organization capable of making its laws respected. But this step is, properly speaking, but a means of procedure to the taking of possession, and, therefore, is not identical with the latter.

> There may also be cases where it is unnecessary to have recourse to this method. Thus, if a territory, by virtue of the fact that it was completely uninhabited, is, from the first moment when the occupying state makes its first appearance there, at the absolute and undisputed disposition of that state, from that moment the taking of possession must be considered as accomplished, and the occupation is thereby complete.

France was held to have established effective title in 1858 and subsequently did nothing to evince an intention to relinquish sovereignty over the island reef. Consequently, when Mexico, some 40 years later, sought to take possession of the territory, it was already 'occupied' by France and therefore no longer *terra nullius.*

7.17   Similarly, the Permanent Court of International Justice did not regard Denmark's failure to establish permanent colonies in the vast but highly inhospitable eastern region of Greenland as defeating its claim to occupation dating from about 1721. The Court regarded as significant that Denmark had populated the more habitable parts of Greenland and that, for most of the period of its asserted sovereignty over eastern Greenland, no State contested Denmark's claim.[23]

Furthermore, the International Court of Justice did not regard the United Kingdom's non-establishment of a permanent population on two groups of practicably uninhabitable islets and rocks in the English Channel as fatal to its territorial claim over them.[24]

---

21.   *Arbitral Award on the Subject of the Difference Relative to the Sovereignty over Clipperton Island (France v Mexico)* (1932) 26 *American Journal of International Law* 390.
22.   Ibid, 393–394.
23.   *Legal Status of Eastern Greenland* case *(Norway v Denmark)* PCIJ Rep (1933) Ser A/B No 53.
24.   *Minquiers and Ecrehos Case (France v United Kingdom)* ICJ Rep (1953) 47.

Administration

7.18   The administration element of occupation is characterised by Oppenheim in the following terms:[25]

> After having taken possession of a territory, the possessor must establish some kind of administration thereon which shows that the territory is really governed by the new possessor. If, within a reasonable time after the act of taking possession, the possessor does not establish some responsible authority which exercises governing functions, there is then no effective occupation, since in fact no sovereignty is exercised by any state over the territory.

7.19   The extent of the obligation to establish an administration is, like the requirement to establish and maintain a settled population, relative to the nature of the territory in question.

In the **Island of Palmas Case**,[26] Spain had ceded the Philippines to the United States in 1898 under the Treaty of Paris, at the conclusion of the Spanish–American War. The Treaty indicated that the island of Palmas (also known as Miangas) was part of the Philippines. The island lies about 50 miles off the southern coast of the Philippines island of Mindanao. It is less than two square miles in size. Eight years after assuming sovereignty over the Philippines, a United States official made a visit to Palmas, on the understanding that Spain had ceded the island to the United States along with the Philippines. Upon his arrival, he discovered a Dutch flag flying on the island. Dutch authorities subsequently confirmed to United States officials that the Netherlands regarded Palmas as a Dutch colonial possession. The dispute concerning sovereignty over the island was referred by the two States to the Permanent Court of Arbitration. At the time of the arbitration, Palmas had a population of fewer than 1,000. The United States relied on the cession provisions in the Treaty of Paris, and claimed Palmas as successor to Spain.

The Netherlands claimed that its title derived, inter alia, from a continuous exercise and display of Dutch sovereignty dating from about 1700. The central issue was whether the island was part of Spanish territory in 1898, so that Spain could cede it to the United States, or whether it was a Dutch possession at that date and therefore beyond Spain's authority to cede. The sole arbitrator, Max Huber, made the following remarks in his award:[27]

> Territorial sovereignty … involves the exclusive right to display the activities of a State. This right has a corollary duty: the obligation to protect within the territory the rights of other States, in particular their right to integrity and inviolability in peace and in war, together with the rights that each State may claim for its nationals in foreign territory. Without manifesting its territorial sovereignty in a manner corresponding to circumstances, the State cannot fulfil this duty. …

> International law, the structure of which is not based on any super-State organisation, cannot be presumed to reduce a right such as territorial sovereignty, with which almost all international relations are bound up, to the category of an abstract right, without concrete manifestations. …

---

25.   Sir Robert Jennings and Sir Arthur Watts (eds), *Oppenheim's International Law,* 9th ed, Longman, New York, 1992, § 251, 689.
26.   *Island of Palmas Case (Netherlands v United States)* (1928) 2 RIAA 829.
27.   Ibid, 839–868.

Manifestations of territorial sovereignty assume, it is true, different forms, according to conditions of time and place. Although continuous in principle, sovereignty cannot be exercised in fact at every moment on every point of a territory. The intermittence and discontinuity compatible with the maintenance of the right necessarily differ according as inhabited or uninhabited regions are involved, or regions enclosed within territories in which sovereignty is incontestably displayed or again regions which are accessible from, for instance, the high seas. It is true that neighbouring States may by convention fix limits to their own sovereignty, even in regions such as the interior of scarcely explored continents where such sovereignty is scarcely manifested, and in this way each may prevent the other from any penetration of its territory. The delimitation of Hinterland may also be mentioned in this connection.

If, however, no conventional line of sufficient topographical precision exists or if there are gaps in the frontiers otherwise established, or if a conventional line leaves room for doubt, or if, as, *e.g.* in the case of an island situated in the high seas, the question arises whether a title is valid *erga omnes,* the actual continuous and peaceful display of State functions is in case of dispute the sound and natural criterion of territorial sovereignty. ...

As regards the territory forming the subject of the present dispute, it must be remembered that it is a somewhat isolated island, and therefore a territory clearly delimited and individualised. It is moreover an island permanently inhabited, occupied by a population sufficiently numerous for it to be impossible that acts of administration could be lacking for very long periods. The memoranda of both Parties assert that there is communication by boat and even with native craft between the Island of Palmas (or Miangas) and neighbouring regions.

The inability in such a case to indicate any acts of public administration makes it difficult to imagine the actual display of sovereignty, even if the sovereignty be regarded as confined within such narrow limits as would be supposed for a small island inhabited exclusively by natives. ...

The Netherlands found their claim to sovereignty essentially on the title of peaceful and continuous display of State authority over the island.

Since this title would in international law prevail over a title of acquisition of sovereignty not followed by actual display of State authority, it is necessary to ascertain in the first place, whether the contention of the Netherlands is sufficiently established by evidence, and, if so, for what period of time. ...

The acts of indirect or direct display of Netherlands sovereignty at Palmas (or Miangas), especially in the 18th and early 19th centuries are not numerous, and there are considerable gaps in the evidence of continuous display. But apart from the consideration that the manifestations of sovereignty over a small and distant island, inhabited only by natives, cannot be expected to be frequent, it is not necessary that the display of sovereignty should go back to a very distant period. It may suffice that such display existed in 1898, and had already existed as continuous and peaceful before that date long enough to enable any Power who might have considered herself as possessing sovereignty over the island, or having a claim to sovereignty, to have, according to local conditions, a reasonable possibility for ascertaining the existence of a state of things contrary to her real or alleged rights. ...

Now the evidence relating to the period after the middle of the 19th century makes it clear that the Netherlands Indian Government considered the island distinctly as part of its possessions and that, in the years immediately preceding 1898, an intensification of display of sovereignty took place. ...

There is moreover no evidence which would establish any act of display of sovereignty over the island by Spain or another Power, such as might

> counterbalance or annihilate the manifestations of Netherlands sovereignty. … These circumstances, together with the absence of any evidence of a conflict between Spanish and Netherlands authorities during more than two centuries as regards Palmas (or Miangas), are an indirect proof of the effective display of Netherlands sovereignty. …
>
> The display has been open and public, that is to say it was in conformity with usages as to exercise of sovereignty over colonial States. A clandestine exercise of State authority over an inhabited territory during a considerable length of time would seem to be impossible. …
>
> The conditions of acquisition of sovereignty by the Netherlands are therefore to be considered as fulfilled.

Administration and inhospitable territories

7.20   Palmas was 'an island permanently inhabited, occupied by a population sufficiently numerous for it to be impossible that acts of administration could be lacking for very long periods'. However, public displays of State authority on such a remote and small island did not need to be frequent, provided that they were:

> … enough to enable any Power who might have considered herself as possessing sovereignty over the island, or having a claim to sovereignty, to have, according to local conditions, a reasonable possibility for ascertaining the existence of a state of things contrary to her real or alleged rights.

Where a territory is completely uninhabited, the requirement that the possessing State establish an administration may be satisfied by even less. In such cases, the possessing State need merely perform public and official acts affecting the territory which demonstrate to other States that it is exercising sovereign powers over the territory.

In the *Clipperton Island* case,[28] the arbitrator said that a State wishing to exercise sovereignty over a territory must take 'steps to exercise exclusive authority there'. Establishing in the territory 'an organization capable of making its laws respected' is the usual way a State achieves this result, but it need not go so far in the case of a completely uninhabited territory. The few steps taken by France in that case were considered adequate to establish an administering authority over an uninhabited and remote coral reef lagoon.

The International Court of Justice regarded the unchallenged exercise of judicial and administrative authority over certain uninhabited rocks and islets in the English Channel as conferring title on the United Kingdom.[29]

In the *Legal Status of Eastern Greenland* case, the Permanent Court of International Justice was impressed by the granting of concessions

---

28.   *Arbitral Award on the Subject of the Difference Relative to the Sovereignty over Clipperton Island (France v Mexico)* (1932) 26 *American Journal of International Law* 390. See **7.16**.
29.   *Minquiers and Ecrehos Case (France v United Kingdom)* ICJ Rep (1953) 47.

for trading, hunting, mining and the erection of telegraph lines in the sparsely populated and inhospitable eastern region of Greenland by the King of Denmark. This was regarded as adequate to establish Denmark's exercise of public administration over the region. The Court said:[30]

> It is impossible to read the records of the decisions in cases as to territorial sovereignty without observing that in many cases the tribunal has been satisfied with very little in the way of the actual exercise of sovereign rights, provided that the other State could not make out a superior claim. This is particularly true in the case of claims to sovereignty over areas in thinly populated or unsettled countries.

Discovery

7.21   Occupation was usually preceded by discovery of the territory. In this context, 'discovery' refers to the first encounter with a territory by explorers, traders or soldiers from a European country, usually during the period from the 15th century until the 18th century. Mere discovery, even if accompanied by a symbolic act of taking, was not enough to secure a conclusive title for the discovering State. Discovery conferred, instead, merely an inchoate title — that is, an option to occupy which had to be exercised within a reasonable time. Until that time had passed, other States were not permitted to occupy the territory. If no effective occupation had occurred after the passage of a reasonable time from the date of discovery, the territory reverted to *terra nullius*.

Prescription

7.22   Whereas occupation provides acquisition of State title over *terra nullius*, prescription refers to a situation where a State has been considered the lawful owner even of those parts of its territory of which it originally took possession wrongfully, provided that the possessor has been in undisturbed possession for so long as to create the general conviction that the present condition of things is in conformity with international order.[31]

7.23   Acquisition of title by prescription may occur in one of two forms: immemorial possession or adverse possession. The distinction depends upon the length of time which has elapsed since the territory was taken into possession.

A State will enjoy prescriptive title by immemorial possession where the State acquiring title has been in possession for so long that competing claims by earlier sovereigns have been forgotten. Many older States are in possession of lands the title to which, if enquiry were made, would need to rest on immemorial possession.

---

30.   *Legal Status of Eastern Greenland* case (*Norway v Denmark*) PCIJ Rep (1933) Ser A/B No 53, 46. See 2.11.
31.   Sir Robert Jennings and Sir Arthur Watts (eds), *Oppenheim's International Law*, 9th ed, Longman, New York, 1992, § 269, 706.

Prescriptive title by adverse possession occurs where the identity of the previous sovereign is known, but the State acquiring title has exercised sovereign authority over the territory for so long that the previous sovereign is regarded as having forfeited its title. The concept of forfeiture is appropriate, because prescriptive title by adverse possession cannot arise unless the previous sovereign has acquiesced in the exercise of sovereign functions by the acquiring State.

Protest and acquiescence

7.24   Both occupation and prescription require the exercise and display of State functions over the subject territory. The principal difference between the two modes of acquiring title concerns the response of other States to the exercise and display of official authority by the possessing State.

7.25   Title by prescription is established by the continuous and peaceful display of State functions. 'Peaceful' implies not only the absence of force, but also the absence of protest. In other words, 'peaceful' display is established where other States — and especially any State now contesting the possessor's title — have acquiesced in that display. In the *Chamizal Arbitration,* an international boundary commission unanimously held that the United States was unable to assert a prescriptive title over certain disputed territory as Mexico had 'constantly questioned and challenged' the exercise of political control over the territory by United States authorities. Mexico had protested through its diplomatic agents, and the commission remarked that:[32]

> ... however much the Mexicans may have desired to take physical possession of the district, the result of any attempt to do so would have provoked scenes of violence and the Republic of Mexico cannot be blamed for resorting to the milder forms of protest contained in its diplomatic correspondence.

Prescription and occupation contrasted

7.26   In theory, the exercise and display of State functions need not be peaceful in the case of title by occupation. Because such territory was *terra nullius* at the time of taking possession, protests by other States asserting a prior title must logically be incorrect. This neat distinction between occupation and prescription does not, however, translate into clear practical differences. According to Malcolm Shaw:[33]

> Prescription differs from occupation in that it relates to territory which has previously been under the sovereignty of a state. In spite of this, both concepts are similar in that they may require evidence of sovereign acts by a state over a period of time. And although distinct in theory, in practice

---

32.   *Chamizal Arbitration between the United States and Mexico* (1911) 5 *American Journal of International Law* 782, 807.
33.   Malcolm N Shaw, *International Law,* 6th ed, Cambridge University Press, Cambridge, 2008, 505.

these concepts are often indistinct since sovereignty over an area may lapse and give rise to doubts whether an abandonment has taken place, rendering the territory *terra nullius*.

7.27   In practice, international tribunals actually tend to collapse the theoretical distinction between occupation and prescription, and they are rarely explicit on the issue of whether a possessor's title rests upon one or the other. This is because where:

> ... no conventional line of sufficient topographical precision exists or if there are gaps in the frontiers otherwise established, or if a conventional line leaves room for doubt, or if, as, for example, in the case of an island situated in the high seas, the question arises whether a title is valid *erga omnes,* the actual continuous and peaceful display of State functions is in case of dispute the sound and natural criterion of territorial sovereignty.[34]

Consequently, regardless of whether a possessing State's title is said to rest upon occupation or upon prescription, a tribunal looks for evidence that the contesting State has acquiesced in the possessing State's exercise and display of State functions.

It is possible to reconcile this practice with the theoretical distinction between the two types of title. If the possessing State's title rests upon prescription, the absence of protest by other States establishes that any displays of State functions were peaceful. On the other hand, if the possessing State's title rests upon occupation, the absence of protest by other States is evidence that no State had a prior title and that the territory was *terra nullius* at the time it was taken into possession. In either case, it is relevant to enquire whether the possessing State's displays of sovereignty have been met with protests or acquiescence by other States.

Accretion

7.28   Title by accretion occurs whenever natural forces add to a State's land territory. Examples are where an island emerges in an internal river or in the territorial sea, or where land is extended into the sea by soil deposits from a river. A State does not need to formally claim the new land — title accrues automatically.

7.29   Problems may arise where accretion occurs as a result of the change of course of a river marking an international border. The customary rule is that land acquired by accretion is transferred to the receiving State's territorial sovereignty. Accretion, for this purpose, means a gradual and imperceptible change in the river's course.

If, however, the boundary river is affected by avulsion — a sudden and perceptible change of course, for example, as a result of flooding — the international boundary remains where it was before the change of course.[35]

---

34.   *Island of Palmas Case (Netherlands v United States)* (1928) 2 RIAA 829, 840.
35.   *Chamizal Arbitration between the United States and Mexico* (1911) 5 *American Journal of International Law* 782.

Conquest

7.30   In the past, a State could acquire sovereign title to territory by conquest. This consisted of taking possession of enemy territory in time of war with the intention of acquiring sovereignty over it. Frequently, transfer of title would be effected by a peace treaty in which the conquered territory would be formally ceded — in which case, cession was the proper foundation of title.[36]

Where no formal act of cession occurred, title could pass by conquest where either: (i) the armed forces of the defeated State were completely destroyed, thereby leaving the territory open to possession by the victor State; or (ii) the defeated State abandoned the territory by withdrawing its armed forces, thereby leaving the territory open to possession by the victor State.

7.31   Conquest no longer operates as a valid basis for acquiring sovereign title to territory.

The Kellogg–Briand Pact condemns 'recourse to war for the solution of international controversies' and the States parties renounce war 'as an instrument of national policy in their relations one with another'.[37]

Article 2(4) of the UN Charter similarly requires States to 'refrain in their international relations from the threat or use of force against the territorial integrity or political independence of any state'.

The General Assembly's Declaration on Principles of International Law Concerning Friendly Relations and Co-operation among States in Accordance with the United Nations Charter provides as follows:[38]

> The territory of a State shall not be the object of acquisition by another State resulting from the threat or use of force. No territorial acquisition resulting from the threat or use of force shall be recognised as legal.

This provision reflects customary international law.[39]

7.32   Nevertheless, where a sufficiently large number of States extend *de jure* recognition to an asserted title based on conquest, such recognition may operate to validate the title. An example is the 1961 invasion of the Portuguese enclaves of Goa, Danao and Diu by India.[40] Title founded on conquest prior to the emergence of the prohibitions on resort to war and the threat or use of force remain valid in accordance with the inter-temporal principle.

---

36. See **7.9–7.11**.
37. General Treaty for the Renunciation of War as an Instrument of National Policy (Kellogg–Briand Treaty, or Pact of Paris), Art 1, League of Nations Treaty Series, Vol 94, p 57. See **9.6**.
38. General Assembly Resolution 2625 (XXV) (1970).
39. *Legal Consequences of the Construction of a Wall in the Occupied Palestinian Territory* advisory opinion, ICJ Rep (2004) 136, para 87.
40. Rebecca M M Wallace, *International Law*, 4th ed, Sweet & Maxwell, London, 2002, 95–96.

Uti possidetis juris

7.33 A colony, dependent territory, or sub-national unit of a sovereign State which has achieved independent statehood is in a special position. Its pre-independence territorial boundaries will have been determined by its former sovereign. What is the status of those boundaries when the colony, dependent territory, or sub-national unit achieves statehood?

7.34 The new State will, unless it is a remote island, have neighbours. Can the new State ever be justified in raising territorial claims against its neighbouring States, or vice versa? Some of those neighbours may have been colonies or sub-national units of the same sovereign as the new State. Others may have been colonies or sub-national units of a different sovereign. And yet others may be older States that were never colonies or sub-national units of other sovereigns. The new State may wish to challenge the boundaries determined by its former sovereign on the basis that they fail to accommodate geography, history, religious or ethnic unity, or some social, political or economic reality. The boot might also be on the other foot, and the new State's neighbours may wish to make territorial claims on the new State.

7.35 It is possible to conceive of a legal principle according to which no States would be obliged to accept the territorial boundaries decided by a new State's former sovereign as determinative of the new State's post-independence borders. However, that is not the principle which has emerged. Rather, the principle known as *uti possidetis juris*[41] operates to transform pre-independence boundaries into international borders defeasible only by agreement between the bordering States.

7.36 Originally, *uti possidetis juris* operated to transform the internal administrative boundaries of Spain's American empire into the international borders of the many new States that achieved independence from Spain in the 19th century. This was done with a view to pre-empting European re-colonisation of parts of the former Spanish empire in America on the basis that they might otherwise have been *terra nullius*.[42]

By the mid-20th century, *uti possidetis* was extended. It became a general principle of customary international law encompassing not only internal administrative boundaries of the former colonial sovereign, but also a former colony's international borders with territories belonging to other sovereigns.

---

41. The phrase *'uti possidetis'* originates in the Latin *uti possidetis, ita possideatis,* meaning 'as you possessed, you shall continue to possess'.
42. *Affaire des Frontières Colombo-Vénézuéliennes (Colombia v Venezuela)* (1922) 1 RIAA 223, 228.

In the **Frontier Dispute case**,[43] Burkina Faso and Mali asked a chamber of the International Court of Justice to resolve a border dispute. Both States were former colonies of France which had been separated by an administrative boundary imposed by the French authorities. The parties agreed that, upon decolonisation, the colonial administrative boundary became the international border separating the two new States. There was disagreement between the parties as to the correct location of part of the former colonial administrative boundary and, thus, of the present international border. The Court made the following remarks concerning the status of colonial boundaries in determining the location of post-independence international borders:

> 20. Since the two Parties have ... expressly requested the Chamber to resolve their dispute on the basis, in particular, of the 'principle of the intangibility of frontiers inherited from colonization', the Chamber cannot disregard the principle of *uti possidetis juris*, the application of which gives rise to this respect for intangibility of frontiers. ... [I]t should be noted that the principle of *uti possidetis* seems to have been first invoked and applied in Spanish America, inasmuch as this was the continent which first witnessed the phenomenon of decolonization involving the formation of a number of sovereign States on territory formerly belonging to a single metropolitan State. Nevertheless the principle is not a special rule which pertains solely to one specific system of international law. It is a general principle, which is logically connected with the phenomenon of the obtaining of independence, wherever it occurs. Its obvious purpose is to prevent the independence and stability of new States being endangered by fratricidal struggles provoked by the challenging of frontiers following the withdrawal of the administering power.
>
> 21. It was for this reason that, as soon as the phenomenon of decolonization characteristic of the situation in Spanish America in the 19th century subsequently appeared in Africa in the 20th century, the principle of *uti possidetis*, in the sense described above, fell to be applied. The fact that the new African States have respected the administrative boundaries and frontiers established by the colonial powers must be seen not as a mere practice contributing to the gradual emergence of a principle of customary international law, limited in its impact to the African continent as it had previously been to Spanish America, but as the application in Africa of a rule of general scope.
>
> 22. The elements of *uti possidetis* were latent in the many declarations made by African leaders in the dawn of independence. These declarations confirmed the maintenance of the territorial status quo at the time of independence, and stated the principle of respect both for the frontiers deriving from international agreements, and for those resulting from mere internal administrative divisions. ...
>
> 23. There are several different aspects to this principle, in its well known application in Spanish America. The first aspect, emphasized by the Latin genitive *juris*, is found in the pre-eminence accorded to legal title over effective possession as a basis of sovereignty. Its purpose, at the time of the achievement of independence by the former Spanish colonies of America, was to scotch any designs which non-American colonizing powers might have on regions which had been assigned by the former metropolitan State to one division or another, but which were still uninhabited or unexplored. However, there is more to the principle of *uti possidetis* than this particular aspect. The essence of the principle lies in its primary aim of securing respect for the territorial boundaries at the moment when independence is

---

43.   *Case Concerning the Frontier Dispute (Burkina Faso v Mali)* ICJ Rep (1986) 554.

achieved. Such territorial boundaries might be no more than delimitations between different administrative divisions or colonies all subject to the same sovereign. In that case, the application of the principle of *uti possidetis* resulted in administrative boundaries being transformed into international frontiers in the full sense of the term. This is true both of the States which took shape in the regions of South America which were dependent on the Spanish Crown, and of the States Parties to the present case, which took shape within the vast territories of French West Africa. *Uti possidetis,* as a principle which upgraded former administrative delimitations, established during the colonial period, to international frontiers, is therefore a principle of a general kind which is logically connected with this form of decolonization wherever it occurs.

24. The territorial boundaries which have to be respected may also derive from international frontiers which previously divided a colony of one State from a colony of another, or indeed a colonial territory from the territory of an independent State, or one which was under protectorate, but had retained its international personality. There is no doubt that the obligation to respect pre-existing international frontiers in the event of a State succession derives from a general rule of international law, whether or not the rule is expressed in the formula *uti possidetis.* Hence the numerous solemn affirmations of the intangibility of the frontiers existing at the time of the independence of African States, whether made by senior African statesmen or by organs of the Organization of African Unity itself, are evidently declaratory rather than constitutive: they recognize and confirm an existing principle, and do not seek to consecrate a new principle or the extension to Africa of a rule previously applied only in another continent.

25. … At first sight this principle conflicts outright with another one, the right of peoples to self-determination. In fact, however, the maintenance of the territorial *status quo* in Africa is often seen as the wisest course, to preserve what has been achieved by peoples who have struggled for their independence, and to avoid a disruption which would deprive the continent of the gains achieved by much sacrifice. The essential requirement of stability in order to survive, to develop and gradually to consolidate their independence in all fields, has induced African States judiciously to consent to the respecting of colonial frontiers, and to take account of it in the interpretation of the principle of self-determination of peoples.

7.37   Soon after the *Frontier Dispute* judgment was delivered, a civil war erupted in the Socialist Federal Republic of Yugoslavia (SFRY), which eventually resulted in that State's dissolution. This conflict prompted the European Community to establish an Arbitration Commission (the Badinter Commission) in order to facilitate a peaceful settlement among the warring parties.[44] In commenting upon the new international borders that might emerge from a dissolution of the Yugoslav federation, the Commission remarked that 'whatever the circumstances, the right to self-determination must not involve changes to existing frontiers at the time of independence *(uti possidetis juris)* except where the states concerned agree otherwise'.[45] It further observed that:[46]

---

44.   See **4.50**.
45.   *Opinion No 2* (1992) 92 ILR 167, 168.
46.   *Opinion No 3* (1992) 92 ILR 170, 171.

Once the process in the SFRY leads to the creation of one or more independent states, the issue of frontiers ... must be resolved in accordance with the following principles ... Except where otherwise agreed, the former boundaries become frontiers protected by international law. This conclusion follows from the principle of respect for the territorial status quo and, in particular, from the principle of *uti possidetis*. *Uti possidetis*, though initially applied in settling decolonization issues in America and Africa, is today recognized as a general principle ...

It is, therefore, highly likely that *uti possidetis juris* now reaches beyond the colonial context. If this is correct, it also extends to transform a sovereign State's internal administrative boundaries into international borders upon a successful separation from the State by one of its territorial units. There is ample modern State practice to support a customary rule to this effect — for example, Bangladesh (formerly East Pakistan) (secession); Indonesia and East Timor (secession); the Czech Republic and Slovakia (dissolution); the former Soviet republics (dissolution); the former Yugoslav republics (dissolution); Malaysia and Singapore (expulsion); and Denmark and Greenland (autonomous home rule en route to separation from Denmark).

7.38   Where a disputed international border originates as an internal colonial administrative boundary or a boundary delimiting territorial units within a sovereign State, *uti possidetis juris* will always apply. Where, however, a new State's post-independence international border originates as a colonial or sub-national territory's international border, *uti possidetis juris* will apply only where the new State's previous sovereign and the foreign sovereign with which the border was shared were in agreement as to the border's location. In other words, an international border will not be subject to *uti possidetis juris* to the extent that its location was disputed by one of the sovereigns sharing it prior to the new State attaining independence. This is because the rationale for *uti possidetis juris* is the avoidance of territorial disputes between sovereigns where none previously existed.

Question

Remora and Camoona are neighbouring States. Part of their common border passes through the Merino Alps, a remote region of high, inhospitable and largely barren mountains covering about 100 square kilometres.

The exact border line has long been unclear in sections of the Merinos due to their forbidding topography and inaccessibility.

This lack of certainty in the precise location of the border has not posed a problem for the last 160 years, as the Merino Alps lacked any known resources and possessed little strategic value. Last May, however, a survey team from a mining company discovered a large seam of gold in the Merino Valley which is located within the Merino Alps. Remoran maps usually show the valley as being in Remora, while Camoonan maps usually show the valley as falling on the Camoona side of the international border.

The first known expedition into the Merinos occurred in 1588, when a team led by Hans Polo and commissioned by the King of Naples explored and mapped most of the region. At that time, the Merinos were populated by about 800 Merino tribesmen who hunted and foraged throughout the mountains. Nothing is now known of their political organisation, if any, at the time. Polo found no signs of authority by any State during his explorations. At the conclusion of the expedition, and before he left the region, Polo formally raised his King's flag and claimed the Merinos for the crown of Naples. Upon returning to Naples, Polo reported his acts to the King. There is no record of the King ever taking any action in response to Polo's report. No attempt was ever made by Naples to colonise the Merinos.

In 1688, Naples was defeated in war by a coalition of States which included Remora. The Treaty of Siena, which ended the war, contained a clause 'transferring from the King of Naples to the King of Remora all sovereign rights and titles over the region known as the Merino Mountains'. Naples and Remora were both parties to the Treaty of Siena.

From about 1700, Remora was the scene of violent conflicts between those adhering to the official State religion and a heavily persecuted breakaway sect. During this period, some members of the sect retreated into the Merino Valley and established a self-governing commune there, confident that Remoran authority would not reach them. The Merino tribesmen had, by this time, left the Merino Alps.

When the persecutions ended in 1788, the commune had a population of about 1,500. The commune-dwellers were considered by Remoran law to be Remoran subjects, but they did not acknowledge the authority of anyone except their religious leaders. No agencies of the Remoran crown existed in the commune or elsewhere in the Merino Alps. A team of Remoran tax collectors, sent to the Merino Valley in 1789, fled after being met with violent resistance by the commune-dwellers.

In 1790, a delegation from the Merino Valley commune visited Camoona and petitioned the Queen to grant Camoonan citizenship and protection to the commune-dwellers. The Queen of Camoona issued a decree conferring citizenship on all the commune-dwellers in the Merino Valley and their descendants. She also appointed the commune's leader as her Royal Governor with power to administer Camoona's laws in the Merino Valley.

Shortly thereafter, the new Governor began conspicuously flying the Camoonan flag throughout the valley, and an office of the Royal Camoonan Postal Service was established in the commune. The Remoran ambassador in Camoona made vigorous protests against all these developments, claiming that the Merino Valley belonged to Remora.

The protests were repeated every year until 1840, but Remora refrained from dispatching troops to the valley in order to avoid war with Camoona. In that year, the two States concluded a treaty settling their common border. The treaty divided the Merino Alps about equally between the parties, but was deliberately ambiguous as to whether the Merino Valley fell within Remora or Camoona.

There were no further developments until the discovery of gold in the Merino Valley last May. The valley and the commune are still de facto administered by a Governor appointed by Camoona. The population of the commune is still about 1,500.

Remora has now issued a mining licence to a company wishing to exploit the valley's gold deposits. When the licence was granted, Remora's Prime Minister publicly stated that 'important mineral deposits located in the Merino Valley, which has been Remoran territory since the Treaty of Siena, can now be exploited for the benefit of Remora's people'.

Camoona's Minister for Mines asks you whether International Law entitles Remora to issue the licence, given that Camoona regards the Merino Valley as forming part of Camoona's territory. Advise him.

Suggested answer

Remora 'may not exercise its power in any form in the territory of another State' (*Lotus* case). If the Merino Valley belongs to Camoona, then Camoona has 'the right to exercise therein, to the exclusion of any other State, the functions of a State' *(Island of Palmas Case)*. The granting of licences to conduct economic activities in a territory is an exercise of State powers or functions (*Legal Status of Eastern Greenland* case). Furthermore, a State's exclusive sovereign powers over its territory extend to the subsoil beneath its territory, including all mines and minerals.

Both Camoona and Remora claim the Merino Valley as part of their exclusive sovereign territory. It is therefore necessary to decide which of the two States has the stronger claim (*Legal Status of Eastern Greenland* case).

Remora's claim

Remora's Prime Minister appears to base his State's claim to the Merino Valley on the 1688 Treaty of Siena, whereby Naples purported to cede all of the Merino Alps to Remora. Cession provides a sound basis for asserting title, but the ceding State cannot convey a better title than it already possesses *(Island of Palmas Case)*.

Naples' title rested upon Hans Polo's discovery of the Merino Alps and his making of a formal claim. Where a territory was *terra nullius*, international law provided that State sovereignty could be provisionally established by discovery and the making of a formal claim by some symbolic act of taking. The title thus established was inchoate, and could be perfected only if the claiming State occupied the territory within a reasonable time. Occupation consisted of two elements — possession and administration.

Possession occurred where there was a symbolic or formal act of taking with an intention to occupy *(animus occupandi)*, followed by actual settlement of a population under the authority of the possessing State. Hans Polo's conduct almost certainly established the requirement for a formal act of taking on behalf of Naples.

However, in the 100 years following Hans Polo's expedition, Naples made no effort to settle a population under its authority in the Merino Alps. The requirement to establish a settlement may be relaxed where the territory in question is particularly inhospitable for reasons of climate or topography (*Clipperton Island* case, *Legal Status of Eastern Greenland* case, *Minquiers and Ecrehos* case). The Merino Alps are high, barren and inhospitable, thereby probably relieving Naples of the requirement to settle a population. Consequently, it was still possible for Naples to occupy the Merino Alps simply by establishing an administration over the territory. This normally meant placing in the territory 'an organization capable of making its laws respected' (*Clipperton Island* case). But, where the establishment of a permanent population was not feasible, the requirement of administration could be performed by the exercise over the territory of State functions such as making laws for it, and performing administrative and judicial functions in relation to it.

Naples did not, during the 100 years between discovery and the purported cession, perform any of these functions (apart from the purported cession itself). If the territory had been completely uninhabited, discovery and claiming might have been enough to establish a complete title (*Clipperton Island* case), but the territory was populated by about 800 tribesmen. Consequently, it probably cannot be said that Naples obtained a title over the Merino Alps by occupation. Between 1588 and 1688, Naples failed to occupy the Merino Alps, thereby probably causing its inchoate claim to lapse by effluxion of a reasonable period of time.

If the tribesmen were 'socially and politically organized in tribes and under chiefs competent to represent them' (*Western Sahara* advisory opinion), the Merino Alps were probably not *terra nullius* at the time of their discovery by Hans Polo. This test of *terra nullius* was, however, current some 300 years after Hans Polo's expedition and might not be appropriate to determine the question in 1588.

According to the inter-temporal principle, 'a juridical fact must be appreciated in the light of the law contemporary with it' *(Island of Palmas Case)*. In any event, there is not now any evidence of the social or political structure of the Merino tribesmen in 1588, and so it is not possible to reach a concluded view on this issue.

If the Merino Alps were not *terra nullius* in 1588, Naples' title could have been established by conquest or by agreement with the local population. Neither event occurred in this case. If the Alps were *terra nullius* then, as has been seen, Naples failed to perfect its inchoate title by occupation.

In either case, Naples probably did not possess any title to the Merino Alps in 1688. Consequently, it was unable to cede the Alps to Remora by the Treaty of Siena. As a result, Remora will probably be unable to establish that it ever possessed title over any part of the Merino Alps on the basis of cession.

Remora might argue that its title rests upon occupation as a result of the migration of Remoran citizens to the Merino Valley during the period 1700–88. There would, however, appear to be no *animus occupandi* by Remora in this process. The commune-dwellers were fleeing Remoran authority, and went to the Merino Valley precisely because the power of Remora could not reach them there. Indeed, the commune-dwellers actively rejected Remoran authority, as vividly evidenced by their expulsion of visiting Remoran tax collectors in 1789. Furthermore, according to Judge McNair in the *Anglo-Norwegian Fisheries* case:

> ... the independent activity of private individuals is of little value unless it can be shown that they have acted in pursuance of ... some ... authority received from their Governments or that in some other way their Governments have asserted jurisdiction through them.

In construing the conduct of the commune-dwellers, it is impossible to perceive any exercise of authority or jurisdiction by Remora.

Camoona's claim

Camoona's claim to sovereignty over the Merino Valley rests on prescriptive title. According to the *Island of Palmas Case,* prescriptive title is established by 'the actual continuous and peaceful display of State functions'. This form of title is the 'sound and natural criterion of sovereignty' where, as in the case of the Merino Valley:

> ... no conventional line of sufficient topographical precision exists or ... there are gaps in the frontiers otherwise established, or ... a conventional line leaves room for doubt.

Occupation is not, strictly speaking, the correct basis for establishing Camoona's title because the commune-dwellers were already there when the Camoonan State 'appeared' in the valley. Their level of social and political organisation, as evidenced by the dispatch of a political delegation to Camoona in 1790, strongly indicates that the valley was not *terra nullius* at the time. However, the distinction between title based on occupation and title based on prescription is more theoretical than practical. Both require the actual continuous display of State functions.

Camoonan State authority has been exercised in the valley by a Governor since 1790. Visible external displays of that authority are provided by the flying of Camoona's flag throughout the valley and the functioning of a Camoona government post office in the commune. There is no evidence of other visible displays by Camoona of State functions. Nevertheless, these displays are probably sufficient for the purposes of establishing prescriptive title. The extent of display required varies according to the nature of the territory involved. The more remote, inaccessible and sparsely populated the territory, the less is required in order to demonstrate a continuous display of State functions. What is important, according to the *Island of Palmas Case*, is that:

> ... any Power who might have considered herself as possessing sovereignty over the ... [territory], or having a claim to sovereignty, to have, according to local conditions, a reasonable possibility for ascertaining the existence of a state of things contrary to her real or alleged rights.

Having regard to the remoteness and small population of the Merino Valley, the displays of State sovereignty made by Camoona are probably sufficient. They are almost certainly sufficiently continuous, having been performed since 1790.

If the proper basis of Camoona's claimed title is prescription, then in addition to visibility and continuity, the displays of State functions must also be peaceful. Peaceful displays of sovereignty can be denied not only by forceful measures such as military action, but also by the making of formal protests, at least if the reason from refraining from more forceful action is the avoidance of violent clashes *(Chamizal Arbitration)*. Remora denied peaceful displays of State functions by Camoona between 1790 and 1840 by regular official protests against those displays. In order to avoid war with Camoona, Remora did not resort to armed action. Consequently, it cannot be said that Camoona established prescriptive title over the valley before 1840. Within a reasonable time of Remora ceasing to make protests, however, Camoona's displays of State functions in the valley became 'peaceful'. That position remained unchanged for about 160 years until last May, with the result that Camoona's displays of State functions also became 'continuous'.

Conclusion

Camoona's claim to sovereignty over the Merino Valley is much stronger than Remora's. As there is no third claimant, Camoona's claim would very likely succeed in any arbitration or judicial settlement. Consequently, Remora is not entitled to issue the mining licence in respect of gold deposits in the Merino Valley. Camoona should also make a formal protest against Remora's claim to the Merino Valley, lest a lack of response be interpreted as acquiescence in Remora's asserted title.

Further tutorial discussion

1. Is there any practical utility in maintaining a distinction between prescriptive title and title founded on occupation?
2. What roles do acquiescence and protest play in determining territorial sovereignty?
3. Can prescriptive title prevail over title based on terms in a treaty?
4. How might France have lost title to Clipperton Island?
5. In the event of a dispute over territorial sovereignty, the practice of international courts and tribunals is to compare the two claims to see which is the stronger. What is the strongest basis for claiming territorial sovereignty, and what is the weakest?

6. What is the function of *uti possidetis juris* in determining disputes over territorial sovereignty? Does a title based on *uti possidetis juris* prevail over prescriptive title? Does it prevail over title based on terms in a treaty?

International dispute settlement

8

Objectives

After completing this chapter, you should:

(1) appreciate the reasons why all legal systems require mechanisms for the settlement of disputes;

(2) be aware of the obligation to settle all international disputes by peaceful means;

(3) understand and be able to explain the similarities and differences between the various modes of peaceful settlement — negotiation, enquiry, mediation, good offices, conciliation, arbitration and judicial settlement;

(4) understand and be able to explain the composition and functions of the International Court of Justice (ICJ);

(5) be aware of the ICJ's contentious jurisdiction, and its engagement by special agreement *(compromis)* and optional clause declaration;

(6) understand and be able to apply the rules on reservations (including self-judging reservations) attached to an optional clause declaration;

(7) be aware of the way in which the legal rights of States that are not parties to ICJ contentious proceedings affect the availability of contentious jurisdiction;

(8) understand the legal effect and the limited enforceability of the ICJ's contentious jurisdiction judgements;

(9) understand the ICJ's advisory jurisdiction, the role of various organs and agencies of the United Nations in engaging that jurisdiction, and the juridical character of advisory opinions; and

(10) be aware of other significant international courts and tribunals offering judicial settlement of international disputes.

Key cases

Interpretation of Peace Treaties with Bulgaria, Hungary and Romania advisory opinion, ICJ Rep (1950) 65
Case of Certain Norwegian Loans (France v Norway) ICJ Rep (1957) 9
Concerning East Timor (Portugal v Australia) ICJ Rep (1995) 90
Concerning Certain Phosphate Lands in Nauru (Nauru v Australia) ICJ Rep (1992) 240
Legality of the Use by a State of Nuclear Weapons in Armed Conflict advisory opinion, ICJ Rep (1996) 66
Legality of the Threat or Use of Nuclear Weapons advisory opinion, ICJ Rep (1996) 226

Key treaties and instruments

United Nations Charter (1945): Art 2(3), Art 2(7), Art 33, Art 94, Art 96
Statute of the International Court of Justice (1945): Art 36(1), Art 36(2), Art 59

Dispute settlement generally

8.1 A cardinal function of every legal system is to provide rules and principles by which disputes may be authoritatively determined. Hardly less important is the associated function of applying those rules and principles to facts so that authoritative determinations of disputes may result. This dispute resolution function requires the establishment and maintenance of mechanisms and institutions which are, in turn, governed by just procedures.

The positive law and its dispute resolution machinery are human cultural artefacts which provide a means of dealing with conflicts so that disputes may be resolved either without resort to force, or by resort to force which is authoritatively sanctioned, regulated and limited. They are an important means of maintaining and advancing the common good[1] and for ensuring that relations among people do not degenerate into a state of general violence. In other words, they are an essential foundation for preserving a society.

8.2 A system of rules which did not advance these functions and purposes, however imperfectly, would not deserve the name 'law'. International law lacks a centralised system of law enforcement and adjudication. It has, however, established or evolved institutions and mechanisms for adjudication and enforcement which are reasonably appropriate to a system of international relations characterised by decentralisation and a relatively small number of State-subjects.

Obligation to resolve disputes peacefully

8.3 From at least the 18th century until 1945, international law placed no general prohibition on the use of force in relations among States, although from 1919 certain multilateral treaty obligations existed limiting a party's right to resort to war and imposing obligations to settle disputes peacefully.[2] This is not to say, however, that States possessed no peaceful means for resolving international disputes prior to the end of the First World War. Then, as now, the vast majority of disputes between States were settled by means of negotiation, enquiry, good offices, mediation, conciliation or arbitration.

Although resort to armed force was legally permissible, it remained in practice an exceptional and usually last-resort means of resolving

---

1. See **1.79–1.81**.
2. See **9.1–9.6**.

international disputes. There was, however, no obligation under general international law to use any of these peaceful means.[3]

8.4   At the end of the Second World War, Art 2(4) of the United Nations Charter imposed a reasonably comprehensive prohibition on the threat or use of force in international relations.[4] This prohibition exists in tandem with the following obligation contained in Art 2(3) of the UN Charter:

Article 2

The Organisation and its Members, in pursuit of the Purposes Stated in Article 1, shall act in accordance with the following Principles. ...

3. All Members shall settle their international disputes by peaceful means in such a manner that international peace and security, and justice, are not endangered.

Article 33 of the UN Charter complements these provisions in the following terms:

Article 33

1. The parties to any dispute, the continuance of which is likely to endanger the maintenance of international peace and security, shall, first of all, seek a solution by negotiation, enquiry, mediation, conciliation, arbitration, judicial settlement, resort to regional agencies or arrangements, or other peaceful means of their own choice.

2. The Security Council shall, when it deems necessary, call upon the parties to settle their dispute by such means.

8.5   Given that almost every State is a party to the UN Charter, it can now be said that there is a customary obligation on all States to seek solutions to international disputes by peaceful means whenever the continuation of the dispute would be likely to endanger the maintenance of international peace and security.[5] The means enumerated in Art 33(1) reflect the modes of settlement which States were entitled, but not obliged, to use prior to the UN Charter. They cover a range of options with varying degrees of complexity, from the highly informal (negotiation) through to the highly structured and formal (judicial settlement). Of the options available, only negotiation is ever purely bilateral. All the other options involve a third person in the form of an individual, another State, an international organisation, or an international court or arbitral tribunal.

United Nations procedures

8.6   Article 33 is contained within Pt VI of the UN Charter, which deals with Pacific Settlement of Disputes. There are some other noteworthy provisions in Pt VI. Article 37 requires parties to a dispute

---

3.   *Status of Eastern Carelia* advisory opinion, PCIJ Rep (1923) Ser B No 5, 27–28.
4.   See **9.9–9.10**.
5.   *Case Concerning Legality of Use of Force (Yugoslavia v Belgium)* Provisional Measures ICJ Rep (1999) 124, para 48.

to refer it to the Security Council if the dispute's continuance is likely to endanger the maintenance of international peace and security. In such a case, the Security Council may recommend terms of settlement or it may, pursuant to Art 36, recommend appropriate procedures or methods of adjustment.

Furthermore, any member of the United Nations may bring any international dispute or other situation to the attention of the Security Council or General Assembly if the situation might lead to international friction.[6] The Security Council may also investigate such matters on its own initiative with a view to determining whether the dispute or situation 'is likely to endanger the maintenance of international peace and security'.[7] If such a determination is made, the Security Council's powers under Chapter VII (Acts with Respect to Threats to the Peace, Breaches of the Peace, and Acts of Aggression) will be engaged.[8]

Negotiation, enquiry, good offices, mediation and conciliation

Negotiation

8.7 Negotiation is the oldest, simplest and most common form of resolving international disputes. Negotiation is also the method invariably adopted for agreeing or amending treaties. As a dispute settlement mechanism, negotiations are almost always conducted between two disputing States, though a multilateral dispute may entail negotiations among more than two parties. A defining characteristic of negotiations is that they are conducted directly between or among the disputants without requiring the assistance or involvement of parties outside the dispute. Although third party involvement is not required, negotiations may be assisted by the complementary mechanisms of enquiry, good offices, mediation or conciliation.

8.8 Negotiations are almost always held in secret so that the media, the public and other States are excluded from the proceedings. They are, furthermore, conducted at venues and according to agendas which the parties themselves determine — these preliminary matters are themselves sometimes the subject of extended negotiations. Depending on the importance of the dispute, negotiations may be conducted at a variety of different levels, ranging from diplomats and government functionaries up to Head of Government or Head of State. States occasionally take advantage of forums provided by international organisations, groupings or regular conferences in order to conduct negotiations at higher official levels; some examples are the United Nations and its various

---

6. UN Charter, Art 35.
7. Ibid, Art 34.
8. See **9.49–9.62**.

agencies, the Council of Europe, the Association of South East Asian Nations (ASEAN), Asia Pacific Economic Co-operation (APEC), the South Pacific Forum, the North Atlantic Treaty Organisation (NATO), the Organization of American States (OAS), and the Organisation of African Unity (OAU).

8.9 An attempted negotiation is a prerequisite for submitting a dispute to judicial settlement.[9] Parties to a dispute may also be under an 'obligation so to conduct themselves that the negotiations are meaningful, which will not be the case when either of them insists upon its own position without contemplating any modification of it'.[10]

8.10 The main advantages of negotiations are their informality and the fact that, if they proceed to an agreed settlement, a compromise is probable. Each party is more likely to feel satisfied that they have protected their important interests in the dispute. On the other hand, the absence of an impartial participant means that it is more difficult to resolve disputed issues of fact. It is also easier for a State in a stronger bargaining position to advance its own claims, and to insist upon preconditions for negotiation. Negotiations are also frequently dominated by political considerations, with legal arguments often playing a secondary role.

8.11 Where negotiations are successful in resolving an international dispute, they usually result in a settlement embodied in a binding agreement, sometimes in the form of a treaty.

Enquiry

8.12 It may be that negotiations are impeded by the inability of the parties to reach agreement about issues of fact. In such circumstances, the mechanism of enquiry may be particularly useful. Enquiry occurs where the parties commission a third person or committee to investigate disputed issues of fact and make determinations on those issues. Indeed, enquiry is sometimes referred to as 'fact finding'. In practice, an enquiry will be carried out by persons who are nationals of third States, sometimes assisted by nationals of the disputing States. The disputing States will often agree to be bound by the findings of those carrying out the enquiry.

Notwithstanding that the UN General Assembly has urged greater use of enquiry,[11] it remains a relatively unusual procedure. The Hague Conventions on the Pacific Settlement of Disputes (1899 and 1907)[12] contain provisions facilitating the establishment of commissions of enquiry.

---

9. *Mavrommatis Palestine Concessions* case *(Jurisdiction) (Greece v United Kingdom)* PCIJ Rep (1924) Ser A No 2.
10. *North Sea Continental Shelf* cases *(Germany v Denmark, Germany v Netherlands)* ICJ Rep (1969) 3, para 85.
11. Resolution 2329 (XXII) (1967).
12. See also **1.12**.

Good offices and mediation

8.13   Good offices and mediation are two closely related dispute settlement mechanisms. As with enquiry, they both involve third parties and they are both directed to assisting the parties reach a negotiated settlement. Good offices involve the intercession of a third party with the relatively limited aim of bringing the parties together and, perhaps, providing them with a preliminary agenda. The Secretary-General of the United Nations sometimes employs good offices in order to start disputants talking to each other, but there is no restriction on the identity of the person or institution qualified to use good offices. The Pope has also frequently used good offices to help resolve international disputes. As the name of the mechanism suggests, it will typically be exercised by a person occupying a post enjoying the trust or respect of both disputing States.

Mediation involves a somewhat higher level of involvement for the third party who is seeking to assist the disputing States in their negotiations. In addition to bringing the parties together, the mediator will play a role in the negotiations themselves. This role will fall short of adjudication, but will involve the making of suggestions, alternative proposals and attempts at reconciling conflicting positions. The object is to help the parties reach an agreed settlement.

Conciliation

8.14   Conciliation closely resembles mediation. Indeed, the terms are sometimes used interchangeably. Essentially, conciliation is a more formalised version of mediation and typically involves the appointment of a conciliation commission by the disputing States. It may resemble arbitral or judicial proceedings in some respects, but its conclusions take the form of recommendations or opinions rather than a binding determination, award or judgment. The Hague Conventions on the Pacific Settlement of Disputes (1899 and 1907) contain provisions facilitating the establishment of conciliation commissions by the parties to a dispute.

Arbitration

8.15   The International Law Commission has defined arbitration as 'a procedure for the settlement of disputes between states by a binding award on the basis of law and as a result of an undertaking voluntarily accepted'.[13]

8.16   Arbitration is a formal dispute settlement mechanism which differs importantly from negotiation, enquiry, good offices, mediation

---

13.   *Yearbook of the International Law Commission,* 1952, Vol II, 202.

and conciliation in that it results in a legally binding determination by a person or persons not party to the dispute.

Arbitration resembles judicial settlement inasmuch as it involves a formal adjudication of factual and legal issues according to procedures which are identifiably judicial. It differs from judicial settlement in two important respects.

First, the composition of an arbitral tribunal is determined by the choice of the disputing States. Membership of international courts, by contrast, is generally predetermined so that the parties must accept the court's membership as they find it. Second, arbitration permits the parties themselves to select the law and the rules of procedure applicable to their dispute. International courts are generally bound to apply a predetermined body of law (for example, international law in the case of the International Court of Justice, or European Community law in the case of the European Court of Justice) and their procedures are likewise fixed in their statutes and rules.

8.17   States can never be compelled to submit a dispute to arbitration. Arbitration is always the result of an agreement to arbitrate between the disputing States. In practice, there are two types of agreement.

Disputes can arise in connection with matters which are not regulated by treaty, or where the regulating treaty does not specify an obligation to arbitrate. In such cases, the disputing States may conclude a legally binding agreement known as a *compromis,* whereby the parties commit themselves to arbitrate their differences. A *compromis* specifies a range of important matters, including the questions which the arbitral tribunal is expected to resolve, the law and procedure to be applied, the period within which an arbitral award (that is, a decision or judgment) is to be delivered, and the number and identity of the arbitrators. Finally, a *compromis* contains a binding commitment by the parties to abide by the results of the arbitration.

States may also be in dispute about matters which are regulated by a treaty which already contains a requirement to arbitrate. Where this occurs, the parties must comply with their treaty obligation to submit to arbitration in terms required by the treaty. To the extent that the treaty obligation has not already dealt with matters normally specified in a *compromis,* the parties will conclude a *compromis* regulating those matters and perhaps reiterating matters already required by the treaty.

8.18   Treaties which contain a requirement to arbitrate usually impose such an obligation where a 'dispute' arises concerning the treaty's interpretation or application and negotiations have proved unsuccessful in resolving the matter. Whether a dispute has arisen such as to engage an obligation to arbitrate is a question capable of objective verification.

In the ***Interpretation of Peace Treaties* advisory opinion,**[14] Bulgaria, Hungary and Romania had concluded treaties ending hostilities with the allied powers at the close of the Second World War. Subsequently, some of the allied powers accused the new communist dictatorships in Bulgaria, Hungary and Romania of violating their obligations under the peace treaties 'to secure to all persons under [their] jurisdiction, without distinction as to race, sex, language or religion, the enjoyment of human rights and of the fundamental freedoms, including fundamental freedom of expression, of press and publication, of religious worship, of political opinion and of public meeting'. The treaties provided that in the event of a dispute arising concerning a treaty's interpretation or execution, and negotiations proving unsuccessful, a three-member arbitration commission would be appointed. The commission was to consist of one representative of the allied powers, one representative of Bulgaria, Hungary or Romania (as the case required), and a third member selected by mutual agreement of the two parties from nationals of a third country. In the event that the parties could not agree on the identity of the third member, the Secretary-General of the United Nations would make the appointment. Some of the allied powers sought to establish arbitration commissions, but Bulgaria, Hungary and Romania refused to appoint a representative. The General Assembly asked the International Court of Justice for an advisory opinion on the question, inter alia, as to whether Bulgaria, Hungary and Romania were in breach of their international obligations by refusing to appoint a representative. Bulgaria, Hungary and Romania denied that any dispute existed which obliged them to make an appointment. The Court said:[15]

> Whether there exists an international dispute is a matter for objective determination. The mere denial of the existence of a dispute does not prove its non-existence. In the diplomatic correspondence submitted to the Court, the United Kingdom, acting in association with Australia, Canada and New Zealand, and the United States of America, charged Bulgaria, Hungary and Romania with having violated, in various ways, the provisions of the articles dealing with human rights and fundamental freedoms in the Peace Treaties and called upon the three Governments to take remedial measures to carry out their obligations under the Treaties. The three Governments, on the other hand, denied the charges. There has thus arisen a situation in which the two sides hold clearly opposite views concerning the question of the performance or non-performance of certain treaty obligations. Confronted with such a situation, the Court must conclude that international disputes have arisen.

The Court held that Bulgaria, Hungary and Romania were each under an obligation to appoint a representative to the arbitration commissions required to be established under their respective peace treaties. After delivery of the advisory opinion, the three communist-controlled States continued in their refusal to appoint representatives. The matter was brought back to the court several months later for a second phase hearing.[16] The Court was asked for an advisory opinion on the question of whether, absent the requisite cooperation of the three States, the Secretary-General of the United Nations could appoint the third members of the arbitration commissions. The Court was of the opinion that, as the parties to the treaties had not authorised the Secretary-General to appoint persons in place of a party's representative, he could not do so without that party's consent. According to the Court:[17]

---

14. *Interpretation of Peace Treaties with Bulgaria, Hungary and Romania* advisory opinion, ICJ Rep (1950) 65.
15. Ibid, 74.
16. *Interpretation of Peace Treaties with Bulgaria, Hungary and Romania* advisory opinion, Second Phase, ICJ Rep (1950) 221.
17. Ibid, 229.

> The principle of interpretation expressed in the maxim: *Ut res magis valeat quam pereat,* often referred to as the rule of effectiveness, cannot justify the Court in attributing to the provisions for the settlement of disputes in the Peace Treaties a meaning which ... would be contrary to their letter and spirit.

8.19   The drafting of a *compromis* is facilitated by the existence of certain model rules of arbitration procedure. Most prominent among these are model rules on arbitration contained in the Hague Conventions on the Pacific Settlement of Disputes (1899 and 1907), the General Act for the Pacific Settlement of International Disputes (1928, amended in 1949) and the Model Rules on Arbitral Procedures (1958) which were proposed by the International Law Commission and adopted by the General Assembly of the United Nations.

8.20   Awards resulting from arbitration are ordinarily binding on the parties as a result of their agreement in the *compromis* or treaty under which the arbitration was conducted. It is unusual for a State to reject the legality of an arbitral award. However, it is possible to seek the annulment of an award when it is tainted by certain legal errors. In the *Arbitral Award* case,[18] the International Court of Justice accepted in principle three grounds upon which such an annulment could be sought:

- **Insufficient reasoning:** It is essential that arbitral awards be supported by adequate legal reasons. A succinct statement of reasons is not fatally flawed provided it is clear and precise.
- **Lack of a true majority:** The arbitral award must be supported by a true majority of the Tribunal. If this is not the case, the award will be void.
- *Excès de pouvoir* **(excess of jurisdiction):** Arbitrators must not refuse to decide questions which, on a true construction of the *compromis* or empowering treaty, have been referred to them. If the arbitrators overstep the authority which the parties have bestowed on them, their award may be declared void.

Excès de pouvoir is more commonly alleged where arbitrators exercise powers which have not been conferred on them or decide questions which have not been referred to them.

In the *Boundary Case between Costa-Rica and Panama*,[19] United States Chief Justice Edward Douglass White (1845–1921), acting as sole arbitrator, declared part of an earlier arbitral award to be 'non-existing'. This decision applied only to that part of the earlier award that purported to fix an international boundary line outside the geographical limits authorised by disputing States in their agreement establishing the jurisdiction of the arbitrator.

It is also generally accepted that an arbitral award can be annulled where the Tribunal has failed in its duty to observe procedural rules binding on it, whether under the terms of the *compromis* itself or in violation of certain general principles of law. Examples of the latter include failure to afford each party an adequate opportunity to present

---

18.   *Case Concerning the Arbitral Award of 31 July 1989 (Guinea-Bissau v Senegal)* ICJ Rep (1991) 53.
19.   *Boundary Case between Costa-Rica and Panama* (1914) 11 RIAA 519.

its case, fraud or corruption on the part of an arbitrator, and perhaps bias in the form of an undisclosed personal interest on the part of an arbitrator.

8.21   There are two arbitral tribunals which are specifically worth noting. The Permanent Court of Arbitration was established on the basis of the Hague Conventions on the Pacific Settlement of Disputes (1899 and 1907). It is not a 'court' in the usual sense of that term, but rather an organisation from which arbitral tribunals can be constructed drawing on a panel of some 300 expert nominees from the States parties. It had 17 cases between 1902 and 1935. From 1935 to 1998, the Court had no cases and one may be forgiven for having thought that it had outlived its usefulness. Since 1998, however, there has been a definite revival of the Court's fortunes, with almost 30 concluded or pending cases. The Permanent Court of Arbitration also played an instrumental role in helping establish the Iran–United States Claims Tribunal.

The Iran–United States Claims Tribunal is perhaps the most significant arbitral tribunal in history. It was established by the Algiers Declarations[20] for the purpose of settling numerous outstanding claims between the United States and Iran, and claims by each of their nationals against the other State. More than 3,800 cases have been filed, with a total value of around US$50 billion. The Tribunal consists of nine members, three appointed by each State and three (third country) members appointed by the six members appointed by Iran and the United States. Claims are decided by one of three three-member chambers of the Tribunal, or by the Full Tribunal. The Tribunal conducts its business in accordance with the arbitration rules of the United Nations Commission on International Trade Law (UNCITRAL), as modified by the two States and the Tribunal. Its decisions are published in the *Iran–United States Claims Tribunal Reports*.

Judicial settlement

Prior to 1945

8.22   Judicial settlement of disputes between States is almost a century old. The Central American Court of Justice was established by treaty in 1907 among Costa Rica, El Salvador, Guatemala, Honduras and Nicaragua.[21] Its jurisdiction included disputes in international law among the participating States.

The Court was dissolved in 1918 after hearing only 10 cases, five of which were declared inadmissible and three of which were commenced at the Court's own initiative.

---

20.   (1981) 20 ILM 224.
21.   Marjorie M Whiteman (ed), *Digest of International Law*, US Government Printing Office, 1963, Vol 1, 39.

8.23   The Permanent Court of International Justice (PCIJ) proved to be a somewhat more successful venture. It was established pursuant to Art XIV of the Covenant of the League of Nations. The Court's Statute was opened for signature in 1920 and came into force in 1921. It held its first session in 1922. The seat of the PCIJ was The Hague. After Germany's invasion of the Netherlands in 1940, the Court virtually ceased functioning. Article XIV authorised conferral on the Court jurisdiction 'to hear and determine any dispute of an international character which the parties thereto submit to it' and to render advisory opinions on any dispute or question referred to it by the Council or the Assembly of the League. During the two decades of its functioning existence, the Court issued 27 advisory opinions and 25 judgments on the merits in contentious cases. Many of the Court's opinions and judgments remain important landmarks in international law and are still regularly referred to by courts, tribunals, legal publicists and legal officers of States.

International Court of Justice

8.24   The Permanent Court of International Justice and the League of Nations were formally dissolved in 1946. The functional successor of the PCIJ is the International Court of Justice (ICJ), which is a principal organ of the United Nations[22] and the principal judicial organ of the United Nations.[23] The Statute of the ICJ is annexed to the UN Charter and every member of the United Nations is also a party to the Statute,[24] which is closely modelled on the Statute of the PCIJ. Almost every State in the world is, therefore, a party to the ICJ Statute. States which are not members of the United Nations may, nevertheless, become parties to the ICJ Statute.[25]

8.25   The International Court of Justice consists of 15 judges, all of whom are elected for renewable nine-year terms by the General Assembly and the Security Council.[26] Candidates are elected from nominees put forward by the groupings of States devised for the purposes of the Permanent Court of Arbitration (Australia is in the 'Western Europe and Others' group). The judges' terms are staggered, so that five judges are elected every three years. The practice of the United Nations is to elect a court which is broadly representative of the members' geographic spread. No two judges may be nationals of the same State.[27]

It has also been the practice to elect one judge from each of the Security Council's permanent members (although China has not always had one of its nationals on the Court). The judges themselves elect the ICJ's President and Vice-President.[28] Only one Australian has served as

---

22.   UN Charter, Art 7(1).
23.   Ibid, Art 92.
24.   Ibid, Art 93(1).
25.   Ibid, Art 93(2).
26.   ICJ Statute, Art 4.
27.   Ibid, Art 3(1).
28.   Ibid, Art 21.

a judge of the ICJ pursuant to these arrangements: Sir Percy Spender (1897–1985) was a judge from 1958 until 1967, and President of the Court from 1964 until 1967. All cases are decided by a majority of the judges hearing it, with the President possessing a casting vote in the event of a tie.[29]

Cases may be heard by the Full Court, for which the presence of at least nine judges is required, or by chambers of at least three judges.[30] Judges are free to hear cases involving their own States. Where a State appears as a party before the Court and it does not already have a judge of its own nationality on the bench, it may exercise its right to appoint a *juge ad hoc* (temporary judge) for that hearing.[31] Two Australians have served as *juges ad hoc*: Sir Garfield Barwick (1903–1997) from 1973 until 1974 (*Nuclear Tests* cases[32]) and Sir Ninian Stephen from 1991 until 1995 (*East Timor* case[33]).

8.26 The International Court of Justice possesses two principal categories of jurisdiction: contentious and advisory. It also possesses an incidental jurisdiction, which empowers it to issue certain interim orders.

Contentious jurisdiction

8.27 A function of the International Court of Justice is 'to decide in accordance with international law such disputes as are submitted to it'.[34] There are two crucial limitations *ratione personae* on the contentious jurisdiction of the ICJ.

8.28 First, only States may be parties before the Court. This means that it is not possible for individuals, corporations, non-governmental organisations or even public international organisations to be parties before the Court, even if all parties to a dispute consent. The Court may, however, 'request of public international organisations information relevant to cases before it, and shall receive such information presented by such organisations on their own initiative'. Furthermore, whenever 'the construction of the constituent instrument of a public international organisation or of an international convention adopted thereunder is in question in a case before the Court', the organisation is to be notified of the case and shall be entitled to receive copies of all the written proceedings.[35]

8.29 The other principal limitation is that, as with arbitration, no State may be subjected to the Court's jurisdiction in the absence of its consent. Under Art 36(1) of the ICJ Statute, the Court's jurisdiction 'comprises all cases which the parties refer to it and all matters specially provided

29. Ibid, Art 55.
30. Ibid, Arts 25 and 26.
31. Ibid, Art 31.
32. See **1.199**.
33. See **8.40**.
34. ICJ Statute, Art 38(1).
35. Ibid, Art 34.

for in the Charter of the United Nations or in treaties and conventions in force'. This means that States may either confer jurisdiction on the ICJ by a 'special agreement' (also known as a *compromis*), whereby they refer a specified dispute to the Court, or accept the Court's jurisdiction in advance by reason of a clause in a treaty already binding on them. An example of the latter arrangement is provided by the Convention on the Prevention and Punishment of the Crime of Genocide:[36]

> Article IX
>
> Disputes between the Contracting Parties relating to the interpretation, application, or fulfilment of the present Convention, including those relating to the responsibility of a State for genocide or for any of the other acts enumerated in Article III [conspiracy, incitement, attempt and complicity], shall be submitted to the International Court of Justice at the request of any of the parties to the dispute.

Treaties which predate the United Nations and the International Court of Justice sometimes contain clauses conferring contentious jurisdiction on the Permanent Court of International Justice or other tribunals established by the League of Nations. Where this is the case, Art 37 of the ICJ Statute operates to confer jurisdiction on the ICJ.

Optional clause declarations

8.30   A State may also express its consent to be subjected to the Court's jurisdiction by making a declaration under Art 36(2) of the ICJ Statute, sometimes referred to as the 'optional clause':

> Article 36
>
> 2. The states parties to the present Statute may at any time declare that they recognise as compulsory ipso facto and without special agreement, in relation to any other states accepting the same obligation, the jurisdiction of the Court in all legal disputes concerning:
>
>   a. the interpretation of a treaty;
>
>   b. any question of international law;
>
>   c. the existence of any fact which, if established, would constitute a breach of an international obligation;
>
>   d. the nature or extent of the reparation to be made for the breach of an international obligation.

8.31   If a State makes a declaration under Art 36(2), it will be exposed to proceedings brought against it by any other State which has also made such a declaration. It therefore establishes a form of compulsory jurisdiction, qualified by reciprocity, in respect of legal disputes brought before the Court and concerning the matters listed in paras a–d of Art 36(2). Both the claimant State and the respondent State must have made a declaration under the optional clause before it will provide the Court with jurisdiction. Optional clause declarations made under

---

36.   UNTS, Vol 78, p 277.

the equivalent provisions in the Statute of the Permanent Court of International Justice remain effective for the purposes of the International Court of Justice.[37]

8.32   Fewer than 70 States have declarations currently in force under Art 36(2) or 36(5). Of the five permanent members of the Security Council, only the United Kingdom has such a declaration. Australia's most recent declaration was made in March 2002, the operative terms of which are as follows:[38]

> The Government of Australia declares that it recognises as compulsory *ipso facto* and without special agreement, in relation to any other State accepting the same obligation, the jurisdiction of the International Court of Justice in conformity with paragraph 2 of Article 36 of the Statute of the Court, until such time as notice may be given to the Secretary-General of the United Nations withdrawing this declaration. This declaration is effective immediately.
>
> This declaration does not apply to:
>
> (a) any dispute in regard to which the parties thereto have agreed or shall agree to have recourse to some other method of peaceful settlement;
>
> (b) any dispute concerning or relating to the delimitation of maritime zones, including the territorial sea, the exclusive economic zone and the continental shelf, or arising out of, concerning, or relating to the exploitation of any disputed area of or adjacent to any such maritime zone pending its delimitation;
>
> (c) any dispute in respect of which any other party to the dispute has accepted the compulsory jurisdiction of the Court only in relation to or for the purpose of the dispute; or where the acceptance of the Court's compulsory jurisdiction on behalf of any other party to the dispute was deposited less than 12 months prior to the filing of the application bringing the dispute before the Court.

8.33   The legal character of declarations made under the optional clause has been described by the International Court of Justice in the following terms:[39]

> 59. Declarations of acceptance of the compulsory jurisdiction of the Court are facultative, unilateral engagements, that States are absolutely free to make or not to make. In making the declaration a State is equally free to do so unconditionally and without limit of time for its duration, or to qualify it with conditions or reservations. In particular, it may limit its effect to disputes arising after a certain date; or it may specify how long the declaration itself shall remain in force, or what notice (if any) will be required to terminate it. ...
>
> 60. In fact, the declarations, even though they are unilateral acts, establish a series of bilateral engagements with other States accepting

---

37.   ICJ Statute, Art 36(5).
38.   [2002] Australian Treaty Series 5.
39.   *Case Concerning Military and Paramilitary Activities in and Against Nicaragua (Nicaragua v United States)* Jurisdiction and Admissibility, ICJ Rep (1984) 392.

the same obligation of compulsory jurisdiction, in which the conditions, reservations and time-limit clauses are taken into consideration.

Reservations

8.34   State practice establishes that declarations under Art 36(2) may be made subject to reservations or conditions, as the text of the Australian declaration demonstrates and as the International Court of Justice has recognised. The principle of reciprocity, upon which Art 36(2) rests, means that if a claimant State has made a reservation or condition, the respondent State may also rely on it.

Among the most common reservations are those dealing with disputes arising before a certain date (usually the date of the declaration); arising out of armed hostilities; in which a different dispute settlement mechanism is specified; involving certain other States; and involving matters falling within the declaring State's domestic jurisdiction.

8.35   A State may specify that its optional clause declaration will be terminated upon the giving of a certain period of notice. If the declaration says nothing about notice, then it is terminable only upon the giving of reasonable notice.

In the *Nicaragua* case, the International Court of Justice held that the principle of reciprocity in its application to optional declarations does not extend to the 'formal conditions of their creation, duration or extinction', but only to the 'scope and substance of the commitment entered into'.[40] The United States was unable to rely on a provision in Nicaragua's optional clause declaration reserving to Nicaragua the right to terminate the declaration upon notice. The United States' own declaration provided for termination on six months' notice. The Court held that the United States could withdraw its declaration after giving the notice specified in its own declaration. The giving of such notice did not, however, deprive the Court of jurisdiction in respect of any proceedings commenced between the time the notice was given and the time the notice was to take effect.

8.36   Currently, around 15 States have declarations in effect under the optional clause which expressly withhold matters falling within the declaring State's 'domestic jurisdiction' from the jurisdiction of the Court. This reflects the proviso in Art 2(7) of the UN Charter:

Article 2

7. Nothing contained in the present Charter shall authorise the United Nations to intervene in matters which are essentially within the domestic jurisdiction of any state or shall require the Members to submit such matters to settlement under the present Charter; but this principle shall not prejudice the application of enforcement measures under Chapter VII.

---

40.   Ibid, para 62.

Self-judging reservations

8.37 There can, therefore, be no objection in principle to a State expressly withholding matters which are essentially within its domestic jurisdiction from the jurisdiction of the International Court of Justice. There may, however, be a difficulty where a State declares that it is the sole judge as to whether a matter falls within its domestic jurisdiction for the purpose of applying its optional clause declaration. Five States have current optional clause declarations containing this sort of reservation (Liberia, Malawi, Mexico, the Philippines and Sudan). Mexico's declaration, for example, provides that it does not 'apply to disputes arising from matters that, in the opinion of the Mexican Government, are within the domestic jurisdiction of the United States of Mexico'.

8.38 It is not clear if these self-judging reservations in optional clause declarations are legally valid and, if they are not, what the consequence is. Such a clause, if legally effective, would appear to give the declaring State authority to veto any decision by the Court to accept jurisdiction in a proceedings to which that State is a party. Article 36(6) of the ICJ Statute provides, however, that if there is a 'dispute as to whether the Court has jurisdiction, the matter shall be settled by the decision of the Court'.

> In the **Norwegian Loans case**,[41] France brought proceedings in the International Court of Justice against Norway in respect of Norway's treatment of certain French nationals who held Norwegian government bonds. Both States had made declarations under the optional clause, with France's containing a proviso that it did not 'apply to differences relating to matters which are essentially within the national jurisdiction as understood by the Government of the French Republic'. Norway's declaration contained no similar reservation, but Norway took the view that the subject matter of the dispute concerned matters falling essentially within Norway's domestic jurisdiction. Norway sought to invoke France's reservation on the basis of reciprocity, with a view to depriving the ICJ of jurisdiction to determine the case. The Court said:[42]
>
>> [I]n the present case the jurisdiction of the Court depends upon the Declarations made by the parties in accordance with Article 36, paragraph 2, of the Statute on condition of reciprocity; and that, since two unilateral declarations are involved, such jurisdiction is conferred upon the Court only to the extent to which the Declarations coincide in conferring it. A comparison between the two Declarations shows that the French Declaration accepts the Court's jurisdiction within narrower limits than the Norwegian Declaration; consequently the common will of the parties, which is the basis of the Court's jurisdiction, exists within these narrower limits indicated by the French reservation. …
>>
>> In accordance with the condition of reciprocity to which acceptance of the compulsory jurisdiction is made subject in both declarations and which is provided for in Article 36, paragraph 3, of the Statute, Norway, equally with France, is entitled to except from the compulsory jurisdiction of the Court disputes understood by Norway to be within its national jurisdiction. …

---

41. *Case of Certain Norwegian Loans (France v Norway)* ICJ Rep (1957) 9.
42. Ibid, 23–27.

The validity of the reservation has not been questioned by the Parties. It is clear that France maintains its Declarations, including the reservation, and that Norway relies on the reservation. ...

The Court considers that the Norwegian Government is entitled, by virtue of the condition of reciprocity, to invoke the reservation contained in the French Declaration ...

The Court's judgment would appear to support the proposition that a self-judging reservation in an optional clause declaration is legally valid. However, the Court expressly declined to examine the legality of France's self-judging reservation on the basis that both States supported its validity. This is curious, as courts generally determine issues of jurisdiction objectively and are not bound by the agreement of the parties. Judge Sir Hersch Lauterpacht (1897–1960), in a separate opinion, agreed with the majority that the Court lacked jurisdiction, but did not retreat from scrutinising the legality of France's reservation.

Judge Lauterpacht:[43] ... I consider that as the French Declaration of Acceptance excludes from the jurisdiction of the Court, 'matters which are essentially within the national jurisdiction as understood by the Government of the French Republic' it is for the reason of the latter qualification an instrument incapable of producing legal effects before this Court and of establishing its jurisdiction. This is so for the double reason that: (a) it is contrary to the Statute of the Court; (b) the existence of the obligation being dependent upon the determination by the Government accepting the Optional Clause, the Acceptance does not constitute a legal obligation. That Declaration of Acceptance cannot, accordingly, provide a basis for the jurisdiction of the Court.

Norway has not accepted the jurisdiction of the Court on any other basis. The Court therefore has no jurisdiction. ... If that type of reservation is valid, then the Court is not in the position to exercise the power conferred on it — in fact, the duty imposed upon it — under paragraph 6 of Article 36 of its Statute. ... The French reservation lays down that if, with regard to that particular question, there is a dispute between the Parties as to whether the Court has jurisdiction, the matter shall be settled by a decision of the French Government.

The French reservation is thus not only contrary to one of the most fundamental principles of international and national jurisprudence according to which it is within the inherent power of a tribunal to interpret the text establishing its jurisdiction. It is also contrary to a clear specific provision of the Statute of the Court ...

Now what is the result of the fact that a reservation or part of it are contrary to the provisions of the Statute of the Court? The result is that the reservation or that part of it is invalid. ...

In accepting the jurisdiction of the Court Governments are free to limit its jurisdiction in a drastic manner. As a result there may be little left in the Acceptance which is subject to the jurisdiction of the Court. ... Their right to append reservations which are not inconsistent with the Statute is no longer in question. But the question whether that little that is left is or is not subject to the jurisdiction of the Court must be determined by the Court itself. ...

An instrument in which a party is entitled to determine the existence of its obligation is not a valid and enforceable legal instrument of which a court of law can take cognizance. It is not a legal instrument. It is a declaration of a political principle and purpose. ...

---

43.   Ibid, 43–58.

> ... I consider that it is not open to the Court in the present case to sever the invalid condition from the acceptance as a whole. For the principle of severance applies only to provisions and conditions which are not of the essence of the undertaking. Now an examination of the history of this particular form of the reservation of national jurisdiction shows that the unilateral right of determining whether the dispute is essentially within domestic jurisdiction has been regarded by the declaring State as one of the crucial limitations — perhaps the crucial limitation — of the obligation undertaken by the acceptance of the Optional Clause of Article 36 of the Statute. ... To ignore that clause and to maintain the binding force of the Declaration as a whole would be to ignore an essential and deliberate condition of the Acceptance.
>
> Judge José Gustavo Guerrero (1876–1958), the last president of the PCIJ and the first president of the ICJ, wrote a dissenting opinion in which he agreed with Judge Lauterpacht that the French reservation was invalid. He took the view, however, that the Court could not be deprived of its jurisdiction because a party had unilaterally issued such an instrument.

8.39   Two years later, in the *Interhandel Case*,[44] a case brought by Switzerland against the United States for the taking of a Swiss national's assets, the International Court of Justice encountered a similar self-judging domestic jurisdiction reservation in the United States declaration. The Court declined jurisdiction on grounds of failure to exhaust domestic remedies and did not address the validity of the United States reservation.

However, Judge Lauterpacht once again issued a separate opinion in which he reiterated his views on self-judging domestic jurisdiction reservations in the *Norwegian Loans* case, and Judge Sir Percy Spender (1897–1985) effectively concurred with him on this point. President Helge Klæstad (1885–1965) and Judge Enrique Armand-Ugón (1893–1984) agreed that the United States reservation contravened Art 36(6) and was invalid.

In a dissenting opinion in the *Nicaragua* case, Judge Steven Schwebel expressed approval of Judge Lauterpacht's reasoning, but noted that a number of States had continued to treat this type of reservation as valid — thereby rendering 'Judge Lauterpacht's analysis less compelling today'.[45] Nevertheless, in the period following the *Norwegian Loans* case and the *Interhandel Case*, several States withdrew their self-judging domestic jurisdiction reservations (for example, India, Pakistan and the United Kingdom).

Rights and obligations of third States

8.40   A dispute will occasionally come before the International Court of Justice in which, if the matter were to proceed to final judgment, it would be necessary for the Court to determine the legal rights and obligations of a State which is not party to the proceedings.

---

44.   *Interhandel Case (Switzerland v United States)* ICJ Rep (1959) 6.
45.   *Case Concerning Military and Paramilitary Activities in and Against Nicaragua (Nicaragua v United States)* Jurisdiction and Admissibility, ICJ Rep (1984) 392, 602.

In the *Monetary Gold* case,[46] Italy commenced proceedings in the ICJ against three allied powers in the Second World War regarding a decision made by an arbitral tribunal about the disbursement of monetary gold seized by Germany from a bank in Rome. The gold fell under allied control upon Germany's defeat. It belonged to Albania when it was taken by Germany, and the arbitrator awarded the gold to Albania. Italy claimed the gold as compensation for various acts committed by Albania. The Court declined jurisdiction in the case because Albania had not consented to be subject to the Court's jurisdiction and 'Albania's legal interests would not only be affected by a decision, but would form the very subject-matter of the decision'.[47]

In the **East Timor case,**[48] Portugal commenced proceedings in the International Court of Justice against Australia pursuant to each State's declaration under the optional clause. Portugal alleged that Australia had breached international obligations owed to it when the Australian government concluded a 1989 treaty with Indonesia delimiting the continental shelf between East Timor and Australia. Indonesia had invaded East Timor in 1975 and continued to occupy it in alleged violation of Portugal's sovereign rights over the territory. Australia objected to the Court's jurisdiction because Indonesia was not party to the proceedings. The Court said:

26. The Court recalls ... that one of the fundamental principles of its Statute is that it cannot decide a dispute between States without the consent of those States to its jurisdiction. ...

27. The Court notes that Portugal's claim ... is based on the assertion that Portugal alone in its capacity as administering Power, had the power to enter into the Treaty on behalf of East Timor, that Australia disregarded this exclusive power, and, in so doing, violated its obligations to respect the status of Portugal and that of East Timor.

28. The Court has carefully considered the argument advanced by Portugal which seeks to separate Australia's behaviour from that of Indonesia. However, in the view of the Court, Australia's behaviour cannot be assessed without first entering into the question why it is that Indonesia could not lawfully have concluded the 1989 Treaty, while Portugal allegedly could have done so; the very subject-matter of the Court's decision would necessarily be a determination whether, having regard to the circumstances in which Indonesia entered and remained in East Timor, it could or could not have acquired the power to enter into treaties on behalf of East Timor relating to the resources of its continental shelf. The Court could not make such a determination in the absence of the consent of Indonesia.

29. However, Portugal puts forward an additional argument aiming to show that the principle formulated by the Court in the case concerning *Monetary Gold Removed from Rome in 1943* is not applicable in the present case. It maintains, in effect, that the rights which Australia allegedly breached were rights *erga omnes*[49] and that accordingly Portugal could require it, individually, to

---

46.   *Case of the Monetary Gold Removed from Rome in 1943 (Italy v France, United Kingdom, and United States)* ICJ Rep (1954) 19.
47.   Ibid, para 32.
48.   *Case Concerning East Timor (Portugal v Australia)* ICJ Rep (1995) 90.
49.   See **2.106–2.110**.

respect them regardless of whether or not another State had conducted itself in a similarly unlawful manner.

In the Court's view, Portugal's assertion that the right of peoples to self-determination ... has an *erga omnes* character, is irreproachable. ... [I]t is one of the essential principles of contemporary international law. However, the Court considers that the *erga omnes* character of a norm and the rule of consent to jurisdiction are two different things. Whatever the nature of the obligations invoked, the Court could not rule on the lawfulness of the conduct of a State when its judgment would imply an evaluation of the lawfulness of the conduct of another State which is not a party to the case. Where this is so, the Court cannot act, even if the right in question is a right *erga omnes*.

Accordingly, the ICJ declined jurisdiction in the case.

8.41 The jurisdiction of the International Court of Justice will not, however, be precluded merely because a judgment will indirectly affect the legal position of a State which is not party to the proceedings.

In the **Phosphate Lands case**,[50] Nauru commenced proceedings against Australia in respect of certain environmental damage caused by the mining of phosphate on Nauru. At the relevant times, Australia had been one of three States constituting the Administering Authority in Nauru — the others being New Zealand and the United Kingdom. Neither New Zealand nor the United Kingdom could be compelled to join the proceedings because of the terms of their declarations under the optional clause. Australia objected to the Court's jurisdiction because, inter alia, the other two administering authorities were not parties. The Court said:

55. In the present case, the interests of New Zealand and the United Kingdom do not constitute the very subject-matter of the judgment to be rendered on the merits of Nauru's Application ...

... In the present case, the determination of the responsibility of New Zealand or the United Kingdom is not a prerequisite for the determination of the responsibility of Australia, the only object of Nauru's claim ... In the present case, a finding by the Court regarding the existence or the content of the responsibility attributed to Australia by Nauru might well have implications for the legal situation of the two other States concerned, but no finding in respect of that legal situation will be needed as a basis for the Court's decision on Nauru's claims against Australia. Accordingly, the Court cannot decline jurisdiction.

Legal effect and enforcement of judgments

8.42 The obligation to comply with decisions of the International Court of Justice in contentious proceedings is specified in the UN Charter:

Article 94

1. Each Member of the United Nations undertakes to comply with the decision of the International Court of Justice in any case to which it is a party.

---

50. *Case Concerning Certain Phosphate Lands in Nauru (Nauru v Australia)* ICJ Rep (1992) 240.

2. If any party to a case fails to perform the obligations incumbent upon it under a judgment rendered by the Court, the other party may have recourse to the Security Council, which may, if it deems necessary, make recommendations or decide upon measures to be taken to give effect to the judgment.

A number of judgments of the ICJ in contentious proceedings have never been complied with — for example, the *Corfu Channel Case*,[51] the *Right of Passage* case,[52] and the *Nicaragua* case.[53] The record of compliance is less impressive than for judgments rendered by the Permanent Court of International Justice. Nevertheless, the Security Council has never used its enforcement powers under Art 94(2). States remain free, of course, to use countermeasures as a means of enforcing their legal rights.[54]

Generally speaking, though, judgments of the ICJ have a reasonably good record of being complied with. This is not really surprising, as States which freely submit to the Court's jurisdiction will be likely to comply with its judgments. In practical terms, the main problem for the Court's authority is not non-compliance with judgments, but rather non-submission to its contentious jurisdiction. As we have seen, only about one-third of all States, and only one in five permanent members of the Security Council, have made current optional clause declarations.

In the 65 years since it was established, there have been fewer than 130 proceedings commenced under the Court's contentious jurisdiction.[55] Almost half of the total, however, have been commenced since 1990, so that an increase in the workload of the Court can easily be perceived since the end of the Cold War — albeit from a very low base. Many of the judgments rendered by the ICJ have been highly significant in terms of their impact on international law.

8.43 The doctrine of *stare decisis* does not attach to judgments of the International Court of Justice. This is made clear by the ICJ Statute:

Article 59

The decision of the Court has no binding force except between the parties and in respect of that particular case.

Orthodox doctrine maintains that the ICJ does not create international law; the law is to be found in treaties, customs and the general principles of law. The formal role of the ICJ, as with other tribunals applying

---

51. See **12.51**.
52. See **1.148**.
53. See **9.10**.
54. See **5.66**.
55. These numbers include formally separate proceedings commenced by a single claimant against different State respondents but which are essentially the same dispute — for example, the two proceedings commenced by Germany against Denmark and the Netherlands in the *North Sea Continental Shelf* cases; the three proceedings commenced by the Congo against Burundi, Rwanda and Uganda in the *Armed Activity in the Territory of the Congo* cases; and the 10 proceedings commenced by Yugoslavia against Belgium, Canada, France, Germany, Italy, the Netherlands, Portugal, Spain, the United Kingdom and the United States in the *Legality of the Use of Force* cases.

international law, is to identify the law from these sources and apply it to the dispute in hand. Although the general principles are almost completely static, laws derived from treaties and custom change over time and international lawyers need to be aware that the older a judgment of the ICJ or other international tribunal, the more likely it is to be out of date by reason of changes having occurred in positive international law.

Nevertheless, decisions of the ICJ and the PCIJ are highly influential in terms of shaping the way States and publicists understand international law. Most decisions of the ICJ and the PCIJ are, in practice, widely regarded as being so persuasive as to be virtually conclusive. Indeed, judgments and opinions of the ICJ frequently refer to the Court's own earlier jurisprudence and that of the PCIJ in such a way as to suggest that earlier decisions are virtually binding.

Advisory jurisdiction

8.44 The International Court of Justice also possesses an advisory jurisdiction. The UN Charter provides as follows:

Article 96

1. The General Assembly or the Security Council may request the International Court of Justice to give an advisory opinion on any legal question.

2. Other organs of the United Nations and specialized agencies, which may at any time be so authorized by the General Assembly, may also request advisory opinions of the Court on legal questions arising within the scope of their activities.

8.45 A request for an advisory opinion must come from one of the organs or agencies of the United Nations referred to in Art 96. As the International Court of Justice observed in its *Administrative Tribunal* advisory opinion, it is:[56]

> ... a precondition of the Court's competence that the advisory opinion be requested by an organ duly authorised to seek it, that it be requested on a legal question, and that, except in the case of the General Assembly or the Security Council, that question should be one arising within the scope of the activities of the requesting organ.

8.46 Although the text of Art 96(1) provides that the General Assembly and the Security Council may request the International Court of Justice to give an advisory opinion 'on any legal question', the Court has sometimes examined the relationship between the question posed in the request for an advisory opinion and the activities of the

---

56. *Application for Review of Judgment No 273 of the United Nations Administrative Tribunal* ICJ Rep (1982) 325, para 21.

General Assembly.[57] The ICJ has, however, never declined jurisdiction to respond to a request for an advisory opinion from the General Assembly.

8.47   Where the organ is not the General Assembly or the Security Council, the International Court of Justice will more closely examine the scope of that organ's competence in order to establish the Court's jurisdiction.

In the **WHO Nuclear Weapons advisory opinion**,[58] the International Court of Justice was asked to provide an advisory opinion at the request of the World Health Organization (WHO), an agency of the United Nations. The WHO asked: 'In view of the health and environmental effects, would the use of nuclear weapons by a State in war or other armed conflict be a breach of its obligations under international law including the WHO constitution?' The Court declined jurisdiction to answer the question, saying:[59]

> 21. Interpreted in accordance with their ordinary meaning, in their context and in the light of the object and purpose of the WHO Constitution, as well as of the practice followed by the Organization, the provisions of its Article 2 may be read as authorizing the Organization to deal with the effects on health of the use of nuclear weapons, or of any other hazardous activity, and to take preventive measures aimed at protecting the health of populations in the event of such weapons being used or such activities engaged in.

> The question put to the Court in the present case relates, however, *not to the effects* of the use of nuclear weapons, but to the *legality* of the use of such weapons *in view of their health and environmental effects*. Whatever those effects might be, the competence of the WHO to deal with them is not dependent on the legality of the acts that caused them. Accordingly, it does not seem to the Court that the provisions of Article 2 of the WHO Constitution, interpreted in accordance with the criteria referred to above, can be understood as conferring upon the Organization a competence to address the legality of the use of nuclear weapons, and thus in turn a competence to ask the Court about that.

8.48   Once a request is filed, the Court may invite States and international organisations to appear for the purpose of making written and oral statements and to furnish information.[60]

8.49   Unlike judgments in contentious proceedings, advisory opinions are not legally binding. As their title suggests, they are advisory in nature. As with judgments in contentious proceedings, however, advisory opinions are generally afforded the highest respect by States and

---

57.   For example, *Interpretation of Peace Treaties with Bulgaria, Hungary and Romania* advisory opinion, ICJ Rep (1950) 65, 71; *Legality of the Threat or Use of Nuclear Weapons* advisory opinion, ICJ Rep (1996) 226, paras 11–12; *Legal Consequences of the Construction of a Wall in the Occupied Palestinian Territory* advisory opinion, ICJ Rep (2004) 136, paras 16–17; and *Accordance with International Law of the Unilateral Declaration of Independence in Respect of Kosovo* advisory opinion, 22 July 2010, paras 18–28.
58.   *Legality of the Use by a State of Nuclear Weapons in Armed Conflict* advisory opinion, ICJ Rep (1996) 66.
59.   Emphasis in original.
60.   ICJ Statute, Art 66.

publicists. Indeed, they are usually regarded as constituting authoritative statements of the law to which they relate.

8.50 Sometimes, separate arrangements are made whereby the participants undertake to be bound by an advisory opinion. Where this occurs, the binding force of the advisory opinion derives from the instrument which provides for it. An example of this type of exceptional arrangement is provided by the statute of the International Labour Organization's Administrative Tribunal:

Article XII

1. In any case in which the Governing Body of the International Labour Office or the Administrative Board of the Pensions Fund challenges a decision of the Tribunal confirming its jurisdiction, or considers that a decision of the Tribunal is vitiated by a fundamental fault in the procedure followed, the question of the validity of the decision given by the Tribunal shall be submitted by the Governing Body, for an advisory opinion, to the International Court of Justice.

2. The opinion given by the Court shall be binding.

8.51 The ICJ may answer only a 'legal question'. It is sometimes suggested that the Court will lack jurisdiction, or should decline to exercise jurisdiction, where the question asked is more political than legal.

In the ***Nuclear Weapons* advisory opinion**,[61] the General Assembly requested an advisory opinion in response to the question: 'Is the threat or use of nuclear weapons in any circumstances permitted under international law?' Several States argued that the question was of a political character, and that the Court should therefore not provide an advisory opinion in response to it. The Court said:

13. The Court must ... satisfy itself that the advisory opinion requested does indeed relate to a 'legal question' within the meaning of its Statute and the United Nations Charter. ...

The question put to the Court by the General Assembly is indeed a legal one, since the Court is asked to rule on the compatibility of the threat or use of nuclear weapons with the relevant principles and rules of international law. To do this, the Court must identify the existing principles and rules, interpret them and apply them to the threat or use of nuclear weapons, thus offering a reply to the question posed based on law.

The fact that this question also has political aspects, as, in the nature of things, is the case with so many questions which arise in international life, does not suffice to deprive it of its character as a 'legal question' and to 'deprive the Court of a competence expressly conferred on it by its Statute' (*Application for Review of Judgement No 158 of the United Nations Administrative Tribunal, Advisory Opinion*, ICJ Reports 1973, 172, para 14). Whatever its political aspects, the Court cannot refuse to admit the legal character of a question which invites it to discharge an essentially judicial task, namely, an assessment of the legality of the possible conduct of States with regard to the obligations imposed upon

---

61.   *Legality of the Threat or Use of Nuclear Weapons* advisory opinion, ICJ Rep (1996) 226.

them by international law … The Court moreover considers that the political nature of the motives which may be said to have inspired the request and the political implications that the opinion given might have are of no relevance in the establishment of its jurisdiction to give such an opinion.

14. Article 65, paragraph 1, of the Statute provides: 'The Court *may* give an advisory opinion …' (Emphasis added.) This is more than an enabling provision. As the Court has repeatedly emphasised, the Statute leaves a discretion as to whether or not it will give an advisory opinion that has been requested of it, once it has established its competence to do so. In this context, the Court has previously noted as follows:

> The Court's opinion is given not to the States, but to the organ which is entitled to request it; the reply of the Court, itself an 'organ of the United Nations', represents its participation in the activities of the Organization, and, in principle, should not be refused. (*Interpretation of Peace Treaties with Bulgaria, Hungary and Romania, First Phase, Advisory Opinion*, ICJ Reports 1950, 71) …

The Court has constantly been mindful of its responsibilities as 'the principal judicial organ of the United Nations' (Charter, Art 92). When considering each request, it is mindful that it should not, in principle, refuse to give an advisory opinion. In accordance with the consistent jurisprudence of the Court, only 'compelling reasons' could lead it to such a refusal …

There has been no refusal, based on the discretionary power of the Court, to act upon a request for advisory opinion in the history of the present Court; in the case concerning the *Legality of the Use by a State of Nuclear Weapons in Armed Conflict*[62] the refusal to give the World Health Organization the advisory opinion requested by it was justified by the Court's lack of jurisdiction in that case.

The Permanent Court of International Justice took the view on only one occasion that it could not reply to a question put to it, having regard to the very particular circumstances of the case, among which were that the question directly concerned an already existing dispute, one of the parties to which was neither a party to the Statute of the Permanent Court nor a Member of the League of Nations, objected to the proceedings and refused to take part in any way *(Status of Eastern Carelia, PCIJ, Series B, No 5)*. …

16. … once the General Assembly has asked, by adopting a resolution, for an advisory opinion on a legal question, the Court, in determining whether there are any compelling reasons for it to refuse to give such an opinion, will not have regard to the origins or to the political history of the request or to the distribution of votes in respect of the adopted resolution.

8.52   In the 65-year history of the International Court of Justice, it has received only 26 requests for an advisory opinion. This compares to a total of 27 requests for advisory opinions received by the Permanent Court of International Justice in the 20 years during which it conducted hearings. The ICJ's advisory opinions have dealt with questions ranging over many areas of international law, including the institutional law of the United Nations and its agencies, the interpretation of peace treaties, the status of South-West Africa and the Western Sahara, the threat or use of nuclear weapons, and the status of occupied territories.

---

62. See **8.47**.

Review of acts by the Security Council

8.53   The question of whether the International Court of Justice may review a determination or exercise of power by the Security Council under Chapter VII of the UN Charter is discussed elsewhere.[63]

Other international courts

8.54   The International Court of Justice is not the only international court with jurisdiction to settle disputes between States. The vast majority of cases brought before the European Court of Human Rights and the Inter-American Court of Human Rights involve individual petitioners alleging violation of their rights under the European Convention on Human Rights or the American Convention on Human Rights. However, each court has provision for proceedings between States where an infringement of their respective human rights treaties is alleged.

The European Court of Justice (ECJ) — whose principal role is the interpretation and judicial enforcement of law resulting from treaties establishing the European Coal and Steel Community, the European Community, the European Atomic Energy Community and the European Union — is by far the busiest international court in the world. It has jurisdiction to hear disputes between member States of the European Union, but it is rare for the member States to use this procedure.

The vast majority of cases before the ECJ are commenced by the Commission against member States (the 'enforcement procedure') or involve the ECJ responding to questions about European Community law from the national courts of the member States (the 'preliminary reference procedure').

The dispute settlement procedures of the World Trade Organization (WTO), although not expressed in terms of courts and judges, are in reality an example of the judicial settlement of international disputes.

The procedures may require disputing States to participate in formal hearings of differences arising under the WTO agreements. The States parties are not free to select the members of the Panels which hear the disputes, or of the Appeal Body to which appeals lie from Panel reports, or of the law and procedure to be applied in the hearings. The Panels and Appeal Body make reports which become legally binding after they have been adopted by the Dispute Settlement Body. Adoption is really a formality, as reports are adopted automatically unless rejected by consensus of the more than 140 States represented on the Dispute Settlement Body. This procedure is international judicial settlement in everything but name.

---

63.   See **9.57**.

Question

Lydia and Ephesus are neighbouring States. In January last year, Lydia suddenly adopted a new national flag which bears a striking resemblance to the national flag of Ephesus. When Lydia's new flag was revealed, the government of Ephesus made a vigorous protest through its ambassador in Lydia. Ephesus complained that the new Lydian flag would cause confusion, and that it implicitly resurrected old claims by Lydia to sovereignty over Ephesian territory in breach of the 1973 Treaty of Friendship between the two States.

Over the next three months, Ephesus and Lydia attempted to negotiate a resolution of their differences concerning the new flag. Lydia was adamant, however, that the design of its national flag was a matter entirely internal to itself and there was no dispute between the States that raised any legal issues under the Treaty of Friendship or otherwise.

Lydia also reinforced its Corps of Border Guards near the frontier between the two States. Ephesus has not objected to this measure.

Article 12 of the Treaty of Friendship provides as follows:

Article 12

Dispute Settlement

1. Should negotiations fail to resolve any dispute arising under this Treaty, the parties agree to establish a commission of arbitration to which the dispute shall be referred.

2. A commission of arbitration shall consist of a sole arbitrator appointed by the Secretary-General of the United Nations after consulting the governments of Ephesus and Lydia.

3. The commission of arbitration shall receive evidence and take submissions from both parties.

4. The commission of arbitration shall make an award, including such orders as may be necessary, settling the dispute. The award and orders shall be binding on the parties and the parties agree to implement their terms.

Ephesus approached the Secretary-General, urging him to appoint an arbitrator under Art 12(2) in order to settle the dispute over the flag. After consulting both Ephesus and Lydia, the Secretary-General appointed as arbitrator a retired judge from a third country.

During the course of consultations, Lydia emphasised its opposition to the appointment of an arbitrator on the grounds that no differences existed between itself and Ephesus relating to the subject matter of the Friendship Treaty.

In June last year, the arbitrator conducted hearings into the complaint by Ephesus that the adoption by Lydia of its new flag violated the Treaty of Friendship. The arbitrator invited both States to provide evidence and make submissions.

Ephesus participated in the hearings of the commission of arbitration. Lydia sent a message to the arbitrator declining 'to participate in the proceedings in any way'. According to Lydia's message, the commission lacked jurisdiction in relation to the dispute because the 'issue of Lydia's national flag falls entirely outside the scope *ratione materiae* of the Friendship Treaty, and remains entirely a matter of Lydia's domestic jurisdiction'.

In August last year, and after receiving many volumes of evidence and submissions from Ephesus, the arbitrator delivered his award. The reasons consist of one brief sentence in which he states simply that 'Lydia has violated its obligations under the Friendship Treaty by adopting its new flag and reinforcing its Corps of Border Guards'.

The reasons are followed by two orders: (i) Lydia is to cease using its new flag; and (ii) Lydia must withdraw the recent reinforcements of its Corps of Border Guards.

Lydia is considering making an application to the International Court of Justice to have the arbitrator's award annulled. Both Ephesus and Lydia are members of the United Nations.

Both States have also made declarations accepting the jurisdiction of the International Court of Justice under Art 36(2) of the Court's Statute. The declaration of Ephesus is made without any reservations or conditions. Lydia's declaration is subject to two reservations or conditions. First, the declaration may be withdrawn upon giving notice to the Secretary-General of the United Nations. Second, it withholds from the Court's jurisdiction 'any matter which falls within the domestic jurisdiction of Lydia as determined by the government of Lydia'. Advise Lydia.

Suggested answer

There are two sets of issues associated with Lydia's proposal to apply for annulment of the arbitral award before the International Court of Justice.

- Are there any substantive legal grounds upon which such an application might be made?
- Are there any jurisdictional obstacles which might prevent the Court from hearing the case?

Annulment of the award

States are legally bound by the terms of an arbitral award where they have expressed their consent to that effect. In this case, Lydia has agreed to be bound by the arbitral award by virtue of Art 12 of the Treaty of Friendship under which the commission of arbitration was constituted.

As Lydia's consent is expressed by the terms of a treaty provision, it is also bound to comply with the award by virtue of the principle *pacta sunt servanda*. Lydia is therefore under a prima facie obligation to comply with the terms of the award.

Excès de pouvoir

Although it is unusual for States to regard an arbitral award as a nullity, there are grounds upon which it is possible to do so. One such ground is *excès de pouvoir* — if an arbitrator exceeds the authority conferred on him or her by the parties, the award may be regarded as a nullity (*Arbitral Award* case). This error can occur where the arbitrator exercises powers not conferred upon him or her, or where the arbitrator decides questions not referred to him or her *(Boundary Case between Costa-Rica and Panama)*.

Under the terms of Art 12(1) of the Treaty of Friendship, there needs to be a 'dispute arising under this Treaty' before a commission of arbitration can be established in the first place. Unless such a dispute exists, it must necessarily follow that almost everything a commission of arbitration does will involve it in an *excès de pouvoir*.

It was Lydia's consistent position from the beginning of its disagreements with Ephesus that the issue of Lydia's flag falls entirely outside the scope of matters covered by the Treaty of Friendship. On this view, there was never any 'dispute' within the meaning of Art 12. However, in the *Interpretation of Peace Treaties* advisory opinion, the ICJ emphasised that the existence of a dispute is a matter that is capable of objective verification — the fact that a State denies a dispute exists does not determine the matter. It is enough that one State alleges a violation of a treaty, and the other State denies it. Where such a disagreement exists, there will be a 'dispute' regarding that treaty. In the present case, Ephesus alleged a violation of the Treaty of Friendship, which was denied by Lydia. Notwithstanding Lydia's unilateral view that the design of its flag is not within the scope *ratione materiae* of the Treaty of Friendship, a dispute existed under the Treaty such as to authorise the establishment of a commission of arbitration.

An arbitrator will also exceed his or her powers by deciding a question which was not referred to the arbitrator. In the present case, the only 'dispute' which existed concerned the design of Lydia's flag. Ephesus did not regard Lydia's reinforcement of its Corps of Border Guards as involving a violation of any international legal obligation. Nevertheless, the award purports to decide that Lydia's conduct in this regard violated the Treaty of Friendship and orders the withdrawal of the reinforcements. This probably involved the arbitrator in an *excès de pouvoir,* with the consequence that the Court may nullify the award.

As the *Arbitral Award* case also indicates, an arbitral award may be annulled where it is not supported by sufficient reasons.

A brief statement of reasons is not fatally flawed provided it is clear. In this case, however, the reasons for the arbitrator's award consisted of one brief sentence in which it stated simply that 'Lydia has violated its obligations under the Friendship Treaty by adopting its new flag and reinforcing its Corps of Border Guards'. This is a brief assertion of conclusions, rather than a statement of reasons. It cannot be said that the reasoning by which the arbitrator reached his conclusions has been set out clearly. This provides an additional ground for annulment of the arbitral award.

The Court's jurisdiction

Both Ephesus and Lydia are members of the United Nations. They are both, therefore, parties to the ICJ Statute (UN Charter, Art 93(1)). This entitles Ephesus and Lydia to be parties to proceedings before the Court. Only States may be parties before the Court (ICJ Statute, Art 34), which means that the arbitrator himself may not be a party to any proceedings that Lydia may commence.

The Court is not competent to determine a legal issue in the absence of a State whose 'legal interests would not only be affected by a decision, but would form the very subject matter of the decision' (*Monetary Gold* case; semble *East Timor* case). Any challenge to the validity of the arbitrator's award in this case would involve the legal interests of Ephesus as the very subject matter of the proceedings — that is, the interests of Ephesus in the validity of an arbitral award made in its favour. If Lydia is to challenge the validity of the award before the Court, it will be necessary that Ephesus be made a party to the proceedings.

The fact that States are parties to the ICJ Statute does not mean that they are required to appear as a party before it. The Court's jurisdiction in contentious cases is based on the consent of the States parties to the proceedings. One of the ways in which that consent can be expressed is by making a declaration under Art 36(2) of the ICJ Statute, sometimes known as the 'optional clause'. A State which has made a current optional clause declaration will be exposed to the compulsory jurisdiction of the Court in respect of proceedings commenced against it by any other State that has also made such a declaration. In the present case, both Ephesus and Lydia have made current optional clause declarations, with the result that Lydia may commence proceedings against Ephesus before the Court.

The ICJ has observed that in 'making the [optional clause] declaration a State is equally free to do so unconditionally and without limit of time for its duration, or to qualify it with conditions or reservations' (*Nicaragua* case). The optional clause rests upon a foundation of reciprocity, which extends not only to the declarations themselves, but also to any conditions or reservations forming part of those declarations. This means that a respondent State is entitled to rely both on its own conditions and reservations, and on those contained in the declaration of the claimant State.

The potential respondent State in this case is Ephesus, whose own optional clause declaration has been made without conditions or reservations. However, the principle of reciprocity entitles Ephesus to rely on any conditions and reservations contained within Lydia's declaration. Lydia has made a condition relating to withdrawal of the declaration, and a reservation concerning matters falling within its domestic jurisdiction.

Because Ephesus has not specified any conditions concerning the period of notice to be given for a valid withdrawal of its declaration, it may be withdrawn upon the giving of reasonable notice. Lydia's declaration, on the other hand, permits termination upon giving notice to the Secretary-General of the United Nations. Could Ephesus withdraw its declaration with immediate effect upon giving notice to the Secretary-General, by relying on the withdrawal condition in Lydia's declaration? According to the ICJ in the *Nicaragua* case, the principle of reciprocity in its application to declarations made under the optional clause does not extend to the 'formal conditions of their creation, duration or extinction', but only to the 'scope and substance of the commitment entered into'. The United States was, accordingly, unable to rely on a condition in Nicaragua's declaration permitting withdrawal immediately upon the giving of notice.

Should Ephesus now be considering withdrawing its declaration, it will need to give reasonable notice before such a withdrawal will take effect. The giving of such notice by Ephesus will not deprive the Court of jurisdiction in respect of any proceedings commenced between the time notice was given and the time the notice takes effect.

Lydia's declaration also contains a self-judging reservation withholding any matter falling within Lydia's domestic jurisdiction. The essence of a self-judging reservation is that it purports to confer on the declaring State the exclusive right to determine whether the reservation is operative. In the *Norwegian Loans* case, the ICJ permitted the respondent State to rely on the claimant State's self-judging reservation. The respondent State was able to characterise the subject matter of the dispute as falling within its domestic jurisdiction and therefore outside the scope of its optional declaration. The result was that the Court declined jurisdiction in the case.

The same result was reached by Judge Lauterpacht, albeit on the basis of different reasoning. He took the view that the claimant State's self-judging reservation was invalid because it unlawfully purported to usurp the Court's function under Art 36(6) of its Statute, which provides that if there is a 'dispute as to whether the Court has jurisdiction, the matter shall be settled by the decision of the Court'. He also considered the reservation invalid for the reason that 'the existence of the obligation being dependent upon the determination by the Government accepting the Optional Clause, the Acceptance does not constitute a legal obligation'. It was, instead, 'a declaration of a political principle and purpose'. Judge Lauterpacht took the view that the self-judging reservation was not severable from the claimant State's declaration because such reservations are invariably essential to the consent of the State making the declarations to which they are attached.

The consequence, according to Judge Lauterpacht, was that the whole of the claimant State's optional clause declaration was invalid. As a result, the respondent State's obligation to accept the Court's jurisdiction could not be established on the basis of reciprocity under the optional clause.

Whether one accepts the reasoning of the Court or of Judge Lauterpacht in the *Norwegian Loans* case, the result is likely to be the same for the proposed proceedings by Lydia against Ephesus. If Ephesus chooses to invoke Lydia's self-judging reservation on the basis of reciprocity, and to characterise the subject matter of the dispute as falling within its domestic jurisdiction, the Court is likely to decline jurisdiction to hear and determine the case.

If Lydia wishes to pursue its proposed application before the Court against Ephesus — and if it thinks that Ephesus would be likely to invoke Lydia's self-judging reservation to defeat the Court's jurisdiction — it might consider withdrawing its current optional clause declaration and replacing it with another which did not contain a similar reservation. This could be done immediately, as Lydia's current declaration is terminable upon notice, and the declaration of Ephesus contains no conditions which might prevent Lydia's new declaration being effective in proceedings brought against Ephesus.

Further tutorial discussion

1. Why has the ICJ, in its nearly 70 years of activity, received about the same number of requests for advisory opinions as the PCIJ in its 20 years of activity?
2. Why are States so reluctant to use the ICJ to settle international disputes?
3. What are the main similarities and differences between arbitration and judicial settlement? Which is better?
4. Should nationals of States which do not have a current declaration under Art 36(2) of the ICJ Statute be eligible for election to the Court? Is election by the General Assembly and the Security Council an appropriate way to select ICJ judges?
5. Why has there been, since about 1990, an increase in cases commenced before the International Court of Justice and the Permanent Court of Arbitration?

International use of force

9

Objectives

After completing this chapter, you should:

(1) possess a broad understanding of the modes in which resort to the international use of force was legally regulated prior to 1945;

(2) understand and be able to explain the prohibition on the threat or use of force prescribed by the UN Charter and the parallel prohibition at customary international law;

(3) understand and be apply to apply the defence of self-defence under the UN Charter and at customary international law;

(4) understand and be able to apply the customary international law principle of non-intervention in the internal affairs of States, and be able to contrast non-intervention with the prohibition on the use of force;

(5) understand and be able to explain the powers of the United Nations Security Council and General Assembly to authorise the use of military force and to require the use of non-military sanctions in international relations;

(6) be aware of claims that States may, as a matter of customary international law, unilaterally use force to protect their nationals from certain threats within the territory of other States; and

(7) be aware of claims that States may, as a matter of customary international law, unilaterally use force to protect foreign populations from humanitarian disasters which the territorial State is unable or unwilling to prevent.

Key cases

Military and Paramilitary Activities in and Against Nicaragua (Nicaragua v United States) Merits, ICJ Rep (1986) 14
Caroline case (1841) 29 *British & Foreign State Papers* 1137–1138, (1842) 30 *British & Foreign State Papers* 195–196
Legality of the Threat or Use of Nuclear Weapons advisory opinion, ICJ Rep (1996) 226
Certain Expenses of the United Nations advisory opinion, ICJ Rep (1962) 151

Key treaties and instruments

Charter of the United Nations (1945): Art 2(3), Art 2(4), Art 14, Art 25, Art 39, Art 41, Art 51, Art 103

Declaration on Principles of International Law Concerning Friendly Relations and Co-operation among States in Accordance with the Charter of the United Nations, General Assembly Resolution 2625 (XXV) (1970)
Resolution on the Definition of Aggression, General Assembly Resolution 3314 (XXIX) (1974): Art 1, Art 3
Declaration on the Admissibility of Intervention in the Domestic Affairs of States and the Protection of their Independence and Sovereignty, General Assembly Resolution 2131 (XX) (1965)
Uniting for Peace, General Assembly Resolution 377 (V) (1950): Art 1, Art 8

Use of force before 1945

9.1   Prior to the emergence of the modern State system, relations between European rulers were conceived principally in terms of the *jus gentium*.[1]

Publicists working within that tradition drew a distinction between just wars and unjust wars. A ruler was forbidden from waging a war unless it was a just war. St Augustine (354–430) was among the first writers to discuss the difference between just and unjust wars. St Thomas Aquinas (1225–1274), building on Augustine's work, argued that a just war must satisfy a number of conditions:[2]

> In order for a war to be just, three things are necessary. First, the authority of the sovereign by whose command the war is to be waged. For it is not the business of a private individual to declare war, because he can seek for redress of his rights from the tribunal of his superior. ... Secondly, a just cause is required, namely that those who are attacked, should be attacked because they deserve it on account of some fault. Wherefore Augustine says ... :
>
>> A just war is wont to be described as one that avenges wrongs, when a nation or state has to be punished, for refusing to make amends for the wrongs inflicted by its subjects, or to restore what it has seized unjustly.
>
> Thirdly, it is necessary that the belligerents should have a rightful intention, so that they intend the advancement of good, or the avoidance of evil. ... For it may happen that the war is declared by the legitimate authority, and for a just cause, and yet be rendered unlawful through a wicked intention. Hence Augustine says ... :
>
>> The passion for inflicting harm, the cruel thirst for vengeance, an unpacific and relentless spirit, the fever of revolt, the lust of power, and such like things, all these are rightly condemned in war.

The just war doctrine was central to the *jus gentium*'s regulation of armed conflict among sovereigns, and survived into the early period of modern international law. Indeed, the distinction between just and unjust wars was of pivotal concern to Hugo Grotius (1583–1645), widely regarded as the founder of modern international law, who sought to

---

1.   See 1.7.
2.   St Thomas Aquinas, *Summa Theologica*, I–II, Q 40 A, c 1266.

place the doctrine on a less theological basis and attempted to transform the requirement for a just cause from an objective requirement into a subjective one.

9.2 Assertions by some contemporary publicists that the just war doctrine never found much reflection in the practice of sovereigns are without foundation. On the contrary, medieval European princes almost invariably sought to justify their military campaigns in terms of the doctrine.

Indeed, even in the modern period prior to 1945, States routinely invoked elements of the doctrine, without necessarily naming it as such, in order to more fully justify resort to armed force against other States. This is not surprising, given that the doctrine is part of the *jus gentium* which, in turn, forms part of the supplementary 'general principles of law recognised by civilised nations'.[3] That such invocations were sometimes mistaken or disingenuous does not diminish the fact that States, in practice, have always recognised the necessity of justifying their use of armed force in terms which go beyond the narrower positive law requirements of treaty and custom.

9.3 Almost from the beginning of the modern State system, however, the just war doctrine began to recede in prominence as the body of positive international law, both customary and conventional, began to accumulate, thereby rendering the general principles of law gradually less significant. This growth in positive international law was accompanied by the growing influence of legal positivism, which on the international plane asserts that only law made by and among States is really law.[4] By the 18th century, the just war doctrine had formally given way to a sovereign right of war under which States possessed a legal right to resort to war for any reason, international law being confined to regulation of acts performed in the course of waging war *(jus in bello)*.

By the 19th century, most publicists were of the view that the just war doctrine, not being part of custom or treaty, did not belong to international law. According to W E Hall (1836–1894):[5]

> International law has ... no alternative but to accept war, independently of the justice of its origin, as a relation which the parties to it may set up, if they choose, and to busy itself only in regulating the effects of the relation. Hence both parties to every war are regarded as being in an identical legal position and consequently as being possessed of equal rights.

J L Brierly (1881–1955) observed that as 'long as this was the attitude of the law to war, the rules concerning recourse to lesser forms of force were somewhat illusory, since these could always be placed beyond criticism by the simple process of declaring war'.[6]

---

3.   See **1.152–1.174**.
4.   See **1.58–1.60**.
5.   W E Hall, *A Treatise on International Law,* ed A P Higgins, 8th ed, Scientia Verlag, Aalen, 1924, 82.
6.   J L Brierly, *The Law of Nations,* ed Sir Humphrey Waldock, 6th ed, Oxford University Press, New York, 1963, 398.

9.4 For most of the 18th and 19th centuries, therefore, positive international law effectively abandoned the central duty of any legal system — that is, defining and regulating the distinction between forbidden and permitted acts of force. The burden of preserving the peace was placed almost entirely upon extra-legal devices, most prominently the European 'balance of power' system. Under this system, shifting sets of alliances were supposed to guarantee that no State or combination of States would ever be strong enough to commence armed hostilities without seriously risking defeat. This system, which was reasonably effective in Europe for almost a century, came to an end with the outbreak of the First World War.

9.5 At the end of the First World War, the Versailles Peace Conference established the League of Nations and attempted to re-regulate resort to war. According to the League's Covenant:

Article 12

The Members of the League agree that, if there should arise between them any dispute likely to lead to a rupture they will submit the matter either to arbitration or judicial settlement or to enquiry by the Council [of the League], and they agree in no case to resort to war until three months after the award by the arbitrators or the judicial decision, or the report by the Council.

The Covenant provided that any member State which failed to comply with Art 12 and related provisions 'shall *ipso facto* be deemed to have committed an act of war against all other members of the League'.[7] It also provided that in case of a threat or act of aggression by one member against another, the League Council was to 'advise' upon the means by which the obligation to respect and preserve the territorial integrity and political independence of all League members was to be fulfilled (Art 10). The Covenant also provided for financial and economic sanctions, though this was not linked to the Council's functions under Art 10. It was mainly the vagueness of these provisions which caused the United States Senate to block American ratification of the Covenant, resulting in the United States' non-membership of the League.

The Covenant did not go so far as to forbid resort to war. On the contrary, war was conditionally preserved as a valid instrument of dispute resolution among the League's member States, provided a State failed to comply with any applicable award, judicial decision or unanimous Council report. Failure by the Council to make a unanimous report in the absence of an arbitral or judicial determination also meant that members of the League maintained 'the right to take such action as they shall consider necessary for the maintenance of right and justice'.[8] Furthermore, as it was only resort to 'war' which was subject to limited control, some aggressor States were inclined to argue that their military actions amounted merely to coercion short of war, and that

---

7. Article 16.
8. Article 15.

their obligations under the Covenant were not affected. An egregious case in point was Japan's invasion in 1932 of Chinese Manchuria.

This systemic weakness was compounded by the absence from the League's membership of some of the most powerful States. The United States never joined, while Germany, Japan, Italy, Spain and Brazil (among 11 others) resigned their memberships. The League's last substantive act was to expel the Soviet Union in 1939 for refusing to submit its dispute with Finland to arbitration.

9.6   The United States and France initiated an attempt to achieve a clearer prohibition on resort to war with the General Treaty for the Renunciation of War as an Instrument of National Policy,[9] also known as the Pact of Paris or the Kellogg–Briand Pact after the US Secretary of State and the French Foreign Minister. By the terms of the Kellogg–Briand Pact, the contracting parties condemned 'recourse to war for the solution of international controversies' and renounced war 'as an instrument of national policy in their relations one with another'.[10]

The Kellogg–Briand Pact, like the League Covenant before it, did not define 'war' and so left open the question of its application to the use of armed force without a declaration of war. Furthermore, the Pact provided no effective enforcement machinery, but contented itself with a declaration that 'the settlement or solution of all disputes or conflicts of whatever nature or of whatever origin they may be ... shall never be sought except by pacific means'.[11] Almost every State had become party to the Kellogg–Briand Pact by the outbreak of the Second World War. Germany's adherence formed part of the prosecution's case against the principal National Socialist defendants on charges of crimes against the peace before the International Military Tribunal at Nuremberg in 1945.[12] This Treaty remains in force today.

Use of force prohibited

9.7   The victory of the allied powers at the end of the Second World War created the conditions for a transformation of international law in the realm of armed force. The Allies had begun referring to themselves as 'the United Nations' as early as 1942. An intergovernmental organisation of the same name was formally established on 24 October 1945 under the leadership of the principal allied powers: China, France, the Soviet Union, the United Kingdom and the United States. The principal axis

---

9.   League of Nations Treaty Series, Vol 94, p 57. The original parties were Australia, Belgium, Canada, Czechoslovakia, France, Germany, India, Ireland, Italy, Japan, New Zealand, Poland, South Africa, the United Kingdom and the United States. A further 39 States (including China and the Soviet Union) subsequently became parties.
10.   Article I.
11.   Article II.
12.   Judgment of the Nuremberg International Military Tribunal (1947) 41 *American Journal of International Law* 172.

powers were permitted to join only after various intervals of time: Italy in 1955, Japan in 1956, and Germany in 1973.

9.8   Article 2(3) of the UN Charter essentially reiterates the rule, contained in the Kellogg–Briand Pact, that all international dispute settlement should be peaceful:

Article 2

3. All Members shall settle their international disputes by peaceful means in such a manner that international peace and security, and justice, are not endangered.

9.9   Article 2(4) of the UN Charter is, however, the crucial provision which transformed international law's requirements concerning the international use of force:

Article 2

4. All Members shall refrain in their international relations from the threat or use of force against the territorial integrity or political independence of any state, or in any other manner inconsistent with the Purposes of the United Nations.

This provision goes further than the prohibition on war prescribed by the League of Nations Covenant, in that resort to war is not preserved as a remedy of last resort should peaceful dispute settlement fail. Rather, the prohibition continues even after peaceful mechanisms prove unsuccessful. Furthermore, Art 2(4) goes further than either the League Covenant or the Kellogg–Briand Pact by proscribing not only 'war', but all threats or use of 'force' which are 'directed against the territorial integrity or political independence of any state, or in any other manner inconsistent with the Purposes of the United Nations'. In opting for the language of 'force' rather than 'war', the Charter makes clear that its prohibition applies even if there has been no formal declaration of war or threatened declaration of war. Article 2(4) represented, therefore, the most comprehensive prohibition on the use of armed force among States in the history of international law.

There are some exceptions. Self-defence[13] and the collective use of force under United Nations authority[14] are expressly provided for under the Charter. Some other possible exceptions which might exist in customary law are the protection of nationals abroad[15] and humanitarian intervention.[16]

Otherwise, the prohibition is complete. In particular, the provision makes it reasonably clear that the just war doctrine can no longer be used to justify the unilateral initiation of war or armed force in international relations, though the doctrine may continue a twilight existence as a foundation for the possible customary law exceptions to the Art 2(4) prohibition. The doctrine's substantive requirements will also, no doubt,

---

13.   See **9.19–9.40**.
14.   See **9.49–9.62**.
15.   See **9.63–9.67**.
16.   See **9.68–9.77**.

continue to inform deliberations leading to the adoption of collective measures and most acts of self-defence, even if its name is not always expressly invoked.

9.10   Although the prohibition in Art 2(4) is contained in a treaty and is expressly addressed only to members of the United Nations, it nevertheless binds all States as a matter of customary international law. Thus, the few States which are not parties to the UN Charter are nevertheless bound by a customary prohibition in terms materially identical to Art 2(4). Even UN member States are bound by the prohibition simultaneously under the Charter and as a matter of custom. This simultaneous binding will be significant in the context of peaceful dispute resolution procedures where, for some reason, Art 2(4) of the UN Charter is excluded from consideration.

In the **Nicaragua case,**[17] a leftist insurgency in 1979 led by Sandinista guerrillas overthrew Nicaragua's military government led by President Somoza. The Sandinistas then formed a government in Nicaragua. In 1981, the United States accused Nicaragua of aiding a leftist guerrilla insurgency in neighbouring El Salvador, a country with which the United States enjoyed close relations. According to the United States, Nicaragua's assistance took the form of allowing its territory and ports to be used to transport Soviet weapons and supplies to the El Salvador insurgents. Furthermore, the United States accused Nicaragua of being responsible for a number of cross-border military attacks against Honduras and Costa Rica, with which the United States also enjoyed close relations. The United States terminated economic aid to Nicaragua, blocked or opposed loans to Nicaragua by international financial institutions, reduced Nicaragua's sugar import quota by 90 per cent, and then imposed a complete embargo on trade between Nicaragua and the United States. Nicaragua accused the United States of, inter alia, training, financing, equipping and organising the Contra insurgency movement whose object was the overthrow of the Sandinista government; laying explosive mines in Nicaraguan ports and territorial waters; participating with the Contras in planning, directing and supporting attacks on Nicaraguan oil installations and a naval base; violating Nicaraguan airspace with US military aircraft; engaging in military manoeuvres with the armed forces of Honduras in proximity to the border between Nicaragua and Honduras; and engaging in naval manoeuvres in international waters near the Nicaraguan coast.

In 1984, Nicaragua commenced proceedings against the United States in the International Court of Justice. Nicaragua alleged breaches of Art 2(4) of the UN Charter, and of similar prohibitions in the Organization of American States (OAS) Charter and customary international law. It also alleged that the United States had unlawfully intervened in Nicaragua's internal affairs, contrary to customary international law. Contentious proceedings before the International Court of Justice can be commenced only if the parties have agreed to do so by treaty or special agreement,[18] or if the respondent State has made a declaration under Art 36(2) of the ICJ Statute accepting the Court's compulsory jurisdiction and subject to any applicable conditions placed on that declaration.[19] In 1946, the

---

17.   *Military and Paramilitary Activities in and Against Nicaragua (Nicaragua v United States)* Merits, ICJ Rep (1986) 14.
18.   See **8.29**.
19.   See **8.30–8.39**.

United States made a declaration under Art 36(2) which included a reservation that it excluded from the declaration's scope 'disputes arising under a multilateral treaty, unless (1) all parties to the treaty affected by the decision are also parties to the case before the Court, or (2) the United States of America specifically agrees to jurisdiction'. The United States denied that the Court possessed jurisdiction to hear Nicaragua's application on the basis that it involved the Court hearing a dispute arising under multilateral treaties (that is, the UN and OAS Charters) while all the parties that stood to be affected by the Court's decision — most notably El Salvador — were not parties to the proceedings. The Court accepted (by 11 votes to four) the United States argument that the multilateral treaty reservation to its 1946 declaration precluded the Court's consideration of possible breaches of the UN and OAS Charters. The Court's judgment goes on to consider whether the Court is thereby excluded from considering whether the United States is in breach of any customary rule parallel to Art 2(4):

174. … The Court would observe that, according to the United States argument, it should refrain from applying the rules of customary international law because they have been 'subsumed' or 'supervened' by those of international treaty law, and especially those of the United Nations Charter. …

178. There are a number of reasons for considering that, even if two norms belonging to two sources of international law appear identical in content, and even if the States in question are bound by these rules both on the level of treaty-law and on that of customary international law, these norms retain a separate existence. This is so from the standpoint of their applicability. In a legal dispute affecting two States, one of them may argue that the applicability of a treaty rule to its own conduct depends on the other State's conduct in respect of the application of other rules, on other subjects, also included in the treaty.

… But if the two rules in question also exist as rules of customary international law, the failure of the one State to apply the one rule does not justify the other State in declining to apply the other rule. Rules which are identical in treaty law and in customary law are also distinguishable by reference to the methods of interpretation and application. A State may accept a rule contained in a treaty not simply because it favours the application of the rule itself, but also because the treaty establishes what that State regards as desirable institutions or mechanisms to ensure implementation of the rule. Thus, if that rule parallels a rule of customary international law, two rules of the same content are subject to separate treatment as regards the organs competent to verify their implementation …

The Court tacitly accepted a United States argument that a State cannot be bound simultaneously by divergent treaty and customary norms on the same subject. This is because the parties have substituted a different standard for the one found in customary law and they are bound to observe that treaty-based standard under the principle of *pacta sunt servanda*.[20] In the case of Art 2(4), however, the Court did not think this precluded holding the parties bound by the parallel customary rule:

181. … so far from having constituted a marked departure from a customary international law which still exists unmodified, the Charter gave expression in this field to principles already present in customary international law, and that law has in the subsequent four decades developed under the influence of the Charter, to such an extent that a number of rules contained in the Charter have acquired a status independent of it. The essential consideration is that both the Charter and the customary international law flow from a common fundamental principle outlawing the use of force in international relations.

---

20. At para 180.

Force

9.11 The precise parameters of 'force' for the purpose of the Art 2(4) prohibition are not clear from the text of the provision itself. For instance, although one would expect it to prohibit an armed invasion by regular military forces across national borders, does it extend to arming insurgents in a foreign country, the acquisition of military hardware possessing a primarily offensive capability, or the use of economic embargoes?

Some guidance may be obtained from the Declaration on Principles of International Law Concerning Friendly Relations and Co-operation among States in Accordance with the Charter of the United Nations (General Assembly Resolution 2625 (XXV) (1970)). This resolution was adopted by the General Assembly without a vote, and is evidence of the requirements of Art 2(4) and of the parallel customary law prohibition.[21] According to Resolution 2625, the duty to refrain from the threat or use of force includes the following obligations:

- A war of aggression constitutes a crime against the peace for which there is responsibility under international law.
- States have a duty to refrain from propaganda for wars of aggression.
- Every State has the duty to refrain from the threat or use of force to violate the existing international boundaries of another State or as a means of solving international disputes, including territorial disputes and problems concerning frontiers of States.
- Every State likewise has the duty to refrain from the threat or use of force to violate international lines of demarcation, such as armistice lines.
- States have a duty to refrain from acts of reprisal involving the use of force.
- Every State has the duty to refrain from any forcible action which deprives peoples referred to in the elaboration of the principle of equal rights and self-determination of their right to self-determination and freedom and independence.
- Every State has the duty to refrain from organising or encouraging the organisation of irregular forces or armed bands, including mercenaries, for incursion into the territory of another State.
- Every State has the duty to refrain from organising, instigating, assisting or participating in acts of civil strife or terrorist acts in another State or acquiescing in organised activities within its territory directed towards the commission of such acts, when the acts referred to ... involve a threat or use of force.

The Resolution expressly resiles from 'enlarging or diminishing in any way the scope of the provisions of the Charter concerning cases in which the use of force is lawful'. Thus, it is not intended to affect the scope of the Charter provisions on self-defence[22] and collective use of force under United Nations supervision.[23]

---

21. *Military and Paramilitary Activities in and Against Nicaragua (Nicaragua v United States)* Merits, ICJ Rep (1986) 14, para 188.
22. See **9.19–9.40**.
23. See **9.49–9.62**.

9.12   In the *Nicaragua* case, the International Court of Justice found that the extensive United States naval manoeuvres off the coast of Nicaragua and the numerous joint United States–Honduran military manoeuvres near the Nicaraguan border did not constitute a violation of the prohibition on the threat or use of force.[24] This was so notwithstanding Nicaragua's complaint that the manoeuvres 'formed part of a general and sustained policy of force intended to intimidate ... Nicaragua into accepting the political demands of the United States'.[25] It would therefore seem that, absent an actual threat to transform them into hostilities, the holding of military exercises does not involve an unlawful threat or use of force.

Furthermore, the Court found that the mere supply of funds to the Contra rebels did not violate the prohibition on use of force, although it did violate the customary law principle of non-intervention. On the other hand, the Court found that the United States, in violation of the terms of Resolution 2625, infringed the customary law prohibition on use of force by organising, or encouraging the organisation of, the Contras for incursion into Nicaragua's territory, thereby participating in acts of civil strife in that country.

The Court also held that the armed attacks on the oil installations and naval bases, the laying of mines in Nicaraguan waters, and the arming and training of the Contra rebels for the purpose of launching cross-border attacks into Nicaragua — all of which the Court found attributable to the United States — violated the customary rule against the use of force.

Aggression

9.13   One of the purposes of the United Nations is 'the suppression of acts of aggression and other breaches of the peace'.[26] Resolution 2625 indicates that a 'war of aggression', and the making of propaganda for such a war, are caught by the rule prohibiting the threat or use of force. The Resolution does not define 'aggression', yet its parameters are important as the term clearly refers to the 'most grave forms of the use of force'.[27]

The concept of 'aggression' is also central to the exercise by the Security Council of its powers to deal with 'any threat to the peace, breach of the peace, or act of aggression'.[28]

9.14   Guidance as to the meaning of 'aggression' can be derived from the Resolution on the Definition of Aggression (General Assembly Resolution 3314 (XXIX) (1974)). According to this resolution, aggression is defined primarily as:[29]

---

24.   *Military and Paramilitary Activities in and Against Nicaragua (Nicaragua v United States)* Merits, ICJ Rep (1986) 14, paras 227–228.
25.   Ibid, para 92.
26.   UN Charter, Art 1(1).
27.   *Military and Paramilitary Activities in and Against Nicaragua (Nicaragua v United States)* Merits, ICJ Rep (1986) 14, para 191.
28.   UN Charter, Art 39. See **9.50**.
29.   General Assembly Resolution 3314, Art 1.

... the use of armed force by a State against the sovereignty, territorial integrity or political independence of another State, or in any other manner inconsistent with the Charter of the United Nations.

This does not carry the matter much further than the text of Art 2(4) of the UN Charter. However, Art 3 of Resolution 3314 sets out certain acts which are said to qualify as acts of aggression. These acts are:

(a) The invasion or attack by the armed forces of a State of the territory of another State, or any military occupation, however temporary, resulting from such invasion or attack, or an annexation by the use of force of the territory of another State or part thereof;

(b) Bombardment by the armed forces of a State against the territory of another State or the use of any weapons by a State against the territory of another State;

(c) The blockade of the ports or coasts of a State by the armed forces of another State;

...

(e) The use of armed forces of one State which are within the territory of another State with the arrangement of the receiving State in contravention of the conditions provided for in the agreement ...

(f) The action of a State in allowing its territory, which it has placed at the disposal of another State, to be used by that other State for perpetrating an act of aggression against a third State;

(g) The sending, by or on behalf of a State of armed bands, groups, irregulars or mercenaries, which carry out acts of armed force against another State of such gravity as to amount to the acts listed above, or its substantial involvement therein.

This list is expressly declared to be non-exhaustive, and the resolution recognises that the Security Council may determine other acts to constitute aggression.[30] Article 3 of Resolution 3314 has been recognised by the International Court of Justice as reflecting customary international law.[31]

9.15 Article 3(g) of Resolution 3314 accommodates the reality of much modern international conflict in which wars and armed attacks are made by proxy or stealth. A State will not be able to evade legal responsibility for aggression by using armed bands of mercenaries, irregulars or terrorists with no formal links to the State. Provided the State has 'sent' them, or has been 'substantially involved' in their sending, and provided they carry out acts of armed force against the target State of such gravity as to amount to any of the acts listed in paras (a)–(f), the sending State will have committed an act of aggression.

9.16 There is disagreement among publicists as to whether the phrase 'against the territorial integrity or political independence of any state, or in any other manner inconsistent with the Purposes of the United Nations' limits the prohibition set out in Art 2(4) of the UN Charter.

---

30. Ibid, Art 4.
31. *Military and Paramilitary Activities in and Against Nicaragua (Nicaragua v United States)* Merits, ICJ Rep (1986) 14, para 195.

According to the permissive view, the inclusion of this phrase indicates that armed force is not forbidden by Art 2(4) if such force is not intended to, and does not, jeopardise the target State's territorial integrity or political independence, and if it is consistent with the purposes of the Charter. Accordingly, armed force which has as its sole purpose, and which is reasonably tailored to achieve, the prevention of certain human rights abuses[32] would not violate Art 2(4).

Furthermore, proportionate acts of armed reprisal for a prior breach of international law would be lawful provided there was no attempt to occupy territory or topple the target State's government. This permissive interpretation has the advantage of being more consistent with the ordinary meaning of the language employed in Art 2(4).

The restrictive interpretation, on the other hand, holds that the intention of Art 2(4) was to prohibit completely a State's resort to force unless a specific exception can be found in the Charter (viz, self-defence and collective security under United Nations supervision). On this view, the reference to 'territorial integrity or political independence' merely describes the complete reality of statehood, and there was no intention to permit any use of force which violates these essentials in any way. According to this view, the phrase 'or in any other manner inconsistent with the Purposes of the United Nations' was intended to prohibit the use of force against non-State entities such as colonies, protectorates and trust territories.

The restrictive interpretation has the advantage of being more consistent with the Charter's *travaux préparatoires* from the United Nations Conference on International Organization, held in San Francisco in 1945 (San Francisco Conference), which indicate that the concluding phrase was intended to strengthen the prohibition on the use of force rather than provide exceptions to it. Furthermore, State practice tends to favour the restrictive interpretation. For example, in Resolution 2625,[33] the General Assembly declared that:

> No State or group of States has the right to intervene, directly or indirectly, for any reason whatever, in the internal or external affairs of any other State. Consequently, armed intervention and all other forms of interference or attempted threats against the personality of the State or against its political, economic and cultural elements, are in violation of international law.

9.17   It is sometimes suggested that Art 2(4) of the UN Charter prohibits not only international acts of armed force, but also non-military pressure of an economic, diplomatic or political character. That Art 2(4) is confined to the prohibition of armed force is, however, made reasonably clear by the Charter's *travaux préparatoires*. A Brazilian amendment to include a reference to 'the threat or use of economic measures' in the text of Art 2(4) was rejected at the San Francisco Conference. Furthermore, in the *Nicaragua* case, the International Court of Justice observed that

---

32.   See **9.68–9.77**.
33.   See **9.11**.

it was unable to regard the United States' extensive economic measures against Nicaragua as violating the customary law principle of non-intervention.[34]

Moreover, the preamble to the UN Charter specifies that the members of the United Nations are committed 'to ensure ... that *armed* force shall not be used, save in the common interest ...'.[35] Although non-military pressure will probably not involve a breach of Art 2(4), the Security Council might nevertheless regard it as constituting a 'threat to the peace' for the purposes of exercising its functions under Chapter VII of the Charter.[36]

It should also be noted that shortly after the *Nicaragua* case was decided, the General Assembly adopted without a vote the Declaration on the Enhancement of the Effectiveness of the Principle of Refraining from the Threat or Use of Force in International Relations (Resolution 42/22 (1987)). While this resolution substantially reiterated Resolution 2625, it added that no State:[37]

> ... may use or encourage the use of economic, political or any other type of measure to coerce another State in order to obtain from it the subordination of the exercise of its sovereign rights and to secure from it advantages of any kind.

Consequently, it may be that coercive non-military pressure of the kind proscribed by Resolution 42/22 is in the process of becoming part of the customary law prohibitions on the use of force or non-intervention.

9.18 The prohibition on the threat or use of force by States in their international relations is not absolute. It is subject to two exceptions which are expressly provided for in the UN Charter: self-defence and collective measures authorised by the United Nations. Of less certain legal status are the defence of nationals abroad and humanitarian intervention, both of which might exist in customary international law.

Self-defence

9.19 States may use armed force in their international relations if they are exercising their right of individual or collective self-defence. The UN Charter provides as follows:

Article 51

Nothing in the present Charter shall impair the inherent right of individual or collective self-defence if an armed attack occurs against a Member of the United Nations, until the Security Council has taken measures necessary to maintain international peace and security. Measures taken by Members in exercise of this right of self-defence shall be immediately

---

34. *Military and Paramilitary Activities in and Against Nicaragua (Nicaragua v United States)* Merits, ICJ Rep (1986) 14, para 245. As to the rule against intervention, see **9.41–9.48**.
35. Emphasis added.
36. See **9.63–9.67**.
37. General Assembly Resolution 42/22 (1987), Art I(8).

reported to the Security Council and shall not in any way affect the authority and responsibility of the Security Council under the present Charter to take at any time such action as it deems necessary in order to maintain or restore international peace and security.

9.20   Some publicists have argued that Art 51 is now the sole source of a State's right of individual or collective self-defence. That provision, however, refers to an 'inherent' right of self-defence. The equally authentic French version of the Charter uses the expression *droit naturel*. This language strongly suggests that Art 51 does not create, but merely recognises, the existence of a right of self-defence and accommodates it to the institutional machinery of the Charter. At the very least, as with the prohibition on the threat or use of force, there exists a parallel customary rule in almost identical terms to Art 51.[38]

9.21   That the right of self-defence is indeed 'inherent' or 'natural' is confirmed by reference to its existence in the *jus gentium*, and hence its inclusion among the general principles of law. As a *jus gentium* principle, it applied to all relations between people, including relations between political communities. Furthermore, in signing the Kellogg–Briand Pact,[39] several States made declarations affirming that, although the Pact made no reference to it, self-defence is a natural or inherent right which remained intact.[40]

9.22   As with most general principles of law, the inherent or natural right of self-defence finds a more precise expression in positive international law. Not only is it given a somewhat sharper form in Art 51, it also existed in customary law long before the Charter's adoption.

In the ***Caroline* case,**[41] there was an anti-British rebellion in Canada in 1837. The *Caroline* was a United States steamboat operated mainly by United States nationals who were sympathetic to the rebellion and who supplied and reinforced insurrectionary forces operating in Canadian territory. Although the United States authorities professed their opposition to the pro-rebel forces in their territory, and took certain steps to frustrate their activities, the United States proved either unable or unwilling to stop the activities of the *Caroline*. While the *Caroline* was moored on the United States side of the Niagara River, a force of Canadian militia under British command forcibly seized the vessel, set her alight, and set her adrift over Niagara Falls. Two United States nationals were killed in the process. A British subject was subsequently arrested in the United States and charged with arson and murder in connection with the attack on the vessel. The United Kingdom sought his release and, in the course of negotiating this demand, senior officials of the United States and British governments exchanged correspondence. The following passage is from the letter dated 24 April 1841 of Mr Daniel Webster (1782–1852) (United States Secretary of State) to the British Minister (that is, ambassador) in Washington DC:

---

38.   *Military and Paramilitary Activities in and Against Nicaragua (Nicaragua v United States)* Merits, ICJ Rep (1986) 14, para 176.
39.   See **9.6.**
40.   Hunter Miller, *The Peace Pact of Paris,* G P Putnam's Sons, New York, 1928, ch 9.
41.   *Caroline* case (1841) 29 *British & Foreign State Papers* 1137–1138, (1842) 30 *British & Foreign State Papers* 195–196.

It is admitted that a just right of self-defence attaches always to nations as well as to individuals, and is equally necessary for the protection of both. But the extent of this right is a question to be judged of by the circumstances of each particular case, and when its alleged exercise has led to the commission of hostile acts within the territory of a Power at peace, nothing less than a clear and absolute necessity can afford ground of justification. …

Under these circumstances, and under those immediately connected with the transaction itself, it will be for Her Majesty's Government to show upon what state of facts, and what rules of national law, the destruction of the *Caroline* is to be defended. It will be for that Government to show a necessity of self-defence, instant, overwhelming, leaving no choice of means, and no moment for deliberation.

It will be for it to show, also, that the local authorities of Canada, even supposing the necessity of the moment authorized them to enter the territories of the United States at all, did nothing unreasonable or excessive; since the act, justified by the necessity of self-defence, must be limited by that necessity, and kept clearly within it. …

In a reply dated 28 July 1842, Lord Ashburton for the British government wrote:

[W]e are perfectly agreed as to the general principles of international law applicable to this unfortunate case. Respect for the inviolable character of the territory of independent nations is the most essential foundation of civilization.

9.23   The statement by Mr Webster as to the appropriate test to be applied for a lawful exercise of the inherent or natural right of self-defence, though couched in terms of a general principle of law ('a just right of self-defence attaches always to nations as well as to individuals'), has come to be generally regarded as setting out the customary law requirements.

The test requires that, before an act of force can be justified on grounds of self-defence, the following elements must all be satisfied:

■ There must be a necessity of self-defence, which is both instant and overwhelming.

■ There must be no choice of means.

■ There must be no moment for deliberation.

■ Those relying on a right of self-defence must show that they did nothing unreasonable or excessive.

9.24   The *Caroline* test appears to set a very high standard for acts of self-defence. In particular, it is frequently interpreted as severely limiting the defending State's right to carry a fight to the aggressor State's territory for the purpose of inflicting a military defeat. Such an interpretation finds, however, no support in State practice. On the other hand, annexing any part of the aggressor State's territory after a military defeat has been inflicted will constitute an act of aggression and an infringement of the occupying State's duty to refrain from the use of force.[42]

---

42.   Viz, General Assembly Resolution 3314, Art 3(a). See **9.14**.

9.25 It should also be recalled that Mr Webster's test was expressly limited to circumstances where there have been 'hostile acts within the territory of a Power at peace'; such were the facts in the *Caroline* case. Indeed, the United Kingdom did not allege that the United States itself was engaged in acts of aggression. These, too, were the circumstances in which the test in the *Caroline* case was expressly reaffirmed by the International Military Tribunal at Nuremberg.[43] The defence argued that Germany's 1940 invasion of neutral Norway was justified in order to pre-empt an imminent British invasion. The Tribunal rejected the defence plea on the grounds that no British invasion was, on the facts, imminent.

9.26 In the *Nicaragua* case, on the other hand, the United States was taken to have justified its measures against Nicaragua by relying on its right of collective self-defence with El Salvador, Honduras and Costa Rica in response to alleged acts of aggression by Nicaragua against those three States.[44] The circumstances taken to be alleged by the United States were, therefore, distinguishable from those in the *Caroline* case or before the International Military Tribunal at Nuremberg; the hostile acts were not performed 'within the territory of a Power at peace', but within the territory of a State which allegedly had already performed acts of aggression. In discussing the content of the customary right of self-defence in this context, the International Court of Justice referred to only some of the elements in the *Caroline* test:[45]

> The Court ... finds that Article 51 of the Charter is only meaningful on the basis that there is a 'natural' or 'inherent' right of self-defence, and it is hard to see how this can be other than customary in nature, even if its present content has been confirmed and influenced by the Charter. Moreover the Charter, having itself recognized the existence of this right, does not go on to regulate all aspects of its content. For example, it does not contain any specific rule whereby self-defence would warrant only measures which are proportional to the armed attack and necessary to respond to it, a rule well established in customary international law.

The Court refrained from mentioning the other elements of the *Caroline* test. In particular, it made no mention of the requirement that circumstances leave no choice of means and no moment for deliberation. In other words, the judgment of the Court in the *Nicaragua* case appears to recognise that a State exercising a right of self-defence in the territory of an aggressor State has a wider latitude of action than where it is exercising that right in the territory of a State with which it is at peace. If this is the case, then a State taking defensive measures in the territory of an aggressor State would be free to engage in deliberation and to choose its means, subject always to the overriding requirement that it does

---

43. Judgment of the Nuremberg International Military Tribunal (1947) 41 *American Journal of International Law* 172, 205.
44. *Military and Paramilitary Activities in and Against Nicaragua (Nicaragua v United States)* Merits, ICJ Rep (1986) 14, paras 130 and 163.
45. Ibid, para 176.

nothing disproportionate, unnecessary or excessive to prevent further attacks by the aggressor State. In addition to reflecting the qualitatively different character of the two types of situations, this interpretation would appear to have the advantage of being in harmony with the overwhelming weight of State practice.

9.27   It is sometimes suggested that the use of nuclear weapons, even in self-defence, could never satisfy the requirements of necessity and proportionality.

In the ***Nuclear Weapons* advisory opinion**,[46] the General Assembly requested an advisory opinion from the International Court of Justice in response to the question: 'Is the threat or use of nuclear weapons in any circumstances permitted under international law?' The Court's reply included the following remarks:

41. The submission of the exercise of the right of self-defence to the conditions of necessity and proportionality is a rule of customary international law. As the Court stated in the case concerning *Military and Paramilitary Activities in and against Nicaragua (Nicaragua v United States of America):* ... there is a 'specific rule whereby self-defence would warrant only measures which are proportional to the armed attack and necessary to respond to it, a rule well established in customary international law' (*ICJ Reports 1986,* p 94, para 176). This dual condition applies equally to Article 51 of the Charter, whatever the means of force employed.

42. The proportionality principle may thus not in itself exclude the use of nuclear weapons in all circumstances. But at the same time, a use of force that is proportionate under the law of self-defence, must, in order to be lawful, also meet the requirements of the law applicable in armed conflict which comprises in particular the principles and rules of humanitarian law.

43. Certain States have in their written and oral pleadings suggested that ... the very nature of nuclear weapons, and the high probability of an escalation of nuclear exchanges, mean that there is an extremely strong risk of devastation. The risk factor is said to negate the possibility of the condition of proportionality being complied with. The Court does not find it necessary to embark upon the quantification of such risks; nor does it need to enquire into the question whether tactical nuclear weapons exist which are sufficiently precise to limit those risks: it suffices for the Court to note that the very nature of all nuclear weapons and the profound risks associated therewith are further considerations to be borne in mind by States believing they can exercise a nuclear response in self-defence in accordance with the requirements of proportionality.

In para 2E of its *dispositif* (the actual answers to the requested advisory opinion), the Court made the following reply by seven votes to seven with the President's casting vote:

... the threat or use of nuclear weapons would generally be contrary to the rules of international law applicable in armed conflict, and in particular the principles of humanitarian law ... However, in view of the current state of international law, and of the elements of fact at its disposal, the Court cannot conclude definitively whether the threat or use of nuclear weapons would be lawful or unlawful in an extreme circumstance of self-defence, in which the very survival of a State would be at stake.

This response by the Court drew particularly scathing dissents from Judge Rosalyn Higgins and Judge Steven Schwebel. Judge Higgins said:[47]

---

46.   *Legality of the Threat or Use of Nuclear Weapons* advisory opinion, ICJ Rep (1996) 226.
47.   Emphasis in original.

27.   The meaning of the second sentence of paragraph 2E of the *dispositif*, and thus what the two sentences of paragraph 2E of the *dispositif* mean when taken together, is unclear. The second sentence is presumably not referring to self-defence in those exceptional circumstances, implied by the word 'generally', that might allow a threat or use of nuclear weapons to be compatible with humanitarian law. If, as the Court has indicated in paragraph 42 (and operative paragraph 2C), the Charter law does not *per se* make a use of nuclear weapons illegal, and if a specific use complied with the provisions of Article 51 *and* was also compatible with humanitarian law, the Court can hardly be saying in the second sentence of paragraph 2E that it knows not whether such a use would be lawful or unlawful.

28.   Therefore it seems the Court is addressing the 'general' circumstances that it envisages — namely that a threat or use of nuclear weapons violates humanitarian law — and that it is addressing whether in *those* circumstances a use of force *in extremis* and in conformity with Article 51 of the Charter, might nonetheless be regarded as lawful, or not. The Court answers that it does not know.

29.   What the Court has done is reach a conclusion of 'incompatibility in general' with humanitarian law; and then effectively pronounce a *non liquet* on whether a use of nuclear weapons in self-defence when the survival of the State is at issue might still be lawful, even were the particular use to be contrary to humanitarian law. Through this formula of non-pronouncement the Court necessarily leaves open the possibility that a use of nuclear weapons contrary to humanitarian law might nonetheless be lawful. This goes beyond anything that was claimed by the nuclear weapons States appearing before the Court, who fully accepted that any lawful threat or use of nuclear weapons would have to comply with the *jus ad bellum* [the law on the use of force] and the *jus in bello* [humanitarian law] …

Armed attack

9.28   In order to understand the circumstances in which a State may invoke the right of self-defence, it is important to ascertain what constitutes an 'armed attack' for the purposes of Art 51 of the UN Charter. In this regard, the International Court of Justice said in the *Nicaragua* case:[48]

> There appears now to be general agreement on the nature of the acts which can be treated as constituting armed attacks. In particular, it may be considered to be agreed that an armed attack must be understood as including not merely action by regular armed forces across an international border, but also 'the sending by or on behalf of a State of armed bands, groups, irregulars or mercenaries, which carry out acts of armed force against another State of such gravity as to amount to' (*inter alia*) an actual armed attack conducted by regular forces 'or its substantial involvement therein'.

The Court was quoting from Art 3(g) of General Assembly Resolution 3314, which it took to be reflective of customary international law. By adopting this approach, the Court appears to be equating 'armed attack' for the purposes of Art 51 of the UN Charter and the parallel customary right with 'aggression' as defined by Resolution 3314.

---

48.   *Military and Paramilitary Activities in and Against Nicaragua (Nicaragua v United States)* Merits, ICJ Rep (1986) 14, para 195.

Thus, subject to the 'scale and effects' test,[49] any act proscribed by Art 3 of Resolution 3314 will constitute an 'armed attack' justifying resort to such armed force as is proportionate and necessary to repel the attack and prevent a continuation or repetition of attacks on the defending State's territory.

9.29   In the *Nicaragua* case, the International Court of Justice focused on the circumstances in which a State's support for rebels in another State may constitute an armed attack. This was because the United States was taken to have relied on its collective right of self-defence against the alleged assistance rendered by Nicaragua to the local insurgents in El Salvador. In this regard, the Court said:[50]

> The Court sees no reason to deny that, in customary law, the prohibition of armed attacks may apply to the sending by a State of armed bands to the territory of another State, if such an operation, because of its scale and effects, would have been classified as an armed attack rather than as a mere frontier incident had it been carried out by regular armed forces.

The Court here introduces a 'scale and effects' test which supplements Resolution 3314 for the purpose of equating 'aggression' with 'armed attack'. Accordingly, an act of aggression must be on a scale, and produce effects, greater than a mere frontier incident carried out by regular forces. This qualification will be particularly relevant not only in the context of internal rebellions, but also where the 'armed attack' is said to result from a cross-border bombardment or use of weapons.[51]

9.30   In the same paragraph of the *Nicaragua* judgment, the International Court of Justice went on to say:

> [T]he Court does not believe that the concept of 'armed attack' includes not only acts by armed forces where such acts occur on a significant scale but also assistance to rebels in the form of the provision of weapons or logistical or other support.

The Court thus draws a distinction between 'the sending by a State of armed bands to the territory of another State', and 'assistance to rebels in the form of the provision of weapons or logistical or other support'. Only the former constitutes an armed attack by a State, and then only if the armed bands carry out attacks which satisfy the 'scale and effects' test.[52]

This is not to say that the provision by a State of weapons or logistical support to rebels in another State is lawful; on the contrary, as the Court observed, such assistance may be regarded as an unlawful threat or use of force,[53] or amount to an unlawful intervention on the internal or external affairs of other States.[54] It should be noted that according to

---

49.   See **9.29**.
50.   *Military and Paramilitary Activities in and Against Nicaragua (Nicaragua v United States)* Merits, ICJ Rep (1986) 14, para 195.
51.   General Assembly Resolution 3314 (XXIX) (1974), Art 3(b). See **9.14**.
52.   See **9.29**.
53.   See **9.9**.
54.   See **9.41–9.48**.

Art 3(g) of Resolution 3314,[55] it is enough for a State to be 'substantially involved' in the sending of armed bands into the territory of another State for the sending State to be guilty of aggression.

It would seem to follow that if armed bands are sent into State A with the substantial involvement of State B, and if those armed bands carry out attacks which meet the 'scale and effects' test, then State B will have committed both an act of aggression and an armed attack on State A.

According to the International Court of Justice, however, a right of self-defence does not arise where the armed attack is committed by persons or groups whose conduct is not attributable to another State.[56] Thus, armed attacks committed by terrorists will not justify acts of self-defence against another State unless that other State sent, or was substantially involved in sending, the terrorists into the territory of the victim State.

9.31 Different considerations of attribution apply when the 'armed attack' is carried out by private persons who have not been sent into the victim State by, or with the substantial involvement of, the alleged aggressor State. Before the conduct alleged to constitute the 'armed attack' can be attributed to the alleged aggressor State, it must be shown that the impugned conduct of the private persons was 'directed or controlled' by that State within the meaning of Art 8 of the Draft Articles on State Responsibility.[57]

Thus, where State A sends, or is substantially involved in the sending of, private persons into State B and those persons perform acts whose scale and effects make them equivalent to an armed attack carried out by regular forces, State A will have committed an armed attack on State B. However, where State A is merely supporting private persons within State B to engage in conduct which satisfies the 'scale and effects' test, State A will not have committed an armed attack on State B unless State A had effective control over the very 'operations in the course of which the alleged violations were committed'.[58]

It is therefore easier to attribute the conduct of private insurgents, guerrillas, terrorists, and other such persons to a State where that State has sent them, or been substantially involved in sending them, into the territory of the victim State. Conversely, it is more difficult to establish attribution where the alleged aggressor State is supporting insurgents, guerrillas, terrorists and others whom it has not sent, or has not been substantially involved in sending, into the victim State. In other words, sending insurgents into the territory of another State is more egregious than supporting insurgents who are already there.

9.32 Whether an 'armed attack' has occurred is an objective question, and is not dependent on the subjective assessment of either the putative

---

55. See 9.14.
56. *Legal Consequences of the Construction of a Wall in the Occupied Palestinian Territory* advisory opinion, ICJ Rep (2004) 136, para 139.
57. See 5.29–5.31.
58. *Military and Paramilitary Activities in and Against Nicaragua (Nicaragua v United States)* Merits, ICJ Rep (1986) 14, para 115.

victim State or the accused aggressor State. Nevertheless, evidence that a State did not, at the time of the relevant events, regard itself as being the victim of an armed attack may be taken into account in assessing the true nature of the events in question.

The requirement in Art 51 of the UN Charter that '[m]easures taken by Members in exercise of this right of self-defence shall be immediately reported to the Security Council' is of significance in determining whether the putative victim State regarded itself as being the victim of an armed attack. A failure to make such a report, either at all or until after the relevant events have concluded, will tend to indicate that the putative victim State did not regard itself as being the target of an armed attack. This will, in turn, weigh against a finding that it was in fact the victim of an armed attack.[59]

It is, nevertheless, possible to foresee circumstances in which a failure to make an Art 51 report would be reasonable and justified — for example, if a State was attacked on such a scale that all its attention was necessarily focused on repelling the attack, it would seem perverse to deny it the legal protection of self-defence because it did not file the correct paperwork with the Security Council.

Thus, a failure to comply with the reporting requirements of Art 51 will likely be relevant only where there are other reasons for doubting that the State in question was the victim of an armed attack. This was, in fact, the approach taken by the International Court of Justice to El Salvador's failure to comply with the reporting requirements of Art 51 in the *Nicaragua* case.

Anticipatory self-defence

9.33 As the International Court of Justice has observed, although the right of self-defence existed in customary law prior to the establishment of the United Nations, 'its present content has been confirmed and influenced by the Charter'.[60] On one reading of Art 51, the circumstances in which the customary right may be invoked have been further narrowed by the requirement of 'an armed attack'. A particularly strict reading of this phrase, favoured by some publicists, would mean that no State could resort to force in self-defence until an armed attack had actually commenced.

On such a reading, even strong evidence of an imminent attack would be insufficient for the target State to engage in military action by way of anticipatory self-defence. This interpretation has the advantage of clarity and transparency, since the true intentions of States are frequently difficult to ascertain; a right of anticipatory self-defence would be open to abuse by aggressor States seeking deceptively to justify their unlawful use of force; and the occurrence of an actual armed attack is easily verifiable.

---

59. Ibid, paras 199–200.
60. Ibid, para 176.

On the other hand, denying the existence of an anticipatory right of self-defence deprives the intended victim of international aggression of such military advantages as may attach to an anticipatory strike, while simultaneously strengthening the hand of the intending aggressor.

One alternative to the strict reading of the 'armed attack' requirement is that it simply qualifies the circumstances in which the Security Council may become involved, while preserving intact the pre-existing customary rules of self-defence. On this reading, also favoured by some publicists, anticipatory military action would be legitimate where all the elements of the *Caroline* test are satisfied. Indeed, the *Caroline* case was itself an instance of attempted anticipatory self-defence by British forces, and the United States clearly admitted that there might be circumstances where such action could be justified on self-defence grounds. Such a reading would also be consistent with a view that Art 51 does not override the putative customary law right of a State to use force in protection of its nationals abroad,[61] a right which is usually justified as an expression of self-defence.

9.34 The International Court of Justice in the *Nicaragua* case expressly refused to comment on 'the issue of the lawfulness of a response to the imminent threat of armed attack' on the grounds that it had not been raised by either side in the proceedings.[62] Nevertheless, the Court found that the right of individual self-defence 'is subject to the State concerned having been the victim of an armed attack' and that '[r]eliance on collective self-defence does not remove the need for this'.[63]

It therefore seems that an 'armed attack' is now a prerequisite for invoking the right of self-defence in international relations, with doubt surrounding only whether such an attack may be anticipated by military action. This view precludes recourse to use of force in self-defence where the cause is a threat to national interests not involving, actually or potentially, an armed attack. Such a use of force would now almost certainly fall within the scope of 'aggression' within the meaning of General Assembly Resolution 3314,[64] Art 5(1) of which provides that '[n]o consideration of whatever nature, whether political, economic, military or otherwise, may serve as a justification for aggression'.

9.35 Anticipatory or pre-emptive self-defence was one of the justifications advanced by the United States and its allies in forcibly removing the government of Iraq from power in 2003 (the primary justification rested upon an interpretation placed upon 17 Security Council resolutions covering the period 1991–2002). The United States and the Security Council accused Iraq of developing and maintaining prohibited weapons of mass destruction and of providing support to international terrorist groups. According to the United States and its

---

61. See **9.63–9.67**.
62. *Military and Paramilitary Activities in and Against Nicaragua (Nicaragua v United States)* Merits, ICJ Rep (1986) 14, para 194.
63. Ibid, para 195.
64. See **9.14**.

allies, the Iraqi regime's weapons program, and its involvement with terrorist organisations which regularly performed actual armed attacks on United States and allied targets, justified the Iraqi regime's removal from power as an act of self-defence. The Iraqi regime's systematic and widespread human rights violations in defiance of Security Council resolutions allegedly provided an additional basis for military action.

The United States-led campaign in Iraq was publicly supported by more than 40 other States, though only three of them (Australia, Poland and the United Kingdom) openly provided the United States with military support inside Iraq. The 2003 allied campaign in Iraq strengthens the case for the existence of anticipatory or pre-emptive self-defence, although a number of other States — led by France, Germany and Russia — regarded the campaign as lacking legal authorisation. International law now holds a State responsible for the attacks of armed groups or bands when the attack was carried out with that State's 'substantial involvement'.[65]

The requirement that an attack be 'imminent' before an act of anticipatory self-defence may be justified has usually been understood in the context of classical international relations where military preparations are readily observable (for example, mobilisation, concentration of forces, and so on). Preparations for terrorist attacks are rarely manifested in such observable ways. Nevertheless, a terrorist attack may be just as devastating as an attack by regular armed forces, especially if it is planned or executed with the substantial involvement of a State. In this new security environment, it may be that the 'imminence' of an anticipated attack is manifested by a record of past attacks accompanied by a refusal to refrain from further attacks. Indeed, most terrorist groups make no secret of their intention to continue attacks on targets associated with their victim States. Where a State is substantially involved with the activities of such terrorist groups, it now runs the risk of exposure to acts of anticipatory self-defence by other States which are targets of armed attacks by those groups. Any such acts will, of course, continue to be legally constrained by the requirements of necessity, proportionality and humanitarian law.

Collective self-defence

9.36 The question as to whether a State has been the victim of an 'armed attack' within the meaning of Art 51 of the UN Charter is not only relevant to the ability of the defending State to engage in acts of armed self-defence against the attacking State, it is also important in determining whether third States are entitled to engage in acts of collective self-defence with the State which claims to have been attacked.

9.37 Article 51 of the UN Charter recognises an inherent right of individual and collective self-defence. The Charter's *travaux préparatoires* from the San Francisco Conference show that Art 51 was inserted partly in

---

65.   See **9.15** and **9.30–9.31**.

order to accommodate certain regional security arrangements, for which the Charter makes express provision in Chapter VIII (Arts 52–54).

Among the most prominent regional arrangements is the North Atlantic Treaty Organization (NATO), consisting of 28 member States in Europe and North America. NATO was established in 1949 by the North Atlantic Treaty,[66] which provides as follows:

Article 5

The Parties agree that an armed attack against one or more of them in Europe or North America shall be considered an attack against them all and consequently they agree that, if such an armed attack occurs, each of them, in exercise of the right of individual or collective self-defence recognised by Article 51 of the Charter of the United Nations, will assist the Party or Parties so attacked by taking forthwith, individually and in concert with the other Parties, such action as it deems necessary, including the use of armed force, to restore and maintain the security of the North Atlantic area.

Any such armed attack and all measures taken as a result thereof shall immediately be reported to the Security Council. Such measures shall be terminated when the Security Council has taken the measures necessary to restore and maintain international peace and security.

The 1951 Security Treaty between Australia, New Zealand and the United States (ANZUS)[67] provides similarly as follows:

Article IV

Each Party recognizes that an armed attack in the Pacific Area on any of the Parties would be dangerous to its own peace and safety and declares that it would act to meet the common danger in accordance with its constitutional processes.

Any such armed attack and all measures taken as a result thereof shall be immediately reported to the Security Council of the United Nations. Such measures shall be terminated when the Security Council has taken the measures necessary to restore and maintain international peace and security.

9.38 The right of collective self-defence entitles third States to use armed force in support of a State which has been attacked. An act of collective self-defence must meet all the requirements of an act of individual self-defence: armed attack on the State entitled to engage in individual self-defence; proportionality; necessity; and observance of the *jus in bello*. Third States seeking to rely on a right of collective self-defence in justification of their use of armed force must also satisfy an additional mandatory requirement of an essentially procedural character.

According to the International Court of Justice in the *Nicaragua* case, the State which regards itself as the victim of an armed attack must call upon the third State to come to its defence. Where no such request has been made, the third State will have no entitlement to engage in acts of

---

66. UNTS, Vol 541, p 244.
67. UNTS, Vol 131, p 84.

collective self-defence.[68] The Court found that, because El Salvador had not called upon the United States to come to its aid until well after the alleged attacks had occurred, the United States was unable to rely on a collective right of self-defence in order to justify its measures against Nicaragua.

9.39 Article 51 of the UN Charter requires States relying on a collective right of self-defence to report measures taken in reliance on that right immediately to the Security Council.[69]

A failure to comply with the reporting requirements of Art 51 will likely be relevant only where there are other reasons for doubting that there has, in fact, been an armed attack on the State said to be the target. This was the approach taken by the International Court of Justice to the United States' failure to make timely compliance with the reporting requirements of Art 51 in the *Nicaragua* case.

Security Council action

9.40 The extent to which Security Council action can abridge a State's right of individual or collective self-defence is discussed elsewhere.[70]

Intervention

9.41 According to Brierly, intervention 'means dictatorial interference in the domestic or foreign affairs of another state which impairs that state's independence'.[71] It is a broad concept which embraces both armed and unarmed State activities which seek to dictate another State's conduct in its internal affairs or external relations. Where an act of intervention involves the use of arms, it is also likely to violate the prohibition on the use of force contained in Art 2(4) of the UN Charter. According to the International Court of Justice in the *Nicaragua* case:[72]

> The principle of non-intervention involves the right of every sovereign State to conduct its affairs without outside interference; though examples of trespass against this principle are not infrequent, the Court considers that it is part and parcel of customary international law. ... [T]his principle is not, as such, spelt out in the Charter. But it was never intended that the Charter should embody written confirmation of every essential principle of international law in force. ... It has ... been presented as a corollary of the principle of the sovereign equality of States.

---

68. *Military and Paramilitary Activities in and Against Nicaragua (Nicaragua v United States)* Merits, ICJ Rep (1986) 14, para 199.
69. Semble **9.32** for the identical obligation with respect to acts of individual self-defence.
70. See **9.59**.
71. J L Brierly, *The Law of Nations*, ed Sir Humphrey Waldock, 6th ed, Oxford University Press, New York, 1963, 402.
72. *Military and Paramilitary Activities in and Against Nicaragua (Nicaragua v United States)* Merits, ICJ Rep (1986) 14, para 202.

The Court has also described the principle of territorial sovereignty, of which the principle of non-intervention is an expression, as 'an essential foundation of international relations'.[73]

9.42   In the Declaration on the Admissibility of Intervention in the Domestic Affairs of States and the Protection of their Independence and Sovereignty (General Assembly Resolution 2131 (XX) (1965)) and the Declaration on Principles of International Law Concerning Friendly Relations and Co-operation among States in Accordance with the Charter of the United Nations (General Assembly Resolution 2625 (XXV) (1970)), the General Assembly expressed a number of normative statements concerning the principle of non-intervention:

- No State has the right to intervene, directly or indirectly, for any reason whatever, in the internal or external affairs of any other State.
- Consequently, armed intervention and all other forms of interference or attempted threats against the personality of the State or against its political, economic or cultural elements are illegal.
- No State may use or encourage the use of economic, political or any other type of measure to coerce another State in order to obtain from it the subordination of the exercise of its sovereign rights or to secure from it advantages of any kind.
- No State shall organise, assist, foment, finance, incite or tolerate subversive, terrorist or armed activities directed towards the violent overthrow of the regime of another State, or interfere in civil strife in another State.
- The use of force to deprive peoples of their national identity constitutes a violation of their inalienable rights and of the principle of non-intervention.
- Every State has the inalienable right to choose its political, economic, social and cultural systems, without interference in any form by another State.

Resolutions 2131 and 2625 have been recognised by the International Court of Justice as expressing the requirements of customary international law.[74]

9.43   By including a reference to 'economic, political or any other type of measure', Resolutions 2131 and 2625 might appear to proscribe a very wide range of activities which are, in fact, regular features of international State practice. Oppenheim argues for a somewhat more restricted conception of unlawful intervention:[75]

> It must be emphasised that to constitute intervention the interference must be forcible or dictatorial, or otherwise coercive, in effect depriving the state intervened against of control over the matter in question. Interference pure and simple is not intervention. There are many acts

---

73. *Corfu Channel Case (Merits) (United Kingdom v Albania)* ICJ Rep (1949) 4, 35. See **12.51**.
74. *Military and Paramilitary Activities in and Against Nicaragua (Nicaragua v United States)* Merits, ICJ Rep (1986) 14, para 203.
75. Sir Robert Jennings and Sir Arthur Watts (eds), *Oppenheim's International Law*, 9th ed, Longman, New York, 1992, § 129, 432–34 (footnotes omitted).

which a state performs which touch the affairs of another state, for example granting or withholding recognition of its government, good offices, various forms of cooperation, making representations, or lodging a protest against an allegedly wrongful act: but these do not constitute intervention, because they are not forcible or dictatorial. Similarly, a state may, without thereby committing an act of intervention ..., sever diplomatic relations with another state, discontinue exports to it or a programme of aid, or organise a boycott of its products. Such measures are often in response to actions or policies of which the state taking the measures disapproves or regards as unlawful, and may be presented by it as a form of 'sanctions'. Although such measures may ... be intended ... to persuade the other state to pursue, or discontinue, a particular course of conduct, such pressure falls short of being dictatorial and does not amount to intervention.

9.44   The act of coercion or dictation must, furthermore, 'be one bearing on matters in which each State is permitted, by the principle of State sovereignty, to decide freely', which will include 'the choice of political, economic, cultural and social system, and the formulation of foreign policy'.[76]

An act of coercion which does not bear on one of these matters will not involve an unlawful intervention. Such may be the case where the coercing State is seeking to enforce an international obligation owed to it, though coercive conduct for this purpose may violate the separate obligation to settle disputes by peaceful means.[77]

9.45   In the *Nicaragua* case, the International Court of Justice observed that the:[78]

... element of coercion, which defines, and indeed forms the very essence of, prohibited intervention, is particularly obvious in the case of an intervention which uses force, either in the direct form of military action, or in the indirect form of support for subversive or terrorist armed activities within another State.

The Court said that acts of this kind also violated the prohibition on the threat or use of force.

9.46   Unlawful intervention can, however, take a form which does not involve a threat or use of force. Thus, according to the International Court of Justice, 'the mere supply of funds' to an opposition group in another State, 'while undoubtedly an act of intervention in the internal affairs' of that other State, 'does not in itself amount to a use of force'.[79]

We have already seen that many of the most common kinds of economic, political and other non-military pressure will not constitute an unlawful intervention, and it is to be expected that most violations of the principle of non-intervention will also violate the prohibition on the use of force.

---

76.   *Military and Paramilitary Activities in and Against Nicaragua (Nicaragua v United States)* Merits, ICJ Rep (1986) 14, para 205.
77.   See chapter 8.
78.   *Military and Paramilitary Activities in and Against Nicaragua (Nicaragua v United States)* Merits, ICJ Rep (1986) 14, para 205.
79.   Ibid, para 228.

9.47 A State which has been the victim of an unlawful intervention in its internal or external affairs is entitled to engage in proportionate countermeasures against the intervening State. In the *Nicaragua* case, the International Court of Justice expressly left open the question of whether the victim State would be entitled to employ proportionate armed force as a countermeasure to an unlawful intervention involving armed force.[80]

9.48 The International Court of Justice in the *Nicaragua* case was clear that there is no right for a third State to engage in armed countermeasures against an intervening State.[81] In other words, there is no right to engage in armed countermeasures analogous to collective self-defence. The Court took the view that a collective use of force is permitted only where there is an express exception to the prohibition on the threat or use of force in Art 2(4) of the UN Charter, and such an exception is to be found only in Art 51 of the Charter.

On the question of whether there is a right for third States to engage in countermeasures which do not involve the use of force, the Court was more ambiguous. On the one hand, the Court emphatically eschewed any consideration of the question.[82] Yet, elsewhere in the judgment, the Court remarked that an unlawful intervention involving the use of force 'could not justify counter measures taken by a third State ... and particularly could not justify intervention involving the use of force'.[83]

United Nations authorisation

Security Council

9.49 A State may engage in the coercive use of force against other States if it has received prior authorisation from the Security Council, which has 'primary responsibility for the maintenance of international peace and security'.[84] The Security Council possesses legally binding 'enforcement powers' under Chapter VII of the Charter (Arts 39–51).

9.50 The key which unlocks the authorisation powers of the Security is the following provision of the UN Charter:

Article 39

The Security Council shall determine the existence of any threat to the peace, breach of the peace, or act of aggression and shall make recommendations, or decide what measures shall be taken in accordance with Articles 41 and 42, to maintain or restore international peace and security.

---

80. Ibid, paras 210 and 249. If the use of force is sufficiently grave as to amount to an 'armed attack', the victim State is undoubtedly entitled to use proportionate armed force in self-defence (see **9.28–9.32**).
81. *Military and Paramilitary Activities in and Against Nicaragua (Nicaragua v United States)* Merits, ICJ Rep (1986) 14, paras 211 and 249.
82. Ibid, para 210.
83. Ibid, para 249.
84. UN Charter, Art 24(1).

9.51   Article 41 of the UN Charter empowers the Security Council to 'decide what measures not involving the use of armed force are to be employed to give effect to its decisions'. The Security Council may 'call upon' the member States to apply such measures, which may include 'complete or partial interruption of economic relations, and of rail, sea, air postal, telegraphic, radio, and other means of communication, and the severance of diplomatic relations'.

9.52   The Security Council is also empowered by the UN Charter to use armed force:

Article 42

Should the Security Council consider the measures provided for in Article 41 would be inadequate or have proved to be inadequate, it may take such action by air, sea or land forces as may be necessary to maintain or restore international peace and security. Such action may include demonstrations, blockade, and other operations by air, sea, or land forces of Members of the United Nations.

The means for the Security Council's use of its enforcement powers under Art 42 were intended by the Charter's drafters to be provided in accordance with Arts 43–47. Under Arts 43 and 45, all member States are obliged to enter into special agreements with the Security Council whereby they make available to the Council, and at its call, their armed forces, assistance and facilities to the extent necessary for maintaining international peace and security. These forces are to be under the command of the Security Council itself, with the advice and assistance of a Military Staff Committee drawn primarily from the permanent members' Chiefs of Staff (Arts 46 and 47). States contributing national forces to a Security Council force may participate in the Security Council's deliberations concerning the use of that force (Art 44).

9.53   It is important to note, however, that the scheme envisioned by Arts 42–47 of the Charter has never become operational. This was the consequence of tensions that emerged among the Security Council's permanent members shortly after the establishment of the United Nations. These tensions heralded the four decades of the Cold War which, because of the veto power held by each of the five permanent members, severely impeded the Council's work across the board.

9.54   Although the enforcement scheme envisaged by the Charter's drafters remains dormant, the Security Council has, in practice, evolved a substitute scheme that finds a general legal foundation in Chapter VII. Instead of the Security Council itself using armed force, it has adopted the practice of authorising States to use force for the purpose of maintaining or restoring international peace and security. This practice effectively reads out of Art 39 the words 'in accordance with Articles 41 and 42'. States are thus authorised, but not compelled, to use force in accordance with a Security Council resolution. Although Art 39 provides no express authority, the Security Council also uses Chapter VII to require States which are deemed responsible for threats to the peace, breaches of the peace, or acts of aggression to cease and desist and to perform any acts which the Security Council determines are necessary to maintain or restore international peace and security.

Perhaps the two most famous instances of this procedure are the Security Council resolutions authorising member States to use force to repel North Korea's invasion of South Korea in 1950, and to eject Iraq from the territory of Kuwait in 1990.

In its resolution of 27 June 1950, the Security Council recommended 'that the Members of the United Nations furnish such assistance to the Republic of [South] Korea as may be necessary to repel the armed attack and to restore international peace and security in the area'. In a subsequent resolution dated 7 July 1950, the Security Council recommended that member States provide military forces and other assistance to a 'unified command under the United States', requested the United States to designate a commander of such forces, and authorised the unified command to use the United Nations flag in the course of operations against North Korean forces. The Soviet Union, which would have vetoed these resolutions, was absent because it was boycotting Security Council meetings. Sixteen member States committed forces to combat in Korea under the unified command.

In Resolution 660 of 2 August 1990, the Security Council demanded 'that Iraq withdraw immediately and unconditionally all its forces' from Kuwait, which Iraq had invaded the previous day. After a number of further resolutions reiterating this demand and requiring States to adopt non-military measures against Iraq under Art 41, the Security Council adopted Resolution 678 (1990), in which it invoked Chapter VII of the Charter and authorised member States to cooperate:

> ... with the Government of Kuwait ... to use all necessary means to uphold and implement Security Council Resolution 660 (1990) and all subsequent relevant resolutions and to restore international peace and security in the area.

As a consequence, a 29-member coalition of States under United States command assembled in the Middle East and successfully ejected Iraq from Kuwait by force of arms in February 1991.

9.55 Before acting under Chapter VII of the Charter, the Security Council is first obliged to make a finding that there is a 'threat to the peace, a breach of the peace, or an act of aggression'.

When it does so, it then has a duty to take 'measures to maintain or restore international peace and security'.[85] It is therefore clear that the Security Council's enforcement powers do not exist to enforce international law in general. Unless a breach of the law also constitutes a threat to, or breach of, the peace or an act of aggression, Chapter VII enforcement powers are not available.

Conversely, it is conceivable that a state of affairs which does not involve the threat or use of armed force between States will nevertheless

---

85.   Ibid, Art 39.

constitute a threat to the peace such that the Security Council will elect to make use of its Chapter VII enforcement powers. For example, Resolution 837 (1993) authorised the Secretary-General to take 'all necessary measures' against those responsible for an attack on United Nations forces engaged in humanitarian relief in Somalia. The attack was carried out by one of the factions in the Somali civil war, and UN member States were urged to contribute 'military support and transportation' to confront and deter attacks on those engaged in the relief effort. The resolution asserted that the situation in Somalia was a threat to regional peace and security and Chapter VII of the Charter was expressly invoked.

This resolution provided legal authority for the United States' ill-fated attempt to capture the factional leader thought to be responsible for the attacks.

9.56 The Security Council is an overtly political body and not a judicial one. While it regularly expresses its collective view as to the legalities of disputes and other situations before it, such expressions are, strictly speaking, evidence of the *opinio juris* of the States that support those views. Nevertheless, given the central place of the Security Council in protecting international peace and security, its collective assessment as to the lawfulness of conduct in disputes or situations before it is not to be lightly disregarded.

However, even if its assessment as to the applicable existing law in a particular case is in error, the Security Council nevertheless retains the authority to make binding determinations and valid authorisations to use force under Chapter VII. This is consistent with the political character of the tasks which the Charter entrusts to the Security Council.

9.57 A more difficult issue arises where it is asserted that the Security Council lacks power to act under Chapter VII because it has incorrectly determined that there is a 'threat to the peace, breach of the peace or act of aggression'. As the International Court of Justice has observed, 'the political character of an organ cannot release it from the observance of the treaty provisions established by the Charter when they constitute limitations on its powers or criteria for its judgement'.[86]

It seems very likely, however, that the International Court of Justice will not review the Security Council's determination that there exists a 'threat to the peace, breach of the peace or act of aggression'. The Court has never impugned the validity or applicability of a Security Council resolution on such grounds, and Judge Sir Elihu Lauterpacht has remarked as follows:[87]

> That the Court has some power [of judicial review over the Security Council's acts] can hardly be doubted, though there can be no less doubt

---

86. *Conditions of Admission as a State to Membership in the United Nations* advisory opinion, ICJ Rep (1948) 57, 64.
87. *Case Concerning Application of the Convention on the Prevention and Punishment of the Crime of Genocide (Bosnia and Herzegovina v Yugoslavia (Serbia and Montenegro))* Further Requests for the Indication of Provisional Measures, ICJ Rep (1993) 325, 439.

that it does not embrace any right of the Court to substitute its discretion for that of the Security Council in determining the existence of a threat to the peace, a breach of the peace or an act of aggression, or the political steps to be taken following such a determination.

In Judge Lauterpacht's view, the International Court of Justice may judicially review a Chapter VII resolution only where it requires a State to breach, or assist in breaching, a rule of *jus cogens* such as the prohibition on genocide. In such a case, according to Judge Lauterpacht, States are relieved of their ordinary obligation to comply with Chapter VII resolutions.

9.58   A State acting in response to an authorisation to use armed force under Chapter VII of the UN Charter will be released from any conflicting treaty obligations. Article 25 of the Charter provides that member States 'agree to accept and carry out decisions of the Security Council in accordance with the present Charter'. The UN Charter goes on to provide that:[88]

Article 103

In the event of a conflict between the obligations of the Members of the United Nations under the present Charter and their obligations under any other international agreement, their obligations under the present Charter shall prevail.

9.59   Article 51 of the UN Charter recognises and preserves the inherent right of individual and collective self-defence in the event of an armed attack 'until the Security Council has taken measures necessary to maintain international peace and security'. The inherent right of self-defence in response to an armed attack is therefore, in principle, temporary and terminates once the Security Council has taken the prescribed measures. Article 51 also requires States exercising their right of self-defence to report immediately to the Security Council the measures they have taken, without prejudice to the 'authority and responsibility of the Security Council under the present Charter to take at any time such action as it deems necessary in order to maintain or restore international peace and security'.

It does not necessarily follow, however, that any action taken by the Security Council in response to an act of aggression will deprive a State of its right of self-defence. Article 51 mentions an 'inherent' right of self-defence and the Security Council is responsible to take action which is 'necessary in order to maintain or restore international peace and security'.

The better view is that a State does not lose its right to continue armed acts of self-defence unless the Security Council's action is actually effective in restoring international peace and security. A State's right of self-defence is recognised as 'inherent' or *'naturel'* by Art 51 of the UN Charter.[89] It would be a perverse result if an aggressor State was able to

---

88.   Semble *Case Concerning Questions of Interpretation and Application of the 1971 Montreal Convention Arising from the Aerial Incident at Lockerbie (Libya v United Kingdom)* Provisional Measures, ICJ Rep (1992) 3, para 39.

89.   See **9.19–9.21**.

inflict a military defeat because the victim State unilaterally complied with resolutions made under a treaty which has among its principal purposes the maintenance of international peace and security and respect for the self-determination of peoples.[90]

This view is supported by State practice. When Argentina invaded and occupied the Falkland Islands in 1982, defeating the British garrison and overthrowing British administration of the territory, the Security Council adopted Resolution 502 (1982). That Chapter VII resolution demanded a ceasefire and the withdrawal of all Argentine forces from the territory. Argentina made it clear that no such withdrawal would occur and the United Kingdom dispatched a naval and military taskforce to reclaim the territory. In the ensuing debate in the Security Council, most States expressed the view that the United Kingdom's inherent right of armed self-defence continued intact for as long as the Security Council's resolution remained unheeded by Argentina and provided the United Kingdom's response was as immediate as the circumstances allowed. Similarly, after the Iraqi invasion of Kuwait in 1990, Security Council debates reflected a broad consensus that Kuwait's inherent right of individual and collective self-defence was not abridged by the Security Council's unheeded demand under Chapter VII for Iraq's withdrawal.

These incidents support the view that a right of self-defence continues even after an armed attack is complete, provided the armed response is launched as quickly as circumstances permit. It also supports the view that a State is permitted to engage in deliberation and choice in mounting its response if the armed attack emanates from a State with which the defending State is no longer at peace.[91]

General Assembly

9.60   According to the UN Charter:

Article 14

... the General Assembly may recommend measures for the peaceful adjustment of any situation, regardless of origin, which it deems likely to impair the general welfare or friendly relations among nations, including situations resulting from a violation of the provisions of the present Charter setting forth the Purposes and Principles of the United Nations.

9.61   After the Soviet Union lifted its boycott of the Security Council's proceedings in 1950,[92] a majority of States in the General Assembly formed the view that the Security Council was failing to control UN military action in Korea. This was because the Soviet veto effectively paralysed Security Council oversight of the campaign. In an attempt to fill this political vacuum, the General Assembly passed, by 52 votes to five with two abstentions, the Uniting for Peace Resolution (Resolution 377 (V) (1950)), which provides in part as follows:

---

90. UN Charter, Art 1.
91. See **9.24–9.27**.
92. See **9.54**.

The General Assembly ...

1. Resolves that if the Security Council, because of a lack of unanimity of the permanent members, fails to exercise its primary responsibility for the maintenance of international peace and security, in any case where there appears to be a threat to the peace, breach of the peace, or act of aggression, the General Assembly shall consider the matter immediately with a view to making appropriate recommendations to Members for collective measures, including in the case of a breach of the peace or act of aggression the use of armed force when necessary, to maintain or restore international peace and security. ...

8. Recommends to the State Members of the United Nations that each Member maintain within its national armed forces elements so trained, organised and equipped that they could promptly be made available, in accordance with its constitutional processes, for service as a United Nations unit or units, upon recommendations by the Security Council or the General Assembly ...

9.62   The Uniting for Peace Resolution has been used on a number of occasions to authorise the assembly and deployment of United Nations peacekeeping forces — for example, Suez (1956), the Congo (1960), Bangladesh (1972), Afghanistan (1980), Namibia (1981) and certain territories occupied by Israel (1982). All these operations were conducted with the assent of the State in whose territory they occurred. The resolution has never been used to authorise coercive military action by one State against another. Nevertheless, the terms of Art 1, the debate preceding the resolution's adoption, and the circumstances in which the resolution was proposed suggest that the General Assembly originally intended such authorisation as a possibility. The International Court of Justice has since ruled on the scope of the General Assembly's powers to authorise the use of force by States.

In the ***Certain Expenses of the United Nations* advisory opinion,**[93] several member States of the United Nations had fallen seriously behind in their mandatory financial contributions to the UN's budget, as determined in accordance with Art 17(2) of the UN Charter. The defaulting States argued that they were not obliged to make the required payments to the extent that they were assessed to meet the expenses of the United Nations Emergency Force (UNEF), which was deployed in Egypt after the Suez Crisis of 1956. The General Assembly had authorised the establishment and deployment of UNEF, but the defaulting States argued that the force was unconstitutional because the Charter assigned responsibility for the maintenance of international peace and security to the Security Council. The General Assembly requested the International Court of Justice to provide an advisory opinion. The Court said:[94]

> The responsibility conferred [on the Security Council to maintain international peace and security by Article 24 of the Charter] is 'primary', not exclusive. This primary responsibility is conferred upon the Security Council, as stated in Article 24,

---

93.   *Certain Expenses of the United Nations* advisory opinion, ICJ Rep (1962) 151.
94.   Ibid, 163.

'in order to ensure prompt and effective action'. To this end, it is the Security Council which is given a power to impose an explicit obligation of compliance if for example it issues an order or command to an aggressor under Chapter VII. It is only the Security Council which can require enforcement by coercive action against an aggressor.

The Charter makes it abundantly clear, however, that the General Assembly is also to be concerned with international peace and security. … The word 'measures' in Article 14, implies some kind of action, and the only limitation which Article 14 imposes on the General Assembly is the restriction found in Article 12, namely, that the Assembly should not recommend measures while the Security Council is dealing with the same matter unless the Council requests it to do so. Thus while it is the Security Council which, exclusively, may order coercive action, the functions and powers conferred by the Charter on the General Assembly are not confined to discussion, consideration, the initiation of studies and the making of recommendations; they are not merely hortatory. Article 18 deals with 'decisions' of the General Assembly 'on important questions'. These 'decisions' do indeed include certain recommendations, but others have dispositive force and effect. …

The Court reviewed the General Assembly's resolution establishing UNEF and related materials. It noted that UNEF was stationed in Egypt with the consent of the Egyptian government and for the purpose of policing a ceasefire agreement between Egypt and Israel, the latter also having consented to UNEF's deployment. It then said:[95]

It is not possible to find in this description of the functions of UNEF … any evidence that the Force was to be used for the purposes of enforcement. Nor can such evidence be found in the subsequent operations of the Force …

It could not therefore have been patent on the face of the resolution that the establishment of UNEF was in effect 'enforcement action' under Chapter VII which, in accordance with the Charter, could be authorized only by the Security Council.

On the other hand, it is apparent that the operations were undertaken to fulfil a prime purpose of the United Nations, that is, to promote and to maintain a peaceful settlement of the situation. This being true, the Secretary-General properly exercised the authority given to him to incur financial obligations of the Organisation and expenses resulting from such obligations must be considered 'expenses of the Organisation within the meaning of Article 17, paragraph 2'.

Protection of nationals abroad

9.63 There is some State practice to support the view that a State may use force in the territory of another State in order to rescue its own nationals whose lives or safety are in danger. This right exists either as an expression or extension of the right of self-defence (which presupposes that Art 51 of the UN Charter does not comprehensively codify the 'inherent' right of self-defence), or as a customary law exception to the prohibition on the use of force.

If the right of protection is viewed as an expression or extension of the right of self-defence, then the threat to the intervening State's nationals is assimilated to a threat to, or attack upon, the territory of the State itself. If it is viewed as an exception to the Art 2(4) prohibition on the use of

---

95. Ibid, 171–172.

force, it might be justified as not involving a violation of the 'territorial integrity or political independence' of the State in whose territory it is performed.

9.64   The *locus classicus* of the right of protection is the 1976 Entebbe incident, in which an Air France airliner on a flight between Tel Aviv and Paris was hijacked by armed terrorists and diverted to Entebbe airport in Uganda. The non-Jewish passengers were released, but about 100 Jewish passengers were held hostage aboard the aircraft. The terrorists threatened to kill the hostages unless a number of Palestinians were released from prisons in several different countries. There was evidence that Ugandan authorities were doing little or nothing to rescue the hostages, but instead assisted the hijackers in a number of ways. Six days after the hijacking occurred, Israel dispatched military aircraft and soldiers to Entebbe and rescued the hostages by military force. Uganda's permission for the operation was not obtained. All the hijackers were killed, as were some Israeli and Ugandan military personnel. The Israeli forces immediately left Uganda with the rescued hostages.

Despite Uganda's protests at the United Nations and elsewhere, neither the Security Council nor the General Assembly condemned Israel's military operation as a violation of international law. In the Security Council debate, the United States representative (Mr Scranton) framed the right of protection in the following terms:

> [T]here is a well established right to use limited force for the protection of one's own nationals from any imminent threat of injury or death in a situation where the State in whose territory they are located is either unwilling or unable to protect them. The right, flowing from the right of self-defence, is limited to such use of force as is necessary and appropriate to protect threatened nationals from injury.

9.65   The United States relied on the right of protection in 1980 in launching its unsuccessful attempt to liberate by military force the hostages held at the United States embassy in Tehran.[96] It also relied on the right when it invaded Grenada in 1983 and Panama in 1989. The United Kingdom relied on the right of protection in 1956 when it sent troops to protect property owned by British nationals in the Suez Canal, but no claims based simply on danger to property have since been made.

9.66   Brierly outlined the right of protection as follows:[97]

> [T]he dispatch of troops to another state's territory to prevent an unlawful expropriation of the property of nationals and other acts of a similar kind are outside the principle and are forbidden by Article 2(4) of the Charter. Whether the landing of detachments of troops to save the lives of nationals under imminent threat of death or serious injury owing to

---

96.   *United States Diplomatic and Consular Staff in Tehran* case *(United States v Iran)* ICJ Rep (1980) 3. The Court did not rule on this aspect of the case.
97.   J L Brierly, *The Law of Nations,* ed Sir Humphrey Waldock, 6th ed, Oxford University Press, New York, 1963, 427–28.

the breakdown of law and order may be justifiable is a delicate question. Cases of this form of intervention have been not infrequent in the past and, when not attended by suspicion of being a pretext for political pressure, have generally been regarded as justified by the sheer necessity of instant action to save the lives of innocent nationals, whom the local government is unable or unwilling to protect. Clearly, every effort must be made to get the local government to intervene effectively and, failing that, to obtain its permission for independent action; equally clearly every effort must be made to get the United Nations to act. But, if the United Nations is not in a position to move in time and the need for instant action is manifest, it would be difficult to deny the legitimacy of action in defence of nationals ... ; this is, of course, on the basis that the action was strictly limited to securing the safe removal of the threatened nationals.

9.67   Publicists agree that the protecting State's armed forces must not exceed what is required to rescue the imperilled nationals. Thus, the infliction of unnecessary damage by the intervening forces, or — worse still — their refusal to leave the receiving State's territory once the nationals have been rescued, will place the intervening State in breach of the rule against the threat or use of force in Art 2(4) of the UN Charter[98] and the principle of non-intervention in customary international law.[99]

Humanitarian intervention

9.68   Humanitarian intervention occurs when a State sends its personnel into the territory of another State, without that State's permission, in order to protect the lives or safety of persons who are not the nationals of the intervening State. Indeed, almost all the persons whose life or safety is threatened will usually be nationals of the territorial State. The threat to life or safety might be a natural disaster, civil disturbance or conduct by the territorial State itself. In the case of natural disasters, the dispatched personnel might or might not include armed forces. If the threat to life or safety emanates from civil disturbance or the conduct of the territorial State, the intervening State will almost certainly dispatch its armed forces.

9.69   Controversy surrounds the existence of a right of humanitarian intervention in international law. If no such right exists, then an act of humanitarian intervention will violate the prohibition on intervention in the internal affairs of other States.[100] If it involves the use of armed forces, then it will also violate the prohibition on the use of force under Art 2(4) of the UN Charter.[101] It will not be saved by the right of self-defence, as no threat exists to the territory or nationals of the intervening State.

---

98. See **9.9**.
99. See **9.41–9.48**.
100. See ibid.
101. See **9.9**.

9.70   A right of armed humanitarian intervention was recognised by Grotius:[102]

> If a tyrant ... practices atrocities towards his subjects, which no just man can approve, the right of human social connection is not cut off in such a case. ... [I]t would not follow that others may not take up arms for them.

Much more recently, Sir Hersch Lauterpacht (1897–1960), a former judge of the International Court of Justice and one of the 20th century's most respected publicists, remarked that:[103]

> ... when a State renders itself guilty of cruelties against and persecution of its nationals in such a way as to deny their fundamental human rights and to shock the conscience of mankind, intervention in the interest of humanity is legally permissible.

9.71   Many publicists oppose the existence of a right of humanitarian intervention, mainly on the grounds that supporting State practice is ambiguous, it is open to abuse by States seeking to impose their will by force, and Art 2(4) of the UN Charter does not accommodate it.

Further, it is sometimes argued, a right of humanitarian intervention would seriously undermine territorial sovereignty and the rule against non-intervention in a much more serious way than the right to protect nationals abroad. This is because the right of protection can be discharged by simply rescuing and removing the intervening State's endangered nationals. Most exercises of a right of humanitarian intervention are, however, unlikely to be successful unless the intervening State either installs an occupation force to protect the endangered population or removes the government of the territorial State.

9.72   There is fairly extensive evidence of a right of humanitarian intervention in 19th century State practice, especially arising from interventions by several European powers to protect the lives and safety of persecuted Christian populations in the Ottoman Empire.

Between the end of the Second World War and the end of the Cold War, State practice is more ambiguous. Some publicists point to India's armed intervention in East Pakistan (Bangladesh) during the Pakistan civil war (1971); Tanzania's armed intervention in Uganda, which helped topple Idi Amin from power (1979); and Vietnam's armed intervention in Cambodia, which ended the rule of the Khmer Rouge communist regime (1978).

In each case, the foreign military intervention ended serious and widespread human rights abuses committed by the government of the territorial State against its own nationals. In the Indian and Tanzanian cases, however, the intervening States did not expressly rely on a right of humanitarian intervention.

---

102. Hugo Grotius, *De jure belli ac pacis libri tres,* with an abridged translation by William Whewell, John W Parker, London, 1853, Vol I, 288.
103. Hersch Lauterpacht, *Oppenheim's International Law,* 8th ed, Longman, London, 1955, 312.

In the Vietnamese case, the plea of humanitarian intervention was rejected by a large majority of States participating in the subsequent Security Council proceedings — though this was mainly the result of Vietnam's continued military occupation of Cambodia after the removal of the Khmer Rouge communist regime.

9.73 Since the end of the Cold War, however, there has been additional State practice which strengthens the case for some right of humanitarian intervention.

9.74 Following the end of the first Gulf War, the Security Council adopted Resolution 688 (1991). The Security Council expressed grave concern at the repression by the Iraqi government of Iraq's civilian population, particularly in areas occupied by the Kurdish people, which led to massive refugee flows across international borders and threatened international peace and security in the region.

The resolution demanded that Iraq end the repression and allow access by international humanitarian organisations to all those in need of assistance inside Iraq. It appealed to all States 'to contribute to these humanitarian relief efforts'. Shortly after the resolution was adopted, and despite Iraq's objections, France, the United Kingdom and the United States dispatched troops to Northern Iraq to provide 'safe havens' in which Iraqi civilians could live and receive humanitarian assistance without exposure to attacks by the Iraqi military. These coalition troops were subsequently replaced by United Nations personnel with Iraq's consent.

However, the United Kingdom and the United States then imposed two 'no-fly' zones in the airspace above Northern and Southern Iraq. British and United States warplanes patrolled these zones with orders to attack Iraqi government aircraft, in order to protect the civilian population from Iraqi air attacks on civilian populations and to inhibit Iraqi troop movements in the zones.

The British government took the view that these uses of armed force were not authorised by Resolution 688 (1991), but were nevertheless justified by the customary law right of humanitarian intervention. According to the British government's Foreign and Commonwealth Office, four conditions must be fulfilled for a State to rely on a right of humanitarian intervention:[104]

1. There must be a 'compelling and an urgent situation of extreme humanitarian distress which demanded immediate relief'.
2. The territorial State must be unable or unwilling to deal with the humanitarian distress.
3. There must be no practical alternative to external intervention which would relieve the distress.
4. The action constituting the intervention must be limited in time and scope.

---

104. (1992) 63 *British Yearbook of International Law,* 827–29.

This test is almost identical to one proposed by Brierly, who also specified that it must be impractical for the United Nations to take action.[105]

9.75   In 1998, mounting tension between the ethnic Serb and Albanian communities in Serbia's province of Kosovo escalated into widespread armed confrontations and acts of terrorism. The Serbian and federal Yugoslavian security forces reacted severely, engaging in seemingly indiscriminate attacks on Albanian towns and villages, culminating in the attempted mass expulsion of the province's entire majority Albanian population.

The Security Council adopted Resolutions 1199 (1998) and 1203 (1998), in which it expressed alarm at the 'impending humanitarian catastrophe' inside Kosovo and, acting under Chapter VII of the Charter, directed the parties to take certain steps to avert the catastrophe. When those steps were not taken and the mass expulsion of ethnic Albanians continued apace, several member States of NATO committed armed forces to a campaign of aerial bombing against Serbian and federal military and paramilitary forces and infrastructure inside Serbia.

NATO's stated aim was to end the humanitarian catastrophe and create a situation where some 250,000 displaced Albanians could return to their homes. A number of statements issued by officials of NATO and the United States, which led the NATO campaign, indicate that their operations were based partly on a claimed right of humanitarian intervention in international law. Shortly after the NATO bombing commenced, a draft Security Council resolution condemning NATO's conduct as illegal was defeated by 12 votes to three (with China, Namibia and Russia voting against).

9.76   In both the Iraq and Kosovo cases, the intervening States dispatched forces only after the Security Council had characterised the situation in the territorial State as involving a serious humanitarian crisis for which the territorial State was itself responsible. If such a characterisation by the United Nations or some other international institution is now to be regarded as a customary prerequisite for engaging in acts of humanitarian intervention, then the objection that a right of humanitarian intervention is open to abuse by powerful States seeking a pretext to impose their will largely falls away.

9.77   The objection that Art 2(4) of the UN Charter is incompatible with a right of humanitarian intervention is valid only if one takes the view that the qualifying phrase 'against the territorial integrity or political independence of any state, or in any other manner inconsistent with the Purposes of the United Nations' does not qualify the prohibition in such a way as to permit humanitarian intervention. It is arguable, however, that an act of humanitarian intervention which does not have the purpose or result of annexing or occupying territory does not affect the territorial

---

105. See **9.66**.

integrity of any State. The International Court of Justice, however, rejected a similar interpretation of Art 2(4) as a defence to Britain's naval minesweeping operation in Albania's territorial waters for the purpose of collecting evidence to be used in international proceedings.[106]

That case did not, however, involve an act of humanitarian intervention or any issue of fundamental human rights, which have assumed greater prominence in international law over the last half century.

Nor does an act of humanitarian intervention affect any State's political independence if it is aimed at preventing acts in which, as a matter of international law, no State is free to engage — for example, genocide and certain other widespread and egregious human rights abuses.

Similarly, according to Art 1(3) of the UN Charter, promoting 'respect for human rights and for fundamental freedom for all' are among the primary purposes of the United Nations.

Question

Remora and Camoona are neighbouring States, both of which have historically enjoyed close relations with another State, the Federated Provinces (FP). In 2002, a military coup in Remora brought to power a new government which was ideologically very hostile to the FP and its allies, including Camoona.

Early in 2003, an international religious sect calling itself 'the Brotherhood' moved its headquarters to Remora. The Brotherhood preaches that the FP is the source of all evil in the world, and has long advocated the FP's 'complete annihilation by any and all means'. It has carried out numerous terrorist attacks on FP civilian and diplomatic targets for the last 30 years.

Remora provided the Brotherhood with a right of residence to members of the sect, an office block, a training academy, a large donation of money, and access to Remoran weapons and military advisers. The Brotherhood operates, however, completely independently of the Remoran State and the vast majority of its members are not Remoran nationals. After its relocation to Remora, terrorist attacks by the Brotherhood on FP targets around the world increased dramatically, resulting in the deaths of around 300 FP civilians and diplomats every year. Some of these attacks occurred in the territory of Camoona.

In July 2006, Camoona and the FP began financing the activities of Remoran Renewal, an underground political party in Remora which was pledged to restoring democracy and expelling the Brotherhood. After Remoran Renewal members became the subject of terrorist attacks by the Brotherhood, Camoona's and the FP's intelligence services provided Remoran Renewal with small arms and ammunition, as well as training in their use.

---

106. *Corfu Channel Case (Merits) (United Kingdom v Albania)* ICJ Rep (1949) 4, 35. See 12.51.

On the day after news of Camoona's and the FP's aid to Remoran Renewal was made public, and for a week afterwards, Remora's air force attacked numerous targets inside Camoona's territory, resulting in the deaths of over 1,000 Camoonan nationals. Remora's President declared that his State was acting in self-defence against Camoona's and the FP's arming of Remoran Renewal. On the same day that Remora's air campaign against Camoona commenced, a group of Brotherhood terrorists exploded a nuclear bomb carried in a suitcase in a major FP city, resulting in the deaths of around 7,000 civilians and the destruction of an urban district.

The terrorists had entered the FP on passports in false names issued by Remora, and Remora had donated the nuclear bomb to the Brotherhood. Remora was known to possess several more identical bombs in undisclosed locations. An emergency meeting of the United Nations Security Council was unable to decide on any action against Remora or the Brotherhood because of a single negative vote cast by a permanent member.

One month after the nuclear explosion, the FP launched a full-scale military invasion of Remora. The FP's Prime Minister publicly claimed that his State was exercising its inherent right of individual and collective self-defence in response to the attacks on the FP and Camoona, and notified the Security Council of the steps being taken by the FP. Within three days after the invasion, the Remoran government had collapsed and all members of the Brotherhood had been killed or had fled the country. Remoran Renewal formed a new government in Remora. All FP troops left Remora within a few weeks. Some States have accused the FP of violating international law on the use of force. The FP's Foreign Minister asks your advice on his State's legal position.

You may assume that the FP, Remora and Camoona are all parties to the UN Charter, but that they are not parties to any other treaty which might be relevant.

Suggested answer

The FP's military invasion of Remora involved a prima facie violation of the prohibition on the use of force contained in Art 2(4) of the UN Charter.

According to General Assembly Resolution 2625 (XXV), the duty to refrain from the threat or use of force includes refraining from waging a war of aggression. Article 3 of General Assembly Resolution 3314 (XXIX) defines 'aggression' to include the 'invasion or attack by the armed forces of a State of the territory of another State'. The International Court of Justice has said that Resolution 2625 (XXV) and Art 3 of Resolution 3314 (XXIX) reflect customary international law (*Nicaragua* case). In order for the FP's invasion to be lawful, it must fall within the scope of a recognised exception to the prohibition on the use of force.

At the time the invasion was launched, the FP's Prime Minister claimed to be acting pursuant to the inherent right of individual and collective self-defence, which is one of the exceptions to the prohibition on the use of force. Article 51 of the UN Charter provides that nothing in the Charter 'shall impair the right of individual or collective self-defence if an armed attack occurs against a Member of the United Nations'. In order to rely on Art 51, the FP must show that Remora is responsible for an armed attack against the FP or against its ally Camoona.

Camoona was the subject of an armed attack by Remora's air force. The International Court of Justice has held that 'action by regular forces across an international border' constitutes an armed attack for the purposes of Art 51 (*Nicaragua* case, para 195).

Remora's air strikes will not constitute an 'armed attack' against Camoona if they can be justified as an act of self-defence against Camoona. Remora's President attempted to advance this very justification at the time the strikes were launched. Remora's attempted justification will be successful only if Camoona's assistance to Remoran Renewal itself amounted to an armed attack on Remora. The International Court of Justice has, however, stated that the concept of 'armed attack' does not extend to 'assistance to rebels in the form of provision of weapons or logistical or other support' (*Nicaragua* case, para 195). It follows that Camoona's provision of small arms, ammunition and training to Remoran Renewal does not constitute an armed attack and cannot, therefore, justify a claim of self-defence by Remora.

This is not to say that Camoona's actions were entirely lawful. On the contrary, Camoona has infringed the customary international law principle of non-intervention in the internal affairs of Remora. In Resolutions 2131 (XX) and 2625 (XXV), the General Assembly expressed the view that the principle of non-intervention prevented States from interfering in civil strife in another State. The International Court of Justice has held these resolutions to be reflective of customary international law (*Nicaragua* case, para 203). In para 205 of the same judgment, the ICJ said that the:

> ... element of coercion, which defines, and indeed forms the very essence of, prohibited intervention, is particularly obvious in the case of an intervention which uses force ... in the indirect form of support for subversive ... activities within another State.

The Court said that acts of this kind would amount not only to an unlawful intervention, but also to a violation of the rule against the use of force in Art 2(4) of the UN Charter. It seems likely that Camoona's aid to Remoran Renewal placed Camoona in breach of the principle of non-intervention and also, possibly, the prohibition on the use of force.

It should be borne in mind, however, that a violation of the Charter prohibition on the threat or use of force does not necessarily involve an 'armed attack' within the meaning of Art 51, and does not do so in this case. Remora's remedy for Camoona's violation of the non-intervention principle is the taking of proportionate countermeasures (*Nicaragua* case, paras 210 and 249). A week of air strikes resulting in over 1,000 deaths could hardly be regarded as a proportionate response to Camoona's violation.

It follows, therefore, that Remora's air strikes constituted an armed attack on Camoona, entitling the latter to exercise a right of self-defence. The FP, however, was not entitled to exercise a collective right of self-defence against Remora on the basis of Remora's air strikes without first having received a request from Camoona (*Nicaragua* case, para 199).

If Camoona did not request the FP to join in Camoona's defence, the FP's invasion of Remora was a violation of Art 2(4), unless the FP can show that the invasion was an act of individual self-defence. This would involve demonstrating that Remora was responsible for the nuclear terrorist attack and that its own response was proportionate and necessary. The Brotherhood was the organisation which carried out the nuclear attack, and it was completely independent of the Remoran State.

Nevertheless, the International Court of Justice has equated an 'act of aggression' with an 'armed attack' for the purposes of Art 51 and has held the definition of aggression in Art 3 of General Assembly Resolution 3314 (XXIX) to be reflective of customary international law. The Court remarked that (*Nicaragua* case, para 195):

> ... the prohibition of armed attacks may apply to the sending by a State of armed bands to the territory of another State, if such an operation, because of its scale and effects, would have been classified as an armed attack rather than as a mere frontier incident had it been carried out by regular armed forces.

Paragraphs (a) and (b) of Art 3 define 'aggression' to include an international attack by armed forces or an international bombardment with weapons. According to para (g) of Art 3, 'aggression' also includes:

> ... the sending, by or on behalf of a State of armed bands, groups, irregulars or mercenaries, which carry out acts of armed force against another State of such gravity as to amount to the acts listed above, or its substantial involvement therein.

Consequently, Remora will be guilty of aggression if it was 'substantially involved in' an attack by an armed band on the FP on such a scale and with such effects as to amount to an armed attack had it been carried out by regular armed forces. If it was guilty of aggression in this sense, it also perpetrated an armed attack, and the FP would be entitled to exercise its inherent right of individual self-defence.

Remora provided the Brotherhood with a right of residence to members of the sect, an office block, a training academy, a large donation of money, and access to Remoran weapons and military advisers. Even more importantly, Remora furnished the terrorists who carried out the nuclear attack with official passports in false names and donated the nuclear bomb which killed over 7,000 people and devastated an urban district in the FP. Remora was, therefore, 'substantially involved' in an attack by an armed band on such a scale and with such effects as to amount to an armed attack had it been carried out by regular armed forces. Consequently, and notwithstanding the Brotherhood's independence from the Remoran State, Remora committed an armed attack on the FP, which was entitled to exercise its inherent right of individual self-defence against Remora.

In order for an act of self-defence to be fully compliant with international law, however, it must be consistent with certain additional requirements established in customary international law. In particular, a State responding to an armed attack by another State is obliged to observe the requirement that measures taken in self-defence 'are proportional to the armed attack and necessary to respond to it' (*Nicaragua* case, para 176). In this case, the devastation and loss of life caused by the nuclear terrorist attack were extensive.

Furthermore, there were several more identical bombs under the control of a government which had shown itself quite prepared to see them used against civilian populations in the FP. In the circumstances, a military invasion to remove the government which was substantially involved in the terrorist attack would appear to be neither disproportionate nor unnecessary to the FP's right of self-defence.

The swift withdrawal of FP troops after the Remoran government's removal is also consistent with the requirements of proportionality and necessity.

Security Council authorisation for the FP's invasion of Remora was not obtained. The Security Council has 'primary responsibility for the maintenance of international peace and security' (UN Charter, Art 24(1)). The Charter does not confer sole responsibility for the maintenance of international peace and security on the Security Council. Indeed, Art 51 recognises that States have an inherent right of self-defence. Chapter VII of the UN Charter confers certain powers and duties on the Security Council. In particular, it is obliged to 'determine the existence of any threat to the peace, breach of the peace, or act of aggression' and is required to 'make recommendations, or decide what measures shall be taken ... to maintain or restore international peace and security' (UN Charter, Art 39).

Furthermore, members of the UN are required to 'accept and carry out decisions of the Security Council' (UN Charter, Art 25). In this case, however, the Security Council failed or refused to discharge its responsibilities. In the absence of any effective action by the Security Council for the restoration of international peace and security, the FP was left to rely solely on its inherent right of self-defence (*Falkland Islands* case).

Further tutorial discussion

1. Does the threat from terrorism posed by non-State entities require the revision of the international law on self-defence?

2. In what circumstances might State A violate the prohibition on the use of force against State B, without entitling State B to respond under its inherent right of self-defence?

3. Is an act of aggression, or a threatened act of aggression, a necessary prerequisite for the Security Council to take action under Chapter VII of the UN Charter?

4. What safeguards exist to prevent the Security Council from abusing its powers to maintain and restore international peace and security?

5. 'States are always entitled to take whatever steps are necessary in the territory of other States in order to protect the lives of their nationals and the security of their nationals' property.' Discuss.

6. 'Any right of humanitarian intervention which may have existed before 1945 was definitely extinguished by the adoption of the UN Charter.' Discuss.

International criminal law

10

Objectives

After completing this chapter, you should:

(1) be aware of the stages by which individual criminal responsibility emerged as part of international law and be able to explain the distinctive characteristics of international criminal law;

(2) understand and be able to apply the law on the crime of piracy *jure gentium;*

(3) understand and be able to apply the international criminal law on slavery and the slave trade;

(4) understand and be able to apply the law on the crime of genocide;

(5) understand and be able to apply the law on the crimes of torture and cruel, inhuman or degrading treatment or punishment;

(6) understand and be able to apply the law on crimes against humanity;

(7) understand and be able to apply the law on war crimes; and

(8) understand and be able to apply the law on individual and command responsibility for genocide, crimes against humanity and war crimes.

Key cases

In Re Piracy Jure Gentium [1934] AC 586; [1934] All ER Rep 506
Prosecutor v Akayesu (1998) 9 IHRR 608
Ireland v United Kingdom (1978) 2 EHRR 25
Dikme v Turkey [2000] ECHR 366
Prosecutor v Kunarac, IT-96-23-T & IT-96-23/1-T, 22 February 2001 (ICTY)
Prosecutor v Kupreškić, IT-95-16-T, 14 January 2000 (ICTY)
Prosecutor v Tadić (1995) 105 ILR 419
Prosecutor v Halilović, IT-01-48-T, 16 November 2005 (ICTY)

Key treaties and instruments

Slavery Convention (1926)
Supplementary Convention on the Abolition of Slavery, the Slave Trade, and Institutions and Practices Similar to Slavery (1956)
Convention on the Prevention and Punishment of the Crime of Genocide (1948)
Geneva Convention for the amelioration of the condition of the wounded and sick in armed forces in the field (Geneva Convention I) (1949)
Geneva Convention for the amelioration of the condition of the wounded, sick and shipwrecked members of the armed forces at sea (Geneva Convention II) (1949)

Geneva Convention relative to the treatment of prisoners of war (Geneva Convention III) (1949)

Geneva Convention relative to the protection of civilian persons in time of war (Geneva Convention IV) (1949)

Protocol Additional to the Geneva Conventions of 12 August 1949, and relating to the Protection of Victims of International Armed Conflicts (Geneva Protocol I) (1977)

Protocol Additional to the Geneva Conventions of 12 August 1949, and relating to the Protection of Victims of Non-International Armed Conflicts (Geneva Protocol II) (1977)

Convention against Torture and Other Cruel, Inhuman or Degrading Treatment or Punishment (1984)

Statute of the International Criminal Tribunal for the former Yugoslavia (1993)

Statute of the International Criminal Tribunal for Rwanda (1994)

Rome Statute of the International Criminal Court (1998)

Elements of Crimes of the Rome Statute of the International Criminal Court (2002)

Emergence of individual criminal responsibility

10.1   International law is a system primarily concerned with the rights and obligations of States and of international organisations established by States. The two principal exceptions to this State-centred subject matter of international law are international human rights[1] and international criminal law. Both these branches of international law are concerned with rules and principles applying directly to individuals. Often portrayed as peculiarly modern phenomena, the emergence of these two domains of international law can also be viewed as the partial reappearance of a pre-modern conception of international order in which the *jus gentium* regulated affairs between members of different political communities who were not governed by a common *jus civile*.[2]

Before the Second World War

10.2   Indeed, the oldest of all the international crimes derives directly from the *jus gentium* by which Roman law regarded pirates as *hostis humani generis* (the enemies of mankind) who were liable to be punished by any sovereign who could apprehend them in the sovereign's own territory or in places beyond any sovereign's territorial jurisdiction (such as the high seas).

10.3   Customary laws of war among European sovereigns, such as the prohibition on killing prisoners of war, began to emerge as early as the middle ages, with either the sovereign of the perpetrator or the sovereign in whose service the victims were fighting being entitled to exercise jurisdiction over the crimes.

---

1.   See chapter 11.
2.   See 1.7 and 1.56–1.68.

10.4   During the 19th century, and as a consequence of the formal condemnation of the slave trade at the Congress of Vienna in 1815, Britain's Royal Navy waged a long and ultimately successful campaign on the high seas against the transportation of slaves. In 1820, the United States enacted legislation making the trade in slaves a capital crime equal to piracy. In the 19th century, however, the slave trade did not acquire the status of a crime *jure gentium* and was not subject to universal jurisdiction, as was piracy *jure gentium*. Rather, the campaign against the slave trade was legally underpinned by a number of treaties promoting international cooperation in the suppression of the slave trade and the granting of mutual rights of visit and search of vessels.[3]

10.5   By the close of the 19th century, international law did not impose criminal responsibility on individuals except for piracy and a relatively narrow range of war crimes. Where an individual committed any of these crimes, international law permitted States to exercise jurisdiction over them, there being no international tribunals to perform the function.

After the Second World War

10.6   The 20th century witnessed a significant expansion in the scope of individual criminal responsibility at international law. In particular, at the close of the Second World War the International Military Tribunal at Nuremberg (Nuremberg Tribunal) was established in order to try leading members and associates of Germany's National Socialist regime on charges of crimes against the peace, war crimes, and crimes against humanity. On the existence of individual criminal responsibility in international law, the Nuremberg Tribunal remarked:[4]

> It was submitted that international law is concerned with the actions of sovereign States, and provides no punishment for individuals; and further, that where the act in question is an act of State, those who carry it out are not personally responsible, but are protected by the doctrine of the sovereignty of the State. In the opinion of the Tribunal, both these submissions must be rejected. That international law imposes duties and liabilities upon individuals as well as upon States has long been recognized. ... Crimes against international law are committed by men, not by abstract entities, and only by punishing individuals who commit such crimes can the provisions of international law be enforced. ... The principle of international law, which under certain circumstances, protects the representatives of a state, cannot be applied to acts which are condemned as criminal by international law.

10.7   The United Nations General Assembly subsequently affirmed 'the principles of international law recognised by the Charter of the Nuremberg Tribunal and the judgment of the Tribunal'[5] An International

---

3.   Sir Robert Jennings and Sir Arthur Watts (eds), *Oppenheim's International Law*, 9th ed, Longman, New York, 1992, § 429, 979–80.
4.   International Military Tribunal (Nuremberg), Judgment and Sentences (1947) 41 *American Journal of International Law* 172, 220–21.
5.   General Assembly Resolution 95 (I) (1945).

Military Tribunal for the Far East was later established at Tokyo for the purpose of trying defendants associated with Japan's wartime regime on charges similar to those prosecuted at Nuremberg.

10.8 Although genocide was not among the crimes identified in the Charter of the Nuremberg Tribunal,[6] a crime of genocide attracting individual criminal responsibility was recognised by the Convention on the Prevention and Punishment of the Crime of Genocide[7] (Genocide Convention) in 1948.

10.9 The following year saw the conclusion of the four Geneva Conventions: the Geneva Convention for the amelioration of the condition of the wounded and sick in armed forces in the field[8] (Geneva Convention I); the Geneva Convention for the amelioration of the condition of the wounded, sick and shipwrecked members of the armed forces at sea[9] (Geneva Convention II); the Geneva Convention relative to the treatment of prisoners of war[10] (Geneva Convention III); and the Geneva Convention relative to the protection of civilian persons in time of war[11] (Geneva Convention IV).

10.10 The four Geneva Conventions furnish the foundations of the modern international law regulating the use of force in armed conflict, also known as 'international humanitarian law'. Each of them provides for individual criminal responsibility in certain situations by stipulating that States parties 'undertake to enact any legislation necessary to provide effective penal sanctions for persons committing, or ordering to be committed, any of the grave breaches' defined in the conventions.[12]

10.11 Although the four Geneva Conventions are primarily concerned with regulating international armed conflicts, Common Art 3 extends certain protections also to persons affected by a non-international (or internal) armed conflict, such as a civil war or domestic insurgency. The persons covered by this extended protection are limited to those 'taking no active part in the hostilities, including members of armed forces who have laid down their arms and those placed "hors de combat" by sickness, wounds, detention, or any other cause'. Common Art 3 of the four Geneva Conventions represents customary international law.[13]

10.12 In 1977, the Geneva Convention regime of individual criminal responsibility committed in the context of an international armed conflict was extended, with some additions and refinements, by the

---

6. The Charter of the Nuremberg Tribunal did, however, identify 'extermination' as constituting a crime against humanity: Art 6(b).
7. UNTS, Vol 78, p 277.
8. UNTS, Vol 75, p 32.
9. UNTS, Vol 75, p 86.
10. UNTS, Vol 75, p 136.
11. UNTS, Vol 75, p 288.
12. Geneva Convention I, Art 49; Geneva Convention II, Art 50; Geneva Convention III, Art 129; Geneva Convention IV, Art 146. Semble Geneva Protocol I, Art 85.
13. *Case Concerning Military and Paramilitary Activities in and Against Nicaragua (Nicaragua v United States)* Merits, ICJ Rep (1986), para 218.

first and second protocols to the Geneva Conventions to internal armed conflicts.[14] Under the first protocol (Geneva Protocol I), the scope of the four Geneva Conventions is extended to 'include armed conflicts in which peoples are fighting against colonial domination and alien occupation and against racist regimes in the exercise of their right of self-determination'.[15] This protection applies to combatants who do not wear uniforms or other insignia of their affiliation, provided they carry arms openly in certain situations.[16] The second protocol (Geneva Protocol II) extends and refines the protections afforded by Common Art 3 of the Geneva Conventions to internal armed conflicts which are not covered by Geneva Protocol I.[17] In other words, it develops and supplements the Geneva Convention protections in their application to internal armed conflicts not involving a struggle against colonial domination and alien occupation and against racist regimes in the exercise of a right of self-determination. Geneva Protocol II does not, however, apply to 'situations of internal disturbances and tensions, such as riots, isolated and sporadic acts of violence and other acts of a similar nature, as not being armed conflicts'.[18] 'Many provisions' of Geneva Protocol II represent customary international law.[19]

10.13   Torture was defined and expressly made the subject of individual criminal responsibility in the Convention against Torture and Other Cruel, Inhuman or Degrading Treatment or Punishment[20] (Torture Convention), concluded in 1984.

10.14   The 1990s were the most significant decade for the development of international criminal law since the 1940s. Two episodes were of particular importance. The first was a civil war lasting from 1991 to 1995, costing more than 120,000 lives, and resulting in the emergence of several new States on the territory of what had been the Socialist Federal Republic of Yugoslavia. The second was the 1994 genocide in Rwanda involving the killing of somewhere between 500,000 and one million members of the Tutsi ethnic group.

10.15   In response to these events, the Security Council of the United Nations established two international tribunals to try individuals who had committed crimes against international law while occupied in the Yugoslav civil war or in the Rwandan genocide. The International Criminal Tribunal for the former Yugoslavia (ICTY) was established, and its Statute adopted, by Security Council Resolution 827 (1993). Located at The Hague, the ICTY was given jurisdiction to try persons

---

14. Protocol Additional to the Geneva Conventions of 12 August 1949, and relating to the Protection of Victims of International Armed Conflicts (Protocol I), UNTS, Vol 1125, p 4; Protocol Additional to the Geneva Conventions of 12 August 1949, and relating to the Protection of Victims of Non-International Armed Conflicts (Protocol II), UNTS, Vol 1125, p 611.
15. Geneva Protocol I, Art 1(3).
16. Ibid, Art 44(3).
17. Geneva Protocol II, Art 1(1).
18. Ibid, Art 1(2).
19. *Prosecutor v Tadić* (1995) 105 ILR 419, 2 October 1995, para 117.
20. UNTS, Vol 1465, p 85.

responsible for serious violations of international humanitarian law committed in the territory of the former Yugoslavia since 1991.[21] More than 160 defendants have been indicted before the ICTY. Soon after the establishment of the ICTY, the Security Council established the International Criminal Tribunal for Rwanda (ICTR) by Resolution 955 (1994). Located at Arusha in Tanzania, the ICTR was given jurisdiction to try cases involving genocide, crimes against humanity, and war crimes by any persons committing the offences in Rwanda or by Rwandan citizens charged with committing the offences in States neighbouring Rwanda between January 1991 and December 1994.[22] More than 60 defendants have been indicted before the ICTR.

In establishing both the ICTY and the ICTR by resolution under Chapter VII of the United Nations Charter,[23] the Security Council was able to move more quickly than if it had waited for the results of multilateral treaty-making negotiations. Using Chapter VII also had the advantage of binding States to compliance without their consent, a result that would have been impossible by treaty negotiation.

10.16   The Genocide Convention provided that persons charged with offences under that convention 'shall be tried by a competent tribunal of the State in the territory of which the act was committed, or by such international penal tribunal as may have jurisdiction with respect to those Contracting Parties which shall have accepted its jurisdiction'.[24] The establishment and work of the ICTY and ICTR provided a powerful impetus for the establishment of a standing international tribunal with jurisdiction over genocide and other international crimes attracting individual responsibility.

10.17   In 1998, the General Assembly of the United Nations convened a conference in Rome. The conference was attended by 148 States, which adopted the text of a treaty known as the Rome Statute of the International Criminal Court.[25] After 60 States had ratified the Rome Statute, it came into force on 1 July 2002, thereby bringing into existence the International Criminal Court (ICC).

Any person committing a crime within the jurisdiction of the ICC 'shall be individually responsible and liable for punishment' in accordance with the Rome Statute.[26]

The crimes which may be tried before the ICC are genocide, crimes against humanity, war crimes, and the crime of aggression.[27] The ICC cannot exercise jurisdiction over aggression until a definition of that crime and the conditions under which the ICC may exercise jurisdiction

---

21.   ICTY Statute, Arts 1 and 8.
22.   ICTR Statute, Arts 2, 3, 4 and 7.
23.   See **9.49–9.59**.
24.   Genocide Convention, Art VI.
25.   UNTS, Vol 2187, p 3. The text was adopted by a vote of 120 to seven, with 21 abstentions.
26.   Ibid, Art 25(2).
27.   Ibid, Art 5(1).

over it are settled in accordance with the Rome Statute's amendment and review provisions.[28]

The Rome Statute provides for the adoption of 'Elements of Crimes' which 'shall assist the Court in the interpretation and application of' provisions concerning genocide, crimes against humanity and war crimes.[29] The ICC is required to apply the Elements of Crimes.[30] The foreshadowed Elements of Crimes were adopted by the Assembly of States parties to the Rome Statute in September 2002.[31]

10.18   In order for a crime to be within the jurisdiction of the ICC, it must have been committed after the Rome Statute's entry into force,[32] so that the ICC possesses no retroactive jurisdiction over crimes committed prior to that date.

The ICC will, furthermore, lack jurisdiction unless the accused was a national of a State party to the Rome Statute, or unless the crime was committed on the territory of a State party, or unless the crime was committed aboard a vessel or aircraft registered under the laws of a State party.[33] A State which is not a party to the Rome Statute may confer jurisdiction on the ICC in respect of crimes committed on its territory or by its nationals where it makes a declaration to the Registrar of the Court.[34] A State will also need to make such a declaration if it wishes the ICC to exercise jurisdiction over crimes committed on its territory or by its nationals prior to it becoming a State party;[35] the Court otherwise lacks jurisdiction over crimes occurring before the State becomes a party. In no case, however, can the ICC exercise jurisdiction over offences committed prior to 1 July 2002.

The ICC may also exercise jurisdiction in a situation in which a crime within the Rome Statute is referred to the ICC Prosecutor by the Security Council acting under Chapter VII of the UN Charter,[36] obviating the need for any link to the nationality or territory of a State party.

Characteristics of individual criminal responsibility

10.19   Before turning to consider specific crimes at international law, it is worth considering what characterises international crimes as distinct from other wrongs at international law and other crimes. International criminal law is distinguished principally by two attributes.

First, as indicated above, international crimes give rise to the responsibility of individuals and are therefore not part of the law of State responsibility.[37]

---

28.   Ibid, Art 5(2).
29.   Ibid, Art 9.
30.   Ibid, Art 21(1)(a).
31.   Official Records, ICC-ASP/1/3.
32.   Rome Statute, Art 24(1).
33.   Ibid, Art 12(2).
34.   Ibid, Art 12(3).
35.   Ibid, Art 11(2).
36.   Ibid, Art 13(b).
37.   As to the law on State responsibility, see chapter 5.

Second, and in contrast to non-international crimes, States may exercise jurisdiction over international crimes on a basis other than the territorial, nationality or protective principles.[38] In other words, they may exercise jurisdiction on the basis of the universality principle or some variation on that principle. The universality principle in its most complete form permits or requires States to exercise their criminal jurisdiction over offences regardless of the location of the offence, the nationality of any persons involved, or the impact on any essential security interests of the prosecuting State. Torture is an international crime that attracts this complete form of the universality principle. A more restricted variation on the universality principle of jurisdiction is provided by piracy *jure gentium*, over which a State is permitted to exercise criminal jurisdiction for certain acts committed on the high seas (but not in a place under the jurisdiction of another State, unless the nationality principle or the protective principle can be employed). Another species of variation is provided by offences for which international law requires States either to prosecute a suspect in their territory or to extradite that person to another State with some treaty-designated connection to the crime.[39]

10.20   It should also be noted that individual criminal responsibility is still an exceptional feature of the international legal system. As the Inter-American Court of Human Rights remarked in its *Re-introduction of the Death Penalty* advisory opinion:[40]

> 52. International law may grant rights to individuals and, conversely, may also determine that certain acts or omissions on their part could make them criminally liable under that law. In some cases, that responsibility is enforceable by international tribunals. In that sense, international law has evolved from the classical doctrine, under which international law concerned itself exclusively with states.

> 53. Nevertheless, at the present time individual responsibility may only be invoked for violations that are defined in international instruments as crimes under international law, such as crimes against peace, war crimes, and crimes against humanity or genocide, which, of course, also affect specific human rights.

10.21   Even where international law establishes or acknowledges an international crime, domestic legislation may be required before national courts will exercise jurisdiction over it.[41]

---

38.   See 6.7–6.22.
39.   See 6.28–6.36.
40.   *International Responsibility for the Promulgation and Enforcement of Laws in Violation of the Convention (Arts 1 and 2 of the American Convention on Human Rights)*, Advisory Opinion OC-14/94, 9 December 1994.
41.   For example, *Nulyarimma v Thompson* (1999) 96 FCR 153; 165 ALR 621 (Federal Court of Australia) (see 3.21); *R v Bow Street Metropolitan Stipendiary Magistrate; Ex parte Pinochet Ugarte (No 3)* [2000] 1 AC 147 (House of Lords) (see 6.60).

Piracy *jure gentium*

10.22   Piracy is the oldest of international crimes attracting individual responsibility. Because piracy is a criminal offence under numerous domestic legal orders, the term 'piracy *jure gentium*' is frequently employed to designate the offence in its modality under international law.

10.23   Piracy *jure gentium* is currently defined by Art 101 of the Convention on the Law of the Sea.[42] The crime embraces certain 'illegal acts of violence or detention, or any act of depredation, committed for private ends by the crew or passengers of a private ship ... and directed ... on the high seas against another ship ... or against persons or property on board' that other ship.[43] This definition does not expressly extend to attempts to commit any of these acts.

> Whether an unsuccessful attempted act of robbery can constitute the crime of piracy *jure gentium* was considered by the Privy Council on a special reference from Hong Kong in *Re Piracy Jure Gentium:*[44]
>
> Viscount Sankey LC: On January 4, 1931, on the high seas, a number of armed Chinese nationals were cruising in two Chinese junks. They pursued and attacked a cargo junk which was also a Chinese vessel. The master of the cargo junk attempted to escape, and a chase ensued during which the pursuers came within 200 yards of the cargo junk. The chase continued for over half an hour, during which shots were fired by the attacking party, and while it was still proceeding, the steamship *Hang Sang* approached and subsequently also the steamship *Shui Chow*. The officers in command of these merchant vessels intervened and through their agency, the pursuers were eventually taken in charge by the Commander of H. M. S. *Somme*, which had arrived in consequence of a report made by wireless. They were brought as prisoners to Hong Kong and indicted for the crime of piracy. The jury found them guilty subject to the following question of law: 'Whether an accused person may be convicted of piracy in circumstances where no robbery has occurred.' The Full Court of Hong Kong on further consideration came to the conclusion that robbery was necessary be support a conviction of piracy and in the result the accused were acquitted. ...
>
> Upon November 10, 1933, His Majesty in Council made the following Order: 'The question whether actual robbery is an essential element of the crime of piracy *jure gentium,* or whether a frustrated attempt to commit a piratical robbery is not equally piracy *jure gentium*, is referred to the Judicial Committee for their hearing and consideration.' ...
>
> With regard to crimes as defined by international law, that law has no means of trying or punishing them. The recognition of them as constituting crimes, and the trial and punishment of the criminals, are left to the municipal law of each country. But whereas according to international law the criminal jurisdiction of municipal law is ordinarily restricted to crimes committed on its *terra firma* or territorial waters or its own ships, and to crimes by its own nationals wherever

---

42.   See **12.97–12.100**. An identical definition is provided by Art 15 of the Convention on the High Seas, UNTS, Vol 450, p 11.
43.   Convention on the Law of the Sea, Art 101(a)(i).
44.   *In Re Piracy Jure Gentium* [1934] AC 586; [1934] All ER Rep 506.

committed, it is also recognized as extending to piracy committed on the high seas by any national on any ship, because a person guilty of such piracy has placed himself beyond the protection of any State. He is no longer a national, but *'hostis humani generis'* and as such he is justiciable by any State anywhere: Grotius (1583–1645) *'De Jure Belli ac Pacis,'* vol. 2, cap. 20, 40. ...

The conception of piracy according to the civil law is expounded by Molloy (1646–1690) *'De Jure Maritimo et Navali'* or 'A Treatise of affairs Maritime and of Commerce.' That book was first published in 1676 and the ninth edition in 1769. Chapter 4 is headed 'Of Piracy.' The author defines a pirate as 'a sea thief or *hostis humani generis* who to enrich himself either by surprize or open face sets upon merchants or other traders by sea.' He clearly does not regard piracy as necessarily involving successful robbery or as being inconsistent with an unsuccessful attempt. Thus in para. xiii. he says: 'So likewise if a ship shall be assaulted by pirates and in the attempt the pirates shall be overcome if the captors bring them to the next port and the judge openly rejects the trial, or the captain cannot wait for the judge without certain peril and loss, justice may be done on them by the law of nature, and the same may be there executed by the captors.' Again in para. 14 he puts the case where 'a pirate at sea assaults a ship but by force is prevented from entering her' and goes on to distinguish the rule as to accessories at the common law and by the law marine. ...

... Assume a modern liner with its crew and passengers, say of several thousand aboard, under its national flag, and suppose one passenger robbed another. It would be impossible to contend that such a robbery on the high seas was piracy and that the passenger in question had committed an act of piracy when he robbed his fellow passenger, and was therefore liable to the penalty of death. 'That is too wide a definition which would embrace all acts of plunder and violence in degree sufficient to constitute piracy simply because done on the high seas. As every crime can be committed at sea, piracy might thus be extended to the whole criminal code. If an act of robbery or murder were committed upon one of the passengers or crew by another in a vessel at sea, the vessel being at the time and continuing under lawful authority and the offender were secured and confined by the master of the vessel to be taken home for trial, this state of things would not authorise seizure and trial by any nation that chose to interfere or within whose limits the offender might afterwards be found': Dana's Wheaton, p. 193, note 83, quoted in Moore's Digest of International Law (Washington, 1906) Article 'Piracy,' p. 953. ...

Having ... referred to the two cases, *Dawson* (1696) and *Smith* (1820),[45] which are typical of one side of the question, their Lordships will briefly refer to two others from which the opposite conclusion is to be gathered.

It will be observed that both of them are more recent. The first is the decision in the case of the *Serhassan Pirates*,[46] decided in the English High Court of Admiralty by that distinguished judge, Dr. Lushington (1782–1873), in 1845. It was on an application by certain officers for bounty which, under the statute 6 Geo. 4, c. 49, was given to persons who captured pirates, and the learned judge said (it is not necessary to detail all the facts of the case for the purpose of the present opinion) 'the question which I have to determine is whether or not the attack which was made upon the British pinnance and the two other boats constituted an act of piracy on the part of these prahns, so as to bring the persons who were on board within the legal denomination of pirates.' He held it was an act of piracy and awarded the statutory bounty. It is true that that was a decision under the

---

45.   *R v Dawson* (1696) 13 St Tr col 451; *United States v Smith* (1820) 5 Wheat 153.
46.   *Serhassan Pirates* (1845) 2 W Rob 354.

special statute under which the bounties were claimed, but it will be noted that there was no robbery in that case; what happened was that the pirates attacked, but were themselves beaten off and captured. A similar comment may be made on the case in 1853 of *The Magellan Pirates*,[47] where Dr. Lushington said: 'it was never, so far as I am able to find, deemed necessary to inquire whether parties so convicted of these crimes (i.e., robbery and murder), had intended to rob on the high seas, or to murder on the high seas indiscriminately.'

Finally, there is the American case *The Ambrose Light*[48] where it was decided by a Federal Court that an armed ship must have the authority of a State behind it, and if it has not got such an authority, it is a pirate even though no act of robbery has been committed by it. ...

All that their Lordships propose to do is to answer the question put to them, and ... they have come to the conclusion that the better view and the proper answer to give to the question addressed to them is that ... actual robbery is not an essential element in the crime of piracy *jure gentium,* and that a frustrated attempt to commit piratical robbery is equally piracy *jure gentium.*

10.24 The crime of piracy *jure gentium* is, therefore, committed even when any of the prohibited acts are unsuccessfully attempted. Furthermore, and as the definition in Art 101 confirms, piracy *jure gentium* at sea cannot be committed except by the crew or passengers of one ship against another ship on the high seas. Illegal acts of violence, and so on, committed by the crew or passengers of a ship against the same ship, or against another ship outside the high seas, will not constitute piracy *jure gentium.*

10.25 Article 100 of the Convention on the Law of the Sea requires States parties to 'co-operate to the fullest extent in the repression of piracy on the high seas or in any other place outside the jurisdiction of any State'.[49] Any State into whose custody a pirate falls is entitled to exercise criminal jurisdiction over that person.[50]

Slavery and the slave trade

10.26 In 1926, under the auspices of the League of Nations, an international conference in Geneva adopted the Slavery Convention.[51] The States parties undertook to 'prevent and suppress the slave trade'[52] and to 'adopt the necessary measures in order that severe penalties may be imposed in respect of such infractions'.[53] The 'slave trade' was defined to include 'all acts involved in the capture, acquisition or disposal of a person with intent to reduce him to slavery; all acts involved in the acquisition of a slave with a view to selling or exchanging him; all acts of

---

47. *Magellan Pirates* (1853) 1 Spinks E & A 81.
48. *Ambrose Light,* 25 Fed Rep 408.
49. Semble Convention on the High Seas, Art 14.
50. *Case of the SS Lotus (France v Turkey)* PCIJ Rep (1927) Series A No 10, 70. See 6.11.
51. LNTS, Vol 60, p 254.
52. Slavery Convention, Art 2(a).
53. Ibid, Art 6.

disposal by sale or exchange of a slave acquired with a view to being sold or exchanged, and, in general, every act of trade or transport in slaves'.[54] 'Slavery' was defined to mean 'the status or condition of a person over whom any or all of the powers attaching to the right of ownership are exercised'.

10.27 The Slavery Convention made the slave trade an international crime attracting individual criminal responsibility. It did not, however, clearly criminalise slavery itself. In respect of the status of slavery, the Convention provided merely that States parties were to 'bring about, progressively and as soon as possible, the complete abolition of slavery in all its forms'.[55]

10.28 In 1948, the General Assembly of the United Nations adopted the Universal Declaration of Human Rights[56] (UDHR) which provides that '[n]o one shall be held in slavery or servitude; slavery and the slave trade shall be prohibited in all their forms'.[57]

10.29 The conventional law on slavery and the slave trade was significantly developed in 1956 by the Supplementary Convention on the Abolition of Slavery, the Slave Trade, and Institutions and Practices Similar to Slavery[58] (Supplementary Slavery Convention), which has more than 120 parties including Australia. 'Slavery' and the 'slave trade' are defined in terms materially identical to those in the Slavery Convention.[59]

10.30 The crime of engaging in the slave trade is reaffirmed and amplified by the Supplementary Slavery Convention in the following terms:

Article 3

1. The act of conveying or attempting to convey slaves from one country to another by whatever means of transport, or of being accessory thereto, shall be a criminal offence under the laws of the States Parties to this Convention and persons convicted thereof shall be liable to very severe penalties.

2. (a) The States Parties shall take all effective measures to prevent ships and aircraft authorized to fly their flags from conveying slaves and to punish persons guilty of such acts or of using national flags for that purpose.

10.31 Not only the slave trade, but also slavery itself, is criminalised in the Supplementary Slavery Convention:

Article 6

1. The act of enslaving another person or of inducing another person to give himself or a person dependent upon him into slavery, or of

---

54. Ibid, Art 1(2).
55. Ibid, Art 2(b).
56. General Assembly Resolution 217A (III); UN Doc A/810, 71 (1948).
57. UDHR, Art 4.
58. UNTS, Vol 266, p 3.
59. Supplementary Slavery Convention, Art 7.

attempting these acts, or being accessory thereto, or being a party to a conspiracy to accomplish any such acts, shall be a criminal offence under the laws of the States Parties to this Convention and persons convicted thereof shall be liable to punishment.

10.32 The Supplementary Slavery Convention also makes it a criminal offence to perform the acts proscribed in Art 6(1) in relation to debt bondage, serfdom, or certain practices affecting the status of women and minors that are analogous to slavery.[60]

10.33 Although it requires the abolition of slavery, the Supplementary Slavery Convention provides protections to those who remain enslaved by criminalising certain conduct directed against slaves:

Article 5

In a country where the abolition or abandonment of slavery ... is not yet complete, the act of mutilating, branding or otherwise marking a slave or a person of servile status in order to indicate his status, or as a punishment, or for any other reason, or of being accessory thereto, shall be a criminal offence under the laws of the States Parties to this Convention and persons convicted thereof shall be liable to punishment.

10.34 All major international human rights instruments specify the right of every person to be free from slavery.[61] That the prohibition on the slave trade is part of the *jus cogens* was very strongly indicated by 1966 when the International Law Commission, in its commentaries on the Draft Articles on the Law of Treaties, said that the trade in slaves was contrary to a peremptory norm of international law.[62] By 1970 at the latest, customary international law had developed to the point where the International Court of Justice was able to say that 'protection from slavery' is an obligation of an *erga omnes* character.[63]

10.35 'Enslavement' is now listed among the crimes against humanity falling within the jurisdiction of the ICC, 'when committed as part of a widespread or systematic attack directed against any civilian population, with knowledge of the attack'.[64] It is also listed among the crimes against humanity over which the ICTY has jurisdiction 'when committed in armed conflict, whether international or internal in character, and directed against any civilian population'.[65] The ICTR has jurisdiction over the crime of enslavement as a species of crimes against humanity 'when committed as part of a widespread or systematic attack against any civilian population on national, political, ethnic, racial or religious grounds'.[66]

---

60. Ibid, Arts 6(2) and 1.
61. International Covenant on Civil and Political Rights, Art 8; European Convention on Human Rights, Art 4; American Convention on Human Rights, Art 6; African Charter on Human and Peoples' Rights, Art 5.
62. *Yearbook of the International Law Commission*, 1966, Vol II, 248. See **2.107**.
63. *Case Concerning the Barcelona Traction, Light and Power Company Ltd* Second Phase, ICJ Rep (1970) 4, para 34. See **5.110**.
64. Rome Statute, Art 7(1)(c).
65. ICTY Statute, Art 5(c).
66. ICTR Statute, Art 3(c).

10.36 Although the jurisdictions of the ICC, ICTY and ICTR over 'enslavement' are limited by the contexts prescribed in their respective statutes (as is their jurisdiction over torture), those statutes and the Supplementary Slavery Convention strongly suggest that there is now an international crime of slavery *jure gentium*.

10.37 'Enslavement' (or the crime of slavery *jure gentium*) and certain modes of participation in the slave trade as proscribed by Art 3 of the Supplementary Slavery Convention are now probably international crimes attracting individual responsibility, even when committed outside the contexts conferring jurisdiction on the three principal international criminal tribunals.[67] Australian law, for instance, has already criminalised enslavement and the slave trade outside the context of armed conflicts, even where neither the perpetrators nor the victims are Australian nationals and even where the crime is committed outside Australia.[68]

Genocide

10.38 Perhaps the most egregious feature of the Second World War was the campaign of racial obliteration carried out by the National Socialist regime in Germany against Europe's Jewish population, and the mass annihilation of other victims in concentration camps where an estimated 12 million people perished. This aspect of the war, which was laid publicly bare in the proceedings of the Nuremberg Tribunal, prompted the conclusion in 1948 of the Genocide Convention.

10.39 The term 'genocide' did not enter into general circulation until after the Nuremberg Tribunal had completed its work, when a word was needed to describe the enormity of what had happened in Germany and some of its occupied territories during the war. Nor did the term appear in the Charter of the Nuremberg Tribunal, which instead employed the expression 'extermination'.[69] The Nuremberg Tribunal's judgments likewise did not refer to 'genocide', although the term was used in some of the indictments.

10.40 The crime of genocide is defined in the Genocide Convention as follows:

Article II

In the present Convention, genocide means any of the following acts committed with intent to destroy, in whole or in part, a national, ethnical, racial or religious group, as such:

(a) Killing members of the group;

(b) Causing serious bodily or mental harm to members of the group;

---

67. Semble Malcolm N Shaw, *International Law*, 6th ed, Cambridge University Press, Cambridge, 2008, 673–74; cf Antonio Cassese, *International Criminal Law*, 2nd ed, Oxford University Press, Oxford, 2008, 11–13.

68. *Criminal Code Act 1995* (Cth), Div 270.3.

69. Charter of the Nuremberg Tribunal, Art 6(c).

(c) Deliberately inflicting on the group conditions of life calculated to bring about its physical destruction in whole or in part;

(d) Imposing measures intended to prevent births within the group;

(e) Forcibly transferring children of the group to another group.

10.41 Article III of the Genocide Convention provides that genocide is punishable, as are any attempt, conspiracy, or direct and public incitement to commit genocide and any complicity in genocide.[70] Persons committing these acts 'shall be punished, whether they are constitutionally responsible rulers, public officials or private individuals'.[71]

10.42 Article VI of the Genocide Convention provides that '[p]ersons charged with genocide … shall be tried by a competent tribunal of the State in the territory of which the act was committed, or by such international penal tribunal as may have jurisdiction with respect to those Contracting Parties which shall have accepted its jurisdiction'. On a literal reading of Art VI, States parties to the Genocide Convention were not permitted to exercise jurisdiction over the crime of genocide except on the basis of the territorial principle. The ironic result, on this interpretation, is that genocide was less susceptible to State jurisdiction than were other crimes in respect of which States could also invoke the nationality and protective principles. Nevertheless, by no later than 1961 all States acquired universal jurisdiction over genocide as a matter of customary international law.[72] Alternatively, Art VI properly construed 'simply establishes the minimal obligations on states'[73] and always implied the availability of universal jurisdiction, thereby avoiding the ironic result attaching to the provision's literal interpretation. States must also enact 'effective penalties' for genocide and the adjectival offences.[74]

10.43 Because the National Socialist regime's campaign of racial extermination provides the popular paradigm of genocide, the most striking aspect of the definition in the Genocide Convention is that it encompasses a range of conduct that goes beyond the killing of large numbers of people on racial grounds. The varieties of prohibited conduct must, however, be 'committed with intent to destroy, in whole or in part, a national, ethnical, racial or religious group, as such'.

10.44 The International Criminal Court (ICC) possesses jurisdiction over the crime of genocide (including conspiracy, incitement and attempt to commit genocide, and complicity in genocide),[75] as does the International Criminal Tribunal for the Former Yugoslavia[76] (ICTY) and

---

70. Genocide Convention, Art III.
71. Ibid, Art IV.
72. *Attorney-General of the Government of Israel v Eichmann* (1961) 36 ILR 5 (see 6.22).
73. *Guatemala Genocide Case* STC-2005-237, Naomi Roht-Arriaza (2006) 100 *American Journal of International Law* 207, 210 (Spanish Constitutional Tribunal (Second Chamber)).
74. Genocide Convention, Art V.
75. Rome Statute, Art 5(1)(a).
76. ICTY Statute, Art 4.

the International Criminal Tribunal for Rwanda[77] (ICTR). The statutes of all these tribunals contain definitions of genocide materially identical to that of the Genocide Convention.[78]

The ICTR has convicted a number of defendants of the crime of genocide. In **Prosecutor v Akayesu,**[79] Jean-Paul Akayesu was a local (commune) mayor in Rwanda who, in 1994, organised massacres of ethnic Tutsi residents in his municipality. He became the first person ever to be convicted of the crime of genocide by an international tribunal. Articles 2(2) and 2(3) of the ICTR Statute are materially identical to Arts II and III respectively of the Genocide Convention. Article 2(3)(a) of the ICTR Statute provides that genocide shall be punishable, while Art 2(2) provides as follows:

> Genocide means any of the following acts committed with intent to destroy, in whole or in part, a national, ethnical, racial or religious group, as such:
>
> a)   Killing members of the group;
>
> b)   Causing serious bodily or mental harm to members of the group;
>
> c)   Deliberately inflicting on the group conditions of life calculated to bring about its physical destruction in whole or in part;
>
> d)   Imposing measures intended to prevent births within the group;
>
> e)   Forcibly transferring children of the group to another group.

The judgment of the ICTR's trial chamber included the following observations on the elements of the crime of genocide:

> **Crime of Genocide, punishable under Article 2(3)(a) of the Statute**
>
> …
>
> 495. The Genocide Convention is undeniably considered part of customary international law, as can be seen in the opinion of the International Court of Justice on the provisions of the Genocide Convention,[80] and as was recalled by the United Nations' Secretary-General in his Report on the establishment of the International Criminal Tribunal for the former Yugoslavia.[81] …
>
> 497. Contrary to popular belief, the crime of genocide does not imply the actual extermination of a group in its entirety, but is understood as such once any one of the acts mentioned in Article 2(2)(a) through 2(2)(e) is committed with the specific intent to destroy 'in whole or in part' a national, ethnical, racial or religious group.
>
> 498. Genocide is distinct from other crimes inasmuch as it embodies a special intent or *dolus specialis*. Special intent of a crime is the specific intention, required as a constitutive element of the crime, which demands that the perpetrator clearly seeks to produce the act charged. Thus, the special intent in the crime of genocide lies in 'the intent to destroy, in whole or in part, a national, ethnical, racial or religious group, as such'.

---

77.   ICTR Statute, Art 2.
78.   ICTY Statute, Art 4(2); ICTR Statute, Art 2(2); Rome Statute, Art 6. See also the Elements of Crimes adopted pursuant to Art 9 of the Rome Statute.
79.   *Prosecutor v Akayesu*, ICTR-96-4-T, (1998) 9 IHRR 608. Footnotes in this extract refer to sources cited in the judgment, unless referring to sections of this book.
80.   See **2.60**.
81.   General's Report pursuant to para 2 of Resolution 808 (1993) of the Security Council, 3 May 1993, S/25704.

499. Thus, for a crime of genocide to have been committed, it is necessary that one of the acts listed under Article 2(2) of the Statute be committed, that the particular act be committed against a specifically targeted group, it being a national, ethnical, racial or religious group. Consequently, in order to clarify the constitutive elements of the crime of genocide, the Chamber will first state its findings on the acts provided for under Article 2(2)(a) through Article 2(2)(e) of the Statute, the groups protected by the Genocide Convention, and the special intent or *dolus specialis* necessary for genocide to take place.

Killing members of the group (paragraph a):

500. With regard to Article 2(2)(a) of the Statute, like in the Genocide Convention, the Chamber notes that the said paragraph states *'meurtre'* in the French version while the English version states 'killing'. The Trial Chamber is of the opinion that the term 'killing' used in the English version is too general, since it could very well include both intentional and unintentional homicides, whereas the term *'meurtre'*, used in the French version, is more precise. It is accepted that there is murder when death has been caused with the intention to do so …

501. Given the presumption of innocence of the accused, and pursuant to the general principles of criminal law, the Chamber holds that the version more favourable to the accused should be upheld and finds that Article 2(2)(a) of the Statute must be interpreted in accordance with the definition of murder given in the Penal Code of Rwanda, according to which *'meurtre'* (killing) is homicide committed with the intent to cause death. The Chamber notes in this regard that the *travaux préparatoires* of the Genocide Convention,[82] show that the proposal by certain delegations that premeditation be made a necessary condition for there to be genocide, was rejected, because some delegates deemed it unnecessary for premeditation to be made a requirement; in their opinion, by its constitutive physical elements, the very crime of genocide, necessarily entails premeditation.

Causing serious bodily or mental harm to members of the group (paragraph b):

502. Causing serious bodily or mental harm to members of the group does not necessarily mean that the harm is permanent and irremediable.

503. In the Adolf Eichmann case,[83] who was convicted of crimes against the Jewish people, genocide under another legal definition, the District Court of Jerusalem stated in its judgment of 12 December 1961, that serious bodily or mental harm of members of the group can be caused:

> by the enslavement, starvation, deportation and persecution [...] and by their detention in ghettos, transit camps and concentration camps in conditions which were designed to cause their degradation, deprivation of their rights as human beings, and to suppress them and cause them inhumane suffering and torture.[84]

504. For purposes of interpreting Article 2(2)(b) of the Statute, the Chamber takes serious bodily or mental harm, without limiting itself thereto, to mean acts of torture, be they bodily or mental, inhumane or degrading treatment, persecution.

---

82. Summary Records of the meetings of the Sixth Committee of the General Assembly, 21 September–10 December 1948, Official Records of the General Assembly.
83. See **6.22**.
84. *Attorney General of the Government of Israel v Eichmann*, District Court of Jerusalem, 12 December 1961, quoted in (1968) 36 ILR 340.

Deliberately inflicting on the group conditions of life calculated to bring about its physical destruction in whole or in part (paragraph c):

505. The Chamber holds that the expression deliberately inflicting on the group conditions of life calculated to bring about its physical destruction in whole or in part, should be construed as the methods of destruction by which the perpetrator does not immediately kill the members of the group, but which, ultimately, seek their physical destruction.

506. For purposes of interpreting Article 2(2)(c) of the Statute, the Chamber is of the opinion that the means of deliberate inflicting on the group conditions of life calculated to bring about its physical destruction, in whole or part, include, *inter alia*, subjecting a group of people to a subsistence diet, systematic expulsion from homes and the reduction of essential medical services below minimum requirement.

Imposing measures intended to prevent births within the group (paragraph d):

507. For purposes of interpreting Article 2(2)(d) of the Statute, the Chamber holds that the measures intended to prevent births within the group, should be construed as sexual mutilation, the practice of sterilization, forced birth control, separation of the sexes and prohibition of marriages. In patriarchal societies, where membership of a group is determined by the identity of the father, an example of a measure intended to prevent births within a group is the case where, during rape, a woman of the said group is deliberately impregnated by a man of another group, with the intent to have her give birth to a child who will consequently not belong to its mother's group.

508. Furthermore, the Chamber notes that measures intended to prevent births within the group may be physical, but can also be mental. For instance, rape can be a measure intended to prevent births when the person raped refuses subsequently to procreate, in the same way that members of a group can be led, through threats or trauma, not to procreate.

Forcibly transferring children of the group to another group (paragraph e):

509. With respect to forcibly transferring children of the group to another group, the Chamber is of the opinion that, as in the case of measures intended to prevent births, the objective is not only to sanction a direct act of forcible physical transfer, but also to sanction acts of threats or trauma which would lead to the forcible transfer of children from one group to another.

510. Since the special intent to commit genocide lies in the intent to 'destroy, in whole or in part, a national, ethnical, racial or religious group, as such', it is necessary to consider a definition of the group as such. Article 2 of the Statute, just like the Genocide Convention, stipulates four types of victim groups, namely national, ethnical, racial or religious groups.

511. On reading through the *travaux préparatoires* of the Genocide Convention,[85] it appears that the crime of genocide was allegedly perceived as targeting only 'stable' groups, constituted in a permanent fashion and membership of which is determined by birth, with the exclusion of the more 'mobile' groups which one joins through individual voluntary commitment, such as political and economic groups. Therefore, a common criterion in the four types of groups protected by the Genocide Convention is that membership in such groups

---

85.   Summary Records of the meetings of the Sixth Committee of the General Assembly, 21 September–10 December 1948, Official Records of the General Assembly.

would seem to be normally not challengeable by its members, who belong to it automatically, by birth, in a continuous and often irremediable manner.

512. Based on the *Nottebohm* decision[86] rendered by the International Court of Justice, the Chamber holds that a national group is defined as a collection of people who are perceived to share a legal bond based on common citizenship, coupled with reciprocity of rights and duties.

513. An ethnic group is generally defined as a group whose members share a common language or culture.

514. The conventional definition of racial group is based on the hereditary physical traits often identified with a geographical region, irrespective of linguistic, cultural, national or religious factors.

515. The religious group is one whose members share the same religion, denomination or mode of worship.

516. Moreover, the Chamber considered whether the groups protected by the Genocide Convention, echoed in Article 2 of the Statute, should be limited to only the four groups expressly mentioned and whether they should not also include any group which is stable and permanent like the said four groups. In other words, the question that arises is whether it would be impossible to punish the physical destruction of a group as such under the Genocide Convention, if the said group, although stable and membership is by birth, does not meet the definition of any one of the four groups expressly protected by the Genocide Convention. In the opinion of the Chamber, it is particularly important to respect the intention of the drafters of the Genocide Convention, which according to the *travaux préparatoires,* was patently to ensure the protection of any stable and permanent group. ...

520. With regard to the crime of genocide, the offender is culpable only when he has committed one of the offences charged under Article 2(2) of the Statute with the clear intent to destroy, in whole or in part, a particular group. The offender is culpable because he knew or should have known that the act committed would destroy, in whole or in part, a group.

521. In concrete terms, for any of the acts charged under Article 2 (2) of the Statute to be a constitutive element of genocide, the act must have been committed against one or several individuals, because such individual or individuals were members of a specific group, and specifically because they belonged to this group. Thus, the victim is chosen not because of his individual identity, but rather on account of his membership of a national, ethnical, racial or religious group. The victim of the act is therefore a member of a group, chosen as such, which, hence, means that the victim of the crime of genocide is the group itself and not only the individual.[87]

522. The perpetration of the act charged therefore extends beyond its actual commission, for example, the murder of a particular individual, for the realisation of an ulterior motive, which is to destroy, in whole or part, the group of which the individual is just one element.

523. On the issue of determining the offender's specific intent, the Chamber considers that intent is a mental factor which is difficult, even impossible, to determine. This is the reason why, in the absence of a confession from the accused,

---

86.   International Court of Justice, 1955. See **5.108**.
87.   Nehemiah Robinson, *The Genocide Convention: Its Origins as Interpretation,* p 15, which, as the ICTR judgment notes, 'states that victims as individuals "are important not *per se* but as members of the group to which they belong".

his intent can be inferred from a certain number of presumptions of fact. The Chamber considers that it is possible to deduce the genocidal intent inherent in a particular act charged from the general context of the perpetration of other culpable acts systematically directed against that same group, whether these acts were committed by the same offender or by others. Other factors, such as the scale of atrocities committed, their general nature, in a region or a country, or furthermore, the fact of deliberately and systematically targeting victims on account of their membership of a particular group, while excluding the members of other groups, can enable the Chamber to infer the genocidal intent of a particular act.

524. Trial Chamber I of the International Criminal Tribunal for the former Yugoslavia also stated that the specific intent of the crime of genocide

> may be inferred from a number of facts such as the general political doctrine which gave rise to the acts possibly covered by the definition in Article 4 [of the ICTY Statute, materially identical to Article 2 of the ICTR Statute], or the repetition of destructive and discriminatory acts. The intent may also be inferred from the perpetration of acts which violate, or which the perpetrators themselves consider to violate the very foundation of the group-acts which are not in themselves covered by the list in Article 4(2) but which are committed as part of the same pattern of conduct.[88]

Thus, in the matter brought before the International Criminal Tribunal for the former Yugoslavia, the Trial Chamber, in its findings, found that

> this intent derives from the combined effect of speeches or projects laying the groundwork for and justifying the acts, from the massive scale of their destructive effect and from their specific nature, which aims at undermining what is considered to be the foundation of the group.[89] ...

731. With regard, particularly, to ... rape and sexual violence, the Chamber wishes to underscore the fact that in its opinion, they constitute genocide in the same way as any other act as long as they were committed with the specific intent to destroy, in whole or in part, a particular group, targeted as such. Indeed, rape and sexual violence certainly constitute infliction of serious bodily and mental harm on the victims and are even, according to the Chamber, one of the worst ways of inflict harm on the victim as he or she suffers both bodily and mental harm. In light of all the evidence before it, the Chamber is satisfied that ... acts of rape and sexual violence ..., were committed solely against Tutsi women, many of whom were subjected to the worst public humiliation, mutilated, and raped several times, often in public, in the Bureau Communal premises or in other public places, and often by more than one assailant. These rapes resulted in physical and psychological destruction of Tutsi women, their families and their communities. Sexual violence was an integral part of the process of destruction, specifically targeting Tutsi women and specifically contributing to their destruction and to the destruction of the Tutsi group as a whole.

10.45   The crime of genocide thus requires, as with all international crimes, an *actus reus* and a *mens rea*.

The *actus reus* for genocide may take any one of the five forms specified in Art II of the Genocide Convention, provided it is directed at one or more members of any stable and permanent group — such as a national,

---

88.   *Prosecutor v Karadžić*, IT-95-5-R61 & IT-95-18-R61, Consideration of the Indictment within the framework of Rule 61 of the Rules of Procedure and Evidence, 11 July 1996, para 94.
89.   Ibid, para 95.

ethnic, racial or religious group. The victim or victims must be chosen because of their membership of the target group, and not on the basis of some other factor.

Rape and sexual violence can constitute the *actus reus* of genocide where they cause serious bodily or mental harm (which will always be the case). It is also possible for an omission to constitute the necessary *actus reus*.[90] On the other hand, the forced migration of populations (or 'ethnic cleansing') is not an *actus reus* of genocide, although it may help establish the required *mens rea* when viewed in the context of other conduct.[91]

10.46 The *mens rea* for genocide is an intention to destroy, in whole or in part, the target group of which the particular victim or victims are a component. In *Prosecutor v Krstić*, the ICTY had occasion to consider what it means to destroy a group 'in part':[92]

> [T]he intent to destroy a group, even if only in part, means seeking to destroy a distinct part of the group as opposed to an accumulation of isolated individuals within it. Although the perpetrators of genocide need not seek to destroy the entire group protected by the Convention, they must view the part of the group they wish to destroy as a distinct entity which must be eliminated as such. A campaign resulting in the killings, in different places spread over a broad geographical area, of a finite number of members of a protected group might not thus qualify as genocide, despite the high total number of casualties, because it would not show an intent by the perpetrators to target the very existence of the group as such. Conversely, the killing of all members of the part of a group located within a small geographical area, although resulting in a lesser number of victims, would qualify as genocide if carried out with the intent to destroy the part of the group as such located in this small geographical area. Indeed, the physical destruction may target only a part of the geographically limited part of the larger group because the perpetrators of the genocide regard the intended destruction as sufficient to annihilate the group as a distinct entity in the geographic area at issue. In this regard, it is important to bear in mind the total context in which the physical destruction is carried out.

The required intention could, as with any international crime, be established by confession. In the absence of a confession of genocidal intention, it may be established by inference. Such an inference may be drawn where the impugned conduct forms part of a pattern of culpable acts systematically directed against the same group;[93] where non-members of the target group are excluded or protected from the impugned conduct; where there is repetition of the impugned conduct; where the scale and

---

90. *Prosecutor v Kambanda* ICTR 97-23-S, paras 39–40 (ICTR).
91. *Attorney-General of the Government of Israel v Eichmann* (1962) 36 ILR 5, para 185 (Supreme Court of Israel); *Prosecutor v Brdjanin*, IT-99-36-T, para 982 (ICTY).
92. *Prosecutor v Krstić*, IT-98-33-T, 2 August 2001, para 590.
93. The Elements of Crimes for Art 6 of the Rome Statute provide that the conduct of genocide must take place 'in the context of a manifest pattern of similar conduct directed against that group or [be] conduct that could itself effect such destruction'.

nature of the impugned conduct suggest a genocidal intention; where there is a general political doctrine, of which the impugned conduct is an expression or product, suggesting a genocidal intention; or where the combined effects of speeches or projects laying the groundwork for the impugned conduct suggest a genocidal intention.

Torture and cruel, inhuman or degrading treatment or punishment

Emergence of prohibition on torture and similar conduct

10.47 The prohibition of torture and similar conduct made its initial appearance in international law as 'a common standard of achievement for all peoples and all nations'[94] when the UDHR proclaimed in 1948 that '[n]o one shall be subjected to torture or to cruel, inhuman or degrading treatment or punishment'.[95]

10.48 The following year, the four Geneva Conventions imposed individual criminal responsibility for acts of 'torture and inhuman treatment' committed, in the context of an international armed conflict, against persons protected by those conventions.[96] Common Art 3(1)(a) of the four Geneva Conventions requires States parties to prohibit 'cruel treatment and torture', in the context of an internal armed conflict, against persons taking no active part in the hostilities, including members of armed forces who have laid down their arms and those placed *hors de combat* by sickness, wounds, detention or any other cause. In 1977, the first two protocols to the Geneva Conventions extended the prohibition on torture and similar conduct to the forms of armed conflict newly regulated by those protocols. Geneva Protocol I prohibits 'torture of all kinds, whether physical or mental', and 'humiliating and degrading treatment', regardless of whether the prohibited acts are performed by civilian or military agents.[97] Geneva Protocol II prohibits 'cruel treatment such as torture' and 'humiliating and degrading treatment'.[98]

10.49 The exhortation in the UDHR was transformed into similar conventional obligations in the European Convention on Human Rights (ECHR),[99] the International Covenant on Civil and Political Rights

---

94. UDHR, Preamble.
95. Ibid, Art 5.
96. Geneva Convention I, Art 50; Geneva Convention II, Art 51; Geneva Convention III, Art 130; Geneva Convention IV, Art 147.
97. Geneva Protocol I, Art 75(2).
98. Geneva Protocol II, Art 4(2).
99. Convention for the Protection of Human Rights and Fundamental Freedoms, UNTS, Vol 213, p 221; CETS, No 5. ECHR, Art 3: 'No one shall be subjected to torture or to inhuman or degrading treatment or punishment'.

(ICCPR),[100] and the American Convention on Human Rights (ACHR).[101] A prohibition on 'torture, cruel, inhuman or degrading punishment and treatment' was also proclaimed in the African Charter of Human and Peoples' Rights (ACHPR),[102] and a prohibition on 'physical or psychological torture or to cruel, degrading, humiliating or inhuman treatment' has been prescribed by the Arab Charter on Human Rights.[103] None of these instruments sought, however, to define either 'torture' or the terms describing the related forms of prohibited conduct.

10.50 In 1984, the General Assembly of the United Nations adopted the text of the Torture Convention. This instrument built upon General Assembly Resolution 3453 (XXX) (1975).[104] Entering into force in 1987, the Torture Convention has more than 145 States parties, including Australia. It provides that each State party 'shall take effective legislative, administrative, judicial or other measures to prevent acts of torture in any territory under its jurisdiction'.[105] The Torture Convention also provides that each State party 'shall undertake to prevent in any territory under its jurisdiction other acts of cruel, inhuman or degrading treatment or punishment which do not amount to torture'.[106]

10.51 The following year, the Organization of American States adopted the Inter-American Convention to Prevent and Punish Torture (IACPPT).[107] Entering into force the same year as the Torture Convention, the IACPPT provides that the States parties 'shall take effective measures to prevent and punish torture within their jurisdiction'.[108] The IACPPT also provides that each State party 'shall take effective measures to prevent and punish other cruel, inhuman, or degrading treatment or punishment within their jurisdiction'.[109]

10.52 The ICTY Statute confers jurisdiction on the ICTY to prosecute persons committing 'torture or inhuman treatment' when the impugned conduct constitutes a grave breach of any of the four Geneva Conventions,[110] and 'torture' or 'other inhumane acts' as crimes against humanity 'when committed in armed conflict, whether international or internal in character, and directed against any civilian population'.[111]

---

100. ICCPR, Art 7, UNTS, Vol 999, p 171: 'No one shall be subjected to torture or to cruel, inhuman or degrading treatment or punishment. In particular, no one shall be subjected without his free consent to medical or scientific experimentation.'
101. ACHR, Art 5(2), UNTS, Vol 1144, p 144: 'No one shall be subjected to torture or to cruel, inhuman, or degrading punishment or treatment. All persons deprived of their liberty shall be treated with respect for the inherent dignity of the human person.'
102. ACHPR, Art 5, UNTS, Vol 1520, p 345.
103. Arab Charter on Human Rights, Art 8(1), (2005) 12 IHRR 893.
104. 'Torture and other cruel, inhuman or degrading treatment or punishment in relation to detention and imprisonment.'
105. Torture Convention, Art 2(1).
106. Ibid, Art 16(1).
107. OAS Treaty Series, No 67.
108. IACPPT, Art 6.
109. Ibid.
110. ICTY Statute, Art 2(b).
111. Ibid, Art 5(f), (i).

10.53 The ICTR Statute confers jurisdiction on the ICTR to prosecute persons committing 'torture' and 'humiliating and degrading treatment' when the impugned conduct constitutes a serious violation of Common Art 3 of the four Geneva Conventions,[112] and 'torture' or 'other inhumane acts' as crimes against humanity 'when committed as part of a widespread or systematic attack against any civilian population on national, political, ethnic, racial or religious grounds'.[113]

10.54 The Rome Statute confers jurisdiction on the ICC to prosecute 'Torture' or 'Other inhumane acts of a similar character intentionally causing great suffering, or serious injury to body or to mental or physical health' as crimes against humanity 'when committed as part of a widespread or systematic attack directed against any civilian population, with knowledge of the attack'.[114] The ICC can also prosecute persons performing acts of 'Torture or inhuman treatment' when committed as 'war crimes in particular when committed as part of a plan or policy or as part of a large-scale commission of such crimes'.[115]

Definition of torture

10.55 The Torture Convention contains the first multilateral conventional definition of 'torture':

Article 1

1. For the purposes of this Convention, torture means any act by which severe pain or suffering, whether physical or mental, is intentionally inflicted on a person for such purposes as obtaining from him or a third person information or a confession, punishing him for an act he or a third person has committed or is suspected of having committed, or intimidating or coercing him or a third person, or for any reason based on discrimination of any kind, when such pain or suffering is inflicted by or at the instigation of or with the consent or acquiescence of a public official or other person acting in an official capacity. It does not include pain or suffering arising only from, inherent in or incidental to lawful sanctions.

2. This article is without prejudice to any international instrument or national legislation which does or may contain provisions of wider application.

10.56 Unlike the prohibition on torture in the four Geneva Conventions and their two protocols, the ICTY Statute, the ICTR Statute and the Rome Statute, the prohibition in the Torture Convention does not rely on the existence of an armed conflict or the commission of crimes against humanity. The crime of torture under the Torture Convention, and therefore under customary international law,[116] does not need to

---

112. ICTR Statute, Art 4(a), (e).
113. Ibid, Art 3(f), (i).
114. Rome Statute, Art 7(f), (k).
115. Ibid, Art 8(1), (2)(ii).
116. The definition of torture in the Torture Convention represents customary international law: *Prosecutor v Furundžija*, IT-95-17/1-T, 10 December 1998, para 160 (ICTY).

have been committed as part of a broader campaign or matrix of facts. Rather, the crime of torture is committed under the Torture Convention and customary international law whenever: (i) physical or mental pain or suffering of a *designated intensity* ('severe') is intentionally inflicted; (ii) the pain is inflicted by or at the instigation, or with the consent or acquiescence, of a *designated person* ('a public official or other person acting in an official capacity'); and (iii) the pain is inflicted for a *designated purpose* ('such purposes as obtaining from [the victim] or a third person information or a confession, punishing him for an act he or a third person has committed or is suspected of having committed, or intimidating or coercing him or a third person, or for any reason based on discrimination of any kind').

10.57 In 1992, the Human Rights Committee (HRC) established under the ICCPR[117] issued a General Comment on the interpretation and application of that convention's prohibition in Art 7 on torture and cruel, inhuman or degrading punishment or treatment.[118] The HRC declined to provide more comprehensive guidance on the meaning of torture than that already suggested in the ICCPR and the Torture Convention: 'The [ICCPR] does not contain any definition of the concepts covered by article 7, nor does the Committee consider it necessary to draw up a list of prohibited acts or to establish sharp distinctions between the different kinds of punishment or treatment; the distinctions depend on the nature, purpose and severity of the treatment applied.'[119] The Committee against Torture (CAT), established under the Torture Convention,[120] has yet to issue a General Comment dealing with the definition of torture.

10.58 The European Court of Human Rights has, however, considered what is required in order for conduct to constitute a violation of the prohibition on torture and inhuman or degrading treatment in Art 3 of the ECHR.

In ***Ireland v United Kingdom,***[121] factions of the Irish Republican Army (IRA), in pursuit of their goal of unifying the United Kingdom province of Northern Ireland with the Republic of Ireland, had been conducting a campaign of shootings and bombings against British civilian, police and military targets. Rival paramilitary groups, opposed to the political goals of the IRA, also emerged and engaged in armed violence. In response, the British authorities launched Operation Demetrius, in which about 350 persons suspected of being members of paramilitary gangs were, under emergency regulations, arrested and detained without trial. The Royal Ulster Constabulary (RUC, the police force in Northern Ireland) subjected 14 of the detained suspected paramilitaries to methods of interrogation which came to be known as the 'five techniques'. The government of the Republic of Ireland, on behalf of the men who had been subjected to the five techniques while in British custody, made an application to the European Commission of Human Rights. The

---

117. ICCPR, Art 28. See **11.25–11.29**.
118. General Comment No 20 of 1992. See **11.37**.
119. Ibid, para 4.
120. Torture Convention, Art 17.
121. *Ireland v United Kingdom,* Case 5310/71, (1978) 2 EHRR 25.

Commission reported that the five techniques, taken together, constituted torture in violation of Art 3 of the ECHR. Ireland then applied to the European Court of Human Rights to receive judicial confirmation of the Commission's report. The Court said:

96. Twelve persons arrested on 9 August 1971 and two persons arrested in October 1971 were singled out and taken to one or more unidentified centres. There, between 11 to 17 August and 11 to 18 October respectively, they were submitted to a form of 'interrogation in depth' which involved the combined application of five particular techniques.

These methods, sometimes termed 'disorientation' or 'sensory deprivation' techniques, were not used in any cases other than the fourteen so indicated above. It emerges from the Commission's establishment of the facts that the techniques consisted of:

(a) wall-standing: forcing the detainees to remain for periods of some hours in a 'stress position', described by those who underwent it as being 'spread eagled against the wall, with their fingers put high above the head against the wall, the legs spread apart and the feet back, causing them to stand on their toes with the weight of the body mainly on the fingers';

(b) hooding: putting a black or navy coloured bag over the detainees' heads and, at least initially, keeping it there all the time except during interrogation;

(c) subjection to noise: pending their interrogations, holding the detainees in a room where there was a continuous loud and hissing noise;

(d) deprivation of sleep: pending their interrogations, depriving the detainees of sleep;

(e) deprivation of food and drink: subjecting the detainees to a reduced diet during their stay at the centre and pending interrogations.

...

98. The two operations of interrogation in depth by means of the five techniques led to the obtaining of a considerable quantity of intelligence information, including the identification of 700 members of both IRA factions and the discovery of individual responsibility for about 85 previously unexplained criminal incidents.

...

102. At the hearing before the Court on 8 February 1977, the United Kingdom Attorney-General made the following declaration:

The Government of the United Kingdom have considered the question of the use of the 'five techniques' with very great care and with particular regard to Article 3 of the Convention. They now give this unqualified undertaking, that the 'five techniques' will not in any circumstances be reintroduced as an aid to interrogation.

...

150. Article 3 provides that 'no one shall be subjected to torture or to inhuman or degrading treatment or punishment'.

...

162. As was emphasised by the Commission, ill-treatment must attain a minimum level of severity if it is to fall within the scope of Article 3. The assessment of this minimum is, in the nature of things, relative; it depends on all the circumstances of the case, such as the duration of the treatment, its physical or mental effects and, in some cases, the sex, age and state of health of the victim, etc.

163. The Convention prohibits in absolute terms torture and inhuman or degrading treatment or punishment, irrespective of the victim's conduct. Unlike most of the substantive clauses of the Convention …, Article 3 makes no provision for exceptions and, under Article 15 (2), there can be no derogation therefrom even in the event of a public emergency threatening the life of the nation.

164. In the instant case, the only relevant concepts are 'torture' and 'inhuman or degrading treatment', to the exclusion of 'inhuman or degrading punishment'.

…

165. The facts concerning the five techniques are summarised … above. In the Commission's estimation, those facts constituted a practice not only of inhuman and degrading treatment but also of torture. The applicant Government asks for confirmation of this opinion which is not contested before the Court by the respondent Government.

166. The police used the five techniques on fourteen persons in 1971 …. Although never authorised in writing in any official document, the five techniques were taught orally by the English Intelligence Centre to members of the RUC at a seminar held in April 1971. …

167. The five techniques were applied in combination, with premeditation and for hours at a stretch; they caused, if not actual bodily injury, at least intense physical and mental suffering to the persons subjected thereto and also led to acute psychiatric disturbances during interrogation. They accordingly fell into the category of inhuman treatment within the meaning of Article 3. The techniques were also degrading since they were such as to arouse in their victims feelings of fear, anguish and inferiority capable of humiliating and debasing them and possibly breaking their physical or moral resistance.

On these two points, the Court is of the same view as the Commission.

In order to determine whether the five techniques should also be qualified as torture, the Court must have regard to the distinction, embodied in Article 3, between this notion and that of inhuman or degrading treatment.

In the Court's view, this distinction derives principally from a difference in the intensity of the suffering inflicted.

The Court considers in fact that, whilst there exists on the one hand violence which is to be condemned both on moral grounds and also in most cases under the domestic law of the Contracting States but which does not fall within Article 3 of the Convention, it appears on the other hand that it was the intention that the Convention, with its distinction between 'torture' and 'inhuman or degrading treatment', should by the first of these terms attach a special stigma to deliberate inhuman treatment causing very serious and cruel suffering.

Moreover, this seems to be the thinking lying behind Article 1 in fine of Resolution 3452 (XXX) adopted by the General Assembly of the United Nations on 9 December 1975, which declares: 'Torture constitutes an aggravated and deliberate form of cruel, inhuman or degrading treatment or punishment'.

Although the five techniques, as applied in combination, undoubtedly amounted to inhuman and degrading treatment, although their object was the extraction of confessions, the naming of others and/or information and although they were used systematically, they did not occasion suffering of the particular intensity and cruelty implied by the word torture as so understood.

168. The Court concludes that recourse to the five techniques amounted to a practice of inhuman and degrading treatment, which practice was in breach of Article 3.

10.59 The decision of the European Court of Human Rights in *Ireland v United Kingdom* indicates that torture on the one hand, and cruel, unusual or degrading treatment or punishment on the other, are the same phenomena at different points on a spectrum of seriousness. Both forms of conduct are unlawful, with torture being an aggravated or egregious and intentional manifestation of cruel or degrading treatment. Although the 'five techniques' constituted inhuman and degrading treatment, they did not in the Court's assessment rise to the level of torture because they did not cause 'very serious and cruel suffering'.

> In *Dikme v Turkey*,[122] on the other hand, the European Court of Human Rights held that the treatment to which the applicant was subjected at the hands of the Turkish police was sufficiently aggravated to constitute torture:
>
> > 12. At 7.30 a.m. on 10 February 1992 three police officers stopped and questioned the first applicant [Mr Dikme] and his female companion Y.O. in the Levent district of Istanbul. Both were in possession of false identity papers. They were immediately arrested and, after a wait of several hours at the local police station, were taken to the anti-terrorist branch of the Levent police headquarters in Istanbul ('the branch').
> >
> > They were taken into custody in separate parts of the building. On arrival, the first applicant was blindfolded and a group of police officers who said they were members of the 'anti-*Dev-Sol*'[123] squad began punching and kicking him, threatening to kill him if he did not reveal his true identity. He was then led to a ground-floor room where he was stripped, had his hands tied together behind his back and was suspended by his arms, a method known as 'Palestinian hanging'. For several hours the police officers beat him repeatedly while he was in this position and administered electric shocks through electrodes attached to his feet and genitals.
> >
> > 13. At about 7 p.m. Mr Dikme was carried to another room and made to lie on the floor with his hands still tied behind his back. A man who said he was a member of the secret service told him: 'You belong to *Devrimci Sol,* and if you don't give us the information we need, you'll be leaving here feet first!' The police officers then started to beat him, aiming some of their blows at his genitals. That lasted until 2 a.m., at which point he was taken to a 2-sq. m. cell, where he had to sleep naked on the floor.
> >
> > 14. At about 8 a.m. the next morning he was taken back to the ground floor, tied up and laid on the ground. He suffered a further beating and electric shocks were administered to his feet, the area behind his ears and his tongue. By the time the torturers went to lunch, he had already fainted twice. An hour later he was again subjected to 'Palestinian hanging' and given electric shocks while having cold water poured over him. He was then left lying on the concrete, naked and blindfolded.
> >
> > That evening he was taken back upstairs, where the secret-service agent dragged him by the hair and twice banged his head against the wall. He was then dressed and taken to a forest, where somebody pointed a revolver at his head and urged him to say his 'last prayer' before firing a blank shot. Immediately after

---

122. *Dikme v Turkey*, Case 2086/92, [2000] ECHR 366.
123. A footnote here in the ECHR judgment explains that 'Dev-Sol' (Revolutionary Left) is the term commonly used for the extreme left-wing armed movement Türkiye Halk Kurtuluş Partisi/Cephesi-Devrimci Sol.

this mock execution, he was escorted back to the branch. There he was again blindfolded and stripped and then placed in a bath of ice-cold water. The next day the police officers continued to ill-treat him.

15. The ill-treatment ended on Mr Dikme's fifth day in custody. However, he continued to be questioned while blindfolded, and was subjected to a barrage of abuse.

...

89. As the Court has held on many occasions, Article 3 enshrines one of the most fundamental values of democratic societies. Even in the most difficult circumstances, such as the fight against terrorism and organised crime, the Convention prohibits in absolute terms torture or inhuman or degrading treatment or punishment. Unlike most of the substantive clauses of the Convention and of Protocols Nos. 1 and 4, Article 3 makes no provision for exceptions and no derogation from it is permissible under Article 15 § 2 even in the event of a public emergency threatening the life of the nation ...

90. The Court reiterates that, in respect of a person deprived of his liberty, recourse to physical force which has not been made strictly necessary by his own conduct diminishes human dignity and is an infringement of the right set forth in Article 3 ... In this connection, the requirements of an investigation and the undeniable difficulties inherent in the fight against terrorist crime cannot justify placing limits on the protection to be afforded in respect of the physical integrity of individuals (see, *mutatis mutandis*, the *Ribitsch v Austria* judgment of 4 December 1995, Series A no. 336, p. 26, § 38). It should also be borne in mind that the prohibition of torture and inhuman or degrading treatment or punishment is absolute, irrespective of the victim's conduct and — where detainees are concerned — the nature of the alleged offence ...

91. Having regard to the facts which it regards as established ..., the Court considers that the blows inflicted on Mr Dikme were such as to cause both physical and mental pain or suffering, which could not but have been exacerbated by his total isolation and the additional factor that he was blindfolded. Mr Dikme was therefore treated in a way that was likely to arouse in him feelings of fear, anxiety and vulnerability likely to humiliate and debase him and break his resistance and will.

92. The Court accordingly considers that the violence inflicted on the first applicant was both inhuman and degrading.

In this connection, it points out that in *Selmouni*,[124] in accordance with the principle that the Convention was a 'living instrument which must be interpreted in the light of present-day conditions', it said that certain acts which had previously been classified as 'inhuman and degrading treatment' as opposed to 'torture' might be classified differently in future (see *Selmouni* ..., § 101):

> ... the increasingly high standard being required in the area of the protection of human rights and fundamental liberties correspondingly and inevitably requires greater firmness in assessing breaches of the fundamental values of democratic societies.

It therefore remains to be determined whether the treatment meted out to Mr Dikme can, as he submitted, be classified as torture.

93. The Court must first give due weight to the distinction embodied in Article 3 between the notion of torture and that of inhuman or degrading treatment. It appears that the distinction was drawn in the Convention in

---

124. *Selmouni v France*, Case 25803/94, (1999) 29 EHRR 403.

order to attach a special stigma to deliberate inhuman treatment causing very serious and cruel suffering (ibid., § 96).

94. A similar distinction is made in Article 1 of the [Torture Convention] …

As the Court has previously found, the criterion of 'severity' referred to in [Article 1 of the Torture Convention] is, in the nature of things, relative, like the 'minimum severity' required for the application of Article 3 (ibid., § 100); it depends on all the circumstances of the case, such as the duration of the treatment, its physical and/or mental effects and, in some cases, the victim's sex, age and state of health …

95. In the instant case the first applicant undeniably lived in a permanent state of physical pain and anxiety owing to his uncertainty about his fate and to the blows repeatedly inflicted on him during the lengthy interrogation sessions to which he was subjected throughout his time in police custody.

The Court considers that such treatment was intentionally meted out to the first applicant by agents of the State in the performance of their duties, with the aim of extracting a confession or information about the offences of which he was suspected.

96. In those circumstances the Court finds that the violence inflicted on the first applicant, taken as a whole and having regard to its purpose and duration, was particularly serious and cruel and was capable of causing 'severe' pain and suffering. It therefore amounted to torture within the meaning of Article 3 of the Convention.

97. There has consequently been a violation of Article 3 on that account.

10.60   The European Court of Human Rights in *Dikme v Turkey* held that the treatment meted out to the applicant over five days clearly crossed the threshold qualifying it as degrading within the meaning of Art 3 of the ECHR. Indeed, the mere fact that the applicant was, while deprived of his liberty, subjected to physical force not required as a response to his own conduct was enough to qualify the treatment as unlawfully degrading. The fact that his treatment was likely to arouse fear, anxiety and vulnerability likely to humiliate and debase him, and break his resistance and will, provided additional grounds for holding that the applicant was subjected to unlawfully inhuman and degrading treatment.

10.61   Having thus established that the treatment meted out to the applicant violated the prohibition in Art 3 on unlawful conduct falling short of torture, the next step was to consider whether any of the same conduct was so serious as to amount also to a violation of the prohibition on torture. The Court observed that the reason for dividing the prohibited conducted in Art 3 into torture and the other forms of prohibited conduct was to attach a 'special stigma to [torture as] deliberate inhuman treatment causing very serious and cruel suffering'. Most significantly, the degree of severity required in order for unlawful conduct to rise to the level of torture depends on 'all the circumstances of the case, such as the duration of the treatment, its physical and/or mental effects and, in some cases, the victim's sex, age and state of health'. In this regard, the court noted that the applicant lived for five days in a 'permanent state of physical pain and anxiety' owing to the 'particularly serious and cruel' violence deliberately inflicted on him by public officials in order to extract a confession. The Court found that the pain caused was, in all the circumstances, sufficiently severe as to qualify for the more serious violation of the prohibition on torture.

10.62   Finally, the Court in *Dikme v Turkey* reaffirmed its recently propounded jurisprudence in which the location of the threshold separating torture from the other forms of conduct prohibited by Art 3 is subject to change. According to this view, some forms of conduct which were earlier considered to be insufficiently severe as to constitute torture would now be regarded as violating the prohibition on torture. This is because, in the Court's view, standards of human rights protection are becoming increasingly stringent over time. It is possible, therefore, that some or all of the 'five techniques' employed in *Ireland v United Kingdom* would now be held by the European Court of Human Rights to constitute torture.

Definitional significance

10.63   The four Geneva Conventions and their first two protocols, the ECHR, the ICCPR, the ACHR, the Torture Convention, the IACPPT, the ACHPR, the ICTY Statute, the ICTR Statute, the Rome Statute and the Arab Charter on Human Rights all prohibit or criminalise both torture and similar conduct, such as inhuman and degrading treatment. Why, then, is there any necessity to expend effort deciding whether a particular form of prohibited conduct rises to the level of 'torture'? There are a number of reasons why the distinction matters.

10.64   The first reason is less juridical than socio-psychological. As the European Court of Human Rights pointed out in *Dikme v Turkey*, 'the distinction was drawn in the Convention [ECHR] in order to attach a special stigma to deliberate inhuman treatment causing very serious and cruel suffering'.[125] Put another way, no civilised State wishes to attract the acute diplomatic odium, and no government the acute political odium, of a definitive judicial finding that it has engaged in acts of torture. In the context of individual criminal responsibility, this translates into the juridical reality that torture is a more serious charge even than one of cruel, inhuman or degrading treatment or punishment.

10.65   The distinction is also important in the context of the jurisdiction of domestic courts. States parties to the Torture Convention are obliged to ensure that all acts of torture, including attempts to commit torture and complicity or participation in torture, are offences under their criminal law.[126] They must also make these offences 'punishable by appropriate penalties which take into account their grave nature'.[127] The Torture

---

125. *Dikme v Turkey*, Case 2086/92, [2000] ECHR 366, para 93.
126. Torture Convention, Art 4(1).
127. Ibid, Art 4(2).

Convention requires a State party to establish its jurisdiction over the crime of torture when the offence is committed in its own territory, when the alleged offender is a national of that State party (thereby requiring jurisdiction on the basis of the active nationality principle), and when the victim was a national of that State 'if that State considers it appropriate' (thereby permitting jurisdiction on the basis of the passive nationality principle).[128] A State party to the Torture Convention is also under an obligation to extradite an alleged torturer in its territory and under its jurisdiction to the State on whose territory the offence was committed, to the State of the alleged offender's nationality, or to the State of the victim's nationality. Unless the State party chooses one of these options, it must prosecute the offender itself — even if the only connection between the crime and the State is that the alleged offender is in the State's territory and under its jurisdiction.[129] Where a person alleged to have committed the offence of torture is in the territory of a State party, it must 'take him into custody or take other legal measures to ensure his presence' pending an inquiry into the facts and a decision as to whether he should be prosecuted or extradited.[130] Thus, the Torture Convention establishes, at least for those States party to it and who have adopted any necessary domestic juridical measures giving effect to it,[131] a version of universal jurisdiction for the crime of torture. No such jurisdictional regime is established for cruel, unusual or degrading treatment or punishment.

10.66   States parties to the Torture Convention must also 'afford one another the greatest measure of assistance in connection with criminal proceedings brought in respect of [torture offences], including the supply of all evidence at their disposal necessary for the proceedings'.[132] No similar obligation is prescribed for cruel, inhuman or degrading treatment or punishment.

10.67   States are forbidden to expel, return or extradite a person to any State where there are substantial grounds for believing that he or she would be in danger of being subjected to torture.[133] The Torture Convention contains no similar injunction for the lesser forms of proscribed conduct.

10.68   Where the unlawful conduct is sufficiently severe to constitute torture, it is not possible to rely on 'any exceptional circumstances whatsoever, whether a state of war or a threat of war, internal political instability or any other public emergency … as a justification'.[134] Moreover, where the unlawful conduct of an accused person crosses the threshold of torture, an 'order from a superior officer or a public authority may not be invoked as a justification'.[135] Once again, the Torture Convention

---

128. Ibid, Art 5(1). As to the active and passive personality principles of jurisdiction, see 6.13–6.17.
129. Torture Convention, Arts 5(2), 7 and 8.
130. Ibid, Art 6.
131. *R v Bow Street Metropolitan Stipendiary Magistrate; Ex parte Pinochet Ugarte (No 3)* [2000] 1 AC 147 (House of Lords). See 6.60.
132. Torture Convention, Art 9(1).
133. Ibid, Art 3(1). See *Elmi v Australia* (2000) 7 IHRR 603 (CAT).
134. Torture Convention, Art 2(2).
135. Ibid, Art 2(3).

contains no similar caveat concerning the less severe forms of prohibited conduct.[136]

10.69   Finally, the Torture Convention establishes a procedure whereby the CAT is empowered to conduct an inquiry when it 'receives reliable information which appears to it to contain well-founded indications that torture is being systematically practised in the territory of a State Party'.[137] No power of inquiry is conferred on the CAT in respect of conduct amounting to cruel, unusual or degrading treatment or punishment not rising to the level of torture.

Crimes against humanity

10.70   Crimes against humanity are international crimes attracting individual responsibility. They may be prosecuted before any international tribunal on which jurisdiction has been conferred by or under a treaty. This includes tribunals established by treaty such as the Nuremberg Tribunal or the ICC. It also includes tribunals, such as the ICTY and the ICTR, established under Charter VII of the United Nations Charter. They are also customary law obligations of a *jus cogens* character and may be prosecuted by national courts employing jurisdiction based on the universality principle.[138]

Elements of crimes against humanity

10.71   The Charter of the Nuremberg Tribunal was the first multilateral treaty to codify crimes against humanity. These crimes were constituted by specified acts committed in a prescribed context by a particular pool of potential defendants. The acts were murder, extermination, enslavement, deportation and 'other inhumane acts'. The context was the commission of any of the specified acts 'against any civilian population'. Persecutions on political, racial or religious grounds 'in execution of or in connection with' any crime within the Nuremberg Tribunal's jurisdiction also constituted crimes against humanity. The pool of potential defendants comprised 'persons ... acting in the interests of the European Axis countries, whether as individuals or as members of organizations'.[139]

10.72   The ICTY has jurisdiction over crimes against humanity where specified acts are committed in the context of 'armed conflict, whether

---

136. The major human rights charters provide, however, that States parties may never derogate from the obligation to prevent both torture and the less severe forms of prohibited conduct, even on grounds such as public emergency: ICCPR, Art 4(2); ECHR, Art 15(2); ACHR, Art 27(2).
137. Torture Convention, Art 20.
138. *Attorney-General of the Government of Israel v Eichmann* (1962) 36 ILR 5 (District Court of Jerusalem and Supreme Court of Israel); *Fédération Nationale des Déportés et Internés Résistants et Patriotes v Barbie* (1983–84) 78 ILR 125 (Court of Cassation, France); *R v Finta (No 3)* [1994] 1 SCR 701; (1994) 104 ILR 284 (Supreme Court of Canada); Malcolm N Shaw, *International Law*, 6th ed, Cambridge University Press, Cambridge, 2008, 671.
139. Charter of the Nuremberg Tribunal, Art 6(b).

international or internal in character, and directed against any civilian population'. These acts incorporate and expand upon the list used at Nuremberg: murder; extermination; enslavement; deportation; imprisonment; torture; rape; persecutions on political, racial and religious grounds; and other inhumane acts.[140] The ICTR has jurisdiction over crimes against humanity where the same acts are committed 'as part of a widespread or systematic attack against any civilian population on national, political, ethnic, racial or religious grounds'.[141]

10.73   The Rome Statute confers jurisdiction on the ICC for crimes against humanity[142] and builds upon the Charter of the Nuremberg Tribunal and the Statutes of the ICTY and the ICTR by providing as follows:

Article 7

Crimes Against Humanity

1. For the purpose of this Statute, 'crime against humanity' means any of the following acts when committed as part of a widespread or systematic attack directed against any civilian population, with knowledge of the attack:

    (a) Murder;

    (b) Extermination;

    (c) Enslavement;

    (d) Deportation or forcible transfer of population;

    (e) Imprisonment or other severe deprivation of physical liberty in violation of fundamental rules of international law;

    (f) Torture;

    (g) Rape, sexual slavery, enforced prostitution, forced pregnancy, enforced sterilization, or any other form of sexual violence of comparable gravity;

    (h) Persecution against any identifiable group or collectivity on political, racial, national, ethnic, cultural, religious, gender as defined in paragraph 3,[143] or other grounds that are universally recognized as impermissible under international law, in connection with any act referred to in this paragraph or any crime within the jurisdiction of the Court;

    (i) Enforced disappearance of persons;

    (j) The crime of apartheid;

---

140. ICTY Statute, Art 5. These crimes must also have been committed in the territory of the former Yugoslavia since 1991: ICTY Statute, Arts 1 and 8.
141. ICTR Statute, Art 3. These crimes must also have been committed by any persons in Rwanda or by Rwandan citizens in States neighbouring Rwanda between January 1991 and December 1994: ICTR Statute, Arts 2, 3, 4 and 7.
142. Rome Statute, Art 5(1)(b).
143. Rome Statute, Art 7(3) provides as follows: 'For the purpose of this Statute, it is understood that the term "gender" refers to the two sexes, male and female, within the context of society. The term "gender" does not indicate any meaning different from the above.'

(k) Other inhumane acts of a similar character intentionally causing great suffering, or serious injury to body or to mental or physical health.

10.74 As with the definitions of 'crimes against humanity' in the Charter of the Nuremberg Tribunal and in the Statutes of the ICTY and the ICTR, the Rome Statute defines the term by reference to a range of specified acts committed in a prescribed context.

10.75 The specified acts in Art 7 of the Rome Statute are the same as those identified in the text of the ICTY and ICTR Statutes, but with the following express additions: enslavement; forcible transfer of population (that is, 'ethnic cleansing'); severe deprivation of physical liberty in violation of fundamental rules of international law (as distinct from 'imprisonment'); sexual slavery, enforced prostitution, forced pregnancy, enforced sterilization, or any other form of sexual violence of comparable gravity (as distinct from 'rape'); persecution against any identifiable group or collectivity on national, ethnic, cultural, gender or other grounds that are universally recognised as impermissible under international law, in connection with any crime within the jurisdiction of the ICC (as distinct from persecution on 'political, racial or religious grounds'); enforced disappearance of persons; the crime of apartheid; and other inhumane acts of a similar character intentionally causing great suffering, or serious injury to body or to mental or physical health (as distinct from simply 'other inhumane acts').

10.76 The context required by the Rome Statute is that the specified acts must be 'committed as part of a widespread or systematic attack directed against any civilian population, with knowledge of the attack'. A similar context is also required by the Charter of the Nuremberg Tribunal and by the Statutes of the ICTY[144] and the ICTR. Acts of murder, rape, enslavement, deportation and so on which are not committed as part of a widespread or systematic attack on a civilian population cannot constitute a crime against humanity.

In *Prosecutor v Akayesu* (for the facts of which, see 10.44 above),[145] the ICTR made the following observations concerning both the specified acts and the prescribed context of crimes against humanity:

Crimes against Humanity in Article 3 of the Statute of the Tribunal

578. The Chamber considers that Article 3 of the [ICTR] Statute confers on the Chamber the jurisdiction to prosecute persons for various inhumane acts which constitute crimes against humanity. This category of crimes may be broadly broken down into four essential elements, namely:

---

144. Although Art 5 of the ICTY Statute does not expressly require a 'widespread and systematic attack', the ICTY has interpreted the provision to mean that a crime against humanity can be committed only where the prescribed acts 'occur on a widespread or systematic basis, ... there must be some form of a governmental organizational or group policy to commit these acts and ... the perpetrator must know of the context within which his actions are taken': *Prosecutor v Tadić*, IT-94-1-T, (1997) 112 ILR 1, para 644.
145. *Prosecutor v Akayesu*, ICTR-96-4-T, (1998) 9 IHRR 608. Footnotes in this extract refer to sources cited in the judgment.

(i)   the act must be inhumane in nature and character, causing great suffering, or serious injury to body or to mental or physical health;

(ii)   the act must be committed as part of a wide spread or systematic attack;

(iii)   the act must be committed against members of the civilian population;

(iv)   the act must be committed on one or more discriminatory grounds, namely, national, political, ethnic, racial or religious grounds.

The act must be committed as part of a wide spread or systematic attack

579. The Chamber considers that it is a prerequisite that the act must be committed as part of a wide spread or systematic attack and not just a random act of violence. The act can be part of a widespread or systematic attack and need not be a part of both.[146]

580. The concept of 'widespread' may be defined as massive, frequent, large scale action, carried out collectively with considerable seriousness and directed against a multiplicity of victims. The concept of 'systematic' may be defined as thoroughly organised and following a regular pattern on the basis of a common policy involving substantial public or private resources. There is no requirement that this policy must be adopted formally as the policy of a state. There must however be some kind of preconceived plan or policy.[147]

581. The concept of 'attack' maybe defined as a unlawful act of the kind enumerated in Article 3(a) to (i) of the Statute, like murder, extermination, enslavement etc. An attack may also be non violent in nature, like imposing a system of apartheid, which is declared a crime against humanity in Article 1 of the Apartheid Convention of 1973, or exerting pressure on the population to act in a particular manner, may come under the purview of an attack, if orchestrated on a massive scale or in a systematic manner.

The act must be directed against the civilian population

582. The Chamber considers that an act must be directed against the civilian population if it is to constitute a crime against humanity. Members of the civilian population are people who are not taking any active part in the hostilities, including members of the armed forces who laid down their arms and those persons placed *hors de combat* by sickness, wounds, detention or any other cause.[148] Where there are certain individuals within the civilian population who do not come within the definition of civilians, this does not deprive the population of its civilian character.[149]

---

146. A footnote here in the ICTR's judgment explains:
    In the original French version of the Statute, these requirements were worded cumulatively: 'Dans le cadre dune adieux generalise et systematic', thereby significantly increasing the threshold for application of this provision. Since Customary International Law requires only that the attack be either widespread or systematic, there are sufficient reasons to assume that the French version suffers from an error in translation.
147. Report on the International Law Commission to the General Assembly, 51 UN GAOR Supp (No 10), 94 UN Doc A/51/10 (1996).
148. A footnote here in the judgment states:
    Note that this definition assimilates the definition of 'civilian' to the categories of person protected by Common Article 3 of the Geneva Conventions; an assimilation which would not appear to be problematic. Note also that the ICTY Vukovar Rule 61 Decision, of 3 April 1996, recognised that crimes against humanity could be committed where the victims were captured members of a resistance movement who at one time had borne arms, who would thus qualify as persons placed hors de combat by detention.
149. Protocol Additional to the Geneva Convention of 12 August 1949, and relating to the Protection of Victims of International Armed Conflict, Art 50.

...

The enumerated acts

585. Article 3 of the Statute sets out various acts that constitute crimes against humanity, namely: murder; extermination; enslavement; deportation; imprisonment; torture; rape; persecution on political, racial and religious grounds; and; other inhumane acts. Although the category of acts that constitute crimes against humanity are set out in Article 3, this category is not exhaustive. Any act which is inhumane in nature and character may constitute a crime against humanity, provided the other elements are met. This is evident in (i) which caters for all other inhumane acts not stipulated in (a) to (h) of Article 3.

586. The Chamber notes that the accused is indicted for murder, extermination, torture, rape and other acts that constitute inhumane acts. The Chamber in interpreting Article 3 of the Statute, shall focus its discussion on these acts only.

Murder

587. The Chamber considers that murder is a crime against humanity, pursuant to Article 3 (a) of the Statute. The International Law Commission discussed the inhumane act of murder in the context of the definition of crimes against humanity and concluded that the crime of murder is clearly understood and defined in the national law of every state and therefore there is no need to further explain this prohibited act.

...

589. The Chamber defines murder as the unlawful, intentional killing of a human being. The requisite elements of murder are:

1.   the victim is dead;

2.   the death resulted from an unlawful act or omission of the accused or a subordinate;

3.   at the time of the killing the accused or a subordinate had the intention to kill or inflict grievous bodily harm on the deceased having known that such bodily harm is likely to cause the victim's death, and is reckless whether death ensures or not.

590. Murder must be committed as part of a widespread or systematic attack against a civilian population. The victim must be a member of this civilian population. The victim must be a member of this civilian population. The victim must have been murdered because he was discriminated against on national, ethnic, racial, political or religious grounds.

Extermination

591. The Chamber considers that extermination is a crime against humanity, pursuant to Article 3 (c) of the Statute. Extermination is a crime which by its very nature is directed against a group of individuals. Extermination differs from murder in that it requires an element of mass destruction which is not required for murder.

592. The Chamber defines the essential elements of extermination as the following:

1.   the accused or his subordinate participated in the killing of certain named or described persons;

2.   the act or omission was unlawful and intentional.

3.   the unlawful act or omission must be part of a widespread or systematic attack;

4.   the attack must be against the civilian population;

5.   the attack must be on discriminatory grounds, namely: national, political, ethnic, racial, or religious grounds.

Torture

593. The Chamber considers that torture is a crime against humanity pursuant to Article 3(f) of the Statute. Torture may be defined as:

> … any act by which severe pain or suffering, whether physical or mental, is intentionally inflicted on a person for such purposes as obtaining from him or a third person information or a confession, punishing him for an act he or a third person has committed or is suspected of having committed, or intimidating or coercing him or a third person, or for any reason based on discrimination of any kind, when such pain or suffering is inflicted by or at the instigation of or with the consent or acquiescence of a public official or other person acting in an official capacity.[150]

594. The Chamber defines the essential elements of torture as:

(i)   The perpetrator must intentionally inflict severe physical or mental pain or suffering upon the victim for one or more of the following purposes:

    (a)   to obtain information or a confession from the victim or a third person;

    (b)   to punish the victim or a third person for an act committed or suspected of having been committed by either of them;

    (c)   for the purpose of intimidating or coercing the victim or the third person;

    (d)   for any reason based on discrimination of any kind.

(ii)   The perpetrator was himself an official, or acted at the instigation of, or with the consent or acquiescence of, an official or person acting in an official capacity.

595. The Chamber finds that torture is a crime against humanity if the following further elements are satisfied:

(a)   Torture must be perpetrated as part of a widespread or systematic attack;

(b)   the attack must be against the civilian population;

(c)   the attack must be launched on discriminatory grounds, namely: national, ethnic, racial, religious and political grounds.

Rape

596. Considering the extent to which rape constitute crimes against humanity, pursuant to Article 3(g) of the Statute, the Chamber must define rape, as there is no commonly accepted definition of this term in international law. While rape has been defined in certain national jurisdictions as non-consensual intercourse, variations on the act of rape may include acts which involve the insertion of objects and/or the use of bodily orifices not considered to be intrinsically sexual.

597. The Chamber considers that rape is a form of aggression and that the central elements of the crime of rape cannot be captured in a mechanical description of objects and body parts. The Convention against Torture and Other Cruel, Inhuman and Degrading Treatment or Punishment does not catalogue specific

---

150.   Convention against Torture and Other Cruel, Inhuman or Degrading Treatment or Punishment, Art 1.

acts in its definition of torture, focusing rather on the conceptual framework of state sanctioned violence. This approach is more useful in international law. Like torture, rape is used for such purposes as intimidation, degradation, humiliation, discrimination, punishment, control or destruction of a person. Like torture, rape is a violation of personal dignity, and rape in fact constitutes torture when inflicted by or at the instigation of or with the consent or acquiescence of a public official or other person acting in an official capacity.

598. The Chamber defines rape as a physical invasion of a sexual nature, committed on a person under circumstances which are coercive. Sexual violence which includes rape, is considered to be any act of a sexual nature which is committed on a person under circumstances which are coercive. This act must be committed:

(a)   as part of a wide spread or systematic attack;

(b)   on a civilian population;

(c)   on certain catalogued discriminatory grounds, namely: national, ethnic, political, racial, or religious grounds.

Prescribed context

10.77   The context in which the specified acts must be performed in order to constitute crimes against humanity include, according to the ICTR in *Akayesu*, a requirement that they be committed on grounds discriminating on the basis of nationality, ethnicity, political considerations, race or religion. Although discrimination is required by the terms of the ICTR Statute in order for the ICTR to exercise jurisdiction, it is not required by the ICTY Statute or the Rome Statute. Rather, the requirement of discrimination in the ICTR Statute is explained by the special circumstances which the Tribunal was established to address. Similarly, the identified pool of potential defendants in the Charter of the Nuremberg Tribunal was a creature of the special circumstances with which the victorious powers were confronted in 1945. Neither discrimination nor an association with National Socialist Germany or its European allies is required in order to establish crimes against humanity. Customary international law requires only that the prescribed acts be part of a widespread or systematic attack directed against any civilian population, with knowledge of the attack.

10.78   As the ICTR indicates in *Akayesu*, the prescribed act must be committed as part of a widespread or systematic attack, and not just 'a random act of violence'.[151] There will be an 'attack' when any of the specified violent acts (murder, torture, rape, and so on) are committed. An 'attack' can also occur in the form of non-violent 'pressure' to act in a particular way 'if orchestrated on a massive scale or in a systematic manner'.[152] The imposition of a regime of apartheid is given as an example, but other pressured acts compelling a civilian population to

---

151. *Prosecutor v Akayesu*, ICTR-96-4-T, (1998) 9 IHRR 608, para 579.
152. Ibid, para 581.

act in a way which denies basic human rights would also be covered. An example would be the suppression of religious freedom on a massive scale or in a systematic manner.

10.79   The attack will not be 'widespread' unless it is 'massive, frequent, large scale action, carried out collectively with considerable seriousness and directed against a multiplicity of victims'. It cannot be 'systematic' unless it is 'thoroughly organised and following a regular pattern on the basis of a common policy involving substantial public or private resources' involving 'some kind of preconceived plan or policy'.[153] The attack must be *either* widespread *or* systematic; it need not be both.[154] An entirely spontaneous unorganised attack probably does not suffice. There needs to be, at a minimum, some active promotion or encouragement of the attack from an organised entity. According to the Elements of Crimes for Art 7 of the Rome Statute:[155]

> 'Attack directed against a civilian population' ... is understood to mean a course of conduct involving the multiple commission of acts referred to in article 7, paragraph 1, of the Statute against any civilian population, pursuant to or in furtherance of a State or organizational policy to commit such attack. The acts need not constitute a military attack. It is understood that 'policy to commit such attack' requires that the State or organization actively promote or encourage such an attack against a civilian population.

10.80   The victims of the widespread or systematic attack must be civilians. Indeed, unlike war crimes, there is no requirement for crimes against humanity to have been committed as part of an armed conflict. The perpetrators may indeed be misusing their official powers against their own disarmed and unresisting population (as notoriously occurred during the period of communist rule in Cambodia from 1975 to 1979). Even if there are armed resisters among the civilian population, that does not deprive the population of its civilian status for the purpose of establishing crimes against humanity.[156]

Specified acts

10.81   According to the ICTR in *Akayesu*, the common feature uniting all the acts specified as constituting crimes against humanity is that they are inhumane in character and cause great suffering, or serious injury to body or to mental or physical health.[157] The various acts expressly specified in the ICTR Statute are examples of proscribed conduct. Indeed, the Charter of the Nuremberg Tribunal, the Statutes of the ICTY and the ICTR, and the Rome Statute all expressly leave open the list of specified acts by permitting 'other inhumane acts' to be included. Understood in

---

153. Ibid, para 580.
154. Ibid, para 579.
155. Semble Rome Statute, Art 7(2)(a).
156. *Prosecutor v Akayesu*, ICTR-96-4-T, (1998) 9 IHRR 608, para 582.
157. Ibid, para 578.

this way, there is nothing necessarily unwarranted in the expansion of the specified acts between 1945 and 1998.

Murder

10.82 Murder is one of the modes by which crimes against humanity (and war crimes) may be committed. However, murder per se is not an international crime.[158]

The elements of the act of murder identified by the ICTR in *Akayesu* are more comprehensive, and more helpful, than those contained in the Elements of Crimes for Art 7(1)(a) of the Rome Statute. The latter provide simply that the perpetrator 'killed one or more persons' while noting that 'killed' is interchangeable with 'caused death'. Thus framed, causing the victim's death accidentally would be equivalent to murder. The requirement for an intention to kill, present in all major legal systems for the crime of murder, is missing from the Elements of Crimes.

According to the ICTR, however, murder requires the death of a victim, resulting from an unlawful act or omission by the accused, which he or she was aware was likely to cause death, with an intention by the perpetrator to cause the victim's death or an indifference as to whether the victim lived or died.[159] Although many legal systems regard indifference to the killed victim's fate as constitutive merely of manslaughter, it is sufficient to constitute the specified act of murder as a crime against humanity.

Extermination

10.83 In order to constitute the specified act of extermination, the accused must have participated in the killing of at least one named or described person by an act or omission which was both unlawful and intentional. Although the accused need not personally have committed multiple killings, his or her conduct must have been a participant in the killing of a group of people in an act of mass destruction.[160] The conduct must have 'constituted, or [taken] place as part of, a mass killing of members of a civilian population'.[161] In *Prosecutor v Krstić*, the ICTY said that in order for 'the crime of extermination to be established, in addition to the general requirements for a crime against humanity, there must be evidence that a particular population was targeted and that its members were killed or otherwise subjected to conditions of life calculated to bring about the destruction of a numerically significant part of the population'.[162]

---

158. *R v Bow Street Metropolitan Stipendiary Magistrate; Ex parte Pinochet Ugarte (No 3)* [2000] 1 AC 147.
159. *Prosecutor v Akayesu*, ICTR-96-4-T, (1998) 9 IHRR 608, para 589. Semble *Prosecutor v Rutaganda*, ICTR-96-3, 6 December 1999, para 80 (ICTR); *Prosecutor v Kupreškić*, IT-95-16-T, 14 January 2000, para 561 (ICTY); *Prosecutor v Musema*, ICTR-96-13, 17 January 2000, para 215 (ICTR).
160. *Prosecutor v Akayesu*, ICTR-96-4-T, (1998) 9 IHRR 608, paras 591–592.
161. Elements of Crimes for Art 7(1)(b), Rome Statute.
162. *Prosecutor v Krstić*, IT-98-33-T, 2 August 2001, para 503.

Extermination may include the 'intentional infliction of conditions of life, inter alia the deprivation of access to food and medicine, calculated to bring about the destruction of part of a population'.[163]

Unlike genocide, it is not necessary that there be an intention to destroy any permanent group of persons — such as a national, ethnic, racial or religious group — in whole or in part. It is only necessary that the victims be part of a civilian population.[164]

Enslavement

10.84 The Rome Statute defines 'enslavement' to mean 'the exercise of any or all of the powers attaching to the right of ownership over a person and includes the exercise of such power in the course of trafficking in persons, in particular women and children'.[165] Thus framed, 'enslavement' imports the prohibitions on the slave trade and slavery in the Slavery Convention and the Supplementary Slavery Convention[166] when they are breached in the prescribed context of crimes against humanity.

In ***Prosecutor v Kunarac,***[167] the three accused were members of Bosnian Serb militia forces who, in 1992 and 1993, were engaged in fighting against Bosnian Muslim forces in the area around Foča in southern-eastern Bosnia. Two of the accused each deprived two Muslim women or girls of their freedom and treated them as their property. These two accused were convicted of enslavement as a crime against humanity, contrary to Art 5(c) of the ICTY Statute. The ICTY expounded upon the elements of enslavement:

539. ... [T]he Trial Chamber finds that, at the time relevant to the indictment, enslavement as a crime against humanity in customary international law consisted of the exercise of any or all of the powers attaching to the right of ownership over a person.

540. Thus, the Trial Chamber finds that the *actus reus* of the violation is the exercise of any or all of the powers attaching to the right of ownership over a person. The *mens rea* of the violation consists in the intentional exercise of such powers.

...

542. Under this definition, indications of enslavement include elements of control and ownership; the restriction or control of an individual's autonomy, freedom of choice or freedom of movement; and, often, the accruing of some gain to the perpetrator. The consent or free will of the victim is absent. It is often rendered impossible or irrelevant by, for example, the threat or use of force or other forms of coercion; the fear of violence, deception or false promises; the abuse of power; the victim's position of vulnerability; detention or captivity, psychological oppression or socio-economic conditions. Further indications of enslavement include exploitation; the exaction of forced or compulsory labour or service, often without remuneration and often, though not necessarily,

163. Rome Statute, Art 7(2)(b).
164. *Prosecutor v Krstić*, IT-98-33-T, 2 August 2001, para 499.
165. Rome Statute, Art 7(2)(c).
166. See **10.29–10.33**.
167. *Prosecutor v Kunarac*, IT-96-23-T & IT-96-23/1-T, 22 February 2001.

involving physical hardship; sex; prostitution; and human trafficking. With respect to forced or compulsory labour or service, international law, including some of the provisions of Geneva Convention IV and the Additional Protocols, make clear that not all labour or service by protected persons, including civilians, in armed conflicts, is prohibited — strict conditions are, however, set for such labour or service. The 'acquisition' or 'disposal' of someone for monetary or other compensation, is not a requirement for enslavement. Doing so, however, is a prime example of the exercise of the right of ownership over someone. The duration of the suspected exercise of powers attaching to the right of ownership is another factor that may be considered when determining whether someone was enslaved; however, its importance in any given case will depend on the existence of other indications of enslavement. Detaining or keeping someone in captivity, without more, would, depending on the circumstances of a case, usually not constitute enslavement.

543. The Trial Chamber is ... in general agreement with the factors put forward by the Prosecutor, to be taken into consideration in determining whether enslavement was committed. These are the control of someone's movement, control of physical environment, psychological control, measures taken to prevent or deter escape, force, threat of force or coercion, duration, assertion of exclusivity, subjection to cruel treatment and abuse, control of sexuality and forced labour. The Prosecutor also submitted that the mere ability to buy, sell, trade or inherit a person or his or her labours or services could be a relevant factor. The Trial Chamber considers that the *mere ability* to do so is insufficient, such actions actually occurring could be a relevant factor.

10.85 The Elements of Crimes for the Rome Statute indicate, furthermore, that 'right of ownership' over a person includes the power to purchase, sell, lend, barter or impose a similar deprivation of liberty.[168] However, as the ICTY judgment in *Kunarac* indicates, the power or right to sell, trade, and so on, another person is not enough to constitute enslavement, although actually exercising that power will be strong evidence of enslavement. The more important factor is the existence of forced or compulsory and uncompensated labour. As a United States Military Tribunal said in connection with enslavement as a crime against humanity committed in Germany and its occupied territories during the Second World War:[169]

Slavery may exist even without torture. Slaves may be well fed, well clothed, and comfortably housed, but they are still slaves if without lawful process they are deprived of their freedom by forceful restraint. We might eliminate all proof of ill-treatment, overlook the starvation, beatings, and other barbarous acts, but the admitted fact of slavery — compulsory uncompensated labour — would still remain. There is no such thing as benevolent slavery. Involuntary servitude, even if tempered by humane treatment, is still slavery.

---

168. Elements of Crimes for Art 7(1)(c), Rome Statute.
169. *In Re Pohl* (1947) 14 ILR 290, 291–292. Cited with approval by the ICTY in *Prosecutor v Kunarac*, IT-96-23-T & IT-96-23/1-T, 22 February 2001, para 525.

Deportation or forcible transfer of population

10.86   The Rome Statute defines 'deportation or forcible transfer of population' to mean 'forced displacement of the persons concerned by expulsion or other coercive acts from the area in which they are lawfully present, without grounds permitted under international law'.[170] The Elements of Crimes elaborate by stating that a transfer will be 'forced' if it involves either physical force or a 'threat of force or coercion, such as that caused by fear of violence, duress, detention, psychological oppression or abuse of power against such person or persons or another person, or by taking advantage of a coercive environment'.[171] Deportation involves a transfer across international borders, while forcible transfer means displacement within a State.[172] Deportation and forcible transfer are also synonymous with 'forcibly displaced'.[173]

These specified acts are certainly broad enough to cover the practice which has come to be known as 'ethnic cleansing', although it is not necessary that the victims be targeted on any discriminatory grounds prohibited by international law; it is enough that they are part of a civilian population.

Imprisonment or other severe deprivation of physical liberty

10.87   The Rome Statute does not define 'imprisonment or other severe deprivation of physical liberty in violation of fundamental rules of international law'. The Elements of Crimes, however, state that the perpetrator must have imprisoned one or more persons or otherwise severely deprived one or more persons of their physical liberty. The imprisonment or deprivation of liberty must also have risen to the level of a violation of fundamental rules of international law and the perpetrator must have been aware of the factual circumstances that established the gravity of the conduct.[174]

The ICTY has held that in order to constitute 'imprisonment' as a crime against humanity, there must be a deprivation of liberty without due process of law. Imprisonment of civilians will be unlawful where they are 'detained without reasonable grounds to believe that the security of the Detaining Power makes it absolutely necessary', or where 'the procedural safeguards required by Art 43 of Geneva Convention IV are not complied with in respect of detained civilians, even where initial detention may have been justified'.[175] This means that the imprisoned person must have his or her detention reconsidered as soon as possible by a court or administrative board. Thereafter, the court or administrative

---

170. Rome Statute, Art 7(2)(d).
171. Elements of Crimes for Art 7(1)(d), Rome Statute.
172. *Prosecutor v Krstić*, IT-98-33-T, 2 August 2001, para 521 (ICTY).
173. Elements of Crimes for Art 7(1)(d), Rome Statute.
174. Ibid for Art 7(1)(e), Rome Statute.
175. *Prosecutor v Kordić*, IT-95-14/2-T, 26 February 2001, paras 302–303.

board must give consideration to the case at least twice yearly with a view to a favourable amendment of the initial decision, if circumstances permit.

Torture

10.88   The ICTR in *Akayesu* adopted verbatim the definition of torture contained in the Torture Convention, qualifying it only by the prescribed context for crimes against humanity.[176] Subsequently, however, the ICTY took a different approach. In *Prosecutor v Kunarac,* a distinction was drawn between torture as a violation of human rights law as embodied in instruments such as the Torture Convention and torture as a criminal violation of international humanitarian law:[177]

> 496. The Trial Chamber concludes that the definition of torture under international humanitarian law does not comprise the same elements as the definition of torture generally applied under human rights law. In particular, the Trial Chamber is of the view that the presence of a state official or of any other authority-wielding person in the torture process is not necessary for the offence to be regarded as torture under international humanitarian law.

> 497. ... the Trial Chamber holds that, in the field of international humanitarian law, the elements of the offence of torture, under customary international law are as follows:

> (i)   The infliction, by act or omission, of severe pain or suffering, whether physical or mental.

> (ii)   The act or omission must be intentional.

> (iii)   The act or omission must aim at obtaining information or a confession, or at punishing, intimidating or coercing the victim or a third person, or at discriminating, on any ground, against the victim or a third person.

10.89   The Rome Statute defines 'torture', in its guise as a crime against humanity, to mean 'the intentional infliction of severe pain or suffering, whether physical or mental, upon a person in the custody or under the control of the accused; except that torture shall not include pain or suffering arising only from, inherent in or incidental to, lawful sanctions'.[178] When committed as a crime against humanity, therefore, it is not necessary that torture be committed by a designated person such as a public official. It is enough that the impugned conduct be performed 'upon a person in the custody or under the control of the accused'. Thus, not only public officials but also persons such as members of unofficial militias or insurrectionary forces can be guilty of a crime against humanity when engaged in torture.

---

176. *Prosecutor v Akayesu,* ICTR-96-4-T, (1998) 9 IHRR 608, paras 593–595.
177. *Prosecutor v Kunarac,* IT-96-23-T & IT-96-23/1-T, 22 February 2001.
178. Rome Statute, Art 7(2)(e).

10.90 Torture as a crime against humanity differs from the Torture Convention crime also in not requiring a designated purpose, such as obtaining a confession or information. It is enough to establish torture as a crime against humanity that the severe pain or suffering was inflicted to intimidate, coerce or discriminate against the victim. What remains common to torture under the Torture Convention and torture as a crime against humanity is that there be the intentional infliction of 'severe pain or suffering'. In order to be a crime against humanity, however, the infliction of severe pain or suffering must occur as part of a widespread or systematic attack on a civilian population.

Rape and sexual violence

10.91 The Rome Statute includes '[r]ape, sexual slavery, enforced prostitution, forced pregnancy, enforced sterilization, or any other form of sexual violence of comparable gravity' among the acts specified to constitute crimes against humanity.[179]

10.92 The ICTR in *Akayesu* defined rape in its guise as a crime against humanity as 'a physical invasion of a sexual nature, committed on a person under circumstances which are coercive'.[180] The Tribunal also defined 'sexual violence', which it took to be covered by 'rape', to include 'any act of a sexual nature which is committed on a person under circumstances which are coercive'.[181]

10.93 The Elements of Crimes provide detailed guidance on rape and related specified conduct.

'Rape' is constituted by invasion of 'the body of a person by conduct resulting in penetration, however slight, of any part of the body of the victim or of the perpetrator with a sexual organ, or of the anal or genital opening of the victim with any object or any other part of the body'. An 'invasion' is intended to mean that the proscribed act is 'gender neutral'. The invasion must also be 'committed by force, or by threat of force or coercion, such as that caused by fear of violence, duress, detention, psychological oppression or abuse of power ... or by taking advantage of a coercive environment, or the invasion was committed against a person incapable of giving genuine consent'.[182]

'Sexual slavery' occurs when the perpetrator exercises 'any or all of the powers attaching to the right of ownership over one or more persons, such as by purchasing, selling, lending or bartering such a person or persons, or by imposing on them a similar deprivation of liberty'. The perpetrator must also cause the victim to 'engage in one or more acts of a sexual nature'.[183]

---

179. Ibid, Art 7(1)(g).
180. *Prosecutor v Akayesu*, ICTR-96-4-T, (1998) 9 IHRR 608, para 598. See also *Prosecutor v Delalić*, IT-96-21-T, 16 November 1998, para 479 (ICTY).
181. *Prosecutor v Akayesu*, ICTR-96-4-T, (1998) 9 IHRR 608, para 598.
182. Elements of Crimes for Art 7(1)(g)-1, Rome Statute. Semble *Prosecutor v Furundžija*, IT-95-17/1-T, 10 December 1998, para 160 (ICTY).
183. Ibid for Art 7(1)(g)-2, Rome Statute.

'Enforced prostitution' means causing 'one or more persons to engage in one or more acts of a sexual nature by force, or by threat of force or coercion, such as that caused by fear of violence, duress, detention, psychological oppression or abuse of power, against such person or persons or another person, or by taking advantage of a coercive environment or such person's or persons' incapacity to give genuine consent'. There must also be an actual or expected 'pecuniary or other advantage in exchange for or in connection with the acts of a sexual nature'.[184]

'Forced pregnancy' is defined by the Rome Statute to mean 'the unlawful confinement of a woman forcibly made pregnant, with the intent of affecting the ethnic composition of any population or carrying out other grave violations of international law'.[185]

'Enforced sterilization' means the permanent deprivation of 'biological reproductive capacity' which is 'neither justified by the medical or hospital treatment of the person or persons concerned nor carried out with their genuine consent'.[186]

'Sexual violence' occurs when there is 'an act of a sexual nature against one or more persons … by force, or by threat of force or coercion, such as that caused by fear of violence, duress, detention, psychological oppression or abuse of power, against such person or persons or another person, or by taking advantage of a coercive environment or such person's or persons' incapacity to give genuine consent'. The act must also be of a gravity comparable to that of the other acts prohibited by Art 7(1)(g) of the Rome Statute and the perpetrator must have been aware of the factual circumstances that established the gravity of the act.[187]

Persecution

10.94 Certain kinds of persecution are capable of constituting crimes against humanity. The Rome Statute identifies persecution 'against any identifiable group or collectivity on political, racial, national, ethnic, cultural, religious, gender … or other grounds that are universally recognized as impermissible under international law' committed in connection with any other act specified as constituting a crime against humanity.[188] In this context, 'persecution' means 'the intentional and severe deprivation of fundamental rights contrary to international law by reason of the identity of the group or collectivity'.[189]

10.95 The Elements of Crimes indicate that the deprivation of fundamental rights must be 'severe',[190] but otherwise add nothing to the Rome Statute provisions prohibiting and defining the specified acts.

---

184. Ibid for Art 7(1)(g)-3, Rome Statute.
185. Rome Statute, Art 7(2)(f). The Elements of Crimes cast no additional light on this definition.
186. Elements of Crimes for Art 7(1)(g)-5, Rome Statute.
187. Ibid for Art 7(1)(g)-6, Rome Statute.
188. Rome Statute, Art 7(1)(h).
189. Ibid, Art 7(2)(g).
190. Elements of Crimes for Art 7(1)(h), Rome Statute.

Persecution as a crime against humanity received attention in the judgment of the ICTY in **Prosecutor v Kupreškić.**[191] Two of the six accused were members of Bosnian Croat militia forces who, in 1993, participated in an attack on mostly Muslim civilians in the village of Ahmici-Šantici in central Bosnia. More than 100 Muslim civilians were killed and 169 houses belonging to Muslims were burned. All six accused were charged with and convicted of, inter alia, committing persecutions on political, racial or religious grounds contrary to Art 5(h) of the ICTY Statute. The convictions of four of the accused were subsequently set aside on appeal because the supporting evidence was insufficiently reliable. The Trial Chamber made the following observations on the charges of persecution as a crime against humanity:[192]

3. The Definition of Persecution

616. ... [T]he crime of persecution encompasses a wide variety of acts, including, *inter alia,* those of a physical, economic, or judicial nature that violate an individual's basic or fundamental rights. The discrimination must be on one of the listed grounds to constitute persecution. ...

617. ... [T]his is a broad definition which could include acts prohibited under other subheadings of Article 5, acts prohibited under other Articles of the Statute, and acts not covered by the Statute. The same approach has been taken in Article 7(2)(g) of the ICC Statute, which states that '[p]ersecution means the intentional and severe deprivation of *fundamental rights* contrary to international law by reason of the identity of the group or collectivity' (emphasis added).

618. However, this Trial Chamber holds the view that in order for persecution to amount to a crime against humanity it is not enough to define a core assortment of acts and to leave peripheral acts in a state of uncertainty. There must be *clearly defined limits* on the types of acts which qualify as persecution. Although the realm of human rights is dynamic and expansive, not every denial of a human right may constitute a crime against humanity.

619. Accordingly, it can be said that at a minimum, acts of persecution must be of an equal gravity or severity to the other acts enumerated under Article 5. This legal criterion has already been resorted to, for instance, in the *Flick* case.[193]

620. It ought to be emphasised, however, that if the analysis based on this criterion relates only to the level of seriousness of the act, it does not provide

---

191. *Prosecutor v Kupreškić,* IT-95-16-T, 14 January 2000.
192. Emphasis in original.
193. A footnote here in the ICTY judgment quotes from the US Military Tribunal sitting at Nuremberg in *United States v Flick,* NMT, Vol VI, p 1215, which held that:

> [n]ot even under a proper construction of the section of Control Council Law No. 10 relating to crimes against humanity, do the facts [compulsory taking of Jewish industrial property] warrant conviction. The 'atrocities and offences' listed therein, 'murder, extermination,' etc., are all offences against the person. Property is not mentioned. Under the doctrine of *ejusdem generis* the catch-all words 'other persecutions' must be deemed to include only such as affect the life and liberty of the oppressed peoples. Compulsory taking of industrial property, however reprehensible, is not in that category.

The ICTY notes that this statement was taken up and used by the US Military Tribunal in *United States v Krauch,* NMT Vol VIII, pp 1129–1130 (*Farben* case). The footnote then refers to the UN War Crimes Commission, *Law Reports of Trials of War Criminals,* Vol IX:

> which states at p. 50 that the judgement in the *Flick* case declared that 'A distinction could be made between industrial property and the dwellings, household furnishings and food supplies of a persecuted people' and thus left open the question whether such offences against personal property as would amount to an assault upon the health and life of a human being (such as the burning of his house or depriving him of his food supply or his paid employment) would not constitute a crime against humanity.

guidance on what types of acts can constitute persecution. The *ejusdem generis* criterion can be used as a supplementary tool, to establish whether certain acts which generally speaking fall under the proscriptions of Article 5(h), reach the level of gravity required by this provision. The only conclusion to be drawn from its application is that only gross or blatant denials of fundamental human rights can constitute crimes against humanity.

621. The Trial Chamber, drawing upon its earlier discussion of 'other inhumane acts', holds that in order to identify those rights whose infringement may constitute persecution, more defined parameters for the definition of human dignity can be found in international standards on human rights such as those laid down in the Universal Declaration on Human Rights of 1948, the two United Nations Covenants on Human Rights of 1966 and other international instruments on human rights or on humanitarian law. Drawing upon the various provisions of these texts it proves possible to *identify a set of fundamental rights appertaining to any human being, the gross infringement of which may amount, depending on the surrounding circumstances, to a crime against humanity.* Persecution consists of a severe attack on those rights, and aims to exclude a person from society on discriminatory grounds. The Trial Chamber therefore defines persecution as *the gross or blatant denial, on discriminatory grounds, of a fundamental right, laid down in international customary or treaty law, reaching the same level of gravity as the other acts prohibited in Article 5.*

622. In determining whether particular acts constitute persecution, the Trial Chamber wishes to reiterate that acts of persecution must be evaluated not in isolation but in context, by looking at their cumulative effect. Although individual acts may not be inhumane, their overall consequences must offend humanity in such a way that they may be termed 'inhumane'. This delimitation also suffices to satisfy the principle of legality, as inhumane acts are clearly proscribed by the Statute.[194]

623. The Trial Chamber does not see fit to identify which rights constitute fundamental rights for the purposes of persecution. The interests of justice would not be served by so doing, as the explicit inclusion of particular fundamental rights could be interpreted as the implicit exclusion of other rights *(expressio unius est exclusio alterius)*. This is not the approach taken to crimes against humanity in customary international law, where the category of 'other inhumane acts' also allows courts flexibility to determine the cases before them, depending on the forms which attacks on humanity may take, forms which are ever-changing and carried out with particular ingenuity. Each case must therefore be examined on its merits.

624. In its earlier conclusions the Trial Chamber noted that persecution was often used to describe a series of acts. However, the Trial Chamber does not exclude the possibility that a single act may constitute persecution. In such a case, there must be clear evidence of the discriminatory intent. For example, in the former Yugoslavia an individual may have participated in the single murder of a Muslim person. If his intent clearly was to kill him because he was a Muslim, and this

---

194. An ICTY footnote here quotes from the US Military Tribunal in the *Einsatzgruppen* case (*United States v Ohlendorf*, NMT, Vol VI, p 49):

> Can it be said that international conventions and the law of nations gave no warning to these accused that their attacks against ethnic, national, religious, and political groups infringed the rights of mankind? We do not refer to localised outbursts of hatred nor petty discriminations which unfortunately occur in the most civilised of states. When persecutions reach the scale of nationwide campaigns designed to make life intolerable for, or to exterminate large groups of people, law dare not remain silent (...) The Control Council simply reasserts existing law when naming persecutions as an international offence.

occurred as part of a wide or systematic persecutory attack against a civilian population, this single murder may constitute persecution. But the discriminatory intent of the perpetrator must be proved for this crime to qualify as persecution.

625. Although acts of persecution are often part of a discriminatory policy, the Trial Chamber finds that it is not necessary to demonstrate that an accused has taken part in the formulation of a discriminatory policy or practice by a governmental authority. An example is that of the defendant Streicher: 'In his speeches and articles [...] he infected the German mind with the virus of anti-Semitism, and incited the German People to active persecution'.[195] He did so not in any official capacity but as the publisher of an anti-Semitic journal, *Der Stürmer*. The Tribunal concluded that his 'incitement to murder and extermination at the time when Jews in the East were being killed under the most horrible conditions clearly constitutes persecution' and sentenced him to death.[196]

626. The Trial Chamber observes that in the light of its broad definition of persecution, the Prosecution cannot merely rely on a general charge of 'persecution' in bringing its case. This would be inconsistent with the concept of legality. To observe the principle of legality, the Prosecution must charge particular acts (and this seems to have been done in this case). These acts should be charged in sufficient detail for the accused to be able to fully prepare their defence.

627. In sum, a charge of persecution must contain the following elements:

(a)   those elements required for all crimes against humanity under the Statute;

(b)   a gross or blatant denial of a fundamental right reaching the same level of gravity as the other acts prohibited under Article 5;

(c)   discriminatory grounds.

4. The Application of the Definition set out above in the Instant Case

628. The Trial Chamber will now examine the specific allegations in this case, which are the 'deliberate and systematic killing of Bosnian Muslim civilians', the 'organised detention and expulsion of the Bosnian Muslims from Ahmici-Šantici and its environs', and the 'comprehensive destruction of Bosnian homes and property'. Can these acts constitute persecution?

629. In light of the conclusions above, the Trial Chamber finds that the 'deliberate and systematic killing of Bosnian Muslim civilians' as well as their 'organised detention and expulsion from Ahmici' can constitute persecution. This is because these acts qualify as murder, imprisonment, and deportation, which are explicitly mentioned in the Statute under Article 5.

---

195. IMT judgment, p 302.
196. Ibid, pp 302–304. An ICTY footnote here states:
> This is also demonstrated in cases brought before German courts acting under Control Council Law no. 10. The *Oberster Gerichtshof für die Britische Zone in Köln*, 9 Nov, 1948, StS 78/48 held that denunciation 'is [...] intimately linked to the National Socialists' regime of violence and arbitrariness because, from the very outset, it clearly fitted into the organised campaign of persecution against all Jews and everything Jewish in Germany which all humanity not under the sway of National Socialism perceived as an assault and, although directed against this one victim only, became part and parcel of all the mass crimes committed during the persecution of Jews (translation on file with the ICTY)'. More generally, the *Düsseldorf Oberlandesgericht* stated in a judgment of 20 May 1948 (Criminal Chamber 3/48) that National Socialism has built up a power mechanism in the party and State which could be set in motion against anyone from anywhere. Not only the holder of the power himself who used his own personal position of power against someone weaker can be a perpetrator of a crime against humanity but also anyone who on his own initiative also participated in any way or even only encouraged the commission of such acts. (Judgment of Düsseldorf Regional Appellate Court, 20 May 1948, translation on file with ICTY, p 4).

630. The Trial Chamber next turns its attention to the alleged comprehensive destruction of Bosnian Muslim homes and property. The question here is whether certain property or economic rights can be considered so fundamental that their denial is capable of constituting persecution. The Trial Chamber notes that in the Judgement of the IMT, several defendants were convicted of economic discrimination. For example, Göring 'persecuted the Jews ... and not only in Germany where he raised the billion mark fine ... this interest was primarily economic — how to get their property and how to force them out of economic life in Europe'.[197] Defendants Funk and Seyss-Inquart were also charged with acts of economic discrimination.[198]

631. The Trial Chamber finds that attacks on property can constitute persecution. To some extent this may depend on the type of property involved: in the passage from *Flick* cited above the Tribunal held that the compulsory taking of industrial property could not be said to affect the life and liberty of oppressed peoples and therefore did not constitute persecution. There may be certain types of property whose destruction may not have a severe enough impact on the victim as to constitute a crime against humanity, even if such a destruction is perpetrated on discriminatory grounds: an example is the burning of someone's car (unless the car constitutes an indispensable and vital asset to the owner). However, the case at hand concerns the comprehensive destruction of homes and property. Such an attack on property in fact constitutes a destruction of the livelihood of a certain population. This may have the same inhumane consequences as a forced transfer or deportation. Moreover, the burning of a residential property may often be committed with a recklessness towards the lives of its inhabitants. The Trial Chamber therefore concludes that this act may constitute a gross or blatant denial of fundamental human rights, and, if committed on discriminatory grounds, it may constitute persecution.

10.96 Persecution may therefore be constituted by any of the other acts specified as capable of constituting crimes against humanity. Thus, acts of murder, imprisonment, deportation, and so on, will themselves be crimes against humanity if committed in the prescribed context. They will simultaneously amount to persecution as a crime against humanity where they are a severe deprivation of fundamental rights intentionally directed against any identifiable group or collectivity on political, racial, national, ethnic, cultural, religious, gender or other grounds recognised by international law as impermissible.

10.97 Furthermore, other acts may also constitute persecution as a crime against humanity where they are a gross, blatant or severe denial of a fundamental right reaching the same level of gravity as the other acts prohibited as crimes against humanity, and where they are performed with the same discriminatory intent. Confiscation of industrial property in the Second World War was not regarded as persecution because it was an insufficiently severe violation of fundamental rights, but confiscation or destruction of property essential to support life (such as a house) is a sufficiently severe violation of fundamental rights as to qualify as persecution.

---

197. IMT judgment, p 282.
198. Ibid, pp 305, 328–329.

Enforced disappearance of persons

10.98   The enforced disappearance of persons will constitute a crime against humanity when committed in the prescribed context.[199] The specified act is defined as 'the arrest, detention or abduction of persons by, or with the authorization, support or acquiescence of, a State or a political organization, followed by a refusal to acknowledge that deprivation of freedom or to give information on the fate or whereabouts of those persons, with the intention of removing them from the protection of the law for a prolonged period of time'.[200]

10.99   The Elements of Crimes provide detailed guidance on the conduct required to constitute enforced disappearance.

The perpetrator must either arrest, detain, abduct, or maintain an abduction of a person. The initial arrest or detention itself could be either lawful or unlawful. The arrest, detention or abduction must be followed or accompanied by a refusal to acknowledge the deprivation of freedom, or to give information on the fate or whereabouts of the person. The perpetrator must have been aware that the arrest, detention or abduction would be followed in the ordinary course of events by a refusal to acknowledge the deprivation of freedom or to give information on the fate or whereabouts of the person. The arrest, detention or abduction must be carried out by, or with the authorisation, support or acquiescence of, a State or a political organisation.

Alternatively, the perpetrator must refuse to acknowledge the arrest, detention or abduction, or to give information on the fate or whereabouts of the person so apprehended. The refusal must, to the perpetrator's knowledge, be preceded or accompanied by the deprivation of freedom. The refusal to acknowledge the deprivation of freedom, or to give information on the fate or whereabouts of the person, must be carried out by, or with the authorization or support of, the State or political organization that carried out the arrest, detention or abduction.

In either case, the perpetrator must have intended to remove the person from the protection of the law for a prolonged period of time, and the perpetrator must have known that the conduct was part of, or intended the conduct to be part of, a widespread or systematic attack directed against a civilian population.[201]

10.100   The practice of enforced disappearance is now also the subject of the International Convention for the Protection of All Persons from Enforced Disappearance (Enforced Disappearance Convention),[202] which builds

---

199. Rome Statute, Art 7(1)(i).
200. Ibid, Art 7(2)(i).
201. Elements of Crimes for Art 7(1)(i), Rome Statute.
202. UN Doc A/61/488. C.N.737.2008.Treaties-12 of 2 October 2008 (Proposal of corrections to the original text of the Convention (Arabic, Chinese, English, French, Russian and Spanish texts) and to the Certified True Copies) and C.N.1040.2008.Treaties-20 of 2 January 2009 (Corrections). The text of the Enforced Disappearance Convention was adopted by the 61st session of the General Assembly of the United Nations by Resolution A/RES/61/177. Semble the Inter-American Convention on Forced Disappearance of Persons (1994) 33 ILM 1429.

upon the United Nations General Assembly Declaration on the Protection of All Persons from Enforced Disappearance (Resolution 47/133 (1992)). The Enforced Disappearance Convention provides that '[n]o one shall be subjected to forced disappearance' and that '[n]o exceptional circumstances whatsoever, whether a state of war or a threat of war, internal political instability or any other public emergency, may be invoked as a justification for enforced disappearance'.[203] It also provides as follows:

Article 2

For the purposes of this Convention, 'enforced disappearance' is considered to be the arrest, detention, abduction or any other form of deprivation of liberty by agents of the State or by persons or groups of persons acting with the authorization, support or acquiescence of the State, followed by a refusal to acknowledge the deprivation of liberty or by concealment of the fate or whereabouts of the disappeared person, which place such a person outside the protection of the law.

The Convention also provides for a regime of State jurisdiction based on a variety of the universality principle very similar to that established under the Torture Convention.[204]

Opened for signature in January 2007, the Enforced Disappearance Convention will enter into force after it acquires 20 ratifications.[205]

Other inhumane acts of a similar character and gravity

10.101   The Charter of the Nuremberg Tribunal, the ICTY and ICTR Statutes, and the Rome Statute all state that, apart from the acts specified as constituting crimes against humanity, 'other inhumane acts' committed in a prescribed context are also to be such crimes. The Rome Statute elaborates by requiring the 'other inhumane acts' to be 'of a similar character intentionally causing great suffering, or serious injury to body or to mental or physical health'.[206]

The meaning of 'other inhumane acts', as contained in Art 5(i) of the ICTY Statute, was considered by the ICTY in ***Prosecutor v Kupreškić*** (for the facts of which, see 10.95):[207]

562. The expression 'other inhumane acts' was drawn from Article 6(c) of the London Agreement [the Charter of the Nuremberg Tribunal] and Article II(1)(c) of Control Council Law No. 10.[208]

563. There is a concern that this category lacks precision and is too general to provide a safe yardstick for the work of the Tribunal and hence, that it is contrary to the principle of the 'specificity' of criminal law. It is thus imperative to establish what is included within this category. The phrase 'other inhumane acts'

---

203. Enforced Disappearance Convention, Art 1.
204. Ibid, Arts 7–15.
205. Ibid, Art 39.
206. Rome Statute, Art 7(1)(k).
207. *Prosecutor v Kupreškić*, IT-95-16-T, 14 January 2000.
208. Control Council Law No 10 was 'a legislative act jointly passed in 1945 by the four Occupying Powers [in Germany] and thus reflecting international agreement among the Great Powers on the law applicable to international crimes and the jurisdiction of the courts called upon to rule on those crimes': ibid, para 541.

was deliberately designed as a residual category, as it was felt to be undesirable for this category to be exhaustively enumerated. An exhaustive categorization would merely create opportunities for evasion of the letter of the prohibition. The importance of maintaining such a category was elucidated by the ICRC [International Committee of the Red Cross] when commenting on what would constitute a violation of the obligation to provide 'humane treatment' contained in common Article 3 of the Geneva Conventions:[209]

> [I]t is always dangerous to try to go into too much detail — especially in this domain. However great the care taken in drawing up a list of all the various forms of infliction, it would never be possible to catch up with the imagination of future torturers who wished to satisfy their bestial instincts; and the more specific and complete a list tries to be, the more restrictive it becomes. The form of wording adopted is flexible and, at the same time, precise.

564. In interpreting the expression at issue, resort to the *ejusdem generis* rule of interpretation does not prove to be of great assistance. Under this rule, that expression would cover actions similar to those specifically provided for. Admittedly such a rule of interpretation has been relied upon by various courts with regard to Article 6(c) of the London Agreement. Thus, for instance, in the *Tarnek* case, the District Court of Tel-Aviv held in a decision of 14 December 1951 that the definition of 'other inhumane acts' laid down in the Israeli Law on Nazi and Nazi Collaborators (Punishment) of 1950, which reproduced the definition of Article 6(c), was to apply only to such other inhumane acts as resembled in their nature and their gravity those specified in the definition.[210] This interpretative rule lacks precision, and is too general to provide a safe yardstick for the work of the Tribunal.

565. The Statute of the International Criminal Court (ICC) (Article 7(k)) provides greater detail than the ICTY Statute as to the meaning of other inhumane acts: 'other inhumane acts of a similar character intentionally causing great suffering, or serious injury to the body or to mental or physical health'.[211] However, this provision also fails to provide an indication, even indirectly, of the legal standards which would allow us to identify the prohibited inhumane acts.[212]

---

209. *ICRC Commentary on the IVth Geneva Convention Relative to the Protection of Civilian Persons in time of War*, 1958, reprinted 1994, 39.

210. *Attorney-General v Tarnek* (1951) 18 ILR 540. A footnote here in the ICTY judgment refers also to *Attorney-General v Enigster* (1952) 18 ILR 540, 541–42.

211. With regard to a similar concept, 'inhuman treatment' under Art 2(b) (grave breaches), a footnote here in the judgment quotes the ICTY Trial Chamber in *Prosecutor v Delalić*, which 'noted that "inhuman treatment" was constituted by "an intentional act or omission [...] which causes serious mental or physical suffering or injury or constitutes a serious attack on human dignity"' (see *Prosecutor v Delalić*, IT-96-21-T, 16 November 1998, at para 543). The footnote goes on to state: 'The Trial Chamber also suggested a negative definition, namely that inhuman treatment is treatment which causes severe mental or physical suffering but which falls short of torture, or lacks one of the elements of torture (e.g. a prohibited purpose or official sanction) [ibid at para 542] ... Whether a given conduct constitutes inhuman treatment will be determined on a case-by-case basis and appears ultimately to be a question of fact [ibid at para 544].' Finally, the footnote quotes from *Prosecutor v Kayishema*, ICTR-95-1-A, 21 May 1999, at para 151: '[T]he acts that rise to the level of inhuman acts should be determined on a case-by-case basis.'

212. A footnote here in the judgment quotes from the International Law Commission, commenting on Art 18 of its Draft Code of Crimes:

> [t]he Commission recognized that it was impossible to establish an exhaustive list of the inhumane acts which might constitute crimes against humanity. First, this category of acts is intended to include only additional acts that are similar in gravity to those listed in the preceding subparagraphs. Second, the act must in fact cause injury to a human being in terms of physical or mental integrity, health or human dignity.

(*Report of the International Law Commission on the Work of its Forty-Eighth Session*, 6 May–26 July 1996, UNGAOR 51st Session Supp No 10 (A/51/10) (Crimes Against the Peace and Security of Mankind), 103, para 17.)

566. Less broad parameters for the interpretation of 'other inhumane acts' can instead be identified in international standards on human rights such as those laid down in the Universal Declaration on Human Rights of 1948 and the two United Nations Covenants on Human Rights of 1966. Drawing upon the various provisions of these texts, it is possible to identify a set of basic rights appertaining to human beings, the infringement of which may amount, depending on the accompanying circumstances, to a crime against humanity. Thus, for example, serious forms of cruel or degrading treatment of persons belonging to a particular ethnic, religious, political or racial group, or serious widespread or systematic manifestations of cruel or humiliating or degrading treatment with a discriminatory or persecutory intent no doubt amount to crimes against humanity: inhuman or degrading treatment is prohibited by the United Nations Covenant on Civil and Political Rights (Article 7), the European Convention on Human Rights, of 1950 (Article 3), the Inter-American Convention on Human Rights of 9 June 1994 (Article 5) and the 1984 Convention against Torture (Article 1).[213] Similarly, the expression at issue undoubtedly embraces the forcible transfer of groups of civilians (which is to some extent covered by Article 49 of the IVth Convention of 1949 and Article 17(1) of the Additional Protocol II of 1977), enforced prostitution (indisputably a serious attack on human dignity pursuant to most international instruments on human rights), as well as the enforced disappearance of persons (prohibited by General Assembly Resolution 47/133 of 18 December 1992 and the Inter-American Convention of 9 June 1994[214]). Plainly, all these, and other similar acts, must be carried out in a systematic manner and on a large scale. In other words, they must be as serious as the other classes of crimes provided for in the other provisions of Article 5. Once the legal parameters for determining the content of the category of 'inhumane acts' are identified, resort to the *ejusdem generis* rule for the purpose of comparing and assessing the gravity of the prohibited act may be warranted.

10.102   The acts specified in the instruments establishing the Nuremberg Tribunal, the ICTY, the ICTR and the ICC as constituting crimes against humanity (murder, extermination, and so on) are particular manifestations of a crime which can take many forms. A crime against humanity is any act (when committed in the prescribed context) which is as serious as the acts specified in the instruments.

Any act which violates a fundamental right recognised by international law (such as the right not to be subjected to cruel, inhuman or degrading treatment or punishment, or the right not to be arbitrarily deprived of one's life), and which causes either great suffering or serious injury to health, is capable of constituting a crime against humanity; the act must, however, be committed as part of a widespread or systematic attack directed against any civilian population with knowledge of the attack.

---

213. In a footnote here, the ICTY states:
    As for the specification of what constitutes cruel, debasing, humiliating or degrading treatment, resort can of course be had to the important case-law of the relevant international bodies, chiefly to the United Nations Torture Committee and the European Commission and Court of Human Rights.
214. Inter-American Convention on Forced Disappearance of Persons (1994) 33 ILM 1429.

War crimes

War crimes and crimes against humanity contrasted

10.103   War crimes, like crimes against humanity, are international crimes attracting individual responsibility. There are, however, two important categorical distinctions separating the different types of offences.

10.104   First, whereas crimes against humanity occur in the context of a widespread or systematic attack on a civilian population, war crimes can occur only in the context of an armed conflict. There is obviously scope for overlap between the two different types of offences. Where an armed conflict includes a widespread or systematic attack on a civilian population, it is possible that a particular instance of prohibited conduct (for example, rape or torture) might be simultaneously a war crime and a crime against humanity.

10.105   Second, crimes against humanity are essentially a branch of international human rights law that attaches individual criminal responsibility to certain kinds of human rights violations. War crimes, on the other hand, originate in international humanitarian law (or the *jus in bello*[215]), the primary function of which is to place obligations on States. International humanitarian law has, however, evolved in such a way as also to attach individual criminal responsibility to certain violations of its requirements. As with international human rights, crimes against humanity are not dependent on any reciprocity between States. International humanitarian law, however, has emerged out of a context of express or implied bargains — for example, we will treat your captured troops according to certain rules, in the expectation or hope that you will reciprocate with our captured troops. International humanitarian law is, in a sense, a modern functional equivalent of medieval chivalry. Whereas the penalty for violating the requirements of chivalry was usually dishonour (not a small matter in medieval society), in more recent times violations of the code of warfare have often resulted in the perpetrators facing imprisonment or a firing squad.

Development of war crimes

10.106   The Charter of the Nuremberg Tribunal identified the war crimes with which leading members and associates of Germany's National Socialist regime and its European allies could be charged. War crimes were declared to mean 'violations of the laws or customs of war' and a non-exhaustive list of acts constituting such violations was provided: 'murder, ill-treatment or deportation to slave labor or for any other purpose of civilian population of or in occupied territory, murder or ill-treatment of prisoners of war or persons on the seas, killing of hostages,

---

215. See **9.3**.

plunder of public or private property, wanton destruction of cities, towns or villages, or devastation not justified by military necessity'.[216]

10.107   Individual criminal responsibility was subsequently confirmed for 'grave breaches' of the four Geneva Conventions.[217] When committed against persons or property protected by the Conventions, these grave breaches are 'wilful killing, torture or inhuman treatment, including biological experiments, wilfully causing great suffering or serious injury to body or health' (all four Geneva Conventions);[218] 'extensive destruction and appropriation of property, not justified by military necessity and carried out unlawfully and wantonly' (Geneva Conventions I, II and IV);[219] 'compelling a prisoner of war to serve in the forces of the hostile Power, or wilfully depriving a prisoner of war of the rights of fair and regular trial prescribed in this Convention' (Geneva Convention III);[220] and 'unlawful deportation or transfer or unlawful confinement of a protected person, compelling a protected person to scrve in the forces of a hostile Power, or wilfully depriving a protected person of the rights of fair and regular trial prescribed in the present Convention, [and] taking of hostages' (Geneva Convention IV).[221]

The four Geneva Conventions each have more than 190 States parties, including Australia. Geneva Protocol I and Geneva Protocol II each have more than 160 States parties, including Australia.

10.108   The ICTY has jurisdiction over war crimes as 'Grave breaches of the Geneva Conventions of 1949'[222] and 'Violations of the laws or customs of war'.[223] The ICTR's jurisdiction over war crimes is in the form of 'Violations of Article 3 common to the Geneva Conventions and of Additional Protocol II'.[224]

10.109   Article 8(1) of the Rome Statute succinctly confers on the ICC jurisdiction over war crimes: 'The Court shall have jurisdiction in respect of war crimes in particular when committed as part of a plan or policy or as part of a large-scale commission of such crimes'. Article 8(2) then takes some 1,500 words to define 'war crimes'.

Article 8(2) divides war crimes into four categories. The first two categories relate to war crimes committed in the context of an international armed conflict, while the third and fourth categories relate to war crimes committed in the context of an internal armed conflict.

The four categories of war crimes contain a total of 50 classifications of acts specified as constituting war crimes when committed in the

---

216. Charter of the Nuremberg Tribunal, Art 6(b).
217. See **10.10**.
218. Geneva Convention I, Art 50; Geneva Convention II, Art 51; Geneva Convention III, Art 130; Geneva Convention IV, Art 147.
219. Geneva Convention I, Art 50; Geneva Convention II, Art 51; Geneva Convention IV, Art 147.
220. Geneva Convention III, Art 130.
221. Geneva Convention IV, Art 147.
222. ICTY Statute, Art 2.
223. Ibid, Art 3.
224. ICTR Statute, Art 4.

prescribed context of an international armed conflict and an internal armed conflict. The Elements of Crimes furnish guidance in the interpretation and application of these provisions.[225]

War crimes in international armed conflicts

Grave breaches of the Geneva Conventions

10.110   The first category of war crimes, codified in Art 8(2)(a) of the Rome Statute, corresponds to those 'grave breaches' identified by the four Geneva Conventions as attracting individual criminal responsibility in the context of an international armed conflict. There are eight classifications of act specified as constituting such a grave breach:

2.   For the purpose of this Statute, 'war crimes' means:

   (a)   Grave breaches of the Geneva Conventions of 12 August 1949, namely, any of the following acts against persons or property protected under the provisions of the relevant Geneva Convention:

   (i)   Wilful killing;

   (ii)   Torture or inhuman treatment, including biological experiments;

   (iii)   Wilfully causing great suffering, or serious injury to body or health;

   (iv)   Extensive destruction and appropriation of property, not justified by military necessity and carried out unlawfully and wantonly;

   (v)   Compelling a prisoner of war or other protected person to serve in the forces of a hostile Power;

   (vi)   Wilfully depriving a prisoner of war or other protected person of the rights of fair and regular trial;

   (vii)   Unlawful deportation or transfer or unlawful confinement;

   (viii) Taking of hostages.

These classifications of prohibited acts accurately correspond to the 'grave breaches' identified as giving rise to individual criminal responsibility under the four Geneva Conventions.[226]

Violations of other customary rules

10.111   The second category of war crimes, codified in Art 8(2)(b) of the Rome Statute, corresponds to those other rules of customary international law applicable to international armed conflicts but not codified as grave

---

225. See **10.17**.
226. See **10.10**.

breaches of the Geneva Conventions. There are 26 classifications of act specified as constituting a violation of such rules:

2. For the purpose of this Statute, 'war crimes' means: ...

(b) Other serious violations of the laws and customs applicable in international armed conflict, within the established framework of international law, namely, any of the following acts:

(i) Intentionally directing attacks against the civilian population as such or against individual civilians not taking direct part in hostilities;

(ii) Intentionally directing attacks against civilian objects, that is, objects which are not military objectives;

(iii) Intentionally directing attacks against personnel, installations, material, units or vehicles involved in a humanitarian assistance or peacekeeping mission in accordance with the Charter of the United Nations, as long as they are entitled to the protection given to civilians or civilian objects under the international law of armed conflict;

(iv) Intentionally launching an attack in the knowledge that such attack will cause incidental loss of life or injury to civilians or damage to civilian objects or widespread, long-term and severe damage to the natural environment which would be clearly excessive in relation to the concrete and direct overall military advantage anticipated;

(v) Attacking or bombarding, by whatever means, towns, villages, dwellings or buildings which are undefended and which are not military objectives;

(vi) Killing or wounding a combatant who, having laid down his arms or having no longer means of defence, has surrendered at discretion;

(vii) Making improper use of a flag of truce, of the flag or of the military insignia and uniform of the enemy or of the United Nations, as well as of the distinctive emblems of the Geneva Conventions, resulting in death or serious personal injury;[227]

(viii) The transfer, directly or indirectly, by the Occupying Power of parts of its own civilian population into the territory it occupies, or the deportation or transfer of all or parts of the population of the occupied territory within or outside this territory;

---

227. The distinctive emblem is a red cross on a white background, and 'in the case of countries which already use as emblem, in place of the red cross, the red crescent or the red lion and sun on a white ground', those emblems are also distinctive emblems: Geneva Convention I, Art 38; Geneva Convention II, Art 41. An additional distinctive emblem 'composed of a red frame in the shape of a square on edge on a white ground' is granted equal status to the other distinctive emblems by Art 2 of the Protocol additional to the Geneva Conventions of 12 August 1949, and relating to the Adoption of an Additional Distinctive Emblem (Protocol III), of 8 December 2005.

(ix)   Intentionally directing attacks against buildings dedicated to religion, education, art, science or charitable purposes, historic monuments, hospitals and places where the sick and wounded are collected, provided they are not military objectives;

(x)   Subjecting persons who are in the power of an adverse party to physical mutilation or to medical or scientific experiments of any kind which are neither justified by the medical, dental or hospital treatment of the person concerned nor carried out in his or her interest, and which cause death to or seriously endanger the health of such person or persons;

(xi)   Killing or wounding treacherously individuals belonging to the hostile nation or army;

(xii)   Declaring that no quarter will be given;

(xiii)   Destroying or seizing the enemy's property unless such destruction or seizure be imperatively demanded by the necessities of war;

(xiv)   Declaring abolished, suspended or inadmissible in a court of law the rights and actions of the nationals of the hostile party;

(xv)   Compelling the nationals of the hostile party to take part in the operations of war directed against their own country, even if they were in the belligerent's service before the commencement of the war;

(xvi)   Pillaging a town or place, even when taken by assault;

(xvii)   Employing poison or poisoned weapons;

(xviii)   Employing asphyxiating, poisonous or other gases, and all analogous liquids, materials or devices;

(xix)   Employing bullets which expand or flatten easily in the human body, such as bullets with a hard envelope which does not entirely cover the core or is pierced with incisions;

(xx)   Employing weapons, projectiles and material and methods of warfare which are of a nature to cause superfluous injury or unnecessary suffering or which are inherently indiscriminate in violation of the international law of armed conflict, provided that such weapons, projectiles and material and methods of warfare are the subject of a comprehensive prohibition and are included in an annex to this Statute, by an amendment in accordance with the relevant provisions set forth in articles 121 and 123;

(xxi)   Committing outrages upon personal dignity, in particular humiliating and degrading treatment;

(xxii)   Committing rape, sexual slavery, enforced prostitution, forced pregnancy, as defined in article 7, paragraph 2 (f),[228] enforced sterilization, or any other form of sexual

---

228. See 10.93.

violence also constituting a grave breach of the Geneva Conventions;

(xxiii) Utilizing the presence of a civilian or other protected person to render certain points, areas or military forces immune from military operations;

(xxiv) Intentionally directing attacks against buildings, material, medical units and transport, and personnel using the distinctive emblems of the Geneva Conventions in conformity with international law;[229]

(xxv) Intentionally using starvation of civilians as a method of warfare by depriving them of objects indispensable to their survival, including wilfully impeding relief supplies as provided for under the Geneva Conventions;

(xxvi) Conscripting or enlisting children under the age of fifteen years into the national armed forces or using them to participate actively in hostilities.

War crimes in internal armed conflicts

Common Article 3

10.112   The third category of war crimes is codified in Art 8(2)(c) of the Rome Statute. This category is stated to consist of serious violations of Common Art 3 of the Geneva Conventions committed in the context of an internal armed conflict. There are four classifications of act specified as such serious violations:

2. For the purpose of this Statute, 'war crimes' means: ...

(c) In the case of an armed conflict not of an international character, serious violations of article 3 common to the four Geneva Conventions of 12 August 1949, namely, any of the following acts committed against persons taking no active part in the hostilities, including members of armed forces who have laid down their arms and those placed *hors de combat* by sickness, wounds, detention or any other cause:

(i)   Violence to life and person, in particular murder of all kinds,[230] mutilation, cruel treatment and torture;

(ii) Committing outrages upon personal dignity, in particular humiliating and degrading treatment;

(iii) Taking of hostages;

(iv) The passing of sentences and the carrying out of executions without previous judgement pronounced by a regularly constituted court, affording all judicial guarantees which are generally recognized as indispensable.

---

229. See footnote 227.
230. Murder is one of the modes by which war crimes against humanity (and crimes against humanity) may be committed. However, murder per se is not an international crime: *R v Bow Street Metropolitan Stipendiary Magistrate; Ex parte Pinochet Ugarte (No 3)* [2000] 1 AC 147.

These classifications of prohibited acts accurately correspond to the minimum standards to be observed in internal armed conflicts, as identified in Common Art 3.[231]

Violations of other customary rules

10.113   The final category of war crimes, codified in Art 8(2)(e) of the Rome Statute, corresponds to rules of customary international law not already codified in Common Art 3 and attracting individual criminal responsibility in the context of an internal armed conflict. There are 12 classifications of acts specified as constituting a violation of such rules:

2.   For the purpose of this Statute, 'war crimes' means: ...

   (e)   Other serious violations of the laws and customs applicable in armed conflicts not of an international character, within the established framework of international law, namely, any of the following acts:

   (i)   Intentionally directing attacks against the civilian population as such or against individual civilians not taking direct part in hostilities;

   (ii)   Intentionally directing attacks against buildings, material, medical units and transport, and personnel using the distinctive emblems of the Geneva Conventions in conformity with international law;[232]

   (iii)   Intentionally directing attacks against personnel, installations, material, units or vehicles involved in a humanitarian assistance or peacekeeping mission in accordance with the Charter of the United Nations, as long as they are entitled to the protection given to civilians or civilian objects under the international law of armed conflict;

   (iv)   Intentionally directing attacks against buildings dedicated to religion, education, art, science or charitable purposes, historic monuments, hospitals and places where the sick and wounded are collected, provided they are not military objectives;

   (v)   Pillaging a town or place, even when taken by assault;

   (vi)   Committing rape, sexual slavery, enforced prostitution, forced pregnancy, as defined in article 7, paragraph 2 (f),[233] enforced sterilization, and any other form of sexual violence also constituting a serious violation of article 3 common to the four Geneva Conventions;

   (vii)   Conscripting or enlisting children under the age of fifteen years into armed forces or groups or using them to participate actively in hostilities;

---

231. See 10.11.
232. See footnote 227.
233. See 10.93.

(viii) Ordering the displacement of the civilian population for reasons related to the conflict, unless the security of the civilians involved or imperative military reasons so demand;

(ix) Killing or wounding treacherously a combatant adversary;

(x) Declaring that no quarter will be given;

(xi) Subjecting persons who are in the power of another party to the conflict to physical mutilation or to medical or scientific experiments of any kind which are neither justified by the medical, dental or hospital treatment of the person concerned nor carried out in his or her interest, and which cause death to or seriously endanger the health of such person or persons;

(xii) Destroying or seizing the property of an adversary unless such destruction or seizure be imperatively demanded by the necessities of the conflict;

Armed conflict

10.114   In order for any act to constitute a war crime, it must be committed in the context of an 'armed conflict'. Many acts are war crimes if they are committed in the context of an international armed conflict, while a somewhat narrower range of acts are also war crimes if they are committed in the context of an internal armed conflict. The distinction between international and internal armed conflicts and the different regimes of war crimes applicable to each are reflected in the drafting of Art 8 of the Rome Statute.

10.115   The meaning of these essential contextual requirements was considered by the ICTY in an interlocutory appeal on jurisdiction.

> In *Prosecutor v Tadić*,[234] the accused was President of the Local Board of the Serb Democratic Party in Kozarac, a town in the Prijedor region of northern Bosnia with a population of about 4,000. In 1992, Bosnian Serb forces attacked and occupied Kozarac, killing about 800 civilians in the process. The surviving non-Serb population (mostly Croats and Muslims) was rounded up and expelled from the town. As they were herded out of town along a road, many of these people were singled out by Bosnian Serb forces and shot. The expellees from Kozarac and surrounding localities were relocated to a prison camp at Omarska in the Prijedor region under the guard of Bosnian Serb forces. The camp inmates were subjected to severe mistreatment, which included executions, torture, beatings and sexual assault. Their living conditions lacked basic sanitation (even to an absence of latrines), while food and water were unfit for human consumption and diseases such as dysentery became prevalent and went untreated. Inmates were also subjected to degrading psychological abuse. The accused actively participated with the Bosnian Serb forces in these events. He was ultimately convicted on one count of 'various acts of persecution' as a crime against humanity, five counts of

---

234. *Prosecutor v Tadić* (1995) 105 ILR 419, 2 October 1995.

inhumane treatment as crimes against humanity (ICTY Statute, Art 5[235]), and five counts of cruel treatment as violations of the laws and customs of war (ICTY Statute, Art 3[236]). During the trial, the accused objected to the Tribunal's jurisdiction. The Trial Chamber dismissed the objections, and the accused appealed to the Appeal Chamber on three grounds. The first ground was that the ICTY was founded illegally — that is, by the United Nations Security Council acting *ultra vires*. The second ground was that the ICTY had unlawfully asserted jurisdictional primacy of national courts. The appeal on both these grounds was dismissed. The final ground was that there was no jurisdiction *ratione materiae* because there was no 'armed conflict', either international or internal, in and around the locations of the impugned acts and during the times those acts were alleged to have been committed:

> 65. Appellant's third ground of appeal is the claim that the International Tribunal lacks subject-matter jurisdiction over the crimes alleged. The basis for this allegation is Appellant's claim that the subject-matter jurisdiction under Articles 2,[237] 3 and 5 of the Statute of the International Tribunal is limited to crimes committed in the context of an international armed conflict. Before the Trial Chamber, Appellant claimed that the alleged crimes, even if proven, were committed in the context of an internal armed conflict. On appeal an additional alternative claim is asserted to the effect that there was no armed conflict at all in the region where the crimes were allegedly committed.

> Before the Trial Chamber, the Prosecutor responded with alternative arguments that: (a) the conflicts in the former Yugoslavia should be characterized as an international armed conflict; and (b) even if the conflicts were characterized as internal, the International Tribunal has jurisdiction under Articles 3 and 5 to adjudicate the crimes alleged. On appeal, the Prosecutor maintains that, upon adoption of the Statute, the Security Council determined that the conflicts in the former Yugoslavia were international and that, by dint of that determination, the International Tribunal has jurisdiction over this case.

> The Trial Chamber denied Appellant's motion, concluding that the notion of international armed conflict was not a jurisdictional criterion of Article 2 and that Articles 3 and 5 each apply to both internal and international armed conflicts. The Trial Chamber concluded therefore that it had jurisdiction, regardless of the nature of the conflict, and that it need not determine whether the conflict is internal or international.

> ...

> 66. Appellant now asserts the new position that there did not exist a legally cognizable armed conflict — either internal or international — at the time and place that the alleged offences were committed. Appellant's argument is based on a concept of armed conflict covering only the precise time and place of actual hostilities. Appellant claims that the conflict in the Prijedor region (where the alleged crimes are said to have taken place) was limited to a political assumption of power by the Bosnian Serbs and did not involve armed combat (though movements of tanks are admitted). ...

---

235. Article 5 of the ICTY Statute confers jurisdiction in respect of crimes against humanity and is functionally equivalent to Art 7(1) of the Rome Statute.
236. Article 3 of the ICTY Statute confers jurisdiction in respect of 'violations of the laws or customs of war' without expressly specifying whether such violations may be committed in the context of an internal armed conflict. It is functionally equivalent to Art 8(2)(b), (e) of the Rome Statute.
237. Article 2 of the ICTY Statute confers jurisdiction in respect of grave breaches of the four Geneva Conventions and is materially identical to Art 8(2) of the Rome Statute.

67. International humanitarian law governs the conduct of both internal and international armed conflicts. Appellant correctly points out that for there to be a violation of this body of law, there must be an armed conflict. The definition of 'armed conflict' varies depending on whether the hostilities are international or internal but, contrary to Appellant's contention, the temporal and geographical scope of both internal and international armed conflicts extends beyond the exact time and place of hostilities. With respect to the temporal frame of reference of international armed conflicts, each of the four Geneva Conventions contains language intimating that their application may extend beyond the cessation of fighting. For example, both Conventions I and III apply until protected persons who have fallen into the power of the enemy have been released and repatriated. ...

68. Although the Geneva Conventions are silent as to the geographical scope of international 'armed conflicts,' the provisions suggest that at least some of the provisions of the Conventions apply to the entire territory of the Parties to the conflict, not just to the vicinity of actual hostilities. Certainly, some of the provisions are clearly bound up with the hostilities and the geographical scope of those provisions should be so limited. Others, particularly those relating to the protection of prisoners of war and civilians, are not so limited. With respect to prisoners of war, the Convention [Geneva Convention III] applies to combatants in the power of the enemy; it makes no difference whether they are kept in the vicinity of hostilities. In the same vein, Geneva Convention IV protects civilians anywhere in the territory of the Parties. This construction is implicit in Article 6, paragraph 2, of the Convention, which stipulates that:

'[i]n the territory of Parties to the conflict, the application of the present Convention shall cease on the general close of military operations.' (Geneva Convention IV, art. 6, para. 2 ...)

Article 3(b) of Protocol I to the Geneva Conventions contains similar language. ... In addition to these textual references, the very nature of the Conventions — particularly Conventions III and IV — dictates their application throughout the territories of the parties to the conflict; any other construction would substantially defeat their purpose.

69. The geographical and temporal frame of reference for internal armed conflicts is similarly broad. This conception is reflected in the fact that beneficiaries of common Article 3 of the Geneva Conventions are those taking no active part (or no longer taking active part) in the hostilities. This indicates that the rules contained in Article 3 also apply outside the narrow geographical context of the actual theatre of combat operations. Similarly, certain language in Protocol II to the Geneva Conventions ... also suggests a broad scope. First, like common Article 3, it explicitly protects '[a]ll persons who do not take a direct part or who have ceased to take part in hostilities.'[238] ... Article 2, paragraph 1, provides:

'[t]his Protocol shall be applied [...] to all persons *affected* by an armed conflict as defined in Article 1.' (Id. at art. 2, para. 1 (Emphasis added).)

The same provision specifies in paragraph 2 that:

'[A]t the end of the conflict, all the persons who have been deprived of their liberty or whose liberty has been restricted for reasons related to such conflict, as well as those deprived of their liberty or whose liberty is restricted after the conflict for the same reasons, shall enjoy the protection of Articles 5 and 6 until the end of such deprivation or restriction of liberty.' (*Id.* at art. 2, para. 2.)

238. Geneva Protocol II, Art 4(1).

Under this last provision, the temporal scope of the applicable rules clearly reaches beyond the actual hostilities. Moreover, the relatively loose nature of the language 'for reasons related to such conflict', suggests a broad geographical scope as well. The nexus required is only a relationship between the conflict and the deprivation of liberty, not that the deprivation occurred in the midst of battle.

70. On the basis of the foregoing, we find that an armed conflict exists whenever there is a resort to armed force between States or protracted armed violence between governmental authorities and organized armed groups or between such groups within a State. International humanitarian law applies from the initiation of such armed conflicts and extends beyond the cessation of hostilities until a general conclusion of peace is reached; or, in the case of internal conflicts, a peaceful settlement is achieved. Until that moment, international humanitarian law continues to apply in the whole territory of the warring States or, in the case of internal conflicts, the whole territory under the control of a party, whether or not actual combat takes place there.

Applying the foregoing concept of armed conflicts to this case, we hold that the alleged crimes were committed in the context of an armed conflict. Fighting among the various entities within the former Yugoslavia began in 1991, continued through the summer of 1992 when the alleged crimes are said to have been committed, and persists to this day. Notwithstanding various temporary cease-fire agreements, no general conclusion of peace has brought military operations in the region to a close. These hostilities exceed the intensity requirements applicable to both international and internal armed conflicts. There has been protracted, large-scale violence between the armed forces of different States and between governmental forces and organized insurgent groups. Even if substantial clashes were not occurring in the Prijedor region at the time and place the crimes allegedly were committed — a factual issue on which the Appeals Chamber does not pronounce — international humanitarian law applies. It is sufficient that the alleged crimes were closely related to the hostilities occurring in other parts of the territories controlled by the parties to the conflict. There is no doubt that the allegations at issue here bear the required relationship. The indictment states that in 1992 Bosnian Serbs took control of the Opstina [administrative district] of Prijedor and established a prison camp in Omarska. It further alleges that crimes were committed against civilians inside and outside the Omarska prison camp as part of the Bosnian Serb take-over and consolidation of power in the Prijedor region, which was, in turn, part of the larger Bosnian Serb military campaign to obtain control over Bosnian territory. Appellant offers no contrary evidence but has admitted in oral argument that in the Prijedor region there were detention camps run not by the central authorities of Bosnia-Herzegovina but by Bosnian Serbs ... In light of the foregoing, we conclude that, for the purposes of applying international humanitarian law, the crimes alleged were committed in the context of an armed conflict.

...

96. Whenever armed violence erupted in the international community, in traditional international law the legal response was based on a stark dichotomy: belligerency or insurgency. The former category applied to armed conflicts between sovereign States (unless there was recognition of belligerency in a civil war), while the latter applied to armed violence breaking out in the territory of a sovereign State. Correspondingly, international law treated the two classes of conflict in a markedly different way: interstate wars were regulated by a whole body of international legal rules, governing both the conduct of hostilities and the protection of persons not participating (or no longer participating) in armed violence (civilians, the wounded, the sick, shipwrecked, prisoners of war).

By contrast, there were very few international rules governing civil commotion, for States preferred to regard internal strife as rebellion, mutiny and treason coming within the purview of national criminal law and, by the same token, to exclude any possible intrusion by other States into their own domestic jurisdiction. This dichotomy was clearly sovereignty-oriented and reflected the traditional configuration of the international community, based on the coexistence of sovereign States more inclined to look after their own interests than community concerns or humanitarian demands.

97. Since the 1930s, however, the aforementioned distinction has gradually become more and more blurred, and international legal rules have increasingly emerged or have been agreed upon to regulate internal armed conflict. There exist various reasons for this development. First, civil wars have become more frequent, not only because technological progress has made it easier for groups of individuals to have access to weaponry but also on account of increasing tension, whether ideological, inter-ethnic or economic; as a consequence the international community can no longer turn a blind eye to the legal regime of such wars. Secondly, internal armed conflicts have become more and more cruel and protracted, involving the whole population of the State where they occur: the all-out resort to armed violence has taken on such a magnitude that the difference with international wars has increasingly dwindled (suffice to think of the Spanish civil war, in 1936–39, of the civil war in the Congo, in 1960–1968, the Biafran conflict in Nigeria, 1967–70, the civil strife in Nicaragua, in 1981–1990 or El Salvador, 1980–1993). Thirdly, the large-scale nature of civil strife, coupled with the increasing interdependence of States in the world community, has made it more and more difficult for third States to remain aloof: the economic, political and ideological interests of third States have brought about direct or indirect involvement of third States in this category of conflict, thereby requiring that international law take greater account of their legal regime in order to prevent, as much as possible, adverse spill-over effects. Fourthly, the impetuous development and propagation in the international community of human rights doctrines, particularly after the adoption of the Universal Declaration of Human Rights in 1948, has brought about significant changes in international law, notably in the approach to problems besetting the world community. A State-sovereignty-oriented approach has been gradually supplanted by a human-being-oriented approach. Gradually the maxim of Roman law *hominum causa omne jus constitutum est* (all law is created for the benefit of human beings) has gained a firm foothold in the international community as well. It follows that in the area of armed conflict the distinction between interstate wars and civil wars is losing its value as far as human beings are concerned. Why protect civilians from belligerent violence, or ban rape, torture or the wanton destruction of hospitals, churches, museums or private property, as well as proscribe weapons causing unnecessary suffering when two sovereign States are engaged in war, and yet refrain from enacting the same bans or providing the same protection when armed violence has erupted 'only' within the territory of a sovereign State? If international law, while of course duly safeguarding the legitimate interests of States, must gradually turn to the protection of human beings, it is only natural that the aforementioned dichotomy should gradually lose its weight.

98. The emergence of international rules governing internal strife has occurred at two different levels: at the level of customary law and at that of treaty law. Two bodies of rules have thus crystallised, which are by no means conflicting or inconsistent, but instead mutually support and supplement each other. Indeed, the interplay between these two sets of rules is such that some treaty rules have gradually become part of customary law. This holds true for common Article 3 of the 1949 Geneva Conventions, as was authoritatively held by the International

Court of Justice (Nicaragua Case, at para. 218), but also applies to Article 19 of the Hague Convention for the Protection of Cultural Property in the Event of Armed Conflict of 14 May 1954, and, as we shall show below (para. 117), to the core of Additional Protocol II of 1977.

...

117. Attention must also be drawn to Additional Protocol II to the Geneva Conventions. Many provisions of this Protocol can now be regarded as declaratory of existing rules or as having crystallised emerging rules of customary law or else as having been strongly instrumental in their evolution as general principles. ...

126. The emergence of ... general rules on internal armed conflicts does not imply that internal strife is regulated by general international law in all its aspects. Two particular limitations may be noted: (i) only a number of rules and principles governing international armed conflicts have gradually been extended to apply to internal conflicts; and (ii) this extension has not taken place in the form of a full and mechanical transplant of those rules to internal conflicts; rather, the general essence of those rules, and not the detailed regulation they may contain, has become applicable to internal conflicts. ...

127. Notwithstanding these limitations, it cannot be denied that customary rules have developed to govern internal strife. These rules, as specifically identified in the preceding discussion, cover such areas as protection of civilians from hostilities, in particular from indiscriminate attacks, protection of civilian objects, in particular cultural property, protection of all those who do not (or no longer) take active part in hostilities, as well as prohibition of means of warfare proscribed in international armed conflicts and ban of certain methods of conducting hostilities.

...

128. Even if customary international law includes certain basic principles applicable to both internal and international armed conflicts, Appellant argues that such prohibitions do not entail individual criminal responsibility when breaches are committed in internal armed conflicts; these provisions cannot, therefore, fall within the scope of the International Tribunal's jurisdiction. It is true that, for example, common Article 3 of the Geneva Conventions contains no explicit reference to criminal liability for violation of its provisions. Faced with similar claims with respect to the various agreements and conventions that formed the basis of its jurisdiction, the International Military Tribunal at Nuremberg concluded that a finding of individual criminal responsibility is not barred by the absence of treaty provisions on punishment of breaches. (See The Trial of Major War Criminals: Proceedings of the International Military Tribunal Sitting at Nuremberg Germany, Part 22, at 445, 467 (1950).) The Nuremberg Tribunal considered a number of factors relevant to its conclusion that the authors of particular prohibitions incur individual responsibility: the clear and unequivocal recognition of the rules of warfare in international law and State practice indicating an intention to criminalize the prohibition, including statements by government officials and international organizations, as well as punishment of violations by national courts and military tribunals (id., at 445–47, 467). Where these conditions are met, individuals must be held criminally responsible ...

129. Applying the foregoing criteria to the violations at issue here, we have no doubt that they entail individual criminal responsibility, regardless of whether they are committed in internal or international armed conflicts. Principles and rules of humanitarian law reflect 'elementary considerations of humanity' widely recognized as the mandatory minimum for conduct in armed conflicts of any kind. No one can doubt the gravity of the acts at issue, nor the interest of the international community in their prohibition.

10.116   The context of an 'armed conflict' necessary for the commission of war crimes is therefore present whenever 'there is a resort to armed force between States or protracted armed violence between governmental authorities and organized armed groups or between such groups within a State'.

10.117   When armed force is employed between two or more States, the armed conflict is international. In armed conflicts of an international character, individual criminal responsibility for war crimes applies from the initiation of the conflict and extends beyond the cessation of hostilities until a general conclusion of peace is reached. It also extends to the whole territory of the warring States.

10.118   The existence of 'protracted' armed violence 'between governmental authorities and organized armed groups or between such groups within a State' indicates an internal armed conflict. Where armed groups are involved, they must be 'organized' in order to create an internal armed conflict. As the Rome Statute now clarifies, the fighting must also be of a certain intensity. In particular, neither the serious violations of Common Art 3 nor the other serious violations of customary international law applicable in internal armed conflicts apply to mere 'internal disturbances and tensions, such as riots, isolated and sporadic acts of violence or other acts of a similar nature'.[239] Moreover, the other serious violations of customary international law applicable in internal armed conflicts apply only 'when there is protracted armed conflict between governmental authorities and organized armed groups or between such groups'.[240] Unless the violence rises to the level of at least an internal armed conflict, there is no scope for the application of the law on war crimes. In armed conflicts of an internal character, individual criminal responsibility for war crimes applies until a peaceful settlement is achieved. It also applies to the whole territory under the control of a party, whether or not actual combat takes place there.

10.119   The distinction between international and internal armed conflicts was somewhat downplayed in *Tadić* because of the way the ICTY Statute, and especially Art 3, is drafted. No distinction is expressly drawn between the two types of armed conflict, hence the ICTY's observation that '[i]nternational humanitarian law governs the conduct of both internal and international armed conflicts'. So it does. Nevertheless, the ICTY Appeals Chamber in *Tadić* recognised that the distinction between the two types of armed conflict retained significance in terms of the scope *ratione materiae* of individual criminal responsibility for war crimes. It is only the 'general essence' of the rules on war crimes in international armed conflicts which apply as a matter of customary international law in internal armed conflicts. This understanding of the scope *ratione materiae* of war crimes in the two different types of armed conflict finds its reflection in the careful drafting of the war crimes provisions in the Rome Statute, to which more than 110 States are parties.

---

239. Rome Statute, Art 8(2)(d), (f).
240. Ibid, Art 8(2)(f).

Individual and command responsibility

10.120   There are two modes by which an individual can bear criminal responsibility for the crime of genocide, crimes against humanity and war crimes: responsibility as an individual, and responsibility as a commander or superior.

Individual responsibility

10.121   Individual responsibility for war crimes and crimes against humanity was expressly provided for in the Charter of the Nuremberg Tribunal, the ICTY Statute, and the ICTR Statute.[241] The Rome Statute provides for individual responsibility in the following terms:

Article 25

Individual criminal responsibility

1. The Court shall have jurisdiction over natural persons pursuant to this Statute.

2. A person who commits a crime within the jurisdiction of the Court shall be individually responsible and liable for punishment in accordance with this Statute.

3. In accordance with this Statute, a person shall be criminally responsible and liable for punishment for a crime within the jurisdiction of the Court if that person:

   (a) Commits such a crime, whether as an individual, jointly with another or through another person, regardless of whether that other person is criminally responsible;

   (b) Orders, solicits or induces the commission of such a crime which in fact occurs or is attempted;

   (c) For the purpose of facilitating the commission of such a crime, aids, abets or otherwise assists in its commission or its attempted commission, including providing the means for its commission;

   (d) In any other way contributes to the commission or attempted commission of such a crime by a group of persons acting with a common purpose. Such contribution shall be intentional and shall either:

      (i) Be made with the aim of furthering the criminal activity or criminal purpose of the group, where such activity or purpose involves the commission of a crime within the jurisdiction of the Court; or

      (ii) Be made in the knowledge of the intention of the group to commit the crime;

   (e) In respect of the crime of genocide, directly and publicly incites others to commit genocide;

   (f) Attempts to commit such a crime by taking action that commences its execution by means of a substantial step, but the crime does

---

241. Charter of the Nuremberg Tribunal, Art 6; ICTY Statute, Art 7(1); ICTR Statute, Art 6(1).

not occur because of circumstances independent of the person's intentions. However, a person who abandons the effort to commit the crime or otherwise prevents the completion of the crime shall not be liable for punishment under this Statute for the attempt to commit that crime if that person completely and voluntarily gave up the criminal purpose.

4.   No provision in this Statute relating to individual criminal responsibility shall affect the responsibility of States under international law.

10.122   These different modalities of individual responsibility — personally or jointly committing the crime, ordering or soliciting the crime, aiding or assisting in the crime's commission, contributing to a group's commission of the crime, attempting the crime, and directly and publicly inciting the crime of genocide — reflect customary international law.

Command responsibility

10.123   When the crime of genocide, crimes against humanity and war crimes are committed, it will usually be in the context of conduct by members of military, paramilitary, militia, armed police or similar forces. Those personally responsible for the crimes will therefore usually be part of an organisation in which there are chains of command with persons in positions of superior authority above them. Are commanders or others in a position of superior authority ever criminally responsible for the conduct of their subordinates? It is to be noted in this regard that ordering the commission of a crime gives rise to individual responsibility.[242]

10.124   Even without giving orders or otherwise attracting individual responsibility, it is possible for such persons to be criminally liable for certain failures or omissions which permit, result in, or fail to punish crimes committed by their subordinates. This form of liability is known as 'command responsibility' or 'superior responsibility'.

10.125   Command responsibility received formal recognition in Geneva Protocol I.[243] Both the ICTY Statute (Art 7(3)) and the ICTR Statute (Art 6(3)) provide for command responsibility in terms materially identical to each other:

> The fact that any of the [criminal acts] of the present Statute was committed by a subordinate does not relieve his superior of criminal responsibility if he knew or had reason to know that the subordinate was about to commit such acts or had done so and the superior failed to take the necessary and reasonable measures to prevent such acts or to punish the perpetrators thereof.

10.126   The ICTY has considered the meaning and scope of command responsibility on numerous occasions.

---

242. Rome Statute, Art 25(3)(b).
243. Geneva Protocol I, Arts 85 and 86.

In **Prosecutor v Halilović**,[244] the accused was deputy commander of the Supreme Command Staff of the Army of Bosnia and Herzegovina (ABiH). In 1993, he was appointed to lead an 'inspection team' for the purpose of coordinating a military operation in Herzegovina. During the operation, numerous Bosnian Croat civilians were murdered by units of the ABiH. The accused was charged with these murders in his capacity as commander of the troops who committed the acts, and by failing to prevent the murders or punish the perpetrators. He was acquitted on the basis that there was insufficient evidence establishing that he was in a position to command or exercise authority over the delinquent troops. In the course of dismissing the charges, the Trial Chamber of the ICTY made the following observations:

The Elements of Command Responsibility

55. The principle of individual criminal responsibility of commanders for failure to prevent or to punish crimes committed by their subordinates is an established principle of customary international law.[245] Article 7(3) of the Statute is applicable to all acts referred to in Articles 2 to 5 thereof and applies to both international and non-international armed conflicts.[246]

56. To hold a superior responsible under Article 7(3) of the Statute, the jurisprudence of the Tribunal has established that three elements must be satisfied:

  i. The existence of a superior–subordinate relationship;

  ii. the superior knew or had reason to know that the criminal act was about to be or had been committed; and

  iii. the superior failed to take the necessary and reasonable measures to prevent the criminal act or punish the perpetrator thereof.[247]

(a) Superior–Subordinate Relationship

57. It is the position of command over the perpetrator which forms the basis for the superior's duty to act, and for his corollary liability for a failure to do so.[248] As held by the Trial Chamber in *Čelebići*, the doctrine of command responsibility is 'ultimately predicated upon the power of the superior to control the acts of his subordinates.'[249]

58. The main factor in determining a position of command is the 'actual possession or non-possession of powers of control over the actions of subordinates'.[250] In determining the degree of control required by the superior over the subordinate for command responsibility to be applicable, the Appeals

---

244. *Prosecutor v Halilović*, IT-01-48-T, 16 November 2005. Footnotes in this extract refer to sources cited in the judgment.

245. *Prosecutor v Delalić*, IT-96-21-A, 20 February 2001, para 195; IT-96-21-T, 16 November 1998, para 343.

246. For application of the principle of command responsibility to both international and non-international armed conflicts, see *Prosecutor v Hadzihasanović*, IT-01-47-A, 22 April 2008, para 31.

247. *Prosecutor v Delalić*, IT-96-21-T, 16 November 1998, para 346; *Prosecutor v Blaškić*, IT-95-14-A, 29 July 2004, para 484; *Prosecutor v Aleksovski*, IT-95-14/1-A, 24 March 2000, para 72. See also *Prosecutor v Kordić*, IT-95-14/2-A, 17 December 2004, para 827; *Prosecutor v Blaškić*, IT-95-14-T, 3 March 2000, para 294; *Prosecutor v Kvočka*, IT-98-30/1-T, 2 November 2001, para 401.

248. *Prosecutor v Aleksovski*, IT-95-14/1-A, 24 March 2000, para 76.

249. *Prosecutor v Delalić*, IT-96-21-T, 16 November 1998, para 377. The case is referred to as *Čelebići*, after the prison camp in which the acts alleged in this case took place. A footnote to the judgment adds: 'It is well established that command responsibility is applicable to both military and civilian superiors', *Prosecutor v Delalić*, IT-96-21-A, 20 February 2001, paras 195–196 and 240; *Prosecutor v Aleksovski*, IT-95-14/1-A, 24 March 2000, para 76.

250. *Prosecutor v Delalić*, IT-96-21-T, 16 November 1998, para 370.

Chamber endorsed the concept of 'effective control', which it defined as 'the material ability to prevent and punish criminal conduct'.[251] In this respect, factors indicative of an accused's position of authority and effective control may include the official position held by the accused, his capacity to issue orders, whether de jure or de facto, the procedure for appointment, the position of the accused within the military or political structure and the actual tasks that he performed.[252] The Appeals Chamber in Blaškić held that 'the indicators of effective control are more a matter of evidence than of substantive law, and those indicators are limited to showing that the accused had the power to prevent, punish, or initiate measures leading to proceedings against the alleged perpetrators where appropriate'.[253]

59. A degree of control which falls short of the threshold of effective control is insufficient for liability to attach under Article 7(3). 'Substantial influence' over subordinates which does not meet the threshold of effective control is not sufficient under customary law to serve as a means of exercising command responsibility and, therefore, to impose criminal liability.[254]

60. The jurisprudence of the Tribunal has interpreted the concepts of command and subordination in a relatively broad sense. Command does not arise solely from the superior's formal or de jure status,[255] but can also be 'based on the existence of de facto powers of control'.[256] In this respect, the necessity to establish the existence of a hierarchical relationship between the superior and the subordinate does 'not [...] import a requirement of direct or formal subordination'.[257]

61. Command responsibility applies to every commander at every level in the armed forces. This includes responsibility for troops who have been temporarily assigned to that commander.[258] ...

To hold a commander liable for the acts of troops who operated under his command on a temporary basis it must be shown that at the time when the acts charged in the indictment were committed, these troops were under the effective control of that commander.[259]

...

63. Consistent with the above reasoning, there is no requirement that the superior–subordinate relationship be direct or immediate in nature for a commander to be found liable for the acts of his subordinate.[260] What is required is the establishment of the superior's effective control over the subordinate, whether that subordinate is immediately answerable to that superior or more

---

251. Prosecutor v Delalić, IT-96-21-A, 20 February 2001, para 256.
252. See Prosecutor v Kordić, IT-95-14/2-T, 26 February 2001, paras 418–424.
253. Prosecutor v Blaškić, IT-95-14-A, 29 July 2004, para 69.
254. Prosecutor v Delalić, IT-96-21-A, 20 February 2001, para 266.
255. Ibid, para 193.
256. Ibid, para 195. The ICTY footnote adds:
    The Appeal Chamber in Čelebići stated that a superior vested with de jure authority who does not have effective control over his or her subordinates would therefore not incur criminal responsibility pursuant to the doctrine of superior responsibility, whereas a de facto superior who lacks formal letters of appointment or commission but, in reality, has effective control over the perpetrators of offences would incur criminal responsibility where he failed to prevent or punish such criminal conduct, ibid., para. 197.
257. Ibid, para 303 (emphasis in the original).
258. Prosecutor v Kunarac, IT-96-22-T & IT-96-23/1-T, 21 February 2001, para 399. The ICTY footnote states: 'The temporary nature of a military unit is not, in itself, sufficient to exclude a relationship of subordination, ibid.'
259. Ibid, para 399, citing Prosecutor v Delalić, IT-96-21-A, 20 February 2001, paras 197–198 and 256.
260. Prosecutor v Strugar, IT-01-42-T, 31 January 2005, para 363.

remotely under his command.[261] As to whether the superior has the requisite level of control, this is a matter which must be determined on the basis of the evidence presented in each case.[262]

(b) Mental Element: 'Knew Or Had Reason To Know'

64. The mental element required for a superior to be held responsible under Article 7(3) of the Statute is established where the superior knew or had reason to know that the subordinate was about to commit or had committed a crime.

65. Superior responsibility is not a form of strict liability.[263] It must be proved either that (1) the superior had actual knowledge that his subordinates were committing or about to commit crimes within the jurisdiction of the Tribunal, or that (ii) he had in his possession information which would at least put him on notice of the risk of such offences, such information alerting him to the need for additional investigation to determine whether such crimes had been or were about to be committed by his subordinates.[264]

...

67. A commander will be considered to have 'had reason to know' only if information was available to him which would have put him on notice of offences committed by his subordinates,[265] or about to be committed.

...

69. A superior is not liable for failing to acquire information in the first place.[266] The Appeals Chamber has held that knowledge cannot be presumed if a person fails in his duty to obtain the relevant information of a crime, but it may be presumed where a superior had the means to obtain the relevant information and deliberately refrained from doing so.[267] Furthermore, a commander is not permitted to remain 'wilfully blind' of the acts of his subordinates.[268]

70. The Trial Chamber notes that an assessment of the mental element required by Article 7(3) of the Statute should be conducted in the specific circumstances of each case, taking into account the specific situation of the superior concerned at the time in question.[269] This is a factual assessment to be made on the basis of the evidence presented to the Trial Chamber.

---

261. An ICTY footnote here states: 'The ICRC Commentary to the Additional Protocols, dealing with the concept of a "superior" within the meaning of Article 86 of Additional Protocol I, which provides the basis for the duty in Article 7(3), emphasises that the term is not limited to immediate superiors. ...'

262. An ICTY footnote here states that '[a]s discussed above, the indicators of effective control depend on the specific circumstances of the case', citing *Prosecutor v Strugar*, IT-01-42-T, 31 January 2005, para 392.

263. *Prosecutor v Delalić*, IT-96-21-A, 20 February 2001, para 239.

264. Ibid, paras 223 and 241.

265. *Prosecutor v Blaškić*, IT-95-14-A, 29 July 2004, para 62, citing *Prosecutor v Delalić*, IT-96-21-A, 20 February 2001, para 241.

266. *Prosecutor v Delalić*, IT-96-21-A, 20 February 2001, para 226; *Prosecutor v Blaškić*, IT-95-14-A, 29 July 2004, para 62.

267. *Prosecutor v Delalić*, IT-96-21-A, 20 February 2001, para 226.

268. A footnote in the judgment quotes from the Trial Chamber in *Prosecutor v Delalić*, IT-96-21-T, 16 November 1998, para 387:
    a superior is not permitted to remain wilfully blind to the acts of his subordinates. There can be no doubt that a superior who simply ignores information within his actual possession compelling the conclusion that criminal offences are being committed, or are about to be committed, by his subordinates commits a most serious dereliction of duty for which he may be held criminally responsible under the doctrine of superior responsibility.

269. *Prosecutor v Delalić*, IT-96-21-A, 20 February 2001, para 239.

71. In conclusion, the Trial Chamber must be satisfied that, pursuant to Article 7(3) of the Statute, the accused either 'knew' or 'had reason to know'. In this respect, the Trial Chamber notes that the Appeals Chamber has held that criminal negligence is not a basis of liability in the context of command responsibility.[270]

(c) Failure to Prevent or Punish

72. Article 7(3) contains two distinct legal obligations: to prevent the commission of the offence and to punish the perpetrators thereof.[271] The duty to prevent arises when the commander acquires actual knowledge or has reasonable grounds to suspect that a crime is being or is about to be committed, while the duty to punish arises after the commission of the crime.[272] A failure to take the necessary and reasonable measures to prevent an offence of which a superior knew or had reason to know cannot be cured simply by subsequently punishing the subordinate for the commission of the offence.[273]

10.127 The customary international law on command responsibility therefore consists of two primary elements.

First, the accused must have been in a position to control effectively the conduct of those who were individually responsible for the crimes. A degree of control that does not rise to the level of 'effective control' is not enough. Likewise, it is not enough that the accused exercised 'substantial influence' over the individual perpetrators. On the other hand, the accused does not need to stand in immediate authority above the individual perpetrators in the chain of command; it is enough that he or she exercised effective control over the perpetrators, even if there were one or more levels of command authority between the accused and the perpetrators.

Second, the knowledge of the accused is important. He or she must have known, or had reason to know, that the crimes were about to be committed or had been committed. In this regard, it is important to note that command responsibility is not a form of strict liability — the commander is not automatically responsible for any crimes committed by his or her subordinates. Nor is the commander responsible even on the basis that he or she was criminally negligent. Rather, the commander must have actually known that his or her subordinates had committed, or were about to commit, the crimes, or the commander must have actually possessed information which put him or her on notice. A failure to make inquiries is not enough unless the commander was being wilfully blind to the conduct of his or her subordinates.

10.128 Where the two primary elements of command responsibility are present, the responsibility of the commander or superior is to take such measures as are both necessary and reasonable either to prevent the

---

270. *Prosecutor v Blaškić*, IT-95-14-A, 29 July 2004, para 63, citing *Prosecutor v Bagilishema*, ICTR-95-1A-A, 3 July 2002, paras 34–35.
271. *Prosecutor v Blaškić*, IT-95-14-A, 29 July 2004, para 83.
272. Ibid, para 83; *Prosecutor v Kordić*, IT-95-14/2-T, 26 February 2001, paras 445–446.
273. *Prosecutor v Blaškić*, IT-95-14-T, 3 March 2000, para 336.

criminal conduct of his or her subordinates, or to punish them for such conduct already committed.

10.129   That this conception of command responsibility corresponds to the requirements of customary international law finds support not only in the jurisprudence of the ICTY interpreting Art 7(3) of the ICTY Statute, but also in the text of the Rome Statute:

Article 28

Responsibility of commanders and other superiors

In addition to other grounds of criminal responsibility under this Statute for crimes within the jurisdiction of the Court:

(a) A military commander or person effectively acting as a military commander shall be criminally responsible for crimes within the jurisdiction of the Court committed by forces under his or her effective command and control, or effective authority and control as the case may be, as a result of his or her failure to exercise control properly over such forces, where:

(i) That military commander or person either knew or, owing to the circumstances at the time, should have known that the forces were committing or about to commit such crimes; and

(ii) That military commander or person failed to take all necessary and reasonable measures within his or her power to prevent or repress their commission or to submit the matter to the competent authorities for investigation and prosecution.

(b) With respect to superior and subordinate relationships not described in paragraph (a), a superior shall be criminally responsible for crimes within the jurisdiction of the Court committed by subordinates under his or her effective authority and control, as a result of his or her failure to exercise control properly over such subordinates, where:

(i) The superior either knew, or consciously disregarded information which clearly indicated, that the subordinates were committing or about to commit such crimes;

(ii) The crimes concerned activities that were within the effective responsibility and control of the superior; and

(iii) The superior failed to take all necessary and reasonable measures within his or her power to prevent or repress their commission or to submit the matter to the competent authorities for investigation and prosecution.

10.130   There are two divergences worth noting between the jurisprudence of the ICTY and the drafting of the Rome Statute.

First, whereas Art 7(3) of the ICTY Statute stipulates that the commander must have 'had reason to know' that his or her subordinates had committed, or were about to commit, a crime, Art 28(a)(i) of the Rome Statute requires simply that the commander 'should have known'. The wording of the Rome Statute implies a more stringent standard for the commander than the ICTY Statute upon which judgments such as *Halilović* are based.

Second, in respect of crimes that were already committed, the ICTY Statute requires the commander to take 'necessary or reasonable steps to punish' the perpetrators. Article 28(b)(iii) of the Rome Statute, on the other hand, requires the commander to 'submit the matter to the competent authorities for investigation and prosecution'. The Rome Statute provision makes more explicit the requirement that the punishment meted out to the perpetrators must follow procedures consistent with basic requirements of procedural fairness.

Immunities

10.131   As far as the jurisdiction of the ICC is concerned, immunities and special procedural rules enjoyed by Heads of State, Heads of Government or other government or public officials do not apply.[274] Similar provisions exist in the Charter of the Nuremberg Tribunal and in the ICTY and ICTR Statutes.[275] Although serving and former Heads of State, Heads of Government, Foreign Ministers, diplomatic agents and consular agents enjoy extensive immunities from the jurisdiction of foreign national courts,[276] no such immunities apply before the ICC, the ICTY and the ICTR.

Question

From 2002 until January this year, Kim was the most senior Admiral in the navy of the Popular Republic of Norkia. He was a respected and influential figure throughout all of Norkia's armed forces. Port Norkia is a town in Norkia with a population of about 40,000.

In February and March last year, there was a labour strike of stevedores in Port Norkia. The strikers were demanding better working conditions, an end to official corruption, and the establishment of a democratic political system.

In late February, the Norkian army and navy were ordered to crush the strikes and demonstrations before they spread nationally. An army General was placed in overall command of the operation (code-named Operation Restore Harmony), while Kim's task was strictly limited to ensuring that the navy's role was properly coordinated with that of the army. Operation Restore Harmony went into immediate effect and was scheduled to culminate on 11 March with military operations by 20,000 army troops and six navy vessels.

On 1 March, and in accordance with the first (preparatory) phase of Operation Restore Harmony, the Norkian warship *The Gracchi* anchored in Port Norkia's harbour. The vessel and its crew were under Kim's command.

---

274. Rome Statute, Art 27.
275. Charter of the Nuremberg Tribunal, Art 6; ICTY Statute, Art 7(2); ICTR Statute, Art 6(2).
276. See **6.50–6.61**.

On 9 March, a group of about 50 civilian strikers staged a noisy protest at the docks about 100 metres from *The Gracchi*'s anchorage. The protesters were reiterating the strike's demands. When Kim ordered the ship's crew to fire machine guns directly into the group of protesters, 20 of them were killed before the others escaped.

News of the dockside massacre spread quickly throughout Port Norkia. On 10 March, a general strike erupted throughout Port Norkia and there was a mass demonstration in the town's main square and in other locations in the town calling for an end to one-party rule.

On 11 March, the second (operational) phase of Operation Restore Harmony was launched. Twenty thousand army troops and six navy vessels took up positions surrounding Port Norkia. The army launched an artillery barrage on the main square and the headquarters of the strike movement, killing about 500 people within a few minutes. Immediately after the barrage, the troops assaulted the town, killing a further 1,000 people. The troops met no organised armed resistance.

Over a period of several days, the army systematically entered dwellings throughout the town, looking for indications of support or sympathy for the strikes and demonstrations. Whenever anything was found (leaflets, posters, placards, letters, union membership cards, and so on), all the inhabitants of the dwelling were arrested and removed from the town in army trucks for transportation to labour camps elsewhere in Norkia. About 6,000 people were forcibly transferred. Anyone resisting arrest was immediately shot. About 300 people perished in this way. Suspected leaders and agitators in the strikes and demonstrations — about 100 people in total — were shot by military firing squads in the town's main square.

While these events took place, Kim was usually present in the town observing the proceedings. He never sought to prevent the activities of the troops, or to have the individual perpetrators brought to justice.

In spite of the efforts of Norkia's State-controlled media, news of the military operations in Port Norkia leaked out and became widely known throughout the country. Strikes and demonstrations in sympathy with the inhabitants of the town spread nationwide. The government of Norkia collapsed in December last year and an interim democratic administration assumed control of the re-named Republic of Norkia.

In January this year, Kim was formally dismissed from the navy. The new government of Norkia is deciding how it should deal with him. After many decades of one-party dictatorship, Norkia does not have a rule of law tradition. The new Attorney-General is considering handing over Kim to the International Criminal Court (ICC) for prosecution. Norkia has never been party to the Rome Statute of the ICC.

Kim has never possessed any State's nationality except that of Norkia.

Advise the Attorney-General as to whether:

■ Kim's treatment of the dockside protesters constitutes any international crimes;

- Kim's conduct during Operation Restore Harmony constitutes any international crimes; and
- the ICC can exercise jurisdiction over any such crimes.

Suggested answer

Kim's treatment of the dockside protesters

Kim's order on 9 March to open fire with machine guns at the dockside protesters, resulting in 20 deaths, is an act of murder.

Murder is not, as such, an international crime *(R v Bow Street Metropolitan Stipendiary Magistrate; Ex parte Pinochet Ugarte (No 3))*. Where they are committed in certain contexts, however, acts of murder will constitute the international offences of crimes against humanity (Rome Statute, Art 7(1)(a)) or war crimes (Rome Statute, Art 8(2)(a)(i) ('wilful killing'), Art 8(2)(c)(i)).

There will be a crime against humanity where there is an act: (i) 'inhumane in nature and character, causing great suffering, or serious injury to body or to mental or physical health'; (ii) 'committed as part of a widespread or systematic attack'; and (iii) committed against 'members of the civilian population' *(Prosecutor v Akayesu)*.

The requirements of (i) are satisfied by an act of murder. Murder occurs when the victim is dead; the act or omission was unlawful and intentional; and, at the time of the killing, the accused had the intention to kill or inflict grievous bodily harm on the deceased, having known that such bodily harm was likely to cause the victim's death, and was reckless whether death ensued or not *(Prosecutor v Akayesu)*.

Kim's conduct appears to satisfy requirement (i) because his conduct in ordering his subordinates to fire machine guns into the crowd of dockside protesters, thereby causing deaths, meets the definition of 'murder' for the purposes of establishing a crime against humanity. Requirement (iii) also appears to be clearly satisfied, as the victims were civilians.

The act must also have been 'committed as part of a widespread or systematic attack directed against any civilian population, with knowledge of the attack' *(Prosecutor v Akayesu; Prosecutor v Tadić; Rome Statute, Art 7(1))*. An 'attack' occurs when an act such as murder has been committed. The attack must be either widespread or systematic, but it need not be both. An attack is widespread if it is 'massive, frequent, large scale action, carried out collectively with considerable seriousness and directed against a multiplicity of victims'. It is systematic if it is 'thoroughly organised and following a regular pattern on the basis of a common policy involving substantial public or private resources', and there must be 'some kind of preconceived plan or policy'. An attack that is 'just a random act of violence' cannot constitute a crime against humanity *(Prosecutor v Akayesu)*.

Although Kim did not personally fire any weapon into the demonstration, he ordered marines under his command to do so and they obeyed the order. This will engage his individual responsibility for any resulting crime against humanity committed by the subordinates (Rome Statute, Art 25(3)(b)).

Although Kim will undoubtedly argue that the shooting of the dockside protesters was 'just a random act of violence', it appears to have been committed as part of a widespread or systematic attack. At the time it occurred, there was already a plan or policy to suppress the strike before it spread to other parts of Norkia (Operation Restore Harmony). This plan was both large scale (20,000 troops and six navy vessels) and systematic, as evidenced by the conduct of the operations directed against Port Norkia and its population. Although the second (operational) phase of the plan had not been launched by 9 March, the plan was already in effect and Kim was in Port Norkia's harbour as part of the plan's first (preparatory) phase in order to coordinate the navy's role with that of the army. The demonstration he dispersed was also a manifestation of the very labour unrest which the plan was designed to quell.

Therefore, it is likely that Kim committed a crime against humanity on 9 March when he ordered personnel under his command to fire machine guns into the demonstration, resulting in the deaths of 20 protesters.

Kim's conduct does not simultaneously constitute a war crime. Although murder and wilful killing are potential elements of war crimes, the murders or killings must be committed within a prescribed context. They can occur only in the context of an 'armed conflict' (Rome Statute, Art 8(2); *Prosecutor v Tadić*). An armed conflict exists where 'there is a resort to armed force between States or protracted armed violence between governmental authorities and organized armed groups or between such groups within a State' *(Prosecutor v Tadić)*. No State other than Norkia was involved in the assault on Port Norkia and the Norkian army met no organised armed resistance during its assault on the town.

Kim's conduct during the operational phase of Operation Restore Harmony

While the second (operational) phase of Operation Restore Harmony was under way, Kim was often present in Port Norkia observing the proceedings. He never sought to prevent the activities of the troops, or to have the individual perpetrators brought to justice.

Because the prescribed context for war crimes was absent (see above), no such crimes were committed during the army's execution of Operation Restore Harmony.

On the other hand, we have already seen that the prescribed context for the commission of crimes against humanity was present. Were any such crimes committed during the operational phase of Operation Restore Harmony?

When the troops shot about 300 people resisting arrest, and a further approximately 100 people as suspected leaders and agitators of the strikes and demonstrations, this almost certainly constituted murder (*Prosecutor v Akayesu* (see above); Rome Statute, Art 7(1)(a)).

At the least, these killings constituted 'other inhumane acts of a similar character intentionally causing great suffering, or serious injury to body or to mental or physical health (Rome Statute, Art 7(1)(k)). Any act which violates a fundamental right recognised by international law, and which causes either great suffering or serious injury to health, is capable of constituting a crime against humanity *(Prosecutor v Kupreškić)* when committed in the prescribed context.

The deaths of the 1,500 people killed in the artillery barrage and the subsequent assault on the town also constitute either murder or 'other inhumane acts of a similar character intentionally causing great suffering, or serious injury to body or to mental or physical health'.

The forced removal of about 6,000 people from Port Norkia to labour camps clearly amounted to a criminal 'forcible transfer of population' (Rome Statute, Art 7(1)(d)). This means a 'forced displacement of the persons concerned by expulsion or other coercive acts from the area in which they are lawfully present, without grounds permitted under international law' (Rome Statute, Art 7(2)(d)). A displacement will be 'forced' if it involves, inter alia, physical force or a 'threat of force or coercion, such as that caused by fear of violence' (Elements of Crimes for Art 7(1)(d), Rome Statute).

At least some of this conduct by members of the Norkian army will also simultaneously constitute 'persecution' as a crime against humanity. The Rome Statute identifies as a crime against humanity any persecution against an identifiable group or collectivity on political (and some other) grounds committed in connection with any other act specified as constituting a crime against humanity (Rome Statute, Art 7(1)(h)). Acts which are independently crimes against humanity will simultaneously amount to persecution as a crime against humanity where they are a severe deprivation of fundamental rights intentionally directed against any identifiable group or collectivity on political grounds *(Prosecutor v Kupreškić)*. The 100 people shot as suspected leaders or agitators, the 300 people shot resisting arrest, and the 6,000 people forcibly transferred to labour camps were selected on the basis of their actual or perceived membership of the group or collectivity of persons in Port Norkia who supported the strikes and anti-government demonstrations.

There is nothing to suggest that Kim is individually responsible, within the meaning of Art 25 of the Rome Statute, for what happened in the town after the army launched its assault. There is no evidence that he personally or jointly committed any crime, ordered or solicited any crime, aided or assisted in any crime's commission, contributed to a group's commission of the crime, or attempted any crime. He simply observed the events as they unfolded.

Kim will nevertheless be criminally liable for any of the army's crimes against humanity to the extent that he bore command or superior responsibility for those crimes and where, in certain circumstances, he either failed to prevent those crimes or failed to punish them (Rome Statute, Art 28). In order to attract command or superior responsibility, Kim must have been in a position to control effectively the conduct of the troops who were individually responsible for the crimes. A degree of control that does not rise to the level of 'effective control' is not enough. Likewise, it is not enough that Kim exercised 'substantial influence' over the individual perpetrators *(Prosecutor v Halilović)*.

Kim was the most senior officer in the Norkian navy. The personnel who committed the crimes against humanity during the operational phase of Operation Restore Harmony were members of the Norkian army. An army General was placed in overall command of Operation Restore Harmony, while Kim's task was strictly limited to ensuring that the navy's role was properly coordinated with that of the army. There appears to be no evidence that Kim was in a position of either *de jure* or *de facto* authority over the troops who committed the crimes against humanity in Port Norkia. It is true that Kim was a respected and influential figure throughout all of Norkia's armed forces, but 'influence' is not enough to establish command or superior responsibility *(Prosecutor v Halilović)*.

Although numerous crimes against humanity were committed by members of the army during Operation Restore Harmony, Kim does not appear to be responsible for those crimes either individually or as a commander or superior. Kim's conduct during and after the army's attack on Port Norkia does not constitute an international crime.

Jurisdiction of the International Criminal Court

The ICC's jurisdiction is limited by the terms of the Rome Statute.

Ratione materiae, the jurisdiction of the ICC includes crimes against humanity and also embraces the crime of genocide and war crimes (Rome Statute, Art 5(1)). The crime of aggression will be brought within the ICC's subject-matter jurisdiction once a definition of the crime is adopted (Rome Statute, Art 5(2)). Kim's treatment of the dockside protesters, as a crime against humanity, falls within the subject-matter jurisdiction of the ICC.

Ratione temporis, the jurisdiction of the ICC is confined to crimes committed after the entry into force of the Rome Statute (Rome Statute, Art 11) — that is, 1 July 2002. Kim's attack on the dockside protesters occurred last year and falls within the temporal jurisdiction of the ICC.

The ICC may exercise jurisdiction over a crime where the State on whose territory the crime occurs or whose nationality the accused possesses is a party to the Rome Statute (Rome Statute, Art 12(2)). As Norkia has never been a party to the Rome Statute, the ICC cannot exercise jurisdiction over Kim's crime against humanity unless another basis can be established.

Nevertheless, there are two ways in which the ICC could acquire jurisdiction to prosecute the crimes against humanity committed by Kim in Port Norkia.

First, the United Nations Security Council could refer Kim's crimes to the Prosecutor; the nationality of the accused and the location of the crimes are then irrelevant to the question of jurisdiction (Rome Statute, Art 13(b)).

Second, Norkia could make a declaration to the Registrar of the ICC accepting the Court's jurisdiction over crimes committed by Kim at Port Norkia (Rome Statute, Art 12(3)). Even were Norkia now to become a party to the Rome Statute, such a declaration would be necessary because the ICC otherwise lacks jurisdiction over crimes committed prior to a State becoming a party (Rome Statute, Art 11(2)).

Further tutorial discussion

1. What are the main differences and similarities between international criminal law and the law on State responsibility?
2. What are the main differences and similarities between international criminal law and international humanitarian law?
3. Should international law provide for the criminal responsibility of States?
4. Are international courts and tribunals really necessary in order to prosecute international crimes? Would the international community be better served by relying on national courts exercising universal jurisdiction over such crimes?
5. Should murder be an international crime?
6. Is the International Criminal Court sufficiently accountable for its conduct?
7. Should jurists from States without the rule of law be permitted to serve on international courts and tribunals exercising jurisdiction over international crimes?
8. Should international courts and tribunals exercising jurisdiction over international crimes be permitted to impose the death penalty for crimes such as genocide?
9. Does the United Nations Security Council have the power to halt a prosecution before the International Criminal Court? Should it have such a power?
10. Crimes against humanity should not require the context of a widespread or systematic attack on a civilian population. Do you agree?
11. Should there be trial by jury for international crimes prosecuted before international tribunals?

International human rights

11

Objectives

After completing this chapter, you should:

(1) appreciate that modern human rights law has both natural law and positive law antecedents;
(2) be aware of the existence of both universal and regional institutional architectures for the international protection of human rights;
(3) understand and be able to explain the prohibition on racial discrimination;
(4) understand and be able to apply the law protecting civil and political rights with particular reference to right to life; torture; slavery; arbitrary arrest and detention; humane treatment of detainees; imprisonment for contractual obligations; freedom of movement and residence; expulsion of aliens; equality before the law and fair trial; retroactive criminal laws; recognition as a person before the law; privacy; freedom of thought, conscience and religion; freedom of expression; freedom of assembly and association; protection of the family; protection of the child; participation in public affairs; minority rights; non-discrimination and equality before the law; and permitted derogations;
(5) be aware of the existence of economic, social and cultural rights;
(6) understand and be able to explain the prohibition on discrimination against women;
(7) understand and be able to apply the law protecting the rights of children; and
(8) be able to identify those human rights which, at customary international law, give rise to obligations owed to all other States.

Key cases

Akkoç v Turkey [2000] ECHR 577
Judge v Canada [2003] UNHRC 51
Johnson v Jamaica [1996] UNHRC 20
A v Australia [1997] UNHRC 7
Gridin v Russia [2000] UNHRC 12
Baumgarten v Germany [2003] UNHRC 44
Toonen v Australia [1994] UNHRC 8
Mukong v Cameroon [1994] UNHRC 41
Winata v Australia [2001] UNHRC 24

Key treaties and instruments

Universal Declaration on Human Rights (UDHR), General Assembly Resolution 217A (III) (1948)

International Convention on the Elimination of All Forms of Racial Discrimination (ICERD) (1966): Art 1, Art 5, Art 6

International Covenant on Civil and Political Rights (ICCPR) (1966): Art 2, Art 4, Art 6, Art 8, Art 9, Art 10, Art 11, Art 12, Art 13, Art 14, Art 15, Art 16, Art 17, Art 18, Art 19, Art 20, Art 21, Art 22, Art 23, Art 24, Art 25, Art 27

Optional Protocol to the International Covenant on Civil and Political Rights (1966)

Human Rights Committee, *General Comment No 11* (1983)

Human Rights Committee, *General Comment No 15* (1986)

Human Rights Committee, *General Comment No 17* (1989)

Human Rights Committee, *General Comment No 18* (1989)

Human Rights Committee, *General Comment No 19* (1990)

Human Rights Committee, *General Comment No 20* (1992)

Human Rights Committee, *General Comment No 21* (1992)

Human Rights Committee, *General Comment No 22* (1993)

Human Rights Committee, *General Comment No 23* (1994)

Human Rights Committee, *General Comment No 25* (1996)

Human Rights Committee, *General Comment No 27* (1999)

Human Rights Committee, *General Comment No 28* (2000)

Human Rights Committee, *General Comment No 29* (2001)

Human Rights Committee, *General Comment No 31* (2004)

Human Rights Committee, *General Comment No 32* (2007)

Convention against Torture and Other Cruel, Inhuman or Degrading Treatment or Punishment (1984): Art 1(1)

Slavery Convention (1926): Art 1

International Covenant on Economic, Social and Cultural Rights (ICESCR) (1966)

Convention on the Elimination of All Forms of Discrimination against Women (CEDW) (1979)

Convention on the Rights of the Child (CRC) (1989)

11.1 International human rights are the branch of international law which regulates the obligations of States to the protection and promotion of certain rights possessed by individuals and groups, as recognised in customary international law, treaty law, and the general principles of law. In structural terms, the rights are possessed by the individuals or groups themselves, and the corresponding duties are owed to them by States. This structure sets international human rights apart from almost all other branches of international law (with the principal exception of international criminal law), which are concerned almost exclusively with the rights and duties of States and public international organisations *inter se*.

Antecedents of international human rights

The natural law

11.2 The idea that all human beings possess rights by reason of their humanity, and that earthly sovereigns can neither confer nor revoke those rights, is deeply embedded in the Judeo-Christian religious and philosophical traditions and particularly the Christian tradition of the natural law *(jus naturale)*. That tradition has its roots in classical antiquity and reached its apogee during Europe's high middle ages, with the influential works of the scholastics such as St Thomas Aquinas (1225–1274). Indeed, the main concerns of Aquinas's landmark *Treatise on Law* (1266) are the nature and varieties of law, the relationship between the natural law and the positive law, and the obligations owed to all persons under the natural law simply by virtue of their humanity.

11.3   During the middle ages and prior to the advent of the modern State system in the late 16th and early 17th centuries, relations among European sovereigns were conceived and regulated mainly in terms of the *jus gentium,* which derived partly from the *jus naturale* and partly from the positive law of all civilised peoples. This was true also of relations between European sovereigns and the subjects of foreign sovereigns.[1]

11.4   The medieval conception of the *jus naturale,* sometimes referred to as the *philosophia perennis* (perennial philosophy), began to pass out of favour with the arrival of the intellectual movement known as the Enlightenment which accompanied the emergence of the modern State system. Enlightenment legal theorists of the 'naturalist' school broke with the *philosophia perennis,* which they scornfully rejected as an artefact of a backward age. They did not, however, entirely reject the idea of a natural law.

Indeed, a highly distorted and desiccated version of the *jus naturale* enjoyed considerable intellectual fashionability during the Enlightenment period.

11.5   Enlightenment naturalism in continental Europe was highly individualistic, voluntarist and rationalist, and rested on various conceptions of a state of nature and a social contract (the Enlightenment movements in England and Scotland were more empirical and sceptical, and less inclined to the flights of rationalist fancy which afflicted their continental counterpart). It tended strongly, but in varying degrees depending on the publicist, towards a rejection of custom and tradition as sources of authority or as restraints on personal and political action. Further, the naturalism of the continental Enlightenment cut itself off from the much older and richer tradition of the *philosophia perennis.* That tradition postulated man as an intrinsically social being, and not simply a creature who surrendered his cosmic solitude in some notional contract with his fellows. Rather, the *jus naturale* was ordained to the common good and was man's rational participation in an antecedent eternal law.

11.6   In its earlier stages, Enlightenment naturalism was definitely 'an affair of the ruling class, the nobility and the intellectuals of the age, clerics and men of science'.[2] It was, from the first, primarily political in

---

1.   See 1.7 and 1.156–1.168.
2.   Heinrich Rommen, *The Natural Law: A Study in Legal and Social History and Philosophy,* trans Thomas R Hanley, Liberty Fund, Indianapolis, 1998, 69.

orientation. It served reformist objectives by helping to replace the remnants of feudal society with more rational social arrangements corresponding to the orderly administrative requirements and modernising ambitions of centralised Enlightenment despotism.

As these political objectives were realised and consolidated, and as the logic of its individualist and contractarian foundations were remorselessly worked through, Enlightenment naturalism became an increasingly important component of a popular-revolutionary ideology, particularly in France. Under the influence of Jean-Jacques Rousseau (1712–1778) in particular, the politicisation of Enlightenment naturalism was completed, and by the late 18th century it had become principally an ideological weapon for social revolution and the overthrow of Enlightenment despots. Though it superficially resembled the *philosophia perennis*, Enlightenment naturalism involved a dramatic decay in legal theorising. This decay was only partly offset, during Enlightenment naturalism's later radical phase, by the express recognition of natural rights.

11.7 The Enlightenment's recognition of natural rights was, however, substantially impaired by the distorting conceptual framework of the social contract. In its earlier reformist phase, under the influence of Thomas Hobbes (1588–1679) and the naturalist school, Enlightenment naturalism posited that man had decisively surrendered the rights he possessed in his state of nature when he entered into the social contract. In the later revolutionary phase, these radically individualist 'natural rights of man' were thought, on the contrary, to be preserved intact by the social contract.

There was also a distinct readiness, for narrowly political purposes, to reject established positive law by appeals to a highly abstract, disembodied and revolutionary conception of the natural rights of man.

11.8 The apotheosis of the continental Enlightenment was the French Revolution of 1789, and the ensuing continent-wide series of wars, social upheavals and insurrections which lasted until Napoleon's final defeat at Waterloo 26 years later.

Among the most enduring and influential legal artefacts of this period was the Declaration of the Rights of Man and of the Citizen, the revolutionary charter approved by the French National Assembly in 1789. The American Declaration of Independence of 1776 and the Bill of Rights of 1791 (being the first 10 amendments to the United States Constitution) were also significant manifestations of Enlightenment naturalism. The American examples were, however, more precisely drafted, less given to generalised abstractions, more deferential to established liberties and the requirements of prudence, and significantly tempered by a British empiricism and suspicion of abstract theorising. In this they are in the tradition of earlier English charters of fundamental freedoms, most notably the Magna Carta (1215) and the Bill of Rights (1689). The American Revolution was political, while the French Revolution was political, social and cultural.

Notwithstanding important differences between them, the French and American documents express common commitments to certain basic rights of the human person. The French declaration, for instance, says that '[m]en are born and remain free and equal in rights'[3] and that the 'natural and imprescriptible rights of man' are 'liberty, property, security, and resistance to oppression'.[4] The opening words of the American declaration are: 'We hold these truths to be self-evident, that all men are created equal, that they are endowed by their Creator with certain unalienable Rights, that among these are Life, Liberty and the pursuit of Happiness.'

Both the French declaration and the American Bill of Rights make provision for freedom of religion, freedom of expression, property rights, and rights of the accused in criminal cases.

The French declaration engages in additional generalised abstractions, such as '[t]he principle of all sovereignty resides essentially in the nation',[5] while the American Bill of Rights enumerates further specific guarantees not included in the French document, such as freedom from unreasonable search and seizure.[6] The French and American documents established a burgeoning tradition of liberal constitutionalism which endured and spread throughout the world in the 19th and 20th centuries, and which was to be highly influential on the 20th century's evolving regime of international human rights.

Positive law antecedents

11.9   As the modern State system consolidated and the first great period of globalisation arrived in the 19th century, international law began a steady expansion of its material scope.[7]

The principle of sovereignty, which underpins the State system of international law and relations, generally prohibits any external interference in the way a State treats persons within its territory.[8] Nevertheless, the 19th century witnessed resort to humanitarian intervention[9] by States in the territories of other States with regard to the protection of the lives and safety of persecuted minorities, the suppression of the slave trade on the high seas by Britain's Royal Navy[10] following condemnation of the slave trade by the Congress of Vienna,[11] the continuing emergence and consolidation of a customary law of diplomatic protection of aliens,[12] the conclusion of several important conventions regulating the law of armed conflict,[13] and the treatment of Christian minorities inside the Ottoman Empire. The Versailles Peace Conference at the conclusion of the First World War established an international legal regime for the protection of

---

3.   Article 1.
4.   Article 2.
5.   Article 3.
6.   Fourth Amendment.
7.   See **1.13**.
8.   See **7.1–7.4**.
9.   See **9.68–9.77**.
10.   See **12.96**.
11.   See **1.11** and **10.4**.
12.   See **5.76–5.125**.
13.   See **1.12**.

minority rights after the extensive redrawing of international boundaries left substantial pockets of ethnic, religious and linguistic peoples located in States in which they were a minority. These various currents also contributed to the shaping of the 20th century's system of international human rights.

United Nations human rights system

11.10 The principal issues facing international society at the end of the Second World War were the preservation of international peace and the protection of human rights. These priorities were dictated by the experience of the war itself. The Axis powers' global acts of predatory aggression against other States' territorial sovereignty and political independence triggered a world war costing more than 50 million lives and violations of the standards of human decency on a hitherto unimagined scale.

11.11 These preoccupations found reflection in the Charter of the United Nations, the international organisation established in 1945 to replace the defunct League of Nations. The UN system for preserving international peace and security is discussed in detail elsewhere.[14] The UN Charter lists among its basic purposes and principles 'promoting and encouraging respect for human rights and for fundamental freedom for all without distinction as to race, sex, language, or religion'.[15] The system of human rights protection established by, or under the auspices of, the United Nations provides the international legal framework for the protection of human rights.

The principal rights, and the institutional mechanisms for their protection, are discussed below. Particular attention is paid to developments occurring in the 20 years following the Second World War, during which time the main foundations of international human rights were laid. This important period witnessed the conclusion of conventions against genocide and racial discrimination, and the emergence of a fundamental right to self-determination of peoples. It also embraced the 'International Bill of Rights', consisting of the Universal Declaration of Human Rights (UDHR) and two landmark conventions on civil, political, economic, social and cultural rights.

Regional human rights systems

11.12 It should also be noted that the United Nations system of human rights protection is complemented by three regional systems, all of which are autonomous from the UN system and from each other.

---

14.   See **9.7–9.62**.
15.   UN Charter, Art 1(3).

The European system is based on the Council of Europe (not to be confused with the European Union), under whose auspices was concluded the 1950 Convention for the Protection of Human Rights and Fundamental Freedoms (usually referred to as the European Convention on Human Rights, or ECHR).[16] The ECHR is, in juridical and jurisprudential terms, the most highly developed of all the international human rights instruments. The European Court of Human Rights has furnished thousands of judgments on complaints of violations by States parties of the ECHR. The European Court of Justice has also developed its own case law for the protection of human rights within the context of the law of the European Union.

The Organization of American States (OAS) — which has 35 member States in North, Central and South America and the Caribbean — is host to the 'Inter-American' system of human rights protection. The 1969 American Convention on Human Rights[17] establishes the Inter-American Court of Human Rights, whose jurisprudence has been particularly important in the clarification and elaboration of human rights in developing States often struggling to establish basic freedoms and democratic norms.

There is also a much less developed African system of human rights protection established as part of the African Union. The African Charter on Human and Peoples' Rights[18] is distinctive from the European and American Conventions in that it incorporates in its text not only civil and political rights, but also 'rights to development' and other collective rights. Widely hailed as a bold development in recognising the 'indivisibility' of all human rights, in practice this feature of the African Charter has proved a major factor in its relative lack of success. The African Charter is the least effective and influential of all the major international human rights instruments. Further consideration of the regional systems of human rights protection is outside the scope of this chapter.

Self-determination of peoples

11.13 The self-determination of peoples is among the central political principles in the United Nations system. Not only is it expressly enshrined as one of the basic purposes and principles of the UN itself,[19] it is also one of the specified objectives of the UN system of international economic and social cooperation which all member States are pledged to support.[20] Nevertheless, self-determination was not initially conceptualised as a human right, as evidenced by its inclusion as an institutional purpose and principle distinct from human rights in the drafting of Art 1 of the UN

---

16. UNTS, Vol 213, p 221; Council of Europe Treaty Series, No 5.
17. UNTS, Vol 1144, p 144.
18. UNTS, Vol 1520, p 245.
19. UN Charter, Art 1(2).
20. Ibid, Arts 55 and 56.

Charter. Furthermore, self-determination was entirely omitted from the litany of rights included within the General Assembly's 1948 Universal Declaration of Human Rights (UDHR).[21]

Nevertheless, as decolonisation progressed and new States joined the United Nations, a re-conceptualisation of self-determination as a human right occurred. This process had gone so far by 1966 that Arts 1(1) of both the International Covenant on Civil and Political Rights (ICCPR)[22] and the International Covenant on Economic, Social and Cultural Rights (ICESCR)[23] provide identically as follows:

> All peoples have the right of self-determination. By virtue of that right they freely determine their political status and freely pursue their economic, social and cultural development.

A more detailed consideration of the principle of the self-determination of peoples is undertaken elsewhere.[24]

Genocide

11.14   Perhaps the most singular feature of the Second World War was the campaign of racial obliteration carried out by the National Socialist regime in Germany against Europe's Jewish population, and the mass annihilation of other victims in concentration camps where an estimated 12 million people perished. This aspect of the war, which was laid publicly bare in the proceedings of the International Military Tribunal at Nuremberg, quickly prompted the conclusion of the 1948 Convention on the Prevention and Punishment of the Crime of Genocide (the Genocide Convention).[25] Strictly speaking, genocide (or even 'freedom from genocide') is not a human right at all. It is, rather, an international crime. A more detailed consideration of the crime of genocide is undertaken elsewhere.[26]

Racial discrimination

11.15   The principal element in the ideology of National Socialism which informed almost every aspect of policy in Hitler's regime was a view about the hierarchy of humans based on their race. The racial group of which the German people supposedly formed the main component — the 'Aryans' — was placed at the pinnacle of this hierarchy. On this view, Germany was destined, for its own benefit and also for the benefit of all the 'lesser' races, to dominate the world. This would require an extended

---

21.   General Assembly Resolution 217A (III) (1948).
22.   UNTS, Vol 999, p 171.
23.   UNTS, Vol 993, p 3.
24.   See **4.37–4.56**.
25.   UNTS, Vol 78, p 277.
26.   See **10.38–10.46**.

campaign of conquests in order to unite all Aryans under a single political leadership and in order to secure the land and other resources necessary for a world-leadership role.

It would also require a political and social struggle to purge the Aryan heartlands of all non-Aryan peoples who were not needed to provide labour. According to National Socialist ideology, the Jewish people were a uniquely deadly threat to the achievement of the Aryans' destiny, and exceptionally harsh measures were required against them. In time, these harsh measures escalated to an attempted mass extermination of the Jewish people. After the military defeat of Germany and its allies in 1945, matters relating to racial discrimination assumed a heightened importance in international affairs. Within months of the war's end, the promotion and encouragement of human rights on a racially non-discriminatory basis was identified as a purpose and principle of the United Nations.[27]

11.16 As mentioned above, the campaign of racial extermination conducted by the German State mainly against Europe's Jewish population during the Second World War provided the catalyst for the Genocide Convention. The day after the adoption of the text of the Genocide Convention, the United Nations General Assembly adopted the Universal Declaration of Human Rights, in which a 'common standard of achievement for all peoples and all nations'[28] was prescribed in respect of a range of rights and freedoms. According to the UDHR, each of these rights should apply 'without distinction of any kind, such as race, colour, ... language, ... national or social origin, ... [or] birth'.[29] Thus, in both the UN Charter and the UDHR, racial non-discrimination was identified as a human rights meta-principle which imbued all other human rights.

11.17 In 1963, the General Assembly adopted a Declaration on the Elimination of All Forms of Racial Discrimination.[30] This declaration served as a precursor to the 1966 International Convention on the Elimination of All Forms of Racial Discrimination (ICERD).[31] The ICERD has more than 170 parties, including Australia and all the permanent members of the UN Security Council. Racial discrimination is defined in the ICERD as follows:

Article 1

1. In this Convention, the term 'racial discrimination' shall mean any distinction, exclusion, restriction or preference based on race, colour, descent, or national or ethnic origin which has the purpose or effect of nullifying or impairing the recognition, enjoyment or exercise, on an equal footing, of human rights and fundamental freedoms in the political, economic, social, cultural or any other field of public life.

---

27. UN Charter, Art 1(3).
28. UDHR, Preamble.
29. Ibid, Art 2.
30. General Assembly Resolution 1904 (XVIII) (1963).
31. UNTS, Vol 660, p 195.

11.18   Having defined racial discrimination, the ICERD proceeds to impose certain requirements on States. The cornerstone obligation is to 'prohibit and eliminate' racial discrimination:

Article 5

… States Parties undertake to prohibit and to eliminate racial discrimination in all its forms and to guarantee the right of everyone, without distinction as to race, colour, or national or ethnic origin, to equality before the law, notably in the enjoyment of the following rights:

(a) The right to equal treatment before the tribunals and all other organs administering justice;

(b) The right to security of person and protection by the State against violence or bodily harm, whether inflicted by government officials or by any individual group or institution;

(c) Political rights, in particular the right to participate in elections — to vote and to stand for election — on the basis of universal and equal suffrage, to take part in the Government as well as in the conduct of public affairs at any level and to have equal access to public service;

(d) Other civil rights, in particular:

   (i)   The right to freedom of movement and residence within the border of the State;

   (ii)   The right to leave any country, including one's own, and to return to one's country;

   (iii) The right to nationality;

   (iv)   The right to marriage and choice of spouse;

   (v)   The right to own property alone as well as in association with others;

   (vi)   The right to inherit;

   (vii) The right to freedom of thought, conscience and religion;

   (viii) The right to freedom of opinion and expression;

   (ix)   The right to freedom of peaceful assembly and association;

(e) Economic, social and cultural rights, in particular:

   (i)   The rights to work, to free choice of employment, to just and favourable conditions of work, to protection against unemployment, to equal pay for equal work, to just and favourable remuneration;

   (ii)   The right to form and join trade unions;

   (iii) The right to housing;

   (iv)   The right to public health, medical care, social security and social services;

   (v)   The right to education and training;

   (vi)   The right to equal participation in cultural activities;

(f) The right of access to any place or service intended for use by the general public, such as transport, hotels, restaurants, cafes, theatres and parks.

11.19   This obligation 'to prohibit and to eliminate' is buttressed by a further obligation to provide:[32]

> ... effective protection and remedies, through the competent national tribunals and other State institutions, against any acts of racial discrimination which violate ... human rights and fundamental freedoms contrary to this Convention, as well as the right to seek from such tribunals just and adequate reparation or satisfaction for any damage suffered as a result of such discrimination.

11.20   Some forms of discrimination are not caught by the obligation to prohibit and eliminate. States remain free to maintain 'distinctions, exclusions, restrictions or preferences ... between citizens and non-citizens'.[33]

A State does not violate the ICERD merely because, for instance, it restricts the right to vote to its own citizens or makes it more difficult for non-citizens to enter the country or obtain employment. States are similarly free to maintain distinctions in legal provisions 'concerning nationality, citizenship or naturalisation, provided that such provisions do not discriminate against any particular nationality'.[34]

11.21   States are also free to adopt measures sometimes referred to as 'affirmative action' or 'positive discrimination', provided they are 'measures taken for the sole purpose of securing adequate advancement of certain racial or ethnic groups or individuals requiring such protection', and that they are 'necessary in order to ensure such groups or individuals equal enjoyment or exercise of human rights and fundamental freedoms'. Such exceptional measures must not, however, 'lead to the maintenance of separate rights for different racial groups and ... they shall not be continued after the objectives for which they were taken have been achieved'.[35]

11.22   The ICERD establishes a Committee on the Elimination of Racial Discrimination consisting of 18 experts elected by the States parties.[36] The Committee receives regular reports from the States parties 'on the legislative, judicial, administrative or other measures which they have adopted and which give effect' to their ICERD obligations,[37] and oversees a conciliation procedure for complaints concerning non-observance among the States parties.[38]

11.23   Individuals who claim to be victims of a State's violation of ICERD obligations, and who have exhausted their local remedies in that State, may petition the Committee where the State has made a declaration accepting such a right of petition.

---

32.   ICERD, Art 6.
33.   Ibid, Art 1(2).
34.   Ibid, Art 1(3).
35.   Ibid, Art 1(4).
36.   Ibid, Art 8.
37.   Ibid, Art 9(1).
38.   Ibid, Arts 10–13.

The Committee investigates the petitioner's claims after consulting the State party and then makes non-binding 'suggestions and recommendations' to the State party.[39]

Civil and political rights

11.24   The International Covenant on Civil and Political Rights was drafted by the Economic and Social Council of the United Nations,[40] and its text was adopted by the General Assembly in 1966. Together with the UDHR and the ICESCR, it forms part of the International Bill of Rights. The ICCPR's principal purpose is to transpose into treaty form the first 21 Articles of the UDHR dealing with the classical, or 'first generation', fundamental freedoms, which are typically associated with a liberal and democratic political order. It was the inclusion of these rights which caused the Soviet Union and its communist-ruled satellites to abstain from voting on the UDHR in the General Assembly. The ICCPR has more than 165 parties, including Australia. All permanent members of the Security Council except China are parties.[41] The ICCPR is the most juridically significant of all the human rights instruments in the United Nations system. This is because of the classically justiciable and foundational nature of most of the rights conferred or recognised, and because there exists a relatively mature institutional mechanism for indicating a State's compliance with its obligations under the Covenant. This institutional mechanism revolves around the Human Rights Committee.

Human Rights Committee

11.25   The Human Rights Committee is based in Geneva and is established by Art 28 of the ICCPR. It consists of 18 members who serve in their personal capacity — that is, they are not intended to act as representatives or delegates of any other person or State. Members of the Committee must be nationals of a State party to the ICCPR, but no more than one national of a State party may be elected to the Committee at any one time. They are elected by secret ballot of the States parties for four-year terms.

11.26   All States parties are required to submit reports to the Human Rights Committee on the measures they have adopted which give effect to the rights recognised in the ICCPR and on the progress made in the enjoyment of those rights.[42] The Committee has adopted the practice of making concluding observations on each report, and these provide a useful guide to the Committee's views on the requirements of the ICCPR.

---

39.   Ibid, Art 14.
40.   See 1.48.
41.   China signed the ICCPR on 6 October 1998, but has not ratified.
42.   ICCPR, Art 40.

11.27   The Human Rights Committee has also adopted the practice, under Art 40(4) of the ICCPR, of issuing 'General Comments' on the interpretation and application of particular provisions or aspects of the Covenant. These instruments are neither legally binding nor dispositive, but are frequently treated by States and publicists as authoritative interpretations of the Covenant's requirements. The Committee has issued 33 General Comments.

11.28   A State party may declare that it recognises the competence of the Human Rights Committee to receive and consider communications from other States parties claiming that it is not fulfilling its obligations under the ICCPR.[43]

Only about 50 States parties, including Australia, have made such a declaration. Russia, the United Kingdom and the United States are the only permanent members of the UN Security Council to have done so. This procedure has never been used by any State party. This is probably because inter-State complaints are considered diplomatically aggressive. Further, States rarely have much interest in ICCPR violations inside other States unless their own nationals are involved, in which case they are more likely to respond through the traditional customary law mechanisms of diplomatic protection.

11.29   Perhaps the single most significant source of jurisprudence on the ICCPR is the individual written 'communication' which can be made by persons who regard themselves as victims of violations of their Covenant rights. This procedure exists in respect of any State party when it has made a declaration under Art 1 of the First Optional Protocol to the ICCPR.[44] More than 110 States parties, including Australia, have made such a declaration. France and Russia are the only permanent members of the UN Security Council to have made a declaration under the First Optional Protocol.

Once the Committee has accepted an individual communication as admissible, the State party concerned submits written explanations or statements concerning the alleged breaches in the communication. The Committee meets in private session and operates on the basis of written statements. It is not a court and it does not take oral evidence. It concludes its task by formulating its 'views' on the communication and forwarding them to the author of the communication and the State party concerned. The Committee's views are not binding on any State or person, although they are published and States have a generally good record of compliance with them.

Right to life

11.30   After self-determination,[45] the first substantive right enshrined in the ICCPR is the right to life. The UDHR states simply that '[e]veryone

---

43.   Ibid, Art 41.
44.   Optional Protocol to the International Covenant on Civil and Political Rights, UNTS, Vol 999, p 171.
45.   See 11.13.

has the right to life, liberty and security of the person'.[46] The corresponding provision in the ICCPR reads as follows:

Article 6

1. Every human being has the inherent right to life. This right shall be protected by law. No one shall be arbitrarily deprived of his life.

11.31 It is clear that this provision requires a State's security and police forces to refrain from killing suspected criminals without first meeting violent resistance from the suspected criminals.[47] There may, however, be circumstances where the State's obligation is more onerous, and in which failure to protect a person from murder by private persons can engage the State in a violation of the right to life.

In **Akkoç v Turkey,**[48] a Kurdish school teacher in south-east Turkey was murdered by gunmen on his way to work. He had been active in a trade union thought to be associated with the PKK (Kurdistan Workers' Party), a pro-independence Kurdish paramilitary organisation which carried out armed attacks on Turkish security forces, Turkish officials, and civilian targets. Although there was a suspicion that the deceased was murdered by Turkish security forces, the European Court of Human Rights found insufficient evidence to support such a finding. Instead, the killing was imputed to unknown private assailants. The Court was required to consider whether Turkey's failure to protect the deceased from an act of murder by private persons placed Turkey in violation of its obligation under Art 2(1) of the European Convention on Human Rights, which provides:

Everyone's right to life shall be protected by law. No one shall be deprived of his life intentionally save in the execution of a sentence of a court following his conviction of a crime for which this penalty is provided by law.

The Court said:

77. The Court recalls that the first sentence of Article 2(1) enjoins the State not only to refrain from the intentional and unlawful taking of life, but also to take appropriate steps to safeguard the lives of those within its jurisdiction… . This involves a primary duty on the State to secure the right to life by putting in place effective criminal-law provisions to deter the commission of offences against the person backed up by a law-enforcement machinery for the prevention, suppression and punishment of breaches of such provisions. It also extends in appropriate circumstances to a positive obligation on the authorities to take preventive operational measures to protect an individual whose life is at risk from the criminal acts of another individual (see the *Osman v the United Kingdom* judgment of 28 October 1998, *Reports* 1998–VIII, p. 3159, §115).

78. Bearing in mind the difficulties in policing modern societies, the unpredictability of human conduct and the operational choices which must be made in terms of priorities and resources, the scope of the positive obligation must be interpreted in a way which does not impose an impossible or disproportionate burden on the authorities. Not every claimed risk to life therefore can entail for the authorities a Convention requirement to take operational measures to prevent that risk from materialising. For a positive obligation to arise, it must be

---

46. UDHR, Art 3.
47. *Guerrero v Colombia* [1982] UNHRC 5.
48. *Akkoç v Turkey* [2000] ECHR 577.

established that the authorities knew or ought to have known at the time of the existence of a real and immediate risk to the life of an identified individual or individuals from the criminal acts of a third party and that they failed to take measures within the scope of their powers which, judged reasonably, might have been expected to avoid that risk (see the *Osman* judgment cited above, p. 3159–60, §116). …

80. The Court notes that the applicant's husband, who was a teacher of Kurdish origin, had been involved with the applicant in the trade union Eðit-Sen, which was regarded as unlawful by the authorities. He had been detained a number of times by the police. Following a demonstration in October 1992, in which teachers had claimed that police officers had assaulted and abused them and eleven had been taken into custody, the applicant and her husband had received telephone calls in which it was threatened that they would be killed next. These had been reported to the public prosecutor in petitions.

81. … The Court is satisfied that Zübeyir Akkoç, as a Kurdish teacher involved in activities perceived by the authorities as being unlawful and in opposition to their policies in the south-east, was at that time at particular risk of falling victim to an unlawful attack. Moreover, this risk could in the circumstances be regarded as real and immediate.

82. The Court is equally satisfied that the authorities must be regarded as being aware of this risk. …

83. Furthermore, the authorities were aware, or ought to have been aware, of the possibility that this risk derived from the activities of persons or groups acting with the knowledge or acquiescence of elements in the security forces. A 1993 report by a parliamentary investigation commission … stated that it had received information that a Hizbullah training camp was receiving aid and training from the security forces and concluded that some officials might be implicated in the 908 unsolved killings in the south-east region. …

85. The Court has considered whether the authorities did all that could reasonably be expected of them to avoid any threat to Zübeyir Akkoç from materialising.

86. It recalls that, as the Government submitted, there were large numbers of security forces in the south-east region pursuing the aim of establishing public order. They faced the difficult task of countering the violent armed attacks of the PKK and other groups. …

87. The Court observes, however, that the implementation of the criminal law in respect of unlawful acts allegedly carried out with the involvement of the security forces discloses particular characteristics in the south-east region in this period.

The Court found evidence that Turkish security forces in the south-east of the country were engaged in extra-judicial killings of persons suspected of supporting the PKK.

91. The Court finds that these defects undermined the effectiveness of the protection afforded by the criminal law in the south-east region during the period relevant to this case. It considers that this permitted or fostered a lack of accountability of members of the security forces for their actions which … was not compatible with the rule of law in a democratic society respecting the fundamental rights and freedoms guaranteed under the Convention.

92. Consequently, these defects removed the protection which Zübeyir Akkoç should have received by law. …

94. The Court concludes that in the circumstances of this case the authorities failed to take reasonable measures available to them to prevent a real and immediate risk to the life of Zübeyir Akkoç. There has, accordingly, been a violation of Article 2 of the Convention.

11.32   The general protection of life accorded by Art 6(1) of the ICCPR is accompanied by several further provisions dealing specifically with the death penalty.

> **Article 6**
>
> ...
>
> 2. In countries which have not abolished the death penalty, sentence of death may be imposed only for the most serious crimes in accordance with the law in force at the time of the commission of the crime and not contrary to the provisions of the present Covenant and to the Convention on the Prevention and Punishment of the Crime of Genocide. This penalty can only be carried out pursuant to a final judgement rendered by a competent court.
>
> ...
>
> 4. Anyone sentenced to death shall have the right to seek pardon or commutation of the sentence. Amnesty, pardon or commutation of the sentence of death may be granted in all cases.
>
> 5. Sentence of death shall not be imposed for crimes committed by persons below eighteen years of age and shall not be carried out on pregnant women.
>
> 6. Nothing in this article shall be invoked to delay or to prevent the abolition of capital punishment by any State Party to the present Covenant.

It is clear from the drafting of Art 6 that the death penalty is not forbidden by the ICCPR, although its use is circumscribed. However, the Human Rights Committee has on several recent occasions expressed the view that a mandatory death penalty constitutes an arbitrary deprivation of life in violation of Art 6.[49] Furthermore, although the death penalty itself is not contrary to the ICCPR, certain modes of execution may contravene the prohibition of cruel, inhuman and degrading punishment in Art 7.[50]

11.33   The death penalty has received separate treatment in the 1990 Second Optional Protocol,[51] which requires States parties to refrain from carrying out any executions and to abolish the death penalty.[52] Reservations are not permitted, except where providing for the application of the death penalty in time of war pursuant to a conviction for a most serious crime of a military nature committed during wartime.[53] The Second Optional Protocol has more than 70 parties, including Australia.

11.34   It may be that a State which has abolished the death penalty may not deport or extradite a person to another State where the person stands at risk of being executed, unless the deporting State first receives assurances that the person will not be executed.

---

49. *Thompson v Saint Vincent and the Grenadines* [2000] UNHRC 35; *Kennedy v Trinidad and Tobago* [2002] UNHRC 6; *Ramil Rayos v Philippines* [2004] UNHRC 51; *Chan v Guyana* [2006] UNHRC 1; *Larrañaga v Philippines* [2006] UNHRC 52.
50. See 11.35–11.39.
51. Second Optional Protocol to the International Covenant on Civil and Political Rights, aiming at the abolition of the death penalty, UNTS, Vol 1642, p 414.
52. Ibid, Art 1.
53. Ibid, Art 2.

In **Judge v Canada**,[54] the author of a communication to the Human Rights Committee escaped from a United States prison where he was under sentence of death for murder. He fled to Canada, where he committed a string of robberies for which he received 10 years' imprisonment. The Canadian authorities deported him to the United States at the end of his term of Canadian imprisonment without first obtaining an assurance from United States authorities that he would not be executed. The communication's author claimed that Canada's conduct placed it in violation of Art 6 of the ICCPR. The Human Rights Committee had previously expressed an opinion that a State did not violate Art 6 merely by deporting, without assurances of non-execution, a person to another State where he or she might face the death penalty. On this occasion, the Committee said:

> 10.2 In considering Canada's obligations, as a State party which has abolished the death penalty, in removing persons to another country where they are under sentence of death, the Committee recalls its previous jurisprudence in *Kindler v Canada*,[55] that it does not consider that the deportation of a person from a country which has abolished the death penalty to a country where he/she is under sentence of death amounts per se to a violation of article 6 of the Covenant. The Committee's rationale in this decision was based on an interpretation of the Covenant which read article 6, paragraph 1, together with article 6, paragraph 2, which does not prohibit the imposition of the death penalty for the most serious crimes. It considered that as Canada itself had not imposed the death penalty but had extradited the author to the United States to face capital punishment, a state which had not abolished the death penalty, the extradition itself would not amount to a violation by Canada unless there was a real risk that the author's rights under the Covenant would be violated in the United States. On the issue of assurances, the Committee found that the terms of article 6 did not necessarily require Canada to refuse to extradite or to seek assurances but that such a request should at least be considered by the removing state.

> 10.3 While recognizing that the Committee should ensure both consistency and coherence of its jurisprudence, it notes that there may be exceptional situations in which a review of the scope of application of the rights protected in the Covenant is required, such as where an alleged violation involves that most fundamental of rights — the right to life — and in particular if there have been notable factual and legal developments and changes in international opinion in respect of the issue raised. ... The Committee considers that the Covenant should be interpreted as a living instrument and the rights protected under it should be applied in context and in the light of present–day conditions.

> 10.4 In reviewing its application of article 6, the Committee notes that, as required by the Vienna Convention on the Law of Treaties, a treaty should be interpreted in good faith and in accordance with the ordinary meaning to be given to the terms of the treaty in their context and in the light of its object and purpose. Paragraph 1 of article 6, which states that 'Every human being has the inherent right to life…', is a general rule: its purpose is to protect life. States parties that have abolished the death penalty have an obligation under this paragraph to so protect in all circumstances. Paragraphs 2 to 6 of article 6 are evidently included to avoid a reading of the first paragraph of article 6, according to which that paragraph could be understood as abolishing the death penalty as such. This construction of the article is reinforced by the opening words of paragraph 2 ('In countries which have not abolished the death penalty …') and by paragraph 6 ('Nothing in this article shall be invoked to delay or to prevent the abolition of capital punishment by any State Party to the present Covenant.'). In effect,

---

54. *Judge v Canada* [2003] UNHRC 51.
55. *Kindler v Canada* [1993] UNHRC 23.

paragraphs 2 to 6 have the dual function of creating an exception to the right to life in respect of the death penalty and laying down limits on the scope of that exception. Only the death penalty pronounced when certain elements are present can benefit from the exception. Among these limitations are that found in the opening words of paragraph 2, namely, that only States parties that 'have not abolished the death penalty' can avail themselves of the exceptions created in paragraphs 2 to 6. For countries that have abolished the death penalty, there is an obligation not to expose a person to the real risk of its application. Thus, they may not remove, either by deportation or extradition, individuals from their jurisdiction if it may be reasonably anticipated that they will be sentenced to death, without ensuring that the death sentence would not be carried out.

10.5 The Committee acknowledges that by interpreting paragraphs 1 and 2 of article 6 in this way, abolitionist and retentionist States parties are treated differently. But it considers that this is an inevitable consequence of the wording of the provision itself, which, as becomes clear from the *Travaux Préparatoires*, sought to appease very divergent views on the issue of the death penalty, in an effort to compromise among the drafters of the provision.

The Committee notes that it was expressed in the *Travaux* that, on the one hand, one of the main principles of the Covenant should be abolition, but on the other, it was pointed out that capital punishment existed in certain countries and that abolition would create difficulties for such countries. The death penalty was seen by many delegates and bodies participating in the drafting process as an 'anomaly' or a 'necessary evil'. It would appear logical, therefore, to interpret the rule in article 6, paragraph 1, in a wide sense, whereas paragraph 2, which addresses the death penalty, should be interpreted narrowly.

10.6 For these reasons, the Committee considers that Canada, as a State party which has abolished the death penalty, irrespective of whether it has not yet ratified the Second Optional Protocol to the Covenant Aiming at the Abolition of the Death Penalty, violated the author's right to life under article 6, paragraph 1, by deporting him to the United States, where he is under sentence of death, without ensuring that the death penalty would not be carried out. The Committee recognizes that Canada did not itself impose the death penalty on the author. But by deporting him to a country where he was under sentence of death, Canada established the crucial link in the causal chain that would make possible the execution of the author.

Torture and cruel, inhuman or degrading treatment

11.35   The UDHR provides: 'No one shall be subjected to torture or to cruel, inhuman or degrading treatment or punishment.'[56] Article 7 of the ICCPR adopts exactly the same clause with the additional sentence: 'In particular, no one shall be subjected without his free consent to medical or scientific experimentation.'

11.36   Neither the UDHR nor the ICCPR defines 'torture', and the Human Rights Committee has not adopted a comprehensive definition of the term. Nevertheless, the word suggests mistreatment of a kind that exceeds the merely unpleasant, uncomfortable or embarrassing. An authoritative working definition of 'torture' has been provided by

---

56.   UDHR, Art 5.

the 1984 Convention against Torture and Other Cruel, Inhuman or Degrading Treatment or Punishment:[57]

Article 1

1. For the purposes of this Convention, the term 'torture' means any act by which severe pain or suffering, whether physical or mental, is intentionally inflicted on a person for such purposes as obtaining from him or a third person information or a confession, punishing him for an act he or a third person has committed or is suspected of having committed, or intimidating or coercing him or a third person, or for any reason based on discrimination of any kind, when such pain or suffering is inflicted by or at the instigation of or with the consent or acquiescence of a public official or other person acting in an official capacity. It does not include pain or suffering arising only from, inherent in or incidental to lawful sanctions.

11.37   The Human Rights Committee made the following observations concerning the prohibition of torture and cruel, inhuman or degrading treatment or punishment in its General Comment No 20 (1992):

3. ... [N]o justification or extenuating circumstances may be invoked to excuse a violation of article 7 for any reasons, including those based on an order from a superior officer or public authority.

4. The Covenant does not contain any definition of the concepts covered by article 7, nor does the Committee consider it necessary to draw up a list of prohibited acts or to establish sharp distinctions between the different kinds of punishment or treatment; the distinctions depend on the nature, purpose and severity of the treatment applied.

5. The prohibition in article 7 relates not only to acts that cause physical pain but also to acts that cause mental suffering to the victim. In the Committee's view, moreover, the prohibition must extend to corporal punishment. ...

6. The Committee notes that prolonged solitary confinement of the detained or imprisoned person may amount to acts prohibited by article 7. ... [W]hen the death penalty is applied by a State party for the most serious crimes, it must not only be strictly limited in accordance with article 6 but it must be carried out in such a way as to cause the least possible physical and mental suffering. ...

9. ... States parties must not expose individuals to the danger of torture or cruel, inhuman or degrading treatment or punishment upon return to another country by way of their extradition, expulsion or refoulement. ...

11. ... To guarantee the effective protection of detained persons, provisions should be made for detainees to be held in places officially recognised as places of detention and for their names and places of detention, as well as for the names of persons responsible for their detention, to be kept in registers readily available and accessible to those concerned, including relatives and friends. ... Provisions should also be made against incommunicado detention. ... The protection of the detainee also requires that prompt and regular access be given

---

57.   UNTS, Vol 1465, p 85.

to doctors and lawyers and, under appropriate supervision when the investigation so requires, to family members.

12. It is important for the discouragement of violations under article 7 that the law must prohibit the use of admissibility in judicial proceedings of statements or confessions obtained through torture or other prohibited treatment.

13. ... Those who violate article 7, whether by encouraging, ordering, tolerating or perpetrating prohibited acts, must be held responsible. Consequently, those who have refused to obey orders must not be punished or subjected to any adverse treatment. ...

15. ... some States have granted amnesty in respect of acts of torture. Amnesties are generally incompatible with the duty of States to investigate such acts; to guarantee freedom from such acts within their jurisdiction; and to ensure that they do not occur in the future. States may not deprive individuals of the right to an effective remedy, including compensation and such full rehabilitation as may be possible.

11.38   Although capital punishment is not per se a violation of Art 7 of the ICCPR, certain modes of execution are. In *Ng v Canada*,[58] Mr Ng had been extradited from Canada to the United States on multiple charges of murder. If convicted, he stood to be executed by cyanide gas asphyxiation.

The Human Rights Committee noted that this mode of execution 'may cause prolonged suffering and agony and does not result in death as swiftly as possible, as asphyxiation by cyanide gas may take over 10 minutes', and consequently that it failed to meet the test of 'least possible physical and mental suffering' in para 6 of General Comment No 20.[59] The Committee expressed the view that Canada was in breach of Art 7 of the ICCPR by extraditing Ng to a jurisdiction where he might be executed by cyanide gas asphyxiation without first receiving an assurance that this method of execution would not be used.

11.39   The European Court of Human Rights has held that a State party to the European Convention on Human Rights would be in violation of that Convention's provisions concerning torture and inhuman or degrading treatment (Art 3) were it to extradite a person to face the prospect of an extended period of time on 'death row' prior to execution.[60] The Court's reasoning was that, although capital punishment itself was not a violation of Art 3 and extended time spent on death row was the result of appeals processes, the 'death row phenomenon' did not conform to the Convention's requirements. This was because the prisoner was exposed to 'the anguish and mounting tension of living in the ever-present shadow of death'.[61] The Human Rights Committee has taken a different view in the application of Art 7 of the ICCPR.

---

58.   *Ng v Canada* [1994] UNHRC 1.
59.   Ibid, paras 16.3–16.4.
60.   *Soering v United Kingdom* [1989] ECHR 14.
61.   Ibid, para 106.

In **Johnson v Jamaica,**[62] the author of a communication complained that his detention on 'death row' for over 10 years would make any future execution of his death sentence a violation of Arts 7 and 10 (humane treatment of prisoners) of the ICCPR. The Committee said:

8.2 The question that must be addressed is whether the mere length of the period a condemned person spends confined to death row may constitute a violation by a State party of its obligations under articles 7 and 10 not to subject persons to cruel, inhuman and degrading treatment or punishment and to treat them with humanity. In addressing this question, the following factors must be considered:

(a) The Covenant does not prohibit the death penalty, though it subjects its use to severe restrictions. As detention on death row is a necessary consequence of imposing the death penalty, no matter how cruel, degrading and inhuman it may appear to be, it cannot, *of itself,* be regarded as a violation of articles 7 and 10 of the Covenant.

(b) While the Covenant does not prohibit the death penalty, the Committee has taken the view, which has been reflected in the Second Optional Protocol to the Covenant, that article 6 'refers generally to abolition in terms which strongly suggest that abolition is desirable'. (See General Comment 6 of 27 July 1982; also see Preamble to the Second Optional Protocol to the Covenant Aiming at the Abolition of the Death Penalty.) Reducing recourse to the death penalty may therefore be seen as one of the objects and purposes of the Covenant.

(c) The provisions of the Covenant must be interpreted in the light of the Covenant's objects and purposes (article 31 of the Vienna Convention on the Law of Treaties). As one of these objects and purposes is to promote reduction in the use of the death penalty, an interpretation of a provision in the Covenant that may encourage a State party that retains the death penalty to make use of that penalty should, where possible, be avoided.

8.3 In light of these factors, we must examine the implications of holding the length of detention on death row, *per se,* to be in violation of articles 7 and 10. The first, and most serious, implication is that if a State party executes a condemned prisoner after he has spent a certain period of time on death row, it will not be in violation of its obligations under the Covenant, whereas if it refrains from doing so, it will violate the Covenant. An interpretation of the Covenant leading to this result cannot be consistent with the Covenant's object and purpose. The above implication cannot be avoided by refraining from determining a definite period of detention on death row, after which there will be a presumption that detention on death row constitutes cruel and inhuman punishment. Setting a cut-off date certainly exacerbates the problem and gives the State party a clear deadline for executing a person if it is to avoid violating its obligations under the Covenant. However, this implication is not a function of fixing the maximum permissible period of detention on death row, but of making the time factor, *per se,* the determining one. If the maximum acceptable period is left open, States parties which seek to avoid overstepping the deadline will be tempted to look to the decisions of the Committee in previous cases so as to determine what length of detention on death row the Committee has found permissible in the past.

8.4 The second implication of making the time factor *per se* the determining one, i.e. the factor that turns detention on death row into a violation of the Covenant, is that it conveys a message to States parties retaining the death penalty that they should carry out a capital sentence as expeditiously as possible after it was imposed. This is not a message the Committee would wish

---

62.   *Johnson v Jamaica* [1996] UNHRC 20.

to convey to States parties. Life on death row, harsh as it may be, is preferable to death. Furthermore, experience shows that delays in carrying out the death penalty can be the necessary consequence of several factors, many of which may be attributable to the State party. Sometimes a moratorium is placed on executions while the whole question of the death penalty is under review. At other times the executive branch of government delays executions even though it is not feasible politically to abolish the death penalty. The Committee would wish to avoid adopting a line of jurisprudence which weakens the influence of factors that may very well lessen the number of prisoners actually executed.

It should be stressed that by adopting the approach that prolonged detention on death row cannot, *per se,* be regarded as cruel and inhuman treatment or punishment under the Covenant, the Committee does not wish to convey the impression that keeping condemned prisoners on death row for many years is an acceptable way of treating them. It is not. However, the cruelty of the death row phenomenon is first and foremost a function of the permissibility of capital punishment under the Covenant. This situation has unfortunate consequences.

8.5 Finally, to hold that prolonged detention on death row does not, *per se,* constitute a violation of articles 7 and 10, does not imply that other circumstances connected with detention on death row may not turn that detention into cruel, inhuman and degrading treatment or punishment. The jurisprudence of the Committee has been that where compelling circumstances of the detention are substantiated, that detention may constitute a violation of the Covenant. This jurisprudence should be maintained in future cases.

8.6 In the present case, neither the author nor his counsel have pointed to any compelling circumstances, over and above the length of the detention on death row, that would turn Mr. Johnson's detention into a violation of articles 7 and 10. The Committee therefore concludes that there has been no violation of these provisions.

The Human Rights Committee has had occasion to consider 'compelling circumstances' which might make a prolonged detention on 'death row' a violation of Art 7. In *Francis v Jamaica,*[63] the Committee took the view that several compelling circumstances rendered the prisoner's 13-year detention on death row, prior to commutation of sentence, a violation of Art 7. These included regular beatings at the hands of prison guards, 'ridicule and strain' to which he was subjected in a 'death cell' during five days while awaiting imminent execution, a 13-year failure by an appeal court to issue a written judgment, and a concomitant decline in the prisoner's mental health.

Slavery, servitude and forced labour

11.40   Germany and Japan (and, on the Allied side, the Soviet Union) made extensive use of slave labour and forced labour during the Second World War. Slavery, servitude and the slave trade are condemned by the UDHR.[64]

---

63.   *Francis v Jamaica* [1995] UNHRC 19.
64.   UDHR, Art 4.

11.41   The ICCPR also prohibits slavery and the slave trade[65] and servitude.[66] It also prohibits forced or compulsory labour, subject to a range of exceptions relating to penal servitude, judicial detention, military service, compulsory service in cases of emergency or calamity, or service as part of normal civil obligations.[67]

11.42   Slavery and the slave trade are defined by the 1926 Slavery Convention[68] in the following terms:

Article 1

For the purposes of the present Convention, the following definitions are agreed upon:

(1) Slavery is the status or condition of a person over whom any or all of the powers attaching to the right of ownership are exercised.

(2) The slave trade includes all acts involved in the capture, acquisition or disposal of a person with intent to reduce him to slavery; all acts involved in the acquisition of a slave with a view to selling or exchanging him; all acts of disposal by sale or exchange of a slave acquired with a view to being sold or exchanged, and, in general, every act of trade or transport in slaves.

11.43   Servitude is a broader category than slavery and embraces severe economic exploitation or dominance exercised over one person by another, as well as practices similar to slavery.[69]

11.44   'Compulsory labour' is defined in the 1930 International Labour Organisation Convention Concerning Forced or Compulsory Labour (ILO Convention No 29)[70] to mean 'all work or service which is extracted from any person under the menace of any penalty and for which the said person has not offered himself voluntarily'.[71]

11.45   In recent times, the Human Rights Committee has identified the trafficking in women and children across borders and forced prostitution as practices prohibited by Art 8 of the ICCPR.[72]

Arbitrary arrest and detention

11.46   One of the principal features of any free society is the limited circumstances in which a State's police and security services may arrest and detain citizens and other persons lawfully within the jurisdiction. The UDHR proclaims a right to 'liberty and security of the person'.[73]

---

65.   ICCPR, Art 8(1).
66.   Ibid, Art 8(2).
67.   Ibid, Art 8(3).
68.   LNTS, Vol 60, p 253.
69.   1956 Supplementary Convention on the Abolition of Slavery, the Slave Trade, and Institutions and Practices Similar to Slavery, UNTS, Vol 226, p 3.
70.   UNTS, Vol 39, p 55.
71.   Ibid, Art 2(1).
72.   For example, General Comment No 28 (2000), para 12. See also the 1949 Convention for the Suppression of the Traffic in Persons and of the Exploitation of the Prostitution of Others, UNTS, Vol 96, p 271.
73.   UDHR, Art 3.

Article 9(1) of the ICCPR adopts this phrase and goes further by adding that '[n]o one shall be subjected to arbitrary arrest or detention' or 'deprived of his liberty except on such grounds and in accordance with such procedures as are established by law'.

11.47   Article 9(1) is not confined in its material scope to arrest and detention in criminal cases. Rather, it is 'applicable to all deprivations of liberty, whether in criminal cases or in other cases — such as, for example, mental illness, vagrancy, drug addiction, educational purposes, immigration control, etc'.[74]

In **A v Australia,**[75] the author of a communication to the Human Rights Committee was a Cambodian national who landed in Australia illegally by boat. His application for refugee status was rejected, and he used legal proceedings to avoid deportation pending determination of his appeals. He was, after four years, permitted to remain in Australia on humanitarian grounds. In the meantime, he had been held in immigration detention. The author claimed, inter alia, that his prolonged detention was arbitrary and that Australia was therefore in violation of Art 9(1) of the ICCPR. The Committee said:

9.2. … the Committee recalls that the notion of 'arbitrariness' must not be equated with 'against the law' but be interpreted more broadly to include such elements as inappropriateness and injustice. Furthermore, remand in custody could be considered arbitrary if it is not necessary in all the circumstances of the case, for example to prevent flight or interference with evidence: the element of proportionality becomes relevant in this context. The State party however, seeks to justify the author's detention by the fact that he entered Australia unlawfully and by the perceived incentive for the applicant to abscond if left in liberty. The question for the Committee is whether these grounds are sufficient to justify indefinite and prolonged detention.

9.3. The Committee agrees that there is no basis for the author's claim that it is *per se* arbitrary to detain individuals requesting asylum.

Nor can it find any support for the contention that there is a rule of customary international law which would render all such detention arbitrary.

9.4. The Committee observes however, that every decision to keep a person in detention should be open to review periodically so that the grounds justifying the detention can be assessed. In any event, detention should not continue beyond the period for which the State can provide appropriate justification. For example, the fact of illegal entry may indicate a need for investigation and there may be other factors particular to the individual, such as the likelihood of absconding and lack of cooperation, which may justify detention for a period. Without such factors detention may be considered arbitrary, even if entry was illegal. In the instant case, the State party has not advanced any grounds particular to the author's case, which would justify his continued detention for a period of four years, during which he was shifted around between different detention centres. The Committee therefore concludes that the author's detention for a period of over four years was arbitrary within the meaning of Article 9, paragraph 1.

---

74.   General Comment No 8 (1992), para 1.
75.   *A v Australia* [1997] UNHRC 7.

11.48 There are some further specific guarantees for those arrested or detained on criminal charges. Anyone arrested must immediately be given reasons and must promptly be informed of any charges.[76] Those who have been arrested or detained on criminal charges must be brought promptly before a judicial officer and shall be released unless brought to trial within a reasonable time.[77] Persons deprived of their liberty must be able to take proceedings to test the legality of their detention.[78] There must be an enforceable right to compensation for any person unlawfully arrested or detained.[79]

Humane treatment for detainees

11.49 According to Art 10(1) of the ICCPR, persons held in detention must be treated with humanity and with respect for their dignity. In its General Comment No 21 of 1992, the Human Rights Committee observed:

2. Article 10, paragraph 1, of the International Covenant on Civil and Political Rights applies to any one deprived of liberty under the laws and authority of the State who is held in prisons, hospitals — particularly psychiatric hospitals — detention camps or correctional institutions or elsewhere. States parties should ensure that the principle stipulated therein is observed in all institutions and establishments within their jurisdiction where persons are being held.

3. Article 10, paragraph 1, imposes on States parties a positive obligation towards persons who are particularly vulnerable because of their status as persons deprived of liberty, and complements for them the ban on torture or other cruel, inhuman or degrading treatment or punishment contained in article 7 of the Covenant. Thus, not only may persons deprived of their liberty not be subjected to treatment that is contrary to article 7, including medical or scientific experimentation, but neither may they be subjected to any hardship or constraint other than that resulting from the deprivation of liberty; respect for the dignity of such persons must be guaranteed under the same conditions as for that of free persons.

Persons deprived of their liberty enjoy all the rights set forth in the Covenant, subject to the restrictions that are unavoidable in a closed environment.

4. Treating all persons deprived of their liberty with humanity and with respect for their dignity is a fundamental and universally applicable rule. Consequently, the application of this rule, as a minimum, cannot be dependent on the material resources available in the State party. This rule must be applied without distinction of any kind, such as race, colour, sex, language, religion, political or other opinion, national or social origin, property, birth or other status.

---

76. ICCPR, Art 9(2).
77. Ibid, Art 9(3).
78. Ibid, Art 9(4).
79. Ibid, Art 9(5).

11.50   In addition to the general requirement for humane treatment, the ICCPR stipulates more specifically that accused persons and convicted criminals should be segregated and that the former 'shall be subject to separate treatment appropriate to their status as unconvicted persons'.[80] Accused juveniles are also to be segregated from adults.[81] The essential aim of the penitentiary system must be the 'reformation and social rehabilitation' of prisoners.[82]

Imprisonment for contractual obligations

11.51   No-one may be imprisoned merely for failure to fulfil a contractual obligation: Art 11, ICCPR. Imprisonment of debtors is forbidden, but the prohibition does not extend to violations of statutory or criminal obligations or the non-payment of any resultant fines or the non-performance of any other resultant penalties.

Freedom of movement and residence

11.52   The UDHR proclaims a right to 'freedom of movement and residence within the borders of each State', as well as a right to leave any country and to return to one's own country.[83] Article 12 of the ICCPR is more precise: 'Everyone lawfully within the territory of a State shall, within that territory, have the right to liberty of movement and freedom to choose his residence.'[84] It also confers a right to leave any country, including one's own country.[85] These rights and freedoms may be restricted where it is necessary to protect national security, public order, public health or morals, and the rights and freedoms of others.[86] However, no person may ever be denied the right to enter his or her own country.[87]

11.53   An important qualification on the protection afforded by Art 12 of the ICCPR is that it extends only to those 'lawfully within the territory of a State'. The extent to which aliens are protected was considered by the Human Rights Committee in its General Comment No 27 (1999), which also specifically addressed the rights of women to exercise rights of free movement and residence:

> 4. Everyone lawfully within the territory of a State enjoys, within that territory, the right to move freely and to choose his or her place of residence. In principle, citizens of a State are always lawfully within the territory of that State.

---

80.   Ibid, Art 10(2)(a).
81.   Ibid, Art 10(2)(b).
82.   Ibid, Art 10(3).
83.   UDHR, Art 13.
84.   ICCPR, Art 12(1).
85.   Ibid, Art 12(2).
86.   Ibid, Art 12(3).
87.   Ibid, Art 12(4).

The question whether an alien is 'lawfully' within the territory of a State is a matter governed by domestic law, which may subject the entry of an alien to the territory of a State to restrictions, provided they are in compliance with the State's international obligations. In that connection, the Committee has held that an alien who entered the State illegally, but whose status has been regularised, must be considered to be lawfully within the territory for the purposes of article 12. Once a person is lawfully within a State, any restrictions on his or her rights guaranteed by article 12, paragraphs 1 and 2, as well as any treatment different from that accorded to nationals, have to be justified under the rules provided for by article 12, paragraph 3. It is, therefore, important that States parties indicate in their reports the circumstances in which they treat aliens differently from their nationals in this regard and how they justify this difference in treatment. ...

6. The State party must ensure that the rights guaranteed in article 12 are protected not only from public but also from private interference. In the case of women, this obligation to protect is particularly pertinent. For example, it is incompatible with article 12, paragraph 1, that the right of a woman to move freely and to choose her residence be made subject, by law or practice, to the decision of another person, including a relative.

Expulsion of aliens

11.54 Aliens have no general right to enter the territory of a State or to remain there. This principle is a corollary of the sovereignty which all States enjoy over their own territory. However, once an alien is lawfully within a State's territory, he or she not only enjoys a freedom of movement and a right to choose his or her own residence,[88] but also attracts certain procedural rights which must be satisfied before the State may expel him or her. According to Art 13 of the ICCPR, such an alien:

> ... may be expelled ... only in pursuance of a decision reached in accordance with law and shall, except where compelling reasons of national security otherwise require, be allowed to submit the reasons against his expulsion and to have his case reviewed by ... the competent authority.

This right is procedural, rather than substantive. Provided a State complies with these procedural requirements, it remains free to expel an alien.

11.55 According to the Human Rights Committee in its General Comment No 15 (1986):

> 10. Article 13 directly regulates only the procedure and not the substantive grounds for expulsion. However, by allowing only those carried out 'in pursuance of a decision reached in accordance with law', its purpose is clearly to prevent arbitrary expulsions. On the other hand, it entitles each alien to a decision in his own case and, hence,

---

88. See 11.52–11.53.

article 13 would not be satisfied with laws or decisions providing for collective or mass expulsions. This understanding, in the opinion of the Committee, is confirmed by further provisions concerning the right to submit reasons against expulsion and to have the decision reviewed by and to be represented before the competent authority or someone designated by it.

An alien must be given full facilities for pursuing his remedy against expulsion so that this right will in all the circumstances of his case be an effective one. The principles of article 13 relating to appeal against expulsion and the entitlement to review by a competent authority may only be departed from when 'compelling reasons of national security' so require. Discrimination may not be made between different categories of aliens in the application of article 13.

11.56 The customary international law of diplomatic protection regarding expulsion of aliens is discussed elsewhere.[89]

Equality before the law and fair trial

11.57 The maintenance of human rights and fundamental freedoms is impossible without the rule of law, and an essential component of the rule of law is every person's equality before the law and the courts, and the fairness of trials before those courts. These concerns are addressed in Arts 6, 7, 10 and 11 of the UDHR and are the subject of the most detailed substantive provision in the ICCPR:

Article 14

1. All persons shall be equal before the courts and tribunals. In the determination of any criminal charge against him, or of his rights and obligations in a suit at law, everyone shall be entitled to a fair and public hearing by a competent, independent and impartial tribunal established by law. The press and the public may be excluded from all or part of a trial for reasons of morals, public order *(ordre public)* or national security in a democratic society, or when the interest of the private lives of the parties so requires, or to the extent strictly necessary in the opinion of the court in special circumstances where publicity would prejudice the interests of justice; but any judgement rendered in a criminal case or in a suit at law shall be made public except where the interest of juvenile persons otherwise requires or the proceedings concern matrimonial disputes or the guardianship of children.

2. Everyone charged with a criminal offence shall have the right to be presumed innocent until proved guilty according to law.

3. In the determination of any criminal charge against him, everyone shall be entitled to the following minimum guarantees, in full equality:

    (a) To be informed promptly and in detail in a language which he understands of the nature and cause of the charge against him;

    (b) To have adequate time and facilities for the preparation of his defence and to communicate with counsel of his own choosing;

---

89. See 5.87.

(c) To be tried without undue delay;

(d) To be tried in his presence, and to defend himself in person or through legal assistance of his own choosing; to be informed, if he does not have legal assistance, of this right; and to have legal assistance assigned to him, in any case where the interests of justice so require, and without payment by him in any such case if he does not have sufficient means to pay for it;

(e) To examine, or have examined, the witnesses against him and to obtain the attendance and examination of witnesses on his behalf under the same conditions as witnesses against him;

(f) To have the free assistance of an interpreter if he cannot understand or speak the language used in court;

(g) Not to be compelled to testify against himself or to confess guilt.

4. In the case of juvenile persons, the procedure shall be such as will take account of their age and the desirability of promoting their rehabilitation.

5. Everyone convicted of a crime shall have the right to his conviction and sentence being reviewed by a higher tribunal according to law.

6. When a person has by a final decision been convicted of a criminal offence and when subsequently his conviction has been reversed or he has been pardoned on the ground that a new or newly discovered fact shows conclusively that there has been a miscarriage of justice, the person who has suffered punishment as a result of such conviction shall be compensated according to law, unless it is proved that the non-disclosure of the unknown fact in time is wholly or partly attributable to him.

7. No one shall be liable to be tried or punished again for an offence for which he has already been finally convicted or acquitted in accordance with the law and penal procedure of each country.

11.58 These extensive requirements were originally the subject of the Human Rights Committee's General Comment No 13 (1984), now replaced by General Comment No 32 (2007):[90]

2. The right to equality before the courts and tribunals and to a fair trial is a key element of human rights protection and serves as a procedural means to safeguard the rule of law. Article 14 of the Covenant aims at ensuring the proper administration of justice, and to this end guarantees a series of specific rights. ...

4. Article 14 contains guarantees that States parties must respect, regardless of their legal traditions and their domestic law. While they should report on how these guarantees are interpreted in relation to their respective legal systems, the Committee notes that it cannot be left to the sole discretion of domestic law to determine the essential content of Covenant guarantees. ...

19. The requirement of competence, independence and impartiality of a tribunal in the sense of article 14, paragraph 1, is an absolute right that is not subject to any exception. The requirement of independence

---

90. Most footnotes omitted.

refers, in particular, to the procedure and qualifications for the appointment of judges, and guarantees relating to their security of tenure until a mandatory retirement age or the expiry of their term of office, where such exist, the conditions governing promotion, transfer, suspension and cessation of their functions, and the actual independence of the judiciary from political interference by the executive branch and legislature. States should take specific measures guaranteeing the independence of the judiciary, protecting judges from any form of political influence in their decision-making through the constitution or adoption of laws establishing clear procedures and objective criteria for the appointment, remuneration, tenure, promotion, suspension and dismissal of the members of the judiciary and disciplinary sanctions taken against them. A situation where the functions and competencies of the judiciary and the executive are not clearly distinguishable or where the latter is able to control or direct the former is incompatible with the notion of an independent tribunal. It is necessary to protect judges against conflicts of interest and intimidation. In order to safeguard their independence, the status of judges, including their term of office, their independence, security, adequate remuneration, conditions of service, pensions and the age of retirement shall be adequately secured by law. ...

25. The notion of fair trial includes the guarantee of a fair and public hearing. Fairness of proceedings entails the absence of any direct or indirect influence, pressure or intimidation or intrusion from whatever side and for whatever motive. A hearing is not fair if, for instance, the defendant in criminal proceedings is faced with the expression of a hostile attitude from the public or support for one party in the courtroom that is tolerated by the court, thereby impinging on the right to defence,[91] or is exposed to other manifestations of hostility with similar effects. Expressions of racist attitudes by a jury that are tolerated by the tribunal, or a racially biased jury selection are other instances which adversely affect the fairness of the procedure. ...

28. All trials in criminal matters or related to a suit at law must in principle be conducted orally and publicly. The publicity of hearings ensures the transparency of proceedings and thus provides an important safeguard for the interest of the individual and of society at large. Courts must make information regarding the time and venue of the oral hearings available to the public and provide for adequate facilities for the attendance of interested members of the public, within reasonable limits, taking into account, inter alia, the potential interest in the case and the duration of the oral hearing. ...

29. Article 14, paragraph 1, acknowledges that courts have the power to exclude all or part of the public for reasons of morals, public order *(ordre public)* or national security in a democratic society, or when the interest of the private lives of the parties so requires, or to the extent strictly necessary in the opinion of the court in special circumstances where publicity would be prejudicial to the interests of justice. Apart from such exceptional circumstances, a hearing must be open to the general public, including members of the media, and must

---

91.   A footnote here in the General Comment cites *Gridin v Russia* [2000] UNHRC 12.

not, for instance, be limited to a particular category of persons. Even in cases in which the public is excluded from the trial, the judgment, including the essential findings, evidence and legal reasoning must be made public, except where the interest of juvenile persons otherwise requires, or the proceedings concern matrimonial disputes or the guardianship of children. ...

30. According to article 14, paragraph 2 everyone charged with a criminal offence shall have the right to be presumed innocent until proven guilty according to law. The presumption of innocence, which is fundamental to the protection of human rights, imposes on the prosecution the burden of proving the charge, guarantees that no guilt can be presumed until the charge has been proved beyond reasonable doubt, ensures that the accused has the benefit of doubt, and requires that persons accused of a criminal act must be treated in accordance with this principle. It is a duty for all public authorities to refrain from prejudging the outcome of a trial, e.g. by abstaining from making public statements affirming the guilt of the accused.[92] ...

32. Subparagraph 3 (b) provides that accused persons must have adequate time and facilities for the preparation of their defence and to communicate with counsel of their own choosing. This provision is an important element of the guarantee of a fair trial and an application of the principle of equality of arms. ... There is an obligation to grant reasonable requests for adjournment, in particular, when the accused is charged with a serious criminal offence and additional time for preparation of the defence is needed.

33. 'Adequate facilities' must include access to documents and other evidence; this access must include all materials that the prosecution plans to offer in court against the accused or that are exculpatory. Exculpatory material should be understood as including not only material establishing innocence but also other evidence that could assist the defence (e.g. indications that a confession was not voluntary). ...

34. The right to communicate with counsel requires that the accused is granted prompt access to counsel. Counsel should be able to meet their clients in private and to communicate with the accused in conditions that fully respect the confidentiality of their communications.

11.59 According to the Human Rights Committee, the presumption of innocence in criminal cases guaranteed by Art 14(2) extends beyond the standard requirement that the prosecution must prove its case beyond reasonable doubt and that the court must give the benefit of any such doubt to the defendant. At para 30 of General Comment No 32, the Committee takes the further position that it is 'a duty for all public authorities to refrain from prejudging the outcome of a trial'. This duty extends, according to the Committee, even to the police when publicly commenting on particular cases. A similar observation was made in General Comment No 13, to which the Human Rights Committee referred in stating its views on a communication received from an author in Russia.

---

92. Ibid.

In **Gridin v Russia,**[93] the author of a communication to the Human Rights Committee was arrested and put on trial before a Russian criminal court for attempted rape and murder, and for six other sexual assaults. He was denied access to a lawyer for five days following his arrest, notwithstanding his request for access to legal advice. Within days of his arrest, local radio stations and newspapers declared that the author was the notorious 'lift-boy' murderer who had raped several girls, murdering three of them. At about the same time, the head of the local police announced himself satisfied that the author was the murderer, and these remarks were broadcast on television. The police investigator was also alleged to have addressed public meetings condemning the author as guilty and urging the public to send social prosecutors to the trial (social prosecutors represent members of the public and may join the prosecution of a defendant). As an alleged consequence, 10 social prosecutors joined the trial, while the author was defended by a single social defender who was later forced to leave the courtroom. The author also stated that the courtroom was crowded with people screaming for the death sentence, that the social prosecutors and the victims were threatening the defence and the witnesses, and that the trial judge did nothing to stop any of this behaviour. This was alleged to have resulted in an inability properly to examine the principal witnesses at the trial. The trial court sentenced the author to death, and several appeals to the Supreme Court and the prosecutor's office were all dismissed. The author's death sentence was, however, eventually commuted to life imprisonment. Before the Committee the author made several complaints about the conduct of his trial. In particular, he argued that he was denied a fair trial and that he was effectively denied the presumption of innocence. The Committee said:

8.2. With regard to the author's claim that he was denied a fair trial in violation of article 14, paragraph 1, in particular because of the failure by the trial court to control the hostile atmosphere and pressure created by the public in the court room, which made it impossible for defence counsel to properly cross-examine the witnesses and present his defence, the Committee notes that the Supreme Court referred to this issue, but failed to specifically address it when it heard the author's appeal. The Committee considers that the conduct of the trial, as described above, violated the author's right to a fair trial within the meaning of article 14, paragraph 1.

8.3. With regard to the allegation of a violation of the presumption of innocence, including public statements made by high ranking law enforcement officials portraying the author as guilty which were given wide media coverage, the Committee notes that the Supreme Court referred to the issue, but failed to specifically deal with it when it heard the author's appeal. The Committee refers to its General Comment No 13 on article 14, where it has stated that: 'It is, therefore, a duty for all public authorities to refrain from prejudging the outcome of a trial'. In the present case the Committee considers that the authorities failed to exercise the restraint that article 14, paragraph 2, requires of them and that the author's rights were thus violated. ...

8.5. With respect to the allegation that the author did not have a lawyer available to him for the first 5 days after he was arrested, the Committee notes that the State party has responded that the author was represented in accordance with the law. It has not, however, refuted the author's claim that he requested a lawyer soon after his detention and that his request was ignored. Neither has it refuted the author's claim that he was interrogated without the benefit of consulting a lawyer after he repeatedly requested such a consultation. The Committee finds that denying the author access to legal consent after he had requested

---

93. Ibid.

> such access and interrogating him during that time constitutes a violation of the author's rights under article 14, paragraph 3 (b). Furthermore, the Committee considers that the fact that the author was unable to consult with his lawyer in private, an allegation which has not been refuted by the State party, also constitutes a violation of article 14, paragraph 3 (b) of the Covenant.

Retroactive criminal laws

11.60 Article 15(1) of the ICCPR provides that no person may be convicted of any criminal offence on account of any conduct which was not a crime under domestic or international law at the time it was committed. Similarly, no-one may have a heavier criminal penalty imposed on him or her than was applicable at the time the crime was committed, although if a lighter penalty has subsequently been prescribed the offender shall benefit from the change.

A defendant's rights concerning retroactive criminal liability will not be violated if the impugned act or omission was a violation of 'international law' at the time it occurred, even if the conduct was not criminalised under national law.

11.61 The absence of a relevant national law will not prevent the prosecution of a defendant whose conduct constituted a crime according to the 'general principles of law recognised by the community of nations'.[94]

In *Baumgarten v Germany,*[95] the author of a communication to the Human Rights Committee had been Deputy Minister of Defence in the East German (German Democratic Republic, or GDR) communist dictatorship from 1979 to 1990. In that capacity, he had authorised the use of deadly force by East German border guards against persons attempting to flee East Germany by illegally crossing the border into the territory of the Federal Republic of Germany (FRG). After the collapse of the East German dictatorship and the reunification of East Germany with the FRG, the author was prosecuted under FRG law for the numerous killings and attempted killings of persons crossing the border into the FRG. The author claimed that his prosecution and conviction violated his guarantee against non-retroactive criminal sanction, as all the orders he issued were perfectly regular under East German law. This was submitted to be borne out by the fact that no East German border guard had ever been prosecuted for using unlawful force against those illegally fleeing East Germany at the border. The Committee said:

> 9.3. … the Committee notes that the specific nature of any violation of article 15, paragraph 1, of the Covenant requires it to review whether the interpretation and application of the relevant criminal law by the domestic courts in a specific case appear to disclose a violation of the prohibition of retroactive punishment or punishment otherwise not based on law. In doing so, the Committee will limit itself to the question of whether the author's acts, at the material time of commission, constituted sufficiently defined criminal offences under the criminal law of the GDR or under international law. 9.4. The killings took place in the

---

94. ICCPR, Art 15(2).
95. *Baumgarten v Germany* [2003] UNHRC 44.

context of a system which effectively denied to the population of the GDR the right freely to leave one's own country. The authorities and individuals enforcing this system were prepared to use lethal force to prevent individuals from nonviolently exercising their right to leave their own country. The Committee recalls that even when used as a last resort lethal force may only be used, under article 6 of the Covenant, to meet a proportionate threat. The Committee further recalls that States parties are required to prevent arbitrary killing by their own security forces.

It finally notes that the disproportionate use of lethal force was criminal according to the general principles of law recognized by the community of nations already at the time when the author committed his acts.

9.5. The State party correctly argues that the killings violated the GDR's obligations under international human rights law, in particular article 6 of the Covenant. It further contends that those same obligations required the prosecution of those suspected of responsibility for the killings. The State party's courts have concluded that these killings violated the homicide provisions of the GDR Criminal Code. Those provisions required to be interpreted and applied in the context of the relevant provisions of the law, such as section 95 of the Criminal Code excluding statutory defences in the case of human rights violations ... and the Border Act regulating the use of force at the border. ... The State party's courts interpreted the provisions of the Border Act on the use of force as not excluding from the scope of the crime of homicide the disproportionate use of lethal or potentially lethal force in violation of those human rights obligations. Accordingly, the provisions of the Border Act did not save the killings from being considered by the courts as violating the homicide provisions of the Criminal Code. The Committee cannot find this interpretation of the law and the conviction of the author based on it to be incompatible with article 15 of the Covenant.

The Committee agreed with the FRG courts that the border killings and attempted killings were contrary to East German law properly interpreted, and that there was no issue of retroactivity in the author's trial and conviction. The Committee did not directly address the question as to whether the author's treatment would have violated Art 15 had his conduct actually been consistent with East German law. However, at para 9.4 of the opinion, the Committee implies that the FRG could have prosecuted the author even if GDR law had permitted his conduct, because such conduct 'was criminal according to the general principles of law recognized by the community of nations already at the time when the author committed his acts'.

Recognition as a person before the law

11.62   Article 16 of the ICCPR states simply that: 'Everyone has the right to recognition everywhere as a person before the law.' Subject to exceptional rules relating to minority and insanity, every person must be able to exercise legal rights and assume legal obligations and to commence or defend legal proceedings. The laws of National Socialist Germany restricting the ability of Jews to bear or legally vindicate a wide range of rights were an egregious example of a failure to recognise everyone's legal personality. The old practice of 'civil death' (that is, depriving prisoners and other classes of malefactors of their civil capacities) is not consistent with this right.

11.63   The Human Rights Committee has never issued a General Comment dealing specifically with Art 16 of the ICCPR. In its General Comment No 28 (2000), however, it made the following observation:

> 19.   The right of everyone under Article 16 to be recognized everywhere as a person before the law is particularly pertinent for women, who often see it curtailed by reason of sex or marital status. This right implies that the capacity of women to own property, to enter into a contract or to exercise other civil rights may not be restricted on the basis of marital status or any other discriminatory ground. It also implies that women may not be treated as objects to be given, together with the property of the deceased husband, to his family.
>
> States must provide information [in their periodic reports to the Committee] on laws or practices that prevent women from being treated or from functioning as full legal persons and the measures taken to eradicate laws or practices that allow such treatment.

Privacy

11.64   The ICCPR provides that no-one 'shall be subjected to arbitrary interference with his privacy, family, home or correspondence, nor to unlawful attacks upon his honour and reputation' (Art 17(1)), and that everyone 'has the right to protection of the law against such interference or attacks' (Art 17(2)). The UDHR proclaims an almost identical right.[96]

11.65   Neither the UDHR nor the ICCPR defines 'privacy', and the Human Rights Committee has so far avoided venturing a comprehensive definition in either its cases or its General Comments. Perhaps the closest it has come to formulating such a definition was in *Coeriel v The Netherlands*, where it said that 'the notion of privacy refers to the sphere of a person's life in which he or she can freely express his or her identity, be it by entering into relationships with others or alone'.[97]

11.66   That the right to privacy may, in certain circumstances, extend to protect sexual conduct from State regulation was made apparent in the Human Rights Committee's opinion on a communication involving Australia:

> In *Toonen v Australia*,[98] the author of the communication was an activist for the interests of homosexuals in Tasmania. He complained that two provisions of the Tasmanian Criminal Code violated, inter alia, his right to privacy. Sections 122(a), 122(c) and 123 of the Criminal Code criminalised sexual contacts between men, including such contacts between consenting adult men in private. These provisions

---

96.   UDHR, Art 12.
97.   *Coeriel v The Netherlands* [1994] UNHRC 55, para 10.2.
98.   *Toonen v Australia* [1994] UNHRC 8.

had not been used as the basis of a prosecution for many years, but the Tasmanian Director of Public Prosecutions had recently affirmed that prosecutions would still be commenced if there arose cases supported by sufficient evidence. The Tasmanian authorities submitted that regulation of public morality is a matter for the community to decide through its representatives, and is not a matter for any international law on privacy. They further submitted that the ICCPR does not guarantee privacy per se, but only freedom from arbitrary interferences with privacy. As the ban on male homosexual activity in private was supported by law, it was not arbitrary. The ban was also argued to be justified as a measure necessary to protect public health from the spread of HIV/AIDS. The Human Rights Committee said:

8.2. In so far as article 17 is concerned, it is undisputed that adult consensual sexual activity in private is covered by the concept of 'privacy', and that Mr. Toonen is actually and currently affected by the continued existence of the Tasmanian laws. The Committee considers that sections 122 (a) and (c) and 123 of the Tasmanian Criminal Code 'interfere' with the author's privacy, even if these provisions have not been enforced for a decade. In this context, it notes that the policy of the Department of Public Prosecutions not to initiate criminal proceedings in respect of private homosexual conduct does not amount to a guarantee that no actions will be brought against homosexuals in the future, particularly in the light of undisputed statements of the Director of Public Prosecutions of Tasmania in 1988 and those of members of the Tasmanian Parliament. The continued existence of the challenged provisions therefore continuously and directly 'interferes' with the author's privacy.

8.3. The prohibition against private homosexual behaviour is provided for by law, namely, sections 122 and 123 of the Tasmanian Criminal Code. As to whether it may be deemed arbitrary, the Committee recalls that pursuant to its general comment 16 on article 17, the 'introduction of the concept of arbitrariness is intended to guarantee that even interference provided for by the law should be in accordance with the provisions, aims and objectives of the Covenant and should be, in any event, reasonable in the circumstances'. The Committee interprets the requirement of reasonableness to imply that any interference with privacy must be proportional to the end sought and be necessary in the circumstances of any given case.

8.4. While the State party acknowledges that the impugned provisions constitute an arbitrary interference with Mr. Toonen's privacy, the Tasmanian authorities submit that the challenged laws are justified on public health and moral grounds, as they are intended in part to prevent the spread of HIV/AIDS in Tasmania, and because, in the absence of specific limitation clauses in article 17, moral issues must be deemed a matter for domestic decision.

8.5. As far as the public health argument of the Tasmanian authorities is concerned, the Committee notes that the criminalization of homosexual practices cannot be considered a reasonable means or proportionate measure to achieve the aim of preventing the spread of AIDS/HIV. The Government of Australia observes that statutes criminalizing homosexual activity tend to impede public health programmes 'by driving underground many of the people at the risk of infection'. Criminalization of homosexual activity thus would appear to run counter to the implementation of effective education programmes in respect of the HIV/ AIDS prevention. Secondly, the Committee notes that no link has been shown between the continued criminalization of homosexual activity and the effective control of the spread of the HIV/AIDS virus.

8.6. The Committee cannot accept either that for the purposes of article 17 of the Covenant, moral issues are exclusively a matter of domestic concern, as this would open the door to withdrawing from the Committee's scrutiny a potentially large number of statutes interfering with privacy. It further notes that with the exception of Tasmania, all laws criminalizing homosexuality have been repealed throughout Australia and that, even in Tasmania, it is apparent that there is no consensus as to whether sections 122 and 123 should not also be repealed. Considering further that these provisions are not currently enforced, which implies that they are not deemed essential to the protection of morals in Tasmania, the Committee concludes that the provisions do not meet the 'reasonableness' test in the circumstances of the case, and that they arbitrarily interfere with Mr. Toonen's right under article 17, paragraph 1.

Freedom of thought, conscience and religion

11.67   The UDHR proclaims a universal right to freedom of thought, conscience and religion. This right includes a right to have or adopt a religion or belief of one's own choosing, and freedom to manifest that religion or belief in worship, observance, practice and teaching.[99]

Article 18 of the ICCPR establishes a right in identical terms[100] and adds that no-one shall be subject to coercion which would impair his or her freedom to have or adopt a religion or belief.[101] This freedom may be limited only by law and only to the extent necessary to protect public safety, public order, public health or public morals or other persons' fundamental rights and freedoms.[102] Parents must also be able to ensure the religious and moral education of their children in accordance with the parents' own convictions.[103]

11.68   The Human Rights Committee elaborated on its understanding of the freedom of thought, conscience and religion in its General Comment No 22 (1993):

1. The right to freedom of thought, conscience and religion (which includes the freedom to hold beliefs) in article 18.1 is far-reaching and profound; it encompasses freedom of thought on all matters, personal conviction and the commitment to religion or belief, whether manifested individually or in community with others. The Committee draws the attention of States parties to the fact that the freedom of thought and the freedom of conscience are protected equally with the freedom of religion and belief. ...

2. Article 18 protects theistic, non-theistic and atheistic beliefs, as well as the right not to profess any religion or belief. ...

4. ... The freedom to manifest religion or belief in worship, observance, practice and teaching encompasses a broad range of acts. The concept of worship extends to ritual and ceremonial acts giving direct expression to belief, as well as various practices integral to such acts, including the building of places of worship, the use of ritual formulae and objects, the display of symbols, and the observance of holidays and days of rest. The observance and practice of religion or belief

---

99.   UDHR, Art 18.
100. ICCPR, Art 18(1).
101. Ibid, Art 18(2).
102. Ibid, Art 18(3).
103. Ibid, Art 18(4).

may include not only ceremonial acts but also such customs as the observance of dietary regulations, the wearing of distinctive clothing or headcoverings, participation in rituals associated with certain stages of life, and the use of a particular language customarily spoken by a group. In addition, the practice and teaching of religion or belief includes acts integral to the conduct by religious groups of their basic affairs, such as the freedom to choose their religious leaders, priests and teachers, the freedom to establish seminaries or religious schools and the freedom to prepare and distribute religious texts or publications.

5.   ... the freedom to 'have or to adopt' a religion or belief necessarily entails the freedom to choose a religion or belief, including the right to replace one's current religion or belief with another or to adopt atheistic views, as well as the right to retain one's religion or belief. Article 18.2 bars coercion that would impair the right to have or adopt a religion or belief, including the use of threat of physical force or penal sanctions to compel believers or non-believers to adhere to their religious beliefs and congregations, to recant their religion or belief or to convert. Policies or practices having the same intention or effect, such as, for example, those restricting access to education, medical care, employment or the rights guaranteed by article 25 and other provisions of the Covenant, are similarly inconsistent with article 18.2. The same protection is enjoyed by holders of all beliefs of a non-religious nature.

11.69   The ICCPR also guarantees, at Art 19(1), a 'right to hold opinions without interference'. In *Kang v Korea*,[104] the Human Rights Committee expressed the opinion that the Republic of Korea's 'ideology conversion system' was a violation of this right, and of the right to freedom of thought in Art 18(1). This system was a program of inducements and punishments (for example, increased opportunities for parole and extended periods of solitary confinement) for certain inmates of the State's prisons. It was aimed at converting away from their communist ideology prisoners convicted of subversive activities on behalf of the North Korean regime. The violation arose, in the Committee's view, because the ideology conversion system was both discriminatory and coercive.

Freedom of expression

11.70   An essential feature of any free society is the freedom not only to hold, but also to express, one's beliefs and opinions. Article 19(2) of the ICCPR establishes a right of 'freedom of expression', which includes 'freedom to seek, receive and impart information and ideas of all kinds, regardless of frontiers, either orally, in writing or in print, in the form of art, or through any other media'. According to Art 19(3), this freedom may be restricted only by law and only where necessary to protect the rights and reputations of others or for the protection of national security, public order, public health or morals. The UDHR is to identical effect.[105]

---

104. *Kang v Korea* [2003] UNHRC 23.
105. UDHR, Art 19(2), (3).

11.71   From the perspective of protecting civil and political rights, the right to freedom of expression is at its most important when applied to the protection of political expression and the free flow of public debate.

In **Mukong v Cameroon,**[106] the author of a communication to the Human Rights Committee was a journalist and a longstanding opponent of Cameroon's one-party dictatorship. He claimed that he was arrested and detained because of his advocacy of multi-party democracy and that one of his books criticising Cameroon's regime had been banned. In the author's view, these acts constituted a violation of his freedom of expression. The Committee said:

3.4 The author notes that his arrests on 16 June 1988 and 26 February 1990 were linked to his activities as an advocate of multi-party democracy, and claims that these were Government attempts designed to suppress any opposition activities, in violation of article 19 of the Covenant. This also applies to the Government's ban, in 1985, of a book written by the author (Prisoner without a Crime), in which he described his detention in local jails from 1970 to 1976. ...

6.7 ... the State party argues that the arrest of the author was for activities and forms of expression that are covered by the limitation clause of article 19, paragraph 3, of the Covenant. It contends that the exercise of the right to freedom of expression must take into account the political context and situation prevailing in a country at any point in time. Since the independence and reunification of Cameroon, the country's history has been a constant battle to strengthen national unity, first at the level of the francophone and anglophone communities and thereafter at the level of the more than 200 ethnic groups and tribes that comprise the Cameroonian nation. ...

9.6 The author has claimed a violation of his right to freedom of expression and opinion, as he was persecuted for his advocacy of multi-party democracy and the expression of opinions inimical to the Government of the State party. The State party has replied that restrictions on the author's freedom of expression were justified under the terms of article 19, paragraph 3.

9.7 ... The State party has indirectly justified its actions on grounds of national security and/or public order by arguing that the author's right to freedom of expression was exercised without regard to the country's political context and continued struggle for unity. While the State party has indicated that the restrictions on the author's freedom of expression were provided for by law, it must still be determined whether the measures taken against the author were necessary for the safeguard of national security and/or public order. The Committee considers that it was not necessary to safeguard an alleged vulnerable state of national unity by subjecting the author to arrest, continued detention and treatment in violation of article 7. It further considers that the legitimate objective of safeguarding and indeed strengthening national unity under difficult political circumstances cannot be achieved by attempting to muzzle advocacy of multi-party democracy, democratic tenets and human rights; in this regard, the question of deciding which measures might meet the 'necessity' test in such situations does not arise. In the circumstances of the author's case, the Committee concludes that there has been a violation of article 19 of the Covenant.

---

106. *Mukong v Cameroon* [1994] UNHRC 41.

According to the Human Rights Committee, a developing State will not be able to justify derogations from freedom of expression on grounds of national unity. Only those grounds prescribed in Art 19(3) may be relied on, and then only to the extent necessary to safeguard the interests identified in those grounds. It would seem to follow that derogations from freedom of expression on other grounds sometimes advanced by developing States — such as fostering economic growth or maintaining 'social stability' — would also be inconsistent with Art 19.

11.72 Additional limitations on freedom of expression relate to 'propaganda for war' (ICCPR, Art 20(1)) and 'advocacy of national, racial or religious hatred that constitutes incitement to discrimination, hostility or violence' (ICCPR, Art 20(2)). In each case, the obligation on the State is that the proscribed activity must be 'prohibited by law'. In General Comment No 11 (1983), the Human Rights Committee remarked:

> 2. Article 20 of the Covenant states that any propaganda for war and any advocacy of national, racial or religious hatred that constitutes incitement to discrimination, hostility or violence shall be prohibited by law. In the opinion of the Committee, these required prohibitions are fully compatible with the right of freedom of expression as contained in article 19, the exercise of which carries with it special duties and responsibilities. The prohibition under paragraph 1 extends to all forms of propaganda threatening or resulting in an act of aggression or breach of the peace contrary to the Charter of the United Nations, while paragraph 2 is directed against any advocacy of national, racial or religious hatred that constitutes incitement to discrimination, hostility or violence, whether such propaganda or advocacy has aims which are internal or external to the State concerned. The provisions of article 20, paragraph 1, do not prohibit advocacy of the sovereign right of self-defence or the right of peoples to self-determination and independence in accordance with the Charter of the United Nations. For article 20 to become fully effective there ought to be a law making it clear that propaganda and advocacy as described therein are contrary to public policy and providing for an appropriate sanction in case of violation. The Committee, therefore, believes that States parties which have not yet done so should take the measures necessary to fulfil the obligations contained in article 20, and should themselves refrain from any such propaganda or advocacy.

11.73 According to the Human Rights Committee, States are not required to make it an offence to advocate a war which would be in self-defence[107] or in pursuit of self-determination.[108] It would also seem to follow that Art 20(1) does not require prohibition of other internationally lawful uses of force by States, such as force authorised under the UN Charter[109] or force justified by the requirements of humanitarian intervention[110] and protection of nationals abroad.[111]

---

107. See 9.19–9.40.
108. See 11.11 and 4.37–4.56.
109. See 9.49–9.62.
110. See 9.68–9.77.
111. See 9.63–9.67.

Assembly and association

11.74 Having established a right to hold opinions and then to express them, the ICCPR goes on to guarantee their expression as part of a larger group assembled for that purpose. Article 21 requires States to recognise a 'right of peaceful assembly' and provides that no restrictions may be placed on the right other than those imposed in conformity with the law and which are necessary in a democratic society in the interests of national security or public safety, public order, public health and morals, or the rights and freedoms of others.

11.75 The assembly must be peaceful, so that non-peaceful gatherings (for example, riots) are not protected. Otherwise, restrictions on assemblies must be no more than is required for the State and public interests named in Art 21. In *Kivenmaa v Finland*,[112] the Human Rights Committee considered a Finnish law requiring that police be given at least six hours' notification of many types of outdoor public meetings. The Committee was of the view that the law could not be imposed to prohibit small gatherings which posed no objective threat to national security or public safety; *in casu* about 25 people assembled to protest against a visiting foreign Head of State by displaying a banner denouncing alleged human rights abuses in the visitor's country.

11.76 The UDHR proclaims simply a right 'to freedom of peaceful assembly and association', and that no one may be 'compelled to belong to an association'.[113] The ICCPR is somewhat more detailed concerning the freedom of association:

Article 22

1. Everyone shall have the right to freedom of association with others, including the right to form and join trade unions for the protection of his interests.

2. No restrictions may be placed on the exercise of this right other than those which are prescribed by law and which are necessary in a democratic society in the interests of national security or public safety, public order *(ordre public)*, the protection of public health or morals or the protection of the rights and freedoms of others. This article shall not prevent the imposition of lawful restrictions on members of the armed forces and of the police in their exercise of this right.

3. Nothing in this article shall authorize States Parties to the International Labour Organisation Convention of 1948 concerning Freedom of Association and Protection of the Right to Organise to take legislative measures which would prejudice, or to apply the law in such a manner as to prejudice, the guarantees provided for in that Convention.

11.77 Freedom of association requires States to permit individuals to form and join non-governmental associations of their choosing in order to pursue any social activity. These associations include clubs, societies,

---

112. *Kivenmaa v Finland* [1994] UNHRC 21.
113. UDHR, Art 20.

corporations, charities, trade unions, pressure groups, lobby groups, and political parties.

Freedom of association is completely inconsistent with the types of organising structures imposed on society by a totalitarian State, in which associations that are independent of the State or the ruling party are not tolerated and in which membership of some associations is often mandatory (for example, State- or party-controlled trade unions).

11.78   The International Labour Organisation Convention (No 87) Concerning Freedom of Association and Protection of the Right to Organise,[114] which is referred to in Art 22(3) of the ICCPR, provides for certain rights to be enjoyed by trade unions and their members. Nothing in Art 22 can be construed to prejudice any of those rights. It should be noted, however, that the Human Rights Committee has interpreted freedom of association as not implying a right to strike.[115] It is also likely that the Committee would regard a compulsory requirement of trade union membership as violating freedom of association.[116]

Protection of the family

11.79   The UDHR declares that the family 'is the natural and fundamental group unit of society and is entitled to protection by society and the State'.[117] This formulation is adopted verbatim by the ICCPR at Art 23(1). The ICCPR goes further by recognising a right of men and women of marriageable age to marry and found a family,[118] by providing that no marriage shall be entered into without the free and full consent of the intending spouses,[119] and by requiring States to ensure equality of rights and responsibilities of the spouses as to marriage, during marriage and at its dissolution.[120]

11.80   In its General Comment No 19 (1990), the Human Rights Committee made the following observations concerning the meaning of the provisions on protection of the family:

> 2.   The Committee notes that the concept of the family may differ in some respects from State to State, and even from region to region within a State, and that it is therefore not possible to give the concept a standard definition. However, the Committee emphasizes that, when a group of persons is regarded as a family under the legislation and practice of a State, it must be given the protection referred to in article 23. ...
>
> 4.   ... The Covenant does not establish a specific marriageable age either for men or for women, but that age should be such as to enable each

---

114. UNTS, Vol 68, p 18.
115. *J B v Canada* [1986] UNHRC 87.
116. *Gauthier v Canada* [1999] UNHRC 13.
117. UDHR, Art 16(3).
118. ICCPR, Art 23(2).
119. Ibid, Art 23(3).
120. Ibid, Art 23(4).

of the intending spouses to give his or her free and full personal consent in a form and under conditions prescribed by law. ...

5. The right to found a family implies, in principle, the possibility to procreate and live together. When States parties adopt family planning policies, they should be compatible with the provisions of the Covenant and should, in particular, not be discriminatory or compulsory. Similarly, the possibility to live together implies the adoption of appropriate measures, both at the internal level and as the case may be, in cooperation with other States, to ensure the unity or reunification of families, particularly when their members are separated for political, economic or similar reasons. ...

7. With regard to equality as to marriage, the Committee wishes to note in particular that no sex-based discrimination should occur in respect of the acquisition or loss of nationality by reason of marriage. Likewise, the right of each spouse to retain the use of his or her original family name or to participate on an equal basis in the choice of a new family name should be safeguarded.

8. During marriage, the spouses should have equal rights and responsibilities in the family. This equality extends to all matters arising from their relationship, such as choice of residence, running of the household, education of the children and administration of assets. Such equality continues to be applicable to arrangements regarding legal separation or dissolution of the marriage.

9. Thus, any discriminatory treatment in regard to the grounds and procedures for separation or divorce, child custody, maintenance or alimony, visiting rights or the loss or recovery of parental authority must be prohibited, bearing in mind the paramount interest of the children in this connection. ...

11.81 Issues of family protection frequently arise in the context of immigration law and its impact on family unity. This will occur where a person is deported from, or refused permission to enter, the territory of a State where members of the person's family are lawfully resident. In this regard, the right to family protection will not assist would-be immigrants where there is no effective family life between the lawful resident and the would-be immigrant.

Thus, in *A S v Canada*,[121] the Human Rights Committee was of the view that a refusal to allow the author's adopted daughter to migrate to Canada from Poland did not involve a violation of Art 23. This was because the two people had resided together in Canada for only two years before the adopted daughter freely returned to Poland, where she remained apart from her adoptive mother for a further 17 years. In these circumstances, there was no effective family life and therefore no issue of family protection. Furthermore, a deportation of a family member will not violate Art 23 unless it is unlawful or arbitrary. Where the decision to deport has been made pursuant to law and after giving due consideration to factors affecting family unity, the State may still

---

121. *A S v Canada* [1981] UNHRC 3.

deport a family member where there is a legitimate State interest (for example, protecting the community from repeated criminal offences).[122]

11.82   The disruption of family unity in a migration context may, however, be arbitrary, notwithstanding that the immigration authorities have turned their minds to the issue. In such circumstances, there will be a violation of the right to family protection.

In **Winata v Australia,**[123] the authors of a communication to the Human Rights Committee were Indonesian nationals who entered and resided in Australia legally, but subsequently overstayed their visas and remained in Australia illegally. They met each other in Australia and commenced a de facto relationship, a product of which was the birth of a son. The son grew up in Australia and acquired Australian citizenship on his 10th birthday by automatic operation of law. The next day, his parents applied to regularise their immigration status in Australia, but their applications were unsuccessful and they faced deportation to Indonesia. The authors claimed that their deportation to Indonesia would violate their right to family protection as they would be required to choose between removing their young Australian son to a radically alien environment, and leaving him behind in Australia. According to the Committee:

> 7.3 It is certainly unobjectionable under the Covenant that a State party may require, under its laws, the departure of persons who remain in its territory beyond limited duration permits. Nor is the fact that a child is born, or that by operation of law such a child receives citizenship either at birth or at a later time, sufficient of itself to make a proposed deportation of one or both parents arbitrary. Accordingly, there is significant scope for States parties to enforce their immigration policy and to require departure of unlawfully present persons. That discretion is, however, not unlimited and may come to be exercised arbitrarily in certain circumstances. In the present case, both authors have been in Australia for over fourteen years. The authors' son has grown in Australia from his birth 13 years ago, attending Australian schools as an ordinary child would and developing the social relationships inherent in that. In view of this duration of time, it is incumbent on the State party to demonstrate additional factors justifying the removal of both parents that go beyond a simple enforcement of its immigration law in order to avoid a characterisation of arbitrariness. In the particular circumstances, therefore, the Committee considers that the removal by the State party of the authors would constitute, if implemented, arbitrary interference with the family, contrary to article 17, paragraph 1, in conjunction with article 23, of the Covenant in respect of all of the alleged victims, and, additionally, a violation of article 24, paragraph 1, in relation to [the son] due to a failure to provide him with the necessary measures of protection as a minor.

Protection of the child

11.83   The ICCPR requires States to ensure that every child shall have such measures of protection as are required by his or her status as a minor on the part of the child's family, society and the State. This protection must be available without any distinction as to race, colour,

---

122. *Stewart v Canada* [1996] UNHRC 35.
123. *Winata v Australia* [2001] UNHRC 24.

sex, language, religion, national or social origin, property or birth. Article 24 provides that children shall be registered immediately after birth and shall be entitled to acquire a nationality. The entitlement to special protections for children is the result of their intellectual and physical immaturity. In its General Comment No 17 (1989), the Human Rights Committee observed:

> 2.   ... the rights provided for in article 24 are not the only ones that the Covenant recognises for children and that, as individuals, children benefit from all of the civil rights enunciated in the Covenant. In enunciating a right, some provisions of the Covenant expressly indicate to States measures to be adopted with a view to affording minors greater protection than adults.
>
> Thus, as far as the right to life is concerned, the death penalty cannot be imposed for crimes committed by persons under 18 years of age. Similarly, if lawfully deprived of their liberty, accused juvenile persons shall be separated from adults and are entitled to be brought as speedily as possible for adjudication; in turn, convicted juvenile offenders shall be subject to a penitentiary system that involves segregation from adults and is appropriate to their age and legal status, the aim being to foster reformation and social rehabilitation.
>
> In other instances, children are protected by the possibility of the restriction — provided that such restriction is warranted — of a right recognised by the Covenant, such as the right to publicise a judgement in a suit at law or a criminal case, from which an exception may be made when the interest of the minor so requires.
>
> 3.   In most cases, however, the measures to be adopted are not specified in the Covenant and it is for each State to determine them in the light of the protection needs of children in its territory and within its jurisdiction. The Committee notes in this regard that such measures, although intended primarily to ensure that children fully enjoy the other rights enunciated in the Covenant, may also be economic, social and cultural. For example, every possible economic and social measure should be taken to reduce infant mortality and to eradicate malnutrition among children and to prevent them from being subjected to acts of violence and cruel and inhuman treatment or from being exploited by means of forced labour or prostitution, or by their use in the illicit trafficking of narcotic drugs, or by any other means. In the cultural field, every possible measure should be taken to foster the development of their personality and to provide them with a level of education that will enable them to enjoy the rights recognised in the Covenant, particularly the right to freedom of opinion and expression. ...

11.84   The ICCPR is no longer the primary international instrument concerning the protection of children's rights. This area is now comprehensively covered by the Convention on the Rights of the Child.[124]

---

124. See 11.119–11.124.

Participation in public affairs

11.85   Perhaps the most important civil and political right in structural terms is the right to live in a democratic political system and to participate in the functioning of that system. The ICCPR provides as follows:

Article 25

Every citizen shall have the right and the opportunity, without any of the distinctions mentioned in article 2 and without unreasonable restrictions:

(a) to take part in the conduct of public affairs, directly or through freely chosen representatives;

(b) to vote and to be elected at genuine periodic elections which shall be by universal and equal suffrage and shall be held by secret ballot, guaranteeing the free expression of the will of the electors;

(c) to have access, on general terms of equality, to public service in his country.

11.86   The text of Art 25 does not use the term 'democracy'. Nevertheless, the Human Rights Committee has interpreted the provision as requiring nothing less than a representative democratic political system. In its General Comment No 25 (1996), the Committee said:

1.   ... Article 25 lies at the core of democratic government based on the consent of the people and in conformity with the principles of the Covenant. ...

5.   The conduct of public affairs, referred to in paragraph (a), is a broad concept which relates to the exercise of political power, in particular the exercise of legislative, executive and administrative powers. It covers all aspects of public administration, and the formulation and implementation of policy at international, national, regional and local levels. ...

7.   Where citizens participate in the conduct of public affairs through freely chosen representatives, it is implicit in article 25 that those representatives do in fact exercise governmental power and that they are accountable through the electoral process for their exercise of that power. It is also implicit that the representatives exercise only those powers which are allocated to them in accordance with constitutional provisions. ...

10.   ... It is unreasonable to restrict the right to vote on the ground of physical disability or to impose literacy, educational or property requirements. Party membership should not be a condition of eligibility to vote, nor a ground of disqualification. ...

14.   ... Persons who are deprived of liberty but who have not been convicted should not be excluded from exercising the right to vote. ...

17. The right of persons to stand for election should not be limited unreasonably by requiring candidates to be members of parties or of specific parties. If a candidate is required to have a minimum number of supporters for nomination this requirement should be reasonable and not act as a barrier to candidacy. Without prejudice to paragraph (1)

of article 5 of the Covenant, political opinion may not be used as a ground to deprive any person of the right to stand for election. ...

19. ... Voters should be able to form opinions independently, free of violence or threat of violence, compulsion, inducement or manipulative interference of any kind. ... The results of genuine elections should be respected and implemented. ...

21. ... The principle of one person, one vote, must apply, and within the framework of each State's electoral system, the vote of one elector should be equal to the vote of another. The drawing of electoral boundaries and the method of allocating votes should not distort the distribution of voters or discriminate against any group and should not exclude or restrict unreasonably the right of citizens to choose their representatives freely.

11.87   Possibly the most important component of General Comment No 25 is para 7. A requirement that the people's elected representatives 'do in fact exercise governmental power and that they are accountable through the electoral process for their exercise of that power' is inconsistent with much political practice in modern history. A common feature of dictatorships is that the forms of representative democracy are assiduously cultivated in order to create the impression of popular support for the regime. Thus, the Soviet Union had its Supreme Soviet, National Socialist Germany featured a Reichstag, and the regime controlling mainland China boasts its National People's Congress.

All these bodies, and many similar ones in different States at different times, are or were ostensibly popularly elected with genuine State powers. In fact, they are or were compliant ciphers of their respective dictatorships, exercising no real governmental power. The ICCPR is inconsistent with the establishment or maintenance of such a political system.

Minority rights

11.88   The ICCPR establishes special rights for individuals who are also members of a minority within a State. The relevant provision reads as follows:

Article 27

In those States in which ethnic, religious or linguistic minorities exist, persons belonging to such minorities shall not be denied the right, in community with the other members of their group, to enjoy their own culture, to profess and practice their own religion, or to use their own language.

11.89   The rights of minorities under Art 27 are distinct from the right of peoples to self-determination under Art 1. Minority rights are enjoyed by individuals by virtue of their membership of a minority within a State or of a territory under the jurisdiction of a State, whereas the right of self-determination is enjoyed by the people as a whole who live within a non-self-governing territory.

11.90   The Human Rights Committee made the following observations about minority rights in its General Comment No 23 (1994):

5.2. Article 27 confers rights on persons belonging to minorities which 'exist' in a State party. ... migrant workers or even visitors in a State party constituting such minorities are entitled not to be denied the exercise of those rights. ...

6.1. Although article 27 is expressed in negative terms, that article, nevertheless, does recognise the existence of a 'right' and requires that it shall not be denied. Consequently, a State party is under an obligation to ensure that the existence and the exercise of this right are protected against their denial or violation.

Positive measures of protection are, therefore, required not only against the acts of the State party itself, whether through its legislative, judicial or administrative authorities, but also against the acts of other persons within the State party.

6.2. Although the rights protected under article 27 are individual rights, they depend in turn on the ability of the minority group to maintain its culture, language or religion. Accordingly, positive measures by States may also be necessary to protect the identity of a minority and the rights of its members to enjoy and develop their culture and language and to practise their religion, in community with the other members of the group. ...

7. With regard to the exercise of the cultural rights protected under article 27, the Committee observes that culture manifests itself in many forms, including a particular way of life associated with the use of land resources, especially in the case of indigenous peoples. That right may include such traditional activities as fishing or hunting and the right to live in reserves protected by law. The enjoyment of those rights may require positive legal measures of protection and measures to ensure the effective participation of members of minority communities in decisions which affect them.

11.91 The Covenant does not define 'minority', and the Human Rights Committee has thus far refrained from filling this gap. In *Ballantyne v Canada*,[125] however, the Committee expressed the view that the English-speaking minority in Quebec was not a 'minority' for the purposes of Art 27 because English speakers were a majority in Canada as a whole.

Notwithstanding the absence of a definition, it seems that a minority is an objective phenomenon which cannot be defined in any way a State wishes. Thus, in *Lovelace v Canada*,[126] the Human Rights Committee expressed the view that Canadian legislation which deprived a person of her membership of an Indian tribe violated Art 27. Once she entered into a marriage with a non-Indian, the legislation permanently deprived her of her tribal membership so that she lost her right to reside among her tribe's people on reserved land. The breakdown of her marriage did not restore her legal status as a member of the tribe, and she remained unable to return to her people and tribal lands. The Committee took the view that the Canadian legislation was, in all the circumstances of

---

125. *Ballantyne v Canada* [1993] UNHRC 9.
126. *Lovelace v Canada* [1981] UNHRC 13.

the case, unreasonable and unnecessary to preserve the tribe's identity and that to deny her membership of her tribe was a violation of Art 27.

Non-discrimination and equality before the law

11.92   The ICCPR is clear and repetitive in its insistence on the principle of non-discrimination. Article 2 stipulates that every State party must:

> ... respect and ... ensure to all individuals within its territory and subject to its jurisdiction the rights recognised in the present Covenant, without distinction of any kind, such as race, colour, sex, language, religion, political or other opinion, national or social origin, property, birth or other status.

Article 26 of the ICCPR mandates that all people are equal before the law and are entitled without discrimination to the equal protection of the law. A State party's laws must prohibit any discrimination and guarantee:

> ... equal and effective protection against discrimination on any ground such as race, colour, sex, language, religion, political or other opinion, national or social origin, property, birth or other status.

Whereas Art 2 governs non-discrimination in the enjoyment of rights established or recognised in the ICCPR itself, Art 26 goes further by requiring that the principle of non-discrimination be implemented throughout each State party's domestic legal system. Article 3 of the ICCPR requires all States parties to 'ensure the equal treatment of men and women to the enjoyment of all civil and political rights' contained in the Covenant.

11.93   In its General Comment No 18 (1989), the Human Rights Committee expressed the following views about the nature and scope of these non-discrimination provisions:

1. Non-discrimination, together with equality before the law and equal protection of the law without any discrimination, constitute a basic and general principle relating to the protection of human rights. ...

5. ... the Covenant sometimes expressly requires them to take measures to guarantee the equality of rights of the persons concerned. For example, article 23, paragraph 4, stipulates that States parties shall take appropriate steps to ensure equality of rights as well as responsibilities of spouses as to marriage, during marriage and at its dissolution. Such steps may take the form of legislative, administrative or other measures, but it is a positive duty of States parties to make certain that spouses have equal rights as required by the Covenant. ...

6. ... the Covenant neither defines the term 'discrimination' nor indicates what constitutes discrimination. ...

7. ... the term 'discrimination' as used in the Covenant should be understood to imply any distinction, exclusion, restriction or preference which is based on any ground such as race, colour, sex, language, religion, political or other opinion, national or social origin, property, birth or other status, and which has the purpose or effect of nullifying or impairing the recognition, enjoyment or exercise by all persons, on an equal footing, of all rights and freedoms. ...

10. ... the principle of equality sometimes requires States parties to take affirmative action in order to diminish or eliminate conditions which cause or help to perpetuate discrimination prohibited by the Covenant. For example, in a State where the general conditions of a certain part of the population prevent or impair their enjoyment of human rights, the State should take specific action to correct those conditions. Such action may involve granting for a time to the part of the population concerned certain preferential treatment in specific matters as compared with the rest of the population. However, as long as such action is needed to correct discrimination in fact, it is a case of legitimate differentiation under the Covenant. ...

13. ... not every differentiation of treatment will constitute discrimination, if the criteria for such differentiation are reasonable and objective and if the aim is to achieve a purpose which is legitimate under the Covenant.

Obligations of States parties

11.94   States parties to the ICCPR undertake specific obligations with respect to the rights established or recognised in the Covenant. Article 2(1) requires that parties must 'respect and ensure' rights under the ICCPR to all persons within their territories and subject to their jurisdiction on a non-discriminatory basis. In particular, Art 2(2) requires that States parties must 'adopt such legislative or other measures as may be necessary to give effect to the rights recognised in the ... Covenant'. States must also ensure that those whose ICCPR rights have been violated shall have an effective remedy, even if the violation was committed by a person acting in an official capacity. The remedy shall be given by a competent judicial, administrative or legislative authority, and the State shall ensure that remedies are enforced (Art 2(3)).

11.95   It is apparent that a State must provide an effective remedy for the violation of a Covenant right perpetrated by a State official. A State will not be able to escape liability simply because the delinquent official was acting *ultra vires* in terms of domestic law.[127]

11.96   Generally speaking, the ICCPR does not impose obligations on States parties to prevent 'horizontal' violation of the rights recognised in the Covenant. A horizontal violation is one committed not by an official or agent of the State, but by a private party.

Thus, generally speaking, the State will not be liable for a violation of Art 6 of the ICCPR merely because a private criminal has arbitrarily deprived another person of his or her life. As a general matter of State responsibility, however, there may be exceptional circumstances in which a State is liable for the wrongful and injurious conduct of private parties. This will occur when the State failed to exercise due diligence to prevent the private delinquency from occurring.[128]

---

127. *Jegatheeswara Sarma v Sri Lanka* [2003] UNHRC 27. See also **5.26–5.28**.
128. See **5.32**. See also the judgment of the Inter-American Court of Human Rights in *Velasquez-. Rodriguez v Honduras* (1988) 9 HRLJ 212, para 172.

11.97   A failure properly to investigate or punish a delinquency committed by a private party will also sometimes engage a State's responsibility.[129]

11.98   On the subject of State liability for horizontal violations of rights recognised in the ICCPR, the Human Rights Committee has made the following remarks in its General Comment No 31 (2004):

> 8.   The article 2, paragraph 1, obligations are binding on States Parties and do not, as such, have direct horizontal effect as a matter of international law. The Covenant cannot be viewed as a substitute for domestic criminal or civil law. However the positive obligations on States Parties to ensure Covenant rights will only be fully discharged if individuals are protected by the State, not just against violations of Covenant rights by its agents, but also against acts committed by private persons or entities that would impair the enjoyment of Covenant rights in so far as they are amenable to application between private persons or entities. There may be circumstances in which a failure to ensure Covenant rights as required by article 2 would give rise to violations by States Parties of those rights, as a result of States Parties' permitting or failing to take appropriate measures or to exercise due diligence to prevent, punish, investigate or redress the harm caused by such acts by private persons or entities. States are reminded of the interrelationship between the positive obligations imposed under article 2 and the need to provide effective remedies in the event of breach under article 2, paragraph 3. The Covenant itself envisages in some articles certain areas where there are positive obligations on States Parties to address the activities of private persons or entities. For example, the privacy-related guarantees of article 17 must be protected by law. It is also implicit in article 7 that States Parties have to take positive measures to ensure that private persons or entities do not inflict torture or cruel, inhuman or degrading treatment or punishment on others within their power. In fields affecting basic aspects of ordinary life such as work or housing, individuals are to be protected from discrimination within the meaning of article 26.

Reservations

11.99   The ICCPR does not expressly forbid the making of reservations, and many States parties have made reservations to various of the Covenant's provisions. The law on reservations to treaties is discussed elsewhere.[130]

Derogations

11.100   There may be exceptional situations in which it is necessary, in the general interest, to attenuate or suspend the enjoyment of some civil and political rights.

---

129. See 5.84.
130. See 2.53–2.67 and 2.72–2.74. As to whether these general rules are fully applicable to human rights treaties generally and the ICCPR in particular, see 2.68–2.71.

For example, if a life-threatening epidemic takes hold in a particular place, the public interest may demand that the area be placed under quarantine until the medical emergency is brought under control. This would involve an attenuation of the right of free movement for those outside the quarantine area, and a suspension for those inside. Such a situation might, depending on the epidemiological nature of the threat, also require a suspension of the right of assembly inside the quarantined area.

Similarly, a natural disaster might exceptionally require the public authorities to compel temporarily persons to perform certain sorts of labour in order to save life or restore liveable conditions. For instance, in the event of a major flood which overwhelms the State's resources to respond, private boat owners might be required to assist in a search-and-rescue operation for survivors. This would involve a suspension of the boat owners' right not to perform compulsory labour.

11.101 The ICCPR permits these sorts of attenuations or suspensions in narrowly defined circumstances. The relevant provision reads as follows:

Article 4

1. In time of public emergency which threatens the life of the nation and the existence of which is officially proclaimed, the States Parties to the present Covenant may take measures derogating from their obligations under the present Covenant to the extent strictly required by the exigencies of the situation, provided that such measures are not inconsistent with their obligations under international law and do not involve discrimination solely on the ground of race, colour, sex, language, religion or social origin.

11.102 The public emergency must be an extremely serious one; it must 'threaten the life of the nation'. State practice indicates that a sufficiently serious, but localised, public emergency will justify derogations from civil and political rights.

An example is provided by the United Kingdom's response to the terrorist emergency in Northern Ireland, or Spain's response to a similar emergency in the Basque country.

In each case, it must be conceded, however, that terrorist attacks have also been extensively launched in parts of the country outside the localised epicentres. It would, nevertheless, be a perverse interpretation of Art 4(1) if genuine life-threatening, but localised, public emergencies could not be adequately responded to because they did not threaten the life of people throughout the entire country. In the case of geographically large States such as Australia, nothing short of full-scale foreign invasion, global natural catastrophe, or the appearance of an actual or potential nationwide epidemic would ever permit resort to Art 4.

11.103 It should also be recalled that derogations are permitted under Art 4(1) only 'to the extent strictly required by the exigencies of the situation'.

It is possible, therefore, that the complete suspension of a right might violate the ICCPR where the strictly required response might permit only a partial attenuation. For instance, a quarantine imposed on an epidemic-affected area might, depending on the nature of the epidemic, violate freedom of movement and the right to life if it unnecessarily prevented qualified medical personnel from entering and leaving the affected areas.

11.104 The public emergency must also be 'officially proclaimed'. The Human Rights Committee has observed that the requirement of official proclamation 'is essential for the maintenance of the principles of legality and rule of law at times when they are most needed', and that when making such a proclamation 'States must act within their constitutional and other provisions of law that govern ... the exercise of emergency powers'.[131]

11.105 Perhaps most importantly, Art 4(2) prescribes a range of ICCPR rights from which derogations are never permitted, even in the event of an officially proclaimed public emergency.

These are the right to life (Art 6); freedom from torture and cruel, inhuman or degrading treatment or punishment (Art 7); freedom from slavery and prohibition of the slave trade (Art 8(1)); freedom from servitude (Art 8(2)); non-imprisonment for breach of contractual obligations (Art 11); prohibition of retroactive criminal liability and penalties (Art 15); right to recognition as a person before the law (Art 16); and freedom of thought, conscience and religion (Art 18).

The Human Rights Committee is, however, of the view that this express list of non-derogable rights is not exhaustive. In the words of its General Comment No 29 (2001):

11. The enumeration of non-derogable provisions in article 4 is related to, but not identical with, the question whether certain human rights obligations bear the nature of peremptory norms of international law. The proclamation of certain provisions of the Covenant as being of a non-derogable nature, in article 4, paragraph 2, is to be seen partly as recognition of the peremptory nature of some fundamental rights ensured in treaty form in the Covenant (e.g., articles 6 and 7). However, it is apparent that some other provisions of the Covenant were included in the list of non-derogable provisions because it can never become necessary to derogate from these rights during a state of emergency (e.g., articles 11 and 18). Furthermore, the category of peremptory norms extends beyond the list of non-derogable provisions as given in article 4, paragraph 2. States parties may in no circumstances invoke article 4 of the Covenant as justification for acting in violation of humanitarian law or peremptory norms of international law, for instance by taking hostages, by imposing collective punishments, through arbitrary deprivations of liberty or by deviating from fundamental principles of fair trial, including the presumption of innocence.

12. In assessing the scope of legitimate derogation from the Covenant, one criterion can be found in the definition of certain human rights violations as crimes against humanity. If action conducted under the authority of a State constitutes a basis for individual criminal

---

131. General Comment No 29 (2001), para 2.

responsibility for a crime against humanity by the persons involved in that action, article 4 of the Covenant cannot be used as justification that a state of emergency exempted the State in question from its responsibility in relation to the same conduct. Therefore, the recent codification of crimes against humanity, for jurisdictional purposes, in the Rome Statute of the International Criminal Court is of relevance in the interpretation of article 4 of the Covenant.

13. In those provisions of the Covenant that are not listed in article 4, paragraph 2, there are elements that in the Committee's opinion cannot be made subject to lawful derogation under article 4. Some illustrative examples are presented below.

   (a) All persons deprived of their liberty shall be treated with humanity and with respect for the inherent dignity of the human person. Although this right, prescribed in article 10 of the Covenant, is not separately mentioned in the list of non-derogable rights in article 4, paragraph 2, the Committee believes that here the Covenant expresses a norm of general international law not subject to derogation. This is supported by the reference to the inherent dignity of the human person in the preamble to the Covenant and by the close connection between articles 7 and 10.

   (b) The prohibitions against taking of hostages, abductions or unacknowledged detention are not subject to derogation. The absolute nature of these prohibitions, even in times of emergency, is justified by their status as norms of general international law.

   (c) The Committee is of the opinion that the international protection of the rights of persons belonging to minorities includes elements that must be respected in all circumstances. This is reflected in the prohibition against genocide in international law, in the inclusion of a non-discrimination clause in article 4 itself (paragraph 1), as well as in the non-derogable nature of article 18.

   (d) As confirmed by the Rome Statute of the International Criminal Court, deportation or forcible transfer of population without grounds permitted under international law, in the form of forced displacement by expulsion or other coercive means from the area in which the persons concerned are lawfully present, constitutes a crime against humanity. The legitimate right to derogate from article 12 of the Covenant during a state of emergency can never be accepted as justifying such measures.

   (e) No declaration of a state of emergency made pursuant to article 4, paragraph 1, may be invoked as justification for a State party to engage itself, contrary to article 20, in propaganda for war, or in advocacy of national, racial or religious hatred that would constitute incitement to discrimination, hostility or violence.

14. Article 2, paragraph 3, of the Covenant requires a State party to the Covenant to provide remedies for any violation of the provisions of the Covenant. This clause is not mentioned in the list of non-derogable provisions in article 4, paragraph 2, but it constitutes a treaty obligation inherent in the Covenant as a whole. Even if a State party, during a state of emergency, and to the extent that such measures are strictly required by the exigencies of the situation, may introduce adjustments to the practical functioning of its procedures

governing judicial or other remedies, the State party must comply with the fundamental obligation, under article 2, paragraph 3, of the Covenant to provide a remedy that is effective.

11.106   The Human Rights Committee's reasoning in paras 11 and 12 of General Comment No 29 is clearly sound. If a form of conduct were to constitute a violation of the peremptory norms of international law *(jus cogens)* from which derogations are never permitted under international law, it would necessarily follow that the same conduct could not be a valid derogation under Art 4.[132]

Similarly, because the perpetration of war crimes and crimes against humanity will always result in individual criminal responsibility at international law, it must follow that such crimes cannot be valid derogations under Art 4.[133]

The Committee is, however, on less certain ground in paras 13 and 14. With the exception of genocide mentioned in para 13(c) and unjustified deportation and forcible transfer of populations mentioned in para 13(d), none of the measures referred to in paras 13 and 14 are war crimes, crimes against humanity, or undoubted violations of the *jus cogens*. In the case of these measures, the Committee is implicitly signalling its policy preference that the remaining measures nominated in paras 13 and 14 are such that they could never be 'strictly required to meet the exigencies' of an officially declared public emergency threatening the life of the nation.

Economic, social and cultural rights

11.107   Whereas the ICCPR is concerned primarily with the 'first generation' or classical liberal rights of the 18th and early 19th centuries, the International Covenant on Economic, Social and Cultural Rights is concerned mainly with the 'second generation' of aspirations that characterised many social reform movements of the later 19th century and the 20th century. The ICESCR has around 160 States parties, including Australia.

11.108   The ICCPR remains the premier international human rights instrument partly because the rights upon which it principally focuses require that the State refrain from taking specific actions (for example, unjustifiably interfering with the right of assembly), or that the State establish relatively limited mechanisms or structures which are well within the financial means of modern States (for example, ensuring that trials are fairly conducted).

This renders justiciable most of the rights recognised by the ICCPR, and explains the existence of an authoritative — albeit non-binding — semi-judicial mechanism for indicating a State's violations of the Covenant's obligations.

---

132. As to the *jus cogens,* see **2.106–2.110.**
133. As to war crimes and crimes against humanity, see chapter 10.

The ICESCR is less significant from a juridical perspective because the rights it asserts can, with two exceptions,[134] only be achieved by States committing themselves to the achievement of broadly stated policy goals which usually require the expenditure of large sums of money and a sustained political will over relatively long periods of time. The acceptance of a broad policy goal still leaves open the essentially political questions as to which mix of social and economic policies will be required to achieve and sustain it.

These are matters about which reasonable people of good faith may differ, and they explain the existence of political parties and other non-governmental organisations with mutually exclusive policies to achieve common broadly stated goals. It cannot, for instance, be determined by juridical means whether the rates of infant mortality (ICESCR, Art 12(2)(b)) would be best reduced by expending finite resources on more medical research, educating more health professionals, or upgrading the technical capacity of hospitals (or some mix thereof, or of other alternatives). Perhaps none of these policies would, in a given set of circumstances, result in a reduction of infant mortality rates. In any event, such questions can be determined only by making difficult public policy assessments with the assistance of the best available — but still frequently contradictory — technical advice. Bodies of legal experts are rarely the ideal entities to make such assessments.

11.109   The ICESCR does not possess a specialised quasi-judicial body similar to the ICCPR's Human Rights Committee with the authority to receive and consider communications from individuals and States alleging violations of the Covenant. Rather, States parties to the ICESCR are required to submit reports to the Committee on Economic, Social and Cultural Rights of the UN Economic and Social Council 'on the measures which they have adopted and the progress made in achieving observance' of the rights contained in the ICESCR.[135]

11.110   The central obligation of a State party under the ICESCR is to:[136]

> ... take steps, individually and through international assistance and co-operation, especially economic and technical, to the maximum of its available resources, with a view to achieving progressively the full realisation of the rights recognised in the ... Covenant by all appropriate means, including particularly the adoption of legislative measures.

States parties must also ensure that the rights enunciated in the ICESCR are exercised 'without discrimination of any kind as to race, colour, sex, language, religion, political or other opinion, national or social origin, property, birth or other status'.[137]

---

134. The exceptions are trade union rights (ICESCR, Art 8) and the right of every person to benefit from the protection of the moral and material interests resulting from any scientific, literary or artistic production of which he or she is the author (ICESCR, Art 15(1)(c)).
135. ICESCR, Art 16.
136. Ibid, Art 2(1).
137. Ibid, Art 2(2).

11.111   The rights to which this central obligation applies are the right of all peoples to self-determination;[138] the right to work;[139] the right to just and favourable conditions of work;[140] the right to form and join trade unions;[141] the right to social security, including social insurance;[142] the right to protection of and assistance to the family;[143] the right to an adequate standard of living;[144] the right to the highest attainable standard of physical and mental health;[145] the right to education;[146] and the right of every person to participate in cultural life, to enjoy the benefits of scientific progress, and to benefit from the protection of the moral and material interests resulting from any scientific, literary or artistic production of which he or she is the author.[147]

Discrimination against women

11.112   In 1967, the United Nations General Assembly adopted a Declaration on the Elimination of Discrimination against Women,[148] which was intended as a precursor to a multilateral treaty elaborating upon the declared rights and incorporating them into binding commitments. The result was the 1979 Convention on the Elimination of All Forms of Discrimination against Women (CEDW).[149] The CEDW has more than 185 parties, including Australia.

11.113   The broad goal for States parties to the CEDW is to 'pursue by all appropriate means and without delay a policy of eliminating discrimination against women'. This general objective is stipulated to require the following principal obligations:[150]

- embody the principle of the equality of men and women in national constitutions and other legislation, and ensure practical realisation of the principle;
- adopt legislative and other measures, including sanctions where appropriate, prohibiting discrimination against women;
- establish legal protection of women's equal rights, and ensure through tribunals and other public institutions the effective protection of women against any act of discrimination;
- refrain from any act or practice of discrimination against women;
- eliminate discrimination against women by any person, organisation or enterprise;

138. Ibid, Art 1.
139. Ibid, Art 6.
140. Ibid, Art 7.
141. Ibid, Art 8.
142. Ibid, Art 9.
143. Ibid, Art 10.
144. Ibid, Art 11.
145. Ibid, Art 12.
146. Ibid, Arts 13 and 14.
147. Ibid, Art 15.
148. General Assembly Resolution 2263 (XXII) (1967).
149. UNTS, Vol 1249, p 13.
150. CEDW, Art 2.

- modify or abolish existing laws and practices which constitute discrimination against women; and
- repeal all national penal provisions which constitute discrimination against women.

11.114 The key concept which is the focus of all the principal obligations is that of 'discrimination against women'. The CEDW defines this concept in the following terms:

Article 1

For the purposes of the present Convention, the term 'discrimination against women' shall mean any distinction, exclusion or restriction made on the basis of sex which has the effect or purpose of impairing or nullifying the recognition, enjoyment or exercise by women, irrespective of their marital status, on a basis of equality of men and women, of human rights and fundamental freedoms in the political, economic, social, cultural, civil or any other field.

This definition consists of two parts. The first deals with the practice of discrimination itself, and focuses on the drawing of distinctions, the imposition of exclusions, or the making of restrictions which impair or nullify equal treatment between the sexes to the detriment of women. There will be discrimination if the purpose of the practice is to impair or nullify. It will be enough, however, if the effect of the practice (regardless of the intended purpose) is to impair or nullify.

The second part of the definition deals with the fields in which the impairment or nullification occurs. This is stated so broadly as to be of limited juridical use — 'human rights and fundamental freedoms in the political, economic, social, cultural, civil or any other field'. The CEDW goes on, however, to specify a range of particular human rights fields in which the parties' principal obligations are to be brought to bear.

11.115 States parties to the CEDW are under an obligation to eliminate discrimination against women in the following specific fields: the political and public life of the country;[151] the opportunity to represent governments at the international level and to participate in the work of international organisations;[152] the acquisition, change or retention of nationality;[153] education and vocational training;[154] employment;[155] health care;[156] economic and social life, with particular reference to family benefits, access to financial credit, and participation in recreational, sporting and cultural activities;[157] various aspects of life in rural areas;[158] status before the law in civil matters, such as contract and property rights;[159] and marriage and family relations.[160]

---

151. Ibid, Art 7.
152. Ibid, Art 8.
153. Ibid, Art 9.
154. Ibid, Art 10.
155. Ibid, Art 11.
156. Ibid, Art 12.
157. Ibid, Art 13.
158. Ibid, Art 14.
159. Ibid, Art 15.
160. Ibid, Art 16.

11.116   Apart from these duties to 'eliminate discrimination', the CEDW imposes some more affirmative duties on States parties. There is an extremely broad obligation 'in all fields' to take measures that ensure 'the full development and advancement of women, for the purpose of guaranteeing them the exercise and enjoyment of human rights and fundamental freedoms on a basis of equality with men'.[161] States parties must also suppress the traffic in women and the exploitation of prostitution of women.[162]

Perhaps most ambitiously, the CEDW commits States parties to:[163]

> ... modify the social and cultural patterns of conduct of men and women with a view to achieving the elimination of prejudices and customary and all other practices which are based on the idea of the inferiority or the superiority of either of the sexes or on stereotyped roles for men and women.

11.117   States parties are also free to adopt measures sometimes referred to as 'affirmative action' or 'positive discrimination'. Temporary measures discriminating against men and in favour of women may be implemented where they are 'aimed at accelerating de facto equality between men and women', provided such measures 'in no way entail as a consequence the maintenance of unequal or separate standards' and provided they are 'discontinued when the objectives of equality of opportunity and treatment have been achieved'.[164]

11.118   A Committee on the Elimination of Discrimination against Women is established by Art 17 of the CEDW. The Committee consists of 23 experts elected by States parties to the Convention for renewable four-year terms, but the experts serve in their personal capacity and do not represent States. The main purpose of the Committee is to receive and consider reports from States parties 'on the legislative, judicial, administrative or other measures which they have adopted to give effect to the provisions of the ... Covenant and on the progress made in this respect'.[165] The Committee reports to the UN General Assembly through the Economic and Social Council, and may make suggestions and general recommendations based on examination of the reports and information received from the States parties.[166]

Children's rights

11.119   The international society of States began taking a formal interest in the welfare of children as early as 1924 with the adoption by the League of Nations Assembly of the Geneva Declaration of the Rights of the Child. The UN General Assembly followed up in 1948 with the UDHR, which provides:

---

161. Ibid, Art 3.
162. Ibid, Art 6.
163. Ibid, Art 5(a).
164. Ibid, Art 4.
165. Ibid, Art 18.
166. Ibid, Art 21.

Article 25

> 2. Motherhood and childhood are entitled to special care and assistance. All children, whether born in or out of wedlock, shall enjoy the same social protection.

In 1959, the General Assembly adopted its own Declaration on the Rights of the Child.[167] It was not until 1989, however, that the Convention on the Rights of the Child (CRC)[168] was opened for signature. The CRC came into force just nine months later — a record for multilateral human rights treaties — and, with more than 190 States parties, has the largest participation of any human rights treaty.

11.120   A child is 'every human being below the age of eighteen years unless, under the law applicable to the child, majority is attained earlier'.[169] A central obligation of States parties under the CRC is to:[170]

> ... respect and ensure the rights set forth in the ... Convention to each child within their jurisdiction, irrespective of the child's or his or her parent's or legal guardian's race, colour, sex, language, religion, political or other opinion, national, ethnic or social origin, property, disability, birth or other status.

States parties are also committed to 'undertake all appropriate legislative, administrative, and other measures for the implementation of the rights recognised in the ... Convention', although as regards economic, social and cultural rights, States parties are required only to 'undertake such measures to the maximum extent of their available resources and, where needed, in the framework of international co-operation'.[171]

11.121   A fundamental principle governing the effective discharge of all State party obligations under the CRC is that in:[172]

> ... all actions concerning children, whether undertaken by public or private social welfare institutions, courts of law, administrative authorities or legislative bodies, the best interests of the child shall be a primary consideration.

11.122   The CRC goes on to set out the rights to which the central obligations refer. These children's rights are:

- life, survival and development (Art 6);
- registration at birth, name and nationality (Art 7);
- preservation of identity, including nationality, name and family relations (Art 8);
- freedom from non-voluntary separation from parents, except in closely defined circumstances (Art 9);
- positive, humane and expeditious consideration of applications to reunite children separated from their parents by State borders (Art 10);

---

167. General Assembly Resolution 1386 (XIV) (1959).
168. UNTS, Vol 1577, p 3.
169. CRC, Art 1.
170. Ibid, Art 2(1).
171. Ibid, Art 4.
172. Ibid, Art 3(1).

- freedom of expression (Arts 12 and 13);
- freedom of thought, conscience and religion (Art 14);
- freedom of association and assembly (Art 15);
- respect for privacy, family, home and correspondence (Art 16);
- access to information and material from a diversity of sources (Art 17);
- freedom from violence, injury, abuse, negligence, neglect, maltreatment or exploitation (Art 19);
- special protection for children deprived of their family environment (Art 20);
- full and decent life for disabled children (Art 23);
- enjoyment of the highest attainable standard of health (Art 24);
- periodic review of cases of children placed in care (Art 25);
- social security (Art 26);
- adequate standard of living (Art 27);
- education (Arts 28 and 29);
- enjoyment of minority rights (Art 30);
- rest and leisure (Art 31);
- freedom from economic exploitation and hazardous work (Art 32);
- protection from the use of illicit drugs (Art 33);
- freedom from sexual exploitation and abuse (Art 34);
- protection from 'all other forms of exploitation prejudicial to any aspects of the child's welfare' (Art 36);
- freedom from torture or other cruel, inhuman or degrading treatment or punishment (Art 37(a));
- liberty of the person (Art 37(b)–(d));
- respect for international humanitarian law (Art 38); and
- procedural safeguards in criminal cases (Art 40).

11.123 States parties are also under an obligation to take measures to combat the illicit transfer and non-return of children abroad;[173] use their best efforts to ensure recognition of the principle that both parents have common responsibilities for the upbringing and development of the child;[174] observe certain safeguards and principles with respect to the adoption of children;[175] take measures to ensure that children seeking refugee status shall receive protection and humanitarian assistance applicable to them under the CRC and other human rights and humanitarian law instruments;[176] take measures to prevent the abduction or sale of, or the traffic in, children;[177] and take measures to promote the physical and psychological recovery and social reintegration of children traumatised by certain human rights abuses.[178]

---

173. Ibid, Art 11.
174. Ibid, Art 18.
175. Ibid, Art 21.
176. Ibid, Art 22.
177. Ibid, Art 35.
178. Ibid, Art 39.

11.124   A Committee on the Rights of the Child is established by Art 43 of the CRC. The Committee consists of 10 experts elected by States parties to the Convention for renewable four-year terms, but they serve in their personal capacity and do not represent States.

The main purpose of the Committee is to receive and consider reports from States parties 'on the measures they have adopted which give effect to the rights recognised [in the CRC] and on the progress made on the enjoyment of those rights'.[179]

Customary human rights

11.125   According to the International Court of Justice, some international human rights are obligations owed by States *erga omnes*. Such obligations do not depend on satisfying the rules of diplomatic protection on nationality of claims,[180] and all States can be held to have a legal interest in their protection regardless of the nationality of the persons whose rights have been violated.

Obligations *erga omnes* include the prohibition on genocide and 'rules concerning basic rights of the human person including protection from slavery and racial discrimination'.[181] They also include the right of self-determination of peoples.[182]

11.126   These obligations arise in accordance with the requirements of customary international law and especially the rules governing the transformation of conventional obligations into customary obligations.[183] They are also obligations of a *jus cogens* character, so that any attempt to derogate from them by treaty will be void.[184]

11.127   Not every violation of conventional human rights will simultaneously involve the breach of an *erga omnes* obligation. According to some publicists, the adoption of the UDHR, the ICCPR, the ICESCR and other human rights conventions, and the resolutions and practice of international bodies, have resulted in a 'general principle … prohibiting gross and large-scale violations of basic human rights and fundamental freedoms'.[185] On this view, less egregious or relatively small-scale violations of international human rights obligations will not entitle other States to make international claims under customary international law.

11.128   Other publicists take a somewhat more expansive view. According to the American Law Institute:[186]

---

179. Ibid, Art 44.
180. See 5.99–5.109.
181. *Case Concerning the Barcelona Traction, Light and Power Company Ltd (Belgium v Spain)* ICJ Rep (1970) 3, paras 33–34.
182. *Concerning East Timor (Portugal v Australia)* ICJ Rep (1995) 90, para 29.
183. See 1.138–1.146.
184. See 2.106–2.110.
185. Antonio Cassese, *International Law*, 2nd ed, Oxford University Press, New York, 2005, 59.
186. American Law Institute, *Restatement (Third) of the Foreign Relations Law of the United States*, 1987, Vol 1.

§ 702. Customary international law of human rights

A State violates international law if, as a matter of State policy, it practices, encourages, or condones

(a) genocide,

(b) slavery or slave trade,

(c) the murder or causing the disappearance of individuals,

(d) torture or other cruel, inhuman, or degrading treatment or punishment,

(e) prolonged arbitrary detention, or

(f) a consistent pattern of gross violations of internationally recognised human rights.

11.129   It would therefore appear that 'gross and large-scale violations of basic human rights' or 'a consistent pattern of gross violations of internationally recognised human rights' will engage a delinquent State's responsibility to all other States under customary international law.

However, some human rights obligations are so fundamental that a delinquent State may be responsible *erga omnes,* even if the violation is not gross, large-scale or part of a consistent pattern, provided they are practised, encouraged or condoned as a matter of State policy. These obligations include the prohibitions on genocide; slavery and the slave trade; murder; causing the disappearance of individuals; torture or other cruel, inhuman or degrading treatment or punishment; and prolonged arbitrary detention.

11.130   Where a State violates an obligation owed *erga omnes,* all other States are entitled to protest and seek remedies in accordance with the rules governing State responsibility and international dispute settlement.[187]

There is, however, very little State practice supporting a right to seek remedies for breaches of obligations *erga omnes.* The reality is that, where human rights are concerned, States generally have little motivation to make formal claims against other States. Another reason for such paucity of State practice is that customary international law provides no mandatory arbitral or judicial mechanisms for determining human rights claims between States.

Individuals do not possess remedies under customary international law, but may make claims and seek remedies in accordance with any applicable treaty provision.

11.131   Occasionally, States have sought to exercise the controversial right of humanitarian intervention by taking unilateral military action in the territory of another State in order to protect the lives of persons threatened by extreme humanitarian distress which the territorial State is unable or unwilling to prevent.[188]

---

187. See chapters 5 and 8.
188. See 9.68–9.77.

Question

John and Mary were a married couple who lived all their lives in the Republic of Daaih-gwok. In 2004, Mary gave birth to their first child, Sunny. John, Mary and Sunny were all citizens of Daaih-gwok. John is a clergyman in the Church of Faith, a significant religious denomination in Daaih-gwok. Mary and Sunny are also members of the Church of Faith.

In January 2009, Daaih-gwok experienced a military coup d'état which brought to power the Daaih People's Progressive Party (DPPP). The new regime publicly committed itself to a 'cultural revolution' in Daaih-gwok, including a 'strike-hard policy against all reactionary superstitions'.

One of the first measures of the new regime was the Anti-Superstition Decree, which:

(i) bans the Church of Faith;

(ii) requires all members of the Church to sign a declaration renouncing their religious beliefs and their Church membership;

(iii) imposes a mandatory death penalty on Church clergymen who refuse to sign the declaration; and

(iv) imposes indefinite imprisonment on other Church members until they sign the declaration.

The Decree also stipulates that imprisonment and the death penalty may be imposed by the 'Culture Commissioner', who is authorised to act on 'any information received if he believes it to be sufficiently well-founded'.

The Decree also provides that no decision of the Commissioner is to be challenged before, or reviewed by, any court or tribunal. The Culture Commissioner is a post established by the constitution of the DPPP, and is held by a member of that party's Central Committee.

John used his position as a clergyman to oppose publicly the Anti-Superstition Decree. He preached against the measure, and published articles in the Church press.

John and his family began receiving anonymous death threats, and on one occasion Mary discovered a bomb attached to the family car. The bomb was removed and disarmed by a Church member. Mary reported every incident to the police, but was repeatedly told only that her husband's law-breaking stance made many people understandably angry and that the police would do nothing to protect him or his family.

On the morning of 5 March 2009, a policeman visited John and Mary's family home. He presented John and Mary with declarations under the Anti-Superstition Decree, demanding their signatures. He also ordered John to sign a declaration on behalf of Sunny. When John and Mary refused to sign, the policeman arrested John, took him to the police station, and charged him with refusing to sign a declaration under the Anti-Superstition Decree.

Before leaving the house, the policeman told Mary that she should be careful about her own safety and that of Sunny because the police had received credible reports of further attacks on their family home. He also said that if she were still alive the next day, he would return to arrest her.

During the course of the afternoon, John was interrogated at a police station. He was told that if he did not provide a list of all Church members, the police would do nothing to save the lives of Mary and Sunny, who, they said, were in imminent mortal peril from persons planning to attack them. Upon hearing this assertion, John began sobbing and violently trembling, but refused to provide the requested list.

While John was being interrogated, the national commander of the police issued a widely reported public statement saying that John was a 'core leader of the illegal and subversive Church of Faith and the People will use the Anti-Superstition Decree to strike hard against this unpatriotic criminal'.

That evening, John and Mary's family home was attacked by a masked gang wielding machetes. Mary was hacked to death, but Sunny managed to escape. He fled to the house of a nearby Church member, who smuggled him out of the country on an international flight to the neighbouring State of Bakland. Sunny is now in temporary foster care with a Bakland family, pending a decision on his future status by Bakland's immigration authorities.

Prior to a determination of his fate by the Culture Commissioner, John was sent to a 're-education farm' in Daaih-gwok's remote hinterland. The re-education farm was established specifically for the purpose of receiving persons detained or convicted under the Anti-Superstition Decree. Although temperatures rarely rose above freezing, John and his fellow inmates were housed in unheated tents with only one threadbare blanket each to keep them warm at night. They worked in the fields during all daylight hours, and they were fed only a small quantity of plain rice every day.

Inmates who refused to work were beaten and denied food. The camp had no medical or sanitary facilities. In response to criticism by several foreign States concerning the conditions prevailing in the re-education farm, the DPPP defended the system by saying that Daaih-gwok is a developing country, the re-education farm must be financially self-supporting, and conditions on the farm could improve if the inmates worked harder and generated more income. After two months' detention, John had lost more than one-third of his bodyweight and had become dangerously undernourished.

All inmates of the re-education farm, including John, were required to attend daily re-education sessions before dawn. These sessions consisted of lectures and films aimed at persuading the inmates to abandon their allegiance to the Church of Faith and to sign the declaration under the Anti-Superstition Decree.

The inmates were told that early release would be available for those who signed. John refused all invitations to sign the declaration.

In May 2011, the Culture Commissioner secretly reviewed John's case file. The Commissioner decided that John was guilty of a capital offence under the Anti-Superstition Decree and ordered the re-education farm's commandant to place John in solitary confinement without food or water until he died. The commandant immediately complied with the order and, after four days of solitary confinement, John died of thirst, starvation and exposure to cold.

Under Bakland's current immigration policy, one of the relevant factors in deciding whether a foreign child may be granted a right of permanent residence is whether 'he or either of his parents has suffered abuses at the hands of their State of nationality in violation of international human rights obligations binding on that State'. If such abuses have occurred, they will be a factor in favour of granting permanent residence.

Daaih-gwok was, at all material times, party to the ICCPR and the CRC without reservations. It is not party to any additional protocols to either convention, nor is it party to any other relevant treaty.

The Bakland lawyers acting for Sunny's foster parents ask your advice as to whether Sunny or his parents suffered such abuses. Advise the Bakland lawyers.

Suggested answer

Sunny and his parents all suffered abuses at the hands of Daaih-gwok (their State of nationality) in violation of international human rights obligations binding on Daaih-gwok.

Right to life

Daaih-gwok was obliged to respect and ensure Mary's right to life (ICCPR, Arts 6 and 2(1)). This right will certainly be violated where the State's own forces arbitrarily deprive a person of his or her life *(Guerrero v Colombia)*.

The right to life will also be violated by a State where it fails to take all reasonable steps to protect the life of a person from killing by private persons where it has reasonable grounds to believe that the person's life is at risk. There is probably insufficient basis to conclude that Mary's life was taken by Daaih-gwok's own security forces. However, there is ample reason to conclude that the Daaih-gwok police knew, or ought to have known, at the time of the existence of a real and immediate risk to Mary's life from the criminal acts of a third party, and that they failed to take measures within the scope of their powers which, judged reasonably, might have been expected to avoid that risk *(Akkoç v Turkey)*.

Mary reported all the threats to the police and she reported the planting of a bomb on the family car. Indeed, on the day John was arrested, the police told John and Mary separately of credible reports that Mary and Sunny would be attacked by persons intent on killing them. Yet the police pointedly refused to take any steps whatsoever to protect Mary's life. Daaih-gwok therefore violated Mary's right to life.

Daaih-gwok was also obliged to respect and ensure John's right to life. Although the right to life is not inconsistent with capital punishment per se, sentence of death may be imposed only for the most serious crimes, only if it is not contrary to the requirements of the ICCPR, and only if it is pursuant to a final judgment rendered by a competent court (ICCPR, Art 6(2)). None of these three conditions are satisfied in the present case.

First, failure to sign a declaration renouncing one's religious faith and affiliation can hardly be described as a 'most serious crime'.

Second, the capital crime in this case was directly contrary to the requirements of the ICCPR, which guarantees freedom of thought, conscience and religion (see below).

Third, John's death sentence was not imposed by a competent court, as required by Art 6 of the ICCPR, but by a political official of the ruling party acting extra-judicially.

Fourth, a mandatory death penalty always constitutes an arbitrary deprivation of life, contrary to Art 6 of the ICCPR *(Thompson v Saint Vincent and the Grenadines; Kennedy v Trinidad and Tobago; Ramil Rayos v Philippines; Chan v Guyana; Larrañaga v Philippines)*. John's offence in refusing to sign the declaration as a clergyman in the Church of Faith carried a mandatory death penalty.

Finally, anyone sentenced to death shall have the right to seek pardon or commutation of the sentence (ICCPR, Art 6(4)). The Anti-Superstition Decree makes no provision for appeals from the death sentence, and John was not given any opportunity to make such an appeal.

Daaih-gwok therefore violated John's right to life.

Torture and cruel, inhuman or degrading treatment or punishment

Daaih-gwok was obliged to respect and ensure John's right not to be subjected to torture or to cruel, inhuman or degrading treatment (ICCPR, Arts 7 and 2(1)).

Torture consists of 'any act by which severe pain or suffering, whether physical or mental, is intentionally inflicted on a person for such purposes as obtaining from him … information … [or] punishing him' (Convention against Torture and Other Cruel, Inhuman or Degrading Treatment or Punishment, Art 1).

The Human Rights Committee considers it unnecessary to draw up a list of prohibited acts or to establish sharp distinctions between the different kinds of punishment or treatment, but supports the idea that Art 7 can be violated by acts that cause either physical or mental suffering (General Comment No 20, paras 4 and 5).

In the course of interrogating John on the day of his arrest, the police threatened that they would not save his wife and son from imminent mortal peril unless he complied with their demand to divulge the identities of Church members.

This assertion generated severe mental suffering in John (as evidenced by the sobbing and violent trembling that he immediately exhibited), and was made for the purpose of obtaining information from him.

John's method of execution (deprivation of food and water, and exposure to cold temperature, resulting in death after four days) caused 'prolonged suffering and agony and did not result in death as swiftly as possible' (*Ng v Canada,* in which this test was applied to support the view that gas asphyxiation taking 10 minutes to kill was too prolonged, and constituted a violation of Art 7 of the ICCPR).

Daaih-gwok therefore violated John's right not to be subjected to torture or to cruel, inhuman or degrading treatment.

Forced or compulsory labour

Daaih-gwok was obliged to respect and ensure John's right not to be subjected to forced or compulsory labour (ICCPR, Arts 8(3) and 2(1)). 'Compulsory labour' means 'all work or service which is extracted from any person under the menace of any penalty and for which the said person has not offered himself voluntarily' (ILO Convention No 29, Art 2(1)).

While interned at the re-education farm, John worked in the fields for more than two years under threat of beatings and denial of food. A person may be required to perform compulsory labour during penal servitude or judicial detention (ICCPR, Art 8(3)). However, John's detention was not judicially imposed and he had not been convicted of any crime at the time he was required to perform compulsory labour.

Daaih-gwok therefore violated John's right not to be subjected to forced or compulsory labour.

Arbitrary arrest and detention

Daaih-gwok was obliged to respect and ensure John's right to personal liberty and his right not to be subjected to arbitrary arrest and detention (ICCPR, Arts 9 and 2(1)).

A deprivation of liberty will certainly be arbitrary unless it is on grounds, and in accordance with procedures, established by law (ICCPR, Art 9(1)). Even where these formal requirements are satisfied, a deprivation of liberty will nevertheless be arbitrary if it is inappropriate and unjust in all the circumstances. Moreover, every decision to keep a person in detention should be open to review periodically, so that the grounds justifying the detention can be assessed (*A v Australia*). In John's case, his deprivation of liberty was inappropriate and unjust because it was directly contrary to the requirements of the ICCPR, which guarantees freedom of thought, conscience and religion and freedom of association (see below). The Anti-Superstition Decree makes no provision for review of detention, and John was held in detention for more than two years without any such review occurring.

A person arrested or detained on criminal charges must be brought promptly before a judicial officer and shall be released unless brought to trial within a reasonable time (ICCPR, Art 9(3)). Persons deprived of their liberty must also be able to take proceedings to test the legality of their detention (ICCPR, Art 9(4)). John was never brought before a judicial officer and he was not released, notwithstanding that it took more than two years for the Culture Commissioner to determine his case. Given the harshness of the conditions under which John was detained, this delay must be regarded as unreasonable. The Anti-Superstition Decree makes no provision for proceedings to test the legality of detention. Indeed, it expressly forbids any review of the Culture Commissioner's decisions, and no such review occurred.

Daaih-gwok therefore violated John's right to personal liberty and his right not to be subjected to arbitrary arrest and detention.

Humane treatment in detention

Daaih-gwok was obliged to respect and ensure John's right to be treated with humanity and with respect for his dignity while in detention (ICCPR, Arts 10 and 2(1)).

This requirement complements the ban on torture or other cruel, inhuman or degrading treatment or punishment. Detainees must not be subjected to any hardship or constraint, other than that resulting from the deprivation of liberty; respect for the dignity of such persons must be guaranteed under the same conditions as for that of free persons, subject to the restrictions that are unavoidable in a closed environment (General Comment No 21, para 3).

John's detention at the re-education farm was characterised by especially egregious hardships and constraints which extended far beyond those which were an unavoidable consequence of detention. In particular, John was required to endure for more than two years sub-freezing temperatures with only the shelter of tents and a single blanket. During this time, he was provided with no sanitary or medical facilities and he became malnourished as a result of a meagre diet. The threatened beatings and withdrawal of food were also an unnecessary hardship of his detention.

The essential aim of the penitentiary system must be the 'reformation and social rehabilitation' of prisoners (ICCPR, Art 10(3)). Nothing in the evidence suggests that the re-education farm system is directed to any such aim. On the contrary, the regime on these farms is entirely punitive. The re-education sessions cannot be regarded as 'reformation and social rehabilitation' for the purposes of Art 10(3), because they violate the ICCPR's guarantee of freedom of thought, conscience and religion (see below).

Treating all persons deprived of their liberty with humanity and with respect for their dignity is a fundamental and universally applicable rule. Consequently, the application of this rule cannot be dependent on the material resources available to a State. This rule must also be applied without distinction of any kind, such as religion (General Comment No 21, para 4). The DPPP's defence of the conditions on the re-education farm, on the ground that Daaih-gwok is a developing country, cannot justify those conditions *(Mukong v Cameroon)*. Furthermore, the re-education farm system is reserved for members or suspected members of the Church of Faith. It therefore violates the requirement of non-discrimination on religious grounds (ICCPR, Art 2(1)).

Daaih-gwok therefore violated John's right to be treated with humanity and respect for his dignity while in detention.

Equality before the law and fair trial

Daaih-gwok was obliged to respect and ensure John's right to equality before the law and to receive a fair trial (ICCPR, Arts 14 and 2(1)). In determination of the criminal charge against him, John was entitled to a fair and public hearing by a competent, independent and impartial tribunal established by law (ICCPR, Art 14(1)).

There is also a range of minimum procedural guarantees that must be observed in order for a trial to be considered fair (ICCPR, Art 14(3)). Here, there was no trial of any kind, and none of the minimum guarantees were satisfied. John's case was, instead, dealt with on the basis of a secret review of his file by a political authority.

Everyone charged with a criminal offence shall, furthermore, have the right to be presumed innocent until proved guilty according to law (ICCPR, Art 14(2)). In this connection, it is a duty of all public authorities, including the police, to refrain from prejudging the outcome of a trial and publicly condemning the accused (General Comment No 13, para 7; *Gridin v Russia*). In this case, the national commander of the police publicly accused John of committing offences under the Anti-Superstition Decree while he was still being interrogated.

Daaih-gwok therefore violated John's right to equality before the law and to receive a fair trial.

Freedom, religion and the right to hold opinions

Daaih-gwok was obliged to respect and ensure John's and Mary's freedom of religion and their right to hold opinions without interference (ICCPR, Arts 18, 19 and 2(1)). The freedom of religion includes a right to have or adopt a religion or belief of one's own choosing and freedom to manifest that religion or belief in worship, observance, practice and teaching (ICCPR, Art 18(1)).

It also includes a prohibition of coercion which would impair the freedom to have or adopt a religion or belief (ICCPR, Art 18(2)). This prohibition of coercion includes the use or threat of physical force or penal sanctions to compel believers to recant their religion or belief (General Comment No 22, para 5). John and Mary were threatened with penal sanctions unless they recanted their religious beliefs.

Parents must also be able to ensure the religious and moral education of their children in accordance with the parents' own convictions (ICCPR, Art 18(4)). This right was infringed by Daaih-gwok when it coercively required John and Mary to change Sunny's religious affiliation.

While in detention, John was subjected to daily mandatory 're-education sessions'. These sessions were aimed at persuading John to abandon his allegiance to the Church of Faith and to sign the declaration under the Anti-Superstition Decree. John was told that early release would be available if he signed. Coercive and discriminatory measures of this kind constitute a violation of the right to hold opinions without interference (*Kang v Korea*).

Daaih-gwok therefore violated John's and Mary's right to freedom of religion, and John's right to hold opinions without interference.

Protection of the child

Daaih-gwok was obliged to respect and ensure Sunny's right to protection (ICCPR, Arts 24 and 2(1)). Children are entitled to receive such measures of protection as are required by their status as minors on the part of their family, society and the State. They are entitled to this protection regardless of their religion (ICCPR, Art 24(1)).

These protective measures will include, at the least, preservation of family relations (CRC, Art 8); freedom of thought, conscience and religion (CRC, Art 14); and freedom from violence (CRC, Art 23). Sunny's family relations were destroyed by Daaih-gwok's conduct in breach of the requirements of international human rights.

John was removed from the family and ultimately executed in violation of his right to life, his right to fair trial, his freedom from arbitrary arrest and detention, and his freedom of religion. Mary was killed in a violation by Daaih-gwok of her right to life. Daaih-gwok attempted to coerce Sunny's parents, contrary to the requirements of international human rights, into changing Sunny's religious affiliation. Sunny's freedom of religion was thereby infringed. Sunny was the victim of an attempted murder by assailants whom the Daaih-gwok police took no measures to deter and in circumstances where the police had reasonable grounds to believe that Sunny's life would be at risk. Daaih-gwok thereby exposed Sunny to violence.

Consequently, Daaih-gwok violated Sunny's right to protection under the ICCPR and his right to preservation of family relations, freedom of religion, and freedom from violence under the CRC.

Further tutorial discussion

1. Why have human rights assumed an important place in international law only since the end of the Second World War?
2. Have international human rights made the law on diplomatic protection redundant?
3. Why should States make the treatment of their own nationals the subject of international treaties? Why should a State be concerned about the treatment of foreigners by their own States?
4. Should there be an International Court of Human Rights?

5. Why do economically developing States sometimes claim that they should not be expected to observe the same levels of human rights protection as developed States? Should developing States be permitted greater discretion than developed States in the extent to which they observe human rights?

Law of the sea 12

Objectives

After completing this chapter, you should:

(1 appreciate the pre-modern genesis of the law of the sea, including the contest between freedom of the sea and sovereignty of the sea;

(2) appreciate the role of the Hague Conference and the three United Nations conferences on the law of the sea in the creation of the modern law;

(3) appreciate that maritime zones are the main organising principle of the modern law of the sea;

(4) understand and be able to explain why the rules on baselines are essential to the system of maritime zones, and be able to contrast normal baselines with straight baselines;

(5) understand and be able to apply the rules on internal waters;

(6) understand and be able to apply the rules on territorial sea, especially including innocent passage;

(7) understand and be able to apply the rules on the contiguous zone;

(8) understand and be able to apply the rules on the exclusive economic zone (EEZ);

(9) understand and be able to apply the rules on the continental shelf;

(10) understand and be able to apply the rules on the high seas, with particular reference to the rules on flag State jurisdiction and hot pursuit;

(11) understand and be able to apply the rules on the international seabed; and

(12) be aware of the principles by which maritime boundary disputes are determined

Key cases

Anglo-Norwegian Fisheries case *(United Kingdom v Norway)* ICJ Rep (1951) 116
Corfu Channel Case (Merits) (United Kingdom v Albania) ICJ Rep (1949) 4
M/V 'Saiga' (No 2) case *(Saint Vincent and the Grenadines v Guinea)* (1999) 3 ITLOS Rep No 2, 37 ILM 1202
Case Concerning Maritime Delimitation in the Black Sea (Romania v Ukraine), International Court of Justice, judgment, 3 February 2009

Key treaties and instruments

Convention on the Law of the Sea (CLS) (1982)
Convention on the Territorial Sea and the Contiguous Zone (CTSCZ) (1958)

Convention on the High Seas (CHS) (1958)
Convention on the Continental Shelf (CCS) (1958)
Convention on Fishing and Conservation of the Living Resources of the High Seas (CFC) (1958)

Freedom of the sea and sovereignty of the sea

12.1 International law in every field owes a large debt to those statesmen and scholars who, in the 16th and 17th centuries, painstakingly established the earliest rules and principles by which Europe's leading maritime States coordinated their use of the sea. Together with the law regulating the use of armed force, the law of the sea is one of the twin pillars upon which all subsequent developments in international law have been built.

This foundation provided States with the fundamental techniques, methods and sources of legal reasoning by which their relations could be increasingly regulated by rules and principles possessing a legal character. Indeed, for the 350 years between the early 17th century and the end of the Second World War, the law of the sea and the regulation of armed force dominated the legal dimension of international relations.

12.2 During the Middle Ages, and as part of its prolonged and accelerating recovery from the collapse of the Roman Empire, European traders had increasing contact with China, South East Asia, and India. The origins of these contacts are usually traced to the 20-year journey of the Venetian adventurer Marco Polo (c 1254–1324) through those regions in the late 13th century. Polo's published account of his travels portrayed Eastern societies enjoying economic prosperity and technological prowess in advance of conditions then prevailing in Western Europe. His descriptions of exotic luxuries — particularly silks and spices — spurred others to explore avenues for trade with the Far East. It was soon apparent that substantial profits could be made by merchants importing Asian luxury goods into Europe.

By the late Middle Ages, the Silk Road and other overland caravan routes from Asia fed Europe's demand for Eastern goods in a trade dominated by the Arabs, Venetians and Genoese. Political stability provided reasonably secure conditions within which the overland trade between Europe and Asia could flourish. All this changed in the latter half of the 15th century with the turbulent collapse of Tamerlane's vast Mongol empire and the apparently inexorable rise of the Ottoman Turks, which was starkly evidenced by the Ottoman seizure of Constantinople in 1453.

The roads eastward ceased to provide a sufficiently economical or secure route for the Asian imports in respect of which increasingly prosperous Europeans had developed a firmly acquired taste, and for which they were prepared to pay handsomely.

It was against this background that the nascent maritime powers of Spain and Portugal — located far from the overland routes to Asia and facing the wide ocean — began their quests for a sea route to the Asian goods for which Europe's increasingly prosperous inhabitants clamoured.

12.3   The 1490s were a fateful decade for the modern law of the sea. In 1492, a Spanish expedition led by Christopher Columbus (1451–1506) discovered the Americas while on a quest to open a sea route to the East Indies. Six years later, the Portuguese navigator Vasco da Gama (c 1460–1524) succeeded in reaching India via Southern Africa. Columbus's discovery was mistakenly thought to have encroached upon Portugal's claims in East Asia and gave rise to jurisdictional questions concerning different Catholic religious orders engaged in missionary activities.

In 1493, in an attempt to settle these canonical issues, Pope Alexander VI issued a papal bull dividing between Spain and Portugal the entire non-European world which was accessible by sea. The Pope's determination was, with an alteration favourable to Portugal, given legal effect in 1494 by the Treaty of Tordesillas, which placed the dividing line at a north–south meridian which runs through present-day Brazil (and later extended to an anti-meridian on the opposite side of the world along a north–south line running through eastern Australia). Everything to the east of the meridian was to be Portugal's, and everything to the west, Spain's.

Neither the papal bull nor the Treaty of Tordesillas in terms divided the seas between Spanish and Portuguese sovereignties. Nevertheless, both Spain and Portugal subsequently gave the documents this interpretation when they sought to exclude foreign ships from trading in areas within their claimed areas. It was Portugal's claims to exclusive trading rights in India and East Asia, with an asserted concomitant right to exclude foreign shipping from the surrounding seas, that sparked the great struggle between proponents of freedom of the seas and sovereignty of the seas. This struggle gave birth to the modern law of the sea and, indeed, to much of modern international law generally.

12.4   The main challenge to Portuguese pretensions came from the Netherlands. In 1580, Spain and Portugal were effectively unified when the King of Spain assumed the Portuguese throne. The northern region of the Spanish Netherlands declared independence the following year. Up until that time, Dutch merchants had benefited from Spain's claimed maritime hegemony with Portugal, but now they were treated as foreigners and Portugal sought forcibly to exclude Dutch vessels from its lucrative trading routes in Asia. The Dutch, in turn, vigorously resisted Portugal's efforts to enforce its claimed exclusive trading rights.

In legal terms, matters came to a head in 1604. The Portuguese armed merchant vessel *Catharina* and its hugely valuable cargo, which had been captured by Dutch forces near Malaya, were declared forfeit by a Dutch prize court (the law of prizes is a branch of admiralty law which determines the status of a vessel and its cargo which have been seized by force in armed conflict). Hugo Grotius (1583–1645), widely regarded as the founder of modern international law, appeared in the prize court proceedings and was instrumental in securing the *Catharina*'s forfeiture.

Drawing on his pleadings in the *Catharina* case, Grotius wrote one of the great classics of international law, *De jure praedae commentarius (A Commentary on the Law of Prizes)*. The *Commentarius* was probably written in 1605 or 1606, although it was not published in Grotius's lifetime. It extended to matters well outside the immediate issues in the *Catharina* case, such as the jurisprudential foundations of law among sovereigns and the rules and principles regulating the international use of force.

12.5   The long war between Spain and its rebellious former provinces in the Netherlands drew to a conclusion in 1609 with a formal armistice. As part of the armistice negotiations, Spain and Portugal demanded that the Dutch refrain from trading in India, East Asia and the West Indies. Their argument was that the seas connecting Europe to these trading destinations were under the sovereign jurisdictions of Spain and Portugal, at least insofar as navigation for commercial purposes was concerned (Portuguese claims to sovereignty over the Indian Ocean extended to navigation for all purposes).

This maritime sovereignty was said to rest not only on the division effected by Pope Alexander VI, but also on discovery and prescription.[1] The idea that sovereign authority could extend to the seas was a credible element in the ideology of State sovereignty which had been gaining steady momentum in Europe since the late 16th century, and which was to win a major institutional victory in the 1648 Peace of Westphalia.[2]

Concerned that the Dutch government might concede to the Spanish and Portuguese demands in order to secure an armistice, the United East India Company (which enjoyed semi-official powers and a monopoly of Dutch trade in India and East Asia) requested Grotius to publish a chapter from the *Commentarius* which dealt with an asserted right to Dutch freedom of navigation for the purposes of trade with the Far East. Grotius's *Mare liberum sive de jure quod Batavis competit ad Indicana commercia dissertatio (The Freedom of the Seas or the Right which Belongs to the Dutch to Take Part in the Indian Trade)* was published in 1609. *Mare liberum* rejected claims to exclusive use of the seas and proved to be a work of monumental significance in the development of the law of the sea and of international law generally.

12.6   In rejecting Spanish and Portuguese claims, *Mare liberum* also engaged the interests of England, which had, since the defeat of the Spanish Armada in 1588, begun to supplant the Iberian kingdoms as the world's dominant maritime power. England had its own claims to

---

1.   See 7.21–7.23.
2.   See 1.10.

sovereignty over the seas. These claims were based mainly on a desire to exclude or restrict foreign fishing in waters claimed as English, but were also sometimes invoked to prevent ships trading with England's enemies during times of war.

Much less ambitiously than the Spanish and Portuguese claims over the broad oceans, England claimed sovereign rights over the seas abutting England's land territory (similar claims were made for Scotland, which shared a monarch with England after the accession to the English throne of Scotland's James VI in 1603).

England's claims to sovereignty embraced a ribbon of sea — of various widths at different times — immediately adjoining the land. Sometimes claims of a more extensive nature were made, so that the whole of the North Sea, the Irish Sea and the English Channel were included. The most influential English proponent of sovereignty over the seas was John Selden (1584–1654), who, in about 1618, wrote *Mare clausum sive de domino maris (The Closed Seas or the Sovereignty of the Seas)* as a rebuttal to *Mare liberum*. Initially suppressed for diplomatic reasons, *Mare clausum* was eventually published in 1635 with royal patronage.

12.7 The 17th-century controversy over whether the seas were inherently *free (mare liberum)* or subject to sovereignty *(mare clausum)* eventually resulted in a synthesis around which a broad consensus formed. By 1700, it was generally accepted that a claim to sovereignty over land or sea was justified by the fact of effective occupation, and not mainly by resort to arguments of a theological or philosophical character of the sort that tended to predominate during the earlier part of the century.

Initially, it was widely considered that effective occupation of the sea could be established by naval domination. However, the limited technological sophistication of ships in the 17th century, the endemic naval rivalry and warfare of the period, and the sheer scale of the world's oceans exposed the impossibility of using naval domination as a test for establishing effective maritime occupation. It came to be broadly accepted in European writings and practice that sovereignty could be exercised only in those parts of the sea where State power could be effectively projected. This meant, in practice, the seas immediately adjacent to a State's territory. Different claims were made as to the width of this 'territorial sea' or 'national sea'.

A frequently expounded rule was that States could claim sovereignty over so much of the sea as lay within range of cannon-shot from the shore. A claim of three miles[3] became common, although other claims of up to 100 miles were also sometimes made. Widespread disagreement over the maximum permissible width of the territorial sea endured until well into the 20th century, and unanimity does not exist even now.

12.8 By the turn of the 18th century, *mare clausum* had prevailed in relation to the territorial sea, but *mare liberum* was victorious in relation

---

3. All references to 'miles' in this chapter are to nautical miles. One nautical mile is equivalent to 1.15077945 statute miles, or 1.8520000031807997 kilometres.

to the vastly larger portion of the seas which lay beyond. Freedom of the seas had become freedom of the high seas. The United Kingdom, in full bloom as the dominant maritime power of the 18th and 19th centuries, emerged as the pre-eminent champion of freedom of the high seas.

Under this evolving regime, all States enjoyed a freedom to navigate the high seas for any purpose — although the rule did not require States to abandon the policy of mercantilism, in pursuance of which domestic laws were frequently enacted restricting international trade. Furthermore, the freedom of navigation on the high seas was not always respected, even by States which were its energetic advocates — for example, the United Kingdom's sustained campaign in the early 19th century to suppress the international slave trade by having the Royal Navy interdict suspect vessels of any nationality in the Atlantic Ocean.

The successful conclusion of the British naval and diplomatic campaign against the international slave trade coincided with the decline of mercantilism, the rise of international free trade, and the advent of steam-powered navigation. These developments heralded, in the mid-19th century, the apogee of the freedom of the high seas. This period also saw an erosion of sovereign powers in the territorial sea with the emergence of a right of innocent passage.

Codification of the law of the sea

12.9   From its origins at the end of the 15th century until the second half of the 20th century, the international law of the sea was almost entirely customary. A reasonably clear, stable and comprehensive set of customary rules and principles had emerged by the late 19th century. The establishment of the League of Nations after the First World War provided an opportunity for treaty codification and, in so doing, possible resolution of remaining points of disagreement among States.

Hague Conference

12.10   After six years of preparatory work by a League of Nations Committee of Experts, codification of the law on the territorial sea was among the tasks placed before the 1930 Hague Conference on the Codification of International Law. Although broad agreement was reached on the right of innocent passage and the extent of sovereign rights in the territorial sea, the Conference failed to produce a draft convention because of disagreement on the issue of the maximum permissible width of the territorial sea.

The main sticking point was fisheries conservation. The prevailing view was that jurisdiction over fisheries had to be co-extensive with the territorial sea, so that States which preferred more vigorous efforts to conserve fisheries desired a broader territorial sea than the three miles on offer at the Hague Conference. Many States favoured six miles, some wanted 12, while others made even larger claims extending out as far as the continental shelf. These more ambitious claims encroached on the high seas and, thereby, stood to diminish the geographical scope of the freedom to navigate and harvest resources which were enjoyed by all States in those waters.

UNCLOS I and UNCLOS II

12.11 No further substantive progress on codification was made until after the Second World War and the establishment of the United Nations. The codification and progressive development of the law of the sea were taken up by the International Law Commission,[4] which, after six years of work, submitted draft Articles on the law of the sea to the General Assembly in 1956. Two years later, the first United Nations Conference on the Law of the Sea (UNCLOS I) was held in Geneva. The result was four conventions dealing with different aspects of the law of the sea: the Convention on the Territorial Sea and the Contiguous Zone (CTSCZ);[5] the Convention on the High Seas (CHS);[6] the Convention on the Continental Shelf (CCS);[7] and the Convention on Fishing and Conservation of the Living Resources of the High Seas (CFC).[8] Australia ratified the four conventions in 1963, and they had all entered into force by 1966.

12.12 The four Geneva Conventions attracted reasonably widespread adherence by States, mainly because each Article was adopted by a two-thirds majority vote of the States participating in UNCLOS I. Nevertheless, the juridical stability which might have been expected to flow from UNCLOS I did not materialise. There were three principal reasons for this.

First, as with the 1930 Hague Conference, UNCLOS I did not produce agreement on the width of the territorial sea. This was a significant weakness in the UNCLOS I regime. A second United Nations Conference on the Law of the Sea (UNCLOS II) was convened in 1960 in order to settle this matter and the closely related issue of State jurisdiction over fisheries. However, UNCLOS II failed to produce an agreement, as leading maritime States continued to favour a three-mile territorial sea while many others continued to press their more ambitious claims. The Conference narrowly rejected a compromise proposal for a six-mile territorial sea and an adjacent six-mile fisheries zone.

Second, UNCLOS I was concluded during the early stage of decolonisation. Within 15 years of the Conference, there was a dramatic increase in the number of the world's States. The United Nations had 82 members in 1958, but by 1974 that number had grown to 138. Almost all the new States were coastal. Although many of these States accepted

---

4.   See **1.54**.
5.   UNTS, Vol 516, p 205.
6.   UNTS, Vol 450, p 11.
7.   UNTS, Vol 499, p 311.
8.   UNTS, Vol 559, p 285.

the results of UNCLOS I and became parties to the Geneva Conventions, many others embraced the ideological position that they should not be required to accept treaty terms 'imposed' by older developed States allegedly against the interests of newer developing States.

In particular, many new States sought to resurrect the spirit of *mare clausum* by asserting sovereign or exclusive economic rights over natural resources located in the high seas but proximate to their territories, even where they lacked the technological expertise or capital to exploit those resources. This revision of the international maritime order was vigorously asserted to be a cure for economic underdevelopment. In this cause, many new States took a political lead from the Soviet bloc and the rulers of the Chinese mainland.

The implausibility of the asserted link between economic under development and the prevailing freedom of the high seas was obscured by the international politics of the Cold War. The strengthening political influence of the Soviet Union, Mainland China, and their clients in the 'Non-Aligned' movement of numerous developing and socialist-orientated States during this period provided a powerful impetus for revising UNCLOS I. The increasing possibilities for exploiting the mineral resources of the international seabed were a third factor in favour of a revision of UNCLOS I. Up until the 1960s, it remained virtually impossible to access minerals in deeper waters economically, but technology was by then beginning to make significant progress against the barriers placed by nature in the way of mining the international seabed.

The exploitation of international seabed mineral resources became increasingly feasible. These scientific developments were used to buttress the political campaign tendentiously associating the plight of underdeveloped States with their lack of exclusive rights to the exploitation of resources located in the high seas.

UNCLOS III

12.13 The third United Nations Conference on the Law of the Sea (UNCLOS III) began its work in 1973, and held its first major session in Caracas the following year. Its deliberations were to span 11 major sessions and were not concluded until 1982. The protracted nature of the process was consistent with the difficult task confronting the Conference, whose brief was the preparation of a comprehensive treaty on all important aspects of the law of the sea. This involved brokering numerous complex and difficult compromises among a large number of States with differing, and frequently contradictory, interests.

The result was the 1982 United Nations Convention on the Law of the Sea (CLS),[9] a comprehensive treaty of 320 articles and nine annexes. It is without doubt one of the most important artefacts of international

---

9. UNTS, Vol 1833, p 3.

law. Because of the delicate and interlocking nature of the numerous compromises which the CLS incorporates, it was drafted as a package. Parties are generally not permitted to make any reservations or enter any exceptions.[10]

The CLS covers all the topics of the four Geneva Conventions, and establishes new legal regimes concerning the exclusive economic zone (EEZ) and the international seabed. In relation to the matters covered by the Geneva Conventions, the CLS sometimes merely repeats the earlier provisions, and sometimes lays down different or more detailed requirements.

12.14   The early life of the CLS was not without its difficulties. As noted earlier, the Convention's genesis lay largely in the international politics of the Cold War. Its more controversial provisions were not harmonious with the interests of developed States which favoured a more liberal regime in relation to non-territorial seas and the international seabed. These differences meant that it was difficult to attract ratifications of the CLS from developed States. Indeed, almost all the ratifications before the Convention's entry into force in 1994 were from developing States.

The main obstacles to ratification for most developed States were the original CLS provisions on the international seabed, which, in the view of most developed States, unreasonably sought to lock maritime resources away from those most able to extract them. This obstacle was, however, effectively overcome by 1994.[11]

12.15   The law of the sea is now a patchwork. All States are bound by the customary rules, except in their relations with other States with which they have concluded one or more of the 1958 and 1982 conventions — in which case, the treaty provisions will prevail if they are inconsistent with custom. The Convention obligations will apply concurrently with custom if the conventional rule codifies or reflects customary law.

As between States which are parties to the same Geneva Conventions, there is also the impact of any reservations which they may have made.

Some new customary rules, binding on all States, may also have crystallised as a result of the widespread ratification and implementation of the conventions and as a result of non-parties adopting the conventional rules in their State practice out of a sense of legal obligation.[12]

Some States are parties to one or more of the Geneva Conventions but not the CLS, and other States are parties to the CLS but not all of the Geneva Conventions. Their relations *inter se* will be governed by customary law as modified by the impact of the conventions on State practice and *opinio juris*. There are about 160 parties to the CLS, but that

---

10.   CLS, Art 309: 'No reservations or exceptions may be made to this Convention unless expressly permitted by other articles of this Convention.'
11.   See **12.106–12.108**.
12.   *North Sea Continental Shelf* cases *(Germany v Denmark, Germany v The Netherlands)* ICJ Rep (1969) 3, paras 71–74. See **1.140**.

means there are about 30 States which are not parties to it — including the United States. In Australia's region, East Timor has not acceded to the CLS, while Cambodia, North Korea and Thailand have signed but not ratified it. The CTSCZ, the CHS and the CCS each have between 50 and 60 parties, while the CFC has fewer than 40 parties.

In addition to all this, there are numerous bilateral and regional treaties relating to maritime matters (for example, maritime boundary treaties and regional treaties on fisheries and maritime pollution), and the possibility of local customary law of the sea.

Maritime zones

12.16   The modern law of the sea deals with the competing interests of States in the world's seas and submerged lands by dividing them into several zones defined by their geographical relationship to a State's territory, the uses to which they may be put, and the conditions attached to such uses. Indeed, maritime zones furnish the organising principle around which the modern law of the sea is structured. The seven maritime zones recognised in, or established by, the CLS are internal waters; territorial sea; contiguous zone; exclusive economic zone; high seas; continental shelf; and international seabed. There are also special legal regimes for straits and archipelagic States.

Baselines

12.17   The baseline is a legal device upon which almost the whole system of maritime zones depends. The locations of all maritime zones, except the international seabed, are completely or partly determined by reference to baselines.

Baselines are drawn by reference to a State's land territory. For this purpose, islands and even exposed rocks may frequently be useful in extending the geographic scope of a State's claims to the sea.[13] A valid claim to sovereignty over an island can, therefore, vastly extend the reach of a State's rights to regulate navigation and exploitation of the sea's resources. It is this feature of the law of the sea which usually explains the considerable effort occasionally exerted by States in establishing sovereignty over sometimes small, uninhabited, remote and inhospitable islands or rocky outcrops.

Normal baselines

12.18   The 'normal baseline' is 'the low-water mark along the coast as marked on large-scale charts officially recognised by the coastal State'.[14]

---

13.   See 12.31.
14.   CLS, Art 5 and CTSCZ, Art 3.

Baselines will, therefore, usually follow the contours of a coast at its low-water mark. Such baselines will never be perfectly straight, unless perhaps a section of the coast has been artificially altered.

12.19   Using normal baselines will generally present no difficulties where the coast is not excessively indented, fringed by islands, or pitted by bays, harbour works and rivers flowing into the sea. In such cases, States may be permitted to draw baselines according to different rules.

Straight baselines

12.20   In localities 'where the coastline is deeply indented and cut into, or if there is a fringe of islands along the coast in its immediate vicinity, the method of straight baselines joining appropriate points may be employed in drawing the baseline from which the breadth of the territorial sea is measured'.[15] In such cases, the:[16]

> ... drawing of straight baselines must not depart to any appreciable extent from the general direction of the coast, and the sea areas lying within the lines must be sufficiently closely linked to the land domain to be subject to the regime of internal waters.

This rule reflects customary law, as formulated in a judgment of the International Court of Justice.

> In the ***Anglo-Norwegian Fisheries* case** (for the facts of which, see 1.119), the International Court of Justice said:[17]
>
> > The Court has no difficulty in finding that, for the purpose of measuring the breadth of the territorial sea, it is the low-water mark, as opposed to the mean between the two tides, which has generally been adopted in the practice of States. This criterion is the most favourable to the coastal State and clearly shows the character of territorial waters as appurtenant to the land territory. The Parties also agree that in the case of a low-tide elevation (drying rock) the outer edge at low water of this low-tide elevation may be taken into account as a base-point for calculating the breadth of the territorial sea ...
> >
> > The Court finds itself obliged to decide whether the relevant low-water mark is that of the mainland or of the 'skjaergaard'. Since the mainland is bordered in its western sector by the 'skjaergaard' which constitutes a whole with the mainland, it is the outer line of the 'skjaergaard', which must be taken into account in delimiting the belt of Norwegian territorial waters. This resolution is dictated by geographic realities.
> >
> > Three methods have been contemplated to effect the application of the low-water mark rule. The simplest would appear to be the method of the *tracé parallèle*, which consists of drawing the outer limit of the belt of territorial waters by following the coast in all its sinuosities. This method may be applied without difficulty to an ordinary coast, which is not too broken. Where a coast is deeply indented and cut into ... or where it is bordered by an archipelago such as the 'skjaergaard' ..., the baseline becomes independent of the low-water mark, and can only be determined by means of geometric construction.

---

15.   CLS, Art 7(1) and CTSCZ, Art 4(1).
16.   CLS, Art 7(3) and CTSCZ, Art 4(3).
17.   *Anglo-Norwegian Fisheries* case *(United Kingdom v Norway)* ICJ Rep (1951) 116, 128–142.

In such circumstances the line of the low-water mark can no longer be put forward as a rule requiring the coast line to be followed in all its sinuosities. Nor can one characterise as exceptions to the rule the very many derogations which would be necessitated by such a rugged coast; the rule would disappear under the exceptions. Such a coast, viewed as a whole, calls for the application of a different method; that is, the method of baselines which, within reasonable limits, may depart from the physical line of the coast. ...

The principle that the belt of territorial waters must follow the general direction of the coast makes it possible to fix certain criteria valid for any delimitation of the territorial sea; these criteria will be elucidated later. The Court will confine itself at this stage to noting that, in order to apply this principle, several States have deemed it necessary to follow the straight baselines method and that they have not encountered objections of principle by other States. This method consists of selecting appropriate points on the low-water mark and drawing straight lines between them. This has been done, not only in the case of well-defined bays, but also in case of minor curvatures of the coastline where it was solely a question of giving simpler form to the belt of territorial waters.

It has been contended, on behalf of the United Kingdom, that Norway may draw straight lines only across bays. The Court is unable to share this view. If the belt of the territorial waters must follow the outer line of the 'skjaergaard', and if the method of straight baselines must be admitted in certain cases, there is no valid reason to draw them only across bays ... and not also to draw them between islands, islets and rocks, across the sea areas separating them, even when such areas do not fall within the conception of a bay. It is sufficient that they should be situated between the island formations of the 'skjaergaard', *inter fauces terrarium*.[18] ...

The Court now comes to the question of the length of the baselines drawn across the waters lying between the various formations of the 'skjaergaard'. ... [T]he United Kingdom ... maintains on this point that the length of straight lines must not exceed 10 miles. In this connection, the practice of States does not justify the formulation of any general rule of law. The attempts that have been made to subject groups of islands or coastal archipelagoes to conditions analogous to the limitations concerning bays ... have not got beyond the stage of proposals. Furthermore, apart from any question of limiting the lines to 10 miles, it may be that several lines can be envisaged. In such cases the coastal State would seem to be in the best position to appraise the local conditions dictating the selection. ...

The delimitation of sea areas has always an international aspect; it cannot be dependent merely upon the will of the coastal State as expressed in its municipal law. Although it is true that the act of delimitation is necessarily a unilateral act, because only the coastal State is competent to undertake it, the validity of the delimitation with regard to other States depends upon international law. In this connection, certain basic considerations inherent in the nature of the territorial sea, bring to light certain criteria which, though not entirely precise, can provide courts with an adequate basis for their decisions, which can be adapted to the diverse facts in question.

Among these considerations, some reference must be made to the close dependence of the territorial sea upon the land domain. It is the land which confers upon the coastal State a right to the waters off its coasts. It follows that

---

18.   Meaning 'between the jaws of the land'.

while such a State must be allowed the latitude necessary in order to be able to adapt its delimitation to practical needs and local requirements, the drawing of baselines must not depart to any appreciable extent from the general direction of the coast.

Another fundamental consideration, of particular importance in this case, is the more or less close relationship existing between certain sea areas and the land formations which divide or surround them. The real question raised in the choice of baselines is in effect whether certain sea areas lying within these lines are sufficiently closely linked to the land domain to be subject to the regime of internal waters. This idea, which is at the basis of the determination of the rules relating to bays, should be liberally applied in the case of a coast, the geographical configuration of which is as unusual as that of Norway. …

The Norwegian Government admits that the baselines must be drawn in such a way as to respect the general direction of the coast and that they must be drawn in a reasonable manner. …

It should be observed that, however justified the rule in question may be, it is devoid of any mathematical precision. In order properly to apply the rule, regard must be had for the relation between the deviation complained of and what, according to the terms of the rule, must be regarded as the *general* direction of the coast. Therefore, one cannot confine oneself to examining one sector of the coast alone, except in the case of manifest abuse.

The Court found that the baselines used by Norway to delimit its 'fisheries zone' were not contrary to international law.

12.21 The International Court of Justice in the *Anglo-Norwegian Fisheries* case also observed that, in drawing baselines, there is another:[19]

... consideration not to be overlooked, the scope of which extends beyond purely geographical factors: that of certain economic interests peculiar to a region, the reality and importance of which are clearly evidenced by a long usage.

The Court was impressed by the fact that, in a particularly contentious section of the internal waters and territorial sea claimed by Norway as a result of the baselines it had proclaimed, Norwegian nationals had long been economically dependent on fishing. According to the Court:[20]

Such rights, founded on the vital needs of the population and attested by very ancient and peaceful usage, may legitimately be taken into account when drawing a line which ... appears to the Court to have been kept within the bounds of what is moderate and reasonable.

Norway had, moreover, for some 80 years made territorial claims to those fishing grounds without any objection from the United Kingdom until after about 60 years of that period had elapsed, and without any objection whatever from other States.

The language used by the Court to emphasise the relevance of long-established and important economic interests in determining the international validity of straight baselines is closely reflected in the drafting of the conventions, which provide that, where the method of

---

19. *Anglo-Norwegian Fisheries* case *(United Kingdom v Norway)* ICJ Rep (1951) 116, 133.
20. Ibid, 142.

straight baselines is applicable, 'account may be taken, in determining particular baselines, of economic interests peculiar to the region concerned, the reality and the importance of which are clearly evidenced by long usage'.[21]

12.22 An important conventional limitation on the use of straight baselines is the requirement that they 'shall not be drawn to and from low-tide elevations, unless lighthouses or similar installations which are permanently above sea level have been built on them'.[22] A 'low-tide elevation' is a 'naturally formed area of land which is surrounded by and above water at low tide but submerged at high tide'.[23] This limitation is intended to prevent States from abusively extending the reach of their maritime zones by using semi-submerged rocks over which they claim territorial sovereignty as a basis for drawing straight baselines. Some low-tide elevations may, however, be used to draw a variant of normal baselines.[24]

Deltas

12.23 Sometimes, a section of coast may be highly unstable because of the presence of a delta which may change shape over relatively short periods of time. The CLS provides that in such a case:[25]

> ... the appropriate points [for drawing straight baselines] may be selected along the furthest seaward extent of the low-water line and, notwithstanding subsequent regression of the low-water line, the straight baselines shall remain effective until changed by the coastal State in accordance with this Convention.

This provision was inserted into the CLS at the behest, and primarily for the benefit, of Bangladesh. The CTSCZ contains no similar provision.

River mouths

12.24 Most rivers flowing into the sea do not create deltas. The conventions provide that, in such cases, 'the baseline shall be a straight line across the mouth of the river between points on the low-water line of its banks'.[26]

Bays

12.25 Bays have customarily been treated as part of a State's internal waters, so that 'closing lines' drawn between the bay's entrance points

---

21. CLS, Art 7(5) and CTSCZ, Art 4(4).
22. CLS, Art 7(4) and CTSCZ, Art 4(3) (the CLS provision addends the phrase 'or except in instances where the drawing of baselines to and from such elevations has received general international recognition').
23. CLS, Art 13(1) and CTSCZ, Art 11(1).
24. See 12.30.
25. CLS, Art 7(2).
26. CLS, Art 9 and CTSCZ, Art 13.

(that is, across the bay's mouth) provided the boundary between the State's internal waters and its territorial sea. Customary international law provided, however, little guidance on when an indentation in a coast properly constitutes a 'bay'.

According to the conventions, a 'bay' is a 'well-marked indentation whose penetration is in such proportion to the width of its mouth as to contain land-locked waters and constitute more than a mere curvature of the coast'. This provides some guidance, but not an accurate measure. The same provisions in the conventions proceed to provide a more geometrically precise test by stipulating that an indentation 'shall not … be regarded as a bay unless its area is as large as, or larger than, that of the semi-circle whose diameter is a line drawn across the mouth of that indentation'.[27]

12.26   Prior to the CTSCZ, it is likely that there was no maximum distance for a closing line across the mouth of a bay at customary international law.[28]

The conventions take a different approach. A closing line not exceeding 24 miles in length may be drawn between the low-water marks of the two natural entrance points to the bay.[29] Where the distance between the two natural entrance points is greater than 24 miles, 'a straight baseline of 24 nautical miles shall be drawn within the bay in such a manner as to enclose the maximum area of water that is possible with a line of that length'.[30]

12.27   In the *Land, Island and Maritime Frontier Dispute* case, the International Court of Justice remarked that these conventional provisions regarding bays 'might be found to express general customary law'.[31]

Harbour works

12.28   Ports and harbours are always host to at least some form of artificial infrastructure, however minimal. Developed ports will usually feature extensive and elaborate installations designed to facilitate the business of shipping. These installations, including breakwaters, will sometimes extend out into the surrounding sea. The conventions provide that 'the outermost permanent harbour works which form an integral part of the harbour system are regarded as forming part of the coast'.[32] Thus, the outermost permanent harbour works are assimilated to the coastline, with the consequence that the baseline will be drawn along

---

27. CLS, Art 10(2) and CTSCZ, Art 7(2).
28. *North Atlantic Coast Fisheries Case (United Kingdom v United States)* (1910) 11 RIAA 167; *Anglo-Norwegian Fisheries* case *(United Kingdom v Norway)* ICJ Rep (1951) 116.
29. CLS, Art 10(4) and CTSCZ, Art 7(4).
30. CLS, Art 10(5) and CTSCZ, Art 7(5).
31. *Land, Island and Maritime Frontier Dispute* case *(El Salvador v Honduras: Nicaragua intervening)* ICJ Rep (1992) 351, 588.
32. CLS, Art 11 and CTSCZ, Art 8 (the CLS provision adds that offshore installations and artificial islands shall not be considered permanent harbour works).

the low-water mark of those works. The tribunal in the *Dubai–Sharjah Border Arbitration* indicated that these conventional rules had entered into customary international law.[33]

Roadsteads

12.29 Roadsteads are installations erected at sea for the purpose of loading and unloading ships and for their anchorage. These installations are not used to draw baselines. Rather, they are included in a State's territorial sea if they would otherwise be outside the territorial sea.[34] Thus, a roadstead located outside the ordinary territorial sea becomes an enclave of territorial sea completely surrounded by non-territorial sea, or an exceptional extension of the territorial sea if only part of it is located outside the ordinary territorial sea.

The installation so affected is, of course, territorial 'sea' only as a legal fiction. The intention is clearly that the State may exercise the same rights and shoulder the same duties of territorial sovereignty over the installation as apply in the territorial sea.

Low-tide elevations

12.30 Although low-tide elevations may not be used to draw straight baselines,[35] their low-water marks may be used to draw baselines where they are wholly or partly within the territorial sea from the mainland or an island.[36] In other words, low-tide elevations within the width of the territorial sea from the mainland or an island generate their own territorial sea. Other low-tide elevations do not generate their own territorial sea, and are of no account in drawing baselines.[37]

Islands and reefs

12.31 Before the conventions, customary international law accepted that an island generates its own territorial sea and that the baseline is the island's low-water mark. In this respect, islands were treated in the same way as coasts for the purpose of generating territorial sea. What was not so clear was whether islands which were so small or barren that they could not support their own human habitation or economic life (for example, 'islands' which were simply exposed rocks) could generate maritime zones in the same way that more substantial or hospitable islands could. The conventions resolve these uncertainties by providing that an island is any 'naturally formed area of land, surrounded by water, which is above water at high tide'.[38] Therefore, even small rocks,

---

33. *Dubai–Sharjah Border Arbitration (Dubai v Sharjah)* (1981) 91 ILR 543, 661–662.
34. CLS, Art 12 and CTSCZ, Art 9.
35. See **12.22**.
36. CLS, Art 13(1) and CTSCZ, Art 11(1).
37. CLS, Art 13(2) and CTSCZ, Art 11(2).
38. CLS, Art 121(1) and CTSCZ, Art 10(1).

provided they are naturally formed, exposed and surrounded by water at high tide, are islands for the purposes of baselines.

According to the conventions, all islands generate their own territorial sea in exactly the same way as coastal areas.[39] The CLS provision goes further by stipulating that all islands generate their own contiguous zone (this is implicit also in the CTSCZ). The question as to whether an island can support its own human habitation or economic life remains alive, however, because the CLS provides that only such islands can generate their own EEZ and continental shelf.[40]

12.32   A special problem is posed by islands situated on reefs (that is, atolls) or islands fringed by reefs. Should the island's baseline be drawn at its low-water mark, or should the baseline be drawn along the reef's edge? In answering this question, should it matter whether the reef is occasionally or permanently submerged? The Geneva Conventions did not address these questions, but the establishment of some island-States in the Pacific and Indian Oceans and the Caribbean Sea after 1958 prompted their inclusion in the work of UNCLOS III. The result was Art 6 of the CLS:

> **Reefs**
>
> In the case of islands situated on atolls or of islands having fringing reefs, the baseline for measuring the breadth of the territorial sea is the seaward low-water line of the reef, as shown by the appropriate symbol on charts officially recognized by the coastal State.

This provision makes it clear that the baseline may be drawn from the reef's edge, rather than from the island's low-water line.

However, the reference to the reef's low-water line strongly indicates that permanently submerged reefs may not provide baselines. From the perspective of marine conservation this is not too problematic, as an EEZ may extend up to 200 miles from the island's low-water line.[41]

Archipelagic States

12.33   Archipelagos were not the subject of separate treatment under the Geneva Conventions, but the establishment after 1958 of a significant number of States based in archipelagos made their status a task for UNCLOS III. Under the CLS, a special regime of baselines exists for archipelagic States, which are defined as States 'constituted wholly by one or more archipelagos and may include other islands'.[42] An archipelago is:[43]

> ... a group of islands, including parts of islands, interconnecting waters and other natural features which are so closely interrelated that such

---

39.   CLS, Art 121(2) and CTSCZ, Art 10(2).
40.   CLS, Art 121(3).
41.   See **12.64**.
42.   CLS, Art 46(a).
43.   Ibid, Art 46(b).

islands, waters and other natural features form an intrinsic geographical, economic and political entity, or which historically have been regarded as such.

The States in Australia's region which have taken advantage of the special archipelagic regime in the CLS are Fiji, Indonesia, Kiribati, the Marshall Islands, Papua New Guinea, the Philippines, the Solomon Islands, Tuvalu and Vanuatu. A State which possesses an archipelago in addition to its main landmass (for example, Australia in relation to the Whitsunday Islands, or the United States in relation to Hawaii) is not entitled to take advantage of the special regime because it does not consist 'wholly' of one or more archipelagos. Where the archipelago fringes the State's coast, however, the State may be entitled to employ the straight baselines system.[44]

12.34   An archipelagic State is permitted to draw straight baselines joining the outermost points of the outermost islands and drying reefs — that is, reefs which are exposed at low tide. In so doing, the archipelagic State must ensure that its main islands are included within the baselines. The term 'main islands' is not defined, but the context indicates that they are the geographically largest islands, as distinct from the most populous or economically important islands. The archipelagic State must also ensure that the area of water contained within the baselines is equal to or greater than the area of land (this requirement renders the special system unavailable to some archipelagos with large islands separated by comparatively small bodies of water, such as Japan and New Zealand, and, if it properly falls within the definition of 'archipelagic State', Australia).

The area of water must also be not more than nine times greater than the area of land[45] (thereby rendering the special system unavailable to encompass all the outer-lying islands in archipelagos with small islands separated by comparatively large bodies of water, such as Fiji). Because archipelagic States may consist of more than one archipelago, they may, however, be able to satisfy the sea-to-land ratio requirements by drawing more than one set of enclosing baselines around different combinations of their islands (as does, for example, the Solomon Islands).

12.35   Archipelagic baselines 'shall not be drawn to and from low-tide elevations, unless lighthouses or similar installations which are permanently above sea level have been built on them or where a low-tide elevation is situated wholly or partly at a distance not exceeding the breadth of the territorial sea from the nearest island'.[46]

12.36   As a general rule, archipelagic baselines must not be more than 100 miles long. An archipelagic State may, however, draw baselines of

---

44.   See **12.20–12.22**.
45.   CLS, Art 47(1).
46.   Ibid, Art 47(4).

up to 125 miles, provided they do not constitute more than 3 per cent of the total number of baselines employed.[47]

12.37   The archipelagic baselines must not 'depart to any appreciable extent from the general configuration of the archipelago'.[48]

Internal waters

Location

12.38   All waters lying on the landward side of baselines are a State's internal waters.[49] This includes the sea falling between the high and low-water lines of the coast, islands, and harbour works; waters lying between an island and the low-water line of its atoll or fringing reef; the sea lying landward of straight baselines drawn between the coast and its fringing islands and low-tide elevations supporting lighthouses or similar permanent installations and across deep coastal indentations; the sea lying landward of the low-tide marks of low-tide elevations lying within 12 miles of the coast; waters lying landward of straight baselines drawn across deltas and river mouths; and waters lying landward of closing lines across bays.

Sovereignty over internal waters

12.39   As a matter of customary international law, a State's internal waters are assimilated to its land territory. Consequently, whatever a State may do in its own lands, it may also do in its internal waters. This includes, subject always to conventional or local customary obligations, the right to exclude persons, vessels or goods from entering or transiting through the State's internal waters. In the *Nicaragua* case, the International Court of Justice observed that States exercise sovereignty over their internal waters and that they may, therefore, regulate access to their ports.[50]

This principle of sovereignty over internal waters and ports is reflected in numerous treaties — such as the 1962 Convention on the Liability of Operators of Nuclear Ships,[51] which provides that nothing in the Convention 'shall affect any right which a Contracting State may have under international law to deny access to its waters and harbours to nuclear ships licensed by another Contracting State'.[52] Subject to conventional or local customary obligations, coastal States are free to

---

47.   Ibid, Art 47(2).
48.   Ibid, Art 47(3).
49.   CLS, Art 8(1) and CTSCZ, Art 5(1).
50.   *Military and Paramilitary Activities in and Against Nicaragua (Nicaragua v United States)* Merits, ICJ Rep (1986) 14, para 213.
51.   UNTS, Vol 922, p 49.
52.   Convention on the Liability of Operators of Nuclear Ships, Art 8.

attach any conditions they like to permission for foreign vessels to enter internal waters. Where such conditions have been imposed, the 'coastal State ... has the right to take the necessary steps to prevent any breach of the conditions to which admission of those ships to internal waters ... is subject'.[53]

Australia is party to the 1923 Convention and Statute on the International Regime of Maritime Ports,[54] which provides conditional rights of entry into internal waters and access to ports, but only 40 States are parties to that treaty. There are also hundreds of bilateral treaties of 'Friendship Commerce and Navigation' which grant conventional rights of access to internal waters and ports. Customary international law has, furthermore, long provided a right for ships to enter ports in order to preserve human life.[55]

Thus, as a matter of general customary international law, there is no right to enter a State's internal waters, no right of innocent passage through those waters,[56] and no right of access to ports except where it is necessary to preserve human life. Under the CLS and CTSCZ, however, there is an exceptional right of innocent passage through internal waters where the drawing of straight baselines in accordance with the conventions' provisions relating to deeply indented coastlines, fringing islands, deltas, and low-tide elevations with permanent installations 'has the effect of enclosing as internal waters areas which had not previously been considered as such'.[57]

12.40 As a corollary of their complete sovereignty over internal waters, States may also exercise jurisdiction over foreign ships located in those waters. This jurisdiction is subject to the rules of sovereign immunity,[58] diplomatic and consular immunity,[59] and diplomatic protection.[60] States usually refrain from exercising their enforcement jurisdiction over foreign ships, except in the case of serious crimes (for example, homicide) where the host State's own interests are directly involved (for example, customs, quarantine and immigration matters), and where non-crew members are involved in breaches of the law either as perpetrators or victims. Otherwise, States are usually content to permit breaches of the law aboard foreign vessels in internal waters to be dealt with according to the law and procedures of the State whose nationality the ship possesses.[61]

---

53.   CLS, Art 25(2) and CTSCZ, Art 16(2).
54.   LNTS, Vol 58, p 285.
55.   *Hoff, Administratrix of the Estate of Allison, Deceased (USA) v United Mexican States* (1929) 4 RIAA 444. See also **5.70–5.73** (Defence of Distress).
56.   See **12.47–12.56**.
57.   Art 8(2), CLS and Art 5(2), CTSCZ.
58.   See **6.37–6.49**.
59.   See **6.50–6.56**.
60.   See **5.76–5.116**.
61.   See **6.18** and **12.90–12.95**.

Territorial sea

Width of the territorial sea

12.41   The existence of a 'national sea' or 'territorial sea', meaning a belt of water adjacent to a State's land territory over which the coastal State exercises substantial jurisdiction, has been acknowledged by virtually all European States since the 17th century.

As we have already seen, neither the 1930 Hague Conference nor UNCLOS I was able to reach agreement on the maximum width of this adjacent belt of sea.

UNCLOS III decided that the maximum width of the territorial sea should be 12 miles as measured from baselines.[62] Consequently, States which are parties to the CLS are not permitted to make claims in excess of 12 miles and are obliged to respect the claims of other States which make similar claims. Australia maintains a 12-mile claim for its territorial sea.

Although a few States (almost all of which are in Africa and Latin America) continue to make more ambitious claims of up to 200 miles, the vast majority of States have maintained or adjusted their claims in accordance with the 12-mile standard prescribed by the CLS. In some cases, the more ambitious claims do not involve an assertion of full territorial sovereignty. Uruguay, for example, claims a 200-mile 'territorial sea', but accepts unrestricted navigation and overflight in the outer-lying 188 miles of that zone.

The position in customary international law is probably now that a claim made by a non-party to the CLS in excess of 12 miles will be invalid unless other States have acquiesced in that claim. Even then, the claim will not be opposable to any State which has persistently objected to the claim.[63]

Juridical nature of the territorial sea

12.42   As the conventions make clear, the 'sovereignty of a coastal State extends, beyond its land territory and internal waters ... to an adjacent belt of sea, described as the territorial sea'.[64] States accordingly enjoy in principle all the rights of sovereignty over their territorial sea, including foreign vessels and persons located therein, that they enjoy in their land territory and internal waters. This sovereignty extends to the airspace above and the subsoil beneath the territorial sea.[65]

12.43   There are, however, some restrictions on States' legislative and enforcement jurisdiction over their territorial sea. In terms of their

---

62.   CLS, Art 3.
63.   See 1.119–1.123.
64.   CLS, Art 2(1) and CTSCZ, Art 1(1).
65.   CLS, Art 2(2) and CTSCZ, Art 2.

legislative jurisdiction, States are restricted in their entitlement to adopt laws which affect the exercise of the right of innocent passage.[66]

12.44 The enforcement by a coastal State of its criminal law is restricted by specific provisions in the conventions. The coastal State is not permitted to:[67]

> ... take any steps on board a foreign ship passing through the territorial sea to arrest any person or to conduct any investigation in connexion with any crime committed before the ship entered the territorial sea, if the ship, proceeding from a foreign port, is only passing through the territorial sea without entering internal waters.

This effectively precludes the operation of the objective territorial principle of State jurisdiction[68] which applies to the State's land territory and internal waters.

Where a crime is committed on board a foreign vessel while it is exercising a right of innocent passage, the coastal State 'should not' ordinarily exercise its criminal enforcement jurisdiction to arrest any person or to conduct any investigation in connection with the crime during the vessel's passage. This recommended restriction is not operative in four situations:[69]

(i)   if the consequences of the crime extend to the coastal State;

(ii) if the crime is of a kind to disturb the peace of the country or the good order of the territorial sea;

(iii) if the assistance of the local authorities has been requested by the master of the ship or by a diplomatic agent or consular officer of the flag State; or

(iv) if such measures are necessary for the suppression of illicit traffic in narcotic drugs or psychotropic substances.

In considering whether and in which manner to exercise its criminal enforcement jurisdiction in these circumstances, the coastal State is obliged to pay 'due regard to the interests of navigation'.[70]

12.45 The enforcement by a coastal State of its civil law is also restricted by specific provisions in the conventions. A coastal State is not permitted to levy execution against or arrest a foreign ship passing through the territorial sea 'for the purpose of any civil proceedings, save only in respect of obligations or liabilities assumed or incurred by the ship itself in the course or for the purpose of its voyage through the waters of the coastal State'.[71] This prohibition is, however:[72]

---

66. See 12.47–12.56.
67. CLS, Art 27(5) and CTSCZ, Art 19(5). The CLS rule includes an exception for provisions in Part XII ('Protection and Preservation of the Marine Environment') and laws adopted in accordance with Part V ('Exclusive Economic Zone').
68. See 6.10–6.12.
69. CLS, Art 27(1); semble CTSCZ, Art 19(1).
70. CLS, Art 27(4) and CTSCZ, Art 19(4).
71. CLS, Art 28(2) and CTSCZ, Art 20(2).
72. CLS, Art 28(3) and CTSCZ, Art 20(3).

... without prejudice to the right of the coastal State, in accordance with its laws, to levy execution against or to arrest, for the purpose of any civil proceedings, a foreign ship lying in the territorial sea, or passing through the territorial sea after leaving internal waters.

A coastal State 'should not', furthermore, 'stop or divert a foreign ship passing through the territorial sea for the purpose of exercising civil jurisdiction in relation to a person on board the ship'.[73] This provision, it should be noted, applies even where the foreign ship is passing through the territorial sea after having left internal waters.

12.46   The recommendatory character of some of these provisions — coastal States 'should not' exercise their enforcement jurisdiction in certain situations — embodies a compromise between two competing views about enforcement jurisdiction in the territorial sea.

Some States traditionally took a restrictive view of their jurisdiction, while other (mostly common law) States took the view that the territorial sea was an almost complete jurisdictional extension of the land territory. This theoretical disagreement had, however, few practical consequences. That which the former States regarded as falling outside a State's enforcement jurisdiction, the latter usually refrained from exercising as an expression of comity. The language adopted in the conventions, however, represents an affirmation of the more expansive view of State enforcement jurisdiction, subject to non-binding considerations of international comity.

Innocent passage

12.47   A major exception to the plenary sovereignty enjoyed by States in their territorial sea is the right of innocent passage. Ships of all nationalities enjoy a right of innocent passage through the territorial sea[74] and the coastal State must not hamper the exercise of that right except on certain legally recognised grounds.[75]

No such right exists in respect of a State's internal waters, and no similar right for foreign persons or conveyances exists in relation to a State's land territory.

12.48   The conventions define 'passage' to mean traversing the territorial sea without entering internal waters or calling at any port facility or roadstead outside internal waters. It also means a journey to or from internal waters or a port facility or roadstead outside internal waters. In each case, the journey must be 'continuous and expeditious', although:[76]

... passage includes stopping and anchoring, but only in so far as the same are incidental to ordinary navigation or are rendered necessary by

---

73.   CLS, Art 28(1) and CTSCZ, Art 20(1).
74.   CLS, Art 17 and CTSCZ, Art 14 (1).
75.   CLS, Art 24(1)(a) and CTSCZ, Art 15 (1).
76.   CLS, Art 18 and CTSCZ, Art 14.

force majeure or distress or for the purpose of rendering assistance to persons, ships or aircraft in danger or distress.

A foreign ship which 'hovers' — that is, lingers — in the territorial sea is not engaged in passage, and therefore not exercising a right of innocent passage.

12.49   Passage will be 'innocent' only if 'it is not prejudicial to the peace, good order or security of the coastal State'.[77] This was already well established in customary international law before UNCLOS I. The States participating in UNCLOS III sought to give greater precision to the rule. The CLS lists (at Art 19(2)) a range of activities which, if undertaken in the territorial sea, shall be considered prejudicial to the coastal State's peace, good order or security:[78]

(a) any threat or use of force against the sovereignty, territorial integrity or political independence of the coastal State, or in any other manner in violation of the principles of international law embodied in the Charter of the United Nations;

(b) any exercise or practice with weapons of any kind;

(c) any act aimed at collecting information to the prejudice of the defence or security of the coastal State;

(d) any act of propaganda aimed at affecting the defence or security of the coastal State;

(e) the launching, landing or taking on board of any aircraft;

(f) the launching, landing or taking on board of any military device;

(g) the loading or unloading of any commodity, currency or person contrary to the customs, fiscal, immigration or sanitary laws and regulations of the coastal State;

(h) any act of wilful and serious pollution contrary to this Convention;

(i) any fishing activities;

(j) the carrying out of research or survey activities;

(k) any act aimed at interfering with any systems of communication or any other facilities or installations of the coastal State;

(l) any other activity not having a direct bearing on passage.

The drafting language employed makes it unclear as to whether this list of activities is exhaustive or inclusive. The practice of at least two major maritime States suggests that it is exhaustive.

In 1989, the United States and the Soviet Union (to which Russia is now the successor) signed an instrument entitled 'Uniform Interpretation of Rules of International Law Governing Innocent Passage'. The two parties expressly agreed that the list of activities in Art 19(2) of the CLS is exhaustive and that passage will be innocent if a ship passing through the territorial sea does not engage in any of the listed activities.

12.50   Even prior to UNCLOS I, innocent passage was a right available to foreign non-military vessels as a matter of customary international law.

---

77.   CLS, Art 19(1) and CTSCZ, Art 14(4).
78.   CLS, Art 19(2).

There was, however, a divergence of State practice on the availability of a right of innocent passage to foreign warships. Broadly speaking, there were three approaches. Some States effectively rejected the existence of such a right by insisting that foreign warships receive prior authorisation before traversing the territorial sea. Some other States accepted the existence of such a right in principle, but made it conditional upon prior notification to the coastal State. A third group of States, consisting mostly of major Western naval powers and their allies, asserted a right of innocent passage for warships without the need for either prior authorisation or notification.

The conventions, by making innocent passage available simply to 'ships of all States'[79] without distinction as to their civilian or military status, indicate that warships attract at least the same rights of innocent passage as non-military vessels. The CLS provides that foreign warships must comply with the coastal State's laws and regulations concerning innocent passage,[80] but does not authorise coastal States to adopt laws and regulations requiring approval or notification prior to exercising the right of innocent passage. Indeed, the CLS expressly forbids coastal States from imposing 'requirements on foreign ships which have the practical effect of denying or impairing the right of innocent passage'.[81]

A requirement of prior authorisation would certainly have the practical effect of denying or impairing the right of innocent passage. One of the major naval States which had long objected to a right of innocent passage for warships without prior authorisation was the Soviet Union. However, in the 1989 Uniform Interpretation of Rules of International Law Governing Innocent Passage which the Soviet Union concluded with the United States, the parties agreed that:

> All ships, including warships, regardless of cargo, armament or means of propulsion, enjoy the right of innocent passage through the territorial sea in accordance with international law, for which neither prior notification nor authorization is required.

Russia ratified the CLS in 1997. The current legal position is probably that, at least as between parties to the CLS, no prior authorisation or notification is required for foreign warships to exercise a right of innocent passage in the territorial sea.

12.51   The manner in which warships are to conduct themselves in order for their passage to be innocent may vary according to the circumstances with which they are confronted.

If there is a reasonable basis for believing that they may be attacked for exercising their right of innocent passage, the warships may adopt a posture which might otherwise deprive their passage of its innocent character.

---

79.   CLS, Art 17 and CTSCZ, Art 14(1).
80.   CLS, Art 30.
81.   Ibid, Art 24(1)(a).

In the **Corfu Channel Case,**[82] two British naval cruisers were passing through the North Corfu Channel in Albanian territorial waters on 15 May 1946 when they were fired upon by an Albanian coastal battery. The United Kingdom protested that the naval vessels were exercising a right of innocent passage through straits used for international navigation, while Albania argued, inter alia, that there was no right of innocent passage without prior authorisation of the coastal State, which was absent in this case. On 22 October 1946, the same two British cruisers, this time accompanied by the British naval destroyers *Saumarez* and *Volage*, were again sent through the North Corfu Channel for the admitted purpose of demonstrating the United Kingdom's asserted right of innocent passage. In proceedings commenced by the United Kingdom for death, injury and loss suffered by its navy in a related incident involving Albanian mines in the Corfu Channel, Albania counter-claimed that the actions of the four British warships violated Albania's territorial sovereignty. Albania contended that the warships were engaged in naval manoeuvres in the North Corfu Channel, that they were in combat formation, and that there were armed soldiers on board. The International Court of Justice rejected these contentions on the evidence, and proceeded to discuss other aspects of the conduct of the British vessels in the context of the United Kingdom's defence that the vessels were exercising a right of innocent passage:[83]

> It is, in the opinion of the Court, generally recognised and in accordance with international custom that States in time of peace have a right to send their warships through straits used for international navigation between two parts of the high seas without the previous authorisation of the coastal State, provided that the passage is *innocent*. … It remains … to consider whether the *manner* in which the passage was carried out was consistent with the principle of innocent passage … The guns were … 'trained fore and aft, which is their normal position at sea in peace time, and were not loaded'. …

> In the light of this evidence, the Court cannot accept the Albanian contention that the position of the guns was inconsistent with the rules of innocent passage. … [T]he passage 'was made with ships at action stations in order that they might be able to retaliate quickly if fired upon again'.

> In view of the firing from the Albanian battery on May 15, this measure of precaution cannot, in itself, be regarded as unreasonable. But four warships — two cruisers and two destroyers — passed in this manner, with crews at action stations, ready to retaliate quickly if fired upon. They passed one after another through this narrow channel, close to the Albanian coast, at a time of political tension in the region. The intention must have been, not only to test Albania's attitude, but at the same time to demonstrate such force that she would abstain from firing again on passing ships.

> Having regard, however, to all the circumstances of the case, as described above, the Court is unable to characterise these measures taken by the United Kingdom authorities as a violation of Albania's sovereignty.

> … In a report of the commander of *Volage* … it is stated: 'The most was made of the opportunities to study Albanian defences at close range. …' With regard to the observations of coastal defences made after the explosions, these were justified by the fact that two ships had just been blown up and that, in this critical situation, their commanders might fear that they would be fired on from the coast, as on May 15. Having thus examined the various contentions

---

82.   *Corfu Channel Case (Merits) (United Kingdom v Albania)* ICJ Rep (1949) 4.
83.   Ibid, 28–32.

of the Albanian Government in so far as they appear to be relevant, the Court has arrived at the conclusion that the United Kingdom did not violate the sovereignty of Albania by reason of the acts of the British Navy in Albanian waters on October 22, 1946.

12.52 There are some additional rules affecting two specific types of vessels. While present in the territorial sea, submarines must navigate on the surface and show their flags.[84] If a vessel is nuclear-powered, or if it is carrying nuclear or other inherently dangerous or noxious substances, it shall 'carry documents and observe special precautionary measures established for such ships by international agreements',[85] and the coastal State may require it to restrict its passage to specially designated sea lanes.[86]

12.53 The coastal State is permitted to adopt laws and regulations relating to innocent passage only with respect to certain nominated subjects. These laws may be for the purpose of navigational safety; the regulation of maritime traffic; the protection of navigational aids; other navigational installations; cables and pipelines; the conservation of living maritime resources; the regulation of fisheries; environmental protection; the conduct of scientific research and surveys; and the enforcement of customs, fiscal, immigration and sanitary laws.[87] In particular, the coastal State may prescribe sea lanes and maritime traffic separation schemes for the safety of maritime navigation.[88]

Foreign ships exercising a right of innocent passage are required to comply with these laws and regulations, as well as generally accepted international regulations relating to the prevention of collisions at sea.[89] The coastal State's laws 'shall not apply to the design, construction, manning or equipment of foreign ships unless they are giving effect to generally accepted international rules or standards'.[90]

Nor may the coastal State impose any financial charge on foreign ships by reason only of their passage through the territorial sea, although it may charge on a non-discriminatory basis for specific services rendered.[91] Furthermore, the coastal State is not permitted to 'discriminate in form or in fact against the ships of any State or against ships carrying cargoes to, from or on behalf of any State',[92] and is obliged to 'give appropriate publicity to any danger to navigation, of which it has knowledge, within its territorial sea'.[93]

---

84. CLS, Art 20 and CTSCZ, Art 14(6).
85. CLS, Art 23.
86. Ibid, Art 22(2).
87. Ibid, Art 21(1).
88. Ibid, Art 22(1).
89. Ibid, Art 21(4).
90. Ibid, Art 21(2).
91. CLS, Art 26 and CTSCZ, Art 18.
92. CLS, Art 24(1)(b).
93. CLS, Art 24(2) and CTSCZ, Art 15(2).

12.54   A coastal State's right to make laws and regulations concerning innocent passage involves a corollary right to enforce them. The conventions put the matter succinctly by providing that the 'coastal State may take the necessary steps in its territorial sea to prevent passage which is not innocent'.[94]

The conventions do not specify the 'steps' which States may take, but customary international law permits the arrest of foreign vessels which are located in the territorial sea and not engaged in innocent passage. It follows that force may be used against vessels resisting arrest, provided such force respects the limits imposed by other branches of international law such as diplomatic protection and human rights.

12.55   The coastal State's right to enforce the requirements of innocent passage are more circumscribed where the vessel is a foreign warship or a foreign government ship engaged in non-commercial activities. A warship is a:[95]

> ... ship belonging to the armed forces of a State bearing the external marks distinguishing such ships of its nationality, under the command of an officer duly commissioned by the government of the State and whose name appears in the appropriate service list or its equivalent, and manned by a crew which is under regular armed forces discipline.

Foreign government ships engaged in non-commercial activities are entitled to the protections of sovereign immunity[96] so that they may not be arrested by the coastal State.

Foreign warships which are present in the territorial sea but not exercising rights of innocent passage may be requested to leave the territorial sea. Where the warship disregards such a request, 'the coastal State may require it to leave the territorial sea immediately'.[97] If the foreign warship still does not leave, the coastal State will be permitted to use such force as would be reasonably necessary to compel it to leave.

Were matters to reach this point, then international law relating to the use of armed force, and particularly the law of self-defence,[98] could also come into play. Although the CLS is silent on the point, it would seem evident that non-military foreign government ships engaged in non-commercial activities are subject to the same rules as warships where such non-military ships are present in the territorial sea and not engaged in innocent passage.

In either case, the flag State bears 'international responsibility for any loss or damage to the coastal State resulting from the non-compliance by a warship or other government ship operated for non-commercial

---

94.   CLS, Art 25(1) and CTSCZ, Art 16(1).
95.   CLS, Art 29; semble CHS, Art 8(2).
96.   CTSCZ, Art 22(2) and CLS, Art 32, which expressly extends the same protection to foreign warships. See generally 6.37–6.49.
97.   CLS, Art 30 and CTSCZ, Art 23.
98.   See 9.19–9.40.

purposes with the laws and regulations of the coastal State concerning passage through the territorial sea'.[99]

12.56 There is no right of passage for foreign aircraft overflying the territorial sea. Coastal States enjoy full territorial sovereignty in the airspace above the territorial sea.[100] The conventions' provisions deal only with a right of passage for vessels including submarines, and no right of overflight above a State's territory has ever emerged in customary international law.

Contiguous zone

Emergence of contiguous zone

12.57 The concept of a contiguous zone as a discrete maritime regime, wedged between the territorial sea and the high seas, emerged slowly during the 18th, 19th and early 20th centuries. Although different terms were used to name it, States increasingly exerted jurisdiction over a belt of sea adjacent to the territorial sea for certain limited purposes. These purposes varied somewhat between States and changed over time, but embraced such matters as the enforcement or preventive enforcement of the coastal State's customs, quarantine and immigration laws; the protection of fish stocks; or the assertion of privileged access to the zone's fisheries and other resources.

State practice was sufficiently well established by the time of UNCLOS I that the contiguous zone received recognition and codification in the text of the CTSCZ. These provisions were, with one significant alteration and a minor addition, replicated in the text of the CLS.

Width

12.58 There was no final agreement in UNCLOS I as to the maximum width of the territorial sea, although many States favoured six miles. It was in this context that the CTSCZ prescribed that the contiguous zone may extend only up to 12 miles from the baselines from which the width of the territorial sea is measured.[101] The CLS provides that the contiguous zone may extend up to 24 miles from the baselines from which the width of the territorial sea is measured.[102] This means that for States with a 12-mile territorial sea, they may claim a further 12-mile contiguous zone. Australia has claimed, in addition to its 12-mile territorial sea, a 12-mile contiguous zone.

---

99. CLS, Art 31, which undoubtedly reflects the requirements of customary international law. See 5.18–5.21.
100. CLS, Art 2(2) and CTSCZ, Art 2.
101. CTSCZ, Art 24(2).
102. CLS, Art 33(2).

Jurisdiction

12.59   The coastal State enjoys a less extensive jurisdiction in the contiguous zone than in its internal waters and territorial sea. Whereas in internal waters the coastal State's jurisdiction is complete, and in the territorial sea the coastal State's jurisdiction is complete subject to specified customary and conventional exceptions, in the contiguous zone the coastal State enjoys only so much jurisdiction as is specifically conferred on it by customary international law or treaty.

However, it should be borne in mind that, in the case of most States including Australia, the 12-mile contiguous zone is also part of the 188-mile EEZ. Consequently, the area subject to the contiguous zone regime will also be subject to the EEZ regime where the coastal State claims both zones.

12.60   The conventions permit a coastal State to exercise control in the contiguous zone necessary to punish infringements of its 'customs, fiscal, immigration or sanitary laws and regulations' which have been committed in its territory or territorial sea. The State may also exercise control in the contiguous zone necessary to prevent infringements of the same laws and regulations in its territory or territorial sea.[103]

This must include a power to arrest vessels and persons and to use such force as is reasonably necessary to execute such arrests. Although the conventions are silent on the point, foreign warships and government vessels engaged in non-commercial activities will be protected by sovereign immunity in the usual way, and so may not be arrested. The conventions do not, however, confer a power to punish infringements of national laws committed in the contiguous zone itself.

12.61   The protection of security is probably not one of the purposes for which coastal States may exercise jurisdiction in the contiguous zone. A proposal to include such a provision among the domestic laws whose territorial infringement or prevention could be controlled was defeated at UNCLOS I and not adopted at UNCLOS III. Nevertheless, a number of States have, apparently without widespread protest from other States with the notable exception of the United States, asserted a right to punish or prevent violations of security laws in the contiguous zone or a 'security zone' outside the territorial sea. It may be that some such special claims have crystallised, or will crystallise, into local customary law binding on other States except persistent objectors.[104] Burma, Cambodia, China and Vietnam are among the States in Australia's region which assert a right to control, in the contiguous zone or a 'security zone' contiguous to their territorial sea, activities bearing upon security.

---

103. CLS, Art 33(1) and CTSCZ, Art 24(1).
104. See generally **1.115–1.123** and **1.147–1.151**.

Protection of historical and archaeological objects

12.62   The CLS also imposes an obligation on States to protect objects of an archaeological and historical nature found at sea and to cooperate for that purpose. In order to control traffic in such objects, coastal States are entitled to presume that their removal from the seabed of the contiguous zone 'would result in an infringement within its territory or territorial sea of the laws and regulations' in respect of which enforcement or preventative controls may be exercised.[105]

Exclusive economic zone

Emergence of the EEZ

12.63   By the middle of the 20th century, fisheries and whaling technology had progressed to the point where numerous States entertained mounting concerns about the sustainability of fish and whale stocks posed by over-exploitation.

In the years immediately following the Second World War, numerous coastal States declared territorial seas, 'exclusive fishing zones', or functionally equivalent zones far in excess of the width of prevailing claims for the territorial sea. They did this in order to exclude foreigners from the exploitation of fish and whale stocks and to conserve living marine resources. Two-hundred-mile claims were not uncommon.

The exclusive economic zone (EEZ) is a maritime zone established as a result of the work of UNCLOS III and represents a compromise between some States making ambitious claims to a very wide territorial sea and others with an interest in maintaining the maximum possible freedom of the high seas.

In terms of its juridical status, however, the EEZ is not simply an extension of either the territorial sea or the high seas. Rather, the EEZ is 'subject to the specific legal regime established in [Part V of the CLS], under which the rights and obligations of the coastal State and the rights and freedoms of other States are governed by the relevant provisions' of the CLS.[106]

The idea of the EEZ was so immediately attractive to many coastal States that within only three years of the CLS being opened for signature, the International Court of Justice was able to say that 'the institution of the exclusive economic zone ... is shown by the practice of states to have become part of customary law'.[107]

---

105. CLS, Art 303.
106. Ibid, Art 55.
107. *Case Concerning the Continental Shelf (Libya v Malta)* ICJ Rep (1985) 13, para 34. See also *Concerning the Continental Shelf (Tunisia v Libya)* ICJ Rep (1982) 18, para 100.

Location

12.64   The EEZ is 'an area beyond and adjacent to the territorial sea',[108] which 'shall not extend beyond 200 nautical miles from the baselines from which the breadth of the territorial sea is measured'.[109] In most cases, including Australia's, where the territorial sea is 12 miles wide, the EEZ will be 188 miles wide. The EEZ and the territorial sea are distinct zones, but the first 12 miles of the EEZ are co-extensive with the contiguous zone. Islands may be used for drawing baselines, but unless they can 'sustain human habitation or economic life of their own'[110] they will not possess their own EEZ.[111]

Rights of coastal State

12.65   Within the EEZ, the coastal State enjoys:[112]

> ... sovereign rights for the purpose of exploring and exploiting, conserving and managing the natural resources, whether living or non-living, of the waters superjacent to the seabed and of the seabed and its subsoil, and with regard to other activities for the economic exploitation and exploration of the zone, such as the production of energy from the water, currents and winds.

In practical terms, this means that the coastal State has the right to harvest fish, whales and other marine creatures, and to prospect for and exploit any oil and minerals lying beneath or on the seabed. Because the right to engage in these activities is 'sovereign', the coastal State may exclude any person and any other State from pursuing the activities, or permit the activities to such persons and on such terms as the coastal State decides.

The coastal State may, in the exercise of these rights, 'take such measures, including boarding, inspection, arrest and judicial proceedings, as may be necessary to ensure compliance with the laws and regulations adopted by it'.[113] Arrested vessels and their crews are to be promptly released upon the posting of a reasonable bond or other security,[114] and penalties for violations of fisheries laws must not include imprisonment or any other form of corporal punishment.[115]

12.66   The coastal State enjoys an exclusive right in the EEZ to construct artificial islands, installations for economic purposes, and other installations and structures which may interfere with the coastal State's EEZ rights.[116]

---

108. CLS, Art 55.
109. Ibid, Art 57.
110. Ibid, Art 121(3).
111. See 12.31.
112. CLS, Art 56(1)(a).
113. Ibid, Art 73(1).
114. Ibid, Art 73(2).
115. Ibid, Art 73(3).
116. Ibid, Art 60(1).

Where it is necessary to do so in order to protect the safety of these constructions and international navigation, the coastal State may establish reasonable safety zones around the constructions.[117] However, these constructions 'may not be established where interference may be caused to the use of recognised sea lanes essential to international navigation'.[118] Although the coastal State enjoys exclusive jurisdiction over these constructions and safety zones, 'including jurisdiction with regard to customs, fiscal, health, safety and immigration laws and regulations',[119] the constructions and safety zones do not possess the status of islands, do not have their own territorial sea, and do not affect the delimitation of the territorial sea, the EEZ or the continental shelf.[120]

Duties of coastal State

12.67   Coastal States also have duties in the EEZ. They are obliged to determine the allowable catch of the EEZ's living resources and adopt such proper conservation and management measures as are necessary to prevent over-exploitation of such resources. These measures must be designed:[121]

> ... to maintain or restore populations of harvested species at levels which can produce the maximum sustainable yield, as qualified by relevant environmental and economic factors, including the economic needs of coastal fishing communities and the special requirements of developing states, and taking into account fishing patterns, the interdependence of stocks and any generally recommended international minimum standards.

12.68   These obligations of conservation are balanced by duties to ensure an effective exploitation of resources. In particular, coastal States must 'promote the optimum utilisation of the living resources' in the EEZ.[122] Having determined the allowable catch, the coastal State must then determine its own capacity to harvest the EEZ's living resources. Where the coastal State does not possess the capacity to exploit the entire allowable catch, it shall give other States access to the surplus in accordance with agreements or other arrangements[123] and nationals of those other States must comply with the coastal State's conservation measures and other terms and conditions in exploiting the surplus.[124] Landlocked States also have the right to participate, on an equitable basis, in the exploitation of the surplus of the region in which they are located.[125] The same is true of 'geographically disadvantaged States', which are defined as:[126]

---

117. Ibid, Art 60(4).
118. Ibid, Art 60(7).
119. Ibid, Art 60(2).
120. Ibid, Art 60(8).
121. Ibid, Art 61.
122. Ibid, Art 62(1).
123. Ibid, Art 62(2).
124. Ibid, Art 62(4).
125. Ibid, Art 69.
126. Ibid, Art 70.

... coastal States, including States bordering enclosed or semi-enclosed seas, whose geographical situation makes them dependent upon the exploitation of the living resources of the exclusive economic zones of other States in the ... region for adequate supplies of fish for the nutritional purposes of their populations or part thereof, and coastal States which can claim no exclusive economic zones of their own.

12.69   These rules do not apply to 'sedentary species'[127] — that is, stationary or non-swimming creatures.[128] The conservation and exploitation of some other marine creatures are also subject to special rules — for example, highly migratory species such as tuna, marlin, dolphins and oceanic sharks;[129] marine mammals such as seals and whales;[130] species which migrate from marine water to rivers in order to breed;[131] and species which migrate from fresh water to marine water in order to breed.[132]

12.70   A coastal State is not obliged to submit to compulsory adjudication or arbitration:[133]

... any dispute relating to its sovereign rights with respect to the living resources in the exclusive economic zone or their exercise, including its discretionary powers for determining the allowable catch, its harvesting capacity, the allocation of surpluses to other States and the terms and conditions established in its conservation and management laws and regulations.

Such disputes may, however, be referred to compulsory conciliation in the case of certain manifest or arbitrary breaches by the coastal State,[134] but the conciliation commission must not substitute its discretion for that of the coastal State[135] and its report is not binding on the parties.[136]

Rights of non-coastal States

12.71   States other than the coastal State enjoy their own specified rights in the EEZ. These are the high seas rights of navigation and overflight, the laying of submarine cables and pipelines (subject to the rules relating to the continental shelf), 'and other internationally lawful uses of the sea related to these freedoms, such as those associated with the operation of ships, aircraft and submarine cables and pipelines, and compatible with the other provisions' of the CLS.[137]

The rules relating to navigation on the high seas also apply to the EEZ, to the extent that they are not incompatible with specific rules relating to

---

127. Ibid, Art 68.
128. Ibid, Art 77(4).
129. Ibid, Art 64.
130. Ibid, Art 65.
131. Ibid, Art 66.
132. Ibid, Art 67.
133. Ibid, Art 297(3)(a).
134. Ibid, Art 297(3)(b).
135. Ibid, Art 297(3)(c).
136. Ibid, Arts 14 and 7(2), Annex V.
137. Ibid, Art 58(1).

the EEZ.[138] In exercising their rights and performing their duties in the EEZ, other States must also 'have due regard to the rights and duties of the coastal State and shall comply with the laws and regulations adopted by the coastal State' in accordance with the CLS.[139]

In the **Saiga case,**[140] the *Saiga* was an oil tanker flying the flag of Saint Vincent and the Grenadines when it was fired upon by a Guinean patrol boat and then boarded by Guinean officers. The master and crew of the *Saiga* were all Ukrainian nationals. Three employees of Senegalese nationality were also on board. The vessel was owned by a Cypriot company and under charter to a Swiss company. After boarding the *Saiga* without resistance, the Guinean officers fired indiscriminately on the deck and used gunfire to stop the ship's engine. Two persons aboard the *Saiga* were seriously injured in the shooting, which also caused extensive damage to the vessel. At the time of the Guinean attack, the *Saiga* was drifting in waters outside the southern boundary of Guinea's EEZ. On the previous day, however, the *Saiga* was inside Guinea's EEZ, where it 'bunkered' (that is, stored and sold) fuel oil to fishing vessels. After being attacked and boarded, the *Saiga* was arrested and taken to a Guinean port, where the ship's master was detained and its cargo seized. The master was charged with violating Guinean law in that he had 'imported, without declaring it, merchandise that is taxable on entering Guinean territory, in this case diesel oil, and that he refused to comply with injunctions by Agents of the Guinean Navy, thus committing the crimes of contraband, fraud and tax evasion'. Guinea's domestic law established a 'customs radius' which included a 'marine area' extending 250 kilometres (that is, 135 miles) from the coast. The *Saiga*'s master was convicted and fined more than 15 billion Guinean francs (about US$3 million), against which the *Saiga* and its cargo were confiscated as a guarantee. On appeal, the conviction was upheld and the penalty increased by the addition of a six months' suspended prison sentence. Saint Vincent and the Grenadines argued, inter alia, that Guinea violated international law by seeking to enforce its customs laws in the EEZ. The International Tribunal for the Law of the Sea said:

119. ... Saint Vincent and the Grenadines contends that the extension of the customs laws of Guinea to the exclusive economic zone is contrary to the Convention. It argues that article 56 of the Convention [on the Law of the Sea] does not give the right to Guinea to extend the application of its customs laws and regulations to that zone. It therefore contends that Guinea's customs laws cannot be applied to ships flying its flag in the exclusive economic zone. Consequently, the measures taken by Guinea against the *Saiga* were unlawful.

120. In the view of the Tribunal, there is nothing to prevent it from considering the question whether or not, in applying its laws to the *Saiga* in the present case, Guinea was acting in conformity with its obligations towards Saint Vincent and the Grenadines under the Convention and general international law. In its Judgment in the *Case Concerning Certain German Interests in Polish Upper Silesia,* the Permanent Court of International Justice stated:

From the standpoint of International Law and of the Court which is its organ, municipal laws are merely facts which express the will and constitute the activities of States, in the same manner as do legal decisions

---

138. Ibid, Art 58(2).
139. Ibid, Art 58(3).
140. *M/V 'Saiga' (No 2) case (Saint Vincent and the Grenadines v Guinea)* (1999) 3 ITLOS Rep No 2, 37 ILM 1202.

or administrative measures. The Court is certainly not called upon to interpret the Polish law as such; but there is nothing to prevent the Court's giving judgment on the question whether or not, in applying that law, Poland is acting in conformity with its obligations towards Germany under the Geneva Convention.

(*Certain German interests in Polish Upper Silesia, Merits, Judgment No. 7, 1926, P.C.I.J., Series A, No. 7, p. 19*)

121. A denial of the competence of the Tribunal to examine the applicability and scope of national law is even less acceptable in the framework of certain provisions of the Convention. One such provision, which is also relied upon by Guinea, is article 58, paragraph 3, … Under this provision, the rights and obligations of coastal and other States under the Convention arise not just from the provisions of the Convention but also from national laws and regulations 'adopted by the coastal State in accordance with the provisions of this Convention'. Thus, the Tribunal is competent to determine the compatibility of such laws and regulations with the Convention.

122. The Tribunal notes that Guinea produces no evidence in support of its contention that the laws cited by it provide a basis for the action taken against the *Saiga* beyond the assertion that it reflects the consistent practice of its authorities, supported by its courts. Even if it is conceded that the laws of Guinea which the *Saiga* is alleged to have violated are applicable in the manner that is claimed by Guinea, the question remains whether these laws, as interpreted and applied by Guinea, are compatible with the Convention.

123. Saint Vincent and the Grenadines claims that, in applying its customs laws to the *Saiga* in its customs radius, which includes parts of the exclusive economic zone, Guinea acted contrary to the Convention. It contends that in the exclusive economic zone Guinea is not entitled to exercise powers which go beyond those provided for in articles 56 and 58 of the Convention. It further asserts that Guinea violated its rights to enjoy the freedom of navigation or other internationally lawful uses of the sea in the exclusive economic zone, since the supply of gas oil by the *Saiga* falls within the exercise of those rights.

124. Guinea denies that the application of its customs and contraband laws in its customs radius is contrary to the Convention or in violation of any rights of Saint Vincent and the Grenadines. It maintains that it is entitled to apply its customs and contraband laws to prevent the unauthorized sale of gas oil to fishing vessels operating in its exclusive economic zone. It further maintains that such supply is not part of the freedom of navigation under the Convention or an internationally lawful use of the sea related to the freedom of navigation but a commercial activity and that it does not, therefore, fall within the scope of article 58 of the Convention. For that reason, it asserts that the Guinean action against the *Saiga* was taken not because the ship was navigating in the exclusive economic zone of Guinea but because it was engaged in 'unwarranted commercial activities'.

125. Guinea further argues that the exclusive economic zone is not part of the high seas or of the territorial sea, but a zone with its own legal status (a *sui generis* zone). From this it concludes that rights or jurisdiction in the exclusive economic zone, which the Convention does not expressly attribute to the coastal States, do not automatically fall under the freedom of the high seas.

126. The Tribunal needs to determine whether the laws applied or the measures taken by Guinea against the *Saiga* are compatible with the Convention. In other words, the question is whether, under the Convention, there was justification for Guinea to apply its customs laws in the exclusive economic zone within a customs radius extending to a distance of 250 kilometres from the coast.

127. The Tribunal notes that, under the Convention, a coastal State is entitled to apply customs laws and regulations in its territorial sea (articles 2 and 21). In the contiguous zone, a coastal State may exercise the control necessary to:

(a) prevent infringement of its customs, fiscal, immigration or sanitary laws and regulations within its territory or territorial sea;

(b) punish infringement of the above laws and regulations committed within its territory of territorial sea.

(article 33, paragraph 1)

In the exclusive economic zone, the coastal State has jurisdiction to apply customs laws and regulations in respect of artificial islands, installations and structures (article 60, paragraph 2). In the view of the Tribunal, the Convention does not empower a coastal State to apply its customs laws in respect of any other parts of the exclusive economic zone not mentioned above.

128. Guinea further argues that the legal basis of its law prohibiting the supply of gas oil to fishing vessels in the customs radius is to be found in article 58 of the Convention. It relies on the reference, contained in paragraph 3 of that article, to the 'other rules of international law' to justify the application and enforcement of its customs and contraband laws to the customs radius. These 'other rules of international law' are variously described by Guinea as 'the inherent right to protect itself against unwarranted economic activities in its exclusive economic zone that considerably affect its public interest', or as the 'doctrine of necessity', or as 'the customary principle of self-protection in case of grave and imminent perils which endanger essential aspects of its public interest'.

129. The Tribunal finds it necessary to distinguish between the two main concepts referred to in the submissions of Guinea. The first is a broad notion of 'public interest' or 'self-protection' which Guinea invokes to expand the scope of its jurisdiction in the exclusive economic zone, and the second is 'state of necessity' which it relies on to justify measures that would otherwise be wrongful under the Convention.

130. The main public interest which Guinea claims to be protecting by applying its customs laws to the exclusive economic zone is said to be the 'considerable fiscal losses a developing country like Guinea is suffering from illegal off-shore bunkering in its exclusive economic zone'. Guinea makes references also to fisheries and environmental interests. In effect, Guinea's contention is that the customary international law principle of 'public interest' gives it the power to impede 'economic activities that are undertaken [in its exclusive economic zone] under the guise of navigation but are different from communication'.

131. According to article 58, paragraph 3, of the Convention, the 'other rules of international law' which a coastal State is entitled to apply in the exclusive economic zone are those which are not incompatible with Part V of the Convention. In the view of the Tribunal, recourse to the principle of 'public interest', as invoked by Guinea, would entitle a coastal State to prohibit any activities in the exclusive economic zone which it decides to characterize as activities which affect its economic 'public interest' or entail 'fiscal losses' for it. This would curtail the rights of other States in the exclusive economic zone. The Tribunal is satisfied that this would be incompatible with the provisions of articles 56 and 58 of the Convention regarding the rights of the coastal State in the exclusive economic zone.

Non-ascribed jurisdiction

12.72 Circumstances may arise where there is a conflict of interests between a coastal State and another State concerning activities in the

EEZ and about which the CLS has not attributed jurisdiction to either of them. In such cases, 'the conflict should be resolved on the basis of equity and in the light of all the relevant circumstances, taking into account the respective importance of the interests involved to the parties as well as to the international community as a whole'.[141]

Continental shelf

12.73   The continental shelf is, like the EEZ, a maritime zone of relatively recent origin. However, unlike the EEZ, which must be actually claimed by the coastal State, the continental shelf maritime zone exists for the coastal State without the necessity of any claim.[142] The continental shelf regime therefore applies whether or not the coastal State has made a claim to an EEZ.

12.74   In geological terms, the continental shelf is a ledge of relatively shallow seabed (up to about 200 metres below sea level) which extends out beyond the shoreline, before dropping away more or less precipitously into much deeper waters, often thousands of metres below sea level.

In some parts of the world's seas, the geological continental shelf is only a few miles wide, whereas in other places it extends for many hundreds of miles (for example, the entire North Sea and Persian Gulf consist of continental shelf). The significance of the continental shelf for legal purposes lies in its economic riches. It is an area generously endowed with oil and gas resources and is frequently host to abundant fishing resources.

Emergence of continental shelf regime

12.75   The reasons for the emergence of the continental shelf as a juridical maritime zone are essentially the same as those which led to the establishment of the EEZ. By the middle of the 20th century, technological advances made access to the continental shelf's economic resources — particularly its oil, gas and mineral resources — technically possible and increasingly economical. This also occurred at a time when demand for such resources was steadily accelerating.

It is, therefore, not surprising that the United States, with its global technological lead at the end of the Second World War, was the first to make a juridical claim to its adjacent continental shelf. President Harry S Truman's (1884–1972) 1945 proclamation on the continental shelf claimed for the United States:[143]

---

141. CLS, Art 59.
142. CLS, Art 77(3) and CCS, Art 2(3).
143. *Proclamation 2667 of September 28, 1945: Policy of the United States with Respect to the Natural Resources of the Subsoil and Sea Bed of the Continental Shelf,* 10 Fed Reg 12,305 (1945).

... the natural resources of the subsoil and sea bed of the continental shelf beneath the high seas but contiguous to the coasts of the United States as appertaining to the United States, subject to its jurisdiction and control.

The Truman proclamation gave four justifications for the claim to national sovereignty of the continental shelf's subsoil and seabed resources:

(i)   'the effectiveness of measures to utilize or conserve these resources would be contingent upon co-operation and protection from the shore';

(ii) 'the continental shelf may be regarded as an extension of the land mass of the coastal nation and thus naturally appurtenant to it';

(iii) 'these resources frequently form a seaward extension of a pool or deposit lying within the territory'; and

(iv) 'self-protection compels the coastal nation to keep close watch over activities off its shores which are of their nature necessary for utilization of these resources'.

12.76   Many other coastal States quickly followed the United States in making their own claims to sovereignty over the resources of the continental shelf. Thirteen years after the Truman proclamation, UNCLOS I produced the Convention on the Continental Shelf (CCS). By 1969, the International Court of Justice was able to say:[144]

... the rights of the coastal state in respect of the area of continental shelf that constitutes a natural prolongation of its land territory into and under the sea exist *ipso facto* and *ab initio*, by virtue of its sovereignty over the land, and as an extension of it in an exercise of sovereign rights for the purpose of exploring the seabed and exploiting its natural resources. In short there is here an inherent right.

Location

12.77   The CCS defines the continental shelf as 'the seabed and subsoil of the submarine areas adjacent to the coast but outside the area of the territorial sea, to a depth of 200 metres or, beyond that limit, to where the depth of the superjacent waters admits of the exploitation of the natural resources of the said areas', and 'the seabed and subsoil of similar submarine areas adjacent to the coasts of islands'.[145]

There are two problems with this definition, one technical and one political. The technical problem is that permitting extension of the geographical scope of the juridical continental shelf by reference to advancing extraction technologies introduces a significant element of uncertainty and a potentially open-ended expansion of the zone. The political problem is that some coastal States have very large areas of adjacent continental shelf down to a depth of 200 metres, while nature has been far less generous to many others.

144. *North Sea Continental Shelf* cases (*Germany v Denmark, Germany v The Netherlands*) ICJ Rep (1969) 3, para 19.
145. CCS, Art 1.

12.78 The depth-extended-by-technology definition of the juridical continental shelf employed by the CCS was abandoned at UNCLOS III. The CLS defines a coastal State's continental shelf as:[146]

> ... the sea-bed and subsoil of the submarine areas that extend beyond its territorial sea throughout the natural prolongation of its land territory to the outer edge of the continental margin, or to a distance of 200 nautical miles from the baselines from which the breadth of the territorial sea is measured where the outer edge of the continental margin does not extend up to that distance.

The continental margin consists of 'the submerged prolongation of the land mass of the coastal State, and consists of the sea-bed and subsoil of the shelf, the slope and the rise' but not 'the deep ocean floor with its oceanic ridges or the subsoil thereof'.[147] The 200-mile continental shelf is now part of customary international law.[148]

Under the CLS and customary international law, therefore, every coastal State possesses a juridical continental shelf extending from the boundary of the territorial sea to at least 200 miles from baselines, subject to valid overlapping claims by other States. This applies even if the continental shelf, in its geological sense, does not extend so far. For the purpose of delimiting the juridical continental shelf, the water's depth within the 200-mile area is irrelevant, as are advances in resource-extraction technologies.

The juridical continental shelf will be wider than the 200-mile minimum where the continental margin is more than 200 miles from baselines. Where this occurs, the outer edge of the continental margin is determined by the application of a complex test involving straight lines not exceeding 60 miles in length, the thickness and distribution of sedimentary rocks and their proximity to the continental slope, and rates of gradient change.[149] The juridical continental shelf cannot, however, be wider than either 350 miles from the baselines or 100 miles from the points at which the water is 2,500 metres deep, whichever provides the wider area.[150]

Rights of coastal State

12.79 The coastal State enjoys sovereign rights to explore its continental shelf and to exploit its natural resources.[151] The conventions make clear that sovereignty in this context means that no-one else may explore or exploit the continental shelf without the coastal State's permission — even if the coastal State does not itself exercise the

---

146. CLS, Art 76(1).
147. Ibid, Art 76(3).
148. *Case Concerning the Continental Shelf (Libya v Malta)* ICJ Rep (1985) 13, paras 29–36.
149. CLS, Art 76(4).
150. Ibid, Art 76(5).
151. CLS, Art 77(1) and CCS, Art 2(1).

rights.[152] These rights inhere automatically in the coastal State and are not dependent on any effective or notional occupation or on any express proclamation.[153]

12.80   Only the coastal State may authorise drilling for any purpose in the continental shelf.[154] The coastal State is also free to exploit the continental shelf's resources by tunnelling into the subsoil.[155]

12.81   In contrast to the EEZ, which involves rights to both the living and the non-living resources of the sea itself, as well as those of the seabed and subsoil, the continental shelf regime involves a more limited range of rights. The right to exploit natural resources in the continental shelf extends only to:[156]

> ... the mineral and other non-living resources of the sea-bed and subsoil together with living organisms belonging to sedentary species, that is to say, organisms which ... either are immobile on or under the sea-bed or are unable to move except in constant physical contact with the sea-bed or the subsoil.

In practical terms, the continental shelf regime does not confer sovereign or exclusive rights to exploit fish and other creatures swimming or floating in the sea. It does, however, confer such rights in relation to fossil fuels and minerals on or beneath the seabed and to non-swimming and non-floating creatures on or beneath the seabed, such as oysters, clams, crabs and sea sponges.

12.82   The CLS provides for a system of payments and contributions to the International Sea Bed Authority for the exploitation of the continental shelf's resources beyond 200 miles from baselines. At any one site, the first five years of production are free, but in the sixth year the coastal State must pay 1 per cent of the value or volume of production, rising annually by single percentage points to 7 per cent in the 12th and subsequent years of production. Special concessionary rules apply to developing States.[157]

12.83   The rights of the coastal State over the continental shelf do not affect the legal status of the waters and airspace above it.[158] Thus, where those waters are part of the EEZ or high seas, all the rights and obligations attaching to the EEZ or the high seas continue to apply to those waters. A coastal State must, furthermore, refrain from exercising its continental shelf rights in such a way that they infringe upon or unjustifiably interfere with other States' navigation rights.[159]

---

152. CLS, Art 77(2) and CCS, Art 2(2).
153. CLS, Art 77(3) and CCS, Art 2(3).
154. CLS, Art 81.
155. CLS, Art 85 and CCS, Art 7.
156. CLS, Art 77(4) and CCS, Art 2(4).
157. CLS, Art 82.
158. CLS, Art 78(1); semble CCS, Art 3.
159. CLS, Art 78(2).

Cables, pipelines, artificial islands and installations

12.84   A coastal State may not impede the laying of submarine cables and pipelines on the continental shelf,[160] although the coastal State may refuse consent to the delineation of the course of pipelines.[161] States laying submarine cables and pipelines on the continental shelf must also pay due regard to the position of existing cables and pipelines, and must not prejudice the possibility of repairing the existing installations.[162]

12.85   The EEZ provisions on the construction of artificial islands, installations for economic purposes, and other installations and structures which may interfere with the coastal State's rights[163] apply in like fashion to the continental shelf.[164]

High seas

Location

12.86   The high seas consist of the world's oceans which lie beyond the internal waters, territorial sea, EEZ and archipelagic waters of coastal States.[165] They represent about 64 per cent of the world's marine surface, or about 45 per cent of the world's entire surface.

Freedom of the high seas

12.87   With the triumph of the principle of the freedom of the seas,[166] the high seas were placed beyond the jurisdiction of any State. This rule of customary international law is reflected in the conventions which provide that no State may subject any part of the high seas to its sovereignty[167] and that every State has the freedom of navigation involving the right to sail ships flying its flag on the high seas.[168]

UNCLOS I identified the other principal freedoms of the high seas as being the freedom of fishing, the freedom to lay submarine cables and pipelines, and the freedom of overflight.[169] UNCLOS III extended this list by adding the freedom to construct artificial islands and other installations permitted by international law, and the freedom to conduct scientific research.[170]

---

160. CLS, Art 79(1), (2) and CCS, Art 4.
161. CLS, Art 79(3).
162. Ibid, Art 79(5).
163. See 12.66.
164. CLS, Art 80.
165. CLS, Art 86; semble CHS, Art 1.
166. See 12.1–12.8.
167. CLS, Art 89 and CHS, Art 2.
168. CLS, Arts 87(1)(a) and 90 and CHS, Arts 2(1) and 4.
169. CHS, Art 2.
170. CLS, Art 87(1)(d), (f).

The freedoms to lay submarine cables and pipelines, to construct artificial islands and installations, and to conduct scientific research were made subject to the rules on the continental shelf, while the freedom to conduct scientific research in the high seas was also made subject to some principles and rules affecting marine scientific research generally.[171] The right to fish was made subject to other treaty obligations, and certain rules relating to the conservation of marine species.[172] In relation to submarine cables and pipelines, States are under an obligation to adopt domestic laws making it an offence by those subject to their jurisdiction to break cables and pipelines wilfully or by culpable negligence.[173] States must also adopt domestic laws requiring the owners of cables or pipelines to bear the cost of repairs when they damage a cable or pipeline belonging to someone else.[174]

12.88   These principal freedoms are to be exercised with 'due regard'[175] or 'reasonable regard'[176] to the interests of other States exercising their high seas rights, and to the rights relating to the international seabed area.[177] Two leading publicists on the law of the sea have observed:[178]

> The requirement of 'due regard' seems to require that where there is a potential conflict between two uses of the high seas, there should be a case-by-case weighing of the actual interests involved in the circumstances in question, in order to determine which use is the more reasonable in that particular case. For example, the stringing out of long lines of fishing nets across a busy shipping lane would not be permissible, although the use of such nets elsewhere might be reasonable and permissible. Arguably, there is a presumption in favour of an established use as against a new use. Such a weighing of interests will normally occur through negotiations between the States concerned … In practice stronger States have often been able to insist upon their own uses of the high seas even if such use may appear unreasonable to other States.

A State's obligation to pay reasonable regard to the high seas freedoms of other States was an issue in the *Nuclear Tests* cases.[179] Although States frequently use the high seas in order to test weapons, safety precautions normally take the form of giving international warnings and urging vessels to remain well clear of the test site. In the *Nuclear Tests* cases, however, France used force to exclude international shipping and aircraft from entering areas of the high seas close to the sites of the nuclear tests. This forceful closure attracted international protests as being an unlawful interference in the freedom of the high seas and was among the issues raised by Australia and New Zealand in the cases. The issue did not

---

171. Ibid, Art 87(1)(c), (f).
172. Ibid, Art 116.
173. Ibid, Art 113.
174. Ibid, Art 114.
175. CLS, Art 87(2).
176. CHS, Art 2.
177. CLS, Art 87(2).
178. R R Churchill and A V Lowe, *The Law of the Sea*, 3rd ed, Manchester University Press, Manchester, 1999, 206.
179. *Nuclear Tests* cases *(Australia v France, New Zealand v France)* ICJ Rep (1974) 253. See **1.199**.

proceed to judgment, however, because the International Court of Justice held that France's unilateral declaration ending future atmospheric nuclear tests terminated the disputes.

Peaceful purposes

12.89   The high seas are also 'reserved for peaceful purposes'.[180] State practice not only supports using the high seas for weapons testing, it also permits them to be used as a venue for naval manoeuvres — for example, the finding concerning United States naval manoeuvres on the high seas near Nicaragua's coast in the *Nicaragua* case.[181] The principle that the high seas be reserved for peaceful purposes is best understood as reiterating, in the context of the high seas regime, the general international law requirements that international disputes be settled by peaceful means[182] and that States refrain from the threat or use of force in their international relations.[183]

Flag State jurisdiction

12.90   Although the high seas are not themselves subject to the jurisdiction of any State, ships traversing the high seas are subject to the exclusive jurisdiction of the State whose nationality they possess.

This fundamental principle of international law found expression in the *Lotus* case, in which the Permanent Court of International Justice observed that 'vessels on the high seas are subject to no authority except that of the state whose flag they fly'.[184]

12.91   Each State determines the conditions for the grant of nationality to ships, for the registration of ships, and for the right to fly its flag. A ship possesses the nationality of the State whose flag it is entitled to fly. A ship is not allowed to change its flag during a voyage or while visiting a port of call, except where there has been a transfer of ownership or a change of registry. Any ship which attempts to sail under more than one flag, using them according to convenience, is not entitled to claim any State's nationality and may be treated as a ship without any nationality.[185]

12.92   The conventions stipulate that there must be a 'genuine link' between a ship and the State whose nationality it possesses, and that the State must effectively exercise its jurisdiction and control over the ship in administrative, technical and social matters.[186] This raises a question as to what constitutes a genuine link, and whether other States are obliged to recognise a ship's nationality if the genuine link is missing.

---

180. CLS, Art 88.
181. *Military and Paramilitary Activities in and Against Nicaragua (Nicaragua v United States)* Merits, ICJ Rep (1986) 14. See **9.10**.
182. See **8.4–8.5**.
183. See **9.9–9.10**.
184. *Case of the SS Lotus (France v Turkey)* PCIJ Rep (1927) Series A No 10, 25. See **6.11**.
185. CLS, Arts 91 and 92 and CHS, Arts 5 and 6.
186. CLS, Arts 91(1) and 94(1) and CHS, Art 5(1).

In the ***Saiga* case** (for the facts of which, see 12.71),[187] the International Tribunal for the Law of the Sea said:

75. The next objection to admissibility raised by Guinea is that there was no genuine link between the *Saiga* and Saint Vincent and the Grenadines. Guinea contends that 'without a genuine link between Saint Vincent and the Grenadines and the M/V *"Saiga"*, Saint Vincent and the Grenadines' claim concerning a violation of its right of navigation and the status of the ship is not admissible before the Tribunal *vis-à-vis* Guinea, because Guinea is not bound to recognise the Vincentian nationality of the M/V *"Saiga"*, which forms a prerequisite for the mentioned claim in international law'.

76. Guinea further argues that a State cannot fulfil its obligations as a flag State under the Convention with regard to a ship unless it exercises prescriptive and enforcement jurisdiction over the owner or, as the case may be, the operator of the ship. Guinea contends that, in the absence of such jurisdiction, there is no genuine link between the ship and Saint Vincent and the Grenadines and that, accordingly, it is not obliged to recognize the claims of Saint Vincent and the Grenadines in relation to the ship.

77. Saint Vincent and the Grenadines maintains that there is nothing in the Convention to support the contention that the existence of a genuine link between a ship and a State is a necessary precondition for the grant of nationality to the ship, or that the absence of such a genuine link deprives a flag State of the right to bring an international claim against another State in respect of illegal measures taken against the ship.

78. Saint Vincent and the Grenadines also challenges the assertion of Guinea that there was no genuine link between the *Saiga* and Saint Vincent and the Grenadines. It claims that the requisite genuine link existed between it and the ship.

Saint Vincent and the Grenadines calls attention to various facts which, according to it, provide evidence of this link. These include the fact that the owner of the *Saiga* is represented in Saint Vincent and the Grenadines by a company formed and established in that State and the fact that the *Saiga* is subject to the supervision of the Vincentian authorities to secure compliance with the International Convention for the Safety of Life at Sea (SOLAS), 1960 and 1974, the International Convention for the Prevention of Pollution from Ships, 1973, as modified by the Protocol of 1978 relating thereto (MARPOL 73/78), and other conventions of the International Maritime Organization to which Saint Vincent and the Grenadines is a party. In addition, Saint Vincent and the Grenadines maintains that arrangements have been made to secure regular supervision of the vessel's seaworthiness through surveys, on at least an annual basis, conducted by reputable classification societies authorized for that purpose by Saint Vincent and the Grenadines. Saint Vincent and the Grenadines also points out that, under its laws, preference is given to Vincentian nationals in the manning of ships flying its flag. It further draws attention to the vigorous efforts made by its authorities to secure the protection of the *Saiga* on the international plane before and throughout the present dispute.

79. Article 91, paragraph 1, of the Convention provides: 'There must exist a genuine link between the State and the ship'. Two questions need to be addressed in this connection. The first is whether the absence of a genuine link between a flag State and a ship entitles another State to refuse to recognize the nationality of the ship.

---

187. *M/V 'Saiga' (No 2)* case *(Saint Vincent and the Grenadines v Guinea)* (1999) 3 ITLOS Rep No 2, 37 ILM 1202.

The second question is whether or not a genuine link existed between the *Saiga* and Saint Vincent and the Grenadines at the time of the incident.

80. With regard to the first question, the Tribunal notes that the provision in article 91, paragraph 1, of the Convention, requiring a genuine link between the State and the ship, does not provide the answer. Nor do articles 92 and 94 of the Convention, which together with article 91 constitute the context of the provision, provide the answer. The Tribunal, however, recalls that the International Law Commission, in article 29 of the Draft Articles on the Law of the Sea adopted by it in 1956, proposed the concept of a 'genuine link' as a criterion not only for the attribution of nationality to a ship but also for the recognition by other States of such nationality. After providing that 'ships have the nationality of the State whose flag they are entitled to fly', the draft article continued: 'Nevertheless, for purposes of recognition of the national character of the ship by other States, there must exist a genuine link between the State and the ship'. This sentence was not included in article 5, paragraph 1, of the Convention on the High Seas of 29 April 1958 (hereinafter 'the 1958 Convention'), which reads, in part, as follows: 'There must exist a genuine link between the State and the ship in particular, the State must effectively exercise its jurisdiction and control in administrative, technical and social matters over ships flying its flag'. Thus, while the obligation regarding a genuine link was maintained in the 1958 Convention, the proposal that the existence of a genuine link should be a basis for the recognition of nationality was not adopted.

81. The Convention [on the Law of the Sea] follows the approach of the 1958 Convention. Article 91 retains the part of the third sentence of article 5, paragraph 1, of the 1958 Convention which provides that there must be a genuine link between the State and the ship. The other part of that sentence, stating that the flag State shall effectively exercise its jurisdiction and control in administrative, technical and social matters over ships flying its flag, is reflected in article 94 of the Convention, dealing with the duties of the flag State.

82. Paragraphs 2 to 5 of article 94 of the Convention outline the measures that a flag State is required to take to exercise effective jurisdiction as envisaged in paragraph 1. Paragraph 6 sets out the procedure to be followed where another State has 'clear grounds to believe that proper jurisdiction and control with respect to a ship have not been exercised'. That State is entitled to report the facts to the flag State which is then obliged to 'investigate the matter and, if appropriate, take any action necessary to remedy the situation'. There is nothing in article 94 to permit a State which discovers evidence indicating the absence of proper jurisdiction and control by a flag State over a ship to refuse to recognize the right of the ship to fly the flag of the flag State.

83. The conclusion of the Tribunal is that the purpose of the provisions of the Convention on the need for a genuine link between a ship and its flag State is to secure more effective implementation of the duties of the flag State, and not to establish criteria by reference to which the validity of the registration of ships in a flag State may be challenged by other States. ...

86. In the light of the above considerations, the Tribunal concludes that there is no legal basis for the claim of Guinea that it can refuse to recognize the right of the *Saiga* to fly the flag of Saint Vincent and the Grenadines on the ground that there was no genuine link between the ship and Saint Vincent and the Grenadines.

87. With regard to the second question, the Tribunal finds that, in any case, the evidence adduced by Guinea is not sufficient to justify its contention that there

> was no genuine link between the ship and Saint Vincent and the Grenadines at the material time.
>
> 88. For the above reasons, the Tribunal rejects the objection to admissibility based on the absence of a genuine link between the *Saiga* and Saint Vincent and the Grenadines.

12.93   A corollary of exclusive flag State jurisdiction is the rule that a warship may not board another State's ship on the high seas unless that other ship is reasonably suspected of being engaged in the slave trade,[188] piracy[189] or unauthorised broadcasting.[190]

The only other circumstances in which a warship may board a foreign ship on the high seas is where the ship is reasonably suspected of being without nationality,[191] or where the ship is reasonably suspected of possessing the same nationality as the warship although the ship is flying a foreign flag or refuses to show its flag.[192] In such cases, however, the right to board is more limited than in cases involving the slave trade, piracy and unauthorised broadcasting. The warship must first seek to verify a ship's right to fly its flag. To this end, the warship may exercise a right of approach by sending a boat under an officer's command to the ship. The warship may board the ship only if suspicion remains after the ship's documents have been checked upon approach.[193] It would seem to follow that if the ship refuses to permit the warship to exercise its right of approach (for example, by attempting to flee), the warship would be permitted to board the ship without first exercising the right of approach.

12.94   Only the flag State, or the State whose nationality the master or a crew member possesses, may take penal or disciplinary measures against the master or a crew member in respect of a collision or other navigation incident on the high seas. Furthermore, only the flag State may seize or arrest the ship as a consequence of any such incident.[194]

12.95   States are under an obligation to require the master of every ship flying their flag to assist or rescue persons in distress at sea, including any other ship and persons involved in a collision at sea.[195]

Slave trade

12.96   During the 19th century, Britain's Royal Navy mounted a long and ultimately successful campaign against the international slave trade.

---

188. CLS, Art 110(1)(b). See **12.96**.
189. CLS, Art 110(1)(a). See **12.100**.
190. CLS, Art 110(1)(c). See **12.102**.
191. CLS, Art 110(1)(d).
192. CLS, Art 110(1)(e) and CHS, Art 22(1)(c).
193. CLS, Art 110(2) and CHS, Art 22(2).
194. CLS, Art 97 and CHS, Art 11; cf *Case of the SS Lotus (France v Turkey)* PCIJ Rep (1927) Series A No 10, 25 (see **6.11**).
195. CLS, Art 98 and CHS, Art 12.

Under the modern law of the sea, all States are under an obligation to take effective measures to prevent and punish the transport of slaves in ships flying their flags, and to prevent the use of their flags for transporting slaves. A slave taking refuge aboard any ship, whatever its flag, is automatically free.[196] A warship may also board any foreign ship, except another State's warship, reasonably suspected of being engaged in the slave trade.[197]

Piracy

12.97   Quite possibly the oldest widely accepted rule of maritime law is the prohibition on piracy. The Romans enacted an anti-piracy law, addressed also to Rome's allies in the eastern Mediterranean, as early as 100 BC. It provided, inter alia, that 'no official or garrison will harbour pirates and should be considered zealous collaborators for the safety of all'. Roman naval and military forces were repeatedly deployed to suppress piracy throughout the maritime areas bounding the empire, and Roman law regarded pirates as *hostes humanis generis* (enemies of all mankind) to be suppressed by all available means, regardless of their citizenship. Piracy has been a more or less permanent problem since ancient times, and has experienced a recent resurgence in areas such as South East Asia, Africa, the Indian Ocean, South America and even the Mediterranean.

12.98   The conventions reflect the longstanding customary international rule that all States 'shall co-operate to the fullest possible extent in the repression of piracy on the high seas or in any other place outside the jurisdiction of any State'.[198]

12.99   Piracy occurs when the crew or passengers of a private ship on the high seas commit illegal acts of violence or detention or any act of depredation against another ship, or any person or property on board that other ship. The acts of violence, detention or depredation must be for private ends if they are to qualify as acts of piracy. Thus, politically motivated acts do not amount to piracy. The requirement that the acts be directed from one ship to another excludes from the scope of piracy acts of mutiny and criminal acts among persons on board the same ship.

Any person who voluntarily participates in the operation of any ship with knowledge of the facts making it a pirate ship is also engaged in acts of piracy. Piracy is also committed by any person who incites or intentionally facilitates acts of piracy.[199] Warships and government ships cannot be engaged in acts of piracy unless their crews have mutinied and taken control of the ship.[200]

---

196. CLS, Art 99 and CHS, Art 13.
197. CLS, Art 110(1)(b) and CHS, Art 22(1)(b).
198. CLS, Art 100 and CHS, Art 14.
199. CLS, Art 101 and CHS, Art 15.
200. CLS, Art 102 and CHS, Art 16.

12.100   A warship may board any foreign ship, except another State's warship, reasonably suspected of being engaged in piracy.[201] On the high seas, any State may seize a pirate ship, or any ship captured by and under the control of pirates, regardless of the ship's nationality. Any property on board may also be seized and any persons arrested. The seizing State's courts may determine the penalties for the persons arrested and the action to be taken in respect of the seized ship and property, subject to the rights of third parties acting in good faith.[202]

Only warships and military aircraft, or other ships and aircraft clearly marked and identifiable as being on government service and authorised to that effect, may seize a ship on account of piracy.[203] Where a ship has been seized on suspicion of piracy without adequate grounds, the seizing State is obliged to make reparation for any loss or damage to the State whose nationality the seized ship possesses.[204]

Drug trafficking

12.101   All States are under an obligation to cooperate in the suppression, by ships on the high seas, of illicit traffic in narcotic drugs and psychotropic substances contrary to international conventions. Under the CLS, there is no general power of States to board, search or seize foreign ships on the high seas and arrest persons on board who are engaged in illicit drug trafficking. Rather, the flag State of a ship reasonably suspected of engaging in illicit drug trafficking may request other States' cooperation in the suppression of the traffic.[205] Thus, other States may board, search and seize a vessel on the high seas and arrest persons on board only if requested to do so by the flag State.[206]

Unauthorised broadcasting

12.102   All States are also required to cooperate in the suppression of unauthorised broadcasting from the high seas. Unauthorised broadcasting is the 'transmission of sound radio or television broadcasts from a ship or installation on the high seas intended for reception by the general public contrary to international regulations, but excluding the transmission of distress calls'.[207]

A person engaged in unauthorised broadcasting may be prosecuted by the flag State of the ship, the State of registry of the installation, the State of which the person is a national, any State where the unauthorised

---

201. CLS, Art 110(1)(a) and CHS, Art 22(1)(a).
202. CLS, Art 105 and CHS, Art 19.
203. CLS, Art 107; cf CHS, Art 21, which does not prescribe clear marking and identification for the seizing ship or aircraft.
204. CLS, Art 106 and CHS, Art 20.
205. CLS, Art 108.
206. Semble United Nations Convention against Illicit Traffic in Narcotic Drugs and Psychotropic Substances, Art 17, UNTS, Vol 1582, p 95; Council of Europe Agreement on Illicit Traffic by Sea, Art 6, UNTS, Vol 2136, p 79.
207. CLS, Art 109(2).

transmissions can be received, and any State where authorised radio communication is suffering interference. Any of these States may arrest any person or ship on the high seas engaged in unauthorised broadcasting, regardless of the nationality of that person or ship.[208] Any of these States' warships may board any foreign ship, except another State's warship, reasonably suspected of being engaged in unauthorised broadcasting.[209]

Hot pursuit

12.103   During the course of the 19th century, a right of hot pursuit emerged as an exception to the freedom of navigation on the high seas. According to this rule, a foreign ship which violated a coastal State's laws in its internal waters or territorial sea could be pursued into the high seas, apprehended there, and forcibly returned to the coastal State's territory in order to be dealt with for the violation of law. As is sometimes the case with customary rules, the precise parameters and conditions of this rule were not always clear. Nevertheless, it was generally accepted that, in exercising the right, the pursuing State could use only 'necessary and reasonable force for the purpose of effecting the objects of boarding, searching, seizing and bringing into port the suspected vessel'.[210]

12.104   UNCLOS I codified the customary international law of hot pursuit, except for the requirements on the use of force.[211] UNCLOS III adopted this provision virtually verbatim, but altered it to accommodate the EEZ and the continental shelf. The relevant provision in the Convention on the Law of the Sea provides, in part, as follows:

Article 111

Right of hot pursuit

1.   The hot pursuit of a foreign ship may be undertaken when the competent authorities of the coastal State have good reason to believe that the ship has violated the laws and regulations of that State. Such pursuit must be commenced when the foreign ship or one of its boats is within the internal waters, the archipelagic waters, the territorial sea or the contiguous zone of the pursuing State, and may only be continued outside the territorial sea or the contiguous zone if the pursuit has not been interrupted. It is not necessary that, at the time when the foreign ship within the territorial sea or the contiguous zone receives the order to stop, the ship giving the order should likewise be within the territorial sea or the contiguous zone. If the foreign ship is within a contiguous zone, as defined in article 33, the pursuit may only be undertaken if there has been a violation of the rights for the protection of which the zone was established.

---

208. Ibid, Art 109(4).
209. Ibid, Art 110(1)(c).
210. *SS 'I'm Alone' case (Canada v United States)* (1935) 3 RIAA 1609.
211. CHS, Art 23.

2. The right of hot pursuit shall apply mutatis mutandis to violations in the exclusive economic zone or on the continental shelf, including safety zones around continental shelf installations, of the laws and regulations of the coastal State applicable in accordance with this Convention to the exclusive economic zone or the continental shelf, including such safety zones.

3. The right of hot pursuit ceases as soon as the ship pursued enters the territorial sea of its own State or of a third State.

4. Hot pursuit is not deemed to have begun unless the pursuing ship has satisfied itself by such practicable means as may be available that the ship pursued or one of its boats or other craft working as a team and using the ship pursued as a mother ship is within the limits of the territorial sea, or, as the case may be, within the contiguous zone or the exclusive economic zone or above the continental shelf. The pursuit may only be commenced after a visual or auditory signal to stop has been given at a distance which enables it to be seen or heard by the foreign ship.

12.105   The requirements of Art 111 are cumulative, and the customary law requirements on the use of force in boarding and arresting the vessel must be observed.

> In the **Saiga case** (for the facts of which, see 12.92),[212] the International Tribunal for the Law of the Sea said:
>
> 139. Saint Vincent and the Grenadines contends that, in arresting the Saiga, Guinea did not lawfully exercise the right of hot pursuit under article 111 of the Convention. It argues that since the Saiga did not violate the laws and regulations of Guinea applicable in accordance with the Convention, there was no legal basis for the arrest. Consequently, the authorities of Guinea did not have 'good reason' to believe that the Saiga had committed an offence that justified hot pursuit in accordance with the Convention.
>
> 140. Saint Vincent and the Grenadines asserts that, even if the Saiga violated the laws and regulations of Guinea as claimed, its arrest on 28 October 1997 did not satisfy the other conditions for hot pursuit under article 111 of the Convention. It notes that the alleged pursuit was commenced while the ship was well outside the contiguous zone of Guinea. The Saiga was first detected (by radar) in the morning of 28 October 1997 when the ship was either outside the exclusive economic zone of Guinea or about to leave that zone. The arrest took place after the ship had crossed the southern border of the exclusive economic zone of Guinea.
>
> 141. Saint Vincent and the Grenadines further asserts that, wherever and whenever the pursuit was commenced, it was interrupted. It also contends that no visual and auditory signals were given to the ship prior to the commencement of the pursuit, as required by article 111 of the Convention.
>
> 142. Guinea denies that the pursuit was vitiated by any irregularity and maintains that the officers engaged in the pursuit complied with all the requirements set out in article 111 of the Convention. In some of its assertions, Guinea contends

---

212. *M/V 'Saiga' (No 2) case (Saint Vincent and the Grenadines v Guinea)* (1999) 3 ITLOS Rep No 2, 37 ILM 1202.

that the pursuit was commenced on 27 October 1997 soon after the authorities of Guinea had information that the *Saiga* had committed or was about to commit violations of the customs and contraband laws of Guinea and that the pursuit was continued throughout the period until the ship was spotted and arrested in the morning of 28 October 1997. In other assertions, Guinea contends that the pursuit commenced in the early morning of 28 October 1997 when the *Saiga* was still in the exclusive economic zone of Guinea. In its assertions, Guinea relies on article 111, paragraph 2, of the Convention. ...

144. Guinea admits that the arrest took place outside the exclusive economic zone of Guinea. However, it points out that since the place of arrest was not in the territorial sea either of the ship's flag State or of another State, there was no breach of article 111 of the Convention. ...

146. The Tribunal notes that the conditions for the exercise of the right of hot pursuit under article 111 of the Convention are cumulative; each of them has to be satisfied for the pursuit to be legitimate under the Convention. In this case, the Tribunal finds that several of these conditions were not fulfilled.

147. With regard to the pursuit alleged to have commenced on 27 October 1997, the evidence before the Tribunal indicates that, at the time the Order for the Joint Mission of the Customs and Navy of Guinea was issued, the authorities of Guinea, on the basis of information available to them, could have had no more than a suspicion that a tanker had violated the laws of Guinea in the exclusive economic zone. The Tribunal also notes that, in the circumstances, no visual or auditory signals to stop could have been given to the *Saiga*. Furthermore, the alleged pursuit was interrupted. According to the evidence given by Guinea, the small patrol boat P35 that was sent out on 26 October 1997 on a northward course to search for the *Saiga* was recalled when information was received that the *Saiga* had changed course. This recall constituted a clear interruption of any pursuit, whatever legal basis might have existed for its commencement in the first place.

148. As far as the pursuit alleged to have commenced on 28 October 1998 is concerned, the evidence adduced by Guinea does not support its claim that the necessary auditory or visual signals to stop were given to the *Saiga* prior to the commencement of the alleged pursuit, as required by article 111, paragraph 4, of the Convention. ... In any case, any signals given at the time claimed by Guinea cannot be said to have been given at the commencement of the alleged pursuit.

149. The Tribunal has already concluded that no laws or regulations of Guinea applicable in accordance with the Convention were violated by the *Saiga*. It follows that there was no legal basis for the exercise of the right of hot pursuit by Guinea in this case.

150. For these reasons, the Tribunal finds that Guinea stopped and arrested the *Saiga* on 28 October 1997 in circumstances which did not justify the exercise of the right of hot pursuit in accordance with the Convention. ...

153. Saint Vincent and the Grenadines claims that Guinea used excessive and unreasonable force in stopping and arresting the *Saiga*. It notes that the *Saiga* was an unarmed tanker almost fully laden with gas oil, with a maximum speed of 10 knots. It also notes that the authorities of Guinea fired at the ship with live ammunition, using solid shots from large-calibre automatic guns. ...

155. In considering the force used by Guinea in the arrest of the *Saiga*, the Tribunal must take into account the circumstances of the arrest in the context of the applicable rules of international law. Although the Convention does not contain express provisions on the use of force in the arrest of ships, international law, which is applicable by virtue of article 293 of the Convention, requires that the

use of force must be avoided as far as possible and, where force is unavoidable, it must not go beyond what is reasonable and necessary in the circumstances. Considerations of humanity must apply in the law of the sea, as they do in other areas of international law.

156. These principles have been followed over the years in law enforcement operations at sea. The normal practice used to stop a ship at sea is first to give an auditory or visual signal to stop, using internationally recognized signals. Where this does not succeed, a variety of actions may be taken, including the firing of shots across the bows of the ship. It is only after the appropriate actions fail that the pursuing vessel may, as a last resort, use force. Even then, appropriate warning must be issued to the ship and all efforts should be made to ensure that life is not endangered (*S.S. 'I'm Alone' case (Canada/United States, 1935), U.N.R.I.A.A., Vol. III, p. 1609; The Red Crusader case (Commission of Enquiry, Denmark – United Kingdom, 1962), I.L.R., Vol. 35, p. 485).* ...

157. In the present case, the Tribunal notes that the *Saiga* was almost fully laden and was low in the water at the time it was approached by the patrol vessel. Its maximum speed was 10 knots. Therefore it could be boarded without much difficulty by the Guinean officers. At one stage in the proceedings Guinea sought to justify the use of gunfire with the claim that the *Saiga* had attempted to sink the patrol boat. During the hearing, the allegation was modified to the effect that the danger of sinking to the patrol boat was from the wake of the *Saiga* and not the result of a deliberate attempt by the ship. But whatever the circumstances, there is no excuse for the fact that the officers fired at the ship itself with live ammunition from a fast-moving patrol boat without issuing any of the signals and warnings required by international law and practice.

158. The Guinean officers also used excessive force on board the *Saiga*. Having boarded the ship without resistance, and although there is no evidence of the use or threat of force from the crew, they fired indiscriminately while on the deck and used gunfire to stop the engine of the ship. In using firearms in this way, the Guinean officers appeared to have attached little or no importance to the safety of the ship and the persons on board. In the process, considerable damage was done to the ship and to vital equipment in the engine and radio rooms. And, more seriously, the indiscriminate use of gunfire caused severe injuries to two of the persons on board.

159. For these reasons, the Tribunal finds that Guinea used excessive force and endangered human life before and after boarding the *Saiga*, and thereby violated the rights of Saint Vincent and the Grenadines under international law.

International seabed (the 'Area')

12.106 The deep ocean floor lying beneath the high seas is the repository of considerable mineral wealth, particularly manganese, cobalt, copper and nickel. UNCLOS III devised a regime for the exploration and exploitation of these resources in what it prosaically named the 'Area'. According to the Convention on the Law of the Sea, the Area is 'the seabed and ocean floor and subsoil thereof, beyond the limits of national jurisdiction'.[213] The Area therefore consists of the entire ocean floor lying beyond the continental shelf.

---

213. CLS, Art 1(1).

12.107 The Area regime devised by UNCLOS III is contained in Part XI (Arts 133–191) of the Convention on the Law of the Sea. The fundamental principles upon which Part XI is based are that the 'Area and its resources are the common heritage of mankind'[214] and that no State or person may appropriate any part of the Area and its resources, or claim, acquire or exercise rights over those resources, except in accordance with the regime established by Part XI itself.[215] That regime was, for the majority of developed States, the sticking point preventing them from ratifying the CLS. The main operational features of the Part XI regime are:

- the establishment of an International Seabed Authority whose function is to organise and control activities in the Area, particularly with a view to administering the Area's resources;[216]
- the establishment of the 'Enterprise', which functions as the Authority's operational arm;[217]
- a detailed production policy giving extensive powers to the Authority and the Enterprise to regulate, authorise and control activities in the area;[218] and
- a system of exploration and exploitation which heavily privileges the Enterprise at the expense of other entities which the Authority permits to engage in mining activities within the area[219] — this system was criticised by developed States as tending to lock up seabed resources, failing to provide adequate incentives for their exploration and exploitation, and entrenching inefficiencies by bureaucratising access to seabed resources and excluding the operation of market forces.

12.108 The impasse drew to a close in the late 1980s and early 1990s as important changes to the international political and economic order brought pressure to bear on the international seabed regime enshrined in the Convention on the Law of the Sea. The collapse of the Soviet bloc, the abandonment of the more egregious aspects of Maoist economic and foreign policies by China, and the acceleration of liberal globalisation created the international climate in which support for the more *dirigiste* features of the Part XI regime diminished and the legal regulation of the Area could be revisited, with a view to attracting more ratifications of the CLS by developed States.

The result was the 1994 Implementation Agreement,[220] under which the original CLS provisions on the Area were substantially modified in ways more acceptable to developed States. In particular, the Enterprise is required to operate according to sound commercial principles and must conduct its initial international seabed mining operations through joint ventures. Furthermore, procedural measures are introduced to strengthen the voice

---

214. Ibid, Art 136.
215. Ibid, Art 137.
216. Ibid, Art 157.
217. Ibid, Arts 158(2) and 170(1).
218. See especially CLS, Art 151.
219. CLS, Art 153 and especially Arts 3, 4, 8 and 9 of Annex III.
220. Agreement relating to the implementation of Part XI of the United Nations Convention on the Law of the Sea of 10 December 1982, UNTS, Vol 1836, p 41.

of developed States in the Authority, and some other rules unattractive to developed States in Part XI, such as compulsory technology transfers to developing States, are modified. The Implementation Agreement was adopted at an international conference of States by 121 votes, with no negative votes and seven abstentions. A number of developed States then felt able to ratify the CLS, which Australia did in 1994. The Implementation Agreement entered into force in 1996.

Delimiting boundaries between maritime zones

12.109   Disagreements sometimes emerge between States concerning the location of boundaries between their maritime zones. These disputes can arise between States with adjacent land territory (for example, Germany and the Netherlands), or between States located opposite each other across a body of water (for example, Australia and East Timor). Usually, these disagreements are resolved by negotiation resulting in a boundary treaty. Where this occurs, the terms of the boundary treaty become binding on the parties and the disagreement is usually resolved. Any future disagreements between the parties concerning the same maritime boundary must, absent a concession by either of them, be settled in accordance with the boundary treaty.

As a practical matter, negotiations are always conducted in the shadow of the international legal rules and principles governing maritime boundary delimitation, although States remain free to settle their boundary dispute however they wish subject to the legal rights of third States.

Negotiation does not always, however, result in an agreed settlement. In such circumstances, States remain obliged to settle their dispute by peaceful means if the dispute would otherwise pose a threat to the maintenance of international peace and security.[221] Where the dispute is resolved in accordance with the procedures prescribed in either Part XV of the Convention on the Law of the Sea ('Settlement of Disputes') or Art 33 of the UN Charter,[222] the international legal rules and principles governing maritime boundary delimitation will be crucial.

12.110   As far as disagreements concerning boundaries between territorial seas are concerned, the principles are relatively straightforward. The conventions provide that, subject to contrary agreement between them, opposite or adjacent States are to demarcate their territorial sea boundary along the 'median line every point of which is equidistant from the nearest points on the baselines from which the breadth of the territorial seas of each of the two States is measured'. This equidistance

---

221. See 8.4–8.5.
222. See 8.4.

principle is subject to requirements of 'historic title or other special circumstances'.[223] This method of demarcation is usually referred to as the 'equidistance/special circumstance principle'.

The International Court of Justice has said that this principle possesses the character of customary international law and that the 'most logical and widely practised approach is first to draw provisionally an equidistance line and then to consider whether that line must be adjusted in the light of the existence of special circumstances'.[224]

12.111 The delimitation of competing claims to the EEZ and continental shelf are governed by Arts 74 and 83 of the Convention on the Law of the Sea respectively. The provision relating to the EEZ reads as follows:

Article 74

Delimitation of the exclusive economic zone between States with opposite or adjacent coasts

1. The delimitation of the exclusive economic zone between States with opposite or adjacent coasts shall be effected by agreement on the basis of international law, as referred to in Article 38 of the Statute of the International Court of Justice, in order to achieve an equitable solution.

2. If no agreement can be reached within a reasonable period of time, the States concerned shall resort to the procedures provided for in Part XV ['Settlement of Disputes'].

3. Pending agreement as provided for in paragraph 1, the States concerned, in a spirit of understanding and cooperation, shall make every effort to enter into provisional arrangements of a practical nature and, during this transitional period, not to jeopardize or hamper the reaching of the final agreement. Such arrangements shall be without prejudice to the final delimitation.

4. Where there is an agreement in force between the States concerned, questions relating to the delimitation of the exclusive economic zone shall be determined in accordance with the provisions of that agreement.

Article 83 of the CLS is identical, except that all references to the EEZ are replaced by references to the continental shelf.

12.112 Articles 74(1) and 83(1) require States to reach agreement on their EEZ and continental shelf boundaries on the basis of Art 38 of the ICJ Statute — that is, on the basis of applicable treaty, custom and general principles of law, the understanding of which may be assisted by judicial decisions and the teachings of the most highly qualified publicists.[225] As far as the continental shelf is concerned, the Convention on the Law of the Sea departs from the rule prescribed by the Convention on the Continental Shelf, which adopts the same equidistance/special

---

223. CLS, Art 15 and CTSCZ, Art 12(1).
224. *Maritime Delimitation and Territorial Questions Between Qatar and Bahrain* case *(Qatar v Bahrain)* ICJ Rep (2001) 40, para 176.
225. See **1.181–1.187**.

circumstances principle that applies to delimitation of the territorial sea.[226]

In the *North Sea Continental Shelf* cases, the International Court of Justice held that this principle did not represent customary international law as far as the continental shelf was concerned. Rather, the Court opined that the continental shelf was to be delimited in accordance with 'the principles and rules of international law';[227] it is this formulation which provides the drafting context of Arts 74(1) and 83(1) of the CLS.

Subsequently, the ICJ has said that the relevant requirements of customary international law are embodied in 'equitable principles', which are actual principles of law and not merely equivalent to resolving the dispute *ex aequo et bono*.[228]

12.113   The Court has recently discussed the application of these legally binding equitable principles in a boundary dispute between Romania and Ukraine.

> In the ***Maritime Delimitation in the Black Sea* case,**[229] Romania commenced proceedings against Ukraine seeking a demarcation of the boundary separating the two States' adjacent EEZs and continental shelfs. The Court explained the equitable principles upon which this part of the dispute was to be resolved:
>
> 115. When called upon to delimit the continental shelf or exclusive economic zones, or to draw a single delimitation line, the Court proceeds in defined stages.
>
> 116. These separate stages, broadly explained in the case concerning *Continental Shelf (Libyan Arab Jamahiriya/Malta) (Judgment, I.C.J. Reports* 1985, p. 46, para. 60), have in recent decades been specified with precision. First, the Court will establish a provisional delimitation line, using methods that are geometrically objective and also appropriate for the geography of the area in which the delimitation is to take place. So far as delimitation between adjacent coasts is concerned, an equidistance line will be drawn unless there are compelling reasons that make this unfeasible in the particular case (see *Territorial and Maritime Dispute between Nicaragua and Honduras in the Caribbean Sea (Nicaragua v. Honduras)*, Judgment of 8 October 2007, para. 281). So far as opposite coasts are concerned, the provisional delimitation line will consist of a median line between the two coasts. No legal consequences flow from the use of the terms 'median line' and 'equidistance line' since the method of delimitation is the same for both.
>
> 117. Equidistance and median lines are to be constructed from the most appropriate points on the coasts of the two States concerned, with particular attention being paid to those protuberant coastal points situated nearest to the area to [be] delimited. The Court considers elsewhere ... the extent to which the Court may, when constructing a single-purpose delimitation line, deviate from the base points selected by the parties for their territorial seas. When

---

226. CCS, Art 6.
227. *North Sea Continental Shelf* cases *(Germany v Denmark, Germany v The Netherlands)* ICJ Rep (1969) 3, para 101. See **1.140**.
228. *Case Concerning the Continental Shelf (Libya v Malta)* ICJ Rep (1985) 13, para 45.
229. *Case Concerning Maritime Delimitation in the Black Sea (Romania v Ukraine)*, International Court of Justice, judgment, 3 February 2009.

construction of a provisional equidistance line between adjacent States is called for, the Court will have in mind considerations relating to both parties' coastlines when choosing its own base points for this purpose. The line thus adopted is heavily dependent on the physical geography and the most seaward points of the two coasts.

118. In keeping with its settled jurisprudence on maritime delimitation, the first stage of the Court's approach is to establish the provisional equidistance line. At this initial stage of the construction of the provisional equidistance line the Court is not yet concerned with any relevant circumstances that may obtain and the line is plotted on strictly geometrical criteria on the basis of objective data.

119. In the present case the Court will thus begin by drawing a provisional equidistance line between the adjacent coasts of Romania and Ukraine, which will then continue as a median line between their opposite coasts.

120. The course of the final line should result in an equitable solution (Articles 74 and 83 of [CLS]). Therefore, the Court will at the next, second stage consider whether there are factors calling for the adjustment or shifting of the provisional equidistance line in order to achieve an equitable result *(Land and Maritime Boundary between Cameroon and Nigeria (Cameroon v. Nigeria: Equatorial Guinea intervening), Judgment, I.C.J. Reports 2002, p. 441, para. 288)*. The Court has also made clear that when the line to be drawn covers several zones of coincident jurisdictions, 'the so-called equitable principles/relevant circumstances method may usefully be applied, as in these maritime zones this method is also suited to achieving an equitable result' *(Territorial and Maritime Dispute between Nicaragua and Honduras in the Caribbean Sea (Nicaragua v. Honduras), Judgment of 8 October 2007, para. 271)*.

121. This is the second part of the delimitation exercise to which the Court will turn, having first established the provisional equidistance line.

122. Finally, and at a third stage, the Court will verify that the line (a provisional equidistance line which may or may not have been adjusted by taking into account the relevant circumstances) does not, as it stands, lead to an inequitable result by reason of any marked disproportion between the ratio of the respective coastal lengths and the ratio between the relevant maritime area of each State by reference to the delimitation line ... A final check for an equitable outcome entails a confirmation that no great disproportionality of maritime areas is evident by comparison to the ratio of coastal lengths. This is not to suggest that these respective areas should be proportionate to coastal lengths — as the Court has said 'the sharing out of the area is therefore the consequence of the delimitation, not vice versa' *(Maritime Delimitation in the Area between Greenland and Jan Mayen (Denmark v. Norway), Judgment, I.C.J. Reports 1993, p. 67, para. 64)*. ...

137. The Court observes that the issue of determining the baseline for the purpose of measuring the breadth of the continental shelf and the exclusive economic zone and the issue of identifying base points for drawing an equidistance/median line for the purpose of delimiting the continental shelf and the exclusive economic zone between adjacent/opposite States are two different issues. In the first case, the coastal State ... may determine the relevant base points. It is nevertheless an exercise which has always an international aspect (see *Fisheries (United Kingdom v. Norway), Judgment, I.C.J. Reports 1951*, p. 132). In the second case, the delimitation of the maritime areas involving two or more States, the Court should not base itself solely on the choice of base points made by one of those parties. The Court must, when delimiting the continental shelf and exclusive economic zones, select base points by reference to the physical geography of the relevant coasts. ...

155. As the Court indicated above (paragraphs 120–121), once the provisional equidistance line has been drawn, it shall 'then [consider] whether there are factors calling for the adjustment or shifting of that line in order to achieve an "equitable result"' (*Land and Maritime Boundary between Cameroon and Nigeria (Cameroon v. Nigeria: Equatorial Guinea intervening), Judgment, I.C.J. Reports 2002*, p. 441, para. 288). Such factors have usually been referred to in the jurisprudence of the Court, since the *North Sea Continental Shelf (Federal Republic of Germany/ Denmark; Federal Republic of Germany/Netherlands)* cases, as the relevant circumstances (*Judgment, I.C.J. Reports 1969*, p. 53, para. 53). Their function is to verify that the provisional equidistance line, drawn by the geometrical method from the determined base points on the coasts of the Parties is not, in light of the particular circumstances of the case, perceived as inequitable. If such would be the case, the Court should adjust the line in order to achieve the 'equitable solution' as required by Articles 74, paragraph 1, and 83, paragraph 1, of [CLS].
...

163. The Court observes that the respective length of coasts can play no role in identifying the equidistance line which has been provisionally established. Delimitation is a function which is different from the apportionment of resources or areas (see *North Sea Continental Shelf (Federal Republic of Germany/Denmark; Federal Republic of Germany/Netherlands), Judgment, I.C.J. Reports 1969*, p. 22, para. 18). There is no principle of proportionality as such which bears on the initial establishment of the provisional equidistance line.

164. Where disparities in the lengths of coasts are particularly marked, the Court may choose to treat that fact of geography as a relevant circumstance that would require some adjustments to the provisional equidistance line to be made.

165. In the case concerning *Land and Maritime Boundary between Cameroon and Nigeria (Cameroon v. Nigeria; Equatorial Guinea intervening)*, the Court acknowledged 'that a *substantial* difference in the lengths of the parties' respective coastlines *may* be a factor to be taken into consideration in order to adjust or shift the provisional delimitation line' (*Judgment, I.C.J. Report 2002, p. 446*, para. 301; emphasis added), although it found that in the circumstances there was no reason to shift the equidistance line.

166. In the case concerning *Maritime Delimitation in the Area between Greenland and Jan Mayen (Denmark v. Norway)*, the Court found that the disparity between the lengths of the coasts of Jan Mayen and Greenland (approximately 1:9) constituted a 'special circumstance' requiring modification of the provisional median line, by moving it closer to the coast of Jan Mayen, to avoid inequitable results for both the continental shelf and the fisheries zone. The Court stated that:

> 'It should, however, be made clear that taking account of the disparity of coastal lengths does not mean a direct and mathematical application of the relationship between the length of the coastal front of eastern Greenland and that of Jan Mayen.' (*Judgment, I.C.J. Reports 1993*, p. 69, para. 69.)

Then it recalled its observation from the *Continental Shelf (Libyan Arab Jamahiriya/ Malta)* case:

> 'If such a use of proportionality were right, it is difficult indeed to see what room would be left for any other consideration; for it would be at once the principle of entitlement to continental shelf rights and also the method of putting that principle into operation. Its weakness as a basis of argument, however, is that the use of proportionality as a method in its own right is wanting of support in the practice of States, in the public expression of their views at (in particular) the Third United Nations Conference on the Law of the Sea, or in the jurisprudence.' (*Continental Shelf (Libyan Arab Jamahiriya/Malta), Judgment, I.C.J. Reports 1985*, p. 45, para. 58.)

In the latter case, the Court was of the view that the difference in the lengths of the relevant coasts of Malta and Libya (being in ratio 1:8) 'is so *great* as to justify the adjustment of the median line' (*ibid.*, p. 50, para. 68; emphasis added). The Court added that 'the degree of such adjustment does not depend upon a mathematical operation and remains to be examined' (*ibid.*).

167. The Court further notes that in the *Delimitation of the Maritime Boundary in the Gulf of Maine Area (Canada/United States of America)* case, the Chamber considered that 'in certain circumstances, the appropriate consequences may be drawn from any *inequalities* in the extent of the coasts of two States into the same area of delimitation' (*Judgment, I.C.J. Reports 1984*, p. 313, para. 157; emphasis added). However, it must be kept in mind that the Chamber did so in the context of discussing what could be 'the *equitable* criteria that may be taken into consideration for an international maritime delimitation' (*ibid.*, p. 312, para. 157; emphasis added). It then further elaborated on this point by stating

'[…] that to take into account the extent of the respective coasts of the Parties concerned does not in itself constitute either a criterion serving as a direct basis for a delimitation, or a method that can be used to implement such delimitation. The Chamber recognizes that this concept is put forward mainly as a means of checking whether a provisional delimitation established initially on the basis of other criteria, and by the use of a method which has nothing to do with that concept, can or cannot be considered satisfactory in relation to certain geographical features of the specific case, and whether it is reasonable or otherwise to correct it accordingly. The Chamber's views on this subject may be summed up by observing that a maritime delimitation can certainly not be established by a direct division of the area in dispute proportional to the respective lengths of the coasts belonging to the parties in the relevant area, but it is equally certain that a *substantial* disproportion to the lengths of those coasts that resulted from a delimitation effected on a different basis would constitute a circumstance calling for an appropriate correction.' (*Ibid.*, p. 323, para. 185; emphasis added.)

185. In determining the maritime boundary line, in default of any delimitation agreement within the meaning of [CLS] Articles 74 and 83, the Court may, should relevant circumstances so suggest, adjust the provisional equidistance line to ensure an equitable result. In this phase the Court may be called upon to decide whether this line should be adjusted because of the presence of small islands in its vicinity. As the jurisprudence has indicated, the Court may on occasion decide not to take account of very small islands or decide not to give them their full potential entitlement to maritime zones, should such an approach have a disproportionate effect on the delimitation line under consideration (see *Continental Shelf (Libyan Arab Jamahiriya/Malta), Judgment, I.C.J. Reports 1985*, p. 48, para. 64; *Maritime Delimitation and Territorial Questions between Qatar and Bahrain (Qatar* v. *Bahrain), Merits, Judgment, I.C.J. Reports 2001*, p. 104, para. 219; *Territorial and Maritime Dispute between Nicaragua and Honduras in the Caribbean Sea (Nicaragua* v. *Honduras)*, Judgment of 8 October 2007, paras. 302 *et seq.*).

It therefore appears that, although the legal formulation for determining boundaries involving the territorial sea on the one hand (equidistance/special circumstances) and the contiguous zone and EEZ on the other (equitable principles) are different, a very similar approach, in fact, operates. The starting point in each case is the equidistance line. In each case, one then must establish whether there are any special circumstances which require a departure from that line.

It appears that it will be easier to establish special circumstances requiring such a departure in cases involving the contiguous zone and the EEZ than in cases involving the territorial sea. This is because of the explicit imperative to achieve an 'equitable solution' in Arts 74(1) and 83(1) of the Convention on the Law of the Sea. In practice, there are significantly fewer disputes concerning boundaries between territorial seas than concerning boundaries between EEZs and continental shelfs.

Question

The M/V *Catharina* is a small cargo vessel owned by nationals of the State of Abacus. Its master and 15 crew have always consisted entirely of Abacus nationals. Nevertheless, the *Catharina* is registered under the law of the State of Bellus as a ship of Bellus nationality with the right to fly Bellus's flag. The *Catharina* flies Bellus's flag at all times.

Bellus and the State of Cadana have both been parties to the Convention on the Law of the Sea since 1994. Cadana's legislation claims a territorial sea, contiguous zone and EEZ to the maximum width allowable under the CLS.

On the morning of 15 October, the *Catharina* entered the territorial sea of Cadana while en route from Port Bellus (in Bellus) to Port Abacus (in Abacus). In addition to its usual complement of master and crew, the *Catharina* was also carrying 30 Bellus nationals. None of these passengers were carrying passports or other travel documents. Over the last few years, Cadana has had a problem of illegal immigrants from Bellus arriving by ship and landing ashore at remote locations on the Cadana coast.

In order to arrive legally in Cadana, foreigners must disembark from a ship or aircraft at a designated seaport or airport, together with a passport and Cadana visa. They must then promptly present themselves at the official immigration checkpoint located at every designated seaport and airport. Failure to comply with this requirement is a criminal offence. It is also a criminal offence knowingly to assist another person to evade the requirement and to perform any act, or assist in the performance of any act, preparatory to the evasion of the requirement.

After sunset on 15 October, the *Catharina* anchored a few metres away from Danger Island, on its seaward side. Danger Island is an uninhabited rocky outcrop belonging to Cadana, the landward side of which is located exactly 12.01 miles from the low-water mark on the nearest part of Cadana's coastline. There are no other islands, rocks, reefs or roadsteads in the vicinity, and no harbour works on the nearby coast. Danger Island is about 10 metres in diameter at low tide and is completely submerged at high tide. It is more than 500 kilometres from any legally designated seaport or airport. Cadana navy maps display Danger Island as generating its own 12-mile territorial sea and a further 12-mile contiguous zone.

After about 20 minutes had passed and it had become almost completely dark, the *Catharina* lowered several rowboats into the water. At this point, a Cadana navy surveillance station on the mainland, receiving a tip-off from someone on board the *Catharina*, sent a radio message to the *Catharina*. The message was immediately received by the ship's master. The message said that the *Catharina* was in Cadana territorial waters, that it must desist from lowering the rowboats, and that it must maintain its position pending the arrival and boarding of a Cadana navy coastal patrol boat.

The *Catharina* immediately hauled its rowboats aboard, raised anchor, and proceeded at maximum speed towards the open ocean. The navy patrol boat despatched from the mainland lost track of the *Catharina* and turned back at 11.00pm on 15 October. By 3.00am on 16 October, the *Catharina* had reached the high seas, but the passengers had become angry at the master's decision to navigate away from the Cadana coast. Two passengers produced pistols and threatened to shoot crew members unless the master turned the *Catharina* around and returned to Cadana. The master refused, and a crew member was shot and seriously wounded by the two armed passengers, who then threatened the remaining crew with death unless the master turned the vessel around. The crew's radio operator managed to send out a distress signal saying that two armed passengers on board the vessel had shot a crew member, and requesting medical assistance.

A Cadana navy destroyer, which had been on the lookout for the *Catharina* since the patrol boat abandoned the chase, responded to the distress call and arrived on the scene within 15 minutes. A detachment of armed marines from the destroyer quickly boarded the *Catharina* without first obtaining permission from the ship's master.

One of the marines shot dead a crew member who did not immediately comply with an order to lie down on the deck. The remaining crew and passengers, including the two armed passengers, immediately complied.

The *Catharina*, with its master, crew and passengers, was taken to Port Cadana (in Cadana). The master and surviving crew were immediately deported to Abacus and the passengers were immediately deported to Bellus. The two armed passengers were arrested by Bellus police upon their arrival in Bellus, where they have been charged with offences relating to the attempted hijacking of the *Catharina*.

Cadana has informed Bellus that, because the *Catharina* has no genuine link to Bellus and because it is not registered as the national of any other State, the vessel is Stateless and no State may raise issues regarding its treatment by the Cadana navy. Cadana asserts that the lack of a genuine link arises from the fact that neither the owners, nor the master, nor the crew of the *Catharina* were nationals of Bellus. The Cadana Minister for Defence has publicly stated that the Cadana navy boarded and arrested the *Catharina* in order to suppress piracy and after a hot pursuit following the ship's attempt to violate Cadana's immigration laws. The *Catharina* has since been judicially declared forfeit to Cadana under Cadana's piracy laws.

The Bellus Ministry of Maritime Affairs asks you whether Cadana has complied with its legal obligations to Bellus. Advise the Ministry.

Suggested answer

The *Catharina*'s nationality

Cadana has refused to accept that Bellus has any legal interest in Cadana's treatment of the *Catharina* on the grounds that there is no genuine link between the vessel and Bellus.

Each State determines the conditions for the grant of nationality to ships, for the registration of ships, and for the right to fly its flag. A ship possesses the nationality of the State whose flag it is entitled to fly. There must also be a 'genuine link' between a ship and the State whose nationality it possesses (CLS, Art 91(1)). Every State is obliged to exercise effective jurisdiction and control in administrative, technical and social matters over ships flying its flag (CLS, Art 94).

According to the International Tribunal for the Law of the Sea, 'the purpose of the provisions of the Convention on the need for a genuine link between a ship and its flag State is to secure more effective implementation of the duties of the flag State, and not to establish criteria by reference to which the validity of the registration of ships in a flag State may be challenged by other States' (*Saiga* case, para 83). It follows that because the *Catharina* is registered as a Bellus ship under Bellus law, Cadana is obliged to accept the *Catharina*'s status as a ship of Bellus nationality.

In any event, the presence or otherwise of a genuine link is determined not by reference to the nationality of the owners, master or crew, but by whether the State of registration carries out its obligations to exercise effectively jurisdiction and control in administrative, technical and social matters over ships flying its flag (*Saiga* case, para 82). There is no evidence that Bellus does not exercise effective jurisdiction and control in administrative, technical and social matters over the *Catharina,* and therefore there is no basis for asserting that the ship does not possess the nationality of Bellus.

Territorial sea and innocent passage

The Cadana navy claims that the *Catharina* was located in Cadana's territorial sea at the time it was ordered to hold its position and await the arrival of a navy patrol boat. If this is correct, then Cadana's sovereign authority extended to the activities of the *Catharina* while it was anchored off Danger Island (CLS, Art 2(1)) and Cadana was entitled to intercept and board the *Catharina* unless it was exercising a right of innocent passage.

Ships of all States enjoy a right of innocent passage through the territorial sea (CLS, Art 17). This right involves traversing the territorial sea without entering internal waters or calling at any port facility or roadstead outside internal waters. The journey must be 'continuous and expeditious', although 'passage includes stopping and anchoring, but only insofar as the same are incidental to ordinary navigation or are rendered necessary by *force majeure* or distress or for the purpose of rendering assistance to persons, ships or aircraft in danger or distress' (CLS, Art 18).

In this case, the *Catharina* stopped and anchored off Danger Island with no apparent connection to the requirements of ordinary navigation or other justifying reason. The *Catharina* was, therefore, probably not engaged in 'passage' while it was anchored off Danger Island.

Furthermore, passage will be 'innocent' only if it is not 'prejudicial to the peace, good order or security of the coastal State' (CLS, Art 19(1)). Passage will be deemed prejudicial to those interests if the vessel engages in any activity not having a direct bearing on passage (CLS, Art 19(2)(l)).

In this case, the *Catharina* began lowering rowboats. By doing so, the *Catharina* was probably not engaged in an activity having a direct bearing on passage. Such conduct is deemed to be prejudicial to the peace, good order or security of Cadana, and deprives the *Catharina*'s putative passage of an innocent character.

Therefore, if the *Catharina* was inside Cadana's territorial sea at the time it was anchored off Danger Island, Cadana was probably justified in requiring the vessel to maintain its position and await the arrival of the navy patrol boat.

However, Cadana's claim that the *Catharina* was inside Cadana's territorial sea while it was anchored off Danger Island is incorrect. The maximum width of the territorial sea is 12 miles as measured from baselines (CLS, Art 3). The normal baseline is the low-water mark along the coast (CLS, Art 5). Straight baselines can replace normal baselines in certain circumstances (CLS, Arts 7, 9 and 10), none of which are indicated on the facts of this case. The *Catharina* was anchored more than 12 miles distant from Cadana's coastal baseline. The *Catharina* was, therefore, not within Cadana's territorial sea as measured from the coastal baseline.

The *Catharina* was, however, anchored only a few metres from Danger Island, which Cadana claims generates its own territorial sea. If this is correct, then the *Catharina* was within Cadana's territorial sea as measured from Danger Island. All islands generate their own territorial sea in exactly the same way as coastal areas (CLS, Art 121(2)). For the purpose of this rule, however, an 'island' is any 'naturally formed area of land, surrounded by water, which is above water at high tide' (CLS, Art 121(1)). Danger Island is completely submerged at high tide, and is therefore not an 'island' capable of generating its own territorial sea. It is actually a 'low-tide elevation' — that is, a 'naturally formed area of land which is surrounded by and above water at low tide but submerged at high tide' — which may generate its own territorial sea only where it is wholly or partly situated within a State's territorial sea as measured from the mainland or an island (CLS, Art 13(1)).

Where a low-tide elevation is not within a State's territorial sea as measured from the mainland or an island, it generates no territorial sea of its own (CLS, Art 13(2)). Danger Island is entirely outside Cadana's territorial sea as measured from the mainland, and therefore cannot generate its own territorial sea. The *Catharina* was, therefore, not within Cadana's territorial sea at the time it was anchored off Danger Island.

Contiguous zone

A State's contiguous zone commences where the territorial sea ends and may extend 24 miles from the baselines from which the width of the territorial sea is measured (CLS, Art 33(2)). Because Cadana has claimed the maximum permissible width for its contiguous zone, that zone extends 12 miles beyond the limits of its territorial sea. The *Catharina* was anchored a few metres from the seaward side of Danger Island, which is located 12.01 miles from Cadana's baselines. Danger Island is only 10 metres in diameter at low tide. The *Catharina* was, therefore, located in Cadana's contiguous zone at the time it was anchored off Danger Island.

Whereas in the territorial sea the coastal State's jurisdiction is complete subject to specified customary and conventional exceptions, in the contiguous zone the coastal State enjoys only so much jurisdiction as is specifically conferred on it by customary international law or treaty. A coastal State may exercise such control in the contiguous zone as may be necessary to punish infringements of its immigration laws which have been committed in its territory or territorial sea. It may also exercise control in the contiguous zone necessary to prevent infringements of immigration laws in its territory or territorial sea (CLS, Art 33(1)). This must include a power to arrest vessels and persons and to use such force as is reasonably necessary to execute such arrests. In this case, however, the *Catharina* had simply weighed anchor and lowered some rowboats. Ships are not obliged to remain in motion in the contiguous zone, and there is probably insufficient evidence of an attempt by any of the *Catharina*'s passengers to reach Cadana in violation of Cadana's immigration laws. Therefore, Cadana was probably not justified in ordering the *Catharina* to maintain its position and await boarding by the navy patrol boat. Accordingly, the *Catharina* was probably within its rights to raise anchor and navigate towards the high seas.

Boarding ships on the high seas

Although the high seas are not themselves subject to the jurisdiction of any State, ships traversing the high seas are subject to the exclusive jurisdiction of the State whose nationality they possess (*Lotus* case).

A warship may not board the ship of another State on the high seas except on several specified grounds, including hot pursuit (CLS, Art 111) and reasonable suspicion of piracy (CLS, Art 110(1)(a)). Cadana seeks to justify the boarding and arrest of the *Catharina* on the high seas on both these grounds.

Hot pursuit

Hot pursuit is available only where several conditions are cumulatively met (*Saiga* case, para 146).

Among these cumulative conditions is the requirement that the coastal State has 'good reason to believe that the ship has violated the laws and regulations of that State' (CLS, Art 111(1)). This means laws and regulations that a State is entitled to adopt in the maritime zone where the suspected violation has occurred (*Saiga* case, paras 127, 149). The CLS, furthermore, specifically provides that if the foreign ship is within a contiguous zone, the pursuit may be undertaken only if there has been a violation of the rights for the protection of which the contiguous zone was established (CLS, Art 111(1)). The *Catharina* was located in Cadana's contiguous zone at the time the alleged violations of immigration law occurred. States are entitled to exercise control in the contiguous zone necessary to prevent infringements of immigration laws in its territory or territorial sea (CLS, Art 33(1)). The lowering of rowboats, however, could give rise to no more than a suspicion that a violation of Cadana's immigration laws might occur, and a mere suspicion does not constitute 'good reason' for the purposes of CLS, Art 111(1) (*Saiga* case, para 147).

Another condition is that pursuit may be continued into the high seas only if it has not been interrupted. In this case, the pursuit was interrupted by the abandonment of the patrol boat's pursuit and its continuation by the navy destroyer some four hours later (*Saiga* case, para 147) and only after the *Catharina* had already entered the high seas.

Use of force in boarding vessels

There are also customary international law requirements relating to the use of force in intercepting and boarding a vessel. In particular, the pursued vessel must be given an internationally recognised signal to stop, and any force used in intercepting and boarding must not exceed the requirements of reasonableness and necessity. Upon boarding the vessel, excessive force must be avoided. Considerations of humanity must apply (*Saiga* case, paras 155, 156 and 158). In this case, the unprovoked shooting of an innocent member of the *Catharina*'s crew by the Cadana marine almost certainly involved a violation of these customary requirements.

Piracy and forfeiture

All States must 'co-operate to the fullest possible extent in the repression of piracy on the high seas' (CLS, Art 100) and a warship may board any foreign ship reasonably suspected of being engaged in piracy (CLS, Art 110(1)(a)). On the high seas, any State may seize a pirate ship, or any ship captured by and under the control of pirates, regardless of the ship's nationality. Any property on board may also be seized and any persons arrested. The seizing State's courts may determine the action to be taken in respect of the seized ship and property, subject to the rights of third parties acting in good faith (CLS, Art 105).

Piracy is, however, carefully defined. Of particular relevance to this case is that piracy occurs when the crew or passengers of a ship on the high seas commit illegal acts of violence or detention or any act of depredation against another ship, or any person or property on board that other ship (CLS, Art 101). The requirement that the acts be directed from one ship to another excludes from the scope of piracy criminal acts among persons on board the same ship.

The navy destroyer had no reasonable grounds for believing that the *Catharina* had been seized and attacked by pirates, because there was no evidence that it had been seized or attacked by the crew or passengers of another ship. Indeed, the *Catharina*'s radio distress signal was clear that the culprits were two of the *Catharina*'s own passengers. It follows, therefore, that the Cadana navy destroyer lacked reasonable grounds for suspecting that the *Catharina* was engaged in piracy — that is, attacking other ships or persons aboard other ships on the high seas. Nor were there reasonable grounds for believing that the *Catharina* was captured by, or under the control of, pirates such that Cadana was justified in seizing the vessel and declaring it forfeit. In any event, forfeiture was a violation of third party rights — namely, the third party rights of the owners of the vessel, who were not party to any illegal acts on board the *Catharina*.

Cadana is therefore in breach of its legal obligations owed to Bellus by:

- requiring the *Catharina,* while located in Cadana's contiguous zone, to maintain its position pending boarding by the patrol boat;
- boarding and arresting the *Catharina* on the high seas without justification of hot pursuit, the suppression of piracy, or other recognised grounds;
- using unreasonable and unnecessary force in the course of boarding and arresting the *Catharina;* and
- declaring the *Catharina* forfeit.

Further tutorial discussion

1. The early history of the law of the sea witnessed a struggle between the advocates of *mare liberum* and *mare clausum*. Which side won?
2. What are the major developments in the law of the sea since 1945, and what factors drove them?
3. Why did the international seabed regime delay widespread ratification of the Convention on the Law of the Sea? Has the problem been completely fixed?
4. Should warships enjoy a right of innocent passage?
5. States which claim the maximum permissible exclusive economic zone enjoy sovereign rights to exploit the zone's natural resources to a distance of 200 nautical miles from baselines. States also enjoy more limited exclusive rights in relation to the resources of the continental shelf. Do you think this is a justified expropriation of wealth that had previously been the common stock of humanity?

Appendix:
Basic documents

Contents

Charter of the United Nations

PREAMBLE

We the Peoples of the United Nations Determined

- to save succeeding generations from the scourge of war, which twice in our lifetime has brought untold sorrow to mankind, and
- to reaffirm faith in fundamental human rights, in the dignity and worth of the human person, in the equal rights of men and women and of nations large and small, and
- to establish conditions under which justice and respect for the obligations arising from treaties and other sources of international law can be maintained, and
- to promote social progress and better standards of life in larger freedom,

And for these Ends

- to practice tolerance and live together in peace with one another as good neighbors, and
- to unite our strength to maintain international peace and security, and
- to ensure by the acceptance of principles and the institution of methods, that armed force shall not be used, save in the common interest, and
- to employ international machinery for the promotion of the economic and social advancement of all peoples,

Have Resolved to Combine our Efforts to Accomplish these Aims

Accordingly, our respective Governments, through representatives assembled in the city of San Francisco, who have exhibited their full powers found to be in good and due form, have agreed to the present Charter of the United Nations and do hereby establish an international organization to be known as the United Nations.

Chapter I: Purposes and principles

Article 1

The Purposes of the United Nations are:

1. To maintain international peace and security, and to that end: to take effective collective measures for the prevention and removal of threats to the peace, and for the suppression of acts of aggression or other breaches of the peace, and to bring about by peaceful means, and in conformity with the principles of justice and international law,

adjustment or settlement of international disputes or situations which might lead to a breach of the peace;

2. To develop friendly relations among nations based on respect for the principle of equal rights and self-determination of peoples, and to take other appropriate measures to strengthen universal peace;

3. To achieve international cooperation in solving international problems of an economic, social, cultural, or humanitarian character, and in promoting and encouraging respect for human rights and for fundamental freedoms for all without distinction as to race, sex, language, or religion; and

4. To be a center for harmonizing the actions of nations in the attainment of these common ends.

Article 2

The Organization and its Members, in pursuit of the Purposes stated in Article 1, shall act in accordance with the following Principles.

1. The Organization is based on the principle of the sovereign equality of all its Members.

2. All Members, in order to ensure to all of them the rights and benefits resulting from membership, shall fulfill in good faith the obligations assumed by them in accordance with the present Charter.

3. All Members shall settle their international disputes by peaceful means in such a manner that international peace and security, and justice, are not endangered.

4. All Members shall refrain in their international relations from the threat or use of force against the territorial integrity or political independence of any state, or in any other manner inconsistent with the Purposes of the United Nations.

5. All Members shall give the United Nations every assistance in any action it takes in accordance with the present Charter, and shall refrain from giving assistance to any state against which the United Nations is taking preventive or enforcement action.

6. The Organization shall ensure that states which are not Members of the United Nations act in accordance with these Principles so far as may be necessary for the maintenance of international peace and security.

7. Nothing contained in the present Charter shall authorize the United Nations to intervene in matters which are essentially within the domestic jurisdiction of any state or shall require the Members to submit such matters to settlement under the present Charter; but this principle shall not prejudice the application of enforcement measures under Chapter VII.

Chapter II: Membership

Article 3

The original Members of the United Nations shall be the states which, having participated in the United Nations Conference on International Organization at San Francisco, or having previously signed the Declaration by United Nations of January 1, 1942, sign the present Charter and ratify it in accordance with Article 110.

Article 4

1. Membership in the United Nations is open to all other peace-loving states which accept the obligations contained in the present Charter and, in the judgment of the Organization, are able and willing to carry out these obligations.
2. The admission of any such state to membership in the United Nations will be effected by a decision of the General Assembly upon the recommendation of the Security Council.

Article 5

A member of the United Nations against which preventive or enforcement action has been taken by the Security Council may be suspended from the exercise of the rights and privileges of membership by the General Assembly upon the recommendation of the Security Council. The exercise of these rights and privileges may be restored by the Security Council.

Article 6

A Member of the United Nations which has persistently violated the Principles contained in the present Charter may be expelled from the Organization by the General Assembly upon the recommendation of the Security Council.

Chapter III: Organs

Article 7

1. There are established as the principal organs of the United Nations: a General Assembly, a Security Council, an Economic and Social Council, a Trusteeship Council, an International Court of Justice, and a Secretariat.
2. Such subsidiary organs as may be found necessary may be established in accordance with the present Charter.

Article 8

The United Nations shall place no restrictions on the eligibility of men and women to participate in any capacity and under conditions of equality in its principal and subsidiary organs.

Chapter IV: The General Assembly

Composition

Article 9

1. The General Assembly shall consist of all the Members of the United Nations.

2. Each member shall have not more than five representatives in the General Assembly.

Functions and powers

Article 10

The General Assembly may discuss any questions or any matters within the scope of the present Charter or relating to the powers and functions of any organs provided for in the present Charter, and, except as provided in Article 12, may make recommendations to the Members of the United Nations or to the Security Council or to both on any such questions or matters.

Article 11

1. The General Assembly may consider the general principles of cooperation in the maintenance of international peace and security, including the principles governing disarmament and the regulation of armaments, and may make recommendations with regard to such principles to the Members or to the Security Council or to both.

2. The General Assembly may discuss any questions relating to the maintenance of international peace and security brought before it by any Member of the United Nations, or by the Security Council, or by a state which is not a Member of the United Nations in accordance with Article 35, paragraph 2, and, except as provided in Article 12, may make recommendations with regard to any such questions to the state or states concerned or to the Security Council or to both. Any such question on which action is necessary shall be referred to the Security Council by the General Assembly either before or after discussion.

3. The General Assembly may call the attention of the Security Council to situations which are likely to endanger international peace and security.

4. The powers of the General Assembly set forth in this Article shall not limit the general scope of Article 10.

Article 12

1. While the Security Council is exercising in respect of any dispute or situation the functions assigned to it in the present Charter, the General Assembly shall not make any recommendation with regard to that dispute or situation unless the Security Council so requests.

2. The Secretary-General, with the consent of the Security Council, shall notify the General Assembly at each session of any matters relative to the maintenance of international peace and security which are being dealt with by the Security Council and shall similarly notify the General Assembly, or the Members of the United Nations if the General Assembly is not in session, immediately the Security Council ceases to deal with such matters.

Article 13

1. The General Assembly shall initiate studies and make recommendations for the purpose of:

   a. promoting international cooperation in the political field and encouraging the progressive development of international law and its codification;

   b. promoting international cooperation in the economic, social, cultural, educational, and health fields, and assisting in the realization of human rights and fundamental freedoms for all without distinction as to race, sex, language, or religion.

2. The further responsibilities, functions and powers of the General Assembly with respect to matters mentioned in paragraph 1(b) above are set forth in Chapters IX and X.

Article 14

Subject to the provisions of Article 12, the General Assembly may recommend measures for the peaceful adjustment of any situation, regardless of origin, which it deems likely to impair the general welfare or friendly relations among nations, including situations resulting from a violation of the provisions of the present Charter setting forth the Purposes and Principles of the United Nations.

Article 15

1. The General Assembly shall receive and consider annual and special reports from the Security Council; these reports shall include an account of the measures that the Security Council has decided upon or taken to maintain international peace and security.

2. The General Assembly shall receive and consider reports from the other organs of the United Nations.

Article 16

The General Assembly shall perform such functions with respect to the international trusteeship system as are assigned to it under Chapters XII and XIII, including the approval of the trusteeship agreements for areas not designated as strategic.

Article 17

1. The General Assembly shall consider and approve the budget of the Organization.

2. The expenses of the Organization shall be borne by the Members as apportioned by the General Assembly.

3. The General Assembly shall consider and approve any financial and budgetary arrangements with specialized agencies referred to in Article 57 and shall examine the administrative budgets of such specialized agencies with a view to making recommendations to the agencies concerned.

Voting

Article 18

1. Each member of the General Assembly shall have one vote.
2. Decisions of the General Assembly on important questions shall be made by a two-thirds majority of the members present and voting. These questions shall include: recommendations with respect to the maintenance of international peace and security, the election of the non-permanent members of the Security Council, the election of the members of the Economic and Social Council, the election of members of the Trusteeship Council in accordance with paragraph 1(c) of Article 86, the admission of new Members to the United Nations, the suspension of the rights and privileges of membership, the expulsion of Members, questions relating to the operation of the trusteeship system, and budgetary questions.
3. Decisions on other questions, Composition including the determination of additional categories of questions to be decided by a two-thirds majority, shall be made by a majority of the members present and voting.

Article 19

A Member of the United Nations which is in arrears in the payment of its financial contributions to the Organization shall have no vote in the General Assembly if the amount of its arrears equals or exceeds the amount of the contributions due from it for the preceding two full years. The General Assembly may, nevertheless, permit such a Member to vote if it is satisfied that the failure to pay is due to conditions beyond the control of the Member.

Procedure

Article 20

The General Assembly shall meet in regular annual sessions and in such special sessions as occasion may require. Special sessions shall be convoked by the Secretary-General at the request of the Security Council or of a majority of the Members of the United Nations.

Article 21

The General Assembly shall adopt its own rules of procedure. It shall elect its President for each session.

Article 22

The General Assembly may establish such subsidiary organs as it deems necessary for the performance of its functions.

Chapter V: The Security Council

Article 23

1. The Security Council shall consist of fifteen Members of the United Nations. The Republic of China, France, the Union of Soviet Socialist Republics, the United Kingdom of Great Britain and Northern Ireland, and the United States of America shall be permanent members of the Security Council. The General Assembly shall elect ten other Members of the United Nations to be non-permanent members of the Security Council, due regard being specially paid, in the first instance to the contribution of Members of the United Nations to the maintenance of international peace and security and to the other purposes of the Organization, and also to equitable geographical distribution.

2. The non-permanent members of the Security Council shall be elected for a term of two years. In the first election of the non-permanent members after the increase of the membership of the Security Council from eleven to fifteen, two of the four additional members shall be chosen for a term of one year. A retiring member shall not be eligible for immediate re-election.

3. Each member of the Security Council shall have one representative.

Functions and powers

Article 24

1. In order to ensure prompt and effective action by the United Nations, its Members confer on the Security Council primary responsibility for the maintenance of international peace and security, and agree that in carrying out its duties under this responsibility the Security Council acts on their behalf.

2. In discharging these duties the Security Council shall act in accordance with the Purposes and Principles of the United Nations. The specific powers granted to the Security Council for the discharge of these duties are laid down in Chapters VI, VII, VIII, and XII.

3. The Security Council shall submit annual and, when necessary, special reports to the General Assembly for its consideration.

Article 25

The Members of the United Nations agree to accept and carry out the decisions of the Security Council in accordance with the present Charter.

Article 26

In order to promote the establishment and maintenance of international peace and security with the least diversion for armaments of the world's human and economic resources, the Security Council shall be responsible for formulating, with the assistance of the Military Staff Committee referred to in Article 47, plans to be submitted to the Members of the United Nations for the establishment of a system for the regulation of armaments.

Voting

Article 27

1. Each member of the Security Council shall have one vote.
2. Decisions of the Security Council on procedural matters shall be made by an affirmative vote of nine members.
3. Decisions of the Security Council on all other matters shall be made by an affirmative vote of nine members including the concurring votes of the permanent members; provided that, in decisions under Chapter VI, and under paragraph 3 of Article 52, a party to a dispute shall abstain from voting.

Procedure

Article 28

1. The Security Council shall be so organized as to be able to function continuously. Each member of the Security Council shall for this purpose be represented at all times at the seat of the Organization.
2. The Security Council shall hold periodic meetings at which each of its members may, if it so desires, be represented by a member of the government or by some other specially designated representative.
3. The Security Council may hold meetings at such places other than the seat of the Organization as in its judgment will best facilitate its work.

Article 29

The Security Council may establish such subsidiary organs as it deems necessary for the performance of its functions.

Article 30

The Security Council shall adopt its own rules of procedure, including the method of selecting its President.

Article 31

Any Member of the United Nations which is not a member of the Security Council may participate, without vote, in the discussion of any question brought before the Security Council whenever the latter considers that the interests of that Member are specially affected.

Article 32

Any Member of the United Nations which is not a member of the Security Council or any state which is not a Member of the United Nations, if it is a party to a dispute under consideration by the Security Council, shall be invited to participate, without vote, in the discussion relating to the dispute. The Security Council shall lay down such conditions as it deems just for the participation of a state which is not a Member of the United Nations.

Chapter VI: Pacific settlement of disputes

Article 33

1. The parties to any dispute, the continuance of which is likely to endanger the maintenance of international peace and security, shall, first of all, seek a solution by negotiation, enquiry, mediation, conciliation, arbitration, judicial settlement, resort to regional agencies or arrangements, or other peaceful means of their own choice.
2. The Security Council shall, when it deems necessary, call upon the parties to settle their dispute by such means.

Article 34

The Security Council may investigate any dispute, or any situation which might lead to international friction or give rise to a dispute, in order to determine whether the continuance of the dispute or situation is likely to endanger the maintenance of international peace and security.

Article 35

1. Any Member of the United Nations may bring any dispute, or any situation of the nature referred to in Article 34, to the attention of the Security Council or of the General Assembly.
2. A state which is not a Member of the United Nations may bring to the attention of the Security Council or of the General Assembly any dispute to which it is a party if it accepts in advance, for the purposes of the dispute, the obligations of pacific settlement provided in the present Charter.
3. The proceedings of the General Assembly in respect of matters brought to its attention under this Article will be subject to the provisions of Articles 11 and 12.

Article 36

1. The Security Council may, at any stage of a dispute of the nature referred to in Article 33 or of a situation of like nature, recommend appropriate procedures or methods of adjustment.
2. The Security Council should take into consideration any procedures for the settlement of the dispute which have already been adopted by the parties.

3. In making recommendations under this Article the Security Council should also take into consideration that legal disputes should as a general rule be referred by the parties to the International Court of Justice in accordance with the provisions of the Statute of the Court.

Article 37

1. Should the parties to a dispute of the nature referred to in Article 33 fail to settle it by the means indicated in that Article, they shall refer it to the Security Council.
2. If the Security Council deems that the continuance of the dispute is in fact likely to endanger the maintenance of international peace and security, it shall decide whether to take action under Article 36 or to recommend such terms of settlement as it may consider appropriate.

Article 38

Without prejudice to the provisions of Articles 33 to 37, the Security Council may, if all the parties to any dispute so request, make recommendations to the parties with a view to a pacific settlement of the dispute.

Chapter VII: Action with respect to threats to the peace, breaches of the peace, and acts of aggression

Article 39

The Security Council shall determine the existence of any threat to the peace, breach of the peace, or act of aggression and shall make recommendations, or decide what measures shall be taken in accordance with Articles 41 and 42, to maintain or restore international peace and security.

Article 40

In order to prevent an aggravation of the situation, the Security Council may, before making the recommendations or deciding upon the measures provided for in Article 39, call upon the parties concerned to comply with such provisional measures as it deems necessary or desirable. Such provisional measures shall be without prejudice to the rights, claims, or position of the parties concerned. The Security Council shall duly take account of failure to comply with such provisional measures.

Article 41

The Security Council may decide what measures not involving the use of armed force are to be employed to give effect to its decisions, and it may call upon the Members of the United Nations to apply such measures. These may include complete or partial interruption of economic relations and of rail, sea, air, postal, telegraphic, radio, and other means of communication, and the severance of diplomatic relations.

Article 42

Should the Security Council consider that measures provided for in Article 41 would be inadequate or have proved to be inadequate, it may take such action by air, sea, or land forces as may be necessary to maintain or restore international peace and security. Such action may include demonstrations, blockade, and other operations by air, sea, or land forces of Members of the United Nations.

Article 43

1. All Members of the United Nations, in order to contribute to the maintenance of international peace and security, undertake to make available to the Security Council, on its call and in accordance with a special agreement or agreements, armed forces, assistance, and facilities, including rights of passage, necessary for the purpose of maintaining international peace and security.
2. Such agreement or agreements shall govern the numbers and types of forces, their degree of readiness and general location, and the nature of the facilities and assistance to be provided.
3. The agreement or agreements shall be negotiated as soon as possible on the initiative of the Security Council. They shall be concluded between the Security Council and Members or between the Security Council and groups of Members and shall be subject to ratification by the signatory states in accordance with their respective constitutional processes.

Article 44

When the Security Council has decided to use force it shall, before calling upon a Member not represented on it to provide armed forces in fulfillment of the obligations assumed under Article 43, invite that Member, if the Member so desires, to participate in the decisions of the Security Council concerning the employment of contingents of that Member's armed forces.

Article 45

In order to enable the United Nations to take urgent military measures Members shall hold immediately available national air-force contingents for combined international enforcement action. The strength and degree of readiness of these contingents and plans for their combined action shall be determined, within the limits laid down in the special agreement or agreements referred to in Article 43, by the Security Council with the assistance of the Military Staff Committee.

Article 46

Plans for the application of armed force shall be made by the Security Council with the assistance of the Military Staff Committee.

Article 47

1. There shall be established a Military Staff Committee to advise and assist the Security Council on all questions relating to the Security Council's military requirements for the maintenance of international peace and security, the employment and command of forces placed at its disposal, the regulation of armaments, and possible disarmament.

2. The Military Staff Committee shall consist of the Chiefs of Staff of the permanent members of the Security Council or their representatives. Any Member of the United Nations not permanently represented on the Committee shall be invited by the Committee to be associated with it when the efficient discharge of the Committee's responsibilities requires the participation of that Member in its work.

3. The Military Staff Committee shall be responsible under the Security Council for the strategic direction of any armed forces placed at the disposal of the Security Council. Questions relating to the command of such forces shall be worked out subsequently.

4. The Military Staff Committee, with the authorization of the Security Council and after consultation with appropriate regional agencies, may establish regional subcommittees.

Article 48

1. The action required to carry out the decisions of the Security Council for the maintenance of international peace and security shall be taken by all the Members of the United Nations or by some of them, as the Security Council may determine.

2. Such decisions shall be carried out by the Members of the United Nations directly and through their action in the appropriate international agencies of which they are members.

Article 49

The Members of the United Nations shall join in affording mutual assistance in carrying out the measures decided upon by the Security Council.

Article 50

If preventive or enforcement measures against any state are taken by the Security Council, any other state, whether a Member of the United Nations or not, which finds itself confronted with special economic problems arising from the carrying out of those measures shall have the right to consult the Security Council with regard to a solution of those problems.

Article 51

Nothing in the present Charter shall impair the inherent right of individual or collective self-defense if an armed attack occurs against a Member of the United Nations, until the Security Council has taken measures necessary to maintain international peace and security. Measures taken by Members in the exercise of this right of self-defense shall be immediately reported to the Security Council and shall not in any way affect the authority and responsibility of the Security Council under the present Charter to take at any time such action as it deems necessary in order to maintain or restore international peace and security.

Chapter VIII: Regional arrangements

Article 52

1. Nothing in the present Charter precludes the existence of regional arrangements or agencies for dealing with such matters relating to the maintenance of international peace and security as are appropriate for regional action, provided that such arrangements or agencies and their activities are consistent with the Purposes and Principles of the United Nations.

2. The Members of the United Nations entering into such arrangements or constituting such agencies shall make every effort to achieve pacific settlement of local disputes through such regional arrangements or by such regional agencies before referring them to the Security Council.

3. The Security Council shall encourage the development of pacific settlement of local disputes through such regional arrangements or by such regional agencies either on the initiative of the states concerned or by reference from the Security Council.

4. This Article in no way impairs the application of Articles 34 and 35.

Article 53

1. The Security Council shall, where appropriate, utilize such regional arrangements or agencies for enforcement action under its authority. But no enforcement action shall be taken under regional arrangements or by regional agencies without the authorization of the Security Council, with the exception of measures against any enemy state, as defined in paragraph 2 of this Article, provided for pursuant to Article 107 or in regional arrangements directed against renewal of aggressive policy on the part of any such state, until such time as the Organization may, on request of the Governments concerned, be charged with the responsibility for preventing further aggression by such a state.

2. The term enemy state as used in paragraph 1 of this Article applies to any state which during the Second World War has been an enemy of any signatory of the present Charter.

Article 54

The Security Council shall at all times be kept fully informed of activities undertaken or in contemplation under regional arrangements or by regional agencies for the maintenance of international peace and security.

Chapter IX: International economic and social co-operation

Article 55

With a view to the creation of conditions of stability and well-being which are necessary for peaceful and friendly relations among nations based on respect for the principle of equal rights and self-determination of peoples, the United Nations shall promote:

a.   higher standards of living, full employment, and conditions of economic and social progress and development;

b.   solutions of international economic, social, health, and related problems; and international cultural and educational co-operation; and

c.   universal respect for, and observance of, human rights and fundamental freedoms for all without distinction as to race, sex, language, or religion.

Article 56

All Members pledge themselves to take joint and separate action in cooperation with the Organization for the achievement of the purposes set forth in Article 55.

Article 57

1.   The various specialized agencies, established by intergovernmental agreement and having wide international responsibilities, as defined in their basic instruments, in economic, social, cultural, educational, health, and related fields, shall be brought into relationship with the United Nations in accordance with the provisions of Article 63.

2.   Such agencies thus brought into relationship with the United Nations are hereinafter referred to as specialized agencies.

Article 58

The Organization shall make recommendations for the coordination of the policies and activities of the specialized agencies.

Article 59

The Organization shall, where appropriate, initiate negotiations among the states concerned for the creation of any new specialized agencies required for the accomplishment of the purposes set forth in Article 55.

Article 60

Responsibility for the discharge of the functions of the Organization set forth in this Chapter shall be vested in the General Assembly and, under the authority of the General Assembly, in the Economic and Social Council, which shall have for this purpose the powers set forth in Chapter X.

Chapter X: The Economic and Social Council

Composition

Article 61

1. The Economic and Social Council shall consist of fifty-four Members of the United Nations elected by the General Assembly.
2. Subject to the provisions of paragraph 3, eighteen members of the Economic and Social Council shall be elected each year for a term of three years. A retiring member shall be eligible for immediate re-election.
3. At the first election after the increase in the membership of the Economic and Social Council from twenty-seven to fifty-four members, in addition to the members elected in place of the nine members whose term of office expires at the end of that year, twenty-seven additional members shall be elected. Of these twenty-seven additional members, the term of office of nine members so elected shall expire at the end of one year, and of nine other members at the end of two years, in accordance with arrangements made by the General Assembly.
4. Each member of the Economic and Social Council shall have one representative.

Functions and powers

Article 62

1. The Economic and Social Council may make or initiate studies and reports with respect to international economic, social, cultural, educational, health, and related matters and may make recommendations with respect to any such matters to the General Assembly, to the Members of the United Nations, and to the specialized agencies concerned.
2. It may make recommendations for the purpose of promoting respect for, and observance of, human rights and fundamental freedoms for all.
3. It may prepare draft conventions for submission to the General Assembly, with respect to matters falling within its competence.

4. It may call, in accordance with the rules prescribed by the United Nations, international conferences on matters falling within its competence.

Article 63

1. The Economic and Social Council may enter into agreements with any of the agencies referred to in Article 57, defining the terms on which the agency concerned shall be brought into relationship with the United Nations. Such agreements shall be subject to approval by the General Assembly.
2. It may coordinate the activities of the specialized agencies through consultation with and recommendations to such agencies and through recommendations to the General Assembly and to the Members of the United Nations.

Article 64

1. The Economic and Social Council may take appropriate steps to obtain regular reports from the specialized agencies. It may make arrangements with the Members of the United Nations and with the specialized agencies to obtain reports on the steps taken to give effect to its own recommendations and to recommendations on matters falling within its competence made by the General Assembly.
2. It may communicate its observations on these reports to the General Assembly.

Article 65

The Economic and Social Council may furnish information to the Security Council and shall assist the Security Council upon its request.

Article 66

1. The Economic and Social Council shall perform such functions as fall within its competence in connection with the carrying out of the recommendations of the General Assembly.
2. It may, with the approval of the General Assembly, perform services at the request of Members of the United Nations and at the request of specialized agencies.
3. It shall perform such other functions as are specified elsewhere in the present Charter or as may be assigned to it by the General Assembly.

Article 67

1. Each member of the Economic and Social Council shall have one vote.
2. Decisions of the Economic and Social Council shall be made by a majority of the members present and voting.

Procedure

Article 68

The Economic and Social Council shall set up commissions in economic and social fields and for the promotion of human rights, and such other commissions as may be required for the performance of its functions.

Article 69

The Economic and Social Council shall invite any Member of the United Nations to participate, without vote, in its deliberations on any matter of particular concern to that Member.

Article 70

The Economic and Social Council may make arrangements for representatives of the specialized agencies to participate, without vote, in its deliberations and in those of the commissions established by it, and for its representatives to participate in the deliberations of the specialized agencies.

Article 71

The Economic and Social Council may make suitable arrangements for consultation with non-governmental organizations which are concerned with matters within its competence. Such arrangements may be made with international organizations and, where appropriate, with national organizations after consultation with the Member of the United Nations concerned.

Article 72

1. The Economic and Social Council shall adopt its own rules of procedure, including the method of selecting its President.
2. The Economic and Social Council shall meet as required in accordance with its rules, which shall include provision for the convening of meetings on the request of a majority of its members.

Chapter XI: Declaration regarding non-self-governing territories

Article 73

Members of the United Nations which have or assume responsibilities for the administration of territories whose peoples have not yet attained a full measure of self-government recognize the principle that the interests of the inhabitants of these territories are paramount, and accept as a sacred trust the obligation to promote to the utmost, within the system of international peace and security established by the present Charter, the well-being of the inhabitants of these territories, and, to this end:

a. to ensure, with due respect for the culture of the peoples concerned, their political, economic, social, and educational advancement, their just treatment, and their protection against abuses;

b. to develop self-government, to take due account of the political aspirations of the peoples, and to assist them in the progressive development of their free political institutions, according to the particular circumstances of each territory and its peoples and their varying stages of advancement;

c. to further international peace and security;

d. to promote constructive measures of development, to encourage research, and to cooperate with one another and, when and where appropriate, with specialized international bodies with a view to the practical achievement of the social, economic, and scientific purposes set forth in this Article; and

e. to transmit regularly to the Secretary-General for information purposes, subject to such limitation as security and constitutional considerations may require, statistical and other information of a technical nature relating to economic, social, and educational conditions in the territories for which they are respectively responsible other than those territories to which Chapters XII and XIII apply.

Article 74

Members of the United Nations also agree that their policy in respect of the territories to which this Chapter applies, no less than in respect of their metropolitan areas, must be based on the general principle of good-neighborliness, due account being taken of the interests and well-being of the rest of the world, in social, economic, and commercial matters.

Chapter XII: International trusteeship system

Article 75

The United Nations shall establish under its authority an international trusteeship system for the administration and supervision of such territories as may be placed thereunder by subsequent individual agreements. These territories are hereinafter referred to as trust territories.

Article 76

The basic objectives of the trusteeship system, in accordance with the Purposes of the United Nations laid down in Article 1 of the present Charter, shall be:

a.   to further international peace and security;

b.   to promote the political, economic, social, and educational advancement of the inhabitants of the trust territories, and their progressive development towards self-government or independence as may be appropriate to the particular circumstances of each territory and its peoples and the freely expressed wishes of the peoples concerned, and as may be provided by the terms of each trusteeship agreement;

c.   to encourage respect for human rights and for fundamental freedoms for all without distinction as to race, sex, language, or religion, and to encourage recognition of the interdependence of the peoples of the world; and

d.   to ensure equal treatment in social, economic, and commercial matters for all Members of the United Nations and their nationals and also equal treatment for the latter in the administration of justice without prejudice to the attainment of the foregoing objectives and subject to the provisions of Article 80.

Article 77

1.   The trusteeship system shall apply to such territories in the following categories as may be placed thereunder by means of trusteeship agreements:

a.   territories now held under mandate;

b.   territories which may be detached from enemy states as a result of the Second World War, and

c.   territories voluntarily placed under the system by states responsible for their administration.

2.   It will be a matter for subsequent agreement as to which territories in the foregoing categories will be brought under the trusteeship system and upon what terms.

Article 78

The trusteeship system shall not apply to territories which have become Members of the United Nations, relationship among which shall be based on respect for the principle of sovereign equality.

Article 79

The terms of trusteeship for each territory to be placed under the trusteeship system, including any alteration or amendment, shall be agreed upon by the states directly concerned, including the mandatory power in the case of territories held under mandate by a Member of the United Nations, and shall be approved as provided for in Articles 83 and 85.

Article 80

1.   Except as may be agreed upon in individual trusteeship agreements, made under Articles 77, 79, and 81, placing each territory under the trusteeship system, and until such agreements have been concluded,

nothing in this Chapter shall be construed in or of itself to alter in any manner the rights whatsoever of any states or any peoples or the terms of existing international instruments to which Members of the United Nations may respectively be parties.

2. Paragraph 1 of this Article shall not be interpreted as giving grounds for delay or postponement of the negotiation and conclusion of agreements for placing mandated and other territories under the trusteeship system as provided for in Article 77.

Article 81

The trusteeship agreement shall in each case include the terms under which the trust territory will be administered and designate the authority which will exercise the administration of the trust territory. Such authority, hereinafter called the administering authority, may be one or more states or the Organization itself.

Article 82

There may be designated, in any trusteeship agreement, a strategic area or areas which may include part or all of the trust territory to which the agreement applies, without prejudice to any special agreement or agreements made under Article 43.

Article 83

1. All functions of the United Nations relating to strategic areas, including the approval of the terms of the trusteeship agreements and of their alteration or amendment, shall be exercised by the Security Council.
2. The basic objectives set forth in Article 76 shall be applicable to the people of each strategic area.
3. The Security Council shall, subject to the provisions of the trusteeship agreements and without prejudice to security considerations, avail itself of the assistance of the Trusteeship Council to perform those functions of the United Nations under the trusteeship system relating to political. economic, social, and educational matters in the strategic areas.

Article 84

It shall be the duty of the administering authority to ensure that the trust territory shall play its part in the maintenance of international peace and security. To this end the administering authority may make use of volunteer forces, facilities, and assistance from the trust territory in carrying out the obligations towards the Security Council undertaken in this regard by the administering authority, as well as for local defense and the maintenance of law and order within the trust territory.

Article 85

1. The functions of the United Nations with regard to trusteeship agreements for all areas not designated as strategic, including the approval of the

terms of the trusteeship agreements and of their alteration or amendment, shall be exercised by the General Assembly.

2.   The Trusteeship Council, operating under the authority of the General Assembly, shall assist the General Assembly in carrying out these functions.

Chapter XIII: The Trusteeship Council

Composition

Article 86

1.   The Trusteeship Council shall consist of the following Members of the United Nations:

   a.   those Members administering trust territories;

   b.   such of those Members mentioned by name in Article 23 as are not administering trust territories; and

   c.   as many other Members elected for three-year terms by the General Assembly as may be necessary to ensure that the total number of members of the Trusteeship Council is equally divided between those Members of the United Nations which administer trust territories and those which do not.

2.   Each member of the Trusteeship Council shall designate one specially qualified person to represent it therein.

Functions and powers

Article 87

The General Assembly and, under its authority, the Trusteeship Council, in carrying out their functions, may:

   a.   consider reports submitted by the administering authority;

   b.   accept petitions and examine them in consultation with the administering authority;

   c.   provide for periodic visits to the respective trust territories at times agreed upon with the administering authority; and

   d.   take these and other actions in conformity with the terms of the trusteeship agreements.

Article 88

The Trusteeship Council shall formulate a questionnaire on the political, economic, social, and educational advancement of the inhabitants of each trust territory, and the administering authority for each trust territory within the competence of the General Assembly shall make an annual report to the General Assembly upon the basis of such questionnaire.

Voting

Article 89

1. Each member of the Trusteeship Council shall have one vote.
2. Decisions of the Trusteeship Council shall be made by a majority of the members present and voting.

Procedure

Article 90

1. The Trusteeship Council shall adopt its own rules of procedure, including the method of selecting its President.
2. The Trusteeship Council shall meet as required in accordance with its rules, which shall include provision for the convening of meetings on the request of a majority of its members.

Article 91

The Trusteeship Council shall, when appropriate, avail itself of the assistance of the Economic and Social Council and of the specialized agencies in regard to matters with which they are respectively concerned.

Chapter XIV: The International Court of Justice

Article 92

The International Court of Justice shall be the principal judicial organ of the United Nations. It shall function in accordance with the annexed Statute which is based upon the Statute of the Permanent Court of International Justice and forms an integral part of the present Charter.

Article 93

1. All Members of the United Nations are ipso facto parties to the Statute of the International Court of Justice.
2. A state which is not a Member of the United Nations may become a party to the Statute of the International Court of Justice on conditions to be determined in each case by the General Assembly upon the recommendation of the Security Council.

Article 94

1. Each Member of the United Nations undertakes to comply with the decision of the International Court of Justice in any case to which it is a party.

2. If any party to a case fails to perform the obligations incumbent upon it under a judgment rendered by the Court, the other party may have recourse to the Security Council, which may, if it deems necessary, make recommendations or decide upon measures to be taken to give effect to the judgment.

Article 95

Nothing in the present Charter shall prevent Members of the United Nations from entrusting the solution of their differences to other tribunals by virtue of agreements already in existence or which may be concluded in the future.

Article 96

1. The General Assembly or the Security Council may request the International Court of Justice to give an advisory opinion on any legal question.
2. Other organs of the United Nations and specialized agencies, which may at any time be so authorized by the General Assembly, may also request advisory opinions of the Court on legal questions arising within the scope of their activities.

Chapter XV: The Secretariat

Article 97

The Secretariat shall comprise a Secretary-General and such staff as the Organization may require. The Secretary-General shall be appointed by the General Assembly upon the recommendation of the Security Council. He shall be the chief administrative officer of the Organization.

Article 98

The Secretary-General shall act in that capacity in all meetings of the General Assembly, of the Security Council, of the Economic and Social Council, and of the Trusteeship Council, and shall perform such other functions as are entrusted to him by these organs. The Secretary-General shall make an annual report to the General Assembly on the work of the Organization.

Article 99

The Secretary-General may bring to the attention of the Security Council any matter which in his opinion may threaten the maintenance of international peace and security.

Article 100

1. In the performance of their duties the Secretary-General and the staff shall not seek or receive instructions from any government or from any other authority external to the Organization. They shall refrain

from any action which might reflect on their position as international officials responsible only to the Organization.

2. Each Member of the United Nations undertakes to respect the exclusively international character of the responsibilities of the Secretary-General and the staff and not to seek to influence them in the discharge of their responsibilities.

Article 101

1. The staff shall be appointed by the Secretary-General under regulations established by the General Assembly.

2. Appropriate staffs shall be permanently assigned to the Economic and Social Council, the Trusteeship Council, and, as required, to other organs of the United Nations. These staffs shall form a part of the Secretariat.

3. The paramount consideration in the employment of the staff and in the determination of the conditions of service shall be the necessity of securing the highest standards of efficiency, competence, and integrity. Due regard shall be paid to the importance of recruiting the staff on as wide a geographical basis as possible.

Chapter XVI: Miscellaneous provisions

Article 102

1. Every treaty and every international agreement entered into by any Member of the United Nations after the present Charter comes into force shall as soon as possible be registered with the Secretariat and published by it.

2. No party to any such treaty or international agreement which has not been registered in accordance with the provisions of paragraph I of this Article may invoke that treaty or agreement before any organ of the United Nations.

Article 103

In the event of a conflict between the obligations of the Members of the United Nations under the present Charter and their obligations under any other international agreement, their obligations under the present Charter shall prevail.

Article 104

The Organization shall enjoy in the territory of each of its Members such legal capacity as may be necessary for the exercise of its functions and the fulfillment of its purposes.

Article 105

1. The Organization shall enjoy in the territory of each of its Members such privileges and immunities as are necessary for the fulfillment of its purposes.

2. Representatives of the Members of the United Nations and officials of the Organization shall similarly enjoy such privileges and immunities as are necessary for the independent exercise of their functions in connection with the Organization.

3. The General Assembly may make recommendations with a view to determining the details of the application of paragraphs 1 and 2 of this Article or may propose conventions to the Members of the United Nations for this purpose.

Chapter XVII: Transitional security arrangements

Article 106

Pending the coming into force of such special agreements referred to in Article 43 as in the opinion of the Security Council enable it to begin the exercise of its responsibilities under Article 42, the parties to the Four-Nation Declaration, signed at Moscow October 30, 1943, and France, shall, in accordance with the provisions of paragraph 5 of that Declaration, consult with one another and as occasion requires with other Members of the United Nations with a view to such joint action on behalf of the Organization as may be necessary for the purpose of maintaining international peace and security.

Article 107

Nothing in the present Charter shall invalidate or preclude action, in relation to any state which during the Second World War has been an enemy of any signatory to the present Charter, taken or authorized as a result of that war by the Governments having responsibility for such action.

Chapter XVIII: Amendments

Article 108

Amendments to the present Charter shall come into force for all Members of the United Nations when they have been adopted by a vote of two thirds of the members of the General Assembly and ratified in accordance with their respective constitutional processes by two thirds of the Members of the United Nations, including all the permanent members of the Security Council.

Article 109

1. A General Conference of the Members of the United Nations for the purpose of reviewing the present Charter may be held at a date and place to be fixed by a two-thirds vote of the members of the General

Assembly and by a vote of any seven members of the Security Council. Each Member of the United Nations shall have one vote in the conference.

2. Any alteration of the present Charter recommended by a two-thirds vote of the conference shall take effect when ratified in accordance with their respective constitutional processes by two thirds of the Members of the United Nations including all the permanent members of the Security Council.

3. If such a conference has not been held before the tenth annual session of the General Assembly following the coming into force of the present Charter, the proposal to call such a conference shall be placed on the agenda of that session of the General Assembly, and the conference shall be held if so decided by a majority vote of the members of the General Assembly and by a vote of any seven members of the Security Council.

Chapter XIX: Ratification and signature

Article 110

1. The present Charter shall be ratified by the signatory states in accordance with their respective constitutional processes.

2. The ratifications shall be deposited with the Government of the United States of America, which shall notify all the signatory states of each deposit as well as the Secretary-General of the Organization when he has been appointed.

3. The present Charter shall come into force upon the deposit of ratifications by the Republic of China, France, the Union of Soviet Socialist Republics, the United Kingdom of Great Britain and Northern Ireland, and the United States of America, and by a majority of the other signatory states. A protocol of the ratifications deposited shall thereupon be drawn up by the Government of the United States of America which shall communicate copies thereof to all the signatory states.

4. The states signatory to the present Charter which ratify it after it has come into force will become original Members of the United Nations on the date of the deposit of their respective ratifications.

Article 111

The present Charter, of which the Chinese, French, Russian, English, and Spanish texts are equally authentic, shall remain deposited in the archives of the Government of the United States of America. Duly certified copies thereof shall be transmitted by that Government to the Governments of the other signatory states.

IN FAITH WHEREOF the representatives of the Governments of the United Nations have signed the present Charter.

DONE at the city of San Francisco the twenty-sixth day of June, one thousand nine hundred and forty-five.

Draft Articles on Diplomatic Protection

Text adopted by the International Law Commission at its Fifty-eighth Session, in 2006, and submitted to the General Assembly as a part of the Commission's report covering the work of that session. The report, which also contains commentaries on the draft articles, appears in Official Records of the General Assembly, Sixty-first Session, Supp No 10 (A/61/10)

PART ONE: GENERAL PROVISIONS

Article 1
Definition and scope

For the purposes of the present draft articles, diplomatic protection consists of the invocation by a State, through diplomatic action or other means of peaceful settlement, of the responsibility of another State for an injury caused by an internationally wrongful act of that State to a natural or legal person that is a national of the former State with a view to the implementation of such responsibility.

Article 2
Right to exercise diplomatic protection

A State has the right to exercise diplomatic protection in accordance with the present draft articles.

PART TWO: NATIONALITY

Chapter I: General principles

Article 3
Protection by the State of nationality

1. The State entitled to exercise diplomatic protection is the State of nationality.
2. Notwithstanding paragraph 1, diplomatic protection may be exercised by a State in respect of a person that is not its national in accordance with draft article 8.

Chapter II: Natural persons

Article 4
State of nationality of a natural person

For the purposes of the diplomatic protection of a natural person, a State of nationality means a State whose nationality that person has acquired, in accordance with the law of that State, by birth, descent, naturalization, succession of States or in any other manner, not inconsistent with international law.

Article 5
Continuous nationality of a natural person

1. A State is entitled to exercise diplomatic protection in respect of a person who was a national of that State continuously from the date of injury to the date of the official presentation of the claim. Continuity is presumed if that nationality existed at both these dates.

2. Notwithstanding paragraph 1, a State may exercise diplomatic protection in respect of a person who is its national at the date of the official presentation of the claim but was not a national at the date of injury, provided that the person had the nationality of a predecessor State or lost his or her previous nationality and acquired, for a reason unrelated to the bringing of the claim, the nationality of the former State in a manner not inconsistent with international law.

3. Diplomatic protection shall not be exercised by the present State of nationality in respect of a person against a former State of nationality of that person for an injury caused when that person was a national of the former State of nationality and not of the present State of nationality.

4. A State is no longer entitled to exercise diplomatic protection in respect of a person who acquires the nationality of the State against which the claim is brought after the date of the official presentation of the claim.

Article 6
Multiple nationality and claim against a third State

1. Any State of which a dual or multiple national is a national may exercise diplomatic protection in respect of that national against a State of which that person is not a national.

2. Two or more States of nationality may jointly exercise diplomatic protection in respect of a dual or multiple national.

Article 7
Multiple nationality and claim against a State of nationality

A State of nationality may not exercise diplomatic protection in respect of a person against a State of which that person is also a national unless the nationality of the former State is predominant, both at the date of injury and at the date of the official presentation of the claim.

Article 8
Stateless persons and refugees

1. A State may exercise diplomatic protection in respect of a stateless person who, at the date of injury and at the date of the official presentation of the claim, is lawfully and habitually resident in that State.
2. A State may exercise diplomatic protection in respect of a person who is recognized as a refugee by that State, in accordance with internationally accepted standards, when that person, at the date of injury and at the date of the official presentation of the claim, is lawfully and habitually resident in that State.
3. Paragraph 2 does not apply in respect of an injury caused by an internationally wrongful act of the State of nationality of the refugee.

Chapter III: Legal persons

Article 9
State of nationality of a corporation

For the purposes of the diplomatic protection of a corporation, the State of nationality means the State under whose law the corporation was incorporated. However, when the corporation is controlled by nationals of another State or States and has no substantial business activities in the State of incorporation, and the seat of management and the financial control of the corporation are both located in another State, that State shall be regarded as the State of nationality.

Article 10
Continuous nationality of a corporation

1. A State is entitled to exercise diplomatic protection in respect of a corporation that was a national of that State, or its predecessor State, continuously from the date of injury to the date of the official presentation of the claim. Continuity is presumed if that nationality existed at both these dates.
2. A State is no longer entitled to exercise diplomatic protection in respect of a corporation that acquires the nationality of the State against which the claim is brought after the presentation of the claim.
3. Notwithstanding paragraph 1, a State continues to be entitled to exercise diplomatic protection in respect of a corporation which was its national at the date of injury and which, as the result of the injury, has ceased to exist according to the law of the State of incorporation.

Article 11
Protection of shareholders

A State of nationality of shareholders in a corporation shall not be entitled to exercise diplomatic protection in respect of such shareholders in the case of an injury to the corporation unless:

    (a) The corporation has ceased to exist according to the law of the State of incorporation for a reason unrelated to the injury; or

    (b) The corporation had, at the date of injury, the nationality of the State alleged to be responsible for causing the injury, and incorporation in that State was required by it as a precondition for doing business there.

Article 12

Direct injury to shareholders

To the extent that an internationally wrongful act of a State causes direct injury to the rights of shareholders as such, as distinct from those of the corporation itself, the State of nationality of any such shareholders is entitled to exercise diplomatic protection in respect of its nationals.

Article 13

Other legal persons

The principles contained in this chapter shall be applicable, as appropriate, to the diplomatic protection of legal persons other than corporations.

PART THREE: LOCAL REMEDIES

Article 14

Exhaustion of local remedies

1. A State may not present an international claim in respect of an injury to a national or other person referred to in draft article 8 before the injured person has, subject to draft article 15, exhausted all local remedies.

2. "Local remedies" means legal remedies which are open to an injured person before the judicial or administrative courts or bodies, whether ordinary or special, of the State alleged to be responsible for causing the injury.

3. Local remedies shall be exhausted where an international claim, or request for a declaratory judgement related to the claim, is brought preponderantly on the basis of an injury to a national or other person referred to in draft article 8.

Article 15

Exceptions to the local remedies rule

Local remedies do not need to be exhausted where:

    (a) There are no reasonably available local remedies to provide effective redress, or the local remedies provide no reasonable possibility of such redress;

    (b) There is undue delay in the remedial process which is attributable to the State alleged to be responsible;

(c) There was no relevant connection between the injured person and the State alleged to be responsible at the date of injury;

(d) The injured person is manifestly precluded from pursuing local remedies; or

(e) The State alleged to be responsible has waived the requirement that local remedies be exhausted.

PART FOUR: MISCELLANEOUS PROVISIONS

Article 16

Actions or procedures other than diplomatic protection

The rights of States, natural persons, legal persons or other entities to resort under international law to actions or procedures other than diplomatic protection to secure redress for injury suffered as a result of an internationally wrongful act, are not affected by the present draft articles.

Article 17

Special rules of international law

The present draft articles do not apply to the extent that they are inconsistent with special rules of international law, such as treaty provisions for the protection of investments.

Article 18

Protection of ships' crews

The right of the State of nationality of the members of the crew of a ship to exercise diplomatic protection is not affected by the right of the State of nationality of a ship to seek redress on behalf of such crew members, irrespective of their nationality, when they have been injured in connection with an injury to the vessel resulting from an internationally wrongful act.

Article 19

Recommended practice

A State entitled to exercise diplomatic protection according to the present draft articles, should:

(a) Give due consideration to the possibility of exercising diplomatic protection, especially when a significant injury has occurred;

(b) Take into account, wherever feasible, the views of injured persons with regard to resort to diplomatic protection and the reparation to be sought; and

(c) Transfer to the injured person any compensation obtained for the injury from the responsible State subject to any reasonable deductions.

Draft Articles on Responsibility of States for Internationally Wrongful Acts

Adopted by the International Law Commission at its Fifty-third Session (2001)

Extract from the Report of the International Law Commission on the work of its Fifty-third Session, Official Records of the General Assembly, Fifty-sixth Session, Supp No 10 (A/56/10), chp.IV.E.1

PART ONE: THE INTERNATIONALLY WRONGFUL ACT OF A STATE

Chapter I: General principles

Article 1
Responsibility of a State for its internationally wrongful acts

Every internationally wrongful act of a State entails the international responsibility of that State.

Article 2
Elements of an internationally wrongful act of a State

There is an internationally wrongful act of a State when conduct consisting of an action or omission:

    (a) Is attributable to the State under international law; and

    (b) Constitutes a breach of an international obligation of the State.

Article 3
Characterization of an act of a State as internationally wrongful

The characterization of an act of a State as internationally wrongful is governed by international law. Such characterization is not affected by the characterization of the same act as lawful by internal law.

Chapter II: Attribution of conduct to a State

Article 4
Conduct of organs of a State

1. The conduct of any State organ shall be considered an act of that State under international law, whether the organ exercises legislative, executive, judicial or any other functions, whatever position it holds in the organization of the State, and whatever its character as an organ of the central government or of a territorial unit of the State.
2. An organ includes any person or entity which has that status in accordance with the internal law of the State.

Article 5
Conduct of persons or entities exercising elements of governmental authority

The conduct of a person or entity which is not an organ of the State under article 4 but which is empowered by the law of that State to exercise elements of the governmental authority shall be considered an act of the State under international law, provided the person or entity is acting in that capacity in the particular instance.

Article 6
Conduct of organs placed at the disposal of a State by another State

The conduct of an organ placed at the disposal of a State by another State shall be considered an act of the former State under international law if the organ is acting in the exercise of elements of the governmental authority of the State at whose disposal it is placed.

Article 7
Excess of authority or contravention of instructions

The conduct of an organ of a State or of a person or entity empowered to exercise elements of the governmental authority shall be considered an act of the State under international law if the organ, person or entity acts in that capacity, even if it exceeds its authority or contravenes instructions.

Article 8
Conduct directed or controlled by a State

The conduct of a person or group of persons shall be considered an act of a State under international law if the person or group of persons is in fact acting on the instructions of, or under the direction or control of, that State in carrying out the conduct.

Article 9

Conduct carried out in the absence or default of the official authorities

The conduct of a person or group of persons shall be considered an act of a State under international law if the person or group of persons is in fact exercising elements of the governmental authority in the absence or default of the official authorities and in circumstances such as to call for the exercise of those elements of authority.

Article 10

Conduct of an insurrectional or other movement

1. The conduct of an insurrectional movement which becomes the new government of a State shall be considered an act of that State under international law.
2. The conduct of a movement, insurrectional or other, which succeeds in establishing a new State in part of the territory of a pre-existing State or in a territory under its administration shall be considered an act of the new State under international law.
3. This article is without prejudice to the attribution to a State of any conduct, however related to that of the movement concerned, which is to be considered an act of that State by virtue of articles 4 to 9.

Article 11

Conduct acknowledged and adopted by a State as its own

Conduct which is not attributable to a State under the preceding articles shall nevertheless be considered an act of that State under international law if and to the extent that the State acknowledges and adopts the conduct in question as its own.

Chapter III: Breach of an international obligation

Article 12

Existence of a breach of an international obligation

There is a breach of an international obligation by a State when an act of that State is not in conformity with what is required of it by that obligation, regardless of its origin or character.

Article 13

International obligation in force for a State

An act of a State does not constitute a breach of an international obligation unless the State is bound by the obligation in question at the time the act occurs.

Article 14

Extension in time of the breach of an international obligation

1. The breach of an international obligation by an act of a State not having a continuing character occurs at the moment when the act is performed, even if its effects continue.
2. The breach of an international obligation by an act of a State having a continuing character extends over the entire period during which the act continues and remains not in conformity with the international obligation.
3. The breach of an international obligation requiring a State to prevent a given event occurs when the event occurs and extends over the entire period during which the event continues and remains not in conformity with that obligation.

Article 15

Breach consisting of a composite act

1. The breach of an international obligation by a State through a series of actions or omissions defined in aggregate as wrongful, occurs when the action or omission occurs which, taken with the other actions or omissions, is sufficient to constitute the wrongful act.
2. In such a case, the breach extends over the entire period starting with the first of the actions or omissions of the series and lasts for as long as these actions or omissions are repeated and remain not in conformity with the international obligation.

Chapter IV: Responsibility of a State in connection with the act of another State

Article 16

Aid or assistance in the commission of an internationally wrongful act

A State which aids or assists another State in the commission of an internationally wrongful act by the latter is internationally responsible for doing so if:

(a) That State does so with knowledge of the circumstances of the internationally wrongful act; and
(b) The act would be internationally wrongful if committed by that State.

Article 17

Direction and control exercised over the commission of an internationally wrongful act

A State which directs and controls another State in the commission of an internationally wrongful act by the latter is internationally responsible for that act if:

    (a) That State does so with knowledge of the circumstances of the internationally wrongful act; and

    (b) The act would be internationally wrongful if committed by that State.

Article 18
Coercion of another State

A State which coerces another State to commit an act is internationally responsible for that act if:

    (a) The act would, but for the coercion, be an internationally wrongful act of the coerced State; and

    (b) The coercing State does so with knowledge of the circumstances of the act.

Article 19
Effect of this chapter

This chapter is without prejudice to the international responsibility, under other provisions of these articles, of the State which commits the act in question, or of any other State.

Chapter V: Circumstances precluding wrongfulness

Article 20
Consent

Valid consent by a State to the commission of a given act by another State precludes the wrongfulness of that act in relation to the former State to the extent that the act remains within the limits of that consent.

Article 21
Self-defence

The wrongfulness of an act of a State is precluded if the act constitutes a lawful measure of self-defence taken in conformity with the Charter of the United Nations.

Article 22
Countermeasures in respect of an internationally wrongful act

The wrongfulness of an act of a State not in conformity with an international obligation towards another State is precluded if and to the extent that the act constitutes a countermeasure taken against the latter State in accordance with chapter II of Part Three.

Article 23

Force majeure

1. The wrongfulness of an act of a State not in conformity with an international obligation of that State is precluded if the act is due to *force majeure*, that is the occurrence of an irresistible force or of an unforeseen event, beyond the control of the State, making it materially impossible in the circumstances to perform the obligation.

2. Paragraph 1 does not apply if:
   (a) The situation of *force majeure* is due, either alone or in combination with other factors, to the conduct of the State invoking it; or
   (b) The State has assumed the risk of that situation occurring.

Article 24

Distress

1. The wrongfulness of an act of a State not in conformity with an international obligation of that State is precluded if the author of the act in question has no other reasonable way, in a situation of distress, of saving the author's life or the lives of other persons entrusted to the author's care.

2. Paragraph 1 does not apply if:
   (a) The situation of distress is due, either alone or in combination with other factors, to the conduct of the State invoking it; or
   (b) The act in question is likely to create a comparable or greater peril.

Article 25

Necessity

1. Necessity may not be invoked by a State as a ground for precluding the wrongfulness of an act not in conformity with an international obligation of that State unless the act:
   (a) Is the only way for the State to safeguard an essential interest against a grave and imminent peril; and
   (b) Does not seriously impair an essential interest of the State or States towards which the obligation exists, or of the international community as a whole.

2. In any case, necessity may not be invoked by a State as a ground for precluding wrongfulness if:
   (a) The international obligation in question excludes the possibility of invoking necessity; or
   (b) The State has contributed to the situation of necessity.

Article 26

Compliance with peremptory norms

Nothing in this chapter precludes the wrongfulness of any act of a State which is not in conformity with an obligation arising under a peremptory norm of general international law.

Article 27

Consequences of invoking a circumstance precluding wrongfulness

The invocation of a circumstance precluding wrongfulness in accordance with this chapter is without prejudice to:

(a) Compliance with the obligation in question, if and to the extent that the circumstance precluding wrongfulness no longer exists;

(b) The question of compensation for any material loss caused by the act in question.

PART TWO: CONTENT OF THE INTERNATIONAL RESPONSIBILITY OF A STATE

Chapter I: General principles

Article 28

Legal consequences of an internationally wrongful act

The international responsibility of a State which is entailed by an internationally wrongful act in accordance with the provisions of Part One involves legal consequences as set out in this Part.

Article 29

Continued duty of performance

The legal consequences of an internationally wrongful act under this Part do not affect the continued duty of the responsible State to perform the obligation breached.

Article 30

Cessation and non-repetition

The State responsible for the internationally wrongful act is under an obligation:

(a) To cease that act, if it is continuing;

(b) To offer appropriate assurances and guarantees of non-repetition, if circumstances so require.

Article 31

Reparation

1. The responsible State is under an obligation to make full reparation for the injury caused by the internationally wrongful act.
2. Injury includes any damage, whether material or moral, caused by the internationally wrongful act of a State.

Article 32

Irrelevance of internal law

The responsible State may not rely on the provisions of its internal law as justification for failure to comply with its obligations under this Part.

Article 33

Scope of international obligations set out in this Part

1. The obligations of the responsible State set out in this Part may be owed to another State, to several States, or to the international community as a whole, depending in particular on the character and content of the international obligation and on the circumstances of the breach.
2. This Part is without prejudice to any right, arising from the international responsibility of a State, which may accrue directly to any person or entity other than a State.

Chapter II: Reparation for injury

Article 34

Forms of reparation

Full reparation for the injury caused by the internationally wrongful act shall take the form of restitution, compensation and satisfaction, either singly or in combination, in accordance with the provisions of this chapter.

Article 35

Restitution

A State responsible for an internationally wrongful act is under an obligation to make restitution, that is, to re-establish the situation which existed before the wrongful act was committed, provided and to the extent that restitution:

  (a) Is not materially impossible;
  (b) Does not involve a burden out of all proportion to the benefit deriving from restitution instead of compensation.

Article 36

Compensation

1. The State responsible for an internationally wrongful act is under an obligation to compensate for the damage caused thereby, insofar as such damage is not made good by restitution.

2. The compensation shall cover any financially assessable damage including loss of profits insofar as it is established.

Article 37

Satisfaction

1. The State responsible for an internationally wrongful act is under an obligation to give satisfaction for the injury caused by that act insofar as it cannot be made good by restitution or compensation.

2. Satisfaction may consist in an acknowledgement of the breach, an expression of regret, a formal apology or another appropriate modality.

3. Satisfaction shall not be out of proportion to the injury and may not take a form humiliating to the responsible State.

Article 38

Interest

1. Interest on any principal sum due under this chapter shall be payable when necessary in order to ensure full reparation. The interest rate and mode of calculation shall be set so as to achieve that result.

2. Interest runs from the date when the principal sum should have been paid until the date the obligation to pay is fulfilled.

Article 39

Contribution to the injury

In the determination of reparation, account shall be taken of the contribution to the injury by wilful or negligent action or omission of the injured State or any person or entity in relation to whom reparation is sought.

Chapter III: Serious breaches of obligations under peremptory norms of general international law

Article 40

Application of this chapter

1. This chapter applies to the international responsibility which is entailed by a serious breach by a State of an obligation arising under a peremptory norm of general international law.

2. A breach of such an obligation is serious if it involves a gross or systematic failure by the responsible State to fulfil the obligation.

Article 41

Particular consequences of a serious breach of an obligation under this chapter

1. States shall cooperate to bring to an end through lawful means any serious breach within the meaning of article 40.

2. No State shall recognize as lawful a situation created by a serious breach within the meaning of article 40, nor render aid or assistance in maintaining that situation.

3. This article is without prejudice to the other consequences referred to in this Part and to such further consequences that a breach to which this chapter applies may entail under international law.

PART THREE: THE IMPLEMENTATION OF THE INTERNATIONAL RESPONSIBILITY OF A STATE

Chapter I: Invocation of the responsibility of a State

Article 42

Invocation of responsibility by an injured State

A State is entitled as an injured State to invoke the responsibility of another State if the obligation breached is owed to:

(a) That State individually; or

(b) A group of States including that State, or the international community as a whole, and the breach of the obligation:

(i) Specially affects that State; or

(ii) Is of such a character as radically to change the position of all the other States to which the obligation is owed with respect to the further performance of the obligation.

Article 43

Notice of claim by an injured State

1. An injured State which invokes the responsibility of another State shall give notice of its claim to that State.

2. The injured State may specify in particular:

(a) The conduct that the responsible State should take in order to cease the wrongful act, if it is continuing;

(b) What form reparation should take in accordance with the provisions of Part Two.

Article 44

Admissibility of claims

The responsibility of a State may not be invoked if:

    (a) The claim is not brought in accordance with any applicable rule relating to the nationality of claims;

    (b) The claim is one to which the rule of exhaustion of local remedies applies and any available and effective local remedy has not been exhausted.

Article 45

Loss of the right to invoke responsibility

The responsibility of a State may not be invoked if:

    (a) The injured State has validly waived the claim;

    (b) The injured State is to be considered as having, by reason of its conduct, validly acquiesced in the lapse of the claim.

Article 46

Plurality of injured States

Where several States are injured by the same internationally wrongful act, each injured State may separately invoke the responsibility of the State which has committed the internationally wrongful act.

Article 47

Plurality of responsible States

1.   Where several States are responsible for the same internationally wrongful act, the responsibility of each State may be invoked in relation to that act.

2.   Paragraph 1:

    (a) Does not permit any injured State to recover, by way of compensation, more than the damage it has suffered;

    (b) Is without prejudice to any right of recourse against the other responsible States.

Article 48

Invocation of responsibility by a State other than an injured State

1.   Any State other than an injured State is entitled to invoke the responsibility of another State in accordance with paragraph 2 if:

    (a) The obligation breached is owed to a group of States including that State, and is established for the protection of a collective interest of the group; or

(b) The obligation breached is owed to the international community as a whole.

2. Any State entitled to invoke responsibility under paragraph 1 may claim from the responsible State:

(a) Cessation of the internationally wrongful act, and assurances and guarantees of non-repetition in accordance with article 30; and

(b) Performance of the obligation of reparation in accordance with the preceding articles, in the interest of the injured State or of the beneficiaries of the obligation breached.

3. The requirements for the invocation of responsibility by an injured State under articles 43, 44 and 45 apply to an invocation of responsibility by a State entitled to do so under paragraph 1.

Chapter II: Countermeasures

Article 49
Object and limits of countermeasures

1. An injured State may only take countermeasures against a State which is responsible for an internationally wrongful act in order to induce that State to comply with its obligations under Part Two.

2. Countermeasures are limited to the non-performance for the time being of international obligations of the State taking the measures towards the responsible State.

3. Countermeasures shall, as far as possible, be taken in such a way as to permit the resumption of performance of the obligations in question.

Article 50
Obligations not affected by countermeasures

1. Countermeasures shall not affect:

(a) The obligation to refrain from the threat or use of force as embodied in the Charter of the United Nations;

(b) Obligations for the protection of fundamental human rights;

(c) Obligations of a humanitarian character prohibiting reprisals;

(d) Other obligations under peremptory norms of general international law.

2. A State taking countermeasures is not relieved from fulfilling its obligations:

(a) Under any dispute settlement procedure applicable between it and the responsible State;

(b) To respect the inviolability of diplomatic or consular agents, premises, archives and documents.

Article 51

Proportionality

Countermeasures must be commensurate with the injury suffered, taking into account the gravity of the internationally wrongful act and the rights in question.

Article 52

Conditions relating to resort to countermeasures

1. Before taking countermeasures, an injured State shall:
    (a) Call on the responsible State, in accordance with article 43, to fulfil its obligations under Part Two;
    (b) Notify the responsible State of any decision to take countermeasures and offer to negotiate with that State.
2. Notwithstanding paragraph 1 (b), the injured State may take such urgent countermeasures as are necessary to preserve its rights.
3. Countermeasures may not be taken, and if already taken must be suspended without undue delay if:
    (a) The internationally wrongful act has ceased; and
    (b) The dispute is pending before a court or tribunal which has the authority to make decisions binding on the parties.
4. Paragraph 3 does not apply if the responsible State fails to implement the dispute settlement procedures in good faith.

Article 53

Termination of countermeasures

Countermeasures shall be terminated as soon as the responsible State has complied with its obligations under Part Two in relation to the internationally wrongful act.

Article 54

Measures taken by States other than an injured State

This chapter does not prejudice the right of any State, entitled under article 48, paragraph 1 to invoke the responsibility of another State, to take lawful measures against that State to ensure cessation of the breach and reparation in the interest of the injured State or of the beneficiaries of the obligation breached.

PART FOUR: GENERAL PROVISIONS

Article 55

Lex specialis

These articles do not apply where and to the extent that the conditions for the existence of an internationally wrongful act or the content or implementation of the international responsibility of a State are governed by special rules of international law.

Article 56

Questions of State responsibility not regulated by these articles

The applicable rules of international law continue to govern questions concerning the responsibility of a State for an internationally wrongful act to the extent that they are not regulated by these articles.

Article 57

Responsibility of an international organization

These articles are without prejudice to any question of the responsibility under international law of an international organization, or of any State for the conduct of an international organization.

Article 58

Individual responsibility

These articles are without prejudice to any question of the individual responsibility under international law of any person acting on behalf of a State.

Article 59

Charter of the United Nations

These articles are without prejudice to the Charter of the United Nations.

International Covenant on Civil and Political Rights

Adopted and opened for signature, ratification and accession by General Assembly Resolution 2200A (XXI) of 16 December 1966

Entered into force on 23 March 1976, in accordance with Article 49 UNTS, Vol 999, p 171

PREAMBLE

The States Parties to the present Covenant,

Considering that, in accordance with the principles proclaimed in the Charter of the United Nations, recognition of the inherent dignity and of the equal and inalienable rights of all members of the human family is the foundation of freedom, justice and peace in the world,

Recognizing that these rights derive from the inherent dignity of the human person,

Recognizing that, in accordance with the Universal Declaration of Human Rights, the ideal of free human beings enjoying civil and political freedom and freedom from fear and want can only be achieved if conditions are created whereby everyone may enjoy his civil and political rights, as well as his economic, social and cultural rights,

Considering the obligation of States under the Charter of the United Nations to promote universal respect for, and observance of, human rights and freedoms,

Realizing that the individual, having duties to other individuals and to the community to which he belongs, is under a responsibility to strive for the promotion and observance of the rights recognized in the present Covenant,

Agree upon the following articles:

PART I

Article 1

1. All peoples have the right of self-determination. By virtue of that right they freely determine their political status and freely pursue their economic, social and cultural development.

2. All peoples may, for their own ends, freely dispose of their natural wealth and resources without prejudice to any obligations arising out of international economic co-operation, based upon the principle of mutual benefit, and international law. In no case may a people be deprived of its own means of subsistence.

3. The States Parties to the present Covenant, including those having responsibility for the administration of Non-Self-Governing and Trust Territories, shall promote the realization of the right of self-determination, and shall respect that right, in conformity with the provisions of the Charter of the United Nations.

PART II

Article 2

1. Each State Party to the present Covenant undertakes to respect and to ensure to all individuals within its territory and subject to its jurisdiction the rights recognized in the present Covenant, without distinction of any kind, such as race, colour, sex, language, religion, political or other opinion, national or social origin, property, birth or other status.

2. Where not already provided for by existing legislative or other measures, each State Party to the present Covenant undertakes to take the necessary steps, in accordance with its constitutional processes and with the provisions of the present Covenant, to adopt such laws or other measures as may be necessary to give effect to the rights recognized in the present Covenant.

3. Each State Party to the present Covenant undertakes:

    (a) To ensure that any person whose rights or freedoms as herein recognized are violated shall have an effective remedy, notwithstanding that the violation has been committed by persons acting in an official capacity;

    (b) To ensure that any person claiming such a remedy shall have his right thereto determined by competent judicial, administrative or legislative authorities, or by any other competent authority provided for by the legal system of the State, and to develop the possibilities of judicial remedy;

    (c) To ensure that the competent authorities shall enforce such remedies when granted.

Article 3

The States Parties to the present Covenant undertake to ensure the equal right of men and women to the enjoyment of all civil and political rights set forth in the present Covenant.

Article 4

1. In time of public emergency which threatens the life of the nation and the existence of which is officially proclaimed, the States Parties to the present Covenant may take measures derogating from their obligations under the present Covenant to the extent strictly required by the exigencies of the situation, provided that such measures are not inconsistent with their other obligations under international law and do not involve discrimination solely on the ground of race, colour, sex, language, religion or social origin.

2. No derogation from articles 6, 7, 8 (paragraphs I and 2), 11, 15, 16 and 18 may be made under this provision.

3. Any State Party to the present Covenant availing itself of the right of derogation shall immediately inform the other States Parties to the present Covenant, through the intermediary of the Secretary-General of the United Nations, of the provisions from which it has derogated and of the reasons by which it was actuated. A further communication shall be made, through the same intermediary, on the date on which it terminates such derogation.

Article 5

1. Nothing in the present Covenant may be interpreted as implying for any State, group or person any right to engage in any activity or perform any act aimed at the destruction of any of the rights and freedoms recognized herein or at their limitation to a greater extent than is provided for in the present Covenant.

2. There shall be no restriction upon or derogation from any of the fundamental human rights recognized or existing in any State Party to the present Covenant pursuant to law, conventions, regulations or custom on the pretext that the present Covenant does not recognize such rights or that it recognizes them to a lesser extent.

PART III

Article 6

1. Every human being has the inherent right to life. This right shall be protected by law. No one shall be arbitrarily deprived of his life.

2. In countries which have not abolished the death penalty, sentence of death may be imposed only for the most serious crimes in accordance with the law in force at the time of the commission of the crime and not contrary to the provisions of the present Covenant and to the Convention on the Prevention and Punishment of the Crime of Genocide. This penalty can only be carried out pursuant to a final judgement rendered by a competent court.

3. When deprivation of life constitutes the crime of genocide, it is understood that nothing in this article shall authorize any State Party to the present Covenant to derogate in any way from any obligation assumed under the provisions of the Convention on the Prevention and Punishment of the Crime of Genocide.

4. Anyone sentenced to death shall have the right to seek pardon or commutation of the sentence. Amnesty, pardon or commutation of the sentence of death may be granted in all cases.

5. Sentence of death shall not be imposed for crimes committed by persons below eighteen years of age and shall not be carried out on pregnant women.

6. Nothing in this article shall be invoked to delay or to prevent the abolition of capital punishment by any State Party to the present Covenant.

Article 7

No one shall be subjected to torture or to cruel, inhuman or degrading treatment or punishment. In particular, no one shall be subjected without his free consent to medical or scientific experimentation.

Article 8

1. No one shall be held in slavery; slavery and the slave-trade in all their forms shall be prohibited.

2. No one shall be held in servitude.

3. (a) No one shall be required to perform forced or compulsory labour;

   (b) Paragraph 3 (a) shall not be held to preclude, in countries where imprisonment with hard labour may be imposed as a punishment for a crime, the performance of hard labour in pursuance of a sentence to such punishment by a competent court;

   (c) For the purpose of this paragraph the term 'forced or compulsory labour' shall not include:

   (i) Any work or service, not referred to in subparagraph (b), normally required of a person who is under detention in consequence of a lawful order of a court, or of a person during conditional release from such detention;

   (ii) Any service of a military character and, in countries where conscientious objection is recognized, any national service required by law of conscientious objectors;

   (iii) Any service exacted in cases of emergency or calamity threatening the life or well-being of the community;

   (iv) Any work or service which forms part of normal civil obligations.

Article 9

1. Everyone has the right to liberty and security of person. No one shall be subjected to arbitrary arrest or detention. No one shall be deprived of his liberty except on such grounds and in accordance with such procedure as are established by law.

2. Anyone who is arrested shall be informed, at the time of arrest, of the reasons for his arrest and shall be promptly informed of any charges against him.

3. Anyone arrested or detained on a criminal charge shall be brought promptly before a judge or other officer authorized by law to exercise

judicial power and shall be entitled to trial within a reasonable time or to release. It shall not be the general rule that persons awaiting trial shall be detained in custody, but release may be subject to guarantees to appear for trial, at any other stage of the judicial proceedings, and, should occasion arise, for execution of the judgement.

4. Anyone who is deprived of his liberty by arrest or detention shall be entitled to take proceedings before a court, in order that that court may decide without delay on the lawfulness of his detention and order his release if the detention is not lawful.

5. Anyone who has been the victim of unlawful arrest or detention shall have an enforceable right to compensation.

Article 10

1. All persons deprived of their liberty shall be treated with humanity and with respect for the inherent dignity of the human person.

2. (a) Accused persons shall, save in exceptional circumstances, be segregated from convicted persons and shall be subject to separate treatment appropriate to their status as unconvicted persons;

   (b) Accused juvenile persons shall be separated from adults and brought as speedily as possible for adjudication.

3. The penitentiary system shall comprise treatment of prisoners the essential aim of which shall be their reformation and social rehabilitation. Juvenile offenders shall be segregated from adults and be accorded treatment appropriate to their age and legal status.

Article 11

No one shall be imprisoned merely on the ground of inability to fulfil a contractual obligation.

Article 12

1. Everyone lawfully within the territory of a State shall, within that territory, have the right to liberty of movement and freedom to choose his residence.

2. Everyone shall be free to leave any country, including his own.

3. The above-mentioned rights shall not be subject to any restrictions except those which are provided by law, are necessary to protect national security, public order (ordre public), public health or morals or the rights and freedoms of others, and are consistent with the other rights recognized in the present Covenant.

4. No one shall be arbitrarily deprived of the right to enter his own country.

Article 13

An alien lawfully in the territory of a State Party to the present Covenant may be expelled therefrom only in pursuance of a decision reached in accordance with law and shall, except where compelling reasons of national security otherwise require, be allowed to submit the reasons against his expulsion and to have his case reviewed by, and be represented for the purpose before, the competent authority or a person or persons especially designated by the competent authority.

Article 14

1. All persons shall be equal before the courts and tribunals. In the determination of any criminal charge against him, or of his rights and obligations in a suit at law, everyone shall be entitled to a fair and public hearing by a competent, independent and impartial tribunal established by law. The press and the public may be excluded from all or part of a trial for reasons of morals, public order (ordre public) or national security in a democratic society, or when the interest of the private lives of the parties so requires, or to the extent strictly necessary in the opinion of the court in special circumstances where publicity would prejudice the interests of justice; but any judgement rendered in a criminal case or in a suit at law shall be made public except where the interest of juvenile persons otherwise requires or the proceedings concern matrimonial disputes or the guardianship of children.

2. Everyone charged with a criminal offence shall have the right to be presumed innocent until proved guilty according to law.

3. In the determination of any criminal charge against him, everyone shall be entitled to the following minimum guarantees, in full equality:

    (a) To be informed promptly and in detail in a language which he understands of the nature and cause of the charge against him;

    (b) To have adequate time and facilities for the preparation of his defence and to communicate with counsel of his own choosing;

    (c) To be tried without undue delay;

    (d) To be tried in his presence, and to defend himself in person or through legal assistance of his own choosing; to be informed, if he does not have legal assistance, of this right; and to have legal assistance assigned to him, in any case where the interests of justice so require, and without payment by him in any such case if he does not have sufficient means to pay for it;

    (e) To examine, or have examined, the witnesses against him and to obtain the attendance and examination of witnesses on his behalf under the same conditions as witnesses against him;

    (f) To have the free assistance of an interpreter if he cannot understand or speak the language used in court;

    (g) Not to be compelled to testify against himself or to confess guilt.

4. In the case of juvenile persons, the procedure shall be such as will take account of their age and the desirability of promoting their rehabilitation.

5. Everyone convicted of a crime shall have the right to his conviction and sentence being reviewed by a higher tribunal according to law.

6. When a person has by a final decision been convicted of a criminal offence and when subsequently his conviction has been reversed or he has been pardoned on the ground that a new or newly discovered fact shows conclusively that there has been a miscarriage of justice, the person who has suffered punishment as a result of such conviction shall be

compensated according to law, unless it is proved that the non-disclosure of the unknown fact in time is wholly or partly attributable to him.

7. No one shall be liable to be tried or punished again for an offence for which he has already been finally convicted or acquitted in accordance with the law and penal procedure of each country.

Article 15

1. No one shall be held guilty of any criminal offence on account of any act or omission which did not constitute a criminal offence, under national or international law, at the time when it was committed. Nor shall a heavier penalty be imposed than the one that was applicable at the time when the criminal offence was committed. If, subsequent to the commission of the offence, provision is made by law for the imposition of the lighter penalty, the offender shall benefit thereby.

2. Nothing in this article shall prejudice the trial and punishment of any person for any act or omission which, at the time when it was committed, was criminal according to the general principles of law recognized by the community of nations.

Article 16

Everyone shall have the right to recognition everywhere as a person before the law.

Article 17

1. No one shall be subjected to arbitrary or unlawful interference with his privacy, family, or correspondence, nor to unlawful attacks on his honour and reputation.

2. Everyone has the right to the protection of the law against such interference or attacks.

Article 18

1. Everyone shall have the right to freedom of thought, conscience and religion. This right shall include freedom to have or to adopt a religion or belief of his choice, and freedom, either individually or in community with others and in public or private, to manifest his religion or belief in worship, observance, practice and teaching.

2. No one shall be subject to coercion which would impair his freedom to have or to adopt a religion or belief of his choice.

3. Freedom to manifest one's religion or beliefs may be subject only to such limitations as are prescribed by law and are necessary to protect public safety, order, health, or morals or the fundamental rights and freedoms of others.

4. The States Parties to the present Covenant undertake to have respect for the liberty of parents and, when applicable, legal guardians to ensure the religious and moral education of their children in conformity with their own convictions.

Article 19

1. Everyone shall have the right to hold opinions without interference.

2. Everyone shall have the right to freedom of expression; this right shall include freedom to seek, receive and impart information and ideas of all kinds, regardless of frontiers, either orally, in writing or in print, in the form of art, or through any other media of his choice.

3. The exercise of the rights provided for in paragraph 2 of this article carries with it special duties and responsibilities. It may therefore be subject to certain restrictions, but these shall only be such as are provided by law and are necessary:

   (a) For respect of the rights or reputations of others;

   (b) For the protection of national security or of public order (ordre public), or of public health or morals.

Article 20

1. Any propaganda for war shall be prohibited by law.

2. Any advocacy of national, racial or religious hatred that constitutes incitement to discrimination, hostility or violence shall be prohibited by law.

Article 21

The right of peaceful assembly shall be recognized. No restrictions may be placed on the exercise of this right other than those imposed in conformity with the law and which are necessary in a democratic society in the interests of national security or public safety, public order (ordre public), the protection of public health or morals or the protection of the rights and freedoms of others.

Article 22

1. Everyone shall have the right to freedom of association with others, including the right to form and join trade unions for the protection of his interests.

2. No restrictions may be placed on the exercise of this right other than those which are prescribed by law and which are necessary in a democratic society in the interests of national security or public safety, public order (ordre public), the protection of public health or morals or the protection of the rights and freedoms of others. This article shall not prevent the imposition of lawful restrictions on members of the armed forces and of the police in their exercise of this right.

3. Nothing in this article shall authorize States Parties to the International Labour Organisation Convention of 1948 concerning Freedom of Association and Protection of the Right to Organize to take legislative measures which would prejudice, or to apply the law in such a manner as to prejudice, the guarantees provided for in that Convention.

Article 23

1. The family is the natural and fundamental group unit of society and is entitled to protection by society and the State.
2. The right of men and women of marriageable age to marry and to found a family shall be recognized.
3. No marriage shall be entered into without the free and full consent of the intending spouses.
4. States Parties to the present Covenant shall take appropriate steps to ensure equality of rights and responsibilities of spouses as to marriage, during marriage and at its dissolution. In the case of dissolution, provision shall be made for the necessary protection of any children.

Article 24

1. Every child shall have, without any discrimination as to race, colour, sex, language, religion, national or social origin, property or birth, the right to such measures of protection as are required by his status as a minor, on the part of his family, society and the State.
2. Every child shall be registered immediately after birth and shall have a name.
3. Every child has the right to acquire a nationality.

Article 25

Every citizen shall have the right and the opportunity, without any of the distinctions mentioned in article 2 and without unreasonable restrictions:
   (a) To take part in the conduct of public affairs, directly or through freely chosen representatives;
   (b) To vote and to be elected at genuine periodic elections which shall be by universal and equal suffrage and shall be held by secret ballot, guaranteeing the free expression of the will of the electors;
   (c) To have access, on general terms of equality, to public service in his country.

Article 26

All persons are equal before the law and are entitled without any discrimination to the equal protection of the law. In this respect, the law shall prohibit any discrimination and guarantee to all persons equal and effective protection against discrimination on any ground such as race, colour, sex, language, religion, political or other opinion, national or social origin, property, birth or other status.

Article 27

In those States in which ethnic, religious or linguistic minorities exist, persons belonging to such minorities shall not be denied the right, in community with the other members of their group, to enjoy their own culture, to profess and practise their own religion, or to use their own language.

PART IV

Article 28

1. There shall be established a Human Rights Committee (hereafter referred to in the present Covenant as the Committee). It shall consist of eighteen members and shall carry out the functions hereinafter provided.
2. The Committee shall be composed of nationals of the States Parties to the present Covenant who shall be persons of high moral character and recognized competence in the field of human rights, consideration being given to the usefulness of the participation of some persons having legal experience.
3. The members of the Committee shall be elected and shall serve in their personal capacity.

Article 29

1. The members of the Committee shall be elected by secret ballot from a list of persons possessing the qualifications prescribed in article 28 and nominated for the purpose by the States Parties to the present Covenant.
2. Each State Party to the present Covenant may nominate not more than two persons. These persons shall be nationals of the nominating State.
3. A person shall be eligible for renomination.

Article 30

1. The initial election shall be held no later than six months after the date of the entry into force of the present Covenant.
2. At least four months before the date of each election to the Committee, other than an election to fill a vacancy declared in accordance with article 34, the Secretary-General of the United Nations shall address a written invitation to the States Parties to the present Covenant to submit their nominations for membership of the Committee within three months.
3. The Secretary-General of the United Nations shall prepare a list in alphabetical order of all the persons thus nominated, with an indication of the States Parties which have nominated them, and shall submit it to the States Parties to the present Covenant no later than one month before the date of each election.
4. Elections of the members of the Committee shall be held at a meeting of the States Parties to the present Covenant convened by the Secretary General of the United Nations at the Headquarters of the United Nations. At that meeting, for which two thirds of the States Parties to

the present Covenant shall constitute a quorum, the persons elected to the Committee shall be those nominees who obtain the largest number of votes and an absolute majority of the votes of the representatives of States Parties present and voting.

Article 31

1. The Committee may not include more than one national of the same State.

2. In the election of the Committee, consideration shall be given to equitable geographical distribution of membership and to the representation of the different forms of civilization and of the principal legal systems.

Article 32

1. The members of the Committee shall be elected for a term of four years. They shall be eligible for re-election if renominated. However, the terms of nine of the members elected at the first election shall expire at the end of two years; immediately after the first election, the names of these nine members shall be chosen by lot by the Chairman of the meeting referred to in article 30, paragraph 4.

2. Elections at the expiry of office shall be held in accordance with the preceding articles of this part of the present Covenant.

Article 33

1. If, in the unanimous opinion of the other members, a member of the Committee has ceased to carry out his functions for any cause other than absence of a temporary character, the Chairman of the Committee shall notify the Secretary-General of the United Nations, who shall then declare the seat of that member to be vacant.

2. In the event of the death or the resignation of a member of the Committee, the Chairman shall immediately notify the Secretary-General of the United Nations, who shall declare the seat vacant from the date of death or the date on which the resignation takes effect.

Article 34

1. When a vacancy is declared in accordance with article 33 and if the term of office of the member to be replaced does not expire within six months of the declaration of the vacancy, the Secretary-General of the United Nations shall notify each of the States Parties to the present Covenant, which may within two months submit nominations in accordance with article 29 for the purpose of filling the vacancy.

2. The Secretary-General of the United Nations shall prepare a list in alphabetical order of the persons thus nominated and shall submit it to the States Parties to the present Covenant. The election to fill the vacancy shall then take place in accordance with the relevant provisions of this part of the present Covenant.

3. A member of the Committee elected to fill a vacancy declared in accordance with article 33 shall hold office for the remainder of the

term of the member who vacated the seat on the Committee under the provisions of that article.

Article 35

The members of the Committee shall, with the approval of the General Assembly of the United Nations, receive emoluments from United Nations resources on such terms and conditions as the General Assembly may decide, having regard to the importance of the Committee's responsibilities.

Article 36

The Secretary-General of the United Nations shall provide the necessary staff and facilities for the effective performance of the functions of the Committee under the present Covenant.

Article 37

1. The Secretary-General of the United Nations shall convene the initial meeting of the Committee at the Headquarters of the United Nations.
2. After its initial meeting, the Committee shall meet at such times as shall be provided in its rules of procedure.
3. The Committee shall normally meet at the Headquarters of the United Nations or at the United Nations Office at Geneva.

Article 38

Every member of the Committee shall, before taking up his duties, make a solemn declaration in open committee that he will perform his functions impartially and conscientiously.

Article 39

1. The Committee shall elect its officers for a term of two years. They may be re-elected.
2. The Committee shall establish its own rules of procedure, but these rules shall provide, inter alia, that:
   (a) Twelve members shall constitute a quorum;
   (b) Decisions of the Committee shall be made by a majority vote of the members present.

Article 40

1. The States Parties to the present Covenant undertake to submit reports on the measures they have adopted which give effect to the rights recognized herein and on the progress made in the enjoyment of those rights:

(a) Within one year of the entry into force of the present Covenant for the States Parties concerned;

(b) Thereafter whenever the Committee so requests.

2. All reports shall be submitted to the Secretary-General of the United Nations, who shall transmit them to the Committee for consideration. Reports shall indicate the factors and difficulties, if any, affecting the implementation of the present Covenant.

3. The Secretary-General of the United Nations may, after consultation with the Committee, transmit to the specialized agencies concerned copies of such parts of the reports as may fall within their field of competence.

4. The Committee shall study the reports submitted by the States Parties to the present Covenant. It shall transmit its reports, and such general comments as it may consider appropriate, to the States Parties. The Committee may also transmit to the Economic and Social Council these comments along with the copies of the reports it has received from States Parties to the present Covenant.

5. The States Parties to the present Covenant may submit to the Committee observations on any comments that may be made in accordance with paragraph 4 of this article.

Article 41

1. A State Party to the present Covenant may at any time declare under this article that it recognizes the competence of the Committee to receive and consider communications to the effect that a State Party claims that another State Party is not fulfilling its obligations under the present Covenant. Communications under this article may be received and considered only if submitted by a State Party which has made a declaration recognizing in regard to itself the competence of the Committee. No communication shall be received by the Committee if it concerns a State Party which has not made such a declaration. Communications received under this article shall be dealt with in accordance with the following procedure:

(a) If a State Party to the present Covenant considers that another State Party is not giving effect to the provisions of the present Covenant, it may, by written communication, bring the matter to the attention of that State Party. Within three months after the receipt of the communication the receiving State shall afford the State which sent the communication an explanation, or any other statement in writing clarifying the matter which should include, to the extent possible and pertinent, reference to domestic procedures and remedies taken, pending, or available in the matter;

(b) If the matter is not adjusted to the satisfaction of both States Parties concerned within six months after the receipt by the receiving State of the initial communication, either State shall have the right to refer the matter to the Committee, by notice given to the Committee and to the other State;

(c) The Committee shall deal with a matter referred to it only after it has ascertained that all available domestic remedies have been invoked and exhausted in the matter, in conformity with the generally recognized principles of international law. This shall not be the rule where the application of the remedies is unreasonably prolonged;

(d) The Committee shall hold closed meetings when examining communications under this article;

(e) Subject to the provisions of subparagraph (c), the Committee shall make available its good offices to the States Parties concerned with a view to a friendly solution of the matter on the basis of respect for human rights and fundamental freedoms as recognized in the present Covenant;

(f) In any matter referred to it, the Committee may call upon the States Parties concerned, referred to in subparagraph (b), to supply any relevant information;

(g) The States Parties concerned, referred to in subparagraph (b), shall have the right to be represented when the matter is being considered in the Committee and to make submissions orally and/or in writing;

(h) The Committee shall, within twelve months after the date of receipt of notice under subparagraph (b), submit a report:

   (i) If a solution within the terms of subparagraph (e) is reached, the Committee shall confine its report to a brief statement of the facts and of the solution reached;

   (ii) If a solution within the terms of subparagraph (e) is not reached, the Committee shall confine its report to a brief statement of the facts; the written submissions and record of the oral submissions made by the States Parties concerned shall be attached to the report. In every matter, the report shall be communicated to the States Parties concerned.

2. The provisions of this article shall come into force when ten States Parties to the present Covenant have made declarations under paragraph 1 of this article. Such declarations shall be deposited by the States Parties with the Secretary-General of the United Nations, who shall transmit copies thereof to the other States Parties. A declaration may be withdrawn at any time by notification to the Secretary-General. Such a withdrawal shall not prejudice the consideration of any matter which is the subject of a communication already transmitted under this article; no further communication by any State Party shall be received after the notification of withdrawal of the declaration has been received by the Secretary-General, unless the State Party concerned has made a new declaration.

Article 42

1. (a) If a matter referred to the Committee in accordance with article 41 is not resolved to the satisfaction of the States Parties concerned, the Committee may, with the prior consent of the States Parties concerned, appoint an ad hoc Conciliation Commission (hereinafter referred to as the Commission). The good offices of the Commission shall be made available to the States Parties concerned with a view to an amicable solution of the matter on the basis of respect for the present Covenant;

   (b) The Commission shall consist of five persons acceptable to the States Parties concerned. If the States Parties concerned fail to reach agreement within three months on all or part of the composition of the Commission, the members of the Commission concerning whom no agreement has been reached shall be elected by secret ballot by a two-thirds majority vote of the Committee from among its members.

2. The members of the Commission shall serve in their personal capacity. They shall not be nationals of the States Parties concerned, or of a State not Party to the present Covenant, or of a State Party which has not made a declaration under article 41.

3. The Commission shall elect its own Chairman and adopt its own rules of procedure.

4. The meetings of the Commission shall normally be held at the Headquarters of the United Nations or at the United Nations Office at Geneva. However, they may be held at such other convenient places as the Commission may determine in consultation with the Secretary-General of the United Nations and the States Parties concerned.

5. The secretariat provided in accordance with article 36 shall also service the commissions appointed under this article.

6. The information received and collated by the Committee shall be made available to the Commission and the Commission may call upon the States Parties concerned to supply any other relevant information.

7. When the Commission has fully considered the matter, but in any event not later than twelve months after having been seized of the matter, it shall submit to the Chairman of the Committee a report for communication to the States Parties concerned:

    (a) If the Commission is unable to complete its consideration of the matter within twelve months, it shall confine its report to a brief statement of the status of its consideration of the matter;

    (b) If an amicable solution to the matter on the basis of respect for human rights as recognized in the present Covenant is reached, the Commission shall confine its report to a brief statement of the facts and of the solution reached;

    (c) If a solution within the terms of subparagraph (b) is not reached, the Commission's report shall embody its findings on all questions of fact relevant to the issues between the States Parties concerned, and its views on the possibilities of an amicable solution of the matter. This report shall also contain the written submissions and a record of the oral submissions made by the States Parties concerned;

    (d) If the Commission's report is submitted under subparagraph (c), the States Parties concerned shall, within three months of the receipt of the report, notify the Chairman of the Committee whether or not they accept the contents of the report of the Commission.

8. The provisions of this article are without prejudice to the responsibilities of the Committee under article 41.

9. The States Parties concerned shall share equally all the expenses of the members of the Commission in accordance with estimates to be provided by the Secretary-General of the United Nations.

10. The Secretary-General of the United Nations shall be empowered to pay the expenses of the members of the Commission, if necessary, before reimbursement by the States Parties concerned, in accordance with paragraph 9 of this article.

Article 43

The members of the Committee, and of the ad hoc conciliation commissions which may be appointed under article 42, shall be entitled to the facilities, privileges and immunities of experts on mission for the United Nations as laid down in the relevant sections of the Convention on the Privileges and Immunities of the United Nations.

Article 44

The provisions for the implementation of the present Covenant shall apply without prejudice to the procedures prescribed in the field of human rights by or under the constituent instruments and the conventions of the United Nations and of the specialized agencies and shall not prevent the States Parties to the present Covenant from having recourse to other procedures for settling a dispute in accordance with general or special international agreements in force between them.

Article 45

The Committee shall submit to the General Assembly of the United Nations, through the Economic and Social Council, an annual report on its activities.

PART V

Article 46

Nothing in the present Covenant shall be interpreted as impairing the provisions of the Charter of the United Nations and of the constitutions of the specialized agencies which define the respective responsibilities of the various organs of the United Nations and of the specialized agencies in regard to the matters dealt with in the present Covenant.

Article 47

Nothing in the present Covenant shall be interpreted as impairing the inherent right of all peoples to enjoy and utilize fully and freely their natural wealth and resources.

PART VI

Article 48

1. The present Covenant is open for signature by any State Member of the United Nations or member of any of its specialized agencies, by any State Party to the Statute of the International Court of Justice, and by any other State which has been invited by the General Assembly of the United Nations to become a Party to the present Covenant.
2. The present Covenant is subject to ratification. Instruments of ratification shall be deposited with the Secretary-General of the United Nations.

3. The present Covenant shall be open to accession by any State referred to in paragraph 1 of this article.

4. Accession shall be effected by the deposit of an instrument of accession with the Secretary-General of the United Nations.

5. The Secretary-General of the United Nations shall inform all States which have signed this Covenant or acceded to it of the deposit of each instrument of ratification or accession.

Article 49

1. The present Covenant shall enter into force three months after the date of the deposit with the Secretary-General of the United Nations of the thirty-fifth instrument of ratification or instrument of accession.

2. For each State ratifying the present Covenant or acceding to it after the deposit of the thirty-fifth instrument of ratification or instrument of accession, the present Covenant shall enter into force three months after the date of the deposit of its own instrument of ratification or instrument of accession.

Article 50

The provisions of the present Covenant shall extend to all parts of federal States without any limitations or exceptions.

Article 51

1. Any State Party to the present Covenant may propose an amendment and file it with the Secretary-General of the United Nations. The Secretary-General of the United Nations shall thereupon communicate any proposed amendments to the States Parties to the present Covenant with a request that they notify him whether they favour a conference of States Parties for the purpose of considering and voting upon the proposals. In the event that at least one third of the States Parties favours such a conference, the Secretary-General shall convene the conference under the auspices of the United Nations. Any amendment adopted by a majority of the States Parties present and voting at the conference shall be submitted to the General Assembly of the United Nations for approval.

2. Amendments shall come into force when they have been approved by the General Assembly of the United Nations and accepted by a two-thirds majority of the States Parties to the present Covenant in accordance with their respective constitutional processes.

3. When amendments come into force, they shall be binding on those States Parties which have accepted them, other States Parties still being bound by the provisions of the present Covenant and any earlier amendment which they have accepted.

Article 52

1. Irrespective of the notifications made under article 48, paragraph 5, the Secretary-General of the United Nations shall inform all States

referred to in paragraph 1 of the same article of the following particulars:

(a) Signatures, ratifications and accessions under article 48;

(b) The date of the entry into force of the present Covenant under article 49 and the date of the entry into force of any amendments under article 51.

Article 53

1. The present Covenant, of which the Chinese, English, French, Russian and Spanish texts are equally authentic, shall be deposited in the archives of the United Nations.

2. The Secretary-General of the United Nations shall transmit certified copies of the present Covenant to all States referred to in article 48.

United Nations General Assembly Resolution 2625 (XXV)

Declaration on Principles of International Law Concerning Friendly Relations and Co-operation among States in Accordance with the Charter of the United Nations

General Assembly Resolution 2625 (XXV), Official Records of the General Assembly, 25th Session, Supp No 28, at 121

UN Doc A/8028 (1971), adopted by consensus on 24 October 1970

The General Assembly,

Recalling its resolutions 1815 (XVII) of 18 December 1962, 1966 (XVIII) of 16 December 1963, 2103 (XX) of 20 December 1965, 2181 (XXI) of 12 December 1966, 2327 (XXII) of 18 December 1967, 2463 (XXIII) of 20 December 1968 and 2533 (XXIV) of 8 December 1969, in which it affirmed the importance of the progressive development and codification of the principles of international law concerning friendly relations and co-operation among States,

Having considered the report of the Special Committee on Principles of International Law concerning Friendly Relations and Co-operation among States, which met in Geneva from 31 March to 1 May 1970,

Emphasizing the paramount importance of the Charter of the United Nations for the maintenance of international peace and security and for the development of Friendly relations and Co-operation among States,

Deeply convinced that the adoption of the Declaration on Principles of International Law concerning Friendly Relations and Co-operation among States in accordance with the Charter of the United Nations on the occasion of the twenty-fifth anniversary of the United Nations would contribute to the strengthening of world peace and constitute a landmark in the development of international law and of relations among States, in promoting the rule of law among nations and particularly the universal application of the principles embodied in the Charter,

Considering the desirability of the wide dissemination of the text of the Declaration,

1. *Approves* the Declaration on Principles of International Law concerning Friendly Relations and Co-operation among States in accordance with the Charter of the United Nations, the text of which is annexed to the present resolution;

2. *Expresses its appreciation* to the Special Committee on Principles of International Law concerning Friendly Relations and Co-operation among States for its work resulting in the elaboration of the Declaration;

3. *Recommends* that all efforts be made so that the Declaration becomes generally known.

Annex

Preamble

The General Assembly,

Reaffirming in the terms of the Charter of the United Nations that the maintenance of international peace and security and the development of friendly relations and co-operation between nations are among the fundamental purposes of the United Nations,

Recalling that the peoples of the United Nations are determined to practise tolerance and live together in peace with one another as good neighbours,

Bearing in mind the importance of maintaining and strengthening international peace founded upon freedom, equality, justice and respect for fundamental human rights and of developing friendly relations among nations irrespective of their political, economic and social systems or the levels of their development,

Bearing in mind also the paramount importance of the Charter of the United Nations in the promotion of the rule of law among nations,

Considering that the faithful observance of the principles of international law concerning friendly relations and co-operation among States and the fulfillment in good faith of the obligations assumed by States, in accordance with the Charter, is of the greatest importance for the maintenance of international peace and security and for the implementation of the other purposes of the United Nations,

Noting that the great political, economic and social changes and scientific progress which have taken place in the world since the adoption of the Charter give increased importance to these principles and to the need for their more effective application in the conduct of States wherever carried on,

Recalling the established principle that outer space, including the Moon and other celestial bodies, is not subject to national appropriation by claim of sovereignty, by means of use or occupation, or by any other means, and mindful of the fact that consideration is being given in the United Nations to the question of establishing other appropriate provisions similarly inspired,

Convinced that the strict observance by States of the obligation not to intervene in the affairs of any other State is an essential condition to ensure that nations live together in peace with one another, since the practice of any form of intervention not only violates the spirit and letter of the Charter, but also leads to the creation of situations which threaten international peace and security,

Recalling the duty of States to refrain in their international relations from military, political, economic or any other form of coercion aimed against the political independence or territorial integrity of any State,

Considering it essential that all States shall refrain in their international relations from the threat or use of force against the territorial integrity or political independence of any State, or in any other manner inconsistent with the purposes of the United Nations,

Considering it equally essential that all States shall settle their international disputes by peaceful means in accordance with the Charter,

Reaffirming, in accordance with the Charter, the basic importance of sovereign equality and stressing that the purposes of the United Nations can be implemented only if States enjoy sovereign equality and comply fully with the requirements of this principle in their international relations,

Convinced that the subjection of peoples to alien subjugation, domination and exploitation constitutes a major obstacle to the promotion of international peace and security,

Convinced that the principle of equal rights and self-determination of peoples constitutes a significant contribution to contemporary international law, and that its effective application is of paramount importance for the promotion of friendly relations among States, based on respect for the principle of sovereign equality,

Convinced in consequence that any attempt aimed at the partial or total disruption of the national unity and territorial integrity of a State or country or at its political independence is incompatible with the purposes and principles of the Charter,

Considering the provisions of the Charter as a whole and taking into account the role of relevant resolutions adopted by the competent organs of the United Nations relating to the content of the principles,

Considering that the progressive development and codification of the following principles:

(a) The principle that States shall refrain in their international relations from the threat or use of force against the territorial integrity or political independence of any State, or in any other manner inconsistent with the purposes of the United Nations,

(b) The principle that States shall settle their international disputes by peaceful means in such a manner that international peace and security and justice are not endangered,

(c) The duty not to intervene in matters within the domestic jurisdiction of any State, in accordance with the Charter,

(d) The duty of States to co-operate with one another in accordance with the Charter,

    (e)   The principle of equal rights and self-determination of peoples,

    (f)   The principle of sovereign equality of States,

    (g)   The principle that States shall fulfil in good faith the obligations assumed by them in accordance with the Charter, so as to secure their more effective application within the international community, would promote the realization of the purposes of the United Nations,

Having considered the principles of international law relating to friendly relations and co-operation among States,

1. *Solemnly proclaims* the following principles:

The principle that States shall refrain in their international relations from the threat or use of force against the territorial integrity or political independence of any State or in any other manner inconsistent with the purposes of the United Nations

Every State has the duty to refrain in its international relations from the threat or use of force against the territorial integrity or political independence of any State, or in any other manner inconsistent with the purposes of the United Nations. Such a threat or use of force constitutes a violation of international law and the Charter of the United Nations and shall never be employed as a means of settling international issues.

A war of aggression constitutes a crime against the peace, for which there is responsibility under international law.

In accordance with the purposes and principles of the United Nations, States have the duty to refrain from propaganda for wars of aggression.

Every State has the duty to refrain from the threat or use of force to violate the existing international boundaries of another State or as a means of solving international disputes, including territorial disputes and problems concerning frontiers of States.

Every State likewise has the duty to refrain from the threat or use of force to violate international lines of demarcation, such as armistice lines, established by or pursuant to an international agreement to which it is a party or which it is otherwise bound to respect. Nothing in the foregoing shall be construed as prejudicing the positions of the parties concerned with regard to the status and effects of such lines under their special regimes or as affecting their temporary character.

States have a duty to refrain from acts of reprisal involving the use of force.

Every State has the duty to refrain from any forcible action which deprives peoples referred to in the elaboration of the principle of equal rights and self-determination of their right to self-determination and freedom and independence.

Every State has the duty to refrain from organizing or encouraging the organization of irregular forces or armed bands including mercenaries, for incursion into the territory of another State.

Every State has the duty to refrain from organizing, instigating, assisting or participating in acts of civil strife or terrorist acts in another State or acquiescing in organized activities within its territory directed towards the commission of such acts, when the acts referred to in the present paragraph involve a threat or use of force.

The territory of a State shall not be the object of military occupation resulting from the use of force in contravention of the provisions of the Charter. The territory of a State shall not be the object of acquisition by another State resulting from the threat or use of force. No territorial acquisition resulting from the threat or use of force shall be recognized as legal. Nothing in the foregoing shall be construed as affecting:

(a)   Provisions of the Charter or any international agreement prior to the Charter regime and valid under international law; or

(b)   The powers of the Security Council under the Charter.

All States shall pursue in good faith negotiations for the early conclusion of a universal treaty on general and complete disarmament under effective international control and strive to adopt appropriate measures to reduce international tensions and strengthen confidence among States.

All States shall comply in good faith with their obligations under the generally recognized principles and rules of international law with respect to the maintenance of international peace and security, and shall endeavour to make the United Nations security system based on the Charter more effective.

Nothing in the foregoing paragraphs shall be construed as enlarging or diminishing in any way the scope of the provisions of the Charter concerning cases in which the use of force is lawful.

The principle that States shall settle their international disputes by peaceful means in such a manner that international peace and security and justice are not endangered

Every State shall settle its international disputes with other States by peaceful means in such a manner that international peace and security and justice are not endangered.

States shall accordingly seek early and just settlement of their international disputes by negotiation, inquiry, mediation, conciliation, arbitration, judicial settlement, resort to regional agencies or arrangements or other peaceful means of their choice. In seeking such a settlement the parties shall agree upon such peaceful means as may be appropriate to the circumstances and nature of the dispute.

The parties to a dispute have the duty, in the event of failure to reach a solution by any one of the above peaceful means, to continue to seek a settlement of the dispute by other peaceful means agreed upon by them.

States parties to an international dispute, as well as other States shall refrain from any action which may aggravate the Situation so as to endanger the maintenance of international peace and security, and shall act in accordance with the purposes and principles of the United Nations.

International disputes shall be settled on the basis of the Sovereign equality of States and in accordance with the Principle of free choice of means. Recourse to, or acceptance of, a settlement procedure freely agreed to by States with regard to existing or future disputes to which they are parties shall not be regarded as incompatible with sovereign equality.

Nothing in the foregoing paragraphs prejudices or derogates from the applicable provisions of the Charter, in particular those relating to the pacific settlement of international disputes.

The principle concerning the duty not to intervene in matters within the domestic jurisdiction of any State, in accordance with the Charter

No State or group of States has the right to intervene, directly or indirectly, for any reason whatever, in the internal or external affairs of any other State. Consequently, armed intervention and all other forms of interference or attempted threats against the personality of the State or against its political, economic and cultural elements, are in violation of international law.

No State may use or encourage the use of economic political or any other type of measures to coerce another State in order to obtain from it the subordination of the exercise of its sovereign rights and to secure from it advantages of any kind. Also, no State shall organize, assist, foment, finance, incite or tolerate subversive, terrorist or armed activities directed towards the violent overthrow of the regime of another State, or interfere in civil strife in another State.

The use of force to deprive peoples of their national identity constitutes a violation of their inalienable rights and of the principle of non-intervention.

Every State has an inalienable right to choose its political, economic, social and cultural systems, without interference in any form by another State.

Nothing in the foregoing paragraphs shall be construed as reflecting the relevant provisions of the Charter relating to the maintenance of international peace and security.

The duty of States to co-operate with one another in accordance with the Charter

States have the duty to co-operate with one another, irrespective of the differences in their political, economic and social systems, in the various spheres of international relations, in order to maintain international peace and security and to promote international economic stability and progress, the general welfare of nations and international co-operation free from discrimination based on such differences.

To this end:
   (a) States shall co-operate with other States in the maintenance of international peace and security;

(b) States shall co-operate in the promotion of universal respect for, and observance of, human rights and fundamental freedoms for all, and in the elimination of all forms of racial discrimination and all forms of religious intolerance;

(c) States shall conduct their international relations in the economic, social, cultural, technical and trade fields in accordance with the principles of sovereign equality and non-intervention;

(d) States Members of the United Nations have the duty to take joint and separate action in co-operation with the United Nations in accordance with the relevant provisions of the Charter.

States should co-operate in the economic, social and cultural fields as well as in the field of science and technology and for the promotion of international cultural and educational progress. States should co-operate in the promotion of economic growth throughout the world, especially that of the developing countries.

The principle of equal rights and self-determination of peoples

By virtue of the principle of equal rights and self-determination of peoples enshrined in the Charter of the United Nations, all peoples have the right freely to determine, without external interference, their political status and to pursue their economic, social and cultural development, and every State has the duty to respect this right in accordance with the provisions of the Charter.

Every State has the duty to promote, through joint and separate action, realization of the principle of equal rights and self-determination of peoples, in accordance with the provisions of the Charter, and to render assistance to the United Nations in carrying out the responsibilities entrusted to it by the Charter regarding the implementation of the principle, in order:

(a) To promote friendly relations and co-operation among States; and

(b) To bring a speedy end to colonialism, having due regard to the freely expressed will of the peoples concerned;

and bearing in mind that subjection of peoples to alien subjugation, domination and exploitation constitutes a violation of the principle, as well as a denial of fundamental human rights, and is contrary to the Charter.

Every State has the duty to promote through joint and separate action universal respect for and observance of human rights and fundamental freedoms in accordance with the Charter.

The establishment of a sovereign and independent State, the free association or integration with an independent State or the emergence into any other political status freely determined by a people constitute modes of implementing the right of self-determination by that people.

Every State has the duty to refrain from any forcible action which deprives peoples referred to above in the elaboration of the present principle of their right to self-determination and freedom and independence. In their actions against, and resistance to, such forcible action in pursuit of the exercise of their right to self-determination, such peoples are entitled to seek and to receive support in accordance with the purposes and principles of the Charter.

The territory of a colony or other Non-Self-Governing Territory has, under the Charter, a status separate and distinct from the territory of the State administering it; and such separate and distinct status under the Charter shall exist until the people of the colony or Non-Self-Governing Territory have exercised their right of self-determination in accordance with the Charter, and particularly its purposes and principles.

Nothing in the foregoing paragraphs shall be construed as authorizing or encouraging any action which would dismember or impair, totally or in part, the territorial integrity or political unity of sovereign and independent States conducting themselves in compliance with the principle of equal rights and self-determination of peoples as described above and thus possessed of a government representing the whole people belonging to the territory without distinction as to race, creed or colour.

Every State shall refrain from any action aimed at the partial or total disruption of the national unity and territorial integrity of any other State or country.

The principle of sovereign equality of States

All States enjoy sovereign equality. They have equal rights and duties and are equal members of the international community, notwithstanding differences of an economic, social, political or other nature.

In particular, sovereign equality includes the following elements:

    (a)   States are judicially equal;
    (b)   Each State enjoys the rights inherent in full sovereignty;
    (c)   Each State has the duty to respect the personality of other States;
    (d)   The territorial integrity and political independence of the State are inviolable;
    (e)   Each State has the right freely to choose and develop its political, social, economic and cultural systems;
    (f)   Each State has the duty to comply fully and in good faith with its international obligations and to live in peace with other States.

The principle that States shall fulfil in good faith the obligations assumed by them in accordance with the Charter

Every State has the duty to fulfil in good faith the obligations assumed by it in accordance with the Charter of the United Nations.

Every State has the duty to fulfil in good faith its obligations under the generally recognized principles and rules of international law.

Every State has the duty to fulfil in good faith its obligations under international agreements valid under the generally recognized principles and rules of international law.

Where obligations arising under international agreements are in conflict with the obligations of Members of the United Nations under the Charter of the United Nations, the obligations under the Charter shall prevail.

General part

2. *Declares* that:

In their interpretation and application the above principles are interrelated and each principle should be construed in the context of the other principles.

Nothing in this Declaration shall be construed as prejudicing in any manner the provisions of the Charter or the rights and duties of Member States under the Charter or the rights of peoples under the Charter, taking into account the elaboration of these rights in this Declaration.

3. *Declares further* that:

The principles of the Charter which are embodied in this Declaration constitute basic principles of international law, and consequently appeals to all States to be guided by these principles in their international conduct and to develop their mutual relations on the basis of the strict observance of these principles.

Vienna Convention on the Law of Treaties

Done at Vienna on 23 May 1969
Entered into force on 27 January 1980
UNTS, Vol 1155, p 331

The States Parties to the present Convention,

Considering the fundamental role of treaties in the history of international relations,

Recognizing the ever-increasing importance of treaties as a source of international law and as a means of developing peaceful cooperation among nations, whatever their constitutional and social systems,

Noting that the principles of free consent and of good faith and the *pacta sunt servanda* rule are universally recognized,

Affirming that disputes concerning treaties, like other international disputes, should be settled by peaceful means and in conformity with the principles of justice and international law,

Recalling the determination of the peoples of the United Nations to establish conditions under which justice and respect for the obligations arising from treaties can be maintained,

Having in mind the principles of international law embodied in the Charter of the United Nations, such as the principles of the equal rights and self-determination of peoples, of the sovereign equality and independence of all States, of non-interference in the domestic affairs of States, of the prohibition of the threat or use of force and of universal respect for, and observance of, human rights and fundamental freedoms for all,

Believing that the codification and progressive development of the law of treaties achieved in the present Convention will promote the purposes of the United Nations set forth in the Charter, namely, the maintenance of international peace and security, the development of friendly relations and the achievement of cooperation among nations,

Affirming that the rules of customary international law will continue to govern questions not regulated by the provisions of the present Convention,

Have agreed as follows:

PART I: INTRODUCTION

Article 1

Scope of the present Convention

The present Convention applies to treaties between States.

Article 2

Use of terms

1. For the purposes of the present Convention:
   (a) 'treaty' means an international agreement concluded between States in written form and governed by international law, whether embodied in a single instrument or in two or more related instruments and whatever its particular designation;
   (b) 'ratification', 'acceptance', 'approval' and 'accession' mean in each case the international act so named whereby a State establishes on the international plane its consent to be bound by a treaty;
   (c) 'full powers' means a document emanating from the competent authority of a State designating a person or persons to represent the State for negotiating, adopting or authenticating the text of a treaty, for expressing the consent of the State to be bound by a treaty, or for accomplishing any other act with respect to a treaty;
   (d) 'reservation' means a unilateral statement, however phrased or named, made by a State, when signing, ratifying, accepting, approving or acceding to a treaty, whereby it purports to exclude or to modify the legal effect of certain provisions of the treaty in their application to that State;
   (e) 'negotiating State' means a State which took part in the drawing up and adoption of the text of the treaty;
   (f) 'contracting State' means a State which has consented to be bound by the treaty, whether or not the treaty has entered into force;
   (g) 'party' means a State which has consented to be bound by the treaty and for which the treaty is in force;
   (h) 'third State' means a State not a party to the treaty;
   (i) 'international organization' means an intergovernmental organization.
2. The provisions of paragraph 1 regarding the use of terms in the present Convention are without prejudice to the use of those terms or to the meanings which may be given to them in the internal law of any State.

Article 3

International agreements not within the scope of the present Convention

The fact that the present Convention does not apply to international agreements concluded between States and other subjects of international law or between such other subjects of international law, or to international agreements not in written form, shall not affect:

(a) the legal force of such agreements;

(b) the application to them of any of the rules set forth in the present Convention to which they would be subject under international law independently of the Convention;

(c) the application of the Convention to the relations of States as between themselves under international agreements to which other subjects of international law are also parties.

Article 4
Non-retroactivity of the present Convention

Without prejudice to the application of any rules set forth in the present Convention to which treaties would be subject under international law independently of the Convention, the Convention applies only to treaties which are concluded by States after the entry into force of the present Convention with regard to such States.

Article 5
Treaties constituting international organizations and treaties adopted within an international organization

The present Convention applies to any treaty which is the constituent instrument of an international organization and to any treaty adopted within an international organization without prejudice to any relevant rules of the organization.

PART II: CONCLUSION AND ENTRY INTO FORCE OF TREATIES

Section 1: Conclusion of treaties

Article 6
Capacity of States to conclude treaties

Every State possesses capacity to conclude treaties.

Article 7
Full powers

1. A person is considered as representing a State for the purpose of adopting or authenticating the text of a treaty or for the purpose of expressing the consent of the State to be bound by a treaty if:

   (a) he produces appropriate full powers; or

   (b) it appears from the practice of the States concerned or from other circumstances that their intention was to consider that person as representing the State for such purposes and to dispense with full powers.

2. In virtue of their functions and without having to produce full powers, the following are considered as representing their State:

   (a) Heads of State, Heads of Government and Ministers for Foreign Affairs, for the purpose of performing all acts relating to the conclusion of a treaty;

   (b) heads of diplomatic missions, for the purpose of adopting the text of a treaty between the accrediting State and the State to which they are accredited;

   (c) representatives accredited by States to an international conference or to an international organization or one of its organs, for the purpose of adopting the text of a treaty in that conference, organization or organ.

Article 8

Subsequent confirmation of an act performed without authorization

An act relating to the conclusion of a treaty performed by a person who cannot be considered under article 7 as authorized to represent a State for that purpose is without legal effect unless afterwards confirmed by that State.

Article 9

Adoption of the text

1. The adoption of the text of a treaty takes place by the consent of all the States participating in its drawing up except as provided in paragraph 2.

2. The adoption of the text of a treaty at an international conference takes place by the vote of two thirds of the States present and voting, unless by the same majority they shall decide to apply a different rule.

Article 10

Authentication of the text

The text of a treaty is established as authentic and definitive:

   (a) by such procedure as may be provided for in the text or agreed upon by the States participating in its drawing up; or

   (b) failing such procedure, by the signature, signature ad referendum or initialling by the representatives of those States of the text of the treaty or of the Final Act of a conference incorporating the text.

Article 11

Means of expressing consent to be bound by a treaty

The consent of a State to be bound by a treaty may be expressed by signature, exchange of instruments constituting a treaty, ratification, acceptance, approval or accession, or by any other means if so agreed.

Article 12

Consent to be bound by a treaty expressed by signature

1. The consent of a State to be bound by a treaty is expressed by the signature of its representative when:

   (a) the treaty provides that signature shall have that effect;

   (b) it is otherwise established that the negotiating States were agreed that signature should have that effect; or

   (c) the intention of the State to give that effect to the signature appears from the full powers of its representative or was expressed during the negotiation.

2. For the purposes of paragraph 1:

   (a) the initialling of a text constitutes a signature of the treaty when it is established that the negotiating States so agreed;

   (b) the signature ad referendum of a treaty by a representative, if confirmed by his State, constitutes a full signature of the treaty.

Article 13

Consent to be bound by a treaty expressed by an exchange of instruments constituting a treaty

The consent of States to be bound by a treaty constituted by instruments exchanged between them is expressed by that exchange when:

   (a) the instruments provide that their exchange shall have that effect; or

   (b) it is otherwise established that those States were agreed that the exchange of instruments should have that effect.

Article 14

Consent to be bound by a treaty expressed by ratification, acceptance or approval

1. The consent of a State to be bound by a treaty is expressed by ratification when:

   (a) the treaty provides for such consent to be expressed by means of ratification;

   (b) it is otherwise established that the negotiating States were agreed that ratification should be required;

   (c) the representative of the State has signed the treaty subject to ratification; or

   (d) the intention of the State to sign the treaty subject to ratification appears from the full powers of its representative or was expressed during the negotiation.

2. The consent of a State to be bound by a treaty is expressed by acceptance or approval under conditions similar to those which apply to ratification.

Article 15

Consent to be bound by a treaty expressed by accession

The consent of a State to be bound by a treaty is expressed by accession when:

(a) the treaty provides that such consent may be expressed by that State by means of accession;

(b) it is otherwise established that the negotiating States were agreed that such consent may be expressed by that State by means of accession; or

(c) all the parties have subsequently agreed that such consent may be expressed by that State by means of accession.

Article 16

Exchange or deposit of instruments of ratification, acceptance, approval or accession

Unless the treaty otherwise provides, instruments of ratification, acceptance, approval or accession establish the consent of a State to be bound by a treaty upon:

(a) their exchange between the contracting States;

(b) their deposit with the depositary; or

(c) their notification to the contracting States or to the depositary, if so agreed.

Article 17

Consent to be bound by part of a treaty and choice of differing provisions

1. Without prejudice to articles 19 to 23, the consent of a State to be bound by part of a treaty is effective only if the treaty so permits or the other contracting States so agree.

2. The consent of a State to be bound by a treaty which permits a choice between differing provisions is effective only if it is made clear to which of the provisions the consent relates.

Article 18

Obligation not to defeat the object and purpose of a treaty prior to its entry into force

A State is obliged to refrain from acts which would defeat the object and purpose of a treaty when:

(a) it has signed the treaty or has exchanged instruments constituting the treaty subject to ratification, acceptance or approval, until it shall have made its intention clear not to become a party to the treaty; or

(b) it has expressed its consent to be bound by the treaty, pending the entry into force of the treaty and provided that such entry into force is not unduly delayed.

Section 2: Reservations

Article 19
Formulation of reservations

A State may, when signing, ratifying, accepting, approving or acceding to a treaty, formulate a reservation unless:

    (a) the reservation is prohibited by the treaty;

    (b) the treaty provides that only specified reservations, which do not include the reservation in question, may be made; or

    (c) in cases not failing under subparagraphs (a) and (b), the reservation is incompatible with the object and purpose of the treaty.

Article 20
Acceptance of and objection to reservations

1.   A reservation expressly authorized by a treaty does not require any subsequent acceptance by the other contracting States unless the treaty so provides.

2.   When it appears from the limited number of the negotiating States and the object and purpose of a treaty that the application of the treaty in its entirety between all the parties is an essential condition of the consent of each one to be bound by the treaty, a reservation requires acceptance by all the parties.

3.   When a treaty is a constituent instrument of an international organization and unless it otherwise provides, a reservation requires the acceptance of the competent organ of that organization.

4.   In cases not falling under the preceding paragraphs and unless the treaty otherwise provides:

    (a) acceptance by another contracting State of a reservation constitutes the reserving State a party to the treaty in relation to that other State if or when the treaty is in force for those States;

    (b) an objection by another contracting State to a reservation does not preclude the entry into force of the treaty as between the objecting and reserving States unless a contrary intention is definitely expressed by the objecting State;

    (c) an act expressing a State's consent to be bound by the treaty and containing a reservation is effective as soon as at least one other contracting State has accepted the reservation.

5.   For the purposes of paragraphs 2 and 4 and unless the treaty otherwise provides, a reservation is considered to have been accepted by a State if it shall have raised no objection to the reservation by the end of a period of twelve months after it was notified of the reservation or by the date on which it expressed its consent to be bound by the treaty, whichever is later.

Article 21
Legal effects of reservations and of objections to reservations

1.   A reservation established with regard to another party in accordance with articles 19, 20 and 23:

(a) modifies for the reserving State in its relations with that other party the provisions of the treaty to which the reservation relates to the extent of the reservation; and

(b) modifies those provisions to the same extent for that other party in its relations with the reserving State.

2. The reservation does not modify the provisions of the treaty for the other parties to the treaty inter se.

3. When a State objecting to a reservation has not opposed the entry into force of the treaty between itself and the reserving State, the provisions to which the reservation relates do not apply as between the two States to the extent of the reservation.

Article 22

Withdrawal of reservations and of objections to reservations

1. Unless the treaty otherwise provides, a reservation may be withdrawn at any time and the consent of a State which has accepted the reservation is not required for its withdrawal.

2. Unless the treaty otherwise provides, an objection to a reservation may be withdrawn at any time.

3. Unless the treaty otherwise provides, or it is otherwise agreed:

(a) the withdrawal of a reservation becomes operative in relation to another contracting State only when notice of it has been received by that State;

(b) the withdrawal of an objection to a reservation becomes operative only when notice of it has been received by the State which formulated the reservation.

Article 23

Procedure regarding reservations

1. A reservation, an express acceptance of a reservation and an objection to a reservation must be formulated in writing and communicated to the contracting States and other States entitled to become parties to the treaty.

2. If formulated when signing the treaty subject to ratification, acceptance or approval, a reservation must be formally confirmed by the reserving State when expressing its consent to be bound by the treaty. In such a case the reservation shall be considered as having been made on the date of its confirmation.

3. An express acceptance of, or an objection to, a reservation made previously to confirmation of the reservation does not itself require confirmation.

4. The withdrawal of a reservation or of an objection to a reservation must be formulated in writing.

Section 3: Entry into force and provisional, application of treaties

Article 24
Entry into force

1. A treaty enters into force in such manner and upon such date as it may provide or as the negotiating States may agree.
2. Failing any such provision or agreement, a treaty enters into force as soon as consent to be bound by the treaty has been established for all the negotiating States.
3. When the consent of a State to be bound by a treaty is established on a date after the treaty has come into force, the treaty enters into force for that State on that date, unless the treaty otherwise provides.
4. The provisions of a treaty regulating the authentication of its text, the establishment of the consent of States to be bound by the treaty, the manner or date of its entry into force, reservations, the functions of the depositary and other matters arising necessarily before the entry into force of the treaty apply from the time of the adoption of its text.

Article 25
Provisional application

1. A treaty or a part of a treaty is applied provisionally pending its entry into force if:
    (a) the treaty itself so provides; or
    (b) the negotiating States have in some other manner so agreed.
2. Unless the treaty otherwise provides or the negotiating States have otherwise agreed, the provisional application of a treaty or a part of a treaty with respect to a State shall be terminated if that State notifies the other States between which the treaty is being applied provisionally of its intention not to become a party to the treaty.

PART III: OBSERVANCE, APPLICATION AND INTERPRETATION OF TREATIES

Section 1: Observance of treaties

Article 26
'Pacta sunt servanda'

Every treaty in force is binding upon the parties to it and must be performed by them in good faith.

Article 27

Internal law and observance of treaties

A party may not invoke the provisions of its internal law as justification for its failure to perform a treaty. This rule is without prejudice to article 46.

Section 2: Application of treaties

Article 28

Non-retroactivity of treaties

Unless a different intention appears from the treaty or is otherwise established, its provisions do not bind a party in relation to any act or fact which took place or any situation which ceased to exist before the date of the entry into force of the treaty with respect to that party.

Article 29

Territorial scope of treaties

Unless a different intention appears from the treaty or is otherwise established, a treaty is binding upon each party in respect of its entire territory.

Article 30

Application of successive treaties relating to the same subject matter

1. Subject to Article 103 of the Charter of the United Nations, the rights and obligations of States Parties to successive treaties relating to the same subject matter shall be determined in accordance with the following paragraphs.
2. When a treaty specifies that it is subject to, or that it is not to be considered as incompatible with, an earlier or later treaty, the provisions of that other treaty prevail.
3. When all the parties to the earlier treaty are parties also to the later treaty but the earlier treaty is not terminated or suspended in operation under article 59, the earlier treaty applies only to the extent that its provisions are compatible with those of the later treaty.
4. When the parties to the later treaty do not include all the parties to the earlier one:
   (a) as between States Parties to both treaties the same rule applies as in paragraph 3;
   (b) as between a State party to both treaties and a State party to only one of the treaties, the treaty to which both States are parties governs their mutual rights and obligations.
5. Paragraph 4 is without prejudice to article 41, or to any question of the termination or suspension of the operation of a treaty under article 60

or to any question of responsibility which may arise for a State from the conclusion or application of a treaty the provisions of which are incompatible with its obligations towards another State under another treaty.

Section 3: Interpretation of treaties

Article 31

General rule of interpretation

1. A treaty shall be interpreted in good faith in accordance with the ordinary meaning to be given to the terms of the treaty in their context and in the light of its object and purpose.
2. The context for the purpose of the interpretation of a treaty shall comprise, in addition to the text, including its preamble and annexes:
    (a) any agreement relating to the treaty which was made between all the parties in connection with the conclusion of the treaty;
    (b) any instrument which was made by one or more parties in connection with the conclusion of the treaty and accepted by the other parties as an instrument related to the treaty.
3. There shall be taken into account, together with the context:
    (a) any subsequent agreement between the parties regarding the interpretation of the treaty or the application of its provisions;
    (b) any subsequent practice in the application of the treaty which establishes the agreement of the parties regarding its interpretation;
    (c) any relevant rules of international law applicable in the relations between the parties.
4. A special meaning shall be given to a term if it is established that the parties so intended.

Article 32

Supplementary means of interpretation

Recourse may be had to supplementary means of interpretation, including the preparatory work of the treaty and the circumstances of its conclusion, in order to confirm the meaning resulting from the application of article 31, or to determine the meaning when the interpretation according to article 31:
    (a) leaves the meaning ambiguous or obscure; or
    (b) leads to a result which is manifestly absurd or unreasonable.

Article 33

Interpretation of treaties authenticated in two or more languages

1. When a treaty has been authenticated in two or more languages, the text is equally authoritative in each language, unless the treaty provides or the parties agree that, in case of divergence, a particular text shall prevail.

2. A version of the treaty in a language other than one of those in which the text was authenticated shall be considered an authentic text only if the treaty so provides or the parties so agree.

3. The terms of the treaty are presumed to have the same meaning in each authentic text.

4. Except where a particular text prevails in accordance with paragraph 1, when a comparison of the authentic texts discloses a difference of meaning which the application of articles 31 and 32 does not remove, the meaning which best reconciles the texts, having regard to the object and purpose of the treaty, shall be adopted.

Section 4: Treaties and third states

Article 34
General rule regarding third States

A treaty does not create either obligations or rights for a third State without its consent.

Article 35
Treaties providing for obligations for third States

An obligation arises for a third State from a provision of a treaty if the parties to the treaty intend the provision to be the means of establishing the obligation and the third State expressly accepts that obligation in writing.

Article 36
Treaties providing for rights for third States

1. A right arises for a third State from a provision of a treaty if the parties to the treaty intend the provision to accord that right either to the third State, or to a group of States to which it belongs, or to all States, and the third State assents thereto. Its assent shall be presumed so long as the contrary is not indicated, unless the treaty otherwise provides.

2. A State exercising a right in accordance with paragraph 1 shall comply with the conditions for its exercise provided for in the treaty or established in conformity with the treaty.

Article 37
Revocation or modification of obligations or rights of third States

1. When an obligation has arisen for a third State in conformity with article 35, the obligation may be revoked or modified only with the consent of the parties to the treaty and of the third State, unless it is established that they had otherwise agreed.

2. When a right has arisen for a third State in conformity with article 36, the right may not be revoked or modified by the parties if it is established that the right was intended not to be revocable or subject to modification without the consent of the third State.

Article 38
Rules in a treaty becoming binding on third States through international custom

Nothing in articles 34 to 37 precludes a rule set forth in a treaty from becoming binding upon a third State as a customary rule of international law, recognized as such.

PART IV: AMENDMENT AND MODIFICATION OF TREATIES

Article 39
General rule regarding the amendment of treaties

A treaty may be amended by agreement between the parties. The rules laid down in Part II apply to such an agreement except insofar as the treaty may otherwise provide.

Article 40
Amendment of multilateral treaties

1. Unless the treaty otherwise provides, the amendment of multilateral treaties shall be governed by the following paragraphs.
2. Any proposal to amend a multilateral treaty as between all the parties must be notified to all the contracting States, each one of which shall have the right to take part in:
   (a) the decision as to the action to be taken in regard to such proposal;
   (b) the negotiation and conclusion of any agreement for the amendment of the treaty.
3. Every State entitled to become a party to the treaty shall also be entitled to become a party to the treaty as amended.
4. The amending agreement does not bind any State already a party to the treaty which does not become a party to the amending agreement; article 30, paragraph 4 (b), applies in relation to such State.
5. Any State which becomes a party to the treaty after the entry into force of the amending agreement shall, failing an expression of a different intention by that State:
   (a) be considered as a party to the treaty as amended; and
   (b) be considered as a party to the unamended treaty in relation to any party to the treaty not bound by the amending agreement.

Article 41

Agreements to modify multilateral treaties between certain of the parties only

1. Two or more of the parties to a multilateral treaty may conclude an agreement to modify the treaty as between themselves alone if:
   (a) the possibility of such a modification is provided for by the treaty; or
   (b) the modification in question is not prohibited by the treaty and:
       (i) does not affect the enjoyment by the other parties of their rights under the treaty or the performance of their obligations;
       (ii) does not relate to a provision, derogation from which is incompatible with the effective execution of the object and purpose of the treaty as a whole.
2. Unless in a case falling under paragraph 1 (a) the treaty otherwise provides, the parties in question shall notify the other parties of their intention to conclude the agreement and of the modification to the treaty for which it provides.

PART V: INVALIDITY, TERMINATION AND SUSPENSION OF THE OPERATION OF TREATIES

Section 1: General provisions

Article 42

Validity and continuance in force of treaties

1. The validity of a treaty or of the consent of a State to be bound by a treaty may be impeached only through the application of the present Convention.
2. The termination of a treaty, its denunciation or the withdrawal of a party, may take place only as a result of the application of the provisions of the treaty or of the present Convention. The same rule applies to suspension of the operation of a treaty.

Article 43

Obligations imposed by international law independently of a treaty

The invalidity, termination or denunciation of a treaty, the withdrawal of a party from it, or the suspension of its operation, as a result of the application of the present Convention or of the provisions of the treaty, shall not in any way impair the duty of any State to fulfil any obligation embodied in the treaty to which it would be subject under international law independently of the treaty.

Article 44

Separability of treaty provisions

1. A right of a party, provided for in a treaty or arising under article 56, to denounce, withdraw from or suspend the operation of the treaty may be exercised only with respect to the whole treaty unless the treaty otherwise provides or the parties otherwise agree.

2. A ground for invalidating, terminating, withdrawing from or suspending the operation of a treaty recognized in the present Convention may be invoked only with respect to the whole treaty except as provided in the following paragraphs or in article 60.

3. If the ground relates solely to particular clauses, it may be invoked only with respect to those clauses where:

    (a) the said clauses are separable from the remainder of the treaty with regard to their application;

    (b) it appears from the treaty or is otherwise established that acceptance of those clauses was not an essential basis of the consent of the other party or parties to be bound by the treaty as a whole; and

    (c) continued performance of the remainder of the treaty would not be unjust.

4. In cases falling under articles 49 and 50, the State entitled to invoke the fraud or corruption may do so with respect either to the whole treaty or, subject to paragraph 3, to the particular clauses alone.

5. In cases falling under articles 51, 52 and 53, no separation of the provisions of the treaty is permitted.

Article 45

Loss of a right to invoke a ground for invalidating, terminating, withdrawing from or suspending the operation of a treaty

A State may no longer invoke a ground for invalidating, terminating, withdrawing from or suspending the operation of a treaty under articles 46 to 50 or articles 60 and 62 if, after becoming aware of the facts:

(a) it shall have expressly agreed that the treaty is valid or remains in force or continues in operation, as the case may be; or

(b) it must by reason of its conduct be considered as having acquiesced in the validity of the treaty or in its maintenance in force or in operation, as the case may be.

Section 2: Invalidity of treaties

Article 46

Provisions of internal law regarding competence to conclude treaties

1. A State may not invoke the fact that its consent to be bound by a treaty has been expressed in violation of a provision of its internal law

regarding competence to conclude treaties as invalidating its consent unless that violation was manifest and concerned a rule of its internal law of fundamental importance.

2. A violation is manifest if it would be objectively evident to any State conducting itself in the matter in accordance with normal practice and in good faith.

Article 47

Specific restrictions on authority to express the consent of a State

If the authority of a representative to express the consent of a State to be bound by a particular treaty has been made subject to a specific restriction, his omission to observe that restriction may not be invoked as invalidating the consent expressed by him unless the restriction was notified to the other negotiating States prior to his expressing such consent.

Article 48

Error

1. A State may invoke an error in a treaty as invalidating its consent to be bound by the treaty if the error relates to a fact or situation which was assumed by that State to exist at the time when the treaty was concluded and formed an essential basis of its consent to be bound by the treaty.

2. Paragraph 1 shall not apply if the State in question contributed by its own conduct to the error or if the circumstances were such as to put that State on notice of a possible error.

3. An error relating only to the wording of the text of a treaty does not affect its validity; article 79 then applies.

Article 49

Fraud

If a State has been induced to conclude a treaty by the fraudulent conduct of another negotiating State, the State may invoke the fraud as invalidating its consent to be bound by the treaty.

Article 50

Corruption of a representative of a State

If the expression of a State's consent to be bound by a treaty has been procured through the corruption of its representative directly or indirectly by another negotiating State, the State may invoke such corruption as invalidating its consent to be bound by the treaty.

Article 51
Coercion of a representative of a State

The expression of a State's consent to be bound by a treaty which has been procured by the coercion of its representative through acts or threats directed against him shall be without any legal effect.

Article 52
Coercion of a State by the threat or use of force

A treaty is void if its conclusion has been procured by the threat or use of force in violation of the principles of international law embodied in the Charter of the United Nations.

Article 53
Treaties conflicting with a peremptory norm of general international law ('jus cogens')

A treaty is void if, at the time of its conclusion, it conflicts with a peremptory norm of general international law. For the purposes of the present Convention, a peremptory norm of general international law is a norm accepted and recognized by the international community of States as a whole as a norm from which no derogation is permitted and which can be modified only by a subsequent norm of general international law having the same character.

Section 3: Termination and suspension of the operation of treaties

Article 54
Termination of or withdrawal from a treaty under its provisions or by consent of the parties

The termination of a treaty or the withdrawal of a party may take place:
- (a) in conformity with the provisions of the treaty; or
- (b) at any time by consent of all the parties after consultation with the other contracting States.

Article 55
Reduction of the parties to a multilateral treaty below the number necessary for its entry into force

Unless the treaty otherwise provides, a multilateral treaty does not terminate by reason only of the fact that the number of the parties falls below the number necessary for its entry into force.

Article 56

Denunciation of or withdrawal from a treaty containing no provision regarding termination, denunciation or withdrawal

1. A treaty which contains no provision regarding its termination and which does not provide for denunciation or withdrawal is not subject to denunciation or withdrawal unless:

    (a) it is established that the parties intended to admit the possibility of denunciation or withdrawal; or

    (b) a right of denunciation or withdrawal may be implied by the nature of the treaty.

2. A party shall give not less than twelve months' notice of its intention to denounce or withdraw from a treaty under paragraph 1.

Article 57

Suspension of the operation of a treaty under its provisions or by consent of the parties

The operation of a treaty in regard to all the parties or to a particular party may be suspended:

    (a) in conformity with the provisions of the treaty; or

    (b) at any time by consent of all the parties after consultation with the other contracting States.

Article 58

Suspension of the operation of a multilateral treaty by agreement between certain of the parties only

1. Two or more parties to a multilateral treaty may conclude an agreement to suspend the operation of provisions of the treaty, temporarily and as between themselves alone, if:

    (a) the possibility of such a suspension is provided for by the treaty; or

    (b) the suspension in question is not prohibited by the treaty and:

        (i) does not affect the enjoyment by the other parties of their rights under the treaty or the performance of their obligations;

        (ii) is not incompatible with the object and purpose of the treaty.

2. Unless in a case falling under paragraph 1 (a) the treaty otherwise provides, the parties in question shall notify the other parties of their intention to conclude the agreement and of those provisions of the treaty the operation of which they intend to suspend.

Article 59

Termination or suspension of the operation of a treaty implied by conclusion of a later treaty

1. A treaty shall be considered as terminated if all the parties to it conclude a later treaty relating to the same subject matter and:

    (a) it appears from the later treaty or is otherwise established that the parties intended that the matter should be governed by that treaty; or

(b) the provisions of the later treaty are so far incompatible with those of the earlier one that the two treaties are not capable of being applied at the same time.

2. The earlier treaty shall be considered as only suspended in operation if it appears from the later treaty or is otherwise established that such was the intention of the parties.

Article 60

Termination or suspension of the operation of a treaty as a consequence of its breach

1. A material breach of a bilateral treaty by one of the parties entitles the other to invoke the breach as a ground for terminating the treaty or suspending its operation in whole or in part.

2. A material breach of a multilateral treaty by one of the parties entitles:

    (a) the other parties by unanimous agreement to suspend the operation of the treaty in whole or in part or to terminate it either:

        (i) in the relations between themselves and the defaulting State; or

        (ii) as between all the parties;

    (b) a party specially affected by the breach to invoke it as a ground for suspending the operation of the treaty in whole or in part in the relations between itself and the defaulting State;

    (c) any party other than the defaulting State to invoke the breach as a ground for suspending the operation of the treaty in whole or in part with respect to itself if the treaty is of such a character that a material breach of its provisions by one party radically changes the position of every party with respect to the further performance of its obligations under the treaty.

3. A material breach of a treaty, for the purposes of this article, consists in:

    (a) a repudiation of the treaty not sanctioned by the present Convention; or

    (b) the violation of a provision essential to the accomplishment of the object or purpose of the treaty.

4. The foregoing paragraphs are without prejudice to any provision in the treaty applicable in the event of a breach.

5. Paragraphs 1 to 3 do not apply to provisions relating to the protection of the human person contained in treaties of a humanitarian character, in particular to provisions prohibiting any form of reprisals against persons protected by such treaties.

Article 61

Supervening impossibility of performance

1. A party may invoke the impossibility of performing a treaty as a ground for terminating or withdrawing from it if the impossibility results from the permanent disappearance or destruction of an object indispensable for the execution of the treaty. If the impossibility is temporary, it may be invoked only as a ground for suspending the operation of the treaty.

2. Impossibility of performance may not be invoked by a party as a ground for terminating, withdrawing from or suspending the operation of a treaty if the impossibility is the result of a breach by that party either of

an obligation under the treaty or of any other international obligation owed to any other party to the treaty.

Article 62

Fundamental change of circumstances

1. A fundamental change of circumstances which has occurred with regard to those existing at the time of the conclusion of a treaty, and which was not foreseen by the parties, may not be invoked as a ground for terminating or withdrawing from the treaty unless:

    (a) the existence of those circumstances constituted an essential basis of the consent of the parties to be bound by the treaty; and

    (b) the effect of the change is radically to transform the extent of obligations still to be performed under the treaty.

2. A fundamental change of circumstances may not be invoked as a ground for terminating or withdrawing from a treaty:

    (a) if the treaty establishes a boundary; or

    (b) if the fundamental change is the result of a breach by the party invoking it either of an obligation under the treaty or of any other international obligation owed to any other party to the treaty.

3. If, under the foregoing paragraphs, a party may invoke a fundamental change of circumstances as a ground for terminating or withdrawing from a treaty it may also invoke the change as a ground for suspending the operation of the treaty.

Article 63

Severance of diplomatic or consular relations

The severance of diplomatic or consular relations between parties to a treaty does not affect the legal relations established between them by the treaty except insofar as the existence of diplomatic or consular relations is indispensable for the application of the treaty.

Article 64

Emergence of a new peremptory norm of general international law ('jus cogens')

If a new peremptory norm of general international law emerges, any existing treaty which is in conflict with that norm becomes void and terminates.

Section 4: Procedure

Article 65

Procedure to be followed with respect to invalidity, termination, withdrawal from or suspension of the operation of a treaty

1. A party which, under the provisions of the present Convention, invokes either a defect in its consent to be bound by a treaty or a ground for

impeaching the validity of a treaty, terminating it, withdrawing from it or suspending its operation, must notify the other parties of its claim. The notification shall indicate the measure proposed to be taken with respect to the treaty and the reasons therefor.

2. If, after the expiry of a period which, except in cases of special urgency, shall not be less than three months after the receipt of the notification, no party has raised any objection, the party making the notification may carry out in the manner provided in article 67 the measure which it has proposed.

3. If, however, objection has been raised by any other party, the parties shall seek a solution through the means indicated in Article 33 of the Charter of the United Nations.

4. Nothing in the foregoing paragraphs shall affect the rights or obligations of the parties under any provisions in force binding the parties with regard to the settlement of disputes.

5. Without prejudice to article 45, the fact that a State has not previously made the notification prescribed in paragraph 1 shall not prevent it from making such notification in answer to another party claiming performance of the treaty or alleging its violation.

Article 66

Procedures for judicial settlement, arbitration and conciliation

If, under paragraph 3 of article 65, no solution has been reached within a period of 12 months following the date on which the objection was raised, the following procedures shall be followed:

(a) any one of the parties to a dispute concerning the application or the interpretation of article 53 or 64 may, by a written application, submit it to the International Court of Justice for a decision unless the parties by common consent agree to submit the dispute to arbitration;

(b) any one of the parties to a dispute concerning the application or the interpretation of any of the other articles in part V of the present Convention may set in motion the procedure specified in the Annex to the Convention by submitting a request to that effect to the Secretary-General of the United Nations.

Article 67

Instruments for declaring invalid, terminating, withdrawing from or suspending the operation of a treaty

1. The notification provided for under article 65, paragraph 1, must be made in writing.

2. Any act of declaring invalid, terminating, withdrawing from or suspending the operation of a treaty pursuant to the provisions of the treaty or of paragraphs 2 or 3 of article 65 shall be carried out through an instrument communicated to the other parties. If the instrument is not signed by the Head of State, Head of Government or Minister for Foreign Affairs, the representative of the State communicating it may be called upon to produce full powers.

Article 68

Revocation of notifications and instruments provided for in articles 65 and 67

A notification or instrument provided for in article 65 or 67 may be revoked at any time before it takes effect.

Section 5: Consequences of the invalidity, termination or suspension of the operation of a treaty

Article 69

Consequences of the invalidity of a treaty

1. A treaty the invalidity of which is established under the present Convention is void. The provisions of a void treaty have no legal force.
2. If acts have nevertheless been performed in reliance on such a treaty:
   (a) each party may require any other party to establish as far as possible in their mutual relations the position that would have existed if the acts had not been performed;
   (b) acts performed in good faith before the invalidity was invoked are not rendered unlawful by reason only of the invalidity of the treaty.
3. In cases falling under article 49, 50, 51 or 52, paragraph 2 does not apply with respect to the party to which the fraud, the act of corruption or the coercion is imputable.
4. In the case of the invalidity of a particular State's consent to be bound by a multilateral treaty, the foregoing rules apply in the relations between that State and the parties to the treaty.

Article 70

Consequences of the termination of a treaty

1. Unless the treaty otherwise provides or the parties otherwise agree, the termination of a treaty under its provisions or in accordance with the present Convention:
   (a) releases the parties from any obligation further to perform the treaty;
   (b) does not affect any right, obligation or legal situation of the parties created through the execution of the treaty prior to its termination.
2. If a State denounces or withdraws from a multilateral treaty, paragraph 1 applies in the relations between that State and each of the other parties to the treaty from the date when such denunciation or withdrawal takes effect.

Article 71

Consequences of the invalidity of a treaty which conflicts with a peremptory norm of general international law

1. In the case of a treaty which is void under article 53 the parties shall:

(a)   eliminate as far as possible the consequences of any act performed in reliance on any provision which conflicts with the peremptory norm of general international law; and

(b)   bring their mutual relations into conformity with the peremptory norm of general international law.

2.   In the case of a treaty which becomes void and terminates under article 64, the termination of the treaty:

(a)   releases the parties from any obligation further to perform the treaty;

(b)   does not affect any right, obligation or legal situation of the parties created through the execution of the treaty prior to its termination, provided that those rights, obligations or situations may thereafter be maintained only to the extent that their maintenance is not in itself in conflict with the new peremptory norm of general international law.

Article 72

Consequences of the suspension of the operation of a treaty

1.   Unless the treaty otherwise provides or the parties otherwise agree, the suspension of the operation of a treaty under its provisions or in accordance with the present Convention:

(a)   releases the parties between which the operation of the treaty is suspended from the obligation to perform the treaty in their mutual relations during the period of the suspension;

(b)   does not otherwise affect the legal relations between the parties established by the treaty.

2.   During the period of the suspension the parties shall refrain from acts tending to obstruct the resumption of the operation of the treaty.

PART VI: MISCELLANEOUS PROVISIONS

Article 73

Cases of State succession, State responsibility and outbreak of hostilities

The provisions of the present Convention shall not prejudge any question that may arise in regard to a treaty from a succession of States or from the international responsibility of a State or from the outbreak of hostilities between States.

Article 74

Diplomatic and consular relations and the conclusion of treaties

The severance or absence of diplomatic or consular relations between two or more States does not prevent the conclusion of treaties between those States. The conclusion of a treaty does not in itself affect the situation in regard to diplomatic or consular relations.

Article 75

Case of an aggressor State

The provisions of the present Convention are without prejudice to any obligation in relation to a treaty which may arise for an aggressor State in consequence of measures taken in conformity with the Charter of the United Nations with reference to that State's aggression.

PART VII: DEPOSITARIES, NOTIFICATIONS, CORRECTIONS AND REGISTRATION

Article 76

Depositaries of treaties

1. The designation of the depositary of a treaty may be made by the negotiating States, either in the treaty itself or in some other manner. The depositary may be one or more States, an international organization or the chief administrative officer of the organization.

2. The functions of the depositary of a treaty are international in character and the depositary is under an obligation to act impartially in their performance. In particular, the fact that a treaty has not entered into force between certain of the parties or that a difference has appeared between a State and a depositary with regard to the performance of the latter's functions shall not affect that obligation.

Article 77

Functions of depositaries

1. The functions of a depositary, unless otherwise provided in the treaty or agreed by the contracting States, comprise in particular:

   (a) keeping custody of the original text of the treaty and of any full powers delivered to the depositary;

   (b) preparing certified copies of the original text and preparing any further text of the treaty in such additional languages as may be required by the treaty and transmitting them to the parties and to the States entitled to become parties to the treaty;

   (c) receiving any signatures to the treaty and receiving and keeping custody of any instruments, notifications and communications relating to it;

   (d) examining whether the signature or any instrument, notification or communication relating to the treaty is in due and proper form and, if need be, bringing the matter to the attention of the State in question;

   (e) informing the parties and the States entitled to become parties to the treaty of acts, notifications and communications relating to the treaty;

   (f) informing the States entitled to become parties to the treaty when the number of signatures or of instruments of ratification, acceptance, approval or accession required for the entry into force of the treaty has been received or deposited;

(g) registering the treaty with the Secretariat of the United Nations;

(h) performing the functions specified in other provisions of the present Convention.

2. In the event of any difference appearing between a State and the depositary as to the performance of the latter's functions, the depositary shall bring the question to the attention of the signatory States and the contracting States or, where appropriate, of the competent organ of the international organization concerned.

Article 78
Notifications and communications

Except as the treaty or the present Convention otherwise provide, any notification or communication to be made by any State under the present Convention shall:

(a) if there is no depositary, be transmitted direct to the States for which it is intended, or if there is a depositary, to the latter;

(b) be considered as having been made by the State in question only upon its receipt by the State to which it was transmitted or, as the case may be, upon its receipt by the depositary;

(c) if transmitted to a depositary, be considered as received by the State for which it was intended only when the latter State has been informed by the depositary in accordance with article 77, paragraph 1 (e).

Article 79
Correction of errors in texts or in certified copies of treaties

1. Where, after the authentication of the text of a treaty, the signatory States and the contracting States are agreed that it contains an error, the error shall, unless they decide upon some other means of correction, be corrected:

(a) by having the appropriate correction made in the text and causing the correction to be initialled by duly authorized representatives;

(b) by executing or exchanging an instrument or instruments setting out the correction which it has been agreed to make; or

(c) by executing a corrected text of the whole treaty by the same procedure as in the case of the original text.

2. Where the treaty is one for which there is a depositary, the latter shall notify the signatory States and the contracting States of the error and of the proposal to correct it and shall specify an appropriate time-limit within which objection to the proposed correction may be raised. If, on the expiry of the time-limit:

(a) no objection has been raised, the depositary shall make and initial the correction in the text and shall execute a procès-verbal of the rectification of the text and communicate a copy of it to the parties and to the States entitled to become parties to the treaty;

(b) an objection has been raised, the depositary shall communicate the objection to the signatory States and to the contracting States.

3. The rules in paragraphs I and 2 apply also where the text has been authenticated in two or more languages and it appears that there is a lack of concordance which the signatory States and the contracting States agree should be corrected.

4. The corrected text replaces the defective text ab initio, unless the signatory States and the contracting States otherwise decide.

5. The correction of the text of a treaty that has been registered shall be notified to the Secretariat of the United Nations.

6. Where an error is discovered in a certified copy of a treaty, the depositary shall execute a procès-verbal specifying the rectification and communicate a copy of it to the signatory States and to the contracting States.

Article 80

Registration and publication of treaties

1. Treaties shall, after their entry into force, be transmitted to the Secretariat of the United Nations for registration or filing and recording, as the case may be, and for publication.

2. The designation of a depositary shall constitute authorization for it to perform the acts specified in the preceding paragraph.

PART VIII: FINAL PROVISIONS

Article 81

Signature

The present Convention shall be open for signature by all States Members of the United Nations or of any of the specialized agencies or of the International Atomic Energy Agency or parties to the Statute of the International Court of Justice, and by any other State invited by the General Assembly of the United Nations to become a party to the Convention, as follows: until 30 November 1969, at the Federal Ministry for Foreign Affairs of the Republic of Austria, and subsequently, until 30 April 1970, at United Nations Headquarters, New York.

Article 82

Ratification

The present Convention is subject to ratification. The instruments of ratification shall be deposited with the Secretary-General of the United Nations.

Article 83

Accession

The present Convention shall remain open for accession by any State belonging to any of the categories mentioned in article 81. The instruments of accession shall be deposited with the Secretary-General of the United Nations.

Article 84

Entry into force

1. The present Convention shall enter into force on the thirtieth day following the date of deposit of the thirty-fifth instrument of ratification or accession.

2. For each State ratifying or acceding to the Convention after the deposit of the thirty-fifth instrument of ratification or accession, the Convention shall enter into force on the thirtieth day after deposit by such State of its instrument of ratification or accession.

Article 85

Authentic texts

The original of the present Convention, of which the Chinese, English, French, Russian and Spanish texts are equally authentic, shall be deposited with the Secretary-General of the United Nations.

IN WITNESS WHEREOF the undersigned Plenipotentiaries, being duly authorized thereto by their respective Governments, have signed the present Convention.

DONE at Vienna this twenty-third day of May, one thousand nine hundred and sixty-nine.

ANNEX

1. A list of conciliators consisting of qualified jurists shall be drawn up and maintained by the Secretary-General of the United Nations. To this end, every State which is a Member of the United Nations or a party to the present Convention shall be invited to nominate two conciliators, and the names of the persons so nominated shall constitute the list. The term of a conciliator, including that of any conciliator nominated to fill a casual vacancy, shall be five years and may be renewed. A conciliator whose term expires shall continue to fulfil any function for which he shall have been chosen under the following paragraph.

2. When a request has been made to the Secretary-General under article 66, the Secretary-General shall bring the dispute before a conciliation commission constituted as follows:

    The State or States constituting one of the parties to the dispute shall appoint:

    (a) one conciliator of the nationality of that State or of one of those States, who may or may not be chosen from the list referred to in paragraph 1; and

    (b) one conciliator not of the nationality of that State or of any of those States, who shall be chosen from the list.

    The State or States constituting the other party to the dispute shall appoint two conciliators in the same way. The four conciliators chosen by the parties shall be appointed within sixty days following the date on which the Secretary-General receives the request.

The four conciliators shall, within sixty days following the date of the last of their own appointments, appoint a fifth conciliator chosen from the list, who shall be chairman.

If the appointment of the chairman or of any of the other conciliators has not been made within the period prescribed above for such appointment, it shall be made by the Secretary-General within sixty days following the expiry of that period. The appointment of the chairman may be made by the Secretary-General either from the list or from the membership of the International Law Commission. Any of the periods within which appointments must be made may be extended by agreement between the parties to the dispute.

Any vacancy shall be filled in the manner prescribed for the initial appointment.

3. The Conciliation Commission shall decide its own procedure. The Commission, with the consent of the parties to the dispute, may invite any party to the treaty to submit to it its views orally or in writing. Decisions and recommendations of the Commission shall be made by a majority vote of the five members.

4. The Commission may draw the attention of the parties to the dispute to any measures which might facilitate an amicable settlement.

5. The Commission shall hear the parties, examine the claims and objections, and make proposals to the parties with a view to reaching an amicable settlement of the dispute.

6. The Commission shall report within twelve months of its constitution. Its report shall be deposited with the Secretary-General and transmitted to the parties to the dispute. The report of the Commission, including any conclusions stated therein regarding the facts or questions of law, shall not be binding upon the parties and it shall have no other character than that of recommendations submitted for the consideration of the parties in order to facilitate an amicable settlement of the dispute.

7. The Secretary-General shall provide the Commission with such assistance and facilities as it may require. The expenses of the Commission shall be borne by the United Nations.

Other important documents

The following documents are also useful primary sources. At the date of publication, they can be accessed on the websites indicated.

International Court of Justice: www.icj-cij.org
- Rules of Court of the International Court of Justice
- Statute of the International Court of Justice

International Criminal Court: www.icc-cpi.int
- Elements of Crimes under the Rome Statute of the International Criminal Court
- Rome Statute of the International Criminal Court

United Nations: www.un.org/en
- Convention against Torture and Other Cruel, Inhuman or Degrading Treatment or Punishment
- Convention on the Prevention and Punishment of the Crime of Genocide
- United Nations Convention on Jurisdictional Immunities of States and Their Property
- United Nations Convention on the Law of the Sea
- Universal Declaration of Human Rights
- Vienna Convention on Diplomatic Relations

Index

References are to paragraphs